To David,
    Who unlike Job's "friends,"
seeks truth beyond conventional
wisdom/theology, understands
YHWH as greater than human
comprehension, and continues
to ask the tough questions.
May this treatise help in
your journey.
    Love, Bob & Wanda (Dad & Mom)
        21 July 2007

SMYTH & HELWYS BIBLE COMMENTARY

JOB

SAMUEL E. BALENTINE

SMYTH&HELWYS
PUBLISHING INCORPORATED · MACON GEORGIA

Smyth & Helwys Bible Commentary: Job
Publication Staff

President & CEO
Cecil P. Staton

Publisher & Executive Vice President
David Cassady

Vice President, Editorial
Lex Horton

Senior Editor
Mark K. McElroy

Book Editor
Keith Gammons

Graphic Designer
Barclay Burns

Assistant Editors
Kelley F. Land
Laura Shirley

Smyth & Helwys Publishing, Inc.
6316 Peake Road
Macon, Georgia 31210-3960
1-800-747-3016
© 2006 by Smyth & Helwys Publishing
All rights reserved.
Printed in the United States of America.

The paper used in this publication meets the minimum
requirements of American National Standard for Information
Sciences—Permanence of Paper for Printed Library Materials.
ANSI Z39.48–1984 (alk. paper)

Library of Congress Cataloging-in-Publication Data

Balentine, Samuel E. (Samuel Eugene), 1950-
Job / by Samuel E. Balentine.
p. cm. — (The Smyth & Helwys Bible commentary ; v.10)
Includes bibliographical references and index.
ISBN 1-57312-067-7 (hardcover : alk. paper)
1. Bible. O.T. Job—Commentaries.
I. Title. II Series.

BS1415.53.B35 2006
223'.107—dc22
Library of Congress Control Number: 2006030845

DEDICATION

For Betty
and Graham and Lauren

ADVANCE PRAISE

Rarely does one find a biblical commentary that is scholarly, in-depth, insightful, theological, and relevant. Balentine's work on Job is a masterpiece!

— *J. Randall O'Brien*
Baylor University

Balentine rises to the challenge of the book of Job in this rich exegetical and theological probing of its mysteries. As good as it gets as a commentary, however, this treatment of Job stands out all the more because of its marvelous collection of literary and artistic representations of the book and the themes with which it deals. The book of Job must have been created for this kind of commentary – or vice versa!

— *Patrick D. Miller*
Princeton Theological Seminary

If God's question to the Adversary, "Have you considered my servant Job?" were put to Samuel E. Balentine, modesty would prevent him from saying more than, "I have." Readers of this richly illustrated commentary, Job, however, will soon recognize that he has thought profoundly, written elegantly, and empathized fully with that object of a gratuitous divine test.

—*James L. Crenshaw*
Duke University

Sam Balentine has written a breath-taking commentary on the book of Job that is sure to be the beginning point of all subsequent Job study. His writing will compel exegetes to pay attention; more than that, it will occupy pastors and theologians with the complexity of articulating the "final truth" about God, and will be an authoritative voice in the great conversation among us concerning our contemporary moral crisis.

Balentine is a first rate exegete. But then, after he reads the text, he moves out in bold and daring ways to make fresh connections. He has digested every commentary, remembered every poem, taken into account every artistic portrayal. There is not a page of this commentary on which I was not led, in generative ways, to where I had not previously been. I cannot imagine a reader who will not find it to be so. Balentine's work is a demanding assurance that the "thickness" of humanity is still available in a way that refuses glib characterization. In this remarkable commentary series, Balentine has set a new standard of excellence . . . of artistic sensibility and of hard-nosed, faithful reading. As I have already said, "breath taking"!

—*Walter Brueggemann*
Columbia Theological Seminary

Samuel Balentine, one of our most sophisticated interpreters of the Old Testament, gives us a fresh and lucid theological reading of the book of Job. Gathering a remarkable array of resources from the wide worlds of art and literature that have been generated by Job, Balentine sensitively weaves this material into his own creative interpretation of the book. Speaking in a post-9/11 world which has been confronted anew with the reality of suffering and the problem of evil, Balentine's insightful and accessible commentary will benefit readers in both church and academy.

—*Terence E. Fretheim*
Luther Seminary

CONTENTS

ABBREVIATIONS USED IN
THIS COMMENTARY

Books of the Old Testament, Apocrypha, and New Testament are generally abbreviated in the Sidebars, parenthetical references, and notes according to the following system.

The Old Testament

Genesis	Gen
Exodus	Exod
Leviticus	Lev
Numbers	Num
Deuteronomy	Deut
Joshua	Josh
Judges	Judg
Ruth	Ruth
1–2 Samuel	1–2 Sam
1–2 Kings	1–2 Kgs
1–2 Chronicles	1–2 Chr
Ezra	Ezra
Nehemiah	Neh
Esther	Esth
Job	Job
Psalm (Psalms)	Ps (Pss)
Proverbs	Prov
Ecclesiastes	Eccl
or Qoheleth	Qoh
Song of Solomon	Song
or Song of Songs	Song
or Canticles	Cant
Isaiah	Isa
Jeremiah	Jer
Lamentations	Lam
Ezekiel	Ezek
Daniel	Dan
Hosea	Hos
Joel	Joel
Amos	Amos
Obadiah	Obad
Jonah	Jonah
Micah	Mic

Nahum	Nah
Habakkuk	Hab
Zephaniah	Zeph
Haggai	Hag
Zechariah	Zech
Malachi	Mal

The Apocrypha

1–2 Esdras	1–2 Esdr
Tobit	Tob
Judith	Jdt
Additions to Esther	Add Esth
Wisdom of Solomon	Wis
Ecclesiasticus or the Wisdom of Jesus Son of Sirach	Sir
Baruch	Bar
Epistle (or Letter) of Jeremiah	Ep Jer
Prayer of Azariah and the Song of the Three	Pr Azar
Daniel and Susanna	Sus
Daniel, Bel, and the Dragon	Bel
Prayer of Manasseh	Pr Man
1–4 Maccabees	1–4 Macc

The New Testament

Matthew	Matt
Mark	Mark
Luke	Luke
John	John
Acts	Acts
Romans	Rom
1–2 Corinthians	1–2 Cor
Galatians	Gal
Ephesians	Eph
Philippians	Phil
Colossians	Col
1–2 Thessalonians	1–2 Thess
1–2 Timothy	1–2 Tim
Titus	Titus
Philemon	Phlm
Hebrews	Heb
James	Jas
1–2 Peter	1–2 Pet
1–2–3 John	1–2–3 John
Jude	Jude
Revelation	Rev

Other commonly used abbreviations include:

BCE	Before the Common Era
CE	Common Era
C.	century
c.	*circa* (around "that time")
cf.	*confer* (compare)
ch.	chapter
chs.	chapters
ed.	edition or edited by or editor
eds.	editors
e.g.	*exempli gratia* (for example)
et al.	*et alia* (and others)
f./ff.	and the following one(s)
gen. ed.	general editor
ibid.	*ibidem* (in the same place)
i.e.	*id est* (that is)
lit.	literally
n.d.	no date
sg.	singular
trans.	translated by or translator(s)
vol(s).	volume(s)
v.	verse
vv.	verses

Selected additional written works cited by abbreviations include the following. A complete listing of abbreviations can be referenced in *The SBL Handbook of Style* (Peabody MA: Hendrickson, 1999):

AB	Anchor Bible
ABD	*Anchor Bible Dictionary*
ANET	*Ancient Near Eastern Texts Relating to the Old Testament*
BibInt	*Biblical Interpretation*
BR	*Bible Review*
BZAW	Beihefte zur Zeitschrift für die alttestamentliche Wissenschaft
CBQ	*Catholic Biblical Quatrerly*
CBQMS	Catholic Biblical Quarterly, Monograph Series
ChrLit	*Christianity and Literature*
DCH	*Dictionary of Classical Hebrew*
ER	*The Encyclopedia of Religion*
FRLANT	Forschungen zur Religion und Literatur des Alten und Neuen Testaments
HBT	*Horizons in Biblical Theology*
HTR	*Harvard Theological Review*

HUCA	*Hebrew Union College Annual*
IB	*Interpreter's Bible*
Int	*Interpretation*
JB	Jerusalem Bible
JBL	*Journal of Biblical Literature*
JNES	*Journal for Near Eastern Studies*
JQR	*Jewish Quarterly Review*
JSOT	*Journal for the Study of the Old Testament*
JSOTSup	Journal for the Study of the Old Testament, Supplement Series
JSS	*Journal of Semitic Studies*
JTS	*Journal of Theological Studies*
KAT	Kommentar zum Alten Testament
KJV	King James Version
LXX	Septuagint
MDOG	Mitteilungen der Deutschen Orient-Gesellschaft
MT	Masoretic Text
NAB	New American Bible
NIB	The New Interpreter's Bible
NICOT	New International Commentary on the Old Testament
NIV	New International Version
NJB	New Jerusalem Bible
NJPS	New JPS Translation (Tanakh)
NRSV	New Revised Standard Version
OTL	Old Testament Library
PRSt	*Perspectives in Religious Studies*
RB	*Revue Biblique*
REB	Revised English Bible
ResQ	*Restoration Quarterly*
RevExp	*Review & Expositor*
SBLDS	Society of Biblical Literature, Dissertation Series
TEV	Today's English Version
TLOT	Theological Lexicon of the Old Testament
TOTC	Tyndale Old Testament Commentaries
VT	*Vetus Testamentum*
VTSup	Supplements to Vetus Testamentum
WBC	Word Biblical Commentary
WMANT	Wissenschaftliche Monographien zum Alten and Neuen Testament
ZAW	*Zeitschrift für alttestamentliche Wissenschaft*

SERIES PREFACE

The *Smyth & Helwys Bible Commentary* is a visually stimulating and user-friendly series that is as close to multimedia in print as possible. Written by accomplished scholars with all students of Scripture in mind, the primary goal of the *Smyth & Helwys Bible Commentary* is to make available serious, credible biblical scholarship in an accessible and less intimidating format.

Far too many Bible commentaries fall short of bridging the gap between the insights of biblical scholars and the needs of students of God's written word. In an unprecedented way, the *Smyth & Helwys Bible Commentary* brings insightful commentary to bear on the lives of contemporary Christians. Using a multimedia format, the volumes employ a stunning array of art, photographs, maps, and drawings to illustrate the truths of the Bible for a visual generation of believers.

The *Smyth & Helwys Bible Commentary* is built upon the idea that meaningful Bible study can occur when the insights of contemporary biblical scholars blend with sensitivity to the needs of lifelong students of Scripture. Some persons within local faith communities, however, struggle with potentially informative biblical scholarship for several reasons. Oftentimes, such scholarship is cast in technical language easily grasped by other scholars, but not by the general reader. For example, lengthy, technical discussions on every detail of a particular scriptural text can hinder the quest for a clear grasp of the whole. Also, the format for presenting scholarly insights has often been confusing to the general reader, rendering the work less than helpful. Unfortunately, responses to the hurdles of reading extensive commentaries have led some publishers to produce works for a general readership that merely skim the surface of the rich resources of biblical scholarship. This commentary series incorporates works of fine art in an accurate and scholarly manner, yet the format remains "user-friendly." An important facet is the presentation and explanation of images of art, which interpret the biblical material or illustrate how the biblical material has been understood and interpreted in the past. A visual generation of believers deserves a commentary series that contains not only the all-important textual commentary on Scripture, but images, photographs, maps, works of fine art, and drawings that bring the text to life.

The *Smyth & Helwys Bible Commentary* makes serious, credible biblical scholarship more accessible to a wider audience. Writers and editors alike present information in ways that encourage readers to gain a better understanding of the Bible. The editorial board has worked to develop a format that is useful and usable, informative and pleasing to the eye. Our writers are reputable scholars who participate in the community of faith and sense a calling to communicate the results of their scholarship to their faith community.

The *Smyth & Helwys Bible Commentary* addresses Christians and the larger church. While both respect for and sensitivity to the needs and contributions of other faith communities are reflected in the work of the series authors, the authors speak primarily to Christians. Thus the reader can note a confessional tone throughout the volumes. No particular "confession of faith" guides the authors, and diverse perspectives are observed in the various volumes. Each writer, though, brings to the biblical text the best scholarly tools available and expresses the results of their studies in commentary and visuals that assist readers seeking a word from the Lord for the church.

To accomplish this goal, writers in this series have drawn from numerous streams in the rich tradition of biblical interpretation. The basic focus is the biblical text itself, and considerable attention is given to the wording and structure of texts. Each particular text, however, is also considered in the light of the entire canon of Christian Scriptures. Beyond this, attention is given to the cultural context of the biblical writings. Information from archaeology, ancient history, geography, comparative literature, history of religions, politics, sociology, and even economics is used to illuminate the culture of the people who produced the Bible. In addition, the writers have drawn from the history of interpretation, not only as it is found in traditional commentary on the Bible but also in literature, theater, church history, and the visual arts. Finally, the *Commentary* on Scripture is joined with *Connections* to the world of the contemporary church. Here again, the writers draw on scholarship in many fields as well as relevant issues in the popular culture.

This wealth of information might easily overwhelm a reader if not presented in a "user-friendly" format. Thus the heavier discussions of detail and the treatments of other helpful topics are presented in special-interest boxes, or *Sidebars*, clearly connected to the passages under discussion so as not to interrupt the flow of the basic interpretation. The result is a commentary on Scripture that focuses on the theological significance of a text while also offering the reader a rich array of additional information related to the text and its interpretation.

An accompanying CD-ROM offers powerful searching and research tools. The commentary text, sidebars, and visuals are all reproduced on a CD that is fully indexed and searchable. Pairing a text version with a digital resource is a distinctive feature of the *Smyth & Helwys Bible Commentary.*

Combining credible biblical scholarship, user-friendly study features, and sensitivity to the needs of a visually oriented generation of believers creates a unique and unprecedented type of commentary series. With insight from many of today's finest biblical scholars and a stunning visual format, it is our hope that the *Smyth & Helwys Bible Commentary* will be a welcome addition to the personal libraries of all students of Scripture.

The Editors

HOW TO USE
THIS COMMENTARY

The *Smyth & Helwys Bible Commentary* is written by accomplished biblical scholars with a wide array of readers in mind. Whether engaged in the study of Scripture in a church setting or in a college or seminary classroom, all students of the Bible will find a number of useful features throughout the commentary that are helpful for interpreting the Bible.

Basic Design of the Volumes

Each volume features an Introduction to a particular book of the Bible, providing a brief guide to information that is necessary for reading and interpreting the text: the historical setting, literary design, and theological significance. Each Introduction also includes a comprehensive outline of the particular book under study.

Each chapter of the commentary investigates the text according to logical divisions in a particular book of the Bible. Sometimes these divisions follow the traditional chapter segmentation, while at other times the textual units consist of sections of chapters or portions of more than one chapter. The divisions reflect the literary structure of a book and offer a guide for selecting passages that are useful in preaching and teaching.

An accompanying CD-ROM offers powerful searching and research tools. The commentary text, Sidebars, and visuals are all reproduced on a CD that is fully indexed and searchable. Pairing a text version with a digital resource also allows unprecedented flexibility and freedom for the reader. Carry the text version to locations you most enjoy doing research while knowing that the CD offers a portable alternative for travel from the office, church, classroom, and your home.

Commentary and Connections

As each chapter explores a textual unit, the discussion centers around two basic sections: *Commentary* and *Connections*. The analysis of a passage, including the details of its language, the history reflected in the text, and the literary forms found in the text, are the main focus of the *Commentary* section. The primary concern of the *Commentary* section is to explore the theological issues presented by the Scripture passage. *Connections* presents potential applications of the insights provided in the *Commentary* section. The *Connections* portion of each chapter considers what issues are relevant for teaching and suggests useful methods and resources. *Connections* also identifies themes suitable for sermon planning and suggests helpful approaches for preaching on the Scripture text.

Sidebars

The *Smyth & Helwys Bible Commentary* provides a unique hyperlink format that quickly guides the reader to additional insights. Since other more technical or supplementary information is vital for understanding a text and its implications, the volumes feature distinctive Sidebars that provide a wealth of information on such matters as:

• Historical information (such as chronological charts, lists of kings or rulers, maps, descriptions of monetary systems, descriptions of special groups, descriptions of archaeological sites or geographical settings).

• Graphic outlines of literary structure (including such items as poetry, chiasmus, repetition, epistolary form).

• Definition or brief discussions of technical or theological terms and issues.

• Insightful quotations that are not integrated into the running text but are relevant to the passage under discussion.

• Notes on the history of interpretation (Augustine on the Good Samaritan, Luther on James, Stendahl on Romans, etc.).

• Line drawings, photographs, and other illustrations relevant for understanding the historical context or interpretive significance of the text.

• Presentation and discussion of works of fine art that have interpreted a Scripture passage.

Each Sidebar is printed in color and is referenced at the appropriate place in the *Commentary* or *Connections* section with a color-coded title that directs the reader to the relevant sidebar. Select Sidebars may be located on the CD-ROM only. These are noted as [CD:] and can be found in a separate collection on the CD-ROM. In addition, helpful icons appear in the Sidebars, which provide the reader with visual cues to the type of material that is explained in each Sidebar. Throughout the commentary, these four distinct hyperlinks provide useful links in an easily recognizable design.

AΩ

Alpha & Omega Language

This icon identifies the information as a language-based tool that offers further exploration of the Scripture selection. This could include syntactical information, word studies, popular or additional uses of the word(s) in question, additional contexts in which the term appears, and the history of the term's translation. All non-English terms are transliterated into the appropriate English characters.

Culture/Context

This icon introduces further comment on contextual or cultural details that shed light on the Scripture selection. Describing the place and time to which a Scripture passage refers is often vital to the task of biblical interpretation. Sidebar items introduced with this icon could include geographical, historical, political, social, topographical, or economic information. Here, the reader may find an excerpt of an ancient text or inscription that sheds light on the text. Or one may find a description of some element of ancient religion such as Baalism in Canaan or the Hero cult in the Mystery Religions of the Greco-Roman world.

Interpretation

Sidebars that appear under this icon serve a general interpretive function in terms of both historical and contemporary renderings. Under this heading, the reader might find a selection from classic or contemporary literature that illuminates the Scripture text or a significant quotation from a famous sermon that addresses the passage. Insights are drawn from various sources, including literature, worship, theater, church history, and sociology.

Additional Resources Study

Here, the reader finds a convenient list of useful resources for further investigation of the selected Scripture text, including books, journals, websites, special collections, organizations, and societies. Specialized discussions of works not often associated with biblical studies may also appear here.

Additional Features

Each volume also includes a basic Bibliography on the biblical book under study. Other bibliographies on selected issues are often included that point the reader to other helpful resources.

Notes at the end of each chapter provide full documentation of sources used and contain additional discussions of related matters.

Abbreviations used in each volume are explained in a list of abbreviations found after the Table of Contents.

Readers of the *Smyth & Helwys Bible Commentary* can regularly visit the Internet support site for news, information, updates, and enhancements to the series at <**www.helwys.com/commentary**>.

Several thorough indexes enable the reader to locate information quickly. These indexes include:

• An *Index of Sidebars* groups content from the special-interest boxes by category (maps, fine art, photographs, drawings, etc.).

• An *Index of Scriptures* lists citations to particular biblical texts.

• An *Index of Topics* lists alphabetically the major subjects, names, topics, and locations referenced or discussed in the volume.

• An *Index of Authors* organizes contemporary authors whose works are cited in the volume.

AUTHOR'S PREFACE

God initiates the drama that sets the compass for this commentary with a question: "Have you considered my servant Job?" (Job 1:8). Perhaps, in some distant time past, such a question was necessary. Personally, I cannot remember a time when I was not thinking about Job. Even before I discovered the book that bears his name, I already knew the basic plotlines of Job's story. The first concrete signpost I can remember was the tragic death of my best friend when I was a boy. Joe had overcome a childhood bout with polio only to meet an opponent on the football field that he could not match. How does one cope with the experience of being a pallbearer at the age of fifteen? Thirty-five years later, equipped with three academic degrees, including a Doctor of Philosophy in biblical studies from one of the most prestigious universities in the world, I walked with another best friend toward his death. His adversary—cancer—was different, but the question that defined my grief was the same as before. "Why?" If anything, this experience has been even more devastating, for now, after a lifetime of study, I concede that theological expertise can be trumped by the hard realities of life. I am confident that I am not the only one who has sat with Job on the ash heap of a life undone by suffering "for no reason" (Job 2:3). On the other side of this commentary, I am also hopeful that others will join me in gratitude for Job's companionship in the journey. Even if immersing ourselves in his story leaves us without definitive answers to the questions that dog our faith, we may be comforted by the biblical affirmation that we are not alone in asking them.

I am grateful to those who have provided support for the journey that results in this book. The Louisville Institute provided a generous Christian Faith and Life Sabbatical Grant that enabled me to spend a year visiting various museums throughout the world in order to view and study how artists "exegete" Job. My former and current institutions, Baptist Theological Seminary at Richmond (1993–2004) and Union Theological Seminary-Presbyterian School of Christian Education (2004–) provided sabbatical leaves that afforded the time for writing and financial support for student research assistants, who helped me find the various bibliographical resources I needed. They deserve to be named: Robin McCall, Woody Jenkins, and especially Richard B. Vinson, Jr., who helped with the preparation of the indices. Special thanks to Jody Rawley, who helped me at the eleventh hour, out of sheer friendship, track down many elusive references. I am also pleased and proud that my former student Marcus Mims has allowed me to include his charcoal drawings—"Seven Days of Silence"—which began as part of an independent study on Job he did with me some years ago.

I owe more than I can say to my family, to my wife Betty, and my children Lauren and Graham, to whom I dedicate this book. No one knows more than they what it means to offer "consolation and comfort" (see Job 2:11; 42:11) to those who sit with Job on the ash heap of suffering. Without their unwavering support, I could have never stayed the course in this wrenching and rewarding journey with Job.

[T]he deepest truth I have learned is that if one accepts the loss, if one gives up clinging to what is irretrievably gone, then the nothing which is left is not barren but is enormously fruitful. Everything that one has lost comes flooding back again out of the darkness, and one's relation to it is new—free and unclinging. But the richness of the nothing contains more, it is the all-possible, it is the spring of freedom.[1]

NOTE

[1] R. Bellah, *Beyond Belief: Essays on Religion in a Post-Traditional World* (New York: Harper and Row, 1970), xx-xxi.

INTRODUCTION

"It is the greatest thing ever written with pen," the Scottish essayist and historian Thomas Carlyle (1795–1881) said of the book of Job. "There is nothing, I think, written in the Bible or out of it of equal merit."[1] This is high praise indeed, especially when considered in the context of the regard most have for the Bible's overall literary excellence. As John Gardner noted in an op-ed piece more than a century later, justifying why the Bible remains on his "recommended reading list," "God is an extremely uneven writer, but when He's good, no one can beat Him."[2]

One of the reasons many consider Job to be the crown jewel of biblical literature is its claim to speak "what is right" about God. In the midst of so many words in this world about God—words inside the Bible and outside, from writers, artists, poets, musicians, and others across the breadth of every medium for creative expression—this book offers a truly astonishing declaration. Thus it begins, "There once was a man in the land of Uz whose name was Job" (1:1). Forty-two chapters later, the story concludes by affirming that of all those in this book who talk about God—Eliphaz, Bildad, Zophar, and Elihu—Job alone has spoken the truth. More remarkable still, this claim comes with God's imprimatur, for it is God who twice dismisses all other contributors by saying, "You have not spoken about me what is right, as my servant Job has done" (42:7, 8). These last words have the ring of a divine commission, freighted perhaps with an imperative equal to that which Jesus gave his disciples (cf. Matt 28:18-20): "Go therefore" and do "as my servant Job has done."

J. Hempel accents this claim and its summons by concluding that the book of Job is "the *struggle* for the *last truth* about God."[3] The word that defines the challenge for every reader of this book is "struggle." It is not only that God's assessment comes at the end of forty-two difficult chapters. Nor is it only because scholars cannot determine with certainty who wrote this book or when, where, how, or for what historical reasons it achieved its present form. The struggle results instead from the fact that whatever Job's truth may be, he was neither the *first* nor the *last* to try to articulate it. The struggle for the truth about what it means to live in a world where order breaks down and chaos runs amok, where the innocent suffer and the wicked thrive, where cries for help go unanswered—by

Job

Jusepe de Ribera (1591-1652). *Job*. Galleria Nazionale, Parma, Italy (Credit: Scala/Art Resource, NY)

powers divine or human—is universal and, as far as we can know in this world, ongoing. If the book of Job has something of import to say about the "*last* truth about God," it does so by contributing its witness to an abiding, ever-vexing, existential conundrum. From the philosophical ruminations of David Hume (1711–1766), to the dramatization of the Joban story in *J.B.* (1956) by the playwright Archibald MacLeish, to the ruminations of Rabbi Harold Kushner in *When Bad Things Happen to Good People* (1981), the question that dogs human existence remains essentially unchanged: If God is just and good, why do the innocent suffer and the guilty thrive? As the British novelist Muriel Spark has observed, the Joban problem is "the only problem, in fact, worth discussing."[4] [The Only Problem] In short, the Joban drama is perhaps the longest-running

---

The Only Problem

The protagonist in *The Only Problem* is Harvey Gotham, who is writing a monograph on the book of Job. As the project proceeds, Harvey finds his own life turned upside down by unexpected calamities, which heighten his appreciation for the issues addressed in this biblical story. Muriel Spark introduces the plot with these words:

> Harvey was a rich man; he was in his mid-thirties. He had started writing a monograph about the book of Job and the problems it deals with. For he could not face that a benevolent Creator, one whose charming and delicious light descended and spread over the world, and being powerful everywhere, could condone the unspeakable sufferings of the world; that God did permit all suffering and was therefore, by logic of his omnipotence, the actual author of it, he was at a loss how to square with the existence of God, given the premise that God is good.
> "It is the only problem," Harvey had always said. Now, Harvey believed in God, and this was what tormented him. "It's the only problem, in fact, worth discussing." (22)

Harvey's friend, Edward Janzen, shared his long-standing interest in the book of Job, and so it did not surprise him when Harvey retreated to his cottage to immerse himself in reflection upon its issues. But, like Job's biblical friends, when Edward paid his friend a visit and saw the stress of the work written in his face, he was taken back. He reflected on a conversation they had once shared in their university days, which now seemed to say as much about Harvey as about Job:

> "Did you know," Edward remembered saying, "that when Job was finally restored to prosperity and family abundance, one of his daughters was called Box of Eye-Paint? Can we really imagine our tormented hero enjoying his actual reward?"
> "No," said Harvey. "He continued to suffer."
> "Not according to the Bible."
> "Still, I'm convinced he suffered on. Perhaps more."
> "It seems odd, doesn't it," Edward had said, "after he sat on a dung-heap and suffered from skin sores and put up with his friends' gloating, and lost his family and his cattle, that he should have to go on suffering."
> "It became a habit," Harvey said, "for he not only argued the problem of suffering, *he suffered the problem of the argument. And that is incurable.*" (32, emphasis added)

Muriel Spark, *The Only Problem* (New York: G. P. Putnam's Sons, 1984).

story in the history of human experience. The biblical Job is but one, even if one of the best, of a cast of characters who has played this role.

JOB BEFORE THE BIBLE

Whatever date we assign to the book of Job, we can be sure the biblical writer(s) did not create the story out of whole cloth. From the second millennium Sumerian composition known as "Man and His God" to the fragmentary Job manuscripts from Qumran (second–first century BCE: 2Q15, 4Q99, 4Q100, 4Q101; cf. two portions of an Aramaic Targum of Job: 4Q157; 11QtgJob), textual evidence confirms that innocent suffering, random disorder, divine injustice, and the futility of life were issues of major concern throughout ancient Egypt, Mesopotamia, and Syria-Palestine. Indeed, we would be hard pressed to find a corpus of texts from any place or time in ancient history where such issues are not present. By the time biblical writers penned this book, others had been exploring similar issues for more than 2,000 years.[5]

This wider context for encountering the Bible's version of the story keeps us mindful that the Joban problem is no aberration; instead, it stands at the center of what it means to be human. For as long as men and women have walked this earth, they have shared the journey with someone, somewhere, named Job. ["Job Is No Longer Man; He Is Humanity!"] We cannot do justice to the full range of ancient Near Eastern texts that are pertinent to this discussion, but a sampling may be sufficient to show that the biblical Job's arrival in the "land of Uz" (1:1) had been long anticipated.

"Job Is No Longer Man; He Is Humanity!"

Alphonse de Lamartine (1790–1869), a poet and outspoken statesman of French romanticism, read the book of Job as the words of a poet who spoke "from the depths of the centuries."

In this epic poem of the soul . . . Job speaks in the tongue of the greatest poet who ever uttered human speech. His language is eloquence and poetry fused together all at once into all the cries of mankind. He narrates, discusses, listens, replies; he grows angry, challenges, apostrophizes, rants, and scolds; he cries out, sings, weeps, jeers, implores; he reflects, he judges himself, he repents, he grows calm, he worships, and soars on the wings of his religious enthusiasm far above his own anguish; from the depths of his despair he justifies God against his own self; he says: "It is good! "

And then, these words in conclusion: "Job is no longer man; he is humanity! A race which can feel, think, and speak in such a voice is truly worthy of a dialogue with the divine; it is worthy of conversing with its creator."

Cours familier de littérature (Paris, 1956), II, 441; cited in N. Glatzer, ed., *The Dimensions of Job: A Study and Selected Readings* (New York: Schocken Books, 1969), 42-43.

Sumerian Jobs

"The Sumerian Job," properly known as "Man and His God," is a second millennium (c. 1750 BCE) copy of a text that may be several centuries older.[6] The composition records the lamentations of a righteous sufferer who has inexplicably lost his health, wealth, and respect. The burden of the lament is a god who appears indifferent to the sufferer's plight:

> My companion says not a true word to me,
> My friend gives the lie to my righteous word.
> The man of deceit has conspired against me,
> (And) you, my god, do not thwart him.
> You carry off my understanding,
> The wicked has conspired against me.
> Angered you, stormed about, planned evil. . . .
> I, the discerning, why am I counted among the ignorant? . . .
> On the day shares were allotted to all, my allotted share was suffering.
> (ll. 35-46)

This "Sumerian Job," unlike his biblical counterpart, accepts the counsel of the sages, who instruct him to give up his lament for the truth of conventional wisdom: all suffering is the result of sin.

> They say—the sages—a word righteous (and) straightforward:
> "Never has a sinless child been born to its mother,
> . . . a sinless workman has not existed from of old". . .
> My god, now that you have shown me my sins, . . .
> I, the young man, would confess my sins before you. (ll. 101-104, 113)

The end of the text reports that when the sufferer confessed his sins, the god rewarded him for proper conduct and turned his "suffering into joy" (l. 125).

Mesopotamian Jobs

A number of Mesopotamian texts anticipate issues addressed in the book of Job. Of these, two may be singled out for special mention.

"I Will Praise the Lord of Wisdom" (*Ludlul bel nemiqi*), sometimes referred to as the "Babylonian Job," comprises four tablets from Ashurbanipal's library in Nineveh. The texts date to the seventh century BCE, but they are likely copies of texts composed in the second millennium.[7] The text records the monologue of a noble person who has undergone a reversal of fortunes and has become a social outcast. He asks why the god Marduk has allowed his servant to suffer, in the process probing a number of Joban issues. For example, he complains that his fidelity counts for nothing because his gods have abandoned him:

My ill luck has increased, and I do not find the right.
I called to my god, but he did not show his face,
I prayed to my goddess, but she did not raise her head.
The diviner with his inspection has not got to the root of the matter,
Nor has the dream priest with his libation elucidated my case. . . .
Like one who has not made libations to his god,
Nor invoked his goddess at table,
Does not engage in prostration, nor takes cognizance of bowing down;
From whose mouth supplication and prayer is lacking,
Who has done nothing on holy days, and despised sabbaths,
Who in his negligence has despised the gods' rites,
Has not taught his people reverence and worship,
But has eaten his food without invoking his god,
And abandoned his goddess by not bringing a flour offering,
Like one who has grown torpid and forgotten his lord,
Has frivolously sworn a solemn oath by his god,
   (like such an one) do I appear.
For myself, I gave attention to supplication and prayer:
To me prayer was discretion, sacrifice my rule.
The day of reverencing the god was a joy to my heart;
The day of the goddess's procession was profit and gain to me.
   (ii.3-7, 12-26)

Given his plight, the sufferer concludes that the will of the gods is simply inscrutable; divine justice is not comparable to human justice:

I wish I knew that these things were pleasing to one's god!
What is proper to oneself is an offense to one's god,
What in one's own heart seems despicable is proper to one's god.
Who knows the will of the gods in heaven?
Who understands the plans of the underworld gods?
Where have mortals learnt the way of a god? (ii.33-38)

In a world full of misery, the only thing this sufferer can know with certainty is that the deity is part of the problem, even if the plaintiff is too fearful to make the accusation explicit: "His [i.e., Marduk's] hand was heavy upon me, I could not bear it. My dread of him was alarming" (iii.1-2). Only when Marduk's mercy replaces his wrath does the sufferer experience relief, whereupon praise replaces lament:

After the mind of my Lord had quietened
And the heart of merciful Marduk was appeased, . . .
The Lord took hold of me,
The Lord set me on my feet,
The Lord gave me life . . .
Mortals, as many as there are, give praise to Marduk! (iii.50-51;
   iv. 2-4, 42)

Although the "blasphemous implications"[8] in the Babylonian Job's wonderments about innocent suffering are similar to those of his biblical counterpart, the poem's dominant concern is the sufferer's eventual restoration. There is no attempt to explain the problem or to offer a solution, other than to affirm that the deity makes all things right in the end. [CD: "The Babylonian Job " or "The Babylonian *Pilgrim's Progress*"?]

A second Mesopotamian text with strong similarities to Job is the "Babylonian Theodicy," an acrostic poem of twenty-seven stanzas, eleven lines each, written c. 1000 BCE.[9] The poem is cast as a dialogue between a sufferer and his companion. The sufferer complains that he was abandoned as an orphan at an early age and left vulnerable to all manner of oppression and affliction. The friend responds by assuring him that while suffering is the common lot of all, those who remain steadfast will ultimately be better off for the experience:

Respected friend, what you say is gloomy.
You let your mind dwell on evil, my dear fellow. . . .
When you consider mankind as a whole,
. . . it is not . . . that has made the impoverished first-born rich. . . .
He who waits on his god has a protecting angel,
The humble man who fears his goddess accumulates wealth. (ll. 12-13,
   18-19, 21-22)

The sufferer counters by complaining that his friend has not understood. If he will but look around, he will see that nature itself offers proof that the wicked prosper at the expense of the righteous:

My friend, your mind is a river whose spring never fails,. . .
Pay attention for a moment; hear my words. . . . (ll. 23, 26)

The onager, the wild ass, who filled itself with. . [.]
Did it pay attention to the giver of the assured divine oracle?
The savage lion who devoured the choicest flesh,
Did it bring its flour offering to appease the goddess's anger?
[. .].the nouveau riche who has multiplied his wealth,
Did he weigh out precious gold for the goddess Mami?
[Have I] held back offerings? I have prayed to my god,

[I have] pronounced the blessing over the goddess's regular sacrifices,
   (ll. 48-55)

The friend responds by citing a conventional maxim: the wisdom of the gods is simply incomprehensible to humans. In the end, the friend contends, the wicked always get their just reward:

O palm tree of wealth, my precious brother,
Endowed with all wisdom, jewel of [gold,]
You are as stable as the earth, but the plan of the gods is remote.
Look at the superb wild ass on the [plain;]
The arrow will follow the gorer who trampled down the fields.
Come, consider the lion that you mentioned, the enemy of cattle.
For the crime which the lion committed the pit awaits him.
The opulent nouveau riche who heaps goods
Will be burnt at the stake by the king before his time. (ll. 56-64)

The sufferer finds the friend's explanation unacceptable and insists that piety is truly meaningless; if anything, devotion makes the faithful even more vulnerable to the whims of the deity:

Your mind is a north wind, a pleasant breeze for the peoples.
Choice friend, your advice is fine.
Just one word would I put before you.
Those who neglect the god go the way of prosperity,
While those who pray to the goddess are impoverished and dispossessed.
In my youth I sought the will of my god;
With prostration and prayer I followed my goddess.
But I was bearing a profitless corvee as a yoke.
My god decreed instead of wealth destitution. (ll. 67-75)

And so the dialogue continues, through repeated exchanges. The sufferer asserts the inexplicable reality of his plight. The friend responds with disputation and counter-arguments. By the end of the poem, the two reach a resolution of sorts. The sufferer thanks his friend for his companionship and asks him to join in a petition to the gods for mercy:

You are kind, my friend; behold my grief.
Help me, look on my distress; know it. . . .
May the god who has thrown me off give help,
May the goddess who has [abandoned me] show mercy,
For the shepherd Samas guides the people like a god. (ll. 287-88, 295-97)

While there are clear parallels between the "Babylonian Theodicy" and Job, there are also notable differences.

• The "friend" in this Babylonian text maintains respect and sympathy for the sufferer to the very end. In their initial approach, Job's friends are also kind and sympathetic (Job 4–14), but the more Job refuses their counsel, the more they stiffen their resolve to wrench a confession of guilt from him (Job 15–21). When this fails, they give up all pretense of listening to his side of the case. Acting as both judge and jury, the friends get the outcome they seek by simply pronouncing Job guilty (Job 22–27).

• The sufferer in the "Babylonian Theodicy" implies that the gods responsible for maintaining justice in the world have failed him, but he never directly challenges them. In the end, he is satisfied to air his grievances before his friend and to wait, in contrition, for the merciful return of the god who has abandoned him. Job, by contrast, becomes increasingly dissatisfied with the friends who will not listen to him and ever more determined to address his complaints and accusations directly to the God he holds responsible for his misfortune (e.g., 7:7-21; 10:1-17; 13:20-28; 30:20-31; 31:35-37). In the end, Job speaks of a change of heart (42:5-6), but as the commentary below will suggest, it is far from clear that his words express contrition.

• The "dialogue" in the "Babylonian Theodicy" is between the sufferer and his companion. The gods never speak, never intervene, never have more than a spoken-about presence in this debate about innocent suffering. By contrast, the *first* and *last* "character" to speak in the biblical Job's story is God (1:7; 42:7). Moreover, although the dialogue between Job and his friends is extensive (Job 4–27), the dialogue on which the book turns is that between God (who, speaking with hurricane force, most clearly does intervene) and Job (Job 38–42).

Egyptian Jobs

Joban issues of innocent suffering and divine injustice, to the extent they were explored at all in ancient Egypt, were addressed somewhat differently. This may be so for a number of reasons. [Egyptian Wisdom Literature] Even so, two texts deserve mention when considering possible Egyptian models for the biblical Job.

"The Protests of the Eloquent Peasant" (20th–18th centuries BCE), records the story of a peasant who appeared before the court of justice to complain about being robbed by a corrupt official. [10] His repeated

Egyptian Wisdom Literature

AΩ Two explanations have been offered as to why Egyptian literature takes a somewhat different approach to Joban issues.

T. Jacobsen has suggested that Egyptians regarded justice as more a "favor" or "privilege" than a "right." As most laws were by and large made by and for the king, who was considered divine, ordinary people did not have access to them and thus had no reason to expect that they were entitled to any justice other than that which they received at the king's pleasure. A second reason may be connected to the Egyptian belief in the afterlife. When rewards and punishments were not forthcoming in this life, one might trust that the problem would be rectified in the future life.

Whatever buffers such explanations may have provided in ancient Egyptian culture, it is clear that Egyptians devoted much time and thought to the exploration of a wide range of justice issues conventionally associated with what we find in the Wisdom Literature of the Old Testament. Broadly speaking, these explorations are found in two kinds of texts: "teachings" or "instructions" (e.g., "The Instruction of Amen-em-opet"), which essentially affirm traditional values, and "lamentations," comprised of complaints, protests, satire, and other reflective forms, which submit established values to pessimistic scrutiny (e.g., "The Protests of the Eloquent Peasant").

For further reading on the connections between Egyptian wisdom literature and the Old Testament, see R. J. Williams, "Egyptian Wisdom Literature," vol. 2 of *ABD*, ed. D. N. Freedman (New York: Doubleday, 1992), 395-99; G. E. Bryce, *A Legacy of Wisdom: The Egyptian Contribution to the Wisdom of Israel* (Lewisburg PA: Bucknell University Press, 1979).

T. Jacobsen, *The Intellectual Adventure of Ancient Man* (Chicago: University of Chicago Press, 1946), 208.

Papyrus from "The Instruction of Amen-emo-pet"
Third Intermediate Period, 1000 BC. Lines from a poem which lacks a narrative framework; instead it is divided into thirty sections or maxims, each concerned with one topic.

British Museum, London, Great Britain. (Credit: HIP/Art Resource, NY)

appeals to the chief steward, who administers the judicial system on the king's behalf, raise a number of social justice issues that resonate with those the biblical Job expects God to address (e.g., Job 21:7-26; 24:1-25; 30:9-15).

O Chief Steward, my Lord, greatest of the great. . . . Because thou art the father of the orphan, the husband of the widow, the brother of the divorcee, and the apron of him that is motherless. Let me make thy name in this land according to every good law: a leader free from covetousness, a great man free from wrongdoing, one who destroys falsehood and brings justice into being, and who comes at the cry of him who gives voice. When I speak, mayest thou hear. Do justice, thou favored one whom the favored ones favor! Dispose of my burdens. Behold me, (how) burdened I am! Count me: behold I am lacking!

Do justice for the sake of the Lord of Justice, the justice of whose justice exists. Thou reed-pen, papyrus, and palette of Thoth, keep apart from doing evil!

Do not delay . . . Be not partial . . . Do not veil thy face against him whom thou knowest. Do not blind thy face against him who thou hast beheld. Do not rebuff him who petitions thee. (ll. 54-71, 305-306; B2: 105-107)

A second Egyptian text, "The Instruction of Amen-em-opet," dating between the tenth and sixth centuries BCE, is cited primarily for its similarities to the biblical book of Proverbs, especially Proverbs 22:17–24:22. As is the case with many of the biblical proverbs, these instructions do not question but instead affirm traditional beliefs about the rewards of the moral life. Nonetheless, the advice concerning how the righteous should respond to suffering echoes the conventional wisdom Job's friends urge him to accept:

Do not spend the night fearful of the morrow.
At daybreak what is the morrow like?
Man knows not what the morrow is like.
God is (always) in his success,
Whereupon man is in his failure;
One thing are the words which men say,
Another is that which the god does.
Say not, "I have no wrongdoing,"
Nor (yet) strain to seek quarreling.
As for wrongdoing, it belongs to the god;
It is sealed with his finger. (XIX, ll. 10-21)

The textual evidence from Sumeria, Mesopotamia, and Egypt does not prove that the biblical author of Job knew or was directly influenced by these prototypes. It does confirm, however, that the problem of righteous suffering did not emerge for the first time in Israelite thought. Whatever safeguards any society's institutions—religious, political, or academic—may use to mute its threat to stability, no civilization can avoid addressing the Jobs in its midst. [CD: "A Shadowy Figure in the Stains on an Old Wall"]

JOB IN THE BIBLE

If the biblical writers did not *create* Job, they certainly did flinch at the problem he posed for their view of God and the world. Exactly when they produced a "book" bearing Job's name is uncertain. Most would date the final composition between the seventh and fifth centuries BCE, that is, sometime within the exilic or early post-exilic period, when in the aftermath of the Babylonian exile, hard questions about the justice of God and innocent suffering were acute.[11] Whenever the biblical story of Job achieved its final form, it is clear that it is a composite, a collection of parts assembled through various stages into a whole. Concerning the "parts," there is widespread agreement. How, when, where, and why the parts eventually became a "whole" remains much debated.[12] Although it may be unsettling to discover that the book of Job was not written by Job, or by any other single "author" for that matter, we need not conclude that it is only a hodgepodge that lacks structure and coherence. As G. K. Chesterton (1874–1936) observed in his introduction to the book of Job, when we enter into any of the grand cathedrals of the world, each one constructed over many years by different artisans, we do not measure their beauty or their abiding witness to truth by the dates when their individual sections were completed. ["When You Deal with Any Ancient Artistic Creation, Do Not Suppose That It Is Anything Against It That It Grew Gradually."]

The Frame and the Center

The *frame* of the book consists of a prose prologue (1:1–2:13) and epilogue (42:7-17) that utilize a combination of speech and action to tell

---

"When You Deal with Any Ancient Artistic Creation, Do Not Suppose That It Is Anything Against It That It Grew Gradually."

When you deal with any ancient artistic creation, do not suppose that it is anything against it that it grew gradually. The book of Job may have grown gradually just as Westminster Abbey grew gradually. But the people who made the old folk poetry, like the people who made Westminster Abbey, did not attach that importance to the actual date and the actual author, that importance which is entirely the creation of the almost insane individualism of modern times. We may put aside the case of Job, as one complicated with religious difficulties, and take any other, say the case of the Iliad. Many people have maintained the characteristic formula of modern skepticism, that Homer was not written by Homer, but by another person of the same name. Just in the same way many have maintained that Moses was not Moses but another person called Moses. But the thing really to be remembered in the matter of the Iliad is that if other people did interpolate the passages, the thing did not create the same sense of shock as would be created by such proceedings in these individualistic times. The creation of the tribal epic was to some extent regarded as a tribal work, like the building of the tribal temple. Believe then, if you will, that the prologue of Job and the epilogue and the speech of Elihu are things inserted after the original work was composed. But do not suppose that such insertions have their obvious and spurious character which would belong to any insertions in a modern, individualistic book

Without going into questions of unity as understood by scholars, we may say of the scholarly riddle that the book has unity in the sense that all great traditional creations have unity; in the sense that Canterbury Cathedral has unity.

G. K. Chesterton, "Introduction to the Book of Job," *G. K. Chesterton as M.C., A Collection of Thirty-Seven Introductions by G. K. Chesterton*, selected and edited by J. P. de Foneska (Freeport NY: Libraries Press, 1967), 34.

the story of a righteous man who patiently suffers horrendous misfortune "for no reason" (2:3) and in the end is doubly rewarded for his unfailing fidelity. Taken as a set piece, this story, which many regard as the oldest part of the book, reads like an ancient version of a nineteenth-century Brothers Grimm fairy tale: "Once upon a time". . . "and they all lived happily ever after." Its enduring appeal is perhaps best illustrated by the single reference to Job in the New Testament, which has long seeded the popular estimation of Job's contribution to the faith community: "You have heard of the patience of Job, and have seen the end of the Lord; that the Lord is very pitiful, and of tender mercy" (Jas 5:11, KJV).[13]

The *center* of the book consists of a lengthy series of dialogues between Job and his friends (chs. 3–31) and between Job and God (38:1–42:6), most likely from a later author who found the "all's-well-that-ends-well" frame story unsatisfying. These dialogues are written in poetry, not prose, and are dominated by the speech of the characters, not their actions. Drawn primarily from the genres of disputation and lament, these speeches offer different profiles for the friends, Job, and God. The friends, who are silent and sympathetic in the prologue, become increasingly strident interlocutors; when they conclude their speeches, it is clear their primary objective is not to comfort Job but to condemn him. Job, whose prologue piety is undisturbed by either doubts or questions, fills the center of the book with curses, laments, and direct challenges to the moral order of the world and to the God who created it. And God, who is content to speak *about* Job's fidelity in the prologue while delegating the day-to-day details, whatever they may entail, to the *satan*, speaks *directly to* Job; indeed, by inviting Job into a dialogue that is both frightening and compelling, God takes extraordinary measures to discuss with him the intricate details of creation's day-to-day rhythms. Whether God's objective is to minimize Job's contribution to God's hopes and expectations for the world or to enhance it remains a matter for debate, but there can be little question that the whirlwind speeches (38–41) constitute a dramatic exchange between Creator and creature.

The structural relationship between the frame and the center effectively creates a story within a story. From a rhetorical standpoint, this results in a debate or, more properly speaking, a dialogue between different ways of addressing a nexus of issues anchored to the principle of retribution, which, simply stated, affirms that God can be trusted to prosper the righteous and punish the wicked. Whereas the prologue/epilogue essentially confirms this principle, the dialogues between Job and his friends contest it. The contrasting perspectives of the frame and the center bring into view an important but typically

Judaism as a Levitical Religion

My use of the term "levitical religion" draws upon the work of William Scott Green, who has been an important conversation partner for me as I have tried to think through Job's importance for Judaism. Green offers the following baseline assessment of Judaism:

Judaism is a levitical religion. It is grounded in a priestly vision of reality, as expressed in the Pentateuch, itself edited by priests. According to the Pentateuch, the central institution of covenant maintenance was the Temple cult. Levitical religion aims to create an order on earth—ethical, social, and physical—that is congenial to God's presence. It supposes that because human beings must build that order, there will be breaks in it. Israel and Israelites will transgress against commandments, either deliberately or unintentionally. In addition, there are other ruptures, which are not classified as sin but as uncleanness or ritual impurity. . . . Through its cultic system, levitical religion provides concrete means through which Israel and Israelites can repair a breach in the covenant relationship.

Measured against this baseline, the book of Job, Green suggests,". . . conforms neither neatly nor fully to the religious structure of Judaism. Rather, it stretches the levitical framework and sets it on altered footing."

William S. Green, "Stretching the Covenant: Job and Judaism," *RevExp* 99 (2002): 572, 573. See further Green's "Levitical Religion," *Judaism from Muhammed. An Interpretation: Turning Points and Focal Points*, ed. J. Neusner, A. J. Avery-Peck, W. S. Green (Leiden: Brill, 2006).

overlooked tension between "levitical religion," with its cult and rituals, and the challenge posed by those who question its adequacy for everyday life experiences. [Judaism as a Levitical Religion] The prologue/epilogue profiles Job as a blameless and devout mediator who offers efficacious sacrifices for his family and friends, thereby securing their good standing with God (1:5; 42:8). Although the cultic imagery is oblique, N. Habel has rightly noted that Job "plays the part of the perfect priest."[14]

By all accounts, Job's reliance upon the sacrificial system works, at least until he is himself afflicted with "loathsome sores" (2:3, 7), which according to priestly perspectives render him unclean and needful of the rituals he has offered to others (Lev 13–14). In short, the dialogues turn the table. The "priest" who once ministered to family and friends now becomes the one who needs the rituals of ministry extended to him. Job's condition, however, presents an enormous challenge to those who would be his priests, for by God's own admission Job suffers "for no reason" (2:3). The presumptive causal connection between sin and misfortune does not apply in his case. How can the conventional cultic rituals "console and comfort" (2:11; 42:11) an innocent sufferer like Job?

Inside the frame story, the dialogues explore this question. The friends urge Job to stay inside the affirmations of their retribution theology. If Job suffers, he must be guilty of sin, in which case the cult promises restoration in exchange for his confession and repentance (e.g., 8:5-7; 11:13-20; 22:21-27). Job counters that he cannot repent of sin he has not committed (6:28-30; 9:21; 10:7; 16:17; 19:6-7; cf. especially Job's oaths of innocence in ch. 31), which in turn threatens to

"Unless" and Other "Worry Words" in the Grammar of Faith

AΩ The Pulitzer Prize-winning author Carol Shields learned that she had stage 3 breast cancer just before Christmas 1998. On the other side of a mastectomy, followed by rounds of chemotherapy and radiation, she progressed to stage 4. As she looked squarely in the face of the death that stalked her, her publisher invited her to write something that might draw upon her life's journey. Shields responded by writing *Unless*, a fictional story published in 2002 some months before she died in July 2003. She begins on page 1 with the following words:

It happens that I am going through a period of great unhappiness and loss just now. All my life I've heard people speak of finding themselves in acute pain, bankrupt in spirit and body, but I've never understood what they meant. To lose. To have lost. I believed these visitations of darkness lasted only a few minutes or hours and that these saddened people, in between bouts, were occupied, as we all were, with the useful monotony of happiness. But happiness is not what I thought. Happiness is the lucky pane of glass you carry in your head. It takes all your cunning just to hang on to it, and once it's smashed you have to move into a different sort of life.

These are the words Shields gives to the protagonist of her story, Rita Winter, an accomplished writer who shares "useful monotony of happiness" with her husband Tom and their three accomplished children, Natalie, Christine, and Norah. In the midst of her happiness, something unpre-dictable and unforeseen happens. Her eldest daughter, Norah, nineteen years old, inexplicably drops out of college, moves out of her apartment, and opts outs of life. She now sits on a Toronto street corner, blank-eyed and begging, wearing around her neck a handmade sign that says simply, of all things, "Goodness." Rita and Tom conduct weekly drive-bys, hoping to catch a glimpse of Norah's face. Sometimes they stop and sit on the sidewalk with her; when they leave they try to be unobtrusive in slipping her money or food or warm clothing. Norah never speaks, never responds, never acknowledges their presence.

When Rita tries to return to her writing, she finds that the only words she can produce say "My heart is broken" (44). She now knows that life is not one continuous, flowing narrative, unimpeded by distraction or disappointment. It is instead full of isolated, often random events. To construct a coherent narrative of the pieces, Rita must learn how to use "little chips of grammar" (208), mostly adverbs and prepositions that are hard to define, like the ones Shields uses so deftly in the chapter titles that tell Rita's story, words like "nearly," "nevertheless," "so," "otherwise," "insofar as," and "despite." Of all these little words, none is more important or more required for her life's grammar than the word that bears the freight of the book's title, "unless." As Rita puts it, "unless" is the "worry word of the English language" (149). We will all be happy, unless . . . We will all be safe, unless . . . We will all believe *X*, unless . . .

The book of Job is constructed from its own "little chips of grammar." In the prologue, the most important of these is the little phrase "for no reason" (2:3).

C. Shields, *Unless* (London/New York: Fourth Estate, 2002).

nullify his place in the cult, *unless* somehow its rituals can be stretched to embrace his complaints and challenges to the God it serves. ["Unless" and Other "Worry Words" in the Grammar of Faith] William S. Green sharply states the problem Job presents:

F]rom a cultic . . . perspective, there is nothing concrete Job can do to repair his relationship with God. Sacrifice, repentance, and religious behaviors that develop from them are nugatory under these circumstances. Job cannot atone for a transgression he did not commit. No offering, no change of heart, can appease divine caprice or undo an affliction that happens for no reason.[15]

Chapter 28: "Where Shall Wisdom Be Found?"

At the end of the dialogues, chapter 28 introduces a lengthy meditation on the elusiveness of wisdom. Unlike the previous speeches, which typically begin by identifying the speaker, this poem is an anonymous soliloquy. It addresses no one directly, and it receives no response from the other speakers in the book. With a twice-repeated question, "Where then does wisdom come from?" (v. 28; cf. v. 12), the poem presents a typical reflection on a proverbial issue.[16] On the one hand, it answers its own question in a conventional way: "mortals do not know" (v. 13), "God knows" (v. 23). On the other, its last verse serves rhetorically and structurally to return the story to its framing compass: "the fear of the Lord, that is wisdom; and to depart from evil is understanding" (v. 28). "Fearing God" and "turning away from evil" are the virtues that define Job's prologue piety (1:1, 8; 2:3), *before* suffering silenced convictions he once had no reason to question.

Perhaps a later author, having considered Job's complaints in the center of the book, concluded that he had transgressed the boundary between God's inscrutable wisdom and human hubris. If so, then the rhetorical objective of this soliloquy may be to bring Job (and his readers) back full circle to original commitments. Because mortals cannot know what God knows, the better course of wisdom is simply to accept, without question or doubt, whatever God gives or takes away (1:21). As attractive as this counsel may be, its contribution to the book's plotline effectively *increases* the tensions already present, for on the other side of chapter 28, Job takes up his discourse "again" (Job 29–31). Once again, he defends his integrity, protests his mistreatment, and demands that God respond to his quest for wisdom, however arrogant and inadequate it may be.

Chapters 32–37: The Speeches of Elihu

The dialogues with the three friends climax with a closing speech from Job in which he issues a formal challenge to God: "Let the Almighty answer me!" (31:35). When "The words of Job are ended" (31:40), the stage is fully set for God's response to the challenge. When a fourth friend named Elihu, elsewhere unmentioned, preempts God's appearance with his own lengthy discourse on the meaning of suffering, we may be reasonably certain that his words represent a still later addition to the book. The presence of the Elihu speeches in the Job manuscripts discovered at Qumran confirms that they had been added at least by the first century BCE. In terms of their linguistic characteristics and thematic focus, Elihu's speeches likely provide "the first commentary" on what had become, in effect, the "book" of Job.[17]

Here too, however, the insertion of Elihu effectively *increases*, rather than *diminishes*, the preexistent tensions within the book. Both Elihu's authorial creator/narrator (32:1-5) and Elihu as a character in his own right (32:6-22 + Job 33–37) suggest that what this story needs is one who can definitively "answer" (vv. 1, 3, 5, 6, 12, 17, 20) Job's questions. According to the narrator, it is Elihu's anger at the friends' failure that compels him to step into this story (32:2, 3, 5). When the constructed Elihu speaks for himself, he claims that he is motivated not by *anger* but by *divine inspiration* (32:8, 18; cf. 33:4). Thus, when Elihu claims to have *the* answer to questions about the meaning of suffering (Job 33), Job, and we readers, must decide whether his *anger is righteous*, thus worthy of emulation, or simply *rage masquerading as a virtue* that we should avoid at all costs.

Given the tension between the frame and the center, it is little wonder that early tradents thought it necessary to splice in these additional parts. Whether the objective was to tilt the balance in favor of one view and away from another, to add a clarifying perspective, or simply to bridge gaps in the story deemed awkward or unacceptable, we cannot know with any certainty. Of one thing we can be reasonably sure. Once the story beginning with the question "Have you considered my servant Job?" (1:8) made its appearance in Israel's journey with God, there were multiple respondents who dared to answer "Yes," even if their contributions only added to the difficulty of deciding "what is right."

JOB BEYOND THE BIBLE

There is deep irony in the truth that Job lives on, well past the biblical text that conveys his story. A legendary character out of the hoary past, Job cursed the day he was born, expressed repeatedly the wish to die, and yet he seems to live forever in the minds and imaginations of his countless interpreters. As E. Wiesel has said, "through the problems he embodied and the trials he endured, he seems familiar—even contemporary."[18] One does not have to look far to find the evidence of Job's perduring claim on us. Two twentieth-century works, both reflecting the struggle for meaning in the aftermath of war, suffice to make the case.

In *The Undying Fire* (1919), H. G. Wells recreates the Joban figure in order to address a regnant despair concerning the human capacity for good, which seemed forever buried in the meaningless destruction wrought by World War I. The hero of the story, Job Huss, addresses his friend, Sir Eliphaz Burrows, with a twentieth-century version of the conundrum experienced by his biblical counterpart:

> I have been forced to revise my faith, and to look more closely than I have ever done before into the meaning of my beliefs and into my springs of action. I have been wrenched away from that habitual confidence in the order of things which seemed the more natural state for a mind to be in. . . . Suddenly, swiftly, I have had misfortune following upon misfortune—without cause or justification. I am thrown now into the darkest doubt and dismay; the universe seems harsh and black to me; whereas formerly I believed that at the core of it and universally pervading it was the Will of a God of Light.
>
> Many men and women have lived and died happy in that illusion of security. But this war has torn away the veil of illusion from millions of men. . . . Mankind is coming of age. We can see life at last for what it is and what it is not.[19]

Why turn to Job in the aftermath of experiences centuries removed from his biblical story? ["Turning to Job "] Wells offers an answer with his version of the prologue's dialogue between God and Satan:

> "There was a certain man in the land of Uz whose name was Job."
> "We remember him."
> "We had a wager of sorts," said Satan. "It was some time ago. . . ."
> "Did I lose or win? The issue was obscured by discussion. How those men did talk! You intervened. There was no decision. . . ."
> Satan rested his dark face on his hand, and looked down between his knees through the pellucid floor to that little eddying in the ether which makes our world. "Job," he said, "lives still. "
> Then after an interval: "The whole earth is now—Job."

"Turning to Job "

Gail Godwin recounts an experience in her parish that drove the community to the book of Job. A young couple's only child was diagnosed with a rare and fast-growing liver cancer a month before his second birthday. Tracking the child's journey through hospitalizations and rounds of chemotherapy, Godwin keeps returning to the question that defined her community of faith for more than two years: "God, where are you? What are you doing here?"

At the end of the journey, as she reflects on what she has learned, Godwin recalls a scene from her novel *Evensong* (New York: Ballantine Books, 1999). A young seminarian, working in a New York hospital, is disheartened by the suffering she feels powerless to alleviate. She writes to an older priest who has been her mentor, "Where is God in all this?" He writes back,

> Your question may be the only one that matters. Despite the convoluted guesswork by theologians ever since Job's friends hunched beside him on the dung heap, "Where is God in this?" (just the question alone, I mean) may be enough to keep us busy down here. Maybe the thing we're required to do is simply keep asking the question as Job did—asking it faithfully over and over—until God begins to reveal himself through the ways we are changed by the answering silence.

G. Godwin, "Turning to Job," *RevExp* 99 (2002): 520.

Then, these concurring words from God: "A thousand years in my sight are but as yesterday when it is past. I will grant what you seek to prove; that Job has become mankind."[20]

"Job has become mankind." Almost forty years later, a different war triggers a similar assessment of Job's ubiquitous presence in the modern world. Archibald MacLeish's Pulitzer Prize-winning play *J.B.* (1956) prepares for the entrance of the Joban figure with a heavenly dialogue between Mr. Zuss, whose name evokes an association with the god Zeus, and Mr. Nickles, a popcorn vendor whose name is apparently a formalization of the traditional nickname for Satan, "Old Nick." Together they view the empty stage on which they will soon reenact the Joban drama. But first they must decide whether there is sufficient interest in the old story to attract a modern audience. Zuss votes to go forward with the production, for as he says, "there's always Someone playing Job." Mr. Nickles agrees, although he wonders if he still has a role to play. The following exchange then occurs:

> *Nickles:* There must be
> Thousands . . .
> Millions and millions of mankind
> Burned, crushed, broken, mutilated,
> Slaughtered, and for what? For thinking!
> For walking around in the world in the wrong
> Skin, the wrong-shaped noses, eyelids:
> Sleeping the wrong night in the wrong city
> London, Dresden, Hiroshima.
> There never could have been so many
> Suffered more for less. But where do
> I come in?
>
> *Zuss:* All we have to do is start.
> Job will join us. Job will be there.
>
> *Nickles:* I know. I know. I know. I've seen him.
> Job is everywhere we go,
> His children dead, his work for nothing,
> Counting his losses, scraping his boils,
> Discussing himself with his friends and physicians,
> Questioning everything—the times, the stars,
> His own soul, God's providence.[21]

If "there's always someone playing Job," if, indeed, the whole world, all of humankind, has in effect become Job, then we should not be surprised that Job's interpreters are also everywhere. At least since the early Middle Ages,[22] the book of Job, perhaps more than any other biblical text, has been the subject of an enormous number of "readings" by scholarly, usually ecclesiastical, "insiders" for whom it is sacred Scripture, and by "outsiders," or to use Cynthia Ozick's term, "common readers,"[23] for whom its existential issues are compelling, irrespective of scholarly puzzles and clerical commentary. [From Biblical Scholars to Literary Critics] The sheer quantity of the work "inspired" or "influenced" by the biblical story confirms its abiding importance for our world.[24] What is especially striking, however, is how different the assessments of Job's contributions to our thinking may be, depending on the historical, cultural, and religious perspectives readers bring to the text. In significant ways, *all readers*, whatever their social location, have a chronic inclination to *read themselves into Job's story*.

At the risk of over-simplifying the complexity of these matters, I venture the following generalizations about Jewish and Christian readings of Job, which may be instructive for the primary audience this commentary addresses.

Jewish Readings of Job

In view of the tensions within the biblical book, which portrays Job as both pious and uncomplaining and as raging and defiant, it should not be surprising to find that Judaism's view of Job is not uniform. As Judith Baskin notes in an overview of rabbinic interpretation, "one could say that there are almost as many Jobs as rabbis who speak about him."[25]

On one hand, one may conclude, as Israel Ta-Sh'ma says in his entry on the book of Job in the *Encyclopedia Judaica*, that "the book of Job is unrelated to Judaism—even though it contains nothing contrary to its

---

From Biblical Scholars to Literary Critics

R. Gordis, a noted Job scholar, observes that just as every actor "harbors a secret ambition to play Hamlet, so every biblical student nurtures the hope of some day writing about Job."

Making the same point from a different perspective, M. Radzinoicz notes Job has become a fashionable topic in modern literary criticism. She suggests that the book of Job has four qualities that make it particularly amenable to literary deconstruction and reconstruction:

(1) Indeterminacy: nobody wrote the book for any clearly ascertainable purpose, thus its meaning is indeterminate.

(2) Generic disunity: the book is a pastiche of genres that by inclusion, exclusion, recombination, redaction, and edition have been forged into a canonical whole.

(3) The book lends itself to political readings. Thus, a large readership has venerated the book, interpreted it, co-opted special parts of it, and "with respect to the Christian Bible used half of it to trivialize the other half in general and to over-interpret Job."

(4) Its witness to a mode of writing that is self-consciously subversive (e.g., Job's protest and rebellion against God) models a way of transgressing and subverting the foundations of society.

R. Gordis, *The Book of God and Man: A Study of Job* (Chicago/London: The University of Chicago Press, 1965), v.
M. Radzinowicz, "How and Why the Literary Establishment Caught Up with the Bible: Instancing the Book of Job," *ChrLit* 39 (1989): 77-89.

teachings, consisting as it does of theoretical and general speculation on the problem of 'the suffering righteous.'"[26] In reflecting on this comment, William S. Green confirms its essential merit: "Although Job is undeniably part of Judaism's scripture, it has no place in the synagogue liturgy . . . is not part of the scriptural repertoire of regular worshippers and therefore is not an obvious touchstone for their religious imagination."[27] On the other hand, as Ta-Sh'ma goes on to say, "the rabbis showed a great love for the book, studied it to a great extent, and extracted moral instruction from it in their usual manner."[28] If we ask what "moral instruction" the rabbis extracted from Job's innocent suffering, the answer is a mixed bag.[29] The talmudic-midrashic literature (primarily first century) devotes considerable attention to Job as a model of righteousness, but it generally defines this righteousness as forbearance, not as complaint or rebellion. As one Midrash puts it, if Job had not complained, his memory would have been revered, along with that of other ancestral heroes of faith; whenever people prayed, they would invoke the "God of Abraham, God of Isaac, God of Jacob, *and* God of Job" (*Pesiq. Rab.* 47 [emphasis added]; see further [Job, the Righteous Gentile] and [Job and Abraham]).[30] At the same time, Judaism, both ancient and modern, has long regarded arguing with God as a time-honored, Scripture-sanctioned characteristic of the people of God. ["From Inside His Community [a Jew] May Say Anything"] We need only consider Franz Kafka's *The Trial* (1937), Joseph Roth's *Job: The Story of a Simple Man* (1974), and Elie Wiesel's *The Trial of God* (1979) to confirm that the defiant Job who dominates the center of the biblical story has been an important template for modern Jewish fiction.

"From Inside His Community [a Jew] May Say Anything"

From inside his community [a Jew] may say anything. Let him step outside it, and he will be denied this right. The revolt of the believer is not that of the renegade; the two do not speak in the name of the same anguish.

E. Wiesel, *Souls on Fire* (New York: Vintage Books, 1973), 111.

Christian Readings of Job

Christian interpreters also typically focus on the "patience of Job " as exemplified in the prologue, which requires glossing over the impatience, anger, and rebellion that characterizes the Job who dominates the center of the biblical story. The precedent for this is no doubt the New Testament, which typically transforms the major characters of the Old Testament (historical or not) into timeless "moral exemplars (e.g., Jas 5:11; 1 Pet 3:6; 1 John 3:11-12)."[31]

A strong case can be made that what Job has most often exemplified for Christians is a Christ-like witness to the promise of resurrection for those who endure suffering faithfully. From third- and fourth-century Joban frescoes in the Roman catacombs to eighteenth-century Joban epitaphs on tombstones, vaults, and mausoleums, Christians who have suffered persecution or affliction have clung to the hope that if they die with Job's faith in God's ultimate deliverance, they will be raised to life everlasting with Christ (see [CD: Buried with Job, Raised Like Christ]).[32] This connection between Job and Christ has long been emphasized in Christian rites and liturgies for the dead, which couple Job's words in 19:25—"I know that my Redeemer lives"—to New Testament texts affirming the promise vouchsafed to the faithful in Christ's resurrection. The most enduring and influential exposition of this promise is no doubt Handel's *Messiah*, first performed in Dublin in 1742. The first part of the soprano aria takes as its text Job 19:25; the second part of the aria, sustained by the glorious Hallelujah Chorus, "exegetes" Job's hope for a redeemer by appealing directly to Paul's declaration in 1 Corinthians 15:20: "For now Christ is risen from the dead, the first fruits of them that sleep" (see further [CD: "I Know That My Redeemer Liveth . . . For Now Christ Is Risen from the Dead"]).

The rather singular focus on selective texts (19:25) and themes (patience) from Job in Christian liturgy may be contrasted with the larger, fictive, presence of this biblical character in the imaginations of those who work outside ecclesiastical orthodoxy. We need only consider the different Joban accents in Robert Frost's *A Masque of Reason* (1945), Carl Jung's *Answer to Job* (1954), Neil Simon's *God's Favorite* (1975), Peter Shaffer's *Amadeus* (1980), and William Safire's, *The First Dissident: The Book of Job in Today's Politics* (1992) to see that outside the church it is Job's defiance of conventional religious maxims that often takes center stage.

The issue here may be framed by returning to the observations of Ta-Sh'ma and Green above. *Outside the synagogue rituals*, they suggest, Job receives frequent comment and reflection. *Inside the synagogue's liturgy*, however, the Job who is clearly part of Judaism's Scripture has little or no presence. A similar conclusion might be drawn with respect to Job's role in Christian faith and practice. *Inside the church's liturgy*, the patient Job of the prologue and the restored Job of the epilogue occupy a place of honor among the great heroes of faith; the Job at the center of the book who curses, complains, and rebels, however, is largely silent. *Outside the liturgy*, the Job who lives on in the fiction, poetry, and drama of everyday life speaks with far less restraint and models a quite different sort of heroism. The full scriptural testimony to Job, it seems, is in a real sense largely "unrelated" to what goes on inside the places for worship in both Judaism and Christianity. As P. Rouillard has noted, commenting on the reduction of Joban texts in the Roman liturgy of the Matins for the Dead after Vatican II, the "over-catechised Job is no longer the Job of the Bible."[33] [Matins for the Dead]

Matins for the Dead

📖 From the 7th century until the middle of the 20th century, when Vatican II initiated significant changes in Roman liturgy, the Matins for the Dead appropriated nine readings from the book of Job, which were recited in this order: 7:16-21; 10:1-7; 10:8-12; 13:22-28; 14:1-6; 14:13-16; 17:1-3, 11-15; 19:20-27; 10:18-23. The sequence is noteworthy because it begins and ends with the same testimony to Job's abject despair: "I loathe my life; I would not live forever. Let me alone, for my days are but a breath" (7:16); "Why did you bring me forth from the womb? Would that I had died before any eye had seen me. . . . Are not the days of my life few? Let me alone, that I may find a little comfort" (10:18, 20). It is only in the penultimate reading from 19:20-27 that the liturgy recognizes Job's astonishing move toward the hope for a redeemer. Yet, having imagined that possibility, the liturgy returns to the world of Job's unrequited suffering. After Vatican II the Roman liturgy breaks with what had been a 1,000-year-old tradition. In the revised Liturgy for the Dead, the nine readings are reduced to one, Job 19:25-27. This text is in turn repositioned as a response to three readings from the Epistle to the Corinthians, each of which proclaims the resurrection of Christ.

A similar practice occurs in other confessional traditions, for example, in the Episcopal liturgy for the Burial of the Dead, which appropriates the following sequence of texts: John 11:25; Job 19:25-27; and Rom 14:7-8. (See further **[CD: "I Know That My Redeemer Liveth . . . For Now Christ Is Risen from the Dead"]**.)

P. Rouillard, "The Figure of Job in the Liturgy: Indignation, Resignation or Silence," *Job and the Silence of God* (Concilium 169, 9/1983) ed. C. Duquoc, C. Floristan (New York: Seabury, 1983), 8-9.

We may press this last point a bit further. The biblical story holds in tension the Job who blesses God's goodness and the Job who curses God's injustice. Both Jobs are models for faith that has integrity. When this story is translated into the liturgy offered to those who gather for worship in synagogues and churches, the tension is removed, the possibilities for addressing God are reduced, and the definition of what constitutes authentic faith is thinned: one may praise but not lament, trust but not doubt, affirm but not question. If this generalization has merit, then our entry into the book of Job will likely require a serious rethinking of its message for the Jobs of this world. If they were to sit beside us on the pew, would the songs we sing, the creeds we recite, the prayers we pray, or the sermons we preach provide any more comfort for them than Job's biblical friends offered to him? As we consider the question, the sad image of Job sitting on the ash heap *outside our sanctuaries*, beyond the reach of orthodox certainties, hovers over the answers we must ponder. ["Inside . . . an Archaic Rule; Outside, the Facts of Life"]

"Inside . . . an Archaic Rule; Outside the Facts of Life"

📖 The narrator in Saul Bellow's short story, "Something to Remember Me By," is a "high-minded Jewish boy" who chafes under the orthodoxy imposed on him at home. He offers the following telling discernment about the gap between religious affirmations and the grim realities of life outside their sanctuary: "At home, inside the house, an archaic rule; outside, the facts of life. The facts of life were having their turn. Their first effect was ridicule."

S. Bellow, "Something to Remember Me By," *Saul Bellow: Collected Stories* (New York: Viking, 2001), 431.

ABIDING THEOLOGICAL ISSUES AND
LINGERING JOBAN PERSPECTIVES

Surely one reason the book of Job continues to find readers is its connection to universal issues that have abiding importance. Three large matters may be singled out for special attention.

Cosmology and the "Grammars of Creation"

As E. Durkheim noted almost a century ago, "there is no religion that is not a cosmology."[34] Ancient Israel is no exception. Three exemplars of Israel's "grammars of creation" suffice to make the point.[35] (1) The opening credo in Genesis 1—"In the beginning God"—announces God's creation of a "very good" world in which every creature, free from the random intrusion of evil, may attain and enjoy its fullest potential. Such an edenic world, this cosmology affirms, invokes, sustains, and rewards unceasing celebration. (2) On the heels of this account, Genesis 2–3 shifts the emphasis from the perfection of God's creation to deficiencies in the garden of Eden that invite and require attention if the world is to fulfill God's hopes and expectations.[36] Although God supplies what is necessary to overcome some of these deficiencies—the lack of vegetation, rain, and humans to cultivate the ground (Gen 2:5)—one limitation presents a much more complex challenge. In the midst of paradise, God plants the "tree of the knowledge of good and evil (*rāʿ*)" (Gen 2:9), then blocks access to it with a primordial prohibition that carries a severe penalty: "You shall not eat, for in the day you eat of it you shall die" (Gen 2:17). When humans succumb to the temptation to disregard this prohibition, they forfeit their place in the garden. The grammars of creation must now be enlarged by the word "sin," which escalates from Cain and Abel to Noah, when "every inclination of the thoughts of their hearts was only evil (*raʿ*)" (Gen 6:5). A grieving God's only recourse, according to this cosmology, is to subsume the world in a flood and start over again. [The Adamic Myth] While readers know that the temptation to transgress God's limitations comes from the serpent, we also know that it was none other than God who created both the forbidden tree and the serpent. The possibility, however remotely conceived, that God is somehow implicated in the evil that undoes the world has now inched its way onto the radar. (3) The anonymous poet of Isaiah 40–55, addressing an audience submerged in a world fractured by Babylonian exile, offers hope by accenting God's promise to "create" a new Eden, resplendent with trees (note the seven species listed in Isa 41:17-20) bearing fruits of "justice" and "righteousness" (Isa 45:8).[37] For all its promise, this

The Adamic Myth

Paul Ricoeur notes that, of all human experiences, evil is most clearly rooted in myths of creation. When life convulses with suffering, whatever its source, the universal existential response is "Why?" Creation myths, which convey explanations of the way the world works and therefore of how human beings may understand and order their lives, offer the first and most generative resource for addressing the question. As Ricoeur puts it, "The intention of the Adamic myth is to separate the origin of evil from that of the good, in other words, to posit the radical origin of evil distinct from the more primordial origin of the goodness of all created things; *man commences evil but does not commence creation.*"

P. Ricoeur, "Evil," *ER*, vol. 5, ed. M. Eliade (New York: MacMillan, 1986), 203 (emphasis added).

God Reprimanding Adam and Eve

Bronze relief on doors. Cathedral St. Mary, Hildesheim, Germany. (Credit: Foto Marburg/Art Resource, NY)

new vision of Eden includes an unsettling affirmation that must now be factored into the grammars of creation. As "Creator of the ends of the earth" (Isa 40:28), God declares, "I form light and create darkness, I bring prosperity (*šalōm*) and create disaster/evil (*rāʿ*); I am the Lord who does all these things" (Isa 45:7). Whatever interpretive strategy we may employ to exegete these words, it is difficult to excise what appears to be their primary implication: God is ultimately responsible for whatever merits the label "evil."[38] In Isaiah's cosmology, the primordial summons to "tend and keep" God's garden of possibilities (cf. Gen 2:15) still hovers over all, but the commission is much more freighted now. Who can faithfully till such a garden as this? It is little wonder that the ancient audience responded with incredulity: "Who can believe what we have heard?" (Isa 53:1).

The book of Job connects with each of these creational accounts, but none of them is fully adequate to explain the world in which Job lives. Like the six-day account of God's creation of "the heavens and the earth" in Genesis 1, Job 1–2 describes Job's life in the "garden of Uz" in a sequence of six scenes alternatively set in heaven and on earth (1:1-5; 1:6-12; 1:13-22; 2:1-7a; 2:7b-10; 2:11-13). At the outset (vv. 1-5), Job's world is a seemingly perfect recapitulation of primordial Eden. There is no intrusion of evil anywhere. Even if there were, as the narrator reports and God confirms, Job always "turns away from evil (*rāʿ*)" (1:1, 8; 2:3). By the end of the prologue, Job's seven sons and three daughters are dead, and it is painfully clear that "evil" (2:11: *rāʿāh*; NRSV: "trouble") has fallen upon his world. Through six scenes Job steadfastly refuses to do anything other than bless the God who concedes to having been "provoked to destroy him for no reason" (2:3). When the curtain rises on the seventh scene, however, Job curses a world that is no longer "very good" (3:1-10). The language of praise and blessing is no longer adequate to express what he feels; he now turns, with no less passion, to the grammar of lament and protest (3:11-26).

As in Genesis 2–3, temptation also plays a role in Job's world. Now, however, its source is not the serpent but one of God's heavenly messengers named "the satan," who serves God by investigating the claims of those who profess fidelity to God. God, not the satan, initiates the conversations that result in the temptations (1:7; 2:2). Twice God yields to the satan's suggestion that Job's world be turned upside down (1:12; 2:6). Unlike Adam, who chose his own course by deciding to eat the forbidden fruit, Job has no say in what is about to happen in his world. He is an unknowing chip in a high stakes poker game in which he holds no cards. The outcome of the temptation leaves Job in much the same situation as the primordial couple, only worse. Like them he is left to sit among the ashes, perhaps as the Septuagint suggests, outside the city, where society consigns the destitute and the rejected. Unlike them, Job is innocent of any wrongdoing. By God's own admission, Job is "blameless and upright" (1:8; 2:3; cf. 1:1). What constitutes authentic faith for the blameless and upright who suffer the loss of everything precious in life "for no reason"? This is the question Job puts to his world, and more importantly, to his God.

Job's story also connects with Isaiah's insights concerning the enigma of evil. Addressing an audience whose faith in the goodness of God's creation has been forcibly pruned by the horrors of exile, the prophet dares to affirm that God lends an extra pair of shoulders to the task of bearing the burden of evil, effectively claiming responsibility for "all these things" (Isa 45:7). Even this stretching of Israel's creation theology, however, fails to address adequately the suffering that defines Job's world. When God says, "I create evil," there is no advance warning that the words "for no reason" are part of the equation. When Job looks on the dead bodies of his children, what comfort can he take from the knowledge that the fingerprints on the assault weapon belong to God?[39]

Tuning himself to the ancient yet abiding dilemma of the Jobs in this world, G. Steiner introduces his exploration of the "grammars of creation" with this pained assessment: "We have no more beginnings." As we embark on the twenty-first century, Steiner looks back on the corpse of centuries swallowed up in the hideous barbarity of warfare, disease, ethnic cleansing, and political murder, to name only a few of the headline evils that define the modern world. He concedes that we now limp through our days with a "core-tiredness," a fatigue of dashed hopes that leaves us sitting at the bar after the last call for drinks, demanding yet another round that time refuses us: "Time, ladies and gents, time." As he says, "Valediction in the air."[40] And yet, Steiner cannot resign himself to valediction. Thus, he closes his search for the grammars of creation with these words: "We have long been, I believe we still are, guests of creation. We owe to our host the courtesy of questioning."[41] Though it may strain our imagination to think of Job's thundering "Why?" questions as a "courtesy," they remain nonetheless an essential part of the language of faith that is somehow folded into God's assessment of "what is right" when "servants" like Job speak. ["Each of His Words Was Like a Splinter"]

Anthropology and Questions about Human Existence

What does it mean to be a human being in a world of suffering like Job's? Job's first words from the ash heap place the question of human identity and vocation at the forefront of his struggle. Why was he born if life promises nothing more than misery (cf. 3:11-12, 16, 20, 23)? Throughout the dialogues, Job's friends use a variety of counter-questions to urge him toward answers they believe are mandatory. Eliphaz sets the agenda that Bildad and Zophar will follow: "Can mortals be righteous before God?" (4:17); "What are mortals that they can be clean?" (15:14); "Can a mortal be of any use to God?" (22:2; cf. Elihu in 33:12; 35:1-8). The only legitimate answer in each case, Eliphaz argues, is "No." Simply put, "human beings are born to trouble" (5:7). No human being can claim to approach God with the integrity of innocence, as Job repeatedly insists he is doing, for every person is but a flawed and sinful image of the Creator. To believe otherwise risks a foolish and dangerous breach of the boundary that separates the divine and the human. When suffering comes, therefore, humans have but one option: "Agree with God, and be at peace; in this way, good will

---

"Each of His Words Was Like a Splinter"

In "All That Glisters Isn't Gold," Doris Betts tells the story of a young girl whose faith is unsettled by the blasphemous pronouncements of Granville. Granville had gone off to university and learned that great chunks of the catechism he had parroted in his youth were vulnerable to critique. The girl knew she should be able to counter Granville's arguments, yet she could not ignore the possibility that he knew something about the faith she professed that she had been unable to see. Betts describes the girl's ruminations as follows:

Each of his words was like a splinter and each slid invisibly inside me. There was a sore spot wherever one penetrated; soon there were bruises all over my religion it was not safe to touch. I preferred the soreness of those splinters to the painful operation of having them removed.

D. Betts, "All That Glisters Isn't Gold," *The Astronomer and Other Stories* (Baton Rouge and London: Louisiana State University Press, 1965), 97.

come to you" (22:21). The *agreement* Eliphaz insists upon must be conveyed in words that praise the inscrutable wisdom of God (5:8-16). The afflicted should not despise their suffering but should instead wear it a badge of honor, for the God who disciplines by "wounding" and "striking" can be trusted to "bind up" and "heal" (5:17-18; cf. 8:6-7 [Bildad]; 11:15-19 [Zophar]; 33:19-22; 36:5-15 [Elihu]).

Job knows the language of praise that Eliphaz commends, but suffering pushes him to question its relevance. An untroubled psalmist may offer astonished praise to the God who creates human beings as near-equals of the Almighty, then elevates them to royalty with the commission to take responsibility for God's world (Ps 8:4-5). In a world defined by suffering like Job's, however, the psalmist's words— "What are human beings that you [God] should be mindful of them?"—convey a doxology of sarcasm, not praise (Job 7:17-18; see further [CD: Psalm 8 and Job 7]). Why, Job wonders, would God exalt human beings as kings, then strip them of the very "glory" and "crown" (19:9) that signifies their God-given nobility? Can it be that God has only lifted him up in order to make him a better target for harassment? If, as his friends insist, all human beings are of little or no use to God, then why does God not just leave him alone (7:19)? Why has God "fashioned and made" him in the divine image, then turned on him with a sinister intent to "destroy" the very creature God has worked to bring into being (10:8)? Why has God has fashioned him "like clay" only to return him to "dust" (10:9), like a potter's vessel that is cast "into the mire" (30:19) because it is flawed beyond repair? Job can only conclude that to be created as "dust and ashes" in God's world amounts to nothing more than consignment to a life of slavery (7:1-6) before a taskmaster who is both "cruel" and indifferent to those who cry out for relief (30:20-21).

And yet, it is God's seemingly excessive preoccupation with him that causes Job to wonder if human beings have more significance in God's world than either he or his friends have understood. Is it possible that Job has the potential of Yam and Tannin (7:12), primordial creatures whose power to impact the world God judges to be real and worthy of attention? Job does not believe this can be the case, and he quickly dismisses the possibility. Slaves may rebel against their masters, but they will not win. Servants of God may contend with their Creator, but they take their life into their hands in doing so (13:14-15). They must know before they risk the first challenge that God will not answer one in a thousand questions they may ask (9:3). Even so, Job insists on his right to complain. As he puts it, "I will speak, and let come on me what may" (13:13). God's response to Job's challenge is in many ways enigmatic, leaving open the possibility that Job's worst fears about confronting the Almighty are right.

Still, there are hints in what God says from the whirlwind that the objective is neither to silence Job's complaints nor to condemn him for daring to express them. One clue is God's evocative summons to Job to put on the regalia of "majesty and dignity," like a king, and live fully into the "glory and splendor" that is his divine calling (40:10). The latter part of this summons is only a slight variation on the affirmation celebrated in Psalm 8:5: "You have made them a little lower than God, and crowned them with glory and honor." A second clue is God's commendation of Behemoth (40:15-24) and Leviathan (41:1-34 [MT: 40:25–41:26]). Both are models of creaturely courage and pride that may teach Job something about his identity and vocation in relation to God. In Behemoth, Job sees one whom God has made "just as I made you" (40:15). In Leviathan, he sees a creature that will not be domesticated by a "covenant" that requires "soft words" (41:3-4 [MT: 40:27-28]). Its power and dignity command recognition, not disregard, for it rules its world like "king" (41:34 [MT: 41:26]). What does God wish Job to learn from Behemoth and Leviathan? How should he respond when God repeats for a second time the imperative, "Declare to me" (38:3; 40:7; cf. 42:4)? [CD: "What Kind of Discussion Does a Man Expect to Have with His Creator?"] The answer comes in 42:6, which constitutes the crux of the book. In advance of the commentary that follows, we note simply that Job claims now to see something new about himself, something that invites and requires a reconsideration of what it means to be created as "dust and ashes" (cf. 30:19). [A Relationship of Defiance, Rejection, and Confrontation?]

Theology and Joban Perspectives on the Character of God

The multiple and divergent portrayals of Job (patient and defiant) and the friends (comforters and accusers) may be negotiated as little more than rhetorical teasers. The different portrayals of God, however, are more problematic.[42] [CD: "I Read the Book of Job Last Night"] In the prologue, the *satan* "incites" a presumably sovereign God to afflict Job with unimaginable suffering "for no reason" (2:3), leaving us to wonder if God can be trusted. In the dialogues between Job and his friends, a presumably compassionate God remains distant and silent, leaving us to wonder if God genuinely cares about those who cry to the heavens for relief. In the whirlwind speeches, God speaks with such self-conscious pride and at such monopolizing length about so many things that seem, at least on first blush, to be irrelevant to Job's plight, we are left to wonder if mere creatures like Job matter at all to the Creator. In the

---

A Relationship of Defiance, Rejection, and Confrontation?

If one stands eye-to-eye with God, like Job does at the end of his long journey, what might the relationship on the other side of the encounter be like? When he says, "now my eye sees you" (42:5), what does Job *see* that is different than before? K. Paffenroth answers the question by comparing Job to the character of Ahab in Herman Melville's *Moby Dick* (1851). At the outset of his quest to find the great sperm whale that has crippled him by biting off one of his legs, Ahab is "dismembered," "stricken, blasted," and "mutilated"; in short, he is an "ungodly, god-like man," trying to claw his way back up to human dignity (109). In order to do so, he must confront the very thing that has harmed him. As he closes in on the elusive whale, which he calls "the grand god" (107), Ahab describes his obsession to confront his enemy, despite all risks and dangers, in sacramental terms. As Paffenroth notes, Ahab's quest is an "act of worship, the deepest expression of the relationship he chooses to have with his God, a relationship of defiance, rejection, and confrontation" (110). To buttress his point, Paffenroth cites the following speech by Ahab, spoken in the aftermath of the typhoon that has left his ship a wreck:

Oh, thou clear spirit of fire, whom on these seas I as Persian once did worship, till in the sacramental act so burned by thee, that to this hour I bear the scar; I now know thee, thou clear spirit, and *I now know that thy right worship is defiance*. To neither love nor reverence wilt thou be kind; and e'en for hate thou cans't but kill; and all are killed. No fearless fool confronts thee. I own thy speechless, placeless power; but to the last gasp of my earthquake life will dispute its unconditional, unintegral mastery in me. In the midst of the personified impersonal, *a personality stands here*. Though but a point at best; whencesoe'er I came; wheresoe'er I go; yet while I earthly live, the queenly personality lives in me, and feels her royal rights. (110; from *Moby-Dick*, ch. 119, "The Candles," emphasis added)

K. Paffenroth, "The Meaning of Suffering in Job and *Moby-Dick*," *In Praise of Wisdom: Literary and Theological Reflections on Faith and Reason* (New York/London: Continuum, 2004), 101-33.

---

epilogue, the God who indicts the friends and restores Job seems more fickle than just, more arbitrary than predictable. If after all that has transpired, Job is indeed a faithful "servant" (1:8; 2:3) who has "spoken what is right" (42:7-8), then why must seven sons and three daughters die before God feels compelled to confirm what God seems already to know? Even if *Job has passed God's test* for fidelity, we must wonder if *God has not failed Job's test* for what is required for God to be God. ["Success Is Itself but a Form of Failure"] We may wince at the words Robert Frost gives to Job in his creation of an imaginary forty-third chapter to the book, but we cannot dismiss the ring of its disturbing authenticity. Having heard the explanation for why God has tortured him so—"I was just showing off to the Devil"—Frost's Job says, "'Twas human of You," but "I expected more. . . ."[43]

How should we piece together these separate snapshots of the God who so elusively and so ambiguously appears in the book of Job? To return to Hempel's observation, if Job's story is "the struggle for the *last* truth about God," then what is this truth? We may construct an overarching umbrella out of the mystery of God's providential wisdom, under which Job's ultimate restoration provides all the assurance we need to sustain belief in *God's inscrutable compassion*. As T. Fretheim argues, the negative portrayals of God as "lord, warrior, judge" in effect "stand in the service of a more positive point," namely, "God's responsiveness to Job in his suffering," which "gives him a renewed vision of God."[44] If,

---

"Success Is Itself but a Form of Failure"

When it comes to assessing great works of literature, ancient or modern, Joyce Carol Oates notes that writers, "perhaps more than most people, inhabit failure, degrees of failure and accommodation and compromise." She makes the point as follows:

It seems reasonable to believe that failure may be a truth, or at any rate a negotiable fact, while success is a temporary illusion of some intoxicating sort, a bubble soon to be pricked, a flower whose petals will quickly drop . . . . From this pragmatic vantage point, "success" is but a form of "failure," a compromise between what is desired and what is attained.

Muriel Sparks writes from another perspective but offers a similar assessment that applies specifically to the "happy" ending of the book of Job: "So the Lord blessed the latter end of Job more than his beginning." Harvey, the character in Sparks's novel who has now completed his monograph on Job, three hard years in the making, has lingering doubts about the ending of both the biblical story and his own book (see [*The Only Problem*]). "In real life," Harvey asks himself, would Job "be satisfied with this plump reward?" Sparks provides her character with this conclusion: "His [Job's] tragedy was that of the happy ending."

Joyce Carol Oates, *The Faith of a Writer: Life, Craft, Art* (New York: HarperCollins, 2003), 52-53.
M. Spark, *The Only Problem* (New York: G. P. Putnam's Sons, 1984), 176.

---

however, we formulate the question as Jack Miles does—"What is it that makes God godlike? What is it that makes the protagonist of the Bible so weirdly compelling, so repellent and so attractive at once?"— we may be constrained to place the accent on *God's capriciousness*, not God's compassion.

> The climax is a climax for God himself and not just for Job or for the reader. After Job, God knows his own ambiguity as he has never known it before. He now knows that. . . he has a fiend-susceptible side and that mankind's conscience is finer than his. With Job's assistance, his just, kind self has won out over his cruel capricious self just as it did after the flood. But the victory has come at an enormous price. . . . The world still seems more just than unjust, and God still seems more good than bad; yet the pervasive mood, as this extraordinary book ends, is one not of redemption but reprieve.[45]

A third option is to follow J. L. Crenshaw and simply admit that "no one can bring together such vastly different perspectives"[46] on whatever may be the *last truth* about God.

> The book reminds readers that every depiction of the deity is a literary construct. They may be drawn to the picture of God in the book, or repulsed by its coldness approaching the demonic, but readers need to be reminded that the portrayal is a human product, like all theological speculation. For some, the removal of human beings from center stage accords well with reality, as does the rejection of a moral force governing all things. Life is too complex, and events too random, to justify belief in a

deity who matches events with conduct. Justice concerns human society, and it will be established, if ever, by people of flesh and blood. The deity, if one can postulate such a being, is not bound by human notions of right and wrong. The theist may claim no more than that God is lord of life, which includes both good and evil. To the extent that mortals set limits and impose them on God, they have constructed an idol. The beauty of the book of Job is that the author excels as an iconoclast, breaking all forms of idolatry. Job's deity may not be lovable, but he is definitely no idol. [47]

Given these multiple and divergent perspectives on the world, human existence, and God, we readers are left to ponder what we are to learn from this book. In the face of innocent suffering, Job asks "Why?" We wait with him for answers, but when all the dialogues end, whether between Job and his friends or between Job and his God, we may be more vexed than satisfied. No doubt the anxiety would be lessened if the book spoke with one clearly authoritative voice, not several that simultaneously vie for our attention. Even so, if the tradents of this book had settled for monologue rather than dialogue, then we would have to weigh the gain of certainty against the loss of debate. In fact, the only time the book yields to this temptation—in the speeches of Elihu (32–37), who claims to have *the* answer to the problem of suffering—the truth offered by way of monologue seems to violate the truth about the hard realities of life as Job and we readers know it. [48] When it comes to suffering "for no reason," this book seems intent on reminding us that questions about the world, human existence, and God necessarily remain open ended. To settle for anything less is to deny the pain that punctuates every faith assertion with a question mark. [CD "Who Can Contemplate Simultaneous, a-Billion-Times-Multiplied Pain?"] ["Seven Days of Silence"]

NOTES

[1] In *On Heroes and Hero Worship* (1841), cited in S. B. Freehof, *The Book of Job* (New York: Union of American Hebrew Congregations, 1958), 3. I am indebted to J. Levenson's masterful essay (*The Book of Job in Its Time and in the Twentieth Century* [Cambridge MA: Harvard University Press, 1972], 1) for calling this citation to my attention.

[2] J. Gardner, "Reading List," *Richmond Times-Dispatch*, 5 January 1996, A.10.

[3] J. Hempel, "The Contents of the Literature," *Record and Revelation: Essays by the Members of the Society for Old Testament Study*, ed. H. Wheeler Robinson (Oxford: Clarendon Press, 1938), 73 (emphasis added). For reflections on Hempel's comment, see the essays by R. E. Murphy, J. L. Crenshaw, and J. Gerald Janzen in "Job," *RevExp* 99 (2002): 581-605.

[4] M. Spark, *The Only Problem* (New York: G. P. Putnam's Sons, 1984), 22.

[5] A. von Soden has convincingly argued that the social, cultural, and historical situations that gave rise to the questioning of divine justice, which emerged so sharply for Israel in the days of the exile (586–538 BCE), were already present in the ancient Near East as least as early as the second millennium ("Das Fragen nach der Gerechtigkeit Gottes im Alten Orient," MDOG 96 [1965]: 41-49; cf. H. H. Schmid, *Wesen und Geschichte der Weisheit* [Berlin: Töpelmann, 1966]).

[6] For the English text and discussion, see S. N. Kramer, "Man and His God: A Sumerian Variation on the 'Job' Motif," *VTS* 3 (1960): 170-82. Kramer's translation, with abbreviated commentary, may also be consulted in *ANET*, 3rd ed. with supplement, ed. J. B. Pritchard (Princeton: Princeton University Press, 1969), 589-91.

[7] For the full text in English, with commentary, see W. G. Lambert, *Babylonian Wisdom Literature* (Oxford: Clarendon Press, 1960), 21-62; cf. Pritchard, *ANET*, 434-37.

[8] Lambert, *Babylonian Wisdom Literature*, 27.

[9] For the full text in English, with commentary, see Lambert, *Babylonian Wisdom Literature*, 63-91; cf. Pritchard, *ANET*, 601-604.

[10] For the English text, see Pritchard, *ANET*, 407-10.

[11] Some have argued on linguistic grounds that both the prose and poetic sections contain a style of Hebrew that may be quite early, perhaps 10th century BCE. Whether this points to a genuinely archaic style or only to a deliberate imitation of this style remains unclear. See, for example, N. Sarna, "Epic Substratum in the Prose of Job," *JBL* 76 (1957): 13-25; D. Robertson, *Linguistic Evidence in Dating Early Hebrew Poetry* (SBLDS 3; Missoula, Mont: Society of Biblical Literature, 1972), 153-156; A. Hurvitz, "The Date of the Prose Tale of Job Linguistically Reconsidered," *HTR* (1974), 17-34. For a full discussion of the literary conventions, see Y. Hoffman, *A Blemished Perfection: The Book of Job in Context* (JSOTSup 213; Sheffield: Sheffield Academic Press, 1996), 46-83.

[12] There are many different hypotheses about the stages in the history of transmission. For a plausible account, see C. Newsom, "The Book of Job," in vol. 4 of *NIB* (Nashville: Abingdon Press, 1996), 320-25.

[13] See, for example, S. Garrett, "The Patience of Job and the Patience of Jesus," *Int* 53 (1999): 254-64.

[14] N. Habel, *The Book of Job: A Commentary* (OTL; Philadelphia: Westminster Press, 1985), 88. Cf. J. Hartley, *The Book of Job* (NICOT; Grand Rapids MI: William B. Eerdmans, 1988), 69-70. Note, however, D. J. A. Clines's cautionary caveat: "the story's setting in place and time lies beyond the horizon of the priestly law" (*Job 1–20* [WBC; Dallas: Word Books, 1989], 16).

[15] William S. Green, "Stretching the Covenant: Job and Judaism," *RevExp* 99 (2002): 574.

[16] C. Westermann, *The Structure of the Book of Job* (Philadelphia: Fortress, 1981), 135-38.

[17] F. I. Anderson, *Job: An Introduction and Commentary* (TOTC; Downers Grove IL: Inter-Varsity, 1976), 50.

[18] E. Wiesel, "Job: Our Contemporary," *Messengers of God: Biblical Portraits and Legends* (New York: Touchstone, 1976), 211.

[19] H. G. Wells, *The Undying Fire: A Contemporary Novel* (New York: The Macmillan Company, 1919), 103, 106.

[20] Ibid., 8-9, 10.

[21] A. MacLeish, *J.B.* (Boston: Houghton Mifflin Co., 1956), 12-13.

[22] E.g., L. Besserman, *The Legend of Job in the Middle Ages* (Cambridge MA/London: Harvard University Press, 1979).

[23] C. Ozick, "The Impious Impatience of Job," *Quarrel and Quandary* (New York: Alfred A. Knopf, 2000), 59-73.

[24] The bibliography dealing with the history of Job's interpretation is far too massive to survey adequately. To date, the most extensive effort to catalogue this material is that of Clines, whose first of a projected three-volume commentary devotes no less than nine pages to works dealing with "Job and Its Influence," including, for example, "Job in Art," "Job in Music," "Job in Dance," and "Job in Film" (*Job 1–20*, civ-cxii). (In personal conversation, Clines has informed me that volumes 2 and 3, currently in press, will significantly expand these entries.) For an introduction to the history of Job interpretation, readers may find it helpful to consult the following: *The Dimensions of Job: A Study and Selected Readings*, ed. N. Glatzer (New York: Schocken Books, 1969), 51-193; *The Voice from the Whirlwind: Interpreting the Book of Job,* ed. L. Perdue, W. Clark Gilpin (Nashville: Abingdon Press, 1992), 99-156; and C. A. Newsom, S. E. Schreiner, "Job, Book of," vol. A-J of *Dictionary of Biblical Interpretation*, ed. J. A. Hayes (Nashville: Abingdon Press, 1999), 587-99.

[25] J. Baskin, "Rabbinic Interpretations of Job," *Voice from the Whirlwind*, 101. For a comprehensive study of the range of Jewish commentary on Job, see J. Baskin, *Pharaoh's Counsellors: Job, Jethro, and Balaam in Rabbinic and Patristic Tradition* (BJS 47; Chico CA: Scholars Press, 1983).

[26] Israel Ta-Sh'ma, "Job, The Book of, In the Aggadah," *Encyclopedia Judaica* (Jerusalem: Keter, 1971), 125. I am indebted to William S. Green, both for calling this citation to my attention and for his perceptive exploration of its implications ("Stretching the Covenant," 569).

[27] Green, "Stretching the Covenant," 570.

[28] Ta-Sh'ma, "Job," 125.

[29] Cf. D. Kraemer (*Responses to Suffering in Classical Rabbinic Literature* [Oxford: Oxford University Press, 1995]), who shows that the Talmud both condemns and praises Job.

[30] For an overview of Job in "Classical Judaic Interpretation," see Glatzer, *Dimensions of Job,* 16-24. For further discussion with extensive bibliography, see R. Eisen, *The Book of Job in Medieval Jewish Philosophy* (Oxford: Oxford University Press, 2004).

[31] See, for example, G. Josipovici, *The Book of God: A Response to the Bible* (New Haven, London: Yale University Press, 1988), 274.

[32] For discussion of the frescoes in the Roman catacombs, see S. Terrien, *The Iconography of Job through the Centuries: Artists as Biblical Interpreters* (University Park PA: Pennsylvania State University Press, 1996), 17-23. For Joban epitaphs on 18th-century tombstones, see J. Lamb, *The Rhetoric of Suffering: Reading the Book of Job in the Eighteenth Century* (Oxford: Clarendon Press, 1995), especially 274-300.

[33] P. Rouillard, "The Figure of Job in the Liturgy: Indignation, Resignation or Silence," *Job and the Silence of God* [Concilium 169, 9/1983] ed. C. Duquoc and C. Floristan (New York: Seabury, 1983), 10.

[34] E. Durkheim, *The Elementary Forms of Religious Life* (New York: Macmillan, 1915), 21. For a concise summary of the importance of cosmology in biblical religion, see R. A. Oden, "Cosmogony, Cosmology," in vol. 1 of *ABD*, ed. D. N. Freedman (New York: Doubleday, 1992), 1162-71.

[35] I appropriate this term from G. Steiner, *Grammars of Creation* (New Haven and London: Yale University Press, 2001). My comments here draw upon and receive further discussion in S. E. Balentine, "For No Reason," *Int* 57 (2003): 349-69.

[36] On the importance of deficiency and provision as defining themes in Gen 2–3, see T. Boomershine, "The Structure of Narrative Rhetoric in Genesis 2–3," *Semeia* 18 (1980): 113-29; W. P. Brown, *The Ethos of the Cosmos: The Genesis of Moral Imagination* (Grand Rapids MI: Eerdmans, 1999), 135-37.

[37] Commentators have long noted that creation language and creation imagery is important in Isa 50–55. Words for "create," "make," or "form" occur with frequency, e.g., *bārā'*

(17x), *yāṣar* (14x), *'āśah* (24x), *pā'al* (5x). The word for "chaos" (*tōhû*), which occurs for the first time in Gen 1:2, occurs in Isa 40–55 more frequently than in any other book. For further discussion, see, e.g., C. Stuhmueller, *Creative Redemption in Deutero-Isaiah* (Rome: Pontifical Biblical Institute, 1970); B. C. Ollenburger, "Isaiah's Creation Theology," *Ex Auditu* 3 (1987): 54-71; R. Clifford, "The Unity of the Book of Isaiah and Its Cosmogonic Language," CBQ 55 (1993): 1-17.

[38] More than three decades have passed since C. Westermann noted, "It is hard to see why this verse does not bother commentators more than it seems to do" (*Isaiah 40–66* [OTL; Philadelphia: Westminster, 1969], 161). More recent work indicates that this verse has indeed vexed a number of commentators, some of whom have offered interpretations that effectively mute God's responsibility for evil, especially in any ontological sense. T. Fretheim, for example, has stressed God's use of specific and less than perfect human agents, in Isaiah's case Babylon, to shape divine justice. See, for example, "Divine Dependence Upon the Human: An Old Testament Perspective," *Ex Auditu* 13 (1997): 6-9; "Divine Judgment and the Warming of the World: An Old Testament Perspective," *Word and Way*, Supplement Series 4 (2000): 25-27.

[39] As Brown notes (*Ethos of the Cosmos*, 319), Job's world is "etched in the blood of a crime scene," which means, from Job's perspective, that it is a world "rife with moral outrage."

[40] Steiner, *Grammars of Creation*, 3.

[41] Ibid., 338.

[42] For a cogent discussion of these matters, see T. Fretheim, "God in the Book of Job," *CurTM* 26 (1999): 85-93.

[43] R. Frost, "A Masque of Reason," *The Poetry of Robert Frost*, ed. E. C. Lathem (New York: Henry Holt and Company, 1969), 484-85.

[44] Fretheim, "God in the book of Job," 89-90, 91.

[45] J. Miles, *God: A Biography* (New York: Alfred A. Knopf, 1995), 327, 328.

[46] J. L. Crenshaw, "Some Reflections on the book of Job," *RevExp* 99 (2002): 595.

[47] Ibid., 593. In *Defending God: Biblical Responses to Evil* (Oxford: Oxford University Press, 2005), Crenshaw reformulates his previous observation in a still more pointed way:

> No one can bring together such vastly different perspectives as the heavenly and the earthly. We are capable of understanding the view from below, as it were; how can we possibly perceive things from above? Creating dialogue for the deity runs the risk of hubris; having that fictional character laud a human as perfect in every way is hubris in the extreme. *Neither Job nor his maker deserves such praise. Both are flawed beings*. That insight may be the permanent legacy of the ancient poet. (186-87) (Emphasis added)

[48] See C. Newsom (*The Book of Job: A Contest of Moral Imaginations* [Oxford: University Press, 2003]), who concedes that "like a latter day Elihu," she began her commentary on Job with the assumption that she would be able to bring some resolution to the debate about innocent suffering. Immersing herself in the dialogue, she discovered that polyphony, not monologue, is the essence of the wisdom this book offers. As she puts it,

> In the postmodern, multicultural world, one cannot escape the reality of the multiplicity of differently situated consciousnesses that continually engage one another over questions of meaning and value. There is no culture, no tradition, no society—indeed, no person—that is not itself composed of multiple voices, dialogically situated. (261)

Because the final form of the book of Job models the interaction of multiple speakers, she ends her quest for definitive answers with these words: "The only conclusion to a study of the dialogic structure of Job can be the advice to go and reread the book in the company of others who will contest your reading" (264).

SEVEN DAYS OF SILENCE

Marcus Mims

The first drawing comes out of Job 2:8. In this scene there is a large figure, centrally located, seated on ash, naked, scared, and in a fetal position. The viewer is abruptly introduced to Job and his story with God. With his transparent stare and his suffocating space, the discomfort of Job's story is forced onto the viewer. His eyes cut through our securities and tell a story of hopelessness and mystery.

Job's feet breach the boundaries of the drawing and into a verse that reveals a contrasting story. Here is where the religious dilemma begins. The author of these words is as important as what the verse declares about Job. It is important to remember throughout this art series, which offers an interpretation of the book of Job, that in verses 1:8 and 2:3 God declares Job to be a "Blameless and upright man, who fears God and shuns evil," even in the face of enormous and undeserved pain. The traditional theological view found in Psalm 1, which shows the faithful prospering and the wicked perishing, is here brought into question.

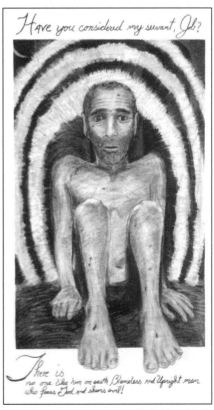

After God's declaration of Job's integrity, what can be said about suffering? Can it be connected with one's innocence or guilt? Can suffering offer a testing ground to one's faithfulness, or lack of faithfulness? Whatever the case, Job's suffering is real, earth shattering, and Job does not understand it.

Job is unaware of the verse that surrounds his picture in the first drawing, as he is unaware of God's pronouncement that brings about all of Job's misfortune. Through our reading of God's dialogue with the adversary, God not only permits but initiates this painful birth for Job. Job's suffering appears to be the catalyst, or tool, that leads him to a new vision of how he is to be in relationship with God and others.

(Credit: Marcus Mims)

The second drawing reveals a large circular image with rows of jagged objects leading the viewer's attention upward toward a skinny, lifeless tree. At the bottom, outside the circle, Job wades, naked, waist deep in the murky waters. With his back to the viewer, it is as though we are invited to look with him at a structure that doesn't offer any answers. At the top of the drawing, the heavens mirror the frantic motion of the rhythm or order onto the large circle. The circle is divided into seven sections. Once again, the intention here is to reflect ironically how the religious order Job has accepted as law did not lead him to prosperity, wisdom, and abundant life, but instead to meaninglessness, which for Job is worse than death. Job feels like a target for God, fenced in on all sides, and waiting for an inevitable death that cannot come soon enough.

(Credit: Marcus Mims)

In the third drawing, Job's naked image with his back still toward the viewer has moved into the central circle. The circle has become tighter and more defined. In the four corners of the drawing, outside the circle, four haunting figures appear: Job's three loving friends and his faithful wife. Whereas all four have good intentions to comfort Job during his dark nights of the soul, only his wife appears to stand by him. His friends' comforting words are more like words of judgment, intensifying Job's turmoil and building his case against God. The fences bearing down on him have become more organic, womb-like, and solid, limiting his sight and increasing upward toward his inevitable end, a catacomb. The eyes of Job's three friends, Eliphaz, Bildad, and Zophar, shift from one to another in judgment over Job as they offer a defense for God, for their own belief system, and for their pride. Job remains faithful to God as he approaches his pain openly and honestly.

(Credit: Marcus Mims)

In the next drawing, the story picks up after 40:3, where God blesses Job with a vision revealing how Job is to live as he has been created to live, in honest relationship with God. Here we see Job's hand over his mouth, eyes wide open, legs distorted, almost appearing dislocated, as he is spellbound by the wonders he has seen. The circle containing Job with the silhouette of his faithful wife behind him now contains the images of two awesome beasts: the Leviathan in the water and the Behemoth on land. God speaks of their ferociousness, strength, and design. Only God can defeat them, yet they face God nonetheless.

If viewers carefully observe the sky from the top of the mountain to the tip of the Leviathan's tail, an expression of God's face in the flashing lightening proceeding from the mountain can be seen. The two mythical beasts face God as Job sits motionless in the beard of God, awestruck by the things this vision has disclosed to him. At the top left of the drawing, outside the circle, the hand of God offers benediction. The boundaries of the circle have become thin and now burst forth with streams of water, possibly embryonic fluids. A new understanding, a new way to live with God, has been realized by Job, and with it comes a means by which his three spiritually blind friends will be cleansed and find redemption, restoration, and ordination.

The final drawing of the series images God as a winged being, appearing out of a whirlwind. Where this series started out with God's alien words of worth for Job and Job's scared feet interrupting the verse, now God's hands protrude out of the drawing, signifying blessing and ordination for Job and outwardly to those who risk seeing and understanding. Now, Job's words of praise for God from 42:3b are written down and speak of his personal experience with the Living God and his limited knowledge of God. This verse is placed behind him as he reaches upward to God and toward the future with God.

(Credit: Marcus Mims)

God is pictured here as dynamic in nature with arms stretched out wide, desiring to be in relationship with all. From the mouth of God flows the tabernacle of God. Here, inside, Job dwells at the head of the table, now clothed, with arms stretched out wide mirroring God's expression. On his lap rest the open Torah, and around the table kneels his restored family. This vision of reconciliation is different from the earlier image in the beginning of the book of Job. Now the daughters' names have been offered, showing them as a vital part of the restored family. The three figures in the dark to the right of the tent represent Job's friends whom God said spoke untruthfully. Job's priestly role of praying for his friends bridged them to the left side of the tent, which is an expression of worship and commissioning. The view is what one might see looking out of the Holy of Holy, beyond the Alter and into the crowds standing outside the entrance to the Tent of Meeting. Like the reference to the sores made in the first drawing, here Job's crucifix expression speaks of One who supplied that bridge for New Testament Christians.

PROLOGUE: LIFE IN THE "GARDEN OF UZ"

Job 1:1–2:13

The book of Job begins with a cryptic but deft announcement: "a man there was in the land of Uz." The man's name, of course, is Job. The prologue will describe his character and life experiences in due course. But the first datum that is given about this man is his locale. He resides in "the land of Uz." To encounter Job, this story suggests, one must enter into a world where a place called Uz centers life in particular ways.

The precise location of Uz is elusive. On a map it is somewhere in "the east" (1:3), but for the Joban story it is likely that this orientation is more theological than geographical. In Hebraic tradition, the east is the direction that orients the entire cosmos in the ways of its Creator. The primeval garden of Eden was planted "in the east" (Gen 2:8), thus marking the place on earth where humankind was first introduced to God's cosmic design and charged with the responsibility "to till it and keep it" (Gen 2:15). The revelation and the summons came first to Adam and Eve. The prologue to the book of Job invites the reader to understand that the world of God's design, with all of its promise and mystery, has now been entrusted to Job and his wife.

This theological orientation suggests that the book of Job functions somewhat like a sequel to the book of Genesis. In contemporary terms, we might

The Story of Job

Taddeo Gaddi (c.1300-1366). *View of the city*, (detail). Camposanto, Pisa, Italy (Credit: Scala/Art Resource, NY)

think of it as "The Creation Story: Part Two." The question the sequel will explore is, "How will Job's life in the garden of Uz be different from life in the paradise of Eden?"

At the outset, a number of verbal and thematic parallels between the prologue and Genesis 1-2 suggest that life in the land of Uz will conform to what we would expect based on the primeval account. Job's world is idyllic, a seemingly perfect recapitulation of primordial Eden. Like Adam, Job is a unique human being. He is "blameless" and "upright," one who "fears God" and "turns away from evil. " By God's own assessment, "there is no one like him on the earth" (1:8; 2:3). His exemplary status is confirmed by his full family and his contingent of servants and possessions (1:2-3). Like Adam, Job has received and realized the creational commission to "be fruitful and multiply" and to have "dominion" over that which has been entrusted to him (cf. Gen 1:22, 28). In Job's world, everything seems to be in place for building a life that is in complete harmony with God's cosmic design.

Job's paradise, however, is unexpectedly shattered, and his story of what it means to live in accordance with God's design for life takes a radical turn. The loss of his wealth and his possessions, the inexplicable death of his children, and the affliction of horrible physical suffering suggest that the forces of the cosmos have been unleashed against this servant of God. Still more unsettling is the report that unlike Adam, whose transgressions justified God's punishment, Job's world has been undone "for no reason," other than that God has been "provoked" by the *satan* (2:3). It is not Job's sin that merits divine reprisal. It is rather Job's righteousness that makes him the target for a divine gambit.

How will Job respond to *this* world of brokenness and loss, where the harmony of creation's design yields to unexpected and unwarranted assault? The prologue strains to insist that Job blesses, not curses, God (1:21). Even so, it acknowledges that Job's journey from prosperity to affliction winds its way finally past blessing to silence (2:13).

The drama of this journey is presented in six scenes alternately set in heaven and on earth. The structure recalls the six-day sequence of creation and thus evokes a further connection between the "genesis" of Job and the pristine beginnings prepared for all of humankind. [Structure of Job 1:1–2:13] However, precisely at the juncture where the parallels with

---

Structure of Job 1:1–2:13

(Day 1) (Scene 1)	1:1-5	On **Earth**: Job's unparalleled piety
(Day 2) (Scene 2)	1:6-12	In **Heaven**: God's first dialogue with "the *satan*"
(Day 3) (Scene 3)	1:13-22	On **Earth**: Disasters befall Job's family and possessions
(Day 4) (Scene 4)	2:1-7a	In **Heaven**: God' second dialogue with "the *satan*"
(Day 5) (Scene 5)	2:7b-10	On **Earth**: Job's personal affliction
(Day 6) (Scene 6)	2:11-13	On **Earth**: The friends arrive to "console" and "comfort" Job
(Day 7) (Scene 7)	?	

Genesis 1-2 lead one to expect a seventh scene that will celebrate the completion of the Joban creation story with a divine blessing, the drama of the prologue comes to an abrupt stop. The friends are so appalled by the suffering they see in Job that they sit in silence for seven days (2:11-13). Job's world has been turned upside down. Order yields to chaos. Silence replaces sound. It is as if Job's suffering has brought creation itself to a standstill. No one can speak further, not even God, until full account is taken of what has happened to Job. It is our first clue as readers that suffering like Job's changes everything, *in heaven and on earth.* ["From Heaven Through the World to Hell"]

COMMENTARY

Scene 1—Job's Unparalleled Piety, 1:1-5

The prologue introduces Job in six scenes that alternate between heaven and earth (1:1-5; 1:6-12; 1:13-22; 2:1-7a; 2:7b-10; 2:11-13). The story is told by an omniscient narrator who provides authoritative evaluation at the beginning (1:2-3) and ending (2:13) of the account and at critical points in between (1:22).[1] The effect of this narration is to impart to the reader information and judgments that require no further verification or analysis. What the narrator says is presumed to be correct: Job *is* "the greatest of all the people of the east" (1:3); he *is*

"From Heaven Through the World to Hell"

At the conclusion to the "Prelude in the Theatre," which introduces Goethe's *Faust,* the Director observes the stage that has been prepared for Faust's Job -like journey:

We have enough analyses,
Now I am eager to see deeds; (214-15)

Tonight, therefore, I say to you,
Do not spare our machinery.
Employ the sun and moon, do not hold back!
Use all the stars we have in stock;
Of water, fire, walls of rock,
And beasts and birds there is no lack.
In our narrow house of boards, bestride
The whole creation, far and wide;
Move thoughtfully, but fast as well,
From heaven through the world to hell. (234-42)

Faust and Mephisto

Gustav Eberlein (1847-1926). Detail of *Faust* from the Monument to Goethe. Villa Borghese, Rome, Italy. (Credit: Timothy McCarthy/Art Resource, NY)

W. Kaufmann, *Goethe's Faust: The Original German and a New Translation and Introduction* (New York/London: Anchor Books/Doubleday, 1961), 79, 81.

'blameless and upright" (1:3); he "*did not* sin" (1:22); his suffering *was* very great (2:13). This evaluation is twice substantiated by none other than God (1:8; 2:3). The reader is invited to join with God in accepting this report as true and reliable. Unlike the dialogues between Job and his friends (4–27), where perceptions are debated at length but without resolution, the prologue reports on matters that are understood to be settled. The community may (should?) appropriate the story as unquestionably normative.

The narration of Job's "genesis" begins in Scene 1 by describing the circumstances and qualities of his life that are constant. These "givens" will in turn provide the context for the enactment of the particular events in the ensuing drama. Three facts about Job are established in v. 1: his homeland, his name, and his extraordinary piety.

The location of the "land of Uz" is uncertain. The Bible associates it with both Edom (Lam 4:21; cf. Gen 36:28) and Aram (Gen 10:23; 22:21). Both designations are tenuous, however, and it is likely that Uz simply represents a place outside Israel that lies somewhere in "the east" (v. 3). Such an origin portrays Job as a non-Israelite, a Gentile, who was a worshipper of Israel's God, YHWH (e.g., 1:21). The book of Job accords no special significance to Job's status as a Gentile. For post-bib-lical Jewish and Christian interpreters, however, Job's origins figured prominently in discussions about the place of Gentiles among God's chosen people. [Job, the Righteous Gentile]

The orientation of the Joban story towards the east suggests that the horizon of its importance lies beyond any specific geographical boundary that defines Israel or its neighbors. The "east" may signify more than a specific location on the map. Of special import is the creation story that reports the garden of Eden was planted "in the east" (Gen 2:8).[2] Hebraic tradition affirms that at this primordial site God's design for the cosmos, entrusted to the stewardship of human beings, began to take concrete shape on earth. Like his Edenic counterpart Adam, Job's life in "the east," in the land of Uz, is connected to a drama that is paradigmatic for creation itself. The name Job (*'iyyob*) is also elusive and invites multiple associations. In second millennium West Semitic texts, an earlier form of the name, *'ayya- abum*, means "where is my father?" That name appears to signify an appeal to a deity, a divine father, for help.[3] In the Hebrew Bible, the only reference to the name outside the book of Job is in Ezekiel. Twice this prophet ranks Job, along with Noah and Danel (a legendary Canaanite king), as one of the righteous heroes in the culture's lore (Ezek 14:14, 20).[4] It has also been suggested that the Hebrew word for Job is connected to the root *'yb*, "to hate," and that the form *'iyyob* is a passive participle meaning "the hated one," "the persecuted one," or simply "the enemy."[5] Given this

Job, the Righteous Gentile

Rabbinic interpretations devote considerable discussion to the question of Job's origins, without arriving at a consensus view. Some rabbinic traditions honor Job as a righteous Gentile, who demonstrates that it is possible to be a faithful worshipper of the one true God even outside the boundaries of Israel. So, for example, Job is regarded as one of the seven Gentile prophets who prophesied to the nations before the Torah was given to Israel. These seven are identified as "Balaam and his father; Job from the land of Uz; and Eliphaz the Temanite; and Bildad the Shuhite; Zophar the Naamathite; and Elihu the son of Barachel the Buzite" (*S. Olam Rab.* 21). Further, some rabbinic accounts consider Job, along with two other Gentiles, Jethro and Balaam, to have been among the counselors living in the court of Pharaoh, who offered instruction concerning the treatment of the enslaved Israelites (see *b. Sotah* 11a, *b. Sanh.* 106a, *Exod. Rab.* 27:3). Balaam is said to have persuaded Pharaoh to issue the decree that all male Israelite children be drowned. For this, Balaam becomes the model of wicked Gentiles who seek the oppression and destruction of the people of Israel. When the decree was issued, Jethro is said to have fled Pharaoh's court and subsequently to have renounced his former life in order to join the Jewish community. For this, Jethro becomes the model for the Gentile who becomes a Jewish proselyte. Job is said to have been silent in the face of Pharaoh's decree, and for this he is punished by God, because he did nothing to prevent Israel's affliction. But at the same time, Job's punishment becomes a distraction

The Prophet Job

Fra Bartolomeo (1472-1517). *The Prophet Job*. Accademia, Florence, Italy. (Credit: Nicolo Orsi Battaglini/Art Resource, NY)

for Pharaoh, and while his attention is turned away from the Israelites, they are enabled to escape through the sea. In this way, Job's suffering ultimately serves to preserve the people of Israel.

Other commentators, however, are more ambivalent about Job's origins and his righteousness. Some traditions stipulate that Job was an Israelite, not a Gentile. *b. B. Bat.* 15b reports that Job was among the Israelites who returned from Babylonian exile, and that he founded a house of study in Tiberias. Some accounts connect Job to the household of Israel through association with the patriarchs. *The Testament of Job,* for example, describes Job as a descendant of Abraham whose wife was Dinah, the daughter of Jacob and Leah (1:5; cf. Pseudo-Philo 8:7; Targum on Job 2:9; *Gen. Rab.* 57:4; 73:9; 80:4).

Even where rabbinic tradition recognizes Job's status as a Gentile, it often seeks to establish the limits of his righteousness by comparing him unfavorably to Israel's patriarchs. It is said, for example, that only if Job had endured his trials without complaint, like Abraham, could his righteousness be regarded as truly comparable to that of Israel's heroes of faith (cf. *Pesiq. Rab.* 47). Such assessments indicate that while some rabbis did not deny the possibility of a righteous Gentile, few would accept the idea that a Gentile could be more righteous than a Jew.

Rabbinic debate concerning Job's righteousness and his origins responds in part to controversies between Jews and Christians that began in the first centuries of the Common Era. A prominent part of the Christian message was that the community of Christian believers, drawn from among the Gentiles, had displaced the Jews as the new Israel. In Christian biblical exegesis, Job became an important part of this message. The Fathers of the Church, for example Jerome, Augustine, and Gregory the Great, regarded Job, the righteous Gentile, as a saint who was part of the true Christian community (in Augustine's terms, "the fellowship of the heavenly city"; *Civ.* 18.47), even though he lived before the time of Christ. Further, as one who endured his sufferings patiently, Job not only exemplified Christian virtue; he also prefigured Christ.

For further reading on rabbinic interpretations of Job, see H. Kaufmann, *Die Anwendung das Buches Hiob in der Rabbinishen Agadah* (Frankfurt, 1893); I. Wiernikowski, *Das Buch Hiob nach der Aufassung der rabbinischen Literatur in den ersten fünf nach Christlichen Jahrhunderten* (Breslau: Freishman, 1902); N. Glatzer, "The Book of Job and Its Interpreters," *Biblical Motifs: Origins and Transformations*, ed. A. Altmann (Cambridge MS: Harvard University Press, 1966), 197-220; N. Glatzer, ed., *The Dimensions of Job: A Study and Selected Readings* (New York: Schocken, 1969), 16-24; J. Baskin, *Pharaoh's Counsellors: Job, Jethro, and Balaam in Rabbinic and Patristic Tradition* (Chico CA: Scholars Press, 1983).

connection, it is possible that there is a play on words in Job 13:24 where Job complains that God treats him like an enemy (*'ôyēb*).

It is impossible to determine precisely how these various associations might have informed the Hebrew story that came to be known simply by the name Job. One might reasonably conjecture, however, that ancient readers would have readily discerned multiple connections, both literal and symbolic, between this archaic name and this story. Job is the legendary paragon of righteousness whose life is marked by both invocation ("Where is God?") and accusation ("You treat me like an enemy"). His stance before God is that of the innocent sufferer whose petition for help is representative of the unjustly persecuted across the ages.

Job's defining characteristic is his extraordinary piety. Four attributes are specified, two adjectives that describe Job's character—"blameless" and "upright"—followed by two verbal phrases that describe how Job's character defines his actions—"feared God" and "turned away from evil. " The adjective "blameless" (*tām*) derives from a verbal form (*tmm*) that means to be "complete" or "finished." A related term, *tummah*, "integrity," which is also important in the book (2:3, 9; 27:5; 31:6), helps to clarify the meaning. Job is a person who is complete, whole, sound; he is not flawed, partial, or impaired in any way. "Upright" (*yāšār*) means "straight" and in the broadest sense has to do with ethical propriety.[6] In secular terms, an upright person is "honest," "true." In religious terms, the equivalent expression is "righteous." It is sometimes suggested that the words *tām* and *yāšār* do not describe two different features of Job's character but rather one single quality. One might say that Job is "scrupulously moral,"[7] or that he is a person of "perfect integrity."[8]

A "blameless" and "upright" person lives accordingly. That is, character is manifest in concrete acts and deeds. Job lives by "fearing God" and by "turning away from evil. " The "fear of God" is a common expression in wisdom literature that means in general to display total devotion to God by living in accord with the Creator's design for the world (e.g., Prov 9:10; 10:27; 14:27; 19:23; Pss 34:11; 111:10). The term refers to religious devotion, or piety, but is not limited to this. One who lives in total commitment to God will follow paths that lead toward good and "turn away from evil (*rā'*)." The prologue stipulates that Job does not choose evil or follow paths that lead to evil. Rather, evil (*rā'āh*) "comes upon him" (2:11). It is not a dimension of life that he determines for himself. It is an experience imposed on him by external forces.

The specific combinations of virtues ascribed to Job are not given to any other person in the Hebrew Bible. Ezekiel compares Job with Noah

(Ezek 14:14, 20), but Noah displays only two of these attributes (Gen 6:9).[9] Abraham is hailed as one who "fears God" (Gen 22:12). But unlike Job, who holds this distinction from the very outset of his story, Abraham is so recognized only after he demonstrates his willingness to sacrifice Isaac. [Job and Abraham] By elevating Job over all other biblical persons, the prologue makes the case that there is *truly* "no one like him in all the earth" (1:8; 2:3).

Verses 2 and 3 continue the description of Job's status as "the greatest of all the people of the east." Both his family and his possessions are reported with symbolic numbers (seven, three, ten) that indicate the completeness of Job's world: 7 sons + 3 daughters = 10; 7, 000 sheep + 3,000 camels = 10,000; 500 oxen + 500 donkeys = 1,000. The description of Job's children and his commodities is introduced in Hebrew with a grammatical construction called a *waw consecutive*, a feature that is not reflected in most translations. When this construction is taken into account, the beginning words of vv. 2 and 3 are more properly translated as follows: "*and so* there was born to him"; "*and so* he had seven thousand sheep." The grammar invites consideration of a question that is central in the prologue: what is the connection between Job's piety and his prosperity? Is piety the *precondition* for Job's prosperity? Or is prosperity the *motivation* for Job's piety? In the next scene, the *satan* will put the question sharply: "Does Job fear God for nothing?" (1:9).

Verses 4 and 5 complete the initial presentation of Job by describing one particular practice that consistently defines his life in the land of Uz. *It was the custom* of his seven sons, "each on his day," to hold a feast and to invite the sisters to join them for a banquet of eating and

---

Job and Abraham

In rabbinic discussion, Job and Abraham are sometimes juxtaposed as competitors for the distinction of "most righteous" person. In the *Testament of Abraham* (c. 100 CE), God sends the archangel Michael to inform the patriarch of his impending death and to instruct him to make a last will and testament before surrendering his soul. Abraham is reluctant, however, and Michael, who is having trouble persuading him, asks God for further instructions:

Lord Almighty, thus he speaks, and I refrain from touching him because from the beginning he has been your friend and he did everything which is pleasing before you. And there is no man like unto him on earth, not even Job, the wondrous man. And for this reason I refrain from touching him. Command, then, immortal king, what is to be done. (15:14-15)

In this account, the elevation of Abraham above Job may reflect the concern among the rabbis that a Gentile's righteousness not be equated with that of the Israelite ancestors. It may also be that in the eyes of some rabbinic commentators, Job's reputation as one who complained to God rendered him less than fully suitable for recognition as the most righteous person in Jewish tradition (see [Job, the Righteous Gentile]). As one Midrash puts it, if Job had not complained he would have been listed along with the ancestors of Israel in the daily prayers of the faithful. People would have prayed "God of Abraham, God of Isaac, God of Jacob and God of Job " (*Pesiq. Rab.* 47).

On rabbinic discussion of the relationship between Job and Abraham, see further A. Buchler, *Studies in Sin and Atonement in the Rabbinic Literature of the First Century* (Oxford: Oxford University Press, 1928), 130-50.

drinking. The days of these feasts are likely associated with the birth-
days of the brothers (see 3:1 where the expression "his days" is
translated "the day of his birth"). What is envisioned are seven annual
times of celebration when Job's children regularly affirm the good
fortune of their lives and the general goodness of the world that the
Creator has provided. As part of this same unbroken pattern of existence, *it was the custom* of Job, upon the completion of each of the
seven banquets, to offer preemptory sacrifices on behalf of his children,
just in case they had unwittingly sinned and "cursed God in their
hearts." [Blessing/Cursing in Job 1–2]

This recurring heptadic pattern of celebration creates an idyllic
picture of life in the land of Uz that recalls the primordial paradise of
Eden. ["Thus Did Job Continually"] Genesis 2:3 reports that upon completion
of that creation week, when the world that would make possible the
fulfillment of God's intentions and hopes had been established, God
"blessed the seventh day and hallowed (*wayĕqaddēš*) it." Job's celebration of life and his concern to honor and sustain the world that makes
it possible images God's activity. When the seven feast days were completed, Job would send for the children and "sanctify them"
(*wayĕqaddĕšēm*).

Once life had been celebrated and sanctified, Job (and his family)
would presumably return to the steady rhythms of everyday behavior.
From information already provided, the narrator expects the reader to
know what this means. Job is "blameless and upright." This is who Job
is always, without exception. He is "one who feared God and turned
away from evil. " In the words of the narrator, "this is what Job always
did."

Scene 2—In Heaven: God's First Dialogue With the Satan, 1:6-12

Scene 2 transports the reader from earth to heaven. The focus now
shifts from the regular routines that define life for Job and his family in
the land of Uz to the particular events of "one day" when a heavenly
council gathers to discuss God's governance of the cosmos (v. 6). The
identity of the participants in this council is not disclosed. They are
called simply by their group name, "sons of God" (*bĕnê haʾĕlōhîm*;
NRSV: "heavenly beings"). [Divine Council] They come to "present themselves before the Lord." The imagery is that of royal attendants who
stand before a king in order to report on their activities and to receive
instructions at the king's pleasure (cf. Prov 22:29; Zech 6:5). In
Mesopotamian and Canaanite religion, the divine council gathers on
New Year's Day to assess the year that has passed and to decide the des-

Blessing/Cursing in Job 1–2

ΑΩ The Hebrew text of Job 1:5 has the word "bless" (*bārak*), not "curse," as most English translations imply. A literal translation would be "It may be that my children have sinned and *blessed* God in their hearts." Virtually all translations (e.g., NRSV, REB, NAB, TEV, NJPS) and commentators have assumed that the verb *bārak* is used euphemistically in place of a word for "curse" (presumably *qālal*). The conventional reasoning behind this translation is that the original author (or a later editor) regarded a text that mentioned cursing God as blasphemous and unacceptable. To avoid this situation, the author substituted the word "bless" for "curse." Later readers would be expected to recognize that the original text had been changed and to re-substitute the word "curse" at the appropriate place.

The prevailing assumption that "bless" (*bārak*) is a euphemism for "curse" is, however, open to question. There is no clear evidence that "bless" is a standard or automatic substitution for "curse," either in the language of the ancient Near East or in the Hebrew Bible. Apart from Job, three additional examples of this substitution are sometimes cited (1 Kgs 21:10, 13; Ps 10:3), but serious questions in each text make the translation less than certain. Within Job 1–2, there are six occurrences of the word *bārak*. Two are routinely translated with the normal meaning "bless" (1:10, 21), four are conventionally translated with the opposite meaning "curse" (1:5, 11, 2:5, 9). If one examines these four texts without assuming that "bless" automatically means "curse," a reasonable case can be made in each instance for reading the text as it stands, without any substitutions. For example, Job 1:5 could be rendered literally, "perhaps my children have sinned, and blessed God." The intended meaning could be that because (or if) the children sinned, it would be inappropriate to offer blessing to God until they sought forgiveness. (E.g., Good takes the verb "sin" [*ht'*] and the verb "bless" [*brk*] as a hendiadys, that is, two words used together to convey a single idea. He translates Job 1:5 as follows: "Perhaps my children have blessed Elohim sinfully"

[*In Turns of Tempest: A Reading of Job with a Translation* (Stanford: Stanford University Press, 1990), 51]). In sum, there are no clear criteria for deciding whether to read *bārak* in Job 1–2 as "bless" or "curse." Either translation may be appropriate, and the different meanings have to be appropriated within the overall context of the prologue.

The ambiguity in the meaning of "bless" in Job may in fact be more than a mere linguistic peculiarity. Each time the word "bless" occurs in the prologue—six times in all—the reader must discern whether the meaning is "bless" or "curse." Such ambiguity is representative of the book of Job, as the debates between Job and his friends will make clear. What does it mean to bless God or to be blessed by God? What does it mean to curse God or to be cursed by God? By the conclusion of the prologue, the reader comes to understand that for Job, being blessed by God (cf. 1:11) is bound up with opposite and unexpected consequences (cf. 1:13-19; 2:7). For the innocent sufferer, is blessing God the only legitimate response of faith (cf. 1:21)? Or is cursing God also within the limits of faithful encounter between the innocent sufferer and God, as a literal rendering of the wife's counsel suggests (2:9)?

In keeping with the six scenes of the prologue, which do not move automatically to a seventh and decisive scene, the six occurrences of "bless" in the prologue do not move unambiguously to final meanings. In the prose narrative (Job 1–2; 42:7-17), which provides one version of the Job story (see Introduction), the seventh and last occurrence of "bless" is in Job 42:12: "The Lord blessed (*bārak*) the latter days of Job more than the beginning . . . ." The reader who follows Job through the long journey from the "beginning" to the "latter days" will have embarked on an important re-examination of what it means to bless and to be blessed by God.

For further reading, in addition to the standard commentary discussions, see T. Linafelt, "The Undecidability of בָּרַךְ in the Prologue to Job and Beyond," *BibInt* 4 (1996): 154-72.

tinies of nations and peoples for the year that approaches. The day marks a pivotal turning point when the rhythmic patterns of created order are suspended in the breach between past and future, old and new. The fate of the cosmos for the next year depends on what the assembly decrees and enacts. The prologue utilizes the imagery of the divine council as the backdrop for the drama that awaits an unsuspecting Job. His world is under review. Decisions will be made, without his consultation, concerning his fate and that of his family.

"Thus Did Job Continually"

William Blake (1757–1827), an English engraver, painter, and poet, was concerned with the book of Job for most of his professional life. His first drawing of Job has been dated to 1785, when he was 28 years old. His last completed masterpiece was the *Illustrations of the Book of Job,* a set of twenty-one engravings produced in several editions between 1821 and 1826. Three months after they were completed, just before his seventieth birthday, Blake died.

Blake's art and poetry is a product of and a response to the eighteenth century and the Age of Reason. He believed there was an eternal truth that joined the natural world and the spiritual world in a harmony that reflected God's design for creation. But given the excesses of human corruption and barbarity, all too manifest in the French Revolution, Blake was convinced that the intended symmetry between God and humankind had been lost. It was recoverable, he believed, by embarking on a journey guided by art and imagination that led one back to the paths of truth. The journey towards truth comprised five critical steps: awaking to the sense of divine reality; a consequent purification of self; the return of an enhanced sense of divine order; a dark night of the soul in which the self is crucified in the absence of the divine; and a complete reunion with the divine. At the end of his life Blake felt that he had completed this journey. In the *Illustrations of the Book of Job* he sought to report back from the last stage of the journey the ultimate truth that he had learned.

Illustration no. 1 shows Job and his wife and their family, seven sons and three daughters, serene and secure in an idyllic setting. Job and his wife hold an open book in their lap, presumably the "Book of the Law" that centers their life. The children are kneeling in a position of prayer. In the foreground, sheep are resting peacefully; there is no need to keep guard for all is calm and quiet. In the background to Job's right is a Gothic church, symbol of religion and conventional piety. To Job's left there is a crescent moon and an evening star shining over tents and storehouses, symbols of Job's considerable material possessions and wealth. In the center stands a tree, emblematic of Eden's tree of life, with branches that extend to encompass the entire scene. On first glance, the scene depicts Job's life as complete and whole, a perfect combination of piety and prosperity. Blake has reinforced this impression by placing a citation from Job 1:1-2 in the bottom border.

On further inspection, however, it becomes apparent that in the midst of Job's ordered world there are already signs forewarning some imminent disaster. The signs of the Zodiac (from left to right: the bull and the ram) that appear in the bottom corners of the border are in reverse order.

Job and His Family

William Blake (1757-1827). *Job's Happy Family*. 1823-1825. Engraving from Blake's *Illustrations of the Book of Job*.

The musical instruments hanging from the tree (tambourine, trumpet, lute) are silent and unused. Finally, Blake inscribes on the altar in the bottom border a citation from 2 Cor 3:6 that offers a negative Christian assessment of Job's fidelity to the sacrificial laws: "The Letter Killeth, the Spirit giveth Life. It is Spiritually Discerned."

For further reading on Blake's interpretation of Job, see J. Wickstead, *Blake's Vision of the Book of Job,* 2nd ed. (New York: E. P. Dutton and Co., 1924); J. Hagstrum, *William Blake Poet and Painter: An Introduction to the Illuminated Verse* (Chicago: Chicago University Press, 1964), 119-35; S. Damon, *Blake's Job: William Blake's Illustrations of the Book of Job* (Providence RI: Brown University, 1966); A. Wright, *Blake's Job: A Commentary* (Oxford: Oxford University Press, 1972); S. Terrien, *The Iconography of Job Through the Centuries: Artists as Biblical Interpreters* (University Park: The Pennsylvania University Press, 1996), 194-228.

Divine Council

The concept of a divine council comprised of a ruling god and an assembly of gods is attested in Egypt, Babylon, and Canaan. In Canaanite religion, for example, the god who held the power of decree was El, and the "assembly of El," comprised of ones referred to as the "sons of god" or the "family of god," are described as El's physical descendants. The assembly convened on El's mountain, which was envisioned to be the center of the cosmos. Through El's decrees, which would be enacted by the assembly, the order of the cosmos was maintained against the threat posed by hostile powers who sought to claim kingship over the earth.

The concept of the divine council is never fully articulated in the Hebrew Bible, although numerous references and allusions make clear that the idea was part of Hebraic thought. For example, the Hebrew Bible refers to the divine assembly as the "council of El" (Ps 82:1 [MT 82:2]) or the "council of the holy ones" (Ps 89:7 [MT Ps 89:8]). It describes the participants in the assembly as "sons of the Most High/Elyon" (Ps 82:6), "holy ones" (Deut 33:2, 3; Job 5:1), or as in Job 1:6 and 2:1, "sons of God" (NRSV: "heavenly beings"). Some post-exilic texts provide the names of members of the divine council ("Michael" in Dan 10:13, 21; 12:1; "Gabriel" in Dan 8:16; 9:21). Perhaps the clearest pictures of the divine council are in 1 Kgs 22:19-22 and in Dan 7:9-14. In the former, YHWH is described as "sitting on a throne" with royal-like attendants to the right and the left.

In the latter, the "ancient of days" sits on a throne of judgment attended by thousands of courtiers. For one depiction of God and the celestial court, see **["Then Went Satan Forth from the Presence of the Lord"]**.

In the intertestamental period, the idea of the divine council develops in different ways. The deities of the assembly are ranked in a hierarchy of angels and archangels who have assigned responsibilities for maintaining the cosmos (Jub 2:2; *1 En.* 20:1-8). Some become intercessors for humans (*1 En.* 15:2; Tob 12:15); some serve as guardians of the righteous (*1 En.* 20:5; Jub 35:17); some serve in the heavenly army that appears at the end of time (1QH 3:35-36; 1QM 15:14). Within this hierarchy, the one called the *satan* becomes a more distinct figure (e.g., Jub 49:2; CD 4:13; 5:18; 8:2). There also gradually emerges a more distinct concept of heavenly beings who are hostile to the will of the supreme deity of the heaven (*1 En.* 40:7; 53:3; 54:6; 61:1; etc.; cf. Jub 10:8; 11:5; 17:16; 49:20). The New Testament reflects this development in its own distinct ways, for example, in the depiction of the angel Gabriel who serves as a heavenly messenger (Luke 1:11-20; cf. 2:8-14) and in the depiction of Satan as the personification of evil.

For further reading see, M. Pope, *El in the Ugaritic Texts* (Leiden: E. J. Brill, 1955); E. T. Mullen, *The Assembly of the Gods* (Chico CA: Scholars Press, 1980); idem, "Divine Assembly," *ABD*, ed. D. N. Freedman (New York: Doubleday, 1992), vol. 2, 214-17.

How he responds will contribute, for good or for ill, to the maintenance of the new creation that God and the heavenly council has designed.

Among the divine beings who are present is one called in Hebrew הַשָּׂטָן. When the Hebrew characters of this word are transposed into equivalent English letters, the resultant form is *haśśāṭān*. The majority of English translations unfortunately render this word as "Satan," a designation that misleadingly associates this one with "the Devil" or "Satan" of later Christian theology. The single Hebrew word comprises two elements (*ha* + *śāṭān*). The word *śāṭān* is a common noun meaning "adversary," "accuser." It is used to describe both human (1 Sam 29:4; 2 Sam 19:22 [MT 19:23]; 1 Kgs 11:14, 23, 25) and superhuman beings (Num 22:22; Zech 3:1) who confront, contend with, or challenge someone. The second element is the definite article "the" (*ha*), which precedes the noun here and in each of its occurrences in Job (1:7, 8, 9, 12; 2:1, 2, 3, 4, 6, 7). The definite article signifies that this word should be understood not as a personal name but rather as a title that is descriptive of one's function and responsibility. *Hassātān* is "the adversary," "the accuser," that is, the heavenly being whose designated role in the divine council is to serve as a kind of prosecuting attorney who brings charges against another in court. The *satan* is not God's opponent; his intentions are neither evil nor opposed to God's purposes. Instead, the *satan* serves as God's advocate, probing human behavior according to God's directives in search of truth and faithfulness.[10] [The Satan]

The drama of Scene 2 focuses on the dialogue between God and the *satan*. God initiates the conversation, and hence the action that follows, by asking the *satan* if in his going back and forth on the earth he has considered the case of the one named Job. Before the *satan* can offer a report of his own, God affirms Job's status with the same unqualified praise that the narrator has already provided in v. 1: Job is "a blameless and upright man, one who fears God and turns away from evil. " God's assessment, however, is even more laudatory. Job is not only a "servant" of God, a designation that ranks him among such honored persons as Abraham (Gen 26:24), Moses (Exod 14:31), and David (2 Sam 7:5). He is in a class of his own: "there is no one like him on the earth" (v. 8). The phrase "no one like him" is normally applied only to God (only here and in 1 Sam 10:24 with reference to humans).[11] By God's estimation Job is righteous beyond comparison. On earth he is a near-equal to God. More than anyone else, he embodies what it means for humankind to be created "in the image of God" (Gen 1:26-27).

The *satan* does not challenge God's assessment of Job's incomparable piety. Instead, he raises two questions that shift the discussion to a consideration of what motivates Job's loyalty to God. First, there is a general probe of Job's motives: "Does Job fear God for nothing (*hinnām*)?" (v. 9), or as one translation puts it, "Doesn't Job have a good reason for being so good?"[12] The question presumes the answer that should follow: "Of course, Job serves God for a good reason." But like God, who had preempted the *satan's* initial response with a follow-up question, the *satan* does not wait for an answer to his query. He proceeds directly to a second question and to particular areas in Job's case that merit further examination. "Have you not placed a hedge around him and around his family and around all that he has?" (v. 10). The "hedge" is an image of divine protection and safety, which if removed leaves one vulnerable to the chaos that ranges freely beyond its borders (Isa 5:1-7; cf. Ps 80:8-13 [MT: 80:9-14]). The most suggestive analogue of an earthly hedge is the firmament with which God holds back the primal waters of chaos in order to create a space where humankind can live and prosper (Gen 1:6-9; cf. Job 38:8-11).[13] The *satan's* question implies that God has so defined Job's world and so pro-

The *Satan*

AΩ The verb *śāṭān* occurs six times in the Hebrew Bible (Pss 38:20 [MT Ps 38:21]; 71:13; 109:4, 20, 29; Zech 3:1). Five of the six occurrences are in lament psalms, which refer to human opponents of the righteous, who "accuse" or act adversarially to defame character or bring duress. Only in Zech 3:1 is the verb used with reference to the activity of "the *satan*." The noun *śāṭān*, "accuser, adversary," occurs twenty-six times in the Hebrew Bible. Of these, seven refer to earthly *satans* (1 Sam 29:4 (David); 2 Sam 19:22 [MT 19:23] (Abishai); 1 Kgs 5:4 [MT 5:18] (an anonymous military adversary of Solomon); 11:14 (Hadad); 11:23, 25 (Rezon); Ps 109:6 (an anonymous accuser of the psalmist). Nineteen of the twenty-six occurrences refer to celestial *satans*. Sixteen of the nineteen, including all of the references in Job 1–2, use the noun with the definite article, that is, "the *satan*." The three exceptions are Num 22:22, 32 and 1 Chr 21:1.

The Hebrew Bible depicts the relationship between God and *satan* in different ways. Three passages, each describing a heavenly or celestial *satan*, are especially pertinent to the occurrences in Job 1 and 2: Num 22:22-35; Zech 3:1-7; and 1 Chr 21:1-22:1. In Num 22, "*satan*" (NRSV: "adversary") is a subordinate figure sent by God to convey God's own disposition and decision concerning Balaam In Zech 3, "the *satan*" is a subordinate of God who brings challenges against the high priest Joshua that God rejects. 1 Chr 21 is somewhat different. This account is based on an earlier version in 2 Sam 24, which reports that "the anger of the Lord was kindled against Israel, and he incited David against them" by instructing him to take a census of the people (v. 1). Having taken the census, however, David is subsequently punished by God for having done what God had instructed (vv. 15-17). The later, parallel story in 1 Chr alters this report and shifts the responsibility for the census away from God to *satan*: "Satan (*sātān*) stood up against Israel, and incited David to count the people of Israel (21:1). In this account, David is punished not for obeying the directives of God, but for obeying one who incites an act God opposes. The text of 1 Chr 21:1 is the only place in the Hebrew Bible where the word *satan*, without the definite article, appears to be used as a proper name for an independent celestial figure who is an adversary of God.

The *satan* in Job 1–2 shares certain features with the figures in both Num 22 and Zech 3. God commissions and authorizes Job's *satan*, as in the case with Balaam And God questions Job's *satan*, thus suggesting there may not be complete agreement between God and the *satan* concerning the objectives of the divine commission. In this respect, both Job 1–2 and Zech 3 depict the divine council as the place where such contrasting perspectives are debated and resolved. There is no indication in Job 1–2, however, that the *satan* is an independent figure who exercises power in opposition to God's intentions, as in 1 Chr 21.

Post-biblical literature gives more attention to the figure of the *satan* than does the Hebrew Bible and typically makes a clearer distinction between the power of the *satan* and the sovereign rule of God. The conventional explanation attributes this concern to distinguish between the forces of evil and the forces of God to Israel's exposure to Persian dualism. In this view, the world becomes a battleground where the good god (Ahura Mazda) and the evil god (Angra Mainyu) contend for sovereignty. In the Book of Jubilees (2nd C. BCE), the chief of evil spirits is called Mastema (lit., "enmity, hatred, hostility"; 10:1-14; 11:1-5). It is Mastema, for example, who is said to have caused Abraham's testing (Jub 17:16; cf. Genesis 22:1) and to have attacked Moses on his way to Egypt (Jub 4:2; cf. Exod 4:24). In Qumran texts, the leader of the forces of darkness is most often identified as Belial (lit., "wickedness" or "worthlessness"). As the prince of the kingdom of wickedness (1QM 17:5-6), Belial leads his troops against the Sons of Light in an effort to control the world (1QM 1:1, 13; 11:8; 15:3).

The Septuagint and the New Testament translate *satan* with the word *diabolos*, "devil. " In general all the features of *satan* in the Hebrew Bible and in Judaism are present in the Devil of the New Testament, although they are obviously developed and presented in a distinctive Christian context. The Devil is a superhuman adversary of God whose power to seduce humankind earns him such titles as "ruler of the demons" (Matt 12:24), "god of this world" (2 Cor 4:4), and "ruler of the power of the air" (Eph 2:2). Although his powers are formidable and will increase in the last days (2 Thess 2:9-10), the New Testament asserts that God will ultimately defeat the Devil and cast him into an eternal fire (Rev 20:1-10).

Given this long development of thought concerning the role of the *satan*, it is important to keep the Job texts in proper perspective. In Job, the figure of the *satan* is not depicted as one who is independent and opposed to God. He is instead one of God's heavenly beings, who at God's initiative and with God's permission embarks on a mission to destroy a righteous man named Job. The conundrum this creates for readers of this story, both ancient and modern, is both the challenge and the invitation of this book. The increasing amount of attention given to this shadowy figure called the *satan*, who apart from Job 1–2 enjoys only brief appearances in the Hebrew Bible, is but case in point.

For further reading see, R. S. Kluger, *Satan in the Old Testament* (Evanston IL: Northwestern University Press, 1967); P. L. Day, *An Adversary in Heaven: Satan in the Hebrew Bible* (Atlanta GA: Scholars Press, 1987); V. Hamilton, "Satan," *ABD*, ed. D.N. Freedman (New York: Doubleday, 1992), vol. 5, 985-89.

tected his life that he has been assured unmitigated blessing. All other fortunes have been denied entrance to his domain. If, however, God would remove this protective border and "stretch out" the hand to afflict Job rather than to protect him, the *satan* wagers that Job would respond in kind. When blessed, Job will bless. And when cursed, Job will curse. [CD: "A Rich Man's Piety Stinks"]

The *satan's* questions are double-edged probes. On the one hand, they invite scrutiny of *Job's piety*. Suffering, the *satan* implies, will change the calculus between God and humans. Will Job worship God for nothing, for no reward? The wager is that without the reward, there will be no devotion. On the other, the questions invite scrutiny of *the nature and character of God*. It is God who has sheltered Job behind a protective hedge; God who has determined the boundaries within which piety can flourish without distraction; and God who has chosen to respond to piety with blessing. But what if God construed another world, with different boundaries and other fortunes? If God did not create the conditions that make devotion natural and prosperity the norm, would God hear the praises of human beings who have other choices to make and different reasons for making them? Is God alone, apart from any reward or retribution, worthy of loyalty and devotion? The question is theological in the most profound way. What kind of God is God? J. Gerald Janzen has framed the critical issues clearly:

> Is God intrinsically worshipful? Is deity capable of creating a creature who, somehow, attains to such freedom and independence, such spiritual and moral maturity, as to be in a position to choose to offer God worship and service because of God's intrinsic worthiness to be loved?[14]

The initial exchange between God and the *satan* concludes (v. 12) with divine consent and a conferral of authority. God agrees to the *satan's* proposal and sets the terms for its enactment. Twice in the preceding dialogue, the *satan* has established that God has put a protective hedge around Job and "all that he has" (vv. 10, 11). Now God consents to remove this hedge and relinquish Job and "all that he has" into the *satan's* power. There is one restriction. The *satan's* hand may extend to all that Job possesses, but it must stop short of Job himself. With delegated power and an agreed agenda, the *satan* "went out from the presence of the Lord."

Scene 3—On Earth: Disasters Befall Job's Family and Possessions, 1:13-22

Scene 3 resumes the account of Job's full and satisfying life in the land of Uz as if nothing has changed since the first report (1:1-5). The reader knows that the decisions made in the divine council have set in motion catastrophic changes for Job, but Job himself is not privy to this information. He and his family go about their normal routines secure and unaware. The sons and daughters are eating and drinking and celebrating the goodness of life, as is their custom. Job, presumably, observes everything with proud satisfaction and prepares the purgative sacrifices, as is his custom. The arrival of the messengers signals that all is about to change. ["And I Only Am Escaped to Tell Thee"]

"And I Only Am Escaped to Tell Thee"

Blake depicts a series of three messengers bringing Job and his wife the news of their misfortune. The first has already arrived with the report that the Sabeans have fallen on his oxen. A second, who comes with news that the "fire of God" has burned up the flocks, can be seen in the middle distance. A third, barely visible under the darkening sky of the far horizon, is on the way with the word that a final catastrophe has struck the children.

In the midst of these reports Job's world remains essentially in tact. He and his wife are still sitting under the tree that centers their life, although Blake has now moved the tree off center and to Job's left. The Gothic church can still be seen in the foreground. Some of Job's possessions are still present, although his barns are gone, and there is now only a remnant of his flocks. Job's wife raises her arms over her head, perhaps in supplication, while keeping her gaze on her husband. Job clasps his hands in prayer and looks toward the heavens, as if preparing to utter the blessing recorded in Job 1:21.

The figure standing astride the heavens towards which Job looks, however, is Satan, not God. His back is turned toward Job. A sword is his in his left hand. He has returned from "going to and fro in the earth." The calamitous results of his mission on earth now swirl around one who remains focused on a God no longer visible.

The Messengers Tell Job of His Misfortunes

William Blake (1757-1827). *The Messengers Tell Job of His misfortunes*. 1823-1825. Engraving from Blake's *Illustrations of the Book of Job*.

Four messengers (vv. 14-19) come in rapid succession to announce a series of calamities that now suddenly "fall" (*nāpal*; repeated in vv. 15, 16, 19) upon Job's world. The report is artfully stylized to heighten its dramatic effect. The use of the number four (four messengers, four disasters) symbolizes the completeness of Job's losses (cf. Ezek 14:12-23; Zech 1:18-21 [MT 2:1-4]). The enumeration of the disasters follows a pattern of ascending gravity (3 + 1) that recalls the sequence of Job's blessings in vv. 2-3, but reverses its order: first, the destruction of the oxen and the donkeys (vv. 14-15), symbols of Job's agricultural interests; second, the destruction of the sheep, symbols of Job's pastoral interests (v. 16); third, the destruction of the camels, signifying the loss of Job's trading and transport enterprises.[15] The fourth and last report—the death of Job's children (vv. 18-19)—brings the dreadful account to its climax. The disasters fall on Job from the four points of the compass, conveyed by agents of destruction identified alternately with earth and heaven: the Sabeans (v. 15), a people connected with southern Arabia; the "fire of God" that "fell from heaven" (v. 16), perhaps associated, from a Palestinian standpoint, with thunderstorms coming from the west; the Chaldeans (v. 17), unsettled nomads of Aramean stock who are depicted as attacking Job from the north; and finally, a "great wind (*rûaḥ gĕdôlah*) from the other side of the desert" (v. 19). Like the khamsin that blows in from the east, it is a force of such enormous power as to suggest parallels with the primordial "wind from God" (*rûaḥ ʾelōhîm*; Gen 1:2) that drives creation itself. The form and substance of these sequenced reports invites the reader to understand that the forces of the cosmos, heaven and earth, have been unleashed almost simultaneously on an unsuspecting Job.

The pace of the presentation allows no time for Job to respond to the individual episodes. Not until Job's losses have their cumulative impact are we permitted to watch and listen to his reaction (vv. 20-22). He expresses himself in two ways. First, he engages in ritual acts of mourning that embody thought and feeling without words (v. 20). He tears his robe (cf. Gen 37:34; Josh 7:6; 2 Sam 1:11; 3:31; 13:31; Ezra 9:3, 5; Esth. 4:1), shaves his head (cf. Isa 15:2; 22:12: Jer 7:29; 16:6; Ezek 7:18; Amos 8:10; Mic 1:16), and falls on the ground (cf. Josh 7:6; 2 Sam 13:31). To these gestures a fourth is added: "and worshipped." The verb means literally "to prostrate oneself" and signifies the act of lying or kneeling and touching the face to the ground in homage to a superior. Job's prostration connects his mourning with conventional postures of worship, reverence, and obeisance (cf. Exod 34:8; 2 Chr 7:3, 20).

Second, Job speaks words that give audible expression, and thus clarity, to what he has bodied forth (v. 21). His gestures convey

mourning; hence the reader prepares to hear words of grief and lamentation. But in mourning Job remains persistently reverent. He
appropriates a traditional wisdom saying that acknowledges the reality
of death without succumbing to despair or fatalism: "Naked I came
from my mother's womb, and naked shall I return there" (cf. Eccl 5:15;
Sir 40:1). The perspective of the maxim is anthropological. The
journey of every human being begins in the mother's womb, with life
defined not by possessions but by intimate dependence on the one who
gives life itself. It ends in the womb of the grave, where one is stripped
of possessions and intimately reconnected with "mother earth" (for the
imagery of earth as womb and grave, see Ps 139:13-15). There are no
exceptions; every life must move between these two boundaries. The
assertion that all mortals rise from the dust of the earth and return to
that dust connects Job's personal journey with primordial images of life
in the post-Eden world (Gen 3:19). At this point in the Joban story, the
assertion is a neutral one, a statement of fact that is neither positive nor
negative. As the book develops, however, what it means to be a mere
mortal, a creature of dust and ashes, will emerge as an important question (see 4:19; 10:9; 17:16; cf. 30:19; 42:6).

To the insight gleaned from human wisdom, Job adds a distinctly
theological assertion: "The Lord has given, and the Lord has taken
away; let the name of the Lord be blessed." The substance of the assertion has to do with the domain of God's activity—giving and taking.
As the human journey from birth to death signifies the totality of life,
so giving and taking signifies the totality of God's dominion in Job's life
and in all creation (cf. Ps 104:27-30). The form of the assertion is that
of a conventional blessing offered in the context of a congregation at
worship. The same form—"let the name of the Lord be blessed"—
occurs in Ps 113:2, accompanied by the words "from this time on and
forevermore." Job's blessing, like that of the psalmist, expresses the conviction that in all of life, in birth and in death, in what is given and
what is taken away, God is worthy of praise and adoration. [CD: "The Lord
Gave; the Lord Has Taken Away"]

The narrator concludes Scene 3 with an assessment of what has transpired (v. 22). The *satan* wagered that if God gave to Job affliction
rather than prosperity, Job would in turn give to God cursing rather
than blessing (v. 11). But Job has not responded to God in kind. He
has not sinned, and he has not "given *tiplāh* (NRSV: "wrong-doing") to
God." The latter phrase is uncertain, but the general context of its
usage in Job suggests that it signifies a form of cursing.[16] Job did not
curse God, even when God had taken away his blessing. Given the
ambiguity of blessing and cursing in the prologue, this additional note
from the narrator reinforces the affirmation of Job's piety. Job remains

what he has always been, a righteous and reverent exemplar of humankind, even though his world (and the God who presides over it) seems no longer attuned to his efforts.

Scene 4—In Heaven: God's Second Dialogue with the Satan, 2:1-7a

The second round of dialogue between God and the *satan* begins with preliminaries that repeat almost verbatim the first meeting of the divine council (2:1-2; cf. 1:6-7). The repetition serves to return the drama to a sense of narrative calm after the calamities that have just been reported. In spite of all that has transpired on earth, God's assessment of things remains the same as before. Job remains "blameless and upright." He continues to "fear God" and "turn away from evil. " He "holds fast" (*ḥāzaq*) to his integrity (*tummah*; see the commentary on 1:1). Job's soundness is reason for God to boast. On earth there may still be found one who exemplifies what it means to live in happy harmony with God's governance of creation.

But if the repetition in this scene restores a sense of balance and calm to the story about life in Job's world, it also encourages the reader to listen carefully for any new details that may once again send the story spinning in a new direction. One such detail is added at the end of v. 3 with God's candid admission to the *satan*, "you incited me against him" The verbal construction "incite against" (*sut* + *bĕ*) carries a negative connotation, as in stirring up someone to an action against another that would not have occurred without provocation (1 Sam 26:19; 2 Sam 24:1; Jer 43:3). Job 2:3 is the only place in the Hebrew Bible where this construction is used with God as the object of the verbal action. God says to the *satan, you* have provoked *me*.

The concession heightens interest in the story in two ways. First, in the opening scene of the heavenly council it is God, not the *satan*, who initiates the conversation about Job, thus setting in motion the course of actions that followed. By all indications, God is in full control of what has transpired. This second council scene, however, suggests that the conversation about Job is more complex than it appears. As the titular head of the divine council, God now seems to be *receiving* instructions from the *satan*, not *giving* them. The two versions of what is going on in heaven stand in tension with each other. Who exercises the controlling influence in the divine council, God or the *satan*? Second, the suggestion that God can be provoked to do something that might not have occurred without some external pressure invites reflection on the character of God. Can God be coerced, manipulated, perhaps even tricked? The prologue does not linger over such questions, for it is principally concerned with the test of *Job's* character, not *God's*.

But in the dialogues between Job and his friends, Job will repeatedly insist that innocent suffering necessarily places God on trial, not the victim (e.g., Job 9-10). The tremor of this approaching debate can be felt already in this unsettling little admission of Scene 4. [Can God Be Incited?]

A second detail from the end of v. 3 contributes further to the reader's suspicion that the drama of the prologue is about to take off in a new direction. God admits to having been provoked to act against Job "for no reason." The Hebrew word (*ḥinnām*) is the same as the word used in the *satan's* question in 1:9: "Does Job fear God for nothing?" The implication of the *satan's* question is that there is a reasonable connection between Job's piety and God's benevolence towards him. Because of this connection, the *satan* argues, it makes sense for Job to love God. In 2:3, God puts the question of the causal connections between human behavior and divine action back on the table for inspection. God now concedes that there is no connection between Job's conduct and God's treatment of him. God has brought him to ruin (*bālaʿ*; lit., "swallowed him up") for no reason, other than to use him as a chip in a wager with the *satan*. On earth, Job believes that his given world, though presently in disarray, offers good reason for him to yield in happy fidelity to the God who "gives" and "takes away" (1:22). In heaven, the second dialogue between God and the *satan* now hints at just how demanding such an unconditional commitment to God may be. ["For No Reason"]

The *satan* responds to God's boast by suggesting that the test of Job has not yet gone far enough for anyone to claim victory (vv. 4-5). He challenges God to take Job's affliction to another level of intensity. "Skin for skin" is a proverbial saying that is open to several interpretations. The most convincing proposal is that the saying originated in ancient practices of bartering where trading one skin for another required careful assessment of relative values. The preposition "for" (*bĕʿad*) is perhaps better translated in this context as "up to." In bartering for an item (skins or other commodities) one would presumably be willing to offer anything of value up to a certain point. This seems to be the general sense of the *satan's* proposal, for in his next statement he goes on to say that "everything a man has he will give, *up to* (*bĕʿad*) his life."[17] Once more the *satan* challenges God to "stretch out" the hand, this time extending affliction to Job's bone and flesh. The wager is that if God exacts the price of physical pain and suffering in exchange for Job's love, Job will refuse to pay. He will curse God openly.

Can God Be Incited?

The suggestion that God was "incited" or provoked by the *satan* presented a challenge to later interpreters. The Septuagint translators softened the text by rendering the phrase "you incited me" as "you have told me." The Talmud states, "Were it not written in the Bible it would be impossible to say: God is like a man whom someone tries to incite and who in the end is incited."

Cited in M. Weiss, *The Story of Job's Beginning* (Jerusalem: Magnes Press, 1983), 37.

"For No Reason"

AΩ The little phrase "for no reason" is one of the "worry words" in the grammar of faith, to use the apt description of Carol Shields (see **["Unless" and Other "Worry Words" in the Grammar of Faith]**). The assessment below, which I appropriate from my previous essay, provides a beginning for further reflection. For supporting notes and additional discussion, readers may consult the full essay.

The adverb *ḥinnām*, "needlessly, without purpose, fro nothing," occurs 32x in the Old Testament. In the majority of cases, the word occurs in contexts that are theologically benign, e.g., in commercial transactions with the meaning "at no cost" or "gratis" (Gen 29:15; Num11:15; Isa 52:3; Jer 22:13), actions that are "in vain" because they do not accomplish the intended results (Ezek 6:10; 14:23; Mal 1:10; Prov 1:17), or actions that are "without warrant" because they are illegal or unjust (Pss 35:7; 109:3; 119:161). The occurrence of *ḥinnām* in Job 2:3, far from being theologically benign, sets in motion an act that would elsewhere be associated with sin and therefore discouraged and condemned. The wisdom admonition in Proverbs 1 clarifies the matter (cf. Prov 3:30; 24:28; 26:2):

My child, if sinners entice you, do not consent. If they say, "Come with us, let us wait for blood; let us wantonly (*ḥinnām*) ambush the innocent; like Sheol, let us swallow (*niblā'êm*) alive." (vv. 10-12a)

my child, do not walk in their way, keep your foot from their paths for their feet run to evil (*ra'*).(vv. 15-16)

The report that God has set about to destroy Job for no reason, like a nefarious sinner who ambushes the innocent, is in my judgment perhaps the single most disturbing admission in the Old Testament, if not in all scripture. The hermeneutical space it leaves open for interpretations that explain or exonerate God's behavior is small indeed. Seven sons and three daughters are dead—at God's instigation and with God's permission—for no reason. Perhaps Coleridge was right. The very existence of the book of Job proves that the Bible is an utterly human production, because God would never have written such a powerful argument against himself!

Samuel. E. Balentine, "For No Reason," *Int* 57 (2003): 360-61.
C. Shields, *Unless* (London, New York: Fourth Estate, 2002), 149.

Once more God agrees to the challenge and places Job at the *satan's* disposal (v. 6). Once more God imposes a condition. The *satan* may afflict Job, but he must "guard" (*šāmar*; NRSV: "spare") his life. Once more the *satan* departs from God's presence to enact a decision that has been mutually agreed upon.

Scene 5—On Earth: Job's Personal Affliction, 2:7b-10

The pace of the presentation in the fifth scene accelerates. There is no repetition of the formalized introduction "one day" that begins Scenes 2, 3, and 4, thus the careful delineation between events in the heavenly realm and those in earthly realm is missing here. Now the *satan* is depicted as simply stepping over the narrative border. With one step he remains in the presence of God, with the next he enters directly into the world of Job. As the *satan* takes his leave, God remains behind, ostensibly uninvolved in what is about to take place. But with the dissolving of the narrative borders between heaven and earth, Scene 5 draws God ineluctably into the process of Job's affliction in a new way. ["Then Went Satan Forth from the Presence of the Lord"]

"Then Went Satan Forth from the Presence of the Lord"

William Blake depicts the moment when Satan leaves God's presence to pour his phial of poison directly into Job's ear. For his part, Job remains virtuous in suffering as he shares his bread with a beggar. The inscription at the top of the frame endorses his well-deserved reputation for caring for the poor and the needy: "Did I not weep for him who was in trouble? Was not my soul afflicted for the Poor?" (Job 30:25; see also 29:12-16).

Although Job's demeanor remains essentially unchanged in the midst of suffering, Blake suggests the same may not be true for God. After giving Satan permission to strike Job—"Behold he is in thy hand"—God's sits on the throne in a posture that suggests sorrow and mourning. With furrowed brow and downcast eyes, God looks away from the sight below, even as the left side of God's body is dragged downward into the swirl of Satan's acts. Shadows now encroach on the aureole around God's head. The hands hang limp at God's side, the right hand resting on a book that is now closed. Twelve angels are floating away from Job, their hands and their eyes signaling an anxious retreat. They are surrounded by flames like those that accompany Satan, as if they and the heavens have become embroiled in Job's affliction.

At the bottom of the frame, Blake has spliced together three biblical texts that offer additional perspective on the moment:

Then went Satan forth from the presence of the Lord (Job 2:7)
And it grieved him at his heart (Gen 6:6)

Satan Going Forth from the Presence of the Lord

William Blake (1757-1827). *Satan Going Forth from the Presence of the Lord*. 1823-1825. Engraving from Blake's *Illustrations of the Book of Job*.

Who maketh his Angels Spirits & his Ministers a Flaming Fire (Ps 104:4)

The citation from Gen 6:6 is particularly intriguing. We cannot know for certain whether Blake was making an intentional connection between God's grief over Job and God's grief over the destruction of the world by the flood. The suggestion is nevertheless quite appropriate and provides good commentary on the creation imagery that is so important in Job 1–2. Suffering like Job's turns everything upside down. It leaves nothing unchanged, either in earth or in heaven.

The *satan* strikes Job with "loathsome sores" that cover his body "from the sole of his foot to the crown of his head." The extent of his affliction is clear—it is the *whole* of his body that now suffers. He must now contend with a personal pain that corresponds with the loss of *all* of his children and *all* of his possessions. Further, it is clear that the narrative depicts an affliction that is physical, not mental. The physicality of Job's pain is important, not only here, but throughout the book where repeated, although imprecise, references will be made to the various ways in which Job's body, his corporeal being, manifest the breakdown in his relationship with God (e.g., 7:5: "my body is clothed with worms and dirt"; 16:16: "my face is red with weeping"; 30:30: "my skin turns black and falls from me"). What is not clear from this brief summary of Job's affliction is the precise identification of Job's malady. The Hebrew word for "loathsome sores" (*šĕḥîn*) is a general term for skin disease that may be rendered in a variety of different ways: "running sores" (NEB); "severe inflammation" (NJPS); "severe boils" (NAB). The imprecision must be accepted as part of the narrative art of the presentation. Enough has been disclosed to make clear that Job suffers a devastating physical affliction, which the *satan* brings to him—with God's permission and "for no reason." [*"The Proof of Pain"*]

Job's response to this affliction is noticeably different than in 1:20-21. He responds physically but not verbally. He acts, but he does not speak. He takes a potsherd and scrapes himself. From a practical standpoint, the scraping offers a counterirritant to soothe itching skin. The Septuagint says that Job took a potsherd "to scrape away the pus." But the symbolism of this act may be more important for the story than any literal therapeutic effect it may have. Job takes a shard, a broken piece of pottery remaindered from something that once was whole, and with brokenness he scrapes his brokenness. The symmetry suggests that Job finds an identity and hence a kind of solace in connection with that which is no longer whole and complete. The broken comforts the broken; a place of discarded bits and pieces becomes home for one whose life is shattered and torn. The syntax of the Hebrew further indicates that Job was already "sitting among the ashes." The indication is that Job has been in the traditional posture for mourners since the conclusion of Scene 3 (1:13-22). The text does not specify the location of this place, although most interpreters assume that the ash-heap or the "dung-heap" (LXX: *koprias*) is a public place outside the city where society consigns the rejected and destitute.

Job's wife enters the scene in v. 9 and speaks her one and only line in the book of Job. Her statement to Job is curiously ambiguous and invites multiple interpretations. Her first words repeat almost verbatim the words of God in 2:3: "still you are holding fast (*ḥāzaq*) to your

"The Proof of Pain"

In the play *J.B.*, Nickles chides Mr. Zuss for exacting from J.B. a "wounded and deliberate Amen." He goes on to argue that Mr. Zuss is not content with "this poor crawling victory." He requires even more proof of J.B.'s devotion:

Nickles: Still He must pursue, still follow
Hunt His creature through his branching veins
With agony until no peace is left him—
All one blazing day of pain:
Corner him, compel the answer.
He cannot rest until He wrings
The proof of pain, the ultimate certainty.
God always asks the proof of pain.

A. MacLeish, *J.B.* (Boston: Houghton Mifflin Co., 1956), 92, 94.

integrity (*tummah*)." Most interpreters take this to be a question and suggest that it carries negative, even sarcastic, overtones: "After all that has happened, do you still hold on to your integrity, even though it is patently futile and meaningless to do so?" (cf. NRSV). The Hebrew text, however, may just as legitimately be taken as an assertion, not a question. In this reading, the statement may mean that Job's wife, like God, has looked on as he has endured his trials, and now she too affirms that Job is a truly righteous person whose fidelity to God remains as strong as ever.

The final words of the wife's statement are equally ambiguous. The conventional interpretation takes the words "Curse God and die" as an echo of the *satan's* speech in 1:11 and 2:5. Thus, one may understand Job's wife to be imploring him to do what the *satan* had predicted any reasonable person would do in circumstances like this: give up your integrity, curse God, accept the consequences of death, and put yourself out of your misery. Where most English translations use the word "curse," however, the Hebrew text has the word "bless." The usual reasoning behind the substitution of "curse" for "bless," here and regularly throughout the prologue, is that the verb *bārak* ("bless") is a euphemism for "curse" (see [Blessing/Cursing in Job 1–2]). But if one reads the text without assuming that this substitution is required, then the wife's counsel to Job may be interpreted in a different light. She may be understood as saying something like: "You have indeed maintained your integrity through everything thus far; now continue on, bless God, even though you may die."

The biblical text, therefore, subtly aligns Job's wife with the objectives of both God and the *satan*. Because of the ambiguity in her one-line speech, or perhaps in spite of it, biblical and non-biblical exegetes offer both positive and negative depictions of Job's wife.[18] The popular interpretation is almost always negative. The statement "Curse God and die" has been understood as a temptation of Job that identifies the wife with the *satan* as one who confronts and challenges Job and expects him to fail. In this tradition of interpretation, she is often depicted as the handmaiden of the Devil. On the other hand, an enormous amount of interpretive work depicts the wife far more sympathetically. She may be understood as an agent of comfort and compassion; indeed, she represents for some an angelic presence that mediates God's love for Job. [Job's Wife as Friend and Comforter] [CD: "I Am a Little Queen of Mercy"]

The prologue, however, is not focused on the character of Job's wife or the motivation behind her words. It moves instead directly to report that Job rejects her advice. He concludes that she speaks like a "foolish" person (v. 10). The term in Hebrew (*nābāl*) has both a moral and a social connotation. It refers to those who renounce God (Ps 14:1) and

Job's Wife as Friend and Comforter

At Job 2:9, the Septuagint adds a description of the wife's prolonged suffering as a result of Job's affliction. While Job has been consigned to the ash heap, she has been reduced to wandering the streets. In this account, her counsel to Job wells up out of weary compassion:

When a long time had passed, his wife said to him, "How long will you endure, saying, 'Behold, I will wait yet for little while, looking for the hope of my salvation?' Behold, the memory of you has been blotted out from the earth, those sons and daughters, the travail and pain of my womb, whom with toil I reared for nothing. And yet you sit in the decay of worms, passing the nights under the open sky, while I roam and drudge about from place to place, waiting for the sun to go down so that I may rest from the toils and sorrows that now grip me. Now, say some word against the Lord, and die."

The Testament of Job (1st C. BCE–1st C. CE) follows the Septuagint and adds details that contribute further to a sympathetic portrait of the wife. In this account, Job spends forty-eight years on the dung-heap (21:1), during which time his wife Sistis is driven to impoverished slavery in order to support him. (P. W. van der Horst notes that whereas in biblical texts women appear in approximately 1 percent of the verses, in *The Testament of Job* they occur in 107 of 388 verses ["Images of Women in the Testament of Job," *Studies in the Testament of Job,* ed. M. W. Knibb, P. W. van der Horst (Cambridge: Cambridge University Press, 1989), 93-116]). When Satan recognized her vulnerability, he disguised himself as a bread seller and persuaded her to sell her hair in exchange for three loaves of bread (23:1-11). Having concluded the deal, Sistis then speaks words that recall the biblical account:

"Job, Job! Although many things have been said in general, I speak to you in brief: In the weakness of my heart, my bones are crushed. Rise, take the loaves, be satisfied. And then speak some word against the Lord and die. Then I too shall be freed from weariness that issues from the pain of your body." (25:9-10).

Various artists have also depicted Job's wife sympathetically. William Blake, for example, consistently portrays Job's wife as a loving and devoted companion who will not leave Job's side whatever the circumstances (see **["Thus Did Job Continually"]**, **["And I Only Am Escaped to Tell Thee"]**, **["Then Went Satan Forth from the Presence of the Lord"]**). One of the most poignant portraits may be that of Georges de la Tour (c. 1635) (see following page).

S. Terrien has noted that this painting was originally misidentified as "Saint Peter Delivered from Prison by an Angel. " In 1936, the association with Job was recognized and the title was changed, interestingly, to "Job Mocked by His Wife." It appears that the conventional assessment of the biblical presentation of Job's wife—as one who rebuked Job—was strong enough to convince interpreters that if the woman in this painting was Job's wife, she must be demonically mocking him not delivering him as an angel. Terrien has rightly challenged this interpretation. He points to numerous details that convey not antagonism or impatience, but love, compassion, and tenderness: the graceful extension of the wife's finger, the gentle parting of her lips, the intent gaze of her right eye, the delicate positioning of the candle that connects her womb and Job's right shoulder in suggestive illumination. He concludes that if this depiction does indeed connect the wife to the biblical words "Curse God and die," then the words are spoken with the infinite sadness of a nurse who seeks to shorten the sufferings of the man she loves. "She is asking for his end through the merciful art of theological euthanasia." (S. Terrien, *The Iconography of Job Through the Centuries: Artists as Biblical Interpreters* [University Park, PA: Pennsylvania State University Press, 1996), 166-69. For the full discussion of the painting see 166-69.

For an interesting perspective on how the conventional assessment of the wife exercises a strong and often misplaced influence on all interpreters, see Muriel Sparks, *The Only Problem* [New York: G. P. Putnam's Sons, 1984]. Harvey, the central character of this novel, is writing a book on Job. He comes across this very painting by Georges de la Tour and is struck by how different the portrait is from that suggested by the text of the Bible. "In Harvey's mind there was much more in the painting to illuminate the subject of Job than in many of the lengthy commentaries that he knew so well. It was eloquent of a new idea." [76].)

heap scorn on the righteous (Ps 39:8 [MT 39:9]). It also refers to the socially disreputable who are shunned and disregarded (Isa 32:5; Prov 17:7; cf. Job 30:8). With either connotation, it is clear that Job seeks to dismiss his wife and discount her words.

One notes, however, that Job's next words no longer assume the simple declarative tone of 1:21. He now speaks a question that strains to remain merely rhetorical: "Surely, if we accept the good from God, should we not also accept the evil?"[19] At one level, the statement expresses the same trust in God's sovereignty that has characterized Job's previous assertion. As one moves through life from birth to death, God gives and takes away, God dispenses good and evil (Isa 45:7; cf. Deut 32:39). For the faithful, the journey need not occasion the questioning of God. It requires instead constant fidelity in order that one's behavior may always be worthy of the Creator's inscrutable objectives. At another level, these words invite the reader to ponder what Job is affirming and what he may now be less than certain about. Job's question conveys the last words we hear from him in the prologue. When next Job speaks (ch. 3), his words will sound very much like the curse that his wife seems to urge. As the poetic dialogues unfold, the balance in Job's speech between assertion and question that is characteristic of the prologue (one assertion [1:21], one question [2:10]) will be less and less apparent. The deeper Job probes for the meaning of his experience, the more frequent and the more intense his questions will become. From a narrative standpoint, therefore, Job is to learn that the ambiguity and turmoil posed for him in his wife's speech cannot be so easily dismissed.

Although questions and uncertainties may be hinted at here, they are clearly not the prologue's primary agenda. To insure that readers stay on target with the principal emphases of the story, the narrator concludes Scene 5 with another evaluative statement: "In all this Job did not sin with his lips" (v. 10). The first half of the statement repeats verbatim the assessment already reached in 1:22. Neither in the loss of his family nor in the loss of his physical wholeness has Job succumbed to sin. In

Job and His Wife

Georges de La Tour (1593-1652). *Job and His Wife.* Early 1630s. Musee Departemental des Vosges, Epinal, France. (Credit: Erich Lessing/Art Resource, NY)

1:21, the narrator went on to stipulate that Job had not given to God even the mildest form of a curse (*tiplah*). In 2:10, the narrator adds that Job has not sinned "with his lips." The latter expression is most likely intended as an unqualified affirmation: the purity of Job's speech is but a window onto the integrity of his whole life (see Ps 39:1 [MT 39:2]; Prov 13:3; 18:4; 21:23). The narrator's attempt to provide an unassailable report concerning Job's piety did not always convince later exegetes. Some rabbinic commentators stipulate that although Job did not sin with his lips, he considered the possibility "in his heart" (*b. B. Bat.* 16a). And if he did not at first actualize these thoughts, Ibn Ezra suggests, he would soon do so.[20]

Scene 6—On Earth: The Friends Arrive to Console and Comfort Job, 2:11-13

In Scene 6, the transactions between heaven and earth break off. There will be no further word from the heavens until God speaks out of the whirlwind in Job 38. Until that point, the drama of Job's afflicted life in the land of Uz will be played out in the interchanges between Job and his friends—without the benefit (or the handicap) of divine assessment.

Having learned of Job's misfortune, three friends journey together to Uz to be with him. [The Far Reach of Job's Affliction] The names of the friends and their places of origin suggest an Edomite background, which means that they, like Job, come from the east. Eliphaz ("God is fine gold") comes from Teman, a region of northern Edom (Amos 1:12; Jer 49:20; Ezek 25:13). Bildad ("son of Hadad") is associated with a place called Shuah. The location is unknown, but biblical genealogies indicate that a certain Shuah, along with other descendants of Abraham and Keturah, was sent away to live in "the land of the east" (Gen 25:2, 6; cf. 1 Chr 1:32). Zophar ("young bird") is associated with Naamah, perhaps a region in northwest Arabia. The friends' origins in the east not only identify them with Job, "the greatest of all the people of the east" (1:3), it also connects them with the tradition that recognizes Edom as the source of great wisdom (Jer 49:7; Obad 8; cf. Bar 3:23). As Scene 6 opens, three "wise" friends journey towards Uz, where Job's life had exemplified Edenic harmony. Now, "evil" (2:11: *rāʿāh*; NRSV: "troubles") has fallen upon this once paradisiacal world, and the one who had always "turned away from evil" (*rāʿ*; 1:8; 2:3) is "sitting among the ashes." With such a scenario,

The Far Reach of Job's Affliction

The biblical text does not disclose how the friends learned of Job's misfortune. The Targum, however, notes that the friends discerned something was wrong when they saw the trees in their garden wither, the meat they were eating turn into raw meat, and their wine turn into blood. The suggestion that all aspects of life reflect the agonies of Job's affliction, though literally unsubstantiated in the biblical text, is consistent with the overall use of creation imagery in the prologue.

D. Clines, *Job 1–20* [WBC; Dallas: Word Books, 1989], 56-57].

the prologue suggests that a world like Job's requires the best insights that wisdom can offer.

The visitors come as friends (*rēʿê*), not just as detached "messengers" (*malʾāk*; 1:14). The narrative presents them as embarking on a mission motivated by loyalty and compassion. Their objective is to "console" and "comfort" Job. The verb "console" (*nûd*) means to "move back and forth" and by extension to "show grief" or to "express sympathy" by nodding the head (Jer 15:5; 22:10). The form of the verb "comfort" (*nḥm*; piel) that is used here means to "show compassion/sorrow" (2 Sam 12:24; 1 Chr 19:2; Ruth 2:13; Job 29:25). Job 42:11 (cf. Ps 69:20 [MT 69:21]; Isa 51:19; Nah 3:7) uses the same two expressions— "comfort" and "console"—to describe the friends and family members who offer Job concrete expressions of sympathy and support ("a piece of money and a gold ring"). The prologue, then, presents Job's friends as acting pastorally towards him. They seek to enter sympathetically into his sorrow and affliction and then to help him come out of it with renewed energies for moving on with his life.

In the ensuing dialogues, what it means to offer "comfort" that enables Job to move beyond his grief will become an important issue. The same verb "comfort" in a passive form (*nḥm*; niphal) means to "be sorry." In this form, the verb is a standard term for "repent," that is, to be sorry or grieved about one's actions. In this sense, *nḥm* is used with the verb "turn" or "return" (*šûb*) to signify the act of expressing deep sorrow that effects a turning away from one course of action towards another that is more desirable (Jer 4:28; 31:19; Jonah 3:9). It is this second sense of *nḥm* that the friends later press upon Job. Eliphaz makes the case for repentance that is representative of the others: "If you will return (*šûb*) to the Almighty, you will be restored" (22:23; cf. 8:5-6; 11:13-14). Job responds consistently to this counsel by maintaining his innocence and rejecting the notion that he must repent of sin in order to move beyond his present plight. His final words in the book, however, indicate that he has in fact undergone a change of some sort when he says, "I repent (*nḥm*; niphal) concerning dust and ashes" (42:6). A full analysis of this verse, which represents the crux of the book of Job, must be delayed until it can be considered in its proper context. At this point, it is sufficient to notice that what the friends offer as comfort and compassion may be received by Job as something quite different.

When the friends "lifted up their eyes" to see Job, they saw a figure whose affliction had made him almost unrecognizable (v. 12). The Job they knew was identified by virtues and possessions that made him the "greatest" (1:3: *gādôl*) of all their countrymen. The Job they see sitting among the ashes has acquired a "greatness" of a different kind. Now it is suffering that is "becoming great" (2:13: *gādal*), that is, growing greater and greater, that distinguishes Job from all others.[21] The friends respond not with words but with conventional gestures of mourning that allow them as onlookers to embody Job's suffering second-hand. They "wail," "tear" their outer robes (see Job's similar act in 1:20), and "throw dust over their heads toward heaven." The meaning of the latter expression is uncertain. Putting dust on one's head is a traditional way of expressing grief (e.g., Josh 7:6; 2 Sam 13:19; Ezek 27:30), but the verb "throw" and the adverbial expression "heavenward" are not used in this particular connection. Some commentators find a parallel in Exodus 9:10, where Moses throws ashes into the air, an act producing a plague of "boils" (*šeḥîn;* the same word is used for "loathsome sores" in Job 2:7) that Pharaoh's magicians cannot duplicate. If the friends' gesture is seen in this connection, they may be symbolically invoking an affliction upon themselves that is similar to Job's as a way of identifying with him.[22] An attractive suggestion is that the act of throwing the dust toward heaven signifies an appeal to God to intervene in the life of this sufferer.[23] In the sixth and final scene of the prologue, where the interchange between heaven and earth has ceased and there is no discernable word from God, such an appeal would not be out of place. ["And When They Lifted Up Their Eyes Afar Off and Knew Him Not"]

The friends perform one other act. They sit on the ground in silence for a period of seven days and seven nights. This too enacts a conventional rite of mourning (Lam 2:10; Isa 3:26; Ezek 8:14), although in the present context its meaning seems to carry extra weight. The period of seven days is the traditional time for mourning the dead (Gen 50:10; 1 Sam 31:13; Sir 22:12). The symbolism of the friends' gesture stands in tension with the stated objective of consoling and comforting Job. They have met together to help a friend move on with his life in the aftermath of a great loss. They perform a ritual, however, that signifies they have come not to look for paths toward life but to acknowledge a journey that has ended in death.

The prologue concludes by insisting that Job has passed the test that has been devised in heaven—he has not cursed God; his devotion to God has remained consistent. The reader who has followed this journey from heaven to earth to ashes must know, however, that Job cannot simply resume his life in the land of Uz as if nothing has changed. Evil is now present in this world. The heavens are now silent. And Job's pain and suffering grow greater and greater with each passing moment. When the seven days and nights of mourning the dead have ended, what will the one who lives in the midst of death and loss do? What

7

What! shall we recieve Good
at the hand of God & shall we not also
recieve Evil

And when they lifted up their eyes afar off & knew him not
they lifted up their voice & wept.& they rent every Man his
mantle & sprinkled dust upon their heads towards heaven

Ye have heard of the Patience of Job and have seen the end of the Lord

WBlake inven & Sculpt

London. Published as the Act directs March 8.1825 by William Blake N3 Fountain Court Strand

Job, His Wife, and Friends

William Blake (1757-1827). *Job, His Wife, and Friends*. 1823-1825. Engraving from Blake's *Illustrations of the Book of Job*.

"And When They Lifted Up Their Eyes Afar Off and Knew Him Not"

Job sits on a mound of straw, his head resting on his wife's breast. His hands, palms downward, extend by his side. His wife kneels behind him, her body providing a pillar of support, her uplifted hands gesturing the prayer Job himself seems now too exhausted to offer. The six uplifted hands of the friends mimic the wife, although their reach heavenward is more extended and their facial expressions convey more intensity and emotion. It is as if by the force of their gestures they wish to lift Job out of his distress. At the top and bottom of the frame, Blake has inscribed the words from Job 2:12. To these he adds a quotation from Jas 5:11 and thus provides the catchword "patience" that captures the popular understanding of the lesson to be drawn from Job. Given the symbolism in the four pair of raised hands that Blake positions around Job, a full citation of the New Testament text may be instructive: "Ye have heard of the patience of Job and have seen the end of the Lord, that the Lord is very pitiful, and of tender mercy" (AV).

will he say? The preliminary presentation of life in the afflicted land of Uz has concluded, but the real drama has just begun.

CONNECTIONS

The language and imagery of the prologue invite the reader to return imaginatively to the garden of Eden, there to reflect once again on primordial questions concerning God, the world, and humankind. The journey back to Eden is of course metaphorical. In literary terms, it is an image conveyed through the artistic manipulation of words and ideas. But it is also more than this. In a world where change is constant, where every belief, institution, and relationship must undergo seemingly endless mutations in order to survive for another day, the journey back to Eden, holds a seductive promise. In the memory of our "beginnings," we may uncover an abiding reality that summons and enables a durable excellence. The lure of returning to our beginnings comes eventually to one and all.

For those gifted with an appreciation for the game of baseball, for example, the trip back to beginnings leads to Cooperstown, a small rural hamlet on the shore of Otsego Lake in upstate New York. There, according to baseball lore, a young boy named Abner Doubleday sat down one day in 1839 and drew up the rules for a new game. Every year the baseball season begins with a gathering of friends and family in Cooperstown. The official reason for the gathering is to celebrate a new class of inductees into the Hall of Fame. But the real reason for returning to Cooperstown each year is to reestablish contact with the roots of the game. It is of little significance to those who make this journey that Doubleday cannot be verified as the game's founder or that Cooperstown may not be the actual place of the first pitch. Committed baseball people know the game's origins are more complicated than that. They know those who have played and preserved the game since 1839 (or whenever) have been frauds and bigots as well as genuine heroes. All have left their distinctive marks on the game. But we return to Cooperstown to remember and celebrate the heroes, for they keep alive the vision of what the game can be at its best.

In Hebraic tradition, Eden orients the community of faith toward its beginnings. The design of the created order is no doubt more complex and more complicated than the brief account in Genesis 1–2 suggests. The unexpected intrusion of evil into Job's world of Uz, otherwise so reminiscent of Eden's paradise, seems an intentional reminder of just this reality. And surely the men and women who have lived within the ebb and flow of creation's order comprise a motley group of saints and

sinners. One does not need to consult the biblical record alone to verify this fact. There are, however, some genuine heroes to whom the community of faith may turn for instruction. The prologue presents Job as one of these heroes of faith. His resolute fidelity to God in the midst of suffering instructs us to remember what faith can be at its best. When we enter into Job's world and reexamine the "archives of Eden," as G. Steiner has so aptly phrased it, we reconnect with our "mastering original. " The hope and the promise is that by returning to primordial issues, we may rekindle the wondrous obsession with the Creator's design that keeps us "vulnerable to the anarchic shock of excellence."[24]
[CD: "Obsession" with the "Mastering Original"]

Job 1–2 invites reflection on three questions that are foundational for the faith community: (1) what kind of world do we live in? (2) what kind of God is God? (3) what kind of relationships, with God and with others, are we created for? The answers to these questions are more complex than any one teacher can impart, even if his name is Job. But as every good teacher knows, and as every serious student must learn, getting the answers right depends first on asking the right questions.

What Kind of World Do We Live In?

Job's story claims that the world we live in is a place where Uz can exist. Although the geographical location of this place may be indeterminate, we should not make the mistake of assuming that its possibilities and promises are merely fictional or illusory. In every life, at every point on the compass, there exists the possibility that Uz may be found. When it is, we discover that the world we have imagined and hoped for and the world we live in can in fact be one and the same. Uz is every place where human beings experience the happy harmony of living in full accord with creation's design. For Job and his wife this means a life that is completely full and completely satisfying. Their investment in their family and in their work is rewarding in every sense. Life has about it a stability, an equilibrium; happiness is the norm, not the exception. In the land of Uz, confidence and security provide the context for struggling with disorder, not the other way around. This is an important assertion about the world, which we are often tempted to reverse.

There is much in the modern world that rightly makes us suspicious of any claim to unadulterated happiness and joy. And certainly one cannot read the prologue of Job, let alone the entire book, without knowing that at least some of our misgivings are justified. Even so, it is one thing to know that we live in a world that causes us at times to question whether all that passes for happiness is real. It would be quite a different thing to conclude that ours is a world in which the bliss of uncorrupted happiness is never possible. For too many people the grind of daily existence has produced just such an understanding of the world. They are resigned to a world flattened by hard experiences. They have been coerced to the assumption that what is is what will be, forever. Such a world yearns for a sacred place called Uz, which shows the way back to Eden's larger vision for life. Without this vision people may learn to be at home with suffering like Job's, which can indeed sometimes be "very great" (2:13), but they will miss the banquets of eating and drinking that celebrate the sheer goodness of life. The preacher's task is to keep the road toward Uz clearly marked.

Job's story claims that happiness and joy, not hurt and grief, is the normal setting for life in the land of Uz. It does *not* claim that the world is immune to suffering. Even the paradisiacal world of Uz is not exempt from evil that falls unawares and "for no reason." Job learns that no amount of faith, however fervent, and no practice of piety, however disciplined, can insulate one from hurt and brokenness. Indeed, his story suggests that there is an inverse relationship between faith and suffering. Faith does not lessen one's vulnerability to pain, instead it intensifies the experience. The deeper one's conviction is that the world is orderly, the more disruptive are the intrusions of random chaos. The more fervent one's belief, the more intense one's love, the deeper one hurts and grieves, precisely because there is so much at stake. Where little is invested, there will always be only minimal losses. Job has sunk his roots deep into the soil of Uz. Those roots cannot spare him misfortune, but they do nurture his abiding faith in the steady rhythms of creation that order and reorder life.

What Kind of God is God?

At the outset, it is important to acknowledge that this is the reader's question, not Job's. Job does not reflect on God's nature and character; he simply accepts conventional maxims about who God is and what God does (1:21; 2:10). When tragedy befalls him, the instincts that takeover are those of the survivor, not the theologian. [CD: Other Things to Think About] The reader may find this presentation of Job unsatisfactory. It may be judged too extreme to be authentic or too fanciful to be believed. But such is the very nature of the Joban story. It asks us to think about possibilities that conventional expectations may long since have discarded.

If Job has not listened in on the deliberations of the divine council and wondered about what he was hearing, the reader has. This too is part of the dramatic design of the story. In our own lives, we are very much like Job, at least in one respect. We must go through the experiences that come to us without the benefit of sitting in the presence of a visible God who speaks audibly about divine intentions. In this ancient story, we are permitted to play another role, figuratively of course. We are invited to eavesdrop on the conversations that take place in the inner sanctum of God. In a dramatic sense, our role as readers elevates us to the position of being almost like one of the heavenly beings who gather around the throne of the Creator of the cosmos. We are permitted to see and hear things about God that are not ordinarily available to us. Why? Perhaps so that in real life, not only figuratively in the divine council, we may image God as near-equals, as ones who have been summoned and commissioned to enact the hopes and intentions of the Creator of the world. Perhaps when the time comes that suffering assigns to us the role of Job, these glimpses of God's internal deliberations can become sources of revelation.

The first picture we get when we look into the divine council is of God holding court, like a king with royal attendants coming and going at his pleasure. The representation of God as a king is a common one in the Hebrew Bible (see, for example, Pss 93, 95–99). It conveys the understanding that God is the sovereign ruler of the universe. The second image we have from the divine council, however, introduces another element into this standard frame. This sovereign ruler engages attendants in substantive conversation about matters of governance. God not only directs, orders, and instructs those who stand before the throne; God also questions, listens, and responds. Moreover, God can be questioned, challenged to review prior decisions, and influenced to consider new proposals for obtaining divine objectives. The suggestion is that God's governance is more than a matter of divine decree or fiat. Subordinate beings have something of importance to contribute to God's decisions. This conceptualization of God's sovereignty is profound. The king of the universe chooses to relinquish absolute control and devolve power to lesser beings.

This picture of God's shared governance is of course complicated by the fact that the one with whom God interacts in this story is called the *satan*. Our first challenge as readers will be to set aside the popular understanding of this figure as the Devil who works against God to secure evil purposes. In Job 1–2, the *satan* is one of God's heavenly beings, one who serves God by investigating the merit of all claims of loyalty and righteousness. He acts only with God's permission, and his objectives are only to serve God's interests. He is not evil, and he does not wish evil on others. However the figure of *satan* may have developed in later thought, it is a mistake to import these notions into the story of Job (see [The Satan]).

This story makes it clear that the *satan's* opinions are important to God. When it comes to assessing the way God has chosen to coordinate divine blessing and human fidelity, the *satan* is able to persuade God that perhaps there is a better way. Is it possible, the *satan* asks, that God has created a world in which blessing (prosperity) is automatic? Is it possible that God has created a human creature in whom the love of God is automatic? If so, can God be certain that when Job (or any human being) says "I love you," it is a genuine expression and not merely a reflex response? The question the *satan* asks is really only secondarily concerned with Job. The real thrust of the question is directed to God. The *satan* in essence asks God to be introspective: are you intrinsically worshipful? Are your qualities, irrespective of the power you possess to give and take at will, sufficiently strong to evoke the free adoration and love of humankind? The prologue is bold to suggest that God is not only open but responsive to this manner of address.

There is one further complication in this story that no discerning reader can ignore. Does God know the answer to the *satan's* question already, or does God need to learn the answer by watching Job? The story begs the question, but it does not answer it. The subtle suggestion that the *satan* has "incited" God to alter Job's world, perhaps against God's best judgment, does little to alleviate our anxieties. This too is part of the dramatic design of the prologue that invites the reader to be a full participant in the Joban story. If God allows subordinates to have a substantive influence in the council, is this an indication that God is weak and susceptible to coercion? Or does it signify that God is strong and unthreatened by input from subordinates that may call for a change in the divine plans? What is perhaps most dramatic and most inviting about the *satan's* question, however, is that according to the prologue it can finally be answered neither by God nor by the *satan* alone. Is God intrinsically worshipful? The prologue stipulates that this question can be answered fully only when Job has had his say. Of all the images of God that we readers glean from eavesdropping on the divine council, the most provocative is that God chooses ultimately to entrust the decision about who God is to human beings.

What Kind of Relationships, with God and with Others, Are We Created For?

The prologue shows Job in a variety of relationships: with God, his children, his wife, and his friends. At the beginning of the story, Job seems confident that these relationships are always predictable and purposeful. In each case, he enjoys connections with others that are unbroken by the caprice of questions and doubt, hurt and pain. Indeed, in the initial scene (1:1-5), the narrator pictures Job going through the routines of life without once speaking directly to anyone. He is self-absorbed in devotion to God and family. The final scene of the prologue (2:11-13) shows Job still going through the routines of his life in silence, but by this point both Job and the reader know that in reality life is too full to be "routine," and genuine relationships are always too complex, and too important, to be conducted only in silence.

At the outset, Job's relationship with God is a mirror image of his relationship with his family. Job is the loving parent who provides all that his children need. He is attentive to their every deed and thought and regularly intervenes directly in their lives to insure that they are protected from anything that might harm them. The children have little role to play in this relationship, other than to enjoy what has been given and to accept what has been arranged. Job seems to expect God to relate to him as he relates to his family. In essence, he sees God in his own image, as a divine parent who provides abundantly for dependents and intervenes regularly to preempt danger or misfortune. By the end of the prologue, however, Job and the reader know that this understanding of God is too small. God does not preempt the suffering that falls on Job, and God does not intervene directly to tell Job what to say or how to act. These are responsibilities God entrusts to Job himself. He must discern on his own, without a direct word from God, how to relate to misfortune and how to respond to the One who not only "gives" but also "takes away." What he learns about relationship with such a God, of course, cannot be fully assessed without considering the book as a whole. But already the prologue makes it clear enough that faith and trust in God—indeed, "heroic" faith and trust—can be legitimately expressed by both affirmation and silence. It may be proclaimed with equal passion by both praise that speaks one's adoration of God (1:21) and by grief that cannot speak even a word (2:8, 13).

Just as one's relationship with God is multidimensional and cannot be adequately expressed without the full range of human emotion and response, so too relationships with family and friends are most authentic when they are open and honest. Although she has only a small part in the story, Job's wife plays an important role in shaping the presentation of what it means to be a true friend and companion. Her brief conversation with Job (2:9-10) is the prologue's only example of interpersonal dialogue. She speaks directly to him. He listens to her and responds. What he says indicates that his perspectives have been enlarged by what he has heard. When Job initially responded to his broken world, he drew only upon the deposit of his own resources and managed no more than a repetition of a traditional religious maxim (1:21). He addressed no one in particular. His assertions did not have to face the test of another's scrutiny. When his wife engages him in dialogue, he moves from detached statements about God to tense wonderments about God *and* good and evil (2:10). In the give and take of dialogue, Job's horizons for encountering God expand. Even when the move is from simple assertions to imponderable issues and questions, such as those that now emerge on Job's horizon, the promise of genuine dialogue is that one may find a true partner for the journey.

In the commentary, we have noted that the wife's speech is ambiguous and open to multiple interpretations. Her words curiously echo the objectives of both God and the *satan*. Interpreters portray her as both angelic and demonic (see [Job's Wife as Friend and Comforter]). This ambiguity will continue to invite analysis, but it does not necessarily demand or yield to resolution. One heuristic approach for the interpreter would be to focus on the importance of ambiguity in the life of faith. The issue presents itself nowhere more intensely than in the matter of innocent suffering. In this respect, Job's wife, whose speech introduces ambiguities that cannot be simply dismissed, is particularly instructive. Two observations may invite further reflection.

First, Job's wife is the only woman who speaks in this book, which is otherwise dominated by debates and discussions between men. The under-representation of feminine perspectives in Job, as elsewhere in Hebrew Scripture, reflects the patriarchal order that existed in biblical antiquity. Contemporary interpreters should be aware of this characteristic of scripture and work diligently to insure that biblical exposition invites both women and men to discover their full partnership with God. The presence of Job's wife in this story, brief as it is, serves as a subtle but important reminder that no discussion of God, the world, and humankind can ever be complete without the female voice.

Second, Job's wife invites reflection because of the particular perspective that the female voice brings to this story. In a world defined by patriarchal arrangements, women are especially vulnerable to abuse and affliction. The cultural and social values of patriarchy assign authority and power to males. In a typical family household, it is the husband who provides for the wife and children. Should they become widowed or orphaned, they may lose not only their identity but also their means for survival. In such a world, a woman knows that loss, abandonment, insecurity, ruin, is always as close as the death of her spouse.[25]

When Job's wife speaks, therefore, we may understand that she brings to their shared grief a pathos that sees suffering with different eyes. She speaks as one well acquainted with brokenness and loss. She knows first-hand the slim margin that separates the blessed and the cursed. It is her insight as a woman, a wife, and especially a mother that connects Job directly to the anguish of having lost something—seven sons and three daughters—that can never be replaced. Thus she takes up the

"The Test Is Always How We Treat the Poor"

In Robert Frost's "A Masque of Reason," Job's wife defends herself against God's implied charge that she has somehow failed her husband. She responds as follows:

I stood by Job. I may have turned on You.
Job scratched his boils and tried to think what he
Had done or not to or for the poor.
The test is always how we treat the poor.
It's time the poor were treated by the state
In some way not so penal as the poorhouse.
That's one more thing to put on Your agenda . . . .

All You can seem to do is lose Your temper
When reason-hungry mortals ask for reasons.
Of course, in the abstract high singular
There isn't any universal reason;
And no one but a man would think there was.
You don't catch women trying to be Plato.
Still there must be lots of unsystematic
Stray scraps of palliative reason
It wouldn't hurt you to vouchsafe the
  faithful.
You thought it was agreed You needn't give them.
You thought to suit yourself. I've not agreed
To anything with anyone.

R. Frost, "A Masque of Reason," *The Poetry of Robert Frost*, ed. E. C. Lathem (New York: Henry Holt and Company, 1969), 477-78.

issue of what it means to have "integrity" in the midst of suffering, even if Job has not yet recognized that this is what is now at stake in his persistent reliance on unaffected piety. She knows, and she would teach her spouse, that inexplicable suffering always requires that faith assertions be forged within the crucible of irresolvable questions. ["The Test Is Always How We Treat the Poor"] Only when Job understands his world from this perspective will he be prepared to pursue fully the connection between God and good and evil that he begins to conceptualize with his final words in the prologue.

NOTES

[1] C. Newsom notes that "the narrator's relation to Job is one of utter transcendence," which leaves room for the reader's "ethical disquiet," precisely because the narrator claims to have the final say about Job (*The Book of Job: A Contest of Moral Imaginations* [Oxford: Oxford University Press, 2003], 68-69). J. Watts makes a similar point by arguing that the author of the book has created Job's "omniscient narrator" as a "foil" to make the problems addressed in the rest of the book more apparent ("The Unreliable Narrator of Job," *The Whirlwind: Essays on Job, Hermeneutics, and Theology in Memory of Jane Morse*, ed. S. L. Cook, C. L. Patton, and J. W. Watts [JSOTSup 336; Sheffield: Sheffield Academic Press, 2001], 168-80).

[2] On Genesis as the primary literary and theological matrix for interpreting the reference to Uz, see S. Meier, "Job I-II: A Reflection of Genesis I-III," VT 39 (1989): 184-85.

[3] M. Pope, *Job* (AB; Garden City NY: Doubleday, 1979), 5-6; cf. D. Clines, *Job 1–20* (WBC; Dallas: Word Books, 1989), 10-11.

[4] See S. Spiegel, "Noah, Daniel, and Job. Touching on Canaanite Relics in the Legends of the Jews," *Louis Ginsburg Jubilee Volume 1* (New York: American Academy for Jewish Research, 1945), English section, 305-56.

[5] R. Gordis, *The Book of Job: Commentary, New Translation, and Special Studies* (New York: Jewish Theological Seminary of America, 1978), 10-11.

[6] Clines, *Job 1–20*, 12.

[7] E. M. Good, *In Turns of Tempest: A Reading of Job with a Translation* (Stanford: Stanford University Press, 1990), 48-49.

[8] S. Mitchell, *The Book of Job* (New York: Harper Collins, 1992), 5.

[9] A. Brenner, "Job the Pious? The Characterization of Job in the Narrative Framework of the Book," *JSOT* 43 (1989): 39-41.

[10] Clines (*Job 1–20*, 25) compares the satan figure with the *advocatus diaboli*, the functionary in Christendom, "whose task is to raise objections to the canonization of a saint: his office and his appointment owe their existence to the body that actively supports the canonization, and his role is to ensure that no potential criticism for the candidate remains unheard and unanswered."

[11] Cf. Clines, *Job 1–20*, 24.

[12] Mitchell, *Book of Job,* 6.

[13] J. Gerald Janzen, *Job* (Atlanta: John Knox, 1985), 39.

[14] Ibid., 41.

[15] See N. Habel, *The Book of Job: A Commentary* (OTL; Philadelphia: Westminster Press, 1985), 92.

[16] Clines (*Job 1–20*, 40; cf. Pope, *Job,* 17) notes that the pattern of the phrase "to ascribe *tiplah* to God" is similar to the common expression "to ascribe glory (*kabod*) to God" (1 Sam 6:5; Jer 13:6; Prov 26:8). On this basis he suggests that *tiplah* is a virtual antonym to "glory."

[17] Good, *In Turns of Tempest*, 198. For a survey of other interpretations, see Clines, *Job 1–20*, 43-45.

[18] On Job's wife, see further Z. Gitay, "The Portrayal of Job's Wife and Her Representation in the Visual Arts," *Fortunate the Eyes that See: Essays in Honor of David Noel Freedman*, ed. A. Breck, A. Bartlett (Grand Rapids MI: Wm. B. Eerdmans, 1995), 516-26; E. Van Wolde, *Mr. and Mrs. Job* (New York: Trinity Press International, 1997); D. Penchansky, "Job's Wife: Satan's Handmaid," *Shall Not the Judge of All the Earth Do What Is Right? Studies on the Nature of God in Tribute to James L. Crenshaw*, ed. D. Penchansky, P. Redditt (Winona Lake IN: Eisenbrauns, 2000), 223-28.

[19] The sentence in Hebrew contains no clear interrogative markers, although most translators assume it should be interpreted as a rhetorical question. For an alternative approach see Good, *In Turns of Tempest*, 200-201. The clause begins in Hebrew with a particle (*gam*; "surely," "indeed") that typically indicates emphasis. The translation of S. Mitchell captures this nicely with a slightly different word order: "We have accepted good fortune from God; surely we can accept bad fortune too" (*Book of Job,* 8).

[20] For discussion see Gordis, *Book of Job,* 22; Clines, *Job 1–20*, 55.

[21] On the significance of the grammatical shift from the adjective *gādôl* ("greatest") to the verbal form *gādāl*, here translated "becoming great," see Janzen, *Job,* 60.

[22] So Habel, *Job,* 97; cf. M. Weiss, *The Story of Job's Beginning* (Jerusalem: Magnes Press, 1983), 76.

[23] Cf. C. Houtman, "Zu Hiob 2:12," ZAW 90 (1978): 269-72.

[24] G. Steiner, "The Archives of Eden," *No Passions Spent* (New Haven/London: Yale University Press, 1996), 292.

[25] On the "moral world of biblical patriarchy" in Job see C. Newsom, "Job," *The Women's Bible Commentary*, ed. C. Newsom, S. Ringe (Louisville KY: Westminster/John Knox Press, 1992), 133-35.

JOB'S ASSAULT ON CREATION

Job 3:1-26

The prologue anticipates a seventh scene that will bring the account of Job's life in the land of Uz to a satisfying conclusion. Given the parallels between Job 1–2 and Genesis 1–2, the reader might well expect that Job will emerge from the seven days of silent suffering (2:13) with a renewed and enlarged sabbath-like celebration of his world and his God. It is this very expectation that chapter 3 stands on its head. When Job breaks the silence of pain, his first words speak curse and lament, not celebration and praise. On the primordial seventh day, God reviewed the whole of creation's design and "sanctified" it (Gen 2:3). In his seventh scene, Job reviews the entirety of what God has done and "curses" it.

After a brief introduction (vv. 1-2), Job's opening speech divides into two major units: a curse directed at the day of his birth and the night of his conception (vv. 3-10) and a lament that thunders a repeating question about the "why?" of existence (vv. 11-26). Both the curse and the lament are grounded in Job's clear sense that life is now inescapably and inexplicably governed by "misery" (v. 10; NRSV: "trouble") and "turmoil" (v. 26; NRSV: "trouble"). [Structure of Job 3:1-26] Job's descent into spoken rage and despair necessitates and generates the ensuing drama. He presses the questions and issues that every subsequent speaker in the book, including God, must address. From Job's perspective, at least, there is much at stake. He contends that suffering like his calls the whole of the created order into question. If there is no response to Job, or if the response is inadequate, his words suggest that suffering will continue to rip and tear at the fabric of life until creation itself is undone. [What Price "All the Soul-and-Body Scars"?]

One further observation is pertinent before embarking on the drama that begins with Job 3. It is not only the nature of the language that changes in this chapter and in those that follow. It is also the manner of its presentation. In

> **Structure of Job 3:1-26**
> 3:1-2 Introduction
> 3:3-10 Curses on day and night
>   vv. 4-5 Curses on "that day"
>   vv. 6-9 Curses on "that night"
>   v. 10 Reason for curses
> 3:11-26 Lament
>   vv. 11-19 Why did I not die?
>   vv. 20-26 Why must I live?

> **What Price "All the Soul-and-Body Scars"?**
> A voice said, Look me in the stars
> And tell me truly, men of earth,
> If all the soul-and-body scars
> Were not too much to pay for birth.
>
> R. Frost, "A Question," in *The Poetry of Robert Frost*, ed. E. C. Lathem (New York: Henry Holt and Company, 1969), 362.

the prologue, a narrator guides the reader through Job's story and provides the proper evaluation of the events. Although issues and questions may arise, the strategy of the prologue is to diminish the reader's level of discomfort and to remove ambiguity by supplying an authoritative guide for interpretation. Beginning with Job 3:1 and continuing through Job 42:6 this changes. The narrator no longer has a voice in these chapters; neither does God. The only ones who speak are Job and his friends. Their words will be introduced with such flat statements as, "After this Job opened his mouth and cursed" (3:1), "Then Eliphaz the Temanite answered" (4:1), "Then Job answered" (6:1), "Then Bildad the Shuhite answered" (8:1). There will be no third party who steps into the middle of these vexed conversations to interpret or critique them for us. In effect, the dialogues now invite the reader to become a third party participant in this drama. It is now our responsibility to listen, to ponder, to discern. If we are to enter fully into this part of Job's journey, the dialogues suggest, we, like Job, must learn to grapple with issues that will not be resolved simply by pronouncement or fiat.[1]

[Learning to Be at Home with the "Obscurities of Parables"]

COMMENTARY

Introduction, 3:1-2

The chapter begins with two statements. The first (v. 1) connects with events described in the prologue: "after this Job opened his mouth." After seven days and nights of silence (2:13), Job speaks the drama into its next scene. The language deftly retains the prologue's focus on Job's mouth. We know that to this point Job has not sinned "with his lips"

Learning to Be at Home with the "Obscurities of Parables"

Israel's wisdom tradition commends the truly "wise" and the truly pious as those who learn to be at home with the enigmas of life:

How different the one who devotes himself
to the study of the law of the Most High!
He seeks the wisdom of all the ancients,
and is concerned with prophecies;
he preserves the sayings of the famous
and penetrates the subtleties of parables;
he seeks out the hidden meanings of proverbs
and is at home with the obscurities of parables. (Sir 39:1-3)

Flannery O'Connor makes a similar argument in an essay on the teaching of literature. She laments the fact that "a generation has been made to feel that the aim of learning is to eliminate mystery." She counters that mystery is not something to be eliminated, but rather something to be valued as "a gift of God," for "without it we have no choice but self-intoxication." "The task of the novelist," she argues, "is to deepen mystery." O'Connor's discernment places her squarely within the company of those who follow the biblical admonition to "be at home" with the mysteries of life.

F. O'Connor, "The Teaching of Literature," *Mystery and Manners: Occasional Prose*, sel. and ed. Sally and Robert Fitzgerald (New York: Farrar, Straus & Giroux, 1969), 124-25.

(2:10). We wait to hear what will come forth from these lips that have now been opened by brokenness and loss. The second statement (v. 2) provides the conventional introduction to the individual speeches in the dialogues that will follow: "and Job answered and said" (cf. 4:1; 6:1; 8:1; and so on). As a transitional piece, verses one and two seem at first sight simply to advance the story to its next logical step. With closer scrutiny, however, it becomes apparent that what Job now says is anything but routine or conventional.

Job "opened his mouth" to curse. The first to speak out of the depths of pain and brokenness is Job, the sufferer, not the friends who are merely onlookers. It is his profound anguish, not their detached reflection, which sets the agenda for what follows. The voice of pain speaks "curse" not blessing. Throughout the prologue, the prospect that Job might curse rather than bless God was only thinly masked by employing a euphemistic translation of the word "bless" (*bārak*) in place of the word for "curse" (see [Blessing/Cursing in Job 1–2]). Now the ambiguity is resolved. Job curses (*qālal*) the day of his birth (lit., "his day"; cf. 1:4-5).

Two dimensions of what it means to "curse" are important for understanding Job's actions. [The Language of Cursing] First, in the Hebrew Bible, to speak a curse (or a blessing) is to utter words that are understood to set in motion the very action the curse articulates. When Job curses the day of his birth, he expresses the wish that that day had never existed (vv. 3-5); that it had never been included among the days of the year (v. 6); in essence, that he had never been born (vv. 10-12). His wish intends to be more than an utterance. It is an act that seeks to bring

---

The Language of Cursing

AΩ Three principal Hebrew roots and their derivatives comprise the language of cursing: '*rr*, *qll*, and *'lh*. The first, which occurs frequently in the participial form *'ārûr* ("cursed"), regularly functions as an antonym to *bārûk* ("blessed"). It is used, for example, in the context of covenant ceremonies to stipulate the kinds of behavior that are "cursed" or "banned" and which if enacted make one subject to punishment (see Deut 27:15-26). The second, *qll*, carries the basic connotation of "make light, treat as worthless or trifling." With the exception of its appearance in Job 3:1, this verb is always used to designate a curse against a person, not a thing or an event. It is most often directed against persons in authority such as a king, or a parent (e.g., Lev 20:9). It is possible, but virtually unthinkable, that one would curse God (Lev 24:11, 14, 15, 23). Because this verb normally conveys curses against persons, not things, some have suggested that Job should be understood to be cursing God implicitly. Against this, it may be countered that it is the very ambiguity in Job's use of conventional language that the text represents. Job comes as close to cursing God, without doing so, as he can. The third term, *'lh*, carries the basic sense of a written or vocal imprecation. It is used in the context of swearing an oath or entering into a legal contract to prove guilt or protect property (e.g., Judg 17:2; 1 Kgs 8:31).

For all these fine distinctions between the various terms, there is a general consensus that it is not the words in and of themselves that convey the power of the "curse." It is rather the power and the status of the person who utters them. On this point, see especially A. Thiselton, "The Supposed Power of Words in the Biblical Writings," *JTS* 25 (1974): 283-99.

For further reading on the general issues, see W. J. Urbock, "Blessings and Cursings," *ABD*, ed. D. N. Freedman (New York: Doubleday, 1992), vol. 1, 755-61.

about the very death that his misery has forced him to contemplate but has not allowed him to experience. In this context, Job's curse raises an interesting question. How can his words reverse something that has already happened in the past? He cannot "unbirth" himself. Such considerations have lead to the suggestion that this curse expresses an empty wish. It is not only a rhetorical utterance; it is also a hopeless one, perhaps even an absurd one.[2] At most, Job's curses may be simply giving expression to the extremity of his grief.[3]

A second consideration should also be brought to bear on understanding Job's curse. Curses (and blessings) are only effective when they are spoken by authorized persons (e.g., kings, prophets, priests, elders) under proper conditions (e.g., in times of family or national crisis, in the liturgies of the cult). The power of the utterance rests not in the words themselves, but in the authority and status of the person who speaks them. Here too the conventional understanding of "cursers" and their potential to effect change raises interesting questions with respect to Job. Job has no official title; he is neither king, nor priest, nor prophet. He has no official standing in the community, other than that which God has provided—"the greatest of all the people of the east"—and even this distinction has been replaced by another that would seem to diminish rather than enhance his stature. Job's "greatness" is now defined by what he has lost, not by what he possesses. By what authority, then, and with what power does Job speak these words? Can one whose status is defined only by suffering that is "very great" expect to challenge and change anything in heaven or on earth?

These two understandings of what it means to curse stand in some tension when applied to Job. He speaks words that would call into being that which he says, and yet what he wishes for seems patently impossible. He speaks as one whose authority and power would command attention and respect, and yet he sits among the ashes, where no person of stature would normally be found. If Job's curses are only rhetorical, then these tensions invite the reader to appreciate this chapter, and the responses that follow from the friends and from God, as a masterful example of the Bible's literary artistry. If, however, Job's afflicted, powerless curses and questions do effect change in his world (and perhaps in God), then these tensions invite us to prepare for more than simply a good read.

Damn the Day, Damn the Night, 3:3-10

Job begins his curse by identifying two objects that he wishes to attack and destroy: the day of his birth and the night of his conception (v. 3) His movement against these two is developed with a series of curses that address each one separately (vv. 4-5, day; vv. 6-9, night). Verse 10 concludes this first unit by stating the reason for Job's curses: "because it [the night] did not shut the doors of my mother's womb."

The Hebrew Bible preserves one other example of a curse on the day of one's birth in Jer 20:14-18. The parallels between the two texts suggest that both Jeremiah and Job are drawing upon a common tradition that includes four basic motifs:

• A curse of the day of birth　　　　　　　Job 3:3a; Jer 20:14a
• The announcement of a male child's birth　Job 3:3b; Jer 20:15
• The blocking of the womb　　　　　　　Job 3:10a; Jer 20:17
• Being born to see "trouble" (*ʿml*)　　　Job 3:10b; Jer 20:18

What is most striking about Job's curse, however, is not its similarity with Jeremiah. Job's words appropriate the language and imagery of Genesis 1 in a manner that suggests he is cursing not only the particular day of his beginnings but also the primordial day of creation that set in motion all beginnings. [Job 3 and Genesis 1] The structure of Job's speech comprises seven curses—three against the day, four against the night—that generally counteract the order of events in the seven days of creation. These seven curses in turn are conveyed through sixteen jussive and negative verbs that counterbalance the fifteen jussives and prohibitions that occur in Genesis 1. The best example of this feature is also the most dramatic. In his first specific curse of "that day," Job says, "let there be darkness" (3:4: *yĕhî ḥošek*). His words effectively call for a reversal of God's first creative act: "let there be light" (Gen 1:3: *yĕhî ʾôr*). In sum, Job's first words from the ash-heap have the force of a "counter-cosmic incantation."[4] With lips no longer silent, he launches into a death wish for himself and the whole of creation. ["Let the Day Perish Wherein I Was Born"]

Job begins with three curses directed against the day of his birth (vv. 3-5). The first (v. 3) is general: "let the day perish." The next two (vv. 4-5) specify the means by which Job seeks the day's destruction. His wish is that that day would be overwhelmed with darkness. Five different words in vv. 4-6 recall and embellish the image of the primordial darkness (*ḥošek*; Gen 1:2) that once governed creation: "darkness" (*ḥošek*), "deep darkness" (*ṣalmāwet*), settling "clouds" (*ʿănānāh*), "blackness of the day" (*kimrîrê yôm*; sometimes understood as "eclipse"), "thick darkness" (*ʿōpel*). The imagery of darkness defeating day is reinforced by three additional expressions. Job hopes that God will not "seek out" (*dāraš*) the day. The word is used in association with seeking an oracle from God, which if granted is a sign that God cares for and attends to the needs of those who call (e.g., Job 5:8). The implication

---

Job 3 and Genesis 1

M. Fishbane has suggested that the sequence and rhythm of Job's seven curses are "exactly paralleled" by the seven-day pattern in Genesis 1. The thrust of these curses, he argues, is to call for a systematic "reversal" of creation (152, 154). To make these parallels work out, however, he must go beyond the natural break that occurs after Job 3:10 and treat vv. 3-13 as the basic pericope that contains the curses. If one stays within vv. 3-10, the parallels with Genesis 1 are not exact, but they remain significant and determinative for interpretation. The seven curses and their general connection to Genesis 1 may be illustrated as follows: (Note: the seven curses are listed in order, one per v., beginning with curse 1 in v. 3; the jussives and negatives are translated with "Let" or "Let not.")

Job 3:3-10	Genesis 1
v. 3 Let the day perish	
v. 4 Let that day be darkness	v. 3 The first day—Let there be light
Let not God *above* seek it	v. 7 The waters *above* the firmament
Let not God light shine on it	
v. 5 Let gloom and deep darkness claim it	v. 2 Darkness was upon the face of the deep
Let clouds settle upon it	
Let the blackness of the day terrify it	
v. 6 Let thick darkness seize that night	v. 14 Lights to separate day and night . . .
Let it not rejoice among the days of the year	for seasons and for days and for years
Let it not come into the number of months	
v. 7 Yes, let that night be barren	
Let no joyful cry be heard in it	
v. 8 Let those curse it who curse the Sea	
those who are skilled to raise up Leviathan	v. 21 God created great sea monsters
v. 9 Let the stars of its dawn be dark	
Let it hope for light, but have none	v. 15 Lights to give light upon earth
v. 15 Let it not see the eyelids of the morning	

For further reading on the parallels between Job 3 and Gen 1, see M. Fishbane, "Jeremiah IV 23-26 and Job III 3-13: A Recovered Use of the Creation Pattern," VT 21 (1971): 151-67. L. Perdue has appropriated and expanded upon Fishbane's work in several significant studies. The seminal article, from which I have taken the title for this chapter, is "Job's Assault on Creation," HAR 10 (1987): 295-315. See further his *Wisdom in Revolt: Metaphorical Theology in the Book of Job* (JSOTSup 112; Sheffield: Almond Press, 1991), 96-98, and *Wisdom and Creation: The Theology of Wisdom Literature* (Nashville: Abingdon Press, 1994), 131-37.

---

seems to be that if God does not seek out the day, then it will languish because of God's indifference. The expression "let no light shine on it" suggests that the deprivation of light will rob the day of something vital for its purposes. Finally, Job asks that gloom and deep darkness will "claim" or "reclaim" (*gāʾal*) the day. The word is also used with reference to the responsibility of the next of kin to "redeem" property or family members from conditions that imperil survival (see Lev 25:25-55). Job's curse ironically reverses that meaning. His hope is that night will reclaim day, not to insure its survival, but to guarantee its oblivion. These multiple images intensify the objective of Job's curse. His desire is not just that the day "perish" (v. 3) in darkness. He intends that what

"Let the Day Perish Wherein I Was Born"

Job sits at the center of this frame. His face is the only one that can be seen, one indication of his isolation from his wife and friends. His arms are outstretched, palms extended upward, and his mouth is opened, as if he is in the process of speaking the words from Job 3:3 cited in the lower margin of the illustration. It is unclear whether Job speaks in anger or despair, but the tears streaming down his cheek indicate a pronounced level of anguish.

Blake's rendering hints that nature itself is undone by Job's suffering. Two mountains form the backdrop. The one to Job's right is leaning as if its foundations are shaken. The skies have darkened, and clouds swirl downwards from the heavens in a manner reminiscent of the tears falling from Job's eyes. The vegetation in the bottom suggests a withering creation. A fruit tree in the bottom left is uprooted and pulled down by the weight of its own produce. A vine of thorns or briars pushes up from the soil, uprooting an assortment of toadstools and plants. To the bottom right, another tree or fruit bush bends down, some of its berries falling like tears. These various images exegete the text that Blake uses to provide the scene's last words: "his grief was very great" (2:13).

Job Curses the Day of His Birth

William Blake (1757-1827). *Job Curses the Day of His Birth*. 1823-1825. Engraving from Blake's *Illustrations of the Book of Job*.

---

darkens the day will "take up residence" in it (v. 5: *šākan*; NRSV, "settle") and "terrorize" it (v. 5: *bāʿat*).

As if trying to seek out root causes, the focus of Job's curse moves backwards from the day of his birth to the night of his conception (see v. 3b). "That night" now becomes the object of four curses (vv. 6-9). The imagery of darkness continues to frame these curses. Verse 6 stipulates that the night be "seized" or "carried away" (*lāqaḥ*) by the sinister forces of "thick darkness" (*ʾōpel*; in Job 30:26 the same word is parallel with "evil" (*raʿ*), and the two words together are used as antonyms for "light" and "good"). Verse 9 expresses the hope that the "stars of twilight" will be "darkened" (*ḥāšak*). Night will wait for light that will not come; it will not see the first blinkings of the dawn.

Within these framing verses, Job's curses appropriate additional imagery that shifts the focus away from the particularities of one night and one conception to wider cosmic objectives. He asks that night no longer be counted among the days and months of the year (v. 6b). In the creational design, night is the first part of day (Gen 1:5: "And there was evening and there was morning, the first day"). If there is no night, there is no day. Without the day, there can be no months or years. In effect, Job calls for a cancellation of the regular cycles (day, night, months, year) that order cosmic time. The idea that night should no longer beget day is strengthened by the wish that night should be "barren" (v. 7: *galmûd*). The word draws upon images of fertility and reproduction to suggest that night should be incapable of conceiving, birthing, and caring for new life. Night is to be sterile; its ability to create life cancelled. Finally, Job names the mythological sea monster Leviathan, symbol of the primordial chaos waters that threaten to destroy the orders of creation (v. 8b).[5] He summons those who are skillful in rousing this slumbering beast to attend to their tasks. The suggestion is that once awakened, Leviathan will devour the night and return creation to the regnant powers of chaos. [Leviathan]

The reason for Job's curse is stated in one line: "because it [the night] did not shut the doors of my mother's womb, and hide trouble from my eyes" (v. 10). Night's crime is that it did not block Job's entrance into life. It is guilty of permitting him to embark on a journey that leads only to "trouble." Job invokes a punishment that fits the crime. Because night did not stop Job from seeing the agony that makes life unbearable, Job would prevent night from seeing the dawn that makes its journey complete (v. 9). Here, as throughout the preceding verses, Job personifies night (and day) as life forces that he wishes to negate. He has not cursed God, at least not directly, and so the reader may understand that even now, when he speaks in the extremity of his affliction, he has not sinned "with his lips."

But rumbling just beneath these curses is an undertone suggesting that Job's words may include God as an unnamed co-conspirator in his indictment. His specific charge is that the night did not close his mother's womb. In Israelite thought, however, it is God who opens and closes the womb (e.g., Gen 29:31; 1 Sam 1:5). Who then is really culpable for his birth? Is it *night*, or *night's Creator*? Further, who or what is really responsible for the "trouble" (v. 10: *ʿāmāl*) that attends Job's life outside the womb? Subsequently, the friends will argue that "trouble" (*ʿāmāl*) is what people reap for the sins they sow (4:8; cf. 5:6). Job will insist that "trouble" (*ʿāmāl*) is assigned to him in the same way that a master assigns hard labor to a slave (7:3). Is night to be condemned for allowing life to proceed into trouble? Is Job to be rebuked for bringing

Leviathan

In Canaanite literature, Leviathan (lit., "twisting one") is the name of the mythological sea serpent who personifies the waters of chaos. It is Baal's defeat of Leviathan that secures creation. A number of texts in the Hebrew Bible appropriate this imagery. Ps 74:12-17 depicts YHWH "crushing the heads of Leviathan" (v. 14) as one of several acts that secured the boundaries of creation. The suggestion that Leviathan has "heads" is particularly interesting in view of Canaanite texts that describe Leviathan as having seven heads. A seven-headed dragon identified as Satan is also described in the New Testament (see further below). Ps 89:9-13 offers a similar affirmation of God, who "crushed Rahab like

Antichrist Riding Leviathan

Antichrist Riding Leviathan. Twelfth century. Illumination. Bodleian Library, University of Oxford.

a carcass" (v. 10). It is likely that Rahab is similar, if not identical, to Leviathan. In Ps 104:26, the psalmist suggests that YHWH "formed" or "created" (*yāṣar*) Leviathan as a plaything. Isaiah 27:1 describes an eschatological day when YHWH will defeat Leviathan, although here the allusion is probably to a historical enemy, perhaps Assyria or Egypt.

In addition to Job 3:8, Leviathan also receives significant attention in God's second speech from the whirlwind in Job 41:1-34 [MT 40:25–41:26]. The latter text offers a lengthy description of Leviathan's strength and power. Its skin is like a warrior's garment (41:13-17); it spews forth fire and smoke (41:18-21); it is a "creature without fear," a "king" in its own realm (41:33-34). God's description of Leviathan offers a curious counterpart to Job 3:8. God commends Leviathan to Job as one of two representatives of the animal world (the other is Behemoth [40:15-24]) who have something positive to teach Job about God's design for creation. In Job 3:8, Job invokes Leviathan, not to learn something of God's world, but to destroy that world. For further discussion see the commentary on Job 41:1-34.

Leviathan is also mentioned in later Jewish literature, almost always, as in Job 40-41, in association with Behemoth. Leviathan is depicted as female and is associated with the "abyss of the ocean"; Behemoth is male and is associated with the "dry desert" (*1 En* 60:7-10 [2nd C. BCE to 1st C. CE]). 2 Esd 6:49-52 (also known as 4 Ezra), which dates to the latter part of the first century CE, and 2 Bar 29:1-8 (early second C. CE) envision Leviathan being devoured in the final judgment. This eschatological reference is further attested in the New Testament, which depicts Christ doing battle in the last days with a seven-headed dragon who is identified as Satan (Rev 12:3, 9; cf. 13:1; 17:3).

The use of Leviathan as a metaphor for all that threatens the church became a prominent feature in Christian exposition. Origen, Jerome, Augustine, Calvin, Luther, and others use both Leviathan and Behemoth as symbols of evil, death, fallen humanity, and the Devil himself. The connection between Leviathan and the AntiChrist, for example, is depicted in this mid-sixteenth century miniature illustration of the book of Job.

Leviathan also has a significant presence in modern literature. For example, Thomas Hobbes's political tractate, *Leviathan* (1651), describes the state that is willing to give up its sovereignty as "the Generation of that great Leviathan." The "Introduction" to *Leviathan* states the agenda: "By art is created that great Leviathan, called a Commonwealth or State—(in Latin, *Civitas*) which is but an artificial man." In several works, William Blake describes Behemoth and Leviathan as the powers of fallen humanity that war against God's creation (e.g., *Marriage of Heaven and Hell* [1790–1793]). Herman Melville's classic novel *Moby Dick* (1851) describes whales as "leiviathans." He appropriates in his own distinct way the dark and ambiguous properties of the mythical monster to depict the terrors and the wonders of the vast creation encountered by Ishmael.

For further reading, see J. Day, *God's Conflict with the Dragon and the Sea* (Cambridge: Cambridge University Press, 1985); T. K. Beal, *Religion and Its Monsters* (New York, London: Routledge, 2002), 47-56, 89-102. For discussion of "AntiChrist Riding Leviathan" see I. Hutter, *Corpus der Byzantinischen MiniaturenhandsChriften*, Band 2 (Stuttgart: Anton Hiersmann, 1978), 54-66. For a survey of Leviathan in literature, see T. Sorell, L. Foisneau, eds., *Leviathan After 350 Years* (Oxford: Clarendon Press, 2004).

trouble on himself? Is there a "master" who doles out trouble at will to those who have no power to resist? Could this one who apportions "trouble" to suffering servants be God, as is indicated elsewhere in Hebrew Scripture (see Isa 53:11, which also uses the word *ʿāmāl*; NRSV: "anguish")?

Such questions lurk beneath the surface of Job's first words from the ash heap, but in the absence of a narrator to provide instruction, the reader must sort through the interpretive options without a definitive answer. Several things, however, are now clear. The Job who was silent in the face of suffering will now speak. The Job who once accepted the ebb and flow of life's journey from birth to death now rejects that journey and condemns the forces that permitted it to begin. The Job whose mouth once only blessed now curses. At the very least, the reader is now keenly aware that the one who "opens his mouth" in chapter 3 has moved a long way from the one who spoke the words recorded in 1:21. [Job 3 and Job 1:21]

Why? Why? Why? 3:11-26

To curse, Job adds lamentation. The lament is a weaving together of both self-lament, i.e., mournful interior reflection (vv. 11-19, 24-26)

Job 3 and Job 1:21

AΩ   R. Moore has suggested that Job 3 is a step-by-step reversal of Job's affirmation in 1:21. In his judgment, the opening soliloquy of the poetic Job (Job 3–42:6) has been written to "confute" the opening soliloquy of the prologue. He illustrates with the following diagram:

Job 1:21	**Job 3**
(1:21a)	(3:1-10)
A. Reverent acceptance of the womb:	Job denigrates the womb:
"Naked I came from my mother's womb"	"It did not shut the doors of my womb"
(1:21b)	(3:11-19)
B. Reverent acceptance of the tomb:	Job regrets delay of the tomb:
"and naked shall I return"	"I should have been at rest"
(1:21c)	(3:20-23)
C. Reverent acceptance of deity:	Indirect questioning of deity:
"The Lord gives and the Lord takes away"	"Why is light *given* to him that is in misery"
(1:21d)	(3:24-26)
D. Theocentric praise:	Egocentric lament:
"Blessed be the name of the Lord"	"The thing I fear comes upon me"

R. Moore, "The Integrity of Job," CBQ 45 (1983): 26.

and God-lament, i.e.,complaint addressed, at least implicitly, to God (vv. 20-23). In both instances, the key word is "why?" (vv. 11, 12, 20; implied in vv. 16, 23). A number of Hebrew terms convey this question, but the repetition of the word *lāmmāh* in vv. 11 and 20, a word typically conveying a strong note of protest, gives to the lament a tone of angry despair. That despair is the governing motif of these words is further indicated by the recognition that even in lament Job remains alone. He appropriates the language, but not the true spirit, of lament. Typically, laments address God directly, include a petition for God to answer, and end with a note of confident expectation that God has heard and will respond. Job refers to God only indirectly (v. 23) and ends up where he began, in the painful solitude of grief searching for an echo that does not come (vv. 24-26). He does not appeal to God, and he does not seem to expect that there will be a response to his plight from any source.

The lament begins with a series of "why" questions (vv. 11-12) that uses three different Hebrew interrogatives to ask essentially the same question: Why did I not die at birth? The first interrogative, *lāmmāh* (v. 11), sets the tone for the entire lament. The word typically introduces lament situations where hard questions, heavy-laden with protest and accusation, are addressed to God, as for example in Ps 10:1: "Why, *O Lord*, do *you* stand far off? (cf. Exod 32:11-12; Pss 22:1; 74:1; Jer 20:18; Lam 5:20). Job's questions are just as freighted, but at most they address God only indirectly. He does not ask, "Why, *O Lord*?" but rather, "Why did *I* not die at birth?" Job's complaint moves him deeper and deeper into the solitude of his own suffering. He begins by asking why he came forth from the *womb*. Then he wonders why, if he had to leave the womb, were there *knees* to receive him as a newborn. And finally, once received into this world, why were there *breasts* to feed him and so to strengthen him for a life journey that he now wishes had never begun (cf. v. 16). ["To Be, or Not to Be"]

Job continues his lament in vv. 13-19 with an evocative description of Sheol and a reflection on why existence in the depths of this netherworld is more desirable than life as he knows it. Israelite tradition typically depicts Sheol as the lowest part of the underworld to which the dead descend in unremitting darkness and gloom. Those confined there may cry out for relief, but normally there is no answer, no exit, no hope for anything beyond their permanent confinement in the dismal abode of the dead (Pss 6:5 [MT 6:6]; 30:9 [MT 30:10]; 88:10-12 [MT 88:11-13]; 115:17). Job's description of Sheol ironically reverses this picture. He desires to escape *to* Sheol, not *from* it. In the darkness of its domain, he imagines that he will "lie down" (*šākab*), be "undisturbed" (*šāqaṭ*; NRSV: "quiet"), "sleep" (*šākan*), and be at "rest" (*nûaḥ*). The

---

"To Be, or Not to Be"

That grief can be so profound as to compel one to prefer death to life is a staple of literature, both biblical and non-biblical. Consider the following examples:

- And I thought the dead, who have already died, more fortunate than the living, who are still alive; but better than both is the one who has not been, and has not seen the evil deeds that are done under the sun. (Eccl 4:2-3)
- Blessed is he who was not born, Or he who was born and died. (2 Bar10:6)
- It would have been better if the earth had not produced Adam, or else, when it had produced him, had restrained him from sinning. (2 Esd. [4 Ezra] 7:46[116])
- Death is better than a life of misery, And eternal sleep than chronic sickness. (Sir30:17)
- Not to be born is the most
  To be desired; but having seen the light,
  The next best is to go whence one came

As soon as may be. (Sophocles, *Oedipus at Colonus*, 1224-1227)

Of numerous other examples that might be cited, surely one that will be easily recognized is Hamlet's opening soliloquy in Act III. In a clever and effective exposition, J. Janzen has drawn upon Hamlet's words as a way of introducing Job's opening soliloquy in ch. 3, which he titles "To Have Been or not to Have Been."

To be, or not to be: That is the question:
Whether tis nobler in the mind to suffer
The slings and arrows of outrageous fortune,
Or to take arms against a sea of troubles,
And by opposing end them? To die: to sleep;
No more; and by a sleep to say we end
The heart-ache and the thousand natural shocks
That flesh is heir to, tis a consummation
Devoutly to be wish'd. To die, to sleep (*Hamlet*, III, i, 56-64)

J. Gerald Janzen, *Job* (Atlanta: John Knox, 1985), 61-70.

---

notion that one should prefer the oblivion of Sheol to life is virtually unprecedented in the Hebrew Bible (cf. Eccl 4:3; 6:3-6). It serves here as a reminder that extreme suffering like Job's invites and requires extreme measures. [Sheol]

The restfulness that Job expects Sheol to offer is presented with different images. He begins by imagining Sheol as a final resting place for kings, counselors, princes, and others who in life enjoyed authority, status, and wealth (vv. 14-15). As one who was himself once revered as "the greatest of all the people of the east" (1:3), Job seems initially to anticipate that in death, if not in life, he may be reunited with his former peers. Verses 17-19, however, indicate that Job no longer identifies with the titled and the prosperous. His affiliation now lies with those whose status in life places them at the bottom of the social scale. He describes with different terms two groups of persons who will inhabit Sheol: the "wicked" and the "weary," the "prisoners" and the "taskmasters," the "small" and the "great," the "slave" and the "master." In each case the relationship between these groups is characterized by inequality and oppression. Job longs for Sheol, because he believes that there these skewed relationships will no longer exist. The wicked will no longer be "raging" (v. 17, *rōgez*; NRSV: "troubling") like thunder against victims whose power to resist has been exhausted. The prisoners will sleep, because they will no longer have to heed the commands of their overseers (v. 18). The small and the great will be together in Sheol,

Sheol

AΩ Several terms are used in the Hebrew Bible to refer to the place of the dead. The most frequent is *šĕ'ôl*, which occurs approximately 65 times. The word refers both to the *place* where the dead reside and to *death personified*. There are no full descriptions of the *place* of Sheol in the Hebrew Bible, but several characteristics are frequently mentioned. It is a place in the depths of the underworld (Deut 32:22; Isa 7:11), often associated with the chaotic waters of the deep (Jonah 2:3-6; cf. Pss 69:1-2, 14-15 [MT 69:2-3, 15-16]; 88:6-7 [MT 88:7-8]. It is associated with darkness (Job 17:13; cf. Job 18:18; Lam 3:6), dust (Job 17:16; 21:26; Pss 7:5 [MT 7:6]), and silence (Pss 31:17 [MT 31:18]; 115:17). It is conventionally understood to be the final gathering place of all the dead, righteous and wicked alike (e.g., Ps 89:48 [MT 89:49]), although it is most often associated with the wicked alone. As *death personified*, Sheol is described as having an appetite (Isa 5:14; Hab 2:5; Prov 27:20), and as having powers to hold persons in its grasp (Hos 13:14) or to make covenants with people (Isa 28:15, 18).

In the New Testament *šĕ'ôl* is typically translated by the word *hades* ("Hades"). Hades shares many of the same characteristics of Sheol. For example, it also designates both a *place* in the depths of the world (e.g., Matt 11:23; Luke 10:15) and the *personified* powers of death that desire to hold sway over the Church (Matt 16:18). Further, Hades is sometimes depicted as being the place of repose for both the righteous and the wicked (e.g., Luke 16:23). Other texts describe it as the place for the wicked alone, with the righteous being assigned to a place called "paradise" (Luke 23:43).

What is striking about Job's desire for Sheol is that it is virtually without parallel in the Hebrew Bible. Only Eccl 6:3-6 and to a lesser degree Eccl 4:3 express a comparable idea. As D. Clines has concluded, "Job's words must be judged eccentric by OT standards." One frequently cited comparable text from the ancient Near East is the Egyptian text "Dispute Over Suicide," which dates to the Middle Kingdom (c. 2nd millennium). The tale reports the dialogue between a sufferer who is weary with life and his own soul.

Death is in my sight today
(Like) the recovery of a sick man,
Like going out into the open after a confinement.
Death is in my sight today
Like the color of myrrh,
Like sitting under an awning on a breezy day . . .
Death is in my sight today
Like the longing of man to see his house (again),
After he has spent many years held in captivity.

For further reading, see T. J. Lewis, "The Abode of the Dead," *ABD*, ed. D. N. Freedman (New York: Doubleday, 1992), vol. 2, 101-105; N. Tromp, *Primitive Conceptions of Death and the Nether World in the Old Testament* (Rome: Pontifical Biblical Institute, 1969).

D. Clines, *Job 1–20* (WBC; Dallas: Word Books, 1989), 92. "Dispute over Suicide," in *ANET*, 3rd ed. with supplement, ed. J. B. Pritchard (Princeton: Princeton University Press, 1969), 407.

but no longer in relationships that make one a "slave" and the other a "master" (v. 19).

In several ways, the language and imagery of Job's curses indicate that suffering has turned his perception of the world upside down. Death is more desirable than life. The underworld of Sheol is more appealing that the upper world of Uz. The one whose station in life once gave him reason to believe that good and evil were matters to be adjudicated only by the "managers" of society (kings, counselors, princes, "great ones" like Job), now knows that for some this arrangement means life is an endless and futile struggle of "slaves" against "masters."

This last image is particularly intriguing and perhaps suggests the most radical reversal of all in Job's perception of his world and his God. The Hebrew word translated "slave" in v. 19 is *'ebed*, which means both "slave" and "servant." The same word occurs for the first time in Job1:8

(cf. 2:3), when God asks the *satan*, "Have you considered my *servant* (*'abdî*) Job?" God's perspective is that Job has a place of honor among those (like Moses), who have distinguished themselves by serving God faithfully. However, between 1:8 and 3:19, the first occurrence of *'ebed* in the poetic sections of the book, Job's world undergoes catastrophic changes. His window on to that world is now the ash heap, and from this vantage point what it means to be an *'ebed* looks very different. His perspective is that he is no more than a common "slave" who has been assigned to onerous labor, with no promise of relief short of his death (see further Job's speeches in 7:1-6; 14:1-6).[6] Also significant is the ambiguity encoded in the last word of v. 19, "masters." The Hebrew word is *'ādōn*. When used with reference to God, this word is normally translated "Lord." When used of humans who exercise power, the word may be translated as "lord" or "master." Like a slave, Job longs to be free from his "master." Given the way suffering has eroded Job's former certainties, he is no longer clear whether his oppressor is human or divine.

The latter half of Job's lament (vv. 20-26) begins with the same interrogative (*lāmmāh*) that introduced the "why" question in v. 11. With the first question, Job asked *why he had not died* at birth, and he proceeded to imagine how different things might have been if he could only have rested peacefully in Sheol. His longing for Sheol, however, is fanciful, and so with the second half of his lament he returns to painful realities. If he could not die at birth, *why must he continue to live?* With this question, he proceeds to describe the actual—not imagined—life of misery and toil that he experiences.

Job's questioning now moves him a step closer to naming God as the party responsible for his suffering. Most translations obscure this move with a passive and impersonal rendering of the verb "give" in v. 20, e.g., "Why is light *given* to one in misery?" (NRSV; cf. REB, NIV, NAB). The Hebrew verb form (*yittēn*), however, is active, not passive. NJPS captures both the sense and the implication of this with its translation: "Why does *He give* light to the sufferer?" Job does not yet explicitly identify God as the one he holds accountable for his plight, but the tone of his language indicates that he understands there is an active agent somewhere behind his suffering. Someone or something "gives" what has come to Job; it is not merely "given." Verse 23 continues this line of questioning (the interrogative beginning of v. 20 is implied) and moves Job yet another step closer to naming God. He asks, "[Why does He give light] to one whose way is hidden, one whom God (*'ĕlôah*) has hedged in (*yāsek*)?" The name Job uses for God is the more impersonal word "Eloah" (the same word occurs in 3:4 and elsewhere more than forty times in Job). [Names for God] Nonetheless, the action that he

Names for God

In the poetic dialogues, Job and his friends always speak of God by using generic terms like El, Eloah, Shaddai, Elohim, but never the distinctive name revealed to Moses, YHWH (Exod 3:14). Job 12:9, where the MT has YHWH, may be the only exception, but most regard this as a secondary insertion. By contrast, the Prologue (1–2), Epilogue (42:7–17), and the divine speeches from the whirlwind (38:1–42:6) use almost exclusively the special name YHWH. The distribution of the divine names throughout the book may be illustrated as follows:

Names for God	Number of Occurances in Job				Total
	Job 1-2 and 42:7-17	Job 3-31	Job 32-37	Job 38-42:6	
El (*'el*)	0 .	33	19	3	55
Eloah (*'eloah*)	0	6	6	2	41
Shaddai (*šadday*)	0	6	6	1	31
Elohim (*'elohim*)	8	2	2	1	14
The elohim (*ha'elohim*)	3	0	0	0	3
Lord (*YHWH*)	23	1 (Job 12:9?)	0	5	29

For these statistics see S. R. Driver and G. B. Gray, *A Critical and Exegetical Commentary on the Book of Job* (Edinburgh: T and T. Clark, 1921), xxxv.

ascribes to Eloah, "hedging in," or "fencing in," is the same as that which the *satan* attributed to YHWH in 1:10 (cf. 38:8). The *satan* had argued that God hedged in Job in order to *protect* him from the chaos of life. Job intimates that God hedges him in in order to *confine* him to a life that is full of nothing but chaos (cf. Hos 2:6 [MT 2:8]).

On both sides of these two probing questions (vv. 20, 23), Job presses his description of the "misery" (v. 20: *ʿāmāl*; NRSV translates the same word as "trouble" in 3:10) that life brings to one and all. He speaks first of the collective fate of all who are "bitter of soul" (v. 20b; the same expression is used of Job himself in 7:11; 10:1). Why must people continue to live, when pain reduces life to no more than a "longing" for a death that will not come (v. 21) or to "digging" like a treasure hunter for a tomb that cannot be found (vv. 21b-22)? Under such circumstances life becomes meaningless. One can neither live fully nor die completely; all that remains is simply to exist. Job speaks next of his own personal experiences (vv. 24-26). Pain and suffering can never be fully assessed if it is understood only in the abstract. Job himself gives a face to misery. It looks like one whose bread and water is "sighing" and "groaning" (v. 24; the word for "groaning" may also be translated "roaring"; e.g., 4:10). It looks like one who lives in persistent "fear" and "dread" (v. 25), as S. Mitchell has put it, like one whose "nightmares have come to life."[7] In the end, it looks like one whose life is defined completely by negatives and absences: there is no "ease," no "quiet," no "rest." There is only "turmoil" (v. 26: *rōgez*; NRSV, "trouble"). The only place where this turmoil will cease, as Job has already discerned (see v. 17, where the same word occurs) is in Sheol, and even the hope for Sheol is vain. ["Grief"]

"Grief"

Eyes
That are frozen
From not crying.

Heart
That knows
No way of dying.

L. Hughes, "Grief," *The Collected Poems of Langston Hughes*, ed. A. Rampersad (New York: Vantage Books, 1994), 334.

CONNECTIONS

It may happen in a moment or in a prolonged sequence of events, but life sometimes comes undone. The world falls apart. Everything we believe in, work towards, hope for is negated. So it was for Job, and so it has been for countless others whose journeys have led them to ash heaps of their own. In his memoirs, Elie Wiesel, a survivor of Auschwitz and Buchenwald, reflects on the day his world changed forever:

> I see images of exodus and uprooting, reminiscent of a past buried in memory; ravaged, dazed, disoriented faces. Everything changed overnight. A few words uttered by a man in uniform, and the order of Creation collapsed. Everything was dismantled; ties were severed, words were emptied of their meaning. Homes became unrecognizable; my house was no longer my own. Everything a family had managed to accumulate in a lifetime had to be left behind.[8]

Experiences that "ravage," "daze," and "disorient" require an agonizing process of reappraisal. When suffering is so great that creation itself seems to buckle under its weight, everything comes under review, including and especially God the Creator. Job Huss, the Joban character in H. G. Wells's fiction *The Undying Fire*, sees clearly what is at stake for the faith enterprise when we "look squarely at the world about us." He reflects on a walk through the woods, where he encountered example after example of cruelty, suffering, and untimely death in the animal kingdom: a young rabbit dragged from its burrow, its head bitten open, torn and bloody; a mouse, spiked on the quills of a hawthorn bush, its limbs twisted horribly, as if challenging Mr. Huss "to judge between it and its creator." Finally, a "villainous-looking" cat unclenched its teeth and deposited at his feet a small crested bird, mangled and flapping in flat circles on the ground. His first impulse was to chase the cat, but upon further thought he decided the kinder act would be to stay and put the bird out of its misery. Wells describes the scene and the confession it exacts from Mr. Huss with a chilling simplicity:

> I hit it with my stick, and as it still moved I stamped it to death with my feet. I fled from its body in agony. "And this," I cried, "this hell revealed, is God's creation!"

> Suddenly it seemed to me that scales had fallen from my eyes and that I saw the whole world plain. It was as if the universe had put aside a mask it had hitherto worn, and shown me its face, and it was the face of boundless evil. [9]

From his ash heap Job looks at his world squarely—"this hell revealed"—and what he sees evokes a similar agony and a comparable cry. What do people do or say when life pushes them beyond Eden into a borderland of hurt? For those who have crossed this border already, and for those who may yet do so, Job's journey from chapters 1 and 2 to chapter 3 invites reflection on three dimensions of the faith that may be required of us: (1) pain must find a voice; (2) that voice is likely to be an anguished but generative combination of curse, which seeks to deny and negate, and (3) lament, which probes restlessly for meaning where none seems available.

Job's journey from chapter 2 to chapter 3 is from silence to speech. Both are necessary, and neither is complete or adequate without the other. Job's seven days and nights of silence signal his full entry into the brokenness and loss that defines his world. He had spoken once in the midst of his travails, an earnest effort to affirm past truths in the face of present grief (1:21). Ultimately, his grief outdistances his affirmation,

---

"Pain Doesn't Travel in Straight Lines"

In Pat Conroy's novel *Beach Music*, Jack McCall, an American living in Rome, returns home to Charleston, South Carolina to try to put the pieces of his life back together after his wife's suicide. His mother Lucy, now afflicted with leukemia, reflects on the suffering that has been the lot of their family: "You think you know what to look out for in life, Jack. You think your childhood teaches you all the traps you need to worry about. But that's not how it works. Pain doesn't travel in straight lines. It circles around and comes up behind you. It's the circles that kill you."

P. Conroy, *Beach Music* (New York: Doubleday, 1995), 339.

---

however, and silence becomes the only response that can take full account of the truth about life in the land of Uz (2:13). The silence is important, for without it Job may be tempted to feign confessions that are no longer connected to reality and so are no longer compelling. Some life experiences are simply too much, the disruption they bring is too extensive, the pain that follows in their wake is too overwhelming, their assault on what is precious is too threatening. Neither life nor faith can go on as usual. ["Pain Doesn't Travel in Straight Lines"] Job learns this lesson, and he yields to a hard truth: suffering that is "very great" can (and perhaps should) silence praise that is too glib, too pat, too disconnected from all that is real.

But in that submission to the reality of pain, there is still another truth to be learned. Silence is not the end of faith; indeed, it may be its true beginning. As Wiesel goes on to observe concerning the darkness of Auschwitz that threatened to eclipse all belief, "Sometimes we must accept the pain of faith so as not to lose it."[10] Job enters into the fullness of pained silence not to lose faith, but to find it. The silence is a way of connecting with the reality of suffering and of searching for some wider truth than he has previously grasped that will make sense of that reality. As long as one stays in silence, however, one searches alone. It is when silence gives way to speech that sufferers begin a journey that advances faith to a new level. Once spoken, pain can be named for what it is. It can be addressed, engaged, questioned, refuted, attacked. The very act of speaking in the midst of pain and suffering is an act of faith. It signals a fierce resolve to believe that someone will listen, someone will care, someone will come.

From his ash heap, Job looks at his world squarely, and he opens his mouth to *curse* and *lament*. These two forms of speech are not unrelated, and the fact that Job uses them in this sequence invites reflection on how pain pushes faith to new levels of passion and desire. The objective of curse is to negate, to speak with such fervor that one's words become armed weapons against targeted opponents. When Mr. Huss looks at the chewed-up bird the cat dropped at his feet, his first impulse is to destroy the one who has inflicted the pain: "A fit of weak and reasonless rage came upon me . . . and seeing the cat halt some yards away and turn to regard me and move as if to recover its victim, I rushed at it and pursued it, shouting."[11]

When Job looks at his mangled life, his grief speaks first as a curse that seeks to spy out root causes and eliminate them. His loss and broken-ness is deep and abiding—seven sons, three daughters. Their senseless deaths rob him of life, and he searches for words that will match his anguish. Damn the day, damn the night, damn the world and everything in it that conspires to make life a masquerade of dead children and destroyed families. To speak in any other way of a world like this would be less than honest. Perhaps Job's words will not change anything— this must for now remain an open question—but they do signal his resolve not to be a passive bystander in the face of death and destruction. To curse the forces of death and destruction may be extreme. It may be futile, even absurd. It is also an act of faith, because it refuses to believe that this is the way life is sup-posed to be. ["I Know Why the Caged Bird Sings"]

Job also laments, and this too is important for those who will, or must, take up his journey into suffering inexplicable. In Israelite tradition, lament is a recognized form for dealing with what is wrong in life. Laments typically follow a pattern: invocation of God, lamentation, petition, and a concluding expression of confidence. Job dares to take up this way of dealing with his afflicted world, although he seems uncertain as yet just how far into this process to go. He laments, but he does not address the laments directly to God. He questions intensely (vv. 11, 12, 16, 20, 23), but he does not petition for improvement or deliverance. His best hope is that death will come quickly. He does not express one word of confidence and ends with a string of negatives that seems to slam the door on any further discovery. But he does question, and these questions are the key to where he is going. They are a sign of his restlessness (cf. vv. 13, 17, 26), his unwillingness to accept that what is is what must be. Questions always harbor the hope for change, even if only implicitly. They call for recalculating, refiguring, reimagining the status quo.

Job seems as yet uncertain whether to address his questions to God. Perhaps this is but an indication of where suffering has taken him. He is now east of Eden, somewhere in the hinterland between curse and

"I Know Why the Caged Bird Sings"

I know what the caged bird feels, alas!
    When the sun is bright on the upland slopes;
When the wind stirs soft through the springing grass,
And the river flows like a stream of glass;
When the first bird sings and the first bud opens,
And the faint perfume from its chalice steals—
I know what the caged bird feels!

I know why the caged bird beats his wing
Till blood is red on the cruel bars;
For he must fly back to his perch and cling
When he fain would be on the bough a-swing;
And a pain still throbs in the cold, old scars
And they pulse again with a keener sting—
I know why he beats his wing!

I know why the caged bird sings, ah me,
When his wing is bruised and his bosom sore, —
When he beats his bars and he would be free;
It is not a carol of joy or glee,
But a prayer that he sends from his heart's deep core,
But a plea, that upward to Heaven he flings—
I know why the caged bird sings!

Paul Laurence Dunbar, "Sympathy," *Black Poets of the United States, from Paul Laurence Dunbar to Langston Hughes* (Urbana: University of Illinois Press, 1973), 356.

"It Must Be Lonely to Be God"

I think it must be lonely to be God.
Nobody loves a master. No. Despite
The bright hosannas, bright clear dear-Lords, and
bright
Determined reverence of Sunday eyes.

Picture Jehovah striding through the hall
Of his importance, creatures running out
From servant-corners to acclaim, to shout
Appreciation of His merit's glare.

But who walks with Him?—dares to take His
arm,
To slap Him on the shoulder, tweak his ear,
Buy Him a Coca-Cola or a beer,
Pooh-pooh his politics, call Him a fool?

Perhaps—who knows?—He tires of looking
down.
Those eyes are never lifted. Never straight.
Perhaps sometimes He tires of being great
In solitude. Without a hand to hold.

Gwendolyn Brooks, "The Preacher Ruminates Behind the
Sermon," *Selected Poems* (New York: Harper and Row, 1944), 8.

lament. He is caught in a nexus of contradictions that make it exceedingly difficult to have clarity. He is caught between God and the *satan*. His world has been targeted for both good and evil. He is hailed as a distinguished "servant," but he is treated as an abused "slave." Given such turmoil, it is understandable that Job curses life and seeks to end it, even as he questions life and probes for meaning that will sustain it. To follow Job's journey through this maze of uncertainties and ambiguities, interpreters should keep their eyes on the questions. The questions will move Job inexorably closer to God, step by step (see vv. 20, 23). Such is the promise of lament.

There is at least one other issue that Job 3 presents to readers. Does pain that risks speaking in vexed blends of curse and lament still count as an authentic expression of faith? At the end of the prologue, we are told that Job "did not sin with his lips" (2:10). The verdict seems to commend praise as the acceptable response to suffering, and if not praise, then silence. Job has now broken silence, and his words are far from praise. The narrator is no longer present, so we have no authoritative guide to tell us whether it is still true that Job's lips have not sinned. When Job curses and laments, does he remain for us a model of faith? The friends are now ready to offer their response to this question. It will come as no surprise to most readers that they will answer with a loud and lengthy "No." That "No" to curse and lament is more pervasive in our faith traditions than we perhaps want to admit. The New Testament's singular focus on the "patience" of Job (Jas 5:11), a characteristic that hardly applies to the one who speaks in Job 3, is but one example of how the community of faith may reduce Job to a more orthodox, less unsettling figure.

But what if God were to make an appearance at the end of chapter 3? What would be the divine assessment of Job's speech? Would God still point to Job and boast that "there is no one like him on earth, a blameless and upright man who fears God and turns away from evil"? Would God still be proud to count Job as one of heaven's most loyal servants? ["It Must Be Lonely to Be God"] Or would God rebuke Job and send him back to the ash heap until he learns how to respond in some more appropriate manner? ["The One Thing God Can't Stomach"] It is a measure of the drama of this book that God declines to resolve these questions at the end of chapter 3. Indeed, God will not speak again until 38:1. In the

"The One Thing God Can't Stomach"

Nickles, who plays the role of Satan in A. MacLeish's play *J.B.*, articulates how suffering shapes the confession that comes from the ash heap:

I heard upon his dry dung heap
That man cry out who cannot sleep:
"If God is God He is not good,
If God is good He is not God;
Take the even, take the odd,
I would not sleep here if I could . . .

Nickles believes that this is precisely the sort of address that God will not, cannot, tolerate. He makes the case as follows:

The one thing God can't stomach is a man
That scratcher at the cracked creation!
That eyeball squinting through into His Eye,
Blind with the sight of Sight!

A. MacLeish, *J.B.* (Boston: Houghton Mifflin Co., 1956), 10-11.

---

meanwhile, the reader must ponder well the ongoing debate between Job and his friends, for much is at stake. From Job's perspective, how we understand creation itself and along with it, at least by implication, the Creator, hangs in the balance. We may think we already know the ultimate outcome of this drama, but like Job himself we must now suspend our conclusions until all the characters, including God, have had their say. At the very least, we must know that the final verdict on whether we are to follow Job in his cursing and lamenting, as well as in his patience, has not yet been reached.

NOTES

[1] On the different reading strategies of the prologue and the dialogues and the moral and social world they imply, see C. Newsom, "Cultural Politics and the Reading of Job," *BibInt* 1 (1993): 119-38; idem, *The Book of Job: A Contest of Moral Imaginations* (Oxford: Oxford University Press, 2003), 70-71.

[2] D. Cox has suggested that Job's desire for oblivion places him in the literary context of modern writers like Sartre, Camus, and Beckett; *The Triumph of Omnipotence: Job and the Tradition of the Absurd* (Roma: Universita Gregoriana Editrice, 1978), 37-52.

[3] See D. Clines, *Job 1–20* (WBC; Dallas: Word Books, 1989), 79: "It is a vain wish and the curses it includes are inconsequential and ineffective because it is too late to do anything about it. . . . The language is fierce, but the curse has no teeth and the wish is hopeless. Its power is wholly literary, its extravagance the violence of Job's feeling."

[4] Fishbane, "Jeremiah IV 23-26 and Job III 3-13: A Recovered use of the Creation Pattern," *VT* 21 (1971): 153.

[5] There may be another allusion to primordial sea monsters in v. 8a. The Hebrew text is "Let the cursers of *day* (*yôm*) curse it." Some commentators suggest a substitution of the word "sea" (*yam*) for "day." This emendation would suggest that "sea" (NRSV: "Sea") is a reference to the sea god known in Canaanite mythology as Yam. For this interpretation see, for example, M. Pope, *Job* (AB; Garden City NY: Doubleday, 1979), 30; R. Gordis, *The Book of Job: Commentary, New Translation, and Special Studies* (New York: Jewish Theological

Seminary of America, 1978), 34-35; N. Habel, *The Book of Job: A Commentary* (OTL; Philadelphia: Westminster Press, 1985), 108-109.

[6] On the metaphor of "slave" in Job 1–2 and its reversal or "destabilization" in Job 3 and elsewhere, see L. Perdue, *Wisdom in Revolt: Metaphorical Theology in the Book of Job* (JSOTSup 112; Sheffield: Almond Press, 1991), 106-108.

[7] S. Mitchell, *The Book of Job* (New York: Harper Collins, 1992), 14.

[8] E. Wiesel, *All Rivers Run to the Sea: Memoirs* (New York: Alfred A. Knopf, 1995), 64.

[9] H. G. Wells, *The Undying Fire* (New York: The Macmillan Company, 1919), 84-85. For discussion of the ways in which this novel recreates the Job story, see J. Levenson, *The Book of Job in Its Time and in the Twentieth Century* (Cambridge: Harvard University Press, 1972), 30-39.

[10] Wiesel, *All Rivers Run to the Sea*, 84.

[11] Wells, *Undying Fire*, 84.

ELIPHAZ'S FIRST RESPONSE TO JOB: "THINK NOW, WHO THAT WAS INNOCENT EVER PERISHED?"

Job 4:1–5:27

The First Cycle: God's Moral Governance of the World, Job 4:1–14:22

In the first cycle, the speeches of all three friends follow a common pattern comprised of three parts: (1) an introduction that presents a rhetorical question (4:2-6; 8:2-7; 11:2-6); (2) the body of the speech that offers general and theoretical observations and admonitions (4:7–5:7; 8:8-19; 11:7-12); and (3) a concluding word of comfort and hope (5:17-27; 8:20-22; 11:13-20).

The general theme sounded by each of the friends is God's moral governance of the world, especially as this is manifest in God's care for the righteous and punishment of the wicked (4:7-11; 8:8-19; 11:11). There are indications, however, that the friends approach their shared interests in different ways and with attitudes toward Job that fluctuate between sympathy and irritation. For example, Eliphaz concludes his first speech (5:17-27) with a lengthy and unequivocal assurance: "You shall *know* that your tent is safe. . . . You shall *know* that your descendants will be many. . . . we have searched this out; it is true. Hear and *know* it for yourself" (vv. 24-27). Bildad also concludes with words of encouragement (8:20-22), although what he offers is briefer, and the happy ending he foresees for Job is more ambiguous and qualified. He assures Job that "God will not reject a blameless person" and that God will "fill your mouth with laughter and your lips with joy." But he laces these assurances with words about the punishment of the wicked—God will not "take the hand of evildoers" and "the tent of the wicked will be no more"—subtly reminding Job that if his status before God is not what he claims, then he can expect a very different fortune. Zophar couches his assurances still more conditionally: "*If* you direct your heart rightly. . . . *If* iniquity is in your hand, put it far away. . . . surely *then* you will lift up your face without blemish." (11:13-15). Whereas Bildad only hints at the alternatives that awaited the wicked, Zophar concludes his speech with three pointed statements that seem more menacing than comforting: "the eyes of the wicked will fail; all way of escape will be lost to them, and their hope will is to breathe their last" (11:20).

Job listens carefully to each of these presentations, then rejects them one by one. He insists he is innocent (6:28-30; 9:21; 10:7), and accuses the friends of "whitewashing the truth" (13:4) in order to insulate themselves and their God from further scrutiny. He charges that God is more absent from the world than present (9:11; 13:24), more hostile than compassionate (10:1-17). Thus, from Job's perspective, God's moral governance of the world is very much in question. One need only "ask the animals. . . the birds of the air. . . the plants of the earth. . . and the fish of the sea" (12:7-8) to know the truth about God's world. God exercises power, without restraint and without purpose, to destroy the very creation the friends claim God has so wondrously and justly fashioned (10:8-12). Why? To pursue the question, Job dares to imagine summoning God—as a defendant—to a court trial, where he could ask, "What are you doing?" (9:12). But then, having considered the possibility, Job yields to despair, for he realizes that God would not answer even one of the questions he might ask (9:3). When the first round of dialogues end, the question that Job asked from the ash heap—"Why did *I* not die at birth?" (3:11)—remains on the table, although now the despair it conveys is heavier, and the accusation it directs against God is more direct: "Why did *you* bring me forth from the womb?" (10:18). ["They Desired to Make Me Truthful"]

"They Desired to Make Me Truthful"

Reflecting on his upbringing in evangelical Christianity, James Wood notes that his childhood "was centrally planned, all negotiations had to pass by Jesus' desk." Even so, he was aware of another, largely unspoken, concern that clouded the convictions of parents and others who sought to keep him in the straight and narrow paths of piety:

Sometimes it seems that my childhood was the noise around a hush, the hush of God. And at times an actual hush: I recall episodes when my parents talked quietly and on their own about someone they knew who had "lost his faith," and the silent vibrations would fill the house at these times, as if a doctor were visiting. Similarly, my childhood was marked by the deaths of friends who were members of their congregation, people for whom the full evangelical panoply—prayer, the laying on of hands, anointing with oil—did not seem to have worked.

As an adult, Wood looks back on these early days and comments on their lasting effect on him:

[I]t was perhaps the wrong kind of religion for a child, because it excited in me two childish responses: fear and shyness. I feared being called out to give testimonials to the congregation. At times, we would all have our heads bent in prayer, and the vicar . . . would announce that he was certain that there was someone here who "had not turned to Christ." His voice scathed me like a searchlight. With the self-consciousness of adolescence, it was always I who had not turned to Christ. The fear produced shyness, or suspicion. "They desired to make me truthful; the tendency was to make me positive and skeptical. . ."

J. Wood, "The Broken Estate: The Legacy of Ernest Renan and Matthew Arnold," *The Broken Estate: Essays on Literature and Belief* (New York: Random House, 1999), 249, 250. The quote (250) "They desired to make me truthful . . . ," which Wood cites as an appropriate assessment of his own experiences, is from Edmund Gosse, *Father and Son*.

COMMENTARY

Since the friends first appeared to "console and comfort" Job (2:11-13), the imperative of their mission has changed considerably. As long as Job endured his suffering with unflinching faith, the friends could be content to sit with him in sympathetic silence. Even though his world had been shattered, they offer calm support, confident in their own eventual return to ordered and secure lives. However, when Job breaks this silence by cursing not only his life but also the cosmic design that perpetuates the misery of all life, the friends know that they can no longer remain passive ministrants. Job has endeavored to set in motion a negation, which if successful, threatens to undo not only his world but theirs as well. When chapter 4 begins, therefore, both Job and the friends embark on a journey into the netherland of grief, where silence yields to other ways of expressing what it means to be "blameless and upright" in the presence of God. [Moving Beyond "Grief's Wordless Catalogue of Loss"]

All of the friends are presented as older than Job. They are elder statesmen who represent the best of seasoned and proven counsel (cf. 12:12; 15:10). In each of the three cycles Eliphaz is the first to speak, a hint that he is the oldest and most respected one of the group. His speeches are generally longer and more developed than those of Bildad and Zophar and as a rule set forth the major issues that the other two basically repeat and review. This is especially true of Eliphaz's opening speech in chapters 4-5, which introduces the notion of retribution—God will punish the wicked and prosper the righteous (4:7-11)—that provides the foundation for all the arguments the friends will employ in the three cycles. A further confirmation of Eliphaz's status as the lead spokesperson for the group may be found in the Epilogue, where God addresses him directly: ". . . the Lord said to Eliphaz the Temanite, 'My wrath is kindled against you and against your two friends; for you have not spoken of me what is right, as my servant Job has'" (42:7).

Eliphaz draws upon a variety of traditional sayings from wisdom, prophetic, and psalmic traditions. The structure of his speech has three primary foci: words of assurance based on Job's personal situation (4:1-6); a lesson about the fate of the righteous and the wicked in the world of God's design (4:7–5:7); and words of assur-

---

Moving Beyond "Grief's Wordless Catalogue of Loss"

To long for what eternity fulfils
Is to forsake the light one has, or wills
To have, and go into the dark to wait
What light may come—no light perhaps, the dark
Insinuates. And yet the dark conceals
All possibilities: thought, word, and light,
Air, water, earth, motion, and song, the arc
Of lives through light, eyesight, hope, rest, and
  work—

And death, the narrow gate each one pass
Alone, as some have gone past every guess
Into the woods by a path lost to all
Who looks back, gone past light and sound of day
Into grief's wordless catalogue of loss.
As the known life is given up, birdcall
Becomes the only language of the way,
The leaves all shine with sudden light, and stay.

Wendell Berry, "Poem XII," *Sabbaths* (San Francisco: North Point Press, 1987), 23.

[Structure of Job 4:1–5:27]

Structure of Job 4:1–5:27

4:1-6 Words of assurance based on Job's personal situation

4:7–5:7 A moral lesson about the treatment of the righteous and the wicked in the world of God's design

    4:7-11 The fate of the righteous and the wicked, a frequent theme in Job (5:2-5; 8:13-19; 15:20-25; 18:5-21; 20:5-29; 27:13-23) and in the teaching of the wisdom tradition (e.g., Prov 12:7-21)

    4:12-21 Eliphaz's special revelation, which draws upon prophetic traditions of receiving a word directly from God (e.g., Amos 7:7-9)

    5:1-7 The fate of the fool, a theme frequent in the wisdom tradition (e.g., Prov 10:8, 14; 12:15, 16; 14:7, 29-30)

5:8-27 Words of assurance based on God's nature

    5:8-16 Hymnic praise of God's power to Rev the fortunes of both the "lowly" and the "crafty" (cf. Pss 113:7-8; 147:2-3, 6)

    5:17-27 Assurance of restitution for the "one whom God approves." At a number of points, this speech draws upon themes and forms common to the wisdom tradition (e.g., v. 17 and Prov 3:11-12; v. 19 and Prov 6:16-19; 30:15-16, 18-19, 21-31; Eccl 11:20)

---

ance based on God's nature (5:8-27). [Structure of Job 4:1–5:27] On first impression, Eliphaz's words remind one of a pastoral counselor who gently ministers to the distraught with equal measures of comfort and sympathetic advice.

- He is sensitive to Job's status in life and thus addresses him with proper respect and deference: "If one ventures a word with you, will you be offended?" (4:2).
- He expresses empathy for Job's present affliction (4:3-5).
- He relates to Job personally, drawing upon his own experiences to offer observations that might prove helpful for his friend: "As I have seen . . ." (4:8); "I have seen . . ." (5:3); "As for me . . ." (5:8).
- He offers the professional insight that is specially vouchsafed to the learned and wise but is presumed to be unavailable to the general public, apart from credentialed mediators like himself (4:12-21).
- He displays the calm confidence of the expert who knows that he is absolutely right in all that he says: "See, we have searched this out; it is true. Hear, and know it for yourself" (5:27).

Despite the sophisticated certainty of his counsel, Eliphaz seems trapped within a world of petrified traditions and unaffected slogans for life. He is content to respond to suffering by stringing together bits and pieces of accumulated wisdom, as if this will substitute for thinking through the particulars of Job's situation for himself. In this respect, he is more like a dogmatic theologian than a pastoral counselor. His approach is that of one who is so addicted to formulas for life's problems that he is unable to feel his way into ideas and experiences alien to his own.[1] He espouses a "cocksure fundamentalism" that brooks no questions and harbors no doubts.[2] As the spokesperson for the first and best counsel the friends can offer to Job, Eliphaz models a way of responding to suffering that makes God's final assessment in 42:7 all the more weighty for those who will be instructed by this drama.

Words of Assurance Based on Job's Personal Situation, 4:1-6

Eliphaz begins with a question, as if cautiously probing for an appropriate way to respond to this one who has now broken silence with such grieved vehemence: "If one ventures a word with you, would you be able to bear it (*til'eh*)?" (v. 2). The expression in Hebrew has to do with concern for Job's weariness more than his impatience, as some English translations suggest (e.g., NRSV, REB). Job has endured a series of catastrophic intrusions into his life. Has he the strength to withstand one further intrusion, if it comes in the form of a "sympathetic" word? Like a good sage, Eliphaz recognizes that there are some situations in life when "the prudent are restrained in speech" (Prov 10:19). Still, the wise teacher also knows that a word rightly spoken can cheer the heart (Prov 12:25; 15:23; 25:11). [CD: "Apt Words Have Power to Swage"] Eliphaz believes that he has just such a word for Job. Both his conviction and Job's need are so imperative that he is unable to keep from speaking.[3]

Eliphaz invites Job to recall former times, before his world was turned upside down, when there was clarity about who he was and what he was about (vv. 3-4). Job had once been a revered counselor whose instruction enabled others to understand and cope with their own suffering. He once knew well how to help those who faltered under the burden of their affliction: he had strengthened "weak hands" and stiffened "feeble knees." The term translated "instructed" (v. 3: *yāsar*) refers to moral and religious instruction that keeps one oriented through both discipline and correction to the proper paths in life. It describes the disciplinary instruction with which a parent nurtures a child (Prov 19:18; 29:17) or with which God admonishes those who have strayed from the correct way (Jer 30:11; 31:18; Pss 6:1; 38:1; 39:11). Such instruction is, "both sympathetic and confrontational."[4] Eliphaz suggests that as a friend and counselor to others, Job has displayed just these qualities. Now the counselor must have the wisdom to be befriended in his own suffering. The teacher must put into practice his own lessons.

Eliphaz's review of Job's former clarity seeks to reorient this one who has now experienced for himself what it means to be "weary" (v. 5a: *tēle'*; the same verb that occurs in v. 2) and "terrified" (v. 5b: *tibbāhēl*;

NRSV: "dismayed") by affliction. [CD: What Is Easy When You Are Well Is Hard When You Are Sick] Eliphaz's assessment of Job's misfortune is curiously impersonal and abstract: "it" happened (*tābôʾ*) to him; "it" struck (*tiggaʿ*) him. The indefinite pronoun "it" that serves as the subject of these verbs does not specify who or what caused Job's demise. In Eliphaz's view "it," broadly and vaguely conceived as adversity like Job's, simply happens. It is a common experience in the world that may come to one and all, irrespective of particular situations and circumstances.

What should Job do when adversity strikes? Eliphaz asks the question (v. 6) and assumes that the answer is self-evident. Job should trust in his "piety" (*yirʾāh*, "fear," an ellipsis for "fear of God," as in NRSV) and in the "integrity" (*tōm*) of his ways. These are the same virtues that the prologue has affirmed for Job (1:8; 2:3), hence Eliphaz, albeit unknowingly, now adds his confirmation of Job's character to those already offered by both the narrator and God. But whereas Job has challenged the notion that piety and integrity secure one's fortunes, Eliphaz continues to press the case that these virtues remain the key to Job's future. Indeed, in his view there is a direct and immutable link between piety and "confidence" and between integrity and "hope," a link that may be tested by suffering but will not ultimately be broken.

Two things, however, may cloud this assertion for the reader, if not also for Job. First, the root word from which the promise of "confidence" (*kisleh*) derives is susceptible to a double meaning: "foolishness" / "folly" (Eccl 7:25; Ps 49:13 [MT 49:14]; Prov 9:13) and "confidence" (as rendered here and in Job 8:14; 31:24, where the word is paralleled by "trust").[5] Eliphaz clearly intends the latter meaning, but one suspects that Job is tempted toward the former. Second, the promise Eliphaz offers is for the future; it offers but distant comfort for those faltering under the weight of immediate grief. For Job, it is precisely this distant lure of rest unrealized (cf. 3:20-26) that defines life in the present as an insufferable ordeal. [CD: "Extolling Patience as the Truest Fortitude"]

A Lesson about the Fate of the Righteous and the Wicked in the World of God's Design, 4:7–5:7

The center of Eliphaz's counsel to Job and the basis for his words of assurance (4:1-6; 5:8-27) is the reliability of the world's moral order. In the world of God's design, both the righteous and the wicked receive their just rewards. Eliphaz supports this assertion in two ways. First, he draws upon personal experience, cloaked as conventional wisdom, which he believes to be universally valid (4:7-11). Second, he claims a special revelation that gives him privileged insight into God's assessment of human nature (4:12–5:7).

Eliphaz begins (4:7-11) by posing a rhetorical question that subtly invites Job to shift his focus away from the troubling specifics of his own suffering to more settled general principles concerning the righteous and the wicked: "Think now (*zĕkor nā*ʾ; lit., "remember now"), who that was innocent ever perished? Where were the upright ever annihilated?" (v. 7). The assertion implicit in the question is not that the righteous do not *suffer*, but that they do not prematurely die or meet with total destruction.[6] Eliphaz's primary concern, however, is not to explain why the righteous suffer, which is clearly the problem that Job presents, but rather to argue that the wicked are certainly punished (vv. 8-11). Towards this end, he employs an agricultural metaphor to show that there is an organic connection between wicked deeds and their consequences. Those who plow the ground and sow "iniquity" (ʾāwen) predictably reap "trouble" (ʿāmāl). They do so not because they exercise any control over the processes of nature, but because God, the architect of the moral order in the world, is personally engaged in executing the divine master plan of retribution. [Retribution] It is the "breath (nĕšāmāh) of God" and the "blast (rûaḥ; lit., "wind, spirit") of his anger" that consummates the destruction of the wicked (v. 9). Verses 10-11 complete this initial review of the doctrine of retribution with a saying about the lion, a conventional symbol for the wicked (e.g., Pss 7:2; 17:12; 58:6; Prov 28:15; Nah 2:10-12). Despite its predatory powers, the lion is doomed to perish (v. 11: ʾōbēd; the same verb occurs in vv. 7, 9).

Eliphaz's use of the doctrine of retribution as a response to Job's suffering invites reflection on several points. First, Eliphaz emphasizes the negative side of the doctrine's assertion—the certain punishment of the wicked (vv. 8-11)—rather than its positive side—the good fortune that is secured for the righteous who suffer (v. 7). The imbalance in his presentation signals at the outset that Eliphaz will concern himself with the particularities of Job's situation only minimally and indirectly. As a person of piety and integrity, Job suffers and asks why. Eliphaz concedes Job's virtues (v. 6) but avoids his question. Job seeks justice for the innocent. Eliphaz suggests that punishing the guilty delivers that justice, as if a verdict *against* the wicked equates to a verdict *for* the falsely condemned who await a full and proper restoration of their life.

Second, Eliphaz appropriates the doctrine of retribution in a selective way. His opening words, "Remember now" (v. 7), suggest that when one reviews the tradition there will be no examples of righteous persons who ever failed to receive their just reward. Such a claim can be made only if one does not recognize evidence to the contrary or does not

---

Retribution

📖 The idea that God "repays" (Lat.: *re* ["back"] + *tribuere* ["to pay"]) virtue with reward and vice with punishment is a staple of Old Testament theology. Each section of the Hebrew canon—Torah, Prophets, Writings—appropriates the idea as an essential part of the argument that the world is morally coherent and assured by God's governance. In the Torah, Deuteronomy places the retribution principle within the context of covenant, thus insisting that blessing and cursing is God's way of sustaining the covenantal partnership with Israel:

> See, I have set before you today life and prosperity, death and adversity. If you obey the commandments of the Lord your God that I am commanding you today, by loving the Lord your God, walking in his ways, and observing his commandments . . . then you shall live and become numerous, and the Lord will bless you . . . But if your heart turns away and you do not hear . . . I declare to you today that you shall perish . . . (Deut 30:15-18).

The prophets appeal to covenantal sanctions in announcing that God has punished Israel because its disobedience violates the partnership with God and jeopardizes the moral foundations of creation:

> Hear the word of the Lord,
> O people of Israel;
> for the Lord has an indictment
> against the people of the land.
> There is no faithfulness or loyalty,
> and no knowledge of God in the land.

> Swearing, lying, and murder,
> and stealing and adultery break out;
> bloodshed follows bloodshed.
> Therefore the land mourns,
> and all who live in it languish;
> together with the wild animals
> and the birds of the air,
> even the fish of the sea are perishing (Hos 4:1-3; cf.
>   Amos 4:1-3, 6-13; Mic 3:9-12).

The Writings articulate the principle of retribution with different voices. Nevertheless, the assumption that God secures the world's moral order by dispensing fair and equitable justice to the righteous and the wicked remains axiomatic. A classic example is Psalm 1; which brings together perspectives from the Torah and the wisdom tradition (note especially Proverbs 10-15) to affirm the certain destiny that God prepares for the righteous and the wicked:

> Happy are those
> who do not follow the advice of the wicked . . .
> but their delight is in the law (*torah*) of the Lord,
> and on his law (*torah*) they meditate day and night.
> They are like trees
> planted by streams of water,
> which yield their fruit in its season,
> and their leaves do not wither.
> In all that they do, they prosper.
> The wicked are not so,
> but are like chaff that the wind drives away . . .
> for the Lord watches over the way of the righteous,
> but the way of the wicked will perish (vv. 1-4, 6).

---

accord such evidence any real significance. Israel's tradition preserves ample memory of persons who either perished in innocence (2 Kgs 21:16; 24:4; cf. Ps 106:38; Isa 59:7; Jer 22:17) or feared they would if God did not intervene to deliver them (e.g., Pss 44:23-26; 59:1-5; 69:1-4). In the face of this evidence, and in virtual disregard of Job who is the immediate embodiment of it, Eliphaz dismisses the plight of the righteous sufferer as if it is neither urgent nor consequential. In his calculations, "isolated cases" of innocent suffering, what we might call "exceptions to the rule," are not important enough to change fundamental doctrines of faith.[7]

A third issue is the way Eliphaz uses doctrine to blur the lines between personal observation and universal truth. He introduces the argument for the connection between deeds and consequences as one

Despite the strong insistence upon God's equitable retribution by Israel's official leadership—prophets, priests, and sages—serious voices of dissent were raised when the enigmas of suffering rendered belief in God's justice suspect. Here too the challenge comes from every part of the Hebrew canon. In the Torah, Abraham (Gen 18:25) and Moses (e.g., Exod 32:11-12) raise hard questions about divine judgment that seems ill-advised and inappropriate. Among the prophets, Jeremiah (Jer 12:1-4; 15:18; 17:15-18; 20:18) and Habakkuk (Hab 1:1-4, 12-17) rail against God's indifference, if not hostility, toward the righteous with the thunderous questions "Why?" and "How long?" Within the Writings, the Psalms provide daring models for lament that insists worship itself is a proper arena for loyal interrogation of God (e.g., Pss 10:1; 13:1-4; 22:1-2; 44:17-26; 74:1, 10-11; 79:5; 88:13-14; 89:46-49).

The book of Job preserves the most sustained challenge to the validity of divine retribution in Hebrew scripture. Job's "Why?" questions articulate the inexplicable suffering that drives one to hurl curses far and wide, damning life and indicting God in the process (see Job 3). As the first of the friends to respond to this challenge, Eliphaz appeals to the doctrine of retribution (4:7-11) in the hope that Job will accept its long-term truth as a sufficient counter to his misplaced rage. Before his speech is completed, Eliphz will expand this doctrine by summoning Job to understand suffering not as a curse but as a blessing, for God disciplines with wounds those whom God desires to heal with love (5:17-18). This initial exchange sets the stage for the ensuing debates between Job and the friends. Job will continue to make his case for the inadequacy of the doctrine of retribution; the friends will continue to affirm it. With different arguments and varying strategies, the friends insist that God's governance of the world is just. From their perspective, it is only Job's impatience or ignorance or willful resistance that keeps him from seeing the truth in what they are saying.

The persistent voices of dissent in Hebraic tradition—Abraham, Moses, Jeremiah, Habakkuk, the anonymous pray-ers of the lament psalms, and especially Job—challenge orthodoxy with the problem scholars call theodicy. Suffering inevitably raises questions about God (*theos*) and justice (*dike*), which defenders of the faith are compelled to answer. Theodicies come from those who, like Job's friends, seek to counter questions that impugn divine justice by pronouncing God "Not guilty" (J. Crenshaw, "Introduction: The Shift from Theodicy to Anthropodicy," *Theodicy in the Old Testament*, ed. J. Crenshaw [Philadelphia: Fortress Press, 1983], 6). Such a verdict may of course be entirely justified, for as the witness of the scriptures makes clear, God will certainly punish the wicked. However, as the dialogues unfold, Eliphaz and the friends exemplify how this truth may be overstated or misapplied. Theirs is the approach of those who maintain a safe distance from the suffering of others in order to defend doctrine at the expense of compassion.

For further reading on the issues of retribution and theodicy in the Hebrew Bible, see J. Crenshaw, ed. *Theodicy in the Old Testament* (Philadelphia: Fortress Press, 1983); idem, *Defending God: Biblical Responses to the Problem of Evil* (Oxford: Oxford University Press, 2005).

that he has discerned through personal experience (v. 8: "As I have seen"). Yet what he reports as his own experience is a conventional and widely appropriated maxim concerning the natural linkage between sowing and reaping (Prov 22:8; cf. Hos 8:7; 10:13; Eccl 7:3; Gal 6:7-8). There is clearly truth in the saying that "you reap whatever you sow," as the Galatians text puts it. The problem arises when this truth is applied across the board and without discrimination to every case of suffering and affliction. Eliphaz employs this maxim, wittingly or not, in a way that collapses Job's particular situation into a general and abstract truth. Job has complained that "trouble" (*'āmāl*; 3:10) has defined his life, through no fault of his own, since the day of his birth. Eliphaz now stipulates a causal connection between all "trouble" (*'āmāl*; 4:8) and iniquity (*'āwen*). Without attending to Job's complaint, Eliphaz has already subtly judged him and found him guilty. [CD: "You Make a Mountain of a Concept"]

In addition to personal observations, Eliphaz claims a privileged revelation that gives him special insight concerning the nature of humankind (4:12–5:7). As a result of what he has seen and heard from God (4:12-16), he proceeds to teach Job that humans are intrinsically frail, mortal creatures who are (1) morally inferior to God (4:17-21) and (2) "born to trouble" (5:6-7). With both assertions, Eliphaz invokes creation imagery that encourages Job to (re)consider the primordial question of what it means to be a human being before God.

The account of Eliphaz's revelation comprises a description of the experience (4:12-16) and a disclosure of its substance (4:17-21). The details of the experience are described with an array of terms and images that interpreters take to be evocative of not only the "numinous," and the "mysterious," but also the "eerie," the "bizarre," and the "spooky." In a "deep sleep" there comes to Eliphaz a "vision." There is something to be seen—a "spirit" (v. 15), an "appearance" (v. 16), a "form" (v. 16)—but it is elusive, unrecognizable. It effects physical sensations ("my bones shake"; "the hair of my flesh bristled") and psychic responses ("dread," "trembling"). ["Then a Spirit Passed Before My Face"] For all these details describing what is seen and felt, however, the primary emphasis is on what is heard. There is a "word" (*dābār*), though Eliphaz catches but a "whisper" (*šēmeṣ*; v. 12) of it; there is a "voice" (*qôl*), though it speaks out of silence (*dĕmāmāh*; v. 16). Such features are reminiscent of theophany experiences in which the presence of God and the intentions of God are revealed with an intensity that exceeds "ordinary" channels of revelation. Like Moses, who was privileged to see the "form (*temunah*) of the Lord" (Num 12:8), and Elijah, who was permitted to hear God speak with "a sound of sheer silence" (*qôl dĕmāmāh*; 1 Kgs 19:12), Eliphaz would deliver to Job a message imprinted with divine authority. ["Did Not Some God Go By?"]

The content of the message is quoted in v. 17, then elaborated in vv. 18-21. Translators have rendered the Hebrew text of v. 17 in different ways, but the context and imagery of this and the following vv. suggest that the question Eliphaz puts to Job is best conveyed as follows: "Can mortals (*ĕnôš*) be righteous (*yisdāq*) in relation to God? Can humans (*geber*) be pure

---

"Did Not Some God Go By?"

D. Clines has noted that Eliphaz's dream experience has a number of Near Eastern parallels. He calls attention to the following account of Gilgamesh, a Mesopotamian king said to rule in the city of Uruk around 2600 BCE:

Sleep, which is shed on mankind, fell on him.
In the middle watch, he ended his sleep.
He started up, saying to his friend:
"My friend, didst thou not call to me? Why am I awake?
Didst thou not touch me? Why am I startled?
Did not some god go by? Why is my flesh numb?
My friend, I saw a third dream,
And the dream that I saw was wholly awesome!
The heavens shrieked, and the earth boomed,
[Day]light failed, darkness came.
Lightning flashed, a flame shot up"

D. Clines, *Job 1–20* (WBC; Dallas: Word Books, 1989). "The Epic of Gilgamesh," Tablet V, iv 7-17, in *ANET*, 3rd ed. with supplement, ed. J. B. Pritchard (Princeton: Princeton University Press, 1969), 83.

"Then a Spirit Passed Before My Face"

Blake visualizes Eliphaz's revelatory experience. Job and his wife are seated on the ground surrounded by the friends. All look upward, toward the vision to which Eliphaz directs them with an uplifted left hand. As their eyes remain fixed on the vision, Eliphaz maintains a stern focus on Job. The scene above depicts Eliphaz startled out of a "deep sleep" (4:13) by the God who now suddenly appears before him. Eliphaz's eyes are bugged; his left hand is crooked upright, as if trying to defend himself against the force that pins him against the bed; his hair stands on end. The citation of Job 4:15 in the lower margin provides the narrative that informs the picture: "Then a Spirit passed before my face / the hair of my flesh stood up."

God stands upright and erect, arms folded against the chest and concealed by a body-length mantle. The divine head is surrounded by a halo, the light from which flashes outward in pulsating rays that cover the lower portion of Eliphaz's body and flicker toward his head. The appearance of God is not only overwhelming but also terrifying. It is the moment just before God speaks the words from Job 4:17-18, which Blake records in the upper part of the frame. Before such a God, no

The Vision of Eliphaz

William Blake (1757-1827). *The Vision of Eliphaz*. 1823-1825. Engraving from Blake's *Illustrations of the Book of Job*.

creature can be justified. Indeed, before such a God, even creation itself withers and collapses. The leafless trees in the margins, blasted and bent to the ground, share with Eliphaz a common fright in the presence of this God.

Interpreters have noted that the face of God and the face of Eliphaz in the lower half of the frame are virtually identical. Eliphaz understands God in his image, as a reflection of his own beliefs. The depiction seems a subtle reminder that if Job is to realize his own destiny as one created in the image of God, he should be less like the person he has become—defiant, restless, cursing—and more like Eliphaz—submissive . . . and terrified.

(*yiṭhar*) in relation to their Maker?" (cf. NAB). [CD: The Syntax of Job 4:17] The issue is not whether human beings can be *more* "righteous"/"pure" than God, as some translations suggests (e.g., KJV), for this would be an argument that neither Eliphaz nor Job would likely have considered plausible. Rather, the point that Eliphaz presses is whether any creature, *in relation to* God, can be "righteous" and "pure." The words "righteous" and "pure" convey a range of meanings both forensic (e.g., legally "innocent") and cultic (e.g., ritually "clean"). Because Eliphaz introduces both with reference to the relationship between Creator and creature, they may be understood here as roughly synonymous expressions for "moral imperfection."[8] The thrust of God's question, which Eliphaz now relays to Job, may be roughly paraphrased as follows: "Who are you, in relation to me? When you measure your righteousness and purity against mine, can you stand before me and raise questions about who suffers and why?" Presumably Eliphaz considers this question, like his previous one (4:6), to be only rhetorical. From his perspective, one may assume that the answer is self-evident: Job is a mere mortal in relation to God; his moral imperfections necessarily mean that he cannot stand before God and raise questions about God's moral governance of the world. Although this may well be Eliphaz's take on this question, in the end the book of Job insists that it is God's question not Eliphaz's, and this raises the possibility that perhaps the question is not rhetorical after all. [9]

The question about humanity's moral capacity is extended in vv. 18-21 with a negative comparison between heavenly beings and human beings. *If* God does not trust even heavenly servants and does not find reason to praise even the angels (v. 18), *then how much less* human creatures whose origins are "clay" (*ḥōmer*) and "dust" (*'āpār*; v. 19)?[10] Eliphaz understands "clay" and "dust" as images of human frailty and limitation. They signify that human existence is precarious. Like the "moth," human beings may be "crushed" (v. 19). So vulnerable are they that between morning and evening they may be "destroyed"; they may "perish" before anyone takes note of their absence (v. 20). In the midst of apparent security, their tent pegs may be pulled up, and their abode (i.e., their place in the world) will collapse on them. They will "die" without ever having acquired the wisdom to live (v. 21).

The lesson on human nature continues in 5:1-7, although the connection between this part of Eliphaz's speech and what precedes is not immediately clear. He begins (v. 1) with a rhetorical question that underscores the futility of appealing to "holy ones" (*qĕdōšîm*) for help. The reference is presumably to the same "servants" and "angels" in 4:18, who are said to be unworthy of such trust. Job has given no indication that he is tempted to appeal to heavenly intercessors, although subsequently he will venture to explore this possibility (9:33; 16:19-21). Verse 2 introduces a proverbial statement concerning the fatal vexation and anger of the "fool" (cf. Prov 14:29-30), which Eliphaz then seeks to illustrate through personal observation (vv. 3-5). Some interpreters take this to be a veiled rebuke of Job's unrestrained outburst in chapter 3.[11] If so, then Eliphaz's description of the fate of the fool's children—"crushed in the gate" with "no one to deliver them" (v. 4)—provides another example of how conventional sayings may condemn the innocent with hurtful generalities. Job's own children lie dead beneath the rubble of their house (1:19). Eliphaz insinuates that their demise is the result of their father's foolishness.

It is not until vv. 6-7 that Eliphaz takes up issues that clearly connect with and advance his teaching about human nature. In 4:8-9 he argued from personal experience that there is an organic connection between sowing "iniquity" and reaping "trouble." He went on to indicate, however, that the connection cannot be determined or controlled by human ingenuity, as if one might intentionally cultivate evil but engineer a harvest of good reward. God is the architect of the retributive system that defines these connections, and God is the undisputed guarantor of the system's final results. In 5:6-7, Eliphaz returns to the connection between "iniquity" and "trouble." Now, however, he abandons the agricultural metaphor for another that suggests an even stronger linkage between "trouble" and "human beings" (*ʾādām*). "Iniquity" (*ʾāwen*) and "trouble" (*ʿāmāl*) do not sprout from the "earth" (*ʿāpār*; lit., "dust") and the "ground" (*ʾădāmah*) like crops that humans have planted and cultivated for harvest (v. 6). Instead, human beings "are born (*yûllad*) to trouble" (*ʿāmāl*; v. 7). The metaphor is not "sowing" and "reaping" but "birthing." With this change of imagery, Eliphaz shifts the argument about the human condition in important new directions.

First, he replaces the connection between "iniquity" and "trouble" with a connection between "trouble" and "human beings." That is, he links humans and trouble without reference to iniquity. Second, he no longer describes this linkage as one that humans initiate with conscious acts like plowing and sowing. Human beings are not *cultivators of* trouble, they are *cultivated for* trouble. In his terms, they "are born" for trouble. The shift from active to passive verbs expresses a certain fatalism about the human condition. From the day of their birth human beings are destined for trouble. Who or what is responsible for this destiny? Eliphaz's assertion begs the question but hints at the answer only obliquely. It is not nature that decides on its own initiative what crops it will yield, just as it is not the child who makes the decision to conceive itself. Behind everything in creation, Eliphaz suggests, there is a master plan devised and implemented by the Creator (cf. 4:9). The implication is that God has ordained a connection between humans and trouble, irrespective of sin and iniquity, which is as inevitable as the sparks that fly upward from a fire (v. 7b).[12] ["Greatly to Live Is Greatly to Suffer"]

Eliphaz's view of humankind as doomed to suffering and affliction has troubled interpreters. Despite the fact that similar assertions occur in a number of ancient Near Eastern texts, such fatalism has seemed to some inappropriate as a response to Job. [CD: Doomed by Divinity?] On one hand, Job's complaint is precisely that he has been born to trouble (3:3-10), and so it is unlikely that Eliphaz intends to agree with Job, or that

---

"Greatly to Live is Greatly to Suffer"

That humans are destined to suffer is a common motif in Athenian tragedies. Thus, for example, the Chorus reproves Antigone for passing the "outermost limit of daring" (l. 865) when he presumes to go beyond what the gods have decreed:

As in the past,
This law is immutable:
For mortals greatly to live is greatly to suffer.
Roving ambition helps many a man to good,

And many it falsely lures to light desires,
Till failure trips them unawares, and they fall
On the fire that consumes them. Well was it said,
Evil seems good
To him who is doomed to suffer;
And short is the time before that suffering comes.
(*Antigone*, ll. 617-20)

Sophocles, *The Thebian Plays*, trans. E. F. Watling (New York: Penguin Books, 1947), 143.

---

if he agreed, Job would be comforted. On the other, the general principle of a predetermined destiny for human beings seems inconsistent with Israel's creation theology, which insists that human beings are endowed by God with the freedom to choose between evil and good.[13] For these and other reasons, some commentators seek ways to "lighten the load" that Eliphaz seems to have placed on the shoulders of human beings with this argument.[14] One solution is to change the Hebrew verb in v. 7a from a passive form, "is born" (*yûllad*; pual), to an active form, "begets" (*yōlîd*; hiphil).[15] A number of modern translations adopt this alternative rendering, e.g., "man himself begets mischief" (NAB); "man brings trouble on himself" (TEV). Such a translation effectively removes the notion that human beings have been capriciously destined for trouble and suggests instead that humans are morally culpable for whatever fortunes befall them. It is Job—not nature, not God—who must bear responsibility for the trouble that has overturned his world. ["God, the Sadness of Creation!"]

Despite the support for this rendering of the text, there is good reason to question whether it conveys accurately what Eliphaz is really saying or only what interpreters wish he were saying. At several places in his speech, Eliphaz does indeed argue that God is the hidden cause of Job's misfortune. Both in this pericope (4:9) and in the one to follow (5:8-27), Eliphaz stipulates that God's involvement in human affairs is the critical factor in determining final outcomes. In both instances, the argument is that God will ultimately consummate divine judgments irrespective of any efforts humans may make to avoid or thwart them.

Moreover, in support of the argument for God's sovereignty over human affairs, Eliphaz appeals to creation theology in ways that suggest he is willing to bend faith traditions to fit his own agenda.[16] Two cases invite comment. In 4:17-19, as previously noted, he uses the affirmation that God forms humans from the "dust of the ground" (Gen 2:7) to buttress the argument that human beings are not only frail but also morally deficient creatures. In Genesis, God creates human beings out of fragile substances and commissions them to image and sustain the

"God the Sadness of Creation"

In *A Month of Sundays*, John Updike chronicles the recuperation of the Reverend Thomas Marshfield, who has been ordered by his bishop to spend a month in therapy for a condition officially diagnosed as "distraction." Thomas' own diagnosis is that he suffers from "nothing less virulent than the human condition" (8), which rather than disguise, he dares to preach. His therapy requires that he write a month of sermons in the hope that this will restore a proper understanding of the nature of God and humanity. In fact, his therapy leads him to focus with increasing clarity on one abiding and impenetrable question: "God, the sadness of Creation! Is it ours, or Thine?" (242). When his month is over and he has completed his last sermon, Thomas wonders out loud whether this could really be the intended objective of his restoration: "Have you really been preparing me for a return to the world and not translation to a better? Is the end of therapy, a reshouldering of ambiguity, rote performance, daily grits, hollow vows, stale gratifications, receding illusions? Yes, is your answer, stern." (253)

J. Updike, *A Month of Sundays* (Greenwich CT: Fawcett Crest Publications, 1974).

Creator's dominion in the world (Gen 1:26-28; cf. 2:15). For Eliphaz, however, to be created of "clay" and "dust" means to be too blemished to stand before the Creator and too weak (and too ignorant) to withstand the destructive forces of creation. What creation theology affirms as God's empowering endowment of humanity, Eliphaz construes as God's calculated limitation of humanity's worth and potential. By the time he completes the report of the revelation he has received, Eliphaz has equated humankind not with the pinnacle of creation, which images God, but with its lowest forms, which exemplify not only mortality but also insignificance.

In 5:6-7, Eliphaz again takes up creation imagery, this time drawing on the tradition in Gen 3:17-19 that connects human hardship with the cursed ground. In Genesis, God curses the ground (ʾădāmāh) because of human sin, and as a result it brings forth (ṣāmāḥ) thorns and thistles that signify the hard labor it will impose on human existence. The tradition that preserves this story stresses that while God's sentence is justified, it is not irrevocable. Following the flood, God removes the curse and opens the door to new possibilities for humankind (Gen 8:20-22). Eliphaz appeals to this tradition, but when he applies it to Job, he alters it in two subtle ways. First, he argues that trouble *does not* sprout (ṣāmaḥ) from the ground (ʾădāmāh). When compared with Gen 3:17-19, this is an elliptical statement that leaves open the question whether sin is at the root of human misfortune. Presumably Eliphaz would not wish to dispute the notion that humans are morally culpable (see, for example, 4:8), but curiously such an argument seems not to be his primary concern here. Second, his focus is not on the ʾădāmāh, "ground," but on the ʾādām, "human being," and in this connection he is less concerned with the fortunes that human beings may bring on themselves than with the "trouble" they find waiting for them when they emerge from the womb. Whereas the Genesis tradition regards the destiny of humankind as inevitably (sometimes undeservedly) open to the decisions of a gracious God, Eliphaz suggests that humans are destined for trouble by decisions that are fixed and permanent. Both here and in 4:17-19, Eliphaz appropriates the traditions of faith in support of theological arguments so extreme and so inflexible that they leave little room for substantive input either from Job or God.

Words of Assurance Based on God's Nature, 5:8-27

With the last section of the speech, Eliphaz turns away from his sobering assessment of the human condition to offer words about God that are meant to encourage and comfort Job. He models for Job a doxology in praise of God's power and providence (5:8-16). In a world where humans are ever vulnerable to trouble, Eliphaz assures Job that these divine virtues offer a reliable basis for hope, justice, and restitution (5:17-27).

Once more, Eliphaz attempts to offer Job careful counsel that will not offend or show disrespect (5:8-16; cf. 4:1-6). He does not presume to tell Job directly what he should do. Instead, Eliphaz demonstrates how he would deal with suffering, should the occasion ever arise. As the model sufferer, he will image for Job the proper way to respond to the question posed in 4:17. How can frail and afflicted mortals be "righteous" and "pure" before God? Eliphaz sees himself as the perfect answer. "Now if it were me, I would seek God [in my distress], and to God I would entrust my cause" (v. 8). He envisions for himself a "hypothetical" piety that would be absolutely undaunted by experiences like Job's. If he should suffer calamity and affliction, then he would turn to God in prayer. The Hebrew expression for "seek God" (*dāraš* + *'el*) is used of inquiries addressed to God in the midst of crisis situations. One commonly thinks of prayers of lament in which a suppliant turns to God in distress with plaintive questions and fervent petitions for deliverance (cf. Gen 25:22; 2 Kgs 8:8; Pss 34:4; 77:2 [MT 77:3]). Under the circumstances, one might well anticipate that a lament prayer would be a most appropriate model for Eliphaz to recommend to Job. But Eliphaz fancies himself as one whose piety is heroic, not ordinary; hence what he means by seeking God is different. When others lament, he would praise. When suffering tempts the weak to question God and appeal for relief, he would have the strength of confidence to yield happily to God.

In the midst of suffering, Eliphaz would praise God as if he were safely ensconced in the worship of the sanctuary (vv. 9-16). He would sing of the God who does "great" and "marvelous things" (v. 9). Such language typically refers to God's wondrous acts in creating the world (e.g., Ps 136:4) and in sustaining its moral orders with incomparable deeds of redemption and restoration (e.g., with the exodus: Pss 78:4; 106:22). Apparent deficiencies and disorders—drought, oppression, poverty, injustice—do not negate the imperative to sing this song, Eliphaz now suggests, for with a marvelous providence God is continually transforming the status quo. When the earth is parched and barren, God "gives" and "sends" rain to replenish its resources (v. 10). When the "lowly" lose their place in the world and the "mourners" despair of relief (v. 11), when the "needy" falter in the grip of the "mighty" (v. 15), God is ever present to lift up, secure, and save. The compulsion to praise also arises when one looks beyond the needy, who recognize their dependence on God, to the "crafty" and the "wise" who do not (vv. 12-14). Here too God is at work, thwarting ill-begotten schemes for success and ensnaring those who devise them in their own machinations. Eliphaz would entrust himself in praise to this God, who continually creates new possibilities out of life's limitations and distortions. From his perspective such undaunted praise not only honors God; it also engenders the "hope" (v. 16: *tiqwah*) that Job seems to have lost (cf. 4:6, with the same word for "hope").

Eliphaz proceeds to describe the restitution that God will effect for sufferers, who will entrust themselves to the praise he has modeled (5:17-27). He begins with a beatitude that both declares the positive effect of divine discipline and exhorts Job to submit himself to it happily: "Blessed ['*ašrê*; NRSV: "Happy"] is the one whom God reproves; therefore do not reject the discipline of the Almighty" (v. 17). [CD: "The World Is All One Vast Intention"] Statements beginning with '*ašrê* are frequent in Psalms (26x) and Proverbs (8x). In this particular case, Eliphaz draws upon a common tradition that associates the discipline of God with the corrective love of a devoted parent (Prov 3:11-12). As a parent's discipline may require both reward and punishment (cf. Prov 13:24; 22:15; 23:13-14), so God's discipline may initiate pain (v. 18: *yakʾîb*; NRSV: "wound") and inflict injury (*yimḥaṣ*; NRSV: "strike"). As J. Hartley has put it, "Misfortune is God's rod of discipline."[17] Eliphaz encourages Job to yield confidently to his "great pain" (see 2:13, which uses a nominal form of the same word for "pain" [*kěʾēb*]), for the God who wounds and strikes may be expected to "bind up" and "heal"; cf. Deut 32:29; Hos 6:1. [The Two Faces of God]

Verses 19-22 elaborate on the beatitude by enumerating the troubles and dangers from which God may be expected to deliver the faithful. The listing follows the typical pattern of an ascending numerical saying (number/number + 1; e.g., Prov 6:16-19; 30:15-31; Amos 1:3-13; Mic 5:5 [MT 5:4]; Ps 62:11-12 [MT 62:12-13]). Such a saying cites a number that would be sufficient by itself and then increases this number by one as a way of emphasizing the comprehensiveness of the statement. Eliphaz speaks of "six troubles" and "seven" (v. 19). Although there is some question whether this list identifies seven spe-

The Two Faces of God

The prologue (Job 1–2) indicates that heaven is of two minds when it comes to assessing human nature. Will/can a blameless and upright person love God for nothing? God and the *satan* take up the conflicted question. In the dialogues (Job 3-37), heaven's two minds about human nature is matched by humanity's two minds about God's nature. Will/can God bless and prosper the righteous and punish the wicked? Eliphaz is only the first of the friends to take up the issue, but one sees already in his initial speech a consideration of the two-sided character of God: the God who both wounds and heals. As one who looks on the wounding of another from a safe distance, Eliphaz can affirm such a God with little risk to himself. As one who is wounded, however, Job's affirmation of the two faces of God cannot be so glib. He will wait and pray, but until God answers he must be content with what R. S. Thomas calls an "infinitesimal deflection" of God's presence:

> With the cathedrals thundering
> At him, history proving
> him the two-faced god, there were
> the few who waited on him
> in the small hours, undaunted
> by the absence of an echo
> to their Amens. Physics' suggestion
> is they were not wrong. Reality
> is composed of waves and particles
> coming at us as the Janus-faced
> chooses. We must not despair.
> The invisible is yet susceptible
> of being inferred. To pray, perhaps, is
> to have part in an infinitesimal deflection.

R. S. Thomas, "Nuance," *No Truce with the Furies* (Newcastle upon Tyne: Bloodaxe Books, 1995), 32.

cific troubles, the following general distinctions can be observed: famine (v. 20a), war (v. 20b), slander (v. 21a; NRSV: "scourge of the tongue"), destruction (v. 21b), destruction and famine (v. 22a), and wild beasts (v. 22b). The force of this numerical saying, however, lies not in the specifics of the examples that may be added up, but rather in the symbolism of the number seven itself. The prologue stipulates that the friends sat in silence with Job for seven days (2:13). The period of time suggests not only the severity of Job's affliction but also their need to comprehend the full extent of his devastation. As the first to speak out of that silence, Eliphaz invokes once again the symbolism of the number seven. His rhetoric suggests that he has considered the full complement of calamities that may befall the Jobs of the world. In every conceivable case, he has found the promise of God's "binding" and "healing" to be true.

What Eliphaz envisions as Job's restitution is tantamount to a return to the paradisiacal harmony of Eden (vv. 23-26). With a "lyrical interplay of images from the natural and human worlds,"[18] he describes the primordial bliss that God has prepared for Job on the other side of his misfortune. He will be in "covenant" (v. 23: *bĕrît*; NRSV: "league") with the stones of the field and at "peace" (*šelēmāh*) with the wild animals. Such a "covenant" is of course metaphorical, but its promise evokes the hope of a union between creation and creature that will restore Job's world to Edenic perfection (cf. Hos 2:18, 21-22 [MT 2:20, 23-24]).[19] As a party to this covenant, Job can "know "(vv. 24, 25) that his life will be full and rewarding: his dwelling will be secure; his estate will lack nothing; his offspring will grow and flourish like the grass of the earth. Like the sheaf of grain that grows resolutely towards harvest maturity, Job will go to his death at a "ripe old age" (v. 26). As a final reminder that what he has modeled for Job is universally true, Eliphaz once more claims that his counsel has been verified by the wisdom of the sages (v. 27). If Job is wise, then he will conform to accepted standards of piety and appropriate this model for himself.

CONNECTIONS

The book of Job introduces the reader to Job by describing first his virtues—he is "blameless and upright, one who fears God and turns away from evil" (1:2, 8; 2:3)—then his words—he blesses (1:21) and curses (3:3-10). From the outset, we are to know that what comes from his lips, both the blessing and the cursing, can be measured against the confirmed qualities of his life. He models in a positive way the truth of the adage that a person's character can speak so loudly we may not hear what they are saying. When we meet the friends of Job, we must be content with more ambiguous characters and less certain equations of virtue and life. The introduction to Eliphaz is typical of the way each of the friends enter this drama: "Then Eliphaz the Temanite answered" (4:1). We may infer that he comes from the east, hence that he speaks as a representative of the wisdom tradition. Beyond this, we know nothing specific about the character of the man behind the words. There is no narrator to fill in the gaps or to provide evaluation. We, like Job, must listen carefully and search for the credibility of these words on our own.

One heuristic entry into the character of Eliphaz and the validity of his counsel is the portrait of Sir Eliphaz Burrows in H. G. Wells's fictional recreation of the Joban drama *The Undying Fire*. Sir Eliphaz and his companions, William Dad (Bildad) and Joe Farr (Zophar), arrive at the small apartment in a village called Sundering-on-Sea to visit a despairing Job and his wife. Sir Eliphaz's appearance suggests "scholarship and refinement." On first encounter, his manners are "elaborately courteous," but after listening to Job's strange ruminations about God and the world, Sir Eliphaz comes to his appointed task "like a soaring vulture to his victim." His expertise is in construction, for he has made his mark in the world as the patentee and manufacturer of Temanite blocks that have revolutionized the building industry. It is the building metaphor that conveys his counsel to Job:

> I want you to get my view that if an enterprise, even though it is fair and honest-seeming. . . begins to crumble and wilt, it means that somehow, somewhere you must have been putting the wrong sort of clay into it. It means not that God is wrong and going back on you, but that you are wrong.[20]

It is instructive to reflect on Eliphaz as a builder of new worlds. Job believes that suffering has crumbled his world. Eliphaz will teach him how to rebuild it. He is certain that he is qualified to offer this instruction, because God has revealed to him the blueprint for creation. He reviews the drawings step by step, from the first stage to the finished product, beginning with the structural foundations. God has built into the world a failsafe system of rewards and punishments. The upright may have confidence that the system will work to their good. The wicked must know that it will work to their demise. There are no exceptions and no loopholes, because God guarantees both the system's design and its performance. Next, he reviews the design for the human creature that God has assigned to live within this system. Created of clay and dust, human beings are by definition both fragile and limited. Their vulnerability means that they are susceptible to forces they cannot control: they may be crushed, destroyed, plucked-up in the midst of security without knowing why. Their limitation means that they are born into a world that they did not make and cannot change. They must entrust themselves to a God who wounds and heals and believe that both these acts advance the system of governance that God ordains. The final stage is the finished product: a world that has been built and now functions according to God's master plan. The system of rewards and punishments works flawlessly to effect a perfect harmony between creation and Creator. Whatever is needed, God provides; whatever is distorted, God corrects and restores. In this Edenic world, the designated language of faith is praise: "Praise God who does great and marvelous things."

The challenge for the interpreter is to look at this account of the way the world works *with Job.* If our vantage point is the ash heap, then we look with the eyes of the sufferer and ponder the gap between the world we know and the world we have been shown. The world Eliphaz envisions summons Job to praise, but the broken world in which Job lives invites only lament. If doxology alone is acceptable in God's world, where then is the place for those who cannot as yet (if ever) speak this language? The world Eliphaz celebrates uses human beings as cogs in a machine that bends and shapes materials to a specified end. From the ash heap, Job ponders the design of a machine that chews up human beings and spits out dead children. Eliphaz is certain that the system driving this machine works to perfection. Job looks at the shattered fragments of his world and wonders how this can possibly be construed as what God means by the promise to reward the righteous.

When one sits *with Job,* the gap between his world and the one Eliphaz would build for him is enormous. It is too soon and too simple to conclude that Eliphaz is wrong or that the gap cannot be bridged. Still, for those who suffer like Job, the journey from misery to comfort can seem endless, even impossible. The journey is made more difficult when the vision mandates that the afflicted silence honest lament, deny the pang of irreparable loss, and believe in a system so perfect that the truly tragic never triumphs. [CD: "Dreaming of Systems So Perfect"] Is *this* the world God has created, or is it only the world Eliphaz would build to protect himself and his world from Job's assault?

There are hints in Eliphaz's speech that when he looks at the world he finds confirmation for his own simplistic version of creation's design. He suggests that the "breath of God" (4:9) brings death not life, as Israel's creation tradition affirms (Gen 2:7). He sees "clay" and "dust" as symbols of humanity's intrinsic corruption, which negates the possibility of being righteous and pure in relation to God (4:17, 19). In Genesis, however, formation out of the dust of the ground connects humans intimately to God (Gen 2:7) and to the commission to image God's dominion and stewardship of creation (Gen 1:26-28; 2:15). Eliphaz concludes that humans are "born to trouble" (5:7) in a world rigidly fixed at creation with God's curse (Gen 3:17-19). He makes no reference to God's gracious revocation of that curse (Gen 8:21-22), nor to the promise of the "everlasting covenant" that signals God's larger creational purposes (Gen 9:16). This subtle alteration of God's design for creation suggests that Eliphaz sees God in his own image. When Job argues that innocent suffering calls creation into question, Eliphaz creates another world, in God's name, which denies his innocence and forbids his complaint.

Job must now ponder his place in the world built by Eliphaz. Is he created "in the image of God"? If so, what does this mean? Or should he recreate himself in the image of Eliphaz, and if so, will this restore his praise of God and calm his anguished lament? If we as readers have sat with Job on the ash heap, his questions will be ours, and we will know that we must give them full play. Before we take up the ministry of comforting others, it is wise to ask ourselves if our intent is to help them find their place in God's world or in ours. ["Our Little Systems"]

"Our Little Systems"

Our little systems have their day;
They have their day and cease to be.
They are but broken lights of thee.
And thou, O Lord, art more than they.

A. Tennyson, "In Memoriam A. H. H.," *Tennyson's Poetry,* selected and edited by R. W. Hill, Jr. (New York/London: W. W. Norton and Co., 1971), ll. 17-20, p. 120.

NOTES

[1] K. Fullerton, "Double Entendre in the First Speech of Eliphaz," JBL 49 (1930): 336-37.

[2] L. Perdue, *Wisdom in Revolt: Metaphorical Theology in the book of Job* (JSOTSup 112; Sheffield: Almond Press, 1991), 111.

[3] The expression "who can keep (*yukal*) from speaking?" is similar to the one used of the prophet Jeremiah whose impulse to speak is "like a burning fire" within his heart that he is unable (*lo' `ukal*) to contain (Jer 20:9). In both texts the compulsion to speak is described as admirably irresistible, since it is driven by an intense love and devotion. In this connection, N. Habel has noted that "Eliphaz' *compassion* is matched by his *compulsion* to speak" (*The Book of Job: A Commentary* [OTL; Philadelphia: Westminster Press, 1985], 124; emphasis added).

[4] C. Newsom, "The Book of Job," in vol. 4 of *NIB* (Nashville: Abingdon Press, 1996), 376.

[5] E. Dhorme, *A Commentary on the Book of Job* (Nashville: Thomas Nelson Publishers, 1967), 44.

[6] Cf. S. R. Driver and G. B. Gray, *A Critical and Exegetical Commentary on the Book of Job* (Edinburgh: T and T. Clark, 1921), 43; D. Clines, *Job 1–20* (WBC; Dallas: Word Books, 1989), 124.

[7] Newsom notes that Eliphaz is not interested in "isolated cases" or "counterexamples," because his moral perception of the world does not allow him to take them seriously. He sees the world through a filter that confirms what he already believes and discounts or eliminates anything that might challenge his beliefs ("The Book of Job," 376-77).

[8] Habel, *Book of Job,* 129-30.

[9] Cf. Clines, *Job 1–20*, 133.

[10] The Hebrew word translated "error" in NRSV, *tŏhŏlā*, occurs nowhere else in the Hebrew Bible in this form; hence its meaning is uncertain. Scholars propose numerous emendations, e.g., *tiplah*, "folly" (cf. 1:22; NRSV: "wrong-doing"), *ḥattalāh*, "deception," *holēlāh*, "madness" (cf. Eccl 1:17; 2:12). A. Blommerde's suggestion that the word be revocalized as *tĕhillah*, "praise," offers a more plausible reading; cf. A. Blommerde, *Northwest Semitic Grammar and Job* (Rome: Pontifical Biblical Institute, 1969), 41-42.

[11] E.g., G. Fohrer, *Das Buch Hiob* (KAT; Gutersloh: Gerd Mohn, 1963), 146; Newsom, "The Book of Job," 379.

[12] The second half of v. 7 has occasioned much debate. The Hebrew expression that NRSV translates "sparks" is "sons of flame" (*bĕnê rešep*). A number of scholars understand *rešep* as a reference to Resheph, a Near Eastern god of pestilence and death (cf. M. Pope, *Job* [AB; Garden City NY: Doubleday, 1979], 42-43). Habel, for example, understands the "sons of Resheph" as an allusion to the chthonic forces of disease and death that fly forth from the underworld to plague human beings (*Book of Job,* 132). For further discussion of the interpretive possibilities see H. H. Rowley, *Job* (The Century Bible; Ontario: Thomas Nelson, 1970), 61.

[13] E.g., R. Gordis, *The Book of Job: Commentary, New Translation, and Special Studies* (New York: Jewish Theological Seminary of America, 1978), 54-55.

[14] Clines, *Job 1–20*, 142.

[15] The arguments for this alteration are cited in most critical commentaries. For a convenient summary, see Rowley, *Job,* 60-61.

[16] On these issues, see further Perdue (*Wisdom in Revolt*, 111-20), who argues that Eliphaz's "abuse" and "misuse" of creation language exemplifies how rigid fundamentalism "misdirects faith's search for understanding towards a blind avowal of its own simplistic propositions" (112).

[17] J. Hartley, *The Book of Job* (NICOT; Grand Rapids MI: William B. Eerdmans, 1988), 125.

[18] Habel, *Book of Job,* 136.

[19] Cf. Newsom ("The Book of Job," 381), who interprets the covenant with the stones of the fields as a reversal of the conflict between human cultivation and the earth's resistance that is described in Gen 3:17b-18.

[20] H. G. Wells, *The Undying Fire* (New York: The Macmillan Company, 1919), 73.

JOB'S RESPONSE TO ELIPHAZ: "I WILL SPEAK IN THE ANGUISH OF MY SPIRIT"

Job 6:1–7:21

With the entrance of Eliphaz there are now three parties who have a stake in this drama: Job, the sufferer, the friends who would "console and comfort" him, and God, whose presence is palpable but as yet undefined. Job's response in chapters 6-7 reflects this triangulation. Driven by suffering to an existence in which there is no "ease," no "rest," no "quiet" (3:26), he now finds himself in a world where would-be friends are disloyal and a would-be God is oppressive. In such a world, Job finds no merit in restrained speech. His words to the friends are "rash" (6:3); his words to God speak the "anguish" of his spirit and the "bitterness" of his soul (7:11).

Given such passion, it is no surprise that Job's speech in these chapters does not yield to simple outlines and neat definitions, for nothing has yet been settled in this struggle between Job, the friends, and God. The measure of Job's vexation is that he is pulled in multiple directions but can find no comfort anywhere he turns. He looks within himself, measures the weight of his suffering against the reservoir of his personal strength, and finds that he is too weak to help himself (6:1-13). He looks to his friends for loyal companionship to help him stay the course, but he finds that they have abandoned him just when he needs them most (6:14-30). He looks within himself again, and in the absence of any evidence to the contrary, he concludes that "emptiness," "misery," and life "without hope" is simply the sad destiny of the whole human race (7:1-6). He looks finally to God, but the extremity of his suffering blunts his expectations and empties his appeal (7:7-21). Because the master plan for creation seems to have targeted humans for destruction, Job hopes for death, not life; he asks no more of God than to be left alone. The movement in Job's speech suggests that he is caught in the middle of failed relationships, both human and divine. Friends who would be comforters will not look at him (6:28). God, whose presence is hostile, will not look away from him (7:19). [CD: "What Balance Is Needed at the Edges of Such an Abyss"]

COMMENTARY

"I Cannot Help Myself," 6:1-13

Job begins where he left off in chapter 3, immersed in the reality of his pain and suffering. At several points, his speech makes contact with what Eliphaz has said to him, hence it is clear that Job has listened to his friend and wants to be in dialogue with him. [Connections Between Job and Eliphaz] Nonetheless, he insists that if the dialogue is to be genuine, it must take full account of his grief; anything less is dishonest and irrelevant.

Job is by necessity preoccupied with his "vexation" (*ka'aś*) and "calamity" (*hawāh*; vv. 2-3). The two words are roughly parallel expressions for the unmerited hardships that persons may experience at the hands of another. The lead term, "vexation," or, more generally, "despair," is particularly instructive. The lament tradition recognizes vexation as one of the burdens of life that compels the suppliant to cry out to God for relief (cf. 1 Sam 1:16; Pss 6:7 [NRSV: "grief"; MT 6:8]; 10:14 [NRSV: "grief"]. The wisdom tradition, however, warns that the expression of *ka'aś* is not only foolish (cf. Prov 12:16) but also dangerous. Its counsel is to refrain from excessive outbursts of pain and misery, for as Eliphaz has already argued, "vexation kills the fool" (5:2). Job now responds to this counsel by insisting that excessive suffering demands excessive speech. If somehow his grief and sorrow could be objectively weighed, then it would be Eliphaz's counsel of restraint that would be judged foolish, not Job's "rash" words. ["Give Sorrow Words"]

Connections Between Job and Eliphaz

Job's speech in chapter 6 picks up a number of key words from Eliphaz's address: "vexation" (*kā'aś*, 6:2; 5:2), "hope" (*tiqwāh*, 6:8 [NRSV: "desire"]; 4:6), "success" (*tûsiyyāh*, 6:13 [NRSV: "resource"]; 5:12), "crush" (*dākā*, 6:9; 4:19), "fear" (*yir'ah*, 6:14; 4:6). In most cases, Job gives to these words an ironic twist, indicating that what Eliphaz says and what he means are not the same. For example, Eliphaz urges Job to withstand adversity by placing his "hope" in his integrity (4:6). Job's "hope," however, is not to survive but to die (6:8-9). His wish is for God to kill him, not restore him.

There are also thematic connections that suggest Job is responding to Eliphaz's speech. For example, Eliphaz urges Job to *seek God* and models for him a prayer of *praise* (5:8-16). Job understands God to be *seeking him* with sinister intent (6:4); he offers a prayer of *lament* that uses the language of praise to indict God for crimes against humanity (7:7-21). Both Eliphaz and Job ask what it means to be a human being and to be in relationship with God, although they come to the question from different perspectives. Eliphaz views the human condition "from above," as if he were God, and chides Job for assuming that his place in creation's hierarchy gives him the moral stature to stand before his Maker (4:17-21). Job views the human condition "from below," as a sufferer, and wonders why God assigns such importance to human creatures that they become the primary "targets" of divine harassment and abuse (7:17-21).

For further discussion of the literary and theological connections between these speeches, see N. Habel, *The Book of Job: A Commentary* (Philadelphia: Westminster Press, 1985), 141-44; W. A. M. Beuken, "Job's Imprecation as the Cradle of a New Religious Discourse: The Perplexing Impact of Semantic Correspondences between Job 3, Job 4–5 and Job 6–7," in *The Book of Job,* ed. W. A. M. Beuken (Leuven: University Press, 1994), 58-67; Y. Hoffman, *A Blemished Perfection: The Book of Job in Context* (JSOTSup 213; Sheffield: Sheffield Academic Press, 1996), 116-31.

Job wishes for a set of cosmic scales, perhaps the kind that consists of two pans suspended from a center pole. On one pan, he would pile up the sands of the sea, under ordinary circumstances an object too numerous to be counted, too heavy to be weighed (cf. Gen 22:17; Hos 1:10 [MT 2:1]; Prov 27:30). On the other, he would stack up the sadness of his life: the cumulative losses of his possessions, his livelihood, and his seven sons and three daughters. The tilt of the scales in the direction of his pain would make clear that life in the land of Uz is terribly out of balance. Suffering and misery have overwhelmed all other experiences. [CD: "God's Roguery, Juggling with the Scales"]

"Give Sorrow Words"

In Shakespeare's *Macbeth*, Ross delivers to Macduff the tragic news of the murder of his wife and children. He describes his report as words that "would be howl'd out in the desert air, where hearing should not latch them." Overhearing the report, Malcolm makes the following observation (IV, iii, 209):

> Give sorrow words: the grief that does not speak
> Whispers the o'er-fraught heart, and bids it break.

The embedded question in Job's assessment of his life is "Why?" Why are his losses so much greater than his gains? Why does despair outweigh all other emotions? It is essentially the same question with which Job pierced the silence of the ash heap in chapter 3 (see vv. 11-26). In that first lament, Job referred to God only indirectly (3:23). Now for the first time, Job explicitly names God as the cause of his life's disproportionate pain and misery: "For the arrows of the Almighty (*šadday*) are in me; my spirit drinks their poison; the terrors of God (*ĕlôah*; the same word occurs in 3:23) are arrayed against me" (v. 4).

Two images give definition to Job's understanding of God's intentions toward him. Neither is elaborated at this point, but both will reappear in later speeches. He envisions God as a *warrior*, armed for hostile engagement (cf. 10:1-17; 16:6-17; 19:6-12; 27:7-12), and he envisions himself as having been targeted, inexplicably, as *God's enemy* (cf. 13:24). God wages the assault with poisoned "arrows" and "terrors." The image of God as an archer is a common one (e.g., Deut 32:23-24; Ezek 5:16; Lam 3:12-13; Pss 7:13; 38:2; 64:7). Although poisoned arrows are not elsewhere mentioned in the Hebrew Bible, it is likely that this too is a conventional part of the imagery that Job appropriates. [CD: "Resheph of the Arrow"] The expression "terrors (*biûtîm*) of God" is likely a metaphorical allusion to the entourage of troops that God dispatches against the opponent (cf. Ps 88:13-18; note v. 15, "terrors" [MT, v. 17: *biûtekā*]). With these interrelated images, Job responds indirectly to the portrait of God that Eliphaz has offered in 5:17-27. Eliphaz understands "wounding" and "striking" as essential tools of the "discipline of the Almighty." In his view, Job should happily submit to this discipline, for it is administered out of love, and its intent is salutary. From Job's perspective, however, the "discipline" of this warrior God is toxic. It breaks down the body, then slowly, painfully, destroys it.

When he imagines himself standing on the battle line opposite this warrior God, Job cannot see the wisdom in remaining silent and passive. His "wild words" (v. 3; TEV, NEB) should not surprise Eliphaz. Indeed, to respond in any other way would be absurd. In defense of his complaint, Job uses two rhetorical questions (vv. 5-6). He assumes that the *answer* and the *implication* of both will be obvious to Eliphaz. Does a wild ass bray or an ox bellow when it has the food it requires? Obviously not. But if that food is lacking, then both animals will instinctively cry out until they find it. Does food that is tasteless or without flavor have any appeal? Obviously not. But if it is seasoned properly, then one will not have to be coerced into eating it. The food God has prepared for Job is undeserved suffering. It sickens him. He will not touch it (v. 7). He will cry out "No!"[1]

In the second half of his introspection (vv. 8-13), Job muses once more about the desirability of death for those whose misery renders them too weak to live. His wish is that God will fulfill his one remaining "hope" (v. 8: *tiqwāh*). It is not the "hope" that Eliphaz holds for him, because he can no longer draw comfort from his piety and integrity (4:6; cf. 5:16). He hopes instead for death. If God would but "loose his hand," freeing the forces of destruction to "crush" him and "cut" him off (vv. 8-9), then death would be a welcome relief.

Verse 10, which completes this unit concerning Job's hope and "consolation," is open to multiple interpretations. The most critical issue is the meaning of the last phrase. NRSV adopts the conventional translation: "for I have not denied the words of the Holy One." On this reading, Job would seem to be saying that he will face his death as the long-suffering and ever-pious hero we have seen in the prologue. Come what may, he will not curse God, and he will not "charge God with any wrong-doing" (1:22).[2] The verb translated "deny" (*kāḥad*), however, normally means "hide." Elsewhere in Job, it refers to the hiding or concealing of a thought or a teaching (cf. 15:18; 27:11). This meaning is also appropriate for v. 10. The phrase "words (*ʾimrê*) of the Holy One" may refer broadly to the ordinances and decrees of God that govern human existence.[3] In this sense, Job can be understood to say that even though he may go to his death in unrelieved suffering, he will take comfort in knowing he has not hidden the truth about the God who has decided "to destroy him for no reason" (2:3).[4] Job's journey towards speaking the truth about God is far from complete. At this point, we may understand that he has committed to more than he knows. We must await the epilogue's last words on these matters (cf. 42:7-8) before we can evaluate the full disclosure of what this truth is and of what it means for both Job and God to have someone in creation who will dare to speak it.

Having committed to stand his ground by saying "No" to undeserved suffering and "Yes" to speaking the truth about God, Job is nevertheless convinced that he does not have the resources, physically or mentally, to do either (vv. 11-13). He does not have the strength to wait for death. He can not imagine any future (*qēṣ*, "end") that provides the incentive to "prolong his life" (v. 11; *kî ʾaʾrîk napšî*; lit., "that I should lengthen my soul"; NRSV: "that I should be patient"). His body is not hard like "stones." His flesh is not durable like "bronze." He has no power to help himself. He senses that he is completely empty, that every "resource" (*tûšîyyāh*; perhaps "success," as in 5:12) has been drained out of him.

The Failure of Friends, 6:14-30

Job can draw nothing more from his own resources. He now looks to the friends for the strength that he cannot provide for himself. He begins with a statement about what true friendship means, followed by a rebuke of his "friends" for failing to measure up to his expectations (vv. 14-21). He then raises a series of questions that issue forth in an appeal for Eliphaz and his cohorts to be for him the friends they profess to be (vv. 22-30).

Job sets forth his expectations concerning true friendship in v. 14. The text is unfortunately difficult, and scholars have proposed a variety of emendations and syntactical rearrangements. [CD: Translations of Job 6:14] The following is a plausible translation of the text as it stands:

> The despairing (*lammās*) needs loyalty (*ḥesed*) from a friend, even if (perhaps "when") they forsake the fear of the Almighty.

Despite the ambiguity in the text, the major emphasis of the first line is relatively clear. Job expects *ḥesed* from a friend. The conventional translation of this word is "kindness" or "steadfast love." A better rendering is "loyalty." *Ḥesed* describes both an attitude and an action that binds two parties together in an unbreakable partnership. Its fullest meaning is exemplified by God for whom "loyalty and faithfulness" (*ḥesed weʾĕmet*) are constant attributes (e.g., Pss 25:10; 57:3; 89:14;138:2). God's loyalty is enacted; it is a disposition that is demonstrated. God "does" (*ʿāśah*) *ḥesed* (e.g., Gen 24:12, 14; Exod 20:6 [= Deut 5:10]; 2 Sam 2:6; 1 Kgs 3:6; Jer 9:24 [MT 9:23]), the most tangible evidence of which is God's commitment to "keeping covenant and steadfast love" (*šōmēr habbĕrît wĕḥaḥesed*; Deut 7:9, 12; 1 Kgs 8:23 [= 2 Chr 6:14]; Neh 1:5; 9:32; Dan 9:4). When humans fail God and break the covenant partnership, it is "loyalty and faithfulness" that motivates God to restore it (Exod 34:6).

God's loyalty is the perfect model of the relentless love that pursues relationship with others, even when they fail. Created in the image of God, humans aspire to this ideal of "loyalty and faithfulness" in their relationships with each other (e.g., Gen 24:49; 32:11; Josh 2:14; Prov 3:3), even though they cannot fully attain it. Even when human relationships fall short of the ideal, the goal remains the same: "deal loyally and compassionately with one another" (*ḥesed wĕraḥămîm ʿaśu*; Zech 7:9 [NJPS]). ["Fireflies in the Garden"] As H. J. Stoebe has put it, *ḥesed* expresses a "magnanimity," which enacts a "sacrificial, humane willingness to be there for the other." It is a commitment to relationship that "surpasses the obligatory."[5]

What Job hopes for from his friends is a loyalty that will not let go of him, even if suffering pushes him beyond the boundaries of conventional piety ("the fear of the Almighty"). What he receives from them is quite different (vv. 15-21). His friends are "treacherous" (*bagĕdû*). The imagery suggests "deceit." They are "brothers" (*ʾaḥîm*), which implies that they are connected to him by a familial affection and solidarity, but they have abandoned him. They are inconsistent and unreliable. Job compares them to the seasonal wadis of Palestine. In the rainy season when water is plentiful, they are full to overflowing. But when the heat of summer arrives, and water is needed and scarce, they dry up and disappear (vv. 15-17). Job compares his own disappointment at their failure to provide what he needs to that of parched caravaneers who spy out the promise of water in the desert but upon arrival find it to be only a mirage (vv. 18-20). Like these dried up, empty water beds, the friends have become for Job a non-existent resource. The Hebrew of v. 21 says, literally, "you have become nothing (*lōʾ*)." With a final play on words, Job adds, "you see (*tirʾû*) a calamity, and you are afraid (*tîrāʾû*)." [CD: "Bear One Another's Burdens"]

Job uses a series of rhetorical questions to make clear what he does and does not expect of his friends (vv. 22-27). He has not asked of them a "gift" of money to pay off a loan or a "bribe" to pay off some

---

"Fireflies in the Garden"

R. Friedman has suggested that the paradox of being human is to be created "enough like God to aspire to the divine, but not enough like God to achieve it." A similar thought is expressed by Robert Frost:

Here come the real stars to fill the upper skies,
And here on earth come emulating flies
That, though they never equal stars in size
(And they were never really stars at heart),
Achieve at times a very starlike start.
Only, of course, they can't sustain the part.

R. Friedman, *The Disappearance of God: A Divine Mystery* (Boston/New York: Little, Brown, and Company, 1995), 99.
R. Frost, "Fireflies in the Garden," in *The Poetry of Robert Frost*, ed. E. C. Lathem (New York: Henry Holt and Company, 1969), 246.

"Neither a Borrower Nor a Lender Be"

M. Pope notes that "Lending and borrowing among friends was a sure way to spoil friendship long before Shakespeare put the famous observation in the mouth of Polonius." The speech to which he refers is from *Hamlet* (I, iii, 75-77):

Neither a borrower nor a lender be:
For loan oft loses both itself and friend;
And borrowing dulls the edge of husbandry.

Jeremiah expresses a similar thought when he says, "I have not lent nor have I borrowed, yet all of them curse me" (Jer 15:10). To these examples may be added a Babylonian proverb, which states the same principle from a different perspective: "Friendship lasts for a day, business connections forever."

M. Pope, *Job* (AB; Garden City NY: Doubleday, 1979), 54-55.
Proverb from W. G. Lambert, *Babylonian Wisdom Literature* (Oxford: Clarendon Press, 1960), 259.

---

official. This would have jeopardized their wealth. ["Neither a Borrower Nor a Lender Be"] He has not asked them to rescue him from his adversaries. This would have exposed them to danger. What he has hoped for is that his friends would help him to understand what unconscious or unintentional "error" (v. 24: *šāgag*; NRSV: "wrong"; cf. Lev 4:13; Num 15:22) he has committed.[6] Instead, they have been distressed (v. 25: *nimrĕšû*, lit., "sickened, afflicted") by his "honest words." They regard their own words as proof that Job is wrong; they regard his "words of despair" (v. 26: *ʾimrê nōʾāš*; NRSV: "the speech of the desperate") to be as empty as wind.[7] Job accuses them of being not only indifferent but hardhearted. They dismiss him as little more than an orphan who could be sold into slavery to pay off a debt (v. 27; cf. 2 Kgs 4:1). They haggle over the worth of his friendship as if he were no more than a commodity to be bartered (v. 27b: *kāra* + *ʿal*; "make a bargain over") at market prices (cf. Job 41:6 [MT 40:30], where the same expression describes bargaining over the price of a fish).

"Words of despair" speak a truth that must not only be heard but also seen and felt. If Job's friends would only pay attention to him as a person, if they would only look at him "face to face," then his face would make a moral claim on them that would change both their words and their attitudes (v. 28).[8] He takes a solemn oath that he will not lie to them (cf. Ps 89:35 [MT 89:36]. He knows what he knows through suffering, not through research into the ancient doctrines (cf. 5:27). It is his clear-eyed truth about the "calamity" (v. 30; cf. v. 2) that has befallen him that keeps him honest. It will do the same for the friends if they will "turn" (v. 29: *šub* [2x]; lit. "return") and see that in everything he has said, his "innocence" or "integrity" (*ṣedeq*; NRSV: "vindication") remains intact.

A Sufferer's View of Human Existence, 7:1-6

Job returns once more to the themes of chapter 3, as if nothing that has transpired since his opening assault on creation has changed his assessment of the nullity of life. In 7:1-6 he returns specifically to 3:17-19 and to the imagery of God as "master" (*ʾādōn*) and humans as "slaves" (*ʿebed*). He now employs three terms that expand upon his previous description of the miserable state of human existence: "hard service" (*ṣābāʾ*); "hired laborer" (*śākîr*); and, again, "slave" (*ʿebed*; vv. 1-2).

The lead term, *ṣābāʾ*, sets a particular horizon of meaning for what follows. The term normally applies to compulsory military service (e.g., Num 1:3, 20, 22; 1 Chr 5:18; 7:11). In three texts, however, it refers to the hard, onerous labor imposed on a slave by an overlord: Job 7:1; 14:14; and Isa 40:2 (cf. Dan 10:1). The connection between Job and Deutero-Isaiah is particularly evocative, because it invites a comparison between Job's "hard service" and the suffering of the Israelites in Babylonian exile.[9] The painful difference in Job's case, however, is that the one who sentences him to a life of pain and misery is not Nebuchadnezzar; it is God. Like an owner who exercises absolute control over his property, God treats him like a "hired hand." He works for subsistence wages, knowing full well that at the end of his service God may decide not to pay what he is owed (cf. Deut 15:15; 24:14-15; Lev 19:13). He is like a "slave" who can be bought and sold at the owner's whim. He pants for the relief of the evening shade when the day's work will cease, but he knows full well that he can have no real rest until he dies, for "slaves are free from their taskmasters" only in Sheol (cf. Job 3:19).

Life as a slave is characterized by time that is unbearable and pain that never heals (vv. 3-6). The calendar consists of "months," "nights," and "days" when nothing in life is like it should be. [The Length of Job's Ordeal] The months are full of "emptiness"; they add up to a life that is hollow and counts for nothing. The nights are full of "trouble" (*ʿāmāl*; cf. 3:10; 5:7) and are unbearably long. When Job lies down he

---

The Length of Job's Ordeal

The biblical text does not give dates or time periods that establish the length of Job's suffering. In 7:1-6 and elsewhere, Job speaks of his ordeal in metaphorical terms. The references to "months," "nights," and "days" are evocative, but not literal. Job's perspective is not unlike that of Bolingbroke in *Richard II*: "Grief makes one hour ten" (I, iii, 273).

The *Testament of Job,* the oldest surviving interpretation of the biblical book (first century BCE), embellishes the story by stating that Job spends forty-eight years on the ash heap (21:1). After eleven years (22:1), his food rations are reduced. After six years of near-starvation, his wife Sistis invites him to "speak some word against the Lord and die" so that he might finally have some relief from his pain (25:10; 26:1). Job refuses. In the twentieth year of his suffering, his friends arrive (28:1, 8). They spend twenty-seven days reviewing his situation (41:1). Eliphaz is the first (31:1) and last to speak (43:1), and after an unspecified period of time Job is restored (44:1-5).

wonders, "How long will it be before I arise?" for he knows that he will twist and turn until dawn. The days are methodical, meaningless, and intolerably swift. One day follows another with no variation in what it brings, like a weaver's shuttle passing constantly back and forth across the loom. When the "thread" (v. 6: *tiqwāh*; the same word can be translated "hope"; cf. 4:6; 5:16; 6:8) runs out, the whole process comes to an abrupt stop, whether or not the product has reached its finished state. ["Hope"] Job's plight is to exist minute by minute, day after day, month after month in a body clothed with "worms and dirt" (v. 5). Some understand this expression as a metaphor for death and mortality (cf. Job 21:26).[10] Others suggest that it refers to a medical condition of some sort. Clines, for example, translates "My flesh is covered with *pus* and *scabs*."[11] This rendering fits well with the second line, which says "my skin hardens and then breaks out (oozes)." With either reading, it remains clear that Job's physical pain, like his general existence, is an endless cycle of unrelieved misery.

"Hope"

AΩ The word *tiqwāh* derives from the verb *qāwah*, which may mean both "wait," and "hope." The etymology of the Hebrew verb suggests that it derives from an Akkadian word *qum*, which means "thread, cord." The basic meaning, therefore, is "to be tense," that is, to "wait" or "hope" with intense concentration. The verb *qāwah* occurs 47 times in the Hebrew Bible, including five times in Job (3:9; 6:19; 7:2; 17:13; 30:26; all in the *piel* stem). The noun *tiqwāh* occurs some 32 times, 13 times in Job (4:6; 5:16; 6:8; 7:6; 8:13; 11:18, 20; 14:7, 19; 17:15, 25; 19:10; 27:8).

In Job, the friends and Job have contrasting understandings of hope. The friends have a clear and consistent understanding of hope that is based on the doctrine of retribution (see **[Retribution]**). The truly pious always have hope (4:6; 5:16; 11:18); the wicked do not (8:13; 11:20). If Job is righteous, then he can be confident that God will reward his persistent hope for vindication. Theirs is the time honored perspective of the wisdom tradition, which insists that "the hope (*tôhelet*) of the righteous ends in gladness, but the expectation (*tiqwat*) of the wicked comes to nothing" (Prov 10:28; cf. 11:23; 23:18). Such hope is commendable and has retained its appeal through successive generations of theologians and poets alike:

"Hope" is the thing with feathers—
That perches in the soul—
And sings the tune without the words—
And never stops—at all—

Extreme suffering, however, places a heavy burden upon those who would strain to keep hope alive by "singing the tune without the words." Job is perhaps the parade example of such suffering, hence it is little wonder that his perspective on hope is quite different from the friends. His plight is to hope for that which does not come. In Job 7, for example, he describes himself as "waiting" (v. 2: *yĕqawweh*) for wages that do not come, the end result of which is life "without hope" (v. 6: *tiqwāh*). Similarly, in Job 17 he laments that if his destiny is to "wait" (v. 13: *'ăqawweh*) for Sheol, where then is his "hope" (v. 15: *tiqwātî* [2x])? More troubling still is his sense that it is none other than God who has uprooted his hope (*tiqwātî*) like a tree (19:10; cf. 14:7, 19). To live with only disappointed hope may mean that death, not life, becomes the ultimate objective. Such is the case with Job. His "hope" (*tiqwātî*) is that God will "crush" him and "cut him off" (6:8-9; cf. 3:9).

Job's hope is born of pain, not research. Like the positive hope advanced by the friends, Job's candor about hope that fails also continues to resonate with those who know suffering. His is the "wisdom" so pithily captured in Benjamin Franklin's maxim: "He that lives upon hope will die fasting."

For further reading, see C. Westermann, "Qwh, pi. 'to hope,'" *TLOT*, vol. 3, trans. M. E. Biddle (Peabody MS: Hendrikson Publishers, 1997), 1126-32.

T. H. Johnson, ed., *The Complete Poems of Emily Dickinson* (Boston/New York: Little, Brown and Company, 1960), 116.

B. Franklin, *Poor Richard's Almanac* (1758), cited in *The Oxford Dictionary of Quotations*, 3rd ed. (Oxford: Oxford University Press, 1980), 218.

To describe human existence as slavery is to call into question God's design for creation. Israel's creation theology affirms that human beings are created "in the image of God." Their divine commission comprises two primary responsibilities: (1) to exercise "dominion" (*rdh*) over the earth's resources (Gen 1:26, 28); and (2) to "till" (*'abad*; "serve") and "keep" (*šāmar*) the ground (Gen 2:15). These twin commissions underscore Israel's belief that human beings have been given the noble assignment of acting like God's near-equals. They are stewards of the divine power (dominion) and nurture (serving and keeping) that enables creation to realize its maximum potential. Israel's creation theology represents an intentional departure from the traditions honored by its near Eastern neighbors. In the Mesopotamian creation story *Enuma Elish*, for example, Marduk, the head of the divine council, decides to create humankind as slave and servant of the gods:

I will establish a savage, man shall be his name.
Verily, savage-man I will create,
He shall be charged with the service of the gods
That they might be at ease! (Tablet VI, ll. 6-9)[12]

Job suggests that Israel's theologians should reexamine their understanding of creation. In his experience, the world that God has created is no different than the world designed by Marduk. The gods—YHWH included—have decreed one eternal destiny for humankind: hard and debilitating labor that yields no more than unremitting pain and misery. ["Tired"]

Job's Prayer: "Let Me Alone," 7:7-21

Job has no doubt who holds the contract on his service. He is under no illusion about the identity of his "master." In vv. 7-21, he addresses God directly for the first time in his speeches thus far. Eliphaz has offered Job a model for praising God in the midst of suffering (5:8-16). Job, however, employs a different model. He turns to the tradition of lament in which suppliants address God with prayers that are typically comprised of four primary elements: invocation, lament, petition, and vow of praise. The objective of such a prayer emerges most clearly in the petition for God to hear and respond, for this signals that the suppliant's primary concern is not with the *articulation* of suffering but with its *removal* or *alleviation*. The structure of the

"Tired"

I am so tired of waiting,
Aren't you,
For the world to become good
And beautiful and kind?
Let us take a knife
And cut the world in two—
And see what worms are eating
At the rind.

Langston Hughes, "Tired," in *The Collected Poems of Langston Hughes*, ed. A. Rampersad (New York: Vintage Books, 1994), 135.

prayer signifies the hope and expectation that lament is a journey, not a final destination. As C. Westermann has argued, lament in its fullest form is always "on the road to praise."[13] Job will address God with words that recall each of the parts of a typical lament prayer. Suffering has so blunted Job's hope, however, that the language and objectives of conventional lament must be modified if he is to give adequate expression to his "anguish" and "bitterness" (v. 11).

Job's *invocation* (vv. 7-8) addresses God as the "Seeing Eye" (v. 8: *'ēn rō'î*; lit., "the eye seeing me").[14] A similar epithet, "El-roi" ("God of seeing") occurs in Gen 16:13. Although one cannot posit a direct connection between the two expressions, there is a thematic, but ironic, linkage between them. Hagar is a person marked by suffering and sorrow. As Sarah's maidservant, she becomes an object to be bartered in exchange for children. When she flees to the desert to escape further affliction from her mistress, the "angel of the Lord" finds her and bestows on her a divine promise that opens her future to new possibilities (Gen 16:7-12). She responds by becoming the first person in the Hebrew Bible to name God. God is El-roi, a "God of seeing." In the context of her affliction, she confesses that God has seen her plight and come to her rescue.

Job suggests that he has been similarly marked and similarly sought out by God's seeing eye. In his case, however, suffering has reduced him to a near nothing, a fragment of a person so infinitesimally small that even God cannot locate him. The God who sees all may search for him, but he will be gone (*'ênennî*; lit., "I will not be"). Like Enoch who walked with God and then "was no more" (*'ênennû*; Gen 5:24), Job will simply have vanished into thin air. Later in his address, Job will return to the image of God's extraordinary surveillance of him (vv. 17-21). At that point, he will declare that if he could in fact escape the "Watcher of Humanity" (v. 20), then he would count this as reason to celebrate, not lament.

Job's *lament* and *petition* are joined together in vv. 9-16. He laments that life has become for him a meaningless, irreversible journey into oblivion. Like a cloud that "breaks up and disperses" (REB) without leaving a trace behind, he descends into the nothingness of Sheol (see [Sheol]) with no possibility of ever returning to his "house" or his "place" (vv. 9-10). His journey toward death is interrupted only by the constant harassment of God, who misses no opportunity to terrorize him. Even in the privacy of his sickbed, God frightens him with nightmares and terrifies him with visions that add psychic pain to bodily affliction (vv. 13-14; cf. 7:3-6). ["With Dreams Upon My Bed Thou Scarest Me"] A life of endless persecution is no life at all. Given the option, Job would "choose strangling and death" (v. 15) and "reject" (v. 16: *mā'as*; NRSV:

"With Dreams Upon My Bed Thou Scarest Me"

William Blake depicts the God who terrifies Job in the night as Satan-like. His feet are cloven; entwined around his legs is the primordial serpent, whose head is visible behind and to the right of God's head. God's left hand points to two arched stones, presumably the tablets of the Law, on which can barely be discerned Hebrew words. God's right hand extends downward, beyond Job's head, pointing towards and almost touching the flames of hell that threaten to engulf Job's body. Job lies upon a narrow bed as if asleep, but his eyes are wide open, and his face is turned away from God. His hands are raised, palms upward, elbows braced against the bed, as he tries in vain to fend off his demonic assailant. Even as he pushes away from the assault from above, however, three claw-fingered, demon-like figures from below pull him down toward the abyss. One grabs his legs, one grabs his waist, the third approaches with a chain, perhaps to shackle Job to the flames of fire.

Blake's imagery suggests his distinctly Christian interpretation of Job's dilemma. Both Job and the friends have relied on the Law that cannot save: Job, by expecting that his innocence entitles him to God's blessing; the friends (represented at this point in the drama by Eliphaz), by clinging to a doctrinaire understanding of divine retribution. Both are guilty of creating God in their own image. In Blake's view, Job (and the friends) must die to this reliance on the Law if he is to be reborn by the grace of the Spirit available in Christ. Although the symbolism in this scene is different, the message is essentially the same as that which Blake conveys in the first illustration with the citation from 2 Cor 3:6: "The Letter Killeth, the Spirit giveth Life."

The marginal texts articulate the physical horror and the spiritual travail that suffering brings to Job. By using a collage of texts from both the Old Testament and the New, Blake reinforces his view that Job's suffering leads toward a "conversion" experience. Three citations from the book of Job, each describing some aspect of affliction, are placed at the top of the border (from left to right: Job 30:17; 20:5; 30:30). Along the top edge of the design, there is a fourth citation from 2 Cor 11:14-15: "Satan himself is transformed into an Angel of Light . . ." At the bottom of the border, another citation from the New Testament completes this thought: "Who opposeth and exalteth himself above all that is called God or is Worshipped" (2 Thess 2:4).

Immediately below the design is a compilation from Job 7:13-14 ("With Dreams upon my bed . . .") that identifies this scene with Job's first reply to Eliphaz. Beneath this citation is a longer one from Job 19:22-27, part of which includes Job's declaration "I know that my Redeemer liveth." Blake follows the conventional Christian interpretation of these words (e.g., in Handel's *The Messiah*) by identifying the Redeemer as Jesus Christ, the true God "and not another" that Job will ultimately see. To convey his meaning more clearly, Blake has altered the last words in this citation by substituting the phrase "my wrought image" for "my reins . . . within me" (19:27, KJV). The "wrought image" apparently refers to Job's false image of God, which he is now learning must be transformed by a new revelation. Job's initial movement toward this new discernment is visually depicted by placing the words "my wrought image" within the consuming flames that are already beginning the purification of his understanding.

For further reading on the complex imagery in this illustration and especially on Blake's appropriation of themes and images from John Milton, see K. Raine, *The Human Face of God: William Blake and the Book of Job* (New York: Thames and Hudson, 1982), 193-202.

"loathe") life that is nothing more than mere "breath" (*hebel*; for the range of meanings associated with this term see Ecclesiastes; e.g., 1:2; 2:1, 11, 19; 6:12; 8:10; 11:8, 10).

Job's lament provides the ground for two petitions. They are separated from each other in the speech, but they are logically related. The first occurs in v. 7: "Remember (*zĕkōr*) [O God] that my life is mere wind (*rûaḥ*)." Calling upon God to remember is a common motif in prayers of lament (e.g., Judg 16:28; Jer 15:15; Ps 74:2). At critical points in life persons call on God to remember their good deeds (2 Kgs 20:3 [= Isa 38:3]; Jer 18:20; Neh 5:19) and their particular sufferings (Pss 74:18, 22; 89:50; Lam 5:1), as well as God's own promise to sustain the covenant partnership (Exod 32:13; Deut 9:27; Jer 14:21)

Job is Haunted by Nightmares

William Blake (1757-1827). *Job is Haunted by Nightmares* 1823-1825. Engraving from Blake's *Illustrations of the Book of Job*.

and to show mercy (Hab 3:2; Ps 25:6). The closest parallel to Job's petition is the call for God to remember the frailty of human life (Ps 89:47), the promise of which, in turn, undergirds the assurance that God will act with compassion toward those who need it most (Pss 78:38-39; 103:13-14). Job's address to God, however, is but an imitation of the conventional petition. His call for God to remember the sad state of his life is not an appeal for God to be more *present* with him, for in his judgment divine presence equates with human misery. What he seeks instead is for God to be more *absent*.

The second petition (v. 16) expresses this ironic appeal in stark terms: "Leave me alone (*hădal mimmennî*; lit., "stop [everything you are doing] with reference to me"). What "ordinary" sufferers fear most, namely that God might abandon them in their misery, is precisely what Job longs for. His appeal extends the hope he has previously expressed in 6:9 that God would simply "loose his hand" and permit the forces of death to complete their work with him. This appeal is virtually unprecedented in Hebrew Scripture, although Job will make the same request again in 10:20 (the only other instance is Isa 2:22). Pain and suffering are now taking Job farther and farther beyond the boundaries of conventional piety. Eliphaz's model of praise will not work for Job, and ordinary lament cannot express adequately the truth about God and about life that he has come to know. He must find a new language and a new way of being in relationship with this God, although what this means is still far from clear to him.

Perhaps the most remarkable feature of Job's lament is his decision not to remain silent, for this launches him on a course of confrontation with the Almighty that seems fraught with peril (vv. 11-12). Three first person declarations announce his resolve: "I will not restrain (*hăśak*) my mouth; I will speak in the anguish of my spirit; I will complain in the bitterness of my soul. " His determination to speak may signify only a normal, acceptable expression of deep emotion. [CD: The Privilege of the Anguished] It is the case, however, that such speech may place one beyond the boundary of what is socially acceptable. The wisdom tradition urges the prudent to be "restrained (*hăśak*) in speech" (Prov 10:19; 17:27). Those who give free rein to the "bitterness of soul" may be regarded as "desperate people," even "outcasts" (Judg 18:25; 1 Sam 22:2; 2 Sam 17:8).[15]

Verse 12 suggests that Job is aware he has embarked on a dangerous course. He wonders if God regards him as allied with the mythical figures Yam (*yām*; NRSV: "Sea") and Tannin (*tannîn*; NRSV: "Dragon"). Ancient Near Eastern texts from Mesopotamia and Canaan describe the primordial conflict between the gods who create and govern the cosmos and the forces of chaos who oppose them. [Ancient Near Eastern Creation Accounts] The closest parallels to Job are in the Ugaritic poems about Baal and his consort Anath. Baal defeats Yam, the sea god, and Anath "muzzles" the dragon Tannin, thus securing cosmic order. The Old Testament describes YHWH's creation and governance of the world in terms that are reminiscent of these mythological accounts. Psalm 74:13-14, for example, asserts that God divided the "sea" (*yām*), broke the heads of the "dragons" (*tannînîm*), and crushed Leviathan (cf. Isa 27:1; 51:9; on Leviathan see [Leviathan]). By appropriating this imagery, Job raises the question whether God sees him as a hostile opponent who must be defeated in order to protect creation's design.

Ancient Near Eastern Creation Accounts

A number of ancient Near Eastern texts describe a primordial battle between the deities who create and govern the universe and the forces of chaos represented by sea-gods. In the Mesopotamian text *Enuma Elish*, for example, Marduk, the patron god of Babylon, defeats Tiamat ("Sea") and her group of followers. After Tiamat is slain, Marduk splits her body into two halves out of which he creates the heavens and the earth, and sets a boundary that prevents any further disruption of the chaotic waters:

> Then joined issue Tiamat and Marduk, wisest of gods.
> They strove in single combat, locked in battle . . .

> He released the arrow, it tore her belly,
> It cut her insides, splitting her heart.
> Having thus subdued her, he extinguished her life.
> He cast down the carcass to stand upon it.

> He split her like a shellfish into two parts:
> Half of her he set up and ceiled it as sky,
> Pulled down the bar and posted guards.
> He bade them to allow not her waters to escape.
> (Tablet IV, ll. 93-94, 101-104, 137-140, in *ANET*, 67)

The imagery of placing a "bar" as a boundary for the waters of chaos is similar to the limits God is said to impose on the sea (cf. Prov 8:27, 29; Pss 104:9; 148:6; Jer 5:22). It is noteworthy that the fullest account of God's limiting the sea occurs in Job 38:8-11. This text curiously describes God as wrapping the sea with "swaddling bands" (38:9) that not only restrain but also protect. For further discussion, see the commentary on Job 38–41.

A number of texts from Ugarit refer to the defeat of the mythological creatures Yam and Tannin. In one account the high god Baal strikes Yam with a club. The defeat is celebrated with the cry "Yam is indeed dead! Baal shall be king!" (CTA 2.4.32; in J. C. L. Gibson, *Canaanite Myths and Legends*, 2nd ed. [Edinburgh: T. & T. Clark, 1977], 45). The text that has been most closely linked with Job 7:12 occurs in the Baal-Anath cycle of poems. Anath, Baal's consort and ally, boasts that she has crushed Yam and "muzzled" Tannin:

> What enemy's ris[en] 'gainst Baal,
> What foe 'gainst the Rider of Clouds?
> Crushed I not El's Belov'd Yamm?
> Destroyed I not El's Flood Rabbim?
> Did I not, pray, muzzle the Dragon? (CTA 3.3.35-37;
> in *ANET*, 137)

Some have suggested that the meaning of the Ugaritic word *sbm*, "muzzle," is appropriate also for the word *mišmār* (NRSV: "guard") in Job 7:12. N. Habel, for example, suggests that *mišmār* functions here with a double meaning of "muzzle/watch." Since Job has indicated his refusal to keep silent (7:11), he may now be protesting that God intends to control or silence him by muzzling his mouth (cf. Pss 39:2 [MT 39:1]; 141:3 where the verb *šmr* is used with reference to controlling or muzzling the "mouth").

ANET, 3rd ed. with supplement, ed. J. B. Pritchard (Princeton: Princeton University Press, 1969).

N. Habel, *The Book of Job: A Commentary* (OTL; Philadelphia: Westminster Press, 1985), 61; cf. M. Pope, *Job* (AB; Garden City NY: Doubleday, 1979), 61. The seminal proposal, which comes from M. Dahood, "*Mismar* 'muzzle' in Job 7:12," JBL 80 (1961): 270-71, is evocative but not certain. For further discussion, see D. Diewert, "Job 7:12: *Yam, Tannin* and the Surveillance of Job," JBL 106 (1987): 203-15.

The conventional interpretation of Job's question is that it is purely rhetorical. Is he the equivalent of Yam and Tannin? Job clearly believes that he is not, and for God to confront him as if he were suggests that God has totally miscalculated his significance in the cosmos. Job's own assessment of his role in creation is that he can aspire to be nothing more than a "slave" (7:1-6). He estimates that his strength to stand opposite this God is no more than that of the "wind" (*rûaḥ*; 7:7), a cloud (7:8), a mere "breath" (7:16; cf. 6:11-13). Given this self-understanding, it is plausible that his *question* is actually an *indictment* of God for treating him "with an intensity wholly disproportionate to his significance."[16]

Job's question leaves open the possibility of another interpretation however. What is *God's* assessment of Job's importance? How does *God* understand Job's role in creation? Has God created a world in which the innocent suffer without redress? Job suspects this is the case. He believes that when he opens his mouth to speak anguish and bitterness, God will place a "guard" (*mišmār*) over him (v. 12). The imagery may suggest either a boundary beyond which God will not permit Job to go or a "muzzle" that will restrict Job's speech (cf. Pss 39:1 [MT 39:2]; 141:3). With either reading the general idea is clear. Job believes God will not tolerate his charge that the world is not functioning properly as long as there is one innocent sufferer whose cry goes unanswered. But will God respond to Job as he predicts?

Job's ruminations about Yam and Tannin harbor the idea that God considers him, a mere mortal, to have a significance that is somehow decisive for the establishment of cosmic order. What if, like these primordial combatants, Job's role is to challenge God to take him and the suffering he exemplifies into account *so that* the cosmic order can be what God intends? What if Job *is* like Yam and Tannin, a force whose claim on creation God judges to be real and worthy of response? Such questions may well seem far-fetched on first reflection. Surely Job would not find much merit in them at this juncture in his story. Two considerations, however, argue against dismissing them too quickly. First, Job's probing questions about his identity and his status before God have only begun. In the final words of his present address (vv. 17-21), he will take up the issue once more in a different way: "What are human beings, that you make so much of them?" Although Job's suffering seems to be pushing him toward negative answers to these questions, it is instructive to remember that the questions are in fact *not answered*. Even when the friends respond to Job (e.g., 15:7-16; 22:1-11), his questions remain fundamentally open, until God answers from the whirlwind. Second, when God finally speaks about creation and the role of humanity within it, God instructs Job to consider two creatures—Behemoth and Leviathan—who require his special attention (40:15–41:34). These two primordial creatures, like Yam and Tannin, are mythical forces of chaos that God must engage in order to secure the stability of creation. What is striking is that God presents them to Job as proud figures of power and dominion that are justly deserving of praise. A full discussion of these matters must await the commentary on the relevant texts. In anticipation of that discussion, it is wise to withhold final judgment on whether Job's question in v. 12 is merely rhetorical.

Lament prayers typically conclude with a note of praise or at least with an expression of confidence indicating that God has heard and can be trusted to respond. Job also uses words of *praise* to conclude his address to God (vv. 17-21). In his case, however, suffering has turned the world upside down: human existence is miserable and meaningless; God is hostile and oppressive; servanthood is slavery. What does it mean in a world like Job's to praise God? The model for Job's praise is Psalm 8:4-5 (cf. Ps 144:3-4).[17] For the psalmist, the hierarchy of the created order, which exalts humankind as a near-equal to God (as in Gen 1), witnesses to God's wondrous attention and beneficence. God elevates mere humans to royal status and gives them dominion and responsibility for creation. In the world of the psalmist, such a design is cause for astonished praise: "What are human beings that you should be mindful of them, mortals that you care for them." In the world of Job, however, these words are laden with vexed ambiguity. They evoke astonishment, but not praise. ["There's Nothing in This World Can Make Me Joy"]

Job submits the language of Psalm 8 to a sufferer's critique. [CD: Psalm 8 and Job 7] He begins with the psalmist's reflection on God's creational intentions for humankind: "What are human beings that you exalt them, that you set your mind on them, visit them every morning, test them every moment?" (vv. 17-18). On the lips of the sufferer, these words speak a doxology of sarcasm, not praise. Virtually every assertion is turned inside out. The interrogative (*mah*) that introduces the psalmist's wonderment evokes from Job a cry of despair instead. When he considers the special attention that God devotes to human beings, he discerns a sinister intent. God "exalts" (*gādal*; lit., "makes great") human beings in order to humiliate them. God's "mind" (*lēb*; lit., "heart") is fixed on harassing and terrifying. God's "visit" (*pāqad*) is for Job a daily reminder that he has been singled out for punishment (cf. Jer 6:15; Hos 1:4; Amos 3:2), not compassion (cf. Gen 21:1; Pss 65:9 [MT 65:10]; Jer 27:22; 29:10). God's "testing" (*bāḥan*) is not for the purpose of proving his innocence (cf. Jer 12:3; Pss 17:3; 26:2; 139:23) but of declaring him guilty, regardless of the evidence that would acquit him. God's relentless scrutiny, morning by morning, moment by moment, serves not to build him up but to break him down. God's presence is oppressive, not gracious. Unlike other sufferers who yearn for God to "look" (*rā'ah*) on them (e.g., 1 Sam 1:11; Isa 37:17; 63:15) in the sure conviction that this will bring relief and restoration, Job longs for God to look anywhere other than at him, for only this would provide a respite from God's painful surveillance: "Will you not look away (*šā'ah*) from me, leave me alone long enough to swallow my spit?" (v. 19; cf. 7:16).

"There's Nothing in This World Can Make Me Joy"

There's nothing in this world can make me joy:
Life is as tedious as a twice-told tale
Vexing the dull ear of a drowsy man;
And bitter shame hath spoil'd the sweet world's taste,
That it yields nothing but shame and bitterness.
(*King John*, III, iv, 107-111)

The first word of v. 20 is a simple declarative in Hebrew: "I sin" (*ḥāṭāʾtî*). It is possible to interpret the expression as a confession of guilt, in which case Job would seem to be admitting finally that he does in fact deserve to be the object of God's assault (cf. KJV; NAB). It is more likely, however, that Job's words continue to convey sarcasm, not confession. Indeed, nothing in the Joban story thus far contradicts the narrator's statement that "Job did not sin with his lips" (2:10), or God's assertion that Job is "blameless and upright" (1:8; 2:3).[18] The logic of Job's lament suggests rather that the sin of which he speaks is only hypothetical. NRSV, with most modern translations, captures this sense nicely by adding the word "if": "*If* I sin, what do I do to you. . ." (cf. 35:6 where Elihu's consideration of the same possibility includes the word "if" [*ʾim*]). The epithet "Watcher of Humanity" (*nōzēr hāʾādām*), like the title "Seeing Eye" (7:8), continues Job's parody of conventional language about God. Elsewhere the verb *nāzar*, "guard, watch," describes God's care and concern for people (Deut 32:10: "like the apple of his eye"; cf. Isa 27:3; Pss 31:23 [MT 31:24]; 140:1, 4 [MT 140:2, 5]). For Job, however, God's watching fixes him as an object for attack. He is God's "target" (*mipgāʿ*), a defenseless victim spied out by an invincible warrior. ["Job's Sad Song"]

Job follows the hypothetical confession of sin with a mock petition for forgiveness (v. 21). *If* I have sinned, Job asks, what would it cost God simply to "lift up" (*nāśaʾ*) my transgression and cause my iniquity to "pass away" (*ʿābar*, Hiphil; cf. 2 Sam 24:10 [= 1 Chr 21:8]; Zech 3:4)? The two verbs are conventional terms for forgiveness, but it is possible that in the present context they mean something more general. E. Dhorme, for example, translates as follows: "Why dost thou not *tol-*

"Job's Sad Song"

Joni Mitchell's ballad, "The Sire of Sorrow (Job's Sad Song)," recreates the Joban drama. As Job rehearses the catalogue of his grief, his friends ("Antagonists") respond by rote with a catch phrase based on Eliphaz's speech in 5:7: "Man is the sire of sorrow." Job, however, persists with his complaint, the repeating refrain of which paraphrases Job 7:20. The first two verses are representative of the whole:

Let me speak, let me spit out bitterness—
Born of grief and nights without sleep and
    festering flesh.
Do you have eyes?
Can you see like mankind sees?
Why have you soured and curdled me?
Oh you tireless watcher! What have I done
    to you?

That you make everything I dread and everything I fear come
    true?
Once I was blessed; I was awaited like
    the rain,
Likes eyes for the blind, like feet from the lame.
Kings heard my words, and they sought my
    company.
But now the janitors of Shadowland flick their brooms at
    me.
Oh you tireless watcher! What have I done to you?
That you make everything I dread and everything I fear
    come true?
(Antagonists: Man is the sire of sorrow)

J. Mitchell, "The Sire of Sorrow (Job's Sad Song)," from the album *Turbulent Indigo*, Reprise/Wea, 1994.

erate my transgression, and *overlook* my fault" (emphasis added).[19] With either rendering, Job's question is more a taunt of God than a genuine plea for mercy. Job's existence on earth is only brief (cf. 7:7-10). Soon (*'atah*, "now," i.e.,"immediately"), he will lie down in the dust and go to his rest in Sheol (cf. 17:16). Surely nothing in the master plan for his life will be lost if God simply suspends the assault on him long enough for him to complete his appointment with death.

Job began his address to God with the recognition that he was destined for nonexistence (v. 8: *'ênennî*). From that pained perspective, he has asked God a series of questions that probe for the meaning of life in the world to which he has been assigned: "Am I the Sea, or the Dragon?" (v. 12); "What are human beings?" (v. 17); "Will you not look away from me?" (v. 19); "What do I do to you?" (v. 20); "Why have you made me your target?" (v. 20); "Why do you not pardon my transgression?" (v. 21). God is silent, and Job is left with questions that remain urgent but unanswered. At the end of his prayer, he winds up where he began, with the abiding conviction that his fate is fixed and unalterable: "I shall not be" (v. 21: *'ênennî*).

CONNECTIONS

With his second speech, Job continues his free fall into suffering that seems to have no end. The two soliloquies that introduce chapters six and seven track his descent. His life is painfully out of balance (6:1-7). Sorrow outweighs joy, losses erase every gain, misfortune cancels all accomplishments. As far as Job can see, misery is the norm for human existence, not the exception. Human beings are created for a life of hardship (7:1-6). Like slaves, they serve a cruel and oppressive master. There is no reward adequate for their toil; there is no relief equal to the fatigue that drains life of every hope. If anyone is to "console and comfort" Job, they must descend with him into *this* world where life is wearisome and meaningless. ["How Weary, Stale, Flat, and Unprofitable . . . the Uses of This World"]

What distinguishes this particular speech is not the description of Job's plight, although this remains the ever present frame within which interpreters must search for meaning. It is rather Job's desperate attempt to find a toehold in suffering by reaching out in two directions with seemingly opposite appeals. He appeals to the friends, who have abandoned him, to return to his side (6:14-30), and he appeals to God, whose presence he can no longer bear, to leave him alone (7:7-21). The challenge for Eliphaz and indeed for all who would minister to the Jobs of this world is to recognize that both these appeals can be important

---

**"How Weary, Stale, Flat, and Unprofitable . . .
the Uses of This World"**

Job's perspective, though tied to the specifics of the biblical drama, is nonetheless characteristic of those who see the world through the lens of depression. Shakespeare's Hamlet offers a classic expression of such depression (I, ii, 129-37):

O, that this too solid flesh would melt,
Thaw, and resolve itself into dew!
Or that the Everlasting had not fix'd

His canon 'gainst self-slaughter! O God! O
   God!
How weary, stale, flat, and unprofitable
Seem to me all the uses of the world!
Fie on't. O fie! 'tis an unweeded garden,
That grows to seed; things rank and gross in
   nature
Possess it merely. That it should come to
   this!

---

and authentic. Not always, but sometimes, a good friend may be more needed and more welcomed than God. Not always, but sometimes, those hollowed out by suffering may fear that the promise of God's presence will only add misery to misery, emptiness to emptiness.

When a Friend is Needed Most

From Job's perspective, the only friendship worthy of the name is that which proves itself in the crucible of suffering. Those whose suffering pushes them into despair need "loyalty" from a friend (v. 14). Job understands this to mean that friends will not let go of friends no matter what. In good times and bad, in success and failure, in joy and in sorrow, friends should be present with equal commitment and passion. Job's criticism of Eliphaz and his cohorts offers a graphic description of what we call "fairweather friends." They are present when it does not cost them anything and their resources are not needed, but when the stakes are high and the cost could be dear, they retreat and wait for better times to appear.

What is particularly intriguing is the suggestion that friendship is most severely tested in matters of faith. When despair pushes one beyond the boundaries of conventional piety, what Job calls "forsaking the fear of the Almighty," then what it takes to be a true friend may be costly indeed. Sufferers like Job are threatening. Their hurt and broken-ness remind the unafflicted of what may be lurking for them around them the next corner. Their cry for help disturbs the serenity of safe and predictable discourse, insisting that life's grammar is punctuated with screams of pain that cannot be ignored and will not be silenced. Job doubts that he has the strength to endure what God ordains (6:11-12); he doubts that life is either meaningful or just (7:1-6); he doubts his identity, his self-worth, his very status as a human being in the world God creates (7:17-21). Honest doubt always threatens belief. When expressed by the truly "blameless and upright," such doubt can be not only dangerous but also contagious. When Job asks "What is my strength?" those who sit with him must wonder about their own reserves. When he asks "What are human beings?" those who sit with him know that the question is not abstract. Now it is personal: "What am I?" [CD: "Alas, What Am I?"]

What if Job's wonderments about these questions are right? This is the constant, if unspoken, anxiety that strikes fear in those who would befriend Job. Perhaps to identify too closely with Job's questions renders one more susceptible to his uncertainties. Perhaps to enter too deeply into his pain leaves one more vulnerable to the hurt that thus far comes only to others. Anyone who has ever encountered someone whose suffering is extreme and seemingly irreversible knows the fear of sitting with Job. The temptation is first to ignore, then to silence through arguments, explanations, answers, and finally, if all else fails, to retreat in self-defense and abandon the suffering to suffering. In short, the temptation for those who would be Job's friends is to act like Eliphaz and his companions.

Job expects and hopes for something more from his friends. He is not closed to honest advice and sound instruction (7:24), but what he most needs is companionship, not to ease the pain, but to improve the quality of suffering. In *A Whole New Life*, Reynolds Price offers personal reflections that speak to those who would sit with the Jobs of this world. He writes about his mid-life war with the cancer that invaded his body and grew up his spine like an eel. He survived, although with a paralysis that bears witness to the battle, and from the "far side of catastrophe," what he calls "the dim other side of that high wall that effectively shuts disaster off from the unfazed world," he articulates the sufferer's need: "In that deep trough I needed companions more than prayers or potions that had worked for another."[20]

Too often what he received from those who wanted to care was something very different. Some of his friends provided "would-be helpful books" that explained why he had cancer—perhaps his own unhealthy habits?—how some new treatment might miraculously cure it—had he tried "moon-rock dust and beetle-wing ointment"?—and, as a last resort, what kind of deal he might cut with God to salvage any life he could: if I give You all the feeling in my legs, and all the control of my upper body, will You permit me a few extra years? His physicians, highly skilled professionals who were trained to treat cancer patients, sometimes offered little or no real comfort. His oncologist turned away from him when he attempted casual conversation in the halls. He seemed unable to offer an unscripted word of encouragement or a spontaneous expression of comradeship. Price's wonderment about such treatment places him in the company of Job:

Did he think I was brewing my grievance against him, some costly revenge in the crowded market of malpractice suits? Did he shy from involvement with one more face that was hungry for life though already stamped *Dead?* My best guess from here is, he didn't know how to act otherwise; and he hadn't tried to learn. It's often said by way of excuse that doctors are insufficiently trained for humane relations. For complex long-range interaction with damaged creatures, they may well need a kind of training they never receive; but what I wanted and needed badly, from that man then, was the frank exchange of decent concern. When did such a basic transaction between two mammals require postgraduate instruction beyond our mother's breast?[21]

Perhaps there is no adequate training for long-range, complex friendships with "damaged creatures" like Job. It is true that such friendship is never easy and may be costly, for the more intimate we become with those whose hurt, the more their pain becomes our own. But Job insists that when such friendship is lacking everyone is diminished, not just the afflicted. Friends who do not hold on to friends who suffer, whether because of fear or indifference, forsake the summons and the opportunity to image God by dealing "loyally and compassionately with one another" (Zech 7:9). The summons and what is at stake when we fail to heed it is not different in the New Testament:

> Beloved, let us love one another, because love is from God; everyone who loves is born of God and knows God. . . Those who say, "I love God," and hate their brothers and sisters, are liars; for those who do not love a brother or a sister whom they have seen, cannot love God whom they have not seen. (1 John 4:7, 20)

When God's Presence Seems Hurtful and Unwanted

Job yearns for the friends to be more authentically present for him. With a similar desperation, he longs for God to be more absent from him. His desire to be beyond the reach of God is harsh, jolting, unsettling. . . and real. Those hollowed out by suffering speak this way. They would hope and believe more if they could, but grief has the capacity to diminish life and deaden the soul. For those who have descended into the abyss of nothingness, even God can seem an unwelcomed intruder. Indeed, for those whose former certainties are tied to expectations of God's abiding love and care, extreme suffering may render God terrifying, oppressive, hostile. Job vows to his friends that he will not hide the truth about the God who has inexplicably targeted him for destruction. It is *his* truth, even if it is not theirs. It is truth informed by *his* experience, even if they cannot fully connect with it. It is the *sufferer's truth about God* that Job insists the friends must hear if they truly want to "comfort and console" him. ["If Thou Wilt Weep My Fortunes"]

On this matter, Reynolds Price has a further word that is pertinent. He observes that in his struggle to carve out a new life for himself in the world of suffering, what he needed was some story, however distant, that might connect with his "unfolding bafflement." He needed "some honest report from a similar war, with a final list of hard facts learned and offered unvarnished."[22] This would have been a comfort to him, a real form of sustenance that would help him stay the course until some further clarity provided new options. ["The Absence of Optimism"] Interpreters may find it instructive to think of Job as providing an authentic report of "hard facts" and "unvarnished" truth about the way God sometimes looks to the sufferer. To minister to the Jobs of this world, it is not required that we agree with them, still less that we chastise or correct them. What is required is that we listen to them and take them seriously, even if they ask that we be willing to join them in a world where God seems no longer relevant. It may be that in that world real friends offer the most accessible and the most concrete image of God that can be found.

It is important to note, finally, that even in despair, Job continues to address God. The irony of his situation is that even as he asks God to leave him alone (7:16), he is in fact reaching out to God. When pushed to the limits, perhaps this is the ultimate expression of faith: to pray without the certainty of a hearing, to believe when experience does not warrant it, to carve out life, step by painful step, even when death seems more desirable. George Herbert (1593–1633), the English poet and rector, includes among his "outlandish proverbs" the following observation: "He that lives in hope danceth without musick."[23] Such is the witness of Job's free fall into suffering. The music for him has ceased, but there remains the passion for the dance.

"If Thou Wilt Weep My Fortunes"

If thou wilt weep my fortunes, take my eyes.

(*King Lear*, IV, vi, 180)

"The Absence of Optimism"

In *Souls Raised from the Dead*, Doris Betts follows the tragic journey of Mary, a young girl whose life is suddenly derailed by an incurable kidney disease. On her thirteenth birthday, she wearily contemplates the transplant that will at best keep her a member of the chronically ill. Her friend Cindy Scofield comes to visit and gives her a gift of two book-tapes, which she can listen to on her portable player.

"They're by African-American women. People who've been through hard times." Cindy showed her the names: Lucille Clifton, Maya Angelou, Nikki Giovanni, Alice Walker, Gwendolyn Brooks. "Black poetry just reads aloud so well," she added nervously . . .

Mary flipped pages of the small accompanying pamphlet, letting words break loose from the printed poems: "My mother is jelly-hearted and she has a brain of jelly. " "Hope is a crushed stalk." The absence of optimism cheered her up instantly.

D. Betts, *Souls Raised from the Dead* (New York: Simon & Schuster, 1994), 268-69.

NOTES

[1] Cf. D. Clines, *Job 1–20* (WBC; Dallas: Word Books, 1989), 172.

[2] See, for example, Clines (*Job 1–20*, 174) who compares Job to a prisoner under torture who refuses to renounce his convictions.

[3] For discussion of these matters see N. Habel, *The Book of Job: A Commentary* (OTL; Philadelphia: Westminster Press, 1985), 147; E. Dhorme, *A Commentary on the Book of Job* (Nashville: Thomas Nelson Publishers, 1967), 82.

[4] Cf. C. Newsom, "The Book of Job," in vol. 4 of *NIB* (Nashville: Abingdon Press, 1996), 388.

[5] H. J. Stoebe, "*Hesed* 'Kindness, '" in E. Jenni, C. Westermann, *Theological Lexicon of the Old Testament*, vol. 2, trans. M. E. Biddle (Peabody MS: Hendrikson Publishers, 1997), 456.

[6] On the meaning of the root *šgg* in this text see J. Milgrom, "The Cultic *segaga* and Its Influence in Psalms and Job," JQR 58 (1967): 115-25.

[7] Cf. R. Gordis, *The Book of Job: Commentary, New Translation, and Special Studies* (New York: Jewish Theological Seminary of America, 1978), 77: "Do you regard (your) empty words as proof, but as mere wind, a despairing man's speech?"

[8] Cf. Newsom, "The Book of Job," 390.

[9] J. Gerald Janzen, *Job* (Atlanta: John Knox, 1985), 80-81.

[10] So, for example, Habel, *Book of Job,* 159.

[11] Clines, *Job 1–20*, 157.

[12] *ANET*, 3rd ed. with supplement, ed. J. B. Pritchard (Princeton: Princeton University Press, 1969), 68.

[13] C. Westermann, *Praise and Lament in the Psalms* (Atlanta: John Knox, 1981), 154.

[14] Cf. Habel, *Book of Job,* 160.

[15] C. Westermann, "*Nephes* 'Soul, '" in *TLOT*, vol. 2, 749; cf. Newsom, "The Book of Job," 395.

[16] Ibid. Similarly Clines, who interprets v. 12 as an ironic appropriation of the doctrine of retribution: "A person is requited *according to* one's works. But in Job's case there is, as it seems to him, a ludicrous and hugely unjust lack of proportion" (*Job 1–20*, 188).

[17] On the rhetorical links between Job 7 and Psalm 8, see M. Fishbane, *Biblical Interpretation in Ancient Israel* (Oxford: Clarendon Press, 1985), 285-86; idem, "The Book of Job and Inner-biblical discourse," *The Voice from the Whirlwind: Interpreting the Book of Job*, ed. L. Perdue, W. Gilpen (Nashville: Abingdon Press, 1992), 87-90; P. E. Dion, "Formulaic Language in the Book of Job: International Background and Ironical Distortions," *SR* 16 (1987): 187-93. For a cautionary appraisal, see R. C. Van Leeuwen, "Psalm 8:5 and Job 7:17-18: A Mistaken Scholarly Commonplace," *The World of the Arameans I: Biblical Studies in Honour of Paul-Eugène Dion*, ed. P. M. Daviau et al. (JSOTSup 324; Sheffield: Sheffield University Press, 2001), 205-15.

[18] Cf. Clines, *Job 1–20*, 194.

[19] Dhorme, *Commentary on the Book of Job,* 111.

[20] R. Price, *A Whole New Life* (New York: Atheneum, 1994), 180.

[21] Ibid., 56.

[22] Ibid., 181.

[23] G. Herbert, *Outlandish Proverbs*, cited in *The Oxford Dictionary of Quotations*, 3rd ed. (Oxford: Oxford University Press, 1980), 246.

BILDAD'S FIRST RESPONSE TO JOB: "DOES GOD PERVERT JUSTICE?"

Job 8:1-22

Bildad's first response offers a marked contrast to the "wild words" of Job's last speech. Job has spoken words born of "anguish" and "bitterness"; Bildad responds with calm, reasoned words that assert simple truths. Job has turned first in one direction, then another, in a desperate search for understanding; Bildad has no doubt about where to turn for authoritative instruction, and he moves swiftly to inform Job of the wisdom that he has neglected. Job has indicated his willingness to be taught by the friends, although he doubts that the words they offer will settle anything. Bildad is pleased to accept the invitation. He makes his case in three parts: (1) God is just (vv. 1-7); (2) God's justice is manifest in fair and predictable principles of reward and retribution (vv. 8-19); and (3) Job can rest assured that God's justice will work for him (vv. 20-22).

If Eliphaz's words have the tone of a pastoral counselor (see commentary on Job 4–5), Bildad's remind one of a professor who moves systematically from premise to illustration to application. He leads with a question that invites the pupil to discover the answer the teacher already knows: "Does God pervert justice?" (v. 3). He appeals to the research of the ancestors (vv. 8-10) and illustrates it with practical examples from the natural world (vv. 12-15, 16-19). He applies the lesson specifically to Job, who should now have sufficient understanding to affirm for himself that "God will not reject a blameless person" (v. 20). [Structure of Job 8:1-22] Like a good teacher, Bildad's objective is to move his student from an inadequate perspective on life to one that is more informed and therefore

> **Structure of Job 8:1-22**
>
> 8:1-7 Premise: God is just
>   v. 3 The general premise that is *not* in question: "Does God pervert justice?"
> 8:8-19 Illustration: God's justice is manifest in just principles of reward and retribution
>   vv. 8-10 Appeal to the wisdom of the ancestors
>   vv. 11-19 Two examples from nature
>   v. 11 A proverbial truth
>   vv. 12-15 The plant that withers
>   vv. 16-19 The plant that survives
> 8:20-22 Application: God's justice will work for Job
>   v. 20 The restatement of the general premise as an assertion: "See, God will not reject a blameless person"

The Rhetoric of Disputation

The rhetorical technique of criticizing an opponent's words as mere "wind" occurs frequently in Job (cf. 6:26; 15:2; 16:3; 32:18). Similar strategies are employed in the disputation literature of the ancient Near East. In the Mesopotamian text Babylonian Theodicy, for example, a friend rebukes his fellow sufferer and accuses him of blaspheming the deity:

My reliable friend, holder of knowledge, your thoughts
     are perverse . . .
You have forsaken right and blaspheme against your
     god's design.

In your mind you have an urge to disregard the divine
     ordinances. (77)

On another occasion the friend offers a similar criticism and admonishes the sufferer to be obedient to his god:

You have let your subtle mind go astray.
     [. . .] you have ousted wisdom,
You despise propriety, you profane ordinances.

Follow in the way of the god, observe his rites. (83)

W. G. Lambert, *Babylonian Wisdom Literature* (Oxford: Clarendon Press, 1960).

better suited for success. In Job's case, this means that he must relinquish the words that spill from his mouth (v. 2: *pikā*) of bitterness and reproach—in order that God may make good on the promise to fill his mouth (*pikā*) with "laughter" and his lips with "shouts of joy" (v. 21).

COMMENTARY

God is Just, 8:1-7

Bildad begins with a question that expresses both his exasperation and his anxiety about the progress of the discussion thus far: "How long will you say these things?" (v. 2). The question rebukes Job for speaking too much and too dangerously. [The Rhetoric of Disputation] Job has complained that the friends treat his words as mere "wind" (*rûaḥ*; 6:26), implying that they consider what he says to be empty and meaningless. Bildad does not make this mistake. He describes Job's words as a "mighty wind" (*rûaḥ kabbîr*). They are forceful and potentially destructive. Their power is like that of a "destroying tempest . . . a storm of *mighty*, overflowing *waters*" (Isa 28:2; cf. Isa 17:12). Bildad understands that if Job's words are left unchecked, the friends' theology and the God for whom they speak will necessarily be compromised.

Bildad's first question sets the stage for his second, which now makes clear the threat he understands "these words" of Job to present. "Does God pervert justice (*mišpaṭ*)? Or does the Almighty pervert the right (*ṣedeq*; v. 3)?" For Bildad, the question is purely rhetorical. ["Can't We Just Have Faith?"] He will in due course provide the only legitimate answer that can be given (v. 20; cf. Elihu's similar response in 34:10-12), but for now he is content to assume that the truth of orthodoxy is simply too strong to deny. *Mišpaṭ* and *ṣedeq* are the foundations of God's

---

"Can't We Just Have Faith?"

Bildad's namesake in H. G. Wells's novel *The Undying Fire* is Mr. William Dad, formerly the designer of the "Dad and Showhite car de luxe" and now a chief contractor for airplanes in England. As an engineer, he is not particularly interested in big, unresolvable God-questions. His preference is for the simple, straightforward approach: "Give me the Bible and the simple religion I learnt on my mother's knee. That's good enough for me. Can't we just have faith and leave all these questions alone?" (80).

When pushed to respond to the calamities that had befallen Job Huss, Mr. Dad uses this "simple religion" to construct a world view that essentially eliminates extreme suffering like Job's from serious consideration: "For my part I don't think there is such a thing as misfortune . . . I don't hold with it. Miscalculation if you like" (41).

H. G. Wells, *The Undying Fire* (New York: The Macmillan Company, 1919).

---

throne (Pss 89:15; 97:2), the principles of God's governance (Ps 99:4), the basis of God's covenant fidelity (Hos 2:19 [MT 2:21]). God loves justice and righteousness (Ps 33:5) and expects the same from those who would sustain God's work in the world (Amos 5:24; cf. 5:7; 6:12). From Bildad's perspective, it is unthinkable that God would "pervert" (*yĕʿawwēt*; lit., "bend, twist") the very qualities that define God as God. Such a notion would turn Israel's ancient confessions upside down:

The Rock, his work is perfect,
and all his ways are just (*mišpaṭ*).
A faithful God, without deceit,
righteous (*ṣaddîq*) and upright is he. (Deut 32:4)

J. Hartley states bluntly what Bildad implies but cannot bring himself to articulate:

Since justice is the cornerstone of God's relationship with humanity, any accusation that God is perverting justice is tantamount to accusing him of acting demonically. If the charge is true, then God is not God. Such a deity would be a devil, unworthy of a person's devotion.[1]

Job has not explicitly accused God of injustice, although his complaint about God's inexplicable hostility towards him (7:7-21) clearly seems to harbor just this thought. It is in fact Bildad who first identifies what is at stake in this drama as a matter of divine justice. The tenor of his question in v. 3 suggests that he knows where Job's discontent is likely to lead and hopes to quash the indictment before it begins. His strategy will not succeed. In Job 9–10, the issue of God's justice will emerge as a primary and specific focus of Job's complaint. In subsequent speeches, he will announce his intent to file a legal case against God (cf. 13:3, 18), a case which he refuses to settle until he secures a verdict that establishes his innocence (cf. 27:2-6) or God's guilt (cf. 31:35-37).[2]

Bildad's absolute certainty concerning God's just and moral governance of the world provides the basis for his interpretation of Job's
situation (vv. 4-7). Like Eliphaz (cf. 4:7-11), he appeals to the doctrine
of retribution as the fundamental explanation of Job's misfortune (see
[Retribution]). In vv. 4, 5, and 6, he uses a sequence of "if . . . then" sentences, which are designed to teach Job that for every consequence
there is a cause, for every cause or act there is a corresponding consequence. This "if . . . then" theology enables him to argue from *cause to
effect* and from *effect to cause*, applying the same rigid linkage between
the two sides of the equation to every situation in life. The subtle, but
virtually automatic, connection between cause and effect is apparent in
v. 4. On first impression, Bildad seems to be speaking hypothetically
about sin that results in death: "*If* your children sinned against him,
then. . . ." In reality, however, he is deducing the cause that lies behind
what has already occurred. Job's children are dead. Given Bildad's theology, their sin cannot be hypothetical; it must be actual. ["They Are Dead
and They Were Innocent"] For Bildad, "if" is equivalent to "since,"[3] a subtle
conclusion obscured by the NRSV but clarified by other translations:

When your children sinned against him,
He gave them over to the penalty of their sin. (NIV)

Your children must have sinned against God,
and so he punished them as they deserved. (TEV)

"They Are Dead and They Were Innocent"

Job does not respond to Bildad's callous equation of
his children's death with sin, even though the reader
can hardly fail to wonder what he might have said. In *J.B.*
Sarah, Job's wife, articulates one possible response that
gives some insight into how Bildad's "if . . .then" theology
sounds to a sufferer. Having listened patiently to Job's
grievous insistence that God is just, she finally reaches her
limit when it comes to linking the death of her children to
sin:

God is just!
If God is just our slaughtered children
Stank with sin, were rotten with it!

Oh, my dear! my dear! my dear!
Does God demand deception of us?—
Purchase His innocence by ours?
Must we be guilty for Him?—bear
The burden of the world's malevolence
For Him who made the world?

When Job persists in seeking for some connection
with sin, she continues:

I will not stay here if you lie—
Connive in your destruction, cringe to it:
Not if you betray my children . . .

I will not stay to listen . . .

They are
Dead and they were innocent: I will not
Let you sacrifice their deaths
To make injustice justice and God good.

Although perhaps it was not MacLeish's intention to do
so, the words he gives Sarah provide a poignant rebuttal to
Bildad. He argues, in effect, that because the children are
dead, therefore they must have sinned. Sarah protests,
"They are dead and they were innocent."

A. MacLeish, *J.B.* (Boston: Houghton Mifflin Co., 1956), 109-10.

In vv. 5-6, Bildad applies the same theology to Job himself, this time reversing the argument in order to teach him how he can move from effect to consequence. If Job fulfills certain conditions, then he can expect and secure the appropriate outcomes. Bildad identifies two requirements. First, Job's piety must be genuine: he must "seek" (*šāḥar*) God earnestly, and he must "make supplication" (*ḥānan*) to God (v. 5). Bildad does not spell out what he means by these acts of piety. The terms he uses may be only general expressions for worship (cf. *šāḥar* in Ps 63:1 [MT 63:2]; Isa 26:9) and prayer (cf. *ḥānan* in Pss 30:9; 142:1 [MT 142:2]). Still, the prologue has already established that Job's piety is defined by such acts (cf. 1:5, also with *šāḥar* [NRSV: "rise early"]). Elsewhere in the Hebrew Bible, to "seek" (*šāḥar*) God involves repentance (cf. Hos 5:15), and the prayer of supplication (*ḥānan*) is a request for forgiveness (cf. 1 Kgs 8:33, 47 [= 2 Chr 6:4, 37]). One suspects it is this more specific understanding of what is required of Job that lies just under the surface of Bildad's words.

Second, Job's piety must be exemplified in behavior that is "pure" (*zak*) and "upright" (*yāšar*; v. 6a). Here too, Bildad seems to be asking Job to demonstrate virtues that God has already affirmed (cf. 1:8; 2:3). Nothing that has transpired in the story thus far refutes God's assessment of Job, and in subsequent speeches Job will insist that he does indeed stand before God as one who is "upright" (*yāšar*; 23:7) and as one whose prayer is "pure" (*zak*; 16:17; 11:4; 33:9). Bildad suggests, however, that these are conditions yet to be fulfilled. While he does not explicitly deny that Job possesses these qualities, he seems far less certain than God that Job is who he claims to be.

If Job is truly devout and morally pure, *then* he can know with certainty that God will restore him (vv. 6b-7). Job will receive his "rightful place" (*nĕwat ṣidqekā*). The expression is ambiguous. It may be taken in a literal sense to mean the home or habitation that is rightfully his (cf. Jer 23:5), in which case the promise would be that Job's estate, his possessions, will be restored. The phrase may also be used poetically to describe the place where "righteousness" dwells, in which case the focus would be more on the restoration of Job's status. The substance of v. 7 may tilt the interpreter toward the former option rather than the latter. If he proves himself worthy, then Job's "beginning" (*rēšît*), that is, his past, will be small when compared with his "latter days" (*ʾaḥărît*), that is, his future. Bildad's prediction turns out to be true, although the outcome may raise more questions than it answers. According to the epilogue, God "blessed the latter days (*ʾaḥărît*) of Job more than his beginning (*mērēʾšitô*)" by doubling his former possessions (42:12). The irony of this final scene, however, is that Job receives God's blessing without fulfilling the conditions spelled out for him by Bildad and his friends. The question thus becomes, "Does God bless Job *in spite of* his refusal to follow the tenets of retribution theology, or *because* of it?"

Examples of God's Justice, 8:8-19

Bildad buttresses his argument concerning God's justice by appealing to the wisdom of the ancestors (vv. 8-10). He then illustrates the truth about the destiny of the wicked and the righteous with two examples drawn from the world of nature (vv. 11-19).

Bildad directs Job to search for the wisdom bequeathed by the "first generation" (*dor rîsôn*; v. 8). [Appeal to Ancient Tradition] The language suggests that Job is to study not only the teaching of previous generations but also the primordial wisdom that inheres in the origins of the cosmos (cf. Deut 4:32; Isa 40:21). Bildad designates that primal wisdom as *ḥēqer*. The verbal root from which this noun derives (*ḥāqar*) refers to searching out a subject by probing to the very limits for its fullest meaning (e.g., Job 28:3). It is this probing of the outermost boundaries of creation's truth that informs the teaching of the ancestors. NRSV misses the literality of the expression but captures its essential thrust nicely: "consider what the ancestors have found (*ḥēqer 'ăbôtām*)." Like Eliphaz (6:27), Bildad claims to be an authoritative spokesperson who can provide Job access to knowledge that will enlarge and correct his limited understanding.

The rationale for appealing to the ancestors is that every individual's experience is limited (vv. 9-10). Human beings (presumably Bildad

Appeal to Ancient Tradition

The appeal to ancient tradition is a genre found in the Hebrew Bible (e.g., Deut 4:32-35; 32:7-9; Isa 40:21-24; 46:8-11; Jer 18:13) and in ancient Near Eastern texts. One example is the Mesopotamian text *Instructions of Shuruppak*, which recounts the instructions of the survivor of the flood to his son. One part of these instructions resembles the admonitions of Bildad:

Every day worship your god.
Sacrifice and benediction are the proper accompaniment of incense.
Present your free-will offering to your god,
For this is proper toward the gods.
Prayer, supplication, and prostration
Offer him daily, and *you will get* your reward.
Then you will have full communion with your god.

The seminal study of this genre is that of N. Habel, "Appeal to Ancient Tradition," ZAW 88 (1976): 253-63; see further *The Book of Job* (OTL; Philadelphia: Westminster Press, 1985), 170-71. He identifies the major features of the form as follows: (1) an opening formula of appeal, such as "inquire now" (Job 8:8); (2) the designation of the past as ancient and authoritative; (3) the citation of a known tradition, often in proverbial form, as in Job 8:1; and (4) the application of the traditional teaching to a specific situation, as in Job 8:20-22.

W. G. Lambert, *Babylonian Wisdom Literature* (Oxford: Clarendon Press, 1960), 105.

included) are but frail creatures who live a few years and die. They are creatures of "yesterday" whose lives are too short to acquire the wisdom that has been accumulated since the beginnings of time. Their knowledge is limited to one lifetime; their insights are informed by one set of experiences, which is to say, Bildad suggests, that left to their own personal resources individuals "know nothing." Job has claimed to know something about life that is as ephemeral as a "shadow" (*ṣēl*; 7:2; the same word occurs in 8:9), but Bildad senses that Job's personal affliction has distorted his perspective. Job has made the mistake of assuming that his experience provides the only lens through which to view the whole of human existence. As one who looks on suffering from a safe distance, Bildad believes he has the advantage of a more dispassionate perspective. Pain is for him something more to be studied and analyzed than felt. He is confident that if Job will but listen, the sages will teach him how to contextualize his misfortune with "words out of their understanding."

The understanding that Bildad would impart is couched in the form of a proverbial saying (v. 11), which he then proceeds to develop with a parable of two plants (vv. 12-15, 16-19) that illustrates the respective fates of the wicked and the righteous. In keeping with his previous strategy, Bildad presents the truth of the proverb in the form of a rhetorical question (cf. v. 3), which invites Job to reach an expected answer. "Can papyrus grow where there is no marsh? Can reeds flourish where there is no water?" The obvious answer to both questions is "No." Neither the papyrus nor the reed, both aquatic plants, can survive without a constant source of water to sustain them. From this general observation, Bildad turns to a more specific illustration that begins to sharpen the imagery with respect to what Job needs to learn. He describes a plant, still fresh and uncut, that withers and dies unexpectedly (v. 12). In the context of the proverb, the *cause* that explains this *effect* is a lack of water. Verse 13 applies this illustration to those who "forget God" (*šōkhê 'ēl*) and are "godless" (*ḥānēp*). To "forget" God is not a failure to remember; it is rather an act of opposing or abandoning God (e.g., Isa 65:11; Hos 2:13 [MT 2:15]. The parallel expression "godless" derives from a root word meaning "to be perverted." In this context, the noun describes those whose lives are a "perversion" or a "distortion" of what God intends. All such persons deprive themselves of the source of their existence. The "paths" (*'orḥôt*; cf. LXX: *ta eschata*, "the destiny") they follow lead to certain destruction. Several images embellish this thought. The "hope" (*tiqwāh*; see [Hope]) of the wicked perishes (v. 13b); their "confidence" collapses (v. 14a);[4] their trust is a "spider's house" (v. 14b); the house upon which they lean "will not stand" (v. 15).

Verses 16-19 are problematic. Some have interpreted them as a continuation of the description of the godless (cf. vv. 12-15) who initially thrive but ultimately perish.[5] A strong case can be made, however, in favor of seeing here a reference to a second plant that provides a contrasting image of the blameless person who may suffer adversities but will ultimately thrive. Similar comparisons of the wicked and the righteous to two plants occur in both ancient Near Eastern and biblical traditions, suggesting that Bildad is drawing upon a common practice to reinforce what he considers to be a traditional teaching. [The Tradition of the Two Plants]

The Tradition of the Two Plants

R. Gordis has presented a convincing argument in support of interpreting vv. 16-19 with reference to a second plant that symbolizes the destiny of the righteous person. Among the reasons he cites are the following: (1) v. 12 describes a plant that has withered; v. 16, a plant that remains fresh and moist; (2) v. 17 continues the imagery by describing the plant's vigor; (3) v. 19 advances the imagery by describing the resilience of a plant that can grow, even in a new environment; and (4) v. 20 provides a summary of the two plants by depicting the first (vv. 12-15) as an analogue for the destiny of the righteous, the second (vv. 16-19) as an analogue for the fate of the wicked. In literary terms, v. 20 completes a chiastic parallelism (which takes the shape of the Greek letter *chi*, X) that begins with v. 12:

vv. 12-15 the plant that withers   v. 20a the blameless person

vv. 16-19 the plant that survives   v. 20b the evildoers

A similar interpretation was offered by the medieval Jewish commentator Saadiah. Further, the rhetorical strategy of using two plants to describe the destinies of the righteous and the wicked occurs also in Jer 17:5-8 and Psalm 1. In the former text, the wicked are cursed "like a shrub in the desert" (v. 6); the righteous, by contrast, are blessed "like a tree planted by water" (v. 8). Habel calls attention to a similar parable in *The Instruction of Amenemope*:

As for the heated man of a temple,
He is like a tree growing in the open.
In the completion of a moment (comes) its loss of foliage,
And its end is reached in the shipyards . . .
(But) the truly silent man holds himself apart.
He is like a tree growing in the *garden*.
It flourishes and doubles its yield;
It stands before its lord.
Its fruit is sweet; its shade is pleasant;
And its end is reached in the garden . . . (Habel, *Book of Job*, 171-72; the text may be consulted in *ANET*, 3rd ed. with supplement, ed. J. B. Pritchard [Princeton: Princeton University Press, 1969], 422)

R. Gordis, *The Book of Job: Commentary, New Translation, and Special Studies* (New York: Jewish Theological Seminary of America, 1978), 521. Gordis's interpretation has been followed by a number of scholars, e.g., N. Habel, *The Book of Job: A Commentary* (OTL; Philadelphia: Westminster Press, 1985), 177-78; J. Hartley, *The Book of Job* (NICOT; Grand Rapids MI: William B. Eerdmans, 1988), 162-63; J. Gerald Janzen, *Job* (Atlanta: John Knox, 1985), 85-86; C. Newsom, "The Book of Job," in vol. 4 of *NIB* (Nashville: Abingdon Press, 1996), 402-403. Saadiah ben Joseph al-Fayyumi, *The Book of Theodicy*, trans. L. E. Goodman (New Haven: Yale University Press, 1988), 217, 220.

Verse 16 introduces the contrast with what has preceded by describing a second plant that remains lush (*rāṭōp*; "moist, juicy") even in the hot sun. Its shoots spread out beyond the borders of its garden (v. 16b); its roots twine around piles of rocks, as if they are spying out foundations for the construction of a "house of stone" (*bēt ʾăbānîm*; v. 17). The imagery suggests that this plant is a metaphor for the righteous who are well nourished and solidly grounded, unlike the godless whose abode is as flimsy as the "house of a spider" (v. 14). Verses 18-19 focus the metaphor in ways that apply more specifically to Job's circumstances. When a strong plant appears to be "swallowed up" (*bālaʿ*; "devoured, destroyed"), its former place in the garden not only eliminated but "denied," it may nevertheless find "joy in its way" (v. 19a: *mĕśôś darkô*; NRSV: "happy ways"). It is difficult to determine precisely what constitutes this joy because of ambiguity in the word *ʾaḥēr*, which occurs in the latter half of v. 19. If we are correct in understanding this second plant as a metaphor for the righteous, then two possible interpretations may be considered. The word may be taken as an adjective that describes some "*other* soil" in which the plant will emerge in defiance of all obstacles to its growth, e.g., "from some other soil it will sprout again."[6] It may also be taken as an adverb designating some "*later* time" when the plant will thrive, despite its initial difficulties, e.g., "from the soil later it will sprout."[7] With either reading, Bildad seems to be promising Job a restoration, *if* he is truly righteous. Like the plant so deeply rooted that it survives every adversity, Job can expect to endure and overcome his calamity, *provided* his faith remains fixed on God. [Those Who Are Just Need Have No Fear]

Those Who Are Just Need Have No Fear
Cardinal Wolsey offers similar advice to his servant Cromwell:

Be just, and fear not.
Let all the ends thou aim'st at be thy country's,
Thy God's, and truth's; then, if thou falls't, O Cromwell,
Thou falls't a blessed martyr. (*Henry VIII*, III, ii, 446-449)

God's Justice Will Work for Job, 8:20-22

Bildad closes his teaching on reward and punishment by offering a positive response to the question he had first posed only rhetorically in v. 3. "Does God pervert justice?" Two affirmations (v. 20) provide an unequivocal answer. God will not reject a "blameless" (*tām*) person, and God will not strengthen the hand of "evildoers" (*mĕrēʿîm*). The term "blameless" recalls the prologue's initial presentation of Job, hence Bildad (unwittingly) echoes a truth about Job that endorses what both the narrator (1:1) and God (1:8; 2:3) have already concluded. On this side of the prologue, however, Bildad's words have a tin sound to them. While it may be true enough in theory that *God* does not "reject" (*māʾas*) the blameless, Bildad seems oblivious to the fact that he now addresses one whose suffering has driven him to "reject" (*mā'as*, 7:16; NRSV: "spurn") the life offered him by this God. In practical terms, Job has expressed his disdain for life with words that are vexed and grievous. They are hammered out on the anvil of "anguish" and "bitterness" (7:11) until they conform to his experience. Bildad has listened, but he remains confident nonetheless that God will fill Job's mouth with the more appropriate sounds of "laughter" and "joy" (v. 21). The promise is consistent with Bildad's strategy of keeping Job focused on *past* convictions and *future* possibilities (cf. v. 7). In his "objective" assessment, the *present,* so often a painful hiatus that erases former certainties and thwarts future hopes, has little or no bearing on the life of faith.

He concludes with a final promise that seeks to move Job from where he is to where he should be. In the previous speech, Job reached such a level of despair about life that he concluded by expressing the expectation, indeed the hope, that he would simply die. If he could obtain this one objective, then he would claim his victory with a stark finality: "I shall not be" (*'ēnennî*; 7:21; cf. 7:8). Bildad counters that it will be Job's enemies (lit., "those who hate you") who will be "no more" (*'ēnennû*; v. 22). They will be "clothed with shame" (*yilbešû bōšet*). The metaphor envisions shame as a garment that signifies disgrace and humiliation (cf. Jer 14:3; 22:22, both cases with the parallel term *klm*, "to be humiliated"). It is likely that Bildad simply intends to draw upon conventional images to describe Job's enemies, but once again (cf. vv. 6-7) his choice of terms makes him more of a prophet than he intends to be. In psalms of lament, the enemies are those who look upon the suffering of the righteous and infer that they have sinned. Against those who "hate without cause" the innocent may appeal to God for the very outcome that Bildad has predicted for Job's enemies:

Do not let my treacherous enemies rejoice over me, or those who hate me without cause (*ḥinnam*; cf. Job 1:9; 2:3) wink the eye.

Let all those who rejoice at my calamity be put to shame and confusion; let those who exalt themselves against me be clothed with shame (*yilbešû bōšet*) and dishonor. (Ps 35:19, 26; cf. 109:29)

When we reach the end of the dialogues, it will become clear that in Job's case the ones who are his enemies, the ones who will be judged by God as having not spoken the truth about him, will be none other than Bildad and his friends (cf. 42:7-8).[8] ["Hoist with His Own Petard"]

> **"Hoist with His Own Petard"**
>
> 📖 The Joban poet may be subtly hinting that Bildad's theology is in reality more a criticism of himself and the friends than of Job. If so, the strategy resembles the famous words of Hamlet concerning those who conspire against him:
>
> There's letters seal'd: and my two schoolfellows, —
> Whom I will trust as I will adders fang'd, —
> They bear the mandate; they must sweep my way,
> And marshal me to knavery. Let it work;
> For 'tis the sport to have the engineer
> Hoist with his own petard. (*Hamlet*, III, iv, 203-207)
>
> In popular usage, to be "hoist with one's own petard" has become a metaphor for being snared in the trap of one's own thinking. Two additional notes sharpen the meaning in a delightfully wicked way: (1) a "petard" is a metal cone used in ancient warfare as an explosive device for creating holes in fortress gates and walls; and (2) the word "petard" derives from the French *peter* and ultimately from the Latin *peder*, both of which mean "to break wind," or, less euphemistically, "to fart."

CONNECTIONS

Commentators rightly observe that the presentation of Bildad in chapter 8 is hardly flattering. C. Newsom's assessment is representative. She notes that the poet depicts him as a "rigid, doctrinaire moralist who loses his humanity in his desire to perceive the world according to a set of rules."[9] Even so, the Joban drama intends that the merits of Bildad's retribution theology be considered carefully. The question that invites reflection is not, "Why is Bildad wrong?" but rather, "What if Bildad is right?" What if God is a God who operates according to the guarantees that are implicit in an "if . . . then" theology? Further, what would faith look like if its sole objective was to satisfy the preexisting conditions of a contractual God? These and other issues related to retribution theology require more attention than can be given in a single exposition. Subsequent speeches by the friends (e.g., 11:13-20; 22:21-30) will articulate this theology from other angles and will provide opportunities for additional reflection. At this juncture, two issues will be examined: (1) the God of "if . . . then" theology; and (2) faith construed by the claims of "if . . . then" theology.

The God of "If . . . Then" Theology

Bildad's first articulation about God occurs in v. 3: "Does God pervert justice?" For him, the question is purely rhetorical, which is to say it is not a real question. It is not a request for information. It is rather an assertion, veiled as a question, which serves to rebuke the questioner. God is just. Any probings that look beyond this assertion are not only unthinkable, they are illegitimate. Such a theology is both a comfort and a burden. It is surely a comfort, if not a necessity, to be able to say with conviction that God is just, or as Bildad puts it, that "God will not reject a blameless person, nor take the hand of evildoers" (v. 20). Without this plank in the foundation, any house that faith would build could hardly be secure. Nonetheless, it is Bildad's unfazed certainty about God that the Jobs of this world may find heavy and perplexing.

Is it true that God cannot be questioned? Are all questions about God's justice only rhetorical, imaginary puzzlements that one may ponder for a moment before dismissing them with guaranteed answers? Bildad implies as much, but his confidence bears the stamp of one whose reservoir of "truths" about God has thus far not been seriously unsettled by the vagaries of suffering. His freedom from pain affords him the luxury of an analytical certainty about God that Job's experience cannot match. Bildad's God is safely ensconced in principles and maxims that invite no scrutiny and brook no doubt. If there is suffering, then there must be sin. The linkage between cause and effect is consistent and predictable, effectively removing God from direct involvement in the deliberative process. *If* X occurs, *then* Y is the automatic response. The question of God's justice is not only not in play, it is also off limits, for when one strays into such matters, the very nature of God may become suspect, compromising the entire system of divine governance. ["God Is Unthinkable if We Are Innocent"] Bildad warns Job against such misdirected ventures by advocating a quid pro quo theology that shields God's decisions against protest or appeal.

Job's suffering, however, has collapsed the prearranged boundaries of faith that Bildad so fearfully guards. His are the convictions of one whose encounters with life forge a credo of tenuous assertions and unrelenting questions. What kind of God will Bildad's God be for Job? Bildad seems certain that he speaks for God when he rebukes Job by asking impatiently, "How long will you say these things?" (v. 2). As the spokesperson for orthodoxy, he is no doubt justifiably anxious about the threat that Job represents to him and his world. Questioning is indeed a profoundly dangerous act, for it dares to contemplate that the status quo can, perhaps should, be changed, corrected, even rejected. When Job persists in asking "Why?" and "What?" and when he insists that these questions are not rhetorical but real and deserving of God's attention, he pokes at "given truths," which Bildad presumes are necessary, solid, and permanent.

"God Is Unthinkable if We Are Innocent"

Bildad would presumably be satisfied to elicit from Job a response like that of J.B., who struggles with any conclusion other than that he suffers because he is guilty:

God is God or we are nothing—
Mayflies that leave their husks behind—
Our tiny lives ridiculous—a suffering
Not even sad that Someone Somewhere
Laughs at as we laugh at apes.
We have no choice but to be guilty.
God is unthinkable if we are innocent.

A. MacLeish, *J.B.* (Boston: Houghton Mifflin Co., 1956), 111.

So the question remains. What if Bildad is right about God? What if God is the system, and the system is God? What if it is true that God will not be questioned and will not tolerate those who try? What if the sum total of who God is can be calculated within the equation *if* X *then* Y? If readers are to enter fully into what is at stake in the book of Job, then they must be willing to take these questions seriously. To *assume* that Bildad is simply wrong would be to treat his arguments with the same disdain that he shows for Job. Furthermore, should there be any doubt that Bildad's theology continues to enjoy widespread support among clergy and parishioners alike, one need look no further than last Sunday's sermon in "Anytown" USA. What if Bildad *is* right? Contemporary readers, like Job, must come to their own conclusions. When those conclusions have been reached, then two further questions will demand attention. If God *cannot* be questioned, what price does this truth exact from the Jobs of this world whose questions are imperative, not optional? If God *can* be questioned, not only rhetorically but actually, then what price does this exact from orthodoxy, which endeavors to speak a truth about God that will stand the test of life? ["Whatever Else God May Be, He Shouldn't Be Pat"]

"Whatever Else God May Be, He Shouldn't Be Pat"

In *Roger's Version*, John Updike describes a conversation between Robert Lambert, a divinity school professor, and Dale Kohler, a graduate school student in computer science who wants to secure his help in procuring a grant that will enable him to prove scientifically that God exists. Like all good professors, Dr. Lambert is trained to be comfortable with ambiguity. He is more than reluctant to encourage what he perceives in this student to be misplaced and immature fervor:

> For myself, I must confess that I find your idea aesthetically and ethically repulsive. Aesthetically because it describes a God Who lets Himself be intellectually trapped, and ethically because it eliminates faith from religion, it takes away our freedom to believe or doubt. A God you could prove makes the whole thing immensely, oh, uninteresting. Pat. Whatever else God may be, He shouldn't be pat. (24)

The student is undaunted by the professor's wisdom. He senses that Dr. Lambert has grown so comfortable with ambiguity that he not only distrusts certainty, he also fears it.

> You don't want God to break through. People in general don't want that. They just want to grub along being human, and dirty, and sly, and amusing, and having their weekends with Michelob, and God to stay put in the churches if they decide ever to drop by . . . (21)

> But sir, think of the comfort to all those who want to believe but don't dare, because they've been intellectually intimidated. Think of the reassurance to all those in trouble or in pain and wanting to pray. (24)

The conundrum explored by these two illustrates nicely the issues that Bildad's theology presents. On the one hand, God "shouldn't be pat"; on the other, "think of all the comfort" that certainty offers.

J. Updike, *Roger's Version* (New York: Alfred A. Knopf, 1986).

Covenant and Blessing

From the Old Testament perspective, one may reflect on the truth of covenant theology, with its promise of blessing or cursing. A classic example occurs in Deut 28 (for further discussion see **[Retribution]**):

If you will obey the Lord your God, by diligently observing all his commandments that I am commanding you today, the Lord your God will set you high above the nations of the earth; all these blessings shall come upon you and overtake you, if you obey the Lord your God . . .

But if you will not obey the Lord your God by diligently observing all his commandments and decrees, which I am commanding you today, then all these curses shall come upon you and overtake you. (Deut 28:1-3, 15)

From a Christian perspective, one may consider numerous examples of assurance theology from hymnody. One example is "Blessed Assurance, Jesus is Mine":

Blessed assurance Jesus is mine! Oh what a foretaste of
glory divine! Heir of salvation, purchase of God,
Born of His Spirit, washed in His blood.

Faith Construed by the Claims of "If . . . Then" Theology

If Job were to put into practice Bildad's "if. . . then" theology, what would his faith look like? The question invites reflection on a number of issues, two of which may be singled out. First, Bildad proposes that faith exercises a contractual relationship with God. If Job practices piety and moral purity, then God will restore him (vv. 5-6). On the surface, the promise seems both logical and attractive. It affirms that religion works, as we moderns might say. The life of faith is not only good, it is also good for you. If you practice its requirements, then you will reap its benefits. Because rewards and punishments are spelled out clearly in relation to behavior that is prescribed and prohibited, one can enter into relationship with God knowing full well that if the conditions are met, then the end result is guaranteed. Moreover, the idea that faith is a sort of contractual relationship with God has a firm foundation in the biblical tradition and in the model of piety that it bequeaths to us. In religious terms, we designate the contract as a "covenant." The blessings that equate with obedience we receive as the "assurances of faith." [Covenant and Blessing] The Bible commends numerous exemplars of such faith, none more compellingly than Job himself, especially as he is portrayed in the prologue. Job is "blameless and upright" *and* "There were born to him seven sons and three daughters. He had seven thousand sheep, three thousand camels. . ." (1:1ff.).

It is the connection between Job's piety *and* his prosperity, however, that the *satan* calls into question. "Does Job fear God for nothing?" (1:9). The *satan's* observation is precisely that faith based solely on the promise of reward is no faith at all. If Job loves God because of what he gets in return, then his love is conditional, not free. God seems to agree that the matter is worthy of investigation and hands Job over to the *satan* to see what Job will do when the linkage between "if" and "then" is broken. At this point in the drama, it is fair to assume that Job himself now has serious questions about whether the rewards of faith are worth the costs. Bildad would reassure him that they are. But what if Job follows Bildad's counsel? *If* he seeks God *in return for* a blessing, *if* he is righteous *in exchange for* restoration, *then* will he not be validating the *satan's* suspicion that piety is little more than a camouflage for what might otherwise be called merely a "wise investment"? If Job does what Bildad tells him to do, will he model the piety God hopes for, or not?[10] The resolution of this question is made more difficult, not less, by the fact that at the end of the story God does in fact restore Job (42:7-17). The *satan's* question remains central, thus reminding interpreters that the requirements of faith can seldom, if ever, be equated with simplistic calculations (*if* X . . .) and guaranteed results (. . . *then* Y).

A second issue for reflection is Bildad's construal of faith in terms of past experiences and future hopes. Job's perspective on life is framed and focused by deep anguish that is relentlessly present (7:1-6). His days are too short to provide relief; his nights are too long and offer no rest. Suffering affords him no point of view beyond the sad constraints of the present. ["Depression Is Atemporal"] Bildad subtly avoids dealing with Job's present. His hope remains resolutely focused on the future, what he calls Job's "latter days," which he is confident will provide restoration that will erase the memory of what he has experienced (v. 7). In effect, he summons Job to a faith in what will be, but he gives him no word that connects with where he is.

In his novel *A Place on Earth*, Wendell Berry describes the tragedy that defines the world of the Feltners. Their only son, Virgil, went off to war and has been listed as "missing in action." He has been missing so long that the family must now admit to themselves that Virgil is dead. Into this scene of death and loss comes their minister, Brother Preston. Upon his arrival, the family dries up its tears and listens for the word from God that might speak to their grief. Brother Preston speaks to them about heavenly things, truths about the "Hereafter," but his words seem oddly disconnected from the hurt that gnaws away at their insides. They listen patiently and respectfully, until the minister has had his say. When he finishes he excuses himself and returns to the church to prepare Sunday's sermon.

After he leaves the Feltners resume their crying. Matt, the father, reflects on the gap between the words of heavenly hope that Brother Preston offered to them and the hurt they feel so deeply that they cannot hear. Matt comes to this conclusion: "In the preacher's words the Heavenly City has risen up, surmounting [our] lives, the house, the town—the final hope, in which all riddles and ends of the world are gathered, illuminated, and bound." But, Matt continues, "This is the

"Depression Is Atemporal"

Writing from personal experience essayist and novelist Andrew Solomon provides one example of how the Jobs of this world might struggle to find the wisdom in Bildad's counsel:

When you are depressed, the past and the future are absorbed entirely by the present, as in the world of a three-year-old. You can neither remember feeling better nor imagine that you will feel better. Being upset, even profoundly upset, is a temporal experience, whereas depression is atemporal. Depression means that you have no point of view.

A. Solomon, "Anatomy of Melancholy," *The New Yorker*, 12 January 1998, 49.

"Let Us Stand, Then, in the Interval of Our Wounding"

The archer with time
as his arrow—has he broken
his strings that the rainbow
is so quiet over our village?

Let us stand, then, in the interval
of our wounding, till the silence
turn golden and love is
a moment eternally flowing.

R. S. Thomas, "Evening," *No Truce with the Furies* (Newcastle upon Tyne: Bloodaxe Books, 1995), 19.

preacher's hope, and he has moved to it alone, outside the claims of time and sorrow."[11]

Such is the nature of "if . . . then" theology. It is sometimes better fitted to analyze the past and predict the future than to enter into the "claims of time and sorrow" that so constrict the present of sufferers like Job. ["Let Us Stand, Then, in the Interval of Our Wounding"]

NOTES

[1] J. Hartley, *The Book of Job* (NICOT; Grand Rapids MI: William B. Eerdmans, 1988), 156.

[2] Janzen observes that Bildad's rhetorical question likely rings "unrhetorically" in Job's ears, inviting from him the very charge Bildad hopes to block. In this respect Bildad plays a role similar to that of Job's wife, whose question in 2:9 draws out feelings that will not for long remain unspoken by Job (J. Gerald Janzen, *Job* [Atlanta: John Knox, 1985], 87-88).

[3] D. Clines, *Job 1–20* (WBC; Dallas: Word Books, 1989), 203. For the argument that the word *'im* ("if") in v. 4 is used to express emphasis ("indeed," "surely"), not conditionality, see R. Gordis, *The Book of Job: Commentary, New Translation, and Special Studies* (New York: Jewish Theological Seminary of America, 1978), 88.

[4] The meaning of v. 14a is uncertain. The MT has the word *yaqot,* presumably from the root *qwt,* which seems to mean "break, snap." Because this is the only occurrence of the word, however, commentators have proposed a variety of emendations. NRSV follows a common approach by understanding the word as a noun that refers to some form of "thread," as in a thin gossamer-like string. Although such a rendering provides a nice parallel with "spider's house" in the latter half of the verse, it remains conjectural.

[5] E.g., S. Terrien, "The Book of Job," *IB,* vol. 3, ed. G. Buttrick (New York: Abingdon Press, 1954), 974; G. Fohrer, *Das Buch Hiob* (KAT; Gutersloh: Gerd Mohn, 1963), 193; Clines, *Job 1–20*, 209-10; E. M. Good, *In Turns of Tempest: A Reading of Job with a Translation* (Stanford: Stanford University Press, 1990), 219-20. NRSV adopts this interpretation by adding the phrase "the wicked" to the beginning of the verse and translating the adjective *ratop,* "moist, juicy," as a verb: "The wicked thrive."

[6] So Gordis, *Book of Job,* 93; cf. N. Habel, "That from the dust it shoots up elsewhere" (*The Book of Job: A Commentary* [OTL; Philadelphia: Westminster Press, 1985], 168).

[7] So Janzen, who notes further that the word "later" (*'aḥēr*) echoes Bildad's description in 8:7 of Job's restoration in the "latter (*'aḥărît*) days" (*Job,* 86).

[8] Cf. Clines, *Job 1–20*, 211; C. Newsom, "The Book of Job," in vol. 4 of *NIB* (Nashville: Abingdon Press, 1996), 403.

[9] Newsom, "The Book of Job," 401.

[10] Clines makes the point similarly. If Job follows Bildad's prescription for faith, "he will have proved that he does not 'fear God for nought' (1:9); he will have allowed his desperate need to determine his behavior toward God and made his piety into a means from improving his sorry lot" (*Job 1–20,* 212).

[11] W. Berry, *A Place on Earth* (San Francisco: North Point, 1983), 94.

JOB'S RESPONSE TO BILDAD: THE IMPERATIVE AND THE IMPOSSIBILITY OF PUTTING GOD ON TRIAL

Job 9:1–10:22

Job's first response to the friends (chs. 6–7) was a cacophony of "anguish" and "bitterness of soul" (7:11) that was passionate but uncentered. In the throes of his suffering, Job sought desperately, but futilely, for some stabilizing perspective that would enable him to hold his ground and fight for his vin-

dication. In his second response, Job's "bitterness of soul" (10:1) remains unabated, but he now begins to grope towards a centering idea that will provide the basis for sustaining the passion, hence the hope, which resides so tenuously inside his grief. [CD: "Hopeless Grief"] What organizes his anguish in these chapters is

Structure of Job 9:1–10:22

	9:1-13	The impossibility of challenging God in court
	9:14-24	In God's court might makes right
	9:25-35	Job considers other possibilities
	10:1-17	Job rehearses the case he will bring against God
	10:18-22	A return to lament: "Why did *you* bring me forth from the womb?"

the daring notion that he might put God on trial. [Structure of Job 9:1–10:22]

He imagines entering into a lawsuit in which he is the plaintiff and God is the defendant (9:2-4). He would question God about the actions that have been taken against him. Did God hand him and his family over to affliction? What are God's motives in consigning innocent children to death and innocent parents to bereavement and torment? Can these motives be justified? Is God right to deal with human beings in this manner? As the defendant, God would be expected to answer the questions, explain divine actions, and counter with questions that Job himself would have to address. Through examination and cross-examination, the two litigants would argue their respective positions until one or the other could prove their case satisfactorily before an impartial jury.

Job knows all too well that putting God on trial is impossible. God is the sovereign Creator of the world (9:5-10). Who can say to God "What are you doing?" (9:12). Who can summon God into court (9:19)? The idea that God and Job "should come to trial together"

(9:32) is transparently absurd, for God is not a mere mortal like Job who can be questioned and summoned to respond. Job, quite logically, considers other options for addressing his situation (9:25-35).

Nonetheless, the idea of confronting God in a court of law continues to hold Job's imagination, and he proceeds to envision the case he would make, if only he had the chance (10:1-17). Having seized on the notion of a trial as his best hope, Job nevertheless concedes that it will not happen, and he descends once more into the abiding despair that defines his miserable existence (10:18-22). For failed litigants like Job, dispute with the Judge of the world yields only unanswered questions ("Why?"), plaintive petitions ("Let me alone"), and an empty future in Sheol, where "light is like darkness."

COMMENTARY

The Impossibility of Challenging God in Court, 9:1-13

Job offers a two-pronged critique of God's justice that responds to both Eliphaz (9:1-13; cf. 4:17-21) and Bildad (9:14-24; cf. 8:3). He begins with what initially seems to be an unqualified affirmation of Eliphaz's argument that it is impossible for mortals to be righteous before God (4:17): "Truly, I know that this is so; how can a mortal be just (*ṣdq*) before God?" The opening word "truly" (*'omnām*) comes from a Hebrew root that means "to be trustworthy, reliable, firm." A more familiar form of this adverb is *'āmēn*, "amen, truly," a solemn oath formula used to indicate that something which has been said is accepted as true and valid (e.g., Deut 27:15-27 [12x]). Job *agrees* that is impossible to be *ṣdq* before God, but his affirmation is different, and it is made on other grounds. Eliphaz interprets *ṣdq* to mean "righteous" in a moral and religious sense (cf. Gen 38:26). His argument is that no human being can be considered righteous in relation to God, because mortals are by definition sinful, morally flawed, creatures. As a consequence, they cannot stand before a perfectly righteous God and raise questions about who suffers and why (see commentary on 4:7–5:7). Job, however, interprets *ṣdq* to mean "innocent" in a legal sense (cf. Exod 23:7; Deut 25:1). His affirmation is that human beings could not obtain a legal verdict of "innocent" if they were so bold as to enter into a lawsuit with God. The sense of Job's statement is captured by REB: "no one can win his case against God" (cf. NJPS, TEV). The impossibility of being innocent before God, Job contends, is not because *humans* are morally imperfect, but because *God* skews the legal processes for obtaining justice.

Job makes his first tentative exploration of the idea of putting God
on trial in vv. 3-4. He will take up the idea once again in 9:14-24 and
in 10:1-17. In subsequent speeches, the image of a trial with God will
increasingly emerge as a central objective in Job's quest for justice. [The
Trial Metaphor in Job] Job's initial consideration of the idea focuses on the
futility of filing a suit against God.

He acknowledges at the outset that two fundamental characteristics
of God present any would-be litigant with insurmountable problems.
First, if one were to "contend" (*rîb*, "hold a trial") with God, "one
could not answer him once in a thousand times" (v. 3). Because the
Hebrew text uses pronouns ("one," "him") rather than proper nouns, it
is possible to interpret Job's words in different ways. The translation in
NRSV understands the phrase to mean that a *person* (i.e., Job) could
not answer one of the charges that God would bring against him. Such

---

The Trial Metaphor in Job

Legal language describing God and people as litigants in a trial occurs frequently in the Hebrew
Bible. A variety of terms convey the idea, especially the
word *rîb*, "strive, contend" (e.g., Job 9:3; 10:2), which is
used in both verbal and nominal forms to describe the
process by which two opposing parties settle a dispute. The
process envisioned is a lawsuit in which one person presents charges against another. The case proceeds through
examination and cross-examination until the charges are
proven true or false. Normally, God is depicted as the plaintiff (and judge) in such cases, and God's adversaries (e.g.,
individuals, Israel, foreign nations) are the defendants.
Prophetic judgment speeches, for example, frequently use
the trial metaphor to describe the process by which God
indicts, examines, and ultimately judges Israel for failing to
obey the covenant. Micah 6:1-4 is a representative text.

Apart from Job, only Jeremiah dares to imagine so boldly
that he will reverse the process and become the plaintiff
who summons God into court to answer the charges that
God, not he, is the one who is guilty of injustice (Jer 12:1-4).

What for Jeremiah is but a fleeting thought becomes for
Job a primary objective. A number of studies have called
attention to the importance of the trial motif in Job. The
most comprehensive analysis is that of N. Habel, who
argues that this metaphor is a major literary device, which
integrates the plot of the book and the theological motif of
Job's quest for justice. In his view, the coherence of the
book may be discerned if it is viewed as a form of "ring
composition," which moves from beginning to middle to
end, with each major stage matched by its complement (A
is matched with A1, B with B1, and so forth). The turning

point in the development of the legal process, according to
Habel's analysis, is in Job 29–31, where Job declares an
oath of innocence (29–30) and formally challenges his
adversary (God) to appear in court (31:35-37).

One need not agree with every detail of Habel's analysis
to appreciate the argument that the trial motif is of major literary and theological importance in the book of Job. Its
dominance in the book suggests that Job expects justice to
be a primary quality of the relationship with God. Without
justice, can there be a meaningful relationship with God?
Job's perspective is not unlike that of Abraham who,
sensing that God may no longer be concerned to distinguish
between the righteous and the wicked, also urges God to
remember that justice is a fundamental requisite of the
"Judge of all the earth": "Far be it from you to do such a
thing, to slay the righteous with the wicked, so that the
righteous fare as the wicked! Far be that from you! Shall not
the Judge of all the earth do what is just?" (Gen 18:25).

For further reading on the trial motif in Job, see J. J. M.
Roberts, "Job's Summons to Yahweh: The Exploitation of a
Legal Metaphor," ResQ 16 (1973): 159-63; M. B. Dick, "The
Legal Metaphor in Job 31," CBQ 41 (1979): 37-50; S. H.
Scholnick, "The Meaning of *mispat* (Justice) in the Book of
Job," JBL 101 (1982): 521-29; C. Schultz, "The Cohesive
Issue of *mispat* in Job," *'Go To the Land I will Show You':
Studies in Honor of Dwight W. Young*, ed. J. E. Colson, V. H.
Matthews (Winona Lake IN: Eisenbrauns, 1996), 159-75; R.
Sutherland, *Putting God on Trial: The Biblical Book of Job*
(Victoria: Trafford, 2004).

N. Habel, *The Book of Job: A Commentary* (OTL; Philadelphia:
Westminster Press, 1985), 54.

a rendering depicts God as the plaintiff in the case, Job as the defendant, a view that is consonant with the dominant use of the trial metaphor elsewhere in the Hebrew Bible (e.g., Isa 3:13; Jer 2:9; Hos 4:1; Mic 6:2). But is also possible, and in this case more likely, to interpret the phrase as meaning that *God* would not answer the charges that Job would bring (cf. REB). That Job imagines himself, not God, as the plaintiff in this case is a daring, but not unprecedented, reversal of the roles normally assigned to the parties in such lawsuits. Elsewhere in the book of Job, both Elihu (33:13) and God (40:2) affirm that this is precisely the role that Job has claimed for himself. While Job is keenly aware that he would be hard pressed to respond to God's cross-examination of him (cf. vv. 14-15), his greater concern is that God will not answer him when he pleads for justice. Both his need to challenge God and his awareness that it is futile to do so places Job in the company of Jeremiah, the one other person in the Hebrew Bible who also dares to imagine that he will take God to court, even if he is certain to lose the case: "You will win, O Lord, if I make claim (*ʾārîb*) against You, / Yet I shall present charges against You" (Jer 12:1; NJPS).

The second obstacle to bringing God to trial is God's superior wisdom and strength (v. 4). Under normal circumstances, one might expect that wisdom and strength are precisely the characteristics one looks for in a just God, but Job's suffering has left him vulnerable and fearful of an encounter with a God like this. He suspects that God will use these attributes not to redeem him but to destroy him. Faced with the prospect of such an overwhelming adversary in court, Job wonders what chance he has to prevail. Who can "resist" (*hiqšāh*) such a God and "succeed" (*yišlām*)? The figurative nature of Job's language is highly suggestive. The word "resist" means literally to "harden" or "stiffen." It generally occurs with "neck" as the object, in the sense of "stiffen the neck," a metaphor often used to describe those who stubbornly defy or oppose God (e.g., 2 Kgs 17:14; Jer 7:26; 17:23; 19:15; Neh 9:16). The word "succeed" translates a Hebrew verb (*šālam*) that means to "be safe, intact, whole." The force of Job's rhetorical question may be rendered thusly: "Who can oppose God and survive to tell about it?"

The divine attributes of wisdom and power now trigger in Job a doxology of praise (vv. 5-10), which on first impression seems to conform to the response that Eliphaz has modeled for him (5:9-16). On close inspection, however, it becomes apparent that the characteristics of God that evoke praise from Eliphaz prompt something very different from Job. Job's doxology adopts the hymnic form that is common in the Psalter. It is composed of seven participial verbs (rendered in English by relative clauses beginning with "who") that suggest Job's review of God's way of dealing with the world intends to be complete and comprehensive. The twin themes of wisdom and power, which Job treats in reverse order, provide the basis for his characterization of the God he believes he will encounter if he persists in going to trial. [CD: The Structure of Job 9:5-10]

Verses 5-7 focus on God's awesome power, which Job perceives to be destructive and brutal. God overthrows mountains, shakes the earth from its place until the pillars upon which it rests threaten to collapse, commands the sun not to rise in the day and the stars not to shine in the night. That God has the power to shake the foundations of the cosmos and convulse nature is not in itself a reason for dread. Indeed, such a description normally signals the coming of God to save the oppressed from their enemies (Nah 1:1-6; Hab 3:3-13) and to deliver the afflicted from their distress (Ps 18:6-16). Job, however, can discern nothing positive in such raw demonstrations of divine force. He can see that God is empowered to turn creation upside down and to replace order with chaos, but like the mountains (v. 5a), he does not know what God is doing or why. He senses that God's power is motivated by anger (v. 5b; cf. v. 13), but that such anger should be used to destroy creation, with no hint of compassion or redemption, offers little reason to believe that an encounter with this God will effect his restoration.

Verses 8-10 complete Job's doxology by shifting the focus from God's destructive power to God's inscrutable wisdom. He begins by cataloguing three specific examples of God's primordial creation and ordering of the world. The act of "stretching out the heavens" refers to God's unfolding the vast cosmic firmament like a tent that will provide the venue for constructing and sustaining the universe (Ps 104:2; Isa 42:5; 45:12; 51:13; Jer 10:12; Zech 12:1). It is an act that God "alone" can accomplish (cf. Isa 44:24), a fact which Elihu will subsequently use to solicit from Job an admission that he is no match for this awesome God (35:5; 36:29-30; 37:1-13, 14-20). "Trampling on the waves of the Sea (*yām*)" is an allusion to God's victory over the primordial forces of chaos represented by sea-gods (see [Ancient Near Eastern Creation Accounts]). Normally, God's defeat of Yam signifies that creation is safe and secure from the forces that seek its destruction. Job, however, fears that God has targeted him as an opponent like Yam (see commentary on 7:12); hence his praise belies the suspicion that God's creative purposes make him a marked man. The making of the constellations, an integral act through which God establishes the temporal rhythms of creation (cf. Gen 1:14), is also a conventional motif of doxologies in praise of the Creator (Amos 5:8; cf. Job 38:31-32). [The Constellations]

These specific examples are followed in v. 10 with a general statement that correlates them with the great and marvelous acts of the Creator, whose wisdom is "beyond understanding." The verse is almost a verbatim repetition of the line that Eliphaz used to introduce his model praise in 5:9. Where Job ends up, however, is not where Eliphaz intended him to be. When Job applies the conventional reasons for praising the Creator to his own life, he concludes that in his world God can neither be comprehended nor resisted (vv. 11-13). God "passes by" (*'ābar*), but Job cannot see; God "glides past" (*ḥālap*), but Job cannot discern or know who it is that has come and gone. Both verbs are used elsewhere to describe revelations in which God's presence is made available in extraordinary ways. The first describes God's appearances to Moses (Exod 33:18-23) and Elijah (1 Kgs 19:11-12), the second, the visionary encounter with God claimed by Eliphaz (4:15). For Job, such experiences disclose only that God is more absent than present. And yet Job has felt a divine presence in his life that is all too painfully real. God snatches things away at will, and there is no one who can intervene to say, "What are you doing?" (cf. Eccl 8:4; Dan 4:35 [MT 4:32]).

Job's final words return to the theme of divine anger, which he discerned at the outset to be the primary motivation behind God's frightful ways with creation (v. 13; cf. v. 5). God's anger is relentless and irresistible. It is satisfied by nothing less than total submission, the proof of which is that even the "helpers of Rahab," another of the great primordial chaos monsters (see [Leviathan]), bow the knee in helpless surrender. We might paraphrase by saying that Job concludes his doxology thusly: "Praise God whose anger rages until all creatures, earthly and cosmic, lie prostrate before the throne of divine power."[1]

Such praise may be adequate for one like Eliphaz, who seems untroubled by the mysterious ways in which God governs the world. But for one like Job, whose pain makes the quest for justice imperative, such praise evokes more questions than affirmations. Eliphaz looks on the suffering of another and is content to say, "How happy is the one whom God reproves" (5:17). Job weighs his innocence against the invincible might of the One who afflicts him arbitrarily and wonders, "How can a mortal be just before God?"

In God's Court, "Might Makes Right," 9:14-24

Job turns next to the issue triggered by Bildad's question in 8:3: "Does God pervert justice?" For Bildad, the question is merely rhetorical. Job has reason to be far less confident of the answer, and so he begins to explore matters that his friend would leave unexamined. Given God's incomparable power and impenetrable wisdom, Job ponders the interrogation that would take place in a courtroom where might makes right (vv. 14-16).[2] If the primordial forces of chaos are humbled into submission before the withering anger of this adversary, "how then" (v. 14) can a mere mortal like Job stand up to God's questions? Even though he is innocent (v. 15: *ṣādaqtî*), Job fears that he would be able to do nothing more than plead for mercy, which is precisely what Bildad had recommended he do (8:5). Bildad's counsel, however, implies that Job should adopt the stance of one who is guilty and in need of forgiveness. Job has no doubt that he is innocent (cf. vv. 20, 21), thus to be faced with only this manner of responding to God means that he must simply speak the words that he is given, whether they adequately reflect the truth of his situation or not. Similarly, when Job contemplates the prospect of examining God, he does not believe that God will answer his questions or take seriously his right to ask them.

Job's experience leads him to believe that the God he will encounter seeks his destruction (vv. 17-18). God "crushes" him with the force of a whirlwind (*śĕʿārāh*; cf. 38:1), leaving him gasping for breath. God wounds him again and again "without cause" (*ḥinnām*), until he is satiated with bitterness. The *satan* asked if Job is capable of loving God "for nothing" (1:9: *ḥinnām*), in response to which God agrees to test Job by afflicting him "for no reason" (2:9: *ḥinnām*). In the prologue, it is Job who is on trial. Now Job reverses the charges. When God assaults the innocent without reason, it is divine justice, not human fidelity, which must be put on trial. But how does one bring charges against an adversary who will not be bound by reason or logic, whose way of dealing with persons is motivated by anger (cf. vv. 5, 13) that is capricious and malevolent? ["Pain That Has But One Close"]

Job envisions two possibilities, neither of which advantages him (vv. 19-21). If justice is to be determined on the basis of power, then

---

"Pain That Has But One Close"

In "The Trial by Existence," Robert Frost reflects on the decree from God mandating that sorrow be the unavoidable test of life on earth:

> And from a cliff top is proclaimed
> The gathering of the souls for birth,
> The trial by existence named,
> The obscuration upon earth. (ll. 17-20)

Humans may "choose" how to respond to the test, but in the end they must know that the choice is only that which is offered by a cryptic deity whose objectives cannot be understood:

> 'Tis of the essence of life here,
> Though we choose greatly, still to lack
> The lasting memory at all clear,
> That life has for us on the wrack
> Nothing but what we somehow chose;

> Thus we are wholly stripped of pride
> In the pain that has but one close,
> Bearing it crushed and mystified. (ll. 65-72)

In the opening stanza of the poem, however, Frost hints that those willing to take the test of this "obscuration on earth," even if it means ultimately to be defeated by it, possess a Job-like courage that is its own reward:

> Even the bravest that are slain
> Shall not dissemble their surprise
> On waking to find valor reign,
> Even as on earth, in paradise;
> And where they sought without the sword
> Wide fields of asphodel fore'er,
> To find that the utmost reward
> Of daring should be still to dare. (ll. 1-8)

R. Frost, "The Trial by Existence," *The Poetry of Robert Frost*, ed. E. C. Lathem (New York: Henry Holt and Company, 1969), 19-21.

---

who can match the invincible strength of God? If it is to be settled on the merits of law, then who will summon God into court? Even if God were to appear in court, Job is convinced that he could not effectively argue his case. Truth would not win out, because Job's own mouth would lie against him, declaring that he was guilty, even though he knows himself to be innocent. God would prove him wrong, even though he knows himself to be "blameless" (*tām*; vv. 20, 21). The word "blameless" recalls both the narrator's and God's assessment of Job's integrity (1:1, 8; 2:3). If Job were to go to court with God, he would lose more than a legal case. He would lose his identity and his self-worth; in essence, he would lose himself. He would cease to be the righteous person that God knows him to be and would become instead someone that he could no longer recognize. The expression "I do not know myself" may be an idiom for a mental disorder of some kind, [3] but a literal rendering fits the context nicely. Job's encounter with God would leave him a shell of his former self. If to be in the presence of God means one must live a lie, then life itself becomes a thing to be despised (v. 21b; cf. 7:16). ["You Can't Pray a Lie"]

From God's failure to honor the innocence of his life, Job infers that God's governance of the cosmos disrespects fundamental distinctions between the righteous and the wicked (vv. 22-24). If a calamity like a plague or a flood brings sudden and indiscriminate death, God mocks the anguish of the innocent by failing to intervene. If a land is given into the hands of the wicked, God makes the judges indifferent to the claims of the innocent. Bildad has claimed with absolute certainty that

> **"You Can't Pray a Lie"**
>
> Job's dilemma bears some similarity to a scene that Mark Twain describes in *The Adventures of Huckleberry Finn*. In the midst of their wondrous journey down the Mississippi, Huck and Jim, the runaway slave, have once again fallen into trouble. Jim has been captured, and his captors are preparing to return him and claim the reward promised by the law of the land, unless Huck intervenes to save his friend. The situation poses a crisis of conscience for Huck. Should he accede to the law, admit that he has been wrong to steal a slave, and so betray his friend? Or should he break the law, be true to his deeper loyalties, and come to Jim's rescue? Huck decides to pray. He will confess to God his wrongdoing and promise to reform, the first evidence of which will be his complicity with the plan to return Jim to slavery.
>
> But having knelt to pray, Huck discovers that he cannot make his mouth say words that betray his heart. He cannot tell God that he is giving up on sin by returning his friend to slavery, because Huck knows, and he knows that God knows, that a trumped-up prayer is the biggest sin of all. In his moment of decision, Huck sees the matter very clearly: "Deep down in me I knowed it was a lie, and He knowed it. You can't pray a lie."
>
> M. Twain, *The Adventures of Huckleberry Finn* (New York: Signet Classic, 1959), 209.

God does not pervert justice and does not reject the claims of a blameless person (8:3, 21). Yet, when Job ponders the injustice of his own life and that of the world in which he lives, he wonders who is responsible for such undeserved and unattended misery. If it is not God, then who is it? Bildad absolves God by indicting Job's children (8:4). Zophar defends God by accusing Job himself (11:13-14). Job cannot accept either explanation as true. If he is innocent and suffers, then it must be God's integrity, not his, that is suspect.

Job Considers Other Possibilities, 9:25-35

Having considered the characteristics of his adversary at law, Job succumbs once more to lament about the hopelessness of his plight (vv. 25-26). His life races by with no good end in sight. He compares the passing of his days to the speed of a runner who covers long distances quickly (cf. 2 Sam 18:19-23), to reed boats skimming along the surface of the waters (cf. Isa 18:1-2), and to eagles swooping down out of the sky to snatch their prey (cf. Hab 1:8). The general theme is the same as that of 7:6, 16. In that context, Job wished simply to be left alone so that he might enjoy what life was left to him. Now that he has begun a quest for justice, the brevity of his life confronts him with a different urgency. If he cannot obtain vindication by taking God to court, then are there other possibilities for resolving his situation before his life expires?

He considers three options that might provide some measure of relief (vv. 27-35). (1) He could forget his complaint (v. 27: *śîḥî*; cf. 7:11: "I will complain [*ʾāśîḥāh*]") and twist his countenance from sadness to feigned cheerfulness, but this would not relieve his suffering or restore his innocence. He knows that no matter what he tries, God has already decided that he is guilty (v. 28b; cf. v. 20). Why then should he exhaust himself in an effort that God has predetermined to be futile (v. 29b)?

(2) He could wash himself with potent cleansing agents, perhaps as a symbolic ritual that would declare his purity (cf. Deut 21:6-7; Pss 26:6; 73:13), but even if he did so, God would plunge him, freshly cleaned, into a filthy pit so that his very clothes would consider him too disgusting to be near (vv. 30-31). (3) Finally, since he recognizes that God is no ordinary litigant who can be summoned to trial by a mere mortal (v. 32), Job might search for an impartial "arbiter" (*môkîaḥ*; NRSV: "umpire") who could mediate the differences between them fairly (vv. 33-35). Elsewhere in the Hebrew Bible, the *môkîaḥ* is described as a third party, who listens to disputes between two persons and offers a judgment that both accept as appropriate (cf. Gen 31:37). Job envisions one who will lay his hand on both God and himself so that the inequalities between the two will be negated. From Job's perspective, this requires that the arbiter remove the rod that God uses to afflict and terrorize him (v. 34). If the arbiter could insure that Job can stand before his accuser without fear of intimidation or reprisal, then Job could argue his case with at least a measure of confidence.

The latter half of v. 35 is obscure. The Hebrew text is literally "for not thus I am with myself." NRSV follows the interpretation of the medieval Jewish commentator Ibn Ezra, who understood Job to be saying, "In my soul I am not as you think." LXX offers a similar reading: "For I do not think myself unjust with Him."[4] The ambiguity in the text is at most only a minor distraction. Whatever confidence Job *might* take from the presence of an arbiter is voided by his announcement at the outset that no such option exists for him. There *is no umpire* who can guarantee a fair encounter with this God. If Job persists in taking God to court, he will do so alone. He will enter the battle armed with his integrity and nothing more.

Job Rehearses the Case He Will Bring Against God, 10:1-17

Job has twice stated that life as he knows it is not worth living. In 7:16, his despair gives rise to the empty hope that God will simply leave him alone. In 9:21, his conviction that God can not be successfully challenged in court evokes a similar sense of futility. In 10:1, he declares once more that he abhors life (lit., "my soul despises [*nāqĕṭāh*] my life"), but now he announces a resolve to move beyond lament and present his case against God. He will let the bitterness of his soul, which will not be quieted (cf. 7:11), run its course, even it means that he finds himself addressing an absent God in an empty courtroom. He imagines himself beginning with two imperatives that would lay the groundwork for his suit (v. 2). He will say to his absent adversary, "Do not condemn me," that is, do not declare me guilty without evidence.

And he will insist that God give him a statement of the alleged charges against him, which he stands ready to dispute. ["Do Not Condemn Me"]

Like a plaintiff interrogating a defendant, Job rehearses three questions he would oblige God to answer (vv. 3-7). Under normal circumstances, Job might assume that the questions are only rhetorical, that the response to each is obvious and beyond dispute. But since Job is no longer clear about God's character or intent, the questions are now open-ended. First, Job asks if God has decided that it is "good" to be an agent of oppression (v. 3). That God should "oppress" (*ʿāšaq*) should be unthinkable, for such behavior involves a cruel mistreatment of others that God routinely condemns (Amos 4:1; Mic 2:1-2; Jer 7:6; Ezek 22:29; Zech 7:10) and promises to judge harshly (Pss 103:6; 105:14; 146:7). Indeed, this is the only instance in the Hebrew Bible where God is the subject of this negative verb. Yet, when Job considers the evidence before him, he is no longer certain that God is acting like God. What is the rationale for God's rejecting the careful designs of God's own handiwork, then smiling with approval on the designs of the wicked?

With a second (v. 4) and third (v. 5) question, Job presses this line of interrogation by asking if God is limited by the same conditions that apply to humans. Does God have the imperfect vision of human eyes, so that what God sees is only partial and subject to error? Is God's life span fixed by days and

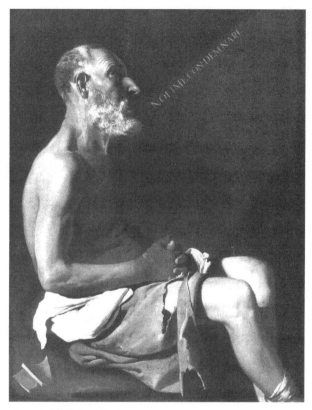

Seated Job in Profile

Diego Velásquez (?). *Seated Job in Profile*. c.1618-1630. Oil on canvas. The Art Institute of Chicago.

"Do Not Condemn Me"

This work has long been attributed to Diego Velásquez (1599–1660), although it is currently ascribed to an anonymous painter of the Velásquez school from the early seventeenth century. The work depicts Job seated alone in the dark. A faint light from behind illuminates his back, shoulders, neck, and face. The profile suggests a middle-aged man who remains in good physical condition, despite the ordeal to which his tattered clothes bear witness. His head is held high, his jaw his firm, his gaze is fixed heavenwards. In Roman letters, the words NOLI ME CONDEMNARE, "Do not condemn me," are written on an ascending angle, as if they have just been spoken to God by this one who now awaits a response. Job's hands are clasped together in his lap. The pose suggests not so much supplication as resolve. Job will pray, but he will not relinquish his claim to be innocent and deserving of a fair hearing from the God of justice in whom he still trusts.

For further discussion of this painting, see S. Terrien, *The Iconography of Job Through the Centuries* (University Park PN: The Pennsylvania State University Press, 1996), 180-82.

years, so that, like humans, God has only a limited time in which to accomplish a task? The questions *ought* to be absurd. Surely God "does not see as mortals see" (1 Sam 16:7). Surely the One who is "from everlasting to everlasting" (Ps 90:2; cf. Gen 21:33; Deut 32:40; Isa 40:28) is not bound by the normal constraints of the calendar. Why then does God search so obsessively for Job's sin, when it should be clear that no such sin exists? Why then does God press so to destroy Job before he has had a chance to defend himself? If there is no one who can ever deliver Job from God's hand, is there not time enough for God to hear and respond to his case (vv. 6-7)?

Job's fear that God is acting in ways that are contrary to the divine nature leads him once more to question God's intentions as Creator (vv. 8-12; cf. 9:5-10). He opens with two statements that invite God to respond to the incongruity he discerns in the creative design for human life. God's own hands formed and shaped him, and yet now God has turned to destroy (*bālaʿ*; lit., "swallow"), not sustain, the very creature that God worked to bring into being (v. 8). According to the prologue, God has already acknowledged to the *satan* that "destroying" (*bālaʿ*) Job "*for no reason*" is not beyond what the Creator is willing to do (2:3). Job, of course, was not privy to that admission, but without realizing it, he now presses God to speak with a similar candor. Job calls on God to remember that he has been fashioned out of clay (v. 9), an image that recalls the potter who molds a vessel with great care from beginning to end (cf. Jer 18:5:12). Job suspects, however, that his end is to be returned to dust, like a vessel that is flawed and cannot be fixed (cf. Jer 18:1-4) or like sinful human beings who have violated God's instructions and must be punished (cf. Gen 3:19). NRSV treats the expression as a question, but the Hebrew puts it as a simple declaration. God has decided to discard him, although there is no evidence that he is blemished or sinful. What kind of Creator destroys the creation without bothering to check if it is worthy of the initial investment? [CD: "A God All Mercy"]

Job strengthens his case by using a sequence of similes that describe God's intimate involvement with every stage of his birth and maturation (vv. 10-12). Is it not true that God poured out the semen like milk and caused the embryo to solidify in the mother's womb like cheese (cf. Wis 7:1-2)? Did not God clothe the fetus with skin and flesh and knit the skeleton together with bones and muscles (for similar descriptions see Ps 139:13-18; Ezek 37:5-8)?[5] Is it not the case that when Job emerged from the womb, God bestowed upon him the gift of life and relentless love (*ḥesed*)? And is it not God's providential care that has sustained (*šāmar*, "guarded") Job's life since he first drew breath?

And God Said, "All This I Will Do"

And God said, I will build a church here
And cause this people to worship me,
And afflict them with poverty and sickness
In return for centuries of hard work
And patience. And its walls shall be hard as
Their hearts, and its windows let in the light
Grudgingly, as their minds do, and the priest's
    words be drowned
By the winds caterwauling. All this I will do,

Said God, and watch the bitterness in their eyes
Grow, and their lips suppurate with
Their prayers. And their women shall bring forth
On my altars, and I will choose the best
Of them to be thrown back into the sea.

And that was only one island. ·

R. S. Thomas, "The Island," *Poems of R. S. Thomas* (Fayetteville: University of Arkansas Press, 1985), 76-77.

Job completes his interrogation by charging that God's meticulous attention to him masks sinister intentions (vv. 13-17). [And God said, "All This I Will Do"] Hidden within God's heart is a strategy to seek and destroy the very life that God has so carefully wrought. Job knows that this is so, and he presents the evidence that compels his adversary to agree with him. God "watches" (*šāmar*) his every move, not to find ways to love and uphold him, but to spy out each and every misstep he might make (cf. 7:20). If he should sin, which he denies having done, God will not forgive him. If he is innocent (*ṣādaq*; NRSV: "righteous"), which he insists he is, God will ensure that his affliction is so heavy, his shame so overwhelming, that he cannot lift his head to assert his integrity or to defy his mistreatment (cf. Judg 8:28; Ps 83:2 [MT 83:3]; Zech 1:21 [MT 2:4]). The imagery of v. 16 may suggest that like a lion, God stalks Job (so NRSV), but in view of ancient Near Eastern parallels which depict lion hunting as a royal sport, it is more likely that Job perceives himself to be the lion, that is, the victim of God's ruthless aggression (cf. NJPS, REB). [Royal Sport] Job's sense of God's violent

King Ashurnazirpal Hunting Lions

9th C. BCE. British Museum, London, Great Britain (Credit: Erich Lessing/Art Resource, NY)

Royal Sport

Although some texts describe God as a lion whose ferocity may be used to attack helpless victims (Hos 5:14; 13:7) or to defend them (Isa 31:4; Hos 11:10), it is common to describe the persecuted as those who are hunted like a lion by their enemies (e.g., Pss 7:2 [MT 7:3]; 10:9; 17:12; 22:13, 21 [MT 22:14, 22]; 35:17; 57:4 [MT 57:5]). In the ancient Near East, lion hunting was a sport of the kings and is frequently depicted in art. In addition to being a sport, lion hunting appears also to have been conceived as a ritual act by which the king could imitate the gods' defeat of the forces of chaos that threaten the cosmic order (cf. O. Keel, *Jahwes Entgegnung an Hiob* [Göttingen: Vandenhoeck & Ruprecht, 1978], 62-63; L. Perdue, *Wisdom in Revolt: Metaphorical Theology in the Book of Job* [JSOTSup 112; Sheffield: Almond Press, 1991], 146). In view of this background, Job may be understood to be saying that God stalks him as though he were a lion that must be captured and slaughtered, because for some reason he has become a threat to creation.

"When Sorrows Come"

📖 O, this is the poison of deep grief . . .
    When sorrows come, they come not as
        single spies,
    But in battalions! (*Hamlet*, IV, v, 78)

intentions toward him spill over into his description of the adversary that will confront him in court. God will send witness after witness to testify against him. Like a general whose passions for defeating the enemy have reached fever pitch, God will order fresh troops against him until he succumbs. ["When Sorrows Come"]

"Why Did You Bring Me Forth from the Womb?" 10:18-22

Job's resolve to move forward with litigation against God only drives him back into the lament from which he started. So it is in the world of affliction, where each step forward may be countered by yet one more obstacle that blocks, denies, and stifles. Job closes this speech with questions and a petition that echo words he has already spoken in chapters 3 and 7. Although the words are similar, the despair they articulate is heavier, because Job now has a pained clarity about God that he did not have before suffering became his teacher. His question is no longer, "Why (*lāmmāh*) did *I* not die at birth, why did *I* come forth from the womb?" (3:11) but rather, "Why (*lāmmāh*) did *you* bring me forth from the womb?" (v. 18). He knows that his birth was neither accidental nor simply the end result of a biological process. God orchestrated everything, including the affliction and the misery that awaited him when he emerged from the womb. The life the Creator designed for him is not worth living. It would have been better if God had not acted at all, for then he could have died in the womb and been spared the scrutiny of the "eye" that so relentlessly spies him out for destruction (cf. vv. 4, 14).[6] His days are but a "few" (*mĕʿaṭ*), so too the "little" (*mĕʿaṭ*) comfort that they afford. Even so, Job's anguish is such that he believes suffering in God's absence may be more tolerable than the ceaseless oppression that comes from living in God's presence. Once more Job asks for nothing more than for God simply to leave him alone (v. 20; cf. 7:16).

Job's longing for death is described with multiple images of the darkness of Sheol (see [Sheol]) that recall his bleak words of 3:4-9 (vv. 21-22). Now, however, this darkness promises a different comfort than before. He has yearned for death because life was unbearable, an endless existence of "misery" (3:10, 20) without "rest" (3:26). Here, he wants to be dead, because the world in which he lives is not only unbearable, it is also perverse. The order of creation has collapsed. The innocent are indicted as guilty, and God laughs at their despair. The wicked run amok, and God favors their schemes over the desperate pleas of the righteous for justice. In a world where justice is not only denied but rendered impossible, Sheol's unremitting gloom promises less hypocrisy. There, darkness without "order" (v. 22: *sĕdārîm*; NRSV: "chaos") and light that "shines like darkness" (*tōpaʿ kĕmô ʾōpel*) is the expected norm. There, Job could at least live in harmony with a world that delivers exactly what it promises. ["No Light, But Rather Darkness Visible"]

CONNECTIONS

The dominant theme of chapters 9–10 is Job's decision to put God on trial. That decision is crucial, for it represents a dramatic shift in Job's understanding of how he must engage God. These reflections will explore some of the theological issues such a decision raises. But first it is instructive to recognize that how Job came to this decision may be as important as the decision itself. The vehicle for Job's aggressive move toward God is the practice of lamentation, a speech-act that typically involves four elements: invocation of God, lament, petition, and a concluding expression of confidence that God will hear and respond.

Job's first words from the ash heap were a vexed combination of curse and lament. So deep and devastating were his losses that he cursed the forces that had conspired to sentence him to life (3:3-10). Yet, even as he cursed life and sought to end it, he groped for some reason to go on living. His first probes took the shape of questions, like those honed over time in the practice of lamentation by sufferers who believed and expected that God would respond to their call for help (3:11-26). Job's questions—Why? Why? Why?—hinted that he too believed God holds the key to what he was searching for (cf. 3:20, 23), but at least initially he seemed unprepared or unwilling to enter fully into the practice of lamentation by addressing God directly. In his next speech, Job moved a step further into lament by resolving to speak his anguish and bitterness directly to God (7:7-21). Here too, however, his lament only approaches its potential for engagement with God. He addresses God, but his petition is that God grant him relief by agreeing to be less present with him, not more (7:16). In chapters 9-10, Job takes yet a further step into the world of lamentation. He resolves not only to address God directly but also to petition God to be present, not absent. Even if God remains distant and silent, Job insists that he will stay in the process of lamentation, until God yields to his demand for a free and fair hearing.

"No Light, But Rather Darkness Visible"

Job's sentiments find a parallel in John Milton's description of the "darkness visible" that defines a "paradise" irretrievably lost:

A dungeon terrible, on all sides round
As one great furnace flam'd; yet from those flames
No light, but rather darkness visible
Serv'd only to discover sights of woe,
Regions of sorrow, doleful shades, where peace
And rest can never dwell, hope never comes that comes to all.

J. Milton, "Paradise Lost," bk. I, ll. 61-67, in *The Portable Milton*, ed. D. Bush (New York: Penguin Books, 1977), 234. Pope cites the same parallel; M. Pope, *Job* (AB; Garden City NY: Doubleday, 1979), 82.

Job's halting but resolute movement toward engagement with God bears witness to the importance of lamentation. At its core, lamentation is an act of hard faith that insists on believing the relationship with God permits and often requires radical dialogue. On the one hand, God *speaks* and *acts* toward humanity; on the other, God *listens for* and *invites* human response. Without this response, the communication breaks down, and the relationship that God desires is incomplete. Sometimes the response is conveyed with words of praise and thanksgiving, which signal not only consent to God's will but also grateful submission. At other times, the hurt and pain of life cannot be honestly expressed with a simple "Yes" or a manufactured "Hallelujah." On these occasions, the language of faith is lament. This too is directed to God with a fervent trust that suffering makes an authentic claim on God's compassion. It is an act of faith that dares to believe life in relationship with God always remains open-ended, not settled or closed. Lament may be accented by doubt and despair, even anger, but it steadfastly resists the temptation to succumb to resignation. Lament is restless for change. In the midst of affliction that would rob life of meaning and hope, lament presses God to speak more clearly and act more decisively.

Job's journey from chapter 3 to chapter 10 underscores both the promise and the mystery of lamentation. The promise of lament is that suffering matters to God. Eliphaz would have Job believe that his suffering is insignificant in the vast scheme of things. It is simply the fate decreed by a God whose ways human beings can neither understand nor question (5:7-8). Bildad would have Job believe that his words of grief and anguish will not be permitted, for they harbor an assault on divine justice that exceeds what a proper relationship with God will bear (8:1-3). Job's reluctance to enter fully into the lamentation process suggests that he may be tempted by both arguments. Yet, his conviction that God will hear and respond is greater than the friends' doubt that God is interested in his plight or available to his complaint. Lament is the means by which Job acts on a promise that he will not relinquish, even if it means that in speaking *to* God he must also speak *against* God.

But if the promise of lament is that *God can be addressed and questioned,* its abiding mystery is that *it cannot guarantee God will answer.* The biblical witness is that God does not resist the restless, sometimes unorthodox, questions that sufferers bring to the dialogue of faith; indeed, God honors such questions as a necessary and vital part of the divine-human relationship. But the biblical record is equally clear that God seldom answers questions, at least not in the simple and straightforward way that suppliants may want and need. Especially in times of acute suffering, the dialogue with God that one yearns for may seem painfully one-sided. One may trust that God hears and believe that God is responsive, but when the questions end, faith must bear the burden of the silence that follows. Job has arrived at precisely this juncture in his relationship with God. He has cursed life and questioned the justice of the One he holds accountable for it, but he remains mired in grief that finds no response. His friends urge him to turn back from an approach to God they regard to be both futile and dangerous. For his part, Job can find no hard evidence to dispute their counsel. He too senses that he is no match for this God, whose ways he can neither contest nor comprehend. But what options does he have? The praise Eliphaz urges on him (5:9-16) will not connect with his pain. The plea for forgiveness that Bildad recommends (8:5-6) will not speak the truth about his innocence, which Job knows, and God knows, is unassailable. If he is to stay in relationship with God and remain true to his self, then he must chart his course by way of lament.

Faith communities may find it instructive to reflect on the importance of lament as an act that binds the afflicted to God. When churches and synagogues invite and nourish the practice of lament, they become sanctuaries for the Jobs of this world who yearn to believe, to speak, and to live as if they matter to God. Conversely, when lament is denied its place in the language of faith, when questions are discouraged as inappropriate or condemned as rebellious, it is likely that the only ones who will find God to be a sanctuary for them will be the modern-day friends of Job. When they gather to praise God, they will speak and act as if suffering makes no real claim on them or on God. For those who may be tempted toward faith that disallows lament, Job represents the importunate rebel at the door of the sanctuary. He knocks and awaits entry, for he dares to believe that the voice of anguished piety belongs in the discourse of faith.

Lament becomes for Job more than simply a way of addressing God. It becomes a means of imagining new ways of encountering God. Like all mortals, Job recognizes that there is a vast difference between God and himself. God is the Creator, he is the creature. Job cannot possibly have equal standing in such a relationship. Nonetheless, he refuses to believe that he has no voice, that his only option is mute submission to whatever God decrees. He imagines putting God on trial. He envisions a face-to-face encounter in a courtroom where the rules of law would negate all inequalities between the litigants. He and God would be free to argue their positions without threat of intimidation or violence. At least in the eyes of the court, the two parties would engage one another as if they were equals. It is a radical thought to be sure, but it is nonetheless an idea that enables Job to imagine, hence to live, like he has something to contribute to this relationship that matters. In thinking that he might stand before God as a near-equal partner, Job is emboldened to live as if the impossible were possible. It is perhaps the most daring way of imagining that humankind really is created in the image of God.

In Jewish tradition, Job becomes a model for those who dare to think that humans have a right and responsibility to stand up to God, in faith, and question, protest, and defy random acts of violence and abuse. One example of this model for contending with God is Elie Wiesel's play *The Trial of God*.[7] The setting is an inn in the village of Shamgorod in 1649. The village has suffered a pogrom. Only two Jews survived, Berish, the innkeeper, and his daughter Hanna. They are both scarred victims. Berish's two sons Hayim ("Life") and Sholem ("Peace") were killed. Hanna ("Grace") was tortured and raped. One night three minstrels arrive at the inn. They have come to perform a play for the holiday of Purim, a carnival time when people play games, wear masks, and pretend. Berish makes it clear that he is not interested in celebrating anything that has to do with God: "I resigned from membership in God—I resigned from God. Let Him look for another innkeeper, let Him find another people, let Him push around another Jew—I'm through with Him" (I, 15).

As the night wears on, Berish finally agrees to participate in a play, provided the minstrels allow him to choose the subject. He insists that they stage a mock trial in which the Master of the universe will have to answer for the shameful silence that hovered over Shamgorod while innocent people were slaughtered. Berish states his intentions clearly: "Listen: either He is responsible or He is not. If He is, let's judge Him; if He is not, let Him stop judging us" (I, 54).

The idea seems cold and frightening to the minstrels. They are understandably hesitant even to pretend that God can be treated as a defendant, charged with a crime, and possibly indicted. What if the verdict is guilty, they ask.

Berish pushes them to agree to his idea. Of course, it will take courage to enact such a drama, but Berish argues that Purim is an invitation to believe that at least on some occasions it is permissible to reverse roles with the Supreme Judge of the world:

You agree? Do you? You have the courage to do my kind of Purimschpiel? And go to the end of things—and utter words no one has ever uttered before? And ask questions no one has ever dared ask before? And give answers no one has ever had the courage to articulate before? And to accuse the *real* accused? Do you have that kind of courage? Tell me! (I, 56)

At first reluctantly and then with growing enthusiasm, the minstrels take up the challenge. As the curtain falls on Act I, one of them,

Mendel, announces their resolve: "Tonight we will be free to say every-thing. To command, to imagine everything—even our impossible victory" (I, 56).

The outcome of Berish's trial, like Job's, is both dramatic and sur-prising. We will have occasion to reflect on both in subsequent sections of this commentary. At this juncture, however, readers may want to ponder the courage that is required to believe that in relationship with God one is free to say and think and imagine everything. The issue may be framed with several questions. What if God is not only open to but desirous of relationships in which hard questions are raised about matters of divine justice? What if it is given to humankind to take innocent suffering so seriously that even God can be challenged to respond more decisively, more justly, one might say, more humanely? On the other hand, what if God only invites relationships in which certain things cannot be said, cannot be examined or even imagined? What if innocent suffering is simply a given, a fact of life that makes no claim on God or on those who would be stewards of God's justice in the world? It is wise to consider that such questions are not merely rhetorical, that the answers are not simple or self-evident. Anyone who has ever stood on Job's side of the divine-human encounter will appreciate what is at stake here.

It is the idea of putting God on trial that centers Job's thoughts in chapters 9 and 10. What is striking about Job's quest for personal justice is the way in which it leads him to ponder once again the larger issue of the justice of God's design for creation. The One he would interrogate is none other than the Creator of the world whose wisdom and power determines both the order and the disorder of the cosmos (9:5-10). Job is but one minor creature within the vast universe God has constructed. He concedes that he can neither discern God's intentions nor dissuade God from doing whatever God pleases. Still, if, as Job surmises from his review of creation's design, God wounds the innocent "without cause" (9:17) and "destroys both the blameless and the wicked" without discrimination (9:20) and "mocks the despair of the innocent" (9:23), then what kind of God is God? Such concerns return Job to the questions that he first raised in chapter 3. Once again he intimates that innocent suffering like his calls all of creation into question. If God's creational purposes towards him are sinister, what conclusions should he draw about the principles of justice that undergird the foundations of the cosmos? If God has created and designed the world to be a place where innocent suffering does not matter, then both God and creation seem indifferent, if not hostile, to the claims of justice and righteousness.

One final observation is pertinent to these reflections. Job's curse has led him to lament and his lament has in turn led him to imagine putting God on trial. But having explored this idea, even to the point of rehearsing the arguments he would make in court, he succumbs once again to lament (10:18-22). On first sight, the closing words of chapter 10 seem to signify that Job has only returned to where he was at the beginning. He questions the meaning of life, longs for death, and petitions an absent God to let him be. Although his despair is similar to what he expressed in chapter 3, Job has in fact moved a step closer to God. To lament is not the same as to curse. To curse is to negate. To lament is to hope, in the midst of negation, that there yet remains some possibility of new beginnings. The telltale sign of Job's move toward God is in the changed trajectory of his question.

"Evil"

Looks like what drives me crazy
Don't have no effect on you—
But I'm gonna keep on at it
Till it drives you crazy, too.

Langston Hughes, "Evil," in *The Collected Poems of Langston Hughes*, ed. A. Rampersad (New York: Vintage Classics, 1994), 227.

He no longer asks "Why did *I* come forth from the womb?" (3:11) but instead "Why did *you* bring me forth from the womb?" (10:18). The shift from *I* to *you* is more than simply a grammatical change. It is an indication of Job's fierce resolve to hold on to God against God. If God is absent, then Job will clamor for God to be present. If God is silent, then Job will cry out until God responds. More remarkable still, even if Job indicts God as guilty, he will continue to believe that the future remains open for new acts of divine justice and compassion. ["Evil"]

NOTES

[1] Cf. J. Hartley, *The Book of Job* (NICOT; Grand Rapids MI: William B. Eerdmans, 1988), 173.

[2] G. Fohrer suggests that Job senses humans can never be right in God's court of law, because God possesses all power. God makes the laws and executes them according to divine prerogatives that can neither be challenged nor resisted. As he puts it, God is always right, because for him might is right" ("Ist Gott im Recht. . . Gott aber immer recht hat, weil bei ihm Recht gleich Macht ist" *Das Buch Hiob* (KAT; Gütersloher Verlagshaus Gerd Mohn, 1963), 201.

[3] S. M. Paul notes that in an Akkadian medical text a similar expression describes a loss of consciousness; "An Unrecognized Medical Idiom in Canticles 6, 12 and Job 9, 21," *Biblica* 59 (1978): 545-47.

[4] For further discussion of these and other interpretive options, see M. Pope, *Job* (AB; Garden City NY: Doubleday, 1979), 76; R. Gordis, *The Book of Job: Commentary, New Translation, and Special Studies* (New York: Jewish Theological Seminary of America, 1978), 111.

[5] For further discussion of this imagery, see Gordis, *Book of Job,* 522; E. Dhorme, *A Commentary on the Book of Job* (Nashville: Thomas Nelson Publishers, 1967), 149-50. Similar descriptions of the formation of the embryo occur in later literature, e.g., Koran, Sura 22:5; 36:76; 40:69; 80:19; 96:2; Aristotle, *Generation of Animals*, 739 b21; Pliny, *Naturalis Historia*, 7.13.

[6] The "eye" may refer to any human eye, but Habel notes that in view of the surveillance motif that has been used in previous speeches (7:8, 17-22; 10:4, 6, 14) this seems to be an allusion to God, the "watcher of humanity" (7:20) (N. Habel, *The Book of Job: A Commentary* [OTL; Philadelphia: Westminster Press, 1985], 200-201).

[7] E. Wiesel, *The Trial of God* (New York: Schocken Books, 1979).

ZOPHAR'S FIRST RESPONSE TO JOB: "CAN YOU FIND OUT THE DEEP THINGS OF GOD?"

Job 11:1-20

In his last speech, Job expressed the hope, futile as it seemed, that God would "answer" him (9:3, 16). If he could just address God in a court of law, then he would insist that God state clearly the reason he had been targeted for affliction (10:2). Zophar, like his friends before him, now steps up to "answer" Job. It would of course be more dramatic if *God* would answer Job, but Zophar does not believe that that will happen, nor, he dares to imagine, is it really necessary. Zophar understands himself to be God's spokesperson. *He* can and will speak for God. Eliphaz relied on a "word" from God that was cloaked in mystery, a "whisper" that disclosed truth by vision and psychic sensations (5:12-16). Bildad appealed to the accumulated wisdom of the ages, from which he distilled the truth about God's moral governance of the world (8:8-10). Zophar claims that he can speak for God even more directly than his friends, because he knows the "secrets of wisdom" (v. 6) that are locked away in the very mind of God. If Job wants to know what God thinks about his situation, then Zophar can tell him. God would say to him three things: (1) know that your punishment is less than you deserve (vv. 2-6); (2) know that you cannot know or contest the justice of God (vv. 7-12); and (3) know that if you repent there is hope, but if you do not, your fate will be no different than that of the wicked (vv. 13-20).

Structure of Job 11:1-20		
	11:1-6	"But oh, that God would speak"
	11:7-12	"What can you do?" "What can you know?"
	11:13-20	Zophar's "if . . . then" theology

[Structure of Job 11:1-20]

Like Eliphaz, Zophar strikes the pose of a theologian who is able to draw upon a variety of theological traditions to buttress what he presumes to know about God. He uses the rhetoric of disputation to quote the words of Job in order to rebut them (vv. 2-4), the language of the psalmist to praise God's inscrutable wisdom (vv. 7-9), the language of wisdom to construct proverbs (v. 12) and to contrast the fates of the righteous and the wicked (vv. 16-20), and the language of the prophets to announce salvation to those who repent of their sin

(vv. 13-15). Unlike Eliphaz, however, Zophar wastes little time with the subtleties of pastoral care. His is the approach of the professional academic who sees suffering as a classroom topic that invites exegesis more than empathy. He will teach Job that when properly examined, human misery is simply a fact of human experience. It can be contextualized within larger truths, then dismissed as a temporary, now forgotten episode in the necessary journey toward submission to God (v. 16).

COMMENTARY

"But Oh, That God Would Speak," 11:1-6

Like Eliphaz (4:2) and Bildad (8:2), Zophar begins with a rhetorical question that lays the groundwork for his rebuke of Job. Can a man of "many words" go unanswered? Will a "man of lips" (NRSV: "one full of talk") be judged innocent simply because he is clever enough to monopolize the conversation? Job's ceaseless talk not only marks him as a fool (Eccl 5:2; cf. Prov 10:19). It also signals that he is unwilling to be a silent sufferer, even after Eliphaz and Bildad have given him good reason to quit his complaining. Job's proud "boasting" (v. 3; cf. Isa 16:6; Jer 48:30; NRSV: "babble") may render others mute. He may "mock" the wisdom of some without rebuke. But Zophar will not let such irreverence go uncontested. He feels a moral obligation to defend God against such aggression by silencing Job. ["Upon Some Issues It Is Impossible to Keep Silence"]

His strategy is to quote Job's words in order to refute them (v. 4). The words Zophar attributes to Job, however, are a subtle but telling misrepresentation of what Job has actually spoken. Job has said "I am

---

"Upon Some Issues It Is Impossible to Keep Silence"

In H. G. Wells's recreation of the Job story, *The Undying Fire*, Zophar's character is played by Mr. Joseph Farr. Mr. Farr is the head of the technical section of the Woldingstanton School, which Job Huss serves as headmaster. Mr. Huss has long wanted to dismiss Mr. Farr from the faculty but finds it difficult to do so because of his undisputed accomplishments in technical chemistry. But now that the school has fallen on hard times, Mr. Farr, along with his friends Sir Eliphaz Burrows and Mr. William Dad, finally moves to replace Job. They all fear that his "wild and wicked" ravings about divine injustice will corrupt the students at Woldingstanton and further weaken the school's prized reputation. Mr. Farr speaks "with a sort of restrained volubility," because, as he puts it, "upon some issues it is impossible to keep silence":

> Think of what such teaching as this may mean among young and susceptible boys! Think of such stuff in the school pulpit! Chary as I am of all wrangling, and I would not set myself up for a moment to wrangle against Mr. Huss, yet I feel that this cavilling against God's universe, this multitude of evil words, must be answered. It is imperative to answer it, plainly and sternly. It is our duty to God, who made us what we are.

H. G. Wells, *The Undying Fire* (New York: The Macmillan Company, 1919), 96.

innocent" (9:15, 20) and "I am blameless" (9:20, 21). He has not said "My teaching (*liqḥî*; see the marginal note in NRSV) is pure." The word "teaching" is a frequent term in Proverbs for the "precepts" or "doctrines" of the sages that are handed on, studied, and accepted as truth (Prov 1:5; 4:2; 9:9; 16:21, 23). But Job has not *studied* affliction, he has *experienced* it. He has not constructed a *doctrine* of grief, he has *cried out* in anguish, because seven sons and three daughters are dead. Zophar is unwilling to engage Job at the level of felt anguish. He prefers to abstract from the real pain of Job's world some theology that can be scrutinized, dismantled, and reformed. Clines aptly compares Zophar's strategy to that of "the professional theologian who uses human misery as the raw data for academic point-scoring."[1]

Job hopes that God will "answer" him (9:3, 16) and tell him specifically the charges that are laid against him (10:2). Zophar shares this hope. He envisions a personal confrontation in which God "opens his lips" (v. 5) and speaks truth to the "man of lips" (v. 2) that establishes once and for all the proper basis for their discourse. God does not in fact speak here, but that has little effect on Zophar, for he is confident that he knows what God would say and can speak on God's behalf. God would teach Job two lessons, from which he would be expected to reach a certain conclusion. First, God would instruct Job in the "secrets of wisdom." Wisdom (*ḥokmāh*) refers to the principles of order by which God creates and sustains the universe. It is given to humankind to search for this wisdom, even to attain it in part, because it holds the key for living in harmony with God's design for creation. But God would remind Job that wisdom has a hidden dimension, which places it beyond the reach of human comprehension. To be truly wise means that one seeks what God discloses and yields to what God withholds. Second, "wisdom (*tûšîyyāh*) is many-sided." The second word for wisdom is a close parallel to the first, but it conveys a more specific connotation. It refers to "efficient wisdom," that is, to the sound judgment that enables one to solve practical problems and achieve successful outcomes (Prov 2:7; 3:21; 8:14; 18:1; cf. Job 5:12).[2] Such wisdom, Zophar maintains, is "many-sided," or better, "double-sided" (*keplayim*; cf. Isa 40:2), by which he implies once again that God's way with the world is both manifest and mysterious.[3] Mortals must make the most of what God reveals to them and accept the rest on faith. [CD: "Excuses Trumped Up by You for Theologians"]

What God knows, and Zophar presumes to know, Job must now learn. He must "know" that in reality God's punishment is less than he deserves (v. 6). Hidden within God's mysterious justice is an unfathomable mercy. The Hebrew text is somewhat ambiguous. The NRSV translation—"God *exacts* of you"—understands the verb *yašše* to be from a root meaning "to lend, become a creditor" (cf. Deut 15:2; Neh

5:11-12). A root with the same spelling, however, means "to forget," and in this case would carry an equally plausible meaning: "God has overlooked for you some of your iniquity" (NJPS). With either reading, the basic sense of what Job must learn is clear. He *is* guilty. God *is* just. Job must yield both to the justice he has experienced and to the compassion that has already tempered that justice, which he has failed to understand. For the reader who has paid attention to the prologue's unqualified affirmation of Job's innocence (1:1, 8; 2:3) and the equally unqualified assertion that God has afflicted him "for no reason" (2:3), Zophar's assertion will seem utterly unconnected to the reality of Job's situation. But Zophar is not concerned with the "minor details" of real life that may give pause to theological certainty. He operates much more comfortably in the abstract realm of hidden truths that apply regardless of what is seen or felt or experienced. ["In the Court of Justice"]

"In the Court of Justice"

In *The Merchant of Venice*, Portia, disguised as lawyer, argues the case against Shylock, who insists that he has been denied justice:

> The quality of mercy is not strain'd;
> It droppeth as the gentle rain from heaven
> Upon the place beneath: it is twice bless'd;
> It blesseth him that gives and him that takes
>
> It is an attribute to God himself;
> And earthly power doth then show likest
>   God's
> When mercy seasons justice . . .
> Though justice be thy plea consider this—
> That in the course of justice none of us
> Should see salvation: we do pray for mercy
> (V, iv, 183-186, 194-199)

"What Can You Do?" "What Can You Know?" 11:7-12

With a second round of rhetorical questions (cf. v. 2), Zophar seeks to elicit from Job the confession that what he claims to know about God pales in comparison with what he does not know (vv. 7-9). Can Job find the "mystery" (*ḥēqer*; REB) of God? Can he reach the "limit" (*taklît*) of God? The two questions ask essentially the same thing. Is Job able to grasp the full extent, the outermost boundaries, of who God is and what God does? The obvious answer is "No." The same point has already been made by Eliphaz (5:9) and acknowledged by Job (9:10). Job has no illusions about the hiddenness of God's wisdom or the limits of human understanding, a point which he will subsequently reiterate at length in chapter 28. But Zophar presses Job to other and still more important concessions. He wants to teach Job his proper place in the universe that God has created. Toward that end he directs Job's attention to the cosmic map (vv. 8-9). The height, depth, length, and breadth of the world correspond to the four geographical regions that provide the arena for God's work at creation: heaven, Sheol, land, and sea (in Gen 1: heaven/firmament, sea, land; cf. Pss 135:6; 139:8-9; Hag 2:6). If God exceeds the very boundaries that define Job's world, then how can he, a mere creature, expect to find the full truth about God? What can he know, except that he is ignorant? What can he do, except to admit that he is powerless? Zophar's questions are neither subtle nor sympathetic. He insists that Job will find his proper place in the world only when he acknowledges that he has no real standing with God.

Having pressed Job to see that he is no way God's equal, Zophar now directs him to recant the challenge to God's justice that he made in 9:11-12 (vv. 10-11). Job has charged that God "passes by" (*ḥālap*), and he can neither "see" (*rā'ah*) nor "discern" (*bîn*) what God is doing. Zophar counters that when God "passes by" (*ḥālap*), God "sees" (*rā'ah* and "discerns" (*bîn*) everything, especially those who have sinned. Job argues that God uses power abusively, even criminally, to "snatch away," and there is no one "who can stop him" (*mî yĕšîbennû*). Zophar contends that God uses power judiciously. What no one can "hinder" (*mî yĕšîbennû*) is God's just procedures for bringing the guilty to account. God places the suspect in custody (*yasgîr*, "confines"; NRSV: "imprisons") until the proper course of action can be decided (cf. Lev 13:4, 5, 21, 26, cases where the priest "quarantines" [*hisgîr*] those suspected of having a skin disease). God then calls a legal assembly (*yaqhîl*; cf. Neh 5:7; Ezek 23:46; Prov 5:14; 26:26) to adjudicate the charges. If a verdict of guilty is declared, it is because God "knows" and executes judgment on those whose testimony before the court has been proven false (*šaw'*; NRSV: "worthless"; in legal contexts the word describes those who have lied or given "false witness/report"; e.g., Exod 20:16; 23:1; Deut 5:20).

The capstone of Zophar's argument is presented in the form of a proverb (v. 12). Like all proverbs, it conveys a truth that must be puzzled out. The saying is composed of two statements that invite Job to reflect further on the impossibility of discovering the wisdom of God. It is as likely that Job can know the full truth about God as it is that a hollow-headed person will become a genius. Or, to state the same thing in a different way, Job has just as much chance of comprehending the mysteries of God as a wild ass has of being born human. In Hebrew, the syntax of the second statement is unfortunately ambiguous, even by the normal standards of a proverb, and different renderings have been proposed (cf. REB, NAB, TEV). [The Syntax of 11:12b] Nonetheless, there is little uncertainty about the basic thrust of what Zophar intends Job to learn from the proverb. Job has embarked on a foolish and futile mission. When he contends with God, he is like a stupid person who pretends to be intelligent. He is like an ass who defies its genetic make-up.

Zophar's "If . . . Then" Theology, 11:13-20

Zophar's counsel is couched in the same "if . . . then" terms that Bildad offered in 8:4-6 (vv. 13-14). But whereas Bildad offered such counsel in

The Syntax of 11:12b

AΩ The Hebrew of v. 12b is difficult. A literal rendering produces something like the following: "and an ass an ass is born a human" (*wĕʿayir pereʾ ʾādām yiwwālēd*). NRSV understands the two words for "ass" to be in apposition with one another, with the second (*pereʾ*) as a delimiting or explanatory term for the first (*ʿayir*), thus: "an ass, that is, a wild ass. . . ." Some other translations treat the two terms as a construct relationship (the ass *of* an ass), so for example, NIV: "a wild donkey's colt" (cf. REB). With either reading, the sense would be generally the same. S. Mitchell's paraphrase emphasizes the impossibility that seems to be implicit in this rendering of the text: "a stupid man will be wise when a cow gives birth to a zebra."

M. Pope offers a different possibility. He notes that the two words for "ass" are not synonyms. The first (*ʿayir*) refers to the domesticated ass, the second (*pereʾ*) to the wild ass. Further, he argues that the phrase *pereʾ ʾādām* is elsewhere a fixed phrase (cf. Gen 16:12: "wild ass of a man"), which in this instance should be modified slightly to read *pereʾ ʾadāmāh*, "a wild ass of the ground." His preferred translation is "when a wild ass is born tame." The general sense then would be: a stupid person will get understanding when a wild ass is born a tame donkey.

S. Mitchell, *The Book of Job* (New York: Harper Collins, 1992), 31.
M. Pope, *Job* (AB; Garden City NY: Doubleday, 1979), 86.

the presumption of Job's innocence, Zophar assumes Job's guilt and his consequent need of repentance. For both friends, it is the doctrine of retribution that provides the explanation as well as the solution for Job's misfortune. *If* Job suffers, *then* he must have sinned. *If* Job will repent, *then* he will be forgiven and restored (see [Retribution]). Zophar places the emphasis on the promise of restoration (vv. 15-19), but he will remind Job pointedly that if he fails to remove himself from the company of the wicked, then the promise of negative consequences is equally certain (v. 20).

Zophar specifies four conditions Job must meet if he is to secure God's promise of restoration (vv. 13-14). (1) He must "set his heart" (*kûn* [Hiphil] + *lēb*) on God. The expression has to do with concentrating one's full energies on God. Such preoccupation with God prepares one for unqualified commitment and obedience (cf. 1 Sam 7:3; 1 Chr 29:18; 2 Chr 30:19). [The Principle of *Kawwanah*] (2) He must spread out his palms (*pāraš* + *kap*) to God in prayer (cf. Ezra 9:5; Ps 143:6; Jer 4:31). The posture is that of one who stands before God with hands raised, palms upwards and close together. The symbolism of the gesture is uncertain, although it is conventionally understood as a sign of supplication or surrender. (3) He must remove iniquity from his hand. The juxtaposition of this expression with the one preceding it suggests that what is required of Job is more than a fervent piety. If the hands are turned to evil acts, then what one says in prayer is rendered null and void (cf. Isa 1:15). Job must not only renounce sin; he must also put it away and eliminate it from his life. (4) He must not let wickedness live in his tent. This expression, like the previous one, admonishes Job to be as morally pure in the affairs of his everyday life as in his religious devotion. Elsewhere in the Hebrew Bible, "to dwell in the tent" of someone is to take over that person's property and possessions, in essence, to seize control of their lives (cf. Gen 9:27; 1 Chr

<table>
</table>

The Principle of *Kawwanah*

In rabbinic teaching *kawwanah* (from the root word *kun*) is a technical term used particularly with reference to prayer. It designates the element of "intention" or "concentration" that is essential for the truly devout. The Mishnah states, for example, that the pious men of old used to wait for an hour before praying in order that they may "direct their heart toward God" (*Berakoth* 5.1; *kûn* + *lēb*, as in Job 11:13). The objective is to pray in such a way that what one what *says* is matched by what one is committed to *do*.

In commenting on this principle, G. F. Moore cites two examples of the obstacles to such prayer. Although he is not commenting on the book of Job, his examples are pertinent:

The learned, on their part, should not go directly to their prayers from trying a case in court or from the discussion of legal norms (Halakah), which would run on in their mind while they were praying. Even the excitement or returning form a journey may so occupy a man that it will be two or three days before he can concentrate his mind on prayer, and it is better that he should not pray at all than go through the empty form.

G. F. Moore, *Judaism in the First Centuries of the Christian Era, The Age of the Tannaim*, vol. 2 (Cambridge MS: Harvard University Press, 1927), 224-25.

5:10; Ps 78:55).[4] Such imagery suggests that Job must not let wickedness take up residence in his home (or in his world) and become the master of his life.

The conditions Job must meet are introduced in v. 13 with the words "*if* you . . ." (*'im 'attāh*). The rewards for compliance with these conditions are introduced in v. 15 with the words "Surely *then*" (*kî 'āz*). The rewards cited in vv. 15-19 are similar to conventional descriptions of the fortunes of the righteous found elsewhere in the Hebrew Bible (e.g., Deut 28:1-6; 30:1-10; Pss 91, 128; Prov 2:6-12; 3:21-27). Nevertheless, Habel has noted that Zophar has not simply repeated traditional theology. He has *used* it to construct a personal word of assurance that addresses specific elements of Job's complaints in the previous speeches. [Allusions to Earlier Speeches] The rewards are grouped around two general themes: the promise of restoration (vv. 15-17) and the promise of security and honor (vv. 18-19).

If Job repents, *then* he will "lift up" his face without "blemish" (*mûm*; v. 15a). Job has complained that if he lifted up his head, God would hunt him down like a lion (10:15-16). Zophar counters that once Job confesses his sins, he can rise in God's presence without fear of being a marked man. The word for "blemish" is especially frequent in ritual texts as a term for physical defects that render a priest unworthy of approaching the altar (Lev 21:17, 18, 21, 23) or an animal unsuitable for sacrifice (Lev 22:20, 21, 25). Zophar probably uses the word in the moral sense of "shame" or "disgrace." Nonetheless, it is inviting to reflect on the possibility that his words carry the subtle hint that Job's sins have disfigured him both morally and physically, thus rendering him unfit for entry into the presence of God.[5] ["Sin Is a Thing That Writes Itself Across a Man's Face"] Job is also assured that repentance leads to being "secure" (v. 15b) The Hebrew word (*mūṣāq*) means literally to be "poured out" and refers to the process of pouring out metals that are

Allusions to Earlier Speeches

N. Habel notes that Zophar makes numerous allusions to specific themes and idioms in Job's previous speeches with what may be described as "compassionless precision." His outline of these connections, slightly modified to reflect the NRSV translations, is reproduced below.

Zophar's Speech (11:13-20)	Job's Speeches
"mind/heart" (*lēb*), 13a Job urged to redirect his "heart" to God	10:13 Job claims to know the "heart" of God
"wickedness" (*'awlāh*), 14b Job urged to dismiss "wickedness" from his tent	6:29, 30 Job claims to be free from "wrong/wickedness" and urges the same from his friends
"lift up" (*nasa'*), 15a Job will be able to "lift up" his face	10:15 God prevents Job from "lifting up" his head
"face/countenance" (*pānîm*), 15a Job's uplifted "face" will be free from blemish	9:27; cf. 29 Job claims it is futile to put off his sad "countenance" and purge his "hands" (cf. 11:13)
"misery/trouble" (*'āmāl*), 16a Job will be able to forget his past "misery"	3:10, 20; 7:3 Life is characterized by "misery/trouble"
"darkness" (*tā'upāh*), 17b The "darkness" of Job's world turned to morning	10:22 "gloom" (*'epatah*) Job anticipates Sheol, where light is darkness
"hope" (*tiqwāh*), 18a; cf. 20c Job can expect confidence and hope	6:8; 7:6 Since life is meaningless, Job's "hope" is to be crushed
"lie down/rest" (*škb*), 18b Job will be able to "rest" in safety	7:4, 21 When Job "lies down" it is misery, but he will soon lie "lie down" in the dust
"search/dig" (*hpr*), 18b (NRSV: "be protected," but see marginal note) Job will "search out" his rest and find it	3:21 Job is like those who "dig" for death as for buried treasure
"fail/fade" (*klh*), 20a The eye (*'ayin*) of the wicked "fails	7:9 "The life of mortals "fades" like a cloud (*'ānān*)

N. Habel, *The Book of Job: A Commentary* (OTL; Philadelphia: Westminster Press, 1985), 205-206.

cast, hence hardened, into solid vessels or statutes (e.g., Exod 25:12; 26:37; 36:36). Zophar's promise of security is set in the context of a deliverance from fear, which is what Job had hoped would make possible his free and full encounter with God (9:35).

If Job repents, *then* he will be able to "forget" all the troubles (*'āmāl*; "misery"; cf. the same word in 3:10, 20) that have destroyed his life and

"Sin Is a Thing That Writes Itself Across a Man's Face"

In *The Picture of Dorian Gray*, Oscar Wilde tells the story of the portrait painted of Dorian Gray by Basil Hallward. Upon seeing that Hallward has portrayed him as having the beauty of an Adonis, Dorian begins to despair that as time passes he will grow old and wrinkled while the painting retains its original beauty. He wishes that it could be the other way—that he might remain forever young and beautiful and the painting reflect the ravages of time and experience. He gets his wish. He gives himself freely to a life of sin and debauchery, but no matter how much pain he inflicts on himself or others there is not a trace of it in his physical appearance. It is the painting that degenerates, and with each sinful deed on Dorian's part, it is gradually transformed until the face it shows is like that of a devil. Dorian locks the painting away in the attic.

The rumors of Dorian's life are rampant, however, and one evening Basil catches up with him to express his concern over what he has been hearing. Basil does not believe the rumors, for as he put it, "Sin is a thing that writes itself across a man's face" (166), and one look at Dorian's face would suggest to anyone that he is as pure as the day he was born. Still, Basil knows something is wrong, and he persists in trying to get to the bottom of things. Finally Dorian invites him to the attic. When Basil sees the painting he cannot believe

The Picture of Dorian Gray

Illustration from *The Picture of Dorian Gray*. British Library, London, Great Britain (Credit: HIP / Art Resource, NY)

the grotesque figure that stares back at him. "This is the face of a satyr," he cries. "It is the face of my soul," Dorian replies. "Each of us has Heaven and Hell in him, Basil" (174).

Both Zophar and Wilde have discerned a truth about sin and its effects that is worthy of consideration. Sin surely does write itself across a person's life in concrete and tangible ways. In some sense then Zophar speaks the truth. His theology is sound and cannot be simply dismissed out of hand. The problem is that his truth does not apply to Job. Job's situation is virtually the opposite of Dorian Gray's. His disfigurement comes as result of his unswerving commitment to God, not to sin. It is punishment that is written across his face, even though his life is a testimony to moral excellence. Zophar's rigid adherence to disconnected truth recalls the observation of T. S. Eliot, who in another context suggests that Thomas Becket's prideful martyrdom is a tragic example of "doing the right thing for the wrong reason." Such actions, he continues, may be "the subtlest form of treason."

O. Wilde, *The Picture of Dorian Gray* (New York: Penguin Books, 1949). T. S. Eliot cited in G. Steiner, "On Kierkegaard," *No Passion Spent: Essays 1978–1995* (New haven/London: Yale University Press, 1996), 262.

driven him to curse and lament (v. 16). He will "remember" tragedy as if it were "waters that have flowed past," leaving little more than a ripple in their wake. In modern parlance, one might say it becomes "like water under the bridge." Clines has noted that the use of "forget" and "remember" as *synonymous* parallels is not only unique, it is also suggestive of the psychological truth that even when pain is forgotten its residual effects linger in the memory.[6] If Zophar is at all cognizant of this truth, he gives little indication of it here. It is more likely that he believes deep anguish, even that occasioned by the innocent death of children, can be simply erased from memory, *if* one's relationship with God is in order. Such a notion brings to mind another modern cliché, which when applied to the losses of sufferers like Job, is particularly insensitive and cruel: "out of sight, out of mind." [CD: "It's Human Nature to Forget What Hurts You, Isn't It?"] That repentance is the key to a reversal of even life's most tragic experiences is evident in the accompanying promise of v. 17. Job despairs that his fate is to dwell in a land of unremitting gloom (*'êpāh*) where "light is like darkness" (10:21-22). Zophar envisions for him "life" (*ḥeled*; "duration"; the word may also mean "world," cf. Pss 17:14; 49:1) that will outlast the pain he has known. Where repentance will lead him is to an existence where even "gloom" (*tā'upāh*) will be bright "like the morning."

If Job repents, *then* he will enjoy both security and honor (vv. 18-19). He will trust in his future, because there is "hope" (*tiqwāh*). We have noted previously that the friends and Job have different understandings of hope (see [Hope]). Eliphaz directed Job to place his hope in the integrity of his past life (4:6). Bildad spoke of the fragile hope of the wicked, which he compared with the thinness of a spider's web (8:13-14). Job complains that his past integrity is more a reason to despair than hope. Like a laborer who does the work and then is denied the wage, Job has been faithful, but his life speeds to an end "without hope" (7:2, 6). The hope upon which he leans is no less fragile than what Bildad ascribes to the wicked. Zophar insists there is hope that will enable Job to find the peace for which he longs. It is *not* based on Job's past integrity, for Zophar is far less convinced of such claims than Eliphaz. It *is*, however, tenuous, for it stands or falls upon Job's satisfactory compliance with a prerequisite. *If* Job transforms his life, *then* there is hope for the future. Whereas normally one thinks of hope as the resilience to believe in the unexpected, the unimagined, perhaps even the impossible, Zophar sees it as a consequence that can be predicted and secured. It is characteristic of retribution theologians like Zophar that even hope becomes a victim of rigid quid pro quo systems that reduce life to a game of sums and products.

The security that repentance promises will be coupled with a restoration of Job's honor. Many will come "to seek his favor" (v. 19b). The expression in Hebrew is literally "to soften/sweeten the face" (*ḥillah pānîm*). When applied to God, the expression describes the intent of supplicants who hope to gain God's favor, in metaphorical terms, to induce God to smile upon their requests (e.g., Exod 32:11; Jer 26:19; 1 Kgs 13:6). When applied to humans, the intent is much the same, namely, to show the respect and honor that wins the approval of persons in high places (e.g., Ps 45:12; Prov 19:6). When this imagery is applied to Job, it suggests that the shame and disgrace that have caused him to be shunned and ostracized by his community will be reversed. Subsequently, Job will complain that once he had been regarded as a paragon of virtue whose advice and leadership was sought by everyone in his community (29:7-17). In the aftermath of his suffering, however, the same people look upon him with utter contempt (30:1-15). Zophar promises that this will change and Job will be restored to his rightful place of respect, *if* he meets the conditions that God has set.

If Zophar had concluded his speech with v. 19, *then* one might conclude that his primary goal was to comfort and encourage Job. But he does not end with this verse, and the addition of v. 20 hints that his intent is as much to warn Job as to assure him. Job must take care not to conduct himself in the ways of the wicked, for their end is very different than what Zophar has thus far been describing for him. With three pointed images, he spells out for his friend the certain consequences that await those who do not forsake their evil ways. Their "eyes will fail," an idiom signifying an agonizing decline in which all passions and desires languish unfulfilled (cf. Lam 4:17).[7] Escape from trouble and destruction will be lost to them (cf. Job 5:4; Jer 25:35; Amos 2:5). And their only "hope" (*tiqwāh*) will be the "breathing of breath." The image suggests exhaling that is heavy with sorrow (cf. Jer 15:9) and perhaps imminent death (cf. Job 31:39). Zophar does not address Job directly in v. 20, as he has done throughout vv. 13-19. He now speaks of the wicked in the language of third-person ("they," "them"), as if he knows that they, like Job, are unlikely candidates for the hopes and promises he envisions for the righteous.

CONNECTIONS

Zophar is a theologian. His expertise lies in studying the traditions of faith and distilling truths that inform and instruct others in the ways of God. It is to Zophar's credit that what he offers to Job is in a real sense truth that carries the stamp of approval of orthodox theology. He is neither a fool nor a heretic. Neither Job nor his readers can simply dismiss what he says about God as irrelevant or unworthy. Still, even good theologians must be subject to peer review, lest their theology become disconnected from the real lives of those they would teach. Two truths in Zophar's theology invite scrutiny from all who would ponder

"Trust and Obey"

The words of the hymn "Trust and Obey" provide but one example of a common theology that nurtures faith in the inscrutable providence of God. V. 2, which speaks of the burden of suffering, exemplifies (from a Christian perspective) the encouragement such theology offers to persons like Job:

Not a burden we bear, Not a sorrow we share
But our toil He doth richly repay; Not a grief or a loss,
Not a frown or a cross, But is blest if we trust and obey.

his counsel as if they lived in Job's world: (1) the mystery of God; and (2) the promise of restoration.

Zophar grounds much of his theology on his understanding of the mystery of God (vv. 6-12). For this he is to be commended. Many who claim to speak for God are unprepared or unwilling to be as honest or as courageous. Zophar has learned well a profound truth of the sages: the truly wise are those who know how to be at home with the enigmas of life (Sir 39:1-3; see further, [Learning To Be at Home with the "Obscurities of Parables"]). The truth of this lesson is of course deeply rooted in Christian theology as well. "Now we see in a mirror dimly," Paul says, "but then we will see face to face. Now I know only in part; then I will know fully, even as I am known" (1 Cor 13:12). Like Paul, Zophar would teach Job that there are some things about God we are not given to know this side of a full encounter with the Creator of the world. The wisdom of God is indeed "many-sided." In the words of the gospel hymn, the faithful must learn to "trust and obey." ["Trust and Obey"]

Despite the legitimacy of its claim, the mystery of God may also afford theologians a means of avoiding reality rather than confronting it. The temptation to retreat to ambiguity is nowhere so alluring as in the issues presented by innocent suffering. The Jobs of the world ask hard questions that defy simple answers. Each plaintive "Why, O Lord?" chips away at the delicate balance between faith and doubt that theologians work so diligently to construct and sustain. Zophar can hardly be faulted for trying to deflect Job's questions with others that remind him how little about God he can truly know or understand. He opts to strengthen faith in what is known and to limit doubt about what is hidden. The problem arises when a theology of the mystery of God becomes a means of denying the claims on that mystery by those who suffer and ask "Why?" Job dares to believe that innocence can be a reality of human existence that makes a claim on God's justice *in this* world. Zophar is little interested in the claims of the innocent, perhaps because if and when they are not realized, they threaten to tilt the balance of life in relation to God more toward doubt than faith. It is safer, for God and for God's spokespersons, to focus on the reality of human guilt. The Zophar character in Archibald MacLeish's *J.B.* describes what is at stake when theology relaxes its preoccupation with guilt:

Guilt is reality!—
The one reality there is!
All mankind are guilty always!

If it were otherwise we could not bear it . . .
Without the fault, without the Fall,
We're madmen: all of us are madmen.[8]

Zophar uses the mystery of God to confirm Job's guilt rather than to ponder the possibility of his innocence. For him, a theology of divine mystery assumes an anthropology of human corruption. The real question is not, "Can mortals be righteous before God?" (4:17). The answer to that is obviously "No." Nor is it the question, "What are human beings?" (7:17), for the answer to that is equally self-evident. Human beings are flawed creatures limited by powerlessness and ignorance (11:8, 12). The real question is rather, "Who is God?" Zophar's answer to this is that God is hidden and mysterious. Both God's justice and God's mercy are beyond the pale of human comprehension and influence. Such theology elevates the mystery of God at the expense of human integrity. It is a partial truth that deadens the soul and robs the spirit. It construes faith as mindless submission to the incomprehensible, not as a journey into the unknown that is open and pregnant with possibility. When theology becomes no more than an endeavor to cloak God in unfathomable mystery, then the Jobs of the world are sentenced to suffer alone. They are invited neither to believe nor disbelieve. Neither the question of their reality nor God's is any longer a burning one. Their only option is to abdicate, surrender, and endure. When confronted with the mystery of God on these terms, it is little wonder that the afflicted are not so much awed as bewildered. [Mystery, But Not Hope]

A second truth in Zophar's theology is the promise of restoration for those who entrust themselves to God's providence (vv. 13-20). The book of Job ends by describing Job's restoration in ways that recall Zophar's promise (42:10-17), hence the reader may know once again that Zophar has in some sense spoken the truth about God. What calls for scrutiny is not Zophar's promise, nor even that he makes this promise contingent on Job's repentance. Even though he *presumes* sin that is not in evidence,

Mystery, But Not Hope

Those—dying then,
Knew where they went—
They went to God's Right Hand—
That hand is amputated now
And God cannot be found—
The abdication of Belief
Makes the Behavior small—
Better an ignis fatuus
Than no illumine at all—

A. Kazin has noted that in her personal life, Emily Dickinson was always circling around God in the hope of an encounter. At times the pursuit drove her to silence; on other occasions it drove her to a "bitterness not always resigned." The poem above perhaps reflects the latter experience. Kazin summarizes Dickinson's enigmatic hope as follows: "Better to be deceived by a light where there is no light than to have no light at all."

E. Dickinson, "# 1551," *The Complete Poems of Emily Dickinson*, ed. T. H. Johnson (Boston/New York/London: Little, Brown and Company, 1961), 646.

A. Kazin, *God & the American Writer* (New York: Alfred A. Knopf, 1997), 142, 145.

Zophar's "if . . . then" theology stands well within conventional understandings of the requirements for restoration. It is rather that Zophar instructs Job to believe that if and when he is delivered from his ordeal, his pain will be forgotten as if it had not happened (v. 16).

Zophar's dismissal of Job's tragedy marks him as one who knows about pain from only secondhand experience. Job's world has been turned upside down. He has not been merely inconvenienced. He has watched sons and daughters die for no reason. Such loss, even when inexplicable, does not render one forever incapable of knowing joy and fulfillment. But it does mean necessarily that life can never be same again. The truly tragic experiences one endures leave scars that cover but do not contain the memory of brokenness. When theologians (or others) glibly promise healing that erases the reality of hurt, they run the risk of expressing contempt, not compassion, for the misfortune of those they would teach (cf. Job 12:5). For those whose lives have been indelibly shaped by tragedy, a silenced memory is not only impossible, it is unwanted. It is the dulled but abiding ache of what has been lost that provides the necessary score for future songs of faith that are genuine. Without that score, the "restored" may live to sing again, but their song will not resonate with the full and rich sounds of life's truth and passion. If a theology of restoration takes away more than it restores, then one must ask if the cost is worth the gain. ["If the Violin Is to Sing"]

"If the Violin Is to Sing"

Elie Wiesel often writes of the sufferer's imperative not to forget or imprison the experiences of pain and loss. A particularly poignant image of this imperative is the following observation, which he offers as one way of explaining why writing as a survivor of the Holocaust is a "painful pleasure": "If the violin is to sing, its strings must be stretched so tight as to risk breaking; slack, they are merely threads."

E. Wiesel, *All Rivers Run to the Sea: Memoirs* (New York: Alfred A. Knopf, 1995), 321.

NOTES

[1] D. Clines, *Job 1–20* (WBC; Dallas: Word Books, 1989), 260.

[2] M. Fox ("Words for Wisdom," *Zeitschrift für Althebräistik* 6 [1993]: 164-65) describes *tusiyyah* as "clear, proficient thinking in the exercise of power and practical operations."

[3] Cf. M. Pope, *Job* (AB; Garden City NY: Doubleday, 1979), 84-85; E. Dhorme, *A Commentary on the Book of Job* (Nashville: Thomas Nelson Publishers, 1967), 159.

[4] G. Fohrer, *Das Buch Hiob* (KAT; Gütersloh: Gütersloher Verlagshaus Gerd Mohn, 1963), 230.

[5] Cf. C. Newsom, "The Book of Job," in vol. 4 of *NIB* (Nashville: Abingdon Press, 1996), 421.

[6] Clines, *Job 1–20*, 269. Clines notes that "remember" is typically paralleled by "*not forget*" (e.g., Pss 9:12 [MT 9:13]; 74:18-19, 22-23) and "forget" by "*not* remember" (e.g., Job 24:20; Prov 31:7; Isa 17:10; 54:10). Only here are these "polar opposites" used as if they were synonyms.

[7] G. Gerleman, "*Klh* to be at an end," *TLOT*, vol. 2, trans. M. E. Biddle (Peabody MS: Hendrikson Publishers, 1997), 617.

[8] A. MacLeish, *J.B.* (Boston: Houghton Mifflin Co., 1956), 122, 126-27.

JOB'S RESPONSE TO ZOPHAR: "I DESIRE TO ARGUE MY CASE WITH GOD"

Job 12:1–14:22

Chapters 12–14 bring to conclusion the first cycle of discourses between Job and the friends. A number of key terms link this speech to Job's opening lament in chapter 3 (e.g., "trouble" [*rōgez*] in 3:17, 26 and 14:1; "deep darkness" [*ṣalmāwet*] in 3:5 and 12:22), thus suggesting that Job is continuing his charge that suffering like his must make some claim on God's moral governance of the creation. Each of the friends has tried to steer Job away from what they believe is a misguided and dangerous reaction to suffering. Eliphaz has argued that no human being can be righteous before God (5:17). Bildad has warned Job against even contemplating that God perverts justice (8:3). Zophar has reminded his friend that God's justice is certain, even if it is beyond human comprehension (11:6). Each in his own way offers the same counsel to Job: *if* he will but seek God, by which they clearly mean that he must repent of his sin, *then* God will restore him (5:8-16; 8:4-6; 11:13-14).

Job now stands at a crossroad. Will he finally yield to this counsel and submit to God, which his friends insist is the only appropriate response for one in his situation? Or will he persist in what they all agree, Job included (cf. 4:18-19; 7:11-16; 9:2-3; 11:7-9), must be a futile challenge to the justice of the Creator of the world? Against all odds, Job chooses the latter option. He will argue his case with God, even if it means that in doing so he takes his life in his hands (13:14). "Trouble" and "deep darkness" remain the lens through which Job struggles to see God. Nothing the friends have said has changed this fact or lessened its burden for Job. Indeed, the tenor of this speech indicates that both his misery and his resolve to protest it have escalated dramatically since chapter 3. ["I Must Stay Here With My Hurt"]

This is the longest of Job's speeches thus far (75 verses; cf. ch. 3: 26 verses; chs. 6–7: 51 verses; chs. 9–10: 57 verses). Only Job's last speech in the third cycle, chapters 29–31 (96 verses) is longer. It is also the most complex of Job's speeches. Some

---

"I Must Stay Here with My Hurt"

It is too late to start
For destinations not of the heart.
I must stay here with my hurt.

R. S. Thomas, "Here," *Poems of R. S. Thomas* (Fayetteville: University of Arkansas Press, 1985), 42.

scholars, noting what appears to be contradictions or inconsistencies with other speeches of Job, suggest that much if not all of chapter 12 (e.g., vv. 7-11, 12-25) as well as portions of chapter 13 (e.g., vv. 1-2) should be regarded as later expansions. Others, while differing on how to delineate the major divisions within the speech, argue for the integrity of the text as it stands.[1] It is the latter option that will be followed here, although it must be conceded that the question about how the various parts fit together can be answered in more than one way.

Most would agree that the speech divides into two primary parts: 12:1–13:12, Job's address to the friends; and 13:20–14:22, Job's address to God. Job 13:13-19, which describes Job's resolve to turn away from the friends and to address God directly, provides the crucial transition between these two divisions. Within these major divisions, both the form and the tone of Job's speech are richly varied. His words are formed by elements drawn primarily from wisdom (e.g., 12:2-3; 13:1-2), psalmody (praise: 12:13-25; lament: 14:1-22), and the courtroom (13:4-28). His mood ranges from sarcasm (12:7-12) to sincerity (13:13-18), from bold imagination about what might be (14:13-17) to mournful despair over what can never be (14:18-22). A general outline of the speech is given below (sub-units will be noted at the appropriate places within the commentary). It is instructive to remember, however, that these structural boundaries are more for the reader of this drama than for its principal actor. The anguish that drives one like Job to contend with God does not readily yield to neat and predictable patterns.

• Job understands . . . and he will speak (12:1–13:3)
• The friends claim to understand, but they should be quiet (13:4-12)
• Job resolves to argue his case with God, come what may (13:13-28)
• Job laments that God has appointed boundaries beyond which no humans can go (14:1-22)

COMMENTARY

Job Understands . . . and He Will Speak, 12:1–13:3

Job's initial address is framed at the beginning and the end by the claim that his understanding is not inferior to his friends' (12:2-3; 13:1-2). What he knows is the hard truth taught by suffering, truth that the friends seem prepared only to scorn (12:4-6). He contends that if the friends will but pay attention to the way the world works, then creation itself will teach them what they have been unable to see for themselves

(12:7-12). They will learn that everything is indeed in "the hand of the Lord" (12:9), a fact which from the sufferer's perspective subverts conventional words of praise into a "doxology of terror" (12:13-25).[2] [Structure of Job 12:1–13:3]

Job's opening words suggest that he has moved beyond mere disagreement or disappointment with his friends. What he feels now is disgust. He begins with the same oath formula that introduced his response to Bildad in 9:2: "Truly (*ʾomnām*; NRSV: 'No doubt') you are the people with whom wisdom will die" (v. 2). In the previous response, Job "agreed" with what his friends had said only to "disagree" on a larger point: it is true that it is impossible to be "innocent" (*ṣdq*) before God, *not because* humans are imperfect creatures, *but because* God's justice is flawed. Now Job "agrees" that the friends consider themselves to be the embodiment of wisdom, but his words convey only a left-handed affirmation. As Shakespeare's Marcius Coriolanus puts it, Job's words are "praises sauced with lies" (*Coriolanus* I, ix, 53). [Advice to Would-be Critics] The truth is that wisdom is larger than the friends; they are not its only custodians. Job has understanding that is equal to theirs, and the truth he discerns is in no way inferior to what they claim for themselves (v. 3). Zophar compared Job to a "stupid person" who has as much chance of understanding the wisdom of God as a wild ass has of being human (11:12). Job now retorts that the "impossible" has happened. He has been transformed. The changes wrought by suffering have endowed him with a wisdom that means he is no longer the person he used to be.

Suffering has taught Job two truths that seem beyond the grasp of his "wise" friends (vv. 4-6). First, he has learned that it is indeed possible for a righteous sufferer, one who is "just and blameless" (*ṣadîq tāmîm*), one who is accustomed to calling on God and being answered, to become a "laughingstock" in the eyes of his friends (v. 4). Both these descriptions of the righteous sufferer recall the "former" Job known to

Structure of Job 12:1–13:3

12:1-3 "I am not inferior to you"
12:4-6 The truth taught by suffering
12:7-12 The truth taught by creation
12:13-25 Job's praise of God's destructive "wisdom and strength"
13:1-3 "I am not inferior to you"

Advice to Would-be Critics

In "An Essay on Criticism" (1711), Alexander Pope offers cogent advice to those who, like Job's friends, pride themselves in being able to discern the faults in others:

But you who seek to give and merit fame,
And justly bear a critic's noble name,
Be sure yourself and your own reach to know,
How far your genius, taste, and learning go;
Launch not beyond your depth, but be discreet,
And mark that point where sense and dullness meet. (l. ll. 46-51)

A. Pope, "An Essay on Criticism," *Essay on Man and Other Poems*, Dover Thrift Editions, ed. S. Appelbaum (New York: Dover Publications, 1994), 5.

us in the prologue. *That* Job was "blameless and "upright" (*tām wĕyāšār*; 1:1, 8; 2:3). *That* Job was one who constantly called on God on behalf of his children (1:5). And *that* Job was honored by both his peers and God as one whose piety was unmatched by anyone on earth (1:8; 2:3; cf. 1:3). But now everything has changed. Although Job remains "just and blameless," he is now ridiculed and scorned, and what is worse, it is those who would be his friends who laugh loudest (cf. Ps 55:12-15). Second, he has learned that it is indeed possible that peace and security belong not to the righteous but to those who despoil and devastate others (v. 6). The last line of v. 6 is ambiguous. NRSV's translation—"who bring their god in their hand"—suggests the arrogance of the wicked who believe they can manipulate God by their own power. A literal translation, however, seems more appropriate in this context: "who *God* brings in *his* hands." By this rendering what Job has learned is that God has the power to punish the wicked but, inexplicably, does not do so.[3]

Why do those who claim to be wise make a laughingstock of an innocent sufferer who seeks honest dialogue with God? Job concludes that such mockery is due to the friends' insulation from suffering: "in the mind of those who are at ease there is contempt for misfortune" (v. 5). Although the line in Hebrew is difficult and susceptible to more than one translation, the general sense is clear enough. [The Difficulties in Job 12:5] Those who have never known hurt and brokenness for them-

---

The Difficulties in Job 12:5

AΩ Two difficulties in 12:5 have elicited different resolutions from scholars. (1) The first word in the Hebrew text is *lappîd*, literally "torch, lamp," which seems to make little sense in the context. A number of scholars propose that it should be corrected and read as the word *pid*, "calamity, misfortune" (the same word occurs in Job 30:24 [NRSV: "disaster"] and 31:29 [NRSV: "ruin"]), a proposal already offered by Ibn Ezra (1092–1167) (see R. Gordis, *The Book of Job: Commentary, New Translation, and Special Studies* [New York: Jewish Theological Seminary of America, 1978], 136; E. Dhorme, *A Commentary on the Book of Job* [Nashville: Thomas Nelson Publishers, 1967], 170). (2) In the second half of the verse, the word *nākôn* may mean "fixed, ready" (from the root *kwn*) or "blow, beating" (from a different root *nkh*). With the former, the sense of the last phrase is that the complacent think misfortune is "established" or "fitting" for the one who is already stumbling. With the latter, the sense is that those who are complacent think it appropriate to "strike" the one already afflicted. The following translations are representative of the different ways the verse can be read:

He that is ready to slip with his feet is as a lamp despised in the thought of him that is at ease. (KJV)

The undisturbed esteem my downfall a disgrace such as awaits unsteady feet. (NAB)

Men at ease have contempt for misfortune as the fate of those whose feet are slipping. (NIV)

Those at ease look down on misfortune, on the blow that fells one who is already reeling. (REB)

In the thought of the complacent there is contempt for calamity;
It is ready for those whose foot slips. (NJPS)

You have no troubles, and yet you make fun of me; you hit a man who is about to fall. (TEV)

selves are often dismissive of others who have not been so spared. It is perhaps only natural that the secure are often complacent about the dangers in life, that those who have never seriously been wronged have an exaggerated confidence in justice. But what Job knows, and the friends have yet to learn, is that such attitudes "add insult to injury." The wound becomes particularly grievous when it comes from those who claim to speak for God, for then too often the message conveyed to the innocent victim is that suffering automatically marks one as a sinner whose pain is self-inflicted. Job argues that the friends' unexamined retribution theology means they speak with a deficient understanding. Until their platitudes are informed by the real-life experience of inexplicable tragedy, their wisdom will make little or no difference in the world of Job. [The Broken and the Whole]

> **The Broken and the Whole**
>
> But Love has pitched his mansion in
> The place of excrement;
> For nothing can be sole or whole
> That has not been rent.
>
> William Butler Yeats, "Crazy Jane Talks with the Bishop," in *The Collected Poems of W. B. Yeats*, rev. 2nd ed., ed. R. Finneran (New York: Scribner, 1989), 259-60.

Job proceeds to demonstrate that his wisdom is not inferior to that of the friends by giving them a lesson on creation (vv. 7-12) that sounds much like the one Zophar gave him in 11:8-9. The similarity between the two discourses has suggested to some that Job is actually quoting his friend.[4] It is more likely that he is paraphrasing conventional wisdom rhetoric, that is, he is only *pretending* to quote what he has heard.[5] The tenor of Job's speech is that of parody. In effect, Job sets a trap for his friends by inviting them to listen to *his* words and hear how *they* sound. But as Newsom has rightly noted, the effectiveness of parody lies in its proximity to the truth.[6] Job intends to mock the wisdom of his friends. But in imitating their words he skirts along the edges of truth that neither he nor they have yet fully discerned. [Job's Friends in Dunce Cap]

Verses 7-10 raise two as yet *ambiguous* truths that Job and the friends must strive to understand. First, does creation *reveal* truth about God or *conceal* it? Zophar appealed to the extreme boundaries of the cosmos—the height of the heavens, the depths of Sheol, the width of the earth, the breadth of the sea—in order to persuade Job that the wisdom of God is beyond his grasp (11:7-9). Job now mocks Zophar by appealing to the same general boundaries within creation in order to teach his friends that the truth about God is accessible to all creatures. One need only ask the "beasts" (*běhēmôt*; NRSV: "animals") of the field, or the "birds of the air," or the "plants of the earth," or the "fish of the sea," and they will teach the truth about God's world (vv. 7-8).

In a real sense, both Zophar and Job are right, although neither has as yet full clarity on these matters. When one considers the vast expanse of the universe that God has created, it is transparent that mere mortals

Job's Friends in Dunce Cap

📖 The Collegium of Champeaux, founded in 1113 by Guillaume de Champeaux (1070–1122), was a celebrated center for theology and sacred music. In 1520/1521, the canons of Champeaux commissioned some fifty-four choir stalls or "mercy seats" for the church. The stalls were decorated with various scenes from the book of Job, one of which depicts the three friends in a single, elongated dunce cap, with donkey ears pro-

Job's Friends in Dunce Cap

truding from each side (for a similar depiction, see **["Job and His Friends"]**). The Archbishop of Paris judged this depiction to be a blasphemous caricature of orthodox theology and sought to have it removed and destroyed. S. Terrien notes that according to a local tradition the canons were able to save the work by relocating it to a less conspicuous place in the church. Terrien offers the following observation about the threat to theologians and ecclesiastical authorities, past and present, represented by this rendering of Job's critique of the friends:

> Whether the three men thus exposed were recognizable theologians at the Sorbonne, as local memory would have it, should be a matter of conjecture. The fact is that the artist, Robert Falaise, made caricatures of the three faces. Like the friends of Job, who upheld orthodoxy with great learning but were devoid of pastoral concern, they are dull and self-satisfied academics. They betray the ignorance and the arrogance of mere religiosity.

S. Terrien, *The Iconography of Job Through the Centuries: Artists as Biblical Interpreters* (University Park: Pennsylvania State University Press, 1996), 124.

can never fully fathom what God has done. This is a truth widely attested in biblical traditions (e.g., Isa 40:12-14; Prov 30:4); indeed, within the book of Job, God will extensively develop this argument to question Job's knowledge of creation (38:1–39:30). It is also true, however, and widely attested, especially in the wisdom tradition, that God endows creation with order and principles that permeate the world and offer instruction for human behavior (e.g., Isa 1:3; Jer 8:7; Prov 6:6; 27:8; 30:24-28). When Job appeals to creation, he is in fact searching for truth in the same way that Bildad has done in 8:11-19. Given the sarcasm in his speech, he appears to be taking the argument a step further for the sake of making his point: *even* the animals know the truth about what he has experienced!

But if Zophar is wrong to think that creation only serves to hide the mysteries of God, Job is also wrong to assume that what creation teaches is simple and elementary. The tell-tale clue that Job also has yet to learn all that creation would teach him lies in the use of the word *bĕhēmôt* in v. 7. The term refers to large land animals, usually "cattle." In the present context, it is best taken in a general sense, as NRSV has done. Subsequently, however, God will instruct Job to pay special attention to the creature called Behemoth (40:15-24). At that point, God will suggest that Job should look again at creation, for this particular animal, "which I made just as I made you" (40:15), has something to teach him that he has not yet understood.

Second, *what* does creation teach about God? Job's answer to this question is straightforward but still oblique. Creation teaches "that the hand of the Lord (YHWH) has done this" (v. 9). What does creation teach about being in "the hand of the Lord"? If the "life" (*nepeš*) and "breath" (*rûaḥ*) of every living creature is in the hand of God, as Job goes on to say (v. 10), is this a good thing or a bad thing? On the one hand, the biblical tradition affirms that to be in the hand of God is to be protected and cared for. A particularly pertinent example occurs in Isaiah 49:2, which describes how God hides the "suffering servant" "in the shadow of his hand." On the other hand, the biblical witness also recognizes that there is some uncertainty that comes with being in the hand of God, for one cannot always be sure of God's intentions. As Qohelet observes, both the righteous and the wicked may be in the hand of God, but "whether it is for love or hate one does not know" (Eccl 9:1). The reader suspects that Job is inclined to agree with Qohelet. From the prologue we know that the *satan* urged God to stretch out the "hand" and test Job's piety (1:11; 2:5). When the test of affliction comes to Job, it is because God delivered him into the *satan's* "hand" (2:6). It would occasion little surprise then if being in the hand of God is for Job a truth that evokes terror and dread, not joy. ["Lodged"]

Even so, Job's choice of words hint that he has tapped into a truth larger than he can presently see. The words of v. 9 are a verbatim repetition of Isaiah 41:20b. As others have noted, it is likely that both Job and the prophet are simply repeating a well known affirmation.[7] One clue that this is so in the present context is the occurrence of the divine name YHWH, which otherwise never appears in the poetic sections of this book (see [Names for God]). What may go unnoticed, however, is that the citation from Deutero-Isaiah is part of a far-reaching and imaginative promise addressed to the exiles in Babylon

"Lodged"

The rain to the wind said,
"You push and I'll pelt."
They so smote the garden bed
That the flowers actually knelt,
And lay lodged—though not dead.
I know how the flowers felt.

Robert Frost, "Lodged," *The Poetry of Robert Frost*, ed. E. C. Lathem (New York: Henry Holt and Company, 1969), 250.

(Isa 41:1-20). Their circumstances are not unlike Job's. They too find themselves trapped in a world of inexplicable suffering. Like Job, they despair that God does not see, does not care, and does not heed their cries for justice (e.g., 40:27). The prophet responds by assuring them that the God upon whom the cosmos depends (note the creation imagery in 41:18-19) is about to act:

> Do not fear, for I am with you,
> do not be afraid, for I am your God;
> I will strengthen you, I will help you,
> I will uphold you with my victorious right hand. (41:10)

For the exiles, as for Job, the promise awaits fulfillment. Between "now" and "then" the words must linger in the hearts and minds of those who have no reason to believe. All they have are words, ambiguous, freighted words that say more than the present allows them to hear.

Job concludes the lesson on creation with two further traditional sayings, which he feels confident the friends agree with (vv. 11-12). Is it not the case, he asks, that a truly wise person will "test" (v. 11) what creation teaches? The imagery draws upon a proverbial saying that compares the functions of the ear and the mouth (Elihu will use the same expression in 34:3; cf. Sir 36:24). The mouth (or the palate) is designed not simply to swallow food but to taste and decide which foods are worthy to be eaten and which are not. So too the ear does not simply receive sounds, it processes them, decodes them, and renders them intelligible. Job is sure that the truth of this statement is self-evident; he expects no disagreement from his friends. He then proceeds, however, to rebuke them for failing to use the critical thinking that they pretend to endorse. As Bildad has already demonstrated (8:8-10; cf. Eliphaz in 15:10), the friends rely on the assumption that wisdom and understanding come from studying the traditions of the aged (v. 12). Job argues that conventional wisdom must be tested by experience, against which it may be validated, revised, or dismissed. What Job discerns when he applies his critical faculties to the lessons of creation is vastly different from what the friends claim they have learned. They look at the world through the lens of retribution theology and conclude that everything is in order. Job looks at the same world through the lens of suffering and concludes that something has gone terribly wrong. His contends that what he sees and knows, *his wisdom*, is not inferior to *theirs* (cf. v. 3). ["Call to Creation"]

Job now offers his own version of *discerning praise* to the Creator of the world that he has come to know (vv. 13-25). Eliphaz has modeled for him the praise that traditional wisdom expects (5:8-16). Job has

"Call to Creation"

Langston Hughes (1902–1967) was an American writer and poet known for his imaginative use of jazz and black folk rhythms. With other African-Americans, like Paul Robeson and Louis Armstrong, Hughes was a major figure during the Harlem Renaissance (1920–1930). Beginning in the 1930s he used poems like "Call to Creation" as a vehicle for social protest. Looking with the eyes of the suffering, Hughes has a perspective on the world that summons all those who see *only* beauty to look again and "see where the murmur runs":

Listen!
All you beauty-makers,
Give up beauty for a moment.

Look at harshness, look at pain,
Look at life again.
Look at hungry babies crying,
Listen to the rich men lying,
Look at starving China dying.
Hear the rumble in the East:
"In spite of all,
Life must not cease."
In India with folded arms,
In China with the guns,
In Africa with bitter smile—
See where the murmur runs . . .

Langston Hughes, "Call to Creation," *The Collected Poems of Langston Hughes*, ed. A. Rampersad (New York: Vantage Books, 1994), 135.

already indicated that such praise will not work for him (9:5-10). Nothing in what the friends have said thus far has persuaded him to change what he believes is the praise God deserves. Indeed, he is more convinced than ever that in a world where innocent sufferers are mocked, the One who holds creation "in his hand" cannot be praised "as usual." What Job offers instead, is *painful praise.* His words are an amalgam of various conventional doxologies, but in his mouth they sound dissonant and out of tune. [CD: Job's Constructed Doxology] In one sense, his praise continues to parody what the friends urge on him. In a more important sense, the friends are no longer the real object of his sarcasm. The one who should feel the sting of these words is none other than God.

Job's praise divides into three strophes (vv. 14-15, 17-21, 23-25), each introduced by a thesis statement (vv. 13, 16, 22). The general theme throughout is God's wisdom, which Job describes in various ways. The three thesis statements mark a strategic development in the way Job comes to understand what this wisdom means to him. Verse 13 speaks of God's "wisdom and strength." Verse 16 retains the same general focus, but reverses the primary emphasis: "strength and wisdom." Verse 22 makes no mention of wisdom at all, although wisdom remains the assumed topic. What focuses Job's thought in this and the following verses is the imagery of "darkness." When Job looks at creation through the eyes of the suffering, the God he sees is characterized by three primary qualities, none of them positive, as far as he can tell: wisdom, strength, and darkness.

Verse 13 introduces the first strophe by attributing to God four qualities: "wisdom" (*ḥokmāh*), "strength" (*gĕbûrāh*), "counsel" (*ʿēṣāh*), and "understanding" (*tĕbûnāh*). The same qualities are used in Isa 11:2 to describe the ideal ruler who will be specially endowed with the "spirit of the Lord." In that context, these qualities are manifest by the ruler's execution of justice and righteousness, specifically on behalf of the poor and the afflicted (Isa 11:3-5). In the litany of reasons for praising God that Job offers, justice and righteousness are noticeably lacking. Verses 14 and 15 explain why. On earth, God "tears down" structures (e.g., cities, 2 Sam 11:25; Isa 14:17) and people (e.g., Exod 15:7; Isa 22:19) but does not "rebuild" them. God "shuts in" or "imprisons" people (cf. Zophar in 11:10) but does not "open up" the doors for their release or deliverance. In nature, God "withholds" the waters until there is too little to survive, then "sends them out" with flood-like force until they "overwhelm" the land. That God has authority and power to curse as well to bless is not what Job finds bewildering. It is rather that God does so without respect to the merits of innocence or guilt, neither of which is mentioned in these verses.

Verse 16 introduces the second strophe and continues the focus on what we may now refer to as God's "so-called" wisdom.[8] The emphasis shifts to the "power" (ʿōz) and "efficiency" (tûšîyāh; see the commentary on 11:6) that accompanies God's wisdom. God exercises power over both the "deceiver" and the "deceived." The "deceiver" (šōgēg) is the one who causes another to go astray or become lost. The "deceived" (mašsgeh) is the one who is the victim of such an effort. In a court of law, an impartial judge would make a distinction between the claims of these two kinds of people. Job implies that God does not. If there is no distinction between the innocent and the guilty, or on the larger scale between good and evil, then God's governance can hardly be just or effective.

Verses 17-21 provide examples of the power God exercises over the leaders of the social order. In each case, Job identifies God as the "deceiver." The designated leaders of society, and the people who look to them for principled governance, are the ones who are "deceived." They discover that God has *used* them as administrators of divine caprice. They are chosen not to govern but to be denied the possibility of governing. Such a display of "wisdom" on God's part is unprecedented. Typically, persons are not only warned against leading others astray (Prov 28:10), they are cursed when they do so (Deut 27:18). Only in Psalm 119:10 is God ever identified as the One who may lead people astray, and in this text the psalmist implores God *not to* engage in such action.

Job lists nine categories of persons who are entrusted with leadership responsibilities in the social, political, and religious spheres of communal life. The details of how God destroys their capacities to govern vary, but the cumulative effect from reading through the list is more than sufficient to communicate the general point:

- God leads away *counselors* (*yō'ăṣîm*) naked
- God makes *judges* (*šōpĕṭîm*) act foolishly
- God removes the symbols of authority from *kings* (*mĕlākîm*)
- God leads away *priests* (*kōhănîm*) naked
- God overthrows the *well-established* (*'ētānîm*; NRSV: "mighty"; the reference is likely to the first ranks of the priests)
- God deprives the *trustworthy* (*ne'ĕmānîm*) of speech
- God takes away the discernment of the *elders* (*zĕqēnîm*)
- God pours contempt on the *nobles* (*nĕdîbîm*)
- God loosens the girdle of the *strong* (*'ăpîkîm*)

The third strophe (vv. 22-25) completes the description of God's manipulation of the moral orders of the cosmos by adding two further examples: God makes nations great only to destroy them (v. 23); God strips leaders of understanding, leaving them to wander aimlessly, like a drunken person, along paths they are too impaired to navigate (vv. 24-25). Job adds a new charge, however, that places these last examples and the preceding ones in a different and most disturbing context. Zophar has rebuked Job for pretending to understand the "depths" (*'ămuqqāh*; 11:8) of God's wisdom. Job counters that he has plumbed these "depths" (*'ămuqôt*; v. 22), and he now understands what they reveal about God's intentions. His charge strikes at the very heart of God's design for creation. When God created the world, the intent was not to impose order on "chaos" (*tōhû*) or to dispel "darkness" (*ḥōšek*; Gen 1:2) with light. Instead, Job claims, the objective was to bring forth darkness (*ḥōšek*; vv. 22a; cf. v. 25a) in its most threatening form (*ṣalmāwet*, "deep/deathly darkness"; v. 22b), and then to give it free reign to impose "chaos" (*tōhû*; v. 24: NRSV: "pathless waste") on every human endeavor.

From the ash heap, Job asked why God gives life to those whose suffering makes it no longer worth living (3:11, 12, 20). He suspected that God's hidden purposes were sinister, not benevolent, that God created only to destroy (10:13-17). Now, despite every effort by the friends to dissuade him from the charge, he declares that his suspicions are true. From the ash heap, he uttered a curse, which called for a reversal of God's first creative act: "Let there be darkness" (3:4; cf. Gen 1:3). He now understands that his curse was not only futile—he certainly has no power to cancel what God has done—it is also pathetically unnecessary. God's so-called blessing of creation is far worse than any curse Job himself can conjure. God has created a world in which leaders and followers alike are destined to "grope in darkness without light" (v. 25a).

["Design of Darkness to Appall"]

Job concludes the first part of his speech by stating once again that what he knows about God is not inferior to what his friends claim to know (13:1-3). What is remarkable is that "all this" (v. 1), that is, the preceding critique and condemnation of God's wisdom and power, does not lead Job to resign in silent despair. Despite the friends' warning that he is pursuing an improper and ultimately dangerous confrontation with God, despite his own recognition that it is foolish to think God will engage him in serious dialogue, Job will "speak to the Almighty" (v. 3). The second line of v. 3 is more than a simple parallel expression. Job's resolve has now become a fervent "desire" (*ʾaḥpāṣ*; NJPS: "I insist"). His intent is not simply to "speak" to God but to "argue" (*hôkēaḥ*) with God. The root form of the verb (*ykḥ*), which means "to determine what is right," signifies a process in which persons rebuke or correct one another until they come to the truth of matter (cf. Prov 19:25; 28:23). Previously, Job has conceded that there will be no "umpire" (9:33: *môkîaḥ*; the noun derives from the same verbal root *ykḥ*, "argue") to settle the dispute between himself and God, thus guaranteeing that if he argues with God he will be overmatched and under-powered. In the face of that reality, Job decides to go it alone.

The Friends Claim to Understand, But They Should Be Quiet, 13:4-12

Job warns the friends that the case he is preparing against God will indict them as well, unless they change their position. In a court of law, where strict rules of evidence apply, they will be vulnerable, because they are "plasterers of lies" (*ṭopĕlê šeqer*) and "worthless physicians" (*rōpʾē ʾĕlil*; v. 4). The first expression is an idiom for "cover-up." To "plaster" is literally to paint over something that is rough and ugly with a mixture of lime, water, and sand, which when it hardens, will leave it looking smooth and white. The process is often referred to as "white-washing." In a figurative sense, Job accuses his friends of trying to cover-up the ugly truth of what he has been saying by smearing him with a concoction of lies (cf. Ezek 13:10-12 with Ps 119:69). The second expression develops this image with reference to doctors (NJPS:

"quacks") who apply worthless medicines, what we might call place-boes, that cannot heal or comfort their patients. S. Mitchell's rendering is a paraphrase, but it captures well the gist of what Job is saying: "For you smear my wounds with ignorance and patch my body with lies."[9] Job cautions the friends to keep quiet (v. 5). If they are truly wise, they will pay close attention to the "argument" (v. 6: *tôkaḥtî*; from *ykḥ*, as in v. 3; NRSV: "reasoning") and the "pleadings" (*ribôt*) that he is about to present in his legal brief against God. As the traditional proverb puts it, "Even fools who keep silent are considered wise" (Prov 17:28; cf. Prov 10:18-19; 15:28).

Job addresses his friends as witnesses who will be called to testify in his case against God (vv. 7-10). When they are sworn in and take the stand, he will put to them a series of questions. Will they speak "falsely" (*'awlāh*) and "deceitfully" (*rĕmiyyāh*) *for God* (v. 7)? In a legal context, the two terms refer specifically to "perjury," that is, to lying under oath, the penalty for which is carefully prescribed (cf. Deut 19:16-19). Job has insisted that there is no falsehood (*'awlāh*) in his speech (6:30; NRSV: "wrong"), and subsequently he will state under oath that his testimony is free of "falsehood" (*'awlāh*) and "deceit" (*rĕmiyyāh*; 27:4). Can the friends say the same? When they take the stand to argue the case for God, will they be biased or impartial witnesses to the truth (v. 8)? Job's question implies that their testimony will be prejudiced. They will seek to gain favor with God by skewing the facts of the case to support what they believe is God's version of the story. Job warns them that they can expect to be cross-examined not only by him but also by God (v. 9). Job's observation is discerning and will require further comment in the "Connections." As Clines notes, those who speak in defense of God must realize that they leave themselves open to divine inspection.[10] When God gets to the bottom of what the friends are saying (*ḥqr*; NRSV: "searches you out"; cf. 5:27), will their testimony hold up? Do they think they can "deceive" (*tālal*) God as easily as one fools an ordinary human being (cf. Jer 9:5)?

Like a good lawyer, Job asks questions to which he believes he already knows the answers (vv. 10-12). Just as he "argues" (*hôkēaḥ*; v. 3) his case against God, he has no doubt that God will "vigorously argue" (NRSV: "surely rebuke"; the verbal construction, *hôkēaḥ yôkîaḥ*, indicates intensity) the case against the friends. When God confronts them, they will cower in fear, because their version of the truth will not stand up. Their "maxims" (*zikkarōn*; lit., "memorials") may be time-honored, but their time has passed (v. 12). They bear witness to old sayings that Job's reality has reduced to "empty (lit., "ashen") platitudes" (NJPS). Their "responses" are like "clay" pots (cf. 4:19: "clay houses").[11] They can be easily shattered beyond repair.

Commentators rightly note that this part of Job's address seems highly ironic. He has already clearly expressed his belief that God does not operate by the rules of law (9:14-24). In God's hands, he believes, there is no difference between the "deceiver" and the "deceived" (12:16-21). And yet, when he warns the friends about the dangers of giving false or prejudiced testimony, he suggests that God will judge them according to the very standards that he has argued God ignores. In fact, Job is right about God's commitment to truth, although he does not yet know it, or if he does, he cannot yet believe it. In the epilogue, God will judge the friends' version of truth in very much the same way that Job has anticipated: "the Lord said to Eliphaz the Temanite: 'My wrath is kindled against you and against your two friends; for you have not spoken of me what is right . . .'" (42:7). What is most curious, and likely to Job's ears most remarkable, is the second part of God's assessment: "you have not spoken of me what is right . . . as my servant Job has" (42:7, 8). The greatest irony of all for Job will be the discovery that he and God share a common perspective on what it means to be an innocent sufferer who speaks "what is right." A crucial part of this discovery is the painful lesson that the route toward common ground with God may lead one to confrontations with the Almighty that the "wise" will regard as forbidden, impossible, and blasphemous. [CD: Truth and Blasphemy] Job has now headed down the road toward this kind of confrontation. The measure of his courage, or his stupidity, is that he does so without the benefit of the reader's advance knowledge of the ultimate outcome of the story.

Job Resolves to Argue His Case with God, Come What May, 13:13-28

Job will begin his direct address to God in 13:20-28, but first he reminds his friends that what he intends to say to God is meant for their ears as well. He admonishes them once more to be silent (v. 13; cf. v. 5) and "listen carefully" (v. 17; cf. v. 6) to the case he is preparing to argue before God. He will speak the truth as he sees it, "come what may" (v. 13b). His resolve is fixed, so too are his suspicions about "what may come" of his decision. God will "kill" him (v. 15), and when his failed lawsuit is over, he predicts that his only remaining option will be to die in silence (v. 19).

He describes his determination to challenge God with two graphic images (v. 14). The expression "take my flesh in my teeth" occurs nowhere else in the Hebrew Bible, hence its meaning is uncertain. The image may be that of an animal that carries its young (or perhaps its prey) between its teeth. When confronted by another animal, it will fight to the death to keep what it has. The second expression, "put my life in my hand," is less ambiguous and helps to clarify what Job is saying. The closest parallel occurs in 1 Sam 19:5, which describes how David, under-armed and overmatched, "took his life in his hand" when he fought the giant Goliath (cf. Judg 12:3; 1 Sam 28:21; Ps 119:109). Together the two expressions convey the same message: Job will enter into the fray with God, even if it means that it costs him his life.

One of the most famous and important lines in the book of Job occurs in v. 15. Two dramatically different interpretations of the text are possible. The more traditional reading is reflected in KJV, which a number of other translations continue to follow: "Though he slay me, yet will I trust in him" (cf. NAB, NIV). The Hebrew word translated as "trust," *yāḥal*, is one of a number of verbs that means "wait," and by extension, "hope."[12] Elsewhere, *yāḥal* describes Job's endurance or perseverance (6:11; 14:14; 30:26), and this would seem to be the sense of KJV's translation in 13:15 as well. Even though God may slay him, Job will persevere in faith. He will wait and hope, or as KJV puts it, he will "trust" in God. This rendering offers a pietistic understanding of Job's resolve that has been enormously influential. Indeed, for many readers, this assertion of faith provides the credo that most clearly articulates what it means to have the proverbial "patience of Job." In the prologue, Job rebukes his wife for suggesting that he respond to what has befallen him by cursing God. His last words from the ash heap are framed as a question: "Shall we receive the good at the hand of God and not the bad?" (2:10). The traditional rendering of 13:15 portrays Job as answering his own question. No matter what he receives from the hand of God, whether it is "good" or "bad," Job will cling to the hope that God will ultimately vindicate the righteous sufferer (for one portrayal of this conventional interpretation, see ["The Just Upright Man Is Laughed to Scorn"]).

It is instructive to note, however, that the traditional rendering of v. 15 is based on a small, but critical, alteration of the text. In the Hebrew text, the word that precedes the verb *yāḥal*, "hope/trust," is clearly written as the negative particle "no/not" (*lōʾ*). NRSV renders this appropriately with the translation "I have *no* hope" (cf. NJPS). A marginal note in the Hebrew text indicates that the word for "no" may be read as if it were a different word, *lô*, which means "to/for him." It is this marginal notation that traditional translations like KJV reflect. The pronunciation of the words *lōʾ* and *lô* is the same, but the spelling, and more importantly, the meaning is different. *What is written* in the body of the text is that Job has *no hope. What can be read,* if one substitutes the word in the margin of the text, is that Job *will hope "to (= in) him."*

Choosing Between "What is Written" and "What is Read"

AΩ The Masoretic tradition preserves a way of noting variations between "what is written" (*Ketib*) in the consonantal text and "what is read" (*Qere*) according to the tradition of vocalization. Such variations arose over the centuries of the transmission of the text and were likely caused by a number of different factors. In Job 13:15, the *Ketib* is *lōʾ ʾăyaḥēl*, "I have *no* hope," or "I will *not* hope." The *Qere*, which represents an orthographic change in the first word of one letter, is *lô ʾăyaḥēl*, "I will hope *to* (= *in*) him."

Traditional translations like KJV have chosen the *Qere* and thus have translated the text *as emended*: "Though he slay me, yet will I trust in him." This choice cannot be simply equated with a desire to convey a more positive portrait of Job, although it clearly does so, for there is substantial evidence in ancient manuscripts and versions of Job to support the proposed emendation. Moreover, it is likely that ancient manuscripts are preserving a tradition of reading Job that was established at least as early as the first century CE (e.g., *Testament of Job* 27:7; Jas 5:7, 11).

Such evidence suggests, then, that the Masoretes were aware that ancient tradition preserved two different understandings of Job 13:15 and thus two quite different interpretations of the way Job responded to his suffering. An interesting passage in the Mishnah frames the crucial question that has long confronted those who look to Job as a model for faith. In the tractate *Sotah* 5.5, it is reported that R. Joshua ben Hyrcanus (second century CE) discussed the difficulty of Job 13:15 and concluded "The matter is undecided—do I trust in him (*lô*) or do I not trust (*lōʾ*)?" (See the discussion in R. Gordis, *The Book of Job: Commentary, New Translation, and Special Studies* [New York: Jewish Theological Seminary of America, 1978], 144.)

The rabbi's question invites reflection on what is perhaps the most enduring cliché associated with this book: the patience of Job. Do people of faith best exemplify Job's legacy when they endure suffering patiently, or when they protest it with radical impatience? In view of the evidence, there is no easy answer to this question. On the one hand, Masoretes determined that it was not only permissible but necessary to *change* the text in order to preserve its *correct* meaning. (See the discussion of B. Zuckerman, *Job the Silent: A Study in Historical Counterpoint* [New York: Oxford University Press, 1991],

170-74.) The model of the "patient Job" surely offers an important word of encouragement to those who throughout history have longed to find in scripture some reason to hope for restoration in the midst of great suffering and loss. As John Chrysostom, patriarch of Constantinople (4th C.), observed, Job "exhausted the misfortunes of the universe" without yielding to the temptation of disbelief. Therefore, when sorrow and suffering strike unawares, "let us always flee to this book."

On the other hand, one can also reasonably suppose that the author of the Joban dialogues intended to criticize and subvert the stereotype of the "patient Job." In contrast to the pietistic ideal embodied by the Job of the prologue, this Joban poet sees no hope of vindication. Like the character of Jenny in Henry Fielding's *The History of Tom Jones*, Job has learned the hard truth that patience "is a virtue which is very apt to be fatigued by exercise." When hope wanes, Job clings to his integrity. When all else fails, he remains true to his conviction that he is innocent, even if it means arguing for justice before a silent God. A model of faith that values honest protest over submission also has an appeal to those who would "flee to this book" in the midst of suffering. For everyone who summons the courage to hope in the midst of adversity, there is someone else who has tried to do so but has failed. For those whose suffering is too great to be patient, the heroic figure of Job screaming against the heavens for relief may provide the only model of faith that is credible.

Instead of choosing one of these portrayals of Job and rejecting the other, it is instructive to recognize that both are deeply rooted in the biblical tradition. Perhaps, like the Masoretes, we must preserve the memory of both the "patient Job" and the "impatient Job," for both have an authentic role to play in the life of faith. Depending on the severity of our suffering and sorrow, either the one or the other will move from the margins of our experience to the center.

For discussion of Chrysostom's presentation of Job, see N. Glatzer, *The Dimensions of Job: A Study and Selected Readings* (New York: Schocken Books, 1969), 24-27.

H. Fielding, *The History of Tom Jones, A Foundling*, vol. 1 (New York: P. F. Collier & Son, 1917), 19.

Even though there is strong evidence in ancient manuscripts and versions of Job for following the marginal notation, the text as written is much more consistent with what Job has said in previous speeches. [Choosing Between "What Is Written" and "What Is Read"] He has cursed and lamented (ch. 3) but to no avail. The friends have urged him to be patient and to trust in God's eventual justice (4:5-7; 11:18), but Job despairs that he does not have the strength to wait on God that long (6:11-13). He has resolved to take God to court, but he does not expect justice, for he knows that God will not answer his charges (9:16, 19-20). Now Job dares to take another risky step toward confrontation with God. Against all odds, he will argue his case face to face with the Creator of the world (13:15b). His "salvation" (v. 16a) will come not from winning the case against God, for there is no hope of that, but from knowing that he has been true to his convictions. A "sinner" (v. 16b: *ḥānēp*, lit., one "perverted by wickedness"; NRSV: "godless") would not dare to stand before God as Job prepares to do.

Job summons his friends to "listen carefully" (v. 17) to the case he is preparing to make against God. He will "order" (v. 18a: *ʿārak*; NRSV: "prepare") his arguments carefully so as to give himself the best chance for success, as if he were he were a general positioning battle troops for strategic advantage (cf. Judg 20:22, 30; 1 Sam 17:8; 2 Sam 10:8). One assumes that Job will present various pieces of evidence, but his defense hangs on one simple assertion, which he states emphatically at the outset (note the repetition of the pronoun "I"): "*I* know that *I*, *I* am innocent (*ʾeṣdāq*)" (v. 18b). It is grammatically possible to translate this phrase as NRSV has done: "I know that I shall be *vindicated.*" Such a rendering suggests that Job still holds out the hope that God will acquit him. Both the syntax and the general context indicate, however, that at this point Job is far more focused on *his innocence* than on *God's justice*. If God (or anyone else) can prove an innocent person guilty (v. 19a: "Who can argue [*yārîb*] with me?"), then Job will concede that he has gone as far as he can go in the pursuit of truth. It will be time then for him to be silent and die (v. 19b). Until that time, however, Job will confront innocent suffering not with patience, as the proverbial cliché would have it, but with naked courage.[13] ["The Supreme Vow"]

In 13:20-28, Job initiates at long last the direct address to God that has been his objective throughout this speech (13:3, 13). He begins by trying to negotiate "pretrial preliminaries" with God.[14] Two conditions must be stipulated, if his case is to go forward (v. 21). First, God must

"The Supreme Vow"

The supreme vow is no vow but a concession to anger at the exigencies of language. The hero

is he who advances
with all his vocabulary
intact to his final
overthrow by an untruth.

R. S. Thomas, "The Vow," *Poems of R. S. Thomas* (Fayetteville: University of Arkansas Press, 1985), 173.

agree to withdraw the divine hand (*kap*) that has laid heavy and unmerited suffering on Job (cf. *yad*, "hand," in 1:11; 2:5; 6:9; 10:7; 19:21). Second, God must agree to give up terrorizing Job so that he can think and speak clearly without the threat of preemptory intimidation. Both conditions are a virtual restatement of the conditions that Job has previously hoped an impartial arbitrator might impose on God (9:33-34). Since he realizes that there is no such person who can adjudicate these matters, Job now implores God to exercise voluntary self-constraint. If God will agree to these conditions, then the mutual interchange that Job desires can happen. When God "calls," Job will be prepared to "answer." When Job "speaks," God must be ready to "reply" (v. 22).

Job presses on with what he wishes to say to God. Two questions set the agenda for the dialogue he seeks. First, he asks God to make explicit the charges that have been brought against him (v. 23). The nature of his question indicates that God must clarify both the number ("how many"; *kammāh*) of his sins (note the plural nouns "iniquities," "sins") as well as their specific nature (note the singular nouns "transgression," "sin").[15] Job has repeatedly declared his innocence, so his question is not an admission that he has in fact sinned. To the contrary, Job assumes that God cannot produce any evidence of his wrongdoing. In actuality, the question only thinly disguises an implicit charge that it is God, not Job, who is guilty of wrongful conduct. A close parallel occurs in Jer 2:5, where God's clearly rhetorical question lays the foundation for an indictment of Israel: "What wrong did your ancestors find in me that they went far from me?"

Job's second question is equally reproachful: "Why (*lāmmāh*) do you hide your face, and count me as your enemy?" (v. 24a). "Hide the face" (*histîr pānîm*) is an idiom for divine absence, which is used in Hebrew scriptures in two principle ways. The prophets understand God's hiddenness as a just punishment of sin (Isa 59:2; Jer 33:5; Mic 3:4). The psalmists, on the other hand, lament and despair that God is inexplicably absent (Pss 13:1 [MT 13:2]; 30:7 [MT 30:8]) and petition God not to abandon them in their time of need (Pss 69:17 [MT 69:18]; 102:2 [MT 102:3]). [God's Hiddenness] Job's question is like that of the psalmists but with a paradoxical twist. For him, God's *absence* is more than inexplicable; it is a sinister and perverted form of *hostile presence*. God abandons him and assaults him at the same time. Job has previously complained that God attacks him as if he were some dangerous opponent who must be targeted for defeat (7:12; 10:16). Now he asks God to explain why it is that he has been labeled as the "enemy" (v. 24b). It is possible that there is a play on the words "Job" (*ʾiyyôb*) and "enemy" (*ʾōyēb*; see the commentary on 1:1). If one views the matter through Job's eyes, one might speculate that he believes God no

God's Hiddenness

AΩ The phrase *histîr pānîm* ("hide the face") occurs twenty-nine times in the Hebrew Bible. Of all the Hebrew verbs that mean "hide," only this verb *(sātar)* takes the word *pānîm* ("face") as an object. In twenty-six of the twenty-nine occurrences, the reference is to God's hiding the face. The lexical evidence indicates that this phrase was used over a relatively long period of time—at least from the sixth century until the mid to late post-exilic period—as *the* particular expression for the absence of God.

The distribution of the phrase in the Hebrew Bible may be illustrated in the chart below. The three occurrences in which a person other than God is the subject of the verb are identified with an asterisk (Samuel E. Balentine, *The Hidden God: The Hiding of the Face of God in the Old Testament* [Oxford: Oxford University Press, 1983], 45).

Pentateuch	*Psalms*	*Prophets*	*Wisdom*
(4x)	(12x)	(11x)	(2x)
*Exod 3:6	Pss 10:11; 13:1 [MT 13:2];	Isa 8:17;	Job 13:24;
(Moses);	22:24 [MT 22:25];	*50:6 (suffering servant);	34:29
Deut 31:17, 18;	27:9; 30:7 [MT 30:8];	*53:3 (suffering servant);	
32:20	44:24 [MT 44:25];	54:8;	
	51:9 [MT 51:11];	59:2; 64:7 [MT 64:6];	
	69:17 [MT 69:18];	Ezek 39:23, 24, 29;	
	88:14 [MT 88:15];	Mic 3:4;	
	102:2 [MT 102:3];	Jer 33:5	
	104:29; 143:7		

longer recognizes him for who he is. He is no longer the "blameless" and "upright" servant who merits God's unqualified endorsement (cf. 1:8; 2:3). Now he is the "enemy" whom God feels compelled to eliminate "for no reason" (cf. 2:3).

With a series of graphic images, Job describes what it feels like to be God's enemy (vv. 25-27). He is weak and feeble; like a "windblown leaf" or "dry chaff," he is cut off from the source of life that gives him strength. He has no chance of withstanding the God who is bent on "terrifying" (cf. Isa 2:19, 21) and "harassing" him (NRSV: "pursue"; cf. Pss 69:26 [MT 69:27]; 109:16; 119:86, 161) with such power. God "writes bitter things against" him, like a judge who issues a decree that mandates harsh treatment for an offender (cf. Isa 10:1). No crime is specified, however, so Job can only surmise that he is being punished for what he may have done when he was but a child. Even if he is culpable for adolescent indiscretions, God's punishment seems wholly disproportionate to the offense. God places his feet in "stocks," like a prisoner. God "watches" his every move (cf. 7:20; 10:13). God sets a boundary around his feet so that his movement in any direction is restricted. In sum, to be God's enemy is to be the target of relentless assault, excessive punishment, and terminal imprisonment.

Many commentators, noting that verse 28 seems to fit more naturally with what follows in the next chapter, have suggested that its original location was after 14:2.[16] If one reads it in its present context, it may be understood to extend and develop the imagery of God's disproportionate attention to Job.[17] Job's life is falling apart. He is worn out, like something that is rotten (LXX: "like a wine-skin") and cannot be repaired. He is tattered and torn like a moth-eaten garment. Why should God expend such energy on one so pitifully weak? Such despair is similar to the way Job has concluded previous speeches (cf. 7:17-21; 10:18-22).

Job Laments that God Has Appointed Boundaries Beyond Which No Human Can Go, 14:1-22

Job's closing words of the first cycle return the drama to it beginnings. When the friends first arrived on the scene, they sat in silence, because they saw that Job's "pain" (*kĕʾēb*, 2:13; NRSV: "suffering") was exceedingly great. Job was the first to break that silence with words of curse and lament that announced "trouble" (*rōgez*, 3:26) had overwhelmed his life. He has listened to three speeches by the friends who have tried to explain that trouble. In response to all that he has heard, however, his basic perspective on life remains unchanged. Human beings are born to a life "full of trouble (*rōgez*, 14:1)." When all is said and done, they know nothing beyond the "pain" (*kāʾab*, 14:22) of their own miserable existence.

Job now retraces the tracks of this "trouble" and "pain" in a mournful lament comprised of three primary sections. Verses 1-12 describe the hopeless condition of human existence from birth (v. 1: mortals are "born" to trouble) to death (v. 10: they "die" and "expire"). In vv. 13-17, he imaginatively explores the possibility that the hope denied in life might be realized in some post-mortem existence (v. 14: "If mortals die, will they live again?"), where God is less abusive and more compassionate. But having dreamed of what might be, Job returns to the hard realities of how things really are (vv. 18-22). One sentence summarizes his numbing assessment of life in the world God has created: "you [God] destroy the hope of mortals" (v. 19).

Job's last speech in the first cycle, like his first (chapter 3), continues to look to creation for some analogue that would explain how suffering like his fits into God's design for the cosmos. He looks to the "flower" and the "shadow" (v. 2), the "tree" (vv. 7-9), the "water" of lakes and rivers (v. 11), the "mountain," the "rock," the "stones," and the "soil" (vv. 18-19), yet he discerns in none of these any message that lessens his despair. The one section of his speech that makes no mention of analogies

Structure of Job 14:1-22

	14:1-12	The hopeless condition of human existence from birth to death
	vv. 1-6	Mortals are born to trouble
	vv. 7-9	There may be hope for a tree
	vv. 10-12	But mortals die
	14:13-17 Job explores the possiblity of a post-modern hope	
	14:18-22	God destroys the hope of mortals

from nature is vv. 13-17, where Job dares to imagine that in another place and time, when "the heavens are no more" (v. 12), life might be different. But this, after all, is only a vision, and there is no evidence anywhere in the world that Job can see to corroborate it. [Structure of Job 14:1-22]

The first section of Job's speech divides into three sub-units (vv. 1-6, 7-9, 10-12). The first and third, which focus on the unalterable human journey from birth (vv. 1-6) to death (vv. 10-12), are thematically related. Every human being (v. 1: *'ādām*), Job observes, is destined from birth for life that is too short on time and too long on misery. Two conventional examples from nature provide a point of comparison for human existence (v. 2): the flower, which blossoms for a time, then wilts and fades away (cf. Ps 103:15-16; Isa 28:1, 4; 40:6-8); and the shadow, which lengthens as the day wanes, then suddenly disappears without leaving a trace behind (cf. Job 8:9; Pss 102:11 [MT 102:12]; 144:4; Eccl 6:12). Like the flower and the shadow, the days and months of every human life are "fixed" (*ḥărûṣ*; NRSV: "determined") by God with prescribed "limits" (*ḥōq*; NRSV: "bounds") that cannot be exceeded (v. 5). If God *would* but see humans for the weak creatures they are, then surely even God must concede the folly of bringing one such as Job to judgment (v. 3). The point is made even sharper by the fact that, from Job's perspective at least, there is no possibility that he can change his status. That which is unclean cannot be clean; by extension, frail human beings can never be equal to the task of one-on-one confrontation with God.[18] The only option open to humans is to implore God to leave them alone, so that they might serve out their days[19] without the added burden of God's constant surveillance (v. 6). If God will cease and desist, then humans will make the steady trek from birth to death (v. 10). Like water that evaporates from lakes and streams and does not reappear (v. 11), they will die and stay dead. They will not "rise again"; they will not "awake; they cannot be "roused" (v. 12). ["Nothing Happens"]

Sandwiched between vv. 1-6 and 10-12 is a brief interlude on the "tree" (vv. 7-9) that temporarily distracts Job from his sweeping review of the unalterable human journey from birth to grave. Whereas Job has no hope (7:6: *tiqwāh*; cf. 13:15), there is "hope" (v. 7a: *tiqwāh*) for a tree. If it is "cut down," it can "sprout again" (v. 7b: *yaḥălîp*). If its roots grow old and it dies, water will revive it, and it will put forth new growth like a tree that has just been planted (vv. 8-9). It is possible that the image has to do with the practice in the Transjordan of cutting off old fig

"Nothing Happens"

The hopelessness of finding God in a fallen world is a major theme in the work of the Irish poet and playwright Samuel Beckett (1906–1989). In *Waiting for Godot*, the play that many regard as Beckett's masterpiece, the character Estragon articulates a Joban-like understanding of the utter wretchedness of a life that is emptied of every sign of transcendence: "Nothing happens, nobody comes, nobody goes, it's awful."

S. Beckett, *Waiting for Godot* (New York: Grove Press, 1954), 27.

The Symbolism of the Tree

The tree, along with other special plants, is a common symbol of the gift of immortality in ancient Near Eastern myths. In the Mesopotamian text "The Epic of Gilgamesh" (second millennium BCE), for example, Gilgamesh tries to avert death by obtaining the secret of immortality from Utnapishtim, the survivor of the great flood of long ago. Utnapishtim offers him a plant by which he can "regain his life's breath." Gilgamesh names the plant "Man Becomes Young In Old Age," and determines that he will eat of it, because it will enable him to "return to the state of my youth" (Tablet XI, 279, 282-84). Unfortunately for Gilgamesh, a serpent smells the fragrance of the plant and carries it off before he can eat from it.

The image of the tree as a source of life carries over into the Old and New Testament and the intertestamental literature. References to the "tree of life" occur in the creation story (Gen 2:9; 3:22, 24) and in Prov 3:18, 11:30, 13:12, 15:4, where it functions as metaphor for the good life that is offered by Wisdom. In Ezekiel's description of the restored Jerusalem, a fresh stream of water flows out of the city and towards the east, bringing fertility in its wake as far south as the Dead Sea. The signs of that fertility are the evergreen trees that grow on the banks of the stream, which are a constant source of fresh fruit that provides food and healing (Ezek 47:1-12; cf. the "trees planted by streams of water" in Ps 1:3). The "tree of life" in Revelation is also associated with the vision of the new Jerusalem (21:9–22:5). In this vision, the fruit of the tree is reserved for the righteous (22:14). A similar scene is described in *1 En* 25:4-5, which reports that on the day of judgment, those who rise to new life in God's presence will eat of the fruit of the tree (cf. T. Levi 18:10-11; 4 Ezra 7:123-124).

For the ancient text see *ANET*, 3rd ed. with supplement, ed. J. B. Pritchard (Princeton: Princeton University Press, 1969), 96.

---

trees, pomegranates, and vines close to the ground, so that in the next year new growth may sprout forth freely.[20]

It is more likely that the tree should be understood against the mythopoetic background of its use as a symbol for life, longevity, and rejuvenation. In ancient Near Eastern literature, the tree is a common fertility symbol representing the source of life that grants one wisdom and power comparable to the gods. [The Symbolism of the Tree] The most pertinent biblical allusion to this myth is in Genesis 2–3, which describes two trees, the "tree of life" and the "tree of the knowledge of good and evil" (Gen 2:9), which were planted in the garden of Eden. The first tree is emblematic of life in its fullest possible scope. The second represents a God-like knowledge of "good and evil" (the phrase is idiomatic for the totality of what can be comprehended about ethical and moral choices). Although the "tree of life" is mentioned at the beginning and ending of the story (2:9; 3:22, 24), the principle focus lies on the "tree of the knowledge of good and evil" (2:9, 17; 3:2-6, 11-12). It is this tree that is expressly forbidden the first couple (2:17), not only because it holds radical possibilities for immortality, but also because it invites what this story clearly understands to be the misguided notion that human beings can attain the understanding that makes them in some sense "like God" (3:22).

It is interesting to speculate on the possible echo of Genesis 2–3 in Job's reflections on the hope of the tree. It is reasonable to suggest that the tree is an alluring symbol of the hope for rejuvenation that temporarily fixes Job imagination.[21] It is also instructive to consider that

Job's hope is not only for life, as if he would be satisfied simply to go on drawing breath. Even more than life, Job desires to understand what is happening to him. On the far side of the "garden of Uz," Job is no longer content simply to accept whatever "good" and "evil" God may assign him (2:10; see further the commentary on Job 1–2). He insists on asking "Why?" He has invited the friends to teach him what his failures are (6:24), but they are convinced that Job simply cannot understand the ways of God (11:7-8). He has repeatedly implored God to make known to him what he has done wrong (7:20; 10:2; 13:23), but he is convinced that no matter how persistently he may call, God will not answer (9:2, 16; 13:22). Like the primordial couple, Job has been denied knowledge of "good and evil," and like them, he has been barred from the fullness of life in the garden. The reason for their banishment was sin. The reason for his is unknown. At issue in both cases is what it means, finally, to be created in the image of God. If the wicked and the righteous alike are denied the possibility of attaining Eden's promise, then how can human beings ever hope to fulfill the divine commission to image God (cf. Gen 1:26-27)? Job looks at the tree and reflects on *life* and *understanding* as divine gifts that have been irretrievably and inexplicably lost. East of Eden/Uz, Job concludes that the only "hope" for humankind is to be born, live in misery, and die. When that sad sequence of events is complete, all that remains is for someone to say a final word: "Human beings (*'ādām*) expire, and where are they?" (v. 10).

From the depths of abject hopelessness, Job reaches far beyond anything he can see or believe to search for some other alternative to life as he knows it (vv. 13-17). Is it possible, he wonders, that after human beings die, they may live again (v. 14)? The logical answer to this question is "No," for the traditional understanding in Israelite thinking is that at death one descends to Sheol, there to remain forever, cut off from the presence of God. [Resurrection?] But Job is not focused on facts. He dreams of possibilities that exceed what traditional knowledge can establish or verify. Perhaps Sheol is not in fact a final destination but instead a place of temporary asylum. He envisions the possibility that God might hide him there until God's anger has passed. Then, at the appointed time God would remember him (*zākar*), summon him back to the land of the living, and resume the relationship (v. 13). God's remembrance would signal a new beginning, like the time when God "remembered" (*zākar*) Noah after the flood waters had passed and summoned him forth into a new world with fresh possibilities for realizing the objectives of creation's design (Gen 8:1).[22] If this were possible, then Job would be willing to endure the "hard service" (v. 14: *ṣābā'*; cf. 7:1) of time spent in Sheol. Whereas in life as he presently knows it,

Resurrection?

In the Hebrew Bible, the common lot of every human being is to die and descend to the place of the dead called Sheol (see **[Sheol]**). There is no concept of life after death, although in one or perhaps two late passages there may be some movement in this direction (see below). There are a few cases in which individuals escape death. Enoch (Gen 5:24) and Elijah (2 Kgs 2:11) were "transferred" from life to heaven. Elijah and Elisha both performed miraculous healings that resuscitated individuals who had died (1 Kgs 17:17-24; 2 Kgs 4:31-37; cf. 2 Kgs 13:20-21). Other texts promise a future restoration for the people of God following some national disaster or particularly difficult period (e.g., Hos 6:1-3; Ezek 37:1-14). Each of these cases describes singular and specific events. They do not speak of resurrection as the promise or hope for all human beings.

Two texts, both from the post-exilic period when apocalyptic views were becoming prominent in Jewish communities, envision something different. The most explicit is Dan 12:1-3, which dates to the time of the persecution of the Jews by Antiochus Epiphanes (167–164 BCE). The angel Michael announces a coming time of great distress, which those who are "found written in the book" will survive (v. 1). Those who do not survive will experience two different "after death" fates. Some will awake to "everlasting life"; others, presumably those who betrayed the cause, will find themselves bound for "everlasting contempt" (v. 2). The promise of life to those who "sleep in the dust of the earth" (v. 2a) is similar to a second, more obscure, passage in Isa 26:19: "O dwellers in the dust, awake and sing for joy!" Both these texts suggest that believers who are faithful in times of torment will experience a resurrection from the dead. The purpose of the resurrection, however, is not to effect the salvation or the immortality of the human soul, which subsequently will emerge as a central concern in the New Testament, but rather to demonstrate the justice of God.

The New Testament concept of resurrection clearly post-dates the book of Job. Nevertheless, in Christian theology Job has come to be viewed as a forerunner of Christ, one who suffers righteously and after death is vindicated and restored by God.

For a convenient summary of the concept of resurrection in the Hebrew Bible, see R. Martin-Achard, "Resurrection," *ABD*, ed. D. N. Freedman (New York: Doubleday, 1992), vol. 5, 680-84; J. Day, "The Development of Belief in Life After Death in Ancient Israel," *After the Exile: Essays in Honour of Rex Mason*, ed. J. Barton, D. J. Reimer (Macon GA: Mercer University Press, 1996), 231-58.

Job has "no hope" (13:15: *lōʾ ʾăyaḥēl*), in the refuge of Sheol, he could "wait/hope" (*ăyaḥēl*) for a post-mortem renewal (*ḥălîpāh*; NRSV: "release"; the same root in 14:7 describes the tree that will "sprout again").

What is most striking about Job's vision is not that he contemplates life after death, as radical as this idea is. He dares to imagine that the purpose of his time in Sheol is not so much to give *him* an opportunity to change as to give *God* the chance to change. He thinks of God hiding him until God's "anger" passes (v. 13; cf. 9:13). Once this has occurred, perhaps a new and different God will emerge (vv. 15-17). *This* God would not have to be summoned; instead, God would take the initiative to "call" Job, and Job would "answer." *This* God would no longer "despise" the handiwork of creation (cf. 10:3) but would instead "yearn" (*kāsap*; NRSV: "long") for it with the same intensity that equals the human quest to be with God (Ps 84:2 [MT 84:3]; cf. Gen 31:30). *This* God would "number" Job's steps not to spy out every possible sin but to find where he may have fallen short of the mark and "cover over" (cf. 13:4) his failure with compassion that exceeds the need for judgment.

But the world Job dreams of does not exist; neither does the God who might bring it into being (vv. 18-22). In the real world, even the strongest are gradually worn down to nothing. When one looks to nature, the truth is that even the most solid and resilient objects of creation—mountains, rocks, stones—can be destroyed by the relentless erosion of water. When one looks to human beings, the truth is that God destroys every "hope" with the same irresistible force (vv. 18-19). In the end, the fate of all human beings is the same. God overpowers them in life, and when at last their face has been disfigured by age and suffering, God dispatches them to the hopeless permanence of death (v. 20). Once banished, the dead are forever cut off from the land of the living. They cannot know whether their children live to be "honored" (*yikbĕdû*) or "belittled" (*yiṣʿărû*; NRSV: "brought low"; v. 21). All that is left to them is the lingering "pain" of flesh (*bāśār*) that can no longer feel, and the mournful lament of a soul that can no longer cry (v. 22).

With these poignant images of death, Job concludes his last speech in the first cycle in the same manner as he has done in each of his previous speeches (3:20-26; 7:19-21; 10:18-22). For the one who insists on asking "Why?" there remains no answer. For the one who dares to hope for a life beyond this life, and for a God beyond this God, there is only the deepening conviction that the boundaries imposed on humankind render both yearnings null and void.

CONNECTIONS

This long and complex speech is enormously rich and invites theological reflection on a variety of issues. Three issues will be singled out in the discussion that follows, with the understanding that they in no way exhaust the claims this text will make on those who will examine it thoughtfully.

Bearing Witness to the Truth of Suffering

Suffering has taught Job things about life and about God that he must speak honestly. Although the friends prefer to deny or discount the importance of what he has to say, Job insists that his understanding is not inferior to theirs (12:3; 13:2). It deserves equal standing in the marketplace of truth that both informs and confounds every quest to be fully human. The strong and the secure may believe that their good fortune equals the sum of truth, but the weak and the vulnerable will calculate things differently. Persons who fall into the former category will be inclined to accept the wisdom of the friends with little or no reservation. Those whose experiences land them in the latter group will likely seek other perspectives that speak more knowingly of different realities. Such persons may find in the wisdom of Job a truth that connects with their lives. They will not have to look in a dictionary to know what it means to be a "laughingstock" (12:4). They will not have to conduct a survey of public opinion to decide whether it is true that the "robbers are at peace" or "that those who provoke God are secure" (12:6). Their own experience will be sufficient to confirm that it is so. Even though Job's discernment may not lessen the burden they bear, they will be comforted to discover that someone is speaking truth that does not require them to wear a mask "that grins and lies." [CD: "We Wear the Mask"]

The truth of suffering, as Job discerns it, is larger than personal experience. Creation itself bears witness to the fact that "the hand of the Lord" (12:9) imposes boundaries and limits on every creature (14:9). God gives life and takes it away, and there is no one who can intervene to block or alter what God determines to do. Here too creation's truth is embraced differently, depending on whether one is favored with life or afflicted with misery. The friends look at the world and conclude that God's wisdom and strength secures justice for one and all (5:8-16; 8:8-19; 11:7-12). Job looks at the world and despairs that God's wisdom and strength permits the forces of darkness to run amok, dealing out random abuse and destruction that leaves nothing in its wake but chaos (12:13, 16, 22-25). Flowers bloom, then inexorably fade and die. Shadows come and go, leaving no sign that they ever existed (14:2). Mountains rise majestically, then disintegrate (14:18). The same water that revives the dead roots of a vulnerable tree (14:9) destroys the hardest stone and washes away soil that once was firm and productive (14:19). From the perspective of the flower, the mountain, the stone, the soil. . . and sufferers like Job, creation testifies that life in the world God has made is at best fraught with cruel ambiguities. At worst, it is manipulated by sinister decree. In either case, Job insists, suffering is a reality that nothing in creation, however strong, can endlessly forestall. [Creation Groans and Waits]

Job's truth about suffering belongs not only in the marketplace but also in the pulpit, because the world is full of people who are hurt and

Creation Groans and Waits

Paul speaks of the glory that will *one day* be fully manifest in the eschatological redemption of the world. *Until that time*, however, creation itself groans in travail and waits to be set free from the decay and futility that God has allowed the cosmic forces to impose on the world:

The creation was subjected to futility, not of its own will but by the will of the one who subjected it, in hope that the creation itself will be set free from its bondage to decay and will obtain the freedom of the glory of the children of God. We know that the whole creation has been groaning in labor pains until now; and not only the creation, but we ourselves. (Rom 8:20-23)

broken like him. Philip Roth recounts the story of one such person in the novel *American Pastoral.* [23] Seymour Irving Levov once lived the American dream In high school, he had been a star athlete in football, basketball, and baseball. After the war, he married a former Miss New Jersey, took over his father's business, and settled into the idyllic and prosperous world that was Old Rimrock, New Jersey. There was never a need to ask why things were they were: "Why should he bother, when the way they were was always perfect? Why are things the way they are? . . . he was so blessed he didn't even know the question existed" (70).

In 1968, everything changed. His beloved teenage daughter Merry unexpectedly left home, joined a terrorist group, and participated in a bombing that resulted in the death of an innocent bystander. He was instantly transported out of the "longed-for American pastoral," with all of its "carefully calibrated goodness" and into its very antithesis, the "counterpastoral—into the indigenous American berserk" (86). Roth describes Levov's encounter with the hard truth that forever changed his life as follows:

> He had learned the worst lesson that life can teach—that it makes no sense. And when that happens the happiness is never spontaneous again. It is artificial and, even then, bought at the price of an obstinate estrangement from oneself and one's history. The nice gentle man with his mild way of dealing with conflict and contradiction, the confident ex-athlete sensible and resourceful in any struggle with an adversary that is fair, comes up against the adversary who is not fair—the evil ineradicable from human dealings—and he is finished. He whose natural nobility was to be exactly what he seemed to be has taken in far too much suffering to be naively whole again. (81)

Job's truth is for those who, like Levov, have lived too much, seen too much, hurt too much to be "naively whole again." Their world will not be restored by what Job says. Their brokenness will not be automatically mended. Their burden will not be any less heavy. But they will know that they are not alone in this world of too much suffering and grief. And that is a truth that offers its own mysterious kind of comfort and sustenance so long as they live in a world where they must "grope in the dark without light" (12:25). ["Lonely"]

"Lonely"

A pen appeared, and the god said:
'Write what it is to be
man.' And my hand hovered
long over the bare page,

until there, like footprints
of the lost traveller, letters
took shape on the page's
blankness, and I spelled out

the word 'lonely.' And my hand moved
to erase it; but the voices
of all those waiting at life's
window cried out loud: 'It is true.'

R. S. Thomas, "The Word," *Poems of R. S. Thomas* (Fayetteville: University of Arkansas Press, 1985), 86.

In the Face of the Truth about Suffering, Retribution Theology Can Be a Cover-up.

Job admonishes his friends to realize that the principles of retribution theology (see [Retribution]) can be overgeneralized to the point of becoming little more that platitudes. It is not that there is no truth in the theology that God blesses the righteous and punishes the wicked. It is rather that this truth is not all sufficient. Sometimes things happen to people that cannot be explained by this theology. Sometimes, to quote Rabbi Kushner, bad things happen to good people.[24] In such circumstances, retribution theology can be sustained only at the expense of a cruel indifference to the facts.

Job charges that those who cling to such theology in the face of suffering like his are engaged in a massive cover-up. They plaster over the truth rather than admit that their theology is inadequate. Perhaps they are uncomfortable when they encounter something they cannot understand. Perhaps they are fearful of letting go old certainties on which they have built their lives. Perhaps the zeal of their religious commitment compels them to treat every sufferer's question as an assault on God, which they must counter with a stiff defense. [CD: "If You Are Not Immune, You Risk Infection"] Whatever the reasons may be, Job warns all would-be retribution theologians that when they presume to speak on God's behalf, they can expect to be interrogated by God (13:7-12). If God finds that they have failed to take seriously another's misery, then God will rebuke them as false theologians.

Religious leaders and lay people alike would do well do consider what changes in their theology might be mandated if God were to subject their words and their practice to close inspection. If God were to evaluate the sermons, lessons, and counsel that people of faith offer to the Jobs of the world, would our words and our actions be judged worthy embodiments of God's compassion? When we examine our sanctuaries and our communities, will we find that Job has been welcomed into our company, or that he has been assigned to the ash heap outside the sacred walls that protect us from those of his type? Has our conduct aligned us with the friends, who point and stare and condemn? Or have we been willing to sit alongside Job as comforters who know that suffering like his means that we all must think carefully before we say anything, lest we are found guilty of speaking "falsely for God" (13:7)? When people of faith fail to measure carefully what they offer to the Jobs of the world, they run the risk of becoming like the persons Joseph Conrad describes in *Tales of Unrest*, who "talk with indignation and enthusiasm . . . about oppression, cruelty, crime, devotion, self-sacrifice, virtue, and . . . know nothing real beyond the words."[25] To all such would-be comforters, Job's question invites a moment of considered pause and introspection: "Will it be well with you when he [God] searches you out?" (13:9). [What Can We Say About God in the Presence of Job?]

Hard Hope in the Midst of Hard Suffering

Job's brief but daring effort to hope (14:13-17) comes in the midst of his deepest despair about the impossibility of hope (14:1-12, 14-22). The hope toward which he struggles is radical, that is, it is proportionate to the brokenness and hurt that has torn his world apart. Job dares to hope that God is as committed to the truth about suffering as he is, hence his warning to the friends that God will judge them harshly if their theology is too small to deal honestly with him. He dares to hope that he can cling both to his innocence and to his questions and still expect God to hear and respond (14:15). He dares to hope that even the boundaries of life and death are not fixed and immovable (cf. 14:5), that in the face of suffering God will provide relief and justice (14:14). More radical still, he dares to hope that God will change. He has encountered the God of anger, but he hopes that God is more than this (14:13). He hopes there is a God beyond this God, a God who ultimately leaves anger behind in order to embrace the needy with love and compassion. Job can see no reason to sustain any of these hopes, however, and he appears ready to relinquish them in the face of the overwhelming silence of the heavens.

It is a curious oddity of Hebraic faith that suffering is the writhing womb from whence radical hope is born. Once birthed, such hope continues to work in hidden ways to find some toehold in reality. It will risk everything, even annihilation, to find a place where it can grow, mature, and procreate itself. Elie Wiesel offers one poignant example of such hard hope in his play *Ani Maamin: A Song Lost and Found Again.*[26] *Ani maamin* is the Hebrew phrase for "I believe." These are also the first words of an old Jewish song, "I believe in the coming of the Messiah, and though he tarry yet will I wait for him." The song originated in the thirteenth century and then was lost for a very long time, until it resurfaced in perhaps the most unlikely of places—in

What Can We Say About God in the Presence of Job?

Irving Greenberg has suggested that the unspeakable horror of the holocaust forever confronts all theological discourse with an unavoidable question. Whatever we might think to say about God in the aftermath of such suffering, it must be examined to see if it will be credible "in the face of burning children."

A personal experience will perhaps illustrate the tremendous pause such counsel warrants with respect to the book of Job. As a classroom exercise the writer once invited students to enact the Joban drama by assuming the role of either the friends or Job. One student played the role of Job and sat at the front of the class. One by one others came to the front of the class and spoke the words of one of the friends. Initially, these students spoke with their backs turned to Job, as if they were addressing the class. They articulated the friends' perspective on Job's suffering accurately and with little or no difficulty. Then the classroom was rearranged so that the ones playing the friends sat facing Job. They were then instructed to say the same speeches while looking directly into Job's eyes. Each one, without exception, became silent. They found that they could not simply repeat the words of the friends if they had to look at Job's suffering full in the face.

Hitler's concentration camps, on the lips of Jews who faced ruthless and systematic extermination. *Ani maamin*, the victims sang, even as they marched to their death, "I believe in the coming of the Messiah, and though he tarry yet will I wait for him."

Wiesel, himself a survivor of these camps, takes up this old song and writes a play that dramatizes how it has lingered in the memory of those who continue to wait and hope for the coming of the Messiah. The major characters are the biblical ancestors Abraham, Isaac, and Jacob. They are charged with the responsibility of pleading the cause of the Jews during the Holocaust before God in heaven. Their task is to articulate the pain and suffering of their fellow citizens and to secure some word of assurance or explanation that will indicate that God knows and cares. First Abraham, then Isaac, then Jacob recount the horrors they have seen: a child bludgeoned to death with a soldier's rifle-butt; a father shot before a grave he has been forced to dig for himself; a mother whose child hides under her skirts from the fiery ovens. In the background, the choir offers support by singing the old song of hope: "Ani maamin, I believe in the coming of the Messiah, and though he tarry yet will I wait for him."

They plead and pray and petition God, one by one, but through it all God remains silent, seemingly indifferent. Finally, they decide that this is the way it is with God. Killers kill and killers laugh, and God is silent; men stumble, mothers falter, and God is silent; a child is frightened, the doors of the furnace open, and God is silent. Abraham, Isaac, and Jacob prepare to give up their praying in heaven and return to the suffering ones on earth. They will tell them the truth about God that vanquishes every hope: "The decision is irrevocable: God looks on, and God is silent" (83). And then Wiesel pens these words:

> Having spoken, Abraham takes another step backward. He does not, cannot, see that God for the first time permits a tear to cloud his eyes. (93)

> Having spoken, Isaac, too takes another step backward. And he does not, cannot, see that for a second time a tear streams down God's somber countenance, a countenance more somber than before. (97)

> Having spoken, Jacob withdraws, and he does not, cannot, see that God . . . weeps and this time without restraint, and with—yes—love. (103)

They leave heaven, Abraham, Isaac, and Jacob, but they "do not, cannot, see that they are no longer alone. God accompanies them, "weeping, smiling, whispering" the comfort of divine presence in their midst (105). The chorus sings the final words of the play a last time:

"Ani maamin, I believe in the coming of the Messiah, and though he tarry yet will I wait for him."

When Job concludes this last speech in the first cycle, he has said virtually all he has to say. He has hoped all he can hope. He will not speak to God again at any length or so directly until he speaks his last words in the book (40:3-5; 42:1-6). Until God speaks and grants him more clarity than he has now, he can only repeat what he has already said. The reader knows that God will indeed speak and that Job's perspective will ultimately be changed. But this is more than Job knows. At this point, his understanding is not different than that of Wiesel's Abraham, Isaac, and Jacob. Like them, Job believes that he has seen the truth about God. Like them, the reality of his suffering has choked out the best hope he can muster. Nothing remains now but the memory of words fast fading away: "Oh that you would hide me . . . then. . . ." Yet, these words linger in Job's imagination, as if he is still waiting for what he does not, cannot, see. And the drama goes on.

NOTES

[1] For a survey of these options, see D. Clines, *Job 1–20* (WBC; Dallas: Word Books, 1989), 285 and R. Gordis, *The Book of Job: Commentary, New Translation, and Special Studies* (New York: Jewish Theological Seminary of America, 1978), 523-24, both of whom argue, albeit in different ways, for the integrity of the speech as it stands.

[2] L. Perdue, *Wisdom in Revolt: Metaphorical Theology in the Book of Job* (JSOTSup 112; Sheffield: Almond Press, 1991), 153.

[3] Clines, *Job 1–20*, 291.

[4] So Gordis, *Book of Job,* 523-24. For a fuller treatment see Gordis, "Quotations as a Literary Usage in Biblical, Oriental and Rabbinic Studies," HUCA 22 (1949): 157-219.

[5] Cf. Clines, *Job 1–20*, 292-293.

[6] C. Newsom, "The Book of Job," in vol. 4 of *NIB* (Nashville: Abingdon Press, 1996), 427.

[7] Similar language is found in Ps 109:27, Isa 66:2, and Jer 14:22. In view of such occurrences, Clines suggests that what Job cites is an "all-purpose phrase" (*Job 1–20*, 294; cf. Newsom, "The Book of Job," 428).

[8] Cf. J. Gerald Janzen, *Job* (Atlanta: John Knox, 1985), 103.

[9] S. Mitchell, *The Book of Job* (New York: Harper Collins, 1992), 34.

[10] Clines, *Job 1–20*, 308.

[11] The word *gab*, which occurs twice in v. 12, is difficult. NRSV's translation, "defenses," treats both occurrences as a form of the word that means "back." In Job 15:26, the same word appears to describe the "boss" or "knob" of a shield, thus the traditional idea of "defenses" (cf. NIV). If this is the correct rendering, however, it provides an odd parallelism with "maxims" and "proverbs," things that are spoken. A homonym of *gab* means "response" or "answer," which provides a better fit with the present context, as a number of translations have noted, e.g., NJPS and NEB: "your arguments." For the lexical discussion, see D. Clines, ed., *DCH*, vol. 2 (Sheffield: Sheffield Academic Press, 1995), 297.

[12] The most important of these parallel verbs is *qāwah*, "hope," which occurs in various forms some eighteen times in Job (as a verb: 3:9; 6:19; 7:2; 17:13; 30:26; as a noun: 4:6;

5:16; 6:8; 7:6; 8:13; 11:18, 20; 14:7, 19; 17:15, 25; 19:10; 27:8. For further discussion, see [Hope]).

[13] Cf. Janzen (*Job,* 107-108), who suggestively contrasts Job's courage with that of the friends. Whereas their fear of falling out of favor with God leads them to "whitewash" the truth (13:4, 7-8), Job's fear leads him to face certain defeat by God with the "courage of absolute vulnerability."

[14] N. Habel, *The Book of Job: A Commentary* (OTL; Philadelphia: Westminster Press, 1985), 231.

[15] Cf. E. Dhorme, *A Commentary on the Book of Job* (Nashville: Thomas Nelson Publishers, 1967), 190; Clines, *Job 1–20,* 319.

[16] E.g., Dhorme, *A Commentary on the Book of Job,* 193; H. H. Rowley, *Job* (The Century Bible; Ontario: Thomas Nelson, 1970), 126; M. Pope, *Job* (AB; Garden City NY: Doubleday, 1979), 106.

[17] Gordis suggests that verse 28 may be regarded as the conclusion of the question raised in v. 25, with vv. 26-27 as an extended parenthesis. Thus one may read, "Will you frighten a windblown leaf. . . that wastes away like a rotten thing?" (*Book of Job,* 146). For a slightly different possibility, see Clines, *Job 1–20,* 323.

[18] See Newsom ("The Book of Job," 440-41), who understands the enigmatic imagery of v. 4 as a figure of speech for expressing "an impossible transformation." "Clean" and "unclean" are opposite qualities that share nothing in common. She compares the possibility that something clean can be gotten from something unclean—or that Job can share common ground with God—to the popular saying that one cannot "make a silk purse out of a sow's ear."

[19] The Hebrew verb is *rāṣah,* which may be translated "enjoy" (so NRSV) or "finish, complete" (cf. Lev 26:34; 2 Chr 36:2). The latter seems more suitable in this context. Cf. Dhorme, *A Commentary on the Book of Job,* 197-98.

[20] Cf. S. R. Driver and G. B. Gray, *A Critical and Exegetical Commentary on the Book of Job* (Edinburgh: T and T. Clark, 1921), 128; Rowley, *Job,* 128; Pope, *Job,* 107; Clines, *Job 1–20,* 328. Each of these commentators references the description of such a practice by J. G. Wetzstein, as cited in F. Delitzsch, *Biblical Commentary on the Book of Job,* 2 vols. (Grand Rapids MI: Wm. B. Eerdmans, 1949).

[21] Cf. Newsom, "The Book of Job," 441.

[22] G. Fohrer, *Das Buch Hiob* (KAT; Gütersloh: Gerd Mohn, 1963), 258; A. Weiser, *Das Buch Hiob,* Das Alte Testament Deutsch (Göttingen: Vandenhoeck & Ruprecht, 1974), 105.

[23] P. Roth, *American Pastoral* (New York: Houghton Mifflin Company, 1997).

[24] H. Kushner, *When Bad Things Happen to Good People* (New York: Schocken Books, 1981).

[25] J. Conrad, *Tales of Unrest* (Harmondsworth: Penguin Books, 1977), 100.

[26] E. Wiesel, *Ani Maamin: A Song Lost and Found Again* (New York: Random House, 1973).

ELIPHAZ'S SECOND RESPONSE TO JOB: THE FATE OF THOSE WHO "BID DEFIANCE TO THE ALMIGHTY"

Job 15:1-35

The Second Cycle: The Place of the Wicked in a Moral World, Job 15:1–21:34

In the second cycle, the speeches of the friends follow much the same pattern as in the first cycle.[1] They begin with rhetorical questions that set the agenda for their concern (15:2; 18:2; 20:4-5) and then proceed with focused observations to describe the world as they understand it. There are, however, some noticeable differences in the way they address Job:

- The range of their concerns now narrows to focus exclusively on one theme: the fate of the wicked (15:17-35; 18:5-21; 20:6-29), with no parallel treatment of the fate of the righteous.
- Their tone is now much sharper, indicating that they are stiffening in their response to Job (e.g., 15:7-9; 18:3; 20:3).
- They offer no word of encouragement to Job, only increased warning, rebuke, and opposition (e.g., 15:5-6; 18:4; 20:4-11).
- There is considerable repetition in their speeches, an indication that they are increasingly mired down in intransigent dogma and theory that will not, and cannot, deal with the substance of Job's charges.

For his part Job, continues, at least in his first two speeches, to focus on God's violence towards him (16:6-17; 19:6-12). Only in his last speech (e.g., 21:17-26) does he address the friends' retribution theology directly and once more rebuts it. He is, he continues to insist, innocent (10:7; 16:17), thus his question is this: Is there any place in heaven or on earth where the cries of the innocent are heard and addressed (16:18-19; 19:23-27)? Absent any clear answer from either the friends or God, Job must conclude that neither can offer him the "consolation" and "comfort" he seeks and deserves (21:2, 34).

COMMENTARY

The second cycle of speeches begins much the same as the first, with Eliphaz taking the lead and setting the agenda that Bildad and Zophar will follow. Eliphaz's second speech, however, is more narrowly focused than his first and introduces a harsher, less sympathetic approach to Job. Initially he had appealed to the doctrine of retribution in order to defend God's moral governance of the world. Towards that end, he argued that God punishes the wicked (4:8-11; 5:12-14) *and* rewards the righteous (4:7; 5:11, 15-16). Now he focuses exclusively on one part of this theology—the punishment of the wicked (15:17-35). This will also be the single theme that dominates the second speeches of both Bildad (18:5-21) and Zophar (20:4-29). Although there is some variation in the way the friends deal with this theme, they each abandon their previous efforts to assure Job that the righteous will receive justice in God's world. Their primary concern is to equate divine justice with punishment, not reward, a shift that signals they now regard Job a more likely candidate for the former than the latter.

Furthermore, Eliphaz began by addressing Job with deference, gently encouraging him to remember that if he is indeed innocent he can trust God to deliver him (4:6; 5:17-27). Bildad and Zophar initially showed a similar respect for Job, and though their encouragement was couched in more conditional terms, they too expressed a sympathetic hope that Job could yet obtain a positive release from his ordeal (8:5-7; 11:13-15). Now each of the friends becomes more aggressive in their rebuttal of Job. ["The Just Upright Man Is Laughed to Scorn"] In their view Job has crossed the line. What he most needs and deserves now is not sympathy but firm reprimand. Once again Eliphaz sets the tone that his friends will follow. Job has turned his "spirit against God" (15:13). If he is not stopped, then he will jeopardize the basis of faith ("the fear of God"; 15:4) upon which the whole enterprise of religion rests.

Eliphaz's speech divides into two parts. The first, vv. 2-16, is a lengthy introduction, which rebukes Job for claiming too much for himself and his perspective. The argument is carried by a series of rhetorical questions (vv. 2-3, 7-9, 11-14), the practical effect of which is to solicit Job's agreement to conclusions Eliphaz has already reached. The second, vv. 17-35, is a vivid description of the fate of the wicked. Although Eliphaz addresses Job directly only in v. 17, he clearly intends this part of the speech to serve as an explicit warning to him. Verse 35 ties the fate of the wicked to Eliphaz's opening remarks in v. 2. If Job insists on filling his "belly" (v. 2: *beṭen*; NRSV: "fill themselves") with wind, then his "belly" (v. 35: *beṭen*; NRSV: "heart") will bring forth deceit that targets him for destruction just like the wicked. [Structure of Job 15:1-35]

"The Just Upright Man Is Laughed to Scorn"

William Blake depicts Job according to the conventional understanding as mournful, submissive, and trusting (for a different portrayal. Job is kneeling, but he holds himself upright. His spotted skin is wrapped from the waist down with the traditional sackcloth. His head is tilted backward. His tear-stained eyes are fixed on the God above whom he cannot see but will not cease to trust. Job's disposition is suggested by the three citations of scripture at the top of the frame:

> But he knoweth the way I take
> when he hath tried me I shall
> come forth like gold (Job 23:10)

> Have pity upon me! Have pity
> upon me! O ye my friends
> for the hand of God hath touched
> me (Job 19:21)

> Though he slay me yet will I trust
> in him (Job 13:15)

The friends have ceased to play the role of comforter; they are now Job's inquisitors. With outstretched hands they point fingers of ridicule in Job's direction. In contrast with Job, their expressions are cold and hard, as is particularly clear in the face of the friend to the fore, presumably Eliphaz. Job's wife, whose hand right hand is also partially extended, seems now to have joined in the reproach. Two further citations in the bottom of the frame from Job's last speech in the first cycle indicate what has drawn the friends' ire:

> The Just Upright man is laughed to scorn (Job 12:4)

> Man that is born of a Woman is of few days & full of trouble
> he cometh up like a flower & is cut down, he fleeth also as a shadow
> & continueth not. And dost thou open thine eyes upon such a one
> & bringest me into judgment with thee (Job 14:1-3)

The figures in the border add to the bleakness of Job's situation from the friends' perspective. Two angels, each weighed down with chains, appear to be holding on with some difficulty to the picture of Job. In the bottom left-hand corner, a bird (a raven? a cuckoo?), perhaps symbolic of slander, steps on a serpent. In the bottom right-hand corner, an owl, perhaps symbolic of false wisdom, grasps a helpless mouse in its talons.

Job Laughed to Scorn

William Blake (1757-1827). *Job Laughed to Scorn.* 1823-1825. Engraving from Blake's *Illustrations of the Book of Job.*

Job's Destructive Words, 15:1-6

In his previous speech, Job claimed to have wisdom equal to that of the friends (12:3; 13:2). In response, Eliphaz now asks whether a truly wise person would speak the way Job does. Job argues (*hôkĕaḥ*; cf. 13:3, 6) with words that are "not profitable" (*lōʾ yiskôn*) and "not useful" (*lōʾ yôʿîl*; v. 3). He speaks with the "tongue of the crafty" (v. 5b; cf. 5:12), hence his own mouth proves him guilty, and his own lips testify against him (v. 6). Eliphaz hardly needs to make the case against Job, for Job's own words provide sufficient proof that "iniquity" (v. 5a), not wisdom, is the source of his discernments. But Eliphaz believes that Job's words are more than simply wrong. They are dangerous and destructive. They have the force of the "east wind" (v. 3), an allusion to the khamsin that blows in off the desert, leaving everything in its path scorched and withered (cf. Ezek 17:10; 19:12).

What Eliphaz fears most is that Job's words have the potential to destroy religion as he knows it *and needs it* to be (v. 4). Job's manner of addressing God "undermines" or "subverts" (*pārar*; NRSV: "does away with") the essence of piety (*yirʾāh*, "fear"; an ellipsis for "fear of God" as in NRSV; cf. 4:6). In wisdom literature, "the fear of God" refers to the devotion and reverence that the faithful exhibit when they order their lives in accord with God's design for the world (Ps 111:10; Prov 9:10; 14:27; 19:23). When Job sat patiently on the ash heap, content to receive both the good and the bad from God without complaint, both the narrator and God judged him to be the perfect example of one "who fears God" (1:1, 8; 2:3). As long as he maintained that posture, Eliphaz also recognized that Job's piety needed no correcting word from him (2:13). But now that Job's blessing has given way to curse, lament, and protest, Eliphaz believes he has abandoned the piety that God expects and commends. ["We Mock Thee When We Do Not Fear"]

Job's present way of speaking "diminishes" (*gāraʿ*, "reduce," "subtract"; cf. Deut 4:2; Eccl 3:14) what it means to engage in "meditation before God." The word for "mediation," *śîḥāh*, is curiously ambivalent. It may refer to "prayer" (cf. Ps 102:1 [MT 102:1]; NRSV: "cry") or to the practice of musing or meditating aloud on God's *torah* (cf. Ps 119:15, 23, 27, 48, 78, 97, 99). In both cases, it signifies a mode of speaking that conveys the deep inner feelings of a pious person. One might describe such speech as a form of "communion with God."[2] The same term may also refer to plaintive speech, that is, to complaint, as in Psalm 77:3 [MT 77:4]: "I think of God, and I moan; I meditate

"We Mock Thee When We Do Not Fear"

"In Memoriam A.H.H." is Alfred Lord Tennyson's poem reflecting on the sudden death of his dear friend Arthur Henry Hallam The poem was composed over a period of seventeen years and shows Tennyson's struggle to come to terms with the abiding sorrow of his loss. The son of a clergyman, Tennyson dealt with his spiritual depression in a way that Eliphaz presumably would endorse:

> Let knowledge grow from more to more,
> But more of reverence in us dwell;
> That mind and soul, according well,
> May make one music as before,
>
> But vaster. We are fools and slight;
> We mock thee when we do not fear:
> But help thy foolish ones to bear;
> Help thy vain worlds to bear thy light. (Prologue, ll. 25-32)

Tennyson understood, however, that those who believe "doubt is Devil-born" make poor counselors for sufferers like himself:

> You tell me, doubt is Devil-born.
>
> I know not: one I knew
> In many a subtle question v. d,
> Who touch'd a jarring lyre at first,
> But ever strove to make it true;
>
> Perplext in faith, but pure in deeds,
> At last he beat his music out.
> There lives more faith in honest doubt,
> Believe me, than in half the creeds. (Section 96, ll. 4-12)

To such a conviction, one suspects Eliphaz might respond differently.

A. Tennyson, "In Memoriam A.H.H.," *Tennyson's Poetry*, sel. and ed. R. W. Hill, Jr. (New York/London: W. W. Norton and Co., 1971), 120, 171.

(*ʾaśîḥāh*), and my spirit faints" (cf. Pss 55:2, 17 [MT 55:3, 18]; 64:1 [MT 64:2]; 142:2 [MT 142:3]). It is this latter sense of "complain" that consistently describes Job's "meditation" (7:11, 13; 9:27; 10:1; 21:4; 23:2).

Eliphaz warns Job that what he offers as meditation to God is not only disrespectful; it is destructive. It does not nurture faith, it diminishes it. He suggests that speech which conveys the will to be trusting, obedient, and submissive is the true measure of reverent piety. Words that express doubt, criticism, and challenge are the mark of one who would attack God and dismantle true theology. [Asking Too Many Questions] In the prologue, God commends Job for his patience and his submission, hence readers are encouraged to understand this mode of faith as proper and exemplary. In the dialogues, however, God is silent, and readers must ponder for themselves whether Eliphaz's assessment of what constitutes true piety is correct or not. The issue may be framed with a question. If God does not permit speech like Job's, then what kind of God is God? If God is open and receptive to speech like Job's, then what are the dogmas of "true theology" that require reexamination, modification, or elimination?

Who Are You to Challenge God? 15:7-16

Job speaks as he does because of what his eyes have seen and his ears have heard (13:1). On the basis of personal experience, he claims to

Asking Too Many Questions

In Elie Wiesel's play *The Trial of God*, Berish, an innkeeper who has lost two sons in a pogrom, announces his intentions to put God on trial for crimes against humanity (see further Job 9–10, "Connections"). Berish will play the role of the prosecuting attorney who interrogates God. He knows all too well that the trial will not be successful: "the outcome won't change anything: the dead will not rise from their graves." Even so, he persists with the notion. As he puts it, "We judge because we wish to know. To understand" (II, 86). He tries to persuade three minstrels who have come to his inn to join him in staging the play. They indicate that they share his sense of outrage, his need to protest, but once they see the full scope of what Berish intends, they grow cautious, fearful that their friend is about to go too far. Yankel, one of the minstrels, states clearly the Eliphaz-like counsel that all who would question God should bear in mind: "Questions are like trips; we must know when to stop" (II, 89).

E. Wiesel, *The Trial of God* (New York: Schocken Books, 1979).

"The Democracy of the Dead"

Tradition means giving votes to the most obscure of all classes, our ancestors. It is the democracy of the dead. Tradition refuses to submit to the small and arrogant oligarchy of those who merely happen to be walking about.

G. K. Chesterton, "The Ethics of Elfland," *Orthodoxy* 4.

understand the sinister secrets of God's design for creation (see the commentary on 12:22-25). Eliphaz counters that Job claims far too much for his experience and his perspective. True knowledge is based not on one individual's observations but on the collective consensus of the "gray-haired and the aged" whose wisdom has stood the test of time (v. 10). It is this wisdom that informs and substantiates Eliphaz's perspective. ["The Democracy of the Dead"] Job has forgotten that no single person can discern the full truth about God's creational intentions. When trouble strikes unawares, the best thing to do is to rely on the accumulated truths that tradition bequeaths to successive generations. ["None of Us Lives in the Light"]

Job has not only rejected the wisdom of the ages, he has also spurned the "consolations of God," which Eliphaz has conveyed in "words that deal gently" with him (v. 11). Eliphaz likely refers to his words in chapters 4–5, words that he claims are divinely inspired (4:12-16). He has urged Job to look on suffering as a form of divine discipline. It is not to be despised or resisted. It is to be embraced happily as a sign of God's corrective love (5:17-18). But Eliphaz sees now that Job regards such "consolations" as "too small" for him. What has happened to change Job's "heart," such that he no longer trusts God to do right by him? What has happened to skew his vision, such that he no longer sees clearly the truth of his situation (v. 12)? Why has Job now turned on God with an angry spirit, spewing forth words of challenge and condemnation (v. 13)? Eliphaz can only conclude that Job has forgotten who he is and how he must act if he is to stand in the presence of God.

To make his case, Eliphaz directs Job once again to think hard about what it means to be a human being before God (vv. 14-16). He first addressed the issue in 4:17: "Can mortals (*'ĕnôš*) be righteous before God? Can human beings be pure (*yiṭhar*) before their Maker?" Prompted by Eliphaz, Job himself took up the same issue in 7:17: "What are human beings (*'ĕnôš*), that you [God] make so much of them?" Given his experience, Job concluded that humans are no more than hapless creatures who are targeted by God for destruction, irrespective of their righteousness or purity (7:18-21). Eliphaz disputes this conclu-

"None of Us Lives in the Light"

In his novel *In the Beauty of the Lilies*, John Updike traces the struggles of faith that befall Clarence Wilmot, the Princeton-educated minister of the Fourth Presbyterian Church located on the corner of Straight Street and Broadway in Patterson, New Jersey. Reverend Wilmot has been well-trained in the pastoral art of balancing like a "trapeze artist" (15) between traditional affirmations of piety and the problems of the modern world. Nonetheless, over time the old certainties wear thin, and the balancing act fails. Clarence succumbs to the only reality that he can see: the world is full of "bombast and deviltry" (23); it is "as empty of divine content as a corroded kettle" (7). He can no longer preach the traditional affirmations, which he now concludes are no more than a "self-promoting, self-protecting tangle of wishful fancy and conscious lies" (19). He submits his resignation and schedules the obligatory meeting with Thomas Dreaver, the moderator of the Presbytery of Jersey City, who would have to give his approval before the resignation could become official.

Reverend Dreaver comes to the meeting wearing a blue, single-breasted business suit, instead of his ordinary clerical collar. He is businesslike in his manner, "save for an extra smoothness, a honeyed promissory timbre to his voice that marked him as an executive of Christian business" (72-73). As Clarence recounts his reasons for resigning, Dreaver deflects them easily by directing him to the Book of Discipline. Clarence begins to feel like a "circus trainer must, tossing a ball to a seal who effortlessly, shimmeringly balances it on his nose" (77). The wisdom of the elders stipulate that he must continue his pastoral duties for a one-year probationary period, in order to see if he can recover his faith and his calling. The one-year period seems to Clarence an unbearable length of time to have to wait, given the hollowness he feels. Was the Presbytery suggesting that he simply go through the motions? Surely his parishioners expect and deserve more than this. To this, too, Dreaver has a ready-made response: "Going through the motions, not at all. Walking toward the light. None of us lives *in* the light; we can only walk toward it, with the eyes and legs God has given us" (80).

Clarence is bewildered, and a little relieved at the same time. The prospect of continuing in ministry is not repugnant to him. Indeed, in some respects to continue to do the only thing he is really trained for would be easier than the other option, which would place his whole family at risk. "How easy it is," he thought, "to use the word 'God' when the reality has been construed out of existence" (80). He finds a new courage to hope that as long as the Presbytery can sustain itself with the counsel of bright young theologians like Reverend Dreaver, perhaps "the church was not utterly dead" (80).

When the year of probation concluded, Clarence resigned his pulpit and became an encyclopedia salesman.

J. Updike, *In the Beauty of the Lilies* (New York: Alfred A. Knopf, 1996).

sion and summons Job to rethink the question, this time with a subtle shift of emphasis that returns the focus to where Eliphaz believes it belongs: "What are mortals (*ĕnôš*), that they can be clean (*yizzkeh*)?" (v. 14). From Eliphaz's perspective, the proper question is not whether God is just but rather whether any human being can be sufficiently "righteous" and "pure/clean" to stand before God and raise questions about who suffers and why. Eliphaz reiterates his previous argument. If even the "holy ones" (see the commentary on 5:1) in heaven are not without contamination, then how much more must this be true of mere mortals who are "abominable and corrupt" (vv. 15-16; cf. 4:18-19).

On first inspection, Eliphaz's argument is a simple one: human beings are sinful. They cannot claim to approach God in innocence, as Job repeatedly insists he is doing (9:15, 20-21; 10:15; 12:4), because they are obviously flawed and imperfect reflections of the Creator. To insist otherwise portends both a foolish and arrogant breach of the boundary that distinguishes the holy from the common, the divine

The Myth of the Primal Human

The figure of the "primal human" is rooted in ancient Near Eastern creation traditions that describe the first heroic figures who were created by the gods and endowed with extraordinary wisdom and power. One Mesopotamian text, for example, describes how the god Ea created Adapa as the "model of men":

Wide understanding he had perfected for to him to
Disclose the designs of the land.
To him he had given wisdom; eternal life he had not
    given him.
In those days, in those years, the sage from Eridu,
Ea, created him as the model of men. (*ANET*, 3rd ed. with supplement, ed. J. B. Pritchard [Princeton: Princeton University Press, 1969], 101)

These mythic figures came to be used to describe the origins of kingship. The assumption of the myth is that the king, as the first human created by the gods, was present at creation and participated in the divine decisions that ordered the cosmos. The myth is never fully appropriated in the biblical tradition, although traces of it may be detected in Gen 2–3 and in Ezek 28. In both cases, the tradition takes on a negative connotation in association with the temptation of humans to rebel against divine rule by arrogating to themselves authority and wisdom that belongs only to God. Ezek 28:2, which reports God's judgment on the king of Tyre, states clearly the sin and its consequent judgment.

It is presumably this tradition of criticizing the hubris of those who would supplant God as king that informs Eliphaz's rebuke of Job for comparing himself to the "firstborn of the human race." There is, however, a latent ambiguity in this tradition. As Prov 8:22-31 suggests, the biblical tradition sometimes *celebrates* the possibility that human beings are created with the capacity to be near-equals of God (see the commentary on 15:7).

For further reading on the myth of the Primal Human in relation to Job, see R. Gordis, "The Significance of the Paradise Myth," AJSL 52 (1936): 86-94; L. Perdue, *Wisdom in Revolt: Metaphorical Theology in the Book of Job* (JSOTSup 112; Sheffield: Almond Press, 1991), 165-70; D. E. Callander, Jr., *Adam in Myth and History: Ancient Israelite Perspectives on the Primal Human* (Harvard Semitic Studies 48; Winona Lake IN: Eisenbrauns, 2000).

from the human. Eliphaz warns Job that he risks stepping over this boundary by invoking an old creation tradition about "the firstborn (*rîʾyšôn*) of the human race" (v. 7a). [The Myth of the Primal Human] Does Job dare to imagine that he was present at creation, privileged by birth and by status to participate in the decisions of the divine council (see [Divine Council]) that ordered the cosmos and all life (v. 8)?

It is interesting, however, that as a part of the argument against Job's hubris Eliphaz challenges him with a question: "Were you brought forth before the hills?" (v. 7b). The question is a quotation of Prov 8:25, where it used with reference to the origin and vocation of personified Wisdom. The context for the verse is Prov 8:22-31, a hymn in which Wisdom exults in being the "first" (*rēʾšît*) of God's creative acts. The hymn does not suggest that Wisdom's exultation is arrogant or disrespectful. It gives no indication that Wisdom should be regarded as figure for rebuke or condemnation. Instead, Wisdom celebrates its role as the firstborn child who works as a co-creator alongside YHWH, the divine parent and principal architect of the cosmos (Prov 8:27-29). Indeed, the parent Creator and the begotten co-creator are intimately linked by their mutual delight in one another (Prov 8:30-31). Joyfully

"Yet Do I Marvel"

Countee Cullen (1903–1946) was a prominent contributor to the Harlem Renaissance (1920–1930), along with other African-American artists such as Langston Hughes, Paul Robeson, and Louis Armstrong. "Yet Do I Marvel" deals with themes that are expressive of life in the black community of his day. But like the tragic figures from Greek mythology that he appropriates, Cullen's poetry speaks with a clarity that transcends temporal and cultural limitations.

I doubt not God is good, well-meaning, kind,
And did He stoop to quibble could tell why
The little buried mole continues blind,

Why flesh that mirrors Him must some day die,
Make plain the reason tortured Tantalus
Is baited by the fickle fruit, declare
If merely brute caprice dooms Sisyphus
To struggle up a never ending-ending stair.
Inscrutable His ways are, and immune
To catechism by a mind too strewn
With petty cares to slightly understand
What awful brain compels His awful hand.
Yet do I marvel at this curious thing:
To make a poet black, and bid him sing!

C. Cullen, "Yet Do I Marvel," *Black Voices: An Anthology of African-American Literature*, ed. A. Chapman (New York: Signet Classic, 2001), 383.

partnered with God in the work of creation, Wisdom invites all who will to take up the life it models: "Happy are those who keep my ways. . . . For whoever finds me finds life" (Prov 8:32-33).

Eliphaz clearly intends his question about the "firstborn" to rebuke of Job for failing to recognize his proper place in the hierarchy of creation. But the tradition from which he draws his challenge perhaps says more than he intends. Is it *misguided hubris* or *radical faith* to believe that human beings are created and commissioned by God for full communion and shared partnership in the work of sustaining creation? Eliphaz asserts the former, but the evidence he presents ironically invites consideration of the latter. At this juncture in the drama, therefore, the debate between Eliphaz and Job concerning the question "What are human beings?" produces no clear answer. When one speaks in a broken world with words like Job's, does this *violate* God's design for human identity and vocation or *fulfill* it? Until God speaks in chapters 38-41, the question, at least insofar as this book is concerned, must remain open.[3] ["Yet Do I Marvel"]

The Fate of the Wicked, 15:17-35

The second part of Eliphaz's speech is a lengthy description of the terrible fate of the wicked. The speech may be outlined as follows: an introduction setting forth the authoritative basis of Eliphaz's instruction (vv. 17-19); a description of the troubles the wicked experience in the present (vv. 20-26); a description of the future troubles that await the wicked (vv. 27-34); and a final summation (v. 35).

Eliphaz begins with the imperative that Job "listen" to the instruction he offers (v. 17). What he is about to say is based both on "what he has seen" and on "what the sages have declared" (vv. 17b, 18). In other words, the source of his knowledge has an authority that is superior to

Job's. Like Job, he has a reservoir of personal experience that informs his perspective. Unlike Job, however, his experience is consistent with and confirmed by the collective wisdom of the sages. It has the weight of tradition behind it.

Moreover, Eliphaz insinuates that the wisdom he imparts has the advantage of being pure and free of foreign ideas. It comes from the time when the ancestors lived in a world in which "no stranger passed among them" (v. 19). It is not clear what specific time Eliphaz refers to. Perhaps the reference is to the time when Israel was in sole possession of the land of Canaan. If so, the statement is not factually true, for even when Israel controlled Canaan, the population was clearly not completely homogenous. Perhaps the reference is to some unknown Temanite traditions of their origins. It is more likely that Eliphaz has in mind simply an ideal time in the primordial beginnings of the human community when discernments about life and about God were exactly as God intended them to be. Such an idyllic period invokes the memory of primordial Eden, or in Job's case, the "garden of Uz" (see commentary on Job 1–2), when piety was always rewarded and trust in God always exceeded doubt. If Job would but remember how he had once conducted himself in that world, then he would realize how far he has strayed into foreign ways of thinking that are radically inconsistent with God's plan for him. The problem with Eliphaz's attempt to return Job to such a world, at least from Job's perspective, is that on this side of the ash heap that former world no longer exists.

Job's perspective, however, is not Eliphaz's primary concern. He is focused instead on abstract principles of divine retribution whose inviolable truth places them above the fray of Job's particular circumstances. He describes the inevitable judgment that shadows every day in the life of the typical wicked person (vv. 20-24). He does not connect this judgment directly to Job. Nevertheless, through inference and innuendo he warns Job that much of what he has himself said indicates that he is dangerously close to becoming just like the persons that are described here. [The Inferred Connections Between Job and the Typical Wicked Person]

Eliphaz begins not by claiming that the wicked will *in the end* get what they deserve, as Bildad has done (8:13-19), but rather by arguing that they are tormented in their *present state*, even though outward circumstances may indicate otherwise. In the midst of seeming prosperity, the wicked live all their "days" and "years" (v. 20) with a "neurotic fear" of what awaits them.[4] They imagine every sound they hear to be that of the "terrors" announcing a disaster lurking just around the corner (v. 21). They despair that there is no escape from "darkness" (v. 22a). They are marked for destruction, whatever they do, for somewhere a sword is raised to kill them (v. 22b; cf. TEV), and vultures are waiting

The Inferred Connections Between Job and the Typical Wicked Person

The demise of the wicked is a prominent theme in the first and second cycle of the friends' speeches (Eliphaz: 4:7-11; 5:2-7, 12-14; 15:20-35; Bildad: 8:11-19; 18:5-21; Zophar: 11:11, 20; 20:4-29). The motif is common, especially in the wisdom tradition (e.g., Prov 12:7-21; see further **[Retribution]**), suggesting that Eliphaz is appropriating traditional language in a conventional way. Nonetheless, as Habel has noted, this conventional language connects with many of the things Job has said in his previous speeches. These connections suggest that Job's words bear the characteristics of a typical wicked person. Hence, even though Eliphaz speaks of the wicked in a rather abstract way, he warns Job that the judgment he describes will apply to him in a very concrete way, if he does not alter his course. Habel notes the following connections and allusions between 15:20-35 and Job's previous speeches:

"writhe in pain" (*ḥwl*)	15:20 (6:10)
"terrifying sounds" (*pāḥad*)	15:21 (3:25)
"the destroyer" (*šôdēd*)	15:21 (12:6)
no "return" (*šwb*) from Sheol	15:22 (7:9-10)
"distress" (*sar*)	15:24 (7:11; NRSV: "anguish")
"terrify" (*bʿt*)	15:24 (7:14)
"prevail against" (*tqp*)	15:24 (14:20)
"play hero" (*gbr*; NRSV: "bid defiance")	15:25 (3:3; NRSV: "man-child; 10:5; NRSV: "human")
"emptiness" (*šaw*)	15:31 (7:3)
"barren" (*galmûd*)	15:34 (3:7)
"fire" (*ʾēš*)	15:34 (1:16)
"mischief" (*ʿāmāl*)	15:35 (3:10; NRSV: "trouble")
"belly" (*beṭen*; NRSV: "heart")	15:35 (3:10-11; NRSV: "womb")

N. Habel, *The Book of Job: A Commentary* (OTL; Philadelphia: Westminster Press, 1985), 251. I have modified Habel's list slightly in order to make clear the translations in NRSV.

to devour their corpse (v. 23).[5] Even though they are secure and healthy, they are overwhelmed by "distress" and "anguish," as if a mighty king had ordered his troops to swoop down upon them (v. 24).

The battle imagery of v. 24 connects with the reason for the wicked person's fear in vv. 25-26. The wicked have "stretched out their hands" (*nāṭāh* + *yad*) against God (v. 25a). The phrase conveys the idea of striking someone with the intention of inflicting harm or injury. It is often used to describe God inflicting judgment on sinful people (e.g., Isa 5:25; Ezek 6:14; 14:9, 13; Zeph 1:4; 2:13). The idea of humans striking at God, however, is exceptional and occurs nowhere else in Hebrew scripture in just this way.[6] Eliphaz suggests that the wicked, and by inference Job as well, are so infatuated with their power that they try to do the impossible. They engage God in combat like warriors who "play the hero" (v. 25b, *yitgabbār*; NRSV: "bid defiance"). They run against God with a stiff "neck," that is, stubbornly (cf. Ps 75:5 [MT 75:6]), assuming that the thickness of their shields is adequate defense for a battle against the Almighty (v. 26).

Eliphaz's reasoning here invites a brief caveat. His premise is that "heroic" defiance of God is not only futile; it is also a sure sign of wicked rebellion. When such behavior is attributed to persons such as he describes in vv. 20-24, there can be little disagreement with his argument. But readers may ponder a different premise. [Starting from Other Premises] Is defiance of God by one who is "blameless and upright" always an act of faithless rebellion? When God at last speaks from the whirlwind, Job will be twice challenged to "gird his loins like a hero (*geber*)" who is preparing to go into battle (38:3; 40:7). The conventional interpretation is that God is rebuking Job, with instruction not unlike Eliphaz offers here, for arrogating to himself privilege and power that rightly belongs only to God. A good case can be made, however, for suggesting that God's intentions are decidedly more positive than the conventional view allows. Are there situations in life when heroic engagement with God is not only necessary but also invited and commended by God? The full consideration of this question must await the commentary on Job 38–41. In anticipation of that discussion, readers may find it instructive to allow Job's pained wonderment from the ash heap to remain an open question: Why is a hero (3:3, *gāber*; NRSV: "man-child"; cf. 3:23) born?

> ### Starting from Other Premises
>
> In "Everything That Rises Must Converge," Flannery O'Connor describes Julian's frustration with his mother's simplistic and self-serving view of the world:
>
> > The old lady was clever enough and he thought that if she had started from any of the right premises, more might have been expected of her. She lived according to the laws of her own fantasy world, outside of which he had never seen her set foot.
>
> *The Complete Stories of Flannery O'Connor* (New York: Farrar, Straus and Giroux, 1971), 411.

Verses 27-34 continue the description of the fate of the wicked, now with a focus on the miserable future that is prepared for them. The meaning of v. 27 is unclear. Some take the reference to "fat" as another description of the would-be warrior's unfitness for battle.[7] Others interpret "fatness" as a symbol of the material prosperity enjoyed by the wicked, which cannot protect them against the destruction that is coming.[8] The latter reading may be preferable, since it is consonant with the theme of vv. 28-29: the houses of the wicked are destined for ruin; what they have acquired in wealth "will not endure."

The vulnerability of the wicked is further illustrated with a plant metaphor that recalls Bildad's imagery in 8:11-15. Their "shoots" and "blossom" will wither and die in the scorching heat (v. 30). Their "branch" will not grow to be strong (v. 31b). Like a diseased vine, they will drop their fruit before it ripens; like an olive tree they will shed all their blossoms without producing any fruit (v. 33). Verse 34 shifts the imagery by using metaphors for emptiness and unfulfillment more naturally associated with humans. The "godless" (cf. 8:13) and those who concert with them are "barren." The point is not that they cannot literally procreate, but rather that their hopes and dreams are impotent; they cannot bring forth life that is full and durable.

In a final summation Eliphaz reiterates the thesis of retribution theology (v. 35). Those who conceive "trouble" (*'āmāl*; NRSV: "mischief') inevitably bring forth "iniquity" (*'āwen*; NRSV: "evil"). The connection Eliphaz makes between "trouble" and "iniquity" is virtually identical to his first articulation of this theme in 4:8, with two exceptions. Previously, he encouraged Job to remember that the other pole to this theology—the connection between righteousness and reward—applied to him. That encouragement is missing here, suggesting that Eliphaz now believes Job needs a very different word. Previously, Eliphaz had argued that the wicked reap what they sow, but the observation was cast in general terms, for at that point he presumed that Job had sown "integrity" and would surely reap "hope" (4:6). Now Eilphaz's presumption of Job's innocence has changed. Job has filled his "belly" (v. 2: *beṭen*; NRSV: "fill themselves") with dangerous and destructive words. And this means that Job must take special care to observe what happens to the wicked whose "belly" (v. 35b: *beṭen*; NRSV: "heart") nurtures "deceit." As far as Eliphaz can see, "hope" is fast vanishing from Job's horizon.

CONNECTIONS

In the reflections on the first speech of Eliphaz, I suggested that one entry into his counsel was through H. G. Wells's portrait of him as a manufacturer of Temanite building blocks (see Job 4–5 "Connections").[9] That metaphor remains an instructive lens for interpreting this speech as well. Eliphaz is intent on building a different world for Job to inhabit, one that in his view is more consonant with the world God has created, one that demands of Job a different enactment of faith than he is presently displaying. The foundation of this world is a theology of retribution, which Eliphaz has already described. He has respectfully sketched the kind of faith this foundational theology requires of Job—he must accept his limitations (4:17-19), trust God who "wounds" and "strikes" (5:17), and praise God's justice, even in the midst of suffering (5:9-16). But Job has not responded the way Eliphaz has hoped, so now he hardens his approach and speaks more directly. True faith, Eliphaz insists, requires of Job three affirmations: (1) communion with God requires speech that is constructive, not destructive; (2) relationship with God requires that humans recognize their proper place in the hierarchy of creation; and (3) commitment to God requires that conventional wisdom take precedence over personal experience.

Communion with God Requires Speech That Is Constructive, Not Destructive

Eliphaz rebukes Job for speaking words that are "not profitable" and "not useful" (v. 3). Presumably he refers to Job's persistence in "arguing" (cf. 13:3, 15) with God over what is right and wrong, over what is just and unjust. Eliphaz believes that God is unassailably just, thus arguing with God, by definition, is equal to rebellion. Rebellion does not add to faith, it subtracts from it. It makes "communion" (v. 4: *śîḥāh*; NRSV: "meditation") with God less than it ought to be. In the fullness of Israel's traditions, communion with God may include the possibility of lament and complaint, as the witness of the Psalms makes clear (see commentary). But Eliphaz is less concerned with what *might be* than with what *ought to be*. He has in mind a purer form of piety, one that he insinuates is free of inferior forms of expression like these (vv. 18-19). In the world he envisions, faith is ideally expressed with profitable and useful language that nurtures the "fear of God" upon which true communion depends.

Eliphaz's argument has two prongs. First, arguing with God is useless. If God will not answer the questions that ones asks, then there is no sense in asking them. If one cannot win the argument, then it is an exercise in futility to begin it. The counsel is logical and prudent. In common parlance, we might say, "Don't start what you cannot finish" or "Don't fight battles you cannot win." It is counsel that business executives and employees, religious leaders and parishioners have likely offered and heeded at one time or another. Those who do not face the facts are unlikely to survive long enough to accomplish their goals and objectives. The argument is clearly utilitarian, *and* it is *genuinely seductive* for just that reason. ["Creative Principledness"] Job does not deny that it

"Creative Principledness"

George Will is an intelligent baseball analyst who earns his keep primarily as a political columnist and television commentator. In a column written in 1984, he describes the "creative principledness" that informs his evaluation of the "designated hitter-rule":

I planned to use the winter to hone a new argument against the American League's designated-hitter rule. The argument was to be that the rule is a middle-class entitlement program (it entitles some men to play extra years) and hence is partly to blame for the federal deficit. But Baltimore's DH, Ken Singleton, is one of Nature's gentlemen, and helps the Orioles win, so a theory I favor must yield to a fact I love. I support the DH until Singleton retires.

That is creative principledness. I learned it in Washington.

Will understands that baseball is surely not unconnected to Job. His decision to spend the winter reflecting on how to argue against the DH begins as follows:

The Bible, which devout baseball fans consider the *Baseball America* of religion, counsels patience. But what did Job and other supposed sufferers know of the interminable cultural drought of the baseball off-season? My patience is exhausted—with the deficit, the Mondale administration (no point writing on that one) and all sports that are not baseball.

G. Will, "Speaking Stengelese," *Bunts, Curt Flood, Camden Yards, Pete Rose and Other Reflections on Baseball* (New York: Scribner, 1998), 59.

is futile to argue with God (9:3, 12, 14, 16, 19, 33). He insists nonetheless that some fights are worth the price of losing.

Second, Eliphaz suggests that arguing with God destroys true piety. His description of Job's approach to God as "crafty" (v. 5: *ʿărûmîm*) recalls the tactics of the "crafty" serpent (Gen 3:1: *ʿārûm*) who sought to cast doubt on God's motives by tempting the first couple to believe that they were a better judge of what was good for them than God. The implication is that when one moves to challenge and question the intentions of the Creator of the world, one steps across the boundary of what God allows. Such arrogance not only subjects the individual to punishment and banishment; it also subverts God's creational design and tilts the cosmos toward chaos instead of order. [Job, His Wife, His Friends, and the Devil] Eliphaz judges Job's words to be a serious threat to the world in which he (and he presumes God) finds meaning and fulfillment. True piety respects its limitations. It exercises faith decisions within carefully prescribed borders that invite compliance with what God requires and discourage what God forbids. From Eliphaz's perspective, Job is like the serpent who looks on these borders and asks, with sinister intent, "*Did God say* that this is what is required of those who would live faithfully in God's world?" (cf. Gen 3:1b). As God's self-appointed spokesperson, Eliphaz confronts this challenge with a stern rebuke: "What is this that you have done?" (Gen 3:13). The next word, unless Job recants, will be one of judgment.

Relationship with God Requires That Humans Recognize Their Proper Place in the Hierarchy of Creation

The proper place of humans in the hierarchy of creation, according to Eliphaz, is closer to the bottom of the stackpole than to the top. Human beings are not the "firstborn" of creation (v. 7). They have not stood in the "council of God" (v. 8), where the design for the world has been crafted with skill and precision. They cannot know and they should not challenge the divine wisdom that directs life to its intended goal. When Job turns his "spirit against God" and "lets such words" escape from his mouth (v. 13), he condemns himself as one who has forgotten his place. His proper role is to recognize that there is a vast, unbridgeable gap between God and himself. If he is to stay in relationship with God, then he must stay on his side of the great divide that separates the Creator from the creature. In theological terms, Eliphaz's argument construes this divide as the boundary between God's sovereignty and humanity's submission. In relational terms, this boundary insists that God is the sole decision-maker; what is required of the human partner is to hear and comply.

Dorothee Soelle describes two experiences that invite reflection on Eliphaz's understanding of what relationship with God requires. In one,

Job, His Wife, His Friends, and the Devil

The Job sculpture in the North Transept at Chartres divides into two halves. In the top half, God, flanked by two angels, surveys the trial of Job from heaven. The angels bow in reverence before the scene they witness, but the expression on God's face suggests that what is happening is an occasion for sadness and grief. The bottom half depicts Job's affliction on earth. To Job's left are the three friends. Two face each other and appear to be engaged in thoughtful discussion. One strokes his beard,

Job, His Wife, His Friends, and the Devil
(Credit: Jane Vadnal)

pondering how to address to Job. The third, presumably Eliphaz, bends down to look at Job and extends his right hand, in the process making connection with the right hand of Satan that rests on Job's head. Job lies on a bed of shells, perhaps symbolic of the hope of rebirth (Terrien, 75). Satan stands over him, his right hand on Job's head, his left on Job's foot (cf. Job 2:7: "from the sole of his foot to the crown of his head"). His posture suggests that he has his victim in a vice-like grip and is ready to squeeze out his life. Satan turns a gruesome face in God's direction, as if waiting for the signal to begin. To Job's right is his wife. Like Eliphaz she looks at Job. Her left arm extends toward God, her right toward Job. Perhaps her posture suggests sympathy and comfort. But the position of her arms suggests that she may also be trying to explain to Job the reason for his punishment by directing his attention to God.

The relation of this scene to the five others that appear in the North and South Porches of the cathedral indicates that it serves to depict Job's patient suffering as a prefiguring of Christ's suffering and the suffering of the persecuted Church. But the imagery of the scene is highly suggestive and invites consideration of other connections as well. Especially intriguing are the two trees that stand behind Job and Satan, which undoubtedly represent the tree of life and the tree of knowledge (cf. Gen 2:9). Both are bent and tilted toward the right, in the direction toward which Satan is pulling Job, as if they are about to be uprooted. The implication is that suffering like Job's weighs heavily on creation, pulling it from its moorings and jeopardizing its survival (see the commentary on Job 1–2).

More suggestive still is the position of Job's left arm. He reaches toward the tree of knowledge on his left, which is bending away from him. Is he *pushing* the tree so as to hasten its destruction or *reaching for it* in order to straighten it and save it? His open palm suggests the latter, and if so one may imagine that Job understands his words to God—his curses, questions, complaints, and arguments—as authentic parts of this effort. Eliphaz, however, presumes the former. He regards Job's words as a threat to piety and a revolt against God's moral governance of creation.

It is generally thought that the sculpture of Job was commissioned by Pierre de Roissy, chancellor of the Chartres Cathedral School from 1208–1213. Roissy, who wrote a commentary on the book of Job, interpreted the biblical figure as a forerunner of the suffering Christ and as a symbol of the Church, which like Job must endure the attacks of Satan and his minions (Terrien, 76). In this connection, it is instructive to reflect on how the contemporary community of faith regards Job's search for understanding and knowledge. Are the Jobs of the world a threat to institutional religion, because they violate conventional expectations of what is right and proper in God's established order? So Eliphaz suggests. Or are they essential for the survival of faith, even if their reach may exceed their grasp?

For further discussion of this sculpture, see S. Terrien, *The Iconography of Job Through the Centuries. Artists as Biblical Interpreters* (University Park PN: The Pennsylvania State University Press, 1996), 73-78. On the sculptures and windows of Chartres in general, see E. Mâle, *Chartres*, trans. S. Wilson (New York: Harper and Row, 1983).

she recounts a conference in which a group of women were exploring religious questions. One woman asked where God had been at Auschwitz. Another, a fervent evangelical, answered that "Auschwitz was willed by God." The answer was shocking, and she was asked to explain what she meant. She responded by saying that "if God had not willed it, it would not have happened. Nothing happens without God." Soelle reflects on the comment as follows:

> The Wholly Other has so determined it, and though we cannot under-stand it we must accept it in humility. God's authority, lordship, and omnipotence may not be placed in doubt, it is not for us to inquire about God's providential will. The God who is completely independent from all God's creatures has willed everything that happens. God and God alone could have hindered it. But God's ways are not our ways.[10]

From another experience, Soelle reports on a church meeting in Hamburg in which the discussion focused on *Kristallnacht* (the "night of broken glass"), November 9, 1938, when the Nazis torched syna-gogues throughout Germany and vandalized Jewish homes and businesses. A young woman told how she had struggled to understand this event in light of her faith convictions about God. She ended by saying, "when I understood Auschwitz, I joined the peace movement." Soelle reflects on this comment as follows:

> In this statement I found a different God from the omnipotent Lord of heaven and earth who is completely independent of us. This woman had understood that in the Nazi period in Germany. . . God was in fact pow-erless because God had no friends, male or female. God's spirit had no place to live; God's sun, the sun of righteousness, did not shine. The God who needs people in order to come into being was a nobody.

She continues by turning the woman's statement over in her mind one more time:

> When I understood Auschwitz, I joined the peace movement. That is to say: I did not rid myself of God like many who had handed over responsibility to God alone; rather I grasped that God needs us in order to realize what was intended in creation. God dreams us, and we should not let God dream alone.[11]

"God dreams us, and we should not let God dream alone." Soelle's discernment does not deal with the solitary suffering of the legendary figure named Job but with the unspeakable horrors of the Holocaust. Nothing is properly analogous to this event, and one must therefore pause before any and all comparisons. Still, we may be permitted to imagine a discussion, similar to the ones Soelle describes, in which Eliphaz and Job seek to understand the suffering that turned the world of Uz upside down. Eliphaz might say, with genuine conviction, something like, "If God had not willed it, it would not have happened. It is not for us to doubt or question God's providential will." Job can be expected to say, with an equally genuine conviction but different passion, something like, "When I understood what happened in Uz, I joined the resistance movement. I grasped that God needed me in order to realize what was intended in creation." Readers may ponder what they would discern from these conversations, if they were to put themselves in the place of Soelle. What are God's dreams for us and for creation? Is it our responsibility to participate in these dreams or only to accept the assignment of living in them?

Commitment to God Requires that Conventional Wisdom Takes Precedence Over Personal Experience

The foundation of Eliphaz's counsel is "what the sages have told" (vv. 17-35). The collective wisdom of the sages, he believes, offers a truer perspective on God's moral governance of the world than the personal experience of Job. Indeed, personal experiences with suffering may skew perspectives by encumbering them with emotion that clouds judgment and prevents one from seeing larger realities that place them in proper context. The larger truth that Job must trust is that God's justice is alive and well. . . and fair. Job's suffering, however grievous, does not change this fact. The wicked are certainly punished, not only by some distant future judgment but also by the anticipation of that judgment, which makes them live in the present with psychic dread. This should serve as Job's "consolation" (v. 11). It should also warn him that if he continues his defiance of God, then he risks joining the ranks of the wicked and sharing their demise (cf. vv. 25-26).

This truth, hammered out by the collective wisdom of the sages and tested over time, enables Eliphaz to trump Job's complaint with theology that he believes cannot be invalidated by personal experience. Such theology assures Eliphaz, who stands at a safe distance from the pain he analyzes, that sufferers like Job should not "despise the discipline of the Almighty" who "wounds" but also "binds up" (cf. 5:17-18). It will do the same for Job, if he will but submit personal experience to the consensus truth that is vouchsafed by majority opinion. [Truth Preserved in "Caskets of Close-hammered Steel"]

William Safire, a prominent political columnist, has noted that the strategy of appealing to consensus plays a necessary but often misguided role in politics as well as religion. Too often the objective of consensus decisions is to camouflage controversy by constructing agreements based on nothing more than the lowest common denominator of truth. He compares the results to the practice of handicapping a horse race. One can bet on the horse that most experts believe will finish first. The problem is that the consensus pick rarely wins. He illustrates what may be lost when politicians and religious leaders insist on "consensing" with an anecdotal experience:

> The trouble with consensus decision-making today is that everyone has to agree to some watered-down version of any move. I dropped in at a meeting of the Planning Commission of the town of Frederick, Maryland, and I was told that I could not observe their discussion before a vote—that behind closed doors, "They're consensing." If this actionless verb describes the emerging voice of the people, we could look forward only to weak bleats of hesitant agreement in place of the healthy roar of controversy. Fortunately, Jobans refuse to consense.[12]

Truth Preserved in "Caskets of Close-hammered Steel"

William Cowper (1731–1800) was an English poet who suffered acute depression throughout his life, which was exacerbated by religious doubt. In his poem "Retirement," he gives his opinion of Job's comforters and those he had endured in his own time:

> Blest, rather than curst, with hearts that
>   never feel,
> Kept snug in caskets of close-hammered
>   steel,
> With mouths made only to grin wide and
>   eat,
> And minds that deem derided pain a treat.
>   (ll. 307-10)

W. Cowper, "Retirement," cited in *A Dictionary of Biblical Tradition in English Literature*, ed. D. Jeffrey (Grand Rapids MI: Wm. B. Eerdmans, 1992), 405.

When chapter 15 concludes, Eliphaz and Job are squarely focused on a common question: "What are mortals?" (15:14; cf. 7:17). That is to say, what are human beings in relation to God? More specifically, what is their proper identity, vocation, and destiny in a world where Jobs collide with good and evil that is neither fully predictable nor fully comprehensible? Eliphaz remains confident that he knows the answers to these questions, and he states them with authority in the three affirmations discussed above. Job has heard the argument before. He remains unconvinced, although he has as yet no clarity sufficient to offer an alternate answer. Until he does, he will hold his position. He will question and complain. *And* in the process he will dream of a God different from the One Eliphaz speaks for, a God who, *perhaps*, desires that the dream be more of a reality than either he or Eliphaz has yet to grasp. In the meanwhile, it is better to ponder deeply the question that focuses Eliphaz and Job than to resolve it too quickly. [The Importance of Serious Thinking]

The Importance of Serious Thinking

In an interview on National Public Radio, a prominent business executive described the motto that hangs on his wall as a constant reminder of his responsibility: "Our task is not to decide for others but rather to insure that the decision making process is so intense that one cannot escape without serious thinking" (4 March 1998).

NOTES

[1] Y. Hoffman notes that the portraits of the friends are not clearly developed in the second cycle of speeches, except for Eliphaz, who "fulfils the role of constituting a clear antithesis to Job " (*A Blemished Perfection: The Book of Job in Context* [JSOTSup 213; Sheffield: Sheffield Academic Press, 1996], 131-42).

[2] R. Gordis, *The Book of Job: Commentary, New Translation, and Special Studies* (New York: Jewish Theological Seminary of America, 1978), 160.

[3] See further, Samuel E. Balentine, "'What Are Human Beings, That You Make So Much of Them?' Divine Disclosure From the Whirlwind: 'Look at Behemoth, '" *God in the Fray: A Tribute to Walter Brueggemann*, ed. T. Beal, T. Linafelt (Minneapolis: Augsburg Fortress, 1998), 259-78.

[4] D. Clines, *Job 1–20* (WBC; Dallas: Word Books, 1989), 357. See further N. Habel (*The Book of Job: A Commentary* [OTL; Philadelphia: Westminster Press, 1985], 258), who suggests that Eliphaz's description of the mental anguish suffered by the wicked reflects a "psychology of fear."

[5] The Hebrew of v. 23a reads "He wanders about for bread, where is it?" (cf. NRSV). If the text is correct, then it suggests that the wicked will search in vain for food. Such a meaning is not inappropriate in this context, but many commentators follow the LXX and read *'ayyah*, "vulture," instead of *'ayyeh*, "where?" A number of translations adopt this alternate rendering, e.g., NIV: "He wanders about—food for vultures "; cf. REB, TEV, NAB.

[6] Clines, *Job 1–20*, 359.

[7] E.g., Habel: "The wicked man who puts his trust in his own capacity to defy God is nothing more than a fat fool clumsily attempting to play the warrior" (*Book of Job,* 259). Cf. H. H. Rowley, *Job* (The Century Bible; Ontario: Thomas Nelson, 1970), 140; Gordis, *Book of Job,* 164; J. Hartley, *The Book of Job* (NICOT; Grand Rapids MI: William B. Eerdmans, 1988), 252.

[8] Cf. G. Fohrer, *Das Buch Hiob* (KAT; Gütersloh: Gerd Mohn, 1963), 275; Clines, *Job 1–20*, 360; C. Newsom, "The Book of Job," in vol. 4 of *NIB* (Nashville: Abingdon Press, 1996), 452.

[9] H. G. Wells, *The Undying Fire* (New York: The Macmillan Company, 1919), 39.

[10] D. Soelle, *Theology for Skeptics: Reflections on God* (Minneapolis: Fortress Press, 1995), 13-14.

[11] Ibid., 15-16.

[12] W. Safire, *The First Dissident: The Book of Job in Today's Politics* (New York: Random House, 1992), 195. For the full discussion, which he titles "Beware consensus," see 192-95.

JOB'S RESPONSE TO ELIPHAZ: PORTRAIT OF GOD AS ENEMY

Job 16:1–17:16

Eliphaz introduced the second cycle of speeches with an aggressive rebuttal of Job's open rebellion against God. Job has turned his "spirit against God" (15:13). Eliphaz warned him that if does not cease his assault on the Almighty, he risks aligning himself with the wicked who stiffen their necks and run head-first into a battle with God they cannot win (15:25-26). Job now responds with similar aggressiveness.

Eliphaz has got it half-right. There is a battle underway, but the assailant is not Job. It is God. It is not Job whose spirit has turned against God. It is God who has attacked Job with such ferocity that he is "worn out" (16:7), and his "spirit is broken" (17:1). Eliphaz argued that those who oppose God always lose. Job counters that although God will always defeat hapless victims like himself, God wins no honor in the process (see the commentary on 17:4). When God acts as an enemy of the innocent, rather than as their defender, it is *God's justice* that is called into question. Job argues that the "upright are appalled" by the victimization of the innocent (17:8). He dares to believe that creation itself, earth and heaven, will lend its witness to the cry for justice that places God, not the victim, on trial (16:18-19). Eliphaz has warned Job that he is letting his emotions get the better of him. The intensity and the passion of Job's speech in these chapters does little to disprove this charge. But when one is torn, broken, dashed to pieces, slashed open, and poured out again and again (cf. 16:9-13), there is little incentive to remain calm and reasonable. ["Job's Scream to the Four Winds"]

There is a disjointedness to this speech that perhaps reflects the unruly passion of its speaker. Job speaks as if he is reeling back and forth between his complaint against the friends (16:2-6; 17:1-10) and his complaint against God (16:7-17). He searches imaginatively for some alternate source of comfort and vindication (16:18-22) but concludes, as he has done in previous speeches, that he is destined to find nothing more than the dust and death that awaits him in Sheol (17:11-16; cf. 3:20-26; 7:19-21; 10:18-22; 14:18-22). Once Job had dared to hope that Sheol might provide a respite from misery while he waited for some yet undefined post-mortem renewal (14:13-17). Now he concedes that Sheol promises no answers for innocent suf-

"Job's Scream to the Four Winds"

Nelly Sachs (1891–1970) emigrated from Germany to Sweden in 1940. During World War II, she began writing poems about the Holocaust that reflected her twofold legacy of suffering as a Jewish poet. On the one hand, she was heir to an ancient tradition of suffering like Job's; on the other, she was a contemporary witness to the atrocities that left only "skeletons in Hiroshima and Maidanek." Lawrence Langer has described her as a "poet picking through the rubble to rescue separate words that may have survived the disaster, while sadly confessing that their place in the moral structure of meaning would never be the same." The poem "Landscape of Screams" is representative of her efforts to stitch these words, Job's screams included, back together.

At night when dying proceeds to sever all seams
the landscape of screams
tears open the black bandage,

Above Moria, the falling off cliffs to God,
there hovers the flag of the sacrificial knife
Abraham's scream for the son of his heart,
at the great ear of the Bible it lies preserved . . .

This is the landscape of screams!
Ascension made of screams

out of the bodies grate of bones,
arrows of screams, released
from bloody quivers.

Job's scream to the four winds
and the scream from Mount Olive
like a crystal-bound insect overwhelmed by
impotence.

O knife of evening red, flung into the throats
where trees of sleep rear blood-licking from the
ground,
where time is shed
from the skeletons in Hiroshima and Maidanek.

Ashen screams from the visionary eye tortured
blind—

O you bleeding eye
in the tattered eclipse of the sun
hung up to be dried by God
in the cosmos—

L. Langer, ed., *Art from the Ashes: A Holocaust Anthology* (New York/Oxford: Oxford University Press, 1995), 636. "Landscape of Screams," which is included in this anthology (651-52), first appeared in English in N. Sachs, *O the Chimneys* (New York: Farrar, Straus & Giroux, 1967).

ferers. It only makes their questions heavier with despair: "Where now is my hope?" (17:15).

COMMENTARY

"Miserable Comforters," 16:1-6

Job begins, as is his custom, by criticizing the arguments of the friends. The friends see themselves as "comforters" (*nḥm*) who are trained in the pastoral art of "nodding the head" (*nwd*; 2:11) to express sympathy and support for the afflicted. Job has argued that they are not good pastoral counselors, they are "worthless physicians" (13:4) whose medicines cannot relieve the patient's misery. He now adds to that criticism by labeling them "miserable comforters" (*měnāḥămê ʿāmāl*). Not only do they *not comfort*, they actually *increase* one's "misery/trouble" (*ʿāmāl*; cf. 3:10; 4:8) by offering theological platitudes that add guilt to suffering. ["Yours Is the Cruelest Comfort of Them All"]

"Yours Is the Cruelest Comfort of Them All"

In Archibald's MacLeish's play *J.B.*, the friends try to comfort J.B. with the traditional maxims of retribution theology. J.B. insists on maintaining his integrity and his innocence. They insist that as a "miserable, mortal, sinful" man, he has no integrity. As Zophar puts it in one such exchange, "Your sin is simple. You were born a man!" J.B. responds that such comfort condemns not only him and not only them; it also condemns God:

Yours is the cruelest comfort of them all,
Making the Creator of the Universe
The miscreant of mankind—
A party to the crimes He punishes.

A. MacLeish, *J.B.* (Boston: Houghton Mifflin Co., 1956), 126.

Job has heard it all before. If he were in their place, looking on suffering from a safe distance, he might easily say the same things. Like the friends, he might question those who complain about suffering by asking, "Is there no limit to your 'windy words'? What has so disturbed you that you talk this way?" (v. 3; cf. Bildad in 8:2; Eliphaz in 15:2).[1] Job knows how to nod his head (v. 4b: *nwʿ*; cf. 2:11) as a gesture of sympathy. He knows how to string together encouraging words, and he knows how to maintain sympathetic silence when the occasion calls for it (vv. 4-5).[2] But unlike the friends, Job has first-hand experience with suffering. He knows that conventional forms of either speech or silence are not enough for those who grieve like him. He has tried silence (2:10; cf. 9:27), and he has tried speaking in the anguish of his spirit (7:11; cf. 13:3, 13). Neither strategy has reduced his pain or assuaged his grief (v. 6). What is the alternative? Is there another way, something beyond speech and silence, beyond traditional responses that require innocent sufferers either to repent of sins they have not committed or accept passively judgment they do not deserve? Job's dilemma forces him to ponder the question. If there is an answer, he does not yet know what it is. ["I Am No Longer Sure of the Goodness of the World"]

"I Am No Longer Sure of the Goodness of the World"

Job Huss, the lead character in H. G. Wells's fictional recreation of the Joban story, admits to his friends that at one time he would have agreed with their counsel. In the aftermath of his suffering, however, the old answers no longer seem so convincing:

I have sat here through some dreary and dreadful days, and lain awake through some interminable nights; I have thought of many things that men in their prosperity are apt to dismiss from their minds; and I am no longer sure of the goodness of the world without us or in the plan of Fate. Perhaps it is only in us within our hearts that the light of God flickers—and flickers insecurely. Where we had thought a God, somehow akin to ourselves, ruled the universe, it may be there is nothing but black emptiness and a coldness worse than cruelty.

H. G. Wells, *The Undying Fire* (New York: The Macmillan Company, 1919), 78.

God the Enemy, 16:7-17

As painful as the friends' scorn is for him, Job knows that it is God who is his real assailant. God has "worn him out" and "shriveled him up," leaving him too weak to resist and too despised to be comforted by his community (vv. 7-8). The implication is that his affliction, when viewed through the lens of retribution theology (see [Retribution]), only confirms the community's worst suspicions about him. He suffers greatly, *therefore*, he must be exceedingly guilty. If he were to present his case in court, then his very appearance would encourage a jury to presume him guilty, not innocent. As Habel puts it, "His innocent inner self cannot be heard because the court sees only his gaunt outer self."[3]

Over against this description of Job's vulnerability and isolation, vv. 9-14 depict the savagery of God's attack as wholly disproportionate. In anger God "tears" (*ṭārap*) Job, like a lion or wolf mauling its prey (cf. Gen 37:33; 44:28; 49:27; Ps 17:12; Ezek 22:27). The attacker's intent is made clear by the grinding of its teeth and the murderous focus of its eyes (v. 9). While God attacks, others who have spied out the victim are emboldened to join the assault (vv. 9-10). They open their mouths wide, hungry to gobble up whatever they can (cf. Isa 5:14). They strike at Job's cheek, a gesture of ridicule that signals they know he does not have the power to resist them (cf. Ps 3:8; Lam 3:30; Isa 50:6). When the time is right, God delivers (*yasgîr*; cf. Ps 78:48, 50, 62) the hapless victim into their midst so they can scavenge among the remains.

Verses 12-14 shift the imagery so that God is now depicted not as a savage beast but as an invincible warrior. ["When the Blast of War Blows in Our Ears"] While Job was "at ease," that is, tranquil and unsuspecting, God launched a surprise attack. The force of the assault is conveyed by the use of two intensive verbs in Hebrew that suggest God comes at Job again and again. God "breaks and breaks" (*yĕparpĕrēnî*), then grabs Job by the neck and "shatters and shatters" (*yĕpaspĕṣēnî*; NRSV: "dashes") until there is nothing left but bits and pieces (v. 12a). The force is not only constant, it is also overwhelming. It is comparable to the power God displays in conquering the waters of primordial chaos (cf. *pārar* in Ps 74:13) and splitting mountains and rocks (cf. *pāṣaṣ* in Jer 23:29; Hab 3:6).

"When the Blast of War Blows in Our Ears"

In war, the savagery of the attack may bear resemblance to both the bestial and the militant. In *Henry V* the king summons his troops into battle against Harfleur with an intensity not unlike that which Job ascribes to God:

But when the blast of war blows in our ears,
Then imitate the action of the tiger:
Stiffen the sinews, conjure up the blood,
Disguise fair nature with hard-favour'd rage;
Then lend the eye a terrible aspect.
Let it pour through the portage of the head
Like the brass canon . . .

Now set the teeth and stretch the nostril
   wide;
Hold hard the breath, and bend up every
   spirit
To his full height! (*Henry V*, III, i, 5-11, 15-17)

Complementary images describe God setting Job up as a "target" (v. 12b: *maṭṭārāh*; cf. 7:20, with a different word), then commanding the archers to train their bows on him. Their arrows pierce his kidneys; the bile from his liver spills out on the ground (v. 13). The damage is more than physical, for the kidneys represent not only a vital internal organ, they are also the symbolic center (like the heart) of one's emotions and passion (cf. Ps 16:7 [MT 16:6]; Prov 23:16; Jer 12:2; in all but Prov 23:16 NRSV translates "heart"). The cruelty of the assault is signaled by a brief phrase sandwiched in the middle of v. 13: as Job's life and passions drain away, God looks on *without compassion* (*lō' yaḥmôl*).

A final image depicts God running at Job like a "warrior" (*gibbôr*) laying siege to a city (v. 14). Not once but repeatedly, literally "breach upon breach," God breaks down Job's defenses and penetrates to the center of his world, a world now teetering on the brink of final collapse. Eliphaz has argued that it is the wicked, and by inference Job, who run against God as "warriors" (15:25: *yitgabbār*; NRSV: "bid defiance"). Job counters that the roles in this war are exactly the opposite. It is God who comes as the enemy of the innocent. It is a charge that calls into question one of Israel's basic affirmations about the way God uses power. Elsewhere in Hebrew scripture, when God is described as a mighty warrior it is typically an affirmation that God fights *for* Israel and *for* suffering individuals, who would not otherwise survive against their enemies (e.g., Exod 15:3-4; Hab 3:9-15; Ps 64:7-10). Job's experience suggests that God has betrayed this allegiance. The divine warrior now fights *against* the righteous. One might think of Job pondering the traditional song of the pilgrims who make their way to the festal celebration in Jerusalem: "If it had not been the Lord who was on our side . . . then they [our enemies] would have swallowed us up alive" (Ps 124:2-3). In Job's case, however, the occasion is no call for celebration, for God is not on his side, and the One whom the pilgrims praise as redeemer (Ps 124:6-8) is none other than his deadly opponent. [The Warrior God]

This graphic description of the brutality of God is followed by an equally vivid description of its effects on Job (vv. 15-17). He "sews sackcloth on his skin," an image suggesting that the traditional mourner's garb is virtually stitched into his body. He buries his strength (*qeren*; lit., "horn"; cf. 1 Sam 2:1; Pss 75:4-5 [MT 75:5-6]; 112:9) in the dust, a clear sign that the one who was once powerful and justly proud now concedes a humiliating defeat. His eyes are red-raw from weeping and ringed with dark shadows (*ṣalmāwet*) that signal death is at the door. [Disfiguring Judgment] Under other circumstances, his appearance might suggest penitence and remorse for having been rightly judged as one who is guilty. His friends have presumed as much with

The Warrior God

The image of God as a warrior is embedded deeply within Israel's traditions and occurs in different genres throughout the biblical period. From Israel's earliest literature, a number of victory hymns acclaim God's defeat of the enemy with the military imagery of war (cf. Exod 15, Deut 33, Judg 5, Hab 3). Exod 15, perhaps the oldest of these hymns, celebrates God's victory over Pharaoh as follows:

The Lord is a warrior;
The Lord is his name.
Pharaoh's chariots and his army
he cast into the sea;
his picked officers were sunk in
the Red Sea. (Exod 15:3-4)

Frequently, God is depicted as armed with the forces of nature: storm clouds provide God's chariot (Judg 5:4; Hab 3:8; Ps 68:4); wind and lightning are God's weapons (Exod 15:8-10; Hab 3:9-12); the stars, the sun, the moon, and other celestial forces are God's armies (Judg 5:20; Hab 3:5, 11). Such imagery suggests that Israel's understanding of God as warrior was rooted in ancient Near Eastern myths that portray deities defeating the cosmic forces of nature (e.g., *Enuma Elish*; see **[Ancient Near Eastern Creation Accounts]**; for a depiction of "Resheph of the Arrow," see **[CD: "Resheph of the Arrow"]**). Ancient Israel understood that God's primordial victory over these cosmic forces not only ensured the stability of creation, it also established God's kingship in Zion and the defeat of Israel's enemies who dared to oppose God's rule (Pss 18:8-16; 89:6-14; cf. Ps 79:6-7). Israel's prophets used the image of the divine warrior to empha-size God's concern for justice, which was not limited to Israel's enemies. The prophets warned that when Israel sinned and violated social, political, or moral sanctions, God would attack with the same ferocity that was directed against their foes (Amos 2:4-5, 9:7-10; Mic 1:2-9; Zeph 1:14-18).

The common thread that binds all these accounts together is God's use of power to redeem the innocent, punish the wicked, and thus secure the moral foundations of the world. On occasion, people petition God not to punish them so vigorously and to accept their confession of sin as a commitment to mend their ways (e.g., Pss 32:4-5; 38:1-4). Other times people complain that God's aggression has been misdirected against innocent victims (e.g., Pss 44:9-12, 17-19; 88:13-18; see further below **[Connections with Lamentations 3]**).

The friends clearly understand God's attack of Job to be justified. They are confident that the weight of tradition backs up their claim. Job insists that he is innocent and that if God is genuinely concerned with justice, then God must call a halt to the assault. He too has the tradition of lament to back up his claim that the righteous can and must complain about unjust affliction. The tension between their differing perspectives reflects the difference between onlookers and victims. Beyond that, it is a reminder that the use of power to enforce justice, human and divine, may have conflicted results, especially when the innocent are ensnared in a judgment they do not deserve.

For further reading on God as warrior, see M.C. Lind, *Yahweh as Warrior* (Scotsdale PA: Herald Press, 1980); P. D. Miller, Jr., *The Divine Warrior in Early Israel* (Cambridge MA: Harvard University Press, 1973).

their steady call for him to repent of his sin and return to God (5:8; 8:5-6; 11:13-15). But for Job it is innocence, not guilt, that compels such grief. He has been assaulted by a violent God, even though there is "no violence" in him. His prayer for justice has gone unanswered, even though he knows it has been honorable and "pure."

Job's graphic description of God as enemy invites comment on two points. First, the language he uses is hard and unsettling. Viewed from within the context of faith, the temptation is to judge it as not only irreverent but also as unacceptable and forbidden. The rebuke of Job's friends, earnest spokespersons for orthodoxy, serves as a clear reminder that those who speak like Job can expect to be confronted and challenged. It is therefore instructive to note that Job's words, harsh as they are, are consonant with Israel's traditional practice of lament. Such

Disfiguring Judgment

William Blake's depiction of the horrors of divine judgment that disfigure Nebuchadnezzar provides a suggestive analogue for reflecting on the devastating effects of God's attack on Job. Like Job, Nebuchadnezzar was a proud and powerful person who suffered the wrath of an angry God. Unlike Job, the reason for Nebuchadnezzar's judgment was that he had sinned (Dan 4:27). In this respect, the analogue both illumines and clouds our understanding of what has befallen Job. He is attacked like one of God's enemies, yet even God has declared him to be "blameless and upright" (Job 1:8; 2:3). If we associate the horrified look on Nebuchadnezzar's face with Job, then we might well hear the echo of his repeating question: "Why?"

Nebuchadnezzar

William Blake (1757-1827). *Nebuchadnezzar*. Colour print finished in ink and watercolour on paper. Tate Gallery, London, Great Britain. (Credit: Tate Gallery, London/Art Resource, NY)

practice provides the afflicted an authentic way of stating the conviction that what has befallen them comes from the hand of God. This conviction is often coupled with a strongly worded protest that it is God, not the victim, who is guilty of wrongful conduct. [CD: "Righteous Anger"] One poignant example occurs in Psalm 44, a communal lament:

> All this has come upon us,
> yet we have not forgotten you,
> or been false to your covenant.
> Our heart has not turned back,
> nor have our feet departed from your way,
> yet you have broken us in the haunt of jackals,
> and covered us with deep darkness. (vv. 17-19; cf. Pss 17:3-5; 26:4-10)

Like those who complain that they are falsely accused and wrongfully broken, Job laments. And like them, his words convey the hard hope that when God acts like God, the innocent will be redeemed and restored to their rightful place in the community of faith. Even when, one suspects *especially when* God seems more like an enemy than a friend, it is the practice of lament that sustains faith against all odds. ["Ah, My Dear Angry Lord"]

"Ah My Dear Angry Lord"

George Herbert (1593–1633) was an English poet who spent most of his career as rector in Bemerton. His poem "Bitter-Sweet" bears witness to the truth that one may image God faithfully in both complaint and praise:

Ah my dear angry Lord,
Since thou dost love, yet strike;
Cast down, yet help afford;
Sure I will do the like.

I will complain, yet praise;
I will wail, approve:
And all my sour-sweet days
I will lament, and love.

George Herbert, "Bitter-Sweet," in *The Complete English Poems*, ed. John Tobin (London: Penguin Books, 1991), 161.

Second, the practice of lament, though traditional, seldom observes convention and formality. The catalyst for lament is pain, and pain will inevitably chart its course without regard for boundaries. It does not say, "I will go this far, but no farther," or "I will invade only one part of the body or mind, but exempt the rest." Instead, it is random and unpredictable, sometimes brief, sometimes lasting, sometimes responsive to treatment, sometimes resistant. For this reason, we may know that lament is also unmanageable. Lament follows the pain and seeks to match its intensity with a comparable passion for release and healing. Job knows that pain is like an assailant that penetrates the body wherever and however it can. He describes it as a physical assault that strikes at his cheek (v. 10), seizes his neck (v. 12), ruptures his kidneys (v. 13), and breaks open his skeleton (v. 14). It is the conventional language of lament that enables him to describe this assault and by describing it to prevent its pain from outdistancing his resistance to it.

Connections with Lamentations 3

Scholars have noted a number of verbal and thematic connections between Job 16:7-17 and Lam 3. The following table identifies the principle similarities:

Job 16:7-17		Lamentations 3
v. 9	God as attacking animal	vv. 10-11
v. 10a	Gaping mouths	v. 46
v. 10b	Striking the cheek	v. 30
vv. 12b-13a	Attacking with bows and arrows	vv. 12-13
v. 13b	Slashing vital organs	v. 13
v. 13b	God shows no mercy	v. 43
v. 13c	Pours out my gall	vv. 15, 19
v. 14	Besieging a city	vv. 5-9
v. 15	Laid in the dust	vv. 16, 29
v. 16	Eyes weeping	vv. 48, 49

Newsom has correctly noted that in v. 17 Job's lament turns in a different direction from Lamentations 3. After lamenting God's brutal attack, Zion turns to express hope in God's mercies (3:20), which in turn leads to accepting the punishment quietly (3:25-30) and confessing the sin that justifies it (3:40-42). Job, however, moves from lament (16:7-16) to a protest of innocence (16:17) and a strong petition for justice (16:18-22). Newsom concludes that Job has broken off from the conventional lament pattern because it is no longer able to express adequately his response to affliction. While her observation about the differences between the two texts is surely correct, it may be suggested that Job has not broken with the practice of lament but instead has enlarged it. It is his pain, not the conventional pattern, which decides where lament must go.

C. Newsom, "The Book of Job," in vol. 4 of *NIB* (Nashville: Abingdon Press, 1996), 460.

Job's lament is perhaps most similar to Lamentations 3, which depicts God's violent assault on Zion with some of the same graphic images that Job uses. [Connections with Lamentations 3] Zion laments the assault but concedes the sin that explains it as the punishment of a righteous God (Lam 3:31-42). Zion's lament is in this respect an affirmation of traditional retribution theology. It laments *toward repentance,* for once suffering is understood as just punishment, then the plea for forgiveness becomes the objective of the prayer. In Job's case, God's assault is similarly savage, but the traditional theology does not work for him, because he is innocent. The objective of his lament, is not *repentance,* but *justice.* He dares to believe that innocent suffering makes a moral claim on God's justice. And so he laments, *not to prove himself sufficiently penitent to remain in God's company* but rather *to insist that God must remain in the company of the righteous as the moral agent of justice.* For such a bold and daring endeavor, Job "pushes the envelope" of lament toward a radically litigious faith-partnership with God (see below on vv. 18-22). Like Abraham, he will stand face to face with the Creator of the world and ask, "Shall not the Judge of all the earth do what is just?" (Gen 18:25).

"Let My Outcry Find No Resting Place," 16:18-22

Job's lament now transposes into legal discourse. In his view, innocent suffering calls into question the moral order of the universe along with the Creator who is responsible for overseeing it. He has appealed to God to hear his complaint and judge it fairly (13:20-23), but God has not responded. Now he calls on creation itself to join in his suit against God. First, he petitions the *earth* not to cover up the evidence of God's violation of justice (v. 18). Secondly, he summons a "witness" in *heaven* to recognize the legitimacy of his cry for justice (v. 19) and to argue his case "with God" (v. 21). In order to understand the full thrust of his appeal for a heavenly witness, it is important to recognize how much is at stake on earth if the cry of innocent blood remains unheard.

Job's cry invokes important memories from Israel's testimony about God's creational intentions. The imagery of innocent blood "crying out" (*zāʿaq*) from the earth for justice recalls the story of Cain's murder of his brother Abel (Gen 4:8-10). Because Abel's blood was "crying out" (*zāʿaq*) from the ground, God interrogates, then punishes Cain for engaging in an act that violates God's intentions for human relationships. Beyond that, however, God determines that such violence subverts the moral order of the cosmos and renders it incapable of sustaining God's creational objectives. As a result, God not only punishes Cain but also subjects the world to the harshest judgment recorded in scripture (Gen 6:11-13). In the post-flood world, God moves to establish a new moral order, which will be sustained by an unconditional divine promise—"Never again" (Gen 8:21-22). This promise becomes the foundation upon which God then reissues the creational commission to "be fruitful and multiply and fill the earth" (Gen 9:1, 7; cf. Gen 1:28). There is, however, one important addition to the post-flood mandate, which signals God's earnest desire that previous violations not be repeated: the lifeblood of human beings should not be shed; if it is, God will require a reckoning (Gen 9:5-6).

God's concern for human life in the post-flood world involves two stipulations. First, it is God who issues the mandate, but God expects human beings to participate in executing the justice God requires: "whoever sheds the blood of a human, *by a human* shall that person's blood be shed "(Gen 9:6a; emphasis added). The context of this admonition has less to do with the thorny issue of capital punishment—concerning which it is important to note that in this text God remains the final authority on the value of human life—than with the commission for humans to exercise responsibility as moral agents of divine justice. Second, the rationale for this commission is that human beings have been created in the image of God (Gen 9:6b).[4] That is to say, whenever human blood is shed, human beings are summoned to image God by seeking justice for the victim. One important example of what this mandate for justice requires of humans is Abraham. When informed *by God* of the divine response that was planned to the "outcry" (*zāʿaq*) from Sodom and Gomorrah, Abraham was emboldened to stand before God and argue that justice would not be served by condemning the righteous as if they were the wicked (Gen 18:20-33).

Job has summoned the earth not to cover the evidence of his blood, which cries out for justice. The suggestion is that he hopes for one like Abraham who is willing to image God by pleading his case, even if it means interrogating God about what has happened to him in a manner similar to the way God interrogated Cain. In view of the creational imagery that echoes in the background of this hope, his plea has broad implications. What is at stake is more than the restitution of a single person. Instead, what hangs in the balance is the new moral order of the world, which has been vouchsafed by God's unconditional promise.

[Blood Still Crying]

From Job's perspective, however, there is no Abraham anywhere on earth who will stand up for him before God. The friends have shown that they are unable or unwilling to argue his case. Job therefore directs his appeal toward heaven in the hope that there may be some voice from on high that will champion his cause. Many commentators interpret the heavenly witness as none other than God.[5] A close reading of

Blood Still Crying

The innocent blood of Abel crying from the ground (Gen 4:10) has become an enduring symbol of the cry for justice that will not and must not be silenced. The Gospel writers appropriated Abel as the prototypical martyr whose murder foreshadowed the rejection of the "prophets, sages, and scribes" sent by God (Matt 23:35; Luke 11:51). The Letter to the Hebrews lists Abel as the first of the righteous who acted "by faith" (Heb 11:4; cf. 1 John 3:12). The shedding of his blood prefigures the "sprinkled blood" of Christ, even though it is inferior to it (Heb 12:24).

Milton reflects at length on the meaning of Abel's death in Paradise Lost. When Adam is shown Abel's death, he is instructed to understand it as testimony to the effect of his original sin. Dismayed at what he sees, and incredulous that it should mean what he is told, he responds:

O teacher, some great mischief hath befallen
To that meek man, who well had sacrificed;
Is piety thus and pure devotion paid?

O sight
Of terror, foul and ugly to behold,
Horrid to think, how terrible to feel! (*Paradise Lost*, XI, ll. 450-52, 463-65)

Shakespeare included numerous allusions and references to Abel's blood. Among them was *Richard II*, in which Bolingbroke vows with his life to avenge the murder of the Duke of Gloucester. Like Abel, the Duke's blood cries for justice from the "tongueless caverns of the earth" (I, i, 97-108).

A final example serves to reinforce the truth that the crying of innocent blood is more than merely a biblical or literary image. It is a profound and ever contemporary summons to humanity to see and hear and respond to innocent victims so that split blood will not be the only voice that cries out to heaven. In *Holocaust Poetry* (New York: St. Martin's Press, 1995), Hilda Schiff has collected 119 poems from 59 contributors that bear witness to the more than six million human beings who died at the hand of the Nazis and their collaborators. In the "Introduction" she states her motivation and her hope:

This is a book to mourn with, to weep with, to show solidarity with, perhaps to pray with. For us Jews it offers an opportunity to recover more fully that part of our heritage which the paralysis of pain has prevented us from making fully our own until this time of grace. (xxiv)

It may be suggested that a sufferer's journey from "the paralysis of pain" to a "time of grace" is long, arduous, and fraught with realties that hinder, block and deny. Perhaps this is in part the explanation for Schiff's choice of words on the frontispiece: "O earth, cover not thou my blood, and let my cry have no resting place" (Job 16:18).

the text, however, suggests that Job's hope is for some third party who will serve as an intermediary *between* himself and God (v. 21).[6] Job expressed a similar hope in 9:33 by appealing for an "arbiter" (*môkîaḥ*; NRSV: "umpire") who could judge impartially between the claims of God and himself. Here he speaks not of a judge but of a "witness," one who will side with him in God's court and bear testimony to the truth of his claim. A similar figure in Zech 3:1 is described as the "angel of the Lord" who stands at the side of Joshua, the high priest, and successfully defends him before the heavenly court against the baseless charges of the *satan* (*hasāṭan*). Eliphaz has warned Job that he cannot expect the "holy ones" to come to his rescue (5:1). Nevertheless, Job clings to the hope that somewhere there is a "redeemer" who will rise and testify on his behalf (19:25). Subsequently, Elihu will also invite Job to hope for an angelic mediator (*melîṣ*) who will be his advocate before God, although Elihu adds that this one's purpose will be to lead Job toward a confession of sin (33:23-28).

As usual there is a vast chasm between what Job hopes for and what his friends predict he will receive. While he "pours out tears to God"

(v. 20), they promise that his cry is in vain. When he hopes for an advocate to defend him, they warn that his only legitimate defense is to plead guilty and accept the judgment of the court. In either case, it seems to Job that he is already beyond the pale of any just recourse. "Even now" (v. 19), as he struggles to hope for the "witness" who does not appear, he is walking down the path of no return (v. 22). Soon he will finish his days in the land of Sheol, and then it will be too late for anyone who might speak on his behalf to do any good.

"My Spirit Is Broken" and "I Cannot Find a Sensible Person Among You," 17:1-10

Job is utterly alone. His friends have abandoned him. God will not answer him. And though he longs for a heavenly witness, there is no reason to believe that any such advocate will come to his defense. He is a broken man in every sense of the word; physically and psychologically he feels as if he is already dead, even though he continues to draw breath. God's relentless assaults have crushed his desire for life, snuffing out his days, exhausting his eyes with grief, withering his limbs so that they become mere shadows of what he once was. He is destined for the grave (vv. 1, 7). The mockery of his friends adds insult to injury (vv. 2, 6). Eyes dimmed with anguish look for relief but see only the "provocation" of those who jeer at his demise. He has become an object of derision, like one on whom people spit to show their disdain and disrespect. ["Cast Out an Honest Friend, and You Cast Out Your Life"]

"Cast Out an Honest Friend, and You Cast Out Your Life"

To slur a good man's name
With baseless slander is one crime—another
Is rashly to mistake bad men for good.
Cast out an honest friend, and you cast out
Your life, your dearest treasure. Time will teach
The truth of this; for time alone can prove
The honest man; one day proclaims the sinner.

(Sophocles, *King Oedipus*, ll. 634-40.)

Sandwiched in between this account of grief and abuse is a brief address to God (vv. 3-4) coupled with a proverbial saying (v. 5). It is but the second time that Job has addressed God directly in this speech. In the first instance, 16:7-8, he addresses God as the enemy who wages an unjust war against him. Now he addresses God as the victor who has won the battle but can claim no honor from the victory. Job challenges the One who has defeated him to recognize that an innocent person has been falsely condemned and wrongfully punished. He offers a pledge of his integrity and petitions God to receive it as proof that he has been as good as his word. A "pledge" (*'erābōn*) is typically offered by one who wishes to guarantee that the terms of a contractual agreement will be faithfully honored. It is the equivalent of a solemn oath that seals a deal by promising to relinquish personal property (Gen 38:17-20) or even a life (Gen 43:9; 44:32) if the agreement is breached. Job declares that he is willing to pledge his life as the guarantee that he has faithfully upheld his end of the partnership with God. He is completely innocent. He has broken no agreements; he has defaulted on no commitments; and therefore he should not be prosecuted, either legally or morally, like one who is guilty. None of this seems to matter to the friends, who without reason have disregarded the evidence that vindicates him. Neither does it seem to have any bearing on God, who is the One responsible for having "closed their minds," deliberately rendering them incapable of recognizing the truth about his situation. [No "Sense of Obligation"] The last phrase of v. 4 is ambiguous. NRSV emends the text by adding an object ("them") to the verb, thus "you [God] will not let *them* [the friends] triumph." Such a reading subtly preserves God's innocence by condemning the friends, although it is clear from the first half of the verse that they are only following God's directives. A more plausible reading given the context, if also a more troubling one, is to take the text as it stands. Job's charge then would be as follows: "Because you [God] have closed their minds to understanding, therefore you [God] will not be exalted."[7]

Verse 5 is also obscure and open to different interpretations. [A Hard Saying] The saying apparently originates in a traditional proverb about "friends" and "children." NRSV interprets the saying as a rebuke of friends who greedily betray the obligations of friendship for personal gain, while leaving their children to expire from hunger.[8] Given the context of Job's preceding complaint against God, however, the saying

No "Sense of Obligation"

A man said to the universe:
"Sir, I exist!"
"However," replied the universe,
"The fact has not created in me
A sense of obligation."

Stephen Crane, "War Is Kind and Other Lines," *The Oxford Book of Short Poems,* ed. P. Kavanagh, J. Michie (New York: Oxford University Press, 1985), 177.

A Hard Saying

AΩ The meaning of the verses remains obscure, despite all the proposed interpretations. A literal rendering of the Hebrew produces something like the following: "For a portion (*ḥeleq*) he tells friends, and the eyes of his children fail." Some older Jewish commentators took the word *ḥeleq* to be from a verbal root meaning "to be smooth," hence "flattery" (as in Prov 7:21). The implication would be that those who denounce a friend in exchange for flattery will see the judgment enacted on their children (cf. KJV). Others have taken *ḥeleq* to mean a "portion" of either food or property. Gordis opts for the former and suggests that the saying has to do with those who pretend to have much to share—they invite their friends to a "feast"—while in reality their resources are too meager to sustain their own family. If the intent is to refer to "property" rather than food, then the verse may be taken with NRSV (cf. NIV, NJPS, TEV)

to be a rebuke of those who "denounce" (or "speak against") a friend in exchange for a "reward."

An equally critical issue is the question about whom the proverb is directed *against*. The conventional understanding is that Job is rebuking his friends for failing (in some way) to fulfill their obligations of friendship. It is also possible that Job is quoting the proverb against God. One can reasonably imagine that from Job's perspective it is God who fails him by succumbing to the "flattery" or perhaps the "reward" of being affirmed as a righteous Judge, while Job, God's own child and "servant" (1:8), dies from a lack of attention. This is an attractive suggestion, especially given Job's preceding complaint against God (17:4), but it must be conceded that the meaning is not certain.

R. Gordis, *The Book of Job: Commentary, New Translation, and Special Studies* (New York: Jewish Theological Seminary of America, 1978), 182.

may just as well be intended as a rebuke of God's failure. That is, God betrays the obligation to act like God by accepting the flattering, but perjured testimony of the friends (cf. 13:7), while God's own child, Job, starves from lack of attention.[9]

Most commentators take vv. 8-10 to be Job's sarcastic rebuke of the friends for failing to demonstrate the righteousness they so vigorously claim for themselves. If the friends were genuinely "upright" and "innocent," then they would be appalled by Job's treatment, and they would stir themselves to rise up in his defense (v. 8). Job's friends betray their true character by resolutely clinging to the assurances of their still unquestioned retribution dogmas. They look at Job's suffering and take comfort from knowing that their hands are clean, and they remain strong; they need not fear the judgment that comes to the wicked (v. 9). From Job's perspective, such behavior indicts rather than vindicates them. They see another's suffering as confirmation of their innocence. Worse still, their "righteousness" confirms dogma at the expense of honesty and compassion. Job could wish that they will "return" and "come" back to him with a truer understanding of the claim his suffering makes on them and their theology. From what he has seen so far, however, he has more reason to despair than to hope. Even if they should make another effort to console him, he does not to expect any wisdom in what they will offer. In his words, "I shall not find a wise person (*ḥākām*; NRSV: "sensible") among you" (v. 10).

"Where Then Is My Hope?" 17:11-16

In each of his previous speeches from the ash heap, Job ends with a deep and despairing focus on death (3:20-26; 7:19-21; 10:18-22; 14:18-22). This speech is no different. He regards his days as having already passed by (*ʿābar*), his plans for the future already "torn up" (*nātaq*), the "desires" of his heart already squelched (v. 11). Once he dared to hope that the night of his misery would eventually yield to a better day and that the darkness of his despair would be illumined by the brightness of the dawn (v. 12). Those hopes are now gone, and in their place there remains only a distorted "hope" (note the repetition of the root *qwh*, "wait, hope," in vv. 13 [NRSV: "look for"], 15a, 15b) that is tied to nothing more promising than the grim reality of Sheol (vv. 13, 14, 16). He has dared to imagine that Sheol might be a temporary sanctuary for him, a place to wait until God remembers him and summons him forth into a new, post-mortem world where he can at last obtain justice (14:13-17). Now he speaks of Sheol as a termination point, a permanent home in darkness, where he resides in the family of the ruined (v. 14: *šaḥat*; NRSV, "pit"; cf. 9:31; 33; 18) and the rotting (*rimmāh*, NRSV: "worm"; cf. 7:5; 21:26).

The double question of v. 15 adds a new note of despair, and a subtle new resolve, to what is by now a familiar lament. If "hope" resides only in Sheol, where death, not life, is the measure of all existence, then what kind of hope is this? If "hope" takes shape only in Sheol, in the underworld that is hidden from all but those who languish there, then who can see it? Job's hope is now squarely focused on justice. He has argued that there must be some place on earth where his cry cannot be silenced (16:18), and there must be some one in the heavens who will be willing to testify that his cry deserves to be heard and addressed by God (16:19). Sheol cannot be the place for justice, for there the plight of innocent victims is beyond public scrutiny. Whether they are restored or silenced is of little consequence for those who must make their choices about good and evil in the land of the living. No one can pass through the "bars of Sheol" (v. 16) to bring back a clarifying report of God's intentions. If God's justice is to be effective and meaningful, then there must be some tangible demonstration of it on earth's ash heaps, where the cause is righteous and the need is urgent.

Thus, while Job's expectations that he is destined for Sheol are similar to what he has said before, his questions signal a gradually strengthening resolve. There must be some alternative to silence and acquiescence. There must be some place on earth where the innocent can cry and be heard. Job does not yet know what the alternative may be, but he has wondered if for some reason God regards him, a mere mortal, as somehow critically important for the establishment of cosmic order (see the commentary on 7:12). He has wondered why God expends so much energy in shaping human beings (7:17), if the purpose is only to condemn them to a life of misery and suffering that defines creation as more a living hell than a paradisiacal garden. Even now, as he describes the overwhelming force that God brings against him (16:6-17), there is a faint echo of the wonderment that God regards him as such a formidable (and worthy?) adversary.

What *does* it mean for human beings to be created in the image of God? Job has as yet no satisfying answer to this question. But his concluding questions in chapter 17 put the reader on notice that he will not settle for any answer that equates hope with Sheol. One clue that he thinks there must be more than this lies in the recognition that this will be the last of his speeches that ends with a focus on Sheol. From this point forward, his quest will be for some alternative that does not uncouple hope from justice. [CD: "Tis Not Too Late to Seek a Newer World"]

CONNECTIONS

Two critical issues in this speech invite reflection. They are necessarily intertwined and for that reason all the more important and deeply disturbing. The first is Job's portrait of God as enemy; the second is his petition that there must be a witness, both on earth and in heaven, to his cry for justice.

God as Enemy

Job 16:6-17 is a vivid description of *pain's portrait of God.* Two aspects of this portrait invite close scrutiny. First, Job insists that his pain is real, *physically real.* Job describes his affliction in highly metaphorical terms—his body is shriveled up; he is broken in two; he is seized by the neck and dashed into pieces, his kidneys are slashed open, his bile poured out; his eyes are reddened with weeping. The temptation may be to interpret such descriptions as *merely metaphorical,* but such an approach is likely to minimize the truth of what Job says. Minimizing pain is the tactic of the friends, who have the "advantage" of looking at Job's suffering from a safe distance. Eliphaz, for example, sounds entirely too glib when he urges Job to accept hurt and brokenness as if it can be dismissed with a simple credal affirmation: God "wounds, but he binds up; he strikes, but his hands heal" (5:17). For Eliphaz, the pain of being wounded and struck is unfelt and virtually invisible. When he looks at Job, he sees only the promise of healing; he feels nothing so deeply as the conviction that in due course it will go away. But the intensity of Job's description of suffering insists that Eliphaz look again. His wounding is real; it is not imaginary or psychological. It takes concrete shape in the distortion of his body; it can be heard in screams that will not be silenced. Moreover, his pain is continuous, not temporary; it is massive; not minor or trifling. Job reminds Eliphaz *and all contemporary sympathizers who might endorse his approach* that such pain cannot be assuaged by religious platitudes that gloss over the truth about being broken in two.[10] [The Scream of Pain]

Second, and still more disturbing is Job's contention that his affliction comes at the hand of One who is supposed to love him. The friends, of course, reject Job's argument as both irreverent and wrong. They exonerate God by proving Job guilty. As much as one might *want* and *need* them to be right in this assessment, the unsettling insistence of this book is that Job is God's servant, he is innocent, *and* he suffers horribly at the hands of the One who "breaks and breaks" and "shatters and shatters" (16:12). Job's pain threatens to break more than his body; it reaches to the depths of his soul where convictions about God's character, God's justice, God's trustworthiness begin to splinter and crack. God has inexplicably become his enemy. He asks "Why?" (cf. 13:24) but receives no answer at all from God and none from the friends that is credible. If Job's question is dismissed as inappropriate, misdirected, or simply unanswerable, then the anxieties that gather round conventional understandings about God will no doubt be lessened. But the one whose pain has forced the question will remain neither healed nor comforted. If the question is embraced and pursued, then trusted certainties are vulnerable, and that constitutes an equally unbearable pain. Sufferers like Job remind us that inside pain's portrait of God, faith is deeply conflicted. The questions are hard . . . and real. What do the faithful do when they feel that God has targeted them for suffering "without compassion" (16:13) and "for no reason" (2:3)?

The Scream

Edvard Munch (1863-1944). *The Scream*. 1893. Tempera and pastels on cardboard. National Gallery, Oslo, Norway. (Credit: Scala/Art Resource, NY)

There Must Be a Witness, on Earth and in Heaven, to the Cry for Justice

Job serves notice once again that pain speaks the language of faith with the words of lament. In ancient Israel, the practice of lament is a bold and variegated expression of faith. In many cases, suppliants acknowledge before God that they have sinned and thus deserve the punishment that signals God's displeasure with them. The object of such lament is to petition God to forgive and to restore (see, for example, the discussion above of

The Scream of Pain

Emily Dickinson speaks on behalf of those whose lives have been twisted and distorted by pain:

Give little anguish—
Lives will fret—
Give avalanches—
And they'll slant—

In a painting titled *The Scream*, the Norwegian artist Edvard Munch (1863–1944) offers a powerfully suggestive rendering of the cry of one whose life is "slanted" by grief. Those who would be counselors of Job do well to consider that their words may be addressed to one like this. Such a recognition may serve as an important caution, without which we may be judged guilty of having become no more than "miserable comforters" (Job 16:2).

E. Dickinson, "#310," *The Complete Poems of Emily Dickinson* (Boston/New York: Little, Brown and Company, 1960), 145-46.

Lam 3). In other cases, suppliants protest before God that they suffer unjustly at the hands of their enemies. The object of lament in these cases is to petition God to redeem the righteous and punish the wicked, for redemption is always consonant with God's "steadfast love" (e.g., Ps 6:5; cf. Pss 3, 5). In still other cases, suppliants dare to say to God that they suffer unjustly because *God* has turned against them, in effect assuming the role of the enemy that one normally associates with the wicked. In such cases, the object of lament is to petition God to be just, for justice must also be a constant characteristic of God's "steadfast love." One example of such a daring lament is Psalm 44, a portion of which has been cited above, but bears repeating again:

> All this has come upon us,
> yet we have not forgotten you,
> or been false to your covenant.
> Our heart has not turned back,
> nor have our feet departed from your way,
> Yet you have broken us. . . .

The concluding petition of this psalm provides additional testimony to what lamenters expect of God and why:

> Rouse yourself! Why do you sleep, O Lord?
> Awake, do not cast us off forever!
> Why do you hide your face? . . .
> Rise up, come to our help.
> Redeem us *for the sake of your steadfast love.* (vv. 23-24a, 26; emphasis added)

Like his psalmic counterpart, Job laments because he desperately needs God to be just. Justice is a requisite of covenant fidelity. It is required of humans, who are expected to be obedient and faithful to the covenantal stipulations that secure the partnership with God. *And* it is required of God, who has chosen to be bound by the same covenant to "steadfast love" that is righteous, moral, and just. It is covenantal fidelity that compels the sinner to lament and seek God's forgiveness. Lamentation is thus a *means of keeping individuals and communities in covenant partnership with God. And* it is that same covenantal fidelity that compels the innocent victim to lament, protest, and petition the Judge of all the earth to turn away from infidelity and unrighteousness. Lamentation is thus also a *means of keeping God in faithful covenantal partnership with the human community.* Job's lamentation puts God on trial (16:18-22). His objective is not to break covenant, but to keep it, or die trying, for he knows that radical faith sometimes requires that one challenge God with their life in their hand (cf. 13:13-15).

The Imperative of Testimony That Disturbs

Elie Wiesel has relentlessly argued that surviving the Holocaust marks both his life and his literature with an ethical mandate to bear witness that disturbs believers who may be tempted toward silence in the face of seemingly invincible injustice. In his memoirs he explains his motive:

I don't believe in art for art's sake. For me literature must have an ethical dimension. The aim of the literature I call testimony is to disturb. I disturb the believer because I dare to put questions to God, the source of all faith. I disturb the miscreant because, despite my doubts and questions, I refuse to break with the religious and mystical universe that has shaped my own. Most of all, I disturb those who are comfortably settled within a system—be it political, psychological, or theological. If I have learned anything in my life, it is to distrust intellectual comfort. . . . Survivors are a bit like parchments. So long as they exist, so long as some of them are still alive, the others know—even though they don't always admit it—that they cannot trespass certain boundaries.

E. Wiesel, *All Rivers Run to the Sea: Memoirs* (New York: Alfred A. Knopf, 1995), 336-37.

Job demands justice of God, because something more than his personal vindication is at stake. God's assault of him has been so extreme, God's unresponsiveness toward him has been so complete, that Job summons creation itself to join his suit against God. Inside pain's portrait of the quest for justice, Job appeals to the earth not to cover the outcry of his innocent blood (16:18). Somewhere on earth there must be a witness to injustice that will not be silenced and cannot be ignored. And somewhere in heaven there must be one who will bear testimony to the truth and the imperative of Job's cry (16:19), even if it means standing in the dangerous breach between Job's gaunt and worn out body and the awesome power of the Almighty (16:21). It is a radical hope, because Job dares to believe that *as long as one righteous plea for justice* goes unanswered, the *moral foundation of creation itself*, earth and heaven, totters on the brink of collapse. It is precisely this assumption that Bildad will soon challenge (cf. 18:4). [The Imperative of Testimony That Disturbs]

That Job ends his speech in these chapters on a note of abject despair only adds to the urgency and the importance of his quest. The friends will not testify for him. God has not responded to him. The earth cries out for relief, but there is as yet no echo in the heavens to keep the cry alive. He is destined for Sheol—that much seems certain—but Sheol cannot be the place for justice. Those who die as victims cannot bear witness to justice in the land of the living. What remains is for Job to ask, "Where then is my hope?" (17:15). Behind that question the reader may know that there is another, which is unspoken but real and persistent: Who will bear witness for Job? [Finding a Place to Stand]

Finding a Place to Stand

The Hebraic affirmation of lament as an authentic act of faith summons the Church to find a place in its liturgy and in its ministries for the cry for justice that keeps God bound to this world of too much suffering and pain. There are clearly strong and persistent voices in Christianity, often cloaked in the Pauline idea that "all have sinned and fallen short of the glory of God" (Rom 3:23), which insist such language is inappropriate and unacceptable. This theological perspective is in itself sound and important to affirm. But when the community of faith allows good theology to harden into rigid and compassionless dogma it runs the risk of speaking like Job's friends. The Church then must resolve whether its place is with the onlookers who condemn by silence or by word, or whether it will join with the afflicted, even it means questioning the Judge of the whole world. Dorothee Soelle states the matter bluntly: "In the face of suffering you are either with the victim or the executioner—there is no other option."

The basis for such a summons is deeply rooted in both Jewish and Christian understandings of what it means to be faithful citizen of the kingdom of God:

He [Jesus] unrolled the scroll [of Isaiah] and found the place where it was written:
"The Spirit of the Lord is upon me,
because he has anointed me
to bring good news to the poor.
He has sent me to proclaim release to the captives
and recovery of sight to the blind,
to let the oppressed go free,
to proclaim the year of the Lord's favor." (Luke 4:17-19;
cf. Isa 61:1-2; 58:6)

D. Soelle, *Suffering* (Philadelphia: Fortress Press, 1975), 32.

NOTES

[1] The pronouns in v. 3 are singular, rather than plural as in vv. 2 and 4-5, suggesting that Job is quoting the friends. He speaks as if he knows exactly what they would say. Cf. R. Gordis, *The Book of Job: Commentary, New Translation, and Special Studies* (New York: Jewish Theological Seminary of America, 1978), 174; D. Clines, *Job 1–20* (WBC; Dallas: Word Books, 1989), 378-79; C. Newsom, "The Book of Job," in vol. 4 of *NIB* (Nashville: Abingdon Press, 1996), 457.

[2] The last line of v. 5 can be translated in different ways (see, for example, NRSV). The Hebrew is literally "and the movement of my lips restrain." Gordis suggests that the phrase provides an antithetic parallel to "encourage you with my mouth" in v. 5a (*Book of Job,* 175). That is, Job knows how to express sympathy in both speech and silence.

[3] N. Habel, *The Book of Job: A Commentary* (OTL; Philadelphia: Westminster Press, 1985), 271.

[4] For suggestive commentary on these texts in Genesis, see T. Fretheim, "The Book of Genesis," *NIB,* vol. 1 (Nashville: Abingdon Press, 1994), 374, 399.

[5] E.g. E. Dhorme, *A Commentary on the Book of Job* (Nashville: Thomas Nelson Publishers, 1967), 239; H. H. Rowley, *Job* (The Century Bible; Ontario: Thomas Nelson, 1970), 150; J. Hartley, *The Book of Job* (NICOT; Grand Rapids MI: William B. Eerdmans, 1988), 264.

[6] So, for example, M. Pope, *Job* (AB; Garden City NY: Doubleday, 1979), 125; Habel, *Book of Job,* 275; Newsom, "The Book of Job," 460.

[7] Cf. Clines (*Job 1–20*, 394-95): "therefore you [God] will win no honor on that account."

[8] Cf. Habel, *Book of Job,* 277; Hartley, *Book of Job,* 269-70.

[9] Cf. G. Fohrer, *Das Buch Hiob* (KAT; Gütersloh: Gerd Mohn, 1963), 294; Newsom, "The Book of Job," 462.

[10] For discerning reflection on religion's temptation to minimize the pain of the Jobs of the world, see Newsom, "The Book of Job," 463.

BILDAD'S SECOND RESPONSE TO JOB: SHOULD THE MORAL ORDER OF THE UNIVERSE BE FORSAKEN ON YOUR ACCOUNT?

Job 18:1-21

Bildad's second response continues the emphasis on the fate of the wicked that dominates the second cycle of the friends' speeches. Like Eliphaz, Bildad begins with a strong rebuke of Job (vv. 2-4), followed by a lengthy lecture on the judgment that is prepared for the wicked in the moral universe of God's design (vv. 5-21). The two parts of the speech are easily recognized, and their respective emphases are relatively straightforward. Moreover, the repetition of the word "place" (*māqôm*) in vv. 4 and 21 suggests that the two parts of the speech address a common concern. The rebuke in vv. 2-4 puts Job on notice that the foundations of the world's moral order are firmly established in their "place." They cannot be removed, and they will not be altered simply because Job has questioned them. The lecture on the wicked (vv. 5-21) reiterates that their "place" of judgment within this moral order is also firmly established and just as certainly unalterable and unavoidable. On a first reading then, Bildad's speech represents what is for the friends a standard defense of the retributive justice that they believe undergirds the world and sustains its moral coherence (see [Retribution]). For every deed and act there is an appointed and inviolable "place" where justice is executed. From Bildad's perspective, the righteous may trust this place, but they cannot challenge it; the wicked may fear this place, but they cannot escape it.

On close inspection, however, two features of this speech caution against a simplistic reading. First, Bildad's rebuke uses second person plural forms of "you" in vv. 2-3 ("you [all] hunt"; "you [all] consider"; "in [all] your sight") rather than singular forms, as one might expect of a response aimed directly at Job. The first phrase in v. 4 uses third person forms to speak of one "who tears himself in his anger." It is not until the second phrase in v. 4 that a singular "you" form addresses Job specifically: "because of you." This one phrase is the only unambiguous direct reference to Job in the entire speech. There

"All the World's a Stage"

In Shakespeare's *As You Like It*, Jacques offers a philosophical assessment of "this wide and universal theatre" in which the Jobs of the world live out their "woeful pageants":

All the world's a stage,
And all the men and women merely players;
They have their exits and their entrances;
And one man in his time plays many parts.
(II, vii, 139-42)

In the end, Jacques concludes, the last scene in life's drama is the same for one and all:

. . . mere oblivion;
Sans teeth, sans eyes, sans taste, sans everything. (II, vii, 165-66)

are a number of possible ways to explain or smooth over this peculiarity (see the commentary below), but even if one follows a standard translation like NRSV, which assumes that all of these verses are addressed to Job, it is curious that Bildad seems so little concerned to identify Job as the principle target of his speech. He is resolutely focused on the larger issue of cosmic order, within which the peculiarities of Job's situation appear to have little significance. The moral foundations of the world are fixed and tuned to the more important principles of cosmic justice. Bildad's language hints that he is distancing himself from Job and his challenge to these principles. Such a tactic invites the interpreter to consider whether there is any concrete "place" in Bildad's construal of the world's justice where the cries of an innocent sufferer like Job are not dismissed as aberrant or marginalized as trivial. ["All the World's a Stage"]

Secondly, just as there is but one explicit reference to Job in this entire speech, there is only one reference to God and this not until the very last word of the chapter: "such is the place of those who do not know God" (v. 21b). The reference occurs as part of Bildad's concluding appraisal of the fate of the wicked, a fate which he describes in vv. 5-20 with a series of graphic images. In sum, he argues that the punishment of the wicked is certain, because God stands behind the moral order of the world that brings them to judgment. Even so, Bildad's lone and long delayed reference to God leaves the impression that the principles of retributive justice are virtually self-sustaining. Once in place, they need little or no further input from God. Indeed, one suspects that the main points of Bildad's lecture would be largely unaffected if v. 21 were omitted altogether. The mention of God seems almost an afterthought, an add-on that hints the system's quid pro quo mechanism for calculating justice can run smoothly with or without God's direct involvement. ["Automatic Law"]

Readers may find it instructive to consider whether the subtle diminishment of both Job and God in Bildad's speech may be more than merely a textual oddity. For all his eloquence and poetic flair, Bildad is curiously obscure about the "place" of both Job and God. For different reasons, both seem more incidental than necessary in Bildad's world and in his theology.

"Automatic Law"

Mark Twain has imagined what it may have been like to be one of the archangels in the Grand Council who were privileged to watch the Creator design the world. Reflecting upon the wonder of the "self-regulating law" that underpins creation, one of the angels offers an appraisal that Bildad might be expected to endorse:

It is a stupendous idea. Nothing approaching it has been evolved from the Master Intellect before. Law—*Automatic Law*—exact and unvarying Law—requiring no watching, no correcting, no readjusting while the eternities endure.

Twain names three of the angels in the Grand Council: Gabriel, Michael, and Satan. The appraisal cited above is that of Satan.

M. Twain, *Letters from the Earth*, ed. B. DeVoto (New York: Harper and Row, 1938), 12.

COMMENTARY

The Rebuke, 18:1-4

Bildad begins with a rebuke comprised of rhetorical questions designed both to reprimand Job and to defend himself. In this respect, his opening words employ the standard strategy that each of the friends has adopted (cf. 4:2; 8:2; 11:2-3; 15:2-3). Bildad's rebuke, however, deviates from the typical pattern by using plural forms of address in vv. 2-3. He does not address Job directly until v. 4 and then only in the single phrase "because of you" (*lĕmaʻanĕkā*). If the text as it stands is correct, then Bildad appears to be addressing his opening remarks to the friends (cf. Elihu in 32:3) and so to be scolding them for not responding more forcefully to Job's arguments.[1] In this case, the gist of the rebuke might be paraphrased as follows: "How long will you all (i.e., Eliphaz and Zophar) go on struggling for the right words to counter this one? Why should we allow Job to treat our wisdom as inferior to his?"

Such a reading is difficult on several counts, however, and the majority of commentators and English translations (e.g., NRSV) opt for emending the plural forms to singular ones.[2] This approach effectively smooths out the difficulties by understanding the entire rebuke as being directed to Job. Bildad can be understood as rebuking Job for playing "word games" (v. 2: "hunting for words")[3] that skirt the truth and mock the friends, as if they are too stupid to know what he is doing (v. 3). Although there is support for such an emendation in LXX, which also has singular forms in v. 2, the presumption that the Masoretic text is corrupt seems to be based more on the need to bring Bildad's words into conformity with the standard pattern than on any persuasive evidence.

Given the irresolvable difficulties with both these solutions, it is preferable to accept the ambiguity in the text as a *clue*, not an *obstacle*, to interpretation. It is instructive to recognize that while Bildad's rebuke is aimed at Job, it addresses him rather obliquely. The one and only clear reference to Job in v. 4 hints that Bildad regards Job's arguments as too insignificant to be addressed directly. Bildad will not alter his theology simply because Job does not agree with it. The lengthy lecture on the fate of the wicked in vv. 5-21 amply illustrates Bildad's resolve not to depart from the party line doctrine of retribution that has become the mainstay in each of the friends' rebuttals of Job.

More importantly, Bildad is certain that God will not alter the primordial design for creation simply because Job complains that it does not work for him. Two freighted rhetorical questions in v. 4 drive home the point: "shall the earth be forsaken because of you, or the rock removed out of its place?" An earth "forsaken" (*ʿāzab*) is an earth without inhabitants (cf. Lev 26:43; Isa 7:16; Ezek 36:4). It is empty, vacant, deserted, and thus vulnerable to whoever or whatever chooses to take up residence in its vacuum. It is in essence an earth vulnerable to chaos, which is precisely what God's creative design seeks to thwart by the placement of careful primordial boundaries (cf. Gen 1) that human beings are commissioned to sustain and nurture (cf. Gen 2:5, 15). The image of the "rock removed (*ʿātaq*) out of its place" recalls Job's charge in 14:18 that even the most solid and durable structures in nature—mountains and rocks—will disintegrate if subjected to enough force. God possesses this kind of force, and Job has complained that God uses it in "anger" (*ʾap*) to "remove" (*ʿātaq*) mountains and shake the earth until the pillars of its foundations buckle and collapse (9:5-6). Bildad discerns that Job is now possessed with what he may believe is a similar "anger" (v. 4a: "you who tear yourself in your anger [*ʾap*]") and perhaps a comparable force that will enable him to play God and remake the world to suit his own needs.

The parallelism of these two images for the world's structures and foundations—earth, rock—suggests that Bildad believes Job is intent on subverting God's blueprint for creation simply to win his personal vindication. If Job were successful, his gain would be the loss of the world that God has so carefully crafted, blessed, and appraised as "very good" (Gen 1:31). Bildad is confident that Job will not be successful, for the issues at stake are far too important, too cosmically consequential, to be reduced to the concerns of any single person, especially one whose perspectives are as distorted as his. Job looks at creation through the eyes of pain and wonders what significance God accords to suffering human beings (7:17). Bildad has the answer for him. In the larger scheme of God's design for the world, persons like Job are little more than a blip on the cosmic screen. [CD: "He Thinks He Is the Creator's Pet"]

The Judgment of the Wicked in the Moral Universe of God's Design, 18:5-21

As in his previous response (Job 8), Bildad composes his lecture with the consummate skill of a professor who is adept at researching the archives of scholarship and marshalling the argument in a manner that is both systematic and poetically persuasive (see [CD: The Poetic Reality of Annihilation]). The source materials for his presentation are found primarily in wisdom and psalmic traditions. [CD: Source Materials] It is instructive to note, however, that Bildad uses these traditions selectively. In Proverbs, for example, maxims about the demise of the wicked are usually coupled with statements about the prosperity of the righteous. The two truths are held together in one sentence, which rhetorically mirrors the perfect balance between reward and punishment that is believed to exist in the moral order of the world. Proverbs 12:21 is a typical example: "No harm happens to the righteous, but the wicked are filled with trouble" (cf. Prov 10:3; 11:5; 12:13; 13:9; 14:11; Pss 1:6; 31:23; 32:10; 37:28). Bildad's lecture focuses only on the latter half of this teaching. Neither in this speech nor in any of the friends' speeches in the second cycle is there one example in which the punishment of the wicked is balanced by a corresponding statement promising the prosperity of the righteous.[4] This exclusive focus on a world where the "harm" that clearly does happen to the righteous has no effect on the balance of justice hints that Bildad and his friends have no place in their theology for an aberration like Job. In the world they construe, the cries of the innocent sufferer make no claim on the objectives of justice. As long as there is punishment for the wicked, justice is served, and the world remains secure. Righteous ones like Job who suffer "for no reason" (2:3) must find their place within a moral order that does not factor in their hurt and brokenness as part of the calculus. ["Truth— with a Capital T"]

Bildad's lecture picks up where his previous one left off (8:22) by resuming the focus on their "tent" (*'ōhel*; vv. 6, 14, 15). He makes essentially the same point here as before, although in this speech "tent" becomes the organizing metaphor for a series of images that depict the vulnerability of the wicked's "place" in the world. The speech comprises two principal sections, vv. 5-13 and 15-20, with v. 14 as the linchpin between the two. [Structure of Job 18:5-20] Verse 21 provides a summary appraisal.

In the first section (vv. 5-13), Bildad describes the tent of the wicked as the "domain of death."[5] Four images convey the same point from different perspectives.

"Truth—with a Capital T"

In *The Plague*, Albert Camus chronicles the various responses of the citizens of Oran to the epidemic of bubonic plague that ravaged their city. Of particular interest is the resolve of the ecclesiastical authorities to assure their parishioners that their suffering does not compromise God's control of the balance between good and evil. Toward that end, Father Paneloux, a Jesuit priest and a distinguished expert on St. Augustine, is selected to preach the keynote sermon in the Week of Prayer that is organized by the church.

If today the plague is in your midst, that is because the hour has struck for taking thought. The just man need have no fear, but the evildoer has good cause to tremble. For plague is the flail of God and the world His threshing floor, and implacably He will thresh out His harvest until the wheat is separated from the chaff . . . now you are learning your lesson, the lesson that was learned by Cain and his offspring, by the people of Sodom and Gomorrah, by Job and Pharaoh, by all that hardened their hearts against Him. And like them you

have been beholding mankind and all creation with new eyes, since the gates of the city closed on you and on the pestilence . . . . And thus, my brothers, at last it is revealed to you, the divine compassion which has ordained good and evil in everything; wrath and piety, the plague and your salvation. The same pestilence which is slaying you works for your good and points your path.

In the aftermath of the sermon Dr. Bernard Rieux, a physician who has lost too many patients to the plague to be indifferent to suffering, offers his appraisal of Father Paneloux's theology:

Paneloux is a man of learning, a scholar. He hasn't come in contact with death; that's why he can speak with such assurance of the truth—with a capital T. But every country priest who visits his parishioners and hears a man gasping for breath on his deathbed thinks as I do. He'd try to relieve suffering before trying to point out its excellence.

A. Camus, *The Plague* (New York: Random House, 1948), 90, 92, 93, 119.

• The wicked live without light (vv. 5-6), which is to say they exist in a world without life, goodness, and joy (cf. Prov 13:9; 20:20; 24:20). The verbal expressions in Hebrew suggest that the world is ordered in such a way that their light flickers for a time and then simply ceases of its own accord: it "goes out" (*yid'āk*), it "does not shine" (*lōʾ yiggah*), it "becomes dark" (*ḥāšak*). As Newsom has put it, "the life and power of the wicked are self-limited because they are cut off from the source of all life."[6]

• The wicked shuffle through life with steps "shortened" by failing strength and diminishing confidence (v. 7a; compare the vigorous gait of the one supported by God in Prov 4:12). The second half of the verse indicates that it is their own "schemes" that "throw them down" or "cause them to stumble" (so LXX).

• The wicked live in a world full of traps that they do not see and cannot avoid (vv. 8-10). Six different synonyms describe various nets, pits, snares, and ropes that are used to capture

Structure of Job 18:5-20

18:5-13 A cloud of death hovers over the "tent" of the wicked
vv. 5-6 They have no light
v. 7 They have no power
vv. 8-10 They are trapped
vv. 11-13 Death stalks them

18:14 Death snatches the wicked from their "tent" and marches them to the underworld

18:15-20 The "tent" they leave behind is destroyed
vv. 15-16 Destroyed "root" and "branch"
vv. 17-19 No memory, no name, no progeny
v. 20 The world is appalled

unsuspecting animals. Although we cannot be certain about the characteristics of each of these devices, the fact that they are designed to ensnare the victim from every conceivable angle—feet, heels, neck—is a clear indication that they seldom fail to catch their prey.[7] ["Thrust Into a Net *by Their Own Feet*"]

• The wicked live in a world where death stalks them, claims them, and devours them no matter what they do to protect themselves (vv. 11-13). The imagery of these verses is open to different interpretations, but it is likely that "terrors," "disaster" (v. 12: reading *ʾawen*; cf. the marginal note in NRSV), "calamity," and "disease" are to be understood as personifications of death. With animal-like savagery, they chase their prey (i.e.,the wicked), wait for it to stumble, then pounce upon it at the most advantageous moment (cf. the descriptions of Death's ravenous hunger in Isa 5:14; Hab 2:5). The reference to the "firstborn of death" (v. 13: *bĕkôr māwet*) draws upon Canaanite mythology and may allude to either the firstborn of the Canaanite deity Mot (Death), who reigns in the netherworld, or to Mot himself, who may bear the title "Firstborn Death." [CD: Mot's Insatiable Appetite] With either understanding the picture of the wicked being devoured in the jaws of death is graphic and gruesome.

"Thrust Into a Net *by Their Own Feet*"

📖 In the Bible, traps, snares, nets, and pits are typically used metaphorically. Such terms frequently describe how the wicked are caught, unwittingly, by the consequences of their own sins, which seems to be the meaning of Bildad's observation that they are "thrust into a net *by their own feet*" (18:8; cf. v. 7: *"their own schemes* throw them down"). A favorite image in this regard is that of the wicked falling into the very pit that they have dug to catch another (Pss 7:14-16; 9:15-16; 35:7-8; 57:6; Prov 26:27; Eccl 10:8; Sir 27:26). This image and variations on it has become a common idiom in English literature, which serves as a reminder that Bildad's theology continues to have widespread appeal and endorsement.

Who by aspersions throws a stone
At th' head of others, hit their own.
(George Herbert, "Charms and Knots")

Violence does, in truth, recoil upon the violent,
 and the schemer falls into the pit which he
 digs for another.
(Arthur Conan Doyle, "The Case of the Speckled Bird")

The verse which Racel had not been able to
 finish finished itself. They have digged a pit
 and fallen into it themselves.
(Patricia Wentworth, *The Lonesome Road*)

For further reading, see C. Tkacz, "He That Diggeth a Pit," *A Dictionary of Biblical Tradition in English Literature*, ed. D. Jeffrey (Grand Rapids: Eerdmans, 1992), 335-36.

Verse 14 provides the climax to death's relentless pursuit of the wicked. Even as the wicked trust in the security of their domain, the agents of death lay siege to their world. They come when least expected and with irresistible force they snatch the wicked from their tents, then compel them to march lock-step (cf. NIV; the Hebrew verb is causative, "make them walk") toward a new and permanent place in a very different world. The "king of terrors" is an epithet that provides a second reference to Mot, the sovereign of the underworld, who has ordered his soldiers to raid the land of the living for new victims (cf. vv. 11-13). This king of death now awaits the arrival of those who will henceforth be captives in a land of no return.

In the second half of his lecture (vv. 15-20), Bildad describes the tents the wicked leave behind once they are "driven out of the world"

(v. 18) and imprisoned in the realm of death below. Once again a series of images combines to drive home one fundamental lesson: every trace of the wicked will be completely erased from the world. [CD: The Poetic Reality of Annihilation] The tents they vacate will be taken over by fire and sulfur (v. 15), an image suggesting they will be destroyed beyond hope of repair (cf. "fire and brimstone [sulfur]" in Gen 19:24; Ps 11:6; Ezek 38:22).[8] That which the wicked produced in their lifetime will be destroyed from "root" to "branch" (v. 16). The metaphor is a general one for total annihilation (cf. Ezek 17:9; Mal 4:1; Sir 23:25), but Bildad applies it more specifically to the wicked's negative legacy. They leave behind no "memory," no "name," no "descendants," and no "survivors" (vv. 17, 19). To die without progeny and progenitors of one's name would be sad in almost any context, but in ancient Israel, where one has no hope of life beyond the grave without descendents, it is particularly tragic. In contemporary terms, we might describe such a total lack of effect as like dipping one's foot in the ocean, then extracting it. The waters immediately close over the opening, leaving behind no trace whatsoever of what had once been there. To witness such an end is a horrible thing. From one end of the earth to the other, from "east" to "west," the human race is (and should be) appalled and terrified at the fate of the wicked (v. 20).

Bildad's closing statement (v. 21) provides a summary appraisal of the lecture's thesis. "Surely" the "place" (*māqôm*; cf. v. 4) of the wicked in the world is just as he has described it in vv. 5-19. In life they are hounded by death. In death they live a meaningless existence. Their unalterable destiny is to reside with those whose disregard for the moral orders of the universe renders them unfit and unworthy for life. With the last word in his speech, Bildad mentions God for the first time. Lest Job miss the point, Bildad reminds him that it is God who sanctions the retributive system of justice that Bildad defends.

Bildad's summation invites the reader to ponder the connection between his rebuke (vv. 1-4) and his instruction (vv. 5-20). He has reprimanded Job for equating his anger with God's and for arrogating to himself power to remake the world to conform to his own needs. It is therefore ironic that he follows this rebuke with a lecture on the fate of the wicked that assumes *his theology* of retribution is *equal* to the moral order of the universe , which, by God's decree, will not be "removed out of its place" (v. 4). Such presumption of authority raises the question, "Who is really playing God here, Job or Bildad?" Bildad is so confident that *his theology* is *God's theology* that he proceeds with his lecture as if God need not be mentioned until the very last word. By this point, however, the unspoken assertion seems to be that God subscribes to the world that *Bildad creates* rather than the other way around.

CONNECTIONS

Bildad's concentration on the "place" (vv. 4, 21) of things in the world God has created invites reflection on what J. Janzen has suggestively called the "ecology of the moral realm."[9] Bildad contends that every part of the cosmos has its appointed place, which by God's decree will not and cannot be altered or removed. He identifies three components of the moral realm—Job, the wicked, God—and seeks to make clear the roles they play in the grand arena of cosmic justice. His appraisal of these components is not always stated directly, but the number of vv. allotted to each one offers a clue for estimating the hierarchy of his passions. At the top of his list of concerns are the wicked, whose place in the world focuses his attention for some seventeen verses (vv. 5-21). Next on the list is Job, who seems to be addressed in three verses (vv. 2-4), although one might argue that he is actually allotted only one phrase ("because of you") in v. 4. By either assessment, Job is a distant second to the wicked. Last on the list is God, who is unnamed until the last word of v. 21.

The Place of the Wicked in Bildad's "Ecology of the Moral Realm."

On this issue Bildad is unambiguous. The wicked have but a diminishing and terrifying place in the land of the living. Their ultimate and permanent place is in the land of the dead, where their past is obliterated and their future is cancelled. In the ecology of justice, their fate is predetermined by principles of retribution that are triggered automatically by evil. The system is failsafe, never missing in its detection of violations, never wrong in its execution of punishment. By this assessment, the moral realm is endowed with an imperative to find and eradicate evil that cannot be controlled and cannot be thwarted. As Bildad states the matter, the wicked will be "driven out of the world" (v. 18).

The picture of a world in which the wicked are punished and evil is expelled is both seductive and satisfying. It beckons the righteous to believe that the moral order of the universe is tuned to good, not evil. Such belief in turn provides incentive to trust in the triumph of light over darkness, right over wrong, virtue over vice. Beyond that, it is morally satisfying and sustaining to be assured that the world's bias toward the good is diamond-hard. The passion with which Bildad focuses on the fate of the wicked and the vividness of his images for their destruction hints that the punishment of others is not only seductive and satisfying. It is also something of an elixir that enables one to swallow life's vagaries while still believing that everything will be alright in the end. As long as the wicked get their just deserts, the line between right and wrong remains etched in the conscience. Like a still small voice it prods and cajoles, warns and cautions.

The importance of clearly identifying the wicked and clearly defining their punishment should not be undervalued, for it serves an essential need in both society and religion. As a social category, "the guilty" provide the community a means to create and strengthen the moral division between "us" and "them." This labeling process is of course often wrong and self-serving. It remains nevertheless a critical way by which a society mobilizes moral consensus in support of conduct that is acceptable and moral censure of behavior that is deviant. One has only to turn on the television during a typical prime time hour to see how attuned the culture is to stories that confirm law and order routinely trumps crime and violence. It has been estimated that the average viewer watches six or more violent crimes during each hour of prime time television. In the vast majority of these cases the plot line is predictable. We see unsavory characters commit crimes, hence we know from the outset that they are guilty. We see them pursued and apprehended by legal authorities, hence we are reassured that there is no perfect crime. We see them brought to court, confronted by irrefutable evidence, and in due course, declared guilty by a justice system that works just like viewers *expect and need.*

It is reasonable to suggest that the expectation and the need of the faith community is little different. It would be instructive to take a sampling of the prime time hour of worship when the minister stands in the pulpit to expound upon law and grace, judgment and mercy, the righteous and the wicked, the promise of heaven and the threat of hell. These religious labels are important and necessary. They remind the gathered community of the difference between being "in faith" and "outside faith." They mobilize and strengthen the community's moral resolve to be faithful, and they do so at least in part by building a case for divine censure that provides a deterrent to sin. [CD: The Appeal of Fire and Brimstone Preaching] The internal solidarity of the religious community, no less than that of society in general, rests in no small measure on an ecology of justice that assigns the wicked a clear and definite place in the world. Bildad's passion for a world where the "light of the wicked is put out" (v. 5) remains a prime time preoccupation.

The problem with Bildad's passion is that it focuses on a world that does not exist, and it does so with energy that is potentially destructive. The end result that Bildad's retribution theology envisions is a world where evil and evildoers do not exist. They are banished, completely eliminated from the land of living. With the erasure of the wicked from society, the righteous are left alone in a paradisiacal world where good is uncontested. On this side of the garden of Eden, however, such an assessment of the world is demonstrably false. Evil and its agents are clearly present in the world, and whatever one believes and hopes about ultimate judgment, evil remains an untiring and often victorious opponent of the good and the right and the virtuous. Job is of course the prime example of the vulnerability of Bildad's theology. The fact that his suffering makes little or no difference in the world that Bildad describes hints that his theology is driven more by illusion than by truth. As Clines has put it, Bildad is a man of dogma, not of faith, and he will run no risks." He can contemplate no world except one that promises "a fairy tale happiness or a sci-fi extermination."[10] Such a world may play well on prime time television. It may evoke a hearty "Amen" in prime time worship. But it does not ring true in a world where Jobs sit on the ash heap.

It is the passion for the "sci-fi extermination" of the wicked that makes retribution theology so potentially mean spirited and destructive. It is one thing to yearn for justice and to work vigorously to make it a reality. Such passion is surely the requisite of all faith that believes what *ought to be can be*. It is another thing to yield to the temptation of thinking that what *ought to be must be*. Too often, such thinking becomes a seed bed for violence that co-opts justice for personal or political agendas. Whether it takes the form of ideology or theology, justice that derives its objectives from "they-get-what-they-deserve" mandates endows itself with the capacity to eliminate almost anyone who does not conform to a rigid definition of what the world *must be*. History is replete with examples of totalitarian regimes that execute justice by squashing dissent. Sadly, the politics of faith are often little different, as an objective analysis of religious warfare and denominational fratricide makes painfully clear. [The Danger of "They Get What They Deserve" Theology]

To be fair to Bildad, he does not advocate violence against the wicked, although he clearly foresees it, and he does not directly identify Job as one of the wicked who is targeted for violence, although one suspects that this is the subtle objective of his instruction. Nevertheless, his passion for punishment is unsettling. He is so certain that the wicked deserve to be eliminated from life, and he is so supremely confident that this is God's will, that he runs the risk of demonizing those who do not conform to his view of what *ought to be*. Once persons are demonized, *for whatever reason*, they become less than human. Once persons are regarded as less than human, the road that leads to their destruction faces few obstacles. Civility, fairness, compassion, and justice become secondary concerns. All that matters is the infliction of pain, punishment, and death.

The Danger of "They Get What They Deserve" Theology

In religion, the temptation to destroy those labeled "wicked" is perhaps more seductive, not less, than in politics, because it can be legitimized under the rubric of "God's will." Even when the charges against the wicked are demonstrably true, there is reason to think carefully before embracing Bildad's position wholeheartedly. If God has vowed "never again" to destroy the world because of the evil in human hearts (cf. Gen 8:21; 9:11, 15), then at the very least one must pause before endorsing a theology that fixates on sanitizing the world by ridding it of the wicked. The need for careful reflection becomes more urgent when one considers that religious fervor may blur the distinction between what is wrong (sinful) and what is only disagreeable to religious authorities. One need only ponder how the Church has struggled for clarity on such issues as slavery, the place of women in society, divorce, abortion, and homosexuality to recognize that decisions to exclude, punish, and banish "the wicked" are in constant need of rethinking. It is perhaps axiomatic that the more rigid one becomes in assessing guilt and assigning blame, the more likely it is that those who "get what they deserve" will include virtually anyone who fails to conform to regnant religious norms.

A personal experience may illustrate how retribution theology may swerve into the absurd and the dangerous. In a former place of employment where fundamentalists had seized control of the Board of Trustees, I served on a search committee that was interviewing prospective candidates for election to the faculty. After a long day of meetings with faculty, students, and trustees, the candidates and the search committee met for dinner. I was sitting next to one of the candidates, and the two of us were sitting across the table from one of the most ardent of the fundamentalist trustees. In the course of our conversations, the trustee asked the candidate why he thought the Jews had been so often persecuted in history. The candidate understandably thought the question was probably a subtle continuation of the interview process and proceeded to formulate an answer that incorporated historical facts with careful theological reflection. After several sentences, the trustee interrupted to offer his own perspective, which only too late the candidate and I realized was the real purpose of the originating question. The trustee stated that the Jews had been persecuted because they had courted persecution throughout their history. They had suffered because they had courted suffering; they needed to suffer to fulfill their God-given destiny. From this he deduced that the Jews got what they wanted and what they deserved. In the span of little more than five minutes the trustee had provided what to his mind was a theological justification for Aushwitz, Dachau, Treblinka, Sobibor . . . and more than six million Jews who were killed because they were guilty of nothing more than being Jews.

I forego comment on this theology except to make two further observations. The trustee who held these views had a fiduciary responsibility to use his judgment in the selection of teachers who would train future generations of denominational pastors and leaders. Further, this trustee was himself a pastor of a large metropolitan church. It is reasonable to suppose that this congregation looked to him for guidance in how to image God in the world. Presumably his "they get what they deserve" theology informed the instruction he offered.

The Place of Job in Bildad's "Ecology of the Moral Realm."

The place in the moral realm that Bildad assigns to the wicked is clear and unambiguous. The same cannot be said of the place he assigns to Job. Is his place among the wicked? One is tempted to read this into Bildad's lecture, but he does not say so directly. Is his place among the righteous? In his previous speech, Bildad suggested as much, and he summoned Job to remain confident that "God will not reject a blameless person" (8:20). In this speech, however, Bildad offers no such promise. In fact, he does not mention the righteous at all, thus suggesting that their destiny has little bearing on what he would say to Job. The only direct mention of Job in the entire speech is the single phrase "because of you" in v. 4. It occurs within the context of a question: "Shall the earth be forsaken *because of you*?"

Job's place in Bildad's ecology of justice is questionable. In a previous speech, Job has pondered his place in the hierarchy of God's creation. When he considered the enormity of his suffering and the extent to which God

The World Is Bigger Than You Think

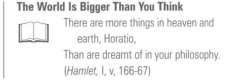

There are more things in heaven and earth, Horatio,
Than are dreamt of in your philosophy.
(*Hamlet*, I, v, 166-67)

seemed preoccupied with his affliction, he wondered why he should attract so much attention: "What are human beings, that you make so much of them, that you set your mind on them, visit them every morning, test them every moment?" (7:17-18). Bildad believes Job has vastly overestimated his importance. God does not order the cosmos to take account of individuals like Job. And God does not alter the grand design of cosmic justice simply because someone somewhere in the universe expresses moral outrage concerning their personal disappointment. God's objectives are too large; Job's plight is too small. In the ecology of God's concerns, Job's place is hardly visible at all. [The World Is Bigger Than You Think]

At one level, Bildad's instruction is important and necessary. Surely it is an axiom of faith that the universal theater of God's activity is larger than the agenda of any one person. If it were otherwise, there would be not one God, sovereign and transcendent over the immediate and the temporary, but many gods, clothed in human nature, whose penultimate concerns would vie for the prize of ultimate dominion. One does not have to argue the merits of Bildad's argument against such faulty thinking on religious grounds alone. In matters of public policy or corporate management or athletic competition, there is widespread support for the premise that "the sum of a thing is greater than its individual parts."

At another level, however, Bildad's view of Job's place in the world invites close scrutiny. Given Job's plight, it hardly seems necessary to remind him that he is virtually invisible to God. He is under no illusion about his place at the bottom of the stackpole of God's concern for justice. His real question is different and much more urgent. He asks if there *is any place* in heaven or an earth where the cries of an innocent sufferer can receive a just and fair hearing (cf. 16:18-19). He struggles against all odds to believe that there is such a place. One does not suspect that he would argue that his suffering is greater than the sum of all creation. But he does dare to believe that creation cannot be all that God intends as long as there is *no place* where injustice can be appealed and rectified. It is just at this point that Bildad's curt dismissal of him is most grievous. Nothing in the universe will be changed "because of you." Everything is fixed and permanent. In Bildad's world, innocent suffering changes nothing. It does not interrupt the steady hum of creation's work. It does not disturb God's fixed focus on cosmic time, cosmic space, cosmic justice.

Grief will speak, even if it is denied a voice. The real question for the community of faith is whether God or those who would image God will pay attention. In his poem "Grief," George Herbert ponders whether there is "provision in the midst of all" for those who cannot stop crying.

> O who will give me tears? Come all ye springs,
> Dwell in my head and eyes: come clouds, and
>   rain:
> My grief hath need of all the wat'ry things,
> That nature hath produced. Let ev'ry vein
> Suck up a river to supply mine eyes,
> My weary weeping eyes too dry for me,
> Unless they get new conduits, new supplies
> To bear them out, and with my state agree.
> What are two shallow fords, two little sprouts
> Of a less world? the greater is small,
> A narrow cupboard for my griefs and doubts,
> Which want provision in the midst of all.

G. Herbert, "Grief," in *The Complete English Poems*, ed. John Tobin (London: Penguin Books, 1991), 154.

As with his first speech, here too the reader may pause to ask, "What if Bildad is right?" (see Job 8, "Connections"). What if there is no place for Job in the ecology of God's justice? What if innocent suffering truly does not have any ultimate bearing on how the world works? What if justice really is only a question of punishing the guilty, not of vindicating the innocent? Would this then be the world that God once blessed and pronounced "very good"? Bildad would likely consider such questions trivial. At the least he would regard them and those who pursue them as aberrations. His dismissal of such questions suggests, however, that he feels more strongly than this. He hints that such questions are arrogant and wrong. They are signals of rebellion, and as such those who ask them are not only to be ignored; they are to be silenced and put in their place among the mute who have no voice and no value in the court of God's justice. In weighing these questions, readers may reflect on the impact of Bildad's argument for every innocent person who has been cheated, abused, betrayed, violated. . . then condemned and ignored. If Bildad is right, then what does justice mean for persons like these? ["O Who Will Give Me Tears?"]

The Place of God in Bildad's "Ecology of the Moral Realm."

As with all who would be God's spokespersons, Bildad may be examined to see what role God plays in his theology. It would be a generous appraisal to say that Bildad has God in the forefront of his thinking from the beginning of his speech to the end. It is striking, however, that Bildad appears to have more passion for speaking about the world he believes God has created than he does for speaking of the God who created the world. He proceeds to describe the way the world works, particularly the judgment it holds in perpetuity for the wicked, with graphic detail. He speaks as one well acquainted with the blueprint for this world. His knowledge is so intimate, his intensity for conveying it so high, that he sounds like one who considers himself the architect of this plan, not simply the one who reads it. By the time he mentions God in this speech—in the last word of v. 21—everything of importance has already been said. God seems quite literally unnecessary. Indeed, from a grammatical perspective, v. 21 depicts God as a noun without a verb, an entity that engages in no action. Bildad simply observes that this is the world Job must learn, and if he does not, then he risks joining the ranks of those who "do not know God."

Bildad's account of the world is at one point reminiscent of the perspective offered by Reverend Clarence Wilmot in John Updike's novel *In the Beauty of the Lilies* (see further ["None of Us Lives in the Light"]). Wilmot sits in his book-lined study at the Fourth Presbyterian Church and looks out on a world that moves from day to day, following "its usual riotous course of bombast and deviltry, with or without God." When subsequently he tries to explain himself to Reverend Dreaver, the moderator of the Presbytery, he sums up his view as follows: "To put it in mathematical terms. . . God is a non-factor—all the equations work without Him." For Clarence, the observation that God is a "nonfactor" in the world is cause for despair. He senses that if this is true, then his place as a minister in God's world is meaningless. As he puts it, "The universe is a pointless, self-running machine, and we are insignificant by-products, whom death will tuck back into oblivion, with or without holy fanfare."[11] He has requested the meeting with Dreaver not to complain or to seek his counsel. What he has come to do is to explain his decision to resign from the ministry.

In Bildad's theology, God stands "behind the scenes" of justice, a silent observer of a retribution system that is designed to work smoothly and efficiently with or without God's direct involvement. In one respect, his view of God is not different than Clarence Wilmot's: "God is a non-factor—all the equations work without Him." In another respect, however, Bildad and Clarence have very different perspectives. For Clarence, a world without God is a world emptied of meaning and purpose. Like Job, he *needs* God to be present, otherwise life is an exercise in futility. For Bildad, a world without God does not seem nearly so frightening. He knows how the system works, and in God's absence he is confident that he can oversee (and administer?) it without any problem. He does not *need* God's input to know who is wicked and deserves to be condemned.

In the final analysis, readers may ponder which moral realm they would rather live in, the one defined by Bildad's confidence, or the one informed by Clarence's despair. Clarence (and Job) longs for God's presence and feels incomplete and insufficient without it. Bildad longs for the judgment of the wicked, and in the absence of God's direct participation in the system, he will render guilty verdicts without reservation or pause. The line between *despair that yearns for God* and *confidence in God that displaces that yearning* is a critical one. Which of these two modes of living is the more faithful depends in large measure on whether life's grammar *needs God* to be a *subject with a verb* or only *the noun at the end of the sentence.* [CD: Faith That Places "Words in Their Best Order"]

NOTES

[1] Cf. G. Fohrer, *Das Buch Hiob* (KAT; Gütersloh: Gerd Mohn, 1963), 300; E. Dhorme, *A Commentary on the Book of Job* (Nashville: Thomas Nelson Publishers, 1967), 257; S. Terrien, "The Book of Job," *IB*, vol. 3, ed. G. Buttrick (New York: Abingdon Press, 1954), 1034-35; E. M. Good, *In Turns of Tempest: A Reading of Job with a Translation* (Stanford: Stanford University Press, 1990), 251-52.

[2] For a discussion and critique of this and other alternatives, see D. Clines, *Job 1–20* (WBC; Dallas: Word Books, 1989), 409-10.

[3] The Hebrew word rendered by "hunting," *qeneṣ*, occurs nowhere else in the Hebrew Bible, hence its translation is uncertain. The translation in NRSV assumes a root word meaning "ensnare, capture." N. Habel (*The Book of Job: A Commentary* [OTL; Philadelphia: Westminster Press, 1985], 281, 285) suggests the equivalent English idiom for engaging in discourse that seeks to "ensnare" or "capture" another with words is playing "word games." He understands Bildad to be rebuking Job for using words and arguments that twist traditional truths to serve his own purposes.

[4] Cf. C. Westermann, *The Structure of the Book of Job* (Philadelphia: Fortress, 1981), 84, 90. Westermann notes that in the first cycle the friends do speak of the good fortune that the righteous may expect *if* they return to God and put away their sins (8:5-7; 11:13-20). In the second cycle the friends abandon even this *conditional* assurance, which is one indication that they are less concerned with the righteous than the wicked. As they move toward this singular emphasis, they necessarily move further away from addressing the issues Job presents, which is the misfortune of the *righteous*, not the *wicked*.

[5] Habel, *Book of Job,* 286.

[6] C. Newsom, "The Book of Job," in vol. 4 of *NIB* (Nashville: Abingdon Press, 1996), 468.

[7] The "rope" (v. 10: *hebel*) that is hidden in the ground seems to be a reference to a noose designed to grab an animal around the neck or perhaps the body when it sniffs the bait and triggers the trap with its head.

[8] The first half of v. 15 is obscure and may be translated in different ways. NRSV attempts to make sense of the phrase *mibbelî-lô*, lit., "things not his," by taking it to mean that nothing that belongs to the wicked remains in their tent. This is a plausible rendering, but many commentators and translations favor a slight emendation of the phrase to a word meaning "fire" (cf. NIV, REB), which provides a good parallel with the word "sulfur/brimstone" (*goprît*) in the second half of the verse. See further, M. Dahood, "Some Northwest-Semitic Words in Job," *Bib* 38 (1957): 312-14.

[9] J. Gerald Janzen, *Job* (Atlanta: John Knox, 1985), 130.

[10] Clines, *Job 1–20*, 425.

[11] J. Updike, *In the Beauty of the Lilies* (New York: Alfred A. Knopf, 1996), 23, 74-75.

JOB'S RESPONSE TO BILDAD: "KNOW THEN THAT GOD HAS PUT ME IN THE WRONG"

Job 19:1-29

In his previous speech, Bildad was ambivalent about Job's place in the world. He was supremely confident that the "tent" (*ʾōhel*) of the wicked would be destroyed (18:6, 14, 15; cf. 8:22), but concerning Job's "tent" he said not a word. Job now insists that if the moral order of the world is to be assessed truthfully, then his place within it must be factored into the judgment. He directs Bildad and his friends to look closely at his "tent" (*ʾōhel*; v. 12), surrounded and under siege by God, and once again he raises hard questions that challenge his comforters and their question-free view of the world: "How long?" (v. 2); "Why?" (v. 22).[1] He begins by rebuking the friends for repeatedly arguing with him as if he were the guilty party (vv. 2-5). He would have them "know" (v. 6) that it is God's behavior that makes a mockery of justice, not his. God has attacked him ruthlessly and without restraint (vv. 7-12), and God has caused his family and friends to abandon him (vv. 13-20). What Job needs from his friends is compassion (v. 21: "have pity," "have pity"), not condemnation, and he would have them "know" (v. 29) that if they continue to attack him, then the judgment they obtain will be their own (vv. 21-29). [Structure of Job 19:1-29]

Two further observations are pertinent as an introduction to this speech.

Structure of Job 19:1-29		
19:1-5	Opening rebuke to the friends: "You are not ashamed to abuse me"	
19:6-20	Job's rebuttal of the friends: *I* am not guilty; *God* is.	
vv. 7-12	God has attacked me	
vv. 13-20	God has destroyed my community	
19:21-29	To the friends: A plea, a hope, a warning	

First, each pericope of the speech is clearly addressed to the friends: v. 2: "How long will you (plural) torment me?" v. 6: "know (plural) that God has put me in the wrong"; v. 21: "Have pity on me. . . . O you my friends." For the first time since he spoke from the ash heap, Job does not address God. He has cursed and complained in God's hearing (Job 3), but God has not answered. He has summoned God to court (Job 9–10), but God has not answered. He has prepared a case against God and presented it as if God were listening (Job

12–14), but God has not answered. He has charged God with criminal assault and appealed to heaven for a witness (Job 16), but God has not answered. Job has much more to say, of course, and he will continue to cock his ear toward heaven for the response that may yet come, but for now he has said all he knows how to to God. When next he addresses God directly, it will be to insist once again on his innocence and to complain once more that when he cries out God does not answer him (30:20-23).

In the midst of friends who listen without compassion and a God who gives every indication of not listening at all, Job would have good reason to give up all hope. Indeed, he now surmises that God has targeted his "hope" for destruction (v. 10). This makes a second feature of his speech all the more surprising. In the middle of the last pericope, sandwiched between vexed contemplation of friends who are "pursuing" and "persecuting" him (vv. 22, 28; in both cases the verb is *rādap*), Job speaks of a "redeemer" who will rise and testify to his innocence (vv. 25-27). These verses are perhaps the most well known in the whole of the book. They are also among the most difficult to interpret. At this juncture, one may suspend discussion of the difficulties in order to appreciate that such verses are present at all. In the midst of everything Job "knows" about brokenness and loss, in the midst of everything he "knows" about God's silence, cruelty, and indifference, Job now declares emphatically that he "knows" something beyond these things as well. However one interprets these verses, it is Job's hope for "something beyond" that makes this speech far more than just another response to one of the friends. ["Hope May Vanish, but Can Die Not"]

"Hope May Vanish, but Can Die Not"

Percy Shelley's poem *Hellas* was written in 1821 in honor of his friend Prince Alexandros Mavrocordato, a Greek aristocrat living in exile in Pisa. When the Greeks revolted and declared their independence from Turkey, who had ruled them for centuries, Mavrocordato returned to his homeland to take part in the fight. Shelley modeled the poem on *The Persians* by Aeschylus, which describes the Greek defeat of the Persian forces led by Xerxes. In the preface to the poem, Shelley states his rationale for appealing to history in order to encourage his friend to believe in the nobility of the fight for freedom: "The modern Greek is the descendant of those glorious beings whom the imagination almost refuses to figure to itself as belonging to our Kind, and he inherits much of their sensibility, their rapidity of conception, their enthusiasm, and their courage." A portion of his poem describes "hope" as one manifestation of the courage that he most admires in his friend:

Life may change, but it may fly not;
Hope may vanish, but can die not;
Truth be veiled but still it burneth;
Love repulsed,—but it returneth! (ll. 34-37)

It was Shelley's conviction that "We are all Greeks." One might extend the argument to say that inasmuch as Job's hope for "something beyond" is faith's legacy to us, the challenge is to *believe* and *act* as if "we are all Jobs."

P. Shelley, "Hellas," *Shelley's Poetry and Prose*, sel. and ed. Donald H. Reiman and Sharon B. Powers (New York/London: W.W. Norton and Company, 1977), 406-40. The citation from the preface occurs on p. 407.

"You Are Not Ashamed to Abuse Me," 19:1-5

Job opens with the same phrase Bildad used to begin both his speeches—"How long?" (v. 2: *'ad 'ānāh*; cf. 8:2; 18:2)—indicating that he too is losing patience with this conversation. While the response may be directed to Bildad, the verbs of rebuke in vv. 2-5 are second person plurals, suggesting that what has worn Job out is the accumulation of words heaped on him by all the friends. They have "tormented" him (*yāgah*; cf. Lam 1:5, 12; 3:32, 33) and tried to "break" him down (*dāka'*; cf. Pss 94:5; 143:3) with arguments that reach to the very center of his existence (v. 2: *nepeš*; NRSV: "me"). With such attacks they would exceed even the *satan's* efforts, for he had aimed at Job's flesh and bones but was ordered to stop short of touching Job's life (*nepeš*; 2:6). "Ten times," that is, "over and over again" (on "ten" as a round number, see Gen 31:7; Num 14:22) they seek to "humiliate" (*kālam*; cf. 1 Sam 20:34) him by publicly ridiculing his claim of innocence; not once do they feel any shame or guilt for what they do (v. 3).

Job has consistently denied that he has sinned (7:20; 9:21; 10:7; 16:17), and he offers no retraction of that claim here. For the sake of argument, however, he is willing to entertain the possibility that he could have erred unintentionally in some way. *If* he has, he is guilty of nothing more than a minor moral lapse, which not even God should regard as worthy of a death penalty.[2] ["Forgive, O Lord ..."] But the friends calculate things differently in order to prove their moral superiority (v. 5a: "you exalt yourselves over me") to Job—and by implication to God! Their retribution theology has no place for discriminating between major and minor infractions. If there is sin, there must be punishment. And if there is punishment, which in Job's case cannot be denied, then sin must be the explanation. Thus they take Job's suffering, his "humiliation" (v. 5b: *ḥerpāh*) at being treated *as if* he were a sinner, and use it to argue from *effect to cause*. In contemporary terms their rationale might be stated as follows: if it walks like a duck and quacks like a duck, it must be a duck!

"Forgive, O Lord . . ."

Robert Frost's poems often suggest that the spiritual quest should not be afraid to risk a little sacrilegious banter. In the following couplet, for example, he imagines there might be an occasion in which one could say to God "turn-about-is-fair-play."

Forgive, O Lord, my little jokes on Thee
And I'll forgive Thy great big one on me.

R. Frost, "[Forgive, O Lord . . .]," *The Poetry of Robert Frost*, ed. E. C. Lathem (New York: Henry Holt and Company, 1969), 428. On Frost and his "spiritual high jinks," see further D. J. Hall, *Robert Frost: Contours of Belief* (Athens: Ohio University Press, 1984), 46-47.

Job's Rebuttal: I Am Not Guilty; God Is, 19:6-20

Job counters the friends' presumption of his sin by demanding that they recognize it is God who is the guilty party, not him. Bildad has argued that God is never guilty of "perverting" (*yĕ'awwēt*) justice (8:3). Job insists that this is precisely what God has done to him: "God has perverted (*ʿiwwetānî*) me" (v. 6; NRSV: "put me in the wrong"). God has declared Job guilty even though he is innocent (cf. 9:20). Beyond that, God has blocked all his efforts to obtain vindication through a fair and just hearing of his case (cf. 9:1-2, 19, 32; 13:13-28). Job now supports the accusation by marshalling the evidence for two additional charges against God: God has ruthlessly attacked him, as if he were an enemy deserving complete destruction (vv. 7-12); and God has caused the social community that once provided his place in the world to abandon him as a stranger and an outcast (vv. 13-20).

The description of God's assault (vv. 7-12) picks up where 16:9-14 left off (see [The Warrior God]). In that account, Job complained that God comes at him again and again; like a savage beast and an enraged warrior God seeks to tear him to pieces. Now Job depicts the warrior God who has finally trapped the hapless victim. God has built a wall across every possible route for escape; any path Job might take to flee, God has so darkened it as to make it invisible and unnavigable (v. 8). God is driven by "anger" (*ʾap*, v. 11a; NRSV: "wrath"), not justice. The objective is to destroy the "adversary" (*ṣar*, v. 11b; cf. 13:24), not to vindicate the "servant" whose piety once earned him God's approval as the most "blameless and upright" person on earth (cf. 2:3). Toward this end, God orders the troops to build a siege ramp and ready themselves for the final breach of Job's defenses (v. 12). The preparations for the attack are massive, suggesting the level of force that is required to defeat an entire city of opponents. The tragic irony is that Job is but a single, frail individual who can mount no more resistance than a "windblown leaf" (13:25) or a "shriveled up" skeleton (16:25); his domain in the world is not a fortress but a mere "tent" (v. 12b; see further ["Lodged"]). As N. Habel puts it, "God's grand assault is a bitter example of divine overkill. "[3]

The language that describes God's assault is largely conventional and likely belongs to a common stock of images and motifs deeply rooted in the lament tradition. [Siege Terminology] At two junctures, however, Job's appropriation of this language is particularly focused and poignant. First, at the outset of God's attack, Job cries out "Violence!" (*ḥāmās*), but there is no answer to his scream (v. 7a). In other contexts, such a cry is a plea for help or deliverance (Hab 1:2; cf. Deut 22:24, 27). Job would no doubt be grateful for deliverance, but his hope is not just to escape punishment, for that in itself would leave his innocence, hence his integrity, an open question. What Job seeks above all is the justice (*mišpāṭ*; cf. 9:19, 32; 14:3) owed one whose hands are free of any "violence" (*ḥāmās*, 16:17). On his lips, the cry of "Violence!" is an indictment of God for presiding over a moral order that is deaf to the claims of the innocent.[4] As the victim of wanton abuse, Job appeals to the Judge of all the world for vindication, but the Judge denies his claim, and the violence against him continues without constraint. Worse still, the perpetrator of the abuse is none other than the Judge, who uses power with reckless abandon for self-serving purposes and has no fear of being held accountable. If "there is no justice" (*mišpāṭ*, v. 7b) for the Jobs of the world, then "Violence!" is no longer an exclamation that disturbs the status quo. It is a summons to join the status quo and profit from the sanctioned abuse of those who have no protection under the law.

Secondly, Job complains that God's abusive treatment strikes him down in a still more serious way. God strips him of his "glory" (*kābôd*) and his "crown" (*ʿăṭeret*, v. 9). At one level, the language suggests that Job is like a king who is humiliated, stripped of his royal insignias, and denied his capacity to rule.[5] At another level, however, Job's charge is far more profound. "Glory" and "crown" are terms signifying the nobility that God bestows on every human being, not just royalty (Ps 8:5 [MT 8:6]). They are divine endowments that summon human beings to exercise "dominion" in the world as near-equals of God ("a little lower than God"). As such, they are the tools by which human beings fulfill the creational commission to *live into* the image of God (cf. Gen 1:26-28). Job's suffering has already forced him to question this creational design for human beings (7:17-19). Now he moves beyond pained questions to unqualified indictment. God singles out human beings for a special blessing, robes them with honor and dignity, and then strips them of every possibility of becoming the very persons God has created them to be. Against this backdrop, Job's charge in v. 10 is particularly unsettling. God has "uprooted his hope (*tiqwāh*) like a tree." It is not only the hope for some post-mortem renewal that God denies Job (cf. 14:7-9, 14-19; see further ["Hope"]). Also denied is the pre-mortem hope that Job can live as fully human. From Job's perspective, the Judge of

---

Siege Terminology

AΩ There are a number of close similarities with Lam 3:5-9, where Zion complains that God has "walled me about so that I cannot escape."

Job 19:7-12			Lam 3:5-9	
v. 7	*ṣaʿq / saw*	"cry out "/ "call"	v. 8	*zaʿaq / sawa*
v. 8	*gādar*	"walled up "/ "blocked"	vv. 7, 9	*gādar*
v. 8	*ḥšk*	"darkness"	v. 6	*ḥšk*
v. 8	*ʾoraḥ / nĕṭîbôt*	"way" / "paths"	v. 9	*derek /nĕṭîbôt*

One further parallel is present. Both Job and Zion refer to God's assault as a form of "subversion." In Job's case, God "subverts" (*ʿāwat*; v. 6) justice; in Zion's case, God "subverts" (*ʿāwat*; Lam 3:9) every path of escape. In both instances, God twists, bends, or makes crooked something which otherwise would have been right and straight and good.

On the similarities between Job and Lam 3, see further **[Connections with Lamentations 3]**.

the world is guilty of destroying every hope for justice in life or death. [CD: "Why Are His Gifts Desirable.?"]

The second piece of evidence Job presents is that God destroys community (vv. 13-20). He identifies some twelve different persons or categories of persons who now exclude him from their company. The list comprises family and kin, guests and servants, children and elders. The clear impression is that the entirety of Job's relational world has collapsed. There is nowhere on earth he can turn to find a friendly face or a sympathetic ear. The breakdown of Job's world can be tracked in the sequence of comments that follows, but the most important and most damning aspect of what these verses report is conveyed by a single verb at the beginning of v. 13, which assigns the responsibility for Job's abandonment to God: [God] *has caused* Job's family *to be removed* (*hirhîq*; the hiphil form indicates causation) from him.[6] [Structure of Job 19:13-20]

Structure of Job 19:13-20

The language and structure of vv. 13-20 suggest that Job intends to give a "detailed map of the relational world from which he is now excluded." He surveys the broad circle of his social network, beginning (vv. 13-14) and ending (vv. 18-19) with those who surround him in the larger community. At the center of this circle of rejection (vv. 15-17) are those who would ordinarily provide his most loyal and intimate support. The structure may be illustrated as follows:

vv. 13-14 Outer circle: Relatives, acquaintances, close friends

vv.15-17 Inner circle: Domestic servants, wife, brothers

vv. 18-19 Outer circle: Neighborhood children, colleagues

See C. Newsom, "The Book of Job," in vol. 4 of *NIB* (Nashville: Abingdon Press, 1996), 476.

• God is responsible for alienating Job's family and friends (vv. 13-14a). Two parallel terms for "family" (v. 13a: *'ahîm*, "brothers"; v. 14a: *qārob*, "near ones") suggest that Job is referring to the general circle of family members and relatives that comprise his clan. Similarly, two parallel terms for "friends" (v. 13b: *yōdĕ'ay*, "ones knowing me"; v. 14b: *mĕyūddā'îm*, "intimates") signify both "acquaintances" and "close friends." Taken together these four terms convey the idea that those who know Job best have now abandoned him.

• The "guests" in Job's house (v. 15a: *gārê bētî*; perhaps "tenants" or "visitors") have forgotten who he is. His domestic servants (v. 15b: *'amahōt*, "maidservants"; v. 16: *'ăbadîm*, "manservants") treat him as if he is a complete stranger. He must beg them for service that under normal circumstances they would offer out of respect or duty. Such complete disregard of Job amounts to a reversal of the social order. The master of the house has no more status than a visitor. The guests and servants of the house act as if they have title and position.

• Job's wife and his brothers (*bĕnê bitnî*; lit., "sons of my belly")[7] find him repulsive (v. 17). Exactly what it is about Job that causes this response is unclear. The text says that Job's *rûaḥ* is strange and disgusting. NRSV takes *rûaḥ* in a literal sense to mean "breath," thus suggesting that Job's mouth odor, perhaps the smell of his disease, is offensive. *Rûaḥ* may also mean "spirit" or more generally "life force." In this sense, what may be repulsive about Job is his life of suffering, which makes even his loved ones want to look away, lest they become infected by his "disease." [The Smell of Death]

• Children (v. 18: *'ăwîlîm*) disrespect Job, colleagues (v. 19a: *mĕtê sôdî*; lit., "men of my confidence/council"; NRSV: "intimate friends") express contempt for him, those whom he loves (v. 19b: *zeh 'āhabtî*) turn against him. In sum, young and old alike, all those who once looked on Job with respect and mutual admiration, now close ranks and turn their backs when he is in their presence.

Verse 20 provides a final graphic image of Job's utter disintegration as a result of God's violent external assault and God's equally injurious internal destruction of his community. The picture of bones clinging to skin and flesh (cf. Ps 102:5) offers a vivid description of a healthy body that has been reduced to the opposite of what it should be. When the body is whole and well nourished, the bones are strong and provide the framework that supports the flesh and skin. When the body is weak, the bones wither and lose their capacity to support life; they cling to skin and flesh in a final effort to avoid total collapse. The imagery is remarkable for its depiction of physical deterioration. But the intent here is likely as much metaphorical as literal. Not only physically but also emotionally, mentally, morally, Job has been reduced to a skeleton of his former self.[8] With what appears to be his last breath, Job says that he has "escaped by the skin of his teeth." The phrase has become idiomatic in English for "narrow escape." A close reading, however, suggests that Job is saying something different. In reality, teeth do not have skin. If Job "escapes" with the skin of his teeth, then he has escaped with nothing. One might say that after all that God has done to him, Job is still alive, but he knows himself to be a "walking dead man."

A Plea, a Hope, a Warning, 19:21-29

Job's closing words begin with a plea (vv. 21-22) and end with a warning (vv. 28-29). Both the plea and the warning are addressed to the friends, who have been Job's principal audience since the beginning of his speech (v. 2: "How long will you [all] torment me?" v. 6: "know [plural] that God has put me in the wrong"). There are also rhetorical links between vv. 21-22 and 28-29 that tie the beginning and end of this last pericope together. Job questions why his friends "pursue" (v. 22: *rādap*) him, then warns them that if they continue "pursuing" (v. 28: *rādap*; NRSV: "persecute") him they will suffer the consequences.

The Smell of Death

Junius Bassus was a Roman prefect who embraced the Christian faith. The sarcophagus that commemorates his death (c. 359) was discovered at the end of the 16th century in the crypt of the Basilica of Saint Peter. The front of the sarcophagus is divided into two panels, each containing five biblical scenes. The lower panel contains four scenes from the Old Testament, which are centered by a scene depicting Jesus' entry into Jerusalem. The upper panel contains five scenes from the New Testament, the center scene depicting the resurrected Jesus. Viewed from left to right and from top to bottom, the ten scenes are (1) the sacrifice of Isaac; (2) Job and his wife; (3) the arrest of Peter; (4) the temptation in the garden; (5) the resurrected Jesus between Peter and Paul; (6) Jesus' entry into Jerusalem; (7) Jesus before Pontius Pilate; (8) Daniel in the lions' den; (9) Pontius Pilate sitting in judgment; and (10) Rebekah with Esau and Jacob.

At the far left end of the lower panel, scene 2 depicts Job seated on stones that form a bench and a footstool. To his right stand one of the friends (or Satan in disguise?) and his wife. With her left hand, Job's wife holds her robe to her nose, perhaps signifying her aversion to his smell. With her right hand, she appears to be offering him bread. The scene recalls the story of Job as presented in the *Testament of Job* (1st century BCE-1st century CE), which reports that Job's wife was reduced to such poverty as a result of his affliction that she was forced to beg for the bread she shared with him (21:1–23:1). A part of her lamentation alludes to Job's malodorous condition: "Job, Job! . . . here you sit in worm-infested rottenness, passing the night in the open air" (24:1, 3; on the similar description in LXX, see further **[Job's Wife as Friend and Comforter]**).

The sarcophagus is an important witness to post-biblical interpretation of Job for a number of reasons. The juxtaposition of the scene depicting Job and his wife with that of Adam and Eve in the garden is particularly intriguing. Not only does it connect Job with creation imagery, it also suggests that Job's display of piety (as described in Job 1–2) provides a positive counterpart to that of the primordial couple. Whereas they succumbed to

Detail of Job from the Sarcophagus of Junius Bassus
Museum of the Treasury, St. Peter's Basilica, Vatican State
(Credit: Erich Lessing/Art Resource, NY)

the temptation to violate God's creational design, Job refused to do so, choosing instead to bear both the good and bad with patience and hope. Beyond that, the inclusion of Job on a relief depicting the hope of life after death shows that by the fourth century Christians viewed this Old Testament figure as a venerated forerunner of Christ and the promise of resurrection (see further **[Buried with Job, Raised like Christ]**).

On the Junius Bassus sarcophagus, see further S. Terrien, *The Iconography of Job Through the Centuries: Artists as Biblical Interpreters* (University Park PN: The Pennsylvania State University Press, 1996), 24-29; E. S. Malbon, *The Iconography of the Sarcophagus of Junius Bassus: Neofitus lit Ad Deum* (Princeton NJ: Princeton University Press, 1990).

Structure of Job 19:21-29

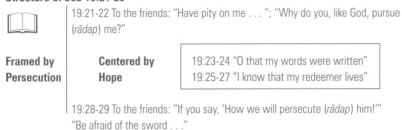

	19:21-22 To the friends: "Have pity on me . . ."; "Why do you, like God, pursue (*rādap*) me?"	
Framed by Persecution	**Centered by Hope**	19:23-24 "O that my words were written" 19:25-27 "I know that my redeemer lives"
	19:28-29 To the friends: "If you say, 'How we will persecute (*rādap*) him!'" "Be afraid of the sword . . ."	

Despite these clues for reading vv. 21-29 as a whole piece, it has long been the practice to isolate vv. 23-27 and to accord them a theological significance that virtually guarantees their relationship to the literary context will be lost. This is especially true for v. 25, which is perhaps the most famous sentence in the book of Job: "I know that my Redeemer lives." Within Christian tradition, this verse can hardly be read apart from the nexus of faith that associates it with Christ and the promise of resurrection. It is surely important to recognize that Job's hope for a redeemer may transcend anything he or the poet of this book may have intended or imagined. But it is also important to bear in mind that in its context Job's hope is framed by persecution. From his perspective, the persecution comes both from God (vv. 6-20) and from friends who act "like God" (v. 22). If it is Job's hope for a redeemer that imagines a transformation of life's framing realities, then it is the persistent claim of these same realities on his life that works to frustrate, confine, and deny this hope. [Structure of Job 19:21-29]

The structure of this last pericope argues against severing the connection between reality and hope. A full appropriation of Job's hope for a redeemer depends on recognizing with him the abiding tension of living between *what is* and *what might be*. The temptation is to weight *what might be* so heavily that *what is* no longer factors into the balance of faith's equations. One strategy for resisting this temptation is to suspend for the moment the discussion of Job's redeemer in order to place his plea (vv. 21-22) and warning (vv. 28-29) at the forefront of our analysis. Once this frame is in place, the hope that *stands at its center* and *yearns for its transformation* can be assessed. [If "the Centre Cannot Hold" Things Fall Apart]

The Frame for Job's Hope (19:21-22, 28-29)
There is a steady and logical progression of thought in these four vv. that invites one to ponder what their meaning would be *if* they were taken as a single unit. Job appeals to the friends for different treatment (v. 21), questions them about their persecution of him (v. 22), cites

If "the Centre Cannot Hold" Things Fall Apart

In "The Second Coming," William Butler Yeats describes the profound tension that exists between the hope of faith and the hard realities against which that hope struggles to assert itself.

Turning and turning in the widening gyre
The falcon cannot hear the falconer;
Mere anarchy is loosed on the world,
The blood-dimmed tide is loosed, and everywhere
The ceremony of innocence is drowned;
The best lack all conviction, while the worst
Are full of passionate intensity.

The force creating the "widening gyre" for Yeats was the sobering reality of World War I. Against the backdrop of what was then a horribly fractured world, Yeats imagines that another world might yet be realizable. In his words, "Surely some revelation is at hand." As the title of the poem suggests, his hope is grounded in a yearning for the "second coming" of Christ. That hope is of course distinctly Christian and for that reason should not be simply equated with Job's hope for a redeemer. Even so, it is not too much to say that given the brokenness of Job's world, he too hopes that some more revelation might be at hand. And, like Yeats, if the center of Job's hope cannot hold, then he too will be forced to scratch for truth in a world where "innocence drowns" in a cacophony of spent convictions and unreciprocated passions.

W. B. Yeats, "The Second Coming," *The Collected Poems of William Butler Yeats* (New York: The Macmillan Company, 1956), 184-85.

their own reasons for persecuting him as evidence against them (v. 28), and then warns them of the penalty they will pay for what they have done (v. 29). Job's lawyer-like movement from appeal to warned punishment is surprising on several counts.

For one who has just described himself as assaulted, stripped, ostracized, and barely clinging to life, Job now seems unexpectedly vigorous. He peppers language with imperatives, questions, and conclusions that suggest he still has the strength and resolve to speak forcefully.

• Because "the hand of God" has "struck" him without cause (v. 21b; cf. 1:11, 19; 2:5), he *demands* that the friends change their way of responding to him. His call for them to "have mercy," or "take pity" (v. 21a: *honnūnî* [2x]) may be only sarcastic. He has never before asked for their mercy, and he has no reason to expect it from them now.[9] It may also be an ultimatum to "Shut up!" As Clines has suggested, "the biggest favor he [Job] can believably ask of them now is to stop hounding him or persecuting him by continuing their speeches. He does not want their pity so much as their silence."[10]

• He *interrogates* them about their reasons for persecuting him (v. 22: "Why?"), then proceeds to *deduce* their motive and *challenge* it as a flat contradiction of the truth. They believe they are acting "like God," and like God they come after him with a vengeance, because they believe "the root of the matter" lies in him (v. 28). The truth is, as Job has tried to make clear to them, it "is God who has put [Job] in the wrong" (v. 6).

• He *warns* them (*gûrû lakem*; "fear for your lives") that persecuting an innocent person is a sin worthy of punishment (v. 29). Previously, Job has admonished the friends to know that if they give perjured testimony in his case they can expect to be cross-examined not only by him but by God (13:7-12). Now he would have them know that their actions against him will be dealt with by the "sword," a symbol for punishment that is comprehensive and fatal (cf. Isa 27:1; Jer 27:8; 44:13).

Even more surprising is what seems to be generating Job's energy. He has already conceded that "there is no justice" (v. 7), and yet with the last word of this speech he indicates that the pursuit of justice is precisely what continues to drive him forward (v. 29: "there is a judgment"). There is a subtle but important tension between Job's concession about the impossibility of justice and his resolve nonetheless to declare it a certainty. He is convinced that there is no justice for an innocent person like himself, because *God* will not answer his petition for vindication. Yet, when he ponders the injustice of his friends' behavior he states without reservation that there will be a judgment that finds them guilty. What is not clear, however, is who will be the agent of this justice. There is no reason to assume that Job believes God will be the agent, for God's silence on these matters seems to be an established fact. Moreover, Job does not once address God in this speech, so if there is to be justice, then Job seems to expect that it will have to come from some other source.

It is instructive to note in this regard that for the first time since chapter 3 Job does not end his speech by longing for death. His desire is now for something different; he yearns for the validation of the words "there is a judgment." With his resolve now focused on justice rather than death, a new possibility, faintly conceived and barely imaginable, begins to suggest itself to Job. In the midst of abandonment by God and persecution by friends, perhaps the one who must assume responsibility for justice is none other than Job himself. Such a thought, of course, seems utterly impossible. The pain of his persecution is too deep. The silence of God is too final. The evidence that there is no justice is too overwhelming. When Job comes to the end of this speech, these are the hard realities that frame his life. If there were not something more, one suspects that these realities would press and squeeze until they exacted from Job a different conclusion than the one with which this speech ends: there is *no* judgment. But these framing realities are not the whole. Something more has inched into the speech, even though there is virtually no room for it in the midst of all that seems to be fixed and settled.

The Center of Job's Hope (19:23-27)

From deep within an existence framed by persecution, Job dares to hope for something more. He articulates this hope in several ways, each of which is shaped by the abiding tension between what he *needs*, what he *knows*, and what he *experiences*.

What Job *needs* is some way to keep his plea for justice alive (vv. 23-24). He has argued the case for his innocence with the friends, but they have been unable or unwilling to accept the merits of his claim. He has appealed to God for a fair and just hearing, but God has refused to answer him. He has screamed out "Violence!" in the hope that somewhere on earth there is a place where the cry of the unjustly accused is not covered up and denied, but "there is no justice" (v. 7; cf. 16:18). What he needs now is a record of his claim on justice that will survive in spite of rejection and denial. He yearns for his testimony to be "written" (*kātab*), "inscribed" (*ḥāqaq*), and "engraved" (*ḥāṣab*; lit., "hewn out"; cf. NJPS: "incised"). Exactly how Job envisions the writing process is unclear, but the sequence of these verbs, each one signifying a means of preservation more permanent than the last, indicates that he desires a record that cannot be erased. It is to last "forever," beyond the friends' rebuke, beyond God's silence, beyond his own unanswered cries for justice. [CD: Tombstone Testimonies]

What Job *knows*, he states emphatically: "I, I know my redeemer lives" (v. 25). Although the grammar that conveys this assertion is clear enough, the meaning of what Job says has been the subject of enormous debate. The unfortunate decision of NRSV and other modern translations (cf. NIV) to capitalize "redeemer" obscures this debate by inviting the Christian community to assume that the one to whom Job refers is Christ. This way of appropriating the text is at least as old the early church fathers (e.g., Clement of Rome, late first century CE; Origen of Alexandria, died 254 CE), but surely its popular hold on the Christian community owes much to Handel's glorious "exegesis" in the *Messiah*, first performed in 1742. [CD: "I Know That My Redeemer Liveth . . . for Now Christ Is Risen from the Dead"] The world in which Job lives, however, and what he "knows" within (and beyond) that world stands at a far remove from what Christians may want to "read back" into his assertion. This is not to deny that Job (or the poet) may have said more than he knew or that a Christian perspective adds faith assertions that may enlarge what Job could have known. Nonetheless, when the community of faith recognizes that what Job "knows" is hard to determine exactly, it keeps itself mindful that the journey from "redeemer" to "Redeemer" is long and complex, not quick and automatic.

Job *knows*, that is, he "firmly believes" a) that his "redeemer" (*gōʾēl*) lives and b) that "at the last he will stand upon the earth" (v. 25). Both assertions merit close attention. The term *gōʾēl* comes primarily from the field of family law.[11] It designates the nearest male relative—brother, paternal uncle, cousin—who acts to protect and preserve the family when his kinsman is unable to do so. The responsibilities of the *gōʾēl* include buying back family property that has fallen into the hands of outsiders (Lev 25:25-28; Ruth 4:3-6; Jer 32:6-8), redeeming a relative sold into slavery (Lev 25:47-49), marrying a widow to provide an heir for her dead husband (Ruth 3:12-13; 4:5), and avenging the blood of a murdered relative (Num 35:19-27; Deut 19:6-12). In religious usage, God is described as the *gōʾēl* of those who have fallen into distress or bondage (e.g., in Egypt: Exod 6:6; 15:13; Ps 74:2; in Babylon: Isa 43:1, 14; 49:7-9). It is noteworthy that God's responsibilities as *gōʾēl* include pleading the case (*ryb*), that is, providing "legal aid,"[12] for those too helpless or too vulnerable to obtain justice for themselves (Ps 119:154; Prov 23:11; Jer 50:34; Lam 3:58).

This range of referents for *gōʾēl* invites an important question: who is the redeemer in whom Job believes? Does he expect a family member to come to his aid? His description of the way family and kin have deserted him (vv. 13-20) indicates that he knows his *gōʾēl* is unlikely to be found among them. Does he expect God to be his *gōʾēl*? What he *knows* about God could hardly give him reason to believe God will be any more help than his family. He *knows* that a mere mortal cannot possibly win a suit against God (9:2), that God will not regard him as innocent (9:28), that God's secret purposes for him are sinister (10:13), and that he can only obtain vindication if God agrees to give up terrorizing him long enough for him to plead his case (13:18).[13] Given his despair over the way both family and God have failed him, it is more likely that Job believes his *gōʾēl* is a third party litigator who will stand between him and his accusers (both divine and human) and argue his case for acquittal. He has explored this possibility on two previous occasions. In 9:33, he imagines that there might be an impartial "arbiter" (*môkîaḥ*; NRSV: "umpire") who can mediate the differences between him and God, but then he dismisses the idea as impossible. In 16:19 he returns to the idea of a heavenly "witness" (*ʿēd*) who would take his side in God's court and give testimony to the truth of his claim. On that occasion, his words were both more urgent and more desperately hopeful: "even now, in fact, my witness is in heaven." Now, Job returns for a third time to the idea that someone, a *gōʾēl*, will come to his defense *against God* and the *friends*. It appears that his hope is again for a heavenly figure, perhaps an intercessory angel similar to the one Elihu mentions in 33:23-24. But it must be conceded that the one who acts as Job's defense attorney is no more precisely identified than is the *satan* who serves as God's prosecutor.[14] What is clear, however, is that for the first time Job does not dismiss the idea out of hand or express it with caution. Now he states emphatically that his redeemer lives and that in the end ("at the last") the redeemer will be successful in obtaining his vindication. [Who Is Job's Redeemer? Details, Debates, and Proposals]

Who Is Job's Redeemer? Details, Debates, and Proposals

The enormous amount of literature on Job's redeemer makes it impossible to survey every interpretation that has been proposed. The major alternative to the position taken in this commentary—the *go'el* is a third party who acts as Job's advocate—is to understand God as Job's redeemer. The principal arguments in support of this interpretation may be summarized and briefly critiqued as follows (For a convenient review of the major positions see N. Habel, *The Book of Job: A Commentary* [OTL; Philadelphia: Westminster Press, 1985], 305-306; Clines, *Job 1–20*, 465):

• The *gō'ēl* Job expects to come to his defense is the same figure as the God he yearns to see (cf. 9:11;13:15, 24; 23:3-7) and ultimately *does* see (42:5). Job, however, longs for a Presence he cannot find God (23:8-9), and he does not expect that God would answer him (9:16) even if he could find where God is hiding. Moreover, Job repeatedly describes God not as his *gō'ēl* but as his enemy (13:24; cf. 16:7-17; 19:7-12), a description he still thinks is justified when he comes to the end of his speeches (31:35: "my adversary [*rîbî*]").

• God is described as the *gō'ēl* of the afflicted in the Psalms (19:14 [MT 19:15]; 77:15 [MT 77:16]; 119:154) and especially in Isa 40–66 (e.g., Isa 44:24; 49:7, 26; 54:5; 63:16). The context for such descriptions is however cultic, not legal, as is the case in Job 19. Unlike the psalmists, Job does not pray for deliverance *by* God; he pleads for justice that will deliver him *from* God.

• The word *'aḥărôn* (19:25) should not be interpreted adverbially ("at the last") but as a noun ("The Last"), which provides a title for God that is synonymous with Redeemer. In support of this argument is the similar usage of *'aḥărôn* in Deutero-Isaiah, e.g., Isa 48:12: "I am He; I am the first and I am the last" (cf. 44:6). It remains the case, however, that "The Last" is not a standard title for God. Furthermore, in Job 19 the context justifies understanding *'aḥărôn* as an adverb, for in the next v. the related preposition *'aḥar*, "after," complements the idea that Job's vindication will occur "at the last," that is, at some future time.

• The word *hay*, "lives" (19:25), is frequently used with reference to God (e.g., "the living God," Josh 3:10; Jer 10:10;

23:36). In Job 27:2, the phrase "As God lives" uses the same term. Such evidence suggests to some that the description of a "living redeemer" can refer to none other than God. It may be countered that Job does not doubt God is a "living God." His question is rather whether the living God is at all concerned with his plight. Moreover, the expression "As God lives" is a standard way of expressing an oath (1 Sam 14;39, 45; 2 Sam 2:27). Job's oath in 27:2 is a means of swearing to his innocence *against the God who insists on declaring him guilty*, not a confession of faith in God's justice.

• It may be argued that Israel's monotheism makes the idea of a third party intermediary who acts as Job's redeemer unlikely, if not unacceptable. But in the book of Job, Israel's monotheism, however this may be construed, does not seem to be so rigid as to deny a role to the *satan*, who is a third party that stands between Job and God. If the *satan* can be a go-between adversary who afflicts Job, it is reasonable to suggest that the redeemer can be a go-between advocate who works for his vindication.

Finally, it is important to acknowledge that the argument in favor of a third party redeemer is not above criticism or challenge. Among recent commentators on Job, J. Gerald Janzen has offered a strong and imaginative defense of the traditional view that God is Job's redeemer. He invites readers to contemplate the possibility that Job implicitly opens the door on a new and alternative world in which God is at work in a way that makes Handel's exegesis more than just a musical fantasy (see **[CD: I Know that My Redeemer Liveth . . . For Now Christ Is Risen from the Dead]**).

Further, D. Clines has recently argued a third alternative: Job's *gō'ēl* is his own cry for justice. His protestation of innocence is personified as the living redeemer who will have the last word. In sum, the cry for justice, however unheeded and seemingly ineffective, is always a witness for truth that cannot be covered up or denied.

Given the ambiguities and uncertainties in the text, and considering the ongoing debate about what Job hopes for and expects, perhaps the better course of wisdom is to linger within the question that refuses to be answered simply: Who will be the redeemer of the Jobs of this world?

J. Gerald Janzen, *Job* (Atlanta: John Knox, 1985), 134-45.
D. Clines, *Job 1–20* (WBC; Dallas: Word Books, 1989), 457-64.

Job *knows* that his redeemer lives. The interpretive question is *when* does he believe the redeemer will rise to his defense? The adverbial expression "at the last" (*'aḥărôn,* v. 25b) indicates that Job's vindication will take place at some future time. The following line—"after (*'aḥar*) my skin has been destroyed "(v. 26a)—suggests a time after Job's death. Job has previously wondered if death might be a temporary state, after which God would summon him to return to a new and fully restored life (14:13-17). It is possible that this idea of a post-mortem renewal finds further expression in 19:26b-27, which can be taken as a description of Job's "re-fleshed" existence after death, when at last he will see God. Such a view has certainly captured the imagination of the Christian community. At least since the third century, Job's "resurrection" has earned him a revered place, alongside Christ, in art and iconography that celebrates the Christian hope of life after death. [CD: Buried with Job, Raised Like Christ]

From a Christian perspective, it may indeed be tempting to interpret Job's vindication "at the last" as an embryonic witness to resurrection. That this is Job's belief, however, is unlikely for several reasons. Although he contemplates renewal after Sheol, he ultimately rejects it as a hope that is utterly without foundation. The truth is that God "destroys" that hope just as certainly as "the waters wear away the stones" (14:18-22). Moreover, Job has become increasingly adamant that a post-mortem vindication cannot satisfy the imperative for justice. Those who die as victims leave a legacy of nothing more than death. There must be some place among the living where the cry for justice gets a hearing (16:18). If there is not, then the voice that speaks from the grave does not celebrate hope; it mourns its loss: "Where then is my hope? Who will see my hope?" (17:15). Finally, it is important to bear in mind that ancient Israelites did not as a rule believe in life after death or the resurrection of the body (see [Resurrection]). Job himself states the representative view: "mortals lie down and do not rise again; until the heavens are no more, they will not awake or be roused out of their sleep" (14:12).

A more satisfactory approach lies along the interpretive lines proposed by Clines.[15] He argues for differentiating between what Job *knows* or *expects* (vv. 25-26a) and what he *desires* (vv. 26b-27). Job knows that a redeemer will rise and vindicate him after his death. But what he most desires is justice while he is alive. He wants to be present when his case comes before the court; he wants to testify on his own behalf; in short, he wants to see God for himself (cf. 13:15-16). The tension between what Job knows and what he desires can be captured by rendering the *conjunction* in the middle of v. 26 (*waw*) as "but" rather than "then" and the following verbs ("imperfects" in Hebrew) as expressing a wish or desire rather than a prediction. The *disjunction* at the middle of vv. 25-27 may then be reflected as follows: "I, I know that my redeemer lives, and that at the last he will stand upon the earth—after my skin has been thus destroyed. *But* I *would see* (*'eḥĕzeh*) God from my flesh. I, I *would see* (*'eḥĕzeh*) for myself. My eyes *would see* (*rā'û*), not another's."

The disjunction between what Job knows and what he desires places the redeemer's role in a different light. Job's certainty about the future does not lessen his desire for the present. At the heart of that desire are two things: the presence of God and justice. From this point forward, Job says no more about arbiters or witnesses or redeemers. Instead, he intensifies his quest to find God (Job 23) and to argue his innocence before the Almighty with a force that requires response (Job 31). It is tempting to jump to the end of Job's story to see the outcome of his quest, for there we learn that at last God appears to Job (chs. 38–41) and at last Job "sees" God (42:5). Whether this ending satisfies his pursuit of justice must remain for now an open question. In the meanwhile, Job must grapple with what he needs and what he knows and *what he desires* in the midst of what he experiences.

Finally, what Job *experiences* is utter exhaustion (v. 27c). "My heart faints within me" is literally, "My kidneys wear out in my bosom."[16] At one level, the expression signifies the overwhelming emotional fatigue that drains Job's passion for carrying on with the struggle, for the kidneys, like the heart, are the symbolic center of intense affections and desires (cf. Ps 16:7 [NRSV: "heart"]; Prov 23:16 [NRSV: "soul"]). At a more basic level, the kidneys are a vital and extremely sensitive part of the human anatomy. They are important in maintaining the balance of fluid and salt that stabilizes the body at a tolerable degree of acidity. When that balance is lost the body is threatened, and if the kidneys cannot act to restore equilibrium the consequences can be fatal. Job of course does not speak with the expertise of a medical internist. His knowledge comes from other sources. He does know, however, what it is like when the kidneys are under attack. God's archers have targeted him for destruction; their arrows pierce his "kidneys" (16:13). It is out of that experience and all that it portends that Job speaks about the dangerous imbalance between God's hostile presence in his life and his emotional and physical capacities to withstand it.

To conclude this discussion of vv. 21-29, we may return once more to the tension between reality and hope that frames Job's closing words. Job is hemmed in by persecution that has no end in sight (vv. 21-22, 28-29). Without some intervening hope, this hard reality will constitute the full measure of what he knows and has already declared to be fixed and settled: "there is no justice." But the structure of this final pericope insists that life must not be read straight through from one reality to the next. Buried deep within Job's consciousness is the hope for something more (vv. 23-27). This hope is real, and it beckons him onward. There is a redeemer, and Job can be certain that in the end the declaration about life will be more than what the present allows him to say.

Even so, a future justice is a justice delayed, and in the meantime the realties that wage war on hope grind away without interruption. Although Job's hope cannot be thwarted, he does concede that there is no obvious stimulus for it to exercise its passions, *unless* somehow *he can sustain its aspirations by his own resolve.* Toward that end, when he turns once more to face the persecution that defines his life, he speaks against it with a new-found imperative: be warned, "there is a judgment" (v. 29). Between the reality that "there *is no* justice" and the determination that "there *is* a judgment" there is a vast chasm. On the far side of that chasm is the redeemer, already proclaiming victory. In the middle of that chasm, where victory is hard to see, is Job. When (not if) the gap between persecution and justice is bridged, Job serves notice that he will have played a role, which is at yet beyond his full comprehension, in pleading for it, believing in it, and working for it. ["To Hope, Till Hope Creates"]

"To Hope, Till Hope Creates"

In the final words of Percy Shelley's *Prometheus Unbound*, Demogorgon addresses the spirits of creatures in the universe and offers them instruction on how to sustain freedom when it is threatened by omnipotent power. His counsel, conveyed with words like "hope," "defy," "bear," "neither to change nor falter nor repent," provides an apt description of Job's resolve inside the breach between persecution and justice:

> To suffer woes which Hope thinks infinite;
> To forgive wrongs darker than Death or Night;
> To defy Power which seems Omnipotent;
> To love, and bear; to hope till Hope creates
> From its own wreck the thing it contemplates;
> Neither to change nor falter nor repent:
> This, like thy glory, Titan! is to be
> Good, great and joyous, beautiful and free;
> This is alone Life, Joy, Empire and Victory.

Prometheus Unbound, IV, ll. 570-78, in *Shelley's Poetry and Prose*, sel. and ed. Donald H. Reiman and Sharon B. Powers (New York/London: W.W. Norton and Company, 1977), 210.

CONNECTIONS

Job makes two moves in this chapter that are important not only for the ongoing drama of this book but also for readers of this book who may share in the enactment of his journey of faith. First, he pronounces the Judge of the world guilty. Second, he declares that the unjustly accused may know that there is something more to believe in than injustice: there is a redeemer, and there is a judgment, and there is work to do. Both these pronouncements are freighted with heavy questions, unyielding realties, and impossible odds. Once Job decides to move in these two directions, he cannot know if the journey can be completed or where it will end. All he knows at this juncture is that this is the course he must follow.

God is Guilty

Job's move toward pronouncing God guilty has been slow, deliberate, and anguished. In chapters 9 and 10, he resolves to move beyond lament and present his case before God, even if it means addressing an absent judge in an empty courtroom. He rehearses the questions he would put to God (10:3-7) and begins to formulate the charge that God harbors secret and sinister intentions to destroy him (10:8-17). The rehearsal fills Job with more despair than courage, however, and he slides back into lament where death, not life, seems the only reasonable objective for the unjustly accused (10:18-22). Out of the depths of lament he resolves again to argue his case with God, "come what may" (13:13). He tries to negotiate the conditions for a fair trial in the hope that God will disclose the charges against him and listen to his defense (13:20-28). But there is no negotiating with a God who predetermines that every human being must take the same unalterable course from birth to death (14:1-6, 10-12). If there is ever a hope for anything more or different, God destroys it (14:19). Once again, Job succumbs to despair. Although there is no reason for Job to continue with his case, his grief will not be silenced. He laments that God is his enemy not his friend, his assailant not his defender (16:7-17). Such charges effectively put God on trial. If God will not appear in court, Job will petition heaven and earth to keep alive the evidence and to bear witness to its truth until God is brought before the bar of justice (16:18-22).

In chapter 19, Job takes yet another step in the long and arduous journey toward justice. He pronounces God guilty. His verdict reads, "God has perverted me" (v. 6). This daring legal sentence gathers together all of Job's words thus far and focuses them with a laser-like intensity on what he believes is God's most egregious injustice. God is guilty of refusing to answer his pleas for justice (9:16), of condemning him without evidence (10:2), of attacking him savagely and without cause (16:7-17; 19:7-12), of destroying his community (19:13-20). Any one of these offenses would be serious enough to justify Job's verdict. But Job's verdict goes still farther. He declares that God is guilty of perverting what it means to be a human being created in the image of God. God has stripped him of his "glory" and "crown" (v. 9), the very attributes that enable him to live out God's own decision to create him as a noble human being with noble responsibilities for the world (cf. Ps 8:5-8). Job has repeatedly questioned what it

"There Is No Truce with the Furies"

The furies are at home
in the mirror; it is their address.
Even the clearest water,
if deep enough can drown.
Never think to surprise them.
Your face approaching ever
so friendly is the white flag
they ignore. There is no truce

with the furies. A mirror's temperature
is always at zero. It is ice
in the veins. Its camera is an X-ray. It is a chalice

held out to you in
silent communion, where gaspingly
you partake of a shifting
identity never your own.

R. S. Thomas, "Reflections," *No Truce with the Furies* (Newcastle upon Tyne: Bloodaxe Books, 1995), 31.

means to be a human being in God's world. He now believes he has the evidence to answer these questions:

"Why did I not die at birth?" (3:11; cf. 10:18). . . Because it was your
  intention to pervert me.
"What are human beings that you make so much of them?" (7:17). . .
  They are your preferred targets for perversion.
"Why do you hide your face, and count me as your enemy?" (13:24). . .
  because you desire to pervert me.
"Do you fix your eyes on such a one?" (14:3). . . Yes, because you are
  determined to pervert me. [CD: The "Sport" of Divine Perversion]

What are readers to make of Job's decision to pronounce God guilty? The first thought will likely be that Job is not only wrong but heretical. In the face of such talk, it seems imperative to come to God's defense. With the friends, we would warn Job that God does not pervert justice, that God's wisdom is beyond his comprehension, that rebellion against God is a sure sign of a lack of faith, love, and obedience. But if we have attended carefully to these dialogues, then we may expect the intrusion of a second, more disturbing thought. It is likely that those who sit with Job on the ash heap will challenge, if not reject, each one of these explanations. They are stiffened by pain that will not be explained away merely by admitting guilt they cannot own. ["There Is No Truce with the Furies"] We should not be surprised to hear them respond with impatience like Job's: How long will you break me in pieces with your words? Are you not ashamed to abuse me like this (vv. 2-3)? The question for Job's comforters then becomes, what will the next word be?

It is wise to linger inside this question long enough to contemplate what it means *both* to sit with Job and declare God guilty *and* to stand with the friends and defend God's innocence. One way to conceptualize these two positions is through the interchange between Berish and Sam in Elie Wiesel's *The Trial of God* (see further the "Connections" in Job 9–10 and Job 16–17). Berish, like Job, determines to put God on trial for the massacre of Jews in Shamgorod in 1649. Sam, like Job's friends, assumes responsibility for acting as God's defense attorney. The major points of their arguments can be traced as follows:[17]

Berish	*Sam*
God is guilty.	God is innocent.
The proof of God's guilt lies in the ruins of the pillaged houses of study, the ashes of the burned synagogue, the mass graves of the innocent.	Suffering is always sad, but it does not necessarily implicate God: "pain does not constitute judicial evidence."

Can God be left out of the conversation
when there is so much inexplicable
suffering? Is God a "neutral bystander"?
"Would a father stand by quietly, silently,
and watch his children being slaughtered?"

"Who are you to make
comparisons or draw
conclusions? Born in dust,
you are nothing but dust."

"I'm not dust. I'm standing up, I'm
walking, thinking, wondering, shouting:
I'm human!"

"The verdict will be worthless!"

Wiesel has clearly constructed this conversation for dramatic effect.
Even so, to listen to Berish and Sam is to recognize that the merits of
their perspectives must be weighed carefully. What hangs in the balance
is the nature of the divine-human relationship. If Berish is right, then
the question of God's justice cannot be left out of the equation of
human suffering. If Sam is right, then the question of human guilt
cannot be left out of the equation of divine justice. Given the arguments that may be placed in evidence for both these perspectives, it is
little wonder that God's accusers and God's defenders often square off
across battle lines fortified against capitulation and compromise. The
Jobs and Berishes of the world know that if they forfeit their innocence
they stand to lose more than an argument. They lose the "glory" and
"crown" that enables them to celebrate and enact the gift of being
created in the image of God. The Sams and friends of Jobs in the world
know that if they yield on the question of God's innocence they risk
losing more than a theological debate. They open a crack in the door
that invites the creature to shape the Creator's gifts in ways that may be
reckless, dangerous, and wrong. Job is willing to run the risk of
shouting "I am human, and I will be no less," even if it means declaring
God guilty. The friends are willing to run the risk of shouting "God is
unassailably just and can be no less," even it means exonerating God by
condemning the innocent. Which of the two runs the greater risk
depends on who is closer to understanding God's creational intentions—the friends who hound Job for a confession of guilt, or Job who
demands that the friends, and God, recognize the nobility of his claim
of innocence? ["Is This Thy Justice, O Father?"]

It is typical of the dialogues to raise this question without answering
it. In the absence of a definitive word from God, Job must decide on
his own whether claiming his creaturely "glory" and "crown" is an act of
obedience or rebellion. Job bets on the former, but he will not know if
he has invested his energies wisely until God speaks. When at last God
does speak, the response will evoke the memory of Job's resolve in this
chapter: "Deck yourself with majesty and dignity; clothe yourself with
glory and splendor" (40:10). At that point, all parties to this drama will

"Is This Thy Justice, O Father?"

In 1906, Atlanta erupted in race riots that took the lives of dozens of innocent black people. Upon hearing the news, W. E. B. Du Bois rushed home from rural Alabama to sit on the steps of South Hall to protect his wife Nina and his daughter Yolanda with a shotgun. On the train ride to the city he wrote "A Litany of Atlanta" in which he challenged God to make sense of such wanton cruelty and to act justly to relieve it. He later admitted that the poem was "a bit hysterical." If so, it remains a truthful witness of the passion that makes one desperate for justice, especially when the silence of God costs too much to be orthodox.

O Silent God, Thou whose voice afar in mist and mystery hath left our ears
a-hungered in these fearful days—
Hear us, good Lord!

Listen to us, Thy children: our faces dark with doubt, are made a mockery in
Thy sanctuary. With uplifted hands we front
Thy heaven, O God, crying:
*We beseech Thee to hear us,
good Lord! . . .*

Is this Thy justice, O Father, that guilt be easier than innocence, and the
innocent crucified for the guilt of the untouched guilty?
Justice, O Judge of men! . . .

Bewildered we are, and passion-tossed, mad with the madness of a mobbed and
mocked and murdered people; straining at the armposts of Thy Throne, we
raise our shackled hands and charge Thee, God, by the bones of our stolen fathers, by the tears of our dead mothers, by the very blood of Thy crucified Christ: What meaneth this? Tell us the Plan; give us the Sign!
Keep not Thou silent, O God!

W. E. B. Du Bois, "A Litany of Atlanta," *The Independent* 61 (11 October 1906): 856-58. The poem was subsequently published with slight modifications in W. E. B. Du Bois, *Darkwater: Voices from within the Veil* (New York: Harcourt, Brace, 1921), 25-28. For further discussion of the background for this poem, see D. Lewis, *W.E.B. Du Bois: Biography of a Race, 1868–1919* (New York: Henry Holt and Company, 1993), 334-36.

have to consider carefully whether Job's way of imaging God is reckless or righteous.

Something More to Believe In Than Injustice: a Redeemer, a Judgment, and Work to Do

In the midst of a life defined by persecution, Job dares to assert that there is something more to believe in than injustice. That "something more" is expressed in terms of the *gōʾēl* (v. 25). Job knows that somewhere, at some undisclosed future time, his redeemer will appear. When that happens, what is wrong will be put right, what is unjust will be rectified, what is broken will be healed. The critical interpretive question is, "Who will be Job's *gōʾēl*?"

The answer proposed in this commentary is that Job looks to some third party who will stand in between himself and God and secure his vindication. The more traditional view is that God will be Job's redeemer. In Christian piety, this view invites the understanding that the agent of God's redemption of Job will be Christ. Both answers may be argued with integrity and passion, and both are open to challenge and correction. The issue is too complex and too confessionally freighted to be resolved by any single interpretive strategy. One observation may provide a useful point of departure for further reflection. Whether Job's redeemer is a third party or God, Job's expects that he will have to *wait* until some future time for the full realization of the vindication he seeks. Given the immediate realties that bear down upon him, Job urgently needs some way to fight for his redemption in the present. He needs some means to keep alive his hope on earth not only in heaven. He needs justice not only later but now. The provocative suggestion of chapter 19 is that in the hard interim between *what is* and *what might be* Job resolves not to be a passive victim of injustice.

Job dares to believe, against all evidence to the contrary, that "there is a judgment" (v. 29). Beyond that, he determines to play a role in calling for that judgment and in working to make it a reality in the here and now. What that role looks like may be deduced from vv. 21-22 and 28-29. It consists of *demanding* a different response to those who are unjustly accused, of *addressing hard questions* to those who believe persecuting innocent victims is ordained by God, of *challenging* the assumption that the root cause of all suffering is the sufferer's own sin, of *warning* that a certain judgment awaits those who will not stand on the side of the victim. Still more provocative is the idea that Job's demands, questions, challenges, and warnings provide a model for justice that may instruct both God and the friends. If God condemns an innocent person, then Job's enactment of justice would dare to effect an indictment: "God has put me in the wrong" (v. 6). If the friends persist in acting "like God" (v. 22), then they too will be judged guilty: "If you say, 'How we will persecute him!'. . . you may know that there is a judgment" (vv. 28, 29).

To claim responsibility for holding both God and God's spokespersons accountable to justice is of course a dangerous move. All creaturely judgments are necessarily flawed and incomplete. On this point the biblical witness is clear: in the vast arena of the cosmic domain, only God can know the full measure of what justice means. If Job is justified in challenging the narrow application of the friends' retributive justice, then he must expect that his own estimate of corrective justice may also be skewed and inadequate. But there is one major difference between Job and his friends that endows his quest for justice with a moral imperative they cannot match. Job speaks as a *victim* of injustice; they speak only as *onlookers*. He cannot survive if the system that sustains his affliction is not changed; they will not question a system that sustains their place within its certainties. Of course, Job may be wrong to contend *with* the friends and *against* God for justice. If he is, he errs on the side of hoping too much, expecting too much, believing too much. Of course, the friends may be right to argue that Job has no claim on *their theology* or on *God's justice*. But if they are, then what Job may hope and believe about the human community and about God is too little to give life meaning in the midst of suffering like his.

Job's resolve to fight for justice invites the understanding that faith may require more than trust in a redeemer who will make all things right in the end. Suffering sometimes so widens the gap between what is and what will be that assurances alone are not enough to sustain one's passion for the journey. What is needed in the interim is a way to pull the future into the present by the sheer strength of commitment. Job determines that crying out "Violence!" makes a down payment on the final purchase of justice. He believes that his redeemer will ultimately honor this commitment and complete its objectives. In the meanwhile, he fights alone, acting on a conviction that yearns to be validated.

It is both Job's resolve to fight for justice and his yearning to have this resolve validated that summons the community of faith to become an active participant in this drama. Inside the trenches, where the hard work of crying for justice goes on, the Jobs of this world await the one who will fulfill the responsibilities of the *gōʾēl.* If Job's readers are satisfied to leave that role to God or some other third party, then they may be content to look on the struggles of the unjustly accused from a distance, confident that the final outcome is not really in doubt. But if it is the commitment to work for justice that somehow hastens its arrival, then readers may want to think again about whether simply looking on is an adequate expression of faith.[18] The critical question that remains to be answered is, "Who will be Job's *gōʾēl?*" How we respond to this question will be an important indication of whether we believe and hope *too much* for the claims of justice on God and the human community or *too little.* ["You Onlookers"]

"You Onlookers"

Nelly Sachs has looked at the role of the "onlookers" through the lens of the Holocaust. To all who would be content with this role she asks, how much killing, how many "dying eyes," how many hands raised in supplication does it take to move one towards the light?

Whose eyes watched the killing.
As one feels a stare at one back
You feel on your bodies
The glances of the dead.

How many dying eyes will look at you
When you pluck a violet from its hiding place?
How many hands be raised in supplication . . .?
How much memory grows in the blood
Of the evening sun? . . .

You onlookers,
You who raised no hand in murder,
But who did not shake the dust
From your longing,
You who halted there, where dust is changed
To light.

N. Sachs, "You Onlookers," in *Art from the Ashes: A Holocaust Anthology*, ed. L. Langer (New York/Oxford: Oxford University Press, 1995), 641.

NOTES

[1] It is noteworthy that in the book of Job it is Job who asks the hard questions about God and the world God has created. The friends are typically willing to question only Job. From their perspective God is beyond question. See further, W.A.M. Beuken, "Job's Imprecation As the Cradle of a New Religious Discourse," *The Book of Job,* ed. W. A. M. Beuken (Leuven: Leuven University Press, 1994), 67.

[2] The verb for "err" in v. 4, *šāgah*, and the noun derivative "error," *mešûgāh*, normally signify unintentional or inadvertent sins, that is, sins committed unknowingly or acciden-

tally. In such cases the transgressor may be cleansed and forgiven by following prescribed acts of ritual purification (cf. Lev 4:13-21, 22-26, 27-31). By contrast, intentional sins, those committed willfully or "highhandedly" (NRSV), are deserving of the most severe punishment (cf. Num 15:30-31). See further, J. Milgrom, "The Cultic Šegaga and Its Influence in Psalms and Job," JQR 58 (1967): 73-79.

[3] N. Habel, *The Book of Job: A Commentary* (OTL; Philadelphia: Westminster Press, 1985), 301.

[4] S. Scholnick has argued that Job's cry of "Violence!" should be understood in a legal sense. She translates v. 7 as follows: "I make a charge "Lawlessness," but I am not answered. I press charges, but there is no litigation." Moreover, she notes that the term *ḥamas*, "violence," is elsewhere "a technical term for wrongdoing" (e.g., Exod 23:1; Deut 19:6) and in some cases (e.g., Prov 4:17) a charge that someone has wickedly seized something that does not belong to them. She notes that "even with a formal charge against him, Yahweh fails to respond [to Job]. . . "; "The Meaning of *Mišpat* in the Book of Job," JBL 101 (1982): 524-25.

[5] Cf. L. Perdue (*Wisdom in Revolt: Metaphorical Theology in the Book of Job* [JSOTSup 112; Sheffield: Almond Press, 1991], 172-74) who interprets this text as a "deconstruction of the metaphor of king."

[6] The MT has a singular form of the verb, thus indicating that God is the subject and causative agent of the verbal action. Some commentators and modern translations favor emending the verb to a plural form, "*they* are distant," thus suggesting that Job's friends and family initiate the ostracism of Job (e.g., NAB: "My brethren have withdrawn from me"; cf. REB). Such an emendation effectively absolves God of responsibility for Job's treatment by others, but there is no textual support for changing the MT.

[7] The phrase is ambiguous. Some (e.g., R. Gordis, *The Book of Job: Commentary, New Translation, and Special Studies* [New York: Jewish Theological Seminary of America, 1978], 202) take it to mean Job's own children. Others (e.g., D. Clines, *Job 1–20* [WBC; Dallas: Word Books, 1989], 449) take it to mean the children born from the same womb as Job, i.e.,his "uterine brothers." It is likely that the term is a conventional expression for those who, like his wife, are Job's closest loved ones.

[8] For a full and convincing discussion of this imagery, see Clines, *Job 1–20*, 450-52.

[9] Cf. Habel (*Book of Job,* 302) who describes Job's appeal as a "sharp sarcastic barb" that asks for sympathy "with tongue in cheek."

[10] Clines, *Job 1–20*, 453.

[11] For further reading on the semantic range of this term and its derivatives, see J. J. Stamm, "*G'l*, to redeem," in *TLOT*, ed. E. Jenni, C. Westermann, (Peabody MA: Hendrikson Publishers, 1997), vol. 1, 288-96.

[12] Ibid., 292.

[13] Cf. Habel, *Book of Job,* 304.

[14] Habel (ibid., 306) suggests that Job's redeemer functions within the heavenly council as the counterpart to the *satan*. A similar figure in Zechariah 3:1-5 is described as the "angel of the Lord" who successfully defends the high priest Joshua against the false charges of the *satan*. See further [The *Satan*].

[15] Clines, *Job 1–20*, 461-62. For a similar approach see Habel, *Book of Job,* 308-309; Newsom, "The Book of Job," 479.

[16] M. Pope, *Job* (AB; Garden City NY: Doubleday, 1979), 147.

[17] E. Wiesel, *The Trial of God* (New York: Schocken Books, 1979), 125-34.

[18] See especially, J. Gustafson, "A Response to the Book of Job," *The Voice From the Whirlwind: Interpreting the Book of Job,* ed. L. G. Perdue, W. Clark Gilpin (Nashville: Abingdon, 1992), 183: "At worst. . . the longing for a Redeemer can focus the eyes of human aspiration on an end in such a way that the realties of human life and the possibilities of participating in them to the benefit of humanity and the world are badly blurred."

ZOPHAR'S SECOND RESPONSE TO JOB: THE FATE OF THE WICKED "EVER SINCE MORTALS WERE PLACED ON THE EARTH"

Job 20:1-29

Like his friends before him, Zophar continues to press the argument concerning the fate of the wicked. His approach to the subject is relatively straightforward. He begins with a rebuke of Job that seeks once again to reframe the discussion in keeping with the friends' primary passion: the inevitable punishment that awaits the wicked (vv. 2-5). The rest of the speech describes that punishment in three different ways: the pride of the wicked may extend to the heavens, but their final resting place is in the dust of the earth (vv. 6-11); their appetite for wickedness may be voracious, but it is also self-destructive (vv. 12-23); they may run from punishment, but they cannot escape the forces of heaven and earth that target them for destruction (vv. 24-28). A concluding summary affirms that the punishment of the wicked is certain, because God has decreed it (v. 29). [Structure of Job 20:1-29]

Zophar's argument concerning the fate of the wicked is largely a conventional one. Like Bildad (8:8-9) and Eliphaz (15:17-18), he appeals to traditional wisdom to authorize his claim to know the truth about the moral order

Structure of Job 20:1-29		
📖	20:1-5	Opening rebuke: "I hear censure that insults me"
	20:6-28	The inevitable punishment of the wicked
	vv. 6-11	Pride goes before a fall
	vv. 12-23	Evil is a deadly delicacy
	vv. 24-28	You can run, but you cannot hide
	20:29	Concluding summary: God decrees the punishment of the wicked

of the world. And like his friends, he seeks to trace this wisdom back to its primordial beginnings, to the time when "mortals were placed on the earth" (v. 4). Zophar, however, reads primordial wisdom in a subtly more negative way than his friends. Bildad argued that from the very beginning of creation there were limits to what mortals could "know" about God's justice (8:9: "we know nothing"). Eliphaz argued that creation sets limits on how "righteous" human beings can be in relation to God (15:14: "What are mortals, that they can be

"We Are the Lost People"

As a Welshman, R. S. Thomas reflects on what it means to live in a land within a land where one's identity is defined more by what must be relinquished than by what can be preserved. The immediate referent in this poem for what is lost is the Welsh identity, but the larger referent—the loss of the potential to be the person one is born to be—is not far removed from Zophar's conclusion about what Job must lose if he is to fit into God's moral order of the world.

We are the lost people.
Tracing us by our language
you will not arrive where we are
which is nowhere. The wind
blows through our castles; the chair
of poetry is without a tenant.

We are exiles within
our own country; we eat our bread
at a pre-empted table. 'Show us, '
we supplicate, 'the way home, '
and they laughingly hiss at us:
'But you are home. Come in
and endure it.' Will nobody
explain what it is like
to be born lost?

The plaintive question—"Will nobody explain what it is like to be born lost?"—may be Job's, but it is not Zophar's. Zophar knows the answer, and for the rest of this speech he will be preoccupied with speaking it.

R. S. Thomas, "The Lost," in *No Truce with the Furies* (Newcastle upon Tyne: Bloodaxe Books, 1995), 14.

clean . . . that they can be righteous?"). Zophar appeals to creational wisdom not to mark the levels of knowledge and goodness that are beyond the reach of mortals but to define the wickedness that marks them for certain punishment. The issue for Zophar is no longer what humans may strive for but never fully attain; it is rather what humans are limited to and can never fully escape. ["We Are the Lost People"]

"I Hear Censure That Insults Me," 20:1-5

Zophar's opening words indicate that he is personally insulted by what Job has said. Job's suggestion that he and the friends will be judged for persecuting an innocent person without cause (19:22, 28-29) strikes at the heart of everything Zophar believes about the inviolable connection between sin and judgment. Such a charge is extremely disorienting and so troubles Zophar that he is compelled by his deepest convictions to refute it (vv. 2-3).

For his rebuttal, he appeals to what he regards as the primordial truth about humankind (vv. 4-5). If Job truly "knows" (19:6, 25) the truth about God's moral governance of the world, then Job must "know" the truth that is as old as Adam, the truth that has been indelibly etched into creation "ever since mortals (*'ādām*) were placed on earth" (cf. Deut 4:32). Zophar locks on that truth with a thesis statement that lays the foundation for everything he has to say: the joy of the wicked is short-lived.

Zophar's discernment about the wicked is hardly novel. That the wicked may prosper, but only for a short duration, is a staple of Israelite teaching (e.g., Pss 37, 73). Both Bildad (8:11-13) and Eliphaz (15:29-33) have made similar arguments already. What is striking is that when

Once Broken, Always Broken

In *Letters from the Earth*, Mark Twain recounts a series of letters written by Satan that report on his visit to earth to examine God's "experiment" with the human race. Letter III assesses the preposterous notion that the descendants Adam and Eve are endowed with "moral sense":

Adam and Eve ate the forbidden fruit, and at once a great light streamed into their dim heads. They had acquired knowledge. What knowledge—useful knowledge? No—merely knowledge that there was such a thing as good, and such a thing as evil, and how to do evil. They couldn't do it before. Therefore all their acts up to this time had been without stain, without blame, without offense.

But now they could do evil—and suffer for it; now they had acquired what the Church calls an invaluable possession, the Moral Sense; that sense which differentiates man from the beast and sets him above the beast. Instead of below the beast—where one would suppose his proper place would be, since he is always foul-minded and guilty and the beast always clean and innocent. It is like valuing a watch that must go wrong, above a watch that can't.

M. Twain, *Letters from the Earth*, ed. B. DeVoto (New York: Harper and Row, 1938), 23.

Zophar reviews the tradition about the time when God "placed" (*śim*, Gen 2:8; the verb is the same as in 20:4) the first human beings in the garden, he focuses exclusively on their journey toward punishment rather than blessing. He omits the primordial truth that God "created humankind in his image" (Gen 1:26), "blessed them" (Gen 1:27), commissioned them for dominion that protects and nurtures the earth (Gen 1:28; 2:15), and pronounced their capacity to fulfill this destiny to be "very good" (Gen 1:31). In Zophar's view, creation teaches that human beings are fated to be like the Adam and Eve of Genesis 3, not of Genesis 1–2. They are more rebels than servants, more wicked than righteous, more deserving of condemnation than celebration. Perhaps Zophar believes his accentuation of this part of the creation story is necessary to correct Job's insistence that he is innocent. Perhaps he is motivated by a determination to prove that the reality of divine punishment is greater than any temporary victory the wicked may claim. In either case, Zophar has construed the truth about creation so narrowly that Job has no place to stand in God's moral order, *until* he admits guilt and accepts punishment. The subtle assertion of Zophar's thesis seems to be that every joy of both the *wicked* and the *righteous* is timed to last "but for a moment" (v. 5). [Once Broken, Always Broken]

Pride Goes Before a Fall, 20:6-11

Zophar's depiction of the fall of the wicked recalls the proverbial estimate of arrogance and hubris: "Pride goes before destruction, and a haughty spirit before a fall" (Prov 16:18). [Pride, Gluttony and the Seven Deadly Sins] The image of reaching for the heavens and the clouds (v. 6) recalls mythological stories about those who aspire to invade God's domain and usurp God's power (cf. Gen 11:1-9; Isa 14:12-20; Ezek 28:1-19).

Pride, Gluttony, and the Seven Deadly Sins

The seven "deadly" sins are popularly known as pride, envy, wrath, sloth, avarice, gluttony, and lechery. They are considered "deadly" not strictly because they lead irrevocably to damnation—there is the possibility of repentance and forgiveness—but because they are the "*capital*" or "*cardinal*" sins that beget other sins. Each of these sins is mentioned in the Bible, although the list is comprised in various ways (e.g., Gal 5:19-21).

Christianity's preoccupation with these sins may be due as much to the way they have been addressed in literature as in the Bible. One example is Chaucer's lengthy discourse in *The Canterbury Tales*. The Parson describes pride as the "root" of the tree from which springs the "branches" and "twigs" of a host of other vices:

> The root of these seven sins is pride, which is the general root of all evils; for from this root spring certain branches . . . And though it be true that no man can absolutely tell the number of the twigs of the evil branches that spring from pride, yet will I show forth a number of them . . . There are disobedience, boasting, hypocrisy, scorn, arrogance, impudence, swelling of the heart, insolence, elation, impatience, strife, contumacy, presumption, irreverence, obstinacy, vainglory; and many another twig that I cannot declare. ("The Parson's Tale," 565-66)

The Parson's elaboration on pride as "presumption" is particularly apt as commentary on Zophar's observation that the wicked try to exceed their limitations by reaching for the heavens: "Presumption is when a man undertakes an enterprise that he ought not to attempt, or one which he cannot accomplish; and that is called over-confidence" (567). The remedy for pride, according to the Parson, is humility or meekness: "That is a virtue whereby a man may come to have a true knowledge of himself, and whereby he will hold himself to be of no price or value in regard to his deserts, but will be considering ever his frailty" (572-73).

The Parson continues by describing gluttony as the sin that corrupted the world "as is well shown by the sin of Adam and Eve." This judgment is further expounded by St. Paul: "For many walk, of whom I have told you often . . . they are the enemies of the cross of Christ: whose end is destruction, whose God is their belly, and whose glory is their shame, who mind earthly things" (602). Like pride, gluttony expresses itself in many ways: drunkenness, indiscretion, bad manners, internal disorders, and forgetfulness. The remedy for gluttony is abstinence, which should be practiced not only for the sake of the body's health but for the sake of virtue (603).

For further examples of the seven deadly sins in the Bible and in literature, see R. Bond, "Seven Deadly Sins," *A Dictionary of Biblical Tradition in English Literature*, ed. D. Jeffrey (Grand Rapids MI: William B. Eerdmans, 1992), 698-701.

G. Chaucer, *Canterbury Tales: Rendered into Modern English* by J. U. Nicolson (Garden City NY: Garden City Publishing Company, 1934).

The account in Ezekiel 28 is particularly striking in this regard. A royal figure, the king of Tyre, is condemned for overstepping his boundaries of being mortal by claiming to have the wisdom and power of a god (28:2, 9). The judgment, however, is followed by a lament in which God grieves over the king's fall from glory (28:11-19). The language of the lament indicates that the king's story is sadly symptomatic of human history "east of Eden." The one who was once "full of wisdom and perfect in beauty" (28:12) has now forfeited wisdom for "the sake of splendor" (28:17); the one who once was "in Eden, the garden of God" (28:13) has now been driven from God's presence by the "garden cherub" (28:16); the one who "was blameless . . . from the day you were created" (28:15) is now cast away as "a profane thing" (28:16).

It is of course too much to say that Zophar has Ezekiel's story in mind when he describes the downfall of the wicked. Nevertheless, it is instructive to reflect on the contrast between God's grief over humanity's loss of Edenic possibilities and Zophar's concern to establish that loss as *the truth* of God's creational design. One clue to Zophar's preoccupation is the way he piles up the images that describe the inevitability of divine judgment that awaits the wicked. They are destined to "perish forever," like "dung" that is discarded as ugly and repulsive (v. 7), like a "dream" that has no external reality (v. 8), like persons who suddenly disappear leaving no trace behind (v. 9), like those whose life work leaves their children so impoverished they must beg for handouts even from the poor (v. 10). A final image completes the picture by making it clear that their destiny is to die before their time. While their bodies are still full of vigor and life, they lie down in the dust and die prematurely (v. 11).

Not once in this litany of judgment does Zophar express a word of lament about what is lost or what might have been if creation's possibilities had been tapped in other ways. From his perspective, the only

Seven Deadly Sins

Hieronymus Bosch (1450-1516). *The Seven Deadly Sins*. Museo del Prado, Madrid, Spain (Credit: Scala/Art Resource, NY)

relevant truth about creation's moral order is that the wicked will be punished. If Job can understand this, then Zophar is confident that the reality of divine judgment is reason enough for him to be more concerned with how *he has failed God* than with how *God may have failed him.*

Evil Is a Deadly Delicacy, 20:12-23

The centerpiece of Zophar's speech is the description of the wicked person's voracious and destructive appetite for evil (see further [Pride, Gluttony, and the Seven Deadly Sins]). With a variety of images, all tied to the metaphor of eating, he depicts evil as a seductively delicious but deadly food. Once ingested, it is like a poison for which there is no antidote. Zophar builds his case around four general assertions: the wicked ingest poisonous food that induces vomiting and death (vv. 12-16); they will not eat wholesome food that sustains life and gives pleasure (vv. 17-18); they are guilty of destroying not only themselves but others as well (v. 19); and they will be punished by God (vv. 20-23).

Zophar begins by comparing evil to food that is savory and sweet to the taste but bitter when swallowed (vv. 12-16). The wicked hold their food in the mouths, hide it under their tongues, and are reluctant to let it pass through to the stomach until they have squeezed every ounce of satisfaction from its taste. When swallowed, however, such food turns sour. It attacks the stomach like the darting tongue of a snake. Its poison shoots through the system until the wicked are forced to vomit it up, but there is no expelling this sickness; when it strikes it kills. The imagery of these verses is largely conventional and thus could be applied to a range of different situations. ["Things Sweet to the Taste"] In v. 15, Zophar steps out of the metaphor to provide two explanations of what he saying. (1) The food of the wicked is an image for ill-gotten "riches" or "wealth." In v. 19, he will define this more specifically as exploiting the poor. (2) The real cause of the wicked person's convulsions is not food, it is God: "God will make his stomach vomit them [riches] up" (NIV). The point of the analogy might be stated as follows: sin disagrees with God's design for the human constitution just as bad food disagrees with the stomach.[1]

The wicked not only eat bad food that sickens and kills; they cannot eat good food that strengthens and nourishes (vv. 17-18). Honey and milk symbolize the promise of prosperity in the land of Canaan. They are gifts of God that summon the faithful to forsake all and share in the blessing of a new life that is more full and more satisfying than can be experienced anywhere else (Exod 3:8, 17; 13:5; 33:3). [Symbols of Divine Blessing] The wicked cannot partake of this gift, for their appetite is for a diet of evil not good. Moreover, what they harvest by their labor they

"Things Sweet to the Taste"

The use of food and drink as a metaphor for things that may be superficially pleasing but ultimately dangerous is used in a variety of ways in literature. Consider the following examples:

With reference to politics and power:
Things sweet to the taste prove in digestion sour.
(*King Richard II*, I, iii, 235)

With eager feeding food doth choke the feeder.
(*King Richard II*, II, i, 37)

With reference to gossip:
The words of a whisperer are like delicious morsels;
They go down into the inner parts of the body. (Prov 18:8; 26:22)

With reference to deceit:
Bread gained by deceit is sweet,

But afterward the mouth will be full of gravel. (Prov 20:17)

With reference to disingenuous piety:
O ye of little faith—this is His cry, for in truth we are insatiable of miracles, and He flees us, as he fled the multitude He had miraculously fed with the five barley loaves and two small fishes; yet we of the multitude pursue Him, though He walk on the water to escape us (this according to John), and on the other shore in exasperation He turns, and delivers the accusation, "Ye seek me, not because ye saw the miracles, but because ye did eat of the loaves, and were filled."

And what a fine judgment . . . this is of our vaunted American religiosity! From the first Thanksgiving, ours is a piety of the full belly; we pray with our stomachs, while our hands do mischief, and our heads indict the universe. (Updike, 122-23)

John Updike, *A Month of Sundays* (Greenwich CT: Fawcett Crest Publications, 1974).

---

cannot swallow, and what they seize by their trading they cannot enjoy. In sum, they cannot sustain life by any means.

In v. 19, Zophar once again leaves behind the metaphor of eating to explain the reason why the wicked are judged to be more deserving of death than life. Their principal offense is that they have abused the poor. Three aspects of this abuse are delineated.[2] It is likely that each one is only an illustration of the multiple ways in which wickedness manifests itself as an economic and social violation of other persons. [CD: Attitudes Toward the Poor as a Definition of Wickedness]

• They "crush" (*rāṣaṣ*; cf. NIV: "oppress") the poor. The verb is used elsewhere to describe forms of economic oppression like fraud or extortion (in 1 Sam 12:3-4 the same verb is parallel to *ʿašaq*, "extort"; cf. Deut 28:33; Amos 3:1).

• They "abandon" (*ʿāzab*) the poor, which suggests that they "neglect" or "ignore" their legitimate demands for fair and equitable treatment under the law (cf. Deut 12:19; 14:27). The next line indicates that what the poor cry out for is the recognition of their property rights.

• They "seize" (*gāzal*; lit., "tear away, "rob," "take violent possession of") houses they did not build (cf. Mic 2:2). The charge hints that the wicked exploit the poor by seizing their property, perhaps because they have fallen in arrears on their rent, or simply because the wicked arrogate to themselves power to take what they want. In either case, they are guilty of taking advantage of persons whose social and economic status provides little means for resistance.

Zophar describes the punishment of the wicked in terms that are particularly appropriate for their crime (vv. 20-23). Even though they indulge their appetite for evil by consuming everything in sight until nothing they crave remains, their bellies are never content. At the very moment when they are most extended by their gluttony (lit., "in the fullness of his sufficiency") they are "narrowed" or "cramped" (v. 22, *yeṣer*; NRSV: "they will be in distress") by unremitting "misery." Their misery is their own making, but Zophar explains once more (cf. v. 15) that God is the true agent of their demise. God "rains "(*māṭar*) anger upon the wicked like food (v. 23). The imagery recalls the "raining" (*māṭar*) of mana from heaven upon Israelites in the wilderness (Exod 16:4; Ps 78:24), but with one important difference. On that occasion, God provided food in such abundance that it secured life against the threat of starvation. In this case, God responds to bloated gluttons by force-feeding them with food that hastens their death.

You Can Run, But You Cannot Hide, 20:24-28

The final section offers a graphic account of the inescapable punishment that befalls the wicked. They may flee from the close range jabs of an iron sword, but they will be pierced from afar by a still stronger bronze arrow.[3] If they manage to remove the arrow from their body (lit., from their "gallbladder"), then they will eviscerate themselves, and their bile will spill on the ground (cf. 16:13). If they attempt to protect their "treasures," literally "things hidden away," then a still more "hidden darkness" (*ḥōšek ṭāmûn*) will find them out. If there is any one left in their tents, then an "unfanned fire," that is, a fire not kindled by human hands, perhaps like the "fire of God" that fell unawares on the rebellious family of Korah (Num 16:35; but cf. Job 1:16!), will devour them. [The Rhetoric of Inescapable Doom] With a final image, Zophar reiterates the utter impossibility that the wicked can escape punishment. Should they survive the sword and the arrow, the darkness and the fire, then heaven and earth will rise up to testify against them (cf. Deut 32.1; Isa 1:2; Mic 6:1-2). The suggestion is that the crimes of the wicked imperil creation itself and trigger the forces of the cosmos to mount a swift and comprehensive response. Once they declare the guilty verdict, they give the climatic order. The flood waters are unleashed, the torrential streams are unloosed, and the house of the wicked is swept away.[4]

A Concluding Summary, 20:29

Zophar closes with a summary appraisal (v. 29) that returns his speech to its beginning thesis. What has been the truth about mortals (*ʾādām*) since they "were placed on the earth" (v. 4)? Zophar's answer contains three affirmations.

• Mortals are grammatically and morally defined by the adjective *rāšāʿ*, "wicked." Zophar's word for the human community is no longer simply *ʾādām*, as in v. 4, but *ʾādām rāšāʿ,* "wicked human." For all intents and purposes the two words now form one. Indeed, most modern translations do not bother with the word *ʾādām*. The gist of what Zophar is saying about *ʾādām* can be adequately rendered simply by translating "the wicked" (NRSV; cf. REB: "the rebel").

• Since "mortals "/ "the wicked" were placed on earth they have been assigned a "portion" (*ḥēleq*) and an "inheritance" (*naḥălāh*; NRSV: "heritage"). Both words commonly refer to the land that a family or clan hands down through successive generations. The "portion" is the tract or parcel of the whole that comes to individuals, which in turn becomes the whole of the land for them and for the life they will carve out within the borders of its possibilities and limitations (cf. Josh 15:13; 18:5-6; 19:9). "Inheritance" is an inclusive term for the life (land, possessions, successes, failures, etc.) that individuals and families leave to their ancestors (cf. Num 27:9-11; 36:3, 8; Ezek 46:16). This then becomes their "portion," and the process of receiving and bequeathing thus begins its next cycle.[5] In the context of Zophar's argu-

The Rhetoric of Inescapable Doom

The idea that a person may escape one disaster only to fall victim to another that is still more threatening appears in several other places, always as an expression of the inevitability of divine judgment:

Terror, and the pit, and the snare
are upon you, O inhabitant of the earth!
Whoever flees at the sound of the terror
shall fall into the pit;
and whoever climbs out of the pit
shall be caught in the snare. (Isa 24:17-18)

Alas for you who desire the day of the Lord!
Why do you want the day of the Lord?
It is darkness and not light;
As if someone fled from a lion,
and was met by a bear;
or went into the house and rested
a hand against the wall,
and was bitten by a snake. (Amos 5:18-19)

ment, the portion allotted to "the wicked" is wickedness and punishment; the inheritance they pass along to the next generation is
wickedness and punishment. Since mortals were placed on the earth,
this is the way it has always been. Wickedness and punishment is the
portion and the whole. The possibilities never get any larger, the limitations never get any smaller.

• The one who establishes and sustains the moral order the way it has
always been is God. Zophar has made this assertion twice before
(vv. 15, 23 ["his anger"]). Now he presses the argument with two final
references. The portion comes from God (*'ĕlōhîm*); the heritage is
ordained by El (*'ēl*).

By framing his response with references to *'ādām* (vv. 4 and 29) and
heaven and earth (vv. 4, 6 and 27), Zophar indicates that like his
friends he wants to teach Job about primordial truths. His objective is
to read creation's design and decode its truth about the nature and
destiny of being human. When he looks to creation, what he sees
compels him to warn Job that the punishment of wickedness is a reality
no human being can afford to ignore. He sees mortals reaching for the
heavens (v. 6), and he draws a line back to primordial temptations to
"be like God" (Gen 3:5, 22; cf. Ezek 28:2, 9). He sees mortals ingesting
wickedness like poisonous food, and he makes a connection with Adam
and Eve eating the fruit that poisons their life in the garden (Gen 3:6).
He sees the wicked vainly fleeing an angry God, and he knows from the
ancient story that there is nowhere they can hide from the judgment of
God (Gen 3:8-10). When punishment returns the wicked to the dust
from whence they came, Zophar is convinced that the primordial curse
continues its hold on the human journey (Gen 3:19).

For all his attention to the story of *'ādām*, however, Zophar's account
of its truth leaves one with the impression that he has started reading
(metaphorically) at Genesis, chapter two. His emphasis on sin, punishment, and banishment is part of the truth, but without the beginning
of the story it cannot be the whole truth. Perhaps Zophar's decision to
skip past the beginning is only a small shift in emphasis. He might well
believe that beginning at a different point is justified by Job's repeated
failure to accept the truth of what each of the friends has tried to show
him. Even if that is the case, Zophar's "exegesis" of the human story
invites the speculation that he is not only rereading it; he is rewriting it
as well. His strict retributionist theology is better served if the story is
changed to emphasize punishment instead of blessing: "So God *created*
human beings in his image" (Gen 1:27-28) . . . and God *cursed* them
. . . (cf. Gen 3:16-19). Everything between these two assertions—the

"O, If This Were Seen"	Oh, if this were seen,
Zophar reads creation's truths like a book of *endings* not *beginnings*. His bleak assessment recalls King Henry's reflections on the "book of fate" that pitches his kingdom into war:	The happiest youth, viewing his progress through, What perils past, what crosses to ensue, Would shut the book, and sit him down and die (*Henry IV, Part Two*, III, i, 53)

divine pronouncement of human goodness, blessing, and possibility—may be glossed over as unimportant or irrelevant. Zophar's edited version of what has been true since the beginning of time suggests that he is not content merely to repeat the traditional wisdom concerning the fate of the wicked. He is reinterpreting the creational plan for judgment in a way that leaves no one, and certainly not Job, unindicted. ["O, If This Were Seen"]

CONNECTIONS

In the second cycle of speeches, each of the friends narrows his focus to one topic: the inevitable punishment of the wicked (15:17-35; 18:5-21; 20:6-29). The preoccupation with this topic suggests that in the face of suffering like Job's those who would speak for God may deem it necessary to resort to one-dimensional theologies. As the last to speak in this cycle, Zophar offers readers an opportunity to assess this theological strategy. Toward that end, a question may be posed. Does innocent suffering require that one's theology be enlarged or reduced?

Zophar's first and second speeches offer a case study for those who would answer this question by choosing the latter alternative. A comparison of the two speeches suggests that when confronted by Job's persistent questions and complaints, Zophar steadily narrows his theology in several ways. He begins by recognizing that wisdom is "many-sided," or better, "double-sided" (11:6). This assertion enables him to construct a theology that is consonant both with what can be known about God and with what cannot be known. It is a theology inclusive of *both* certainty *and* mystery. He ends by focusing on one certainty that overrides all mystery: "know this . . . the exulting of the wicked is short" (20:4). Initially, he speaks as one who understands that theological assertions have to do with those who are "pure" and "clean" (11:4) *and* with those who are "worthless" (11:11). After listening to Job, he speaks as one whose theological lexicon has only one adjective to describe everyone. Each person can be adequately addressed as simply "the wicked" (20:29: *ʾādām rāšāʿ*). His first response addresses Job with a theology of judgment (11:10-11) *and* promise (11:13-19). His second response lacks any word of promise, save that of the promise of judgment (20:6-28). In sum, Zophar cuts and miters his theology in response to the challenge of suffering. He removes *mystery, righteousness, and hope* and builds a finished product exclusively from the materials of *certainty, sin, and punishment.* The question readers must ponder is, does his theology *fit* the dimensions of Job's life?

Anyone who has ever stood on Zophar's side of the dialogue with suffering can appreciate the importance of finding the irreducible minima of faith. When confronted by questions that probe and challenge valued convictions about God, it is instinctive to reach for certainties that can blunt the threat. When pressed to concede that righteousness is too often an unrewarded endeavor, there can be genuine comfort in retreating to an auxiliary truth: wickedness is always punished. When there seems no justification for promising restoration and healing, spokespersons for God may at least cling to the conviction that divine judgment is both deserved and necessary. If we consider these responses from Zophar's side of the encounter with suffering, then we must grant that they sound both reasonable and familiar. Who among us has not responded to tragedy and inexplicable suffering by reducing our theology to one-dimensional affirmations that allow us to go on believing in God's goodness even when we cannot fully explain the reason why? Surely one of the salutary effects of suffering on the faith community is that it forces everyone—theologians, counselors, ministers, teachers, lay persons—to search for bedrock affirmations that provide a place to stand when the ground beneath our feet shifts perilously toward unbelief. [When in Doubt, "Make a Fist" and "Go On with the Ritual"]

It is also the case, as anyone who has ever sat with Job on the ash heap will know, that sufferers yearn for nothing so much as a clear and certain word from God. Sufferers, no less than spokespersons, are compelled to search for the irreducible minima of faith. As defense against the forces that would break life, they too will reach for fragments of conviction that may robe the soul and shelter the spirit. One might think therefore that suffering automatically joins both the healer and the wounded in a mutual search for the truth about God. Zophar's rebuke of Job, however, serves as a sad reminder that this is not always

---

When in Doubt, "Make a Fist" and "Go On with the Ritual"

Gail Godwin describes the "fulfilled melancholy" that sustains the ministry of Father Gower, Rector of St. Cuthbert's, a small church in rural Virginia. It was not a spirit of self-reproachfulness or bitterness or even resignation but of animated sorrowfulness. It provided a "sort of sanity filter against the onslaughts of existence" that bedeviled his work and his faith. Father Adrian, his friend and colleague, recognizes the wisdom in this approach to ministry and confirms it with a personal anecdote:

There was a Jesuit studying with me in Zurich, at the Institute. I once asked him, "What if you as a priest stopped believing? What would you do then?" "Make a fist in my pocket," he said, "and go on with the ritual."

G. Godwin, *Father Melancholy's Daughter* (New York: Avon Books, 1991), 259, 274. On the frontispiece, Godwin dedicates the book to her own Father Melancholy, "the sorrowful but animating spirit who dwells within."

so. Zophar regards Job's quest for truth as a "censure" of his own (v. 2). Job's questions cast a cloud over Zophar's answers; his complaints undermine Zophar's certainties; his insistence that he is innocent plays havoc with Zophar's definition of sin, punishment, and justice. As Clines has put it, "if Job is right, everything Zophar stands for is wrong."[6]

Zophar's strategy for defending himself against the charge that his theology is wrong is to reduce the number of theological assertions that can be right. Absent mystery, Zophar's theology fills up with certainties and absolutes that squeeze out questions and squelch dissent. Absent any need to address the righteous, his theology is free to focus exclusively on the wicked as if they alone are deserving of a word from God. Absent the imperative to create hope, his theology achieves its objective when it establishes the reality of judgment. There can be little doubt that a theology built on the absolutes of sin and judgment is deeply rooted in the biblical tradition. And one does not have to look far to see that Zophar's theology continues to play a prominent role in modern religious life. One need only consider the influence of the "religious right," with its list of social and moral absolutes, to verify that the quest for "truth without any mixture of error"[7] remains very much alive and well. ["Increasing Sales with God and the Gideons"]

"Increasing Sales with God and the Gideons"

Elmer Gantry, the zealous evangelist created by Sinclair Lewis, provides one example of theology focused on the absolutes of sin and judgment. After just two years at the Mizpah Theological Seminary, so named perhaps in honor of the city at which Samuel judged the people of Israel (cf. 1 Sam 7:5-6), he knew "eighteen synonyms for sin, half of them very long and impressive, and the others very short and explosive" (72). He was certain that such a vocabulary would be extremely "useful in terrifying the as yet imaginary horde of sinners gathered before him." Toward that end, he dedicated himself to his studies, confident "of what he might be in twenty years, as a ten-thousand dollar seer" (73). Upon graduation, he embarked on his mission.

His ministry at one preaching venue illustrates the means he used to accomplish his objectives. He arrived in Lincoln, the next stop on his preaching tour, and was pleased to see a poster announcing the title of his sermon: "Increasing Sales with God and the Gideons." He fell into a conversation with the organizers of the revival about the best strategy for a "soul-saving campaign." His host offered the opinion that "even in the most aggressive campaign there is no need of vulgarizing our followers." Gantry preferred a different tactic. He would give them "the good old-fashioned hell. " "Like the hymn says," he continued, "the hell of our fathers is good enough for me." After some further discussion, the matter was resolved in Gantry's favor: "Oh . . . Let him sing it. He's brought in lots of souls on that." Yes indeed, Gantry responded, "Mangy little souls" (171).

At the end of the story, Gantry stands before yet another group of mangy little souls. His last words, offered as both a prayer and a declaration, announce the ultimate objective of his ministry:

Let me count this day, Lord, . . . as the beginning of a crusade for complete morality and the domination of the Christian church through all the land. Dear Lord, thy work is but begun! We shall yet make these United States a moral nation! (432)

S. Lewis, *Elmer Gantry* (New York: Harcourt Brace Jovanovich, 1927). On the frontispiece, Lewis dedicates the book to H. L. Mencken (1880–1956), longtime journalist at the *Baltimore Sun*. It is Mencken who said, "nobody ever went broke underestimating the taste of the American people." The quote refers to the marketing strategies employed by P. T. Barnum, American showman and circus entrepreneur. Lewis's novel hints that Mencken's observation may have other applications as well.

Notwithstanding its prominence and its appeal, Zophar's bare-bones theology invites close inspection. Is a theology without mystery, righteousness, and hope sufficient for the Jobs of the world? Zophar of course believes that it *is* and *always has been,* "ever since mortals were placed on the earth" (v. 4). Indeed, his theology hints that what Milton refers to as the "loss of Eden"[8] is a primordial truth that necessarily limits the possibilities and thins the imaginations of every human being since Adam. Perhaps he is right. Nevertheless, since his speech brings the drama in this book only to the mid-point, it is perhaps wise to withhold judgment until the last scene has been played out. Still, once we leave this chapter we may recognize one fact that will have to be figured into the final assessment. According to the present arrangement of the text, Zophar has nothing further to say after chapter 20. Job, by contrast, continues to question, complain, and search for more than two hundred verses. Therein lies a clue that we must consider carefully before answering the question that was posed at the outset of these reflections: Does innocent suffering require that one's theology be enlarged or reduced?

NOTES

[1] Cf. D. Clines, *Job 1–20* (WBC; Dallas: Word Books, 1989), 490.

[2] This delineation follows Clines (ibid., 491-492), who has discussed it in greater detail.

[3] The MT of verse 24 has "weapon of iron" (*nǎseq barzel*) and "bow of bronze" (*qešet nĕḥûšāh*). The first term may refer to any weapon or armament made of iron; a "sword" is a reasonable conjecture (cf. R. Gordis, *The Book of Job: Commentary, New Translation, and Special Studies* [New York: Jewish Theological Seminary of America, 1978], 220). The second term, if understood literally, is problematic, for one does not ordinarily think of a bow as "piercing" (*ḥālāp,* "passing through;" cf. Judg.5:26) its target. It is more likely that this is an example of synecdoche, a poetic device in which a part of an object represents the whole. In this case bow may be a term inclusive of arrow.

[4] The text of verse 28 is difficult. The word *yĕbûl* is better translated as "flood" (from *nābāl,* "stream, flood;"cf. NIV, REB, NJPS, JB) rather than as "possessions" (NRSV). What NRSV translates as "(things) dragged off" (*niggārôt*) is better translated as "rushing waters" or "torrents" (a participle from nagar, "pouring, flowing;" cf. NIV, REB, NAB), which provides a good parallel with *yĕbûl,* "flood."

[5] On the subtle distinctions between "portion" and "inheritance," see Clines, *Job 1-20,* 499.

[6] Clines, *Job 1-20,* 482.

[7] "Truth without any mixture of error" is the phrase that Southern Baptists used to describe the Bible (see the *Baptist Faith and Message Statement,* which was adopted in1963). It is cited here as only one illustration of how main line Protestant denominations in the United States may envision the absolute truths of God. One caveat may be added. In recent years, Southern Baptists have determined that this phrase is itself not absolute enough. The preferred term now is "inerrant."

[8] J. Milton, "Paradise Lost," Book I, l.4, *The Portable Milton* (New York: Penguin, 1976), 233.

JOB'S RESPONSE TO ZOPHAR: THE TRUTH ABOUT THE FATE OF THE WICKED IN THE MORAL ORDER OF THE WORLD

Job 21:1-34

Throughout the second cycle of speeches, the friends have tried to teach Job the truth about the fate of the wicked in the moral order of God's world (15:17-35; 18:5-21; 20:6-29). To this point, Job has mostly ignored their arguments. His primary concern has been not the wicked but the righteous, not the punishment due the guilty but the justice owed to the innocent. Job's question is this: Is there any place in heaven or on earth where the cries of the unjustly accused are heard and addressed (cf. 16:18-19; 19:23-27)? The friends insist that the answer to Job's question lies in the doctrine of retribution (see [Retribution]). They believe that as long as half of this doctrine can be verified—the punishment of the guilty—then the other half—the vindication of the innocent—should be assumed. Job now responds directly to this argument. He insists that even the half-truth the friends espouse is not really true. By refuting the claim that the wicked are punished, he destroys the single plank that supports the friends' theological house of cards.

Job begins (v. 2) and ends (v. 34) by attacking the friends' misguided efforts to offer him "consolation" and "comfort" (the same root, *nāḥam*, occurs in both places). They have failed him because their theology is wrong. He seeks to demonstrate this by raising three questions (vv. 7, 17, 28), each of which challenges their previous assertions about the wicked. He buttresses the challenge with facts that prove the truth is exactly the opposite of what the friends have claimed (vv. 8-16, 18-26, 27-33). When all the pretense is stripped away from their "comfort," nothing remains but lies (v. 34).

Job does not once address God in this speech, a fact that is consistent with the steady deterioration throughout the second cycle of his hope that God will answer him (see the commentary on Job 19). Even so, buried deep within his speech are two additional questions that suggest there remains a curious intersection between what Job

Structure of Job 21:1-34

21:1-6	Listen, look, and be appalled
v. 4	**"Is my complaint addressed to mortals?"**
21:7-16	Why do the wicked live long and prosperous lives?
21:17-26	"How often is the lamp of the wicked put out?"
v. 22	**"Can anyone teach God knowledge?"**
21:27-34	"You say, 'Where is the tent in which the wicked lived?'"

says to the friends and what he still wants to say to God. [Structure of Job 21:1-34] In v. 4, he asks, "Is my complaint *for adam* (*lĕ ʾādām*)?" Most interpreters take this to be a rhetorical question, which in effect assumes a negative answer: "No, it is not for mortals but for God." The second question is in v. 22: "Can anyone teach knowledge *to* (or *for*) God (*lĕʾēl*)?" This too is usually interpreted as a rhetorical question, which Job only raises in order to rebuke the friends for presuming to impose on God their own rigid version of the doctrine of retribution. Neither question occupies Job for very long, and we may suppose that he regards both as only peripheral to his larger agenda.

Still, the phrasing of the two questions (both with the preposition *lĕ*, "to," "for") invites the speculation that Job says more than he can presently recognize or comprehend. He seems certain that a cry for justice is primarily a cry *to* and *for* God. Can it be also a cry *to* and *for adam*, that is, a cry on behalf of all mortals who suffer as Job suffers? Similarly, Job knows that no one can teach justice *to* or *for* God. But can there be in Job's "rhetorical" question a latent hope that maybe, just maybe, every restless cry for justice somehow *teaches* or *models for* God an imperfect but resolute understanding of what it means for the "Judge of all the earth" to do what is just (cf. Gen 18:25)? Like Abraham, Job seems reluctant to pursue the ramifications of what he *almost* says. Still, he is raising questions, and though he may not know it yet, when one dares to question God's justice there are serious consequences for both creature and Creator. ["I Am an Encloser of Things to Be"]

Listen, Look, and Be Appalled, 21:1-6

When they first looked on Job, the friends were stunned by what they saw. The comfort they offered took the form of sympathetic compassion and respectful silence (2:11-13). Once they began speaking, however, everything changed. Even when Eliphaz couched his sympathy as the "consolations of God" (15:11), all Job heard was "windy words" (16:3) that ran on and on *ad nauseum*. Such words hold no comfort for Job. They only increase his misery by offering hackneyed theological doctrines that add unfounded guilt to innocent suffering. Job has had more than enough of such "comfort." [Comfort That Is Too Little and Too Late] He implores them to "listen" again to

Comfort That Is Too Little and Too Late

That comfort comes too late
'Tis like a pardon after execution.

(*Henry VIII*, IV, ii, 120)

"I Am an Encloser of Things to Be"

In "Song of Myself" (1855), Walt Whitman auda-
ciously envisions himself as a microcosm of life, a
full exemplar of the divinity and the humanity that exists in
every creature. The following excerpts are illustrative of
hubris (or faith?) undaunted by the possibility of striving to
be too much:

I am of old and young, of the foolish as much as the
     wise . . .
Stuff'd with the stuff that is course and stuff'd with
     the stuff that is fine . . .
A learner with the simplest, a teacher of the
     thoughtfullest,
A novice beginning yet experient of myriads of
     seasons,
Of every hue and caste am I, of every rank and
     religion,

A farmer, mechanic, artist, gentleman, sailor, quaker,
     Prisoner, fancy-man, rowdy, lawyer, physician,
     priest.

I am an acme of things accomplish'd, and I an
     encloser of things to be.

To the extent that what Job *almost* says in 21:4, 22
may strike us as no less audacious and unsettling than
Whitman's verse, we may find it instructive to ponder the
observation of the Canadian novelist and playwright
Robertson Davies (1913–1995). In an essay on Greek
tragedy he writes: "We mistrust anything that too strongly
challenges our ideal of mediocrity. But we can admire
nobility when it is safely in the past, in literature and in
art."

W. Whitman, "Song of Myself," *Leaves of Grass*, edited with an introduction by J. Loving (Oxford: Oxford University Press, 1990), 42, 71.
R. Davies, "The Noble Greeks," *Happy Alchemy: On the Pleasures of
Music and the Theatre*, ed. J. Surridge, B. Davies (New York: Viking Press,
1997), 9.

his words (v. 2: *šim'û šāmôaʿ*; cf. 13:17), to "look" again at his suffering
(v. 5a: *pĕnû ʾēlay*; cf. 6:28), and once more to acknowledge the shock of
what they see by placing their hand on their mouth (v. 5b). If they are
to speak meaningfully to his pain, then they must suspend their
mockery long enough (v. 3) to understand calamity from the victim's
perspective. This would provide far more consolation for Job than all
the words they have hurled at him thus far.

If they would make an honest effort to *understand* Job, rather than
only speak *at him*, then the friends might discern a deeper truth about
tragedy. They might see that his complaint is not addressed to them
personally but to the God for whom they speak (v. 4a; see further
below). They might see that suffering like his so taxes one's resources
and "shortens one's spirit" (v. 4b: *qāṣar* + *rûaḥ*; NRSV: "impatient")
that they can never be comforted simply by hollow platitudes.[1] They
might see that from the sufferer's perspective "impatience" is not a vice
(cf. 4:5) but a virtue. It signals a resolve to search for something more
in life, even when there is no reason to believe that it exists. [The
Impatience of Job] And they might see the awful price this resolve exacts
from those who cry out for justice to a silent God. If they will but look
at Job, they will know that to stare into the face of a God who does not
answer is to be overcome with horror that chills the flesh (v. 6).[2]

Job's rhetorical question in v. 4a is worthy of an additional comment.
His immediate concern is to make clear to the friends that his primary

The Impatience of Job

Christian tradition normally reveres Job for the *patience* he exhibits in the prologue not for the *impatience* he shows in 21:4 and throughout the dialogues. This way of appropriating Job has much to do with the classic account in Jas 5:11: "Behold we count them as happy which endure. Ye have heard of the patience of Job, and have seen the end of the Lord; that the Lord is very pitiful, and of tender mercy" (KJV).

It is rather commonly assumed that James either misreads or ignores the Job who protests and complains through nine tenths of the story in order to recommend a supposedly more pious model of faith to the Christian community. By this view, those who truly trust God will endure whatever hardships life may bring without doubting God's mercy or denying God's justice. In other words, faith is sometimes like unrequited love. It requires those who pine for a response to their overtures to sit "like patience on a monument, smiling at grief" (*Twelfth Night*, II, iv, 110).

J. Gerald Janzen has suggested, however, that it is not James who has misread Job but we who have misread James. Janzen compares Job's "turbulent and energetic refusal to give up" on the quest for God's justice to the importunate widow in Luke 18:1-8 (cf. the importunate friend in Luke 11:5-9). From Jesus' perspective the persistent cry for justice from one who has been wrongly treated is a virtue not a vice. It is the mark of an impatience that exemplifies faith by refusing to accept the status quo as what must be or should be. Jesus asks a question of those who hear his teaching that might also be asked of those who are tempted to dismiss or ignore Job's complaints: "When the Son of Man comes, will he find faith [like this] on earth?"

For further discussion of the "patience" and "impatience" of Job, see S. Garrett, "The Patience of Job and the Patience of Jesus," *Int* 53 (1999), 254-264, and **[Choosing Between "What Is Written" and "What Is Read"]**.

J. Gerald Janzen, *Job* (Atlanta: John Knox, 1985), 159.

complaint is addressed to God, not to them. Thus the question—"Is my complaint addressed to mortals (*lĕ 'ādām*)?"—seems to take for granted a negative answer. But given the ongoing exploration within the dialogues of what it means to be a human being before God, it is worth considering whether Job's question might have a second and deeper meaning. [*'ādām*] Although he would speak *to* God, perhaps he also speaks *for* or *with regard to* (the preposition *lĕ* may be used to convey both meanings)[3] every victim of injustice who strains to hear some meaningful word in a theology that assumes their plight is the result of sin and failure. Perhaps his complaint embodies the hopes and dreams of every sufferer who yearns for something more than flat declarations like "human beings are born to trouble" (5:7) or preemptory questions like "Can mortals be righteous before God" (4:17) and "What are mortals, that they can be clean?" (15:14).

There may be a deep irony in v. 4 that even Job does not yet realize or comprehend. He insists that his complaint is addressed to God, yet the remainder of his speech is in fact addressed exclusively to the friends. He says that his arguments are not directed to mortals, yet when he questions the moral foundations of God's justice, he speaks with an anguish that every innocent sufferer recognizes. When Job says "listen" to my words and "look" at my suffering, perhaps he addresses *both* God *and 'ādām*. If this were true then the biggest irony of all would be the suggestion that neither God nor *'ādām* can be all they should be without listening carefully and looking closely.

Why Do the Wicked Live Long and Prosperous Lives? 21:7-16

Job begins his attack on the doctrine of retribution by challenging the claim that the wicked enjoy only temporary prosperity. If this is so, then why do the wicked live such long and prosperous lives (v. 7)? The truth about the wicked is exactly the opposite of what the friends say. The offspring of the wicked are neither cut off nor impoverished (18:19; 20:10); they are securely established (v. 8). The homes of the wicked are not threatened with loss or destruction (15:28; 18:14-15; 20:26, 28); they are peaceful and beyond the reach of God's judgment (v. 9). The possessions of the wicked do not decline or disappear (15:29; 20:15, 18); they multiply without fail (v. 10). The wicked do not live in fear of the terrors that await them (15:21, 24; 18:11; 20:24-25); their lives are carefree, joyous, and filled with the revelry of song and dance (vv. 11-12). [Rejoicing and Recoiling at the Sound of Music] The wicked are not subject to violent and premature death (15:30, 32-33; 18:13-14; 20:11); they complete their days in prosperity, then die peacefully and descend to Sheol (v. 13).

In truth, the fortunes of the wicked are those normally associated with the blessings God bestows upon the righteous, which even the friends seem to recognize (5:23-26; 8:20-21; 11:15b-19). They are in fact very like the blessings of family, home, prosperity, and joy that Job once knew (1:2-5). The prologue reports that it was once Job's custom to regard such blessings as a seamless extension of loving God and turning away from evil. It was not he but the *satan* who wondered if piety was only a down payment on prosperity (1:7). From Job's perspective, righteousness is a way of life not a strategic plan for advancement. Now, in view of what he has lost "for no reason" (2:11), the choice between righteousness and wickedness seems problematic indeed. Perhaps the *satan* was right after all. Perhaps life is a game of

---

'ādām

AΩ The word *'ādām*, "mortal," occurs twenty-seven times in Job. The word *'ĕnôš*, "person," occurs eighteen times. The predominate sense of both these words in Job is that human beings are frail and flawed creatures who cannot be righteous or just in God's eyes (e.g., 4:17; 7:17; 9:2; 14:1; 15:14; 25:4, 6; 34:15). A third word, *geber*, "male" or more generally "person," occurs fifteen times in Job. This word typically carries overtones of "strength" (from the root *gāber*, "be strong, mighty") and thus provides an interesting parallel to the words *'ādām* and *'ĕnôš*. Three texts illustrate the different ways this word is used by Job, the friends, and God: "Let the day perish in which I was born, and the night that said, 'A *geber* is conceived'" (3:3); "Can a *geber* be of use to God?" (22:2); "Gird up your loin like a *geber*, I will question you, and you shall declare to me" (38:3; 40:7).

This range of words for naming and describing the human being provides a window on to an important debate in the book of Job. Are human beings inherently weak or strong? Are they endowed with a capacity to be righteous and just in God's eyes or only wicked and guilty? Job raises the critical question early in the drama: "What are human beings that you make so much of them?" (7:17).

ᾺΛΗ ΠΕϹΩΝ Α΄ΔΑΙΜΟΡΙΑ, ΤΩΝ ΠΑΙΔΩΝ Η ΕΥ ΦΕΟΣΩΙΝ· ΗΝ Α΄ΤΟ ΠΛΗΡΟΙϹΘΗ ΑΙ
ΛΟΙ ΚΑΙ ΚΙΘΑΕΑΙ ΚΑΙ ΤΗΙ ΠΑΜΑ ΥΦΩΙ ΑΙ ΜΒΗ Α΄ΚΟ ΑΙ ΚΑΤΑΥΛΟΩΤΑΙ ΑΙ
ΔΕ ΤΗϹ ΨΥΧΗϹ Η΄ΔΟΝΑΙ, ΔΙΕ ΓΕΙΡΟΝΤΑΙ· ΚΑΙ ΟΙ ΠΑΡΟΝΤΕϹ, ΤΗΙ Α΄ΚΟΛΑϹΩ ΜΕΛΩ
ΔΙΑ ΚΑΤΑΚΗΛΟΩΤΑΙ· ΗΝ ΟΙ ΤΩΝ Α΄ϹΕΒΩΝ ΠΑΙΔΕϹ Α΄ϹΕΛΓΩϹ Ε΄ΞΑΞΟΝΤΑΙ
ΤΑΙϹ ΘΗ ΤΕΤΑ ΜΒΝΑΙϹ Η ΔΕ ΑΙϹ ΤΑϹ ΧΘΕΑϹ ΑΥΤΩΝ Ε΄ΠΙΝΑΙΝΟΝΤΑϹ ΚΑΙ
ΠΡΟϹ ΤΗΝ ΦΩΝΗΝ ΤΩΝ Ο΄ΡΓΑΝΩΝ Ε΄ΠΙΚΡΟΤΟΩΝΤΑϹ:
ϹΥΝΕ ΤΕΛΕϹΑΝ ΔΕ Η΄Ν Α΄ΓΑΘΟΙϹ ΤΟΝ Β΄ΙΟΝ ΑΥΤΩΝ:

Job and Musicians

Job and Musicians (Catena sur Job). 14th C. Illumination. Bibliotéque Nationale, Paris.

Rejoicing and Recoiling at the Sound of Music

In both text and tradition, Job is associated with music in a variety of ways. The prologue pictures Job and his family celebrating the good fortunes of their life by enjoying feasts of great merriment (1:2-5). The biblical text does not mention music specifically, but the *Testament of Job* (1st C. BCE–1st C. CE) adds a report of Job's musical skills as a way of confirming his piety and his ministry to the community:

And I used to have six psalms and a ten-stringed lyre. I would rouse myself daily after the feeding of the widows, take the lyre, and play for them. And they would chant hymns. And with the psaltery I would remind them of God so that they might glorify the Lord. If my maidservants ever began murmuring, I would take up the psaltery and strum payment in return. And thus I would make them stop murmuring in contempt. (14:1-5)

This picture of Job as a "minister of music" is subsequently confirmed in the book of Job. When he prepares the final summation of his case for vindication, Job contrasts his present mourning with former times when his musical instruments were tuned to joy: "My lyre is turned to mourning, and my pipe to the voice of those who weep" (30:31).

In 21:12, Job complains that the wicked also celebrate life with a full symphony of musical sounds from stringed instruments ("lyre," *kinnôr*), wind instruments ("pipe" or flute, *ûgāb*), and percussion instruments ("tambourine" or drum, *tōp*). His complaint indicates that wickedness may be enjoyed with the same revelry of song and dance as righteousness. The only difference is that the righteous seem to be tuned by God for discordant mourning, while the wicked sing merrily along without a care for what God thinks of them or their celebration (21:14-15).

It is perhaps ironic that artists often depict Job's friends as musicians. In some cases, Job is pictured as receiving them gladly, even offering payment in return for the soothing sounds they offer. In other cases, the relationship between Job and the musicians seems more ambivalent and suggests that the friends use music to mock Job rather than to comfort him.

S. Terrien, *The Iconography of Job Through the Centuries: Artists as Biblical Interpreters* (University Park PA: The Pennsylvania State University Press, 1996), 105-26.

calculating means and ends. If so, those who choose evil over good would appear to have made the wiser investment. The wicked are a case in point. Job's quotes them as saying to God that they have no interest in knowing the ways of righteousness and no need for the piety that goes along with it. If God will just leave them alone, then they can secure prosperity by their own power (vv. 14-16a).[4]

It seems rather surprising that after citing such strong evidence in support of the prosperity of the wicked Job should conclude this part of his speech by categorically rejecting their way of life (v. 16b). If his options are either to be righteous and suffer "for no reason" or to be wicked and prosper "for no reason," can there be any compelling motivation for not choosing pleasure over pain? For *reasons* perhaps yet unclear to him, Job has resolved to pursue another option. He will be a *righteous sufferer* who *protests*. He will *love* God by *questioning* God's justice. He will *resist* every theology that promises restoration in return for repentance of sins that have not been committed. Instead, he will *contend* with God, even if it costs him his life (see the commentary on 13:13-28). Job is of course not the first person to recognize that there is often a huge gap between what we want to believe about God and the evidence we expect to see that will confirm our belief. [CD: Job's Kindred Spirits in the Land of Lament] But his persistence in pushing the envelope of what rebellious faith requires suggests that at this mid-way point in the dialogues, he is well on the way to be becoming perhaps *the* parade example of what it means ultimately to be "blameless and upright" (1:1, 8; 2:3) in the eyes of God. ["Who Names Not Now with Honor Patient Job?"]

> **"Who Names Not Now with Honor Patient Job?"**
>
> John Milton accords Job a prominent place in the pantheon of heroes, "the great benefactors of mankind," whose glory and renown compels even God to applaud:
>
> I mention still
> Him whom thy wrongs, with saintly patience borne,
> Made famous in a land and times obscure:
> Who names not now with honor patient Job?
> (*Paradise Regained*, Book III, ll. 92-95)
>
> J. Milton, "Paradise Regained," in *The Portable Milton*, ed. D. Bush (New York: Penguin Books, 1977), 581.

"How Often Is the Lamp of the Wicked Put Out?" 21:17-26

Job directs his second challenge to the claim that the wicked are regularly and predictably punished. Bildad has argued that the "light of the wicked" may flicker for a time, but it will inevitably fail of its own accord (18:5-6). He insists that no matter what the wicked do, "calamity" will find them and bring them down (18:12). Zophar claims that on the "day of anger" God decrees punishment for the wicked (20:28-29). He insists that the wicked are no more endurable than "dung," no more substantial than a fleeting "dream" When one looks for the place they once occupied, there is no trace that they ever existed (20:7-9). Job responds to all of these assertions with a question: "How often?" (v. 17). The implied answer is "Seldom, if ever!" In reality, it is not the wicked, but the innocent, like Job, who are driven like chaff before the wind of God's anger (v. 18; cf. 13:25).

Job continues by citing an objection, which the friends have already hinted they might use to defend their doctrine (vv. 19-21). Should the wicked escape judgment, it is only because God has decided to delay the punishment until it can be administered to their children (v. 19; cf. 5:4; 20:10). Such an argument has some precedent in Israel's traditions (cf. Exod 20:5; Deut 5:9; 2 Sam 12:13-14; Lam 5:7), but it also has to face stiff challenges (Jer 31:29-30; Ezek 18:1-4). Job argues against it not because he can cite precedents as well as the friends, but because he knows from experience that it does not work. When the wicked die, the question of their innocence or guilt goes to the grave with them. They cannot know and they will not care whether their children live to be "honored" or "belittled" (cf. 14:21). If they are to be truly judged, then they must "see" their destruction with their own eyes, they must "drink the wrath of the Almighty" in their own lifetime, before their time ends (vv. 20-21). Once they die, all questions about their injustice are moot. [Justice in the Next Life? "In Your Dreams, Sucker"]

To buttress his argument that death is no substitute for justice, Job adds a further observation (vv. 23-26). Death is no respector of persons. Whether one is righteous or wicked, the end result is the same. One person dies in "full prosperity," like the wicked who have gorged themselves on the cream of life (vv. 23-24; cf. 20:12-17). Another person dies in "bitterness of soul," like Job (3:20), never having tasted the good things of life that the wicked have feasted upon (v. 24). In neither case is there evidence of any correlation between the way they lived and the way they die. Both lie down in the dust; neither is anything more than food for the worms. [Food for Worms]

At the center of this pericope (vv. 17-26) there stands a question that seems at first sight to be an odd interruption of Job's argument. "Can anyone teach knowledge to God?" (v. 22; NIV). Some interpreters suggest that the question is out of place in Job's mouth. Perhaps Job is

Justice in the Next Life? "In Your Dreams, Sucker"

Michael Dorris suggests that justice is one of those "palliative myths," like the tooth fairy, which we cling to in order to believe that every loss will be cancelled out eventually by an equal or better reward. In the theology of the friends, this view of justice promises Job that "what goes around comes around." If he will only be patient, then he will see that the wicked will one day "reap what they sow." Dorris's response to this myth, while perhaps less measured than Job's, may nonetheless not be far removed from Job's thinking: "Uh huh. In your dreams, sucker." Dorris elaborates as follows:

Religion is not the opiate of the people, the conception of justice is. It's our last bastion of rationality, our logical lighthouse on a stormy sea, our anchor. We extend its parameters beyond death—if we haven't found equity in this life, all the great belief systems assure us, just wait till the next. Or the next, or the next. Someday our prince will come.

That may be true, but the paradigm is based on faith, not fact. We can believe in the tooth fairy until the alarm goes off, but unless there's a benevolent parent to value our loss as worth a quarter, we wake up with used calcium, not negotiable currency, under our pillow.

M. Dorris, "The Myth of Justice," in *Outside the Law: Narratives on Justice in America*, ed. S. Shreve, P. Shreve (Boston: Beacon Press, 1997), 77.

Food for Worms

📖 "Worms" and "fire" were common descriptions of the fate prepared for the wicked (e.g., Isa 66:24; Sir 7:17; Jdt 16:17; Mark 9:48). Such descriptions gave rise in the Middle Ages to numerous paintings that used grotesque images of worms to depict God's eternal damnation of lost souls to the tortures of hell. See, for example, this rendering by the Flemmish artist Hieronymous Bosch (1450–1516).

The Garden of Earthly Delights

Hieronymus Bosch (1450-1516). Left panel. Paradise abounds with plants and animals; an owl in the fountain represents knowledge; God between Adam and Eve in the Foreground.

Museo del Prado, Madrid, Spain.
(Credit: Erich Lessing/Art Resource, NY)

quoting what he presumes the friends believe he is guilty of trying to do.[5] Perhaps he is asking the question satirically in order to rebuke the friends for trying to impose their rigid views of retribution on God.[6] Another alternative is to regard the verse as either misplaced from one of the friends' speeches or added by a later scribe who inserted into Job's speech a pious objection to his attitude toward God.[7] On the surface, the question seems clearly rhetorical no matter who the speaker may be. From any perspective, it would be natural to assume that no one can teach God anything (cf. Isa 40:13-14). Beyond that, it would be absurd to think that a mortal could teach the Judge of the world what justice means.

Despite the apparent oddity of this verse, it is plausible to suggest that it is not inconsistent with Job's own thoughts. Indeed, one may consider the question not as an interruption of his argument but rather as the pivot upon which it turns. Job has offered a threefold critique of the moral order the world:[8] (1) God's judgment of the wicked is too infrequent to be regarded as a firm and reliable principle. After all, "how often" does it happen? (vv. 17-18); (2) God's punishment is too slow and too indirect to be effective. If it is reserved for a later generation, then it is impossible to make a clear connection between the sin and the judgment (vv. 19-21); (3) If there is no distinction in life or death between the righteous and the wicked, if these two very different kinds of persons come to one and the same end, then there is a moral randomness in God's governance that leaves no one certain about what constitutes good and evil (vv. 23-26).

Given such an assessment, it is not surprising that Job contemplates the necessity of embarking on an impossible mission: teaching God what it means to do justice.[9] He has previously come to the pained conclusion that "there is no justice" (19:7); yet, rather than yield to despair, he determines to live and work as if "there is a judgment" (19:29). Now he surveys the world that the friends claim is testimony to God's moral governance, and he determines that both they and God need to take another look. Job offers instruction about what really happens in those places where justice is supposed to be so evident. Once more he suggests that the friends *and* God may learn something from looking at the world through his eyes. [Is There "One Moral Law for Heaven and Another for the Earth"?]

"You Say, 'Where Is the Tent in Which the Wicked lived?'" 21:27-34

Job's third challenge continues the argument against the claim that calamity befalls the wicked. He anticipates that the friends will plot new ways to object to his critique (v. 27), and he quotes their argument before they can say it. They will ask "Where is the house of the great

---

Is There "One Moral Law for Heaven and Another for the Earth"?

With the biting satire for which he was so famous, Mark Twain ponders the truism that God is merciful and just and that we, by contrast, must be patient and forebearing. In "Thoughts on God," he asks whether both clergy and parishoners ought not think more carefully about God's moral compass.

It is plain that there is one one moral law for heaven and another for the earth. The pulpit assures us that wherever we see suffering and sorrow which we can relieve and do not do it, we sin, heavily. *There was never yet a case of suffering or sorrow which God could not relieve.* Does He sin, then? If He is the source of Morals He does—certainly nothing could be plainer than that, you will admit. Surely the source of law cannot violate law and stand unsmirched; surely the judge upon the bench cannot forbid crime and then revel in it himself unreproached. Nevertheless we have this curious spectacle: daily the trained parrot in the pulpit gravely delivers himself of these ironies, which he has acquired at second-hand and adopted without examination, to a trained congregation which accepts them without examination, and neither the speaker nor the hearer laughs at himself. It does seem as if we ought to be humble when we are at a bench-show, and not put on airs of intellectual superiority there.

M. Twain, "Thoughts on God," *The Oxford Book of Essays*, chosen and ed. J. Gross (Oxford/New York: Oxford University Press, 1991), 268-69.

one now?"; "Where is the tent in which the wicked man lived?" (v. 28). The parallelism between "great one" (*nadîb*; NRSV: "prince") and "wicked" (*rĕšāʿîm*) suggests that the reference is to those who have attained their high rank in society through violence and extortion.[10] The friends repeatedly assert that the houses of the wicked will not survive the destruction God has prepared from them (15:28, 34; 18:21; 20:26-28). Because they are confident that if they say something, then it is automatically true, they can therefore ask the question with no measure of doubt about its answer.

Job counters that if they ask any traveler who has gone from town to town (v. 29: *ʿôbêrê derek*; NRSV: "those who travel the roads"; cf. Lam 1:12; 2:25; Ps 80:12 [MT 80:13]; Prov 9:15), then they will get contradictory evidence that cannot be denied (vv. 30-33). The truth is that the wicked are "spared" on the day of calamity. No one confronts them with their injustice, no one forces them to make recompense for all they have done. Indeed, instead of being "carried away" (v. 30: *yābal*; NRSV: "rescued") to judgment, they are "carried" (v. 32: *yābal*) in a grand funeral procession to their final resting place where they are buried with great ceremony and celebration. A guard stands watch over their tomb. In death as in life they rest peacefully in the sweetness of the earth. When one truthfully assesses their end, it has nothing of the ignominy the friends have described. In reality, Job insists, when one lives by wickedness, it is much more likely that one will die with honor and public acclaim (cf. Eccl 8:10).

Job closes the second cycle with words that return the drama to its beginning point and at the same time provide an important evaluation of where things now stand (v. 34). The friends have come to offer consolation (2:11). Job has judged them to be "miserable comforters" (16:2). He begins this last speech by imploring them to limit their consolations to listening for the truth in what he is saying about suffering (21:2). Now, after enduring six speeches from them he offers two summary appraisals of their theology of comfort. (1) It is "empty" (*hebel*; cf. 7:16; NRSV: "a breath"). It is the same word Qohelet uses to describe that which is without merit, unreliable, and therefore utterly useless (e.g., Eccl 1:1: "vanity of vanities"). (2) It is *māʿal* (NRSV: "falsehood"). The basic meaning of the root word is "to be unfaithful."[11] On Job's lips, the charge cuts two ways. The friends have been unfaithful *to him*. When he most needed their support, partnership, and loyalty, they broke the sacred trust of their relationship (see the commentary on 6:14). What they have done has a similar effect on him as when a spouse abandons a marriage (cf. Num 5:12, 19-20, 27). More importantly, the friends have been unfaithful *to God*. When persons violate another human being, they violate something sacred, which is the equivalent of breaking faith with God (Num 5:6; cf. Lev 6:2 [MT 5:21]). Job declares the friends' theology to be a form of sacrilege. They treat a friend as an enemy, the truth as a lie, and God as little more than an accomplice in their cover-up of injustice.

CONNECTIONS

In this, his seventh speech from the ash heap, Job offers a summary appraisal of the moral order of the world that flatly contradicts the theology of the friends. The wicked are not punished; they prosper in both life and death. God's justice is not reliable; it is random and too inconsistent to be regarded as a firm moral principle. Even if one grants the premise that judgment comes later rather than sooner, an argument Job rejects, it remains the case that the connection between sin and punishment, righteousness and reward, is too indirect to comfort or instruct those whose misery is all too present. Job's first words about creation from the ash heap were a conflicted amalgam of curse and lament (Job 3). Now, in the seventh speech he surveys the world God blessed and hallowed (Gen 2:3), the world the friends insist bears true witness to the "very good" design of God's creation (Gen 1:31), and he judges it to be a tragic failure. At this mid-point in the dialogues, after he has spoken for more than three hundred verses, Job seems not to have moved very far from the questions that shaped his initial assessment of life in the "garden of Uz": "Why is light given to one in misery, and life to the bitter of soul?" (3:20; cf. 21:25). ["Perhaps His Experiment Went Spectacularly Wrong"]

Despite the despair conveyed by this assessment, Job has in fact made a number of significant moves in the second cycle that signal he is no longer at the same point as he was in chapter 3.

• Echoing Abel's cry for justice, he has petitioned creation itself, heaven and earth, to join him in his suit against God (16:18-22).

• He has ceased to long for death, which seemed to be the one consistent objective of his speeches in the first cycle (7:19-21; 10:18-22; 14:18-22), and has resolved instead that there is something

---

"Perhaps His Experiment Went Spectacularly Wrong?"

In *The Children of Men*, P. D. James's fictional story of the tragedy and sterility of life in the year 2021, Theo Faron, Oxford historian, observes that even God seems to be worn out by the requirements of justice. In an unsettling conversation with a cab driver, he offers the following assessment.

Do you believe God exists? Perhaps His experiment went spectacularly wrong, sir Perhaps He's just baffled. Seeing the mess, not knowing how to out it right. Perhaps He only had enough power left over for the final intervention . . . Whoever He is, whatever He is, I hope He burns in His own Hell.

On first encounter such words are raw and shocking, an audacious attack on God that seems beyond what even Job would say. With a second reading, however, perhaps Theo's candor only speaks Job's curse with different words.

P. D. James, *The Children of Men* (New York: Alfred A. Knopf, 1992), 130.

more to live for and believe in than injustice. There is a "redeemer" who will bring to fruition his quest for vindication (19:25).

• Job has become painfully aware, however, that the fight for justice can never be waged only in the future. There must be some way to make a down payment on justice in the present. If there is not, then the gap between reality and hope is too wide for Job to cross. Job has determined to play a role in bridging that gap. He will stare into the face of the reality that says "there is no justice" (19:7), and he will plead and challenge and question until he transforms its truth into a new assertion: "there is a judgment" (19:29).

The opening words in chapter 21 focus each of these moves with two imperatives that hint at where Job is going: "listen carefully to my words" and "look closely at me." Both imperatives invite a question: *Who* needs to listen to Job and look at him? Three answers may be considered.

(1) The first and obvious answer to this question is that the *friends* need to listen and look at Job. They have built a theology so preoccupied with God's judgment that they have effectively walled out everyone but themselves. The wicked are excluded from their company, because God has judged them unworthy of inclusion. The righteous who suffer, like Job, have no place in their midst, they believe, because their credentials are fraudulent. If they were truly righteous, then they would not be suffering. If their suffering is righteous, then they should not be complaining. If their suffering is unrelieved, then they should be confessing sin and seeking God's forgiveness. Whatever their mistake may be, sufferers like Job must change their ways before they can have communion with the friends and their God.

In the final analysis, when the friends expound their theology, the only ones who will feel at home in their presence are persons who sound like them, think like them, and act like them. In effect, they will be preaching to themselves, courting the affirmation of cloned self-congratulation. Job insists this will not change until their theology is broken open by the truth of tragedy. And this cannot happen until the friends are willing to listen to his questions and complaints and look squarely at the pain that makes them necessary, urgent, and authentic.
["Without Constancy, a Person Cannot Make a Commitment"]

(2) A second and less obvious answer to the question is that *ʾādām, all human beings*, need to listen and look at Job. Job himself gives little consideration to the possibility that he may have something to say to the larger human community. He is conscious only of the need to cry out for help in the desperate hope that someone will respond. When he asks "Is my complaint addressed to mortals (*lĕ ʾādām*)?" (v. 4), it is

---

"Without Constancy, a Person Cannot Make a Commitment"

📖 In assessing the need of speaking in ways that "give voice to the victim," Terence Tilley turns to George Eliot's classic text, *Adam Bede*. Tilley focus on the conversation that takes places in the prison between Hetty, a diarymaid, and Dinah, the devoted friend who "pledges to be [her] sister to the last." Tilley contrasts the constancy that Dinah's friendship offers Hetty with that of a chaplain, who might pretend more than is real:

Of course, a chaplain might drop in and promise to sit with her to the end, but there is little possibility of Hetty seeing him as being able to make the same sort of commitment that Dinah made. Being, and being perceived as, as a person of constancy are necessary conditions for making such a commitment succesfully. *Without constancy, a person cannot make a commitment, only a bargain.*

T. Tilley, *The Evils of Theodicy* (Washington, DC: Georgetown University Press, 1991), 196 (emphasis added).

---

likely that he assumes the answer is "No." He is preoccupied with speaking *to* God. He has no designs on addressing a larger audience.

And yet, because we as readers have the advantage of hindsight, we know that Job was wrong to assume he did not speak to and for us all. For everyone who has suffered and asked "Why?"—for everyone who has asked "Why?" only to hear some spiritual authority say "You must not question God"—Job is no stranger. For everyone who has wanted to believe but could not, tried to fight but failed, hoped for something more only to find endless emptiness and silence, Job is a companion. No doubt Job would have been surprised by his post-mortem fame. He has cursed the day of his birth and repeatedly expressed a wish to die. Yet he lives on through the centuries in the minds and imaginations of countless persons who know his struggle to be theirs as well. Elie Wiesel has with justification referred to Job as "our contemporary." He makes the case as follows:

> Through the problems he embodied and the trials he endured, he seems familiar—even contemporary. We know his story for having lived it. In times of stress it is to his words that we turn to express our anger, revolt or resignation. . . . In him we find the solitary conscience of Abraham, the fearful conscience of Isaac, the torn conscience of Jacob. Whenever the Midrash runs short of examples, it quotes Job, no matter what the topic—and it is always pertinent.[12]

(3) A third possible answer—one Job could hardly contemplate or welcome—is that *God* needs to listen, look, and learn from him. When Job asks, "Can anyone teach knowledge to God? "(v. 22), he knows all too well that the only plausible answer is "No." God is too powerful. Who can coerce a response, if God is unwilling to give it (cf. 9:3)? God's wisdom is too vast, what can a mere mortal do to add to it or correct it (cf. 11:7-12)? God's justice it too inscrutable, God's decisions too unassailable. Who can say to God "What are you doing?" (9:12). And yet, if Job's assessment of the moral order is correct, one could not

fault him for yielding to the temptation of thinking that *someone* needs to tell God that things are not working as they should. Even if he might contemplate such a thought, however, Job must surely consider himself the least likely person to step forward as God's teacher. If he cannot persuade the friends that he has a legitimate perspective of the world, then what are the odds that God will pay attention to him? Still, it is instructive to consider whether it is possible that Job's previous wonderments are still at work shaping the outer edges of his imagination: "What are human beings that you make so much of them?" "Why have you made me your target?" (7:17, 20).

One analogue for reflecting on how these wonderments *might* be weighed from God's perspective is Atticus Finch, the central character in Harper Lee's novel *To Kill a Mockingbird*.[13] Finch is a white attorney in a small Alabama town who accepts the responsibility of defending Tom Robinson, a black man wrongly accused of raping a young white woman. A great number of the people in the town assume Robinson is guilty, and they cannot understand why Atticus would risk his reputation and career on a case that cannot be won. Atticus explains his reasons for taking the case: "Before I can live with other folks I've got to live with myself. The one thing that doesn't abide by majority rule is a person's conscience" (109).

Atticus pours all his energies into Tom's defense, but the jury finds him guilty nonetheless. As he leaves the courtroom, members of the black community seated in the balcony begin rising to their feet. Reverend Sykes, the black preacher, nudges Atticus's daughter who is watching her father make his lonely exit. "Miss Jean Louise, stand up. Your father's passin'" (214). It is their way of honoring a man willing to fight for justice, even when he loses. If we think of God as overlooking the Joban drama from heaven's balcony, then we may ponder what God's response might be to having witnessed Job's refusal to betray his own conscience. Is it possible that God might stand up and applaud Job's efforts? Might God see in Job's resolve a commitment to justice, however frail and fallible, that merits the imperative, "Stand up one and all, Job is passing"? It is of course an impossible thought. Then again, if Job's seventh speech, like God's seventh-day blessing, represents the shouldering of a sacred burden to exercise stewardship of creation's order, perhaps such praise for the one created "in the image of God" is not so far-fetched after all.

NOTES

[1] R. Haak ("A Study and New Interpretation of QSR NPS," JBL 101 [1982]: 161-67) has noted that *qṣr rûaḥ*, "short of spirit" (Mic 2:7; Job 21:4; Exod 6:9; Prov 14:29), and *qṣr nepeš*, "short of soul" (Num 21:4; Judg 10:16; 16:16; Zech 11:8) are used with two connotations: "weakness" and "impatience." Compare, for example, Exod 6:9 where *qṣr rûaḥ* (NRSV: "broken spirit") occurs in synonymous parallelism with *mĕ ʿăbōdāh qāšāh*, "cruel slavery," to indicate the weakness of the Israelites, and Prov 14:29, where *qṣr rûaḥ* (NRSV: "one who has a hasty temper" [i.e., an "impatient one"]) is antithetically parallel to *ʾerek ʾappāyîm*, "whoever is slow to anger." Haak interprets Job 21:4 as a satirical question in which Job announces that he is diminished or weakened because God seems powerless to punish the wicked (164).

[2] See the suggestive paraphrase of 21:6 by Mitchell: "When I think of it I am terrified and horror chills my flesh" (S. Mitchell, *The Book of Job* [New York: Harper Collins, 1992], 52).

[3] On the semantic range of this preposition, see B. Waltke, M. O'Connor, *An Introduction to Biblical Hebrew Syntax* (Winona Lake IN: Eisenbrauns, 1990), 205-12.

[4] Verse 16a is difficult for several reasons, and various proposals have been offered, including deleting the verse altogether (G. Fohrer, *Das Buch Hiob* [KAT; Gütersloh: Gerd Mohn, 1963], 338; cf. M. Pope, *Job* [AB; Garden City NY: Doubleday, 1979], 158-59). NRSV understands these words as a rhetorical question posed by Job. The answer such a question would expect is "Yes, the prosperity of the wicked is in fact their own achievement." The Hebrew text, however, does not contain an interrogative word. An alternative suggestion, plausibly argued by R. Gordis (*The Book of Job: Commentary, New Translation, and Special Studies* [New York: Jewish Theological Seminary of America, 1978], 230), is to interpret these words as a continuation of Job's quotation of what the wicked are saying: "Indeed, our prosperity is not in His hands!"

[5] Gordis, *Book of Job*, 231; J. Gerald Janzen, *Job* (Atlanta: John Knox, 1985), 156.

[6] E. Dhorme, *A Commentary on the Book of Job* (Nashville: Thomas Nelson Publishers, 1967), 318; H. H. Rowley, *Job* (The Century Bible; Ontario: Thomas Nelson, 1970), 189; N. Habel, *The Book of Job: A Commentary* (OTL; Philadelphia: Westminster Press, 1985), 329.

[7] Pope, *Job*, 160; cf. S. R. Driver and G. B. Gray, *A Critical and Exegetical Commentary on the Book of Job* (Edinburgh: T and T. Clark, 1921), 187-88.

[8] The analysis here follows C. Newsom ("The Book of Job," in vol. 4 of *NIB* [Nashville: Abingdon Press, 1996], 493), who argues that throughout ch. 21 Job is not attacking the friends personally but rather their understanding of the moral order of the world.

[9] Similarly, S. Terrien, "The Book of Job," *IB*, vol. 3, ed. G. Buttrick (New York: Abingdon Press, 1954), 1070:

> In a tone not of anxious humility and doubt, but on the contrary of courageous defiance, he [Job] declares that God needs to be taught a lesson. He will reveal to him what actually happens in the world of men. God must be told. Job will offer him some knowledge.

[10] Dhorme, *Commentary on the Book of Job*, 321.

[11] For the range of meanings of this word, see R. Knierim, "*Mʿl* to be unfaithful," E. Jenni, C. Westermann, eds., *TLOT*, vol. 2 (Peabody, MA: Hendrikson Publishers, 1997), 680-682.

[12] E. Wiesel, "Job: Our Contemporary," *Messengers of God: Biblical Portraits and Legends* (New York: Touchstone, 1994), 211, 212.

[13] H. Lee, *To Kill a Mockingbird* (New York: Popular Library, 1962).

ELIPHAZ'S THIRD RESPONSE TO JOB: "CAN A MORTAL BE OF USE TO GOD?"

Job 22:1-30

The Third Cycle: The Dialogue Breaks Down, Job 22:1–27:23

After six speeches and one hundred seventy-five verses the friends have said virtually everything they have to say to Job. It is not surprising, therefore, that the third cycle contains a good deal of duplication, even triplication, of arguments that have already been advanced in the first two cycles of speeches. Eliphaz returns for a third time to his main anthropological argument, this time phrased as "Can a mortal be of use to God?" (22:2-5; cf. 4:17-19; 15:14-16). He also joins Bildad (8:5-7) and Zophar (11:13-20) in promoting a retribution theology that cedes all power to God (22:21-22). Bildad returns to his image of God as incomparably powerful (25:2-6; cf. 18:5-21).

The speeches are not only well-worn, they also seem to be disintegrating. Indeed, the present arrangement of the text suggests that the dialogue between Job and his friends breaks down and breaks off. Bildad's speech (25:1-6) is unusually short—six verses—while Job's response (26-27) is disproportionately long. Zophar's final speech is missing altogether, thus when Job finishes responding to Bildad, there is an awkward pause (27:1), and then Job goes on, as if adding to what he has already said to Bildad. Some try to restore the symmetry of the dialogues, hence the order of the drama by rearranging the text to what is assumed to be its original form. Bildad's speech may be lengthened by subtracting 26:5-14 from Job's words and adding them to Bildad's. Zophar's speech may be reconstructed from parts of Job's speech in 27:13-24. There is, however, no clear evidence that the original text was any different from what the MT preserves.[1] A wiser course is to allow the text as it stands to serve as an interpretive guide. The disarray in the dialogues may be the author's way of suggesting that the dialogue between Job and his friends has reached an impasse where all arguments falter. Indeed, one might even suggest that at this point Job is so familiar with the friends' arguments that he can speak their words for them. They need not bother to speak, because he already knows what they are going to say. Thus for example, it is plausible to read 24:18-25 as Job speaking Zophar's words;[2] 26:5-14 as his parroting of Bildad;[3] and 27:13-24 as his preemption of Zophar's last speech (see further [*Making* the Text Work]).[4]

Job also returns to old issues, but now it is these issues that dominate, as the friends grow increasingly silent and their arguments fall away, one by one. In his seventh and final speech in the dialogues (23-24), for example, Job complains once again about the absence of God (cf. 9:11; 13:24). Once more, he proclaims his innocence, first with the exclamation of an oath (27:2-6), then with a series of formal oaths of innocence (31) that make a legal claim on God's appearance in court (cf. 9-10; 13; 16:18-21; 19:21-29; see further [The Trial Metaphor in Job]). Once more, he concludes that the absent and silent God who assaults him is more an enemy than a savior (27:7-12; cf. 10:1-17; 16:6-7; 19:6-12; 30:16-19). S. Terrien notes that as the dialogues limp to an end, the friends *lose* and Job *gains* focus. The friends become more and more impatient, disconcerted, and angry. Job becomes more and more determined, stable, and resolute in his decision to press the case for justice.[5] Whether Job's resolve is commendable is the question behind the question that hangs over his last words in chapter 27: "Will God hear their [people who have been labeled "wicked"] cry when trouble comes upon them?" (27:9). ["Was He a Brave Man or a Hypocrite?"]

"Was He a Brave Man or a Hypocrite?"

In grayish doubt and black despair
I drafted hymns to the air and the air,
Pretending to joy, although I lacked it.
The age had made lament redundant.

So here's the question—who can answer it—
Was he a brave man or a hypocrite?

Czeslaw Milosz, "In Black Despair," *New and Collected Poems, 1931–2001* (New York: Harper Collins, 2001), 691.

COMMENTARY

As he has done in his two previous speeches, Eliphaz begins his final address with rhetorical questions that lay the foundation for his response to Job (vv. 2-5; cf. 4:2, 6-7; 15:2-3). In this third speech, however, both the tenor and the intent of Eliphaz's questions have changed. In chapter 4, the questions are gentle and sympathetic. Their intent is to encourage Job to hold fast to the promise that his integrity will ultimately result in his vindication: "Is not. . . the integrity of your ways your hope? Think now, who that was innocent ever perished?" (4:6-7). In chapter 15, the questions are sharper and more defensive. They challenge Job's claim to innocence and rebuke him for contesting God's moral governance with arguments that are "not profitable" and "not useful" (15:3). Now Eliphaz's questions move beyond the subtleties of sympathy and challenge and proceed directly to an outright condemnation of Job's arrogance—"Can a mortal be of use to God?" (v. 2)—and a firm declaration of his guilt—"Is not your wickedness great?" (v. 5). Such questions provide the basis for Eliphaz to indict Job on two counts. The first is his moral failure (vv. 6-11), the second, his theological error (vv. 12-20). Eliphaz concludes his speech with a promise of restoration (vv. 21-30), which once again he couches in conditional terms: "*If* you return to the Almighty . . . *then* you will delight yourself in the Almighty." [Structure of Job 22:1-30]

Eliphaz has reached a conclusion about more than just Job's guilt. He speaks as one who knows the bottom-line truth about the role humans are assigned in their relationship to God. In his first response, Eliphaz asked Job to consider whether mortals could be "righteous" and "pure" in relation to God. His assessment was that moral imperfections make it impossible for human beings to question God's governance of the world (see the commentary on 4:17-21). In his second speech, Eliphaz returned to the same issue with a slightly reframed question: "What are mortals that they can be clean?" (15:14). He pressed Job to recognize not only that he is unclean, that is, sinful, but also that he is barred from participating in the divine council, where God's plans for the cosmos are hammered out and implemented (see the commentary on 15:14-16). Eliphaz now raises a third question that indicates he is ready to declare the last truth about the one and only role humans can play in their relationship to God: "Can a mortal be *of use* (*skn*) to God?" (v. 2). The point of the question is to ask whether there is anything a sinful, inferior human being can bring to the relationship with God that will *benefit* or *be of value* to God. In v. 21, Eliphaz uses a different form of the same verb to answer his own question. The one thing humans can do is "*agree* (*skn*) with God," by which Eliphaz means *yield* to God's authority and *submit* to God's judgments. From Eliphaz's perspective, *subordination* is the fundamental prerequisite for relationship with God. *If* Job will give up the pretense of seeing, knowing, and understanding what God is doing (cf. 10:13; 13:1-3; 19:6), *if* he will "*receive* instruction" (v. 22) from God—not *give* it, as Job seems to think is not only possible but necessary (cf. 21:22)—*then* perhaps he can still be of some use to God.

[CD: "Know Then Thyself, Presume Not God to Scan"]

Structure of Job 22:1-30

22:1-5	*Rhetorical* questions: "Can a mortal be of use to God?"
22:6-11	The presumption of guilt: Job's moral failures
vv. 6-9	The alleged crimes
vv. 10-11	The consequent judgment
22:12-20	The presumption of guilt: Job's theological error. "You say, 'What does God know?'" (v. 13)
22:21-30	A final summons: "Agree with God"
vv. 21-22	Agree, be at peace, receive, take it to heart
vv. 23-26	*If . . . then*
vv. 27-30	The benefits of repentance

AΩ Rhetorical Questions

Question	Assumed Answer
#1 "Can a mortal (*gāber*) be of use (*sakan*) to God?"	No
#2 "Can a wise man (*maškîl*) be of use (*sakan*) to him?"	No
#3 "Is there any advantage (*ḥēpēš*) to the Almighty if you are righteous (*tiṣdaq*)?"	No
#4 "Is there any gain (*beṣaʿ*) to him if you perfect (*tattēm*) your ways?"	No
#5 "Is it because of your piety (*yirʾāteka*) that he arraigns you?"	No
#6 "(Is it because of your piety) that he enters into a lawsuit with you?"	No
#7 "Is not your wickedness great?"	Yes
#8 "Is it not rather because there is no end to your iniquities?"	Yes

Rhetorical Questions, 22:1-5

Eliphaz opens with a series of rhetorical questions that provide the foundation for the rest of his speech. He and the friends have routinely used rhetorical questions as a strategy for leading Job to the answers they already know. That is the case here as well. Eliphaz asks questions that he believes can only be answered in the way he has already decided. The first six questions (vv. 2-4) assume a negative answer, the last two (v. 5), a positive answer. [Rhetorical Questions]

It is the case, however, that rhetorical questions are effective only when both the speaker and the addressee agree that the answers are so clear they need not even be spoken. At the most fundamental level, such questions assume and require both silent consent and willing submission. If either of these conditions is lacking, then the questions may quickly spin out of control, inviting unexpected and unwanted detours from the argument they are meant to reinforce. Such is the problem for Eliphaz. His assumptions about God and about Job are not verified either by the narrative framework of the book or by Job's acceptance of their truth. In fact, each of the questions ironically invites an answer that is exactly the opposite of what Eliphaz needs to make his case persuasive. ["Who But Infants Question in Such Wise?"]

"Who But Infants Question in Such Wise?"

Was it a friend or foe that spread these lies?
Nay, who but an infant questions in such wise?
'Twas one of my most intimate enemies.

Dante Gabriel Rossetti, "Fragment," *The Poems of Dante Gabriel Rossetti. Vol. II: The House of Life and Shorter Poems* (New York: Brentano's, 1923), 245.

Does God have an investment in the human condition? Does God derive some benefit from a human being's reverence and fidelity? Can humans contribute something to the relationship with God that sustains and advances God's intentions for the design of creation? Despite Eliphaz's assumptions, the prologue suggests that the answer to each of these questions is "Yes." God initiates the conversation with the *satan* by calling attention to Job's perfection or blamelessness (*tām*) and his unparalleled piety (he "fears [*yērê*] God"; 1:8; cf. 2:3), precisely the attributes Eliphaz dismisses as being of no concern to God. By God's own statement, the *satan's* question about whether one "fears/reverences God for nothing" (1:9) does indeed hang on Job's remaining the faithful and pious person that God has unequivocally declared him to be. If Job does not pass the test that God invites and permits, then God stands to lose more than just the wager with the *satan*; God's own assessment of the human capacity to "turn away from evil" will have proven to be false. In a very real sense, then, the entire Joban drama hinges on the possibility that the answer to Eliphaz's question "Can a mortal be of use to God?" is "Yes."

Similarly, the assumption that Job's "wickedness" is great and that his "iniquities" are beyond number is controverted by both God's assessment and Job's testimony. In the prologue, the narrator introduces Job as someone who resolutely "turns away from evil" (1:1). So preoccupied is he with avoiding even the potential for sin in his household that he offers preemptory sacrifices, just in case his children may have unwittingly erred (1:5). In turn, God twice confirms Job's incomparable piety by declaring that he continues to "turn away from evil" (1:8; 2:3), despite the horrendous calamities that might well have pressed him toward other responses. Moreover, Job is by no means willing to agree to Eliphaz's assumption about his sin. He repeatedly insists that he is innocent (6:28-30; 9:15, 20-21; 10:7; 16:17; 19:6). He vows on his life that God's initial assessment of him is not wrong (13:13-15). The reader knows, therefore, even if Eliphaz does not, that when he asks the question "Is not your wickedness great?" the answer he will *not* accept from Job—"No"—is *precisely what he invites*. ["Let Your 'Yes' Be Yes and Your 'No' Be No"]

The Presumption of Guilt: Job's Moral Failures, 22:6-11

Having presumed Job's guilt, Eliphaz now proceeds to invent the crimes that fit the charge. He calls no witnesses, he produces no evidence. Indeed, in chapter 31 Job will explicitly deny that he is guilty of any of the crimes Eliphaz imputes to him. The compulsion to indict Job is based not on evidence but rather on Eliphaz's commitment to the doctrine of retribution: *if* there is suffering, *then* sin must be the cause. As Gordis puts it, "Finding his theory of Divine justice contradicted by the facts, Eliphaz proceeds to the time-honored device of *adjusting the facts to fit the theory*" (emphasis added).[6]

The list of Job's crimes is presented in the form of a typical prophetic judgment speech.[7] [Imitation May Not Always Be the Sincerest Form of Flattery] The

"Let Your 'Yes' Be Yes and Your 'No' be No"

What Eliphaz seeks to extract from Job is precisely what he will not give: a false confession of guilt. Should Job agree to the answers that Eliphaz expects from him, he would necessarily relinquish his commitment to the truth; he could no longer claim to be one who refuses to lie (Job 6:28). More importantly, he would in effect be denying God's own assessment of him as one whose "integrity" is beyond question (Job 2:3; cf. 27:5; 31:6).

The Letter of James commends integrity of speech as essential for the well-being of the community. "Above all," James says, "let your 'Yes' be yes and your 'No' be no" (Jas 5:12; cf. Matt 5:37; 2 Cor 1:17). If a person's "yes" and "no" can be counted on to be truthful, then not only their speech but their actions can be trusted. One need not

guess or interpret, read between the lines or wonder, whether words harbor some secret agenda that seeks to manipulate the truth for selfish gain. It is surely not insignificant that James's exhortation comes immediately following his recommendation of Job as one of the luminaries of faith whose refusal to give up his integrity is called "blessed" (5:11; see further **[The Impatience of Job]**).

Both Job's integrity and James's exhortation receive fitting commentary in the famous counsel offered by Laertes to his sister Ophelia:

This above all—to thine ownself be true;
And it must follow, as the night the day,
Thou canst not be false to any man. (*Hamlet*, I, iii, 79-80)

offenses (vv. 6-9) are introduced with the particle *kî*, "because" (v. 6; NRSV: "for"), and rounded off in v. 10 with the summative conjunction *ʿal kēn*, "therefore," which stipulates the consequent punishment (vv. 10-11). Eliphaz declares Job guilty of taking pledges from the poor in repayment of debt (v. 6). Israelite law provides a procedure for debt repayment but strictly circumscribes the conditions in order to protect the debtor against unfair and unreasonable burdens that may jeopardize life. For example, a creditor may not seize a debtor's millstones as collateral, because without them a family cannot grind the grain that provides their food (Deut 24:6). Similarly, if a cloak is taken as security against a debt, it must be returned at night, because without it its owner is vulnerable to the ravages of the weather (Exod 22:26-27; Deut 24:12-13). Eliphaz insinuates that Job has abused the practice by exacting gratuitous pledges (*ḥinnam*; NRSV: "for no reason") in order to seize something that he is not owed.

Job's hard-heartedness is further displayed by withholding water from the thirsty and food from the hungry (v. 7; cf. Isa 58:7, 10; Ezek 18:7, 16). His failure to respond positively to even the most basic needs of life marks him as one with the oppressor who uses power and position to possess whatever he wants and to deny whatever he pleases (v. 8).[8] Nothing stands in the way of his greedy and selfish abuse of persons. Widows and orphans are regularly singled out in the Bible as particularly needful of God's compassion (Exod 22:22-23; Deut 10:18; 24:17; Isa 1:17; Jer 22:3). Eliphaz accuses Job of turning them away "empty-handed" and "crushed" (v. 9). If it is true that Job withholds compassion from ones so desperately in need of help, then this proves that he "has reached the depths of degradation and perversity."[9]

Job's alleged crimes fall within the realm of social and economic abuses that are widely condemned in both ancient Near Eastern cul-

Imitation May Not Always Be the Sincerest Form of Flattery

The logic of Eliphaz's argument is, *"Because* X has occurred, *therefore* Y will be the result" (see further **[Retribution]**). His strategy, like that of the prophets he imitates, is to substantiate the causal connection between sin and punishment. The following prophetic speeches illustrate the conventional form:

Because (*kî*) their mother has played the whore . . .
Therefore (*lākēn*) I will hedge up her way with thorns;
and I will build a wall against her,
so that she cannot find her paths. (Hos 2:5-6 [MT 2:7-8])

Because (*kî*) you have forgotten the God of your
    salvation,
and have not remembered the Rock of your refuge;
therefore (*'al-kēn*), though you plant pleasant plants
    . . .
though you make them grow on the day you plant
    them,
and make them blossom in the morning that you
sow; yet the harvest will flee away in a day of grief
and incurable pain. (Isa 17:10-11)

Because (*kî*) the shepherds are stupid,
    and do not inquire of the Lord;
therefore (*'al-kēn*) they have not prospered,
    and all their flock is scattered. (Jer 10:21)

Although his logic is sound and his form for presenting it is consistent with prophetic precedent, there is a major flaw in Eliphaz's indictment of Job. For the prophets, the truth of the "because" section rests on the authoritative discernment of God. For Eliphaz, the "because" section in 22:6-9 is a complete fabrication (cf. E. M. Good, *In Turns of Tempest: A Reading of Job with a Translation* [Stanford: Stanford University Press, 1990], 274). His imitation of the prophets is little more than "smoke and mirrors." As Edmund Burke (1729–1797) once said about Croft, whose style some considered to be a good imitation of the great Samuel Johnson:

"No, no," said he, "it is not a good imitation of Johnson; it has all his pomp, without his force; it has all the nodosities of the oak without the strength; it has all contortions of the Sibyl without the inspiration." (Boswell, *Life of Johnson*, vol. 4, 59, cited in *The Oxford Dictionary of Quotations*, 3rd ed. [Oxford: Oxford University Press, 1979], 112, #14)

tures and in Israel. [CD: Common Condemnations] It is possible that Eliphaz draws upon this traditional understanding in order to portray Job as a typical example of those who build their fortunes on the backs of the poor and the vulnerable. It may be, however, that Eliphaz seeks to discredit Job by indicting him with his own words.[10] Job has accused God of abusing human beings as slaves (7:1-6), of creating a world in which "might makes right" (9:14-24), and of stripping innocent victims of their dignity and their hope (19:9-10). By bringing theses charges, Eliphaz now suggests that Job does not have the moral authority to accuse anyone, certainly not God, of injustice. In political terms, his strategy is similar to an incumbent's attempt to deflect an opponent's challenge by waging a smear campaign that publicly discloses the skeletons in his own closet. ["Let Anyone Among You Who Is Without Sin Be the First to Throw a Stone"]

Once he has defined Job's crimes, Eliphaz pronounces the judgment they require (vv. 10-11). "Snares" are prepared for his capture at every turn, "sudden terror" strikes when he least expects it, darkness obscures every avenue of escape, swelling waters portend his imminent destruction. This litany of judgment recalls the dire predictions that Eliphaz and his friends have previously announced (cf. 15:21-24; 18:8-11;

"Let Anyone Among You Who Is Without Sin Be the First to Throw a Stone"

When the scribes and Pharisees press Jesus on his understanding of how the law applies to a woman caught in adultery, he responds by calling them to accountability for their own actions: "Let anyone among you who is without sin be the first to throw a stone at her" (John 8:7). When Jesus' opponents heard this challenge they gave up their argument and "went away" (John 8:8).

Eliphaz, who fancies himself as specially endowed with God's revelation (cf. Job 4:12-16), condemns Job for accusing God of injustice while covering up his own violations of the law. Unlike the scribes and Pharisees, however, Job will not drop his case. He believes truth is on his side, and he will not simply go away. The ineffectiveness of Eliphaz's strategy is a prudent reminder of the truth Jesus teaches: the condemnation of another succeeds or fails in direct proportion to the merits of the one making the charge.

20:25-26). There is however one important difference between what has already been said and what Eliphaz now solemnly declares. The judgment Eliphaz decrees is no longer an abstract fate only generally applicable to the wicked at large. It is now a concrete reality that is prepared specifically for a wicked person named Job.

The Presumption of Guilt: Job's Theological Error, 22:12-20

With yet another rhetorical question, Eliphaz lays the foundation for imputing to Job theological error. When he asks the question "Is not God high in the heavens?" (v. 12), he knows that Job will answer "Yes." Job's mistake, as Eliphaz sees it, is that he draws the wrong conclusion from the right answer. God is indeed exalted above all things, and this means that God sees all, knows all, and judges the righteous and the wicked with an unerring discernment that is worthy of a mortal's praise and submission (cf. Pss 14:2; 33:13-14; Isa 40:22-23). Eliphaz accuses Job of twisting this truth into a dangerous lie.

He claims to have heard Job say that transcendence is a liability that diminishes God's capacity to judge fairly. God is too remote from the human condition to know what is going on. God "judges," but the "deep darkness" that separates God from those on whom the verdict falls obscures God's adjudication (v. 13). God roams about on the dome-like border (*hug*, "circle, vault," cf. Prov 8:27; Isa 40:22) that connects heaven to earth's horizon, but heavy clouds so veil God's vision that God cannot see clearly what true justice requires (v. 14). It is of little concern to Eliphaz that Job has not said such things about God. In fact, Job has said very nearly the opposite. His claim has been that God sees every move humans make and weighs even the smallest deed with a disproportionate severity (7:19-20; 10:4-6; 13:27; 14:3, 6; 16:9). All that matters to Eliphaz is his conviction that Job is guilty. On that basis, he reads between the lines of Job's complaint to infer that he speaks like the wicked who boast that God cannot see and does not care what happens on earth (Pss 10:11; 73:11; 94:7; Isa 29:15; Zeph 1:12).

Eliphaz believes that Job's flawed theology provides the rationale for his sinful behavior (vv. 15-16). Is it not true that Job has intentionally chosen the "old way (*'ōraḥ 'ôlām*) that the wicked have trod" as the blueprint for his life? The question recalls Jeremiah's plea to those who would be faithful to recognize that when they stand at the moral crossroads of life, they must seek the "ancient paths" (*nětibôt 'ôlām*) that lead to the "good way" and walk in them (Jer 6:16). If they choose wrongly, then they open themselves to certain disaster (Jer 6:19). It is an ancient truth that Eliphaz claims Job now verifies by his own suffering. By following the paths of those whose punishment was to have their life snatched away prematurely and their foundations suddenly washed away by the flood, Job has embarked on a journey that will dead-end in grief.

Verses 17-18 are very similar to what Job has already said in 21:14-16 (compare 22:17a and 21:14a; 22:17b and 21:15a; 22:18b and 21:16b). For this reason, some would delete these verses as a gloss that interrupts the logical connection between vv. 16 and 19.[11] Duplication is not in itself sufficient reason to excise these verses, however, for in the third cycle speakers often resort to repeating arguments that their colleagues have already presented (see the commentary on 24:18-25, 26:5-14, 27:13-24). It is preferable to read through, not around, these verses and thus to consider them as part of Eliphaz's strategy to rebut Job by quoting his own words as evidence of his guilt. In this connection, readers may note two subtle features in the argument, which suggest that like the scribes and Pharisees Jesus rebuked, Eliphaz is "straining out a gnat" in order to "swallow a camel" (Matt 23:24).

First, although Eliphaz quotes Job correctly, he takes his words out of context. Job has not spoken these words as his own thoughts. He has cited them as evidence of what the wicked are saying. They are part of his *complaint* about the wicked, not his *approval*. On close inspection, it is clear that *both* Job *and* Eliphaz are in agreement when they insist that "the plans of the wicked are repugnant" to them (v. 18b). Secondly, Eliphaz embellishes Job's words with a concession that exceeds what Job has said. Eliphaz admits that "he [*God*] filled their houses with good things" (v. 18a), and then, as if he is unwilling to pursue the implications of what he has said, he breaks off his thought almost in mid-sentence. What Job has said is that the wicked believe they can secure their prosperity *by their own hands*, if God will only leave them alone (21:16a). With an irony that perhaps only the reader can appreciate, Eliphaz's indictment of Job has the effect of condemning the accuser, not the accused.

Eliphaz concludes this section with a traditional understanding about the confirmation of divine justice the righteous derive from witnessing the punishment of the wicked (vv. 19-20). When the guilty are found out, the innocent rejoice (*yiśmāhû*; NRSV: "are glad"; cf. Ps 107:42a) and celebrate by adding their ridicule (*yil'ag*; NRSV: "laugh to scorn"; cf. Ps 2:4 with reference to God's laughter) to the wicked person's shame and misery. When their adversaries are eliminated, and the last trace of their ill-gotten rewards is nullified by God's judgment, then the righteous will declare with absolute certainty that justice has been served. Eliphaz's mention of the righteous prepares for his following summons to Job, which holds open the possibility that he too will see justice triumph if he will only repent (vv. 21-30). But once again Eliphaz demonstrates that there is a huge disconnect between what he promises and what Job needs. *The punishment of the wicked* goes only halfway in resolving the equation of Job's grief. Job longs for justice, which to his mind cannot be truly celebrated until the righteous are so "appalled" at the *suffering of the innocent* that they rise up in his defense (17:8-9). [Half of the Law Does Not Equal Justice]

A Final Summons: "Agree with God," 22:21-30

Eliphaz concludes his speech with a summons to repentance that echoes the counsel both Bildad and Zophar have previously offered (8:5-7; 11:13-19). Like them, Eliphaz frames his appeal with the conventional "if . . . then" conditions that anchor his retribution theology (vv. 23-25). Here, however, Eliphaz sets forth a *pre*condition that Job must satisfy even before the process of repentance can begin. Before he enters into dialogue with God, *he must agree to agree* with whatever God says. Four imperatives define what Job must do if the conversation is to go forward.

• Job must "agree" (*hasken*) with God and "be at peace" (*šĕlām*; v. 21). The first verb is a different form of the word *skn* (NRSV: "be of

---

Half of the Law Does Not Equal Justice

In his novel *A Frolic of His Own*, William Gaddis offers a withering critique of the American civil justice system run amok. Far too often the wheels of justice spin out of control, leaving litigants with an unsatisfying forum for telling their story in a way that publicly restores their integrity and honor. One of the principal characters in the novel is Harry Lutz, a corporate lawyer whose candid assessment of the double-dealing greed that characterizes the system he serves has left him with a jaded view of the law and of the world. In a conversation with his step-sister Christina that provides the foundation for understanding the book's title, Harry comments on the foolishness of those who expect the legal system to fulfill their highest hopes for justice: "Justice? You get justice in the next world, in this world you have the law." Gaddis suggests that litigants who expect something more than the punishment of the wicked from self-appointed stewards of justice like Eliphaz may be on a "frolic" that would be laughable . . . if it were not so painful.

W. Gaddis, *A Frolic of His Own* (New York: Scribner Paperback Fiction, 1995), 13. I am indebted to my friend Keat Wiles Ph.D., J.D., for calling this illustration to my attention and for suggesting that sometimes the legal system leaves litigants with the impression that seeking justice in a court of law has the same effect as "banging on the table." It is an exercise of raw emotionalism that has no bearing on the court's response. The characterization of justice as "banging on the table" is cited in R. Marcin, "Justice and Love," *Catholic University Law Review* 33 (1984): 363.

use/service") that occurs twice in v. 2. Initially, Eliphaz asked if there is any way mortals can be of benefit to God. Now he moves to answer his own question. Human beings attain worth in God's eyes by complying with God's terms for relationship. The root of the second verb means to be "complete, sound." It occurs here in a seldom used form (Qal imperative) that is best rendered as "surrender" to God and, by extension, "be complete."[12] Job used a similar form of this verb when he wondered out loud if any one possesses sufficient strength or wisdom to contest God and survive uninjured (9:4, *yišlām*; NRSV: "succeed"). Eliphaz regards even the contemplation of such a question as a sure sign that Job has an exaggerated sense of self-importance. The requirement for relationship with God is submission and unconditional surrender; anything less results in certain defeat. ["Endure. Accept. And say Amen"]

• Job must "receive" (*qaḥ*) what God gives and "take it to heart" (*śîm*; v. 22). What Eliphaz has in mind is informed by the wisdom tradition's understanding of the relationship between teachers and students. The fundamental assumption is that teachers have a monopoly on wisdom and truth. Students are deficient in these matters, but if they are willing to receive "instruction" (*tôrāh*; cf. Prov 4:2; 13:14 [NRSV: "teaching"]) and store up in their hearts the "words" (*'ēmer*; cf. Prov 4:5; 5:7; 7:24; 8:8; in each case paralleled by the word *tôrāh*) of their teachers, then they can obtain the requisite wisdom to live well. Job has dared to ponder a scenario in which the model example of the teacher-student hierarchy might be reversed: "Can anyone *teach God* knowledge?" (21:22). Eliphaz now responds with an unequivocal "No."

Once Job agrees to surrender and not rebel, to learn and not teach, then he will be in the proper position to hear God's conditions for

---

"Endure. Accept. And say Amen"

Eliphaz's counsel bears a close resemblance to the advice offered by Sam to Berish in Elie Wiesel's *The Trial of God* (see further the "Connections" at Job 9–10 and Job 16–17). Berish insists on bringing God to trial for the massacre of Jews in Shamgorod in 1649. Sam, who plays the role of God's defense attorney, warns Berish that God's will and God's reasoning are not subject to human critique. On hearing this argument Mendel, the oldest and wisest of those who look on fearfully as the drama develops, poses a critical question: "What is there left for us to do?" Sam is ready with the answer. From Sam's perspective, Berish has but one real option: "Endure. Accept. And say Amen."

Berish, like Job, refuses this option and chooses another:

He annihilated Shamgorod and you want me to be for Him? I can't! If He insists upon going on with His methods, let Him—but I won't say Amen. Let Him crush me, I won't say Kaddish. Let Him kill me, let Him kill us all, I shall shout and shout that it's His fault. I'll use my last energy to make my protest known. Whether I live or die, I submit to Him no longer.

E. Wiesel, *The Trial of God* (New York: Schocken Books, 1979), 132, 133

Finding Gold in God, Not in Ophir

AΩ Eliphaz speaks of the "gold of Ophir," which in his estimation Job should value less than the gold of God. Ophir was regarded as a source of a particularly fine quality of gold from at least the reign of Solomon (1 Kgs 9:28; 2 Chr 8:18; cf. Ps 45:10; Isa 13:12). The location of Ophir is uncertain, and a number of sites have been proposed ranging from southern Africa to India. Some have suggested that Ophir is a fictional place, not a historical location, perhaps the mythical equivalent of El Dorado ("the guilded one"), the legendary South American city of gold sought by eighteenth century Spanish explorers. Whether real or fictional, Ophir's gold represents for Eliphaz something far less precious than the treasure of a right relationship with God.

There may be more to Eliphaz's counsel than first meets the eye. The name "Eliphaz" may mean something like "God is fine gold." If so, Eliphaz's summons may be an ironic invitation for Job to remake himself in the image of the God Eliphaz believes *he* represents. In a previous speech, Eliphaz has modeled the praise he would offer God if he were ever in Job's place (5:8-16). Perhaps now he envisions himself as the very image of the God to whom that praise should be offered.

repentance (vv. 23-26). The first requirement is the most important: Job must "return" (*šwb*) to God. *If* he will reverse course, that is, turn away from the paths of wickedness (cf. v. 15) and follow the way of righteousness, then he will be "rebuilt" (*tibbāneh*; NRSV: "restored") in the image that God intends.[13] Eliphaz envisions repentance as a reordering of Job's values and priorities. *If* he will remove the "unrighteousness" (v. 23: *ʿawlāh*; cf. 11:14 [NRSV: "wickedness"]) that has taken up residence in his tent, *if* he will reassess what constitutes his greatest good, which is symbolized by returning "gold" to the places where it properly belongs so that God may once again become his most prized possession (vv. 24-25), *then* he will rediscover that submission to God promises more than he can obtain buy any other means. [Finding Gold in God, Not in Ophir] *Then* he will regain the joy that comes from being able to lift his face to God without shame and dishonor (v. 26; cf. Ps 37:4; Isa 58:14).

Eliphaz concludes by assuring Job that repentance benefits him as well as others (vv. 27-30). *For Job* it will mean that when he prays for help (v. 27: *ʿātar*, cf. Gen 25:21; Exod 8:30 [MT Exod 8:26]; 10:18; Judg 13:8), then God will hear and respond positively, for he will have acquitted himself honorably of the promises he has made to surrender himself to God's will (cf. 1 Sam 1:10-11; Ps 61:5 [MT 61:6]). [Vows in the Old Testament] Once Job is in full accord with God's intentions, he will be able to "decide" on a course of action (v. 27: *gāzar*, literally, "divide/cut in two") and know that his choice is right. No longer will he grope about in the terrifying darkness (cf. v. 11); he will walk instead in the confidence of a new light that makes all things clear. Once Job is reconciled to God, he may become a *model and a source of help for others*. When others falter, he can sustain them with a strong word of encouragement: "Be lifted up!" (v. 29a: *gāwāh*; cf. NIV). When the lowly despair of deliverance, they will find in Job one who can save them (v. 29b). Even those who are "not innocent" will be delivered, because when Job stands in the breach between them and God, the purity of his intercessions will change the calculus of divine judgment from punishment to mercy (v. 30).[14]

There is a double irony in Eliphaz's promise that Job will intercede effectively for others. On the one hand, the role he envisions for Job is

Vows in the Old Testament

In v. 27, Eliphaz tells Job that if he meets the conditions of repentance, then he will pray to God, and God will hear him, and he will be able to "complete his vows" (*nĕdārêkā tĕšallēm*). The Old Testament distinguishes between two kinds of vows. The *unconditional* vow is the equivalent of a sworn oath. The maker of the vow promises, for example, to bring to God specific offerings at designated times (Lev 23:37-38; Num 29:39; Deut 12:6, 17; cf. 1 Sam 1:21) or to adhere to certain standards of behavior (Ps 132:2). The promise is not qualified by any variables of volition or circumstance. It represents an unequivocal commitment. The *conditional* vow ties a specific action of the person to a prior specific action of God. The typical form is "*If* God does X, *then* I will do Y in return." Such vows are common, for example, in situations of trouble or distress when one promises to "complete" (*šlm*) an obligation to thank or praise God in return for deliverance (Pss 22:25 [MT 22:26]; 56:12; 61:8 [MT 61:9]; 116:14, 18; Jonah 2:9 [MT 2:10]).

Eliphaz assumes that God will hear and respond positively to Job's prayer, *if* Job is genuinely repentant. When and if Job completes his vow, then it will be confirmation that *Job not God* has fulfilled the conditions necessary for a restoration of the relationship. As elsewhere in Eliphaz's speech, his words of assurance to Job echo with a word of warning. If Job does not follow through with the conditions of repentance, *if* he promises contrition but does not demonstrate it, *then* he dooms himself to still further punishment. The law in such situations is clear: "If you make a vow to the Lord, do not postpone fulfilling it; for the Lord your God will surely require it of you" (Deut 23:21; cf. Prov 20:25; Eccl 5:4-7; Sir 18:22). One may suppose that behind Eliphaz's promise of restoration there is a rebuke waiting to be triggered by an angry God. As Juliet says to Romeo when she is still unsure of the love for her he so gallantly declares,

If thou swearest,
Thou mayst prove false. (*Romeo and Juliet*, II, ii, 91)

For further reading, see C. A. Keller, "*Ndr*, to vow," in *TLOT*, ed. E. Jenni, C. Westermann (Peabody MA: Hendrikson Publishers, 1997), vol. 2, 719-22.

comparable to that of the most revered intercessors in Israel's tradition, Abraham (Gen 18:21-33) and Moses (Exod 32:9-14). Thus, despite his concern to locate Job among the wicked, he concedes that his true place is in the ranks of the famously righteous. Job has in fact dared to wonder if perhaps the objective of his lament, like Abraham's, should be to teach God the true meaning of what justice requires, although he can imagine nothing beyond a plea for personal vindication, and even on that basis he can muster no reason to think he will be successful (see the commentary on 16:18-22 and 21:17-26). On the other hand, the epilogue will ultimately confirm that Eliphaz has foreseen Job's destiny even more clearly than Job himself. What Job is unable to see, however, is that he is destined to prove his capacity to deliver the guilty from God's anger by praying for Eliphaz himself and his friends (42:8-9). [The Efficacious Prayers of "Saint Job"]

CONNECTIONS

Two particular aspects of Eliphaz's last speech invite theological reflection. First, it is instructive to ponder the consequences of holding to a theology of judgment so rigidly conceived that one is willing to invent the crimes that justify the punishment. Eliphaz has tried a pastoral

The Efficacious Prayers of "Saint Job"

Eliphaz's closing words in vv. 29-30 tap into the biblical idea that the prayers of a righteous person may tilt the scales of God's justice away from wrath and towards mercy. This idea is the basis for Abraham's intercession for Sodom in Gen 18:22-33. When God announces the plan to punish Sodom for its transparent wickedness, Abraham insists that justice requires God to pay more attention to the righteous than the guilty. Even if only ten righteous ones can be found in the city, it is incumbent upon God to spare the city for their sake. As Abraham puts it, "Far be it from you . . .to slay the righteous with the wicked, so that the righteous fare as the wicked! Far be that from you! Shall not the Judge of all the earth do what is just?" (Gen 18:25). God shows a remarkable openness to Abraham's plea, for as the text reports God answers him by saying, "For the sake of ten I will not destroy it" (18:32). A similar assumption underlies Ezekiel's argument in Ezek 14:14, even though he cites the possibility only to refute it: "Even if Noah, Daniel, and Job, these three, were in it [the faithless land], they would save only their own lives by their righteousness."

R. Gordis has noted that belief in the efficacy of righteous prayer undergoes extensive development in post-biblical Judaism. The Talmud reports that a saint may even set aside a decree of divine judgment: "Said the Holy One, Blessed be He, 'I rule over man, but who rules over Me? The saint, for when I issue a decree, he sets it aside'" (*b. Moed Qat.* 16b). Similarly, the Talmud attests the traditional Jewish belief that it takes thirty-six saints whose lives glorify the divine presence to preserve the world God has created: "The world cannot endure with less than thirty-six saints who greet the Divine Presence daily" (*b. Sukkot* 45b).

The idea of Job as a saint whose prayers have special claim on God's mercies captured the imagination of numerous artists. One particularly instructive example is

Main Portal to the Church of San Giobbe, Venice.

located above the main entrance to the Church of San Giobbe in Venice. The church was originally associated with a hospital that occupied the same site. The fourteenth century tympanum by Pietro Lombardo depicts two persons kneeling in prayer. The figure on the left, robbed in the traditional garment of the Franciscan monks, is St. Francis of Assisi. With a cross raised by a stigmata-marked hand, he casts his eyes toward the rays of sunshine that extend from heaven. The figure on the right is St. Job (San Giobbe), for whom the church is named. He is naked, except for the cloak that wraps around his waist and drapes freely down his right side. His body is firm, suggesting the physique of a trained athlete. His beard is trim, his jaw is set, his hands are clasped together in prayer. With Francis, he looks toward the light from heaven with a serenity that indicates both resolve and expectation. Both these saints, one canonized, the other still awaiting the recognition (!), offer a marvelously suggestive invitation to all who will to enter this sanctuary and find healing, restoration, and peace.

R. Gordis, *The Book of Job: Commentary, New Translation, and Special Studies* (New York: Jewish Theological Seminary of America, 1978), 251-52. For further discussion see R. Gordis, "Corporate Personality in Job: A Note on 22:29-30," JOHNES 4 (1945): 54-55.

approach to Job. He reasoned that by gently urging Job to reconsider his status in relationship to God, he might persuade him to rethink his claim to be "righteous" and "pure" (4:17). When this proved ineffective, he sharpened his counsel by placing a greater emphasis on the inherent sinfulness that bars every human being from claiming innocence in God's presence (15:14). Now that this strategy has also failed, Eliphaz is left with but two options. He can rethink his own assumptions about Job's guilt—could it be that Job is innocent after all?—or he can find in his own theology the justification to condemn Job without evidence. Eliphaz chooses the latter course.

In so doing, he presents a model of faith that offers a clear antithesis to Job.[15] Job is unwilling to blur or distort the truth about his life in order to conform to theological certainties that someone else believes are inviolable. He will cling to his integrity *and* to his faith in God, despite the heavy uncertainties that call both into question. Eliphaz is unwilling to modify or change his theology simply because it cannot pass the test of truth. In his estimation, it is more important that one's theology be *right* than *credible*. Toward that end, he is prepared to distort reality in order to preserve a theory about God and sin and judgment that he passionately believes is nonnegotiable. *Since* Job suffers, *it must be because* of his sin. *Because* God is just, Job *must be* guilty. Once the first two premises are elevated from belief to law, the other two slide naturally into unassailable decree. Once one obtains the consent of their conscience to regard personal faith as a matter of divine law and decree, then God becomes little more than a silent partner in a game of justice where the rules have already been decided. ["His Own Opinion Was His Law"]

Readers may consider whether Eliphaz or Job is the better model of faith. If one skips ahead to the end of the book, it may be tempting to conclude that the answer to the question is easy and clear. God says to Eliphaz, "My wrath is kindled against you and against your two friends; because you have not spoken of me what is right, as my servant Job has done" (42:7). But to rush to judgment too quickly not only squeezes the tension from this drama, it also minimizes the genuine seductiveness of the faith Eliphaz models. Fervent belief often tilts toward the assumption that passion authenticates coercion. History is littered with examples of those who have yielded to the temptation to believe that their theology/ideology is equivalent to divine law, which must be implemented, even if it means falsifying the truth in order to convert or convict those who see things differently. C. Newsom makes a similar point by cataloguing just a few examples:

"His Own Opinion Was His Law"

Upon hearing the news of Cardinal Wolsey's death, Queen Katharine offers the following post-mortem assessment of his legacy. Her judgment invites one to consider whether Eliphaz might earn for himself a similar eulogy.

He was a man
Of an unbounded stomach, ever ranking
Himself with princes; one that, by suggestion,
Tied all the kingdom: simony was fair play;
His own opinion was the law; i' the presence
He would say untruths; and be ever double
Both in his words and meaning: he was never,
But where he meant to ruin, pitiful:
His promises were, as he then was, mighty
But his performance, as he is now, nothing:
Of his own body he was ill, and gave
The clergy ill example. (*Henry VII*, III, i, 33-44)

The bizarre allegations of anti-Semitic propaganda from the Middle Ages to the present have often found a large audience willing to believe them.

Christians who defended their Jewish neighbors against such egregious slanders were all too rare. In seventeenth century Salem, accusations of witchcraft against well-known and respected persons were widely credited as true. Few who experienced the "red scare" of the 1950s and 1960s can forget how easily the claim that someone was a communist agent could be believed, even when the accused was wholly innocent.[16]

It is indeed tempting to be dismissive of Eliphaz, as if we would never be so arrogant or rigid in our treatment of others as he is of Job. And yet as Newsom reminds us, the faith Eliphaz embodies "is more common than it is comfortable to admit." [CD: How Should One "Weigh a Doubt Against a Certainty"?]

Eliphaz's insistence that Job compromise his innocence for the greater gain of relationship to God invites consideration of a second and still larger question. Eliphaz frames the issue succinctly in his opening words: "Can a mortal be of use to God?" (v. 2). Eliphaz is certain that there can be but one answer to this question. Human beings can only be of use to God if they *agree* that whenever questions arise in matters of faith, God is always right and they are always wrong (v. 21). When humans surrender to God, yield their questions and complaints to God's inscrutable wisdom, then and only then do they become worthy of the relationship God ordains. The irrevocable prerequisite for *partnership* with God, Eliphaz asserts, is *submission*.

Despite the certainty with which he makes this claim, Eliphaz invites the very questions about what God wants and needs from humans that he believes he has put to rest once and for all. Is it true that God tolerates only those who are willing to agree with God, only those who take what God gives (v. 22), in Berish's words, only those who "Endure. Accept. And say Amen" (see ["Let Anyone Among You Who Is Without Sin Be the First to Throw a Stone"])? ["Lord, . . . Is This True?"] And *if* this is what God wants and needs from humans, *then* where do the Jobs of this world find a place to stand in the presence of God? Once again Job's pained question lingers in the background, still awaiting a definitive response from the One who has yet to speak: "What are human beings that you make so much of them?" (7:17).

Those who are inclined to squelch or dismiss Job's wonderment about the value of human beings to God with the theology of Eliphaz and Berish may find it useful to reflect on another question. What may God lose if the divine-human relationship is lived out only as silent acquiescence and submission? One imaginative entry to this question is through the poetry of Walt Whitman, who dares to suggest that somewhere in the cosmos there must be someone who is willing to speak for the "many long dumb voices" of those disfigured and trivialized by agony.[17]

"Lord, . . . Is This True?"

Thomas Hardy (1840–1928) was an English novelist and poet who struggled throughout his life with questions that the orthodoxy of Victorian England viewed as blasphemous and unacceptable. One pertinent example is his poem "A Dream Question," which weighs the "ethic" of human will against the truth declared by a "hosts of theologians" like Eliphaz.

I asked the Lord: 'Sire, is this true
Which hosts of theologians hold,
That when we creatures censure you
For shaping griefs and ails untold
(Deeming them punishments undue)
You rage, as Moses wrote of old?

When we exclaim: "Beneficent
He is not, for he orders pain,
Or, if so, not omnipotent:
To a mere child the thing is plain!"
Those who profess to represent
You, cry out: 'Impious and profane!'"

'Why things are thus, whoso derides,,
May well remain my secret still . . .
A fourth dimension, say the guides,
To matter is conceivable.
Think some such mystery resides
Within the ethic of my will.'

T. Hardy, "A Dream Question," *The Complete Poems of Thomas Hardy*, ed. J. Gibson (New York: Macmillan Publishing Company, 1976), 261-62.

The most likely candidate for this role, Whitman believed, was the poet. In his poem "By Blue Ontario's Shore" (1867), Whitman muses about what America most needed to restore itself in the aftermath of a civil war that had wreaked havoc on a young nation's aspirations for democracy. He imagined an encounter with a "Phantom" that was calling for a poet who would embody a certain kind of justice, a justice that might speak across the great divide of winners and losers. He describes the characteristics of this poet-judge[18] as follows:

> . . . the poet is the equable man,
> Not in him but off from him things are grotesgue, eccentric, fail
>   of their full returns,
> Nothing out of its place is good, nothing in its place is bad,
> He bestows on every object or quality its fit proportion, neither
>   more nor less,
> He is the arbiter of the diverse, he is the key,
> He is the equalizer of his age and land,
> He supplies what wants supplying, he checks what wants checking. . .
> He judges not as the judge judges but as the sun falling around a
>   helpless thing . . .
> He sees eternity in men and women, he does not see men and
>   women as dreams or dots.[19]

Whitman imagines himself interrogating those who might offer themselves as candidates for the role of "the equable man." If one is to embody norms of judgment that counter conventional modes of justice, then these are the questions they must answer satisfactorily:

Are you he would assume a place to teach or be a poet here
    in the States?
The place is august, the terms obdurate.

Who would assume to teach here may well prepare himself body
    and mind,
He may well survey, ponder, arm, fortify, harden, make lithe himself,
He shall surely be question'd beforehand by me with many and
    stern questions . . .
Have you studied out the land, its idioms and men?
Have you learned the physiology, phrenology, politics, geography,
    pride, freedom, friendship of the land? its substratums and
    objects? . . .
Are you faithful to things? do you teach what the land and sea,
    the bodies of men, womanhood, amativeness, heroic angers,
    teach? . . .
Can you hold your hand against all seductions, follies, whirls, fierce
    contentions? are you very strong? are you really of the
    whole People? . . .
Do you hold the like love for those hardening to maturity? for the
    last-born? little and big? and for the errant?[20]

If we were to reflect on these questions as if they were directed by
God to both Eliphaz and Job, then which of the two would we consider to have the better capacity to answer them? Would we decide that
Eliphaz or Job "sees the eternity in men and women"? Is it Eliphaz or
Job who is most "faithful to things"? Is it Eliphaz or Job who holds the
"key" to justice for those who can only speak the "heroic angers" that
life has taught them? Is it Eliphaz or Job who knows how to judge "as
the sun falling around a helpless thing"? When Eliphaz insists that
truth and innocence are virtues God may choose to discredit if one
values them too highly, will God agree or disagree? When Job insists on
clinging fast to his integrity, even if it means contending with the Judge
of the universe, will God smile with approval or rage with anger?
Whoever would assume to teach or be a poet in the land of Uz must
think through these matters carefully before they claim to know God's
answer to the question Job raises in 7:17. Could it be that God does
not wish to leave us alone (cf. 7:16, 19) until the "many long dumb
voices" find someone to plead their case before the throne of justice?

[Does God Laugh or Rage at Human Dissent?]

Does God Laugh or Rage at Human Dissent?

The Talmud records a story that invites reflection on the balance between possibilities and limitations in the divine-human relationship. On a certain occasion, a majority of rabbis rejected the opinion of Rabbi Eliezer. Even when a voice from heaven informed them that Eliezer was right, they still rejected his view. In their defense, the majority cited a piece of a Scripture: "It is not in the heavens" (Deut 30:9). Some time later, Rabbi Nathan has a conversation with the prophet Elijah, who tells him what God said on that day when the rabbis overruled the voice from heaven:

> Rabbi Nathan met Elijah. He said to him, "What did the Holy One Blessed Be He do at that time?"

> He said to him, "He laughed. And He said, 'My children have defeated me.'" (b. B. Mesia 59b)

R. Friedman cites this story in his discussion of how rabbinic Judaism dealt with the long period of divine silence that followed the time the Torah was given to Moses on Sinai. When prophecy ceased and miracles were no more, it fell to the rabbis to keep the Torah alive, and thus to sustain God's presence, through their learned discussions and interpretations of the old traditions. Friedman notes that the oral traditions of the rabbis signify a remarkable shift in the divine-human balance. As the majority group said to Eliezer, the word of God is not any longer only "in the heavens"; it is now entrusted to a democratic vote of human authorities. Friedman makes the case as follows:

> The human authorities, citing a text revealed by God, ruling by the authority of a text revealed by God, reject divine intervention and overrule God. The rabbis have declared that their traditions, decisions, and expositions of texts are Torah—equal to the Torah of the Bible. The Torah is now in the hands of humans, and not even God can change it. (124)

What is still more remarkable than the rabbis claim to near-equal authority with God is God's reported response. God does not rebuke, deny, or rage against those who assume responsibility for seeing to it that Torah is kept. Instead, God "laughed" (see further, **[The Efficacious Prayers of "Saint Job "]**). Friedman concludes that such a portrait of God "is reminiscent of the biblical account of the deity's changing Jacob's name to Israel ('for you have struggled with God and prevailed') as a blessing" (125).

One may consider whether it is Eliphaz or Job who most proves himself worthy of Jacob's blessing.

R. Friedman, *The Disappearance of God: A Divine Mystery* (Boston/New York: Little, Brown, and Company, 1995). For Friedman's discussion of the Talmudic story, see 122-26.

NOTES

[1] As C. Newsom notes, "The earliest translations, the targum of Job from Qumran and the Septuagint, exhibit the same distribution of speeches that one finds in the MT (Newsom, "The Book of Job," in vol. 4 of *NIB* [Nashville: Abingdon Press, 1996]).

[2] J. Gerald Janzen, *Job* (Atlanta: John Knox, 1985), 169; cf. N. Habel, *The Book of Job: A Commentary* (OTL; Philadelphia: Westminster Press, 1985), 357-58.

[3] Cf. Habel, *Book of Job,* 366-68; L. Perdue, *Wisdom and Creation: The Theology of Wisdom Literature* (Nashville: Abingdon,1994), 160-62; *Wisdom in Revolt: Metaphorical Theology in the Book of Job* (JSOTSup 112; Sheffield: Almond Press, 1991), 174-82.

[4] Newsom, "The Book of Job," 522, 524.

[5] S. Terrien, "The Book of Job," *IB*, vol. 3, ed. G. Buttrick (New York: Abingdon Press, 1954), 1072.

[6] R. Gordis, *The Book of Job: Commentary, New Translation, and Special Studies* (New York: Jewish Theological Seminary of America, 1978), 238.

[7] Cf. C. Westermann, *Basic Forms of Prophetic Speech* (Philadelphia: Fortress Press, 1967), 137-68.

[8] Because v. 8 seems more like a benign aphorism or proverb than a moral condemnation addressed specifically to Job, some scholars consider it to be a gloss (an explanatory insertion). An Aramaic fragment from Qumran introduces this verse with the words "and you say," perhaps suggesting that Eliphaz is quoting what he presumes is Job's philosophy.

Gordis (*Book of Job,* 240, 245-46), who follows this line of interpretation, offers the following translation:

> For you [Job] believe,
> 'The man of violence owns the land,
> and he who is powerful lives upon it."

[9] Habel, *Book of Job,* 339.

[10] Cf. ibid.

[11] E.g., S. R. Driver and G. B. Gray, *A Critical and Exegetical Commentary on the Book of Job* (Edinburgh: T and T. Clark, 1921), 196-97.

[12] Cf. G. Gerleman, "Šlm to have enough," in E. Jenni, C. Westermann, eds., *TLOT,* vol. 3, trans. M. E. Biddle (Peabody MS: Hendrikson Publishers, 1997), 1342.

[13] The verb in v. 23 (*bānāh*), which NRSV translates "restored," literally means "build." Its primary meaning has to do with the building or constructing of structures like the temple or the walls of a city like Jerusalem (cf. 2 Sam 7:5, 7; 1 Kgs 6:2, 7; Jer 30:18; Neh 7:1). In some instances, *bānāh* is used idiomatically to mean "obtain children," that is, to "build" a family by providing progeny and descendents. In Gen 16:2, for example, a barren Sarah implores Abraham to take Hagar in her stead in order that she "may obtain children (*'ibbāneh,* lit., "be *built up*") by her" (cf. Gen 30:3). For Sarah, and perhaps for Job as well, being "rebuilt" means the restoration of one's capacities for realizing the fullness of life that God intends.

[14] The Hebrew text of v. 30a, *'î nāqî* (lit., "not innocent"), is difficult. The LXX and the Vulgate omit the word *'î* and translate simply "innocent." Some scholars achieve much the same meaning by emending the text to *'îš nāqî,* "an innocent *man*" (e.g., Driver and Gray, *Book of Job,* 199; G. Fohrer, *Das Buch Hiob* [KAT; Gütersloh: Gerd Mohn, 1963], 352). A number of modern translations adopt a similar reading (cf. RSV, NAB, REB). A case can be made, however, for interpreting the text as it stands (as in NRSV). Gordis (*Book of Job,* 252) notes that the particle *'î* normally carries a negative meaning in Phoenician as well as in post-biblical Hebrew (cf. M. Pope, *Job* [AB; Garden City NY: Doubleday, 1979], 168-69). A similar use of *'î* as a negative occurs in 1 Sam 4:21, where the text explains the meaning of the name Ichabod (*'î-kābôd*), lit. "no glory," by saying that "the glory has departed from Israel."

[15] On the fashioning of Eliphaz and Job as antithetical models of faith, see Y. Hoffman, *A Blemished Perfection: The Book of Job in Context* (JSOTSup 213; Sheffield: Sheffield Academic Press, 1996), 137-40.

[16] Newsom, "The Book of Job," 504.

[17] Whitman, "Song of Myself," *Leaves of Grass,* edited with an introduction by J. Loving (Oxford: Oxford University Press, 1990), 48.

[18] For this appropriation of Whitman's idea of the poet, I am indebted to Nussbaum's provocative discussion of "poets as judges" in *Poetic Justice,* 79-121.

[19] W. Whitman, "By Blue Ontario's Shore," *Leaves of Grass,* 269-70.

[20] Ibid., 270-71.

JOB'S RESPONSE TO ELIPHAZ: GOD IS ABSENT AND EVIL RUNS AMOK

Job 23:1–24:25

When Job declares that his "complaint" (*śîaḥ*; 21:4) against God is too grievous to be born patiently, Eliphaz counsels him to let it go. If Job truly desires relationship with the Almighty, then his only option is to "agree with God" and conform to the model of submissive faith that God requires (22:21). Once again Job refuses to do as he is told. Instead, he launches into one of the most intensive complaints about God's inexplicable absence found anywhere in scripture. Chapter 23 frames this complaint with two statements that insist faith must sometimes be construed as moral rebellion, not silent compliance. In v. 2 Job argues that his "complaint" (*śîaḥ*) is "defiant" (*mĕrî*; NRSV: "bitter"). In v. 17, he announces that despite the way God terrorizes him, he will not "be silenced" or "eliminated" (*lōʾ niṣmattî*; see the commentary below) by the threat of overwhelming darkness. Inside the "claims of time and sorrow" (on this expression, see the "Connections" in Job 8) Job's *compelling hope* is that he might find a God who is more present and more just than the One he now knows (23:3-7). His *lingering fear* is that the unjust and implacable God who terrorizes him is all there is (23:8-16). ["This Great Absence . . . That Compels Me to Address It Without Hope"]

On the heels of this complaint, Job offers the most scathing indictment of God's justice that occurs in the book. He begins with a critical question that authentic faith permits no innocent sufferer to leave unasked: Why do those who know God never see the judgment that God promises (v. 1)? Why do the wicked run free, leaving their victims to

> **"This Great Absence . . . That Compels Me to Address It Without Hope"**
> It is this great absence
> that is like a presence, that compels
> me to address it without hope
> of a reply. It is a room I enter
>
> from which someone has just
> gone, the vestibule for the arrival
> of one who has yet to come.
> I modernize the anachronism
>
> of my language, but he is no more here
> than before. Genes and molecules
> have no more power to call
> him up than the incense of the Hebrews
>
> at their altars. My equations fail
> as my words do. What resources have I
> other than the emptiness without him of my
> whole being, a vacuum he may not abhor?
>
> R. S. Thomas, "The Absence," in *Poems of R. S. Thomas* (Fayetteville: University of Arkansas Press, 1985), 129.

cry out for help to a God who sees nothing wrong with the way the world is working (vv. 2-12)? Why do those who rebel against the light have license to subvert the moral order of the cosmos by using darkness as a cover for their criminality (vv. 13-17)? By any normal definition of justice, such evidence requires God's intervention, yet the abuses pile up, and God remains silent. Given God's apparent indifference to injustice, Job dares to believe that he must speak out on behalf of all those who share his plight and his faith. He will declare the judgment on the wicked that God seems unwilling or unable to do (vv. 18-24).

This last section of his speech is problematic, precisely because the certainty of the judgment Job declares seems on first sight to be more consonant with the views of the friends than with what Job himself seems able to believe. Many interpreters assume that these verses belong either to Zophar or Bildad (see the commentary below). But in view of Job's resolve to walk in the footsteps of God (cf. 23:11), even if it means to *lead* by example rather than to *follow*, it is more plausible to understand these words as Job's courageous effort to model the justice he fervently believes God must enact if God is God. Job is so certain of his position that he challenges anyone, including God, to prove him wrong (v. 25).

Eliphaz has asked Job what he believes and hopes is only a rhetorical question: "Can a mortal be of use to God?" (22:1). He does not expect and cannot accept that faith might construe the answer to this question in terms of a defiant "Yes" instead of a respectful "No." But this is precisely the answer that Job explores. Could it be that rebellion is a form of faith that teaches even God what it means to "love justice" and "not forsake his faithful ones" (Ps 37:28)? [CD: "What Use, After All, Is Man, if Not to Teach God His Lessons?"]

COMMENTARY

Job's Compelling Hope: "Oh, That I Knew Where I Might Find Him," 23:1-7

Job's "complaint" justifies not only impatience (21:4); it is also cause for defiance (v. 2; see the marginal note in NRSV). ["My Lament Is a Revolt"] E. Peterson's paraphrase captures nicely the essence of Job's complaint:

> I'm not letting up—I'm standing my ground.
> My complaint is legitimate.
> God has no right to treat me like this—
> it isn't fair![1]

"My Lament Is a Revolt"

Francis Gruber (1912–1948) was the son of the stained-glass artist Jacques Gruber. In 1916 he moved to Paris, where he distinguished himself as a highly imaginative and visionary painter. He was awarded the Prix National in 1947.

The oil on canvas that he inscribed simply "Job" was painted in 1944 for the Salon d'Automne, which opened in Paris just after the Liberation. It was Gruber's wish to symbolize the heroic courage and hope of those who, like Job, had survived the Nazi occupation. He paints Job as a thinned out young man sitting on a backless chair. His right leg is crossed over his knee. The knee provides a resting place for his right elbow, crooked to support a drooping head. His left arm hangs limply by his side. The posture gives graphic illustration to the biblical description of Job as one whose hand is heavy with groaning (23:2). The red-brick wall opposite Job abuts a make-shift construction of wooden planks that replaces a bombed-out wall. Through the window one sees apartment buildings with broken windowpanes.

The inscription on the paper at which Job is looking reads: "Maintenant encore, ma plainte est une revolte, et pourtant ma mian comprime mes soupirs" ("Even now my complaint is a revolt, and yet my hand restrains my sighs"). The first half of the

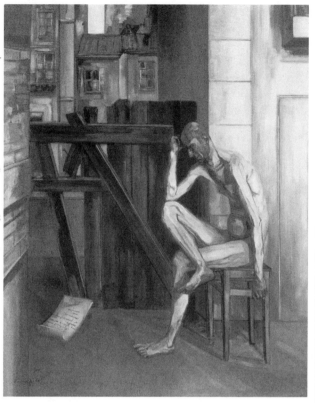

Job

Francis Gruber (1912-1948). *Job*. 1944. Tate Gallery, London, Great Britain (Credit: Tate Gallery, London/Art Resource, NY)

inscription appears to be from Job 23:2 ("My complaint is bitter/defiant (*měrî*; 23:2). The latter half is difficult, but it may echo Job 23:11 ("My foot has held fast to his steps; I have kept his way and have not turned aside"). While one cannot be certain of Gruber's intention, his splicing together of these two texts offers a suggestive comment on the two characteristics that define Job's approach in this chapter. He stands before God as both a *rebel* and a *loyal follower*. The link between these two seemingly dissonant commitments is the critical conjunction "and yet." Gruber appears to suggest that it is the meaning of this "and yet" that the Jobs of this world must ponder carefully.

For the words of the inscription, I am indebted to Mr. Chris Webber of the staff at the Tate Gallery, who provided materials indicating that the information comes from Mme Gruber, October 1958 and January 1975. S. Terrien (*The Iconography of Job Through the Centuries* [University Park PN: The Pennsylvania State University Press, 1996], 250) reads the inscription differently: "Maintenant encore, ma plainte est une *réussite*, et pourtant . . ." ("Even now my lament is a *success*, and yet . . ."). He suggests that the word "réssuite" refers to winning at cards and interprets Gruber to be portraying Job as pondering the realization that "life is a tragic game." When I viewed the painting in 1999, then on display at the Tate Modern Gallery, I was able to confirm that the word in the inscription is "revolte," not "réussite."

Job's hand[2] is heavy with groaning, an indication that his persistence in stretching out his hands in prayer to God brings no relief, despite his innocence (cf. 16:17). Previously, Job acknowledged that the fatigue of grief and despair has drained his strength, leaving him no energy to stay the course with such an intractable God (cf. 6:11-13; 16:7-8). That same despair is now the source of new-found energy. He no longer wishes simply to give up and die (cf. 3:11-13, 20-22; 6:8-9; 7:15, 19-20; 10:18-22; 16:22–17:1); now he determines to find the "fixed place" (v. 3, *tĕkûnāh*; NRSV: "dwelling") where God is hiding and present his case for justice in a one-on-one confrontation. [Job's Changing Wish] If Job is to encounter God, then he will have to be the pursuer, for it seems clear that no amount of suffering moves God to take the initiative to come to him.

Job's resolve to confront God is framed with the legal imagery that has shaped his previous speeches (vv. 4-7; see further [The Trial Metaphor in Job]). He begins by saying that he intends to present his "case" (v. 4: *mišpāṭ*) before God and concludes by saying that his hope is to bring "justice" (v. 7: *mišpāṭ*) to a successful birth.[3] If he is to obtain justice, then several things must happen. He must be able to speak the full range of his "arguments" (v. 4: *tôkāḥôt*; cf. 13:6; NRSV: "reasoning") against God without interruption. He must be assured that God will give up silence (19:7; cf. 9:16; 13:22) and "answer" him with words he can "understand" (v. 5). He must be able to stand before God free from the threat of the "greatness of his power" (v. 6a). Even though Job knows by experience that the odds are against such divine restraint (cf. 9:16-19), he dares to believe that perhaps God can change. Surely God will pay attention (v. 6b) to the arguments of a genuinely "upright" man (v. 7a: *yāšār*; cf. 1:1, 8; 2:3) like Job, for a God of justice must be guided by reason and fair play, not power and petulance.

Job's Changing Wish

AΩ   N. Habel has noted that the formulaic phrase introducing v. 3, *mî-yittēn* ("O that"), occurs more times in Job than in any other biblical book. He suggests that by tracking these occurrences one can plot a progression of thought in Job's "exploratory hopes" to encounter God. Habel's sketch of the major steps in the sequence (see below) indicates that Job's hope to find God (Job 23) comes as his next-to-last best effort to obtain some resolution to his ordeal.

1. The hope to die: "O that I might have my request, . . . that it would please God to crush me" (6:8-9)
2. The hope for a postmortem encounter with a different God: "O that you would hide me in Sheol, that you would conceal me until your wrath is past" (14:13)
3. The hope for a "redeemer" who will defend him against his accusers (both divine and human): "O that my words were written down! . . . For I know my redeemer lives" (19:23, 25)
4. The hope that he could find God's "fixed place" and argue his case: "O that I knew where I might find him . . . I would lay my case before him" (23:3-4)
5. The hope that God would appear in court to hear and answer Job: "O that I had one to hear me! (Here is my signature, let the Almighty answer me!)" (31:35)

On the distribution of Job's hopes and wishes in the overall structure of the book, see further C. Westermann, *The Structure of the Book of Job: A Form-Critical Analysis* (Philadelphia: Fortress Press, 1981), 67-70.

N. Habel, *The Book of Job: A Commentary* (OTL; Philadelphia: Westminster Press, 1985), 347.

Job's Lingering Fear: An Absent and Terrifying God, 23:8-16

Job's hope for justice depends on being able to find God, thus he sets
forth on an imaginative journey to the four points of the compass. He
turns to the east ("forward") and the west ("backward"), then to the
north ("left") and the south ("right"), but the God he seeks is not to be
found anywhere. The sad result of his quest is reported in a sequence of
deadening truths: "he is not there"; "I cannot perceive him"; "I cannot
behold him"; "I cannot see him" (vv. 8-9). The futility of Job's search
for God turns traditional Hebraic affirmations of piety on their end.
The psalmist exalts in the knowledge that there is nowhere in the
cosmos where one is hidden from *God's all-encompassing presence* (Ps
139:7-12). From Job's perspective, it is *God's absence* that is *all-encompassing.* God does not *search* for those who fear they are beyond God's
care and compassion. Instead, God *hides*, perhaps even *flees*, from those
who search the extremities of the globe for any sign whatsoever that
they are not alone in their suffering. ["I Sent a Sigh to Seek Thee Out"]

There is a painful, inexplicable disconnect between Job's yearning
and God's absence (vv. 10-12). Job is confident that the "way" (v. 10a:
derek) he takes is "his [God's] way" (v. 11b: *darkô*), that his feet follow
the footprints made by "his [God's] steps" (v. 11a: *ʾăšurô*), that the
words he speaks and the actions he takes conform to "his [God's] commandments" (v. 12a: *miṣwat śĕpātāw*) and "his [God's] words" (v. 12b:
ʾimrê pîw). Moreover, Job knows that *God knows* he is who he claims to
be. *God knows* that when Job is tried and tested he will "come out like
gold" (v. 10b). [CD: As Good as Gold] If Job is a true and worthy steward of
the gift of God's image, then why does God evade and ignore him?

In vv. 13-16, Job draws a conclusion about the character of the God
he seeks but cannot find. Behind the veil of hiddenness, God "is one"
(v. 13a: *hûʾ bĕʾeḥād*; NJPS; NRSV: "he stands alone"). Under different
circumstances such an assertion might summon the faithful to love
God with a singularity of resolve and commitment that divine sovereignty deserves and invites (cf. Deut 6:4-5). Indeed, even those who
despair that God is absent may be emboldened to hope for new possibilities, *if* they have sufficient reason to believe that God's desire to
deliver them will not be thwarted by any obstacle. The exiles in
Babylon, for example, may take comfort in knowing that God is unal-
terably committed to their rescue: "I am God, and henceforth I am He;
there is no one who can deliver from my hand; I work and who can
hinder it (*yĕšîbennāh*)?" (Isa 43:13).

Job's situation, however, is different, and he can find nothing comforting about God's oneness. Whatever God desires, that is what "he
does" (v. 13b). Whatever destiny God "appoints" for humans, God
works to bring it to completion (v. 14a). No one can "hinder" God

"I Sent a Sigh to Seek Thee Out"

George Herbert's poem "The Search" gives poignant expression to the quest for God whose absence too often seems to exceed the plaintive sigh "deep drawn in pain":

Whither, O, whither art thou fled,
My Lord, my Love?
My searches are my daily bread;
Yet never prove.

My knees pierce th' earth, mine eyes the sky;
And yet the sphere
And centre both to me deny
That thou art there . . .

I sent a sigh to seek thee out,
Deep drawn in pain,
Winged like an arrow: but my scout
Returns in vain . . .

Where is my God? what hidden place
Conceals thee still?
What overt dare eclipse thy face?
Is it thy will? . . .

Since then my grief must be as large,
As is thy space,
Thy distance from me; see my charge,
Lord, see my case.

G. Herbert, "The Search," *The Complete English Poems*, ed. John Tobin (London: Penguin Books, 1991), pp. 152-53, ll. 1-8, 17-20, 29-32, 45-48.

(v. 13a: *yĕšîbennû*; NRSV: "dissuade him"), because God retains exclusive control over divine decisions. No one, not even a righteous person like Job, can say or do anything that might cause God to rethink or alter what has already been determined. As Good has put it, "There is no space between the god's desire and his deed, no thoughtful reflection, no canvassing of implications."[4] As a result Job is "terrorized" (v. 15: *'ebbāhēl*; cf. v. 16b) by the thought of contending with a God whose power is overwhelming and unchallengable. As far as he can see, this God will do nothing to encourage or strengthen him. Instead, God has determined to make his heart so faint (v. 16a: *herek*; lit., "soften") that he becomes too weak and cowardly to do anything but give in and give up.

[Contemplating a Fierce Judge]

By the end of chapter 23, Job's quest for God leaves him facing a critical decision. From the outset Job has been under no illusion about the "darkness" (*ḥōšek*) that threatens to engulf his world and subvert his reason for living (3:3; 10:21; 17:13). As his certainty about this darkness deepens, so too does the despair that his cry for help can ever break through the veil of God's impenetrable silence (9:16; 16:16-18; 19:7). The situation seems so bleak that for a long time Job can do little more than pray that death will come quickly (e.g., 3:20-22; 10:18-21; 16:22–17:1). It is only through an act of courageous defiance that he determines to live for justice rather than death (13:15; 16:18). Now such defiance seems more than merely foolish. It is an act that makes life in pursuit of an absent God even more terrifying than death without vindication. What is Job to do now that he seems to have exhausted all reasonable options? Should he retreat to his first inclination and wait passively for death's final verdict? Or should he accept terror as the only reward for those too stubborn to "agree with God and be at peace" (22:21)?

In v. 17, Job announces that he will accept neither option. He will not be made *invisible* by the "darkness" (*ḥōšek*) that threatens to collapse the boundaries between life and death. Even if "thick darkness" (*'ōpel*) should cover his face so that he can neither see nor be seen, he will be a *presence* that God cannot ignore. The translation in NRSV (cf.

Contemplating a Fierce Judge

Franz Kafka's *The Trial*, which Martin Buber judged to be the most important commentary on the book of Job of our generation (see N. Glatzer, "Introduction: A Study of Job," *The Dimensions of Job: A Study and Selected Readings* [New York: Schocken, 1969], 48), chronicles the terrifying experience of Joseph K., a respected banker who is suddenly arrested "without having done anything wrong" (1). From this point forward, he is consumed by the effort to defend himself against a charge about which he can get no information. Acting on the advice of a colleague, he pays a visit to a painter named Titorelli who works for the Court, in the hope that he might learn something that will help him understand the system arrayed against him. When he arrives at Titorelli's studio, he finds him working on a portrait of what he takes to be a Judge who seems to be rising menacingly from his chair. Behind the Judge's seat was another figure K. can not identify.

"It is Justice," said the painter at last. "Now I can recognize it," said K. "There's the bandage over the eyes, and here are the scales. But aren't there wings on the figure's heels, and isn't it flying?" "Yes," said the painter, "my instructions were to paint it like that; actually it is Justice and the goddess of Victory in one." "Not a very good combina-

Job

Marc Chagall (1887-1985). *Job*. 1975. Private Collection © ARS, NY (Credit: Scala/Art Resource, NY)

tion, surely," said K., smiling. "Justice must stand quite still, or else the scales will waver and a just verdict will become impossible." "I had to follow my client's instructions," said the painter. "Of course," said K., who had not wished to give any offense by his remark. (146)

As the painter works, K. watches a reddish shadow grow around the head of the Judge like a halo. The shadow exaggerated the brightness of the Justice figure, which now seems to be flying right into the foreground, toward K.

It no longer suggested the goddess of Justice, or even the goddess of Victory, but looked exactly like the goddess of the Hunt in full cry. (147)

K.'s perception of the goddess figure that inspires terror is apt commentary on Job's God in ch. 23. Before such a God, one suspects Job's fear and dread might look something like that which Marc Chagall has depicted in the face of "Job at Prayer."

For further reading on comparisons between *The Trial* and Job, see S. Lasine, "Job and His Friends in the Modern World: Kafka's *The Trial*," *The Voice from the Whirlwind: Interpreting the Book of Job,* ed. L. G. Perdue, W. Clark Gilpin (Nashville: Abingdon, 1992), 144-55; M. Wilk, *Jewish Presence in T. S. Eliot and Franz Kafka* (Atlanta: Scholars Press, 1986), 133-67.

F. Kafka, *The Trial* (New York: Schocken Books, 1937). Citations are from *The Trial: The Definitive Edition; Introduction by George Steiner* (New York: Schocken Books, 1992).

NAB) obscures this resolve by changing the Hebrew text from "I am *not* destroyed (*lōʾ niṣmattî*) by the darkness" (see the marginal note) to "*If only* I could vanish (i.e., "be destroyed"; *lû niṣmattî*) in darkness." The verb *ṣāmat*, "destroy, put an end to," is the same word Job uses in 6:17 to rebuke the friends for "disappearing" from him when he most needs their loyalty. They are like river beds too shallow to withstand the changes in weather. When the temperature gets too hot, they simply dry up and go away. Job determines that his resolve to stand before God will demonstrate a different and fiercer presence than the friends have shown him. Moreover, Job will not agree to be a *silent* presence, not even if silence will secure a terrorized peace. What he will do and say instead is the subject of chapter 24. But already the first sound of his stubborn refusal to go quietly into the darkness can be heard in the next word he speaks: "Why?" (24:1). ["Rage, Rage Against the Dying of the Light"]

Why Does God Not See Anything Wrong with the World? 24:1-12

In the second part of his speech, Job turns from the complaint about God's hiddenness to God's indictable failure as a fair and reasonable judge of the world. His first word in a darkened world absent of God is "Why?" (v. 1: *maddûaʿ*). The tenor of the question is similar to that of 21:7 ("Why [*maddûaʿ*] do the wicked live on"), indicating that Job's objective is to raise an issue for the sake of making a counter argument.[5] The translation in NRSV is problematic on several grounds. Gordis provides a better reading: "Why, since times of judgment are not hidden from Shaddai, do His friends not see His day (of judgment)?"[6] Job's concern is not to complain that God "keeps" or "stores up" judgment for a later time, because even if this were true, as the friends have insisted, Job has already rejected this argument as morally indefensible (21:19-20). Instead, he affirms a time-honored truth about God and then asks why God does not live up to this truth. Surely, the times of judgment are *not hidden* from God. God knows *why* judgment is a necessary component of the world's moral order, and God knows *when* judgment must be enacted if the world is to be saved from moral chaos. *Why then* do those who know and entrust themselves to God's truth never see

"Rage, Rage Against the Dying of the Light"

The Welsh poet Dylan Thomas (1914–1953) speaks of the rage one feels when life's days draw to a darkened close, because words can no longer "fork" the lightning. The sentiment belongs not only to the aged.

Do not go gentle into that good night,
Old age should burn and rave at close of day;
Rage, rage against the dying of the light.

Though wise men at the end know dark is right,
Because their words had forked no lightning they
Do not go gentle into that good night.

D. Thomas, "Do Not Go Gentle Into That Good Night," *The Collected Poems of Dylan Thomas 1934–1952* (New York: New Directions Books, 1971), 128.

the judgment that confirms God is God? Job argues that if justice is as hidden as God, then both seem utterly nonexistent. [A Charge of "Cosmic Mismanagement"]

When there are no visible signs of either God or God's justice, the wicked are free to pursue their objectives with impunity. The result, Job argues, is the collapse of the moral order that sustains society (vv. 2-12). [CD: Complaints about Abuse of Power that Remind Rulers of the Need for Social Justice] As evidence of his charge, Job cites a number of civil injustices carried out by the wicked that have the cumulative effect of stealing from people their opportunity to be fully human. The first impression one has from reading this account is that Job's eyes are darting back and forth erratically from oppressor (vv. 2-4, 9) to oppressed (vv. 5-8, 10-12) in a frenzied effort to catalogue what he sees. It is possible, and perhaps helpful, to clarify this description by grouping Job's observations around certain key emphases, but it is wise to remember that in organizing these verses we impose an order of our own making. In a world where the boundaries between good and evil have collapsed, *chaos* not *structure* is closer to what the eye can see.

• People (LXX: "the wicked") steal land and livestock from those too weak to protect what is rightfully theirs (vv. 2-3), leaving them no place to inhabit but the wilderness and no source of food beyond what they can glean from the fields the wicked control (vv. 5-6). The particulars

---

A Charge of "Cosmic Mismanagement"

D. Clines compares the "times of judgment" to the "quarter days" in the English calendar—Lady Day, Midsummer, Michaelmas, and Christmas—which since medieval times have been recognized as times when debts are settled, conflicts are resolved, and a squaring of the record is made public. These quarterly court sessions, called "days of assize," were designed to insure both the rich and the poor that justice could not be denied or delayed. Clines connects this practice to Job's complaint in 24:1 as follows:

Job's complaint is that God holds no such assizes, but allows wrongs to continue unchecked and never brings offenders to book. God's failure to provide regular days for judgment has two harmful outcomes: it dismays the pious who suffer oppression, and it serves to encourage wrongdoers in the belief that they will never be called to account. As an absent governor of the world of humans, standing aloof above the fray of human affairs, God is charged by Job with irresponsibility and cosmic mismanagement. With quarter days gone and the absence of God advertised, scoundrels can prosper and God's own fecklessness can never come to trial.

Building on this analogy, the reader may recall scene 2 in the prologue (see the commentary on 1:6-12), which describes God convening the divine council for the purpose of evaluating the past year and setting the course for the year that approaches. Job's complaint suggests that God is indifferent to the need for establishing times for justice in the rhythmic patterns of the created order. See further **[The Divine Council]**.

D. Clines, "Quarter Days Gone: Job 24 and the Absence of God," *God in the Fray: A Tribute to Walter Brueggemann*, ed. T. Linafelt, T. Beal (Minneapolis MN: Augsburg Fortress, 1998), 242.

of Job's charge center on appropriating property by removing the boundary stones (*gĕbulôt*; NRSV: "landmarks") that divide one person's property from another's, a practice strictly forbidden and condemned in Israel (Deut 19:14; 27:17; Prov 23:10; cf. Hos 5:10). It is not just land that is seized illegally but entire herds of livestock as well. More heinous still is the robbing of the most defenseless persons in society—orphans and widows (see [CD: Common Condemnations]) Such persons cling to life by the barest of threads; the loss of a single donkey or ox can be enough to deny them any chance at all to survive. Stripped of their land and their resources, even their children (v. 9), people are denied the right to live as civilized human beings. They become like "wild assess" foraging in the wasteland. In what is perhaps an ironic twist on Eliphaz's previous argument (11:12), Job charges that injustice has the potential to do the unthinkable. It can turn a human being into a wild animal.

• Injustice drives the destitute out of the public's view (v. 4). They go into hiding, both because they fear the random abuse that awaits them around every corner (cf. Judg 5:6), and because they know they have no one who will hear their appeal for help (cf. Amos 5:12; Isa 10:12). Without clothing and shelter, they are excessively vulnerable to the cold and the rain (vv. 7-8, 10a). If they expect God to be the "Rock" (*ṣûr*) of their salvation (Deut 32:15; cf. Isa 17:10; Ps 18:2 [MT 18:3]), they will be sorely disappointed, for the "rock" (v. 8b: *ṣûr*) they embrace provides neither companionship nor protection.

• Injustice makes slaves of persons whose right is to be free (vv. 10b-11). Job describes those denied land, family, and shelter as day laborers who are forced to produce the goods others enjoy—grain, oil, and wine—without being able to secure for themselves even the basic necessities of life. Deuteronomy 25:4 stipulates that a farmer shall not muzzle an ox while it is treading out the grain, for even an animal deserves the chance to eat while it works (see Paul's application of this verse to human laborers in 1 Cor 9:9). Job charges that those whom injustice turns into outcasts do not even have the rights of an ox.

Since God knows that the world cannot survive without justice, why then does God not respond to the wickedness that frays the moral fabric of creation's design? In v. 12, Job answers his own question (cf. 24:1). The "dying groan," the "soul (*nepeš*; NRSV: "throat") of the wounded cries for help," and God remains indifferent. Why? Because God sees nothing "wrong" with the way the world is working. The word "wrong" (*tiplāh*) is the same word used by the narrator in the pro-

logue (1:22) to affirm that Job did not charge God with any "wrong-doing" when his world was turned upside-down by undeserved affliction.[7] But Job's understanding of this world and of the God who oversees it has now changed. Surely something *is* terribly wrong with a world where innocent victims die unnoticed. If there is not, then the *God of creation's Edenic promise* that the world is "very good" (Gen 1:31) cannot be trusted. Surely something *is* fundamentally wrong with a God who is unaffected by pharaonic-like abuse and oppression. If there is not, then the *God of the Exodus*—the God who hears and heeds the "cry for help" (Exod 2:23-25)—is a dangerous death-dealing myth.
["Where Is the God of the Exodus?"]

The Criminality that Collapses the Creational Boundaries Between Light and Darkness, 24:13-17

To the list of civil injustices that subvert the social order Job now adds the criminal deeds that return creation to primordial chaos. When there is no appointed time for judgment, the governing cycles of the world may be co-opted for sinister purposes. Those who actively "rebel against the light" (v. 13) flout creation's order so that darkness becomes the criminal's playground. Job cites three types of criminals. The "murderer" (v. 14: *rôṣēaḥ*) rises before daybreak to kill the poor and the needy. The "adulterer" (v. 15: *nō'ēp*) watches for the twilight, then veils his face, thinking that no one can see what he is up to. The "thief" (v. 14c: *gānāb*) uses the cover of darkness to burglarize houses, then seals himself up during the day to avoid capture (v. 16). The one thing each of these has in common is a preference for the counterworld of darkness, where night displaces day, and terror becomes an accomplice in crime (v. 17).[8]

"Where Is the God of the Exodus?"

AΩ In a most suggestive exegesis J. Gerald Janzen notes that Job's words in 23:2 (*'anāḥah*; "groaning") and 24:12 (*nā'aq*; "groan"; *šawa'*; "cry for help") contain three of the four terms that occur in Exodus 2:23-25 to describe the cry of the oppressed Israelites in Egypt: "The Israelites groaned (*'ānāḥ*) under their slavery . . . their cry for help (*šawa'*) rose up to God. God heard their groaning (*nā'aq*), and God remembered his covenant with Abraham, Isaac, and Jacob." Over against that successful appeal, Job charges that the God who sees nothing wrong with wounded cries for help that go unanswered cannot be the God of the Exodus. "Where is the God of Exodus? Where is the God of the burning bush? Where is *Yahweh*?" Such questions invite unthinkable thoughts about the nature and character of God. As Janzen puts it, "the unchanging God of 23:13 and the unmoved God of 24:12 resembles unfeeling and unresponsive Pharaoh more than the hearing, remembering, seeing, knowing, and delivering God of Exodus 2:24-25 and 3:7-8."

Job's challenge to the God who no longer keeps faith with the promises of Exodus evokes reflection on Jacob Glatstein's mournful post-Holocaust "tribute" to the God of Sinai. Job might well paraphrase Glatstein's despair as follows: "We received the Torah on Sinai / and in Uz we gave it back."

J. Gerald Janzen, *Job* (Atlanta: John Knox, 1985), 170. The line in Glatstein's poem is "We received the Torah on Sinai / and in Lublin we gave it back" ("Dead Men Don't Praise God," *The Selected Poems of Jacob Glatstein*, translated from the Yiddish and with an introduction by R. Whitman [New York: October House, 1972], 68).

It is interesting to consider why Job cites these three crimes as particular evidence of the moral chaos that threatens to undo the world. Murder, stealing, and adultery are serious covenantal violations (Exod 20:13-15; Deut 5:17-19) that jeopardize Israel's relationship with God. Beyond this, Hosea warns that such crimes infect the cosmos itself. They rob creation of its potential to provide peace and abundance for nature and people. When human wickedness results in murder, stealing, and adultery "the land mourns (*'ābāl*; "dries up"; cf. Joel 1:10) and all who live in it languish" (Hos 4:3). Hosea argues that those who wage such an assault on creation should know that God will change their "glory" into "shame" (Hos 4:7; see the marginal note in NRSV).

Against the backdrop of Hosea's preaching, one can trace a trajectory of thought in Job's vexed contention with the counterworld of darkness that is especially disturbing. His first words from the ash-heap curse creation by calling for "deep darkness" (*ṣalmāwet*, 3:5) to subsume the light of day (see the commentary on 3:3-10). Gradually he resolves to resist this darkness rather than to be complicit in effecting it. He complains that God's secret creational intent (cf. 10:13) is to give the "deep darkness" (12:22: *ṣalmāwet*) free reign to impose its chaos on the light. Now he appears to recognize just how devastatingly successful God can be when darkness not light is the controlling trigger for creation's design. His description of unrestrained criminality in 24:13-17 declares that the world is defined far more by darkness than light. The imbalance is particularly evident in v. 17 where two occurrences of the word for "deep darkness" (*ṣalmāwet*) rhetorically overwhelm the one reference to the morning light.

Implicit in this description is the charge that the wicked have discovered God's *secret* for success in a morally corrupt world. In Job's mind, their *stealthy* wickedness is a true but still perverted image of God's studied indifference to the claims of justice. More unsettling still is Job's determination not to accept this world or to be mute before the God who appears to sanction it. Like Hosea, Job knows that murder, stealing, and adultery are covenantal violations that destroy people and pollute the world. Job has come to believe, however, that the wicked are no more than secondarily culpable for these breeches of covenant fidelity. The One who bears primary responsibility is God. It is none other than God who has inexplicably transmuted *divine glory* (not *human glory*) into divine shame. For the sake of the dying wounded, *and* for the sake of a world that should be more than an open grave, Job believes that covenantal fidelity requires a courageous indictment of injustice, even if it means rebelling against the Creator who sees nothing wrong. ["How Is It Possible for Man to Be Other Than a Rebel in the Face of Such Facts?"]

Speaking Judgment in a World Absent of God, 24:18-25

The interpretation of the last section of chapter 24 is widely disputed. Because these verses announce a judgment on the wicked that is so inconsistent with Job's argument in this chapter, a number of scholars suggest that they comprise part of Bildad's or Zophar's third speech.[9] Other scholars argue that if these are Job's words, then they should be understood as part of his strategy to quote the friends' ideas in order to refute them (see vv. 22-23).[10] Still others take these verses as an independent poem composed by the author of the book, inserted here to provide an apocalyptic-like resolution to the problem of theodicy.[11] In the end times, God's "un-hiding" (the Greek noun *apokalypsis* means "unveiling" or "revelation") will make it clear to all that the wicked prosper "for a little while, and then are gone" (v. 24).[12] Each of these options has merit, but none is without difficulties.

The early versions—the LXX, the Vulgate, and the Peshitta—offer a plausible alternative to the interpretations noted above. By translating these verses as imprecatory wishes, these versions suggest that Job is evoking the judgment he believes God must endorse and enact if God is to act like God. It must be conceded that this approach depends on conjectural emendations that may be challenged.[13] Nevertheless, the picture of Job trying to speak into reality the judgment on the wicked he believes is warranted is consistent with his decision not to be a silent witness to a world where evil runs amok.[14] ["I Do Not Accept . . . This World of God's"] The translation in NJPS, which understands these words as Job's

---

"How Is It Possible for Man to Be Other Than a Rebel in the Face of Such Facts?"

Mr. Job Huss, the Joban character in H. G. Wells's *The Undying Fire*, challenges his friends' counsel with a summons to look squarely at the undeniable evidence of injustice in the world. "What is the true lot of life?" he asks.

Is there the slightest justification for assuming that our conceptions of right and happiness are reflected anywhere in the outward universe ? Is there, for instance, much animal happiness? Do health and well-being constitute the normal state of animals? (81)

He proceeds to inventory the examples of inexplicable suffering he sees everywhere, for example, a rabbit with the back of its head bitten open, the buffalo tormented to panic flight by swarms of flies, the mother penguin who watches helplessly as her eggs freeze to death. When he comes to the end of this survey of stubborn facts Mr. Huss asks a series of questions that he believes drives one to choose between two equally unacceptable answers.

I ask you, how is it possible for man to be other than a rebel in the face of such facts? How can he trust the Maker who has designed and elaborated and finished [these things] in their endless multitude and variety? How can Man trust such a Maker to treat him fairly? Why should we shut our eyes to things that stare us in the face? Either the world of life is the creation of a being inspired by a malignancy at once filthy, petty, and enormous, or it displays a carelessness, an indifference, a disregard for justice. . . . (98-99)

For further discussion of Wells's novel, see the "Connections" on Job 3.

H. G. Wells, *The Undying Fire* (New York: The Macmillan Company, 1919).

"I Do Not Accept . . . This World of God's"

Job's resolve to evoke curses on injustice rather than feign blessing that is a cover-up echoes in the ruminations of F. Dostoevsky's Ivan. In a conversation with his brother Alyosha, Ivan strains to integrate the truth about profound human suffering and the dictums of faith that affirm God is just. "It's not God that I do not accept, you understand, it is this world of God's, created by God, that I do not accept and cannot agree to accept."

A few scenes later Ivan takes his argument a step further. If extreme and inexplicable suffering is the cost of accommodating oneself to the perverted "harmony" of God's world, then Ivan concludes the price is too high.

I don't want harmony, for love of mankind I don't want it. I'd rather remain with my unrequited suffering and my unquenched indignation, *even if I am wrong*. Besides, they have put too high a price on harmony; we can't afford to pay so much for admission. And therefore I hasten to return my ticket. And it is my duty, if only as an honest man, to return it as far ahead of time as possible. Which is what I am doing. It's not that I don't accept God, Alyosha, I just most respectfully return him the ticket.

F. Dostoevsky, *The Brothers Karamazov*, trans. and annot. R. Pevear and L. Volokhonsky (New York: Vintage Books, 1990), 235, 245.

---

curse upon the wicked, gives the reader the best chance of hearing Job's defiant insistence that God knows such judgment is necessary (24:1). If, as Job suspects, God truly sees nothing wrong with the way the world is working (24:12), then God should follow Job's lead. [NJPS: Job's Curse Upon the Wicked]

With a variety of images Job evokes a judgment that nullifies every trace of the corrupting presence of the wicked in the world. He wishes/demands that they become like "floatsom" (v. 18a: *qal*; lit., something "light," "insignificant") that is carried away by the water's current; that their portion in the land be so cursed there will be no grapes to tread in their vineyards (v. 18b); that Sheol consume them like the drought and the heat that destroy the snow-waters of winter (v. 19); that they be utterly forgotten and remembered no more, except by the worms that savor the sweetness of their rotting corpses (v. 20a); that their wickedness be broken like a tree that is split in two (v. 20b);

NJPS: Job's Curse Upon the Wicked

AΩ NJPS, noting that the translation is conjectural, renders Job's words in 24:18-24 as a curse upon the wicked. As with his curse in ch. 3, Job intends these words to be more than mere rhetoric. They constitute a *rhetorical act* that seeks to actualize in God the very judgment that Job declares.

v. 18   May they be floatsam on the face of the water;
        May their portion in the land be cursed;
        May none turn aside by way of their vineyards.

v. 19   May drought and heat snatch away their snow waters,
        And Sheol, those who have sinned.

v. 20   May the womb forget him;
        May he be sweet to the worms;
        May he no longer be remembered;
        May wrongdoers be broken like a tree.

v. 21   May he consort with a barren woman who bears no child,
        Leave his widow deprived of good.

v. 22   Though he has strength to seize bulls,
        May he live with no assurance of survival.

v. 23   Yet [God] gives him the security on which he relies,
        And keeps watch over his affairs.

v. 24   Exalted for a little while, let them be gone;
        Be brought low, and shrivel like mallows,
        And wither like the heads of grain.

See also J. Hartley, *The Book of Job* (NICOT; Grand Rapids MI: William B. Eerdmans, 1988), 350-51.

that their women be barren and thus deprived of the good normally associated with motherhood (v. 21); that their strength be too ineffective to secure their survival (v. 22).

In the midst of this string of curses, Job seems to become uncomfortably aware that he may be calling for a judgment that puts him at odds with God. As far as he can see, it is none other than God who gives the wicked the confidence to flaunt injustice with impunity. Although God sees the way of life the wicked pursue, God seems to discern nothing wrong in their preference for evil instead of good (v. 23). Like Abraham who pleads for the righteous of Sodom, then flinches at the thought that he, a mere mortal, should instruct the Judge of all the earth on how to do justice (Gen 18:27), Job pauses before the possibility that God may be too little concerned with the cries of the innocent to act on their behalf. But also like Abraham (cf. Gen 18:28-32), Job seems to conclude that pressing the case for justice is worth the risk of challenging God. Thus he resumes the call for judgment with a final sequence of demands: "Let them [the wicked] be exalted for a little while and then be no more; let them be brought low and shriveled up like grass; and let them be cut off like the heads of grain" (v. 24). [Hope Founded on Odds of No More Than "a Fraction of One Percent"]

Once he completes his vision of the judgment that is needed, Job issues a defiant challenge to anyone to prove his discernment wrong (v. 25). Who has the moral authority to argue that Job has lied about what he has seen? Surely not the friends, for in Job's estimation they have already shown themselves willing to cover-up the truth about the way the world works (13:4, 7). Who can show that there is nothing worth taking to heart in what Job says? Job knows that *God* can decide his words are worthless, for his experience thus far validates nothing more than that his cries for justice have changed nothing in heaven or on earth (16:18-19; 19:7). But should Job be forced to concede that God does not in fact care about the moral chaos of the world, then he would have to conclude that God is not a God of justice after all. Job's refusal to believe that this is the truth about God rests on the thin edge

---

Hope Founded on Odds of No More than a "Fraction of One Percent"

Job could not be faulted for believing that the odds in favor of his words having any impact on God's decisions are slim and none, perhaps one in a thousand (cf. 9:3, 16). Even so, it is that "fraction of one percent" that stays his tenuous hold on humanity, on God, and on the justice he believes must bind the two together in common cause.

We may doubt the just proportion of good to ill.
There is much in nature against us. But we forget:
Take nature altogether since time began,
Including human nature, in peace and war,
And it must be a little more in favor of man,
Say a fraction of one percent at the very least,
Or our number living wouldn't be steadily more,
Our hold on the planet wouldn't have so increased.

Robert Frost, "Our Hold on the Planet," in *The Poetry of Robert Frost*, ed. E. C. Lathem (New York: Henry Holt and Company, 1969), 349.

of a bold rhetorical move. By calling for the punishment of the wicked, Job seeks to actualize *in God* the truth about justice that now seems hidden away in the deep recesses of God's heart.

The question that ends the chapter may strike the reader as purely rhetorical, but it can hardly be so for Job. If there is nothing of merit in what Job says, then the friends are right, Job is wrong, and the God who listened and responded positively to Abraham is an illusion. When these consequences are carefully weighed, then one begins to sense why Job's complaint is both impatient and defiant (cf. 23:1).

CONNECTIONS

Job's speech in chapters 23–24 holds in tension two seemingly dissonant affirmations: God is absent, and there must be justice. The cotter pin of resolute faith that strains to bind these two affirmations together is 23:17: "But I am not destroyed by the darkness." Readers may find it instructive to reflect on what it means to be stewards of this faith and to be held accountable for acting on it or not acting on it. In pondering the consequences of either choice, it is wise to keep one ear cocked toward God's response, the other toward the cries for help of the wounded and the dying.

Job's deepening sense of the absence of God is hardly his alone. Indeed, a strong case can be made that in "biblical times" and in "modern times" the journey of faith must be plotted in what R. Friedman has described as a "postrevelation world."[15] Whether one reads the Old Testament story from Eve to Esther critically or confessionally, it is in a real sense a story of God's steadily diminishing presence. Friedman notes that at the outset the Pentateuch portrays God as audibly, visibly, at times extraordinarily present in the world (e.g., in the garden of Eden and at Sinai). But after Sinai God appears less and less, speaks less and less, and is less and less actively involved in the affairs of the world and of humankind. For example,

> —the last person to whom God is "revealed" is Samuel (1 Sam 3:21)
> —the last person to whom God "appears" is Solomon (1 Kgs 3:5; 9:2)
> —the last appearance of the cloud and glory as signs of God's presence is at Solomon's dedication of the temple (1 Kgs 8:10-11; 2 Chr 5:14; 7:1-3)
> —the last public miracle is in the story of Elijah at Mount Carmel (1 Kgs 18)
> —the last *appearance* of an angel in the Hebrew Bible is also in the Elijah story (2 Kgs 1:3, 15), and the last *report* of an angel acting on earth is

in the days of Isaiah and Hezekiah (2 Kgs 19:35; Isa 37:36; 2 Chr
32:21)

—the last visible representation of God's presence is in the temple in
Jerusalem, and it is destroyed by the Babylonians in 586 BCE (2 Kgs
25:9; 2 Chr 36:19)[16]

The New Testament's perspective on God's presence is of course different. Critically important is the affirmation in the gospels that God is
incarnate in Jesus. And yet, the New Testament also reports that even
Jesus' faith was shaped by a profound understanding of God's absence.
His last words from the cross—"My God, my God, why have you forsaken me?" (Matt 27:46; Mark 15:34)—are surely enlarged by the
testimony to resurrection, but they are not erased from the story.
Without their lingering echo, the Sunday celebration of Easter is like a
song in search of a tune. As George Steiner has discerned, Christian
faith cannot be Christian without "the long day's journey of the
Saturday" that waits before the "assured" and still "precarious" words of
Jesus' question.[17]

Friedman contends that the witness to God's absence extends far
beyond the Old and New Testaments. Now, nearly 2,000 years after
these canons of scripture were closed, the twentieth century limps to its
end affirming nothing perhaps so strongly as that God has simply dis-
appeared. On the one hand, as the ever expanding domains of science
and technology unlock more and more of the mysteries of the universe,
religious claims about God sound more and more naïve and redundant.
On the other hand, after two world wars, the incomparable evil of the
Holocaust, and the seemingly endless eruptions of violence and barbarity in the world, the sheer quantity of suffering and loss piled on the
scales on the twentieth century suggest that the imbalance between
death and life is more precarious today than ever before. As we stagger
into the twenty-first century under the weight of such misery all
around, Friedman pointedly wonders out loud, "Is there anyone who
does not know that something is wrong here? that something is
missing?"[18]

Job's "friends" in the contemporary world can be expected to respond
to Friedman's questions in predictable ways. *What is wrong,* they will
argue, is that sin has so defiled the place where God wants to be present
that God has determined to depart in judgment. In the words of Isaiah,
"your iniquities have been barriers between you and your God, and
your sins have hidden his face from you so that he does not hear" (Isa
59:2). *What is missing,* therefore, is the repentance that invites a holy
God to take up residence again in the midst of a contrite people (cf.
8:3-6; 11:13-19; 22:23-28). Alternatively, they will argue that *what is
wrong* is that humans want God to be present but not transcendent.

What is missing, therefore, is obedient submission to divine wisdom that is necessarily too deep and too high for mere mortals to comprehend (11:7-9; cf. 26:14; 33:12-14; 34:29; 37:21-24).

Such convictions are important, and the Jobs of this world will rightly be tempted to accept them as the full truth about human nature and divine sovereignty (cf. Job's wonderments in 7:20-21; 9:4-12, 32-33; 12:13-16; 13:23; 23:13-14; 28:20-23). But those who walk in the footsteps of Job (cf. 23:10-11) will not be persuaded that sin and transcendence are adequate explanations for God's absence when evil threatens to become more sovereign than God.[19] With Abraham, Moses, Jeremiah, Habakkuk, the psalmists of lament, and Jesus they will ask "Why?" (see [Retribution]). And like Job they will refuse to be silent in the dark absence of a God who does not respond to "wounded cries for help" (23:17; 24:12). [CD: Is This the Way the World Ends?]

In a world empty of God and full of unrequited suffering, Job demands justice (24:18-24). If God does not see anything wrong when the wicked steal from the poor their right to be free and fully human, then Job will be God's eyes. If God does not hear the cries for help, then Job will speak words that "itch" at God's ears until they are heard and understood. ["I Follow You Whoever You Are from the Present Hour"] If God does not know what justice requires, then Job will describe the punishment that fits the crime of turning the world into a haven for murder, stealing, and adultery. On the chance that he has erred in his discernment, Job takes his stand inside the measureless chasm between what he hopes and believes is the truth about God and his lingering fear that he hopes and believes too much (24:25).

The still unanswered question that haunts Job and his readers is how will God respond to faith that is enacted as moral rebellion rather than reverent submission? Has God determined that human beings are simply "born to trouble," as Eliphaz insists (4:7) and Job suspects (14:1)? Is it God's decision that human beings must do nothing other than "agree with God" and thus submit to a terrorized "peace," as Eliphaz teaches (22:21) and Job increasingly concedes (3:25; 6:4; 7:14; 9:28; 13:21, 25; 16:9; 19:11; 23:15-16)? Job has little reason not to believe that God will ultimately respond to his challenge with a rebuke that ends his defiance once and for all. Indeed, if one accepts the con-

---

"I Follow You Whoever You Are from the Present Hour"

Walt Whitman uses the imagery of words that "itch" at the ear until they are understood to describe the persistent efforts of the teacher who yearns for the student to know and build upon knowledge imparted.

I follow you whoever you are from the present hour
My words itch at your ears till you understand them.

For another appropriation of this poem with reference to Job, see **["I Am an Encloser of Things to Be"]**.

W. Whitman, "Song of Myself," *Leaves of Grass*, ed. with intro. by J. Loving (Oxford: Oxford University Press, 1990), 75.

ventional interpretation of Job 38–41, this is precisely what happens
when God answers Job "out of the whirlwind." Before accepting that
conclusion, however, it is important to suspend final judgment while
we wait with Job in the precarious interval between now and then.

Until God speaks and settles these questions one way or the other, we
may consider one further observation from Friedman about the Bible's
witness to life in a postrevelation world. Perhaps God's hiddenness is
more than only a reaction to human sin. Perhaps it is more than just
the necessary corollary of God's holy otherness. Perhaps God chooses to
hide because to do so is consonant with God's nature and purposes. As
Isaiah so tellingly puts it, God is truly "a God who hides himself
(*mistattēr*)" (Isa 45:15).[20] Friedman suggests that divine hiddenness is
encoded in the world God creates as part of the intentional design for
the divine-human relationship. He finds the clue for the meaning of
this design in the phrase *histîr pānîm*, which typically describes the
hiding of God's face. This expression provides the key metaphor for
divine absence in the Hebrew Bible. Friedman gives particular attention to the imagery conveyed by this language in Deut 32:20, where
just before Moses' death, God announces that the future of the people
of God will be a time of increasing divine hiddenness: "I will hide my
face from them, I will see what their end will be."[21]

The words "I will see what their end will be" hint that Gods hides
purposefully. Friedman suggests that it is part of the divine plan for
God to recede from direct intervention in the affairs of the world in
order to encourage and promote a greater human responsibility for life
on earth. God's disappearance from the stage of human history is therefore only half of the story the Hebrew Bible seeks to impart. The other
half is the steady, intentional shift in the balance of the divine-human
partnership such that humans necessarily have more and more responsibility for the management of their world.[22] Thus when one goes back
over the story from Eve to Esther, it becomes apparent that from beginning to end humans are permitted and expected to exercise an
increasing role in affairs that might well have been the exclusive prerogative of God. Noah builds his own ark (Gen 6:14-16), Abraham
questions God about divine justice (Gen 18:22-33), Moses elicits
"repentance" from God (Exod 32:12-14), in the absence of direct communication between God and humans, the prophets mediate God's
words, and so on. Taken as whole then, the Hebrew Bible affirms an
ironic truth that derives from both the nature of God and the nature of
humankind: the more God is distant, the more humans are *freed* and
required to become fully human, fully faithful. Friedman interprets this
truth as part of God's intentional summons for humans to "grow up,"
that is, humans must learn how to live in a world where the immediate,

Coming of Age in a World Without God

R. Friedman notes that the idea of "growing up" before God is similar to Dietrich Bonhoeffer's notion that humans must "come of age" if they to live in a world where God cannot be found. "So our coming of age leads us to a true recognition of our situation before God. God would have us know that we must live as men who manage our lives without him."

R. Friedman, *The Disappearance of God: A Divine Mystery* (Boston/New York: Little, Brown, and Company, 1995), 215. The citation from Bonhoeffer is found in *Letters from Prison* (New York: Macmillan, 1971), 360.

visible, concrete signs of God's presence may be seriously diminished.[23] In such a world, the creature should not look to the Creator to solve every problem through divine intervention. In such a world, there is much that humans *should do* and *can do* to sustain creation's design in the absence of God. [Coming of Age in a World Without God]

Friedman's observations offer an instructive perspective for reflecting on Job's position at the end of chapter 24. In the absence of God, is he "growing up" into the full image of God when he declares the judgment on the wicked that is deserved but lacking? Or is he perverting that image, as the friends keep insisting, because he refuses to accept silent submission as the only definition of what it means to be a human being? Job has raised two important questions that bear on our consideration of these matters. He has asked "What are human beings, that you make so much of them?" (7:17) and "Why do you hide your face (*pāneka tastîr*), and

"Striving to Embrace the Inhuman Pain"

In his collection of Joban iconography, S. Terrien includes Ossip Zadkine's (1890–1967) eighteen-foot bronze statue of "The City Destroyed," which stands in the center of Rotterdam. Terrien notes that when Zadkine saw this city that had been destroyed by the German Air Force in 1940 and then rebuilt, he determined to sculpt a figure that testified not only to the terror of the city's vulnerability but also to its courage to "embrace the inhuman pain" and to go on living by the grace of God. He depicts a person hollowed out in the center. With broken face and outstretched arms, he strains to push away the violence unleashed from the heavens. This figure provides a striking commentary on the Joban-like faith of those whose hands are heavy with groaning (cf. 23:2) that will not be silenced by the powers arrayed against them.

S. Terrien, *The Iconography of Job Through the Centuries* (University Park PN: The Pennsylvania State University Press, 1996), 269.

The City Destroyed

O. Zadkine. *The City Destroyed*. 1943-1953. Bronze statue. Rotterdam.

count me as your enemy?" (13:24). At this point in Job's story, there can be little question that God has indeed hidden from Job. What is still unclear is why. Does God "make so much" of him because he is God's "enemy," or because "there is no one like him on earth" (1:8; 2:3)? The first answer is Job's, and it represents the candid, pained, unsettling truth that he has determined to defy with his life (cf. 13:14-15). The second answer is the *preliminary* but *untested* assessment of God. This too represents a truth that is pained and vulnerable, because its validation rests on what will happen when God relinquishes full control over Job's life (cf. 2:6). Which of these two truths is left standing at the end of the day will not be finally decided until we unravel the meaning of what Job says in 42:2: "I know that you can do all things, and that no purpose of yours can be thwarted." Until that point, *Job* and *God* and the *reader* must wait to see "what *their* end will be." ["Striving to Embrace the Inhuman Pain"]

NOTES

[1] E. Peterson, *Job: Led by Suffering to the Heart of God* (Colorado Springs: NavPress, 1996), 60.

[2] The LXX has "his hand," implying that it is God's hand of oppression that weighs heavy on Job. A number of modern translations, including NRSV, follow this reading (e.g., NIV, REB, NAB). Although elsewhere it is clear that Job regards the hand of God to be the agent of his affliction (cf. 10:7; 19:21), on this occasion it is God's absence, not God's presence, that is oppressive. For a similar interpretation see E. Dhorme, *A Commentary on the Book of Job* (Nashville: Thomas Nelson Publishers, 1967), 343; M. Good, *In Turns of Tempest: A Reading of Job with a Translation* (Stanford: Stanford University Press, 1990), 112, 276.

[3] This reading follows M. Pope (*Job* [AB; Garden City NY: Doubleday, 1979], 170) and requires a slight emendation of the MT from *miššōpetî*, "from my judge," which NRSV follows, to *mišpatî*, "my judgment." This reading is supported by the LXX and the Vulgate. The verb in v. 7b, *pālat* (NRSV: "acquitted"), occurs in 21:10b where it refers to a cow "birthing" a calf. The imagery suggests that Job hopes his contention with God will give birth to justice, hence to new life, in a similar way. For a comparable argument, see J. Gerald Janzen, *Job* (Atlanta: John Knox, 1985), 166.

[4] Good, *In Turns of Tempest*, 278.

[5] Cf. C. Westermann, *The Structure of the Book of Job* (Philadelphia: Fortress, 1981), 58. The rhetoric of Job's question is also similar to that used by Jeremiah in a number of instances, e.g., Jer 8:22:

> Is there no balm in Gilead?
> Is there no physician there?
> Why then (*maddûaʿ*) has the health of my poor people
> not been restored? (cf. 2:14, 31; 8:4-5, 19; 14:19; 49:1)

For further reading on Jeremiah's questions, see W. Brueggemann, "Jeremiah's use of Rhetorical Questions," *JBL* 92 (1973): 358-74.

[6] R. Gordis, *The Book of Job: Commentary, New Translation, and Special Studies* (New York: Jewish Theological Seminary of America, 1978), 264.

[7] NRSV, following some Hebrew manuscripts, emends *tiplāh* to *těpîllāh*, "prayer." Although this emendation does not radically alter the basic sense of the verse, it fails to capture the ironic interplay between Job's initial absolution of God for wrongdoing in 1:22 and his indictment of God's wrongful indifference in 24:12.

[8] C. Newsom describes Job's words in 23:13-17 as a portrait of the "counterworld of the criminal" ("The Book of Job," in vol. 4 of NIB [Nashville: Abingdon Press, 1996], 511).

[9] Cf. S. Terrien, "The Book of Job," IB, vol. 3, ed. G. Buttrick (New York: Abingdon Press, 1954), 1088-89; Dhorme, *Commentary on the Book of Job*, 366-67; Pope, Job, 179; H. H. Rowley, Job (The Century Bible; Ontario: Thomas Nelson, 1970), 210.

[10] Gordis, *Book of Job*, 531-34. See further RSV, which inserts the words "You say" at the beginning of v. 18.

[11] G. Fohrer, *Das Buch Hiob* (KAT; Gütersloh: Gerd Mohn, 1963), 370-71.

[12] On Job's anticipation of apocalyptic thought and language, see Janzen, *Job*, 170-71.

[13] Cf. S. R. Driver and G. B. Gray, *A Critical and Exegetical Commentary on the Book of Job* (Edinburgh: T and T. Clark, 1921), 211.

[14] For a similar approach, see J. Hartley, *The Book of Job* (NICOT; Grand Rapids MI: William B. Eerdmans, 1988), 350-54; Newsom, "The Book of Job," 511-13.

[15] R. Friedman, *The Disappearance of God: A Divine Mystery* (Boston, New York, Toronto, London: Little, Brown, and Company, 1995), 28. With Friedman, a number of other scholars have noted that in the Hebrew Bible God is depicted as increasingly distant and silent; cf. J. Miles, *God: A Biography* (New York: Alfred A. Knopf, 1995); F. Ferrucci, *The Life of God (as Told by Himself)* (Chicago/London: University of Chicago Press, 1996). I have explored the implications of Friedman's work in more detail in Samuel E. Balentine, *The Torah's Vision of Worship* (Minneapolis MN: Fortress Press, 1998), 219-27.

[16] For these and other examples of the "last" signs of God's presence, see Friedman, *Disappearance of God*, 19-26.

[17] G. Steiner, *Real Presences* (Chicago: University of Chicago Press, 1989), 232. On the importance of this idea for understanding Old Testament theology, see W. Brueggemann, *Theology of the Old Testament: Testimony, Dispute, Advocacy* (Minneapolis MN: Fortress Press, 1997), 400-403.

[18] Friedman, *Disappearance of God*, 208.

[19] See the powerful statement of A. Cohen on contending with the "ultimacy" of evil; *The Tremendum: A Theological Interpretation of the Holocaust* (New York: Crossroad, 1988), 48-52.

[20] On the critical assertions of this text, see Samuel E. Balentine, "Isaiah 45: God's 'I Am, ' Israel's 'You Are, '" HBT 16 (1994): 103-20.

[21] Friedman, *Disappearance of God*, 69-76. On the phrase "hide the face" and other related expressions that comprise the vocabulary of divine hiddenness see further, Samuel E. Balentine, *The Hidden God: The Hiding of the Face of God in the Old Testament* (Oxford: Oxford University Press, 1983).

[22] Friedman, *Disappearance of God*, 30-59.

[23] Ibid., 214.

BILDAD'S THIRD SPEECH AND JOB'S RESPONSE: DOMINION, FEAR, AND A WHISPER OF SOMETHING MORE

Job 25:1–26:14

To this point, the dialogues have proceeded in an orderly and predictable manner, with each of the friends making his case and Job offering his counter response. In the final speeches of the third cycle (chs. 25–27), the steady alternation of speakers ends and the symmetry of the discourses is skewed. Bildad's third speech is disproportionately short (25:2-6); Job's response is long and in two places seemingly inconsistent with what one expects from him (26:5-14; 27:13-23), given his previous arguments. Zophar's third speech appears to be missing altogether. Most scholars have taken a position that puts them in general agreement with R. Gordis, who argues that the third cycle "has suffered great damage" and hence "cannot be meaningfully interpreted in its present form."[1] A variety of proposals for restoring order to these chapters by rearranging them to what may have been their original sequence have been offered. Perhaps the most common suggestion is that Bildad's speech in chapter 25 should be lengthened by adding 26:5-14 and that Zophar's speech should be reclaimed by reassigning 27:13-23 to him rather than to Job. [Making the Text Work]

None of the proposed reconstructions is fully convincing. Moreover, although it is *possible* that the text has suffered some disturbance in transmission, there is *no evidence* that this is so. The earliest translations of the book (the Aramaic Targum of Job from Qumran [11QtgJob] and the LXX) show the same sequence of speeches as the Masoretic Text.[2] A better approach is to wrestle with the text that we have instead of rebuilding a text that conforms to a pattern that may never have existed. It is plausible therefore to understand the disarray in these speeches as an interpretive clue that the dialogue between the friends and Job has finally broken down. Bildad's response in chapter 25 may be shorter than usual, because Job, having grown impatient with arguments that have already been so frequently repeated (cf. 25:4 with 4:17 and 15:14), now interrupts his friend (26:1-4) to show that he has heard it all before. Indeed, the

---

Making the Text Work

AΩ Scholars have offered numerous proposals for restoring order and symmetry to the final speeches in the third cycle (chs. 25–27). The assumption is that the pattern of alternating speakers (Eliphaz-Job, Bildad-Job, Zophar-Job) that dominates the dialogues in cycles one (chs. 4–14) and two (chs. 15–21) was originally present here as well, but for some reason this arrangement has been lost or garbled in the long history of the book's transmission. The proposals typically focus on passages in chs. 26–27 where the subject matter seems inconsistent or inappropriate in the mouth of Job.

For example, 26:5-14 is structurally and thematically a hymn of praise that some regard as more congruent with Bildad's general perspective than with Job's. Indeed, this hymn provides a fitting development of Bildad's opening words in 25:1-5. Similarly, where one expects to find Zophar's third speech, ch. 27 begins instead with the unusual introduction "And Job took up his discourse and said . . ." (27:1). The oath of innocence that follows in 27:2-6 and the curse against the enemy in 27:7-12 sound very much like what Job would say. But the confident description of the punishment of the wicked in 27:13-23 seems to contradict what Job has just said in 21:7-34. Because 27:13 is almost a verbatim of Zophar's concluding words in 20:29, many have suggested that 27:13-23 should be identified as his speech rather than Job's.

The table below gives a representative sampling of the proposals for rearranging chs. 25–27. For discussion of these various proposals, see the following works: S. R. Driver and G. B. Gray, *A Critical and Exegetical Commentary on the Book of Job* (Edinburgh: T and T. Clark, 1921), 215-32; R. Gordis, *The Book of Job: Commentary, New Translation, and Special Studies* (New York: Jewish Theological Seminary of America, 1978), 276-96; E. Dhorme, *A Commentary on the Book of Job* (Nashville: Thomas Nelson Publishers, 1967), 368-98; M. Pope, *Job* (AB; Garden City NY: Doubleday, 1979), 180-96; N. Habel, *The Book of Job: A Commentary* (OTL; Philadelphia: Westminster Press, 1985), 364-87; C. Newsom, "The Book of Job," in vol. 4 of NIB (Nashville: Abingdon Press, 1996), 516-26.

	Bildad	Job	Zophar
Driver	25:1-6	26:1-14; 27:11-12	27:13-23
Gordis	25:1-6; 26:5-14	26:1-4; 27:1-12	27:13-23
Dhorme	25:1-6; 26:5-14	26:1-4; 27:2-12	27:13-23; 24:18-24
Pope	25:1-6; 26:5-14	27:1; 26:1-4; 27:2-7	27:8-23; 24:18-25
Habel	25:1-6; 26:5-14	26:1-4; 27:1-12	27:13-23
Newsom	25:1-6; 26:5-14	26:1-4; 27:1-2	

Each of these proposals has its own strengths and weaknesses. None can be verified by any external evidence. To the extent that interpreters find one or more of these proposals preferable to or more compelling than the text that we have, they must concede that they are working from "a text *made*, not *found*." (On this suggestive phrase for describing the way both ancient writers and modern interpreters have stitched together disparate pieces to *make* the book of Job, see T. Tilley, *The Evils of Theodicy* [Washington, DC: Georgetown University Press, 1991], 90-91 [emphasis added].)

---

friends' way of praising God's dominion and awesomeness (25:2) is by now so predictable that Job can finish Bildad's speech for him (26:5-14). In a similar fashion, there is no need at this late juncture for Zophar to speak again. Job can anticipate what he will say even before he says it (27:13-23).[3]

One further observation may be offered as an introduction to these chapters. Job's speech may be more than simply a mimicking of his friends. His description of the mystery and power of divine governance in the world (26:5-14) foreshadows what God will subsequently spell out in more detail for Job in chapters 38–41. On the one hand, this hints that God's long-awaited response to Job may not be as disconnected from Job's primary concerns as conventional interpretations have suggested (see the commentary on these chapters).[4] God, no less than Job and the friends, is in fact deeply concerned with the question about who human beings will be in relation to the Creator of the world (cf. 4:17, 7:17, 15:14, 25:4 with 38:2: "Who is this?").

On the other hand, Job's words in 26:5-14 invite readers to imagine that he already knows at least some of what God will say about the way the world works even before God says it. Like Eliphaz, Job has heard a "whisper" (*šemeṣ*; cf. 4:12 with 26:14) of God's revelation. But unlike Eliphaz, and Bildad who follows Eliphaz's discernments, Job refuses to believe that partial insights constitute the full sum of what God ultimately intends to disclose. When Job concludes his praise of God with the question "Who can understand the thunder (*ra'am*) of God's power?" (26:14), he knows he has only *begun* the quest for the answer; he will not accept the friends' argument that the search is already *finished*. He will match God thunder for thunder until he has had his full say. Only then can the answer to the question he anticipates from God in response be fully adjudicated: "Can you thunder (*tar'ēm*) with a voice like his?" (40:9). ["Reversed Thunder"]

"Reversed Thunder"

In the Hebrew Bible "thunder" (*ra'am*) is a frequent metaphor for both God's *revelation* (cf. Pss 18:4; 29:3; Job 26:14; 37:4-5) and creation's *praise* of God in response (cf. Pss 96:11; 98:6). Given the reciprocity between the divine and the creaturely that such imagery evokes, it is interesting to consider what lies behind the question God puts to Job in 40:9: "Can you thunder with a voice like his?" (40:9). Is God *rebuking* Job for speaking too much and too presumptuously? Or is God *inviting* Job to enter fully into the dialogue of revelation and response with a creaturely thunder that is worthy of those who have been made in the image of God?

George Herbert, the English rector and poet, uses the suggestive phrase "reversed thunder" to refer to prayer. Sometimes this reversed thunder may offer praise to God; at other times it may roar in lament or protest, like an "Engine against th' Almighty." Herbert invites us to think that in both cases prayer remains "God's breath in man."

Prayer the Church's banquet, Angels' age,
God's breath in man returning to his birth,
The soul in paraphrase, heart in pilgrimage,
The Christian plummet sounding heav'n and earth;
Engine against th' Almighty . . .
Reversed thunder . . .

G. Herbert, "Prayer (1)," *The Complete English Poems*, ed. John Tobin (London: Penguin Books, 1991), 45. I am indebted to J. Gerald Janzen's discussion (*Job* [Atlanta: John Knox, 1985], 178-79) for calling to my attention the provocative parallels between Job 26:14 and Herbert's poetic figure for prayer.

COMMENTARY

Bildad on Dominion, Fear, Mortals, and Maggots, 25:1-6

Bildad laces familiar themes concerning God's unparalleled power and majesty (vv. 2, 3, 5) with images of human impotence and baseness (vv. 4, 6). Like his friends before him, Bildad's view of the moral order of the world is uncompromisingly hierarchical. Alone at the top of the cosmic order is God, whose "dreaded rule" (*hamšēl wāpaḥad*; NRSV: "dominion and fear") imposes a fearsome "peace" in the heavenly realm (v. 2). At the bottom of the order, so far removed from God as to be virtually undetectable on the cosmic screen, is the mortal, the human being (v. 6: *'ĕnôš*). The value of the mortal is even less than that of the "maggot" and the "worm," for long after the human body dies, these flesh-eaters will gorge themselves on the decaying remains (see [Food for Worms]). Patrolling the borders between the top and the bottom of the cosmic order are innumerable "celestial squadrons"[5] (v. 3: *gêdûdîm*; NRSV: "armies"). Their commission is to expose disorder and wickedness wherever it exists with the "light" of God's controlling presence. This military imagery taps into the ancient tradition of God as a divine warrior who uses irresistible force to intimidate foes into submission and when necessary to defeat them in battle (cf. Exod 15:3; Judg 5:20; Joel 2:11; see further [The Warrior God]). Such imagery needs no elaboration for Job. He is well acquainted with what it means to be the target of God's assault "troops" (19:12: *gêdûdîm*; cf. 16:12-14).

Bildad places the primary point he wishes to make with this survey of the world's moral design at the center of his speech (vv. 4-5). Given the permanent hierarchy that defines the created order, how can a mortal (*'ĕnôš*) like Job, one "born of a woman" and therefore destined to die and decay as a mere earthling, ever presume to be "righteous" (*ṣādāq*) or "pure" (*zākāh*) before God? At this point in the fatigued conversations between Job and his friends, Bildad's question hardly advances the discussion. It has been raised twice before by Eliphaz (4:17; 15:14), and twice before Job has pondered it deeply (7:17-21; 9:1-13; cf. 14:1-12).

For the friends, the question is little more than a rhetorical strategy for shifting the focus of the discussion away from Job's troublesome attack on the *morality of divine justice* to less hazardous assertions about *humanity's moral imperfection*. The friends feel completely justified and absolutely confident in insisting on this shift. Even now, as Bildad raises the question for the third time, he simply repeats the answer that Eliphaz gave when the dialogues first began: if even the celestial realms—the "angels" (4:17), the "moon" and the "stars" (25:5)—

cannot be pure before God, how much more is this true for one such as Job? Between 4:17 and 25:5, the friends have spoken at Job for nearly 200 verses. As Bildad now prepares to speak the last words we will hear from him and his colleagues, the best he can do is to return to page one and begin reading again from the same script. The last words Job hears from his would-be comforter are "maggot" and "worm" (v. 6). For all intents and purposes, these words do little more than summon him back to the ash heap, back to the still unanswered questions about why he was ever born (3:11-12, 20, 23), back to an unrequited misery that the friends have only deepened.

Bildad and his friends pose the question about what it means to be a human being in God's universe only as part of a rhetorical tactic. Their singular objective is to bait Job into a confession that he is not who he claims to be (or who *God* claims him to be!). Even so, by raising the question they have unwittingly invited Job to think deeply about traditional affirmations concerning God's design for human vocation. Once Eliphaz places the question on the table (4:17), Job picks it up and examines it through the lens of Psalm 8: "What are human beings (*'ĕnôš*), that you make so much of them.?" (7:17; cf. Ps 8:4). The psalmist asks the question and marvels at the thought that God has endowed human beings with God-like dominion and responsibility for creation. When Job asks the same question, he turns the psalmist's praise inside out in search of any evidence that would prove it true in his case. He can find little or no reason to believe that it is (see the commentary on 7:7-21 and [CD: Psalm 8 and Job 7]). And yet, having looked at the question squarely with a sufferer's eyes, Job cannot let go the possibility that the psalmist may be right after all (cf. 9:2, 32; 10:10-12; 14:1-2). At this penultimate juncture in the third cycle, Job is now approaching the end of what he has to say to the friends. But unlike Bildad, who comes to the end and realizes there is nothing more to say beyond what has already been said, Job has begun to suspect that when one asks the question about the meaning of human existence, the journey toward understanding the "outskirts of his [God's] ways" (v. 14) has not come to an end. It has only just begun. [Endings as Beginnings]

Job Interrupts Bildad, 26:1-4

When Job hears Bildad describe him as a "worm" (25:6: *rimmāh*), he knows that his

Endings as Beginnings

In *Four Quartets*, T. S. Eliot muses on personal memories, what he calls "Time present and time past" and "time future contained in time past." The journey through one's experiences, Eliot suggests, requires the recognition that endings are often beginnings . . . in more than one sense:

> We shall not cease from exploration
> And the end of all our exploring
> Will be to arrive where we started
> And know the place for the first time.

T. S. Eliot, "Little Gidding," *Four Quartets*, in *Collected Poems 1909–1962* (New York: Harcourt, Brace & World, Inc., 1970), 208. The citation that begins is from the first lines of "Burnt Norton," which is the opening poem in *Four Quartets* (see Eliot, *Collected Poems*, 175).

Heard But Not Regarded

King Henry describes his adversary Richard II as having compromised his claim to the throne, because he "Mingled his royalty with carping fools" (*Henry IV, Part One*, III, ii, 63). As a result,

> He was but as the cuckoo is in June,
> Heard, not regarded, —seen, but with such eyes, As . . .
> Afford no extraordinary gaze (*Henry IV, Part One*, III, ii, 75-77)

friend has nothing to say to him that he does not already know. He hardly needs an onlooker to confirm that in his present state he has become little more than food for the worms (cf. *rimmāh* in 7:5; 17:14). But, as Shakespeare's Lord Clifford observes when he cautions King Henry against underestimating his opponent, even "The smallest worm will turn, being trodden on."[6] Thus does Job turn on Bildad with a series of questions that effectively cut off his speech in mid-form (vv. 2-4). The translation in NRSV assumes that Job refers to himself as one "without power," "without strength," and "without wisdom." This reading suggests that Job is mocking Bildad by asking how a defense of God's incontestable power can be construed as "help" or "assistance" or "counsel" for one so obviously already victimized by that same power. Bildad is engaging in overkill; in common parlance we would say he is guilty of "bombing the rubble." The emphasis in Job's complaint may however be placed elsewhere. He might just as well be saying that Bildad is the one who is powerless and simple. NJPS, for example, renders Job's words as a stinging condemnation of advice that is not worth listening to:

> You would help without having the strength;
> You would deliver with arms that have no power.
> Without having wisdom, you offer advice. . .[7] [Heard But Not Regarded]

In 26:4, Job questions Bildad about the source of his so-called wisdom. From whom has he gotten these words? Whose "breath," that is, whose "spirit" inspires him to speak like this? Presumably Bildad

---

Is God's Spirit Always a Guarantee of Truth?

J. Gerald Janzen notes that Job's question in 26:4 may point to the issue of lying spirits, which is raised in 1 Kgs 22. The prophet Micaiah has a vision of the heavenly court in which one of the spirits comes forth and proposes to be a "lying spirit" in the mouths of all the prophets in order to entice King Ahab into making a bad military decision (1 Kgs 22:19-23). As Janzen observes, the text raises the idea that "not all spirit phenomena are a guarantee of truth."

E. Good has cited the same parallel but suggests that in Job's case the issue is more complex and still more unsettling. He notes that Job uses second person singular pronouns in 26:2-4. These "you" words may be addressed to Bildad, in which case Job would be saying that his friend does not have the spirit of God that he claims to possess. But the "you" may also be directed to God, in which case Job's complaint is much more radical. It is God who does not have the spirit to speak the truth to Job, God who perhaps needs help in order to speak more truth than God is able to do alone. Good makes the point as follows: "Job's allusion, denying to the god his own independent breath, condemns his power as immoral and, in effect, collapses chaos and creation together."

J. Gerald Janzen, *Job* (Atlanta: John Knox, 1985), 177.
E. M. Good, *In Turns of Tempest: A Reading of Job with a Translation* (Stanford: Stanford University Press, 1990), 285.

The "Shades"

The term *rĕpā'îm* (NRSV: "shades") is used in two major ways in the Hebrew Bible. First, as in Job 26:5, the *rĕpā'îm* are the dead who are consigned to the netherworld. In Ps 88:10 [MT 88:11], for example, the psalmist asks God not to turn a deaf ear to his plea for life, for once he dies and descends to the underworld, it will be God who has lost a voice from the chorus of human praise: "Do you work wonders for the dead (*mētîm*)? Do the shades (*rĕpā'îm*) rise up to praise you?" (cf. Prov 2:18; 9:18 [NRSV = "dead"]; 21:16 [NRSV = "assembly of the dead"]; Isa 26:14). Isa 14:9 preserves an older and more specific understanding of the *rĕpā'îm* as dead heroes and kings, which is found also in second millennium texts from ancient Ugarit.

Second, the *repa'im* are described as a people with extraordinary physical stature. In Deut 2:10 they are linked to the Anakim, who according to Num 13:33 were feared by Joshua's spies because they were "giants" who made the Israelites feel like "grasshoppers" by comparison. Elsewhere the expression "the Raphites" (*hārāpāh*; NRSV: "the giants") refers to a line of warriors, whose descendents are among those the Israelites drove out from Canaan in order to take possession of the promised land (2 Sam 21:16, 18, 20; 1 Chr 20:4, 6, 8). Deuteronomy (3:11, 13) and Joshua (12:4; 13:12) identify Og, king of Bashan, as one of the last descendants of "the Rephaim."

The New Testament may also preserve some memory of the *rĕpā'îm*. In his speech before the Sanhedrin, Stephen recalls the infidelity that marred Israel's forty years in the wilderness. In Acts 7:43 he cites Amos 5:26 as proof God turned away from Israel, because they "took along the tent of Molech and the star of your god Rephan, the images that you made to worship." The "god Rephan" is not mentioned in Amos and is otherwise unattested in the Hebrew Bible, but some have suggested this god may be identified with the Ugaritic god Rapa'u, perhaps the patron deity of the legendary *rĕpā'îm*.

For further reading, see C. E. L'Heureux, *Rank Among the Canaanite Gods; El, Ba al and the Repha'im* (Missoula MT: Scholars Press, 1979); B. Levine, J. M. de Tarragon, "Dead Kings and Rephaim: The Patrons of the Ugaritic Dynasty," JAOS 104 (1984): 649-59; M. Smith, "Repahim," *ABD*, ed. D. N. Freedman (New York: Doubleday, 1992), vol. 5, 674-76.

---

would answer, if given the chance, that his words and his inspiration come from God. And presumably Job would counter this claim, if he still had the patience to do so, by arguing that if Bildad thinks he speaks for God, then either he is sadly misinformed, or God is in fact the one who is "without power," "without strength," and "without wisdom." Whatever the source of Bildad's counsel, Job rejects it as banal and useless. [Is God's Spirit Always a Guarantee of Truth?]

Job's Version of Bildad's Praise, 26:5-14

Bildad began his paean to the divine warrior by focusing on the "dominion" and "fear," that is, the "dreaded rule," that God imposes on the created order (25:2). Job has heard this speech before (e.g., from Eliphaz in 5:9-16). On two previous occasions he has even given his own version of the praise his friends have urged on him (9:5-10; 12:13-25). Whatever version the friends use to praise God, it always seems to end with the affirmation that human beings are not only a "*little* lower than God" (Ps 8.5), they are a *lot* lower. In the hierarchy of God's creation, human beings rank somewhere in the general area of the "maggot" and the "worm" (25:6). At this point in the drama, Job has good reason to think that he knows where Bildad is going when he begins with words like "dominion" and "fear."

Zaphon

AΩ The word *ṣāpôn* is often used in the Hebrew Bible as a general geographical term for "north" (cf. Gen 13:14; 28:14; Exod 27:11). It is likely that the origin of the term is associated with Mount Zaphon, the cosmic mountain that Canaanite texts identify with the kingship of Baal. Zaphon is the site of Baal's royal palace, the place from which his decrees are issued, and the location of his great cosmic battle with the rival god Mot.

This Canaanite background surely lies behind the Hebrew Bible's association of *ṣāpôn* with the mountain of YHWH in the north. Ps 89:12 [MT 89:13] offers praise to YHWH who created *ṣāpôn* (NRSV: "north") along with Mount Tabor and Mount Hermon. Ps 48:1-2 [MT 48:2-3] identifies Mount Zion "in the far north" (*yarkĕtê ṣāpôn*) with the "city of our God." Isa 2:1-3 describes the nations of the world going up to the "mountain of YHWH, to the house of the God of Jacob," because "out of Zion shall go forth instruction, and the word of the Lord from Jerusalem." Isa 14:13 refers to the "heights of Zaphon" (*yarkĕtê ṣāpôn*) as the location of YHWH's defeat of rival forces, here associated with the king of Babylon. Elsewhere in the Hebrew Bible, particularly in the prophetic literature, the "north" (*ṣāpôn*) is frequently identified as the place from which the enemies of Israel and of God come (e.g., Isa 14:31; 41:25; Jer 4:6; 6:22; 10:22; Ezek 26:7; 32:30; 38:6; 39:2).

For further reading, see R. Clifford, *The Cosmic Mountain* (Cambridge MA: Harvard University Press, 1972); J. Levenson, *Sinai and Zion* (New York: Harper and Row, 1985); W. H. Schmidt, "*sapon* north," in E. Jenni, C. Westermann, *TLOT*, vol. 3 (Peabody MA: Hendrikson Publishers, 1997), 1093-98; H. Alvalos, "Zapon, Mount," *ABD*, ed. D. N. Freedman (New York: Doubleday, 1992), vol. 6, 1040-41.

Job's version of the praise Bildad would offer begins by surveying the created order not from the top down, as his friend prefers to do (cf. 25:2-3), but from the bottom up. He starts (vv. 5-6) with the terrorized peace God imposes on the underworld, here described with the terms "waters" (*mayim*), "Sheol" (see [Sheol]), and Abaddon (*ăbadôn*; from the verb *ābad*, "to perish"; see further [Abaddon]). All the inhabitants of this realm, including the "shades" (*rĕpā'îm*), the spirits of dead warriors and leaders, "writhe in fear" (REB). [The "Shades"] Indeed, the entire underworld itself, personified as Sheol and Abaddon, is "naked" (*ārôm*) and "without covering" (*ēn kesût*) in the presence of God. No corner of this shadowy world is unexposed to whatever judgment God deems appropriate. The friends of course believe that God's judgment is just and that only the wicked need fear it. Job is not so sure. He has looked across the landscape of his world and seen that it is the poor and destitute who are "naked" (*ārôm*) and "without covering" (*ēn kesût*; 24:7) before the wicked. From his perspective, there is no reason to believe that God's "justice" in Sheol is any more deserving of praise than it is on earth.

From this survey of the underworld, Job moves to the mysterious celestial realm that is God's

A Three-storied Universe

domain (vv. 7-9). God stretches out the northern sky to create space for the high heavens, hangs the earth in its place, binds up the waters with thick clouds, and hides the heavenly throne by spreading a cloud over it.[8] At several points, Job's cosmology deviates from the traditional Israelite view. The word "north" (v. 7: *ṣāpôn*) is not normally a parallel for "heaven" (cf. Isa 14:13), although this seems to be what Job means here. Elsewhere in the Hebrew Bible, *ṣāpôn* is associated with Mount Zion, the city of God "in the far north" (Ps 48:2; cf. Isa 14:13), and derivatively with Mount Zaphon (note NRSV), the dwelling place of the god Baal in Canaanite mythology. [Zaphon] Still more curious is the picture of the heavens/*ṣāpôn* suspended over the "void" (*tōhû*; cf. Gen 1:2) and the earth hanging upon "nothing" (*bĕlî-māh*). Most of the Hebrew Bible's cosmological texts suggest that the earth rests on pillars or some such foundational base (cf. Job 38:4-6; Ps 104:5), which in turn keep the earth safely suspended above the watery chaos of the underworld. When Job says the earth on which humanity dwells hangs upon *bĕlî-māh*, he is perhaps only offering a poetic variation of the conventional view. Yet, at this point in the drama it is surely plausible to wonder if he has not purposefully changed the conventional view. Perhaps the "nothing" on which humanity bases its existence in the world is to be taken *literally*, not *poetically*. [Advanced Cosmology or Critical Critique of Traditional Views?]

Job knows that Bildad would praise God for having set a "boundary" (v. 10: *taklît*) to divide the upper world of the cosmos from the underworld. He describes this boundary as a "circle" placed at the farthest edge of the cosmic waters, at the critical intersection where light and darkness have the greatest potential to collapse into one another. The imagery recalls the language of Prov 8:27, where personified Wisdom rejoices in the knowledge that God "drew a circle on the face of the deep." Eliphaz has previously called on this same tradition to rebuke Job for presuming that

The Compass of God

William Blake (1757-1827). *God creating the universe*. Private Collection. (Credit: Art Resource, NY)

Advanced Cosmology or Critical Critique of Traditional Views?

M. Buttenweiser speculated that Job was rejecting traditional Israelite cosmologies in favor of more advanced astronomical views such as those identified with the Greek mathematician Pythagoras (582?–500? BCE). Pythagoras considered the earth to be a globe that revolved with other planets around a central fire-like core. In Buttenweiser's words, "Our author, though naturally ignorant of the law of gravitation, had outgrown the naïve view of his age about the universe , and conceived the earth as a heavenly body floating in space, like the sun, moon, and stars." Buttenweiser's views have not been followed by most commentators.

M. Buttenweiser, *The Book of Job* (New York: Macmillan, 1922). For a brief critique, see M. Pope, *Job* (AB; Garden City NY: Doubleday, 1979), 183-84; J. Hartley, *The Book of Job* (NICOT; Grand Rapids MI: William B. Eerdmans, 1988), 365.

---

he knows anything about the boundaries God has placed in creation or that he has any say-so in how God administers them: "Are you the first-born of the human race? Were you brought forth before the hills? Have you listened in the council of God?" (15:7-8; cf. Prov 8:25). Like Eliphaz, Bildad is certain that the only authentic response Job can make to such questions is "No."

Perhaps by affirming that there are indeed boundaries between light and darkness Job has moved a step closer to conceding the truth of the friends' argument and to offering the praise they insist upon. And yet, if Job is only mimicking his friends in order to rebut them, then we are invited to wonder if perhaps the under-tow of Proverbs 8 is not still pulling Job in a different direction (see the commentary on Job 15:7-16). Is it possible that Job, like Wisdom, dares to imagine that when God drew the primordial boundaries, "I *was there*" and "when he marked out the foundations of the earth, then I *was beside him*, like a master worker" (Prov 8:27, 30)? For the reader, and almost certainly for Job at this point, the question is at best only hypothetical. There is little incentive for lingering over such nonsensical notions, and Job does not do so here. Not until God thunders forth from the whirlwind with similar questions—"Where were you when I laid the foundations of the earth? Tell me if you have understanding" (38:4)—will Job finally have reason to think that the question about his place in the world may be as important to God as it is to himself. ["Why Hast Thou Come on This Far Journey?"]

Having paused only briefly to ponder the boundaries of light and darkness, Job now returns his focus to the underworld, where God's frightful dominion knows no limits (vv. 11-13). As he has done in his previous survey of this part of the cosmos (26:5-6), Job envisions God as an invincible warrior before whom nothing can hold its ground. The distant mountains, which emerged from the primordial waters to support the arch of the heavens (NRSV: "pillars"; cf. 2 Sam 22:8; Ps 18:7, 15), quake at God's rebuke. The mythical forces of chaos that dare to contest God's ordered boundaries—personified as "the Sea" (*hayām*), Rahab, and the "serpent"—are "stilled," "struck," and

---

"Why Has Thou Come on This Far Journey?"

The possibility that Job might consider himself to be welcomed, not rebuked, by the One who oversees the primordial boundaries of the world, has a suggestive parallel in the ancient Mesopotamian story of Gilgamesh (2nd millennium BCE). When Gilgamesh arrives at Mashu, the cosmic mountains that mark the boundary between heaven and earth and the underworld, he is met by scorpion-creatures who are guarding the gate. Their presence strikes terror in Gilgamesh, but after composing himself he engages them in conversation that lays the foundation for his ultimate movement into their domain. The scene is described in Tablet IX, a portion of which is cited below:

When [he arrived] at the mountain range of Mashu,
Which daily keeps watch over sun [rise and sunset]—
Whose peaks [reach to] the vault of heaven
(And) whose breasts reach to the nether world below—
Scorpion-men guard its gate,
Whose terror is awesome and whose glance was death.
Their shimmering halo sweeps the mountains
That at sunrise and sunset keep watch over the sun.
When Gilgamesh beheld them, with fear
And terror was darkened his face.

Regaining his composure, he approached them.
A scorpion-man calls to his wife:
"He who has come to us—his body is the flesh of gods!"
His wife answers the scorpion-man:
"Two-thirds of him is god, one-third of him is human."
[The scorpi]on-man calls to his fellow,
Addressing (these) words [to the offspring] of the gods:
"[Why hast thou come on this] far journey?
[Why hast thou arrived] before me,
[Traversing seas] whose crossings are difficult?
[The purpose of thy com]ing I would learn."

The journeys of Gilgamesh and Job are of course different in many ways, and any parallels between them may owe more to chance than to intention. Nevertheless, when God addresses Job with the questions in 38:4, it is interesting to listen carefully for the distant echo of those ancient guardians of the gate who knew themselves to be in conversation with one whose words were human but whose resolve and purpose might be consonant with that of a god.

Tablet IX, in ANET, 3rd ed. with supplement, ed. J. B. Pritchard (Princeton: Princeton University Press, 1969), 88.

"pierced." [Rahab] Job consistently portrays God's "power" and "understanding" (v. 12) as controlling the unruly forces in creation through diminishment and negation. Indeed, Job has already begun to imagine that for some reason God regards him as an opponent like the "Sea" (*yam*; 7:12), whose contention with creation's order requires the full measure of God's counter-offensive.

It is curious, therefore, that in his next-to-last description of God's dominion Job hints that the divine objective may be more positive than it first appears. The MT in v. 13a says that by God's "wind" or "breath" (*rûaḥ*) "the heavens were made fair (*šiprāh*)." Based on other creation accounts in the Hebrew Bible, one might have expected Job to declare that God uses wind or breath to "rebuke" the sea (Ps 18:15 [MT 18:16]; cf. Exod 15:8). But nowhere do such accounts mention that the breath of divine power makes the heavens "fair" or "beautiful. " Perhaps here, as before, Job is simply offering a poetic variation on a theme (see above on 26:7). Perhaps, as many commentators have proposed, the text we have should be emended to bring it into conformity with a more negative understanding of God's power.[9] Or perhaps we should leave this curious statement as is and ponder what Job could possibly see in this picture of God's purposive plan for creation that deserves the adjective "beautiful. "

Rahab

Rahab (lit., "boisterous one"), like Leviathan, is one of the mythological sea monsters that are identified with the primordial forces of chaos (see **[Leviathan]**). Leviathan is a creature also known in Canaanite literature. A creature named Rahab is not attested in extrabiblical texts.

Rahab appears in the Hebrew Bible primarily in contexts that describe God's defeat of the sea monster at the time of creation. Ps 89:10-11 [MT 89:11-12] declares that heaven and earth belong to God, because "You crushed Rahab like a carcass." The two references to Rahab in Job (9:13; 26:12) occur in a similar context. In both cases, Job affirms the conventional view that God smites Rahab, thus securing its submission to creation's order. The description of God punishing the "fleeing serpent" (Job 26:13) is found in Isa 27:1 with reference to Leviathan. A similar description occurs in Isa 51:9, in this instance paralleled by the statement that God "cut Rahab in pieces." In both Job and Isaiah, it is likely that Rahab and Leviathan are considered to be similar if not identical creatures.

In three places Rahab is used in a wider context as a referent for a country, usually Egypt, that represents a doomed opposition or obstacle to God's plan for Israel. Isa 30:7 makes a specific connection between Egypt, whose "help is worthless and empty" and "Rahab who sits still. " It is likely that Rahab also refers to Egypt in Ps 87:4, where along with other traditional enemies—Babylon, Philistia, Tyre, Ethiopia—it is listed among the nations who recognize God's rule. Isa 51:9-11 seems to combine understandings of Rahab as the sea monster and Rahab as a country. The defeat of Rahab described in v. 9 seems to refer to God's mastery over creation's unruly forces. The description of God's victory over the sea in v. 10 is made within the context of Exodus theology, hence as an affirmation of God's deliverance of Israel from Egypt. V. 11 extends the promise of this deliverance to those exiled in Babylon.

For further reading, see J. Day, *God's Conflict With the Dragon and the Sea* (Cambridge: Cambridge University Press, 1985); idem, "Rahab," *ABD*, ed. D. N. Freedman (New York: Doubleday, 1992), vol. 5, 610-11.

Job's ends this mock-up of the praise he believes Bildad would offer with a summative statement (v. 14). He acknowledges that what he can see of God's governance in the world is no more than the mere "glimpses of His rule" (NJPS; NRSV: "the outskirts of his ways"). Like Eliphaz, he has heard but the "whisper" (*šemeṣ*; cf. 4:12) of what God's creation reveals. For Eliphaz, and for Bildad who is content to borrow truth from his friend, a whisper from God is enough to write the full report about the way creation works. What more does one need to hear in order to know that no mortal, and certainly not Job, can be righteous and pure before the Creator of the world? Job has heard these whispers of truth, and he can spin them forth with eloquence just like his friends.

But Job hints that he has picked up the faint trace of whispers beyond these. He has seen that the earth where he resides hangs precariously on "nothing" (v. 7), but he has also seen that the clouds God hangs overhead are not "torn open" by the waters that would otherwise overwhelm and destroy the earth (v. 8). He has looked hard at the boundary God has put in place between light and darkness (v. 10). He has heard the argument that this boundary marks the difference between what God knows about the foundations of the world and what mortals like Job can never know. But he may also have begun to suspect that on the far horizon of God's plan for humankind, where the boundaries are most vulnerable and most important, there is perhaps a place alongside God for one who will be happily received as a "master worker" (cf. Prov 8:30). He has heard the frightful trembling of the heavens before God; with them he knows what it means to be "astounded at his rebuke" (v. 11). He has also detected something beautiful in the heavens (v. 13), although to this point he can find nothing on earth that provides any explanation for what he sees.

In the midst of these various whispers of something more than Eliphaz and Bildad have heard, Job ends his praise not with an affirmation but with a question. "Who can understand the thunder of his power?" For Job, the question marks a stage in a journey that is not yet complete. Not until God responds to Job with words that turn this question into an issue of mutual concern in heaven and on earth (cf. 40:9) will Job and his friends *and his readers* know which of creation's whispers disclose the most truth.

CONNECTIONS

The most inviting departure for reflection in these chapters is not the theology of dominion and fear that both Bildad and Job know quite well. This has received considerable attention in previous speeches. It is not the assertion that human beings are morally inferior to God, for on this point the friends and Job have little disagreement. It is not Job's rejection of Bildad's counsel as useless, nor his concession that God's governance of creation exceeds anything Job or his friend can comprehend fully. All these issues are simply variations on themes that have already been well rehearsed. What is most curious about these chapters is Job's willingness to speak words of praise that are not his own.

On first encounter, the words of 26:5-14 may not suggest that Job has moved very far from his customary way of responding to the friends. This is not the first time Job has grown so impatient with his friends that he mocks them by mouthing their trivialities for them (cf. 16:1-6). And this is not the first time Job has spoken words of praise that sound very much the same as those the friends have modeled from him (cf. 9:5-10; 12:13-25). On this occasion, however, the words Job speaks sound strangely more like those that we will subsequently hear from God (chs. 38–41) than those we have already heard from the friends.

As God will do, Job begins by looking at the cosmic boundaries that define creation (26:5-10; 38:4-18). Like God, Job pays attention to the provisions for rain (26:8; 38:25-30), clouds (26:8; 38:34-38), and light and darkness (26:10; 38:19-21). Job's survey of creation is brief, and perhaps this explains why there is no mention of a place for human beings in the world he describes. God's survey of creation is extensive. It too makes no mention of a place for human beings, and this in turn invites the question "Why?" Instead of talking about how human beings fit into creation's design, both Job and God end up by focusing on the primordial creatures that appear to command more attention from God than any others. Job concentrates on Rahab (26:12) and sees that *God uses both power and wisdom* to define this creature's place in the world. God concentrates on Behemoth (40:15-24) and Leviathan (41:1-34) and affirms that *they possess such power and determination* as to make their Creator's power all the more formidable and praiseworthy by comparison. When Job comes to the end of a praise that he does not yet fully own, he has sensed that there is something "fair" or "beautiful" in what he has seen (26:13). It is but faintly discerned, more a "whisper" than a "thunder," and it leaves him with a question, not an assertion: "Who can understand?" (26:14). When God comes to the end of the survey of creation that is peculiarly divine, words like "lofty" and "king" (41:34) announce that a speech begun with questions—"Who is this?" "Can you thunder?" (38:2; 40:9)—has achieved its objective.

Readers may ponder what it means for Job to have feigned praise only to end up with questions that place him at the juncture where he can be addressed by God with questions. What does it mean for people of pained faith to go through the motions of speaking words about God and about God's world that they are really not prepared to believe? What does it mean to discover that *your questions* are God's assertions and that *God's questions* invite assertions you can speak but not endorse? The last words of Job's speech in chapter 26 are perplexing, maddening, and . . . irresistible: "Who can understand?"

One entry into Job's question lies along the lines suggested by Leon Wieseltier, whose book *Kaddish* tells the story of how speaking words that he did not own produced surprising results.[10] He begins his book with these words:

> On March 24, 1996, which was Nisan 5, 5756, my father died. In the year that followed I said the prayer known as the mourner's kaddish three times daily, during the morning service, the afternoon service, and the evening service, in a synagogue in Washington and, when I was away from home, in synagogues elsewhere. It was my duty to say it . . .
>
> I was struck almost immediately by the poverty of my knowledge about the ritual I was performing with such fidelity. And it was not long before I understood that I would not succeed in insulating the rest of my existence from the impact of this obscure and arduous practice. The symbols were seeping into everything. A season of sorrow became a season of soul-renovation, for which I was not at all prepared. (vii)

Throughout the year of his mourning, Wieseltier kept a journal. One gets the clear impression that prior to his father's death he had not been a particularly observant Jew. Now he was simply going through the motions of saying the kaddish, because this is what his father would have wanted. He says the words, although he does not understand them and has little reason to think that he would believe them even if he understood them. But something strange happens to him in the course of the year of doing the ritual. The more he repeats the words, the more he feels compelled to find out what they mean. The more he understands, the more he wants to know. And the more he learns, the more he wants to do the ritual. His journal traces his slow and steady trek toward what he calls "soul-renovation."

His initial entries in the diary focus on his sense that the words "Magnified and sanctified may His great Name be" are "nothing but sounds" (4). When he says them, they fall into the pit, smash against his father's coffin, and vanish into the earth. Like his father, they are buried and dead. Magnified and sanctified . . . Magnified and sanctified . . . The more he says the words the more absurd they sound and the more bizarre it seems to mourn things that you cannot change. He stiffens his resolve not to yield: "I do not intend to be inconsolable, but I do not intend to be deceived" (11). He continues the ritual, but with more anger than ease. The only consolation comes from studying the Talmud, which encourages him to think that the rabbis did not consider anger to be a bad thing:

Anger is not apostasy. Quite the contrary. It is another way of acknowledging God's responsibility for the world.
—Nothing could have been done. There is no use beating your head against the wall.
—But I want to know why nothing could have been done. There is a use in beating my brain against the wall. (59)

He continues the ritual and begins to sense something stirring deep within. "I have begun to notice that my prayers are refreshing my life with language. Three times a day, Hebrew music" (62). He increases his study of the tradition in the hope of finding greater clarity. "I study the old texts because I hope to be infected by their dimensions, to attain the size of what I read" (75). About a third of the way through the year he records these words:

A lovely morning, a heavy heart. A few months ago I worried that my mourner's life would interfere with the rest of my life. Now I worry that the rest of my life will interfere with my mourner's life. The temptation is growing to surrender to the drill and the sadness. (131)

Six months into the journey, he concedes that the ritual is seducing him, even though he still cannot find the belief to match the words he repeats:

> It is Labor Day. Washington is a ghost town, but these days I keep company with ghosts. In the stillness of Georgetown in the evening the light is soft, a lowered radiance in which the structures of the brick houses disappear into their surfaces, which are ripe with patterns and textures. I see only small things. When I read the prayers, I can't control my mind. It roams. Small things, small things. My thought and my words have nothing to do with each other. But the words keep coming, unimpeded by my abandonment of them. The triumph of rote. (195-96)

Soul-renovation is hard work. The attempt to impose it on others will almost certainly fail. Comforters like Bildad may confidently urge the Jobs of the world to speak words they cannot believe. Magnified and sanctified. . . May His great Name be blessed. . . . But those who see the world through Job's eyes do not have the patience for mere sounds, and they will not wrap what they know to be true in the cloak of dishonesty. ["Evil's Evil and Sorrow's Sorrow"] Magnified and sanctified . . . May His great Name be blessed . . . "Dominion and fear are with God . . ." Amen! May His great Name be blessed always and forever! Job may say the words. He undoubtedly knows the drill. But who would fault him for feeling like the ritual is more destructive than restorative? Like Wieseltier, we may imagine that at this point in Job's journey he feels like soul-renovation is a prescription for beating your brains against the wall.

And yet Job has for the moment laid down his curse and lament. He has for now suspended his still unanswered cry for justice. To be sure he is not done with these words, for in the chapters that follow he will take up this discourse "again" (cf. 27:1; 29:1). But for now he looks at creation, at an earth hanging on "nothing," at clouds full to breaking yet "not torn open," at heavens that are "fair," even while the pillars upon which they rest "tremble" with fright and astonishment. He strains to understand the thunder of the One whose power makes it so, but he hears only whispers that sound more like silence than revelation. [Testing Faith on Emptiness] And yet, he speaks the praise that Bildad begins with the words "dominion and fear."

Is Job mocking Bildad? Probably. Is he feigning praise as a cynical way of reminding the Almighty that praise may be coerced, but if it is it will not be genuine? Perhaps. Is he speaking the words in the hope that he may yet grow into

---

"Evil's Evil and Sorrow's Sorrow"

The Jobs of the world may be expected to respond to the invitation to give thanks for being bruised and broken "for no reason" with words not unlike those George Eliot's narrator attributes to Adam Bede: "Evil's evil and sorrow's sorrow, and you can't alter its nature by wrapping it up in other words."

G. Eliot, *Adam Bede*, Edited with an Introduction by Stephen Gill (New York: Penguin Books, 1985), 529.

the fullness of understanding that they require to be authentic? We may hope this is the case, but there is no evidence that it is so.

Soul-renovation is hard work. When there are nothing more than whispers to mark the way, the journey is bound to be a series of starts and stops. Still, the mind roams, and the words keep coming, almost as if they are "unimpeded" by Job's abandonment of them. Imitation may not always be the sincerest form of flattery. Then again, if it is true that even sufferers like Job are made "in his image" and "after his likeness," maybe speaking words of praise that sound more like God's than the friends has in fact moved Job a step closer to being able to respond to the One who comes asking, "Can you thunder" with a voice like mine (Job 40:9)?

If we permit ourselves to stay inside the tension of Job's unfinished journey, there is perhaps only one truth that now seems unassailable. The friends started with unexamined certainties about God, and they have ended up exactly where they began. They have nothing more to contribute beyond what has already been said and rejected. [Gone and Forgotten] Job started with questions and complaints and demands for something beyond what he can hear in the "truths" the friends offer. He has come to yet another juncture in his quest. The questions are much the same as when he began:

Testing Faith on Emptiness

Often I try
To analyse the quality
Of its silences. Is this where God hides
From my searching? I have stopped to listen,
After the few people have gone,
To the air recomposing itself
For vigil. It has waited like this
Since the stones grouped themselves about it.
These are the hard ribs
Of a body that our prayers have failed
To animate. Shadows advance
From their corners to take possession
Of places the light held
For an hour. The bats resume
Their business. The uneasiness of the pews
Ceases. There is no other sound
In the darkness but the sound of a man
Breathing, testing his faith
On emptiness, nailing his questions
One by one to an untenanted cross.

R. S. Thomas, "In Church," *Poems of R. S. Thomas* (Fayetteville: University of Arkansas Press, 1985), 54.

Gone and Forgotten

The departure of Job's three friends recalls the words of Auden:

Two friends who met here and embraced are
   gone,
Each to his own mistake . . .

W. H. Auden, "The Quest," *W. H. Auden: Collected Poems*, ed. E. Mendelson (New York: Vintage International, 1991), 286.

"Who can understand?" The only affirmations of God he can endorse still require the words "dominion" and "fear." The only certainties about mortals that he can speak still require the words "maggot" and "worm." And yet, Job has now leaned into his questions and his vexed certainties with a sentence that he knows how to begin but not how to finish: "These are but the outskirts of his ways."

NOTES

[1] R. Gordis, *The Book of Job: Commentary, New Translation, and Special Studies* (New York: Jewish Theological Seminary of America, 1978), 534.

[2] Cf. J. Hartley, *The Book of Job* (NICOT; Grand Rapids MI: William B. Eerdmans, 1988), 4-5; C. Newsom, "The Book of Job," in vol. 4 of NIB (Nashville: Abingdon Press, 1996), 497.

[3] For other efforts to interpret the text as it stands, without reconstruction, see F. I. Anderson, *Job: An Introduction and Commentary* (TOTC; Leicester, England: Inter-Varsity Press, 1976), 214-22; J. Gerald Janzen, *Job* (Atlanta: John Knox, 1985), 171-86; E. M. Good, *In Turns of Tempest: A Reading of Job with a Translation* (Stanford: Stanford University Press, 1990), 281-90. The interpretation offered here is closest to that offered by Janzen.

[4] See also Anderson, *Job*, 216-17.

[5] N. Habel, *The Book of Job: A Commentary* (OTL; Philadelphia: Westminster Press, 1985), 369.

[6] *King Henry VI*, II, ii, 17.

[7] Cf. Habel, *Job*, 375; Newsom, "The Book of Job," 517.

[8] NRSV's translation of v. 9, "He covers the face of the full moon," is based on a proposed emendation of the word *kissēh*, which appears to be a variant spelling of the word for "throne," to the word keseh, which means "full moon." The MT is admittedly ambiguous, but the word "throne" is appropriate given the general context. For supporting arguments see, Gordis, *Book of Job*, 279; Habel, *Job*, 365; Hartley, *Book of Job*, 364.

[9] See M. Pope (*Job* [AB; Garden City NY: Doubleday, 1979], 185-86), who suggests that the word *šiprāh* should be interpreted on the analogy of the Akkadian word *šaparu*, "net." A similar Hebrew word in Ps 56:8 [MT 56:9], *šiprāh*, which Pope takes as a term meaning "bag," suggests to him that the phrase in Job 26:13 should be emended to read "By his wind he bagged the Sea."

[10] L. Wieseltier, *Kaddish* (New York: Alfred A, Knopf, 1998).

JOB AGAIN: "MAY MY ENEMY BE LIKE THE WICKED"

Job 27:1-23

With this chapter, the dialogue between Job and his three friends limps to an end. In chapters 25–26, Job interrupts Bildad's third speech (26:1-4) then proceeds to finish it for him (26:5-14). When that speech is completed, Job appears to pause briefly (note the modified introduction in 27:1), as if waiting for Zophar to respond to his last question: "Who can understand the thunder of his power?" (26:14). Before Zophar can answer, Job pushes ahead with his own agenda.

With a series of oaths, he defends his innocence and, by implication, God's guilt, and he claims that in doing so his conscience is completely clear (27:2-6). Having staked his claim to speak the truth as he knows it, Job invokes a curse on any "enemy" who would contest him (27:7-10). The question on the table is who can understand God's power? Job has something to teach his friends about the "hand" that exercises this power, and what he has learned he will not refrain from speaking (27:11-12). His speech concludes by describing the punishment that a righteous God must necessarily impose on the wicked (27:13-23). [Structure of Job 27:1-23] These last words sound suspiciously like what Zophar might say, and many scholars have in fact suggested that they ought to be assigned to him rather than to Job. It

Structure of Job 27:1-23		
📖	27:1-6	"My heart does not reproach me"
	27:7-12	Job's *māšāl*: "May my enemy be like the wicked"
	27:13-23	"This is the portion of the wicked *with* God"

is more likely, however, that we should understand Job as preempting Zophar by parroting his words for him. The dialogue that Job and his friends have sustained for 551 verses has come to a weary end. As Newsom puts it, "These are persons who finally have no more to say to one another and no desire to hear one another any longer."[1]

For all the signs that the dialogue with the friends has come to a dead end, there are indications that Job is only steadying himself for another conversation that has not yet begun. One clue is the editor's introduction to this speech. Job has begun a "discourse (*māšāl*)." The etymology of the Hebrew word suggests two related ideas: comparison (from *mšl* "to be like") and authoritative word (from *mšl* "to rule"). Both ideas are peculiarly present in the use of the word with reference to the literary form of the proverb, which typically brings together two or more things for comparison in order to establish the vital connections (or disconnections) between them. Properly understood, the comparison becomes in turn an authoritative word that enables one to grasp an essential truth about life. Job's *māšāl* is not as clearly defined as those we find in the book of Proverbs. Nevertheless, he hints in v. 7 that he is pondering a comparison between his "enemy" (*ʾōyēb*) and the "wicked" (*rāšāʿ*). If his enemy could experience what it is like to be treated as one of the wicked, then perhaps he would have more compassion for Job. Job describes the suffering and the punishment he expects to befall the wicked (v. 13: *rāšāʿ*) in vv. 13-23. If the enemy is paying attention to the parallels Job seems to be drawing, then he should know that unless he gives up his assault of this innocent victim, he is destined to be judged severely.

At this point, Job's *māšāl* is ambiguous at best. What is the essential truth he discerns by comparing the "enemy" with the "wicked"? For whom would this truth be instructive and authoritative? At the end of chapter 27, Job's conversation with the friends is over. If the comparison is meant for them, then it has surely failed to have any impact. If the comparison is for Job's own benefit, then there is little evidence that it provides him with any real clarifying truth, for he still seems to have serious doubts about the fate of the wicked. He affirms their punishment here, and then perhaps only sarcastically, for he has repeatedly denied it elsewhere (21:7-16; 24:1-17). Is the comparison meant for God? Is Job perhaps trying to teach God something about the unhappy parallels between the enemy and the wicked? There is one tell-tale sign that such an unimaginable idea may have inched its way toward the edges of Job's thoughts. There has been only previous occurrence of the word "enemy" thus far. It has come from Job, and he has used it to describe the way he believes God regards him: "Why do you hide your face from me and count me as your enemy (*ʾōyēb*)?" (13:24).

At the end of this *māšāl,* Job dares to express the hope that his enemy would somehow come to know what it feels like to be punished as if he were a genuinely wicked person. In chapters 29–31, Job will once again take up his *māšāl* (29:1: NRSV: "discourse"). Only then will we know more certainly who Job thinks his enemy is, how Job expects this enemy to respond to what he has said, and what is at stake if the dialogue about the enemy and the wicked really has dead-ended. [Waiting for Angels or Furies?]

COMMENTARY

"My Heart Does Not Reproach Me," 27:1-6

Job begins his *māšāl* (v. 1; NRSV: "discourse") by swearing an oath of innocence on the life of God. As elsewhere in the Hebrew Bible, such oaths are potentially self-curses. By swearing on the living God, oath makers call on God to bring unspoken calamities on them if their sworn statements are proven false (cf. 1 Sam 20:21; 28:10; 2 Sam 12:5; 14:11; Ruth 3:13). As Habel notes, oaths are more than empty rhetoric; they are a "catalytic action" that forces a response from the one whose name has been invoked.[2]

The measure of Job's conundrum is that the guarantor of justice by whom he swears is none other than the One who has "denied my justice" (v. 2: NIV) and "made my soul bitter" (cf. 7:11; 10:1). Job has repeatedly argued that God denies him the right to present his case before an impartial court of law. Job has protested his innocence (9:20-21), accused God of injustice (9:22, 28), summoned God to answer his charges (13:2, 19, 22-23), and appealed to heaven and earth to stand up as his witnesses (16:18-19; see further [The Trial Metaphor in Job]). For all his efforts, the only truth he can verify is that the odds of getting a fair hearing with God are no better than one in a thousand (9:2). Still, he has searched the far corners of his world in the failing hope that he might find God (23:3, 8-9), "reason with him," and finally "be acquitted forever by my judge" (23:7). In what may be regarded as a desperate act, Job now rests the full weight of his claim to innocence on this conflicted God, his persistent adversary and his chronically absent advocate. [Is This Game Fun for God?]

Following a parenthetical statement (v. 3; see below), Job states the substance of his oath in vv. 4-5 with three "if" clauses (*'im*; untranslated in NRSV). *If* his lips should ever lie (NRSV: "speak falsehood"; cf. 6:30), *if* his tongue should ever be guilty of "deceit" (*rĕmiyyāh*; cf.

Waiting for Angels or Furies?

In "The Waiting," the Welsh poet R. S. Thomas reflects on the choices people of faith must make when life requires them to wrestle with "anonymous" enemies. Which path do the Jobs of the world choose when "the only signs discernable are what no one has erected"? It is instructive that Thomas ends his reflections on a positive note. It is also instructive that he, like Job, leans into the positive with questions that echo with as much incredulity as assertion.

Aré there angels or only
the Furies? We sleep
on a stone pillow
and the troubles of Europe
are the molecules that
compound it. Where is
the ladder or that heavenly
traffic that electrified Jacob?

We wrestle with somebody,
something which withholds its name.
How is the anonymous
disposed? The enemy is without
number; is there an infiltration
of its forces by one not
indifferent to the human?

. . .

Why, then of all possible
turnings do we take
this one rather than that,
when the only signs discernible
are what no one has erected?
Is it because, at the road's
ending, the one who is as a power
in hiding is waiting to be christened?

R. S. Thomas, "The Waiting," *No Truce with the Furies* (Newcastle upon Tyne: Bloodaxe Books, 1995), 64.

Is This Game Fun for God?

In "A Masque of Reason," Robert Frost imagines what kind of conversation God and Job may have had after their years of struggling to understand one another had ended. His Job character now recognizes that it all must have been a great game to God, but he fails to see the fun in it for God. Where is the satisfaction, Job wonders, in watching men and women spend their lives "fumbling at the possibilities" that God refuses to disclose?

I fail to see what fun, what satisfaction
A God can find in laughing at how badly
Men fumble at the possibilities
When left to guess forever for themselves.
The chances are when there's so much pre
  tense
Of metaphysical profundity
The obscurity's a fraud to cover nothing.
I've come to think no so-called hidden
  value's
Worth going after. Get down into things,

It will be found there's no more given there
Than on the surface . . .
We don't know where we are, or who we
  are.
We don't know one another; don't know You
. . . .
Yet You don't speak. Let fools bemuse
  themselves
By being baffled for the sake of being.
I'm sick of the whole artificial puzzle.

The biblical Job does not have the "advantage" of the hindsight that Frost gives to his Job, and so he continues to "guess" that there are some things now hidden that are still "worth going after." To bet your life on a guess is of course a high risk venture. Until the game is over, there is no way to know whether you will come out a champion or a chump.

R. Frost, "A Masque of Reason," *The Poetry of Robert Frost*, ed. E. C. Lathem (New York: Henry Holt and Company, 1969), 483-84.

13:7), *if* he should ever compromise his "integrity" (*tūmmātî*; cf. 1:8; 2:3, 9; 4:6) by saying that his friends are right, *then* may God declare him to be a fake and a fraud. To buttress his claim, he adds a second oath formula that emphatically denies he would ever stoop so low as to lie under oath: "Far be it from me" (cf. Gen 44:7, 17; 1 Sam 12:23; 2 Sam 20:20; 23:17). [Oath Exclamations] Come what may, Job will "hold fast" (v. 6: *ḥāzāq*) to his righteousness. This determination to be true to himself has been one of Job's defining qualities since the days when he first found himself consigned to the ash heap "for no reason." After witnessing his response to the unspeakable death of seven sons and three daughters, even God recognized that Job will not alter his convictions for the sake of convenience: "He still persists (*ḥāzāq*) in his integrity" (2:3; cf. 2:9). It is therefore with a clear conscience that Job claims "my heart does not reproach me for any of my days" (v. 6b). ["They Will Want You to Be Ashamed"]

One of the unsettling paradoxes of Job's oath is that it essentially invokes God against God. Job swears *by God* that he is innocent, a claim that is fully consistent with God's own assessment of him as one who is absolutely "blameless and upright" (1:8; 2:3). His oath puts the burden on God to verify that God is right. And yet it is this same God, according to Job, who denies him justice by pronouncing him guilty even though he is "blameless" (9:20). If God now concedes that Job is in fact innocent, then logically, by implication, God must admit that

Oath Exclamations

AΩ Oaths and wishes in the Hebrew Bible are frequently introduced by exclamations. In Job 27:2, for example, the expression "As God lives" (*ḥay 'ēl*) invokes God's name as a way of reinforcing the oath maker's intent and integrity. Another example is the expression "Far be from me" (*ḥālîlāh lî*) in 27:5, which typically introduces and reinforces a negative oath. Such oaths display a conventional sequence: the phrase *ḥālîlāh* + l ("to," "for"), followed by a dependent clause beginning with *min* ("from") or *'im* ("if"). The dependent clause specifies what the speaker swears under oath not to do. In 27:5 the sequence is as follows: "Far be from me (*ḥālîlāh lî*) if (*'im*) I say that you are right."

The key to understanding the force of this exclamation lies in the word *halilah*, which comes from a root (*ḥll*) meaning to "desecrate" or "profane." The basic meaning has to do with desecrating or profaning something that is holy or sacred. One might paraphrase Job's oath in 27:5 by saying, "Let that which is holy or sacred in me be profaned if I declare that you [friends] are right."

This type of exclamation occurs 21x in the Hebrew Bible. It is used in different circumstances by a variety of persons. In one instance (1 Sam 2:30), even God is described as using this expression. The examples below are representative:

Gen 18:25   Far be it from you to do such a thing, to slay the righteous with the wicked, so that the righteous fare as the wicked! Far be that from you! Shall not the Judge of all the earth do what is just? (Abraham to God)

1 Sam 2:30   Therefore the Lord the God of Israel declares: "I promised that your family and the family of your ancestors should go in and out before me forever"; but now the Lord declares: "Far be it from me; for those who honor me I will honor, and those who despise me shall be treated with contempt." (A "man of God" to Eli)

1 Sam 12:23   Moreover, as for me, far be it from me that I should sin against the Lord by ceasing to pray for you. (Samuel to the people)

1 Sam 26:11   Far be it from me (NRSV: The Lord forbid) that I should raise my hand against the Lord's anointed. (David to Abishai)

God has been wrong to assault him as if he were one of the wicked (9:22). Thus, on the one hand, Job is saying, "Let God curse *me* if *I am guilty* of any wrongdoing." On the other, he is also effectively saying, "Let God curse *Himself* if *God is guilty* of any wrongdoing." Job would seem to be caught in the trap of *logical thinking* that is fundamentally *illogical.* How can God curse God? And if God were to engage in self-cursing, what possible judgment could God impose on Himself?

The whole notion of pitting God against God is made more complicated, not less, by Job's parenthetical statement in v. 3. He resolves to stick by his oath for as long as he has "breath." His determination seems at first to be expressed in nothing more than conventional terms. To have breath (*nĕšāmāh*) means simply to exist, to be alive (cf. Deut 20:20; Josh 11:11; 14; 1 Kgs 17:17). Job's next statement, however, tilts the expression toward a more freighted assertion. He pledges to speak the truth for as long as he is in possession of the "spirit of God" (*rûaḥ 'ĕlôah*). Job's life is the manifestation of the spirit of God in him. He is an extension of the divine life force freely imparted at the dawn of creation, when the *rûaḥ 'ĕlōhîm* (Gen 1:3; NRSV: "wind from God") was moving over what was soon to be. When God formed the first human being from the dust of the ground and "breathed into his nostrils the breath (*nĕšāmāh*) of life" (Gen 2:3), God set in motion a journey that would inevitably lead one day to someone named Job speaking *to* God, even *against* God, with God's own "breath" and "spirit."[3] ["The Most Dangerous Word God Ever Says"]

At the conclusion of his oath making, Job declares with confidence that he has no reason to be ashamed of anything he has done or said. What is not yet clear is whether having heard Job invoke his claim on the spirit of God, God will say with equal conviction that there is no shame in having created one like Job. Not until God finally speaks from the whirlwind will the question be put with definitive clarity: "Will you even put me in the wrong? Will you condemn me that you may be justified?" (40:8). Job's response to this challenge will be the best clue the book provides concerning these matters.

"The Most Dangerous Word God Ever Says"

[T]he most dangerous word God ever says is *Adam*. All by itself it is no more than a pile of dust—nothing to be concerned about, really—but by following it with the words for *image* and *dominion*, God sifts divinity into that dust, endowing it with things that belong to God alone. When God is through with it, this dust will bear the divine likeness. When God is through with it, this dust will exercise God's own dominion—not by flexing its muscles but by using its tongue.

B. Brown Taylor, *When God Is Silent: The 1997 Lyman Beecher Lectures on Preaching* (Cambridge MA: Cowley Publications, 1998), 4.

The Masal Takes Shape: "May My Enemy Be Like the Wicked," 27:7-12

The term *māšāl* refers to a variety of literary forms, most of which are primarily associated with the wisdom tradition. The most common form is the "saying" or the "proverb" (the plural form of the word, *mĕšālîm*, refers to the collection of sayings found in the book of Proverbs). The etymology of the word suggests that a saying has to do with "comparison." A saying therefore is similar to a metaphor; it compares two different objects in order to provide understanding about one or the other. Such understanding in turn enables the wise to discern and act on a truth that enhances the possibility of being successful in life. For example, it is both abnormal and dangerous to honor a fool, or as Proverbs 26:1 puts it: "Like snow in summer or rain in harvest, so honor is not fitting for a fool." [Comparative Sayings]

Job's *māšāl* offers a comparison between the "wicked" (*rāšā'*) and "my enemy" (*ʾōyĕbî*), "my opponent" (*mitqômmĕmî*) and the "unrighteous" (*'awwāl*; v. 7). It is possible that Job refers to his friends as his enemies and opponents or that he is simply using these terms generically to refer to anyone who would abuse an innocent person. The words "enemy" and "opponent" are however singular in form, and this suggests that it is more likely Job is referring specifically to God.[4] He has previously called God his "adversary" (*ṣar*; 16:9) and has accused God of attacking him like a field general who marshals his troops against an "adversary" (*ṣar*; 19:11). He has wondered why God should regard him as an "enemy" (*ʾōyēb*; 13:24; cf. 33:10). Moreover, he has complained that when God "mocks the calamity of the innocent" (9:23), God is culpable for having forsaken the earth "into the hand of the wicked" (*rāšā'*; 9:24).

Job's *māšāl* expresses the wish that God, who inexplicably plays the role of his enemy, could know the experience of being treated "like the

---

Comparative Sayings

ΑΩ The word *māšāl*, is used with reference to a wide variety of literary forms, e.g., taunt songs, beatitudes, allegories, riddles. One type of *māšāl* is the comparative saying. The most common form is typically a short sentence of parallel lines, which compares two different objects in order to gain some insight into one or the other. The sentence is offered by one whose powers of perception are acknowledged to be acute and deserving of both respect and endorsement (e.g., a king, teacher, parent). Comparative sayings are frequent in Proverbs, especially in chs. 25–29, where a large number of sayings either begin with the preposition "like" (*kî*) or juxtapose different images in such a way that comparison is implied. Consider the following examples.

Like the cold of snow in the time of harvest
    are faithful messengers to those who send
    them. (Prov 25:13)

Like a muddied spring or a polluted fountain
    are the righteous who give way before the
    wicked. (Prov 25:26)

Like a dog that returns to its vomit
    is a fool who reverts to folly. (Prov 26:11)

Like a bird that strays from its nest
    is one who strays from home. (Prov 27:8)

Like a roaring lion or a charging bear
    is a wicked ruler over a poor people. (Prov 28:15)

For further reading, see J. L. Crenshaw, *Old Testament Wisdom: An Introduction* (Atlanta: John Knox Press, 1981), 66-79. For a fuller treatment of Prov 25–27, see R. C. Van Leeuwen, *Context and Meaning in Proverbs 25–27* (Atlanta: Scholars Press, 1988).

wicked." If somehow the tables were turned, and the Judge of those who have been condemned as wicked was required to serve their sentence, then perhaps the court would be more sympathetic to appeals from the unjustly accused. [CD: Assessing Judicially Another's Pain] Job describes the plight of those who have been labeled "wicked" from his own firsthand experience. People who have been marked as wicked are without "hope" (v. 8: *tiqwāh*; cf. 14:19; 19:10; see also [Hope]), because God has taken away their life. They may "cry out" (*ṣāʿaq*; cf. 19:7) for help when trouble comes (v. 9). They may even "call" (*qārāʾ*; cf. 9:16) on God "at all times" (v. 10). But will God listen? Does God ever respond? The notion that God might temporarily suffer "like the wicked" is of course hypothetical in the extreme, and the questions Job asks can surely be little more than rhetorical flights of fancy. Still, those who speak in *mĕšālîm* assume their audience will ponder their proposed comparisons carefully. Perhaps there is a deeper truth in the things they are invited to consider than first meets the eye.

In vv. 11-12, Job shifts from singular to plural address, a move that signals he expects no response from his "enemy," who remains as ever silent and indifferent to anything he says. Job turns to his friends instead. They require more direct forms of address, hence he announces his intention to "teach" them in plain terms what it means from his perspective to have to do with the "hand of God" (*yad ʾēl*; v. 11). He has of course covered this ground before. He has told them that God's "hands" have fashioned him as an object targeted for destruction (10:8), that God's "hand" has terrified him (13:21), that God's "hand" has "touched" him nearly to death (19:20-21). If the friends cannot learn the lesson from looking at Job, then they need only look at the world around them, for the truth about God's "hand" is writ large on creation itself (12:9). But having started out to repeat what he has already said and what the friends already know but will not concede, Job stops short. If after all he has said to them, they still choose to "talk such empty nonsense" (v. 12; REB; *hebel tehbālû*; lit., "you blow empty wind"; cf. 21:34), then why bother to say more?

"This Is the Portion of the Wicked with God," 27:13-23

Verse 13 is a topical statement that introduces what has now become a fairly standard description of the expected fate of the wicked. The words of this verse are in fact almost a verbatim repetition of the declaration on the wicked with which Zophar concluded his last speech (20:29). Many scholars have therefore argued that this speech (vv. 13-23) is Zophar's, not Job's, and that he resumes his assertions about the "portion" of the wicked at the very point where he ended before (see further [*Making* the Text Work]). It is just as likely, however, that *Job* is the one who begins where Zophar left off, and that he is parroting the traditional line on the wicked that he has already heard *ad nauseam* from each of his friends. Job's version of the punishment owed the wicked (v. 13: *rāšāʿ*) does however invite close inspection. He has indicated that his *māšāl* has to do with comparing the wicked (*rāšāʿ*) and the enemy (v. 7). Perhaps here too Job is hinting at comparisons that deserve to be carefully considered if one is to have sufficient wisdom to make sense out of life. If so, then Job's words in vv. 13-23 may aim to do more than simply mimic his friend.

Job describes the fate apportioned for the "wicked" (*rāšāʿ*) and the "ruthless" (*ʿārîṣîm*; NRSV: "oppressors"; v. 13) in conventional terms. Their family will be destroyed by sword, famine, and pestilence (vv. 14-15; cf. Jer 14:12; 15:2; Ezek 5:12; 6:12).[5] The principle that justifies such punishment rests on the traditional doctrine of retribution, which argues that the sins of the parents will be visited upon their children (cf. 5:4; 18:19; 20:10; see further [Retribution]). The word translated by NRSV as "pestilence" is *māwet*, lit., "death." The same word occurs in Jeremiah 15:2 where it appears to be appropriately understood as a metaphor for pestilence or plague, perhaps even *the* plague, which is personified by death itself. One analogy noted by commentators is the medieval phrase "the Black Death," which was used indiscriminately for all fatal epidemic diseases.[6] The reference to widows not lamenting points to death so unspeakably tragic that even the most basic obligations to honor the dead are no longer possible or meaningful (cf. Ps 78:64). In Jeremiah 22:18-19, a similar reference applies to King Jehoiakim. Because the king betrayed his claim to royalty by failing to judge "the cause of the poor and the needy" (cf. 22:16), he was to be dishonored with an ignominious burial, which no one would mourn. [To Mourn or Not to Mourn]

The possessions of the wicked are also doomed to destruction (vv. 16-19). Their silver, piled up "like dust" (v. 16a), will be divided among the innocent as if it is their own inheritance (v. 17b). Their clothing, piled up "like clay" (v. 16b), will become the wardrobe of the righteous (v. 17b). "Dust" (*ʿāpār*) and "clay" (*ḥōmer*) are symbols both of abundance and deterioration (cf. Gen 13:16; 28:14 with Job 17:16).[7] Previously, Job has wondered why God would fashion him as "clay" (*ḥōmer*), then dispose of him in the "dust" (*ʿāpār*; 10:9). He does not get an answer to this question, and subsequently he will believe he has no other choice but to admit that God's singular objective is to see him become "dust and ashes" (*ʿāpār waʾēper*; 30:19; cf. 42:6). The houses of the wicked will be no safer than their other possessions (vv. 18-19; cf. 5:3-5; 18:15). They will be destroyed in the blink of an eye, for they are

---

To Mourn or Not to Mourn

Mourning the dead is a conventional way of honoring the legacy of the deceased. The practice of weeping, swinging the arms back and forth, and in other ways bodily displaying grief allows mourners both to identify with the dead and to express the depth of the loss that their passing has created. In like manner, when the community refrains from such practices it publicly declares that the deceased has left no legacy worth remembering or honoring.

The prophet Jeremiah announced that King Jehoiakim, who built his kingdom on "unrighteousness" and "injustice" (Jer 22:13), would have none to mourn his death. The king would be buried, Jeremiah said, with all the pomp and circumstance of an ass that is dragged out of the city and dumped in a field:

The Death Chamber

Edvard Munch (1863-1944). *The Death Chamber*. 1892. Munch Museum, Oslo, Norway. (Credit: Scala/Art Resource, NY)

> They shall not lament for him, saying,
> "Alas, my brother!" or "Alas, my sister!"
> They shall not mourn for him, saying,
> "Alas, lord!" or "Alas, his majesty!"
> With the burial of a donkey he shall be buried—
> dragged off and thrown out beyond the gates of the city. (Jer 22:18-19)

---

as flimsy as a bird's nest, [8] as open to demolition as the temporary booths the watchmen set up in the vineyard (Isa 1:8; cf. Jonah 4:5). When the wicked lie down at night, they will have everything; when they open their eyes the next morning, "it is gone" (v. 19: *ʾēnennû*; cf. Prov 23:4-5). As Habel puts it, "They and their wealth are here today and gone tomorrow."[9]

In the end, the wicked are destined to be banished from the world by destructive forces they cannot resist (vv. 20-23). Death, personified as "terrors" that search and destroy (cf. 15:21; 18:11), erases them from the earth with the force of flood waters (v. 20a). A "storm wind" (*supā*) snatches them away at night (v. 20b). An "east wind" (*qādîm*) blows in from the desert, swirling against them "without mercy"; they are blown out of their place (vv. 21-22). Waters, storm, and wind are traditional symbols of punishment and destruction (cf. Prov 1:27; 10:25; Isa 29:6; 66:15; Nah 1:3). They are also natural forces within creation, which, Job suggests, will not remain passive when the wicked abuse the moral foundations upon which the world depends. Instead, nature itself[10] will rise up not only to punish the wicked, but to "clap" and "hiss" as a way of expressing contempt for their shameful behavior (v. 23; cf. Jer 49:17; Lam 2:15; Zeph 2:15).

There is little reason to doubt that Job is mimicking Zophar by reciting this rather conventional speech about the punishment due the wicked. There are, however, several small but intriguing intimations in this speech that invite readers to consider whether Job may be doing more than simply calling his friend to task. In this regard it is instructive to note that although Job begins in 27:13 where Zophar leaves off in chapter 20, he makes a slight alteration when he recites his friend's concluding words in 20:29. The difference between Zophar and Job may be seen by comparing their two statements:

Zophar (20:29a): This is the portion of the wicked *from God* (*mēʾĕlōhîm*)
Job (27:13a): This is the portion of the wicked *with God* (*ʿim ʾēl*)

Zophar clearly believes that the punishment the wicked deserve comes *from* God, a perspective he reiterates in the second half of his statement: "[This is] the heritage decreed for them *from God* (*mēʾēl*; 20:29b). Job also clearly believes, or at least he *wants* to believe, that the punishment of the wicked comes *from* God, and in the second half of his recitation he repeats his friend's affirmation almost exactly: "[This is] the heritage that oppressors receive *from the Almighty* (*miššadday*; 27:13b). The similarities between the two statements make it all the more curious that Job uses the preposition *with* instead of *from* in 27:13a. The normal meaning of this preposition (*ʿim*) is "accompaniment" or "addition," hence Job appears to be speaking of the punishment the wicked deserve *"along with"* or *"in addition to"* God. Given this meaning, his objective would be not only to describe the just rewards of the wicked, but also to suggest that inasmuch as God, his "enemy," behaves "like the wicked" (v. 7), then God deserves to experience the same fate as the wicked. The idea of *calling on God to judge God* is of course a logical impossibility. It is no less unsettling and paradoxical here than at the beginning of Job's speech, when he effectively calls on God to curse God (vv. 1-6). It is not surprising that most commentators avoid this problem by suggesting that the preposition "with" in 27:13a should be emended to "from" in order to bring it into conformity with Zophar's more orthodox assertion.[11]

There is, however, no convincing textual basis for this change. Despite the difficulties, it is wise simply to wrestle with what Job seems to be saying in the text we have. Like Zophar, Job expects God to punish the wicked, although he can find precious little evidence to sustain this belief. Unlike Zophar, Job is willing to imagine that the principles of divine justice that apply on earth must not be compromised when they are applied to the Judge who sits in heaven.[12]

Two additional observations may be offered in support of the suggestion that Job has set his sights on the expected justice owed the wicked wherever they exist, whether on earth or in heaven. (1) Previously, Job has expressed the fear that God intends to destroy him with a "tempest" (śĕʿārāh; 9:17). He has accused God of attacking him "without mercy" (lōʾ yaḥmôl; 16:13). Now Job foresees a time when the great winds of the east will blow (saʿar; v. 21) "without mercy" (lōʾ yaḥmôl; v. 22), until they sweep the wicked out of their place. Is it possible that Job looks for these winds to be as much a threat to God as they are to the wicked? The end of the book of Job will return to the imagery of the "whirlwind" (saʿar; 38:1; 40:6) as the vehicle for divine revelation. On that occasion, when God at last summons Job to speak what he knows, the reader will have an occasion to reassess which way the winds of divine justice are blowing.

(2) Job has stated with conviction that he has no reason to be ashamed of anything he has done or said (v. 6). With the last words of this speech, he insists with equal conviction that the wicked cannot match his integrity. A part of their punishment will be the shame and contempt heaped on them by the clapping and whistling of the wind (v. 23). Here too Job's anticipation of the shaming of the wicked casts a long shadow towards the end of the book. When God speaks from the whirlwind, Job will be challenged to "look on all who are proud and bring them low" and "to tread down the wicked (rĕšāʿîm) where they stand "(40:12). The conventional view holds that God places before Job an impossible task. Perhaps so. But if God is addressing one who can say with a clear conscience, "May my enemy be like the wicked," then perhaps even God has reason to listen carefully for the clapping and whistling of the wind.

It is important to acknowledge that none of the intimations noted above provides more than a hint that Job may be warning God about the potential ricochet of divine justice. Perhaps Job is doing nothing more than saying what he believes his friends would say if he gave them the chance. Then again, perhaps these small but suggestive allusions to a guilty and punishable God are a fitting note on which to end the dialogues with the friends. What more can the friends say to Job, who having listened to so many of their speeches, still refuses to agree with them? More importantly, now that Job has sworn an oath of innocence that seems to incriminate God, what more can *anyone* say? The drama of this Joban story has reached yet another crucial turning point, and there will now be a substantial pause to allow for its full impact. The rumblings of what comes next lie in the repeating refrain of the following chapter: "Where shall wisdom be found? "(vv. 12, 20).

CONNECTIONS

The dialogue between Job and his three friends has ended. Readers may find it useful to pause in the silence that falls at the end of chapter 27 and take stock of what has happened thus far. [Listening to Silences] Job set the agenda with a series of "Why?" questions in chapter 3 that pressed his friends to reflect on the meaning of life in a world conflicted by innocent suffering. Why is a blameless and upright person like Job born (3:11, 12, 20), if life is to be filled with more misery and turmoil than rest (3:10, 13, 17, 26)? Eliphaz takes the point position for the friends by responding with an affirmation of God's moral governance of the world (4:7–5:7). He urges Job to place his trust in the Creator God and models for him the doxology of praise that ought to define such trust (5:8-16). Job has twice offered his own discerning version of such praise (9:5-10; 12:13-25). Indeed, by the end of the third cycle of speeches he shows that he has learned the standard lines of praise so well that he can speak them just like his friends (26:5-14). At the end of the dialogues, therefore, Job retains in some sense a chronic inclination to praise. He still knows how to say the words "Blessed be the name of the Lord" (1:21), even if they sound a lot more discordant than when spoken from the ash heap.

Listening to Silences

"We hear nothing so clearly as what comes out of silence" (257). This is the realization that comes to author/fisherman David Duncan in the last hours of a September day, as he stands in the middle of the Clark Fork River. He had snagged a magnificent trout and watched it leap and dart in resistance. The catch played itself out, the trout yielded to fatigue and turned over on its side. He unhooked it and released it back into the river. He stands waist-deep in waters now suddenly calm and silent.

In the silence of the moment, Duncan reflects on something he learned about fly fishing as a boy. When trout jump, the rings in the river drift downstream The fisherman must therefore cast not to the visible rings but to the now invisible rings where the trout first appeared. It is called casting to the "memory point." Duncan casts to a memory point, this time not with his fishing rod but with his mind:

In the last hours of a September day, you can't see down into the waters of the Clark Ford. The sun is too low, the light too acutely angled. In the last hours of the day the river's surface grows reflective, shows you blue sky and red clouds, upside-down pines, orange water-birch, yellow cottonwoods. Deer hang as if shot, by their feet, yet keep browsing bright grasses. Ospreys fly beneath you. Everything is swirling. In a snag, way down deep, you might spot a flycatcher. It's hard to believe that these clouds and trees, deer and birds, color grasses are a door. It's hard to believe fish live behind it. Yet it was the clouds at my feet the rainbow troubled by rising. It was into the downward sky that I cast the mahogany mayfly. It was out of inverted pines and cottonwoods that the trout then flew, shattering all reflection, three times speaking its leaping word. (258-59)

Job and his readers must attend to the silences that fall after ch. 27. Perhaps this listening is like casting for memory points, like looking for the now invisible hints and clues that the waters have been seriously and invitingly disturbed. It may be hard to believe that the upside-down world of Uz is a door behind which lies some new word. Then again, knocking on the door, like casting for the invisible rings, may be the only thing to do. As Duncan notes, "Not every cast hits the memory point. But when it does, this word just goes on speaking" (259).

D. Duncan, "A Door," *River Teeth: Stories and Writings* (New York: Bantam Books, 1995).

The friends have also pressed Job to take seriously the doctrine of retribution. They are especially concerned that he stay focused on the truth about the certain judgment that God enacts on the wicked (15:17-35; 18:5-21; 20:6-29). Job has stayed focused on the wicked, and he has twice examined the friends' doctrine and found it wanting (21:7-16; 24:1-17). Still, by the end of the third cycle of speeches, he shows that he can start with the standard line on the wicked and finish at basically the same place as the friends (27:13-23). At the end of the dialogues, therefore, Job retains a keen interest in the truth about divine retribution and punishment. He still knows that he has to deal with a God who gives and takes away (cf. 1:21), a God who dispenses both good and evil (cf. 2:10), even if this is a much more problematic assertion now than when he first made it.

Job has thus affirmed both blessing and cursing as legitimate ways to describe and respond to what God is doing in the world. He has also come to see that neither blessing nor cursing is adequate explanation for what has happened to him. When he contemplates what the Creator God is doing in the world, he has no problem affirming God's wisdom and strength (9:4;12:13), but he cannot see why this should require his praise, for everywhere he looks God's power seems to be used for destructive ends (9:5-12; 12:14-25). He knows that "dominion and fear" are the hallmarks of God's governance (cf. 25:1), but when he uses these as the basis for praise, he cannot help but wonder if there is not something more to God's power than these small terrifying whispers (cf. 25:14). He can celebrate the cursing of the wicked, for they are the enemies of the righteous and hence of God. But when he looks at *his enemy*, he sees *God* (cf. 13:24). If he is to hope that his enemy would be treated like the wicked, that his opponent would experience what it means to be regarded as one of the unrighteous (27:7), then where is the cause for celebration? If he affirms that punishment is the "portion of the wicked *with* God" (27:13), then does he not simply ensnare himself in a hopeless conundrum that only threatens his belief in both God and justice? If blessing and cursing are the *only* legitimate options for describing and responding to what God is doing in the world, then perhaps Job's wife was right after all. He may curse God or bless God; either way something important in him dies (cf. 2:9; see further [Blessing/Cursing in Job]). [Nothing Can Prevent the Descent]

Given the choices that have thus far been presented to Job, it is little wonder that the dialogue breaks down after chapter 27. One might well expect that the drama would simply end at this point, with questions asked, answers offered, pondered, and rejected, and innocent suffering still unchanged by it all. There is however one important clue that signals there is still more to come, and with it, perhaps, a third option.

Job has taken an oath of innocence. He has sworn on the life of God that as long as he embodies God's breath and God's spirit he will not betray himself or God by compromising his integrity (27:2-6). It is Job's integrity that first marks him as the greatest of all the people in the east (1:1, 4). It is his integrity that God applauds, even after God has sacrificed him and his family, for no reason, to the *satan's* test (2:3). It is his integrity that his wife unsuccessfully pushes him to reconsider (2:9). It is his integrity that compels Job to take God to court in order to prove his innocence (9:20-21), even though he knows God will not answer his complaint. It is this same integrity that Job tenaciously reasserts at the end of the dialogues, without shame, as he stares into the face of a silent God and silenced friends.

At the end of chapter 27, it is still unclear what advantage, if any, there is in clinging to one's integrity in a world like Job's. Will filing charges against God really make any difference? Does defending one's honor, with integrity, really count for anything in a world where might makes right (cf. 9:12, 19)? It has become increasingly apparent to Job that integrity may cost him his life (13:14). It may mean that he must appeal to a silent heaven and a scarred earth for support of his claim on justice (16:18-19). It may mean that his ultimate vindication rests in the unseen hands of a distant redeemer (19:25). It may mean that when he has done and said all he can, the only response he will hear is the clapping and hissing of the wind that chases him into shameful exile, along with all others who would contend with the Almighty (27:23).

There is still time for Job to reconsider, and there is good reason to do so, for as the friends have so often reminded him, a mortal, even a mortal with integrity, can never be righteous before God (4:17; 15:14; 22:2; 25:4). Even so, Job has sworn an oath, and here he will take his stand. [CD: "Trial and *Error*" or "Trial and *Rightness*"?]

Nothing Can Prevent the Descent

Ian McEwan begins his novel *Amsterdam* with the friends of Molly Lane reflecting on her tragic and sudden death because of cancer. As the friends gather in the "Garden of Remembrance" just outside the crematorium chapel, they think about what they had witnessed as Molly lived out her last days: "the speed of her descent into madness and pain . . . the loss of bodily function and with it all sense of humor, and then the tailing of into vagueness interspersed with episodes of ineffectual violence and muffled shrieking" (4).

Molly's friend Clive Linley remembers that when the trouble signs first appeared, she had gone to the doctor. Her doctor advised her to get some tests. She had done what they said, submitted herself to the treatment they recommended, and she had died. Clive remembers Molly's journey, and he despairs over what it might mean for him when one day his doctors ask him to act on useless advice: "They could manage your descent, but they couldn't prevent it" (27).

I. McEwan, *Amsterdam* (New York: Nan Talese/Doubleday, 1998).

NOTES

[1] C. Newsom, "The Book of Job," in vol. 4 of NIB (Nashville: Abingdon Press, 1996), 522.

[2] N. Habel, *The Book of Job: A Commentary* (OTL; Philadelphia: Westminster Press, 1985), 380.

[3] Cf. Newsom ("The Book of Job," 523): "Just as Job speaks with God's own breath, he makes his claim *against* God with God's own passion for justice" (emphasis added).

[4] Similarly Habel, *Book of Job*, 381-82; E. M. Good, *In Turns of Tempest: A Reading of Job with a Translation* (Stanford: Stanford University Press, 1990), 287-88.

[5] Cf. E. Dhorme, *A Commentary on the Book of Job* (Nashville: Thomas Nelson Publishers, 1967), 393-94.

[6] R. Gordis, *The Book of Job: Commentary, New Translation, and Special Studies* (New York: Jewish Theological Seminary of America, 1978), 294; Habel, *Book of Job*, 386.

[7] Habel, *Book of Job*, 386.

[8] The word "nest" in v. 18 is difficult and numerous suggestions have been proposed. The Hebrew word (*'aš*) is lit., "moth." The LXX expands on the MT by adding a second word that means "spider." The implication may be that the wicked build houses that are as flimsy as a "moth's cocoon" (cf. NIV) or a "spider's web" (cf. RSV; TEV; NJB). Some scholars cite a comparable word in cognate languages that suggests something more like a "bird's nest" (Dhorme, *Book of Job*, 395; Gordis, *Book of Job*, 295). A number of modern translations adopt this suggestion (cf. NJPS; REB). With any of these readings, the imagery points to the fragility of the structures the wicked build for themselves.

[9] Habel, *Book of Job*, 387.

[10] The subject of the singular verbs in v. 23 ("clap," "hiss") is ambiguous. NRSV (see marginal note) suggests that "God" may be the subject. Some suggest that the subject is indefinite, i.e.,"people" (cf. Dhorme, *Book of Job*, 397; Gordis, *Book of Job*, 296). It is preferable to take the "east wind" (v. 21) as the most logical subject of these verbs (cf. Habel, *Book of Job*, 384).

[11] Cf. S. R. Driver and G. B. Gray, *A Critical and Exegetical Commentary on the Book of Job* (Edinburgh: T and T. Clark, 1921), 229; H. H. Rowley, *Job* (The Century Bible; Ontario: Thomas Nelson, 1970), 223; Dhorme, *Book of Job*, 386; J. Hartley, *The Book of Job* (NICOT; Grand Rapids MI: William B. Eerdmans, 1988), 358.

[12] Good (*In Turns of Tempest*, 289) also prefers to read the text as is. He understands Job to be saying that the wicked receive their portion "with the connivance" of God.

A SECOND SOLILOQUY: "WHERE SHALL WISDOM BE FOUND?"

Job 28:1-28

The structure of this poem on wisdom is relatively easy to discern. Three major sections are clearly marked. The first, vv. 1-14, celebrates the human capacity to mine precious metals from the depths of the earth but concedes that the ultimate gem, wisdom, is not among these treasures. The second, vv. 15-22, provides an extensive catalogue of the earth's treasures, no one of which is equal in value to wisdom, which is the rarest of all jewels in the world. The third, vv. 23-27, affirms that God knows the way to wisdom, because God searched it out when the world was created. A repeating question provides the refrain that connects the three sections: "But where shall wisdom be found?" (v. 12); "Where then does wisdom come from?" (v. 20). The answer toward which the entire poem leads is provided by v. 28: wisdom is a divine possession, which humans may access by fearing God. [Structure of Job 28:1-28]

Despite the clear delineations, Job 28 remains, as N. Habel has observed, "a brilliant but embarrassing poem for many commentators."[1] The terms "brilliant" and "embarrassing" are well chosen, for when one surveys the enormous literature this poem has evoked, it is clear that scholars have been both impressed and perplexed by its contents. On the one hand, there is widespread appreciation for the poem's vivid description of the mining process (vv. 3-4, 9-11), the only such account in the Hebrew Bible, and for the range of poetic

---

Structure of Job 28:1-28

28:1-14	Mining for precious metals
v. 12	"But where shall wisdom *(ḥokmāh)* be found? And where is the place of *understanding (bînāh)*?"
28:15-22	A catalogue of the earth's treasures
v. 20	"Where then does wisdom *(ḥokmāh)* come from? And where is the place of *understanding (bînāh)*?"
28:23-28	God knows the way to wisdom
v. 28	"Truly the fear of the Lord is wisdom *(ḥokmāh)*; and to depart from evil is *understanding (bînāh)*."

images it employs to compare the earth's precious gems and metals to the surpassing value of wisdom (vv. 15-19). On the other, there is little agreement on several issues that are important for understanding what this extraordinary poem means within the context of the book of Job. Who is the speaker of these words? Job? One of the friends? God? Who is the author of the poem, and is the author the same one who is responsible for the rest of the book? Does the poem date to the earliest stages of the book, or is it an independent and later insertion? To these and other questions, scholars have proposed different answers, but like the quest for wisdom itself, final and definitive resolutions remain elusive. [CD: Where Shall Wisdom Be Found among the Scholarly Proposals?]

The absence of consensus on such important questions as date and authorship is instructive, because it suggests that the clues for interpreting this poem may lie along other lines. Two aspects of the poem—its form and its function in its present location—are especially deserving of consideration.

First, the poem has the form of a *soliloquy*. The speaker does not address anyone in particular and does not seek a response. The words are lyrical, even playful, not argumentative and tense like the previous exchanges between Job and his friends. The speaker reflects on matters that have been internalized and now must be spoken in order to hear how they sound and assess their merit. Readers are invited to eavesdrop on this soliloquy and to be alert to any clues that might reveal the identity of the speaker. A number of signs point to Job. The speech does not specify a change of speaker, thus it is plausible that it is a continuation of Job's words in chapter 27. Furthermore, the substance of the speech recalls Job's opening soliloquy in chapter 3, especially his ruminations on the darkness that defines his search for the meaning of life (cf. 3:4-6 with 28:2). Both the beginning and the ending of the dialogues with the friends, therefore, depict Job as thinking deeply about the world in which he lives. In the first soliloquy, he repeatedly asks why there is suffering like his in a world governed by a good and just God. In the second soliloquy, he asks if there is any place in creation where he can obtain wisdom sufficient to answer his questions.

The signs pointing to Job as the speaker are however not unambiguous. When one listens carefully to the tone of these words, there is much that makes them sound discordant on Job's lips. The view that wisdom is ultimately inaccessible to mortals (28:12-13, 20-22) sounds suspiciously like a continuation of the same argument that Zophar makes in 11:7-12. To complicate matters further, the affirmations about the capacity to see, appraise, establish, and search out the totality of creation's mysteries (28:23-27) bear a striking resemblance to what God will subsequently claim as a divine prerogative in chapters 38–41.

In the final analysis, therefore, if Job is the speaker in chapter 28, then it is important to recognize that he remains very much a conflicted person. He is still driven to introspection about the darkness that defies his quest for light. He is still mulling over the friends' seemingly irrefutable argument that his best efforts to find what he seeks cannot succeed. He is still wondering what, if any, of the God-like capacity to understand and rightly appraise the world he might possibly possess.

A second consideration is the function of this poem in its present location. C. Westermann has used the suggestive term *"fermata"* to describe the role this soliloquy plays.[2] In musical terms, a *fermata* is a sign placed above the staff to indicate that a particular note should be held longer than its assigned value in order for the composition to maintain its intended rhythm and pace. Readers may think of Job 28 as playing an analogous role. In literary terms, it is a resting place within the book's drama. The dialogues between Job and his friends have ended. Job's last speech (chs. 29–31) has not yet begun. At this penultimate juncture in Job's discourse, he has blessed and he has cursed (see Job 27, "Connections"), but by neither of these means has he been able to obtain answers to the questions he raised from the ash heap at the outset of this journey. Now he appears to pause in consideration of another question, differently phrased than those first uttered in chapter 3 but similarly freighted: "Where shall wisdom be found?" (28:12; cf. v. 20). The closing verse of this second soliloquy suggests that Job is now ready to reconsider the answer that was posited for him by God at the very beginning of the story. Perhaps wisdom and understanding comes only by embracing the traditional model of piety that is defined by "fear of the Lord" and "departing from evil" (28:28; cf. 1:8; 2:3).

But if this is Job's only recourse, then there should be little surprise that he would want to weigh this matter very carefully. God already knows that Job is the perfect example of this kind of piety. Moreover, Job now has more than enough reason to believe that this kind of piety only makes him a better target for destruction. Given this situation, what should Job do next? Should he return to a kind of piety that asks no questions, offers no complaints, expects no justice? Is such piety the "functional equivalent"[3] of the only wisdom he can hope to obtain? Or should he press on with the search for something more and different, something beyond what either he or the friends have thus far been able to thrash out? The *fermata* that stands over the last word in chapter 28 suggests that the drama now hangs in suspension while Job considers out loud his next move. [Holding the Note on Pain and Mystery]

Holding the Note on Pain and Mystery

In Gail Godwin's novel *Father Melancholy's Daughter*, Margaret reflects on what she has learned about mourning in the aftermath of the sudden death of her father, the Reverend Walter Gower, Rector of St. Cuthbert's, on Good Friday, 1988.

I could write a handbook on mourning: how it weaves in and out of the ordinary traffic of your days, for weeks and months (and maybe years), sometimes diverting you with just a sharp little *blip* of reminder, like the warning blips from Paul's siren ("Pull over to the side of whatever you are doing, and remember!"); other times bringing you to a full stop with a piercing, extended wail, requiring you to leave traffic altogether, turn your ignition off, put your head down on the steering wheel, let yourself be overwhelmed by the incredible words "Never again," and wait for your breath to come back.

And the ache that you treasure, that unique, wrenching ache that you hoard: you go looking for it. Contrary to what so many people try to tell you, people who want to divert you away from the "painful" topic, people who proudly assure you they have "been through it" and "it will get better in time," you want to dwell in its presence, you want to protect it from the heartless, future "time" they promise you is on its way, you want to dwell in the presence of the pain, the mystery of its hold on you.

In words that we may imagine would be just as at home on Job's lips as hers, Margaret concludes that she feels "more at home in the presence of the living mystery than with any strained and false 'wisdom.'"

G. Godwin, *Father Melancholy's Daughter* (New York: Avon Books, 1991), 319-20.

COMMENTARY

The Quest(s) for Wisdom, 28:1-14

Soliloquies are interior musings spoken out loud. Audiences may listen in, and what they hear will provide them a unique perspective on what the speaker is thinking and feeling. But they should not expect the discourse to be systematically organized or the meaning to be transparent on the first hearing. The speaker is reflecting, turning things over and over in the mind, speaking them aloud to hear how they sound, then mulling them over again to find new levels of meaning that may not have been discerned on the mind's first pass through. The first section of Job's soliloquy is a good example of how this works. We must go beyond a first reading, for a traditional verse by verse exposition cannot do justice to the full range of what these verses begin to disclose. As an invitation to this way of reading, the commentary that follows will focus on three levels of meaning in vv. 1-14 that merit close attention: *first*, the general reflection on the mining enterprise and what human ingenuity can and cannot accomplish; *second*, the analogy between the miner's search for precious metals and Job's search for meaning; *third*, the subtle parallels between Job's mining for meaning and God's search for wisdom.

A first level of meaning derives from reflection on mining for precious metals. Job reflects on both the possibilities (vv. 1-11) and the limitations (vv. 12-14) of the mining enterprise. Precious metals and gems have their own special places in the world. Silver has a "source" (v. 1a: *môṣaʾ*; lit., "coming out place") and gold a "place" (v. 1b: *māqôm*). Iron can be extracted from the "dust" (*ʿāpār*, NRSV: "earth"), and copper can be smelted from stone (v. 2). Deep within the bowels of the earth, fire transforms ordinary rocks into precious gems like lapis lazuli (vv. 5-6; see marginal note in NRSV). All of these treasures can be found and they can be obtained, but the process requires extraordinary skill and courage. Miners must search out the farthest and darkest recesses of the earth (v. 3). They must open shafts (v. 4a) and carve out tunnels (v. 10a). They must overturn mountains as if pulling them up by the roots (v. 9), and they must dam up rivers at their source point (v. 11b). All this they must do in isolation, for they work in remote places where ordinary people never go (v. 4b), places the sharp-eyed falcon cannot see (v. 7), places the lion, the most courageous of the wild beasts, has not prowled (v. 8). Miners have the skill and the resolve to meet all these challenges. They see "every precious thing" (v. 10b). Whatever is hidden they bring to light (v. 11b).

For all their expertise, however, miners search in vain for the most prized treasure of all, wisdom (*ḥokmāh*) and understanding (*bînāh*; v. 12). The two terms are often paired in wisdom literature (cf. Prov 1:2; 4:5, 7; 16:16; 23:23), the first as a general reference to knowledge, the second as a more specific designation for the intellectual discernment such knowledge affords.[4] In the context of the mining imagery that sustains vv. 1-11, wisdom and understanding are the rarest and most inaccessible of all jewels, for they are the key that unlocks the "ultimate secret of the world."[5] [Parallels Between Verses 1 and 12] No human being knows the way to the place where such a treasure can be obtained

---

Parallels Between Verses 1 and 12

AΩ Verbal correspondences, which are more readily discerned in Hebrew than in English, suggest that v. 1 comprises the first two parts of a parallelism that are not completed until v. 12 (C. Newsom, "The Book of Job," in vol. 4 of *NIB* [Nashville: Abingdon Press, 1996], 529; cf. J. Gerald Janzen, *Job* [Atlanta: John Knox, 1985], 191-92). Placing these verses side by side helps to make this connection clearer.

Verse 1	Verse 12
Surely there is a coming out place (*moṣāʾ*) for silver, and a place (*māqôm*) for the gold they refine.	But where shall wisdom be found (*timmāṣê*)? And where is the place (*māqôm*) of understanding?

The words "coming out place" and "be found" in vv. 1a and 12a come from different Hebrew roots (*yaṣaʾ* and *maṣaʾ*, respectively), but they have a similar sound. The Hebrew words for "place" in vv. 1b and 12b are identical. The parallelism between the four lines establishes an assertion-question sequence. Thus, there is a *source place* for silver, but where can wisdom *be found*? There is a *place* for gold, but where is the *place* of understanding?

(v. 13a). It cannot be found among the living or the dead (v. 13b; cf. v. 22). Even if one were to search the primordial depths of the cosmos, the watery abyss would stand up and say, "It is not in me" (v. 14).

At a second level the miner's search for buried treasures provides an analogy for reflecting on Job's search for meaning.[6] In his opening soliloquy, Job longs for an end to his misery with a passion like that which drives those who dig for hidden treasures (3:21). If he could but find his own grave, the place where he could lie down and die, then Job would experience a peace and rest equal to the joy of those who discover the riches buried deep within the earth (3:22). Toward that end, he searches for a place where a darkness so thick and so heavy resembles the primordial state of creation (3:4-6), a place where neither day nor night, neither life nor death, neither weariness nor wickedness can exercise any claim on human beings (3:13-19). The "darkness" (3:4: *ḥōšek*) and "gloom" (3:6: *ʾōpēl*) and "deep darkness" (3:5: *ṣalmāwet*) Job seeks corresponds to the "darkness" (*ḥōšek*) and "gloom" (*ʾōpēl*) and "deep darkness" (*ṣalmāwet*) that is the locus for the miner's work (28:3). And like the miner, who dares to work in depths that scare away everyone else (28:4, 7-8), Job has discovered that no one is prepared to join him on his dangerous quest for meaning. His fair-weather "friends" abandon him (cf. 6:14-18), the social community from whom he expects support ostracizes him (19:13-20), the God he expects to come to his aid is nowhere to be found (cf. 23:8-9). "It is as though," Janzen suggests, "in describing the hazardous but worthwhile human quest for the precious resources which lie hidden within the dust, Job unwittingly resorts to the language of his own current experience!"[7]

At this second level, Job's soliloquy invites readers to wonder if perhaps he is searching for some deeper connection between his quest and the miner's work than first meets the eye. It is true that some of earth's treasures—wisdom and understanding—are beyond the reach of all human technological expertise. In this sense, the limitations miners face serve to remind Job that even his best efforts to obtain an answer to his "Why?" questions will not be fully satisfying. In an earlier speech, Zophar chides Job by asking rhetorically "Can you find out the limit (*taklît*) of the Almighty?" (11:7). From Zophar's perspective the only legitimate answer Job can give is "No, of course not." Job himself has been pushed to concede that the full truth about God's work "at the boundary (*taklît*) between light and darkness" (26:10) defies human comprehension.

But now, in contemplating the remarkable accomplishments of the miner, Job appears to be considering the possibility of a different response to Zophar's question. Miners have both the courage and the capacity to reach the farthest limit (28:3b: *taklît*; NRSV: "bound") of

---

Probing the "Sources of the River" Where God Resides

AΩ Job 28:11 refers to the miner's capacity to probe the "sources of the river" (*mibbĕkî nĕhārôt*). A virtually identical phrase is used in Ugaritic texts to describe the warrior goddess Anath penetrating into the sacred domain of El "at the sources of the (two) rivers." The pertinent portion of the text reads as follows:

Forthwith she [Anath] sets face
Towards El at the springs of the (two) rivers (*mbk nhrm*),
Midst the Channels of the (two) deeps.
She penetrates the domain of El and enters
The pavilion of the King, Father of exalted ones.

See M. Pope, *Job* (AB; Garden City NY: Doubleday, 1979), 203; cf. C. Newsom, "The Book of Job," in vol. 4 of *NIB* (Nashville: Abingdon Press, 1996), 530; N. Habel, *The Book of Job: A Commentary* (OTL; Philadelphia: Westminster Press, 1985), 390, 397. For the full text of the Ugaritic poem, see *ANET*, 3rd ed. with supplement, ed. J. B. Pritchard (Princeton: Princeton University Press, 1969), 129-42. The portion of the text cited above may be consulted in Pritchard, 133.

---

what is humanly possible. They can "put an end to darkness" (28:3a). They can cut and carve through almost every obstacle until they come right to the edge of the mysteries that God alone oversees (28:11). [Probing the "Sources of the River" Where God Resides] Even if miners cannot obtain *every* treasure, they can search and find *some* treasures. They can bring to light whatever is hidden (28:11), and in doing so they come as close to the ultimate prize—wisdom and understanding like that which God possesses—as humans can get. Perhaps in pondering the accomplishments of the miner, Job finds a model for the human quest to understand ultimate truths. Perhaps both the limitations and the possibilities of this model are cause for celebration rather than despair. Perhaps such deliberations move Job one step closer to realizing that when human beings are willing to risk reaching for the limits of what is possible, they "approximate the extraordinary powers of God."[8]

At a third level the mining enterprise offers Job a subtle paradigm for reflecting on God's search for wisdom. A number of verbal and thematic connections between what miners do and what God does suggests that for all their limitations humans do in fact possess a certain "godlike ability."[9] When humans "put an end to darkness" (v. 3a) and bring "hidden things. . . to light" (v. 11b), they imitate the creative activity of God, whose word "Let there be light" provides the foundation for the world in which all creatures are to find their place (Gen 1:2-3; cf. Job 12:22).[10] When humans risk probing the "limit points"[11] of their world (v. 3b), they reach for the very boundaries that God sets in place to prevent the collapse of light and darkness (cf. 26:10). The correspondence between God's power and human power extends to the specific measures described in vv. 9-11. The miner's power to "overturn (*hāpak*) mountains" (v. 9) compares with the power that manifests God's peculiar wisdom in governing the world (9:4-5 [note *hāpak* in v. 5]). The ability to "see (*rā'āh*) every precious thing" (v. 10a), even "hidden things" (v. 11b), approximates God's ability to "see (*rāʾāh*) everything under the heavens" (28:24), including wisdom, the most elusive treasure of all (28:27). The capacity to "cut out (*biqqēaʿ*) channels in the rocks" (v. 10) to get to the source of water evokes the image of God "splitting (*bāqāʿ*)" rocks to create water for the people in the wilderness (Ps 78:15; cf. Hab 3:9).

In sum, the first section of this soliloquy indicates that Job has thought deeply and on several levels about what humans can and cannot accomplish in the world. He can see that the world is full of things precious and desirable. Some of the world's greatest treasures—silver and gold—are buried so deeply that their acquisition requires extraordinary human courage and skill. Other treasures—wisdom and understanding—are so elusive that even the best efforts to find them do not succeed. At this juncture, Job remains uncertain about what these possibilities and limitations mean for him. Should he focus on the limitations that humans must live with, as the friends have urged him to do, and resign himself to search only for those things that he has a reasonable chance of obtaining? Should he focus on the possibilities that tempt humans to reach for treasures that inevitably exceed their grasp? Job's experience has provided him ample reason to believe that his friends are right. He understands that at a basic level human beings are slaves to destinies they do not choose. They live and they die, and in between they must simply endure whatever joy or sorrow God apportions to them (cf. 7:1-6; 14:5, 10-12).

Still, even as he is tempted to yield to limitations that cannot be refuted, Job has wondered if in some mysterious way he may be endowed with significance and power that can make a difference in the way the world works (cf. 7:12, 17). Having listened to all the reasons the friends give for why he should abandon such foolish thoughts, Job now contemplates a model for human striving that invites him to hold on to his imagination. It is the miner who fixes Job's reflections on what he can and cannot do. If it is possible for the miner to search inaccessible places and obtain some of the world's most unavailable treasures, then perhaps Job's search for the elusive God who holds the key to his unanswered questions is not so foolish after all. If the miner can reach to the very limits of what is possible and in the process bring what is hidden to light, then perhaps Job can reach for the boundaries between silence and response, absence and presence. In the process, perhaps, he too can see into the hidden things that defy comprehension. And if the miner must concede that some treasures, like wisdom, elude even the most determined efforts, then perhaps the resolve to "overturn" and "split open" and "see" offers Job a model that in fact brings him as close to God as it is humanly possible to be. [CD: Playing Hide and Seek with Wisdom]

Wisdom's Incomparable Value, 28:15-22

In the first part of his soliloquy, Job concedes that wisdom cannot be found by searching for its source in any place on earth. In the second part, he stipulates that wisdom cannot be acquired second-hand through commercial transactions. This second observation, like the first, invites Job (and the reader) to search for meaning at more than one level.

The first impression one gets from listening in on Job's musings is that he sets out to list every precious metal and gem and every type of transaction in which they may be used to acquire wisdom (vv. 15-19). At the top of the list of valuable commodities is gold and silver. Five different Hebrew expressions are used for "gold," which is the most valuable of all metals. The distinctions between these expressions are not clear, a fact conceded by most modern translations, which generally resort to rather vague terms (e.g., NRSV: "fine gold" [v. 17]; "pure gold" [v. 19]) to call attention to the different words. The specific terms are however relatively unimportant, for the primary point seems to be that Job considers every conceivable kind of gold and finds none to have the equivalent value of wisdom. In addition to gold and silver, the list contains seven different gems or stones: onyx, sapphire, glass, coral, crystal, pearls, and chrysolite. Difficulties in understanding the Hebrew words mean that the translations are in some cases only approximate, but here again the limitation is minimal. The number *seven* suggests that the primary objective is to enumerate *all* the precious jewels that exist anywhere in the world. The idea that none of these metals and gems is comparable in value to wisdom is underscored by the use of five different verbs for acquisition, each preceded by the negative particle "no/not" (*lōʾ*). No matter what one may offer in exchange, wisdom cannot be "gotten" (v. 15a: *nātan*), "weighed" (v. 15b: *šāqal*), "paid for" (v. 16a: *sālah*; NRSV: "valued"), "compared/equaled" (vv. 17, 19a: *ʿārak*), or "considered" (v. 18: *zākar*; NRSV: "mention").

Job's meditation on the possibility of acquiring wisdom through commercial transactions draws upon common themes in wisdom literature. The book of Proverbs compares wisdom/understanding with gold/silver (e.g., Prov 3:13-14; 8:10-11, 19; 20:15) and suggests that these are unequal commodities. One may "buy" (*qānāh*) silver and gold, for example, but it is far better to invest in wisdom and understanding (Prov 16:16). One may "buy" (*qānāh*) wisdom and understanding, as well as truth, but it is best not to sell them for things of lesser value (Prov 23:23). In a previous speech, Eliphaz has appropriated these conventional motifs to admonish Job for thinking that his "gold," that is, the exaggerated worth he gives to his personal righteousness, is more valuable than the instruction that comes from God (Job

22:21-26). If Job is truly wise, Eliphaz argues, then he will return his gold to the place where it properly belongs in the common dust of the earth and subordinate his worth to the greater gain of receiving his just reward from God.

Despite these common threads suggesting that gold and other precious jewels give one no purchase on wisdom, Job may once again be thinking on a deeper level than is first apparent. Included among the proverbial sayings about silver and gold is the recognition that these metals must be tested and purified if they are to attain their highest value. The process of refinement is in turn used as a metaphor for the way God tests for the purity of the human heart. In the words of Prov 17:3, "The crucible is for silver, and the furnace is for gold, but the Lord tests (*bāḥan*) the heart" (cf. Prov 27:21). Job is by now well acquainted with the extreme measures God may use to test those who lay claim to righteousness. He has been forced to think deeply about what it means to be a human being in the world God oversees. For what purpose, he wonders, does God "tests" (*bāḥan*; 7:18) human beings so severely? To this point, his best ruminations lead him to believe that God's intentions are sinister, that God's relentless scrutiny is for the purpose of breaking him down, not building him up (10:13-17; cf. 16:7-17; 19:7-12). Even so, Job has not wavered from the conviction that whatever means God uses to "test" (*bāḥan*) him, he will "come out like gold" (23:10).

Against this background, the meditation in 28:15-19 may be read as a playfully serious rethinking of the value of Job's gold. Should Job follow Eliphaz's counsel and give up his gold as no more comparable to wisdom than the five kinds of gold that have been enumerated? Should he hold on to his gold, that is, his personal integrity and righteousness, because this is a treasure that changes the calculation of what humans can and cannot claim in their transactions with God?[12] Job's angle of vision on such questions is still unfocused. The best he can do at this point is to simply think out loud about multiple possibilities.

Verses 20-22 conclude this section of the meditation by returning to the controlling question, "Where then does wisdom come from? And where is the place of understanding?" The words are almost an exact repetition of the question raised in v. 12. The answer that follows in vv. 21-22 is also thematically very similar to that already given in vv. 13-14, although in this case there is a small but important shift in emphasis. In the first attempt to answer the question, the reflection centers on the fact that there is *no place* where wisdom can be found. Now the reflection moves to consider the possibility that wisdom has a *hidden place*. On one level, the difference may be meaningless. For all practical purposes wisdom is *so hidden* that it is beyond the horizon of

Abaddon

AΩ Abaddon is one of several words used to refer to the realm of the dead. The Hebrew word derives from a root meaning "perish," "be destroyed," hence "(the place of) destruction." There are five occurrences of the word in the Hebrew Bible, three of which are in the book of Job (Job 26:6; 28:22; 31:12; Ps 88:11 [MT 88:12]; Prov 15:11). A variant form of the word also occurs in Prov 27:20.

In Job 26:6 Abaddon, along with Sheol (see **[Sheol]**) is depicted as a mysterious place in the underworld. It is hidden from human eyes but clearly not from God, who imposes a terrorizing peace against which Abaddon has no protection. In Job 31:12, Abaddon is a remote place in the underworld where the retaliatory fires of divine judgment punish the sinner. Abaddon is personified in Job 28:22—along with Death (*môt*; see **[Mot's Insatiable Appetite]**), it speaks—and in Prov 27:20—along with Sheol, it is insatiable. A similar personification occurs in Rev 9:11, the single reference in the New Testament, where the king over the demonic locusts is an "angel of the bottomless pit" named Abaddon.

For further reading, see H.G. Grether, "Abaddon," *ABD*, ed. D. N. Freedman (New York: Doubleday, 1992), vol. 1, 6.

Abaddon

Abaddon (on left) with Mammon, god of this world and personification of wealth and miserliness, And Ashtaroth the demon. From Francis Barrett, The Magus, London 1801.

Anonymous. 19th C. Private Collection.
(Credit: Image Select/Art Resource, NY)

what the human eye can see from the ground or what the bird can see from the air (v. 21). It is *so hidden* that even "Abaddon" and "Death," the personifications of the forces located in the depths of the earth, say they can attest to no more than rumors of its existence (v. 22). [Abaddon] On another level, however, the hiddenness of wisdom is paradoxically an invitation to continue the search, not to abandon it, for that which is hidden (v. 21: *ʿālam*) is described as no more inaccessible than the "hidden (*ʿālam*) things" (v. 11) that those with the requisite courage and skill can uncover.

God Knows the Way to Wisdom, 28:23-28

The final section shifts the focus of the meditation from what humans can and cannot do to what God can do. The beginning point for thinking about God in relation to wisdom, according to vv. 23-24, is the *character* of God, more specifically, the *characteristics* of God as Creator. Four verbs spell out the capacities that enable God to acquire wisdom. God "understands/discerns" (*bîn*), "knows" (*yādaʿ*), "looks" (*nābaṭ*), and "sees" (*rāʾāh*). These capacities connect God with everything in "earth" and "the heavens," including wisdom.

It is striking that each of these verbs is generic, that is, each describes a capacity that may apply generally to human beings as well as to God. Within the book of Job, for example, Job claims the capacity to discern (*bîn*) the truth about calamity (6:30), and he insists that what he understands (*bîn*) has the weight of anything the friends can explain to him (13:1; cf. 15:9; 18:2). Where Job's discernment fails him is in understanding the ways of God, but he argues that this is due more to God's inexplicable hiddenness than to any specific limitation on his part (9:11; 23:5, 8). Job "knows" (*yādāʿ*) things about himself (13:18; 19:25) and even about the hidden God (9:28; 10:13; 11:9; 12:9; 23:10), although such knowledge presents him with more questions than answers (9:2). "Looking" (*nābaṭ*) at the world in the hope of finding what one needs is not something God alone does (cf. 6:19; 35:5; 36:25). The problem, at least from Job's perspective, is that there often seems to be a tragic disconnect between what God "sees" and what humans "see" (*rāʾāh*; 10:4; 11:11). If the capacities that connect God to the world—and to wisdom—are in some measure also available to human beings, then why does wisdom remain so inaccessible for seekers like Job? When God understands, knows, sees the world, and lays claim to wisdom, what does God do? Is there something in the way God interacts with the world that offers a clue about the possibilities, however remote, for humans to acquire wisdom?

The overtones of such questions appear to be the catalyst for a second level of reflection on God and wisdom in vv. 25-27. The focus now shifts from God's general characteristics as Creator to God's employment of these characteristics in four specific creative acts. God made the wind and fixed its proper weight in the balance of earth's forces.[13] God made the primordial waters and carefully measured their place in the world (cf. Isa 40:12). God made the rain and set a limit (v. 26: *ḥōq*; cf. Jer 5:22; Ps 148:6; NRSV: "decree") on the amount of water that is to fall. God made the thunderbolt and plotted the way for its travel (cf. Job 38:25). In each of these deeds God interacts with forces in nature that have the potential to be both beneficial and terrifying. In each case God understands, knows, and envisions the proportions that are necessary in order for creation to fulfill its promise.

More importantly, the grammar of these verses indicates that it is "in the act of" (v. 25: *laʿăśôt*; v. 26: *baʿăśōtô*) engaging these forces and determining their role in the world that God obtains wisdom. NRSV captures this sense nicely by rendering vv. 25 and 26 as subordinate clauses that introduce the main clause in v. 27: "*When* he gave to the wind its weight . . . *when* he made a decree for the rain . . . *then* he saw it and declared it; he established it, and searched it out."[14] The implication is that wisdom is not something *in* God, something God possesses *before* God creates the world. It is rather something that God *acquires* in the very act of creative engagement with the world. The reflection on the question "Where shall wisdom be found?" has therefore led to a surprising and strange idea. Wisdom is not found in any one specific *location*. Neither can it be obtained by the proffer of any specific *object of material value*. Wisdom comes from *creatively interacting with the world,* that is, from weighing, measuring, setting limits, and charting courses that offer the best possibilities for the world to become all that it can be. [CD: Wisdom Is as Wisdom Does]

More surprising still is the idea that *God's capacity* to find wisdom by exercising it is in some way *human-like.* The four verbs in v. 27— "saw" (*rā'āh*), "declared" (*sāpar*), "established" (*kûn*), "searched" (*ḥqr*)—are generic. Like the verbs in verbs in vv. 23-24, these four verbs may be used with reference to both divine and human activity. [The Divine/Human Intellectual Process] The root word for "search" (*ḥqr*), which occurs in the climatic position in v. 27, is particularly instructive. The theme of searching out, exploring, or investigating a matter in order to comprehend the full depths of what it discloses and requires occurs frequently in Job. Both the friends (5:9; 36:26; cf. 11:7) and Job (9:10) concede that some things, especially the ways of God, are "unsearchable" (*'ēn / lō' ḥēqer*). Even so, both the friends (5:27) and Job (29:16; NAB:

"the rights of the stranger I studied") are fully engaged in the process of intense exploration. Of all the places this theme appears in Job, the most suggestive occurs in this very chapter with reference to the search for wisdom. According to 28:3, miners have a God-like capacity to search (*ḥqr*) the farthest boundaries of their world in pursuit of its most precious and hidden treasures. Although they cannot obtain every treasure, they work in ways that approximate what God can do. As the soliloquy moves toward its last disclosure concerning the quest for wisdom (v. 28), it suggests that the *miner's God-like capacity* and *God's human-like capacity* are near mirror images of the same search.

Where then, in light of all that has been surveyed in the preceding verses, shall wisdom be found, and how can it be obtained? Verse 28,

Can These Really Be Job's Words?

AΩ Many commentators regard v. 28 as representative of the view of someone other than Job. Two reasons for this are frequently noted. First, the introduction "And he said to humankind" is more typical of prose than poetry. Coupled with the catch phrases "fear of the Lord" and "depart from evil," this rhetoric sounds more like the voice of the narrator of the prologue (cf. 1:1, 8; 2:3) than of Job. If these words are from the narrator, then they function more as an interruption of the soliloquy than a summation. The admonition to return to the simpler, more compliant model of prologue piety does not advance the drama so much as stop it in its tracks. "Moreover," as Newsom observes, "hearing these phrases in the accents of the prose narrator gives them an unbearable smugness, as though chs. 3–27 have meant nothing."

Second, the use of the word "Lord" (*ʾǎdōnāy*) occurs nowhere else in the book of Job, hence some regard it as a later addition to the text (G. Fohrer, *Das Buch Hiob* [KAT; Gütersloh: Gerd Mohn, 1963], 392). In the prologue (1–2), epilogue (42:7-17), and the whirlwind speeches (38:1–42:6) the preferred name for God is YHWH. In the poetic dialogues between Job and his friends, the names for God are El, Eloah, Shaddai, and Elohim (see further **[Names for God]**).

In addition to these specific textual issues, commentators often note that not only v. 28 but also the whole poem on wisdom seems misplaced in the mouth of Job. L. Perdue, for example, has argued that the poem is a later insertion by a pious sage who was uncomfortable with the whole notion of the human quest for wisdom. For this sage, v. 28 is but the thesis statement that undergirds the entire poem: In order to live in compliance with God's teaching, Job must return to the "first naivete" of prologue piety (see **[CD: "Where Shall Wisdom Be Found" Among the Scholarly Proposals?]**).

These challenges to understanding Job 28 as Job's words are substantive and merit careful consideration. The view taken in this commentary is that those who engage in soliloquy may let their minds wander through a variety of ideas and perspectives, some of which they do not endorse but are willing to consider. Perdue himself opens the door on this possibility:

> [The poem on wisdom] does not make sense in the mouth of Job, at least in its current location, *unless* one wishes to argue that Job entertains, at least for a brief moment, the possibility . . . that the proper course of action is to return to the traditional sapiential piety of the prologue in chapters 1–2: "fear God and turn from evil."

C. Newsom, "The Book of Job," in vol. 4 of *NIB* (Nashville: Abingdon Press, 1996), 533.
L. Perdue, *Wisdom and Creation: The Theology of Wisdom Literature* (Nashville: Abingdon Press, 1994), 127 (emphasis added).

---

which provides the climax to the soliloquy, appears on first reading to provide the answer to these governing questions. Simply put, wisdom is equated with "the fear of the Lord"; the prerequisite for its acquisition is the discernment "to depart from evil. " This answer appears to return the drama rather simplistically back to its beginnings. The prologue has stipulated that "fearing God" and "turning away from evil" were the qualities Job exemplified (1:1, 8; 2:3) *before* he filled his mouth with protests and questions. On first impression, then, Job's reflections in chapter 28 seem to have brought him full circle, back to original commitments to accept whatever God gives or takes, back to first forms of piety where blessing—not cursing—is the full measure of the truly wise servant of God. There are, however, a number of considerations that make this interpretation less satisfying than it first appears. [Can These Really Be Job's Words?]

Throughout the dialogues, Job has passionately insisted on his right to question and protest, even if to do so means that he risks a confrontation with God. That he should now suddenly do an about-face and retreat to the ash heap in silent submission to a God who afflicts him for no reason seems curious, if not naïve. Nothing in chapter 28 indicates that Job's passions have substantively changed. To the contrary, there are numerous intimations that he considers striving for wisdom to be a natural and potentially rewarding human exercise. To be certain, the human quest has its limitations, but even these are reminders that searching for hidden, even inaccessible, treasures may model a way of following God that is full of promise. Moreover, if Job is tempted to return to prologue piety, then his inclination to do so is rather short-lived. On the heels of this soliloquy, Job takes up his discourse "again" in chapters 29–31. And once again he defends his integrity, protests his mistreatment, and demands that God respond to his quest for an answer. If this be what it means to "fear God" and "turn away from evil," then perhaps v. 28 signals that it is Job who is transforming prologue piety rather than the other way around.

CONNECTIONS

"Where shall wisdom be found?" This is not only the question posed in an ancient text. It is a, perhaps *the*, perennial question that human beings confront in all ages and times.[15] The answer Job 28 presents begins with these words: God knows (v. 23) . . . mortals do not know (v. 13). In a world like Job's, and ours, where there is too much innocent suffering, too many unanswered cries for help, and too few certainties of God's presence, this "answer" raises at least as many questions as it addresses. If it is true that soliloquies like Job 28 are exercises in thinking out loud about matters that require more than one probe, matters that resist single or simple resolutions, then perhaps it is permissible for reflections on soliloquies like Job 28 to reflect a similar tentativeness and incompleteness. So it is with the questions and ruminations offered below. [Does *Only* Soliloquy Remain?]

Does *Only* Soliloquy Remain?

In his poem "S. K.," R. S. Thomas reflects on the life and work of the Danish philosopher and theologian Soren Kierkegaard (1813–1855).

> Who were his teachers? He learned
> his anonymity from God himself,
>
> leaving his readers, as God
> leaves the reader in life's
>
> book to grope for meaning
> that will be quicksilver in the hand.

Thomas wonders if Kierkegaard's existentialist search for God leads only to soliloquy and self-absorption. Perhaps for S. K., as with Job, soliloquy is but the first step toward prayer, which holds open the possibility of an "exchange of places between I and thou."

> The difficulty
> with prayer is the exchange
> of places between I and thou,
> with silence as the answer
> to an imagined request.
> Is this the price genius
> must pay, that from an emphasis
> on the subjective only
> soliloquy remains? Is prayer
> not a glass that, beginning
> in obscurity as his books
> do, the longer we stare
> into the clearer becomes
> the reflection of a countenance
> in it other than our own?

R. S. Thomas, "S. K.," *No Truce with the Furies* (Newcastle upon Tyne: Bloodaxe Books, 1995), 15, 17.

What Does God Know about Wisdom?

According to Job 28, God knows the way to obtain wisdom. It is acquired through a process of creative engagement with the world (v. 27). Crenshaw has elaborated on this process (see the citation in [The Divine/Human Intellectual Process]), and his comments provide a good starting point for further reflection. The first step, *observation*, involves being attentive to what the eyes can see. Because God sees "everything under the heavens" (v. 24), it may be inferred that God sees both that which is right with the world and that which is wrong, both the good and the evil, the justice and the injustice. Without the capacity to see things for what they are, the route to wisdom could not even begin. The second step is *articulation*, speaking out loud about what has been observed firsthand. When what is seen is declared, personal experience is submitted to public scrutiny, and collective discernment is in turn refracted through new and informed individual decisions. The third step is *establishing hypotheses* that invite preliminary conclusions about what has been observed. Although these hypotheses and conclusions are tentative—they are not only open to but solicitous of additional discovery—they are nevertheless a critical scaffold for the construction of wisdom. As Crenshaw puts it, "the discoverer ultimately bears sole responsibility for any new insight."[16] The fourth step is *searching every idea from as many angles as possible*. Whatever discovery one makes, the process of disclosure is not complete until it has been thoroughly examined for strengths and weaknesses.

What is striking about this description of God's process for obtaining wisdom is that God's capacities are not substantively different than those humans may exercise. To return to the metaphor of vv. 1-11, miners also engage in a process of searching, exposing, extracting, and claiming "every precious thing" (v. 10) their eyes can see. What then is the difference between what God and human beings can acquire when they go in search of wisdom? One answer is that God can search the totality of the cosmos and see "everything under the heavens" (v. 24). Human beings cannot match the vastness of God's search. Because of the "boundlessness of the arena to be explored" there will always be some truth that eludes even the most skilled and persistent human endeavor.[17] After all, God alone has the capacity to work in the cosmic domain of wind, water, rain, and thunder (vv. 25-26). Another answer, which builds on the recognition of the totality of God's search, is that the wisdom God acquires is necessarily of a higher order than human wisdom. There may be a subtle clue in the text that reinforces this distinction. According to a strict reading of vv. 12 and 20, what is hidden from human beings is "*the* wisdom" (*ḥokmāh* with the definite article), that is, the unparalleled wisdom of God. All that is available to human beings is the qualitatively different "wisdom" (v. 28: *ḥokmāh without the definite article*) of the more limited and practical sort expressed in pious devotion ("fear of God") and moral conduct ("depart from evil").[18]

Both of these answers invite close inspection. There is certainly a difference between the wisdom of God and the wisdom of human beings, but as P. Fiddes argues, "it is a difference of scope and extent, not a different kind of thing altogether."[19] Moreover, he makes the case that "the wisdom God possesses. . . is of a completely practical sort."[20] Like miners who apply themselves to the concrete challenges of searching for hidden treasure in the world they inhabit, God focuses divine energy on the extraction of wisdom from the cosmos that is God's domain. Both God and humans plot their course, focus their objectives, and use their capacities in practical—not theoretical—ways.

Does God Want Human Beings to Have Wisdom?

Does God desire that the Jobs of the world remain ignorant of the truths they seek? Does God want human beings like Job to have wisdom sufficient for the world in which they live? Israel's poets and sages wrestled with these questions in different ways (see further [CD: Playing Hide and Seek with Wisdom]).

Job's friends represent the view that God withholds wisdom because God does not trust human beings to use it appropriately or constructively. Eliphaz, for example, urges Job to learn that God places no trust in mere mortals like him (4:18-19; 15:15-16). Creatures of dust are "born to trouble" (5:7) and doomed to die without the wisdom to understand why (4:20-21). If they protest their lot, then they only confirm that they are guilty of having rebelled against the requirement to fear God (15:4, 13). That requirement, Eliphaz argues, is built on the unassailable presumption that human beings are of little or no use to God. As Eliphaz puts it, "Can even the wisest be of service to him?" (22:2). Given this great divide between God and human beings, the best (and only) option for rebels like Job is simply to "agree with God, and be at peace" (22:21).

The idea that human beings cannot be trusted with the things of God is of course deeply rooted in Israel's Eden traditions. The first couple was placed in the garden that provided everything they needed for a full and prosperous life. But when they yielded to the temptation to "be like God, knowing good and evil" (Gen 3:5), they overstepped their boundaries and forfeited their assigned place in the garden (Gen 3:23-24). Some commentators call on the Eden imagery to help explain the hiddenness of wisdom in Job 28. Janzen, for example, calls attention to Ezekiel's condemnation of the king of Tyre (Ezek 28:1-19).[21] This royal figure, "full of wisdom and perfect in beauty" (v. 12) is identified with "Eden, the garden of God" (v. 13). Though the king was "but a mortal, and no god," he dares to compare himself to God (vv. 2, 9). His pride and arrogance lead him to use "wisdom and understanding" to amass great treasures for himself (v. 5). But like the first couple, the king is corrupted by his acquisitions, and like them he is driven from God's presence (vv. 16-18). There is then a significant biblical tradition that affirms that hubris, specifically in terms of the acquisition and corruption of wisdom, is a form of rebellion against God that leads to alienation and judgment.

There is however another way of viewing the quest for wisdom. Israel's sages recognized that wisdom resides with God, hence that it is mysteriously elusive. But they also discerned that God not only could but would make wisdom available to those who seek it. For example, the purpose of the book of Proverbs is to help people acquire "wisdom" and "understanding" (Prov 1:2), which includes instructions in both "the fear of the Lord" (2:5) and in "righteousness and justice" (2:9; cf. 1:3). Toward this end, Proverbs personifies wisdom as a figure crying out for listeners in the public square (1:20-21; 8:1-5; 9:1-6). People are urged not only to stop and hear what wisdom offers, but also to go in search of its instructions. The passion that drives this search should be unquenchable: like that which compels the miner's quest for silver (2:4), the lover's search for his bride (Wis 6:12-15; 8:2; Sir 15:2-6), and the hunter's stalking of his prey (Sir 14:22). As Crenshaw has noted, "In the quest for wisdom one adopts *whatever means are necessary* to accomplish the goal, *whether these happen to be appropriate social conduct or not.*"[22] [Wisdom Is the "Scorn of Consequence"] In view of these different perspectives on the quest for wisdom, the question about whether God wants human beings to have wisdom must be considered an open one. The answer depends in large part on how humans intend to use the wisdom they acquire. If the objective is selfish, if humans seek wisdom in order to subvert God's creational design or to supplant God as Creator, then they can expect to be thwarted and judged. But what if humans seek only that which God has offered? What if their quest is only for the "righteousness and justice" that God promises to those who are "upright" and "blameless" (Prov 2:7; cf. 2:9)? Does God unconditionally withhold wisdom in these circumstances as well? If so,

---

Wisdom Is the "Scorn of Consequence"

Because right is right, to follow right
were wisdom in the scorn of consequence.

Alfred Lord Tennyson, "Oenone," ll. 147-48, in *Tennyson's Poetry*, sel. and ed. R. W. Hill, Jr. (New York/London: W. W. Norton and Co., 1971), 23.

by what principle? By God's own estimation Job is "upright" and "blameless" (Job 1:8; 2:3). If one like Job cannot find wisdom, then in what meaningful sense is wisdom available at all?

Against all odds, it seems, Job has determined to find God and to understand what God is or is not prepared to say to him considering these matters. His only hope is that an "upright person" can reason with God (23:7), even about wisdom, which he concedes "is hidden from the eyes of all the living" (28:21). But then, the very thought of wisdom's inexplicable hiddenness is what lies at the root of this soliloquy. Such a thought must be spoken out loud and turned over and over in the mind before it can be simply relinquished to conventional explanations.

How Do Human Beings Learn What God Wants Them to Know?

Verse 28 proposes an answer to this question: humans may learn wisdom by "fear of the Lord"; they may obtain understanding by "departing from evil." Like most ideas in this soliloquy, however, this "answer" is not as simple as it may appear.

The first issue to be considered is who proposes this answer. The initial impression may be that the speaker is *God*, who for reasons not disclosed has at long last decided to respond to Job's musings with a piece of unanticipated counsel. If God is the speaker, then God seems to be urging Job to hold fast to virtues that God has already confirmed Job has (1:8; 2:3). A strong case can be made that the speaker of these words is either the *narrator of the prologue* or a *later editor* (see further [Can These Really Be Job's Words?]). In either case, the speaker offers counsel that purports to be from God. That is, if God were to respond to Job, God would advise him to "fear the Lord" and "depart from evil." A third possibility is that *Job* speaks these words. If so, then Job may be understood as having returned in his reflections to reconsider the kind of piety that once defined everything he did (cf. 1:5: "This is what Job always did"). Each of these possibilities invites readers to think carefully about what fearing God and shunning evil means from these different vantage points.

What would *God* mean by the admonition to fear God and turn from evil? Does God mean that Job should return to the qualities that defined his life in prosperous times, when his world was in tact and his understanding was undisturbed by suffering and questions? Is God saying that in matters of faith, suffering like Job's—seven sons and three daughters, killed "for no reason"—should have no lasting effect on how one thinks about God and God's providential care? If this is God's definition of faith, *can or should Job embrace it and live with it?*

Or could God be saying that in matters of faith, wisdom sufficient for the times when tragedy strikes "for no reason" is painfully elusive? Could the counsel be that wisdom for such times can only be found in doing (or at least approximating) what God does? That is, should Job follow God's example by being attentive to what his eyes can see, speaking out loud about what he has seen, formulating hypotheses about what he has discerned, and examining his best insights for every possible strength and weakness (cf. v. 27)? If this is God's definition of wisdom and understanding, if reverencing God's way of dealing with the world and walking uprightly in it is the only way for humans to follow God's lead, then *can God embrace Job's effort and live with it?* [The "Mistake" of Finitude]

What would the *narrator of the prologue* or a *later editor* mean by urging Job to fear God and turn from evil? Would they mean that Job should return to the prologue's model of piety, where the credo "Blessed be the name of the Lord" (1:21) is constant in good times and bad? Do they mean that question and doubt, anger and protest, are the marks of rebellion, not devotion? Do they rebuke Job, and any would follow his example, for straying from the straight and narrow paths of fidelity to and trust in God? And if this is their counsel, why do they offer it to Job? Do they accurately reflect God's requirement of sufferers like Job, in which case they should be applauded as defenders of the faith? Or do they reflect the fear of those whose principles and positions are under attack, in which case they may be guilty of betraying God's hopes and expectations for everyone who is created "in the image of God"? ["Where Is the Wisdom We Have Lost in Knowledge?"]

What would *Job* understand fearing God and turning from evil to mean at this juncture in his journey? Does he mean that he has now reconsidered the path he has fol-

---

The "Mistake" of Finitude

"It is a mistake to be embarrassed by finitude, but it is a gorgeous mistake."

L. Wieseltier, *Kaddish* (New York: Alfred A. Knopf, 1998), 583.

"Where Is the Wisdom We Have Lost in Knowledge?"

The friends' advice seems like a counsel of despair. Job may search for wisdom, but he cannot find it. He may strive for knowledge, but he will lose far more than he can gain. The nearer to God he would come, the farther away he removes himself. Both this counsel and the despair it invokes upon hearing resonate with a contemporaneity that keeps us mindful that the friends' perspective cannot easily be discounted. The opening stanza of T. S. Eliot's "Choruses From 'The Rock'" is but one example of how such ideas linger heavily in our consciousness.

The Eagle soars in the summit of Heaven,
The Hunter with his dogs pursues his circuit.
O perpetual revolution of configured stars,
O perpetual recurrence of determined
   seasons,
O world of spring and autumn, birth and dying!
The endless cycle of idea and action,
Endless invention, endless experiment,
Brings knowledge of motion, but not of
   stillness;
Knowledge of words, and ignorance of the
   Word.
All our knowledge brings us nearer our
   ignorance,
All our ignorance brings us nearer to death,
But nearness to death no nearer to GOD.
Where is the Life we have lost in living?
Where is the wisdom we have lost in
   knowledge?
Where is the knowledge we have lost in
   information?
The cycles of Heaven in twenty centuries
Bring us farther from GOD and nearer to the
   Dust.

T. S. Eliot, "Choruses from 'The Rock,'" *Collected Poems 1909–1962* (New York: Harcourt, Brace & World, Inc., 1970), I, 147.

lowed since the question "Why?" first passed his lips? Does he now agree or concede that wisdom sufficient for this question is nowhere to be found? Is he now willing to accept that God gives and takes away for no reason? Does he now understand that when anyone pushes beyond the limits God has imposed they only make matters worse? If so, then he has learned the lesson that faith operates authentically only at the level of first naivete, where blessing, not cursing, is what one must always offer to God. If this is the truth toward which his experiences have led, then will God now single him out for praise with the same words that once defined his place in the world: *"There is no one like my servant Job on the earth"* (cf. 1:8; 2:3)? Or does Job mean that suffering and pain have caused him to rethink the naivete of the faith he once professed? Does he now understand that faith assertions are inevitably vulnerable to question and doubt? Is he now prepared to acknowledge that the pursuit of these questions and the embrace of such doubt is the true measure of faith? Is this is the truth toward which his experiences have led? If he now resolves to act on this truth by pressing forward with the quest for wisdom, *will God still single him out for praise* with the words "There is no one like my servant Job on the earth"?

By the end of chapter 28 Job has come a long way since he first spoke from the ash heap. He has explored a number of options from multiple perspectives. Many things have been considered; nothing has been decided. Like the miners that provide the lens for this reflection, Job has probed to the limits of what it is possible to discover about wisdom. What does God know about wisdom? Does God want humans to have wisdom, and if so how are they to learn what God wants to teach them? Along the way he has discovered that some discoveries are more within his reach than he suspected. Others are more beyond his grasp than he has recognized. The question that remains to be answered is where does he go from here? Should he retreat to pre-suffering expressions of faith, to first levels of naivete, where convictions remain invulnerable to doubt? Or should he press forward to suffering-laden enactments of faith, to second and third and fourth levels of naivete, where doubt pushes and pulls conviction into shapes that neither his friends nor God may recognize or accept? [In This Dark Hour, "a Shower of Facts . . . Uncombined"]

In This Dark Hour, a "Shower of Facts . . . Uncombined"

Job's position at the end of chapter 28 is not unlike that described by Edna St. Vincent Millay:

Upon this gifted age, in its dark hour,
Rains from the sky a meteoric shower
Of facts . . . they lie unquestioned, uncombined.
Wisdom enough to leech us of our ill
Is daily spun, but there exists no loom
To weave it into fabric.

E. St. Vincent Millay, from *Huntsman, What Quarry?* in *Collected Sonnets of Edna St. Vincent Millay*, rev. and exp. ed. (New York: HarperPerennial, 1988), 140.

NOTES

[1] N. Habel, *The Book of Job: A Commentary* (OTL; Philadelphia: Westminster Press, 1985), 391.

[2] C. Westermann, *The Structure of the Book of Job: A Form-Critical Analysis* (Philadelphia: Fortress Press, 1981), 137-38.

[3] Cf. J. Gerald Janzen, *Job* (Atlanta: John Knox, 1985), 188.

[4] M. Fox, "Words for Wisdom," ZAH 6 (1993): 154.

[5] G. Fohrer, *Das Buch Hiob* (KAT; Gütersloh: Gerd Mohn, 1963), 394.

[6] Janzen, *Job,* 192-94.

[7] Ibid., 192-93.

[8] C. Newsom, "The Book of Job," in vol. 4 of *NIB* (Nashville: Abingdon Press, 1996), 531.

[9] Ibid., 530. See also the comment by Habel (*Book of Job,* 396): "the mining exercise is a paradigm for probing a mystery in the natural domain which parallels probing wisdom at a deeper level in the cosmic domain."

[10] Cf. S. A. Geller, "'Where Is Wisdom?': A Literary Study of Job 28 in Its Setting," *Judaic Perspectives on Ancient Israel*, ed. J. Neusner, B. Levine, E. Frerichs (Philadelphia: Fortress Press, 1987), 164.

[11] Habel, *Book of Job,* 395.

[12] Cf. Janzen (*Job,* 194-96), who raises such a possibility on somewhat different grounds.

[13] Cf. Habel, *Book of Job,* 400.

[14] Newsom, "The Book of Job," 532; cf. Janzen, *Job,* 197.

[15] For two examples, see H. Bloom, *Where Shall Wisdom Be Found?* (New York: Riverhead Books, 2004) and K. Paffenroth, *In Praise of Wisdom: Literary and Theological Reflections on Faith and Reason* (New York, London: Continuum, 2004). Both works use Job's quest for wisdom as the touchtone for the ongoing exploration in modern literature.

[16] J. L. Crenshaw, *Education in Ancient Israel: Across the Deadening Silence* (New York: Doubleday, 1998), 217.

[17] P. S. Fiddes, "'Where Shall Wisdom be Found?': Job 28 as a Riddle for Ancient and Modern Readers," *After the Exile. Essays in Honour of Rex Mason*, ed. J. Barton, D. Reimer (Macon GA: Mercer University Press, 1996), 181.

[18] For this argument, see principally R. Gordis, *The Book of Job: Commentary, New Translation, and Special Studies* (New York: Jewish Theological Seminary of America, 1978), 539.

[19] Fiddes, "'Where Shall Wisdom be Found?,'" 179.

[20] Ibid., 175.

[21] Janzen, *Job,* 199-201; cf. L. Perdue, *Wisdom in Revolt: Metaphorical Theology in the Book of Job* (JSOTSup 112; Sheffield: Almond Press, 1991), 165-70, 240-48.

[22] J. L. Crenshaw, *Old Testament Wisdom: An Introduction* (Atlanta: John Knox, 1981), 62 (emphasis added).

PAST BLESSINGS

Job 29:1-25

Job's Summation and the Decision to Move Beyond Blessing and Cursing, Job 29:1–31:40

In chapter 27, Job began a "discourse" (*māšāl*) that explored the options before him. Should he agree with the friends' doctrine of retribution, affirm God's moral governance of the world, repent of his sin, and bless the One who has consigned him to the ash heap "for no reason?" Perhaps, as Eliphaz insists, Job should be happy that God has afflicted him so severely, for this may be confirmation that God loves him enough to discipline him (5:17). ["The Wounds of Possibility"] If so, then his one and only option is to "Agree with God and be at peace" (22:21). Job knows the lines of the praise he has been urged to offer, and he is tempted to speak them (9:5-10; 12:13-25; 26:5-14), even if they sound discordant in his ears. Or should he curse God, as the conventional reading of his wife's demand suggests (2:9)? Job has also dared to explore this possibility (3:3-10), even though he has good reason to suspect that defiance before the Creator of the world is like spitting into the wind. [Standing Before a "Strange God"] It may be bold and courageous to do so, but as far as Job can see, it is ultimately futile and changes nothing. He may curse the day of his birth and wish to die (3:11), but he cannot unbirth himself. He is sentenced to live, which means he has been "born to trouble" (5:7), and the misery that evokes his death wish remains the same, his curses notwithstanding (10:18). Job is certain of but one thing, and on this he takes his stand, for good or for ill. He has sworn on the life of God that whatever course he chooses, he will not betray himself or God by compromising his integrity (27:2-6).

On the heels of this "discourse," indeed perhaps because of it, Job plunges into the soliloquy of chapter 28 and ponders the question that may hold the answer to the decision he should make: "Where shall wisdom be found?" (28:12, 20). Is wisdom so elusive, so hidden

---

Standing Before a "Strange God"

A man went before a strange God—
The God of many men, sadly wise.
And the deity thundered loudly,
Fat with rage, and puffing.
"Kneel, mortal, and cringe
And grovel and do homage
To My Particularly Sublime Majesty."
The man fled.

Stephen Crane, "A Man Went Before a Strange God," *The Oxford Book of Short Poems*, ed. P. Kavanagh, J. Michie (New York: Oxford University Press, 1985), 177.

from the reach of every human being, that Job should abandon the search and settle for the consolation prize, humility before the God who alone possesses such wisdom? Or is wisdom, although never fully accessible, worth the search? Is it possible that risking the effort to gain wisdom is the surest sign that human beings are created in the image of

"The Wounds of Possibility"

Eliphaz and his friends commend suffering to Job with words that echo Kierkegaard's memorable phrase, "the wounds of possibility." H. G. Wells's Joban fiction, *The Undying Fire*, makes a similar point with the question, "Without pain what would life become?" The idea that pain and suffering are not only unavoidable but also necessary, perhaps even part of God's providential "tough love" plan for life, is a common way to explain why bad things happen to good people. Proverbial sayings from both the ancient Near East and the Bible sustain the supposition, for example, Prov 3:11-12: "My child, do not despise the Lord's discipline, or be weary of his reproof, for the Lord reproves the one he loves, as a father the son in whom he delights" (cf. Prov 13:24; 17:10; 19:18; 29:15, 17; Sir 30:1-2, 11-12). As the Letter to the Hebrews puts it, "Discipline always seems painful rather than pleasant at the time, but later it yields the peaceful fruit of righteousness to those who have been trained by it" (12:11).

Thornton Wilder draws upon Eliphaz's counsel to Job in a scene from the end of his novel *The Eighth Day*. After tracking the misfortunes of the Ashley and Lansing families, Wilder concludes the story with an explanation offered by "the Deacon" of the Covenant Church in Kerkommer's Knob. The Deacon points to a homemade woven rug. On one side there is a beautiful but complex design in brown and black. On the reverse side, the rug is "a mass of knots and of frayed and dangling threads" (390). Such is the way of life, the Deacon concludes. God has a pattern for the world that includes the threads of each person's life. The pattern may require that some lives be knotted and frayed in ways that "to our eyes are often cruel and laughable" (392), but from God's perspective the finished product is a beautiful work of art.

Joseph Heller also draws upon Eliphaz's counsel in his novel *Catch-22*, not to commend it, but to mock it. The following conversation between Yossarian and Lieutenant Scheisskopf's wife covers some of the same ground, albeit more irreverently, as the dialogues between Job and his friends.

"Don't tell me God works in mysterious ways," Yossarian continued . . . "There's nothing so myste-

rious about it. He's not working at all. He's playing. Or else He's forgotten all about us. That's the kind of God you people talk about—a country bumpkin, a clumsy, bungling, brainless, conceited, uncouth hayseed. Good God, how much reverence can you have for a Supreme Being who finds it necessary to include such phenomena as phlegm and tooth decay in His divine system of creation? What in the world was running through that warped, evil, scatological mind of His when He robbed old people of the power to control their bowel movements? Why in the world did He ever create pain?"

"Pain?" Lieutenant Scheisskopf's wife pounced upon the word victoriously. "Pain is a useful symptom. Pain is a warning to us of bodily dangers."

"And who created the dangers?" Yossarian demanded. He laughed caustically. "Oh, He was really being charitable to us when He gave us pain! Why couldn't He have used a doorbell instead to notify us, or one of His celestial choirs? Or a system of blue-and-red neon tubes in the middle of each person's forehead. Any jukebox manufacturer worth his salt could have done that. Why couldn't He?"

"People would certainly look silly walking around with red neon tubes in the middle of their foreheads."

"They certainly look beautiful now writhing in agony or stupefied with morphine, don't they? What a colossal, immortal blunderer! When you consider the opportunity and power He had to really do a job, and then look at the stupid, ugly mess He made of it instead, His sheer incompetence is almost staggering. It's obvious He never met a payroll. Why, no self-respecting businessman would hire a bungler like Him as even a shipping clerk!"

. . . "You'd better not talk that way about Him, honey," she warned him reprovingly in a low and hostile voice. "He might punish you." (178)

H. G. Wells, *The Undying Fire* (New York: The Macmillan Company, 1919), 208.

T. Wilder, *The Eighth Day* (New York: Penguin Books, 1967).

J. Heller, *Catch-22: A Critical Edition*, ed. R. M. Scotto (New York: Delta Publishing Company, 1973).

God, whose own quest for wisdom models the virtues of inquiry that humans may emulate? When Job emerges from his musings on these matters, he finds himself standing before an answer that remains both vexed and vexing: "Truly, the fear of the Lord, that is wisdom; and to depart from evil is understanding" (28:28). The answer clearly summons Job backwards, to the prologue piety, the pre-suffering faith, which once defined his integrity (cf. 1:1, 9; 2:3). But does it also invite him to press forward, toward new dimensions of faith that broaden the horizon of old affirmations? [To End Where I Began?]

> **To End Where I Began?**
> But, orderly to end where I begun, —
> Our wills and fates do so contrary run
> That our devices still are overthrown;
> Our thoughts are ours, their ends none of our own
>
> (*Hamlet* III, ii, 192-95)

Chapters 29–31 continue the "discourse" (29:1: *māšāl*) that chapter 27 began but did not complete. Tracking the insights from his musings in chapter 28, Job does indeed return to his beginnings, to the distant but lingering memory of days when faith was unencumbered by doubt, when affirmations could be safely offered without intrusive and unsettling questions, when the promise of prosperity was never tested by adversity. This time, however, we do not have to rely on the narrator's second-hand account (1:1-5). Job offers us his own perspective (Job 29) of what it felt like to live "an utterly blessed life, one that reflects unmarred wholeness in relationship to God, people, and the environment."[1] Job also reflects yet again on his present misery, this time inviting readers behind the curses of chapter 3, where they can feel with him the indignation of being shamed and shunned by friends and God alike (Job 30). The recollection of his former blessings no doubt reminds him of the wisdom in his friends' summons to praise God. The depth of his present misery no doubt invites him to reconsider the wisdom in his wife's summons—and in his own first response—to curse God. Job weighs carefully both options—blessing and cursing—then returns to a third one, one that has been lurking at the edges of his thoughts for some time now (see [The Trial Metaphor in Job]).[2] He declares an oath of innocence (27:2-6) on which he stakes his life, and fortifies it with additional sworn testimony (Job 31) that he believes makes an unassailable claim on God's justice. If God is God, then Job believes he will be vindicated. If God does not respond to the pleas of an innocent person for justice, then God is not God, and all the "words of Job"—praise, curse, contention, and all others—are indeed well and truly "ended" (31:40). [Without Justice, What Is Left?]

COMMENTARY

Remembrance of Past Blessings, 29:1-11

Job begins (vv. 2-11) and ends (vv. 21-25) his recollections of past days with descriptions of the blessings he enjoyed from his relationships. His memory is *framed* by the blessings of friendship, first with God (vv. 2-6), then with his community (vv. 7-11, 21-25). His memory is *centered* by the conviction that authentic friendships depend on indissoluble commitments of "righteousness" and "justice" (vv. 12-17), virtues that seed the hope for a meaningful life (vv. 18-20). [Structure of Job 29:1-25]

Structure of Job 29:1-25

29:1-11   Remembrance of past blessings
29:12-20 Righteousness and justice: the seeds for hope
29:21-25 Remembrance of past blessings

Job's first words, "O that" (*mî-yittēn*; v. 2), employ rhetoric he has used throughout the book to introduce hopes and wishes, often seemingly impossible, that keep his quest for God alive. His memory of former days is thus at the same time a yearning to return to them. He longs for the days when God "watched over" him (v. 2: *šmr*) with compassion, not hostility (10:14; 13:27; 14:16); when God's presence was a "lamp" and a "light" that illumined the darkness (v. 3: *ḥōšek*), not a burden that only made the darkness more impenetrable (10:21-22; 12:25; 19:8; cf. 5:14; 22:11); when God's "friendship" was intimate and enjoyable, like the laughter of his children playing round his table (v. 4; cf. Ps 128:3). These were days of such abundance that he could waste staple foods, like cream, to wash his feet; so plentiful was the yield of his olive trees, it seemed even the rocks poured forth oil (v. 5). The language and imagery is exaggerated and hyperbolic, of course, and still one has the impression that it strains to convey the fullness of the life Job once enjoyed with God.

The blessings of Job's former days extended beyond his relationships with God and family. His life was also full and fulfilling because he enjoyed the respect and admiration of the wider community (vv. 7-11). He had a place of honor at the city gate, where the community gathered to discuss the social, economic, and legal matters on which civic order depended (cf. Deut 21:19; Ruth 4:1). It used to be that when Job arrived, the young would withdraw to the margins, and the elders would rise to acknowledge his presence. The nobles and princes who were holding forth would fall silent, deferring to Job's counsel. Job remembers their assessment of his contribution to their shared lives with deep satisfaction: "whoever heard me spoke favorably of me, and those who saw me bore witness to my merit" (v. 11; REB).

Readers may be tempted, as some commentators have been, to be suspicious of Job's memory. It may be argued that his words betray a sense of self-satisfaction that becomes only the arrogant.[3] Although this interpretation merits consideration, it is prudent to suspend our cynicism—surely no human being was ever this good!—in order to take seriously the integrity of Job's self-understanding.[4] [CD: The "Wisdom" of Self-praise] Perhaps Job has misunderstood his world and his status within it. This possibility applies not only to what he says throughout this chapter but also to the whole of his final summation in 29–30. At the same time, such suspicion necessarily also applies to God's assessment of Job in the prologue: "There is no one like him in all the earth, a blameless and upright man who fears God and turns away from evil" (1:8; 2:3). If we are to avoid the temptation to hear Job only with the suspicious ears of his friends, then we must defer judgment until we have heard God's final assessment of things at the conclusion of the drama. Until then, to paraphrase G. Steiner's cautionary advice about how to read another text with Joban import, F. Kafka's *The Trial*, "it is not so much we who read Job's words, it is they who read us." Can we imagine such a blessed life as Job's? More to the point, can we imagine, with him, what it feels like to have lost it, for no reason? Absent such imagination, the words of Job, Steiner suggests, will read us "and find us blank."[5]

Righteousness and Justice: The Seeds for Hope, 29:12-20

At the center of Job's memory is the conviction that his blessed life was built on relationships cemented by righteousness and justice (v. 14). His discourse moves from the relationships he once enjoyed with God and with his family to those with other, more marginal persons, persons one might suppose would have been beyond (or beneath) the horizon of his concern. Persons who are vulnerable to society's neglect and abuse—the poor, the orphans, the wretched, the widows, the blind, and the lame (vv. 12-13, 15)—direct their cries for help to Job. Even strangers, persons he does not know, trust Job to defend them against victimization (v. 16). Like a shepherd keeping watch over his flock, Job would risk his own life to snatch a helpless victim from the jaws of a wanton predator (v. 17). Job understands his connection to the needy as the extension of core commitments that shape both his character and his conduct. As he puts it, "I wore righteousness, and it wore me; my robe and my turban were the justice I practiced" (v. 14; for "righteousness" as a garment, see Ps 132:9; Isa 59:17). ["Agonies Are One of My Changes of Garments"]

Relationships forged in righteousness and justice are important not only to those who are embraced by another's compassion. They are also meaningful for those who understand that their identity is intrinsically shaped by offering such compassion. Job understands that investment in others nourishes him, like the underground waters that feed the roots of a tree (cf. Ps 1:3; Jer 17:8); it sustains him, like the dew that freshens leaves; it renews his strength, imaged as the "bow" of the warrior who enters no contest empty-handed (vv. 19-20; cf. Gen 49:24; Ps 37:14). Of all these images, the most suggestive occurs in v. 18, where Job seems to associate a life invested in righteousness and justice with the generative powers of the mythical phoenix. [The Phoenix: Guardian of the World]

Remembrance of Past Blessings, 29:21-25

Job enjoyed the friendships of others, because he embodied and acted upon the virtues of friendship himself. With good reason, therefore, the community understands Job's friendship as the key to its security and welfare.

His counsel is decisive (vv. 21-22). When he speaks, people listen, perhaps with the same respect and appreciation accorded to Ahitophel, another reputed wise counselor, whose words had such authority it seemed "as if one had consulted an oracle of God" (2 Sam 16:23).[6] People wait for his words with the urgent expectancy of crops soaking up the life-giving waters of the spring rains (v. 23). Even when they cannot believe, their doubt cannot extinguish the guiding light of his countenance (v. 24). Like Moses, the mediator of the covenant, Job's radiance keeps hope alive (cf. Exod 34:29-35). Like Aaron, the mediator of the cult, Job's "rituals" of friendship embody the benediction that sustains them (cf. Num 6:25-26).[7] Rather than abandon people to their own depleted resources, Job lives among them as a king, marshalling his troops on their behalf whenever they are needed (v. 25a). [King Job] [Job's Royal and Priestly Anthropology] The final image in Job's memory of the community he once fostered may be the most telling of all: he has lived among them as one "who comforts (*yĕnaḥēm*) mourners" (v. 25b). In short, Job offers the friendship of loyal compassion that he expected but has not received from his friends (cf. *nḥm*, "comfort," in 1:11).

Throughout this discourse, Job's memory of how blessed life used to be is seeded with the images of friendship. When we examine this

"Agonies Are One of My Changes of Garments"

In "Song of Myself," Walt Whitman imagines himself into the role of the one who would embody concern for the needy.

Whoever degrades another degrades me,
And whatever is done or said returns at last to me. . . .

Through me many long dumb voices,
Voices of the interminable generations of prisoners and slaves,
Voices of the diseas'd and despairing and of thieves and dwarfs, . . .
And of the rights of them the others are down upon,
Of the deform'd, trivial, flat, foolish, despised . . .

Agonies are one of my changes of garments,
I do not ask the wounded person how he feels, I myself become
the wounded person . . . .

Marc Chagall's *Job with Background of Geometricized Christ* (1975), which depicts Job against the backdrop of a typical Jewish village in Eastern Europe, offers additional commentary on Whitman's Joban words. In the right foreground, Job's body is arced like a bow, as

"Job With Background of Geometricized Christ à la Cimabuë"

Marc Chagall, (1887-1985). *Job*. 1975. Oil on canvas. Private collection, Saint Paul de Vence.

if he is levitating leftwards toward the distant image of the crucified Christ. Job's eyes are downcast, with a single blood red tear running down his cheek. His right hand is clasped over his heart. His head rests on the arm of his wife, whose dress is the same red color that marks Job's cheek. She offers him support, at the same time extending a cup to the crowd that gathers around.

Opposite Job, in the upper-left corner, is the smaller Christ on the cross. He is covered with the same thigh-length garment as Job, and like Job his cross leans him toward the left. To Christ's right an angel flies down from heaven, its feet supported by an unfolding Torah scroll, its hands extended in the direction of Job and his wife. In its mouth, a shofar-like instrument appears to proclaim a message from God. At the base of the cross, between Christ and Job, a crowd of mothers, fathers, children, goats, and lambs move about. The focus of the crowd is about equally divided, half lifting their hands toward Christ, the others toward Job. In contrast with the darkness that covers the top of the painting, Chagall places the crowd in the same light that envelops Job, as if to confirm that the wounded turn instinctively to the wounded for consolation and comfort.

Walt Whitman, "Song of Myself," *Leaves of Grass*, ed. with an intro. by J. Loving (Oxford: Oxford University Press, 1990), 48, 60.
For further discussion of Chagall's painting's connections between Job and Jesus, see Samuel E. Balentine, "Who Will Be Job's Redeemer?" *Perspectives in Religious Studies* 26 (1999): 269-89.

The Phoenix: "Guardian of the World"

📖 The reference in Job 29:18 to the phoenix is lexically ambiguous. The Hebrew word *ḥôl* usually means "sand." Read with the phrase "multiply my days," Job's hope would seem to be defined by the promise of descendants as numerous as the sand. The phrase "I shall die in my nest," however, fits uneasily with this imagery, thus prompting speculation that *ḥôl* should be read as "phoenix," an interpretation already attested in the Talmud (*b. Sanh.* 108b) and perhaps in certain texts from Ugarit and Ebla. (For discussion of the issues, see M. Dahood, "*Ḥôl* 'Phoenix' in Job 29:18 and in Ugaritic," CBQ 36 [1974]: 85-88; L. Grabbe, *Comparative Philology and the Text of Job: A Study in Methodology* [Missoula MT: Scholars Press, 1977], 98-101; R. Gordis, *The Book of Job: Commentary, New Translation, and Special Studies* [New York: Jewish Theological Seminary of America, 1978], 321-22; A. R. Cresko, *Job 29–31 in the Light of Northwest Semitic* [Rome: Biblical Institute Press, 1980], 23.)

While the references to the phoenix in biblical texts are uncertain, there is no doubt that post-biblical Jewish and Christian traditions appropriated the legend of this ancient bird, renowned for its ability to be reborn from the ashes of its burned nest. One text, *3 Baruch [Greek Apocalypse]*; 1st-3rd century CE, may be singled out. The text is an apocalyptic account concerning Baruch, the scribe of Jeremiah. He is sitting by the Kidron River, weeping over the destruction of Jerusalem, when the Lord sends an angel to comfort him and to reveal to him the mysteries of God. The angel leads him through five heavens, the third of which contains a cosmic phoenix identified as "the guardian of the world." This bird runs before the sun and spreads its wings in order to shield the people of the world from the sun's consuming rays, which symbolize the wrath of God.

And [the angel] showed me a chariot drawn by four horses and fire underneath it. And upon the chariot sat a man wearing a fiery crown. The chariot was drawn by forty angels. And behold, a bird runs along before the sun as large as nine mountains.

And I said to the angel, "What is this bird?" And he said to me, "This is the guardian of the world." And I said, "Lord, how is it the guardian of the world? Teach me."

And the angel said to me, "This bird accompanies the sun and spreading its wings absorbs its fire-shaped rays. For if it did not absorb them, none of the race of men would survive, nor anything else that lives, so God appointed this bird."

I Baruch said, "Lord, what is the name of this bird?"

And he said to me, "Phoenix." (*3 Bar* 6:2-6, 9-10)

For text and commentary, see H. E. Gaylord, "3 [Greek Apocalypse of] Baruch," *The Old Testament Pseudepigrapha*, vol. 1: *Apocalyptic Literature and Testaments*, ed. J. H. Charlesworth [Garden City NY: Doubleday and Company, 1983], 653-79. For further reading, see R. van den Broek, *The Myth of the Phoenix According to Classical and Early Christian Traditions* (Leiden: E. J. Brill, 1972); John S. Hall, "Phoenix," *A Dictionary of Biblical Tradition in English Literature*, ed. D. Jeffrey (Grand Rapids, MI: Wm. B. Eerdmans, 1992), 611-613.

---

imagery closely, we should not fail to notice that it challenges not only Eliphaz and his associates but also God. In 6:14 Job states his need of the *ḥesed*, the "loyalty," that God models and humans who would be friends to others should aspire to demonstrate: "The despairing needs loyalty (*ḥesed*) from a friend, even if they forsake the fear of the Almighty" (see the commentary on 6:14-30). Now, in his final summation, he declares that he has done his best to be this kind of friend himself. Like God, he has been a champion for the oppressed (Deut 24:17; Prov 23:10-11), a father to the orphan and a protector of widows (Ps 68:5), and a shepherd who delivers his flocks from the jaws of the wicked (Ps 3:7; cf. Ps 23:1). Like God, Job has clothed himself with "righteousness" and "justice" (Ps 89:14).[8] Still more revealing, and more incriminating, will be Job's subsequent move toward the thinly veiled charge that the friendship he enacts, the justice he embodies, is a critical part of what sustains creation itself (31:38-40; cf. Gen 3:17; 4:10). If God is listening, and Job trusts that this is so, then Job wants God to hear him saying that he has faithfully comforted those who have been entrusted to his care.[9] Can God claim to have offered the same fidelity to Job, who now sits on the ash heap of destruction, bereft of friends and submerged in divine silence?

King Job

The book of Job contains only indirect references to Job's social status. Clearly he was known to be prosperous and respected, but whether he was a king in the literal sense is impossible to say. (On Job's social status, see R. Albertz, "Der sozialgeschichtliche Hintergrund des Hiobsbuches und der Babylonischen Theodizee," *Die Botschaft und die Boten*, ed. J. Jeremias, L. Perlitt [Neukirchen: Neukirchener Verlag, 1981], 349-72.) In any case, perhaps because of the royal imagery in Job 29 and elsewhere throughout the book, early translators and commentators identified Job as a king. The *Testament of Job*, for example, identifies the biblical Job with Jobab, "the king of Egypt" (28:7; cf. LXX Job 42:17b-e). Early Christian artists and medieval miniaturists and iconographers followed suit. For sample images and further discussion of "King Job," see S. Terrien, *The Iconography of Job Through the Centuries. Artists as Biblical Interpreters* (University Park, PN: The Pennsylvania State University Press, 1996), 45-49.

CONNECTIONS

The book of Job is about friendship.[10] For all its heavy hitting on such important theological topics as innocent suffering and the justice of God, it is the theology of friendship that provides the frame for the book's central concerns. At the beginning of the book, Job sits on an ash heap of suffering, surrounded by three friends who come to "console" and "comfort" him, only to find they have no words, at least not at the outset (!), equal to the challenge his suffering presents. They sit with him in silence for seven days and seven nights (2:11-13). At the end of the book, Job is once more surrounded by friends, "brothers and sisters and all who had known him before." They share a meal of communion with him, they "console" and "comfort" him, and they bring him tangible gifts—"a sizeable amount of money and a gold ring"—that contribute to his blessing and his restoration (42:11-12). In between the beginning and ending of the book, the twists and turns of Job's painful journey tracks through the dialogues with various "friends"—Eliphaz, Bildad, Zophar, Elihu, . . . and finally, God—who make their way to his ash heap with words meant to make a difference in his situation. Indeed, of the forty-two chapters that comprise the book of Job, no less than thirty-eight, roughly ninety per cent of the entire story, are forged in the crucible of a lingering, but never articulated question: Who will be Job's friend?

It may be useful to stretch the imagination by reading Job's assessment in this chapter of the friendship he offers to others alongside the New Testament's "Good Samaritan" story (Luke 10:29-37). When the lawyer asks Jesus, "What shall I do to inherit eternal life?" Jesus points him to the abiding summons of Deut 6:4-5: "You shall love the Lord

Job's Royal and Priestly Anthropology

Commentators often note that Job uses royal imagery to describe the role he played in his community (see especially L. Perdue, *Wisdom in Revolt: Metaphorical Theology in the Book of Job* [JSOTSup 112; Sheffield: Almond Press, 1991], 182-95). Comparison with Ps 72, for example, suggests that he judged the poor (vv. 1-4), delivered the needy (vv. 11-14), and enjoyed the blessings of his people (vv. 15-17) like an ideal king.

It is less often noted that Job's ministry in the community is also portrayed with priestly imagery. The prologue (1–2) and epilogue (42:7-17) frame the story of Job with the report that he offers sacrifice. In 1:5 his "burnt offerings" (*'ōlôt*) provide preemptive propitiation for any inadvertent sins his children may have committed. In 42:8 Job receives a "burnt offering" (*'ōlāh*) from his friends, who need his prayer of intercession if God is to forgive them. Even if these are no more than conventional representations of a patriarch's role as head of the family (Gen 8:20; 22:2, 13; 31:54; 46:1), they invite us to imagine that Job "plays the part of the perfect priest" (N. Habel, *The Book of Job: A Commentary* [OTL; Philadelphia: Westminster Press, 1985], 88; cf. J. Hartley, *The Book of Job* [NICOT; Grand Rapids MI: William B. Eerdmans, 1988], 69-70). Job 29:14 may contribute one small, but instructive, detail to Job's priestly profile. Job's word for the "turban" of justice and righteousness he wears is *ṣānîp*. This is not the usual term for the high priestly turban (*miṣnepet*; Exod 39:28; Lev 8:9), but it is clearly related to this garment. Other than Job, the only other person in the Hebrew Bible who wears this turban is Joshua, the high priest, whose integrity is questioned in the heavenly council by the *satan* but confirmed by God (Zech 3:1-10; cf. Isa 62:3 with reference to Zion). (For further discussion of this and other examples of priestly imagery in Job, see Samuel E. Balentine, "Job as Priest to the Priests," *Ex Auditu* 18 [2002]: 29-52.)

Artists and iconographers have long noted Job's priestly role, typically portraying him as a forerunner of Christ, the eternal high priest (cf. Heb 9–10; see further **[Job as Priest]**; **[Inside the Priestly Rituals]**). One particularly evocative example is this sixteenth century wood sculpture in the Mayer van der Bergh Museum in Antwerp. The ecclesiastical turban, the right hand raised in blessing, and the chalice offered with the left hand are conventional priestly symbols. One distinctive feature, however, focuses the viewer's attention. The cup Job offers flames with a fire that appears to have burned a gaping hole in his heart, suggesting that the sacramental blood he offers pours from his own wounds. The image helps to visualize Job's role not only as a proud and powerful king but also as a priest who ministers to the wounded out of his own woundedness (see also **["Agonies Are One of My Changes of Garments"]**).

For further discussion of artistic representations of Job as priest, see S. Terrien, *The Iconography of Job Through the Centuries. Artists as Biblical Interpreters* (University Park PN: The Pennsylvania State University Press, 1996), 149-50.

Saint Job as Priest

Saint Job as Priest, 16 C. Wood sculpture. Mayer van de Bergh Museum, Antwerp. Courtesy Institut Royal du Patrimoine Artistque, Brussels.

your God with all your heart, and with all your soul, and with all your strength, and with all your mind; *and your neighbor as yourself.*" The lawyer presses for more clarity by asking a follow-up question: "And *who is my neighbor?*" Jesus responds by telling a story about "a certain man" who was traveling the dangerous road from Jerusalem to Jericho. Through no fault of his own, he fell victim to random acts of violence and brutality and was left for dead. Three travelers, a priest, a Levite, and a Samaritan, each would-be friends, journey on the same road. The priest and the Levite pass by without offering assistance. The Samaritan, "moved with compassion," stops and pours oil on the beaten man's wounds, bandages him up, and then carries him to an inn, where he pays for his care and safekeeping. When Jesus finishes this story, he asks the lawyer to think about what it means for him: "Which of the three, do you think, was a neighbor to the man?" With one ear cocked toward the words in Job 29, we might pause to reflect on what the meaning of this story would be for us, if the name of the beaten man in the ditch were Job.

In Jesus' story, neither the three travelers on the road to Jericho nor the beaten man in the ditch speaks a word. We do not know what reason the priest and the Levite may have given for neglecting the man, or why the Samaritan was moved with compassion to care for him. By the same token, we do not know what the man may have said to the two passers-by who left him there to die, or how he might have responded to the one who bandaged his wounds and carried him to safety. If his name were Job, however, and if his failed comforters traveled in the company of Job's "friends," Eliphaz, Bildad, and Zophar, then we have a rich deposit of references to friendship from which we may reconstruct the dialogue Luke does not provide.

Job's friends clearly want to "console and comfort him" (2:11). Their initial efforts (4-14) suggest that they have read the required text for Pastoral Care 101. With equal measures of comfort and encouragement, they each gently raise questions they trust will nudge Job to answers they already know (4:2, 6-7; 8:2-3; 11:2-3). When Job fails to respond with a confession of sin, as they had hoped, they stiffen their resolve to coerce repentance from him by focusing on the one truth they are sure he will not deny (15-21): the wicked (read Job) are always punished (15:17:35; 18:5-21; 20:4-9). When Job questions their wisdom (e.g., 21:17), the friends give up their quest for a confession of sin (22-27) and simply announce by fiat that Job is guilty beyond any reasonable doubt (e.g., 22:5). The friends' presumption of Job's guilt effectively leaves him in the ditch with the beaten man on the road to Jericho. They will help him out only if he accepts their terms, unconditional surrender to their theology: to wit, he is suffering, therefore he has sinned; he is guilty, therefore he must repent.

Once the strategy to love Job into conformity with their theology has failed, the friends are left with but two options. They can rethink their definition of friendship. Could it be that Job deserves their loyalty, no matter his guilt or innocence? Or they can decide that their theology is more important than his friendship. When friends run afoul of theological orthodoxy, one must either convert them or condemn them. Eliphaz and his friends choose the latter course. To be charitable, we might imagine that they simply get tired of "being with" Job. Perhaps, as Martin Marty observes, sharing the grief of another, taking into oneself the "agony of the nerves exposed, the plotlessness of pain that never stops," is too much to ask of anyone. Most of those who wear the label of "friend," Marty suggests, will be "tempted to turn their backs" and retreat at some point.[11] [Everyone Can Get Used to Pain, Except the Sufferer] Whether viewed charitably or not, the drama of the book of Job deposits readers on the doorstep of chapter 29 with a thud. His "friends" have condemned him as guilty. Charged and convicted, Job now awaits whatever comes next alone.

Job expects and hopes for something more from his friends . . . and from God. Job expects *ḥesed* from a friend (6:14), which he believes should be manifest in the loyalty of relentless love that will not let go of him, even if suffering pushes him beyond the conventional boundaries of piety ("the fear of the Almighty"). What he receives instead from Eliphaz and his cohorts is what we call "fair-weather" friendship. They stay close when it costs them nothing and their resources are not needed, but when the stakes are high and the cost of befriending Job may be dear, they retreat into pious platitudes that allow them to be little more than voyeurs of suffering. They look at Job from a distance; from the safety of manufactured moral superiority, they theologize about his pain without flinching at its horror.

So far as Job can see at this point, God offers even less than his failed friends. Shrouded in silence, God has not spoken a word since saying to the *satan*, "Very well, he is in your power" (2:6). With these words, to our ears spoken much too casually, God handed Job over to an unimaginable test of piety. *Will Job love God for nothing?* (1:9). Since then, God has stood on the sidelines, watching and listening with a divine indifference that seems neither to contest nor even to deplore what is happening to the servant named Job. Now Job has dared to challenge God with a test of his own: *Will God love him for nothing?*

Everyone Can Get Used to Pain, Except the Sufferer

Alphonse Daudet (1840–1897), novelist, playright, and journalist, kept a journal of his steady descent into disease and death. What the pain felt like to him, and how it was perceived by others, is captured in this entry: "Pain is always new to the sufferer, but loses its originality for those around him. Everyone will get used to it except me."

A. Daudet, *In the Land of Pain*, ed. and trans. J. Barnes (New York: Alfred A. Knopf, 2002), 19.

Tennyson's Theology of Friendship

Alfred Lord Tennyson's (1809–1892) poem "In Memoriam A. H. H." describes the loss he experienced upon the sudden and tragic death of his best friend Arthur Hallam on September 15, 1833, at the age of 22. Hallam had befriended Tennyson at Cambridge. He had introduced Tennyson to the undergraduate literary group, the Apostles, helped him with his first publications of poetry, traveled with him to the Pyrenees and the Rhineland, and counseled him through difficult periods of loneliness and despair. At the time of his death, Hallam was engaged to marry Tennyson's sister, Emily. They were best friends, brothers in the deepest sense of the word. When Tennyson learned of Hallam's death, he began almost immediately to compose the words of this poem. They had shared a friendship for but five years. He worked on this poem, trying to find the words that matched what he had lost, for sixteen years. His hope was to "Let love clasp Grief lest both be drown'd" (1, 10). His lyrics make his loss of Hallam's friendship almost palpable. They are not scripture, but they may be sacred nonetheless:

One writes that "other friends remain,"
That "loss is common to the race"—
And common is the commonplace,
And vacant chaff well meant for grain.

That loss is common would not make
My own loss less bitter, rather more.

Too common! Never morning wore
To evening, but some heart did break . . . . (6, 1-8)

I know that this was Life, —the track
Whereon with equal feet we fared;
And then, as now, the day prepared
The daily burden for the back.

But this it was that made me move
As light as carrier-birds in air;
I loved the weight I had to bear,
Because it needed help of Love;

Nor could I weary, heart or limb,
When mighty love would cleave us twain
The lading of a single pain,
And part it, giving half to him. (25, 1-12)

And then these familiar words, written during the holidays of the first Christmas after Hallam's death,

I hold it true, whate'er befall;
I feel it when I sorrow most;
'T is better to have loved and lost
Than never to have loved at all. (27, 13-16)

Alfred Lord Tennyson, "In Memoriam A. H. H.," *Tennyson's Poetry*, sel. and ed. R. Hill (New York, London: W. W. Norton, 1971), 121, 123, 134 (emphasis added)

Will God come to him, stay by him through thick and thin, even when Job curses and laments and accuses God? Job's abiding hope, yet unrealized, is to find in his friends and in his God a love that will "clasp grief lest both be drown'd." [Tennyson's Theology of Friendship] Until that happens, Job remains in the ditch with the beaten man traveling to Jericho. He is still waiting for the good Samaritan who may be "moved with compassion" to care for him.

Job's discourse on friendship invites us into the ditch of suffering, there to wait and wonder and hope with him. We read of the friendship he has offered to others, and we ask what was going through the minds and hearts of his friends and his God when Job's children were laid in their tombs? What did they feel when they saw Job sitting on the ash heap, deadened himself to anything beyond grief and despair? Did they feel any sense of loss when this faithful servant of God pleaded for a friend who would be loyal, then yielded in despondency to an existence that seemed fated more for death than life?

The movie *Four Weddings and a Funeral* is a raucous, often irreverent, portrayal of the friendships shared by Charles, Tom, Scarlet, Matthew, and Garreth. Each of the friends brings a unique zaniness to the relationship, but it is the unbounded joy for life of middle-aged Garreth that unites and sustains them. When he suddenly drops dead of a heart attack while gamboling at a wedding, the bubble of their unfazed happiness burst. One can almost hear the air leaving the room. Garreth's loss is heavy, especially for his most intimate friend Matthew, who was asked to give the eulogy at his funeral. Matthew chose these words from W. H. Auden:

> Stop all the clocks, cut off the telephone,
> Prevent the dog from barking with a juicy bone,
> Silence the pianos and with muffled drum
> Bring out the coffin, let the mourners come.

> Let aeroplanes circle moaning overhead
> Scribbling on the sky the message He is Dead,
> Put crepe bows round the white necks of the public doves,
> Let the traffic policemen wear black cotton gloves.

> He was my North, my South, my East and West,
> My working week and my Sunday rest,
> My noon, my midnight, my talk, my song;
> I thought that love would last for ever: I was wrong.

> The stars are not wanted now: put out every one;
> Pack up the moon and dismantle the sun;
> Pour away the ocean and sweep up the wood;
> For nothing now can ever come to any good.[12]

We may wonder if either Job's friends or Job's God felt a loss comparable to this when they looked upon his suffering. It may of course stretch the imagination too far, perhaps beyond all boundaries of orthodoxy, to think of God speaking Auden's lines. And yet, the Matthews and Jobs of this world might find it more comforting than unsettling to imagine that God values friendship; that God grieves the brokenness and loss of a loved one at least as much they do. "He was my North, my South, my East and West, / My working week and my Sunday rest, / My noon, my midnight, my talk, my song." Is it really too much for Job to hope that those who would be his friends might be wounded enough by his suffering not only to protest it but also to move to stop it?[13] "Stop all the clocks, cut off the telephone . . . Silence the pianos . . . Pack up the moon and dismantle the sun."

"What Shall I Do to Inherit Eternal Life?"

The *Apocalypse of Paul* (4th C. CE) tells the story of Paul's rapture to "the third heaven" and the saints he met there, including Abraham, Isaac, Jacob, *and* Job. When Paul asked about what his entrance into this company of saints meant for him, an angel explained,

All those who have given hospitality to strangers, when they come forth from the world, first worship the Lord God and are handed over to Michael, and by this route are led into the city, and all the righteous greet them, "Because you have kept humanity and hospitality for strangers, come, receive an inheritance in the city of our God." (II, 776-77)

L. Besserman, *The Legend of Job in the Middle Ages* (Cambridge: Harvard University Press, 1979), 66-67. For the text, see *New Testament Apocrypha*, ed. E. Hennecke, W. Schneemelcher, vol. 2 (Philadelphia: Westminster Press, 1965), 755-59

When Jesus finished his story about those who did and did not care for the beaten man on the road to Jericho, he asked the lawyer, "Which of these three persons, do you think, was a neighbor to the man who fell into the hands of robbers?" It is instructive to imagine that there may have been a pause before the lawyer answered, perhaps long enough for Jesus to buttress the Good Samaritan story with a reminder of Job's legacy of friendship. Perhaps Jesus' citation of Deuteronomy's summons to love your neighbor, coupled with both the "old" and "new" stories of the Good (Joban-like) Samaritan, would be sufficient to make the point.

To return to the question Jesus puts to the lawyer, and now to us, Jesus asks, "Which of these three persons, do you think, was a neighbor to the man who fell into the hands of the robbers?" The lawyer said, "The one who showed him mercy." And the God who was in Jesus said to him, "Go and do likewise." ["What Shall I Do to Inherit Eternal Life?"]

NOTES

[1] J. Wharton, *Job* (*Westminster Bible Companion*; Louisville KY: Westminster John Knox Press, 1999), 121.

[2] Cf. J. Miles, *God: A Biography* (New York: Alfred A. Knopf, 1995), 326.

[3] E. M. Good, for example, suggests that Job's words may be laced with "sardonic images" that are on the whole more negative than positive. The young hide more out of "terror" than respect; the leaders are not only silent but also silenced by Job's overbearing presence. In sum, behind Job's self-satisfaction, "we hear an arrogant man's testimony to the successful exercise of his arrogance" (Good, *In Turns of Tempest: A Reading of Job with a Translation* [Stanford: Stanford University Press, 1990], 299; cf. N. Habel, *The Book of Job: A Commentary* [OTL; Philadelphia: Westminster Press, 1985], 406). See further C. Newsom's critique of the "patriarchy" and "hierarchy" implicit in Job's depiction of his moral world ("The Moral Sense of Nature: Ethics in Light of God's Speech to Job," *The Princeton Seminary Bulletin* 15 [1994]: 9-27; idem, *The Book of Job: A Contest of Moral Imaginations* [Oxford: Oxford University Press, 2003], 183-99).

[4] Cf. Wharton, *Job,* 121.

[5] G. Steiner, *No Passion Spent: Essays 1978–1995* (New Haven, London: Yale University Press, 1996), 251.

[6] C. Newsom, "The Book of Job," in vol. 4 of *NIB* (Nashville: Abingdon Press, 1996), 539.

[7] Cf. J. Gerald Janzen, *Job* (Atlanta: John Knox, 1985), 204.

[8] Newsom, "The Book of Job," 539.

[9] Newsom, following Mikhail Bakhtin, suggests that God is the projected "superaddessee" in Job 29–31. Although the friends may be the logical addressees whose understanding is *sought*, God is the *presumed* hearer, the "ideal listener," whose sympathetic response Job most values and trusts. Implicit in Bakhtin's discussion of these matters, Newsom says, is the idea that "The superaddressee embodies a principle of hope" (*Book of Job,* 186).

[10] Some of the commentary above and the connections here reprise my comments in "Let Love Clasp Grief Lest Both Be Drowned," *PRSt* 30 (2003): 381-97.

[11] M. Marty, *A Cry of Absence* (San Francisco: Harper and Row, 1983), 128.

[12] W. H. Auden, "Twelve Songs," *W. H. Auden: Collected Poems*, ed. E. Mendelson (New York: Vintage International, 1991), 141.

[13] I frame the question with the insights of Susan Sontag, who has thought deeply about what it means to look on the pain of others. See especially her observations in chapter 3, introduced by the evocative question, "What does it mean to protest suffering, as distinct from acknowledging it?" (*Regarding the Pain of Others* [New York: Farrar, Straus and Giroux, 2003], 40).

PRESENT MISERY

Job 30:1-31

In the second part of his discourse, Job's recollections shift from his past blessings to his present misery. The contrast between past and present is jarring. The threefold repetition of the phrase "but now" (*wĕ'attāh*; vv. 1, 9, 16) that punctuates the first half of this chapter (vv. 1-19) makes it read like a "before and after" advertisement for faith that has gone horribly wrong. "Before" suffering wrecked Job's life, God was a constant source of blessing and joy. "After" his life fell apart, God was nowhere to be found, except as the sinister behind-the-scene-presence who pulled the trigger on the assault weapon. In Job's upside down world, the respect he once enjoyed has turned to scorn (vv. 2-8), society's admiration for him has turned to hostile aggression (vv. 9-15), and God, whom Job once knew to be unquestionably gracious and compassionate, has become inexplicably "cruel" (vv. 16-19). Much has changed since Job first spoke from the ash heap in chapter 3, but Job's words in the second half of this chapter (vv. 20-31) make clear that one thing remains constant. Job still "persists in his integrity" (2:3), an integrity that has now solidified in his resolute "cry" to God for help (vv. 20, 24, 28).[1] [Structure of Job 30:1-31]

> **Structure of Job 30:1-31**
>
> I. Job's present misery (vv. 1-19)
> "*But now* they make sport of me" (vv. 1-8)
> "*And now* they mock me in song" (vv. 9-15)
> "*And now* my soul is poured out within me" (vv. 16-19)
>
> II. Job's continuing cry (vv. 20-31)
> "I *cry* to you" (vv. 20-23)
> "Surely one does not turn against the needy, when . . . they *cry* for help" (vv. 24-27)
> "I stand up in the assembly and *cry* for help" (vv. 28-31)

COMMENTARY

"But Now They Make Sport of Me," 30:1-8

Once Job had been among the honored of society, *but now* he is the object of public scorn. To add insult to injury, those who now "laugh" (*śāḥaq*) at him with contempt (v. 1) are among those he once "laughed" with (*śāḥaq*, 29:24; NRSV: "smiled on") when his administration of justice and righteousness made their lives better. He will describe the way they treated him in vv. 9-15, but first he gives voice to the raw human impulse to return insult for insult (vv. 1b-8). Those who hold him in contempt are contemptible themselves. Their social standing is less than that of a dog; they are not even worthy of being entrusted with the care of a shepherd's flock (v. 1b). They have nothing to offer Job, nor would he want anything they give. He would not eat their food, because they scavenge for it among the filth of wastelands where nothing fit to eat can grow (vv. 3-4). He would not keep their company, because they are despised as common criminals who have no place in any human society (v. 5). He would not seek shelter from them, because they live like animals in gullies, holes, rocks, and bushes (vv. 6-7). Job summarizes his disdain in v. 8 by characterizing them as a "senseless and disreputable brood." NRSV's translation is mild compared to the Hebrew, which says they are "foolish" (*nābāl*), thus worthy of nothing more than the same rebuke Job offered his wife (2:10), and "nameless" (*bĕnê bĕlî šēm*; lit., "children of a no-name"), thus utterly lacking any identity worth recognizing.

Job's disdain for those who disdain him is unsettling. Even if we sympathize with his suffering, his dehumanization of those who do him wrong will likely cause our moral and ethical compass to swing toward the red zone, warning us against any facile endorsement. We can applaud his sympathetic assessment of the plight of the destitute in 24:3-8. We can know ourselves challenged by his claim to have cared for the poor and the needy in 29:12-20. But when the victim assumes the characteristics of the victimizer, then we sense that Job's righteous indignation has gone too far. And yet, these are Job's words, his account of what it feels like to have fallen so far that he is now mocked and belittled by the scum of the earth. Just as the prologue invites us to stretch our imagination and think of Job as an unparalleled exemplar of the righteous person, so now Job stretches us to feel with him the indignation, the anger, the impulse to respond to abuse with abuse (see further, Connections). I am persuaded that Wharton is correct when he cautions us not to judge Job's words with a glib sense of moral superiority—we would surely never stoop so low as Job! "We lose all access to chapter 30," Wharton says, if we do not "allow the poet to take us by the hand and lead us into the interior experience of the 'worst-case scenario' of all human suffering."[2] We may want Job to have a "less harsh and uncaring view"[3] of the people who abuse him, but we must remember, if we can, that sufferers like Job "do not have the luxury of patronizing reality."[4] ["It Can Happen Sometimes"]

"And Now They Mock Me in Song," 30:9-15

Job now returns to the description of what his abusers do to him that he had begun in 30:1. His account of what it feels like to sit on the ash heap uses escalating images of cruelty, beginning with verbal aggression (v. 9), then insulting gestures (v. 10), and finally physical violence (vv. 12-14).[5] They taunt him with derisory songs (cf. Lam 3:14) that make him the "butt of their gibes" (NJPS). They express their contempt by spitting in his face, the same face that once radiated the light of God's countenance (29:24). They come against him with strategic aggression, like an army attacking a poorly defended city. They build roads for the siege, break up every escape route, breach his defenses, then roll in upon him with a torrent of destructive force. Their ultimate objective, Job says, is not merely to destroy him but to rob him of his "honor" and "dignity" (NJPS). The contrast between Job's former status and his current position is

stark. The once proud king who marshaled his forces on behalf of the helpless (29:25) is reduced to a prisoner of war who counts for little more than a statistic. Most telling of all is Job's discernment that his opponents employ the same tactics as the God who comes against him to destroy the nobility, the "glory" and "crown" (19:9), that makes human beings fully human (see the commentary on 19:6-20 and [The Warrior God]).

Job interrupts this staccato-like description of the cruelty he experiences at the hands of others only one time, in v. 11. His abusers come at him, and he is vulnerable to their attacks, "because" God has paved the way for his demise. God has loosed his "bowstring" and "afflicted" him (NRSV: "humbled"). The word translated "bowstring" is ambiguous. It may convey the image of the strings on a military weapon that God has disabled, thus leaving Job defenseless (cf. Ps 18:34). It may be an image for a rope or "tent cord" that God has untied, thus causing Job's tent to sag and fall (cf. Job 4:21). With either reading, the effect is the same, from Job's perspective: God has exposed him and made him an easy target for destruction. "Because" God has already decided to make Job vulnerable to abuse, those who now attack him are only following a divinely sanctioned way of treating people like him. They abhor him, because God abhors him. They treat him as less than human, because God treats him as less than human. They legitimate their violence against him by appealing to God's ethical and moral standards. The code of conduct that governs the world Job describes, whether real or only perceived, invites close scrutiny. At issue is what we may call in this post 9-11 world a kind of "terrorist hermeneutics"[6] that appeals to God (or religion) to endorse and bless violence (see further, Connections). [Violence and the Bible]

"It Can Happen Sometimes"

Ian McEwan's character Vernon Halliday is grief stricken over the tragic death of his dear friend Molly, the spiteful indifference of his friends, and, on top of everything else, his wrongful sacking from the editor's job he had held for most of his professional life. "The world was treating him badly, . . . his life was in ruins, no one was treating him worse than his old friend, and . . . this was unforgivable. And insane." He contemplates the wreck his life has become and wonders whether he should simply pretend to make peace with misfortune. McEwan describes Vernon's state of mind with these words: "It can happen sometimes, with those who brood on an injustice, that a taste for revenge can usefully combine with a sense of obligation."

I. McEwan, *Amsterdam* (New York: Nan Talese/Doubleday, 1998), 161-62.

Violence and the Bible

In the wake of the events of September 11, 2001, the issue of religiously inspired violence has forced its way on to our radars with numbing alarm. It is one thing to concede that the Bible often depicts God as a warrior who uses violence as a means of correction and control (see **[The Warrior God]**). It is quite another to countenance the possibility that humans are to image God's use of violence, with God's blessings, to exact revenge on their enemies. A variety of hermeneutical strategies may, indeed must, be employed when reading and interpreting religious texts that use violence to tell the story of the deity and the deity's followers. But at the end of the day, the moral problems posed by such texts remain. As James Barr notes, "the problem is not whether the narratives [of Holy War] are fact or fiction, the problem is that, whether fact or fiction, the ritual destruction is *commended*."

John Collins reflected on these issues and the challenges they present for biblical interpreters in the post 9-11 world in his Presidential address to the Society of Biblical Literature, November 23, 2003.

There is much in the Bible that is not "worthy" of the God of the philosophers. There is also much that is not worthy of humanity, certainly much that is not worthy to serve as a model for imitation. This material should not be disregarded, for it is at least as revelatory as the more edifying parts of the biblical witness. The power of the Bible is largely that it gives an unvarnished picture of human nature and of the

dynamics of history, and also of religion and the things people do in its name. After all, it is only in the utopian future that the wolf is supposed to live with the lamb, and even then the wolf will probably feel the safer of the two. The biblical portrayal of human reality becomes pernicious only when it is invested with authority and assumed to reflect, without qualification or differentiation, the wisdom of God or the will of God. The Bible does not demystify or demythologize itself. But neither does it claim that the stories are paradigms for human action in all times and places.

For further reading on violence in the Bible and in religion, see R. Girard, *Violence and the Sacred* (Baltimore: Johns Hopkins University Press, 1977); P. Trible, *Texts of Terror: Literary-Feminist Readings of Biblical Narrative* (Minneapolis, MN: Fortress Press, 1984); J. G. Williams, *The Bible, Violence, and the Sacred: Liberation from the Myth of Sanctioned Violence* (San Francisco: HarperSanFrancisco, 1991); R. Schwartz, *The Curse of Cain: The Violent Legacy of Monotheism* (Chicago: University of Chicago Press, 1997); C. Kimball, *When Religion Becomes Evil* (San Francisco: HarperSanFrancisco, 2002).

J. Barr, *Biblical Faith and Natural Theology* (Oxford: Clarendon Press, 1993), 209.

J. Collins, "The Zeal of Phinehas: The Bible and the Legitimation of Violence," JBL 122 (2003): 20. For responses to Collins's Presidential address, see the articles by J. Kaminsky, R. Schwartz, D. Kille, and R. Weems in *Religious Studies News/SBL Edition* (June 2003).

"And Now My Soul Is Poured Out Within Me," 30:16-19

Job turns next to the pain and suffering he feels deep within himself, where the long tentacles of social abuse extend their claim on body and soul. ["Pain Finds Its Way Everywhere"] Returning to images of physical and mental anguish he has used before (cf. 7:3-5; 16:8; 19:20), he speaks of pain's relentless assault. The days are full of affliction (v. 16b). At night his body becomes a playground for misery; the pain, which never sleeps, gnaws at him like a dog chewing on a bone (v. 17). More hurtful still is Job's belief that God is the one who has him in a vise-grip. The clothing imagery of v. 18 recalls the royal and priestly garments that once identified Job's place of honor and respect in the community (29:14). Now his tunic serves only as something for God to grab on to, a means for

"Pain Finds Its Way Everywhere"

Pain finds its way everywhere, into my vision, my feelings, my sense of judgment; it's an infiltration.

A. Daudet, *In the Land of Pain*, ed. and trans. J. Barnes (New York: Alfred A. Knopf, 2002), 23.

steadying Job while God lines him up for the final assault. God's intent, it seems, is to hurl Job back into the muck and mire of humanity from which he came (v. 19a; cf. 4:19; 10:9; 33:6).

Job believes that God's ultimate objective is to treat him as "dust and ashes" (*'āpār wā'ēpēr*, v. 19b). The imagery is both simple and freighted. At this juncture in his journey, Job assumes a simple, and profoundly sad, view of God's intent. As far as he can see, to be dust and ashes is to be reduced to abject nothingness, like an object that can be discarded without loss. He counts for nothing more than the dust that covers the ground *before* God breathes life into it (Gen 2:7; 3:19). Forced to sit and remain "among the ashes" (2:8), Job's humiliation is nothing more than the destiny God prepared for him *after* he drew first breath. Job's assessment is that God has made him so contemptible that the mere mention of his name invites others to snicker and sneer. ["I'm a Cliché"]

The words "dust" and "ashes" are also freighted in ways Job does not yet fully understand. As two separate words, their meaning may be simple. Job has heard his friends use both of them and has used them himself many times before.[7] As a pair, however, the words "dust and ashes" constitute a phrase that occurs only three times in the Hebrew Bible, Genesis 18:27, Job 30:19, and Job 42:6. The first occurrence is on the lips of Abraham In the midst of questioning God about the punishment planned for Sodom, Abraham suddenly realizes that he might have overstepped the boundaries of his creaturely status before the "Judge of all the earth": "May I make so bold as to speak to the Lord, I who am nothing but dust and ashes" (REB). The third occurrence constitutes Job's final words in this book. The conventional translation—"I despise myself and repent in dust and ashes" (42:6; NRSV)— suggests that at the end of his journey with God, Job acknowledges, or at least concedes, his own creaturely status.

Two observations about these occurrences, which will require further exploration (see the commentary on Job 42:1-6), may be offered. Although Abraham acknowledges it is risky, perhaps foolish, for a mere mortal to question God, the remainder of his speech indicates that he stays the course, insisting that it is important for God to hear what he has to say. In his last words, Job's "repentance" indicates a change of mind, specifically with reference to what "dust and ashes" means. It is instructive to imagine that in Job 30:19, Job stands inside the tension between these two other occurrences of the words

"I'm a Cliché"

Concerned throughout the dialogue with the use and misuse of words, Job now finds himself reduced to a word: "I'm a cliché, like dust and ashes" (30:19) . . . . I think that the Hithpa'el form of the verb [*msl*, "to be like"] may have the sense not of *being* like something (JPS: "I have become like dust and ashes"), but of the outcome of proverb mongering—"I have become a comparison, a proverb, a dead metaphor," such as those the pseudo-wise and "miserable comforters" bandy about. Job said earlier (v. 9) that he had become a "song" and "word" (*millah*) to his persecutors. Now he has become a cliché to an entire culture. (Yes, indeed. Mention Job, and your interlocutor will almost inevitably speak of patience, so much does the misreading of the book by the author of James 5.11 control our implicit reading.)

E. M. Good, *In Turns of Tempest: A Reading of Job with a Translation* (Stanford: Stanford University Press, 1990), 306-307.

Job's Moral World

Carol Newsom has shown that Job's account of himself in chs. 29–30 offers a picture of the social relationships that define his life and give it moral value. One

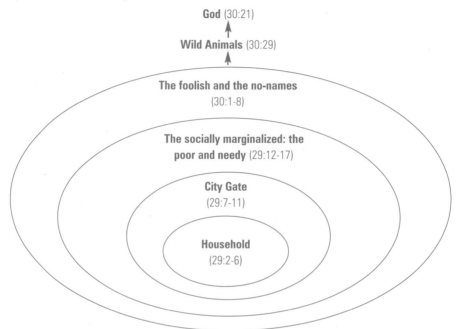

may picture the relationships as a series of concentric circles, moving from most intimate to less intimate and finally to those persons (or creatures) who reside too far beyond the boundaries of society to have significance.

At the center of Job's world is his household, imaged in 29:2-6 as his "tent," which was once graced by the presence of God and the laughter of his children. Next is the social world of the village, especially the relationships he once enjoyed with the elders and nobles who administer justice at the city gate (29:7-11). Then come his relationships with the socially marginalized, for example, the poor and the needy (29:12-17). Within these three spheres, Job's relationships are mutually reinforced by common moral codes of behavior. Job honors others and is honored by them. A commitment to righteousness and justice (29:14) knits each segment of Job's world life into a meaningful whole.

At the outer edges of Job's world are the "senseless, disreputable brood" (30:8) that now heaps abuse upon him. Although they are so contemptible in his eyes that

they deserve to be "driven out from society" (30:5), their insults still have an effect on Job. Newsom describes the dialectic between honor and shame as follows:

The moral world that Job has described in chapter 29 is one in which honor and respect are among the highest goods . . . . The corresponding horror in such a world is to be mocked, shamed, and held in contempt. These are categories that logically imply each other. A society that rewards with honor punishes with shame and contempt. That is precisely what Job speaks of in chapter 30. (189)

Two categories of creatures/persons are beyond even the outer boundaries of Job's moral world: the *wild animals* that inhabit the wilderness, the jackal and the ostrich, who wail far beyond the hearing and the concern of anyone in civilized society (30:29), and the "*cruel*" *God* (30:21), whose "antisocial" character is so extreme as to seem more animal-like than divine. As far as Job can see, this cruel God has broken the social bonds of justice and righteousness that provide the moral foundations of the world.

C. Newsom, *The Book of Job: A Contest of Moral Imaginations* (Oxford: Oxford University Press, 2003), 183-99.

"dust and ashes." As the rest of chapter 30 suggests, Job is tempted to conclude that being "dust and ashes" means that God has little or no regard for him (e.g., v. 20). On the other hand, Job's continuing cries

(vv. 20, 24, 28), coupled with the way he pleads his case in chapter 31, invite the speculation that he intends to model Abraham's temerity, not his caution. The tension—how and why Job does change his mind about "dust and ashes"?—will not be resolved until and unless we walk with him to the end of his journey. ["At the Edge of the Middle of Things"]

"I Cry to You," 30:20-31

Job's present misery, the depth of his physical and psychic anguish, compels him to continue the search for resolution. But what he is to do? Where should he turn? His closing words in this chapter reflect both his uncertainty and his persistence. He is not prepared even now to relinquish the faint hope that God is listening and will, eventually, respond with the friendship he so desperately expects (vv. 20-23). But when Job "cries out" for help, God does not answer. When Job stands silently, God looks on discerningly; whether the look expresses increasing indifference or irritation, Job cannot say (v. 20).[8] Absent a clarifying word from this silent God, all Job has to go on is God's action. He lines out what he sees and feels about God's behavior with a series of heavy and incriminating verbs: you "persecute me" (v. 21b); you "dissolve me" (v. 22b; NRSV: "toss me about"); you "return me" to death (v. 23a). The sum of God's ways adds up to a single conclusion: "You have turned cruel to me" (v. 21). The term "cruel" (*'akzār*) is especially revealing of Job's assessment of who God is. It is used to describe the mercilessness of military foes (Jer 6:23; 50:42; cf. Jer 30:14), the "cruel mercy" of the wicked (Prov 12:10; cf. Prov 11:17), the venom of snakes (Deut 32:33), and the heartlessness of wild animals that refuse to nurse their young (Lam 4:3; cf. Job 39:16). In short, cruelty typifies creatures, human and animal, that hurt others because they do not care; in some species the cruelty is expected, even instinctive. Such a creature, it seems to Job, is God.

There is no place in Job's moral or religious world for a cruel God. [Job's Moral World] Job lives according to the principles of righteousness and justice, which means that he does not turn against the needy who cry to him for help (v. 24). The thought of doing otherwise is virtually unimaginable to him. He can speak the words—"Did I not weep for the unfortunate? Did I not grieve for the needy?" (v. 25; NJPS)—but

"At the Edge of the Middle of Things"

The end occurs not at the end but when I'm still
at the edge of the middle of things.

Toys and plastic chairs lie scattered across the lawn,
the picnic table's spread under an arching beech,

but these human signs can't speak
of the necessary shift, and even the cloud

that cuts the monotonous sky with a brilliant pink
has nothing to do with this change.

The particular, the compelling object, breaks.
And alone, in place, remains

not the common master, waving long flamboyant arms,
but a self subtler and altogether more dangerous.

Out beyond courage and vanity,
I am complete, cut off,
Like the silver-bowled lake
or the deep, impervious dark.

Nadia H. Colburn, "The End," *The New Yorker*, 16 & 23 June 2003, 94.

the questions are rhetorical; Job has already answered them (29:12-17). God appears to follow a different code of conduct. When "blameless and upright" persons like Job look to God for "good," they get "evil" instead. When they expect light, they get darkness (v. 26). The moral and religious coherence of Job's world has been shattered. Like his convulsing bowels, his world is in turmoil (v. 27).

If not to God, then to whom can Job turn? As Job sees it, there remains one option, one place in his world where he might testify to his experiences and get a hearing. He can stand up in "the assembly," among the elders and the supplicants who gather at the city gate in the expectation that justice can be attained (v. 28; cf. 29:7-11). But here too, his expectations seem to be thwarted. His cries sound like nothing more than the wailings of the jackals that inhabit the wastelands (v. 29a), far beyond the boundaries of what civilized society needs care about. He is looked upon as a companion to ostriches (v. 29b), ungainly creatures that are ritually unclean (Lev 11:16; Deut 14:15) and utterly shunned, even by nomads and shepherds (Isa 13:21; 34:13; Jer 50:39). In the assembly that is defined by its execution of justice, Job's presence, the very physicality of his affliction—the look of his skin, the stench of his burning fever (v. 30)—is repulsive (for a visual image, see [The Smell of Death]).

One final image completes Job's description of his present affliction. The music of his life is tuned to mourning. ["Music's Dark Resources"] Driven by pain and suffering to the lower registers on the musical scale, he keeps rhythm with those who weep (v. 31; see further [Job's Sad Song]). Curiously enough, the imagery of Job's "sorrow songs," to use W.E. B. Dubois's language for the slave songs of African-American spirituals, [9] suggests that for all his discomfort and dislocation, he does in fact feel at home with the jackals and ostriches. With one exception, jackals are identified in the Old Testament with piercing shrieks that give voice to the desolateness of their wilderness domain. A lone reference in Isaiah 43:20 envisions a future day when their cries change to praise, because God transforms the wilderness into a garden paradise. Ostriches are routinely described as ugly and undesirable creatures, as noted above, that emit eerie screeches of their own (Mic 1:8). But they are also known for their fearlessness, often taken for stupidity, [10] which enables them to laugh in the face of those who hunt them for sport. [Laughing at the Hunt] Still more suggestive will be the description of the ostrich in the "whirlwind speeches" at the end of this book, when God at last invites Job to see the world from God's point of view. Instead of referring to them by the usual term that Job uses in 30:29 (*ya'ănāh*), God names them *rĕnānîm*, "cries of joy" (39:13). The ostrich, like the jackal, it seems, is a creature with the capacity to cry out at both the lower and upper ends of the register. [The "Secret Arithmetic" of Music]

"Music's Dark Resources"

At least from the time of the Renaissance, Job has been revered as a patron saint of musical guilds (see further **[Rejoicing and Recoiling at the Sound of Music]**) (S. Terrien, *The Iconography of Job Through the Centuries. Artists as Biblical Interpreters* [University Park PN: Pennsylvania State University Press, 1996], 107-26, 146-49). Perhaps Job's identification with music is due, in part, to his familiarity with what Albert Blackwell describes as "music's dark resources." Music has a sacramental capacity, Blackwell says, especially when tuned to the lower registers of the scale, to articulate what William Butler Yeats calls the "'terrible beauty'" of life's realities. Blackwell illustrates with reference to an accordion player named George in Brian Friel's play *Wonderful Tennessee* (1993). Rendered almost mute by a frustrated career, a troubled marriage, and a terminal illness, George articulates his pain by playing the first fifteen seconds of the Third Movement of Beethoven's Sonata No.14 (Moonlight). According to Friel's stage directions, George plays with amazing virtuosity, but so much faster than the piece is scored that the performance "seems close to parody." Then, in the middle of a phrase, he suddenly stops and bows to the other characters on stage, as if he has just given a recital in a concert hall.

Blackwell then cites these words from Frank Rich's review of the play, which bear witness to the theatrical impact of the music George—and Job—plays:

Giving expression to the inexpressible on stage is the most difficult imaginable task, and for all the play's second-hand mythological and religious parables, there are still instances when Mr. Friel creates sacred drama in his own terms. When the dying accordionist . . . , badgered by his friends to tell a story, responds by ripping through a Beethoven sonata, the flaming intensity and tragic futility of an entire life are compressed into a single piece of demented music. There will be better plays than *Wonderful Tennessee* this season, but how many of them will take us, however briefly, to that terrifying and hallowed place beyond words?

A. Blackwell, *The Sacred in Music* (Louisville KY: Westminster John Knox Press, 1999), 132. The reference from William Butler Yeats to "terrible beauty" comes from "Easter 1916," *The Collected Poems of W. B. Yeats* (New York: Macmillan, 1938), 208.

The one constant in the last part of Job's assessment of his present misery is his connection to the cry for help, both his own (vv. 20, 28) and those of fellow sufferers (v. 24). This connectedness to pain, however, appears to have disconnected him from any resource for help. There seems no place for him in God's world, where the ethics of cruelty—not compassion—treat sufferers as objects of contempt. There seems no place for him among his peers in the assembly of justice. Here too the boundaries seem to have been drawn with the objective of excluding those who wail like him. His cries resonate only with the jackals and ostriches, which means that he has been consigned to suffer alone, on the backside of nowhere, out of sight, out of ear, out of mind . . . unless, perhaps, even jackals and ostriches have a place in God's world. ["I Dwell in Possibility"]

CONNECTIONS

In the introductory comments to Job 29–31, I suggested that these chapters offer readers Job's own perspective concerning his experiences. The prologue and epilogue provide the narrator's third-person perspec-

Laughing at the Hunt

In the whirlwind speeches, God compares the ostrich to the horse, which "laughs at fear, and is not dismayed" (Job 39:22). In this depiction of Tutankhamen's hunting, the ostrich is the only one of the targeted prey that looks back, as if mocking, perhaps relishing, the sport.

A Flabellum

A fan-shaped headpiece, depicting Tutankhamun on a chariot aiming his arrow at an ostrich.

1350 BC, New Kingdom. Gold, metal, and wood from the tomb of Tutankhamun. Valley of the Kings, Thebes. Egyptian Museum, Cairo, Egypt (Credit: Erich Lessing/Art Resource, NY)

The "Secret Arithmetic" of Music

Music and the metaphysical, in the root sense of that term, music and religious feeling, have been virtually inseparable. It is in and through music that we are most immediately in the presence of the logically, of the verbally inexpressible but wholly palpable energy in being that communicates to our senses and to our reflection what little we can grasp of the naked wonder of life. I take music to be the naming of the naming of life. This is, beyond any liturgical or theological specificity, a sacramental motion. Or, as Leibniz put it: "music is a secret arithmetic of the soul unknowing of the fact that it is counting."

G. Steiner, *Real Presences* (Chicago: University of Chicago Press, 1989), 216-17.

"I Dwell in Possibility"

I dwell in Possibility—
A fairer House than Prose—
More numerous of Windows—
Superior—for Doors—

E. Dickinson, "# 657," *The Complete Poems of Emily Dickinson*, ed. T. H. Johnson (Boston/New York: Little, Brown and Company, 1960), 327.

tive on Job's life. The dialogues (chs. 4–27) allow readers to listen in on conversations between Job and the friends. We can learn a great deal from these dialogues about the issues the book presents—especially the arguments for and against some coherent theory of moral retribution—but the vantage point is shaped and defined within the conversational matrix of the speakers. Job is speaking primarily to the friends (and to God, on occasion), not to the readers. In the dialogues, we are essentially a third party. In chapter 28, the issue of who is speaking and to whom is more complicated, but even if we take these as Job's words, as I have suggested, we should recognize that they have more the tone of a soliloquy than direct address. Here too, the reader is overhearing words that are both more and less than a simple first-person account. Job's "discourse" in chapters 29–31 is different. Now Job speaks in first-person, and his audience, in effect, is the reader (along with God, Job hopes!). From a literary standpoint, neither the narrator nor the friends act as filters for what Job says. He speaks personally and directly to unknown and unnamed addressees. For the purpose of these reflections, readers are invited to imagine that Job's self-disclosures are addressed to them.

The invitation, such as it is, confronts us as readers with both opportunity and challenge. It may be a gift to be invited to become Job's conversation partner. It will likely also be a challenge to know how to respond. We may respond with automatic affirmation to what Job tells us about his past (ch. 29). When we hear the account of how he invested his life caring for others, we applaud his virtues and instinctively feel challenged to be more like him. But when we hear him speak with such unvarnished rancor about those who abuse him (30:1-8), we justifiably bristle at any suggestion that he should be our role model. David Clines's question about the book of Job is particularly apt for Job's words in chapter 30: "What does it do to you if you read it, what effects does it have?"[11] Does Job persuade us to agree with him or to ignore him? [CD: "One Faces a Text as One Might Face a Person"]

Susan Sontag's *Regarding the Pain of Others* sets the table for our deliberations about how to respond to what we hear Job saying in 30:1-8. She introduces her book by citing Virginia Woolf's reflections on war (the fascist insurrection in Spain) in *Three Guineas*, published in 1938. An eminent lawyer in London had written to her asking, "How in your opinion are we to prevent war?" Woolf responded with a denunciation of war that echoed many others of the time, including the lawyer himself. Referring to the photographic images of war that were constantly being published in the media at the time, Woolf assumed that the pictures could not but unite people of good will in common revulsion. "We are seeing with you the same dead bodies, the same ruined houses." It is this "we" that Sontag scrutinizes. "No 'we' should be taken for granted when the subject is looking at other people's pain."[12]

When looking at Job's pain, and at his contempt for those who inflict it, no "we" should be taken for granted. Two reasons may be suggested. First, it is important to respect the particularity of pain and the way people respond to it. The prologue in fact encourages readers to respect the distance that separates them from Job. Job's origins are located "in the land of Uz." While the geography is imprecise, it clearly places Job somewhere outside the land of Israel. He is portrayed as an outsider, even a Gentile (see [Job, the Righteous Gentile]). His outsider status is important, because it gives us a vantage point for reflection without flinching. This is his story, not ours. The dead children carry his name. The dents in his faith, his struggle to understand, his responses, all come as result of losses we have only read about. To take it all in, we have to be able to stand back and look from a distance. Temporary suspension of empathy is perhaps a prerequisite for looking at the pain of others; otherwise we are likely to become mute and immobilized. [CD: "You Have to Stand Back and Look"]

Job's outsider status, however, comes with a dangerous underside. It encourages us to look at him *only* from a safe distance. Once we bracket his experiences as exceptional and other than our own, we are on the slippery slope toward becoming merely onlookers. We have the luxury, if we choose, to patronize his pain by objectifying, then theorizing about it. Since it did not happen to us, the temptation is to think that it cannot happen to us, or that if it did, we would respond differently, more admirably, than this foreigner named Job. [Preferring "the Evil that Was There"] Sontag illustrates the impulse to insulate ourselves from and against the pain of others with an account about a woman she interviewed for her book:

> A citizen of Sarajevo, a woman of impeccable adherence to the Yugoslav ideal, whom I met soon after arriving in the city the first time in April 1993, told me: "In October 1991 I was here in my nice apartment in peaceful Sarajevo when the Serbs invaded Croatia, and I remember when the evening news showed footage of the destruction of Vukovar, just a couple of hundred miles away, I thought to myself, 'Oh, how horrible,' and I switched the channel. So how can I be indignant if someone in France or Italy or Germany sees the killing taking place here day after day on their evening news and says, 'Oh, how horrible,' and looks for another program. It's normal. It's human."

Sontag makes her point about the woman's comments as follows: "Whenever people feel safe—this was her bitter, self-accusing point—they will be indifferent."[13]

Job does not wish to be patronized. That much should be clear after three rounds of dialogues with his friends. But he also does not want his friends to be indifferent to his suffering. He yearns for them to be more than mere onlookers who tune into his pain for a moment, then shift their sights in search of a more entertaining show. When Eliphaz prefers to *think* about suffering and offer only generic observations about what he sees (4:7–5:7), Job insists on direct encounter: "Look at me" (6:28). When Zophar presses abstract theological discernments about the suffering of the wicked that conveniently ignore the particulars of Job's case, Job is adamant: "*Listen carefully* to my words. . . . *Look at me* and be appalled" (22:2, 5). He does not want his pain to be embalmed in their creeds. He wants friends who will be wounded enough by his pain, even at a distance, not only to deplore it but also to join him in the effort to stop it. Sontag's question is also Job's wonderment: "What does it mean to protest suffering, as distinct from acknowledging it?"[14] "Perhaps," she says, speaking about the photograph of a war victim, "the only people with the right to look at images of suffering of this extreme order are those who could do something to alleviate it—say, the surgeons at the military hospital where the photograph was taken—or those who could learn from it. The rest of us are voyeurs, whether or not we mean to be."[15]

Preferring "the Evil that Was There"

Susan Sontag observes that we build "memory museums" for ourselves as a way of thinking about and mourning the pain of others, e.g., Yad Vashem in Jerusalem, the Holocaust Memorial Museum in Washington, D.C., and the Jewish Museum in Berlin. In such places, photographs and exhibits of suffering testify to the reality of brutality, death, and survival. Gift shops market grief as refrigerator magnets that can be painlessly affixed to the appliances that keep life running smoothly.

But, as Sontag goes on to note, the temples we build to commemorate misery indicate a selective memory and an instinct for survival by denial.

The Disasters of War: Tampoco.

Francisco de Goya (1746-1828). *The Disasters of War: Tampoco.* (Credit: Art Resource, NY)

[W]hy is there not already, in the nation's capital, which happens to be a city whose population is overwhelmingly African-American, a Museum of the History of Slavery? Indeed, there is no Museum of the History of Slavery—the whole story, starting with the slave trade in Africa itself, not just selected parts, such as the Underground Railroad—anywhere in the United States. This, it seems, is a memory judged too dangerous to social stability to activate and to create. The Holocaust Memorial Museum and the future Armenian Genocide Museum and Memorial are about what didn't happen in America. So the memory-work doesn't risk arousing an embittered domestic population against authority. To have a museum chronicling the great crime that was African slavery in the United States of America would be to acknowledge that that the evil was *here.* Americans prefer to picture the evil that was *there*, and from which the United States—a unique nation, one without any certifiably wicked leaders throughout its entire history—is exempt. That this country, like every other country, has its tragic past does not sit well with the founding, and still all-powerful, belief in American exceptionalism.

When viewed against these comments, the picture on the slip-cover of Sontag's book may look like more than merely one of Francisco Goya's eighty-three etchings ("The Disasters of War") of the horrors committed by the soldiers of Napoleon who invaded Spain in 1808. If we dare, we might imagine ourselves in the role of the soldier, who leans in safe repose, looking, without flinching, on the dangling, soon-to-be-dead body of one who might have been named Job.

S. Sontag, *Regarding the Pain of Others* (New York: Farrar, Straus and Giroux, 2003), 87-88.

Perhaps no one, other than God, can ultimately alleviate suffering like Job's. But if we are to avoid the charge of voyeurism, if we wish to be included among those who might "learn" from what Job has to teach us, then we must try hard to "listen carefully" to what he says and "look" closely at his pain. Being "appalled" at what we hear and see may be first step toward positive engagement. [To See "Feelingly"]

There is a second reason why no "we" should be taken for granted when looking at Job's or any other person's pain. At issue is what Emily

Dickinson expresses with simple economy: "Pain—is missed—in praise."[16] Embellishing poetry with commentary risks stripping it of both its power and its truth. I chance these reflections. Pain has its own virtue, which it speaks with a rhetoric comprised of special vocabulary.

To See "Feelingly"

"No eyes in your head," a broken and betrayed King Lear says to the blind Gloucester, who offers him shelter, "yet you see how this world goes."

"I see it feelingly," Gloucester replies.

(*King Lear*, IV, vi, 161-64)

To hear what it says, to respond (at least somewhat) knowingly to the truth it discloses, one must be able to feel the rumblings of hurt below the surface of words that merely audibilize. The words are not equal to felt pain; they merely approximate it. This is no small accomplishment, however, because it places the pain of others at least within the reach of those whose experiences—by luck or divine providence—might have limited their vocabulary to praise.

Job is outraged at the treatment he receives from others, and he says so. At issue for us, his readers, is whether we are persuaded his jibes at the "senseless, disreputable brood" (v. 8) who abuse him are moral, and thus worthy of a place in our code of ethics, or immoral (or amoral), thus deserving only our rebuke and avoidance. On the one hand, we may recognize that pain is a virtue, even if by this we concede no more than its value as a basic biological instinct that sensitizes and warns us of imminent danger.[17] If we did not sense discomfort from the fire's heat, we might not know how to avoid being burned. It is but a short step from this biological verity to the time-honored theological truth Job's friends assert concerning his suffering. Suffering teaches him to do what God requires, to avoid what God prohibits (cf. 5:17). As the Satan character in H. G. Wells's fiction reminds Job, "Without pain what would life become?"[18] [Ingenious Pain] On the other hand, whatever pain's virtues, biological or theological, we likely recoil at the suggestion that it is morally justifiable for Job to respond to pain by inflicting it on others. What is virtuous about holding others in contempt? What is commendable about abusing those who abuse us, whether by word or by deed? As Wells's Satan goes on to remind Job, "Pain is the master only of craven men. It is in man's power to rule it."[19]

Rabbi Meir Soloveichik frames the issue in an article disconcertingly titled "The Virtue of Hate."[20] He focuses on a symposium of prominent theologians, political leaders, writers, and others with diverse religious (Jewish, Christian, Muslim, Buddhist) and non-religious perspectives, who met to discuss Simon Wiesenthal's classic Holocaust text, *The Sunflower*. Wiesenthal's story recounts how he was brought, as a concentration camp prisoner, before a dying SS guard. The man explained his actions, expressed regret and remorse for what he had done, and asked for forgiveness. Wiesenthal listened, contemplated what was being asked of him, and then left without granting the

---

Ingenious Pain

Andrew Miller's novel, *Ingenious Pain*, offers an astute reminder that the capacity to feel pain is a critical virtue for any person who attends to another's grief. The protagonist of Miller's story, James Dyer, is an eighteenth century physician who has a "genius" for surgery. He can cut out tumors and disease, then sew up the holes that he carved in the bodies of his patients with a precision unrivalled by other doctors. His expertise has but one flaw. Because of a freakish accident—when pregnant, his mother fell while ice skating—he had been born with a coldness that manifest itself in imperviousness to pain. He could cut tissue, break bones, and stitch skin without giving so much as a thought to the physical sensation of pain that he was either causing or trying to eradicate. His peculiar gifts served him well as a surgeon. Indeed, his reputation as a doctor rested in large part on his ability to heal others without being distracted by their cries of anguish. And yet, as Reverend Lestrade observes, Dr. James Dyer's extraordinary skills invite questions: "What does the world need most—a good ordinary man, or one who is outstanding, albeit with a heart of ice, of stone?" (41).

On behalf of "good ordinary people," people who remain "flawed" by their sensitivity to pain, Job can be expected to respond as follows: "Those who are at ease have contempt for misfortune" (12:5).

A. Miller, *Ingenious Pain* (New York: Harcourt Brace and Company, 1997).

---

request. He did not condemn the guard, but neither could he bring himself to forgive him. Haunted by the experience and wondering if he had done the right thing, he submitted his story to the symposiasts and asked, "What would you have done?"

Soloveichik notes that Christians and Jews at the symposium responded to the question differently. Christian participants, such as Archbishop Desmond Tutu, typically thought Wiesenthal was wrong not to forgive the repentant soldier. The primary reason for rejecting retributive justice, Tutu argued, was the better model offered by Jesus, who, when he was crucified, said, "Father, forgive them, for they know not what they do." Forgiveness is not only the right thing to do from a spiritual standpoint, Tutu went on to say, it is also prudent from a pragmatic standpoint. Newly empowered South Africans forgave their white oppressors, because it was "practical politics." "Without forgiveness," he explained, "there is no future." Jewish participants, among whom were Rabbi Harold Kushner, Primo Levi, and Cynthia Ozick, were more sympathetic with Wiesenthal's refusal to forgive a Nazi mass murderer. Rabbi Soloveichik identifies with this latter response, and like Bishop Tutu, he justifies it by citing scriptural precedent. He points to Samson's prayer for revenge, "Lord God, remember me and strengthen me only this once, O God, so that with this one act of revenge I may pay back the Philistines for my two eyes" (Judg 16:28); to Samuel's righteous anger against the Amalekite king Agag, "'As your sword has made women childless, so your mother shall be childless among women.' And Samuel hewed Agag in pieces before the Lord in Gilgal" (1 Sam 15:33-34); to Deborah, whose brutal killing of the Philistine Sisera is celebrated in song, "She put her hand to the tent peg . . . she struck Sisera a blow, she crushed his head, she shattered and pierced his temple . . . So perish all your enemies, O Lord!" (Judg 5:26, 31); and to Esther, who, having already defeated Haman, responded to

Does Victimization Justify Violence?

An important caveat is necessary here, which will require exploration at a subsequent point (see the commentary and connections on 42:7-17). For all the similarities between the insults Job levels at his abusers and the biblical precedents Soloveichik cites, Job does not *act* on his outrage. He *speaks* violently, but he *does not engage in acts of violence*, although it might be argued that he would have been justified in doing so.

At issue is what Kim Chernin calls the deeply embedded Jewish sense of victimization. She reflects on why it seems that so many American Jews have difficulty being critical of Israel's treatment of the Palestinians. What justifies the brutality of the Israeli army's policies? In her view, one of the obstacles to a Jew's ability to be critical of Israel is the "hidden belief that a sufficient amount of suffering confers the right of violence" (2).

We call it self-defense, but this is, I suggest, only the surface of our justification. Further down, tucked carefully away in our collective psyche, we find a sense of entitlement about our violence. Our historic suffering, as a people, entitles us to the violence of current behavior. Our violence is not horrendous and cruel like the violence of other people, but is a justified, sacred violence, a holy war. Of curse, we would not want to know this about ourselves—it would make us too much like the perceived enemy whose violence against us we are deploring. When the suicide bomber blows up a hotel full of Passover celebrants, we see clearly that this is an instance of hateful, unjustifiable violence. (And it is, it is.) When we destroy a refugee camp of impoverished Palestinians, this, in our eyes, is a violence purified by our history of persecution. (And it is not, it is not.) We are puzzled that much of the world doesn't see our situation in the same way. (5)

Chernin argues that there is another way, a response to abuse and social injustice that is truer to the truth of Judaism. At its root, the response takes the shape of prayer. "But," she asks, "are we, as a people, still capable of prayer? How will we manage to pray, we who have just seen" yet another bomb explode? She suggests the prayers might sound like this:

Make it possible for us not so seek vengeance.
Help us to find the way that is not the way of violence.
Teach us to grieve without turning into those who have brought us to grief.
Help us to remember the innocence of the innocent.
Teach us to remember ourselves, a holy people.
If compassion is not possible for us,
If love is not possible for us,
Teach us not to hate. (8)

At the end of the book of Job, God's last words indicate why Job remains, even in his anger, a model for us:

After the Lord had spoken these words to Job, the Lord said to Eliphaz the Temanite: "My wrath is kindled against you and against your two friends, for you have not spoken of me what is right, as my servant Job has. Now therefore, take seven bulls and seven rams, and go to my servant Job, and offer up for yourselves a burnt offering; and my servant Job shall pray for you, for I will accept his prayer not to deal with you according to your folly; for you have not spoken of me what is right, as my servant Job has done." So Eliphaz the Temanite and Bildad the Shuhite and Zophar the Naamathite went and did what the Lord had told them; and the Lord accepted Job's prayer. (Job 42:7-9)

K. Chernin, "Seven Pillars of Jewish Denial," *Tikkun* (October 2002): 1-8. The page references are to the version of the article available on the *Tikkun* web site: http://www.tikkun.org/magazine/index.cfm/action/tikkun/issue/tiko209/article/020911a.html.

the question about what more she could possibly want by saying, "If it pleases the king. . . let the ten sons of Haman be hanged on the gallows" (Esth 9:13). Soloveichik does not include Job's name in this list of biblical persons who expressed outrage, spoke of revenge, and sometimes acted violently toward those who abused them, but he might well have. [Does Victimization Justify Violence?]

Soloveichik proceeds with a wide-ranging discussion of the differences in the ways Jews and Christians react to evil. The precedents he cites invite and require more careful exegesis than he applies, but I will not attempt to critique his conclusions here. The critical issue for these reflections is his argument that rage, animosity, and bluntly put, hatred, "can be virtuous when one is dealing with the frightfully wicked." He continues, "Rather than forgive, we can wish ill; rather than hope for repentance, we can instead hope that our enemies experience the wrath of God." How can such sentiments be morally justified? Soloveichik answers by arguing that human beings are created in the image of God, which means (from his Jewish perspective) that we are called to love as God loves *and* to hate as God hates. Obedience to the latter may require that we despise the wicked because God despises the wicked; that we withhold forgiveness, because God has determined that there comes a time in the pursuit of holy justice when forgiveness should be withheld (Exod 34:7). It takes us too far a field to pursue the philosophical and theological ripples of this line of thinking. But if, for example, we feel any connection to the argument offered for the United States' intervention, albeit belatedly, against the Nazi's slaughter of innocent Jews in World War II, then we will pause before the possibility that outrage, not relativism, may sometimes be "not only a morally justified lesser of two evils, . . . it can be a *mitzvah*, a divine imperative."[21] ["Violence Is Never Just, Though Justice May Sometime Require It"]

If, as Theodor Adorno argues, "The need to let suffering speak is the condition of all truth," then Job's panged words in this chapter deserve careful attention.[22] He has arrived at that place "in the land of pain," where, as Daudet puts it, "There are days, long days, when the only part of me that's alive is my pain."[23] ["I Like a Look of Agony, Because I Know It's True"] The rhetoric of pain is the cry for help (vv. 20, 24, 28). The cry may be ignored, it may be criticized, it may be betrayed, but it will not be silenced. The "brother of jackals" and the "companion of ostriches" wails on while others from their respective distances—friends, God, and not least, we his readers—decide whether Job has a place in our world or not.

"Violence Is Never Just, Though Justice May Sometime Require It"

📖 Violence is never just, though Justice may sometime require it: tyrants are persons to whom requisite evil is fun.

W. H. Auden, "Shorts II," *W. H. Auden Collected Poems*, ed. E. Mendelson (New York: Vintage International, 1991), 859.

"I Like a Look of Agony, Because I Know It's True"

📖 I like a look of Agony,
Because I know it's true—
Men do not sham Convulsion,
Nor simulate, a Throe—

The Eyes glaze once—and that is
Death—
Impossible to feign
The Beads upon the Forehead
By homely Anguish strung.

E. Dickinson, "# 241," *The Complete Poems of Emily Dickinson*, ed. T. H. Johnson (Boston/New York: Little, Brown and Company, 1960), 110.

NOTES

[1] J. Wharton, *Job,* (*Westminster Bible Companion*; Louisville KY: Westminster John Knox Press, 1999), 126; cf. N. Habel, *The Book of Job: A Commentary* (OTL; Philadelphia: Westminster Press, 1985), 417.

[2] Ibid., 125.

[3] Ibid.

[4] Cf. S. Sontag, *Regarding the Pain of Others* (New York: Farrar, Straus and Giroux, 2003), 111.

[5] C. Newsom, "The Book of Job," in vol. 4 of *NIB* (Nashville: Abingdon Press, 1996), 546.

[6] For this term, see J. Collins, "The Zeal of Phinehas: The Bible and the Legitimation of Violence," JBL 122 (2003): 3.

[7] The word "dust" (*'āpār*) occurs more than two dozen times in Job (e.g., 4:19; 5:6; 7:21; 10:9; 16:15; 17:16; 20:11; 21:26; 34:15; 42:6). The word "ashes" (*'ēper*) occurs four times (2:8; 13:12; 30:19; 42:6).

[8] The Hebrew phrase that NRSV translates "you merely look at me" is ambiguous. The parallelism of the verse may support either inferring or inserting a negative (*lō'*) before the verb, thus "you do not answer me" // "you do not look at me," a reading followed by the Vulgate. Alternatively, one may read the text as it stands, without the negative, in which case the form of the verb (*titbōnen*) indicates looking *intensely*, that is, *with close scrutiny*.

[9] W. E. B. Du Bois, *The Souls of Black Folk* (New York: Bantam Books, 1989), 177-87.

[10] M. Pope (*Job* [AB; Garden City NY: Doubleday, 1979], 310) cites Pliny, who "thought the bird silly because it imagined that when its head was thrust in a bush, the whole body was concealed." Further, he notes Seneca's account of an incident in which a person was so insulted at being called an ostrich that he wept.

[11] D. J. A. Clines, "Why Is There a Book of Job and What Does It Do to You if You Read It?" *The Book of Job,* ed. W. A. M. Beuken (Leuven: Leuven University Press, 1994), 1-20.

[12] Sontag, *Regarding the Pain of Others*, 7.

[13] Ibid., 99-100.

[14] Ibid., 40.

[15] Ibid., 42.

[16] Dickinson, "# 604," *The Complete Poems of Emily Dickinson*, ed. T. H. Johnson (Boston/New York: Little, Brown and Company, 1960), 296.

[17] On the genetic bases for moral sentiments like fear and outrage, see E. O. Wilson, "The Biological Basis of Morality," *Atlantic Monthly* (April 1998): 53-70.

[18] H. G. Wells, *The Undying Fire* (New York: The Macmillan Company, 1919), 208.

[19] Ibid.

[20] M. Soloveichik, "The Virtue of Hate," *First Things* 129 (January 2003): 41-46.

[21] J. Kaminsky, "Violence in the Bible," *Religious Studies News/SBL Edition* (June 2003): 3.

[22] Cited in *Strange Fire: Reading the Bible After the Holocaust*, ed. T. Linafelt (Sheffield: Sheffield Academic Press, 2000), 267. Within this collection of essays, see further Elie Wiesel's reflections on Adorno's suggestion, "Matters of Survival: A Conversation. Elie Wiesel and Timothy K. Beal," 22-35.

[23] A. Daudet, *In the Land of Pain*, ed. and trans. J. Barnes (New York: Alfred A. Knopf, 2002), 29.

JOB'S DECLARATION OF INNOCENCE

Job 31:1-40

With his lyre "turned to mourning" (30:31), Job sets his last words in this discourse to the tune of innocence. With a series of oaths, he swears that he is not guilty of any wrong, either by act or by attitude, which justifies the treatment he has received from his community and from God. The ethical and moral code by which Job swears is so comprehensive, so lofty, so far beyond most any imaginable reproach that commentators yield to hyperbole in the effort to describe it. It has been esteemed as a "priceless testament"[1] and as "one of the great literary utterances in the Bible and without."[2] It expresses "in exquisite terms the highest moral conscience in the O.T."[3] It "reflects a standard of behavior which is unexcelled either in the Old Testament, the literature of the Ancient Near East and classical Greece, or in the New Testament, not excluding the Sermon on the Mount."[4] "It cannot be disputed," one commentator concludes, "that the Job who utters the oaths of purity in chapter 31 stands almost alone upon an ethical summit."[5] One can only imagine that the words "almost alone" leave room on this summit for God and Jesus.

For all of its appeal, however, Job's ethical and moral code invites careful critique and perhaps a more sober assessment. Job's oath concerning adultery, for example, seeks to validate his innocence by exposing his wife to punishment, if there is sufficient evidence to prove him wrong (vv. 9-10). There is no nobility in Job's self-serving and proprietary view of women. As Good says, "For a speech full of high-flown ethical principles, this one falls with a crash to the earth."[6] It is not only the odd, perhaps aberrant, detail of Job's ethical code that occasions pause; it is also the overall tenor. Job's presumption that innocence guarantees acquittal and restoration suggests that for all his criticisms of the friends, he remains enraptured by their doctrine of retribution. His innocence means that he *deserves* better treatment. Some have seen his retreat to conventional understandings of reward and punishment as an indication that "Retribution is now the heart on Job's sleeve."[7] The upside of Job's moral certitude is his conviction that the random imposition of evil upon good has no place either in his ethics or God's. Wrongs must and will be righted. In Job's world, there are no exceptions, no contradictions, no alternatives. The downside of Job's certitude is that by sacralizing his personal virtues of righteousness and justice (29:14), he risks creating God in his own image. Job's view of what justice requires becomes God's view, de facto.[8] Moreover, Job's appropriation of royal imagery (31:37: "like a prince"; cf. 29:25: "like a king") has suggested to some that he covets God's throne, that, in effect, he believes his administration of justice (29:12-17) makes him more qualified to be the "Judge of all the earth" (Gen 18:25) than God (see further, [King Job]; [Job's Royal and Priestly Anthropology]).[9] Given both the details and the tenor of Job's words, it is perhaps not surprising that even commentators who are ultimately sympathetic describe his claims with phrases like "virulent self-righteousness,"[10] "unbridled presumption,"[11] and "wreckless bravery."[12] In the end, Job's audience, specifically now we readers, must decide whether Job's declaration of innocence is a "manifesto of integrity"[13] or a "comic parody."[14]

Consideration of two matters—the *form* and the *function* of the text—plays a critical role in the interpretive positions readers may take. The text is *formed* by four kinds of expressions: questions (vv. 2-4, 14-15); statements of fact (vv. 11-12, 18, 23, 28, 30, 32); statements of hope/expectation (vv. 35-37); and oaths. The oaths follow two patterns (see further [Vows in the Old Testament]). The conventional oath consists of an "if" clause (protasis), which describes a possible transgression, followed by a "then" clause (apodosis), which stipulates the penalty expected: "*If* I have done X, *then* let Y happen to me." This pattern occurs 4x: vv. 7-8, 9-10, 21-22, 38-40. A second version of this pattern has only the "if" clause, "*If* I have done X. . . ," without any statement of penalty. This abbreviated version of the oath is the rhetorical equivalent of an assertion of innocence so strong that one need not even consider the possibility of punishment: "I *have not* done X!" [Shouting to Make Oneself Clearer] This pattern is more frequent in Job's speech, occurring in vv. 5, 13, 16-17, 19-20, 24, 25, 26, 29, 31, 33.

The diversity of the expressions, plus the possibility for grouping them in different ways, makes it difficult to determine precisely how many oaths Job declares. Proposals range from ten to sixteen. The most persuasive and the most theologically suggestive proposal comes from Robert Gordis, who argues that Job swears his innocence to fourteen sins.[15] ["The Code of A Man of Honor"] The use of seven and its multiples is a fre-

Shouting to Make Oneself Clearer

Robbie Turner, a character in Ian McEwan's *Atonement*, types a letter to Cecilia, his best friend since childhood, to explain his recent behavior. He first tries jokes, then melodrama, and plaintiveness. None of these rhetorical strategies seem sufficient to convey the weight of what he needs to say, so he begins switching back and forth between questions and exclamations, both of which are tactics for communication that give him pause.

The rhetorical questions had a clammy air; the exclamation mark was the first resort of those who shout to make themselves clearer. He forgave this punctuation only in his mother's letters where a row of five indicated a jolly good joke. He turned the drum and typed an *x*. "Cecilia, I don't think I can blame the heat." Now the humor was removed, and an element of self-pity had crept in. The exclamation mark would have to be reinstated. Volume was obviously not his only business.

I. McEwan, *Atonement* (New York: Doubleday, 2002), 80.

"The Code of A Man of Honor"

This Code of A Man of Honor is the noblest presentation of individual ethics in the pages of the Bible. It lists fourteen sins, from which, Job insists, he has been free:

1. lust (vv. 1, 2)
2. cheating in business (vv. 5, 6)
3. taking the property of others (vv. 7, 8)
4. adultery (vv. 9-12)
5. unfairness toward slaves in the courts (vv. 13-15)
6. callousness toward the resident poor (vv. 16-18)
7. lack of pity for the wayfarer (vv. 19, 20)
8. perversion of the just claims of the widow and the orphan (vv. 21-23)
9. love of gold and confidence in wealth (vv. 24-25)
10. the worship of the sun and the moon (vv. 26-28)
11. joy in the calamity of his foes (vv. 29-31)
12. failure to practice hospitality (v. 32)
13. concealing his sins because of the fear of public opinion (vv. 33, 34)
14. the expropriation of land of others within the letter of the law (vv. 38-40)

R. Gordis, *The Book of Job: Commentary, New Translation, and Special Studies* (New York: Jewish Theological Seminary of America, 1978), 542.

---

quent rhetorical device in the Old Testament for setting forth a complete catalogue of items (e.g., Eccl 3:2-8; 7:1-14; Amos 1:3–2:5). Job's double heptad (7 x 2) signals a categorical denial of any conceivable guilt whatsoever. The enumeration of fourteen sins provides a theologically evocative inclusio with Job's seven-fold curse of his beginnings in chapter 3. With his first words from the ash heap, Job cursed life and longed for the relief of death. With his declaration of innocence in chapter 31, he swears by the virtues of his life that he deserves not only to live but also to be respected for his integrity. Both his curse and his sworn declaration of innocence are rhetorical acts of "sevening"[16] that make specific use of creation theology. The former seeks to undo the day of his birth into unjustified suffering, and by implication, the primordial day of the world's beginning, which precipitated a cosmic slide into misery (see the commentary on 3:3-10). The latter appeals to Job's own righteousness and justice as a model for redeeming the afflicted (note, for example, the "womb" imagery in 31:13-15) and restoring the world (31:38-40). The literary envelope provided by chapters 3 and 31 suggests that all that transpires in between—Job's curses and complaints, the friends' counter-arguments, and now Job's final insistence on his personal integrity—has to do, ultimately, with nothing less than the ethical and moral foundation of creation.

Questions of *form* set the table for consideration of the *function* of the text. What does Job hope to accomplish? What is the objective of his various rhetorical moves in this chapter, especially his oaths of innocence? Scholars have advanced a variety of proposals, but two deserve special attention.

(1) A number of clues point to the possibility that Job has adopted legal rhetoric, sworn testimony, which will force his accuser into a formal trial. [17] His oaths of purity, which are similar to well-attested legal practices in the ancient Near East, extend Job's previous explorations of the possibility of litigation (see [The Trial Metaphor in Job]). ["The Protestation of Guiltlessness"] The demand for someone to hear his case, the expectation of a written document or "indictment" from his "adversary at law," and the firm belief in ultimate exoneration appear to bring Job's explorations to a climax with a legal maneuver that forces God to appear in court: "Here is my signature! Let the Almighty answer me!" (vv. 35-37).

"The Protestation of Guiltlessness"

Job's oaths are often compared with similar negative confessions from ancient Near Eastern literature. One prominent example is the Egyptian funerary text "The Protestation of Guiltlessness," which portrays the prayer of the deceased upon entering the hall of judgment. The excerpt below describes what is said before Osiris and the forty-two judges of the dead who will weigh the heart of the suppliant on the balances of truth.

> What is said on reaching the Broad-Hall of the Two Justices, absolving X of every sin which he has committed, and seeing the faces of the gods:
>   Hail to thee, O great god, lord of the Two Justices! I have come to thee, my lord, I have been brought that I might see thy beauty. . . . I have brought thee justice; I have expelled deceit for thee. I have not committed evil against men. I have not mistreated cattle. I have not committed sin in the place of truth. I have not known that which is not. I have not seen evil . . . . I have not blasphemed a god. I have not done violence to a poor man. I have not done that which the gods abominate. I have not defamed a slave to his superior. I have not made (anyone) sick. I have not made (anyone) weep. I have not killed. I have given no order to a killer. I have not caused suffering. I have not cut down on the food (income) in the temples. . . . I have not had sexual relations with a boy. I have not defiled myself. I have neither increased or diminished the grain-measure. . . .

> I have not added to the weight of the balance. I have not weakened the plummet of the scales. I have not taken milk from the mouths of children. . . . I am pure!—[repeated] four times.

The negative confessions are subsequently balanced by affirmations of sinless behavior:

> Behold me—I have come to you without sin, without guilt, without evil, without a witness (against me), without one against whom I have taken action. I live on truth, and I eat truth. I have done that which men said and that with which the gods are content. I have satisfied a god with that which he desires. I have given bread to the hungry, water to the thirsty, clothing to the naked, and a ferry-boat to him who was marooned . . . . (So) rescue me, you; protect me, you. Ye will not make report against me in the presence [of the great god.] I am one pure of mouth and pure of hands, one to whom "Welcome, welcome, in peace!" is said by those who see him . . . . I am one who has a concern for the gods, who knows the nature of their bodies. I have come here to testify to justice and to bring the scales [in which the character of the deceased was weighed] to their (proper) position in the cemetery. (For the full text, see ANET, 3rd ed. with supplement, ed. J. B. Pritchard [Princeton: Princeton University Press, 1969], 34-36.)

For further discussion of these and other ancient Near Easter parallels, see G. Fohrer, "The Righteous Man in Job 31," *Essays in New Testament Ethics*, ed. J. Crenshaw, J. T. Wills (New York: KTAV Publishing House, 1974), 9-19; R. Gordis, *The Book of Job* (New York: Jewish Theological Seminary of America, 1978), 546.

The legal language provides a specific context for assessing Job's objectives. It accents Job's pursuit of *justice*, his need for a *fair and impartial hearing of evidence*, his belief that *innocence and guilt* are not disposable qualities, either in life or in law, and his presumption that *if God is just*, then *God will bear witness* to his truth. [To Exonerate Injustice Is "Precious Service Rendered . . . to the Negators of Truth"]

(2) There are also clues that Job's rhetoric, for all its legal connotations, aims at objectives that cannot be confined to the courtroom. The claims Job makes for himself fall largely outside the realm of what the law can either verify or correct. Of the *actions* Job swears he has not done, only adultery (vv. 9-12) constitutes a punishable offense. The rest of Job's claims concern *attitudes*, e.g., fairness toward slaves (vv. 13-15), generosity toward the poor (vv. 16-18), hospitality to strangers (v. 32), and hypocrisy concerning his own flaws (vv. 33-34). Failure in any one of these areas may occasion personal shame and invite public scorn, but it does not require juridical sanction. "In sum," as Gordis notes, "the sins listed are not the crimes of the lawbreaker; at most they are the offenses of the lawbender."[18]

Job's claims have to do with what J. Gerald Janzen calls "a primal sympathy" for moral and ethical relationships that is prior to and generative of the social customs that are codified in legal statues.[19] Carol Newsom has developed this perspective in a most instructive way. She has shown that Job's rhetoric throughout chapters 29-31 bears witness to his convictions about the moral ethos that seeds and sustains an ethical society. Job's oaths are "preoccupied with the problem of the ethics of power in relationships of inequality."[20] When he claims that he has not used power abusively against his male or female slaves (vv.

To Exonerate Injustice Is "Precious Service Rendered . . . to the Negators of Truth"

The following excerpts are from Clive James's review of Primo Levi's last book, *The Drowned and the Saved*. Levi writes of the horrors he witnessed at Auschwitz and survived, until he died in 1987, apparently having thrown himself into the stairwell of the house in which he had been born.

One of Levi's several triumphs as a moralist—for once the word can be used with unmixed approval—is that he analysed these deep and complicated feelings of unexpungible shame without lapsing into the relativism that everyone was guilty. If everyone was guilty, then everyone was innocent, and Levi is certain that his persecutors were not innocent.

Levi manages to sympathize even with the Kapos, not all of whom were sadists, and all of whom

wanted to live. Levi has no sympathy for the persecutors, but he is ready to understand them, as long as he is not asked to exonerate them. His patience runs out only when it comes close to those who parade their compassion without realizing that they are trampling on the memory of the innocent dead. As a writer, Levi always keeps his anger in check, the better to distribute its intensity, but occasionally you sense that he is on the verge of an outburst . . . . [he] expresses just enough contempt to give us an inkling of what his fury would have been like if he had ever let rip. To confuse the murderers with their victims, he says, "is a moral disease or an aesthetic affectation or a sinister sign of complicity; above all, it is precious service rendered (intentionally or not) to the negators of truth."

C. James, "Primo Levi's Last Will and Testament," *As of This Writing: The Essential Essays, 1968–2002* (New York, London: W. W. Norton and Company, 2003), 261-62.

13-15), or against strangers (v. 32), or even to exploit the land (vv. 38-40), he testifies to his personal investment in what he firmly believes are the moral values that make life peaceable and fulfilling.

The moral and ethical connotations of Job's rhetoric provide another hermeneutical context for assessing his objectives in chapter 31. They accentuate his *personal integrity*, his belief that a solitary individual's *personal ethics* make a vital contribution to *communal solidarity*, his presumption that an honorable declaration of personal virtues gives God the opportunity to affirm God's own commitment to relationships that are moral and ethical. Whereas the legal metaphor envisions a plaintiff, a defendant, and a verdict that vindicates one party by falsifying the claims of the other, the moral formation metaphors that Janzen and Newsom emphasize tilt interpretation in a different, but complementary, direction. Newsom assesses the appeal of this perspective as follows:

> By keeping the focus of the audience upon the judgment to be rendered on his own character, the oath allows Job to negotiate his grievance against God and his community in a way that results in the preservation of the honor of all parties rather than the honoring of one at the expense of the shaming of the other. In modern terms, it allows Job to frame things as a win/win situation rather than a win/lose one.[21]

The commentary below will explore the questions of form and function with one eye cocked to the issues surveyed above. Gordis's delineation of Job's oaths will be primary. The legal and moral claims of Job's words will be held in tension. The comments follow Newsom's outline, not because this settles matters, but because it opens up additional possibilities for reflection. In view of the creation theology that laces the whole of this chapter, her six-part structure invites the thought that the interpretive process may not be complete without a seventh element, which perhaps only God and we, Job's audience, can provide. With this possibility in mind, we read knowing in advance that we may have to decide whether Job's stance here still merits the primordial seventh day assessment that the world is "very good." [Structure of Job 31:1-40]

Structure of Job 31:1-40

C. Newsom identifies five topical groups of oaths, interrupted by Job's wish for a hearing in vv. 35-37. Taken as a whole, the six-part structure may be illustrated as follows.

(1) Sexual ethics and general morality (vv. 1-12)

(2) Justice and social obligation (vv. 13-23)

(3) Ultimate allegiance (vv. 24-28)

(4) Social relations (vv. 29-34)

   (5) Job's wish for a hearing (vv. 35-37)

(6) Land ethics (vv. 38-40)

C. Newsom, "The Book of Job," in vol. 4 of *NIB* (Nashville: Abingdon Press, 1996), 552; *The Book of Job: A Contest of Moral Imaginations* (Oxford: Oxford University Press, 2003), 195.

COMMENTARY

"I Have Made a Covenant with My Eyes," 31:1-12

Job's declaration of innocence derives from the "covenant" he has made (v. 1). The word "covenant" (*bĕrît*) is the most freighted of all the terms the Old Testament uses to describe the commitments and responsibilities that bind God and Israel together in an indissoluble relationship. The word occurs only three times in Job, but these references provide insight into the perspectives of the three major characters in the book: the friends, Job, and God.

• The first occurrence, 5:23, is in Eliphaz's initial counsel to Job. Job's restitution, *if* he can learn to accept misfortune (5:17-18), Eliphaz says, is the promise that one day he shall be in "covenant" (NRSV: "league") with the stones of the field and at "peace" with the wild animals. The promise evokes the hope of a reversal of the primordial punishment that led to banishment from the garden (Gen 3:17-19; see the commentary on Job 5:8-27) and a restoration of the partnership between creatures and creation that returns the world to Edenic harmony.

• The second occurrence is in the present text, where Job declares that he has made a covenant with his eyes. To make a covenant *with the eyes* is an unusual twist on the conventional language. Since the eye symbolizes desire, Job's claim is that he has entered into a covenant with his innermost psychic passions, enumerated in the fourteen oaths to follow, that enables him to be at peace (in union) with himself and with his world. The last of these oaths concerns Job's relationship with the land (vv. 38-40). His claim to have been a good steward of the land's resources also echoes the garden imagery of Genesis 2–3. Job's perspective on these matters is of course not the same as his friends, but his covenant does not ultimately aim at different objectives than those Eliphaz urges upon him in 5:23. Job also yearns for the day when there will be harmony between creature and creation, and he too believes that personal ethics, specifically one's response to misfortune, has a critical bearing on when and how this hope may be realized.

• The third occurrence of covenant is in God's long awaited speech to Job. In a complex survey of creation, God singles out two animals, Behemoth (40:15-24) and Leviathan (41:1-34 [MT 40:25–41:26]), which require Job's special attention. Both are described as creatures that possess extraordinary strength and power. Leviathan's power is associated with its mouth, more specifically with what does and does not come forth from its mouth. What *does not* come forth from its mouth are "soft words," for in the unlikely event that this creature should ever be captured and forced into domestication, it would not even then make a "covenant" with its master that resulted in passivity (41:3-4 [MT 40:27-28]). What *does* come forth from Leviathan's mouth are fire and light, smoke and flames, phenomena elsewhere identified with the strong and compelling appearance of divinity (41:18-21 [MT 41:10-13]). Like Eliphaz, God uses creation imagery, animals, and covenant rhetoric to commend something to Job. Presumably God's objective is to say something that connects with Job's own covenantal instincts, something that enlarges, modifies, and/or corrects his understanding of how to respond rightly to misfortune.

It is instructive to imagine that as Job begins to unfold his oaths of innocence, he finds himself standing in between these three perspectives on what it means to be in covenantal relationship with God. He has heard the friends say that the prerequisite for the restoration he seeks is a covenantal relationship defined by humility and passive acceptance of the misfortunes God may use to discipline him. Readers know, in advance of Job, that God will speak of models that commend other covenantal virtues, including strong words and fierce resistance. Between these covenantal perspectives, both known and yet to be disclosed, Job dares to insert his own views. [The Covenantal Frame for Job's Oaths]

The Covenantal Frame for Job's Oaths

AΩ N. Habel notes that the overall design of Job 31 reflects a "coherent double frame." The outer frame (vv. 1-3, 38-40) consists of covenantal motifs that both ground and define Job's oaths of purity (vv. 7-34). The inner frame (vv. 4-6, 35-37) consists of a double (covenantal) challenge to God. Although I will not follow Habel's outline in this commentary, his understanding of the design of this speech helps to highlight the importance of the covenant theme.

A **Covenant and Curse Motif**—Job's past covenant and expected covenant curses (31:1-3)

　B Challenge—Challenge for God to weigh Job in the balance of justice since he has *counted* (*spr*) Job's *steps* (vv. 4-6)

　　C Catalogue of Crimes (vv. 7-34)

　B1 Challenge—Challenge for God to provide a legal document (*seper*); then Job will repeat the *count* (*spr*) of his *steps* before God (vv. 35-37)

A1 **Covenant Witness and Curse**—Final oath relating to the ground/earth as witness to covenantal oaths (vv. 38-40)

N. Habel, *The Book of Job: A Commentary* (OTL; Philadelphia: Westminster Press, 1985), 427-28.

Job's first four oaths begin (vv. 1-4) and end (vv. 9-12) with claims of innocence in the area of sexual ethics. The violation of a virgin is a punishable offense, because it threatens the rights of the father and jeopardizes the social cohesiveness of the community's organization (Exod 22:16-17 [MT 22:15-16], Deut 22:23-29). Job insists that he has not only not violated the law, he has also avoided every temptation to do so. He has held himself to a higher code. He has not even "looked upon" an unmarried woman (v. 1b), nor has he opened his heart to the possibility of being seduced into the "heinous crime" of committing adultery with another man's wife (vv. 9-12; cf. Exod 20:17; Deut 5:21; Prov 6:20-35). The seriousness with which Job views adultery is made clear in the sanctions he evokes and the consequences he envisions. The sanction, if he has violated another man's wife and thus undermined familial bonds, should be the sexual subjugation of his own wife to another master (v. 10: "let my wife grind for another")[22] and thus the violation of his own family. The consequences of adultery extend far beyond the family, however. Job likens them to a fire burning out of control, consuming everything in its path, ultimately extending its destruction to the cosmic depths of Abaddon, the domain of the dead (v. 12; cf. 26.6; 28:22; see further [Abaddon]). The rationale for Job's adherence to a strict code of ethics is his conviction that the sexual abuse of another, which may be committed secretly, will be seen clearly by God. God numbers every step he takes and factors every move he makes into the blessings and punishments (vv. 2-4: the "portion" and "heritage") apportioned for life on earth. God's accountability to a code of sexual ethics, Job assumes, is the same as his own (see also [Is There One Moral Law for Heaven and Another for the Earth?])

Job's claim not to have abused women frames and is explicated by two additional oaths (vv. 5-6, 7-8) that assert his commitment to ethical relationships in other areas of his life. Because he is a person of "integrity" (*tummāh*; cf. 2:3, 9, 27:5), he has not "walked with falsehood" or hustled toward "deceit" (vv. 5-6). The claim may be a general disavowal of unethical behavior, but the sanction Job invokes—"let me weighed in a just balance"—suggests that he has not cheated in commercial transactions by rigging the scales with false weights and measures. Such a practice is widely condemned throughout the ancient Near East and in the Old Testament by prophets, priests, and sages (e.g., Lev 19:35-36; Deut 25:13-16; Amos 8:5; Mic 6:10-11; Ezek 45:10; Prov 11:1; 16:11; 20:10, 23). [The Scales of Justice] Gordis interprets the following oath (vv. 7-8) as also having to do with business ethics, specifically coveting and taking another's property, the sanction against which is the forfeiture (or failure) of one's own harvest.[23] Other scholars have noted that *ṣe'ĕṣā'îm*, the word used in v. 8 to describe what

The Scales of Justice

Concern for honest business practices is widespread, not only in the ancient Near East and Israel, but also in the New Testament (e.g., Matt 7:2) and in contemporary society (witness the scandal in the United States and abroad that accompanied the corporate meltdown in 2002 of Enron and WorldCom).

In the ancient Near East, the Egyptian *Book of the Dead* describes the heart of the deceased being weighed against a feather, which is the symbol of truth and justice. The god Anubis controls the balance; the scribe Thoth records the verdict and announces it. (Cf. S. Morenz, *Egyptian Religion* [London: Metheuen and Company, 1973], 126-27.) The Babylonian "Hymn to Samas" (c. 900–700 BC) distinguishes between the honest and dishonest merchant as follows:

Anubis/Thoth
Horus supervising the weighing of the heart in the hall of judgment (psychostasis), Thoth and Anubis stand by the scales. Casket for Ushebtis (funerary statuettes).

21st dynasty (1085-950 BC). Wood, stucco, paint. Louvre, Paris, France. (Credit: Giraudon/Art Resource, NY)

The merchant who practices trickery as he holds the corn measure,
Who weighs out loans (or corn) by the minimum standard, but requires a large quantity in repayment,
The curse of the people will overtake him before his time,
If he demanded repayment before the agreed date, there will be guilt upon him.
His heir will not assume the control of the property,
Nor will his brothers take over his estate.
The honest merchant who weighs out loans (of corn) by the maximum standard, thus multiplying
    kindness,
It is pleasing to Samas, and he will prolong his life.
He will enlarge his family, gain wealth,
And like the water of a never failing stream [his] descendants will never fail. (For the text, see W. G. Lambert, *Babylonian Wisdom Literature* [Oxford: Clarendon Press, 1960], 126-38; the lines cited are 112-21.)

Not surprisingly, then, Israel prophets, priests, and sages were similarly concerned with the temptation to unethical commercial transactions. Of particular note is Amos's criticism of the priestly establishment for fostering rituals that feign fidelity to God while turning a blind eye to unethical behavior in the marketplace, e.g., Amos 8:4-5:

Hear this, you that trample on the needy, and bring to ruin the poor of the land, Saying, "When will the new moon be over so that we may sell grain; and the Sabbath, so that we offer wheat for sale? We will make the ephah small and the shekel great, and practice deceit with false balances.

It may be argued that the priests (with whom Job seems to identify; see the commentary throughout this chapter) were alert to the problem and sought to respond to it and correct it by emphasizing that there should be no disconnect between proper rituals offered in the sanctuary and ethical behavior in everyday life, e.g., Lev 19:2, 35-36:

You shall be holy, for I the Lord your God am holy. . . .You shall not cheat in measuring length, weight, or quantity. You shall have honest balances, honest weights, an honest ephah, and an honest hin: I am the Lord your God who brought you out of the land of Egypt.

is rooted out, may refer to "offspring" or "progeny" (as elsewhere in Job: 5:25; 21:8; 27:14), in which case the punishment—loss of children—hardly seems appropriate for the crime.[24] The issue may be more technical than hermeneutically decisive. The various body parts listed ("feet" [NRSV: "steps"], "heart," "eyes," "hands") serve as metaphors for the totality of Job's actions and attitudes (cf. Prov 4:20-27).

The juxtaposition of oaths dealing with legal (adultery) and moral/ethical issues (sexual attitudes, business ethics) invites a return to the questions about form and function introduced above. Whether the sum of Job's oaths is fourteen, as Gordis argues, or another number, there is a general consensus that with the exception of the oath concerning the worship of heavenly bodies (vv. 26-28), the transgressions named have to do with ethical, not ritual, matters. This consensus typically includes two observations: (1) the transgressions are stylistically similar to ancient Near Eastern confessional texts in which worshippers (or a priest as their cultic mediator) stand before the seat of divine judgment and swear their innocence by enumerating sins, intentional and unintentional, that they have not committed (see [The Protestations of Guiltlessness]); and (2) Job's oaths of innocence, while similar in many respects to these Near Eastern models, are fundamentally different from them, because, as G. Fohrer argues, "they seek to put cultic purity on the same level as ethical purity," an equation Fohrer assumes is incompatible with Israelite thought.[25] Fohrer's assumption deserves close scrutiny. If it is unfounded, then the parallels between Job's so-called *ethical* oaths and ancient Near Eastern *ritual* prototypes require further consideration.

The presumption that the Israelites differentiated between cultic purity and ethical purity has a longstanding place in biblical scholarship. Concern for cultic purity has generally been regarded as the responsibility of Israel's priests, who were charged with the stewardship of the rituals, specifically the administration of the sacrificial system, which were observed in the tabernacle and temple. Ethical matters, specifically the requirements for justice and righteousness in everyday life, have been associated primarily with the prophets. Prophetic criticism of the priests served to solidify the notion that a preoccupation with ritual led to their neglect of the weightier matters of social justice (e.g., Isa 1:10-17; Amos 2:1-16; Mic 3:9-12). The book of Job, particularly the oaths in this chapter, offers an interesting vantage point for scrutinizing the assumption that Israel's ethical and ritual codes of conduct were divisible concerns. Three observations invite further reflection.

(1) The prologue (chs. 1–2) and epilogue (42:7-17) suggest a *priestly profile* for Job (see [Job's Royal and Priestly Anthropology]). [Job as Priest] Job 1:5

describes his presentation of "burnt offerings" (*ʿōlôt*) on behalf of his children as a preemptive sacrificial expiation for any inadvertent sins they may have committed. Job 42:8 reports that Job receives the "burnt offering" (*ʿōlôh*) presented by the friends, who require his cultic mediation if God is to forgive their wrongdoings. Although these references are oblique and do not envision a formal ritual setting, they evoke the image of Job as a priest to his family and his community.[26] The priestly frame for the book provides a wider context for reflecting on the internal debate between Job and the friends concerning the doctrine of retribution (see [Retribution]). What is at stake is not only the conventional dogma that God prospers the righteous and punishes the wicked. It is also, and perhaps even more fundamentally, the Priestly tradition's advocacy for the effectiveness of the entire ritual system. Job's reliance on the sacrificial system for maintaining his relationship to God appears initially to work quite satisfactorily, for as the prologue opens, there is no sign of evil's intrusion anywhere in his world. By the end of the prologue, however, this one who always "turned away from evil" (*raʿ*; 1:1) is overwhelmed by "evil" (*rāʿāh*, 2:11; NRSV: "troubles") that has come to him, by God's own admission, "for no reason" (2:3).

This turn of events brings into play a range of critical questions, not least from the priestly perspective. What covenantal code of ethics justifies God's gratuitous punishment of a person God declares is "blameless and upright" (1:8; 2:3)? Of what use is the ritual system to a person who has no sin, known or unknown, to atone for? What rituals, if any, hold God accountable? What sacrifices atone for divine caprice or at least repair the

Saint Job as Priest

16th C. Wood Sculpture. Church of Saint-Martin, Wezemaal, Belgium. Courtesy Institut Royal du Patrimoine Artistique, Brussels

Job as Priest

S. Terrien notes that more than forty statues of "Saint Job the Priest" are preserved in Belgium, Luxembourg, and the Netherlands. This statue in the Church of Saint-Martin in Belgium, a center of Joban pilgrimages in the sixteenth century, shows a priestly robed Job holding in his right hand a placard inscribed (in Flemish) with the words from the prologue that define his piety: "The Lord gave, and the Lord has taken away; blessed be the name of the Lord" (1:21). The object in Job's left hand is likely the host or chalice of the Eucharist.

S. Terrien, *The Iconography of Job Through the Centuries* (University Park PN: The Pennsylvania State University Press, 1996), 149-58.

damage and rehabilitate the innocent victim? Once Job opens the door on these questions, the priestly system that supplies his moral compass for navigating the world must respond effectively or collapse like a house of cards. The epilogue pictures Job ultimately embracing the ritual system and presumably some tethering notion of a covenantal ethic that secures its meaning. How and why he does so is a principal issue in the book.[27]

(2) Inside the priestly frame for the book, Job speaks from the ash heap as one afflicted with "loathsome sores" (*šĕḥîn*; 2:7). The term that describes his condition is one of the words used to identify the skin diseases that make a person unclean and needful of the priestly rituals spelled out in Leviticus 13–14. The text is heavy with details, as one expects from Leviticus, but the pertinent emphases are as follows.[28] Leviticus 13:1-44 describes the steps the priest must take to diagnose various skin diseases that render a person unclean and therefore unable to come near God's holy presence. Leviticus 14:1-32 describes the purification rituals for persons who have recovered from a skin disease and may therefore resume their normal activities within the community. Between these two foci, Leviticus 13:45-46 offers a brief but important description of the behavior prescribed for afflicted persons. The ritual requires that they tear their clothes, dishevel their hair, cover their mouth, and cry out, "Unclean, unclean!" This symbolic enactment of their affliction confirms that they know themselves to be repugnant to the community. They must cry out a warning, lest others inadvertently come too close to their impurity, and they must banish themselves by living alone outside the community for the duration of their affliction (cf. Num 5:1-4). The only thing that stands between them and a final dismissal to the grave of the forgotten is the very ritual that mandates their exclusion. One day, perhaps, the priest will say, "He is clean" (13:6, 13, 17, 23, 28, 34, 35, 37, 38, 40). Until then, they must wait and cry and trust in the efficacy of the ritual.

Job's story provides an insider's perspective on what it means to live in the gap between Leviticus 13:1-44 and 14:1-32. Job is portrayed in the prologue and epilogue as clinging to his faith and to the rituals by which he enacts it. The debate with his friends centers on whether this faith and these rituals can pass muster when tested by suffering that comes "for no reason." The dialogues therefore effectively turn the table. The priestly Job who diligently performs the rituals for his family and friends in the book's frame becomes the one who needs the rituals of restoration that other ministrants may offer him. Simply put, the priest needs a priest. [Inside the Priestly Rituals] The friends, the first to volunteer for ministry to Job, are the spokespersons for religious orthodoxy, and by extension, for the priestly establishment. Eliphaz,

Inside the Priestly Rituals

📖 Jean Fouquet's 15th century illumination depicts Job, lying forlorn on a pile of manure, as one of the oppressed and famished outcasts in French society. His place is outside the walled city, where the Tower of Vincennes (outside Paris) stands opulent and secure. On the manicured grounds just beyond the walls, people go about their normal affairs: a person on horseback sits tall and erect, perhaps surveying his land; two workers amble along in tranquil conversation. Three "friends," dressed in the regalia that identifies their positions of power and privilege, have traveled the long and winding road that leads outside the city to Job. The person to Job's right wears the scarlet that symbolizes the parliament; the person to his left, the royal blue of the monarchy. The figure in the middle, standing before him with hands uplifted to bless, is robed in the white of the church. On first sight the scene suggests concern and sympathy for Job. On closer inspection one notices that the priest who extends the church's blessing does so with eyes closed. Fouquet subtly suggests that the leaders of France's institutional structures, at the center of which stands the church, feign attentiveness to one their own policies have pushed to the margins of society.

Job on the Dung Heap

Jean Fouquet (c.1415/20-1481). *The Hours of Etienne Chevalier, Office of the Dead*.
Musée Condé, Chantilly, France
Photo Credit: Réunion des Musées Nationaux / Art Resource, NY

who always takes the point, tries to convince Job that his affliction is a metaphor for sin and divine judgment. He urges him to accept an understanding of the covenant with God that promises restoration in return for repentance (5:17-27). In his view, there is one and only one option for Job: "Agree with God and be at peace, in this way, good will come to you" (22:21).

Job is not persuaded. Although he knows himself to have become someone the community regards as too repulsive for inclusion in their company (cf. 17:2, 6; 19:13-20; 30:1-15), he persists in believing, against all evidence to the contrary, in a covenant that does not salvage God's justice at the expense of his integrity. No ritual that reduces the vocabulary of faith to the words "Unclean, unclean!" will ever be restorative to victims of innocent suffering. For them, any relationship with God that is worthy of the name "covenant" must include the words "Injustice, injustice!"

(3) Chapter 31 records Job's one and only articulation of an alternative understanding of covenant relationship with God. The covenant he cuts with his eyes emphasizes his belief that ethical behavior and attitudes, no less than religious fidelity (vv. 26-28), demonstrate one's loyalty to God. These same commitments, he insists, lay a sure foundation for a faithful person's appeal to a responding loyalty from God.

Job's fourteen declarations of innocence, as mentioned above, constitute a rhetorical act of "sevening." It is a ritual, no less creative than God's seven primordial declarations ("Let there be"; Gen 1:3, 6, 9, 11, 14, 20, 24) that speaks into being an ethical and moral foundation for the world. It may seem odd that Job begins with sexual ethics, for on first thought such matters seem rather distant from concerns typically associated with covenantal notions of justice and righteousness. Here too, however, Job's identification with priestly concerns opens a window for reflection.

The signature of the book of Leviticus, the *sine qua non* of priestly instruction in the Old Testament, is the summons to "covenantal holiness."[29] The most succinct and memorable expression of this summons occurs in 19:2: "You shall be holy, for I the Lord your God am holy." The inclusio that envelops Leviticus 19 (vv. 2b and 36b) repeats the preamble to the Decalogue (Exod 20:2), thus suggesting that all the explicating instructions for the summons to holiness have the same claim on Israel's obedience as the Ten Commandments. As B. Bamberger has noted, "The ethical component of holiness is not for the priestly writers of the Holiness Code a mere 'extra.'"[30]

Less often noted is the structuring frame of Leviticus 18 and 20, which provides the context for interpreting this all-important summons to holiness.[31] [The Structure of Leviticus 18 and 20] Both chapters begin (18:1-5; 20:7-8) and end (18:24-30; 20:22-26) with exhortations to covenantal obedience. Both chapters extensively explicate the summons to obedience with instructions concerning sexual ethics (18:6-20, 22-23; 20:9-21). Although both chapters include warnings against the

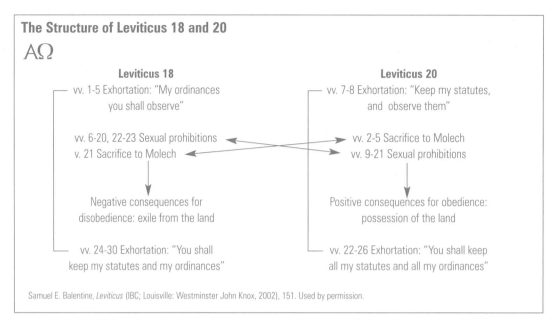

The Structure of Leviticus 18 and 20

AΩ

Leviticus 18	Leviticus 20
vv. 1-5 Exhortation: "My ordinances you shall observe"	vv. 7-8 Exhortation: "Keep my statutes, and observe them"
vv. 6-20, 22-23 Sexual prohibitions	vv. 2-5 Sacrifice to Molech
v. 21 Sacrifice to Molech	vv. 9-21 Sexual prohibitions
Negative consequences for disobedience: exile from the land	Positive consequences for obedience: possession of the land
vv. 24-30 Exhortation: "You shall keep my statutes and my ordinances"	vv. 22-26 Exhortation: "You shall keep all my statutes and all my ordinances"

Samuel E. Balentine, *Leviticus* (IBC; Louisville: Westminster John Knox, 2002), 151. Used by permission.

worship of false gods, they address this concern much more briefly (18:21; 20:2-5). Finally, both chapters warn that moral impurities, principally sexual transgressions, have serious consequences for the land. If the transgressions are committed by individuals, then they will be "cut off" by God from their communities (18:29). But if the transgressions become the norm for the community, then the land will be so sickened by what it has ingested that it will vomit out its abusers (18:25, 28; 20:22). The warning is rooted in creation rhetoric. The first human sin against God's primordial design for a "very good" world was a violation that wounded the land: "Cursed is the ground *because of you*" (Gen 3:17). In sum, the holiness enjoined by Leviticus 19 is framed and defined by instructions that insist covenant fidelity requires more than religious devotion to God. It has also to do with the way human beings treat one another. Given the preoccupation of chapters 18 and 20 with sexual relationships—the most intimate form of human conduct—the texts suggests that the requirement of love for others is equal to, if not greater than, the requirement to love God.

Job's oaths of innocence bear a striking, if tensive, resemblance both to the priestly texts within the Old Testament and to their ancient Near Eastern prototypes. If we imagine him responding to the priestly instructions in Leviticus 18–20, then we may hear him begin the defense of his integrity by affirming that the covenantal commitment that governs the relationships in all areas of his life (e.g., vv. 5-8) is framed and defined by sexual ethics (vv. 1-4, 9-12). If his assertions of innocence are a rhetorical, and potentially creative, act of "sevening," then we are invited to consider that when he imagines himself standing before the throne of divine judgment, like the deceased who claim sinlessness in ancient Near Eastern confessional texts, he would in no way demur from his claim to have lived in ways that sustain the moral foundations of the world, both ritually and ethically (contra Fohrer, see above). There is, however, one major difference between Job's asseverations and those that are highlighted in Leviticus and in the ancient Near Eastern priestly prototypes. Job enumerates all possible transgressions not in order to plead for mercy and forgiveness but instead to claim innocence and demand justice.[32] His demand for justice is clearly couched in legal rhetoric, as commentators have often noted, but it remains quintessentially *ritual* and *ethical.* As Janzen and Newsom have shown, the moral use of power in relationships of inequality is a "primal" instinct that defines righteousness and justice. Job brooks no difference between the mandate to principled love of God and the requirement to live with others in ways that enact this love.

The commentary on the remaining oaths lends itself to the interpretive possibility that the objective of Job's oaths, however they may be delineated, cannot be adequately assessed by separating the legal metaphor of justice from the moral metaphor of personal ethics. Justice requires moral relationships in all areas of life. Moral relationships, whether subject to legal sanction or not, require justice and righteousness that passes muster before God. When Job culminates his oaths with the demand that God appear (31:35-37), he fully expects a response that will exonerate him on legal, moral, ethical, and ritual grounds.

"If I Have Rejected Justice, . . ." 31:13-23

The second group of four oaths is framed by Job's affirmation of justice, both in his household, where his servants look to him to settle their grievances (vv. 13-15), and in the city gate, where the most vulnerable members of the community expect a fair hearing of their cases (vv. 21-23). In both arenas, Job claims to have met and exceeded the legal requirements. The law recognizes only limited rights for male and female slaves (cf. Exod 21:1-11; Lev 25:39-55; Deut 5:14; 15:12-18; 23:15-18). Job recognizes that his servants have a right to justice, not because the law requires it, but because they are human beings. They have been created by the same God and birthed from the same primal womb of compassion as Job, which means their life, regardless of the status assigned them by law or society, carries the full measure of God's hopes and expectations for every human being (v. 15).

The legal requirements of justice extend beyond the private domain of the household to the public arena of the city gate. Here too, in full view of the gathered community, all vulnerable persons in society have a right to a fair and impartial adjudication of their cases. Legal systems can be abused, however, and justice is sometimes a victim. Ruling elders may render verdicts that are influenced by money, politics, or personal ambition. Job swears that he has steered clear of all such compromises. If he has ever raised his hand to condemn (v. 21; cf. Isa 19:16; Zech 2:9) a helpless orphan, simply because his "supporters at the gate" empowered him to do so, then may he be judged with the full weight of the law he has himself corrupted. Verse 22 completes the oath formula with a poetic but palpable quid pro quo expression of the punishment Job would deserve, if he were guilty: let the shoulder that once supported the arm raised in wrongful judgment be separated from its socket; let the arm that extended the hand of a broken justice be broken.

The middle two oaths of this group (vv. 16-18, 19-20) expand Job's affirmations of justice with additional testimony to the moral and ethical integrity of his relationships. Those who live on the margins of society—the poor, the widow, and the orphan—need more than the protection of their legal rights (see further [CD: Attitudes Toward the Poor as a Definition of Wickedness]; [CD: Common Condemnations]). They typically depend on the generosity of others for even the most basic needs. They need a reason to hope, when life's deficiencies cause their vision for the future to dim (v. 16b). They need something to eat, because poverty means they can never guarantee access to food (v. 17). They need clothing and shelter (v. 19), for their own resources are almost never equal to the unpredictable circumstances they face. They need someone like Job has claimed to be (29:12-17), someone who will swear by his own integrity that he is instinctively tuned to their plight (v. 18).

The legal rhetoric of this second group of oaths continues the trial imagery that occurs throughout this chapter. *If* Job is innocent of these transgressions, *then* his accusers, whether the friends (cf. 22:7-9) or God (e.g., 19:6-20), must be judged accordingly. But here too his demand for justice exceeds what any strictly legal verdict can provide. He appeals once more for God's intervention (vv. 14-15, 18, 23; cf. vv. 2-4, 6), not only to acquit him on legal grounds but also to confirm that his conduct is fully in accord with God's own commitment to relationships of justice, not abuse. Two affirmations use loaded language that makes the point. In v. 15, Job grounds his sensitivity to the plight of the helpless in the conviction that he and God share a primal, womb(*reḥem*)-nurtured compassion for those who need their constant care. In v. 18, he calls upon this same womb imagery to explain that he has done his best to image God's model of parental nurture in his own relationships: from his youth God has reared him "like a father"; from his mother's womb (*beten*; lit., "belly") he has learned how to care for those who could not survive without his attention. Job's oaths, therefore, do not seek his personal vindication at the expense of God's guilt (see further the commentary on 40:6-14). They seek God's confirmation that no one who attends to the needs of others, as Job does, can ever be guilty, in any sense of the word, of breaking the only covenant with life that ultimately matters.

"If . . . I Have Been False to God Above," 31:24-28

The third of the five groups, according to Newsom's outline the center of the pentad of oaths, concerns Job's ultimate allegiance. The connection between prosperity and piety is a staple of retributive dogma. The prologue signals the importance of the connection at the very outset when it announces that Job "feared God. . . *and so* he had seven thousand sheep. . ." (1:1-3). The words "and so" invite the suspicion that Job's love of God is motivated by the reward he derives from it. The *satan* asks the critical question that sets in motion the ensuing drama: "Does Job fear God for nothing?" (1:9). The friends tap into the suspicion underlying the question in various ways. Eliphaz, for example, counsels Job to remember that he should place his confidence in the "fear of God" (4:6), because as he later argues, singular allegiance to God promises more than all the material wealth he can acquire (22:24-25). Job has resolutely insisted that when he was a person of means, a situation that clearly no longer exists, he used his resources to improve the lives of the needy, not to leverage power and acclaim (29:12-17; 31:16-20). He reiterates this claim now with an oath repudiating the charge that he is guilty of idolizing wealth. He has neither trusted that his integrity is measured by riches (v. 24) nor boasted because his wealth was great (v. 25). Like his friends, he is in full accord with the wisdom of the sages: "Whoever trusts in riches will fall" (Prov 11:28 [NIV]; cf. Prov 18:11; Pss 49:5-9; 52:7; Sir 5:1-3; 31:1-11).

Idolatry takes many forms; wealth is but one of them. With an additional oath Job swears that he is also innocent of betraying his allegiance to God by worshipping other cosmic powers (vv. 26-28). He has neither looked at the sun or moon nor allowed his heart to be secretly enticed by them. The worship of celestial bodies was widely condemned in ancient Israel (Deut 4:19; 17:2-3; 2 Kgs 21:3-5; Jer 8:1-2). Job's claim not to have done so seems a bit odd, because it is not a serious charge or concern that occurs elsewhere in the book. "Looking" with the eyes and allowing the heart to be "enticed" echoes the language used to describe the temptation to adultery (vv. 1, 9), which perhaps suggests that Job claims to have been faithful to God by refusing to enter into rival relationships of any sort. The meaning of the gesture described in v. 27b—literally, "my hand has kissed my mouth"—is uncertain. The most suggestive proposal comes from Pope, who notes that the kiss, a conventional gesture of intimacy, is associated in the ancient Near East and in the Old Testament with rituals of worshipping gods or idols (Hos 13:2; 1 Kgs 19:18).[33] [Blowing a Kiss to the Gods]

"If I Have Rejoiced at the Ruin of Those Who Hated Me," 31:29-34

Three oaths comprise the fourth group. In the first (vv. 29-31) and third (vv. 33-34), Job grounds his claims of innocence in what he has not done; in the middle oath (v. 32), his innocence rests on the evidence of what he has done. The sequence of these oaths recalls the structural emphases in Leviticus 18–20, which also asserts that covenantal fidelity must be manifest by behavior that says both "no" to what is destructive of the world God has created and "yes" to what sustains this world (see [The Structure of Leviticus 18 and 20]). The summons to holiness in Leviticus 19, like the Decalogue in Exodus 20 that it mirrors, anchors all its negative commands ("You shall not") with two positive exhortations ("You shall"; vv. 19, 37) to keep all God's commandments.

Job's "no" to covenantal infidelity includes two assertions. (1) He has never celebrated the misfortune of others or invoked a curse on those who wish or do him ill (vv. 29-31). Israel's understanding of authentic covenantal piety had a well-worn place for responding to one's enemies in such ways (Pss 52, 59, 64, 69, 109; cf. Jer 11:20; 12:3; 15:15; 17:18; 18:18-23; 20:12; see further [CD: Righteous Anger]). Job has held himself to a higher standard (cf. Prov 14:31; 17:5; 24:17-18; see further the commentary and Connections on 30:1-8). The meaning of v. 31 is uncertain. Habel

The Worshipper of Larsa

Statuette of a kneeling man, known as the "worshipper of Larsa". Dedicated by an inhabitant of Larsa to the god Amurru for the life of Hammurabi.

Early 2nd millenium BC. Bronze and gold. (Credit: Louvre, Paris)

Blowing a Kiss to the Gods

M. Pope notes that the image of placing the hand on the mouth is used to convey both reverent silence (Job 29:9; 40:4; Mic 7:16; Isa 52:15) and adoration of the gods (Hos 13:2; 1 Kgs 19:18). The latter may be indicated in this image from Larsa, which shows the worshipper Awil-Nannar kneeling before the deity, his hand a few inches away from his mouth.

M. Pope, *Job* (AB; Garden City NY: Doubleday, 1979), 235.

notes that similar language describes the friends, who pursued Job like a pack of animals longing to be "sated with his flesh" (19:22). He plausibly suggests that v. 31 should be coupled with v. 32, in which case Job may be denying that he ever gave any members of his household reason to treat him with the same contempt.[34] (2) Job has not pretended to be innocent of any sins he may have committed, for fear of being publicly shamed (vv. 33-34). With a priest's sensitivity to the eroding effects of a guilty conscience, Job knows full well that any sin against God or people, whether intentional or inadvertent, requires confession (Lev 5:1-4; 6:1-7). He does not resist repentance because he hopes to conceal his faults; he resists because he has nothing to confess. The phrase in v. 33a, which NRSV translates "as others do" (*kĕadām*), may also be rendered "as Adam did" (NJPS: "Did I hide my transgressions like Adam"). The creational echo of the rhetoric recalls the primordial garden of Eden, divine promises first entrusted to a woman (Eve) and a man (Adam), and devastating sins that could not be ultimately hidden (Gen 1–3). Job, whose prologue profile invites the reader to understand that he is more than Adam's equal (see the commentary on Job 1–2), now insists that when the burden of creation's promise was bequeathed to him, he did not repeat the mistakes of his forebears. Job's stewardship of the divine commission to protect and nurture creation will be the subject of his final declaration (vv. 38-40).

Job's "yes" to covenant fidelity is an affirmation of his hospitality to strangers (v. 32). The "stranger" (*gēr*) is a resident alien. The status defines persons who have uprooted themselves (or have been forcibly uprooted) from their homeland and have taken up permanent residence in another land. In Israel, such persons generally enjoyed the same civil rights as the Israelites (Exod 12:49; Num 15:16), with some important exceptions. Chief among these were the restrictions against owning property, which in an agricultural economy meant that the strangers worked for Israelite landowners as hired hands. Since they had no land and little or no family of their own in their adopted country, they were almost wholly dependent on the generosity of their employers for adequate food, wages, and shelter. Their vulnerability meant they—along with widows, orphans, and the poor—were members of the population most often subject to exploitation and abuse, therefore most in need of special consideration by the law (Exod 22:20-23; 23:9; Deut 24:17-22). Israel's covenant with God, however, mandates to the stranger more than simply a basic protection of legal rights. It mandates love.[35] More importantly, the covenant insists that love for the stranger is to be comparable to that which God expressed for Israel by delivering them from the oppressive conditions of servitude in Egypt. The mandate is stated succinctly in the priestly

Job and the Golden Rule

The mandate to love one's neighbor as oneself has long been a guideline for ethical and moral conduct for Jews, Christians, and others. One need only consider the following examples:

You shall not take vengeance or bear a grudge against any of your people, but you shall love your neighbor as yourself: I am the Lord. (Lev 19:18; cf. Lev 19:34)

To love each his brother as himself by supporting the poor, the destitute, and the convert. (CD 6:20-21)

What you hate, do not do anyone. (Tob 4:15)

What is hateful to you do not do to your neighbor: that is the whole of the Torah, while the rest is commentary thereon; go and learn it. (Hillel, *b. Sabb.* 31a; cf. *y. Ned.* 9:4)

The way of life is this: First, you should love the Lord your maker, and secondly, your neighbor as yourself. And whatever you do not want to be done to you, you should not do to anyone else. (Did. 31:1-2)

In everything do to others as you would have them do you; for this is the law and the prophets. (Matt 7:12; cf. Luke 6:31; Rom 13:8-10)

When the Pharisees heard that he [Jesus] had silenced the Sadducees, they gathered together, and one of them, a lawyer, asked him a question to test him. "Teacher, which commandment in the law is the greatest?" He said to him, "'You shall love the Lord your God with all your heart, and with all your soul, and with all your mind.' This is the greatest and first commandment. And a second is like it: 'You shall love your neighbor as yourself.' On these two commandments hang all the law and the prophets." (Matt 22:39; cf. Matt 19:19; Deut 6:4-5)

In view of Job's priestly profile, the connections between Job 31:29-34 and Leviticus 19:18, 34 deserve to be singled out. Three comments about the priestly mandate to "love your neighbor as yourself" have particular resonance with Job's claims to covenantal fidelity: (1) The word "love" (*'āhāb*) implies both attitude and act. One must not only feel love but also express it in concrete acts. As one expresses love for God through active obedience to God's commandments, one must demonstrate love for others by reaching out to them with tangible deeds of compassion and concern. Jesus frames the admonition thusly: "*Do* to others as you would have them *do* to you" (Matt 7:12; Luke 6:31). (2) The word "neighbor" refers to a wide range of persons but especially those relegated to the margins of society for political, economic, or physical reasons. Lev 19:9-18 uses no fewer than eight different words to describe the persons included; they are essentially the same persons who receive Job's constant care (cf. Job 29:12-17): "poor" (v. 10), "alien" (v. 10), "neighbor" (v. 13), the "deaf" (v. 14), the "blind" (v. 14), "poor" (v. 15), "fellow citizen" (vv. 15, 17: NRSV: "neighbor/people"). (3). The phrase "as yourself" is open to different interpretations, perhaps the most illuminating of which occurs in the conversation between Rabbi Akiba and Ben Azzai concerning the importance of Lev 19:18:

R. Akiba says: "This is (the most) basic . . . law in the Torah." Ben Azzai says: (Rather) "'When God created man, he made him in the likeness of God' (Gen 5:1), so that you should not say: 'Since I despise myself, let my fellow be despised with me; since I am cursed, let my fellow be cursed with me.' This is a more basic law." (*Sipra* Qedoshim 4:12; cited in J. Milgrom, *Leviticus 17–22* [AB; New York: Doubleday, 2000], 1656)

Ben Azzai's comments turn on the recognition that loving one's neighbor is grounded in creation theology. When one disregards its mandate, it is like saying that God made a terrible mistake in deciding to invest human beings with the divine image.

For further discussion of these matters, see Samuel E. Balentine, *Leviticus* (IBC; Louisville: John Knox Press, 2002), 164-67.

summons to covenantal holiness in Leviticus 19, which as noted above, resonates in various ways with the oaths Job makes: "You shall love the alien (*gēr*) as yourself, for you were aliens (*gērîm*) in the land of Egypt" (Lev 19:34; cf. Deut 10:19).

When Job swears that he has opened his doors to the stranger, he claims to have been more than simply a good host or an observer of the rules of proper etiquette. Portrayed in the prologue as a non-Israelite, thus not bound by Israel's covenantal ethics, and as one who has suffered the loss of his possessions and his family, he lives by a code that places him in the company not only of Israel's paragons of faith, like Abraham (see further [Job the Righteous Gentile]), but also Jesus, whose admonition—"You shall love your neighbor as yourself" (Matt 19:19; 22:39)—has been regarded, since the eighteenth century, as the "Golden Rule" of human behavior. [Job and the Golden Rule]

"O That I Had One to Hear Me!" 31:35-37

At the penultimate point in his discourse, just before the fifth and final oath (vv. 38-40), Job interrupts his declaration of innocence to demand a hearing and a decision. The language is heavy with legal imagery.

• The demand for "one who hears" (v. 35, *šōmēaʿ*) suggests that Job is seeking a formal mediation of a legal dispute (2 Sam 15:3-4).[36]

• The demand is accompanied by Job's "signature" (v. 35, *taw*). The Hebrew word refers to the last letter of the Hebrew alphabet, in ancient times formed like an X, which may indicate a legal certification. The only other occurrence of the word is in Ezekiel 9:4, 6, where God orders a priestly figure clothed in linen garments, with a writing case at his side, to mark the innocent that are to be spared judgment for the violations that have defiled the temple. Those who bear the mark, which Jewish tradition associates with a word beginning with the letter *taw*—"you shall live"—are the ones who "sigh and moan" over abuses that have resulted in the departure of the "glory of the God of Israel" from the temple, and by implication from the world the temple's rituals are meant to sustain.

• Job addresses God as his "adversary at law" (*ʾîš rîbî*, v. 35b; on the lawsuit imagery conveyed by the word *rib*, see [The Trial Metaphor in Job]). He demands from God a "written document" (*sēper kātab*; NRSV: "indictment written"). The contents of the document are not specified. The language refers elsewhere both to legal memoranda, such as divorce decrees (Deut 24:1; Isa 50:1; Jer 3:8) and deeds of sale (Jer 32:11-12), and especially in post-exilic texts, to official, royal edicts (e.g., Esth 1:22; 3:13). Job may be asking for either a formal declaration of the charges God would bring against him or more likely, given his oaths of innocence, an official decree of acquittal. ["God Sees My Name"]

If taken at face value, Job's legal rhetoric sets up a win/lose situation that appears to require God's guilt in order to establish his innocence. Such a move on his part seems *at best* inconsistent with his previous explorations of the legal option. Although he has imagined the possi-

"God Sees My Name"

Arthur Miller's play, *The Crucible*, is a dramatic account of the witchcraft trials in Salem in 1692. The court in Salem, headed by Deputy Governor Danforth, operates on the dictum that when individuals are accused of witchcraft, they are guilty and under sentence of death. By play's end, John Proctor, a hard working Salem farmer who does not attend church regularly, stands accused and faces the maximum penalty. If he wishes to save his life, Proctor will have to plea bargain by confessing guilt, even though he knows himself to be innocent. He is tempted to compromise by offering an oral confession, confident that the God who "sees my name" will know the truth. Danforth insists on a signed confession, which will be posted on the church door for all to see. Proctor refuses. The excerpt below explains why Proctor believes signing one's name to a confession is not a matter for compromise.

Danforth: Come, then, sign your testimony. *To Cheever:* Give it to him. *Cheever goes to Proctor, the confession and a pen in hand. Proctor does not look at it.* Come, man, sign it.

Proctor, *after glancing at the confession*: You have all witnessed it—it is enough.

Danforth: You will not sign it? . . .

Proctor: No . . . .

Danforth: You have not con—

Proctor: I have confessed myself! Is there no good penitence but it be public? God does not need my name nailed upon the church! God sees my name; God knows how black my sins are! It is enough! . . .

Danforth, *with suspicion*: It is the same, is it not? If I report it or you sign it?

Proctor—*he knows it is insane*: No, it is not the same! What others say and what I sign is not the same! . . .

Proctor, *with a cry of his whole soul*: Because it is my name! Because I cannot have another in my life! Because I lie and sign myself to lies! Because I am not worth the dust on the feet of them that hang! How may I live without my name? I have given you my soul; leave me my name!

A. Miller, *The Crucible* (London, New York: Penguin Books, 1976), act 4, 141-43.

bility of bringing God into court (Job 9–10), even rehearsing his speech as plaintiff (13:20-28), he has dismissed the idea as futile. Even if God were to appear before the bench, Job knows that God would not answer even one of a thousand questions Job might ask (9:2-3). At the end of the day, the legal option promises little for persons like Job. They may cry out "Violence!" but there will be no answer from the court. They may seek a fair and impartial trial, but there will be "no justice," whatever legal maneuvers they employ (19:7). *At worst*, summoning God to trial may seem little more than testimony to Job's arrogance. It effectively leaves him open to the same rebuke that he leveled at his wife. Why should he not expect God to respond to him by saying, "You speak as a foolish person" (2:10)?

Even so, we must take seriously the legal rhetoric. For all its weaknesses as a final context for interpreting Job's demand, the legal metaphor insists that justice is not a disposable virtue in covenant relationships, either for God or for human beings. Newsom has opened the door on another possibility for tracking the justice issue. Job's strategy throughout this chapter, she argues, is to "[put] himself on trial in the rhetorical, though not strictly legal sense." The form of the oath—"If *I* have done X . . ."—invokes punishment on *him*, not *God*, at least not directly, if his claims are false. If his claims are true, as he swears by the limits of the legal rhetoric available to him, then a just God "*could not but* declare Job to be righteous and so confirm his honor." [Job's Move Beyond Moral Bitterness] Job's hope and expectation is that God's recognition of his moral, ethical, and ritual fidelity "enhances the honor of both" parties to the covenant. The "brilliance of this rhetorical stance" is that it allows Job to frame the issues not in the zero-sum logic of a win/lose legal trial but instead as the opportunity for a win/win encounter with God.[37] [Affirming Job's Honor Brings No Shame to God]

Verses 36-37, therefore, lend themselves to an interpretation that follows Janzen's lead. Job's demand for a hearing is not a "boast" that condemns him with the charge of "unbridled presumption." It is instead testimony to his "faithful stewardship of a covenanted conscience." "[I]t is not a unilateral self-proclamation, but a self-binding within a relationship."[38] [Job's Self-binding Oaths] When and if God confirms that Job has indeed exhibited the moral and ethical fidelity required by the covenant, then Job will wear the affirmation like a "crown" (v. 36, *ătorā*). This crown, like the garments of righteousness and justice that Job wears (29:14), will validate God's estimation of his worthiness as a holy priest, innocent of any charge the *satan* may ever bring (Zech 6:11, 14; cf. Zech 3:1-10), who can effectively intercede

---

Job's Move Beyond Moral Bitterness

J. Gerald Janzen has argued that Job's oaths in ch. 31 indicate a move beyond the "moral bitterness" that defined his initial outbursts from the ash heap (Job 3). Like Newsom, Janzen understands Job to be reaching toward God, not to hurl an indictment, but to invite an embrace:

One sign of this is the evidence in chaps. 29-30 of an inner transformation. In chapter 3, his bitterness over the loss of everything had moved him to curse the day of his birth and the night of his conception, and to lament that he had ever lived. Now he is able to celebrate the long years when Shadday washed his steps in milk (29:1-6). If in chapter 30 he once again rehearses his present plight, this does not mean that the bitter accusation in 30:20-23 cancels out the sweet memory in 29:1-6. Quite the opposite . . . . [T]he recollection of God's former blessings becomes the rhetorical basis on which the portrayal of present woes is presented to God as an appeal for help. Just as Job had wept and grieved for those in hardship, so Job has looked—and continues to look—for similar solace in his own calamity (30:24-26). It is as such a last-ditch hope, in my view, that Job takes his second oath [Chapter 31]. Though he continues to display a clear conscience, yet in his self-imprecating language he submits his conscience to the judgment of God. This is not an act of moral bitterness. It is an act in which he reaches beyond his bitterness, beyond his own self-knowledge, to God. And the oath that bridges the abyss between his inner self and God becomes the avenue along which God's response can come to him.

J. Gerald Janzen, "Job's Oath," *RevExp* 99 (2002): 603.

Affirming Job's Honor Brings No Shame to God

C. Newsom has helpfully exegeted Job 29–31 with specific reference to the moral values of shame and honor that are deeply rooted in ancient societies like Job's. In arguing that "[W]hat God requires of Job is what Job expects of God," she cites the parallel of Judah and Tamar in Gen 38.

That it would not be a matter of shame is evident in the fact that Job himself uses this example as evidence of his own honorableness. The same dynamics are at work in the narrative account of Tamar and Judah in Genesis 38. When Judah had wrongly accused Tamar of adultery and ordered her death, she showed him the tokens by which he recognized himself as the one who had unknowingly impregnated her. Though Judah had been represented in the story as anything but an honorable man, his public statement, "She is more in the right than I" (Gen 38:26), is an act of honor and is presented as such in the narrative. Indeed, in the context of the larger story, this episode serves as the redemptive moment that marks the transition of Judah's character from one of moral ambivalence to the moral leadership that enables him to resolve Joseph's hesitancy to reconcile with his brothers (Gen 44:18-34).

In advance of reflections that will deserve more comment at a subsequent point in the commentary (see 42:7-17), I note that this parallel may be extended beyond what Newsom has observed. While Job's strategy may offer a win/win situation for God, it may also be the case that it is a daring offer of redemption *to God*. Like Judah, perhaps God welcomes an opportunity to act honorably, especially following the concession that Job suffers "for no reason." (See further Samuel E. Balentine, "My Servant Job Shall Pray For You," *ThTo* 58 [2002], 507-518.)

C. Newsom, *The Book of Job: A Contest of Moral Imaginations* (Oxford: Oxford University Press, 2003), 197.

for the victims of injustice in the world. It will also restore the crown, that is, the nobility, that God bestows on every human being (19:9; cf. Ps 8:5), which Job fears has been stripped from him by humiliation he did not deserve. Thus crowned, robed, and honored, Job anticipates the day when he will recount the steps of his life before the bar of judgment (v. 37), the same steps God also counts (v. 4), and the numbers will come out the same. ["It Cannot Be Replaced . . . But Can Be Ignored, Denied, and Betrayed"]

"If My Land Has Cried Out Against Me," 31:38-40

The fifth oath concerns land ethics. Many commentators consider the

Job's Self-binding Oaths

To lie under oath is to claim to bind oneself in the solitariness of one's heart, to the community and to God while by that very act falsifying that bond, destroying that bridge—and destroying also one's own integrity in speaking with "a double heart" (Ps 12:3 [2]). Robert Bolt gives a modern rendition of these issues in his play, "A Man for All Seasons." The play turns on Thomas More's refusal to take the oath on the Act of Succession, which establishes the right of Henry VIII's offspring by Anne Boleyn to the English throne. When Richard Rich accuses him of having denied the competence of Parliament to make the King Head of the Church in England, More responds: "My lords, if I were a man who heeded not the taking of an oath, you know well I need not be here." For More would long since have taken the oath required of all subjects while in his heart believing otherwise. He then says, "Now I will take an oath! If what Master Rich has said is true, then I pray I may never see God in the face! Which I would not say were it otherwise for anything on earth." When the court believes Rich's testimony, More concludes, "What you have hunted me for is not my actions, but the thoughts of my heart. It is a long road you have opened. For first men will disclaim their hearts and presently they will have no hearts. God help the people whose Statesmen walk your road."

J. Gerald Janzen, "Job's Oath," *RevExp* 99 (2002): 599. The citations are from Robert Bolt, *A Man for All Seasons* (New York: Vintage Books, 1962), 90-91.

placement of these verses after Job's demand for a hearing to be odd and suggest a variety of options for relocating them in closer proximity to the rest of the oaths.[39] Their present location, however, may be defended on both structural and theological grounds. Structurally, they connect Job's last words with his first words. He begins by declaring the covenant he has made with his eyes (v. 1). He ends by invoking the earth, often a witness to covenant treaties (Isa 1:12; Mic 6:2; Deut 30:19), to testify to the truthfulness of all his oaths.[40] Theologically, the placement after v. 37 suggests that these verses provide the words Job would speak when he approaches God "like a prince" and gives "an account" of all his steps.[41]

Job's final oath employs the complete oath formula. Two asseverations (vv. 38, 39) comprise the conditional part of the oath. Verse 40 is the sanction invoked if Job's claims are false. Creation imagery sustains every part of Job's last words.

Job claims first that he has not abused the land (v. 38a). The imagery portrays the land as a sensate human being, crying out when it is wounded, weeping in a concert of furrows or rows when its soil is plowed and planted in injurious ways. Job does not say what he might have done to harm the land, but his words echo the obedience God expects to the commission to "serve" (ʿābad) the land and "nuture" (šāmar) its creational possibilities (Gen 2:15). The second claim (v. 39) focuses on Job's ethical and moral obligation to those who own or work the land. He has neither cheated those who deserve payment for producing the land's goods nor has he selfishly consumed the land's bounty in ways that threaten the livelihood of others who may be more dependent on the land than he is. His stewardship of the land is, as Janzen notes, "a reversed echo of Gen 2:7."[42] By taking care not to "cause its owners to breathe out their life (nepeš)" (v. 39b; NRSV: "caused the death of its owners"), Job has neither violated nor diminished the life (nepeš) that God breathes into human beings as a gift of creation. *If* Job were guilty of such offenses against the land, *then* (v. 40) he invokes God's primordial curse of the land, for he will have been guilty of the same sins as Adam and Eve: "let thorns grow instead of wheat, and foul weeds instead of barley" (cf. Gen 3:17-18).

Upon what theological tradition does Job base his land ethics? To what model of covenantal responsibility does he appeal? The creation

---

"It Cannot Be Replaced . . . But Can Be Ignored, Denied, and Betrayed"

You can hide it like a signature or birthmark but it's always there in the greasy light of your dreams, the knots your body makes at night, the sad innuendos of your eyes, whispering insidious asides in every room you cannot remain inside. It's there in the unquiet ideas that drag and plead one lonely argument at a time, and those who own a little are contrite and fearful of those who own too much, but owning none up takes up your life. It cannot be replaced with a house or car, a husband or wife, but it can be ignored, denied, and betrayed, until the last day, when you pass yourself on the street and recognize the agreeable life you were afraid to lead, and turn away.

P. Schultz, "The Truth," *The New Yorker*, 10 March 2003, 80.

imagery to which he appeals points to the priestly tradition, not only to priestly perspectives on the genesis of the world, but more particularly to the priestly emphasis on faithful stewardship of the land as a fundamental requisite of the holiness mandated by the covenant. The most sustained attention to this requirement in the Old Testament occurs in the "Holiness Code" in Leviticus 17–27. Following on the heels of the detailed instructions for cultic purity in Leviticus 1–16, these instructions make clear that the priests envisioned no disjunction between the requirements for proper rituals *inside* the sanctuary and corollary ethical behavior *outside* the sanctuary, in the everyday affairs of life. The Holiness Code spells out this ethical behavior in a variety of ways, but one warning remains at the forefront throughout: unethical behavior defiles the land and jeopardizes God's promise to bequeath it to human beings in holy trust (Lev 18:24-30; 20:22-26; 22:31-33; 25:18-24; 26:3-45).[43]

This priestly land ethic resonates with all of Job's oaths in this chapter. Beginning with sexual ethics (Lev 18; cf. Job 31:1-12) and ending with the ethics of the sabbatical and Jubilee years, which require "the redemption of the land" from injustices that mar its potential for peace and prosperity (Lev 25; cf. Job 31:38-40), the Holiness Code insists that ultimately God's blessings and curses (Lev 26; cf. Job 42:12) are tied to the responsibility for stewardship of the land. The fulcrum of the Holiness Code, the weight-bearing beam that supports the full load of its land ethic, is Leviticus 18–20, the text to which this commentary has repeatedly returned in search of perspective for understanding Job's oaths of innocence. Here the mandate is first condensed to a single and unalterable requirement—"You shall be holy, for I the Lord your God am holy" (Lev 19:2)—then explicated by the commandments not to harvest at the expense of the poor (19:9-10), not to cheat the laborers of their just compensation (19:13), and not to cheat the land of its yield by prematurely consuming its first fruits (19:23-25). In sum, to be holy as God is holy, means to love the land and treasure it as a sacred trust. This, Job swears with a final oath, is precisely what he has done.

The last words of the chapter are, "the words of Job are ended." The Hebrew word for "ended" (*tammû*) is from the same root that produces the word for the personal "integrity" (31:6, *tummāh*), which Job seeks to defend with each of these oaths. It is also semantically related both to God's prologue affirmation of Job as "blameless" (*tām;* 2:3, 9) and to the priestly term (*tāmîm*) for the unblemished animal that is required for ritual presentation at the altar (e.g., Lev 22:19; Num 19:2; Ezek 43:22-23). When Job "ends" his words, the question that remains unanswered for Job, and for his readers, is, will the presentation of his integrity be an acceptable offering to God or not?

CONNECTIONS

In his final discourse, Job sets out to build what Newsom has called a "working rhetorical world."[44] Speaking in first person, Job testifies to the way he believes the world can and should work. His discernments are informed by his own real-life experiences. He does not rely on the prologue and epilogue's narrator, who has the advantage of abstracting truths *about him* and *about the world he lives in* from the safe vantage point of omniscience. Nor does he feel constrained to trim his testimony to the opinions of his friends. They *live in his world,* but they are *mere onlookers to his experiences.* They may be earnest and sincere, but they are capable of little more than patronizing his reality: they simplify by distorting; they add counsel by subtracting from wisdom. [What Profit the Wisdom of Fools?] Job would of course welcome God's critique of the world he builds, but to this point in his journey, God remains disconcertingly elusive. So, Job presses ahead with the only testimony he knows to be true, awaiting a response from God that is yet to come. ["How Can a Man Get a Voice Out of Silence?"]

Chapters 29–31 unfold the blueprint, as it were, for the world Job wants to build. When the last nail of chapter 31 is driven flush, Newsom argues, Job has built a replica of "the moral world that has made him." It is a persuasive rhetorical construction, because Job is "deeply sincere and utterly committed" to the moral and ethical values that govern his life. And it is a seductively appealing construction, because "in [Job's] world there can be no contradiction in reality, only a wrong to be righted."[45] But in the end such a world, she concludes, is deeply flawed, because Job's "supreme confidence" in his own capacity to right every wrong ultimately reveals "an imperviousness to other perspectives and possibilities," including those God may yet insist deserve to be considered. In short, Job believes he is "in possession of a language that knows how to refuse tragedy,"[46] which seems to trump all other options, *until* God relativizes it with a wider perspective that "reintroduces the tragic as a possibility."[47] Newsom's observations are so strong and generally compelling that isolated details might be allowed to slip beneath the radar of critical scrutiny. However, the suggestion that Job seeks to build a world that refuses tragedy deserves further reflection. A rabbinic maxim provides the catalyst for the comments that follow: "Turn it and turn it again, for everything is in it" (*m. 'Abot* 5:22).

The world Job builds is hammered out on the planks of his past, present, and, he hopes, future. He works from the ground up. First, from the warehouse of his past (Job 29), he constructs a weight-bearing

---

What Profit the Wisdom of Fools?

In a rebuttal to Susan Sontag's suggestion that a certain filmmaker deserves to be assessed against the totality of his films, despite evident weaknesses, Clive James offers a word that may also apply to Job's friends: "[Y]ou will gain no wisdom from a fool's utterance by cancelling the rest of your appointments and listening to him all day."

C. James, "A Whole Gang of Noise: Susan Sontag," *As of This Writing: The Essential Essays, 1968–2002* (New York, London: W. W. Norton and Company, 2003), 359.

"How Can a Man Get a Voice Out of Silence?"

In his essay on Herman Melville, James Wood notes that Melville, born into the Calvinism of the Dutch Reformed Church, constantly struggled with belief. Nathaniel Hawthorne described his friend's persistence in the face of doubts: "He [Melville] can neither believe, nor be comfortable in his unbelief; and he is too honest and courageous not to try to do one or the other" (29).

Picking up on this characteristic, Wood explores Melville's relation to belief, especially his struggle with God's silence, in Joban terms:

Melville . . . was like the last guest who cannot leave the party; he was always returning to see if he had left his hat and gloves. And yet he did not want to be at the party, either. It is just that he had nowhere else to be, and would rather be with people than be alone. He was tormented by God's inscrutable silence. Moby-Dick himself, who is both God and devil, flaunts his unhelpful silence as God does to Job: "Canst thou draw out leviathan with a hook?" . . . Likewise, Melville was gripped by the torment of the pyramids and their emptiness. In 1857, while traveling through Egypt, he visited the pyramids. In his journal he writes, again and again as if, by repetition, to rid himself of the memory of it: It was in these pyramids that was conceived the idea of Jehovah." In *Moby-Dick*, we are reminded by Melville of the "pyramidical silence" of the whale. In *Pierre*, he will not leave alone this torment and fingers it like a wounded rosary, which is partly why the book is so impacted. It is in *Pierre* that he writes, "Silence is the only Voice of our God . . . how can a man get a Voice out of Silence?" He gibes at God: "Doth not scripture intimate, that He holdeth all of us in the hollow of His hands?—a Hollow, truly!" Perhaps, he proposes, all our searches are like this:

By vast pains we mine into the pyramids; by horrible gropings we come to the central room; with joy we espy the sarcophagus; but we we lift the lid—and no body is there!—appallingly vacant as vast is the soul of a man! (30)

Lest Wood's assessment of Melville's struggle (and Job's) with God's silence be taken as a counsel of despair, the last words of his essay deserve to be pondered: "Any true life is a blasphemously exhaustive hunt, and Melville lived a true life. Poor Melville, lucky Melville!" (40).

J. Wood, "The All and the If: God and Metaphor in Melville," *The Broken Estate: Essays on Literature and Belief* (New York: Random House, 1999), 26-40.

---

foundation of intersecting moral and ethical relationships, reinforced by righteousness and justice. Next, he frames the exterior with lumber rough-hewn by brokenness and loss, for present realties (Job 30) have taught him that every habitable world is shaped by these experiences. Finally, he trims out the interior with the personal touches that make the whole structure not only livable but also more desirable and satisfying than other models. Inside Job's world, he accents his hopes for a meaningful life with a covenantal commitment to personal integrity and communal solidarity (Job 31).

When one examines closely the materials Job uses to construct his rhetorical world, it does not seem adequate to conclude that he refuses to build in the possibility of the tragic. His foundation includes not only the titled (29:7-11), who control and administer society's values and goods, but also the socially marginalized—the poor, the orphan, the widow, the blind, the lame, the needy, the stranger—persons whose status makes them targets for tragedy (29:12-17). The exterior that makes his vision for the world apprehensible does not frame a haven free of evil, injustice, or suffering. Instead, its design makes clear that inside one will find persons, like Job, whom the system has failed.

Some will be driven to contemplate vengeance (30:1-8), thus fueling a potential cycle of escalating violence that threatens not only to weaken still further the world they inhabit but also to question the wisdom of the master architect's blueprint (30:20-31). Built into the foundation of Job's world, however, is the promise of righteousness and justice. The promise may be tested; it may be stretched, like garments frayed by constant wear, to and perhaps beyond the breaking point (29:14; 30:16-19). According to Job's design, as long as there is one person who attends to the maintenance of the covenant that constitutes the heart and soul of this world, tragedy will have its impact on the present, it may extend its reach into the future, but it will not have the final say on what life is or can be. ["It Is Impossible to Remove Oneself Totally from Suffering"]

Inasmuch as Job may be understood to be building a world, even if only a rhetorical one, his hopes and aspirations invite comparison with the world spoken into being by God. Newsom suggests that Job's world, constructed, as the voice from the whirlwind will say, from "words without knowledge" (38:2), is "incompatible" with God's world, because ultimately, tragedy cannot be so easily factored out of the calculus.[48] Another perspective may be offered.

Perhaps Job is not so much creating a world in his own image as he is rereading the world God has created and offering his perspective on certain areas that need further attention. His final discourse in chapters 29–31 effectively returns the focus to the prologue, more specifically to the Edenic-Genesis 1-like harmony that provides the narrator's prism for describing Job's world (1:1-5). By all accounts, life in the land of Uz once promised such wholeness and prosperity, such insulation from anything that might be construed as evil, that it resounded with the primordial affirmation "very good." But the "grammar of creation" in that Genesis 1-world changed for Job, if not for the narrator, once the words "for no reason" (2:3) were spoken.[49] As soon as these words became part of the narrative of Job's world, the view of creation advo-

"It Is Impossible to Remove Oneself Totally from Suffering"

C. Newsom, citing Dorothee Soelle, notes, in fact, that "Acceptance of suffering is the correlate of reality."

It is impossible to remove oneself totally from suffering, unless one removes oneself from life itself, no longer enters into relationships, makes oneself invulnerable . . . . The more strongly we affirm reality, the more we are immersed in [suffering]. (D. Soelle, *Suffering* [Philadelphia: Fortress Press, 1975], 88)

Newsom agrees that the Job of the prologue expresses a "radical acceptance" of suffering, but she understands the Job who speaks in ch. 31 to have shifted to a rhetorical stance that "knows how to refuse tragedy." I would argue that Soelle's discernments remain accurate for ch. 31. If anything, Job seems to have deepened and enlarged his understanding of tragedy's place in the world.

C. Newsom, *The Book of Job: A Contest of Moral Imaginations* (Oxford: Oxford University Press, 2003), 60.

cated by the priestly tradition, one of the theological perspectives that shapes, however faintly, Job's self understanding, must per force be rethought. ["I'm Not Stuck in the Past, I've Just Brought It with Me Into the Present"] Job initially responds by trying to conform to the expected code of priestly conduct in this world—offering sacrifice, as he "always did" (1:5) and blessing, not cursing, God (1:22; 2:10)—but by the time he gathers himself to speak from the ash heap, the strain has become too great. From Job 3 onwards, curses, laments, and legal rhetoric that envisions redress and rehabilitation vie for a place in the grammar of a world stuttering with what the words "for no reason" seems now to require. By the time he speaks in chapter 31, Job has hammered out another rhetorical world. He hopes and believes it is a world sturdy enough to survive the vagaries of life, which always explode assertions

"I'm Not Stuck in the Past, I've Just Brought It with Me into the Present"

Julia Alvarez was only ten years old in 1960 when her parents were forced to flee to the United States from the Dominican Republic, shortly before Trujillo was assassinated. Her novel, *In the Time of the Butterflies*, tells the story of what she remembers through the eyes of the four Mirabal sisters, Minerva, Patria, María Theresa, and Dedé. Of the four, only Dedé survived to describe the everyday horrors of life under Trujillo's dictatorship *and* to see that the names of her sisters were not erased from memory. In a scene from the end of the book, Dedé reflects on a conversation with her girlfriend Olga, who has gently rebuked her for getting stuck in the past:

"I'll tell you what I think," Olga says . . . . "You're still living in the past, Dedé. You're in the same old house, surrounded by the same old things, in the same little village, with all the people who have known you since you were this big."

She goes over all the things that supposedly keep me from living my own life. And I am thinking, Why, I wouldn't give them up for the world. I'd rather be dead.

"It's still 1960 for you," she concludes. "But this is 1994, Dedé, *1994!*"

"You're wrong," I tell her. "I'm not stuck in the past, I've just brought it with me into the present. And the problem is not enough of us have done that. What is that thing the gringos say, if you don't study your history, you are going to repeat it?"

Olga waves the theory away. "The gringos say too many things."

"And many of them are true," I tell her. "Many of them." . . .

"After the fighting was over and we were a broken people"—she shakes her head sadly at this portrait of our recent times—"that's when I opened my doors, and instead of listening, I started talking. We had lost hope, and we needed a story to understand what happened to us." (313)

In a "Postscript," Alvarez explains the tension she felt in trying to tell the history and at the same time be true to the truth that history may be unable to provide. As the sisters "became real" to her imagination, she resorted to fiction; she began "to invent them." To the Dominicans "separated by language from the world I have created," Alvarez adds these last words:

. . . what you will find here are the Mirabals of my creation, made up but, I hope, true to the spirit of the real Mirabals. In addition, though I had researched the facts of the regime, and events pertaining to Trujillo's thirty-one year depotism, I sometimes took liberties—by changing dates, by reconstructing events, and by collapsing characters or incidents. For I wanted to immerse my readers in an epoch in the life of the Dominican Republic that I believe can only finally be understood by fiction, only finally be redeemed by the imagination. A novel is not, after all, a historical document, but a way to travel through the human heart. (324)

J. Alvarez, *In the Time of the Butterflies* (Chapel Hill NC: Algonquin Books, 1994)

made by fiat, whether divine or human, that life is simply "very good." It is *not* a world that "refuses tragedy." It is a world in which tragedy may be recognized for what it is, confronted, and perhaps even rectified, by one who refuses to exchange the tattered robes of justice and righteousness for cheaper clothing. Job's constructed world surely invites question. Is his world flawed? Is it fundamentally incompatible with God's? Newsom concludes the answer is "Yes." The rabbinic maxim cited above urges caution: "Turn it and turn it again."

My turnings of the question are instructed by Elaine Scarry's ruminations on the connections between beauty and justice. The first part of her book is devoted mostly to aesthetic and philosophical musings on beauty, generated by the observation that "beauty brings copies of itself into being."[50] Whenever we are in the presence of something beautiful, whether it is the beautiful face of another person, a beautiful crocus in the middle of winter, or an exquisite impressionistic painting by Monet, we instinctively want to linger, to look, to do whatever is possible to keep the beauty sensorialy present for as long as possible. We may paint a picture, write a poem, take a photograph, or simply etch the memory into our minds so that we can retrieve it for future enjoyment. In any event, the beautiful has a forward momentum to it. It summons us to acts of creation, for we know instinctively that what we have beheld is worth preserving. If we lose it, we are diminished, perhaps in ways we cannot fully articulate. [Beauty Creates]

When she turns to the connection between beauty and justice, [51] Scarry invites us to think that she is dialoguing with Genesis and creation, even though there are no references to confirm the suspicion. That which is beautiful inspires the beholder to recognize the beautiful in the world, to ponder and protect it, and to beget by replication beautiful things that sustain the inspiration for others. Further, to stand in the presence of something beautiful is to become acutely aware of the lack of beauty in other places. In other words, beauty sensitizes us to the presence of the ugly, to that which disrupts, distorts, or mars the good that we want to be consistently and permanently available everywhere we look.

In the same way that beauty sensitizes us to the beautiful and its absence, it sensitizes us to justice and its absence, injustice. Beauty has to do with "fairness," fairness in the sense both of something that has a "loveliness of countenance" and in the sense of the ethical requirement to "be fair," or "play fair."[52] That which is beautiful has a right proportion to it; there is a perfect symmetry between the compositional elements, just the right balance between light and dark, bold and muted colors, sharp and smooth angles. The symmetry has to do with relationships, not only the relationships between the compositional ele-

Beauty Creates

Scarry notes that sometimes the beautiful is present, but we cannot see it. We may even have reason to doubt that it exists at all. She recounts the discovery she made by looking at Matisse's paintings of Nice (33-46). She grew up in the northeast, so palm trees were both geographically and aesthetically distant and unfamiliar objects for her. She had had few occasions and still fewer reasons to think that palm trees could be beautiful and deserving of contemplation. So it was with little forethought that one winter, when the garden outside her window was barren of flowers, she decided to place thirteen Matisse prints all over the walls of her house. Throughout the bleak months of winter she applied her empty and unsuspecting eyes to the prints. They became a garden inside her house.

She knew from her study of Matisse that although he had said of his work that he never intended it to save lives, he fervently "wanted to make paintings so serenely beautiful that when one came upon them, suddenly all problems would subside" (33). Only gradually did she recognize that the palm tree was the thing of beauty that captured Matisse's imagination. It was not only the model for his painting; it was also the inspiration behind his compulsion to replicate the way its striped leaves captured the light and refracted it to everything. Matisse's discovery of the beauty of palm trees seems to have been gradual, like that which it prompted in Scarry herself. In his early paintings (1919–1940s), the presence of the palm frond was subtle, sometimes only the bare outline of a leaf in the background of the picture, which then was subtly replicated in the striped light that shined through a louvered window. In these early paintings the palm tree only occupies between one-fiftieth and one sixty-third of the full surface of the composition. It was easily missed, unless of course you were tuned to look for it. In his later paintings, however (beginning in 1947 with *Still Life With Pomegrantes*), the palm fronds become increasingly prominent. They comprise not one sixty-third or one-fiftieth of the composition but one-thirtieth, then one-quarter, then virtually the whole of the composition, until finally Matisse is painting palm fronds on palm fronds on top of palm fronds, literally hundreds of stripes that fill up the entire canvas. By the end of winter, Scarry had discovered beauty where she had previously not known it existed. It had been there all the time, but it was not until she saw the replication that she could see the original that had been its inspiration. Beauty creates. Even replications of beauty create.

E. Scarry, *On Beauty and Being Just* (Princeton: Princeton University Press, 1999).

ments of a particular object that is beautiful, but by extension, also the relationships between all that is beautiful in the world and potential beholders, wherever they exist. When this symmetry is not present, it is unlikely that we feel ourselves to be in the presence of the beautiful. When it is, we know that we have encountered something that captures our imagination. Beauty requires more than an appreciative imagination, however. It "place[s] *requirements* on us for attending to the aliveness or (in the case of objects) quasi-aliveness of our world, and *for entering into its protection*." In sum, "Beauty is, then, a *compact*, or *contract* between the beautiful being (a person or thing) and the perceiver."[53]

So it is, we may imagine, with the primordial beauty of God's creation. The world God creates is "very good." It is paradisiacal, perfect. In biblical terms, the symmetry of its order is perfectly balanced. Everything is in its proper place, nothing is askew, nothing is lacking. There is neither too much nor too little of all that is necessary for the cosmos to be *perfectly* and *justly* attuned, in all its relationships, to the heart of God. The *beauty* and the *justice* of God's creation sensitizes us, not only to what is but to what must be. For beauty to be honored and preserved, we must be alert to its opposite, ugliness. For justice to be honored and preserved, we must be alert to its opposite—injustice, injury, unfair or unethical relationships. In effect, "beauty exerts a pressure toward ethical equality."[54] At the moment we see something beautiful, something happens to us. We are arrested, refocused, transformed, and energized to replicate what we have discovered. We want not only to preserve it for our own pleasure; we also want to insure that it remains available to others. We want beauty to be everywhere present, everywhere available, so that there is no place where it cannot be seen, experienced, and celebrated. From the moment we encounter the beautiful, we cannot imagine its disappearance from our world and all future worlds as anything but a deprivation and loss.[55]

Job has experienced the beauty of the "very good" world that carries God's hopes and expectations for every human being. He also knows first hand the "evil" that can mar this world, "for no reason," and he is arrested by an ethical imperative to resist and repair it, not by fiat, but by hands-on, in-the-trenches acts that keep the promise of righteousness and justice alive and attainable. If Job is to act on the ethical imperative, so crucial to his integrity, what should he do? What options does he have? What possibilities offer the best hope for tangible results?

The legal rhetoric of rhetoric of chapter 31 indicates that Job continues to explore the possibility of a formal trial in which justice is obtained by a court order. But the inadequacies of litigation are all too apparent, especially should one dare to imagine God as the defendant. If Job elects to file as the plaintiff in the suit, it is unclear whether he should be regarded, in literary terms, as Prometheus, the famous Titan in Greek mythology, or Polonius, the dissembling counselor to the king in *Hamlet*. [Job and Prometheus] If the former, then he risks incurring God's wrath by trying to steal a justice for himself and his world that God seems unable or unwilling to bestow. If the latter, then he renders himself ridiculous by the artifice of his discourse; in pretending to have spied out "the very cause of Hamlet's [read God's] lunacy" (*Hamlet*, II, ii, 48-49), he has revealed his own. Either way, a victory in the courtroom means that Job has lost more than he has won. An angry God is not easily assuaged, as Prometheus learned when Zeus chained him to the rocks in the Caucasus, where birds of prey picked away daily at his flesh. A counselor who serves the king by using the "bait of falsehood" (*Hamlet* II, i, 69) should not be surprised when death is ignominious, as Polonius learned when Hamlet discovered him hiding behind the curtain and ran him through with his sword.

Job's exploration of the trial metaphor is important, because it insists that justice matters. Woven through his legal rhetoric, however, are concerns with personal integrity, concerns which require justice but exceed its limitations. He associates these concerns with a primal

Job and Prometheus

In the secondary literature, one often finds a comparison between Job and Prometheus, the heroic figure in Greek mythology. Gilbert Murray, whose article "Prometheus and Job" represents but one example, sets the table for reflection with this opening précis of the myth:

Most religions . . . condemn this temporal world, but swamp its badness in the alleged infinite goodness of some other: only very few arraign the Ruler of the World for his present tyranny. This, however, is the theme of the *Prometheus*. We are shown the pitiful state of mankind. Zeus had hidden away the means of life from man, just as he had hidden away fire. He had let loose innumerable winged evils; the air and sea are full of them; there is no escaping them. Life is hard and lies always under the shadow of death. And, after all, for reasons good or bad, Zeus has from time to time entertained the idea of destroying man altogether, as a noxious and unhappy beast. That is what he sought when he brought the Trojan War. That is what he was going to do when Prometheus thwarted him.

Prometheus Bound

Peter Paul Rubens (1577-1640). Begun 1611-12, completed by 1618 (The eagle was painted by Frans Snyders). Oil on canvas. Purchased with the W. P. Wilstach Fund, 1950. Philadelphia Museum of Art, Philadelphia, Pennsylvania, U.S.A. (Credit: The Philadelphia Museum of Art/Art Resource, NY)

According to the myth, Prometheus ("forethought") and his brother Epimetheus ("afterthought") were assigned the task of providing humans and animals the powers they needed to survive. Epimetheus bestowed on the various animals gifts of courage, strength, speed, and protective coverings, like fur and feathers. When it came time to provide the necessary gifts for human beings, Epimetheus discovered there was nothing left. Feeling compassion for the helpless human creature, Prometheus took over the task. To make humans superior to the animals in strength and stature, he fashioned them in nobler form and enabled them to walk upright. To make them wise, he stole wisdom and fire from the gods. For his efforts, Zeus, the new king in heaven, charged Prometheus with theft and in anger ordered that he be chained to Mount Caucasus. Every day an eagle swooped down and tore away at the lobes of his liver; every night the liver grew back, and the ordeal, said to have continued for thirty thousand years, would begin again. Though chained and tortured, Prometheus continued to use his wits to survive. Ultimately, Heracles killed the eagle and freed Prometheus.

G. Murray, "Prometheus and Job," *Twentieth Century Interpretations of the Book of Job,* ed. P. Sanders (Englewood Cliffs NJ: Prentice-Hall, Inc., 1968), 56

instinct to care for others. It is a womb-formed compassion implanted in him by his mother (v. 18). More importantly, it is a primal compassion Job believes he shares with the God who gave him breath and spirit (v. 15; cf. 27:3). The integrity of such compassion cannot be fully claimed or defended by a legal verdict. Its truthfulness ultimately depends on the solidarity he shares with God. In Scarry's terms, Job has entered into a "contract" with what is beautiful in the world and he pledges to honor it. Job's word for the loyalty he swears and the answering loyalty he expects from God is "covenant" (v. 1).

Job understands his covenant with God to be founded on a mutual obligation, a reciprocal willingness, on the part of both parties to agree. Job bets his life on the promise that covenant partnership does not require God to be less than God. Covenantal validation of his integrity does not compromise God's authority or power. Instead, it offers God the opportunity to be fully God by affirming that God wants what Job wants. The covenant does in fact require the moral and ethical use of power in all relationships, especially those with persons whose God-given right to the beautiful and "very good" world God has created has been diminished "for no reason."

Job's understanding of covenant is deeply rooted in priestly discernments, but it also enlarges them. He insists that God will accept no ritual that reduces those who have been abused "for no reason" to passive compliance. Janzen suggests that Job has engaged in a rhetorical act of "sevening." While that is true, we may fine-tune the idea by suggesting that Job advocates a ritual of "sixing," five oaths of innocence (31:1-34, 38-40) plus a summons for God's affirmation (31:35-37), which requires and merits a seventh act to complete the offering. The seventh act can only be supplied by God—perhaps at the insistence of readers like us who may feel compelled to enter into Job's ritual—whose words "very good," too long absent from Job's world, seem all but impossible, given the reality that seeks to thwart them.

For that word to be spoken, we may pause to wonder whether the God who covenants with Job needs trial lawyers to make the case, or priests. In consideration of the options before us, we might do well to remember that God made the move toward covenant relationship with a specific mandate: "You shall be for me a *priestly* kingdom and a *holy* nation" (Exod 19:6). The parallelism between "kingdom" and "nation" is apparent: both words signify the idea of royal power. The words "priestly" and "holy" describe persons who exercise power in ways distinctively different from conventional politics. Those with whom God covenants are mandated to exercise power not as kings, whose powers cannot be resisted, but as priests, whose empowerment is only exercised in the service of others. Job bets his life on the belief that in matters of

"Another World to Live In"

Thus every living and healthy religion has a marked idiosyncrasy. Its power consists in its special and surprising message and in the bias which that revelation gives to life. The vistas it opens and the mysteries it propounds are another world to live in; and another world to live in—whether we expect to pass wholly into it or no—is what we mean by religion.

G. Santayana, *Reason in Religion*, cited in C. Geertz, "Religion as a Cultural System," *The Interpretation of Cultures: Selected Essays* (New York: Basic Books, 1973), 87.

covenantal fidelity, staying true to the "priestly" and the "holy" are primal requirements, without which there is no possibility that the world of God's hopes and expectations can ever be "very good." He may be wrong, of course, in which case we should expect God to endorse (in some way) the friends' rebuke of him. But if Job is right, if indeed he models another world that God would happily inhabit, then we may expect that neither Job nor God have yet reached the end of this journey. ["Another World to Live In"]

NOTES

[1] F. I. Anderson, *Job: An Introduction and Commentary* (TOTC; Leicester, England: Inter-Varsity Press, 1976), 238.

[2] R. Gordis, *The Book of Job: Commentary, New Translation, and Special Studies* (New York: Jewish Theological Seminary of America, 1978), 546.

[3] S. Terrien, "The Book of Job," *IB*, vol. 3, ed. G. Buttrick (New York: Abingdon Press, 1954), 1117.

[4] Terrien, *Job: Poet of Existence* (Indianapolis: Bobb Merrell, 1958), 186.

[5] G. Fohrer, "The Righteous Man in Job 31," *Essays in Old Testament Ethics*, ed. J. L. Crenshaw, J. T. Willis (New York: KTAV Publishing House, 1974), 19.

[6] E. M. Good, *In Turns of Tempest: A Reading of Job with a Translation* (Stanford: Stanford University Press, 1990), 315.

[7] Ibid., 317; cf. D. Simundson, *The Message of Job: A Theological Commentary* (Augsburg Old Testament Studies; Minneapolis: Ausgburg Publishing House, 1986): "Job cannot let go of the doctrine of retribution. It is too important for his ideas of justice and how God works in the world" (117).

[8] On Job's view that tragedy has no place in his world and should therefore have no place in God's, see C. Newsom, *The Book of Job: A Contest of Moral Imaginations* (Oxford: Oxford University Press, 2003), 196: "The key to the rhetoric [of Job 31] is the way in which Job inscribes and reinscribes God in this moral world. At the same time that Job is constructing his own ethos, he is simultaneously constructing the ethos of God. . . . In Job's construction, God functions in a thoroughly Durkheimian way as the social and moral order writ large."

[9] Cf. L. Perdue on Job 31:35-37: "And now the Primal Man, flushed by the ambition of coveted royalty, steps forth to claim his throne. A human ruler voicing the anguish and pride of all humanity is set to abandon God and the folly of religion for mortal rule. The tale of Job is a redescription of the mythic drama of the fall. Job is the man who would be god" (*Wisdom in Revolt: Metaphorical Theology in the book of Job* [JSOTSup 112; Sheffield: JSOT Press, 1991], 193).

[10] J. Wharton, *Job* (*Westminster Bible Companion*; Louisville KY: Westminster John Knox Press, 1999), 131.

[11] J. Gerald Janzen, *Job* (Atlanta: John Knox, 1985), 215.

[12] J. Hartley, *The Book of Job* (NICOT; Grand Rapids MI: William B. Eerdmans, 1988), 407.

[13] Wharton, *Job,* 130.

[14] Good, *In Turns of Tempest*, 316.

[15] Gordis, *Book of Job,* 542.

[16] For this expression, see Janzen (*Job,* 213), who notes that the Hebrew verb "to swear, take an oath" is semantically related to the word for the number "seven." As he puts it, "the act of swearing involves, in some way, the act of 'sevening.'"

[17] On the importance of the legal metaphor in Job 31, see N. Habel, *The Book of Job: A Commentary* (OTL; Philadelphia: Westminster Press, 1985), 427-31; cf. M. B. Dick, "The Legal Metaphor in Job 31," CBQ 41 (1979): 37-50; idem, "Job 31, the Oath of Innocence, and the Sage," ZAW 95 (1983): 31-53; S. H. Scholnick, "The Meaning of *Mispat* in the book of Job," JBL 101 (1982): 521-29; idem, "Poetry in the Courtroom: Job 38–41," *Directions in Biblical Hebrew Poetry*, ed. E. R. Follis (Sheffield: JSOT, 1987), 185-204.

[18] Gordis, *Book of Job,* 542.

[19] Janzen, *Job,* 210-12; idem, "Job's Oath," *RevExp* 99 (2002): 597-605.

[20] C. Newsom, *Book of Job,* 195; cf. idem, "The Book of Job," in vol. 4 of *NIB* (Nashville: Abingdon Press, 1996), 551-55.

[21] Newsom, *Book of Job,* 195.

[22] The word "grind" (*ṭāḥan;* v. 10) may refer to the humiliation and abuse of slave labor, e.g., being forced to grind with millstones (Exod 11:5; Judg 16:21; Isa 47:2). It also connotes sexual servitude, especially in rabbinic interpretation (Gordis, *Book of Job,* 346).

[23] Gordis, *Book of Job,* 345-46.

[24] M. Pope, *Job* (AB; Garden City NY: Doubleday, 1979), 230; Habel, *Book of Job,* 433; cf. Newsom, "The Book of Job," 553.

[25] Fohrer, "The Righteous Man in Job 31," 10.

[26] Cf. Habel, who notes that although Job acts in accord with conventional patriarchal practice, which understands sacrifice to be the responsibility of the head of the family (cf. Gen 8:20; 22:2, 13; 31:54; 46:1), he nevertheless "plays the part of the perfect priest" (*Book of Job,* 88).

[27] For further discussion of Job's subversive covenantal instincts, see Wm. Scott Green, "Stretching the Covenant: Job and Judaism," *RevExp* 99 (2002): 569-77.

[28] For further discussion of what follows, see Samuel E. Balentine, *Leviticus* (IBC; Louisville: John Knox Press, 2002), 104-17; idem, "Job as Priest to the Priests," *Ex Auditu* 18 (2002): 29-52.

[29] On this term, see Samuel E. Balentine, *The Torah's Vision of Worship* (Minneapolis: Fortress Press, 1998), 167-72.

[30] B. Bamberger, "Leviticus," *The Torah: A Modern Commentary*, ed. W. G. Plaut, B. Bamberger (New York: Union of American Hebrew Congregations, 1981), 890.

[31] For further discussion of what follows, see Balentine, *Leviticus,* 149-67.

[32] Cf. B. Zuckerman, *Job the Silent: A Study in Historical Counterpoint* (New York: Oxford University Press, 1991), n.321, 255.

[33] Pope, *Job,* 235.

[34] Habel, *Book of Job,* 437-38; similarly, Newsom, "The Book of Job," 554. On the difficulties of the text and other interpretations, see Pope, *Job,* 236-37; Gordis, *Book of Job,* 352-53.

[35] See the incisive comments of J. Milgrom, *Leviticus 17–22* (AB; New York: Doubleday, 2000), 1418.

[36] Dick, "The Legal Metaphor in Job 31," 47-49.

[37] Newsom, *Book of Job,* 195, 196.

[38] Janzen, *Job,* 215.

[39] If conformity is the objective, then the proposals of G. Fohrer (*Das Buch Hiob* [KAT; Gütersloh: Gerd Mohn, 1963], 440-42) and Gordis (*Book of Job,* 545) that vv. 38-40 be

relocated after v. 34 have merit. Gordis hypothesizes as follows: "Evidently, a scribe omitted vv. 38-40b by accident and they added at the end of the chapter."

[40] Habel, *Book of Job,* 440.

[41] Janzen, *Job,* 215.

[42] Ibid., 216.

[43] J. Blenkinsopp, *The Pentateuch: An Introduction to the First Five Books of the Bible* (New York: Doubleday, 1992), 224.

[44] Newsom, *Book of Job,* 184.

[45] Ibid., 196.

[46] Ibid.

[47] Ibid., 199.

[48] Ibid. For Newsom's discussion of the "tragic sublime" in God's world, see 234-258.

[49] The phrase "grammar of creation" I take from G. Steiner, *Grammars of Creation* (New Haven and London: Yale University Press, 2001). For discussion of Steiner's arguments in connection with the unsettling grammar in the prologue of Job, see further Samuel E. Balentine, "For No Reason," *Int* 57 (2003): 349-69.

[50] E. Scarry, *On Beauty and Being Just* (Princeton: Princeton University Press, 1999), 3.

[51] Ibid., 57-134, especially 86-124.

[52] Ibid., 91.

[53] Ibid., 90 (emphasis added).

[54] Ibid., 110.

[55] Ibid., 119.

THE INTRODUCTION OF
ELIHU, THE "ANSWERER"

Job 32:1-22

The Speeches of Elihu, Job 32:1–37:24

At this point in the Joban drama, the *problem* of the book, set forth
in the prologue (1:1–2:13)—God's affliction of an innocent person
"for no reason"—has been established. A *debate* about how to address
the problem has run its winding course, from Job's opening curses
and laments (Job 3), to the three friends' responses and Job's counter-
arguments (Job 4–28), and then to Job's final summation (Job
29–31). Once "the words of Job are ended" (Job 31:40), both Job
and his readers wait anxiously for the *resolution*, which the story's plot
line locates in God, who has been palpably silent since speaking the
chilling words to the *satan* that appear to have sealed Job's fate: "Very
well, he is in your power; only spare his life" (2:6).

Instead of God, the book now brings on to the stage Elihu, a new
and unanticipated character. And instead of a divine word that may
resolve the problem, which seems to have been so thoroughly vetted,
we are given a lengthy discourse from Elihu, who claims for himself
the role of "Answerer." On first encounter, Elihu seems both a disappointing and irritating postponement of the expected resolution. His
contribution to the story has in fact been widely dismissed for a
variety of reasons. A majority of scholars regard his words as a later
addition to the book, an assessment that usually includes a decidedly
negative critique. [A Later Addition] At best, some concede that he provides a measure of comic relief, an easing of tensions that may be
compared to the roles of the *alazon* or buffoon in classical Greek
comedy or the fool in Shakespearian tragedy.[1] [CD: "The Great Reservoir of
Comedy"] At worst, others treat Elihu as a figure worthy of ridicule and
contempt, like "someone who has defaced a cultural monument with
his graffiti and forever destroyed a part of the observer's satisfaction."[2]
With either assessment, the inclination of many will be to skip over
Elihu and move on directly to the divine speeches in chapters 38–41,
which seem to hold the better promise of satisfying our pursuit of the
end of the story.

The final form of the book demands more than this. The first clue
is the sheer length of chapters 32–37. Following the narrative intro-

---

A Later Addition

> A variety of historical-critical arguments, both stylistic and substantive, support the near consensus scholarly view that Elihu's speeches are a later addition to the book of Job, most likely composed by a different author than the one(s) responsible for the other speeches. (For the counter argument that Elihu's speeches, if not original to the book, at least function as part of the book's intentional literary design, see N. Habel, "The Role of Elihu in the Design of the book of Job," *In the Shelter of Elyon: Essays on Ancient Palestinian Life and Literature in Honor of G. W. Ahlström*, ed.W. B. Barrick, J. R. Spencer [Sheffield: JSOT Press, 1984], 81-88; J. Gerald Janzen, *Job* [Atlanta: John Knox, 1985], 217-18.) For a full discussion of the debate, readers should consult the standard commentaries. The following discernments are representative:

- Elihu is not mentioned in either the prologue or the epilogue
- Neither the friends (Eliphaz, Bildad, Zophar) nor Job speak *of* or *to* him
- He is the only character in the book who has an Israelite name and a genealogy that suggest Israelite origins (32:2)
- The prose introduction in 32:1-5 differs in tone and style from the introductions of the other characters
- His speeches display a number of distinctive linguistic traits, e.g., an extensive use of the divine name *'el* (19x), a preference for the first-person pronoun *ănî*, "I" (9x), use of particular words not found elsewhere in the book (e.g., *dēaʿ*, "knowledge"), and a preference for addressing Job by name (32:12; 33:1, 31; 34:5; 7, 35, 36; 35:16; 37:14), including more Aramaisms than in the other speeches, which likely suggests a later dating. (For discussion and statistics, see S. R. Driver and G. B. Gray, *A Critical and Exegetical Commentary on the Book of Job* [Edinburgh: T and T. Clark, 1921], xli-xlvii; Y. A. Hoffman, *A Blemished Perfection: The Book of Job in Context* [JSOTSup 213; Sheffield: Sheffield Academic Press, 1996], 187.)
- He cites or alludes to the previous speeches of Job and the friends (e.g., 33:8-13; 34:5-6; 35:2-3), and he anticipates (36:22–37:24) the speeches that God delivers at the end of the book, which suggest that he (or his author) is a later reader of what has already been written.

---

duction (32:1-5), Elihu speaks for 159 uninterrupted verses. As a result, he commands center stage for longer than any of the three friends who preceded him. Indeed, with the exception of Job, Elihu has more lines than any character in the book, including God, whose words from the whirlwind, though surely privileged in important ways, comprise 123 verses. Although length alone does not guarantee the importance of Elihu's words—the numbers may add up to little more than bluster and banality—it does invite, at the very least, what Newsom calls a "deliberately generous curiosity."[3] Even if readers find the arguments for assigning Elihu's speeches to a different author and a later date than the rest of the book to be convincing, it is unlikely that this determination alone can satisfy the curiosity Newsom commends. Other questions require attention, including the following, which stake out a point of departure:

- What role do the speeches play in the overall design of the book?
- Why should an author, at whatever time, have thought it useful to introduce a character who believes that he can offer a better, or at least different, answer to Job than the three friends, and perhaps than even God himself?
- Finally, if we suspend our judgment long enough to grant Elihu the hearing he so persistently demands (32:10; 33:1, 31, 33; 34:2, 10,

16), do his words teach us anything about what is required of those who would be friends to the Jobs of this world?

COMMENTARY

Chapter 32 invites us to meet Elihu, first as the narrator presents him (vv. 1-5), then as Elihu the character presents himself (vv. 6-22). Both introductions profile Elihu as one who is concerned with the "answers" Job's problem requires but has not yet received (vv. 1, 3, 5, 6, 12, 17, 20). The relationship between Elihu as the narrator presents him and Elihu as he sees himself is, however, ambiguous. The narrator provides the credentials—name, family of origin, place of residence, tribal affiliation—that presumably validate Elihu's presence in this story; and yet, by the narrator's own account, it is Elihu's anger, not his pedigree, that compels him to speak (vv. 2 [2x], 3, 5). Elihu describes himself as a youth (v. 6) whose credentials are too insignificant to give him a voice in this story. He is "timid and afraid" (v. 6), not angry. He speaks not because he is overcome by human emotions, but because he is divinely inspired (vv. 8, 18; cf. 33:4). It is this inspiration that defines his *claim to knowledge*, despite his youth (vv. 6-10), his *impatience* with the friends, who despite their age do not possess the wisdom to answer Job (vv. 11-16), and his *compulsion* to speak in the sure conviction that his words alone provide what has been lacking thus far (vv. 17-22). [Structure of Job 32:1-22]

Structure of Job 32:1-22
> 32:1-5 Elihu as the narrator presents him
> v. 2a Elihu "became *angry*";
> v. 2b "He was *angry* at Job"
> v. 3a "He was *angry* also at Job's friends"
> v. 5 Elihu "became *angry*"
> 32:6-22 Elihu as he presents himself
> vv. 6-10 His claim to *inspiration*
> vv. 11-16 His *impatience* with his friends
> vv. 17-22 His *compulsion* to speak

The difference in the two introductions builds into the story a tension that readers must navigate. Are we to understand Elihu as angry or inspired? Does he draw upon a mixed reservoir of reasons characterized by both compulsions at the same time? To sharpen the issue, is Elihu's anger righteous, thus commendable (see [CD: Righteous Anger]), or is his righteousness only rage by another name, a pious mask for a feigned virtue? ["Assume a Virtue, if You Have It Not"] As the journey towards hearing Elihu begins, therefore, the reader senses from the outset that the final assessment of what he says will almost certainly be conflicted.

Elihu as the Narrator Presents Him, 32:1-5

For the first time since the prologue, a narrator steps into the story to set the stage for what follows. In the first instance, the narrator gives but a brief mention of Job's origins "in the land of Uz" (1:1a), then

"Assume a Virtue, if You Have It Not"

Shakespeare's profile of Hamlet has long invited debate concerning whether he is more a *moral idealist*, whose virtue constrains him to implore his mother, Queen Gertrude, to confess her sexual transgressions, or *a self-righteous opportunist*, who is motivated by his own consuming jealousy. In trying to coerce a confession from the Queen, he commends to her the same relationship with virtue that seems to vex his own conscience: "Assume a virtue, if you have it not" (*Hamlet*, III, iv, 161). As he concludes his appeal, he adds this telltale admission:

I must be cruel only to be kind:
Thus bad begins and worse is left remains behind. (III, iv, 179)

spells out the special virtues that both define his character and his importance for the story: he is "blameless and upright, one who fears God and turned away from evil" (1:1b). As the prologue unfolds the story, the congruence of Job's character and his actions (1:21; 2:10), twice affirmed by God (1:8; 2:3), encourages the presumption that this profile of Job is true and reliable. We read believing that this narrator is trustworthy (see the commentary on 1:1-5).

The narrative in chapter 32 likely encourages the same presumption. When the narrator informs us that "these three men" have ceased to answer Job (v. 1a), we know this to be the case. When the narrator adds that Job still believes he is "righteous in his own eyes" (v. 1b), that he still believes he is "more in the right than God" (v. 2b; cf. NJPS: "he thought himself right against God"), and that he does so, despite the friends' persistent claim that Job, not God, is "in the wrong" (v. 3b), we have little difficulty accepting the assessment at face value.

Even so, a close reading of the text may invite an initial suspicion. The affirmation at the end of v. 1—"he was righteous *in his own eyes*"—appears in some ancient versions as "he was righteous *in their eyes*," which suggests that Job has in fact finally convinced the friends with his arguments. Because this reading seems so inconsistent with what the story thus far supports, it may be dispatched without much concern. The affirmation at the end of v. 3 is more complicated. According to an ancient Masoretic tradition, the original text, which reads "and so they declared *God* to be wrong," has been corrected by the scribes, in the interests of piety, to read "and so they declared *Job* to be wrong." [*Tiqqune Sopherim*] Presumably, the scribes wished to avoid the notion that by failing to refute Job's claim to innocence, the friends inadvertently conceded God's guilt. The original "uncorrected" reading, however, is consistent with what Job has argued (27:5), with what seems to have provoked Elihu's anger (e.g., 33:8-12; 34:10-12; 36:5-15), and with what God himself subsequently seems concerned to counter (40:6-8). English translations adopt different approaches to the problem: some adopt the scribal correction and assign the original version to the notes (REB); others do the opposite (NRSV, NIV). Such

---

Tiqqune Sopherim

AΩ The Masoretic text notes that the phrase in Job 32:3, "and so they declared Job to be wrong," is one of eighteen *tiqqune sopherim*, "corrections of the scribes." According to the conventional understanding, the scribes, who are distinguished above all else by their dedication to preserving the received text, believed that exceptions should be made when the text was offensive to God. A parade example occurs in Gen 18:22, where the scribes thought it preferable to change the received text, "while *God* remained standing before *Abraham*," which suggests that Abraham took the lead in communicating to God, to "while *Abraham* remained standing before *God*" (see NRSV), which restores the initiative to God. It is worth noting that the scribal corrections in both Job 32:3 and Gen 18:22 deal with situations in which the received text suggests that humans have raised questions about God's justice.

---

different approaches blur but cannot finally erase the impression that the narrator's words require close scrutiny.

The description of Elihu's family credentials (v. 2) also seems, on first reading, to reinforce the reader's presumptive trust in the narrator's reliability. The name "Elihu," which means, "He is my God," belongs to several Hebrew characters, including the great grandfather of Samuel and the brother of David (1 Sam 1:1; 1 Chr 12:20 [21], 26:7; 27:18). It is also a variant spelling of the name "Elijah" ("YHWH is my God"), which nudges us toward the recognition that Elihu now appears on the scene, like his prophetic forebear, to announce an authoritative word from God. The name of Elihu's father, "Barachel" (*barak'ēl*) means either "He blesses God (El) or "God (El) has blessed." The name is not found in the Bible, but it too is a Semitic name, given to diaspora Jews from Nippur.[4] "Buz" is the name of Abraham's nephew (Gen 22:20, 21), the brother of Uz, the putative founder of Job's tribe (Gen 10:22, 23), and a territory in northwest Arabia whose destiny, according to Jer 25:23, is to yield, ultimately, to God's authoritative judgment. The word "Ram," otherwise unattested as a clan name, is used elsewhere with Judahite connections (1 Chr 2:9, 25, 27) that may be tracked not only to David, but also to Jesus (Ruth 4:19).

The narrator's extensive delineation of Elihu's family origins, which exceeds what we have been given for Job or his three friends, initially tilts readers toward an unquestioning acceptance of this data. On close inspection, however, almost every detail raises at least as many questions as it seems to answer. If the name "Elihu" invites us to think of Elijah the prophet, then we cannot tap into Elijah's story without confronting its candid affirmation of this prophet's doubt about God's ability to prove, in the face of opposition, that God has a demonstrable claim on truth (1 Kgs 19:4-18). If we are to accept that Hebraic tradition associates the name of Elihu's father, "Barachel," with God's "blessing" (*bārāk*), then we must also acknowledge that according to the narrator of the prologue, the distinction between *divine blessing* and *divine cursing* in the book of Job is open to question (see [Blessing/Cursing in Job]). If the word "Buz" suggests a connection to a *positive* trajectory in Hebrew thought, which is anchored to the genealogy of Abraham, then we must also recognize that the same word puns a *negative* word meaning "shame" (*bôš*).[5] If the word "Ram" means "high" or "exalted" in Hebrew, then we must factor into our assessment that the same word may also mean "haughty," which is a disposition typically condemned in Hebraic thought (Deut 8:14; cf. Ps 18:27). The polyvalence in the narrator's genealogical profile of Elihu is best captured by E. Good, who suggests this translation for 32:2: "My-God-he, son of Bless-El, the Contemptible, of the clan of Uppity." With characteristic understatement, Good adds, this phrase "may be at least a subliminal message."[6]

Of all the information the narrator provides, the accent on Elihu's anger is the most curious. The Hebrew word order in v. 2 suggests that the first thing we encounter on meeting Elihu, before any other information is provided, is his emotional state: "And he was angry, Elihu the son of Barachel the Buzite." The idiom *ḥārāh 'ap*, literally "[his] nose burned," occurs four times in the narrative (vv. 2 [2x], 3, 5). The phrase, especially this idiomatic use of the word *'ap*, "nose," which connotes the gesture of "snorting," is a common one and is used throughout the Old Testament to convey both human and divine anger. In the book of Job, for example, the friends frequently warn Job that the wicked bring upon themselves God's anger (4:9; 20:23, 28; cf. 18:4). Job himself senses that God's actions toward him are motivated more by anger than justice (9:5, 13; 14:13; 19:11; 21:17), and he defends himself against the charge that he is guilty of responding to God in kind by insisting that it is the "breath" and "spirit of God," not anger, that fills his nostrils and emboldens him to speak as he does (27:3).

The narrator's description of Elihu's anger, however, appears to set him apart from the other friends. He is the only friend whose response to Job is inflamed by wrath. The phrase that conveys Elihu's anger is in fact applied to only one other character in the book. At the end of the drama, the narrator of the epilogue says that God's "wrath is kindled" (*ḥārāh 'appî*; 42:7) against Eliphaz and his two friends, because they "have not spoken of me what is right." Elihu's narrator hints that Elihu and God draw upon a shared stock of emotions. This in turn invites the presumption that Elihu's inspired anger places him in the esteemed company of Samson and Saul, both of whom are said to be so filled with holy wrath that they execute a violent retribution against those who oppose the mission God has assigned to them (Judg 14:19; 1 Sam 11:6). This presumption, like those reviewed above, also merits close inspection ["Anger as Soon as Fed Is Dead"]

What set of beliefs inform and summon Elihu's anger? How are these beliefs threatened by what has transpired in the story thus far? Are these beliefs and the anger that conveys them in fact consonant with God's character, or are they perhaps incompatible with it? The narrator's fourfold reference to Elihu's anger provides a psychological profile that launches the exploration of these and other questions.

The first reference at the beginning of v. 2 describes Elihu's anger in absolute terms.[7] Anger is an emotion, presumably one among a range of others, like fear, compassion, love, and grief, which Elihu shares with any human being. The second, third, and fourth references connect Elihu's anger to reasons, that is, to a triggering experience that provides both the occasion and the justification for this particular display of emotion. He is angry with Job (v. 2b), because Job has presumed that his claim to justice is more right than God's apparent refusal to honor it. He is angry with the friends (vv. 3b, 5b), because they have failed to provide the answers that refute Job's claim. Depending on which text we read (see above), the friends' failure is cause for anger, either because they have tried to declare that Job was wrong, although they have been unable to state clearly why this is so, or because their failure to prove Job's guilt has left God vulnerable to indictment. With either reading, the narrator seems intent on establishing the fact that Elihu's anger is not trivial or insignificant. It is neither an impulsive nor an irrational response. It is instead a response vitally connected to values that Elihu understands to be deeply rooted in religious belief. [The Intelligence of Emotions] Both Job and the friends, the narrator suggests, are worthy of Elihu's anger, because they do not rightly articulate the connection between human suffering and divine justice.

One further observation concerning Elihu's emotional profile is in order. If the narrator's objective is to connect Elihu's anger to normative religious convictions about suffering and God, then it is interesting to note both what rises to a sufficient level to justify this anger and what does not (see further, "Connections"). From the narrator's perspective, it is appropriate to be angry with those like Job who challenge God's administration of justice, but the innocent deaths of Job's seven sons and three daughters seems insufficient cause for rage. It is appropriate to be angry with those like the friends who fumble the chance to defend God against the charge of injustice, but the unanswered cries of sufferers like Job who claim to be innocent make no comparable demand on the narrator's monitoring of Elihu's passions. It is appropriate to be angry when the religious convictions that provide society's moral compass are compromised by God's spokespersons, whether

"Anger as Soon as Fed is Dead"

> Mine enemy is growing old—
> I have at last revenge—
> The Palate of the Hate departs—
> If any would avenge
>
> Let him be quick—the Viand flits—
> It is a faded Meat—
> Anger as soon as fed is dead—
> 'Tis starving that makes it fat—

Emily Dickinson, "#1509," in *The Complete Poems of Emily Dickinson*, ed. T. H. Johnson (Boston/New York: Little, Brown and Company, 1960), 634.

The Intelligence of Emotions

In making her case for the "intelligence of emotions," Martha Nussbaum argues against the common assumption that emotions are different than beliefs.

A point commonly made about emotions, purportedly in order to distinguish them from beliefs, is that they have a different "direction of fit" : in belief we are trying to fit our mental attitude to the world; in emotion, we are trying to make the world fit our mental attitude. I think there are several confusions with in this picture. First of all . . . emotions do attempt to fit the world—both to take in the events that really do take place, and to get an appropriate view of what matters or has value. Second, they really don't try to get the world to fit them. Emotions may or may not engender desires for action, which might, if successful, make the world a better world for the objects of our emotions . . . . But even if they do engender such desires: does the world thereby fit the emotions better? Fear [or in Elihu's case, anger] says that that there is danger at hand. If that emotion is correct, then the world right now does contain danger. If I change the world by successfully evading the danger, the emotion presumably will change accordingly. Now the world no longer contains that danger, so I don't have fear any longer. But the idea that we are trying to make the world fit the emotions suggests, oddly, that it doesn't fit them already. . . .

In short: the objection denies the evident fact that emotions are responsive to the way the world already is. It does not succeed in establishing any interesting asymmetry between emotions and beliefs.

For further discussion of Nussbaum's views on emotions as intelligent expressions of beliefs and values, see the "Connections" at the end of this chapter.

M. Nussbaum, *Upheavals of Thought: The Intelligence of Emotions* (Cambridge: Cambridge University Press, 2001), 48-49.

---

through ignorance or indifference. But should persons whom God declares to be "blameless and upright" become lost in a world where "evil" (2:11; *rāʿah*; NRSV: "troubles") comes "for no reason" (2:3), Elihu's narrator knows no religious justification for adjusting the moral compass by which they navigate their way. They must head for true north, which given the narrator's orientation seems to mean that they must turn away from anger and towards God, whose charting of the righteous path they must follow is both certain and inscrutable.

The implicit religious beliefs that inform this introductory presentation of Elihu, especially the sense of what does and does not legitimately trigger his anger, raise necessary questions about the provenance of the narrator. If, as a majority of scholars agree, both this narrative introduction and the speeches that follow come from a later author, then can we identify the cultural, historical, and religious context that shapes his understanding? The lack of hard evidence means that we must settle for relative, not absolute, dates for the Elihu speeches. The presence of the speeches in the Job manuscript from Qumran (4QJoba) confirms that they were part of this story at least by the first century BCE. Linguistic evidence suggests a general provenance in the post-exilic period, most likely postdating both the prologue/epilogue and the poetic dialogues.[8] On the basis of comparisons between Elihu's ideas and those of Qoheleth, Ben Sira, and other early Hellenistic literature, H.-M. Wahl has proposed a more specific dating to the third century BCE.[9] In sum, the data we have strongly suggest that the Elihu speeches are among the latest wisdom writings in the Hebrew Bible. If this dating bears up, then the author of the Elihu speeches may be understood as providing "the first commentary" on what was in effect his "book" of Job.[10]

In this respect, as Newsom has noted, "Elihu represents the position of all readers." He, like us, has been listening in on a conversation that has begun without him. Like us, he is an onlooker who finds himself engaged by a story that compels his response (see further the reflections on the "outsider's" perspective on pain in Job 30, "Connections"). Like us, his response is informed and shaped by ideas, beliefs, and values that connect with those he finds in the Job story but which must now be filtered through his own perspective concerning their merit for a later generation of readers. Thus, *as we listen in on this author listening in on Job,* we are invited to examine not only his response and the beliefs that inform it but also *our response to his response.* The question before us is, does the invitation to add responses accented by anger and/or inspiration provide the "answers" the Jobs of the world need, wherever and whenever they speak? ["The Belatedness of All Reading"]

Elihu as He Presents Himself: a Claim to Inspiration, 32:6-10

Elihu (the character) presents himself first to the friends. He begins not by speaking angrily, as the narrator has led us to expect, but rather by declaring that he has been too "timid and afraid" to speak at all (v. 6b). He ends, however, by saying that he can now justify inserting himself

---

"The Belatedness of All Reading"

Newsom appropriates the phrase "the belatedness of all reading" from the literary critic Harold Bloom. In *Agon: Towards a Theory of Revisionism* (Oxford: Oxford University Press, 1982), Bloom argues that every reader comes belatedly to a text that has already served a previous generation and now must be reinterpreted to serve a later one, if it is to continue to have currency. This reinterpretation necessarily enacts what he calls an interpretive "swerve" whereby the present reader effectively usurps the authority of previous readers.

Newsom draws out the implications of this theory for reading the Elihu speeches as follows:

For Elihu's generation, the moral world has tilted, perhaps ever so slightly, on its axis. That tilt, however, is sufficient for moral and religious issues to be configured differently and to require the words that Elihu so urgently wishes to speak. The modern interpretive difficulty is that the axis of our moral own world has tilted considerably more, so that it is hard to measure and appreciate what appear to us extremely subtle differences between Elihu and the Joban dialogue.

In her view, Elihu justifies his "usurpation of authority" by arguing that he represents the views of a younger generation no longer satisfied with the reading of its elders. This observation invites another, in turn. The "mission of true art," Oscar Wilde says, is to "make us pause and look at a thing a second time." Such may be the summons of the book of Job, not only for Elihu, but also for all of us who are belated readers of this drama.

C. Newsom, *The Book of Job: A Contest of Moral Imaginations* (Oxford: Oxford University Press, 2003), 204.

O. Wilde cited in Joyce Carol Oates, *The Faith of a Writer: Life, Craft, Art* (New York: HarperCollins, 2003), 110.

into this drama with authority: "Listen to me, I will speak what I know, I myself" (v. 10b).[11] Elihu's movement from reticence to declaration suggests that he has had to resolve an argument within himself before he gets the consent of his conscience to speak.[12] The reason for his transformation occurs in the middle of this pericope: he understands himself to be inspired (v. 8).

Elihu's *reticence to speak* is informed by his acceptance of a traditional axiom: wisdom resides in the elders, not in the youth. He has therefore respectfully deferred to the expectation that he should be quiet and listen to those who, like his elder friends, have earned the right to speak: "Let days speak, and many years teach wisdom" (v. 7). Nevertheless, having deferred to his elders, he concludes that age alone does not guarantee either understanding or wisdom sufficient to judge Job's story (v. 9).

Elihu's *decision to speak* draws upon stories and affirmations that are also deeply rooted in the Hebraic mindset. Gideon (Judg 6:15), Saul (1 Sam 9:21), and Jeremiah (Jer 1:6) are prime exemplars of persons who were summoned and equipped by God for extraordinary leadership, despite their youth. Thus, on the one hand, Elihu knows that he is right to be respectfully silent before his elders. On the other, he knows that even a youth must speak, when chosen by God. If he does not, he defaults on God's claim on his life. ["Youth May Be Forgiven When It Is Brash and Noisy"] In sum, Elihu must negotiate competing, but presumably equally authoritative, cultural and religious claims on his self-understanding.

Elihu's negotiation of these claims in favor of the decision to speak rests on his appeal to inspiration (v. 8). It is the "spirit (*rûaḥ*) in a person, the breath (*nĕšāmāh*) of the Almighty," not age alone, which gives one wisdom and understanding. Elihu's appeal to inspiration seems relatively straightforward. He, like all human beings, has been created by the God who breathes into the nostrils the breath of life (Gen 2:7). His inspiriting, his source for inner wisdom, is not less than that which exists in his elders. Indeed, there is strong precedence for him to claim that youth often exhibits more God-given wisdom than

---

"Youth May Be Forgiven When It Is Brash and Noisy"

In the foreword to the publication of a second collection of his poems, W. H. Auden muses on what justification he can offer for rearranging and revising works that he had written when he was younger. He notes that when the first collection was published in 1944, he was thirty-seven, and as he admits, "still too young to have any sure sense of the direction in which I was moving." "Youth," he suggests, "may be forgiven when it is brash and noisy." He trusts that the second collection, published in 1965 when he was nearing sixty, will demonstrate that he knows himself and his poetic intentions better. Even so, to the line cited above, he adds an important qualification, "Youth may be forgiven when it is brash and noisy, *but this does not mean that brashness and noise are virtues.*"

"Author's Foreword," in W. H. Auden, *Collected Poems*, ed. E. Mendelson (New York: Vintage International, 1976, 1991), XXV-XXVI (emphasis added).

age: students who meditate on Torah may have "more understanding" than their teachers and elders (Ps 119:98-100); young people called and equipped by God, like Joseph (Gen 41:37-39) and Daniel (Dan 1:17-20; 2:10-23), may possess more wisdom than all the sage counselors in a king's court.

Some have argued that Elihu lays claim to a "rather unique theory of inspiration," perhaps one that appeals to the storied tradition of Israel's prophets (cf. Num 11:26-30).[13] Although he does seem to understand his inspiration to surpass that of the friends, it is not clear, either from Job's perspective or the reader's, exactly why this is so. At the outset of the dialogues, Eliphaz evoked creation imagery to claim an inspiration that he presumed gave him special insight into what God wants to teach Job (see the commentary on 4:7–5:7). Job rejected the claim, countering that he has understanding equal to any his friends offer (cf. 12:1-4). Moreover, when Job draws upon the spirit of God that gives him breath, the same spirit to which Eliphaz and his friends appeal (27:3; cf. 26:1-4), he is convinced that he, not they, has the better claim to wisdom. They claim inspiration but speak "falsely" and "deceitfully" (13:7) in order to salvage God's justice by coercing from Job a confession of sin that compromises his integrity. Job claims that his inspiration justifies a resolute defense of his integrity, and the righteousness that defines it, even if such inspiration puts him at odds with God: "Far be it from me to say that you are right. . . . I hold fast my righteousness, and will not let it go" (27:6).

Even if we grant that Elihu claims to be gifted with a special inspiration, we have cause to wonder if his appearance on the scene does not return us full circle to where the dialogues began. First Eliphaz, now Elihu, claim divine inspiration for teaching Job that he must accept suffering as God's will for him, either by confessing his sin or by submitting to God's inscrutable ways of discipline (see Elihu's speech in ch. 33).[14] Job, drawing upon the same source of inspiration, argues that the Judge of the cosmos honors righteous resistance to innocent suffering, even if requires that God must correct the ways divine justice is executed. For all his claim to inspiration, therefore, Elihu appears destined from the outset to leave both Job and his readers with a still unresolved question. How does anyone know for certain that he or she has rightly discerned the mind of God? [Is Inspiration a Claim to Truth or a Defense for Deception?]

Elihu's Impatience with His Friends, 32:11-16

Whatever ambiguity Job may find in his friends' claim for inspiration, Elihu now makes clear that he has listened long enough to this debate.

Is Inspiration a Claim to Truth or a Defense for Deception?

At several places in this commentary, I have noted connections between Job and the creation imagery in Gen 1–3 (see **[Job 3 and Genesis 1]**) and elsewhere (e.g., **[CD: Psalm 8 and Job 7]**). J. Gerald Janzen suggests that the Elihu speeches may provide additional evidence for this linkage. He points to thematic similarities between Elihu's claim to speak for God and the narrative accounts in Gen 2–3 and 1 Kgs 22:5-22:

Both in the garden story and in the episode in First Kings, a human is confronted with the voice and the directive of God and then with another voice which also claims to speak for God. In the instance of the garden story, the snake's counsel is not offered in direct opposition to that of God, but rather as an alternative communication of what God knows and wishes the humans to know. Similarly, in the scene in First Kings, both Micaiah and the group of prophets claim sincerely to speak on behalf of God—and Micaiah even goes so far as to affirm the group in its claim to inspiration! What he goes on to point out, however, is that their inspiration serves a purpose other than that which they understand.

Given such competing claims to divine truth, the two narratives invite the question, Who can claim to speak the true voice of God? Against this question, the speeches of Elihu invite a similar and perhaps even more complex assessment. Job must decide not only whether Elihu or the friends has the more genuine word from God. He must also decide whether the inspiration that defines Elihu's anger is equal to or less than that which gives authority to God's anger (see the commentary on 32:1-5).

J. Gerald Janzen, *Job* (Atlanta: John Knox, 1985), 222.

He has waited patiently for the friends to make their best case against Job (v. 11); having suffered through their failure to do so, he will wait no longer (v. 16). He has "listened" while they "searched" (*ḥqr*; cf. 5:27; 8:8) for words that would defend God and definitively confute Job, and he has determined that their searching has produced no "answer" worthy of the inspiration they claim (v. 12). The friends have spoken at length, but in the end their words demonstrate only that they do not have the requisite wisdom to be the "arbiter" (v. 12: *mōkîaḥ*; NRSV: the "one that confuted") that Job has demanded (9:33; cf. 16:21). It is not certain that Elihu accepts Job's forensic definition of the arbiter's role, that is, one who insures impartiality in a legal case,[15] but it is clear that he knows that sufferers who raise questions like Job need answering. It is never sufficient, let alone faithful, especially when claiming to speak an inspired word from God concerning the role of suffering in life, to walk away conceding that the questioners have left the answerers psychically "shattered" (v. 15; NRSV: "dismayed").

The friends' failure, Elihu concludes, is the concession that no one but God can successfully answer the arguments of one like Job (v. 13). It is a concession Elihu deems unacceptable. It is one thing to speak God's truths gently; to do otherwise risks the pretension of overwhelming the transcendent with comprehension that claims more than it can ever justify. ["Forceful Hesitation" Is Not the Same Thing as "Bullying"] It is quite another to stand before those who question God and do nothing more than stutter and fumble. To do so is an abdication of one's stewardship of the faith, not humility. Elihu has listened long enough. With

---

"Forceful Hesitation" Is Not the Same Thing as "Bullying"

In his essay on Virginia Woolf, literary critic James Wood comments on her use of metaphor as a means of criticizing fiction. His description of Woolf's concern not to "overwhelm" fiction with "strong comprehension" suggests one way of assessing Elihu's approach to Job:

In her criticism, the language of metaphor becomes a way of speaking to fiction in its own accent, the only way of respecting fiction's ultimate indescribability. Metaphor is how the critic avoids *bullying* fiction with adult simplicities. For it is a language of *forceful hesitation*. Its force lies in the vigor and originality of Woolf's metaphors; its hesitation lies in its admission that in criticism the language of pure summation does not exist . . . . [Woolf] approaches fiction gently, seemingly *anxious not to overwhelm it with strong comprehension*.

J. Wood, "Virginia Woolf's Mysticism," *The Broken Estate: Essays on Literature and Belief* (New York: Random House, 1999), 92-93 (emphasis added).

---

so much at stake, he resolves to wait no longer. To do anything else would mean that when all is said and done, he will be judged with the same severity that he (or at least the narrator) has already reserved for Job's friends (cf. 42:7, 9).

Verse 14 suggests the track he will take. Although the syntax of the verse is somewhat awkward, Elihu seems to have resolved that he will respond to Job with arguments that are different from those of the friends. Commentators often dismiss Elihu's speeches as adding nothing new at all to the conversation. Perhaps this is so. But this is a judgment that must come at the end, after careful consideration of all that he says, not at the outset, before he has a chance to make his case. In the meantime, he insists that for all their long-windedness, the friends have in fact stopped talking too soon. When it comes to the matter of innocent suffering, Elihu now argues, the conversation is never over; there is always more to say.

Elihu's Compulsion to Speak, 32:17-22

Having resolved to speak (v. 10b: "I will speak what I know"), Elihu now readies himself to do just that (v. 17b: "I will speak what I know"). The language and imagery of his words indicates that his resolve has escalated to compulsion. The emphatic idiom for self-assertion, "I myself" (*ʾap ʾănî*; NRSV: "I also"), which Elihu speaks for the first time in v. 10, occurs twice more in v. 17. Words and phrases related to verbal speech repeat throughout: "I will answer" and "I will declare" (v. 17); "I am full of words" (v. 18); "I must speak," "I must open my lips," and "I will answer" (v. 20). Elihu uses a comparable range of terms to describe the friends' speech in vv. 11-16, but once he concludes that they "have nothing further to say" (vv. 15-16), he has no doubt that his words will provide what theirs have not.

The most vivid image Elihu uses to describe his compulsion to speak occurs in vv. 18-20. He is so "full of words" that he likens the internal pressure to that of a wineskin bursting with fermenting wine. If he does not open his mouth and release what is inside him, then he will explode. If we take the image as a genuine representation of what Elihu feels, then we may understand that like the other speakers in this drama, Elihu has both an urgency and passion to speak. Eliphaz begins his address with a rhetorical question that invites affirmation of his passion: "Who can keep from speaking?" (4:2). Zophar speaks "because of the agitation within me" (20:2). Job roils between curses and blessings, because he has no "ease," no "quiet," no "rest" (3:26). He speaks in the "bitterness" of his soul (10:2). He yearns for his "vexation" (6:2) to be heard for what it is, an honest and natural cry for someone to recognize that something has gone terribly wrong. After all, does not a wild ass bray when there is no food (6:5)? Even God, who twice answers Job "out of the whirlwind" (38:1; 40:6), speaks words that seem driven by an irresistible force. Taken at face value, Elihu's passion is commendable, perhaps even worthy of emulation. Like the prophet Jeremiah, who speaks in response to the burning fire raging inside him, we may think of Elihu saying, "I am weary with holding it in, and I cannot" (Jer 20:9). ["Job and Elihu"]

Newsom is probably right, however, when she concedes that most modern readers, including a good number of commentators on Job, will find it almost impossible to listen to Elihu with a straight face.[16] At best, some interpret his passion as little more than empty bombast; he is more fool than prophet, more to be laughed at than regarded. At worst, others read the imagery as grotesque and vulgar. ["A Constipated Fool"] When considering either of these negative views, Newsom's caution is prudent: "What is humorous in one culture, however, is no reliable guide to what is humorous in another. Within the context of ancient values and metaphors, Elihu says nothing absurd."[17]

Elihu concludes this justification for inserting himself into the conversation by affirming that his compulsion to speak is not only passionate but also principled. He will not use passion as an excuse for flattery or partiality (vv. 21-22). With respect to the former temptation, he asserts that he will not "lift his face" (v. 21a: *nāśāʾ pānîm*) to favor one side of an argument over another without persuasive reason for

---

"A Constipated Fool"

The poet's "wry humor," N. Habel suggests, exposes Elihu as both foolish and gross:

Elihu declares that he plans to "answer" with the dictates of his own "mind" or knowledge because he is "bloated" with arguments and has a "belly" bursting with "wind" (vv. 17-18). Unwittingly Elihu characterizes himself as a windbag and a constipated fool . . . . The inner compulsion to speak, which was experienced by Jeremiah as the fire of God's word burning within (Jer 20:9), is transformed by Elihu into a need to relieve himself of the wind building up in his belly (v. 20). "To relieve" (*rwh*) is an obvious wordplay on "wind" (*ruah*). Perhaps the innuendo of this wordplay is captured in the English expression "to pass wind."

N. Habel, *The Book of Job: A Commentary* (OTL; Philadelphia: Westminster Press, 1985), 444-45.

"Job and Elihu"

📖 This illumination, one of forty-three that occurs in a ninth century Greek codex of the book of Job preserved in the Saint John Monastery on Patmos, depicts Elihu and Job as they confront one another. To the right, Job sits on the ash heap, his position slightly elevated. His face, particularly the steady gaze of his eyes and the arched right eyebrow, suggests a resolve that belies the pain of his naked body, which is pock marked from head to toe with sores. To the left and a little lower, Elihu stands before him, wearing garments that indicate he has come to play his priestly role. His legs are bent at the knees, his left foot slightly lifted, as if he is preparing to move, ever so respectfully, a step closer to Job.

Job and Elihu. 9th C. Illumination. Saint John Monastery, Patmos. (Credit: Bibliotheque du Monastere St. Jean le Theologien, Patmos)

The extended right hands of the two persons form the center of the illumination. The fingers on Job's hand, darkened like the rest of his body, are spread and raised, palm upwards. The gesture could indicate both supplication to God and an inviting recognition of Elihu's approach. Elihu's hand is a mirror image of Job's, save for its almost transparent whiteness. Given Elihu's claim to inspiration (32:6-10), his gesture seems a sincere offer to share what illumines him with Job.

S. Terrien has suggested that the extended hands indicate the beginning of an honest exchange between Elihu and Job. Unlike the three friends, who talked *at* Job but never *to* him, Elihu seems to be constructing a "psychological bridge" between himself and Job that "lead[s] to the threshold of the Holy." If so, then we may concur with Terrien when he concludes that Elihu successfully "answered" Job: "Elihu subtly and effectively changed the attitude of Job, preparing him to respond when the Almighty would speak, even from the whirlwind."

Before accepting Terrien's assessment, we do well to let our gaze linger on the two extended hands of Job and Elihu. At the center of the illumination, the artist depicts not a bridge constructed but a space that still separates. Perhaps Elihu does sincerely wish to connect with Job. Perhaps he will be successful in changing Job's attitude if he does. At this point in the drama, however, the distance between the two hands conveys nothing so much as a "wordless proximity." (I take this suggestive phrase from James Wood. His novel *The Book Against God* [New York: Farrar, Straus, and Giroux, 2003], traces the strained relationship between Thomas, a disquieted atheist, and his father, a much beloved parish priest. In a scene from near the end of the book, Thomas mourns the distance, both physical and emotional, between them: "Father sat in his room, and I sat in mine, and I felt stunned by our wordless proximity. The pressure was intolerable" [214].) Elihu concludes his address to Job in ch. 37, after having spoken without interruption for 159 verses. The book records no response at all from Job to Elihu, which invites us to wonder whether there can ever be a bridge between sufferers who ask "Why?" and friends whose first step towards an answer begins with the word "because."

S. Terrien, *The Iconography of Job Through the Centuries: Artists as Biblical Interpreters* (University Park: Pennsylvania State University Press, 1996), 37.

doing so. With respect to the latter, he claims that what he says will not be swayed by any character's claim to a privileged hearing (v. 21b: *wĕʾel ʾādām lōʾ ʾăcanne*, lit., "and to any person I will not confer a title"; cf. Isa

44:5; 45:4). If his passion fails to keep faith with his principles, then he knows that his "Maker" will judge him severely and carry him away (v. 22).

By the end of chapter 32, Elihu appears to have made a strong case for the attention he demands. If Job truly yearns for an arbiter (cf. 9:33) who will grant him a fair hearing, then Elihu has the necessary impartiality that has thus far been missing. If the friends do not have the wisdom sufficient to answer Job, for lack of either inspiration or passion, then Elihu has more than enough of both to command center stage.

There remains, however, the still unresolved matter of the tension between the narrator's introduction of Elihu and his presentation of himself. Is it the raw emotion of anger that defines Elihu's entry into this conversation? If so, then his claim to inspiration, not to mention the impartial wisdom he believes it conveys, seems to be in question. Before he addresses even the first word to Job, which formally begins in the next chapter, we know that he is angry with both him and the friends. Is his anger an inspired emotion in search of a legitimate reason? If so, then what are the values and beliefs that trigger and presumably justify Elihu's anger? Either way, this double-sided introduction to Elihu merely *begins*, not *ends*, our quest to understand whether and why he merits the hearing he demands.

CONNECTIONS

Elihu is widely regarded as an "intruder."[18] He is certainly this. Nothing in the book thus far prepares the reader for his sudden appearance. Moreover, the regnant historical-critical assessment of his speeches as a late addition to the text is too weighty to deny. But Elihu is also more than simply an "intruder." He is more than just another character who wanders accidentally into the story because of vagaries in the transmission history of the text. He is "a reader of the book of Job." As Newsom puts it, he (or his author) "literally writes himself into the text."[19] He does so intentionally, because he has listened to the conversation and now, with the advantage of having considered what has been said by all parties, he believes it is important to add something that has been lacking. If we are to grant him the hearing he demands, then we must suspend suspicions long enough to consider the merits of what he says.

(1) Elihu intrudes *because he believes he is inspired* (vv. 6-10). Inspiration gives him access to understanding that enlarges upon what can be discerned through mere experience. How it does so, however,

---

"Now There Are Varieties of Gifts, but the Same Spirit"

Concerned with the divisions at Corinth, Paul suggests that the discord has been caused by a failure to recognize that the Holy Spirit equips persons in different ways, not to privilege some and diminish others, but to unit all in a healthy body of faith:

Now there are varieties of gifts, but the same Spirit; and there are varieties of services, but the same Lord; and there are varieties of activities, but it is the same God who activates all of them in everyone. (1 Cor 12:4-6)

---

needs explaining. In a secular world, one's claim to be inspired, that is, to have insight beyond what others may offer, is typically linked to a corresponding claim to be uniquely gifted in some way. A person may have a distinguishing intellectual capacity, for example, and thus be recognized as an inspired poet, scientist, economist, and so on. Viewed from this perspective, inspiration separates the extraordinary from the common, usually rewarding the former with honor, title, and other privileges (including, sometimes, monetary compensation) and consigning the latter to a lesser place within the hierarchy of society's values. In a religious world, however, inspiration has a more democratizing effect. God inspires all persons, Elihu claims, with gifts that make each one unique. Every person has worth, every person has a voice, every person has something to contribute. Persons who have no title do not require the counsel or consent of those who do before claiming to have something important to say. Young people are not required because of age to yield to the monopoly of the elders; women are not required because of gender to accept the decisions of men; persons of color are not required to acquiesce to the opinions of someone who is white.

Elihu's claim to inspiration is an important and necessary reminder, especially in a world so easily tempted to confer honor only on those who have a certain status in life, that everyone has something of value to contribute. Elihu's inspiration, like that which both the friends and Job claim for themselves, like that which we readers may also claim for ourselves, means that we all have a voice in the conversation about the meaning of suffering in the life of faith. ["Now There Are Varieties of Gifts, but the Same Spirit"]

(2) Elihu intrudes *because he believes that when it comes to innocent suffering, the conversation is never over* (vv. 11-16). Overcome by suffering that comes "for no reason," Job has raised the thunderous question "Why?" (3:11, 12, 20). Like everyone who has been driven to the ash heap, Job's question has "flushed out the trivial" from his life. [CD: "The Dirty Nurse, Experience"] His friends have tried to fill the vacuum with truth that calls upon the best wisdom they can muster, but their answers and Job's energy for listening to them are spent. As a result, when Job concludes his final summation by conceding that his words

have ended (31:40), the quest for understanding seems to have collapsed in a cul-de-sac. Both questioners and answerers appear too exhausted to find a way out. The best one can do, perhaps, is retreat to clichés: "When we all get to heaven, God will have a lot of explaining to do." Like most clichés, this one claims a victory by straining to deny defeat. [CD: "A Neverending Defeat"]

Questioners *do* grow weary of stumbling along the journey without sufficient resources. Respondents *do* find themselves depleted by the constant drain on their intellectual and spiritual assets. Nonetheless, the question "Why?" remains, for its source is in the abiding issues of human existence. Suffering is almost always more imposed than invited. We do not get to vote on its arrival; we do not have much say about when it leaves. For as long as suffering makes us its home, the only certain thing is that our questions will remain on the table.

The questions linger, even when the conversation flags, waiting for another voice, another perspective, perhaps a new way of thinking about what seems already to be thought out. Elihu adds his voice to a conversation slipping into silence, because he believes there is more to be said. Newsom comments helpfully on the merits of his presence, and why we should welcome him to the table:

> What Elihu touches on here, without being fully aware of it, is the issue of the exhaustion and renewal of human discourse. How is it that human culture never finishes with what it has to say about perennial issues of existence? There are, to be sure, moments of pause, when it seems that everything that can be said has been said, but those moments do not last. The inexhaustible source of human discourse lies in the fundamentally perspectival nature of claims to truth. . . . A stalled conversation is reinvigorated by someone eccentric to the original discourse.[2]

(3) Elihu intrudes *because he believes he can be fair and impartial* (vv. 17-22). When suffering stakes out its targets, it feels like falling under siege. Job has described his experience with military imagery that suggests he knows himself to be overmatched by an opponent that cannot be defeated (e.g., 16:9-14; 19:7-12). He has imagined that his only recourse is to appeal for a legal hearing. If he can get his case into a courtroom, where a judge can neutralize his assailant's power (13:20-28), perhaps then he can secure at least a stay of his execution. Toward that end, he has appealed for an "arbiter," someone who will lay his hand on all parties in the contest, thereby creating a safe zone within which the charges and counter-charges can be adjudicated (9:33-35). Failing this, the assault against him will continue apace. Job's only defense will be conditional wonderments, which invite the contemplation of nothing more than his ultimate destruction: "If it is a contest of

strength, he is the strong one" (9:19); "See, he will kill me, I have no hope" (13:15).

The three friends have heard Job's appeal, and they have offered themselves as the "arbiter" Job seeks. Job, however, considers their commitment to him to be suspect and their counsel to be inadequate. They have predetermined that his best chance to save himself is to cop a plea. Whatever the truth of his claim to innocence may be, they believe that the evidence against him is so strong that his only option is to "agree" that he is guilty (22:21) and plead for mercy (8:5-7; 11:13-20; 22:21-27).

Elihu has listened to both Job's appeal and the friends' counsel. Having deferred to them as long as his conscience will allow, he declares himself impatient with the inability of all parties to resolve the debate. If someone does not step in, then neither the assailant nor the assailed will gain satisfaction. The war of ideas about right and wrong will rage on, the boundaries between what is morally, ethically, and religiously acceptable in a civil world will remain ambiguous, and the number of victims who will pay the price for the indecision will continue to increase. With so much at stake, the price for the indifference of silence is too high. Elihu believes that he must speak. He believes that he has the equanimity to stand between the warring factions, without prejudging the virtue of either. He believes that he can render a decision that all will accept as impartial, fair, and decisive (32:21-22). In the words of the poet Walt Whitman, he believes that he can be "the equable man" this conflict needs and deserves. He will be the "arbiter of the diverse." He will supply "what wants supplying." He will "check what wants checking." As a belated reader of the book, Elihu claims, like Whitman's "equable man," to have the wisdom necessary to "bestow on every object or quality its fit proportion" (for further reflection, see Job 22, "Connections").[21]

In sum, Elihu inserts himself into this stalled conversation because "a work remains, the work of surpassing all that they [read the friends and Job] have done."[22] The merits of his conviction may be considered by asking ourselves a question: Where would the book of Job leave us readers if Elihu, having considered the arguments of Job and his friends, had decided that when it comes to understanding innocent suffering, there is nothing more to say?

For all the merits that Elihu claims for himself (vv. 6-22), we can only assess them by way of the *narrator's presentation* of his character (vv. 1-5). In the *narrator's estimation*, Elihu is angry (vv. 2 [2x], 3, 5). One approach is to take this anger as the interpretive clue for dismissing Elihu as a caricature of the "angry young man." His passion may be more a vice than a virtue. This view of anger is of course deeply rooted in common understanding. [There's No Fool Like an Angry Young Fool] Anger,

There's No Fool Like an Angry Young Fool

📖 William Whedbee identifies the book of Job with the genre of comedy (see [**CD: "The Great Reservoir of Comedy"**]) and suggests that Elihu plays the role of the *alazon* or buffoon.

Just as we find a caricature of the friends in their role as "old" sages, so we have a caricature of the "angry young man" who now aspires to be the one who would defend the ways of God. Though there may be "no fool like an old fool," Elihu as a young fool, comes close.

Whedbee's imagery of the "angry young fool" has currency largely because it resonates with the longstanding correlation of anger with foolishness and self-control with wisdom. Such correlations may be tracked to the ancient Mediterranean world, where the practice of compiling lists of vices and virtues as guides for acceptable conduct was widespread. The Stoics, for example, following Plato, developed a fourfold list of virtues: (1) wisdom (prudence, understanding); (2) moderation (temperance, restraint); (3) justice; and (4) courage. They compiled a similar list of vices: (1) folly; (2) licentiousness; (3) injustice; and (4) cowardice. In the Stoic's view, passions and emotions, such as grief, fear, lust, and anger, were closely linked with vices to be avoided. The abiding influence of such categorizations is evident in the modern world, where a person who exercises self-control may be described as "stoical," whereas one who gives free reign to passions "wears their emotions on their sleeve."

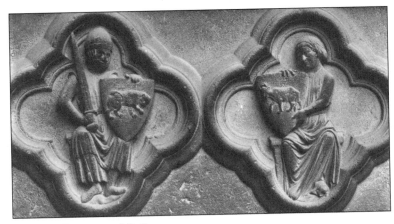

Virtues of Courage and Patience,

West facade, Beau Dieu portal, right wall, Cathedral, Amiens, France (Credit: Foto Marburg/Art Resource, NY)

For persons who look to the Bible for instruction on how to live according to God's wishes, both the Old Testament (e.g., Prov 6:16-19) and the New (e.g., Rom 1:29-31; 1 Cor 6:9-10; Gal 5:19-23) contain similar lists of virtues and vices. If one were to seek justification for avoiding anger, for example, which appears to be Elihu's defining passion, one need look no further than traditional proverbial wisdom:

Whoever is slow to anger has great understanding,
but one who has a hasty temper exalts folly. (Prov 14:29)

One who is slow to anger is better than the mighty,
and one whose temper is controlled than one who captures a city. (Prov 16:32)

With patience a ruler may be persuaded,
and a soft tongue can break bones. (Prov 25:15)

For further reading and additional bibliography, see J. Fitzgerald, "Virtue/Vice Lists," *ABD*, ed. D. N. Freedman (New York: Doubleday, 1992), vol. 6, 857-59.

J. Whedbee, *The Bible and the Comic Vision* (Cambridge: University Press, 1998), 244.

---

however, is a complex emotion, and dismissing Elihu because he expresses it is too simple. It may be nothing more than an unruly display of raw emotion, what we think of as a "knee-jerk" reaction that should be overcome by more a deliberate response. It may also be a thoughtful and appropriate response to what we believe is an unacceptable assault on cherished values. Elihu's narrator invites us to think that this latter view is more accurate for his character. Elihu is angry for reasons that have to with both Job (v. 2) and the three friends (v. 3). These reasons are clues for understanding what Elihu cares deeply about; they say something about the moral values by which he lives. ["Convert to Anger; Blunt Not the Heart"]

"Convert to Anger; Blunt Not the Heart"

When Macduff realizes that Macbeth is behind the death of Duncan, King of Scotland, he sets out on a course of revenge, only to discover that his actions lead indirectly to the slaughter of his own family by Macbeth's henchmen. He is torn between guilt and anger. Malcolm, Duncan's eldest son and the legitimate heir to the throne, urges him to "give sorrow words," otherwise "the grief that does not speak / Whispers the o'er fraught heart, and bids it break" (*Macbeth*, IV, iii, 4-5). Then, Malcolm continues,

Macduff must act; he must "Dispute it like a man" (IV, iii, 219). Macduff agrees on the need to exact vengeance but also insists that whatever he does, "I must feel it like a man" (IV, iii, 220-21).

Malcolm endorses Macduff's decision to yield to anger with these words:

Be this the whetstone of your sword: let grief
Convert to anger; blunt not the heart; enrage it. (IV, iii, 229-230)

Even if we decide to look for the good in Elihu's anger, we may well find that the narrator's introduction increases rather than reduces the complexity of interpretation. The narrator presents his character as angry; the character presents himself as "timid and afraid" (v. 6), even though inspired. The contrast between the two presentations raises a number of slippery questions. If the narrator, the presumed author of all of chapters 32–37, is in full control of the presentation of this character, then has he concluded that anger is the interpretive umbrella for understanding everything Elihu says? If so, then whatever Elihu says in this and the following chapters, the narrator as omniscient creator knows that in the end it all adds up to anger. Or, has the narrator created a character with a certain emotional profile, then stepped aside to watch and listen, in effect giving his character poetic license to emerge on his own before his eyes? If so, then the accent on Elihu's anger may be only the *narrator's* interpretation of where his character winds up at the end of his fictional journey. In other words, perhaps the narrator is reading his character as his character reads Job. He may not be commending (or controlling) the role of anger in this book so much as simply observing that it is a legitimate emotion, for good or for ill, which no discussion of innocent suffering should fail to consider.

"The Riddle We Can Guess / We Speedily Despise"

The Riddle we can guess
We speedily despise—
Not anything is stale so long—
As Yesterday's surprise—

Emily Dickinson, "#1222," T. H. Johnson, ed., *The Complete Poems of Emily Dickinson* (Boston/New York: Little, Brown and Company, 1960), 538.

It is difficult to keep either these questions or the answers that may be offered to them neatly categorized. The considerations they invite seem necessarily to elude a definitive resolution. Perhaps, in the end of the day, this is both the allure and the challenge that confronts every reader who chooses to enter into the stalled conversation between Job and his friends. ["The Riddle We Can Guess / We Speedily Despise"]

We may enter into this conundrum, following Newsom's suggestion, with "a deliberately generous curiosity"[23] about the merits of Elihu's anger. To do so, we take our cue from Martha Nussbaum, who has argued that all emotions are value judgments that reflect cherished beliefs a person regards as important for well being (see [The Intelligence of

Emotions]). With respect specifically to anger, a complex set of beliefs must be present. "In order to have anger," she says, a person must believe:

- That some threat or damage has occurred to the person or to something or someone valued by the person
- That the damage or threat is not trivial but significant
- That it was done by someone, not accidentally, but willingly
- That there is someone to blame, some responsible agent that can be and should be identified, stopped, then corrected and/or punished[24]

If any one of these beliefs is not present—if a person should discover that the threat is only minor, or that nothing of value has been compromised, or that what has happened is accidental and no blame should be assigned—then it is reasonable to expect that either there will be no anger at all, or that anger will dissipate on its own and go away. It is instructive to measure Elihu's anger against this grid of beliefs. In doing so, however, we should not be surprised to discover that there are multiple ways to think about the connections. It will not always be clear whether the connection is with Elihu, or his narrator, or both at the same time.

How has what Elihu heard from Job and his friends threatened or damaged something of value to him? The narrator tells us that Elihu is angry with Job, because "he has justified himself rather than God" (v. 2). He is angry with the friends, because they have failed to refute Job's arguments (v. 3). What appears to be threatened is the belief that God's justice is trustworthy and defensible, even, or perhaps especially, when suffering may cause a person to question it. It is interesting to reflect on the respective values Elihu assigns to human suffering and divine justice. Suffering in and of itself does not seem sufficient reason for Elihu to be angry. After all, people suffer every day, for a variety of reasons. Presumably, Elihu does not become angry every time someone falls ill, or loses property, or experiences a death. There is no hint that even the innocent deaths of Job's seven sons and three daughters rise to a level sufficient to threaten anything Elihu believes. It is only when persons who think suffering gives them permission to challenge God's justice with impunity that Elihu becomes angry. He is angry with Job, not because he has cried out in his suffering, but because he has cried out against God. He is angry with the friends, not because they have failed to comfort Job in his suffering, but because they have failed to condemn him for challenging God. If these convictions about God's justice were not important to Elihu, then we would not expect him to be angry.

Is Elihu's belief concerning God's justice trivial or significant? The assessment of this question is more complicated than it might appear. Nussbaum argues that anger is occasioned and justified when persons believe that an experience threatens something of value to them personally. It is not immediately clear that either Job's questions or the friends' failure to answer them has anything to do with Elihu's personal situation. There is no obvious reason to think that the debate between Job and his friends is anything more than an isolated and irrelevant dispute. Whether they resolve it satisfactorily or not, Elihu would appear to have the same chance to flourish as he would have had had their conversation never happened. It is their problem, not his. Why should he care about what seems important to them?

It is prudent to pause here in order to consider this issue carefully. With so much suffering in this world, it is little wonder that most, if not all persons, feel themselves to be only spectators. We look on or listen in from a distance at someone else's problem. We may flinch at what we see or hear, or not; either way, we move on to more immediate concerns. Someone dies from a terrorist's bomb in Jerusalem or Baghdad, someone is imprisoned for a crime they did not commit in Richmond, Virginia, or Sioux Falls, South Dakota, a gross injustice has occurred in our nation's capital or in Caracas, Venezuela. Ho-hum. However tragic and wrong the event may be, it is not our problem. It has nothing to do with the way we lead our lives or pursue our personal objectives. Given our modern sensibilities, we have good reason to wonder why Elihu should be angry enough at what he has heard from Job and his friends to bother with responding at all.

That he does respond indicates that Elihu or his author is personally affected by what he has heard. This in turn invites the suspicion that his or his author's personal well-being is informed and defined by collective values that have a direct bearing on how every individual lives. When a single innocent sufferer cries out for justice that is unavailable, then the moral compass by which all believe both heaven and earth navigate is suspect. Each and every one may tremble before the consequences, then resolve to speak out in anger, lest everything we believe about the world and our hope for prosperity within it come crashing down on our heads. In sum, Elihu's entry into this conversation suggests we will follow his lead and enter into this debate only if we believe that one person's unanswered cries for justice increases the odds that justice may one day turn a deaf ear to our cries as well.

Has there been intentional damage or threat to Elihu's beliefs, and if so who is to blame? Working backwards from the narrator's affirmation that Elihu is angry, the simple answer to this question would be that Job and his friends are to blame. But if they are the agents of cause for Elihu's anger, it is hard to see how he could conclude that they have intentionally entered into their debate in order to do him harm. This requires an exaggerated subjectivity on Elihu's part that would seem to subvert his own claims to be wise and impartial. Only if he believes that

the world revolves around him, that every conversation going on any-where is not only about him but also has been knowingly structured to hurt him, could he justifiably blame Job and the friends for his anger.
[The Danger of Living Too Much in Our Own Heads]

If we grant the merit of Elihu's anger, then the most important issue to reflect on is the question, who is to blame? Here Nussbaum offers an observation that invites careful attention: "grief, looking about for a cause, expresses itself as anger" (see ["Convert to Anger; Blunt Not the Heart"]).[25] Psychologists tell us that there is a complex relationship between anger and grief. Not in every case, but very often, anger is an expression of an unresolved loss. That we do not know exactly who or what has caused us to be angry does not mean necessarily that the anger is irrational or selfish. It may mean that the assumed cause is inadequate. The more it thins out before our rage, the more we sense how painfully vulnerable we are to the real cause, which is too hidden to be found, too elusive to be identified, stopped, and corrected. As long as the real cause is still out there, we remain a target for further assault, no matter how angry we are at the losses we have already suffered.

Here again, Nussbaum is instructive. She recalls the day in April 1992, when she was lecturing at Trinity College, Dublin. Back home in Philadelphia, her mother was in hospital, recovering from a serious but routine operation. Just before Nussbaum was scheduled to deliver her lecture, she received a call saying that her mother had developed a serious complication and that her life was in jeopardy. Nussbaum stayed to deliver the lecture, out of a sense of obligation to her host and audience, then caught a flight home on the next day. By the time she arrived at the hospital, her mother had died. Thus began a long period of mourning, filled with the unruly emotions of grief, guilt, and a heavy dose of anger. She was angry at the nurses for not prolonging her mother's life until she could be by her side; she was angry at the doctors for letting what was supposed to be a routine surgery go so terribly wrong; she was angry at herself for not abandoning the lecture and heading home the minute she got the word about her mother; she was even angry with the flight attendant for serving her dinner with a smile, as if everything in the world was normal. None of these were adequate causes for her anger, and the route toward identifying the real cause—her complex relationship with her mother—was long and demanding.[26] When Nussbaum moves from this personal experience to her formal analysis of anger and the concomitant need to assign blame, she offers this observation:

> In my case . . . one can see that the very magnitude of . . . grief sometimes prompts a search for someone to blame, even in the absence of any com-

The Danger of Living Too Much in Our Heads

Garret Keizer, an Episcopal priest, reflects on the mentality of anger. "When we live too much in our own heads," he says, "every careless injury is seen as a calculated insult, every tactless boor as a clever sadist, every enemy as the devil himself." To illustrate, he cites the all too common experience of road rage:

Road rage is typically a loss of reality. Both the perceived offense and the response to it are completely out of proportion. Someone cuts you off, and suddenly you want to cut her throat. Someone seizes an advantage, and you're ready to hunt him down like a prey. Surely there's a primitive physiology at work in all this, as in any case where stress triggers our flight-or-fight response. But the response can also be triggered, and indeed is intentionally triggered, by loud music in a gym or in a high action movie. Because the response functions naturally does not mean that its occasions are all natural. It's perfectly natural to scream, for instance, but something's wrong if we're screaming all the time.

Perhaps the best way to grasp the unreality of road rage, its extreme subjectivity, is to notice how selective and relative our sense of justice becomes during the experience. The person poking along in front of me is an idiot; the person on my tail is an idiot too. The person who takes advantage of an opening in traffic is a pushy bastard; the person who checks my doing the same thing is an uptight jerk. If I'm lost, the other driver has no patience; if the other driver's lost, I have no time. The only thing real in this picture is *me.*

G. Keizer, *The Enigma of Anger: Essays on a Sometimes Deadly Sin* (San Francisco: Jossey-Bass, 2002), 75-76.

pelling evidence that there is a responsible agent involved. It seems better that their should be someone to blame *than that the universe should be a place of accident in which one's loved ones are helpless.* Blame is a valuable antidote to helplessness.[27]

I have italicized a part of this quote, because it is so pertinent to Job's story. He has lost loved ones in a world where the words "for no reason" are the semantic equivalent of Nussbaum's description of the universe as a "place of accident." Elihu is angry with Job. He is angry with the three friends. But so far as we know, he is not angry with God. And this is curious, because as a reader of the "book of Job," he should know that God, not Job or the friends, is the one who describes the world Elihu lives in with the words "for no reason." So, where does this leave us in the quest to assess the merits of Elihu as the narrator presents him and Elihu as the character presents himself? Is anger the sum total of his inspiration? Is his inspiration the validation of his anger? The decision, of course, remains with us readers. No commentator can prescribe the one answer that every reader must accept. As readers consider the matters before them, this additional observation invites reflection. Whether angry or inspired or both, Elihu speaks for 159 uninterrupted verses. He neither invites nor receives any response from the friends or from Job. In effect, when he intrudes himself into the story, with his anger and/or his inspiration, the dialogue becomes a monologue. Even though he insists that the conversation must go on, the reader has to wonder if the "conversation" about God and innocent suffering has much of a future when one party claims the right to do all the talking.

NOTES

[1] J. Whedbee, *The Bible and the Comic Vision* (Cambridge: University Press, 1998), 242-45; cf. J. Holbert, *Preaching Job* (St. Louis: Chalice Press, 1999), 114.

[2] C. Newsom, *The Book of Job: A Contest of Moral Imaginations* (Oxford: Oxford University Press, 2003), 200.

[3] Ibid., 201.

[4] M. Coogan, *West Semitic Personal Names in the Murashu Documents* (Cambridge: Harvard Semitic Museum, 1975), 16-17; M. Pope, *Job* (AB; Garden City NY: Doubleday, 1979), 242; cf. C. Newsom, "The Book of Job," in vol. 4 of *NIB* (Nashville: Abingdon Press, 1996), 562.

[5] Newsom, "The Book of Job," 562.

[6] E. M. Good, *In Turns of Tempest: A Reading of Job with a Translation* (Stanford: Stanford University Press, 1990), 320.

[7] Newsom, "The Book of Job," 562.

[8] Cf. A. Hurvitz, "The Date of the Prose Tale of Job Linguistically Reconsidered," *HTR* 67 (1974): 17-34; B. Zuckerman, *Job the Silent: A Study in Historical Counterpoint* (New York: Oxford University Press, 1991), 156-57.

[9] H.-M. Wahl, *Der gerechte Schöpfer: Eine redactions-und theologiegeschichtliche Untersuchung der Elihureden—Hiob 32-37* (BZAW 207; Berlin, New York: Walter de Gruyter, 1993), 182-87.

[10] F. I. Anderson, *Job: An Introduction and Commentary* (TOTC; Downers Grove IL: Inter-Varsity, 1976), 50.

[11] The idiom *ḥāwah* + *dēʿî*, "declare knowledge," provides an inclusio for vv. 6 and 10 (see also v. 17). The word *dēʿî* is not found elsewhere in the book. A number of English translations render this as "opinion" rather than "knowledge," thus inviting the readers' suspicion that Elihu speaks only or merely his own views (cf. NRSV, RSV, KJB, NIV, REB, TEV). Both the substance and the tenor of Elihu's speech, however, give little warrant for such suspicion. Elihu seems intent, rather, on telling the friends what he "knows" (NAB).

[12] Newsom, "The Book of Job," 562-63; idem, *Book of Job*, 205.

[13] L. Perdue, *Wisdom in Revolt: Metaphorical Theology in the Book of Job* (JSOTSup 112; Sheffield: Almond Press, 1991), 248; cf. J. Gerald Janzen, *Job* (Atlanta: John Knox, 1985), 218-19.

[14] Janzen suggests that Elihu's appeal to inspiration in chs. 32–37 "may be taken to form an inclusion" with Eliphaz's similar claims in ch. 4 (*Job*, 218).

[15] So N. Habel, *The Book of Job: A Commentary* (OTL; Philadelphia: Westminster Press, 1985), 452-53.

[16] Newsom, "The Book of Job," 564.

[17] Ibid.

[18] Note R. Gordis's title for his chapter on Job 32–37, "Elihu the Intruder" (*The Book of God and Man: A Study of Job* [Chicago: The University of Chicago Press, 1965], 104).

[19] Newsom, *Book of Job*, 202.

[20] Ibid., 203.

[21] W. Whitmann, "By Blue Ontario's Shore, in *Leaves of Grass*, edited with an introduction by J. Loving (Oxford: Oxford University Press, 1990), 269.

[22] Ibid., 265.

[23] Newsom, *Book of Job*, 201.

[24] M. Nussbaum, *Upheavals of Thought: The Intelligence of Emotions* (Cambridge: Cambridge University Press, 2001), 28-29.

[25] Ibid., 22.

[26] For Nussbaum's account of this event, see *Upheavals of Thought*, 19-22.

[27] Ibid., 29, n. 19 (emphasis added).

THE MEANING OF SUFFERING

Job 33:1-33

Following the lengthy introduction in which both the narrator and Elihu himself seek to justify his role as the "answerer" this story needs, Elihu now addresses Job directly for the first time (v. 1). He begins and ends by reiterating that Job should "hear" (vv. 1, 31, 33; cf. 32:10) what he has to say and respond to him if he can (vv. 5, 32a). The introduction (vv. 1-7) and the summation (vv. 31-33) of what he has to say provide a rhetorical frame that indicates Elihu is sincerely inviting Job into a dialogue.

Elihu hopes to establish this conversation by assuring Job that he has listened carefully, and he understands what he has said (vv. 8-13). He verifies this by citing or summarizing the gist of Job's complaints, especially in chapters 9 and 13, namely, that God does not answer those who cry out in suffering (v. 13). This complaint, Elihu insists, is wrong, and as one who has Job's best interests at heart, he believes Job will want to know why (v. 12). The friends essentially looked past Job's suffering, suggesting by their counsel that piety is more important than pain. Elihu will not make the same mistake. He will address the questions Job is asking about suffering. He will explain how and why God answers people like him.

Elihu frames his answer to Job's questions (vv. 14-30) with the affirmation that God responds in multiple ways to those who suffer (v. 14: "in one way and two"; v. 29: "twice, three times"). Job's problem is not a lack of communication from God; it is rather Job's failure to perceive what God is saying. Elihu spells out God's mode of communication in three steps (vv. 15-18, 19-22, 23-28), a process aimed at securing the sufferer's public confession of sin (v. 27). Each step is accented with a strategically placed assurance that God's abiding purpose is to save a person's life, even when the extremities of suffering push them to believe something else (vv. 18, 24, 28; see also v. 30). [Structure of Job 33:1-33]

Throughout his speech, Elihu draws upon forensic and cultic metaphors—courtroom litigation and prayer—both of which have played an important role in the dialogues between Job and the friends. [Forensic and Cultic Metaphors] On first impression, he seems intent on clarifying the distinctions between these two ways of addressing the problem of suffering, in the process demonstrating to Job and the

Structure of Job 33:1-33

33:1-7   "But now, hear my speech, O Job "

33:8-13   "I have heard the sound of your words"

33:14-30   "God speaks in one way and two . . .
           twice, three times"

  vv. 15-18 Through dreams
           *Purpose: "to spare their souls from
           the Pit"* (v. 18)

  vv. 19-22 Through suffering
           *Purpose: because "their souls draw
           near the Pit"* (v. 22)

  vv. 23-30 Through an angelic mediator
           *Purpose: to redeem souls "from
           going down to the Pit"* (v. 28)

33:31-33 "Listen to me . . . be silent . . . listen to
         me
           *Purpose: "to bring back their souls
           from the Pit"* (v. 30)

friends that he is both a better lawyer and a more informed religious expert than they. If the friends do not have the legal skills to rebut Job's arguments in a courtroom, then Elihu will show them how it is done. If Job resists the friends' summons to pray for forgiveness, then Elihu will show him how and why the cult makes prayers of confession available to him.

On close inspection, however, Elihu's use of legal and cultic terminology seems only to blur the differences between these two ways of addressing Job's complaints. The trial Job seeks and the friends fail to offer is one in which the accused is presumed innocent, until a fair and impartial jury decides that the evidence requires a different verdict. When Elihu invites Job into his courtroom, however, he announces even before the first word is spoken that Job is in the wrong (v. 12). When Elihu summons Job to

---

Forensic and Cultic Metaphors

N. Habel is among those commentators who see the legal metaphor as the primary vehicle for Elihu's discourse (see further **[The Trial Metaphor in Job]**). In his judgment, legal language dominates in vv. 1-11 and 31-33, whereas cultic language is prominent in vv. 12-30. The diagram below, which modifies slightly Habel's discussion, identifies some of the language that sustains the structure.

33:1-11   *Elihu's summons to court*
           Hear my argument (v. 1a)
           Refute me if you can (v. 5a)
           Prepare your case before me (v. 5b)

          33:12-30 *Elihu's summons to cultic prayer*
                    If there is an angel (v.12a)
                    And he pleads for God to be gracious, because he has found a ransom (v.24)
                    And the supplicant prays to God and comes into his presence with joy (v.26)
                    The supplicant sings to others and says, "I have sinned" (v.27)

33:31-30 *Elihu's summons to court*
         Be silent, and I will speak (v. 31; cf. v. 33)
         I desire to justify you (v. 32)

The structure invites this question. Is the legal language, which frames and permeates Elihu's discourse, primary, or is the prayer language, which stands at the center (vv. 12-30), the hub around which the rest revolves?

For further discussion of the legal metaphor in Job 33, see N. Habel, *The Book of Job: A Commentary* (OTL; Philadelphia: Westminster Press, 1985), 459-63; B. Zuckerman, *Job the Silent: A Study in Historical Counterpoint* (New York: Oxford University Press, 1991), 150-53.

prayer, he declares that the cult provides him only one option. He must speak the words his angelic counselor tells him. He must confess and say, "I have sinned and perverted the right" (v. 27). Prayer, at least as Elihu defines it, is simply another word for legal language that presumes Job's guilt and God's innocence. Whether Job presents his case in the courtroom or in the cult, Elihu seems to be saying, the verdict will be the same. ["I Am Circling Around God"]

COMMENTARY

"But Now, Hear My Speech, O Job," 33:1-7

Elihu begins by trying to establish common ground with Job, which he hopes will facilitate the dialogue he desires. Addressing Job by name (v. 1), he summons him once again to "hear" what he has to say (cf. 32:10). His words convey the "uprightness" (*yāšār*; v. 3) of his heart; therefore, he can speak one-to-one (or virtue-to-virtue) with Job, who is the only other character in this story whose "uprightness" (*yāšār*, 1:1, 8; 2:3) has been established. He seems to know that Job has vowed to hold fast to his "righteousness" (*ṣdq*) for as long as the "spirit" (*rûaḥ*) of God is in him (27:3, 6). Elihu assures Job that the same divine "spirit" (*rûaḥ*) has formed him (v. 4), and by the end of his speech, he hopes to persuade Job that he would delight in confirming his "righteousness" (*ṣdq*; v. 32; NRSV: "for I desire to justify you") ["The Pencil of the Holy Ghost"] In short, Elihu invites Job into a conversation where both speakers

---

"I Am Circling Around God"

Rainer Maria Rilke (1875–1926) is considered one of the most influential poets of modern Germany. He is noted for his creation of the "object poem," a form with which he attempted to describe the "silence of the concentrated reality" he saw in physical objects. The search for God, he says, is like circling round the perimeter of an ever-expanding series of orbits. One can never be sure what will be found at the center of the quest.

I live my life in growing orbits,
which move out over the things of the world.
Perhaps I can never achieve the last,
but that will be my attempt.

I am circling around God, around the ancient tower,
and I have been circling for a thousand years,
and I still don't know if I am a falcon, or a storm,
or a great song.

Rainer Maria Rilke, "I Live My Life," in *The Rag and Bone Shop of the Heart: A Poetry Anthology*, ed. R. Bly et al. (New York: Harper Perennial, 1992), 422.

"The Pencil of the Holy Ghost"

 The pencil of the Holy Ghost hath laboured more in describing the afflictions of Job than the felicities of Solomon.

Francis Bacon, *The Essays or Counsels, Civil and Moral, of Francis Ld. Verulam Viscount St. Albans*, "Of Adversity."

---

would have the same standing, not only before each other but also before God. As Elihu puts it, "You and I are the same before God" (v. 6a; NJPS. ["I Too Was Formed from a Piece of Clay"]

The tenor of Elihu's opening words suggests that he is inviting Job into the courtroom, where established principles ensure that both parties have a fair and equal opportunity to present their case. The summons to "hear" (*šĕmaʿ*) and "give ear" (*hăʾazînā*, v. 1; NRSV: "listen") to his words is a common introduction of covenant lawsuits (Deut 32:1-2; Isa 1:2; Mic 6:1).[1] The invitation to "answer" and "set your words in order before me" (v. 5) recalls Job's preparation of his own legal brief against God (13:18, 22; 23:4). The qualifying phrase "if

---

"I Too Was Formed from a Piece of Clay"

Elihu's claim to have equal standing with Job appeals to creation theology. According to Gen 2:7, God forms human beings, like a divine potter, out of the dirt or clay of the earth. Job uses the same imagery to describe himself and his relation to God, although to different ends than Elihu (10:8). The motif of being "nipped from clay" (v. 6b; NJPS) is also found in Mesopotamian and Egyptian literature. In the Gilgamesh Epic, Aruru, the goddess of creation, forms Enkidu to be the equal of Gilgamesh by "pinching off clay and casting it on the steppe."

The great Aruru they called:
"Thou, Aruru, didst create [the man];
Create now his double. . . ."

When Aruru heard this . . .
Aruru washed her hands,

Pinched off clay and cast it on the steppe.
[On the step]pe she created valiant Enkidu.

The Egyptian text, "The Instruction of Amen-em-opet," a collection of maxims often compared to the book of Proverbs, contains similar language. In this case, the equality of human beings, each one created of "clay and straw," is the reason why no one should abuse another.

Do not laugh at a blind man nor tease a dwarf
Nor injure the affairs of the lame.
Do not tease a man who is in the hand of the god,
Nor be fierce against him if he errs.
For man is clay and straw,
And the god is his builder. ("The Instruction of Amen-em-opet," XXV, ll. 9-14; in *ANET*, ed. Pritchard, 424)

"The Epic of Gilgamesh," tablet I, ll. 30-31, 34-36; in *ANET*, 3rd ed. with supplement, ed. J. B. Pritchard (Princeton: Princeton University Press, 1969), 74.

you can" (v. 5a) echoes Job's charge that even if he were to question God in court, God would not answer "once in a thousand times" (9:3). Elihu hints that in the conversation he has in mind, the one who strains for answers will be Job, not God. Even so, Job need not fear this dialogue, for Elihu will not be heavy-handed in what he is about to say (v. 7; NIV: "nor should my hand be heavy upon you"). It is an assurance that should satisfy the conditions for a fair trial that Job himself has insisted upon (13:21).

For all the promises to engage Job in an open, honest, and mutually respectful dialogue, Elihu's words betray a subtle but significant ulterior motive. The Hebrew behind the phrase "See, before God, I am *as you are (kĕpîkā)*" (v. 6a) is literally, "See, before God, I am *like your mouth.*" If we read the expression with NRSV, then Elihu is simply invoking a metaphor for equality. The freight of the words behind the metaphor, however, hints at a different relationship. When and if Job accepts this invitation to dialogue, the only one who will actually have a voice is Elihu, who assumes the responsibility of speaking for them both. After all, as a "belated reader" of the book, Elihu demonstrates in these opening words that he already knows what Job has to say.

"I Have Heard the Sound of Your Words," 33:8-13

As his friends droned on and on, Job repeatedly chastised them for talking *at* him without ever truly listening to what he was saying (6:28; 13:17; 21:2, 5; see further the "Connections" at Job 30). Elihu will not be vulnerable to the same criticism. He has listened carefully to Job (v. 8), and he now restates the gist of what he has heard him say.

He has heard Job make four principal claims to innocence (v. 9), which lay the groundwork for leveling four corresponding charges against God (vv. 10-11).[2] Two sets of parallel phrases affirm that Job claims his innocence is *grounded in character*—"I am clean" (v. 9a) // "I am pure" (v. 9b)—and *enacted in ethical and moral behavior*—"without transgression" (v. 9a) // "no iniquity in me" (v. 9b). This synopsis is generally faithful to what Job has said, although Elihu tweaks Job's actual words in several places. The prologue has described Job's character with the word "blameless" (*tām*; 1:1, 8; 2:3), and Job claims the same thing for himself (9:20, 22; cf. the related word *tummāh*, "integrity," in 27:5). The word Elihu uses for "clean," *zak*, is applied to Job by the friends (8:6; 11:4), but Job himself uses it only with reference to the "purity" of his prayer (16:7). Elihu's word for "pure" (*hap*) occurs only here in the Hebrew Bible; presumably he uses it in this context as a generic synonym for "clean."[3] With respect to his ethical and moral behavior, Job has used the words "transgression" (*pešaʿ*) and "iniquity" (*'āwôn*), although not precisely in the absolute way Elihu claims. Job's fundamental assertion is that even if he has inadvertently erred, he has committed no sin that justifies the punishment he has received (7:20-21; 10:6-7; 13:26; 19:4).

Two additional clusters of phrases, not exactly parallel but clearly thematically linked, summarize Job's charges against God. The first (v. 10) is the accusation that God finds "excuses" or "pretexts" (*tĕnû'ôt*, NRSV: "occasions"; cf. Judg 14:4) to afflict Job. The charge is generally consonant with both God's admission in the prologue (2:3: "for no reason") and with Job's own description of the way God treats him (e.g., 9:11-22). The following phrase, "counts me as an enemy," is a direct reference to Job's words in 13:24b. The second cluster of phrases (v. 11) repeats almost verbatim Job's charge in 13:27. God places his feet in "stocks," as if he were a condemned prisoner, and God "watches" his every move, spying out additional opportunities to abuse him.

In his summation of what he has heard, Elihu focuses on the legal and cultic approaches to suffering that Job has explored thus far. With a single, unqualified response, Elihu declares that in both these approaches Job is wrong (v. 12). Neither his claim to innocence, rooted as much in the blamelessness of his character as in the cultic purity of his prayer, nor his indictment of God for abusing the innocent can withstand scrutiny. The reason is simply this, "God is greater than any mortal" (v. 12b).

It is not immediately clear how this explanation provides any direct answer to Job's complaints. If Elihu has really listened carefully to all that Job has said, then surely he knows there is no need to reason Job *into* an affirmation that he has never tried to reason himself *out of.* [A Satire on Reason] "If it is contest of strength," as Job's puts it, then he has already conceded Elihu's point: "he [God] is the strong one" (9:19). If it is a question of respecting the difference between creatures and Creator, then this too Job has already acknowledged: "he [God] is not a mortal, as I am" (9:32). If we look ahead, however, we have reason to suspect that Elihu's affirmation about God encodes a criticism of Job's understanding of both religion and the law. Job's confusion about prayer has to do with his use of cultic rituals to lament and protest his suffering rather than to express contrition and seek forgiveness for his sins (see below, vv. 23-28). As for the charge that God subverts Job's legal appeal by finding pretexts to condemn the innocent, Elihu defers further comment until chapter 34, where he will vigorously defend the righteousness of God's governance (e.g., 34:10-15).

A Satire on Reason

My comments here play off the Irish satirist, Jonathan Swift (1667–1745), who is perhaps best known as the author of *Gulliver's Travels* (1726). His observation about the use of reason is as follows: "It's useless to attempt to reason a man out of a thing he was never reasoned into" (source unknown).

For now, Elihu concentrates his energies on one specific matter that must be resolved if Job is to learn anything at all about the meaning of suffering. Why does Job say that God does not answer those who cry out in their suffering (v. 13; see the commentary on 9:3)? Elihu has already spoken the first line of his response to this question: "in this you are not right" (v. 12a). The second and succeeding lines of his response now follow in vv. 14-30.

"God Speaks in One Way and Two . . . Twice, Three Times," 33:14-30

Elihu frames the core of his response to Job with an emphatic assertion that God responds to those who suffer not once but multiple times (v. 14: "in one way and two"; v. 29: "twice, three times"). The problem is not God's refusal to communicate. It is rather Job's inability, or perhaps his refusal, to discern what God is trying to say to him. With this affirmation, Elihu places two matters on the table: divine revelation and human response, or in Job's case, the failure to respond. Concerning the former, Elihu lays out three steps in God's revelatory process (vv. 15-18; 19-22; 23-28), each one punctuated by the same clear and consistent statement of God's purpose: to save life (vv. 18, 24, 28). If we were to imagine a classroom setting for this instruction, then our first impressions might be of a master teacher taking a rather slow student by the hand, boiling down the lesson plans to an irreducible minima, and then spelling everything out in artful simplicity: one, two, three. Concerning the issue of discernment, however, Elihu offers nothing beyond his initial one-line statement of the problem in v. 12a. Job has of course offered his own thoughts on the problem of understanding what God is up to, but Elihu gives no indication that he has factored them into his teaching strategies. It is perhaps no cause for surprise, therefore, that when Elihu concludes this lesson, Job remains silent, despite his teacher's invitation to respond (vv. 5, 32). The problem of discernment, it seems, remains measurably unimproved.

The first step in God's revelatory process (vv. 15-18) is to speak through "dreams" (*ḥălôm*), "night visions" (*ḥezôn layĕlāh*), "deep sleep" (*tardēmāh*), and "slumbers" (*tĕnûmût*; v. 15). Job knows about such things, for Eliphaz has already tried to teach him what God has revealed to him in "night visions" (*ḥezyōnôt lāyĕlāh*) and "deep sleep" (*tardēmāh*; 4:13). What Eliphaz knows and what Job must learn is that all humans are "born to trouble" (5:6). Job's only recourse is to submit himself happily to the human condition, assured by the promise that trouble is the rod of God's compassionate discipline (5:17). The revelation that instructs and comforts Eliphaz, however, only frightens Job. It adds psychic terror to bodily pain (7:14).

Dreams and Visions

Hebraic thought recognizes dreams and visions as authentic means of divine revelation, which often require the expertise of someone to interpret the message (e.g., Gen 15:1, 12-15; 28:10-17; 31:10-13, 24; 40:8-18; 41:1-31). The same is true of ancient Near Eastern literature. The poem "Ludlul Bel Nemeqi," often referred to as "The Babylonian Job," describes the dreams Marduk uses to communicate with and ultimately restore one who suffers:

His hand was heavy upon me, I could not bear it.
My dread of him was alarming, it [. . . . . me]
His fierce [.] . . was a tornado [. . . . . . .]
His stride was . . ., it . . . [. . . . . .]
Day and night alike I groan,
In a dream and waking moments I am equally wretched.
A remarkable young man of outstanding physique,
Massive in body, clothed in new garments—
A second time [I saw a dream,]
And in [my night dream which] I [saw]
A remarkable young [man . . . .]
Holding in his hand a tamarisk rod of purification—
"Laluralimma, resident of Nippur,
Has sent me to cleanse you."
The water he was carrying he threw over me,
Pronounced the life-giving incantation, and rubbed [my body.]

"Ludlul Bel Nemeqi," tablet III, ll. 1-4, 7-10, 21-28; W. G. Lambert, *Babylonian Wisdom Literature* (Oxford: Clarendon Press, 1960), 49

Elihu now picks up the thread of truth that Eliphaz had grasped but could not adequately convey to Job. Nocturnal revelations are an important means for divine communication. [Dreams and Visions] God uses such revelations not to terrify people but to "open their ears," then "seal" them (*yaḥtōm*) with warnings (v. 16).[4] The warnings are meant to turn a person away from some hurtful "act" or "deed" that would otherwise destine them for death, imaged here as the "Pit" (= Sheol; see further, [Sheol]) and the "River" (v. 18). [The River of Death] The "act" or "deed" that is the subject of God's warning is the human disposition to "pride" (v. 17).

Pride (*gēwāh* = *gǎʾwāh*) is a complex disposition in Hebraic thinking. In a negative sense, it is associated with arrogance and presumption, and as such it is widely judged to be an attitude displayed by the wicked and rebellious. ["Pride Goes Before Destruction"] Viewed positively, pride includes a cluster of images associated with the basic meaning "to be high" or "exalted." With reference to God, it conveys the sense of "majesty," "nobility," and "glorious power" (e.g., Exod 15:1, 21; Isa 2:10, 19, 21; Mic 5:4 [MT: 5:3]). Precisely because it is godlike, however, human pride is an attitude that must be carefully monitored, for it can easily slide toward hubris. Nonetheless, in appropriate measures, it is right and good (e.g., Ps 47:4 [MT: 47:5]; Nah 2:2 [MT: 2:3]; Isa 4:2). Elihu's use of the word here is rather oblique, but given his

The River of Death

V. 18 employs a parallelism between the "Pit" (*šāḥat*) and the "River" (*šālaḥ*; lit., "channel") that indicates the reference is to the netherworld, most likely to the mythological rivers Styx in ancient Greece, Hubur in Babylon, and perhaps, by extension, to the "Pool of Shelah" (Neh 3:15; NIV: "Siloam"] in the Kidron Valley (cf. M. Pope, *Job* [AB; Garden City NY: Doubleday, 1979], 250). According to this mythology, every soul must cross the river on its journey to join the dead.

"The Babylonian Theodicy" is a poem in the form of a dialogue between a sufferer who complains, like Job, about the injustice of his situation, and a friend, who tries to defend the gods' ordering of the universe. In his first response, the friend refers not only to crossing the river Hubur but also to the promise that "a protecting angel" (see the commentary on Job 33:23-30) will intervene before suffering exacts its ultimate claim.

Pool of Siloam

A water reservoir constructed under King Hezekiah (716-687 BC), to ensure Jerusalem's water supply under a siege.

Siloam, Jerusalem, Israel (Credit: Erich Lessing/Art Resource, NY)

Respected friend, what you say is gloomy.
You let your mind dwell on evil, my dear fellow.
You make your fine discretion like an imbecile's;
You have reduced your beaming face to scowls.
Our fathers did in fact give up and go the way of death.

It is an old saying that they cross the river Hubur . . . .
He who waits on his god has a protecting angel,
The humble man who fears his goddess accumulates wealth. ("The Babylonian Theodicy," ll. 12-17, 21-22; W. G. Lambert, *Babylonian Wisdom Literature* [Oxford: Clarendon Press, 1960], 71)

explicit reference in 35:12 to the "pride of evildoers" whom God "does not answer," there is no doubt that he thinks the warning God intends for Job is aimed at correcting a definite character flaw.

In view of the complexity of the issue, we may pause here to consider whether Elihu has oversimplified the nature of Job's pride. The verbal root for "pride" and its noun derivatives occur eleven times in Job: twice in Job's speeches, four times in the speeches of Elihu and the friends, and five times in God's speeches. Both occurrences in Job's speeches are positive, suggesting that he understands and values the rightness, indeed the instinctive need, for some things "to be high" and "exalted," if they are to survive. "Can papyrus grow (*yigʾeh*) where there is no marsh?" (8:11). Can a lion be a lion, if it is not "bold" (*yigʾeh*; 10:16)? The friends associate *gāôn* with God's "majesty" (37:4), but when they apply the same field of words to humans, they almost always

"Pride Goes Before Destruction"

The negative valuation of pride as the antithesis of humility, as in the contrast between a "haughty spirit" and a "lowly spirit," has a long trajectory, extending from biblical maxims, to Chaucer's *The Canterbury Tales*, and the popular caution concerning the seven "deadly" sins (see **[Pride, Gluttony, and the Seven Deadly Sins]**). This negative critique is perhaps most associated with proverbial wisdom:

> There are six things that the Lord hates,
> seven that are an abomination to him:
> haughty eyes and a lying tongue,
> and hands that shed innocent blood,
> a heart that devises wicked plans,
>   feet that run to evil,
> a lying witness who testifies falsely,
> and one who sows discord in a family. (Prov 6:16-19)

> The fear of the Lord is hatred of evil.
> Pride and arrogance and the way of evil and per-
> verted   speech I hate. (Prov 8:13)

Pride

Hieronymus Bosch (c.1450-1516). Detail of "The Table of the Seven Deadly Sins." Museo del Prado, Madrid, Spain (Credit: Erich Lessing/Art Resource, NY)

> When pride comes, then comes disgrace,
> but wisdom is with the humble. (Prov 11:2)

> The fear of the Lord is instruction in wisdom,
> and humility goes before honor. (Prov 15:33)

> Pride goes before destruction,
> and a haughty spirit before a fall. (Prov 16:18)

adopt the more negative connotation, as the two occurrences in Elihu's speeches confirm (33:17; 35:12).[5]

We might anticipate that the five remaining references, all in God's climatic speeches from the whirlwind, will decisively settle the matter by siding with either Job or the friends. The primary exploration of the issue must be deferred until the commentary on these texts, but first impressions may cause us to wonder whether even God intends to resolve the question. On the one hand, God commends to Job's careful consideration the "proud (*gě'ôn*) waves" of the sea (38:11) and the "pride" (*ga'ăwāh*) displayed in Leviathan's strength (41:15 [MT: 41:7]).[6] On the other, the meaning of God's challenge to Job in chapter 40 is curiously ambiguous. When God summons Job to clothe himself with "glory" (*gā'ôn*) and "splendor" (40:10), then to "look on all who are proud (*gē'eh*)" and bring them down (40:11, 12), is God rebuking Job for his own misplaced aspiration to God-like pride? If so, then God is siding with the friends. Or is God genuinely inviting Job to be proud? Should he aspire to the strength of conviction and character of the sea and Leviathan (see [Leviathan]), whose pride is nothing less than

"You May Be the Bit of Marble That Is Left in the Statue"

In *The Undying Fire*, H. G. Wells's fictional recreational of the Joban story, Elihu's role is played by Dr. Elihu Barrack. As he rebukes the friends for their failure to answer Job, Dr. Barrack describes the complicated "Process" (Wells always capitalizes the word) that rules the world. It is inscrutable to human beings but yet not without purpose. Although Job wants to make moral sense of it all, Dr. Barrack insists that the "Process" has fluctuations, ups and downs, that human beings cannot comprehend.

Some of us are hammer and some of us are anvil, some of us are sparks and some of us are the beaten stuff that survives. The Process doesn't confide in us; why should it? We learn what we can about it, and make what is called a practical use of it, for that is what the will in the Process requires. (140)

Based on this reasoning, Dr. Barrack urges Job to "face facts," that is, to "take the world as it is and take yourself as you are" (144). The bottom line for Dr. Barrack is this:

If the Process wants you it will accept you; if it doesn't you will go under. You can't help it—either way. You may be the bit of marble that is left in the statue, or you may be the bit of marble that is thrown away. You can't help it. Be yourself! (144)

H. G. Wells, *The Undying Fire* (New York: The Macmillan Company, 1919).

God given? If so, then God would appear to be endorsing Job's affirmation of the necessity and importance of pride. To be anything less than proud, God might be saying, would mean that Job is willing to settle for less than God expects of him. ["You May the Bit of Marble That is Left in the Statue"]

This much is clear for now. As far as Elihu is concerned, there is no need for further deliberation. God uses dreams and visions to warn people like Job against the disposition to be proud. If they do not understand the first message, then God will try to get their attention by a second, and decidedly more painful, means of communication. ["What Happens to a Dream Deferred?"]

If the first warning cannot be *heard with the ear*, then God sends a second that conveys a message meant to be *felt by the body* (vv. 19-22; cf. 36:5-15).[7] Once again, Elihu uses legal terminology to suggest that the message comes as a trial: its intent is to "arraign" (*ḥûkaḥ*; NRSV: "chasten") a person in order to "bring a lawsuit" (*rîb*; NRSV: "strife") against him. In this case, however, the venue is not a courtroom; it is a person's flesh and bones. The indictment is not written with words; it is instead scribed on the body with physical pain (v. 19). Elihu spells out pain's effect on the body, but the language he uses is difficult to translate precisely. Some of the words occur nowhere else in the Hebrew Bible; some of the forms are either corrupt or awkward in the present context. One gets the impression that Elihu is trying to describe a level of suffering and anguish for which words are almost

"What Happens to a Dream Deferred?"

What happens to a dream deferred?

Does it dry up
like a raisin in the sun?
Or fester like a sore—
And then run?
Does it stink like rotten meat?
Or crust and sugar over—
like a syrupy sweet?

Maybe it just sags
like a heavy load.

Or does it explode?

Langston Hughes, "Harlem," *The Collected Poems of Langston Hughes*, ed. A Rampersad (New York: Vintage Books, 1994), 426.

Job
Leon Bonnat (1833-1922). *Job*. 1880. Oil on canvas. Musee Bonnat, Bayonne, France.
(Credit: Réunion des Musées Nationaux/Art Resource, NY)

always inadequate. The mere outline of the decimation Elihu invokes may be suggestive enough. Pain's relentless assault first immobilizes persons on their bed, then ravages their body so that their bones shiver. They have no appetite whatsoever; they can stomach neither ordinary bread nor fine foods. Their flesh wastes away; even their bones are withered so thin they can no longer be seen (vv. 20-21).

In his explication of this second mode of divine communication, Elihu demonstrates once again that he has listened carefully to Job's story. From the prologue, he seems to know that God is indeed willing to test a person's fidelity by allowing suffering to claim not only their material possessions and their beloved family but also their own "flesh and bone" (2:4). He seems to know Job's complaint that when persons wind up on the ash heap of suffering, it is because God has consigned them to the ignominy of slavery (7:1-6). Anguish is their master; their role is to submit to life as God gives it, even if "months of emptiness and nights of misery" (7:3) destine them for the "Pit," where death parents them in the lessons about how pain defines hope (cf. 16:13-15). On these points, Job and Elihu seem to be in agreement, although Elihu suggests there is still more to learn. Other modes of divine communication are meant to *spare* a person from the "Pit" (vv. 18; 24, 28, 30). Presumably, this remains God's objective in speaking through pain. But Elihu now seems intent on teaching Job that God is prepared to give suffering free rein, if necessary. Until and unless persons respond as God requires, pain will have its way, even if it means they are brought to the very brink of death, where there seems to be no means of escape (v. 22).

["Death Always Makes People Practical"]

If the chastisement of suffering does not secure the desired response, then God tries a third approach (vv. 23-28). At the pivotal moment when suffering threatens to exact its heaviest price, an angelic mediator appears and stands in the breach between the afflicted person and the specter of death (v. 23). The role of this figure is open to interpretation. The term Elihu uses, *mēlîs*, means primarily "interpreter," that is, one who stands between two parties and interprets what is being said so that both can understand (e.g., Gen 42:23). One venue where this figure appears, especially in post-biblical texts, is the heavenly court, where an angelic defense attorney represents the case of the accused before God.[8] [The High Holy Days] Job himself has used the term in this way (16:20; NIV: "my intercessor is my friend"). Elihu, however, appears to understand the *mēlîs* as functioning more in a cultic setting than a legal one. The cultic context he calls upon is the practice of lament.

The typical form of lament prayer, exemplified most clearly in the Psalms, includes four parts: (1) invocation; (2) lament, usually accompanied by questions and/or protestations of innocence; (3) petition for help; and (4) a concluding statement of praise or thanksgiving. [Psalm 13] The conclusion signals that God has heard the prayer and responded by delivering the suppliant. Such psalms curiously omit, however, any explanation of what actually transpires in the gap between petition (3) and praise (4) to effect the deliverance. True to his understanding of himself as the "Answerer" this story requires, Elihu now supplies the missing link. [Elihu's Explanation of the Lament Process]

Elihu describes a process that consists of two principle steps. The first concerns the work of the angelic mediator, whose primary task is to "interpret" suffering in language the suppliant can understand (vv. 23-25). The second is the work of the suppliant, whose response should demonstrate that he has understood (vv. 26-28). [The Wrath of Elihu]

• NRSV's translation of v. 23b—"declare a person upright"—assumes a forensic setting for the interpretive act, suggesting that the angel defends the innocence of the accused before the heavenly court. The lament tradition to which Elihu appeals, however, assumes a cultic

The High Holy Days

Intercessory angels are well attested in post-biblical literature (cf. 1 En. 9:1-11; 15:1-3; 2 En. 7:1-5; T. Levi 3:5-6). The text from T. Dan 6:1-6 (2nd C. BCE) is illustrative:

And now fear the Lord, my children, be on guard against Satan and his spirits. Draw near to God and to the angel who intercedes for you, because he is the mediator between God and men for the peace of Israel. He shall stand in opposition to the kingdom of the enemy. Therefore the enemy is eager to trip up all who call on the Lord, because he knows that on that day in which Israel trusts, the enemy's kingdom will be brought to an end. The angel of peace will strengthen Israel so that it will not succumb to an evil destiny. (The translation is from H. C. Kee, "Testaments of the Twelve Patriarchs," *The Old Testament Pseudepigrapha*, vol. 1, ed. J. H. Charlesworth [New York: Doubleday and Company, 1983], 810)

The idea of an angelic advocate is fundamental in rabbinic Judaism's concept of the High Holy Days, when each person stands before the judgment of the heavenly court. The rabbis often remind the repentant that Abraham, Isaac, and the ancestors of faith, together with the angels, intercede with God for their forgiveness. The following excerpt from the sermon of Rabbi Shmelke of Nikolsburg (18th century) provides one example:

On Yom Kippur Satan has no permission to act as accuser (Yoma 20a). If we seek God on this day and purify ourselves of our guilt by doing Teshuvah, and with weeping and supplication, he will certainly listen to us . . . .

Therefore come, my beloved brothers, my heart's companions, let us strengthen ourselves with weeping and supplication before our Father who is in heaven, and let us purify ourselves before him, for on this Yom Kippur, when there is no Satan or mishap, His compassion will certainly be moved in our favor . . . . For indeed Abraham our father offered up his life for the sanctification of the Name of God and threw himself into the fiery furnace, and Isaac his son offered himself at the Binding. If we follow their footsteps and do they as they did and sanctify his great Name with love, and cry all together, "Hear, O Israel," with devotion, they will stand and intercede for us on the holy and awesome day. (S. Y. Agnon, *Days of Awe* [New York: Schocken Books, 1948, 1965], 205-206

Job Targum II translates *mēlîṣ* in both Job 16:20 and 33:23 with the Aramaic word *pĕrāqlîtā* (the Targum from Qumran, 11QtgJob, does not contain either passage). This translation connects with the Greek word *parakletos*, thus to the role of the Paraclete or "Advocate" in Johannine literature. The noun has a wide range of meanings, for example, "the one who exhorts," "the one who comforts," "the one who appeals." John's gospel, especially the account of Jesus' farewell discourse in chs. 14–16, employs all these meanings: the Paraclete teaches all things, bears witness to Christ, convinces the world of sin, and guides the wayward to truth and righteousness (John 14:16-17, 26; 15:26; 16:7-11, 12-15).

setting. This makes it more likely that the angel plays a dual role, first with the sufferer on earth, then with God in heaven.[9] With the sufferer, his role is to explain what the cult requires of him, if his appeal to God is to be successful. NIV's translation conveys this sense nicely: "to tell a man what is right for him." Once he has informed the suppliant of his duties, the angel addresses God on his behalf, first appealing to God to be gracious, then petitioning God to "deliver him from going down to the Pit," because "I have a found a ransom" (v. 24).[10] The nature of the "ransom" (*kōper*) is ambiguous, but given the cultic context, a strong case can be made for understanding it in sacrificial terms. It is a ritual offering that atones for sin, thereby averting God's wrath, and effecting the sinner's restoration (v. 25).[11]

Psalm 13

Ps 13 illustrates well the four-part structure of lament. As in many other psalms of this type, the invocation, "O Lord" (v. 1a), follows the first words of an extended lament, in this case articulated by the fourfold repetition of the question "How long?" (vv. 1, 2).

Invocation and lament (vv. 1-2)
How long, O Lord? Will you forget me forever? How long will you hide your face from me? How long must I bear pain in my soul and have sorrow in my heart all day long? How long shall my enemy be exalted over me?

Petition for help (vv. 3-4)
Consider and answer me, O Lord my God! Give light to my eyes, or I will sleep the sleep of death, and my enemy will say, "I have prevailed" . . .

Concluding statement of praise (vv. 5-6)
But I trusted in your steadfast love; my heart shall rejoice in your salvation. I will sing to the Lord, because he has dealt bountifully with me.

• The suppliant's response is to "pray" (v. 26a: *ʿtār*; cf. Eliphaz's use of the same language in 22:27). God "accepts" (*rāṣah*) the prayer in a manner befitting a worthy sacrifice (Lev 1:4; 7:18; 19:7; 22:23, 25, 27), and the suppliant comes into God's presence with a festal shout of joy (v. 26b). God's acceptance is ambiguously phrased (v. 26b: *wayyāšeb leʾĕnôš ṣidqātô*), as Newsom has noted.[12] NRSV translates "and God repays him for his righteousness," suggesting that God confirms the suppliant was and remains, even in his suffering, righteous in all his deeds. NIV's translation—"he is restored by God to his righteous state"—suggests that a transformation has taken place. The suppliant has called his former state of righteousness into question, presumably by failing to respond properly to suffering. Now, on the other side of the angel's interpretation, the suppliant's prayer confirms that he has learned something new. The Hebrew text will support either translation, but the context favors NIV. When the suppliant bears witness to his experience before the congregation, he confesses that he has "sinned and perverted was right (*yāšār*)" (v. 27; cf. v. 23b).

The lesson to be learned, Elihu says, as he completes his description of this third and climatic step of the revelatory process, is this. An ever-gracious God uses suffering not to punish arbitrarily the innocent but to turn persons away from pride, deliver them from the Pit, and restore them to the life-giving presence of the light (vv. 28, 30).

Elihu's shift from legal to cultic metaphors invites scrutiny. On the one hand, he shows himself to be adept at using legal language both to criticize the friends and to correct Job. The aged friends, he says, do not "understand how to judge" (*mišpāṭ*, 32:9; NJPS), which means they do not have what is required to be Job's "arbiter" (*môkîaḥ*, 32:12; cf. 9:33). Because they "have failed to be good lawyers,"[13] Elihu reviews the testi-

---

Elihu's Explanation of the Lament Process

Scholars have long struggled to explain why the mood of suppliants in lament prayers shifts from lament to praise. There is no word in the prayers themselves about God answering the questions or resolving the troubles that precipitate the lament; nevertheless, by the end of the prayer, the suppliant routinely speaks as if God has indeed heard and has already acted to deliver and restore.

The German scholar Joachim Begrich was among the first to propose an answer for the problem, suggesting that in the gap between lament and praise, the cultic process would have typically included a "priestly oracle of salvation." Although the psalms themselves contain no evidence of this, Begrich suggested that the model could be found in the salvation oracles of Second Isaiah. These oracles typically contain such words as "Do not fear," "I will help you," "I have redeemed you," and "I will be with you" (e.g., Isa 41:14-16; 43:1-7; 44:1-2). Begrich theorized that until the priest delivered such words of assurance, the suppliant was unsure whether her lament had been heard.

James F. Ross has argued that Elihu's discourse on lament in Job 33 provides a different and more plausible explanation. In Ross's view, Elihu explains that a sufferer can know, even *before* uttering the lament, that an angelic mediator has already successfully pleaded for his redemption, offered the ransom that secures the outcome, and thus secured the transformation from lament to praise.

Elihu teaches Job that when suffering comes, he can be sure that God has already acted to bring him back from the Pit, if only he will listen and accept the route to deliverance that God has provided.

It is probable that he [Elihu] represents the standard tradition and theology of Hebrew cultic psalmody and that in 33:14-30 he is literally stating the theory, or the phenomenology, of lament. Whereas we have in many of the biblical psalms the text of the words spoken by the sufferer in a cultic context, Elihu provides us not so much with the words themselves as with a description of what actually transpires in the heavenly council before such a psalm is recited. In other words, we have here the rubrics and the theological suppositions of such entreaties. Man suffers; the spokesman interprets the meaning of this, calling him back to his duty; then the angel turns to God in intercession. The former sinner entreats God, i.e., says his psalm of lament. God accepts him; man now enters the cultic presence and tells of his salvation, at the same time confessing his sins and looking to the future ("my life sees the light" [33:28]). Job 33:14-30, in this view, is a treatise on the purpose of the prayer of lament, with a brief quotation of a typical conclusion. The passage is without parallel elsewhere in the Hebrew scriptures, where we have only the laments themselves. (44)

J. Begrich, "Das priesterliche Heilsorakel," ZAW 52 (1934): 81-92. For the full exposition of Ross's argument, see J. F. Ross, "Job 33:14-30: The Phenomenology of Lament," JBL 94 (1975): 38-46.

---

mony Job has put before the court, at times even quoting from the transcript (33:9-11). His rebuttal of the charges suggests that he has resolved to do what the friends could not: he will convict Job and justify God in legal terms (v. 12).

On the other hand, just at the moment when one expects the court to hand down a "Guilty" verdict, Elihu steps outside the legal metaphor to describe a cultic ritual that reframes the issues. Calling upon the tradition of lament prayer, Elihu announces the intervention of an angelic mediator who tells the sufferer what the cult requires of him, in effect persuading him to drop his charges and confess his guilt. Inside the cult, prayer reinterprets the meaning of suffering, shifting the accent from questions about justice to discernments about God's mercy.

On this point, however, Elihu would appear, at least initially, to be more in agreement with both the friends and Job than in conflict with them. The prologue presents Job as one who is at home with the cultic rituals that define life lived in harmony with the blessings of God (1:5). When suffering begins to define his existence in ways the sacrificial

"The Wrath of Elihu"

William Blake's depiction of Elihu follows immediately after his illustration of Job's complaint in 7:14 that God uses dreams and visions to terrify him. To see the connections between the two, readers should compare both images.

Illustration XII depicts a youthful Elihu addressing Job, his wife, and the three friends. His arms are raised, his left hand pointing to twelve stars illumining a blackened sky, his right hand extending toward the friends, palm downward, as if gently correcting them with a bene-dictory blessing from the heavens that makes every-thing right. Beneath his legs are two objects, perhaps rep-resenting the broken potsherds with which Job has scraped himself (2:8). Elihu steps over them as if they are of little consequence for the journey he makes. The three friends sit passively in front of a Druidic altar. Job sits beside them, a slight distance away, his arms folded across his chest, his eyes staring straight ahead, as if he feels

The Wrath of Elihu

William Blake (1757-1827). *The Wrath of Elihu*. 1823-1825. Engraving from Blake's *Illustrations of the Book of Job*.

like little more than an extra in this scene. Only Job's wife shows any response to Elihu's arrival. She buries her face in her knees and clasps her hands together, a prayerful gesture perhaps indicating that she trusts the outcome of this moment to God. Above and below the scene, Blake cites a pastiche of texts, all drawn from Elihu's speeches: at the top, reading clockwise from left to right: 33:14-16, 34:21, and 33:17, 23-24; at the bottom: 32:6, 33:29-30, and 35:5-7.

The most revealing part of this image, especially when compared with the preceding one, is the depiction of Job in the bottom border. The previous illustration (XI) shows Job stretched out on his bed, bracing himself against demon-like figures who are trying to pull him down and

into the terrifying abyss. In Illustration XII, Job rests much more peacefully upon a bed of soft straw. His left hand curls around a scroll, presumably an image for Job's abiding trust in the word of God that he has sought but not yet heard. Across the length of his body and ascending on either side are a series of angels. Their journey towards the heavens symbolizes Elihu's promise that if Job will but heed the instructions of his angelic mediator, he too will rise to see the "light of life" (33:30; cf. v. 28).

rituals seem ill-equipped to address, it is the practice of lament, especially its litany of anguished "Why?" questions (e.g., 3:11, 12, 20; 10:18), which provides Job the words to speak what he feels. Moreover, when God's silence drives Job away from lament to legal brief, it is the friends who urge him not to give up on prayer. Job must continue to pray, but he should change his words from complaint to contrition, for only if he confesses his sins can he expect God to turn and be gracious to him (8:5-7; 11:11-13; 22:21-27). Eliphaz speaks for them all when he asks the question that everyone should already know how to answer: "Can mortals be righteous before God?" (4:17; cf. 8:3). Following this line of reasoning, Zophar adds, "Know then that God exacts of you less than your guilt deserves" (11:5). Job's only recourse, Eliphaz says, is to "Agree with God, and be at peace" (22:21). On this point, at least, Elihu and the friends agree.

How, then, is Elihu's appeal to the cult different from anything that has been said thus far? Newsom has addressed this question in ways that deserve careful consideration. The distinctive feature of Elihu's contribution, she says, is his interest in the *process of moral transformation* that takes place in the cult.[14] The legal process privileges "punctive time," that is, the clarifying moment of the verdict, when one party to the case is judged right, the other wrong. *All that transpired before*, the charges and countercharges, is nugatory; from this moment, it has no recognized significance for what has been judged to be true. *All that follows*, whether the verdict is agreeable to both parties or not, must conform to the court's ruling lest it be judged false. The cult privileges "process time," that is, the journey a person makes, in the midst of charges and countercharges, from flawed understandings of an issue to better-informed ones. The moment of enlightenment is important, but the moral transformation that occurs in route to understanding is decisive. Elihu's contribution is his exploration of how the cult makes it possible for a person like Job to experience restoration by moving from lament to penitence.

Newsom's discernments add a helpful new perspective for assessing the historical context of the Elihu speeches. A precise dating for the speeches remains elusive, but she identifies similarities with texts from the late Persian and early Hellenistic periods that show a decided interest (like Elihu or his author) in issues of character, specifically the importance of repentance in moral formation. The texts of primary interest in this regard are the accounts of King Manasseh (2 Chr 30:10-30), Nebuchadnezzar (Dan 4), and Antiochus IV Epiphanes (1 Macc 6; 2 Macc 9). Of these, Nebuchadnezzar's model of the repentant sinner contains the most striking parallels to Job 33. [CD: Daniel 4 and Job 33] Although she does not pursue the matter, her delineation of the "family resemblances" among these texts deftly lays the groundwork for further exploration of the connection between Elihu's focus on repentance and the gradual displacement of lament by penitential prayer within Israel's cultic practices during the post-exilic period. [The Institutionalization of Penitential Prayer]

However we may assess Elihu's contribution, the fact remains that his "answer" to Job's questions about the meaning of suffering creates an unresolved tension in the story. Job has lamented, but so far as he can see, the heavens remain closed to his prayers, and God's silence makes his suffering more acute not less. He has explored the possibility that he might find the justice he seeks in the court rather than the cult, yet even after having given his imagination free rein to indict God for criminal behavior, he has little reason to hope that justice will be served. Elihu tries to break the impasse by finding some middle ground that seizes on the possibilities of both the court and the cult but avoids

---

The Institutionalization of Penitential Prayer

C. Westermann traces the historical development of lament prayers through three stages.

• The first stage consists of short and spontaneous appeals to God that arise naturally within every day situations of life. The occasion requires no cultic framework, the pray-ers no cultic mediator (e.g., Exod 18:10; Judg 15:18; 2 Sam 15:31).

• In the second or middle stage, these once brief, independent appeals are fused into poetic/psalmic forms, whose setting in life is the temple cult. The formalized structure of these psalms—invocation, lament, petition, and concluding praise—typically accents complaint and protest (e.g., Pss 44: 17-19; 74:1, 10-11, 18-23; 88:8-12; 89:46-51). Confession of sin seldom occurs in this second stage of lament. Ps 51 is the only example of penitential prayer Westermann recognizes.

• The third or late stage in the history of lament coincides with the destruction of the temple, the exile (586–538 BCE), and the consequent loss of the cult and its rituals. The form of prayer shifts from poetry to prose. The content of prayer shifts from complaint and lament that raise questions about God's justice to confession of sin that exonerates God by acknowledging human guilt. The prime exemplar of these transformations is the "prayer of penitence," which appears for the first time in the prose prayers of Neh 9 and Dan 9, then in the post-canonical prayers of 1 Esdr (*3 Ezra*) 8:73-90, the "Prayer of Manasseh," *Pss. Sol.* 9, and Bar 1:15–3:18.

In Westermann's judgment, this shift to penitential prayer signals the dissolution of the lament as a fixed prayer form in ancient Israel. His explanation for why this shift occurred has evoked important review and critique from a new generation of scholars that has focused on the development of penitential prayer in Second Temple Judaism. For a review and assessment of the research, including a preliminary proposal concerning the book of Job's contribution to the discussion, Samuel E. Balentine, "'I Was Ready To Be Sought Out By Those Who Did Not Ask,'" *Seeking the Favor of God: Volume 1: The Origins of Penitential Prayer in Second Temple Judaism*, eds. M. Boda, et al (Scholars Press, 2006), 1-20..

For further reading, the following works may be consulted: R. Werline, *Penitential Prayer in Second Temple Judaism: The Development of a Religious Institution* (Atlanta: Scholars Press, 1998); D. Falk, *Daily, Sabbath, and Festival Prayers in the Dead Sea Scrolls* (Leiden: Brill, 1998); J. Newman, *Praying by the Book: The Scripturalization of Prayer in the Second Temple Period* (Atlanta: Scholars Press, 1999); M. Boda, *Praying the Tradition: The Origin and Use of Tradition in Nehemiah 9* (Berlin, New York: Walter de Gruyter, 1999); R. Bautsch, *Developments in Genre between Post-exilic Penitential Prayers and the Psalms of Communal Lament* (Atlanta: Society of Biblical Literature, 2003).

C. Westermann, "Struktur und Geschichte der Klage im Alten Testament," ZAW 66 (1954): 44-80; English translation: "The Structure and History of Lament in the Old Testament," in *Praise and Lament in the Psalms* (Atlanta: John Knox, 1981), 165-213.

their limitations. In court, Job will get his hearing, but the verdict in the end will be "Guilty." In the cult, Job can and should find comfort in prayer, but the words that trigger the process of transformation Elihu so prizes are not those Job comes to on his own. It is the angelic mediator who tells him what he must say to secure the blessing—"I have sinned and perverted what was right"—even though Job has already resolved that sacrificing his integrity on the altar of manufactured penitence is a price too high to pay for the promise of restoration (13:14; 27:1-6). ["My Mistake, My Mistake"] It remains unclear whether Elihu's contribution has clarified what has already been said or not.

"Listen to Me. . . Be Silent. . . Listen to Me," 33:31-33

Elihu ends where he began. Once more he addresses Job by name

---

"My Mistake, My Mistake"

Thomas Bunting, the main character in James Wood's novel, is the son of a parish priest. Because despair has driven him beyond faith, he hopes to find answers to his questions by pursuing a Ph.D. in philosophy. After seven years, he abandons his dissertation in order to write his masterpiece, an atheistic project tentatively titled "The Book Against God." One of his pet peeves is Kierkegaard's argument for Christianity in the book *Either/Or*. The chapter that draws Bunting's ire is titled, "The Edifying in the Thought That Against God We Are Always in the Wrong." Since we are always sinful and in the wrong, and since God always loves us more than we can possibly love Him, therefore we should want this wrongness. In sum, Kierkegaard insists, being in the wrong is edifying.

Bunting's counter to Kierkegaard is as follows:

Doesn't Kierkegaard's "love sound rather like "hate"? He is exactly like Simone Weil in this regard. Couldn't we substitute "hate" for every use of "love" in Kierkegaard's (or Weil's) work, and get a more accurate picture of the world? God *hates* us more than we can *hate* Him, and we do not deserve that *hate*, therefore, against God we are always in the wrong. Kierkegaard wants us to go about muttering, "My mistake, my mistake," while God lets His earthquakes and Holocausts and famines rage, all the while saying whatever nonsense God feels He wants to say: "Plato was English," perhaps, or "the Holocaust never happened, I, the Almighty, great Jehovah, deny it." (Yes, God would have a *very* good reason to be the first Holocaust-denier.)

Kierkegaard's idea of our relations with God reminds me of a story told by Cicero and several other classical authors, one of those exemplary stories offered as a model of Stoical self-control. Archytas, the owner of a vineyard, discovered that slaves on his estate had behaved offensively and disobediently, and then, realizing that he was feeling too wound up and violent towards them, stopped himself doing anything, except to say mildly, as he walked by them, "You're lucky I'm angry with you."

Well, that's our relationship with God in brief, isn't it? Archytas's idea of "luck" is not far from Kierkegaard's, is it? We are "lucky" that God is angry with us, "lucky" that He made us, and even when we have not behaved badly in the vineyard and have done nothing bad at all, we should still bow and scrape, and murmur, like my father's poor parishioners going down on their knees, "My mistake, my mistake, I am lucky that You are angry with me"—all because Adam, who was anyway created by this hateful tyrant and might not have wanted to be created, this poor Adam, ate the luckless apple. Oh when will humans murder this devilish concept of God? For is God really any more dead now than when Nietzsche told us He was a hundred years or so ago? Until that final day, that real day of murder, of cancellation, of blissful clearing, the holiday of life, an emptied sabbath of repose—until that moment, I propose instead an edifying inversion of Kierkegaard: "the edifying in the thought that against *us* God is always in the wrong."

J. Wood, *The Book Against God* (New York: Farrar, Straus and Giroux, 2003), 117-19.

A Silence that Makes Failure Evident

Andrew Miller's novel, *Oxygen*, revolves around the story of Alec Valentine and his older brother Larry, who have been summoned home to help care for their dying mother. Until Larry arrives, Alec plays host to the friends who come to visit his mother. When Reverend Osbourne shows up, the conversation is strained. They pass small talk, as the Reverend waits for the right moment to slide into his pastoral role.

"The thing about faith," he began, quietly addressing a spider's web that glittered and trembled with rain-drops, a thing of fabulous intricacy under the eaves of the summerhouse, "is that it doesn't have to come all at once. Road to Damascus, et cetera.

You can believe for a morning. Or an hour, if that's all you can manage. It doesn't matter."

"Sorry?" said Alec.

"All I mean is that saying a prayer can help. It's very natural when things are difficult. Some people think it's hypocritical because they don't pray when things are going well. But it's perfectly all right."

"Don't you have to believe that it will make some difference?"

The reverend paused. "Perhaps not even that." He pressed his hair into place with the flats of his hands. "We're not alone."

"No," said Alec, feeling as he spoke the weight of his conviction that quite the opposite was true; that aloneness was what lay at the beginning and end of every argument. "Do you want some tea?" he asked.

When the visit ends, Miller sums up what had been accomplished:

They looked at each other; *a silence that made evident both the purpose and the failure of their conversation.* Then they shook hands again and the reverend made his way towards the stile that led from the garden back to the meadow . . . . He looked up. The clouds now were slashed with a blue as clean as starlight, and he smiled, feeling the grateful inhalation of his soul. It was hard to believe there could be any atheists in Somerset, and by the time he was halfway across the meadow, his coat flapping over his arm, he had quite forgotten his dreams.

A. Miller, *Oxygen* (New York: Harcourt, 2001), 161-62 (emphasis added).

(v. 31; cf. v. 1a). Once again he invites him to hear (*šāma'*; vv. 31, 33; cf. v. 1b) and respond (*hăšîbēnî*; v. 32; cf. v. 5) to what he has said. The near verbatim repetition of the invitation is a rhetorical indicator of sincerity; Elihu speaks as if nothing is more important to him than genuine dialogue with Job. Several subtle additions tacked on to this last appeal, however, betray another agenda. The multiple invitations to Job to speak are now offset by two imperatives to "be silent" (*hahărēš*; vv. 31, 33). Elihu assures Job he would be pleased to confirm that he is "in the right" (*ṣaddĕqekā*; v. 32), but in point of fact he has already decided that Job is "in the wrong" (*lō' ṣādaqtā*; v. 12). The concluding words of the discourse may be the most telling of all: "Be silent, I will teach you wisdom" (v. 33b). In the Hebrew text as in the English translation, the last word on "wisdom" belongs to Elihu. Job, it appears, is little more than a sound of silence in the "dialogue" Elihu offers.

[A Silence That Makes Failure Evident]

CONNECTIONS

Anyone who claims to have the answer to questions about the meaning of suffering will no doubt find an audience. To borrow Terence Mann's famous line from the 1989 film *Field of Dreams*, "if you build it, they will come. . . People will most definitely come." People will come and listen to the Elihus of this world, because suffering has taken up residence in their lives without invitation or so much as a knock at the door before entering. They will come, because the most basic human need, as philosophers, psychologists, and theologians agree, is for meaning. We can bear an enormous amount of *meaningful* sorrow but only very little *meaningless* loss. We can accommodate ourselves, however uncomfortably, to sickness, deprivation, tragedy, even death, so long as we can cling to the belief that life, for all its apparent futility, remains relatively good in the end. When understanding fails us, the assurance that life has purpose can be the elixir we need. Elihu will get the hearing he wants, because he offers hope as a substitute for despair. Trust in this, he says with untroubled conviction, God's hand is in the suffering, knowingly, purposefully monitoring its path along the route that leads to redemption. ["Whose Purpose Was It?"]

Elihu's explanation of the meaning of suffering has strong appeal for several reasons. Unlike the others, who feign pastoral sympathy while treating Job as an object, a *thing* more to be talked about than a *person* to be heard, Elihu claims to have listened carefully and thoughtfully to what Job has said. Unlike the others, whose wisdom derives from nothing more profound than the smug claim to have lived longer and seen more than Job, Elihu speaks sincerely. If there is wisdom in what he offers, then it is because he identifies with Job and with the questions suffering presses upon all God's creatures: "See, before God I am as you are" (v. 5). Moreover, although he is younger and less experienced than his elders, Elihu's insight into the meaning of suffering as divine discipline (33:19-22) echoes a proverbial truth (Prov 3:11-12; 13:24; 15:5). Even when the elders mouth the words of this truth without full understanding (Job 5:17-18), its wisdom remains timeless. As every child knows, loving parents use punishment to admonish and correct their children. Surely it is not hard to understand that both God's love and God's discipline are infinitely greater than anything the best parent can do (Heb 12:6).

Even so, whenever someone proposes to explain suffering by saying it is as simple as this,

---

"Whose Purpose Was It?"

The Universe is but the Thing of things,
The things but balls all going round in rings.
Some of them mighty huge, some mighty tiny,
All of them radiant and mighty shiny.

They mean to tell us all was rolling blind
Till accidentally it hit on mind
In an albino monkey in a jungle,
And even then it had to grope and bungle,

Till Darwin came to earth upon a year
To show the evolution how to steer.
They mean to tell us, though, the Omnibus
Had no real purpose till it got to us.

Never believe it. At the very worst
It must have had the purpose from the first
To produce purpose as the fitter bred:
We were just purpose coming to a head.

Whose purpose was it? His or Hers or Its?
Let's leave that to the scientific wits.
Grant me intention, purpose, and design—
That's near enough for me to the Divine.

R. Frost, "Accidentally on Purpose," *The Poetry of Robert Frost*, ed. E. C. Lathem (New York: Henry Holt and Company, 1969), 425.

"There Is No Truth Which Stupidity Can't Make Use of"

Kinkaid, the youngest of four brothers in the Clarence family, grew up wondering about a lot of things, especially about what happened long ago to his father's baseball career. The only real evidence he had to go on was the look of his father's mangled right thumb, which he understood, from playing backyard baseball with his father, had ruined his slider and curveball. Kinkaid also wondered if this tragedy somehow explained his mother's obsession with religion. For whatever reason, she had become a kind of "religious McCarthyite," waging holy war on the sins of him and his brothers. He knew she loved them all dearly, but the mantra she used to express love—"I come not to bring peace but a sword"—more often than not brought nothing but pain, confusion, and embarrassment.

In David Duncan's novel *The Brothers K*, Kinkaid offers this reflection on the fanatic's brand of salvation.

"What's a little confusion or pain," they ask, "compared to eternal salvation?" And of course this question can't be argued: who wouldn't gladly be robbed of all they own today if they were certain that the thief would "come again" and hand them a billion-dollar compensation payment tomorrow? But this question doesn't address the real problem. In a head-on collision with Fanatics, the real problem is always the same: how can we possibly behave decently toward people so arrogantly ignorant that they believe, first, that they possess Christ's power to bestow salvation, second, that forcing us to memorize and regurgitate a few of their favorite Bible phrases and attend their church *is* that salvation, and third, that any discomfort, frustration, anger or disagreement we express in the face of their moronic barrages is due not to *their* astounding effrontery but to *our* sinfulness?

The Austrian writer Robert Musil summed up the Fanatic's great advantage in just ten words: "There is no truth which stupidity can't make use of."

David James Duncan, *The Brothers K* (New York: Bantam Books, 1993), 250.

---

one, two, three, the only thing the numbers will likely add up to is a zero. Statements about a truth falsely conceived can claim at most to be only half-truths. Elihu wraps his truth in certainty but digesting what he says may feel like eating carpet tacks covered over with chocolate.[15] It may be appealing, even irresistible, but with the first bite you feel your insides being torn apart. How can the innocent deaths of seven sons and three daughters add up to a sum that equals God's love and mercy? If we reverse the logic of such an equation, the horrible error should be clear. Would the long life and happiness of these same innocent children add up to God's wrath and cruelty? Would a world without senseless pain and suffering somehow compromise or diminish God's capacity to love? ["There Is No Truth Which Stupidity Can't Make Use of"]

How we answer this question depends in large part on our vantage point (see further the Connections at Job 30). If we stand with Elihu, looking on Job's suffering from a safe distance, then we may nod with calm agreement, comforted by the assurance that the world we live in, despite the problems of others, remains securely in God's hands. We pray for their restoration, in accordance with God's will, then resume our own satisfying lives. If we sit with Job on the ash heap of suffering, then we may see *and feel* things differently. The pain etched in our souls may yearn for something more than the assurance that God is trying to teach us a lesson. However important that lesson may be, the grief that claims us will likely be impervious to its truth. ["All but Death, Can Be Adjusted"] Elihu's argument *for* God may well clank in our ears as yet

"All but Death, Can Be Adjusted"

All but Death, can be Adjusted—
Dynasties repaired—
Systems—settled in their Sockets—
Citadels—dissolved—
Wastes of Lives—resown with Colors
By Succeeding Springs—
Death—unto itself—Exception—
Is exempt from Change—

Emily Dickinson, "# 749," in *The Complete Poems of Emily Dickinson*, ed. T. H. Johnson (Boston/New York: Little, Brown and Company, 1960), 367.

another piece of evidence in support of our pained case *against* God. It may summon us not to hope but to deepened despair.

James Wood's novel, *The Book Against God*, offers a window on to what the Jobs of the world may feel when they listen to Elihu's sermon on suffering. Thomas Bunting, whose life experiences have driven him to atheism, sits on a pew in the church his father served when he was a young boy. Peter, his boyhood friend and the current minister, offers the pastoral prayer, then the sermon. The litany is familiar, but it invokes in Thomas a cacophony of memories and fraught decisions that lead him to affirm something quite different than the preacher intends.

> Peter, newly plump in his henlike clerical frocks, stood not at the altar but with the congregation, in the middle of the nave. His clean, soft, bald head was filmed in light from several stained-glass windows. On Sundays he wore shoes with rubber soles (no one was quite sure why), so that he had a soundless and pious tread. . . . He acted as if his church had no roof, as if it were an open theatre on which life simply shone its sun: his church, like his head, was uncovered. Into his prayers he folded every human occurrence, triumph, disaster, and banality. . . . He stood, hands clasped and eyes closed, pursing his lips, and enjoined the congregation to pray to God for—everything. For the wonderful weather, for the lunch we will soon go and eat, for Muriel's swift recovery, and so on.
>
> Bowing my head in the pew so that I could smell the gist of the wood. . . I would listen to these prayers. "And we pray," Peter intoned, "for the souls of the three priests murdered this week in El Salvador. Lord, hear our prayer. We pray also for the thousands made homeless by the recent flooding in Bangladesh, and ask you, Lord, to give them succour and shelter. Lord, hear our prayer. At this time, we also pray for Dr. Shields, whose cousin was involved in a car accident in Birmingham last Monday; and for Lance and Angela Menzies, whose son Austin died of leukemia on Friday. Lord, hear our prayer."
>
> I always felt I was hearing a page of atrocious international news and a page of tragic local news, each ripped from the newspaper. When I was a teenager, I used to hear my father with a kind of vindictive horror, my mouth and eyes open with amazement, convinced that such a list of misfortune vandalized the very face of God. . . . Now I realize that, as far Father was concerned, this catastrophe was God's world, vandalized by man. It was because there was so much evil-doing and pain that God's correction was needed. Pain was not an argument against but *for* God. To tell you the truth, this argument still irritates me. Why should we need correction from Him who made us? And why has He made us so very flawed, and then just disappeared? *The most charitable image of this particular God I can produce is that of a father who breaks his*

son's leg just so that he can watch his son learn how to appeal to his dad for help in mending it (emphasis added).[16]

If Elihu's *theology of suffering* leaves us with an unacceptable image of God—a deity infinitely more cruel than compassionate (cf. 30:21)—his *anthropology of prayer* leaves us with an image of a human being more robotic than sentient. Job understands prayer as an invitation to speak his own words, not the words someone else instructs him to say, even if the prompting comes from an angel. ["Speak What We Feel"] Consigned to life's ash heap "for no reason," Job speaks the language of lament, with full-throated questions and complaints, because something has gone terribly wrong in the world God created to be "very good." He is painfully aware that God can choose not to respond to his questions and complaints, but he is unwilling to accept the friends' suggestion that he does not have the right to speak them (cf. 8:2 and 10:1-2). The friends acknowledge that the prayers are offered at the human's initiative. Indeed, they argue that the pivotal point in the experience with suffering comes when a person decides to turn to God and pray. But the friends make it clear to Job that although he is free to pray as he chooses, God responds only to those who confess their sins and plea for mercy (8:6; 11:13-15; 22:23-27).

> **"Speak What We Feel"**
>
> In the final scene of *King Lear*, the king comes center stage holding his dead daughter Cordelia in his arms. By play's end, the once proud and sovereign monarch is broken and despondent. Through his own foolishness his kingdom lies in ruin; through his own scheming, his family is shattered. Holding the limp body of his beloved daughter, Lear moans:
>
> Why should a dog, a horse, a rat have life,
> And thou no breath at all? Thou shalt come
>   no more,
> Never, never, never, never, never!
>
> With these words, the king collapses and dies. Witnessing this grief-filled moment, the Duke of Albany offers a final summation:
>
> The weight of this sad time we must obey;
> Speak what we feel, not what we ought to
>   say.
>
> (*King Lear*, V, iii, ll. 305-307, 322-23)

Elihu's understanding of prayer in relation to suffering is different. *God* takes the initiative, first by sending suffering to get a person's attention, then by sending an angel to tell the person what is right for him to pray. If the sufferer does what he is told, if he prays the prayer of confession he has been given, then a merciful and gracious God will restore him (vv. 22-28). The process of moral and physical regeneration that God offers to sufferers, Elihu says, requires that they tell God what God (or at least Elihu, as the presumptive religious authority) wants to hear. In Elihu's conception of the cult, a confession of sin, even one manufactured by reciting another's words, is more appropriate than honest lament.

Because Elihu arrives at this understanding of prayer by way of appropriating and critiquing legal language, it is important to reflect on what real differences he sees between worship and the courtroom when sufferers need a word from God. Job has himself explored the legal venue, but the reason he has done so is because he despairs of ever getting a word from God through prayer alone. At least in a court-room, each party to a case has a voice to which the other must listen and respond. Both parties are presumed innocent, both have arguments to make that are presumed worthy of the court's time, and both parties have a legal right to expect that no verdict will be rendered without a full and impartial consideration of the evidence. Elihu seems to recognize the merits of the legal approach, with one critical exception. Job can get the hearing he wants in a court of law, but the verdict is prede-termined. In the end, it will be decided that Job is "in the wrong," because "God is greater than any mortal" (v. 12). In Elihu's court, might makes right.

Surely then, worship offers a different context for addressing God, one in which partnership not power, invites an honest exploration of what covenantal relationship requires in order to fulfill the hopes and aspirations of both parties. Elihu's understanding of prayer holds no such promise. All the initiative rests with God. God sends the suffering, because God has determined that a person is heading in the wrong direction. God sends an angel to tell the person his duty, because God has decided that the person, left to his own resources, can only do what is wrong. God provides the words required to make things right, because the sufferer's own words will not do the job, either because they are ineffective, or because, as Elihu himself will soon suggest (34:31-32), God does not want to hear them. The sufferer's only role in prayer is to confirm that he has learned how to say "Yes" to what God requires. In Elihu's cult, as in his court, might makes right.

Faced with an understanding of worship that adds hope by sub-tracting a sufferer's integrity, we might be tempted to decide without further deliberation that Elihu is obviously wrong. Before doing so, however, we should consider that his theology is very much alive and well, even today. The Jobs of this world, in countless numbers, have often discovered that places of worship offer little or no sanctuary for them. Their rants and ravings against the injustice of life have no place in our carefully prescribed litanies. Their anger and their despair, which relentlessly calls for systemic changes in the very institutions that provide for our prosperity, remains unquieted by our traditional bene-dictions of peace. The ancient words, "The Lord bless you and keep you" (Num 6:24), now fossilized in our own sacred rituals, may well sound to their ears more like a threat than promise. How and why do the Jobs of this world so often wind up outside the gates, consigned to suffer alone, until and unless they say the magic words—"I have sinned"—that invite them back into *God's* and *our* good graces?

Elihu's "answer" in chapter 33 provides one clue that invites close inspection. The conventional and seemingly benign translation of v. 6 is, "See, before God, I am as you are" (NRSV; cf. REB, NJPS, NIV, NAB). The Hebrew reads, literally, "See, before God, I am like your mouth." The words Elihu chooses to invite Job's response suggest that what he really desires is monologue, not dialogue. He will speak *to* Job and *for* him.
Subsequently, when he spells out the role of the
mēlîṣ, the angelic *mediator*, who will stand in
between Job and God, he envisions a carbon
copy of himself. The angel, like Elihu, will tell
Job what he must say to God. The words the

> **"A Preacher's Temptation"**
>
> A preacher's temptation
> is the voice persuading
> he is his own message.
>
> R. S. Thomas, "Incarnations," *No Truce with the Furies*
> (Newcastle upon Tyne: Bloodaxe Books, 1995), 35.

angel gives him, "I sinned, and perverted what was right" (v. 27), are Elihu's words, "you are wrong" (v. 12), now wrapped in the sanctity of God's inscrutable will. "A preacher's temptation," Elihu reminds us, albeit inadvertently, is to presume that he and God speak with one voice. ["A Preacher's Temptation"]

At the conclusion of chapter 33, Elihu invites but does not receive a response from Job. From Elihu's vantage point, as both a legal and religious expert, Job's silence matters little, for the outcome of this "dialogue" is already decided. If we have sat with Job on the ash heap, then we too may decide that silence is the only option left to us. If both legal statutes and religious rituals predetermine that we are guilty, then what recourse do we have? ["I No Longer Possess the Courage of My Pessimism"]

"I No Longer Possess the Courage of My Pessimism"

Ian McEwan's novel *Atonement* bears the title that conveys Briony Tallis's quest for absolution. As a young girl of thir-
teen, she saw something that she misinterpreted. As she tries to bring justice to an innocent situation that does not require it, she inadvertently destroys the lives of her sister and her childhood friend, Robbie. She spends the rest of her life trying unsuccessfully to atone for her mistakes. Though her situation is different than Job's—she is guilty, he is innocent—her sense of unease at the end of the novel may well connect with what Job feels at the end of Elihu's discourse in ch. 33: "I no longer possess the courage of my pessimism."

I. McEwan, *Atonement* (New York: Doubleday, 2002), 350.

NOTES

[1] N. Habel, *The Book of Job: A Commentary* (OTL; Philadelphia: Westminster Press, 1985), 463-64; cf. H. Huffmon, "The Covenant Lawsuit in the Prophets," JBL 78 (1959): 285-95.

[2] Ibid., 465; cf. C. Newsom, "The Book of Job," in vol. 4 of *NIB* (Nashville: Abingdon Press, 1996), 568.

[3] In post-biblical Hebrew the verbal root means "to wash, rub," as in washing the hair, for example; see M. Jastrow, *Dictionary of the Targumim* (New York: Judaica Press, 1982 [reprint]), 492.

[4] The Hebrew text is ambiguous. Some scholars, following the LXX, emend _yaḥtōm_, "he seals" (in the sense of "sealing with a signature," as in NJPS; cf. 1 Kgs 21:8; Exod 28:11, 21) to _yĕḥittēm_, "he frightens them," as in NRSV; e.g., R. Gordis, _The Book of Job: Commentary, New Translation, and Special Studies_ (New York: Jewish Theological Seminary of America, 1978), 375; M. Pope, _Job_ (AB; Garden City NY: Doubleday, 1979), 250.

[5] The fourth occurrence in the friends' speeches is Eliphaz's discourse in 22:29. The syntax of this verse is ambiguous. NIV, for example, translates in a positive sense: "When men are brought low and you say, 'Lift them up (_gĕwāh_)!' then he will save the downcast" (see the commentary on 22:21-30). Alternatively, other translations offer a negative connotation, e.g., "but God brings down the pride (_gĕwāh_) of the haughty, and keeps safe those who are humble" (REB; cf. NJPS, NAB). For the syntactical issues, see E. Dhorme, _A Commentary on the Book of Job_ (Nashville: Thomas Nelson Publishers, 1967), 341-42.

[6] The MT's "pride" is often emended to "back." NRSV, for example, translates "its _back_ is made of shields." A literal translation is instructive: "his [Leviathan's] rows of shields are his _pride_ "; cf. Newsom, "The Book of Job," 624.

[7] Cf. Habel (_Book of Job_, 461), who understands _hearing_ to be the mode of experiencing the first warning (vv. 15-18), _feeling_ to be the mode for experiencing the second warning (vv. 19-22), and _seeing_ (that is, seeing the face of God; v. 26) as the mode for experiencing the third warning (vv. 23-29).

[8] Gordis, _Book of Job,_ 377; cf. Habel, _Book of Job,_ 469-70.

[9] C. Newsom, _The Book of Job: A Contest of Moral Imaginations_ (Oxford: Oxford University Press, 2003), 212.

[10] The subject of the verbs in v. 24 is ambiguous. NRSV understands Elihu as the subject of the first verb ("be gracious") and God as the subject of the second ("deliver"): "and he (Elihu) is gracious to that person, and says (to God), 'Deliver him from going down to the pit'" (cf. NIV). NJPS takes God to be the subject of both verbs: "Then He (God) has mercy on him and decrees, 'Redeem him from descending to the Pit.'"

[11] In Priestly literature, especially throughout Leviticus, the verb _kippēr_, from which comes the noun derivative _kōper_, "ransom," is used with reference to sacrifices that "atone for" or "expiate" sin. For an extended discussion, see J. Milgrom, _Leviticus 17–22_ (AB; New York: Doubleday, 2000), 1079-84.

[12] Newsom, "The Book of Job," 570.

[13] B. Zuckerman, _Job the Silent: A Study in Historical Counterpoint_ (New York: Oxford University Press, 1991), 150.

[14] Newsom, _Book of Job,_ 207-16.

[15] This suggestive metaphor I take from Annie Proulx's review of P. Karnezis's book of short stories, _Little Infamies_. Unfortunately, I have been unable to locate the source.

[16] J. Wood, _The Book Against God_ (New York: Farrar, Straus and Giroux, 2003), 54-55.

GOD'S JUST GOVERNANCE OF THE WORLD

Job 34:1-37

In the previous discourse, Elihu declares that Job is "in the wrong" (33:12), specifically with respect to his complaint that God does not answer sufferers who appeal for help. In fact, God answers in multiple ways, including using suffering as a means to get one's attention (33:19-22). The problem is not God's silence; it is Job's failure to hear and heed God's communication. Job has also complained about God's injustice, charging that the Almighty arbitrarily punishes the innocent, all the while turning a blind eye to the wicked who build their fortunes on the miseries of those powerless to resist. On this point also, Elihu has declared that Job is wrong, although he has not yet spelled out why. In chapter 34, he takes up the challenge by offering a vigorous defense of God's moral governance of the world.

The outline of the chapter is relatively straightforward. Elihu begins (vv. 1-9) and ends (vv. 31-37) with an appeal to his audience, addressed as the "wise (men)" and "those who have sense" (vv. 1, 34; cf. vv. 10, 16), to listen to his rebuttal and to concur with his judgment that Job's charges are completely without merit. The core of his speech (vv. 10-30) consists of three principal arguments in defense of God's justice, each one presented as a propositional truth: (1) it is unthinkable that God could be unjust; therefore, anyone who makes such a charge lacks wisdom (vv. 10-15); (2) God is a lover of justice; therefore, God would never do what God hates, namely, pervert justice (vv. 16-20); and (3) God sees and judges everything, including those who try to hide from God's justice; therefore, God's justice is beyond question, even when God's silence and hiddenness suggest otherwise (vv. 21-30). [Structure of Job 34:1-37]

Elihu accents this defense of God's justice in ways that strengthen his arguments but diminish their moral gravitas.

Structure of Job 34:1-37

34:1-9   "Hear my words, you wise men"

34:10-30 "Therefore, hear me, you have sense"

vv. 10-15 It is unthinkable that God could be unjust; therefore, anyone who makes such a charge lacks wisdom

vv. 16-20 God loves justice; therefore, God would never do what God hates, namely, pervert justice

vv. 21-30 God sees everything; therefore, God's justice is beyond question

34:31-37 "The wise who hear me will say"

He continues to address Job by name (vv. 5, 7, 35, 36), thus presumably *speaking directly to him*. At the same time, he uses third person language to *speak about Job*, which indicates that in reality he is objectifying him, treating him as more of an issue than a person. He is more focused in this speech on matters relating to law and *justice* (*mišpāṭ*, 6x: vv. 4, 5, 6, 12, 17, 23; NRSV: "right," justice," "judgment") than any other speaker in the book, save Job. Even so, he defines justice exclusively in terms of God's punishment of the *wicked* (*rešaʿ*; 5x: vv. 8, 10, 17, 18, 29), not God's vindication of the innocent. [CD: The Distribution of Words for Justice and Law] He uses strategically placed rhetorical questions (vv. 7, 13, 17, 29, 33) that *invite a concurring response from Job,* yet he *dismisses any response Job might offer* by declaring in advance that "his answers are those of the wicked" (v. 36). Perhaps most telling of all, he affirms that *God loves justice* (v. 17) and then asserts without flinching that *God renders verdicts "without investigation"* (v. 24). What kind of judge declares people guilty without investigating the truth of the charges against them? More importantly, from Job's perspective, what kind of God loves to administer this kind of justice? ["Doth Not This Justice . . . Stink in Thy Nostrils?"]

COMMENTARY

"Hear My Words, You Wise Men," 34:1-9

Elihu summons the "wise men," "you who know" (v. 1) to hear his words. It is not clear whom Elihu includes among these knowing ones. Presumably the three friends are excluded. If they had demonstrated true wisdom in responding to Job, Elihu would not have needed to enter this conversation. Perhaps he is addressing his peers in the community, those whose claims to wisdom bind them together in an exclusive, members-only fraternity of the knowing. As a "belated reader" of this story, Elihu (or his author) may also be appealing to an imaginary audience of future readers, who will demonstrate their wisdom by agreeing with what he says (see ["The Belatedness of All Reading"]).[1] The critical question within the narrative structure of the book is, does Elihu number *Job* among the wise he wants to hear from? First impression indicates that he does. By citing (v. 3) the proverbial words of wisdom Job used in 12:11, Elihu suggests that he and Job are kindred spirits. Both know that a truly wise person will "test words" before jumping to conclusions about what they mean. Elihu's preemptory dismissal of Job's words as wrong (33:12), however, gives us reason to question whether these two have much in common when it comes

"Doth Not This Justice . . . Stink in Thy Nostrils?"

In his poem, "A Litany of Atlanta," W. E. B. Dubois raises a sharp and pained charge of injustice against the God who seemed indifferent to the wanton cruelty that took innocent lives in the race riots of 1906 in Atlanta (see further **["Is This Thy Justice, O Father?"]**). Although he later conceded that the poem was "a bit hysterical," he refused to apologize for a faith that beseeches God for justice "by the tears of our dead mothers" *and* "by the very blood of Thy crucified Christ":

In the pale, still morning we looked upon the deed. We stopped our ears and held our leaping hands, but they—did they not wag their heads and leer and cry with bloody jaws: *Cease from crime*! The word was mockery, for thus they train a hundred crimes while we do one.
     Turn again our captivity, O Lord!

Behold this maimed and broken thing; dear God, it was an humble black man who toiled and sweat to save a bit from the pittance paid him. They told him: *Work and Rise*. He worked. Did this man sin? Nay, but some one told how some one said another did—one whom he had never seen nor known. Yet for that man's crime this man lieth maimed and murdered, his wife naked to shame, his children, to poverty and evil.
     Hear us, O Heavenly Father!

Doth not this justice of hell stink in Thy nostrils, O God? How long shall the mounting flood of innocent blood roar in Thine ears and pound in our hearts for vengeance? Pile the pale frenzy of blood-crazed brutes who do such deeds high on Thine altar, Jehovah Jireh, and burn it in hell forever and forever!
     Forgive us, good Lord; we know not what we say!

Bewildered we are, and passion-tost, mad with the madness of a mobbed and mocked and murdered people; straining at the armposts of Thy Throne, we raise our shackled hands and charge Thee, God, by the bones of our stolen fathers, by the tears of our dead mothers, by the very blood of Thy crucified Christ: *What meaneth this?* Tell us the Plan; give us the Sign!
     Keep not thou silence, O God!

For further discussion of this poem, see D. Lewis, *W. E. B. Dubois: Biography of a Race, 1868–1919* (New York: Henry Holt and Company, 1993), 334-36.

W. E. B. Dubois, "A Litany of Atlanta," *The Independent* 61 (11 October 1906): 856-58; subsequently published with slight modifications in W. E. B. Dubois, *Darkwater: Voices from Within the Veil* (New York: Harcourt, Brace, 1921), 25-28.

---

to claims about wisdom. The concluding assertion that Job speaks "without knowledge" and "without insight" (v. 35) effectively removes all doubt about Elihu's opinion.

Elihu announces the principal topic for discussion—"what is just" (*mišpāṭ*; NJPS)—in v. 4. The word *mišpāṭ* occurs six times in this discourse (vv. 4, 5, 6, 12, 17, 23), the highest concentration of the term in any chapter of the book. The word has both particular and general meanings. In vv. 5 and 6, Elihu cites Job's use of the word with reference to his specific case, his personal quest for justice. [Quoting or Misquoting Job] In vv. 4, 12, 17, and 23, Elihu himself uses the word in a more general sense, with reference to the process, the system of governance, by which legal judgments are rendered. Although both nuances are often simultaneously conveyed by *mišpāṭ*, Elihu discerns a critical dif-

Quoting or Misquoting Job

While there may be *general* agreement between Job's words and Elihu's citation of them in 34:5-6, the potential slippage may be significant. The following comparison, with differences italicized, invites the thought that Elihu's *quotations* are little more than a "tissue of skewed allusion" (E. M. Good, *In Turns of Tempest: A Reading of Job with a Translation* [Stanford: Stanford University Press, 1990], 327). Elihu's opening summons—"Let us choose what is right" (v. 4a)—may invite a greater scrutiny from his audience than he intends.

Job's Words	Elihu's Quotations
9:15, 10:15 *If/though* ('*im*) I am innocent (*ṣādaqtî*)	34:5a For Job has said, "I am innocent" (*ṣādaqtî*)
27:2a *As God lives* (*ḥay 'ēl*), who has taken away my right	34:5b God has taken away my right
6:28 *Would I lie* ('*im 'ăkazzēb*) to your face? [an oath sworn to the friends]	34:6a in spite of being right I am counted a liar ('*ăkazzēb*)
6:4 The *arrows of the Almighty* (*ḥiṣṣê šadday*) are in me	34:6b my arrow (NRSV: "wound") is incurable

ference between his understanding of the word and Job's. He will demonstrate that *Job argues inductively*, moving from his personal experience of injustice to a negative assessment of God's overall governance of the world. To counter Job's narrow and self-absorbed view, *Elihu will argue deductively*. He begins with an unequivocal affirmation of God's moral governance, then draws the only logical conclusion a truly wise person could make: a God who judges the world righteously could not possibly treat Job or any individual unjustly.[2]

Starting from the premise that God's justice is unassailable, Elihu reasons that any charge brought against God serves only to indict the accuser. To explicate this point, he concludes his opening appeal for a hearing by charging that it is Job's character, not God's, which must be placed under review. With the first of a series of barely rhetorical questions—"Who is there like Job?" (v. 7a)—he spells out three of Job's incriminating flaws: (1) Job "drinks up scoffing like water" (v. 7b), an idiomatic expression that endorses what Eliphaz has already asserted (15:16): Job drinks derision like a man dying of thirst gulps down water; (2) Job keeps company with "evildoers" and with the "wicked" (v. 8); and (3) Job complains that righteousness "profits one nothing" (v. 9). Elihu offers no evidence in support of these charges. He has summoned his wise audience to test words for their claim to truth (v. 3), but he is oblivious to the possibility that his own words may fail to pass the test. The last charge is case in point. Job has in fact spoken the words Elihu cites in v. 9, but he was quoting what the wicked say (21:15). He did so only to insist that he categorically rejected their values. Even though suffering has taught Job the hard lesson that righteousness does not pay, he has refused to give up on its promise to be the better course of wisdom. If we readers are in fact included among the wise ones Elihu invites into this debate, then we should know that Job's wisdom and Elihu's are miles apart.

"Therefore, Hear Me, You Who Have Sense," 34:10-30

Having called Job's character into question, Elihu renews his appeal to all those "who have sense" (vv. 10a) to confirm his assessment. He now buttresses his appeal with three arguments in defense of God's moral governance of the world.

The first argument (vv. 10-15) may be stated simply: God does not pervert justice (v. 12). Two emphatic exclamations punctuate this claim. "Far be it from God" (*ḥālilāh lā'ēl*; v. 10b) is an oath formula that introduces a claim grounded in recognized truths about God. Job has used the expression in 27:5 to validate a series of oaths of innocence he swears on the life of God. The adverbial asseverative "truly" (*'omnām*, v. 12; NRSV: "of a truth") occurs more often in the book of Job than anywhere else in the Old Testament. It always occurs on the lips of either Job (9:2; 12:2; 19:4-5) or Elihu (34:12; 36:4), both of whom use the expression (in Job's case, sometimes sarcastically; e.g., 9:2, 12:2) to underscore the honesty of their words. Elihu employs both exclamations in support of his assertion that it is unthinkable to accuse God of perverting justice. He seems unaware or unfazed by the fact that Abraham, one of Israel's paragons of faith, provides Job with a precedent for making just such a charge (Gen 18:25).

With a second rhetorical question, Elihu begins building his case for God's justice (vv. 13-15). If one truly knows Israel's creation theology, then the question "Who placed the earth in His charge?" (NJPS) requires a simple and unequivocal answer: "No one." God neither seeks nor requires permission from anyone to rule the world that God alone created. The same creation theology undergirds an accompanying assertion. Every person depends on God's animating "spirit" and "breath" (v. 14). When God bestows life, it is a gift. When God withdraws the gift, for whatever reason, life ends, and "all mortals return to dust." We may suppose that Job has no problem in affirming Elihu's claim, for he has already acknowledged that the "life . . . and breath of every human being" is in the hand of God (12:10).

Job, however, discerns a dark underside to God's absolute sovereignty that Elihu's rhetorical question glosses over. The creation theology to which Elihu appeals affirms two primary things about God. First, God's gift of life is motivated by compassion, grace, and providential care. Death is a fact of life, but as the psalmist affirms, it is simply part of the natural and orderly process by which God renews creation (Ps 104:27-30). Secondly, human beings may sin, thereby subverting God's orderly creation and bringing upon themselves a death experienced as divine and righteous punishment (Gen 2–3; cf. Gen 6–9). But where in Elihu's creation *theo*logy (or dare we imagine, in God's *logos*) is there justification for a God who takes away the gift of life "for no reason"?

God Supports the Earth

He's Got the Whole World on His Back

Elihu's creation theology resonates with the simple and affirming words of the traditional gospel song, "He's Got the Whole World in His Hands."

He's got the whole world in His hands.
He's got the whole world in His hands.
He's got the whole world in His hands.
He's got the whole world in His hands.

He's got the wind and the rain in His hands . . . .

He's got the tiny little baby in His hands . . . .

He's got you and me brother in His hands . . . .

He's got the whole world in His hands.

Job agrees, but the tune and perhaps the tenor of his "song" would no doubt be different. Given God's responsibility for securing justice for the whole world, Job has good reason to wonder if the burden is not too great, even for the sovereign Creator. It is an unorthodox thought, to be sure, which explains in part the passion with which Elihu rebukes Job. Even so, Job must surely have his (silent or silenced) supporters.

Robert Falaise may be one of those who sympathize with Job. He was commissioned by the canons of Champeaux, known for theological liberalism, to produce new choir stalls for the collegiate church. He selected, apparently with their permission, the story of Job as the thematic motif for the carvings on the mercy seats. One of the fifty-four seats depicts God bearing the globe of the world. The weight of the world bows God's back, suggesting that the burden of sovereignty can be heavy indeed.

That religious or ecclesiastical authorities typically rebuke those who may hold such views, whether expressed by ancient biblical characters or modern artists, is evident. Falaise's carvings are case in point. In 1783, the Archbishop of Paris sought to have the choir stalls removed from the church and destroyed. According to a local legend, the canons of Champeaux thwarted the Archbishop by relocating the stalls to a less conspicuous place. (For another example of Falaise's work, see the drawing of his sculpture at **["Job's Friends in Dunce Cap"]**.)

For further discussion, see S. Terrien, *The Iconography of Job Through the Centuries: Artists as Biblical Interpreters* (University Park: Pennsylvania State University Press, 1996), 121-26.

From Job's vantage point, when God takes away the breath of life from seven innocent sons and three innocent daughters, every defense of God's justice collapses, especially those built on the foundation of divine sovereignty. [He's Got the Whole World on His Back]

The second argument (vv. 16-20) begins with two rhetorical questions. Both questions assume a propositional truth that Elihu is confident Job must accept. The first truth is that God loves justice. The question "Shall one who hates justice govern?" (v. 17a), therefore, expects the following answer: "No, of course not. Since God loves justice, it is illogical to think that God would do what God hates." The second truth is that God's sovereignty is always just. The question "Will you condemn one who is righteous and mighty?" (v. 17b), therefore, must be answered, "No, it is not proper to doubt the judgments of One who is always right, and it is not possible to challenge One who is all-powerful. "

Elihu supports these two truths by citing examples of God's use of righteous power when dealing with human rulers (vv. 19-20). "Kings," "princes," "nobles," the "rich," and the "mighty" all lay claim to power and privilege by virtue of their place in society. They are expected to use both their position and their resources wisely and unselfishly. Ideally, as Psalm 72 suggests, human rulers validate their power by securing justice for the poor and the needy, protecting the rich and poor alike from oppression, and promoting peace and prosperity for all those in their care. These are precisely the ways Job insists he once used power—"like a king"—when it was entrusted to him (29:12-25; see further [King Job]; [Job's Royal and Priestly Anthropology]). When human rulers abuse power, Israel's prophets, priests, and sages roundly condemn them (e.g., Isa 10:5-19; Jer 22:1-9; Ezek 28:1-10; Sir 9:17–10:18). Although it is surely heartening to believe that one may speak truth to power and be effective, the hard reality is that rulers control the levers of justice. As often as not, they simply choose to ignore the criticism and banish the critics. The parade example may be Amaziah's response to Amos: "O seer, go, flee away to the land of Judah, earn your bread there, and prophesy there; but never again prophesy at Bethel, for it is the king's sanctuary, and it is the temple of the kingdom" (Amos 7:12-13).

Elihu addresses the problem by asserting that as sovereign ruler of the universe, God has the power to say to an unjust king, "You scoundrel," and to corrupt princes, "You wicked men" (v. 18). God not only demands justice; God also personally executes it. The demise of the unjust comes swiftly, "in a moment," and when least expected, "at midnight" (v. 20a). The normal processes of human justice may be ineffective against such rulers, but God's justice suffers no such limita-

Elihu's "Moral Imagination" Concerning Political Power

Carol Newsom has noted that the most distinctive feature of Elihu's discourse is his focus on the contrast between God's just sovereignty and the corruptible political power of human rulers. Elihu's framing of the issues, she suggests, is characteristic of the theological problem posed by Gentile rulers who ruled Israel. A number of texts address this problem, for example, the prophetic judgment against the "king of Assyria" in Isa 10:5-19, but the issue is most clearly developed in Dan 2 and 5 and in Sir 9:17–10:18, which suggest that the specific historical context that shapes Elihu's moral understanding of political power is the Hellenistic period. The verbal and thematic similarities between Elihu's discourse in Job 34 and Dan 2 and 5 are the most noticeable:

	Daniel 2, 5	**Job 34**
(1) It is God who gives human rulers power.	"he deposes kings and sets up kings" (Dan 2:21)	"he shatters the mighty . . . and sets others in their place" (Job 34:34)
(2) Kings are judged to be arrogant and unworthy.	"you [Belshazzar] have not humbled your heart . . . you have exalted yourself against the Lord of heaven!" (Dan 5:22-23)	"You scoundrel . . . You wicked men" (Job 34:18)
(3) As a result, there comes a sudden judgment.	"that very night" (Dan 5:30)	"In a moment they die; at midnight. . ." (Job 34:20a)
(4) Gentile kingdoms are symbolically struck down by God.	"a stone was cut out, not by "human hands" (Dan 2:34)	"the mighty are taken away by no human hand" (Job 34:20b)
(5) God's sovereignty, though hidden, reveals itself in its own time.	"He changes times and seasons" (Dan 2:21a) "He reveals deep and hidden things; he knows what is in the darkness" (Dan 2:22)	"He has no set time for man to appear before God in judgment" (Job 34:23a; NJPS) "there is no gloom or deep where evildoers may hide themselves" (Job 34:22)

Newsom concludes that although Elihu's moral imagination concerning the use of political power may not be substantively different than that of the friends (cf. Bildad in 8:3-4; Eliphaz in 22:13-14), it is shaped by a different set of historical and cultural concerns. She makes the case as follows:

Thus, it is not difficult to see how the author of the Elihu speeches sensed an omission in the dialogue between Job and the friends. He was thus able to provide what the friends could not, namely, an argument persuasive to the tenor of his own times that not only contested Job's sarcastic speech about divine governance in chapter 12 but also allowed him to challenge Job's complaint that times (for judgment) are not reserved by Shaddai (Job 24:1) and that the cry of the oppressed goes unheeded (24:12). For what is the mysterious overthrow of the godless ruler, so often seen in the Hellenistic period, if not a divine response to the cry of the afflicted (34:28, 30)? (219)

C. Newsom, *The Book of Job: A Contest of Moral Imaginations* (Oxford: Oxford University Press, 2003), 216-19.

tions, for it is not dependent on "human hands" (v. 20b; for the expression "without hand," *lōʾ bĕyād*, cf. 2 Sam 23:6; Lam 4:6; Dan 2:34).
[Elihu's "Moral Imagination" Concerning Political Power]

We may wonder if Elihu's second argument actually addresses Job's complaints. Job has no doubts concerning God's absolute power. That God can overturn mountains, shake the world's foundations, and

Can Anyone Summon God to Repentance?

The biblical text only hints at the possibility that humans may call God to repentance for the miscarriage of justice (e.g., Jer 42:10), but the rabbis dare to press the thought. In an editorial written in the aftermath of yet another Palestinian suicide bomber who had killed innocent people in Jerusalem, Rabbi S. Boteach cites one particularly instructive example. As he contemplates the repentance required by the High Holy Days of Yom Kippur, Boteach cannot silence questions that the liturgy does not seem to allow: "Is G-d watching all this?" "Can't G-d prevent it?" "How can He be so silent?" As he ponders such questions, he recalls the story of the Hasidic master, Rabbi Levi Yitzchak of Berditchev.

On the eve of Yom Kippur, while hundreds of people were waiting for him to begin the *Kol Nidre* prayer, Rabbi Yitzchak stood silently facing the holy ark, his back to the congregation, for more than two hours. When the congregation began to grow restless, he turned to them and explained:

I want to bring you into the conversation I was having with G-d. I said to G-d, "I come here before you on Yom Kippur, the Day of Atonement to ask that You atone for my sins." But then it suddenly struck me that in the past year, I haven't brought any plagues upon any part of the world. Nor have I made any woman a widow. Nor have I made any child an

orphan. Nor have I caused anyone to go bankrupt and thereby not be able to sustain and support their children. Yet G-d has done all these things. And then it struck me, why isn't He coming to us and asking *us* for forgiveness? So I said to G-d, "In the past year, I have caused no death. I have brought no plagues upon the world, no earthquakes, no floods. I have made no women widows, no children orphans. G-d, you have done these things, not me! Perhaps You should be asking forgiveness from me. So I'll make a deal. You forgive us, we'll forgive you, and we'll call it even" (68-69)

Boteach then concludes his editorial with these words:

We need more Jewish Jobs who, when afflicted by G-d, not only look internally at what sinful actions might have caused their suffering, but also look outward and rail and thunder against the seeming divine injustice. "By G-d who has deprived me of justice, who has embittered my life, as long as there is life in me … my lips will speak no wrong . . . . Until I die I will maintain my integrity (Job 27:2-5)." (69)

For further reflection, see Samuel E. Balentine, "Turn, O Lord! How Long?" *RevExp* 100 (2003): 465-81.

S. Boteach, "Is It Time For G-d to do Teshuvah?" *Tiqqun* (September-October 2002): 68-70.

snatch away adversaries at will, is all too clear (cf. 9:1-12). Job has already conceded the point: God is "wise in heart, and mighty in strength—who has resisted him and succeeded?" (9:4). Job's complaint raises a different question. How does one bring an unjust God to justice? Given God's unassailable power to create and destroy as God chooses, who can intervene and say to God, "What are you doing?" (9:12). [Can Anyone Summon God to Repentance?] In his second argument, as in his first (v. 13), Elihu's rhetorical questions gloss Job's complaints with truths that console and comfort only if he accepts the propositions upon which they depend.

Elihu's third argument in defense of God's justice (vv. 21-30) picks up on Job's words in chapters 23–24. In chapter 23, Job complains about God's inexplicable hiddenness and silence. Despite searching the universe over, Job despairs of ever finding God (23:3, 8-9), let alone hearing any word from God that might answer his questions (23:5). Hiddenness and silence leave him terrified before the One judging him with a power that he can neither contest nor avoid. In chapter 24, he moves from his personal experience to conclusions about God's governance of the world. In a world where God is absent, Job says, the promise of divine justice is hollow. The wicked are free to pursue their objectives without impunity. They "rebel against the light" (24:13) and revel in "deep darkness" (24:17), where terror becomes their accomplice in a counter world of crime. All the while, they remain supremely confident that "no eye" will see them (24:15). When Job looks on the moral chaos of such a world, he can only scream out "Why?" If God knows there must be a time and place for judgment, why then do those who cry out for help never see the justice that confirms God is God (24:1, 12; see further the commentary on Job 24:1-12)? Elihu now proposes to answer this question.

He addresses Job's complaints in reverse order, arguing first from general truths about God, then teasing out their implications for individuals like Job. In response to Job's charge that "no eye" sees what evil people do, Elihu counters that God sees everything (v. 21a). No step they take (v. 21b), no dark hiding place they seek (v. 22), no wicked deed they do (v. 25), escapes God's surveillance. Against the charge that God fails to establish times for judgment, Elihu asserts that there is "no *set* time for man to appear before God in judgment" (v. 23; NJPS; emphasis added). God acts when God chooses.[3] Human beings cannot schedule God's justice. They must simply wait and see. In due course, God will act decisively to "overturn," "crush," and "strike" the wicked (vv. 25-28).

Next, Elihu moves to Job's personal complaint that God has been silent before his cries and absent from his search (vv. 29-30). Once again, Elihu counters that Job has drawn the wrong conclusion about God by seeing things only through the lens of his limited personal experience. When God is quiet, it is because silence is the response God chooses. To condemn God for not responding as Job demands is to conclude that God's options must conform to what Job alone deems appropriate. When God hides, it is because absence, not just presence, is characteristic of God (cf. Isa 45:15). In sum, silence and hiddenness are vital parts of God's inscrutable sovereignty. ["Truly, You Are a God Who Hides Himself"] The godless should not assume that their impiety escapes the justice God has prepared for them. And more to the point, at least where Job is concerned, those who claim to be righteous should not assume that their piety defines the ways God must be gracious to them.

Elihu's three arguments are characterized by a clear logic that is meant to lead Job to evident conclusions. Two small details, however, merit further consideration, for each in its own way may invite questions Elihu does not intend. (1) For all Elihu's certainty about God's justice, he appears to concede that God makes decisions about a person's guilt "without investigation" (*lōʾ ḥēqer*, v. 24). The verb *ḥāqar* means "to

"Truly You Are a God Who Hides Himself"

Elihu's affirmation invites reflection on Isaiah's discernments concerning the hard confession seared into the memory of Israel in the aftermath of the exile to Babylon: "Truly you are a God who hides himself, O God of Israel, the Savior" (Isa 45:15). This assertion marks a pivotal juncture in Israel's understanding of who God is and how God works in a world that at the time must surely have seemed bereft of divine justice. It is the only place in Hebrew scripture that combines in one taut and indissoluble confession the assertion that the saving God is also the hiding God. From this point forward, the prophet says, Israel must live with the truth that life in relation to God can never be reduced to one part of the confession without the other. Although Pascal likely did not grasp the full import of Israel's understanding, his classic appropriation of the idea remains instructive: "Any religion that does not affirm that God is hidden is not true."

Despite the similarities in their assertions, it is not clear that Elihu is saying the same thing as Isaiah. The hidden ways of God to which Isaiah refers have to do with God's ability to use a foreign king, Cyrus of Persia (Isa 45:1), as the agent of Israel's salvation in a manner that exceeds both comprehension and expectation. However mysterious God's hidden ways of working in the world may be, Israel can rejoice in the assurance that God's ultimate control of history produces a positive result for the faithful.

Elihu's appeal to God's hiddenness appears to buttress a very different claim. When God works for justice in hidden ways, the end result is not only beyond human comprehension, it is also beyond human query, even if Job's "salvation" requires the deaths of seven innocent boys and three innocent girls. In sum, Elihu suggests that God's hiddenness is the modern equivalent to a blank check. The bill for faith is whatever God chooses. If, in fact, Elihu has Isaiah's affirmation in mind, then his appeal to scripture invites reflection on Antonio's famous critique of Shylock's "holy witness":

The devil can cite scripture for his own purpose,
An evil soul producing holy witness
Is like a villain with a smiling cheek—
A goodly apple rotten at the heart:
O, what a goodly outside falsehood hath!
(*The Merchant of Venice*, I, iii, 99-103)

For further reflection on Isaiah 45:15 and its connections to Job, see Samuel E. Balentine, "Isaiah 45: God's 'I Am,' Israel's 'You Are,'" HBT 16 (1994): 103-20; idem, "For No Reason," *Int* 57 (2003): 349-69.

B. Pascal, *Pensees* (London: Penguin Classics, 1966), 103.

search out," as for example in Job's description of his vigorous search for wisdom (28:3; cf. v. 27). The noun derivative, *ḥēqer*, extends this meaning to objects that are "searched out," "investigated," or "examined." There may be some slippage in the words Elihu uses, for a near identical phrase appears in 5:9, 9:10, and 36:26 with the meaning "without number." Following the LXX, some modern translations take this to be the meaning here (e.g., NJPS: "he shatters mighty men without number"). Perhaps Elihu means only that the evidence for God's justice is simply too enormous to be searched out. The times when God shatters the mighty are innumerable, that is, they can never be adequately counted. What Job may well hear Elihu saying, however, is a variation on a theme painfully accented in the prologue. Once God concedes that Job's affliction has occurred "for no reason" (2:3), Job could not be faulted for believing that God wastes little time investigating the facts of a case before rendering a verdict. ["Scared I'd Hafta Face Up to What I Didn't Do"]

(2) The phrase "whether it be a nation or an individual" (v. 29c) is also cryptic, and a range of emendations, including deleting all or some of the words, has been proposed. Taken simply at face value, the meaning appears to be that God's objective when it comes to adminis-

"Scared I'd Hafta Face Up to What I Didn't Do"

Part of Harper Lee's Pulitzer Prize-winning novel, *To Kill a Mockingbird*, is the story of a black man, Tom Robinson, who has been falsely accused of raping Miss Ewell, a white woman. When he is brought to trial, Robinson must answer the questions of Mr. Gilmer, the prosecutor. The following courtroom exchange is pertinent for reflecting on Elihu's attack on Job's claim to be innocent:

(Mr. Gilmer): "Didn't Mr. Ewell run you off the place, boy?"

(Robinson): "No suh, I don't think he did."

"Don't think, what do you mean?"

" I mean I didn't staylong enough for him to run me off."

"You're very candid about this, why did you run so fast?"

"I says I was scared, suh."

"If you had a clear conscience, why were you scared?"

"Like I says before, it weren't safe for any nigger to be in a—fix like that."

"But you weren't in a fix—you testified that you were resisting Miss Ewell. Were you so scared that she'd hurt you, you ran, a big buck like you?"

"No suh, I's scared I'd be in court, just like I am now."

"Scared of arrest, scared you'd have to face up to what you did?"

"No suh, scared I'd hafta face up to what I didn't do."

H. Lee, *To Kill a Mockingbird* (New York: Popular Library Edition, 1960), 200-201.

tering justice, whether dealing with a nation or only one individual, remains the same. Such a claim, however, stands in a curious tension with Elihu's logic. He consistently rebukes Job for arguing from one person's experience to larger truths that apply to the many. The better way to understand God's justice, he insists, is to start from universal truths about God, then conform one's personal experience to what these truths teach. But if God does not dispense one kind of justice to an individual and another kind to a nation, then why should Job's personal complaints be ruled out of order.

Lurking just behind this question is a complaint about divine justice that attained proverbial weight in Israel: "The parents have eaten sour grapes, and the children's teeth have been set on edge" (Ezek 18:2). The complaint is centered in the fear that God has used the guilt of a nation (the ancestors in Israel) to condemn the innocent children now languishing in Babylonian exile. God commands Ezekiel to teach the exiles that this way of thinking is wrong: "this proverb shall no more be used by you" (Ezek 18:3). Neither collective guilt nor collective innocence determines God's justice. God judges each person according to his merits (Ezek 18:4; cf. Deut 24:16). In the words of a colloquialism, one wonders if Elihu got this memo. [Corporate Personality]

"The Wise Who Hear Me Will Say," 34:31-37

Textual difficulties, especially in vv. 31-33, complicate the conclusion of Elihu's speech. Unfortunately, these difficulties occur at strategic points where the choice of one option over another makes a considerable difference. If one reads vv. 31-33 as Elihu's instruction to Job, then this summons to repentance supplements the instruction already given in 33:26-28. Job should say to God, "I have borne my just punishment; I will offend no more."[4] With this reading, the thrust of the rhetorical question in v. 33 is as follows: if *Job rejects God's summons to repentance*,[5] should Job expect God to reward him on his own terms?

Corporate Personality

The distinctive contribution to biblical studies of Henry Wheeler Robinson (1872–1945), a distinguished English pastor, theologian, and Old Testament scholar, is his conception of corporate personality. Arguing that the ancient Hebrews regarded the family, clan, and nation, as the fundamental definition of society, Robinson hypothesized that individuals discerned their identity by looking to the group to which they belonged.

The proverb cited in Ezek 18:2—"the parents have eaten sour grapes, and the children's teeth have been set on edge"—is perhaps the parade exemplar of Robinson's thesis. The thrust of this proverb is the complaint that God is punishing (individual) children for the collective sins of their parents (Ezek 18:5-9, 10-13, 14-19). At issue is the principal of transgenerational retribution, according to which there is believed to be a causal nexus of guilt and punishment that continues to have consequences through several generations.

Although many of the specifics of Robinson's thesis have been widely questioned, there is little doubt that the concern with collective guilt was a staple in both ancient Near Eastern and Hebraic thought. Among ancient Near Eastern examples is the practice described in the Hittite "Instructions for Temple Officials":

If a slave causes his master's anger, they will either kill him or they will injure him . . . or they will seize him, his wife, his children, his brother, his sister, his in-laws, his kin. . . . If ever he is to die, he will not die alone; his kin will accompany him. If then . . . anyone arouses the anger of a god, does the god take revenge on him alone? Does he not take revenge on

his wife, his children, his descendants, his kin, his slaves, and slave-girls, his cattle (and) sheep together with his crop, and will utterly destroy him? Be very reverent indeed to the word of a god! (*ANET*, 3rd ed. with supplement, ed. J. B. Pritchard [Princeton: Princeton University Press, 1969], 207-208)

Within Hebrew Scriptures, the principle is applied inconsistently (cf. Num 26:11; 2 Kgs 14:6), but with enough frequency to indicate its sustained importance. For example, it is used to justify the punishment of Aachan and his family (Josh 7:22-26), Ahimelech and his family (1 Sam 22:16-19), and more broadly God's punishment of Judah because of the "sins of Manasseh" (687–642 BCE; 2 Kgs 21:11-15; 23:6-27; 24:3-4), which in turn buttresses the exilic lament cited not only in Ezek 18:2 but also in Jer 31:29-30 and in Lam 5:7. Given this trajectory, it is perhaps not surprising that Job also charges that God punishes the wicked by killing and starving their children (Job 27:13-14).

For further reading on the contributions of H. W. Robinson, see "Robinson, Henry Wheeler (1872–1945), *Dictionary of Biblical Interpretation*, ed., John H. Hayes, vol. K-Z (Nashville: Abingdon Press, 1999), 407-408. On the theme of individualism in Ezekiel, see P. Joyce, *Divine Initiative and Human Response in Ezekiel* (JSOTSup 51; Sheffield: JSOT Press, 1989). For an analysis of the theory concerning "corporate personality" in Ezekiel, see G. H. Matties, *Ezekiel 18 and the Rhetoric of Moral Discourse* (SBLDS 126; Atlanta: Scholars Press, 1990), 113-25.

H. W. Robinson, "The Hebrew Conception of Corporate Personality," *Werden und Wesen des Alten Testament* (BZAW 66, 1936), reissued as *Corporate Personality in Ancient Israel* (Facet Books, Biblical Series 11; Philadelphia: Fortress Press, 1964).

With a slight emendation in v. 31, however, one might understand Elihu to be rebuking Job for demanding a confession from God: "Should God say to you, 'I have erred, I will offend no more.'"[6] With this reading, the thrust of the rhetorical question in v. 33, no doubt sarcastically put by Elihu, is quite different: if *God rejects Job's summons to repentance*, should Job reward God on God's own terms?[7] The text, then, presents us with these questions: Who should confess to whom? Who is rejecting whom? In view of these complexities, Elihu's summons to Job in v. 33b—"you must decide, and not I"—is freighted in ways that perhaps exceed what either he or his author intended.

Despite the uncertainties in vv. 31-33, the final verses in this speech reiterate the decision that Elihu has not wavered on since 32:12: Job is wrong. Now he seeks to line up support for this verdict from his listeners, both real and imagined. First, he summons once more "those who have sense" and the "wise" (v. 34) to concur that Job has spoken "without knowledge" and "without insight" (v. 35; cf. 35:16), the evidence for which is that his continuing complaints against God have added rebellion to sin (v. 37). Second, and at another level of his imagination, the words he expects to hear from the wise (v. 35) anticipate those God will speak in 38:2. Whether God's meaning will be the same as his is a moot question, from Elihu's perspective. If Elihu has accomplished nothing else thus far, the one truth he believes should be clear to all is that he is supremely qualified to speak for the Almighty. He adds one additional word that suggests his role in this drama is not only to speak for God but also to go beyond what even God may be prepared to do. Elihu desires that Job be "tried to the limit" (v. 36a). The prologue makes clear that God has been willing to test Job with suffering, ever confident that Job's piety will ultimately prove worthy of blessing. Elihu's desire is that Job's testing should not stop until there is nothing more that can be exacted from him. When the test finally plays itself out, however long it may take, Elihu is certain that Job's impiety will prove worthy only of God's judgment. F. I. Anderson's assessment of Elihu's position at the end of chapter 34 is apt: "[God's] justice is safe; but there is no forgiveness."[8] ["Nothing Emboldens Sin So Much as Mercy"]

"Nothing Emboldens Sin So Much as Mercy"

Shakespeare's *Timon of Athens* deals with the problematic virtue of mercy. Timon is virtuous, perhaps to a fault. He delights in giving gifts to persons in need, with no expectation of return, even though his friends constantly worry that his generosity will one day exhaust his resources. That day does indeed come for Timon, and he is shocked to find that his creditors feel no compulsion to show him the mercy he has offered to others. With bills in hand, the creditors surround his home, virtually imprisoning Timon within his now obviously flawed understanding of the virtue of mercy. Enraged, he invites his so-called friends to a banquet of stones and boiling water, curses them for the self-serving flattery they offered him over the years, and then leaves Athens.

The moral of the story is succinctly put in one of the subtle subplots of the play. Inside the Senate House, senators are debating the fate of an honorable soldier who has killed a foe out of passion, but foolishly. The debate concerning the punishment that should be delivered begins with the following exchange between two senators:

(First Senator) My lords, you have my voice to it;
the fault's bloody; 'tis necessary he should die.
Nothing emboldens sin so much as mercy.

(Second Senator) Most true; the law shall bruise him.
(III, v, 1-4)

Alcibiades, a distinguished Athenian general and friend of the accused, responds with the following appeal:

I am an humble suitor to your virtues;
For pity is the virtue of the law,
And none but tyrants use it cruelly. (III, v, 9-11)

At the end of ch. 34, Elihu appears rather like one of the creditors who stand outside Timon's door demanding payment, perhaps also like the senators who fear a show of mercy will compromise the canons of justice. His doctrinaire defense of God's justice leaves little room for considering the virtue of appealing to God's mercy.

CONNECTIONS

The prologue invites readers into the "garden of Uz," this book's theological cipher for the paradisiacal garden of Eden (see the commentary on Job 1–2). The first of the six scenes in the prologue (1:1-5), each one thematically evocative of the six days of creation, uses a telescopic lens to focus our attention on a "blameless and upright" individual named Job. His idyllic life, carefully calibrated to the predictable rhythms of piety and prosperity, is about to be turned upside down. When the *satan* appears, after having gone "to and fro on the earth" (1:7) as God's delegated investigator of all matters relating to divine justice, the story's plotline begins to nudge us, ever so subtly, to anticipate that God's concerns and interests are much larger than the fortunes of any single person in the world. God's first words to the *satan*, however, suggest something different. With the words, "Have you considered my servant Job?" (1:8), God shifts the focus back to one person whose piety has captured God's attention. The question seems strategically designed to raise an issue that originates in God's own imagination. Does God's *cosmic* administration of justice sustain the faith of an *individual* righteous person who experiences unbearable losses and inexplicable suffering? Simply put, are large truths about God's universal justice persuasive for the individual Jobs of the world? The final form of the book invites readers to consider two very different approaches to the question.

The sequence of events in the book of Job suggests that reflection begins with *Job's personal experience*, for he represents the *test case* that either proves or disproves *orthodox assertions* about God's justice. Tracking Job's experience, we are invited to consider that righteous persons may respond to innocent suffering with a vexed combination of blessing and cursing. They may bless God with affirmations, strained but not broken, that celebrate the inscrutable wisdom of divine providence (1:21; 2:10). *And* they may be driven by the extremities of their suffering to curse God (3:3-10), with a strained but fervent conviction that submission to God's cosmic justice does not mandate the sacrifice of personal integrity. The decision to bless or curse plays itself out in Job's ongoing quest to understand his place in God's design for creation. On the one hand, the hard realities of life force him to consider that human beings are created to be nothing more than God's slaves; their only role is to serve a master who consigns them to lives of unending misery (7:1-6). On the other, Job wonders why God seems so preoccupied with human beings. If they are truly of such little significance in the cosmic scheme of things, then why does God single them out for such disproportionate attention? Does God consider them a threat to divine sovereignty? Are they like the primordial monsters that

We Can Only Live *As If* We Are Significant

Reverend Thomas Marshfield, the lead character in John Updike's novel *A Month of Sundays*, has been in a therapy for almost a month. Gradually he begins to realize that even though all people are frail beings, whittled down by the burdens of being merely human, we instinctively cling to the hope that we are more than we seem:

Grains of sand, one by one, make an aeon in the end. . . . A dime held close to the eye eclipses the sun. No matter in how many ways our lives are demonstrated to be insignificant, we can only live them as if they were not.

J. Updike, *A Month of Sundays* (Greenwich CT: Fawcett Crest Publications, 1974), 212-13.

must be constantly muzzled lest they wreak havoc on cosmic order (7:12)? Are they enemies of the Almighty (13:24) who must be targeted for defeat by overwhelming force (16:7-17; 19:6-12)? Job wonders if it really makes any difference to God whether human beings are submissive or rebellious. In the end, God will do what God will do, and neither the righteous nor the wicked can intervene to say, "What are you doing?" (9:12).

The question that hangs over all Job's ruminations is this, "What are human beings, that you make so much of them?" (7:17). He is uncertain whether the answer to the question will evoke a doxology of praise, because he is so important to God, or a doxology of terror, because he is not (see the commentary on 7:7-21 and [CD: Psalm 8 and Job 7]). Try as he might to view the world and his place within it from God's perspective, Job's life requires that he see the world through the eyes of suffering that is painfully personal. His sustaining hope is that even if he cannot see things through God's eyes, somebody—if not God, then perhaps at least his friends—will be able and willing to see things through his (6:28; 22:2, 5). [We Can Only Live *As If* We Are Significant]

The friends take a different approach to the problem Job presents. To the extent that they take Job's personal situation seriously, it is only because they are convinced their doctrine of God's retributive justice applies, without exception, to everyone. Since Job suffers, the only theologically acceptable explanation is that God is punishing him for his sin. This doctrine authorizes but one option for a guilty person like Job: he must confess and appeal to God's merciful forgiveness.

When their doctrinal arguments do not work on Job, they press him with still larger and more generalized assertions about God and humanity that are meant to teach him his place in the world. Eliphaz argues that human beings can never regard themselves as righteous in relation to God (4:17-19); from the day they emerge from the womb, they are destined for trouble by divine decisions that are fixed and permanent (5:6-7). From this truth, Eliphaz urges Job to recognize that human beings can only be of value to God if they agree that whenever questions arise in matters of life and faith, God is always right and they are always wrong (22:1-5). Bildad directs Job to the wisdom of the ages (8:8-10), supremely confident that the long view of time-honored truths prove that God's cosmic plan for justice is far too vast and far too important to be adjusted to any individual's particular concerns (18:4). Zophar invites Job to consider the farthest corners of the cosmic map, then to concede that God's wisdom, which surpasses any boundary imaginable, necessarily exceeds his comprehension. What Job cannot know about God, he must simply accept (11:6-12).

Elihu's arguments in chapter 34 may be more polished and sophisticated than those of his friends, but they are not substantially different. Like them, Elihu's doctrine of God convinces him that Job is wrong (33:12), even before he examines the evidence. And like them, he is convicted that large truths about God provide the only acceptable context for a truly faithful response to personal suffering (34:10-30). In sum, each of the friends, including Elihu, model a theology that insists individuals must conform their personal uncertainties about life in relation to God to unquestioned propositions about divine justice that enlarge and correct them.

"Church Going" and the Hunger for Something "More Serious"

In "Church Going," the distinguished English poet Philip Larkin (1922–1985) views an empty church, with its wilting Sunday flowers, its "tense, musty, unignorable silence," its "shape less recognizable each week." He wonders why people come to such a place at all. For fully three-quarters of the poem, he probes somberly for a "purpose more obscure" than discernible.

Once I am sure there's nothing going on
I step inside, letting the door thud shut.
Another church: matting, seats, and stone,
And little books; sprawlings of flowers, cut
For Sunday, brownish now; some brass and stuff
Up at the holy end; the small neat organ;
And a tense, musty, unignorable silence,
Brewed God knows how long. Hatless, I take off
My cycle-clips in awkward reverence,
Move forward, run my hand around the font.
From where I stand, the roof looks almost new—
Cleaned or restored? Someone would know: I don't.
Mounting the lectern, I peruse a few
Hectoring large-scale verses, and pronounce
"Here endeth" much more loudly than I'd meant.
The echoes snigger briefly. Back at the door
I sign the book, donate an Irish six-pence,
Reflect the place was not worth stopping for. . . .

A shape less recognizable each week,
A purpose more obscure. I wonder who

Will be the last, the very last, to seek
This place for what it was; one of the crew
That tap and jot and know what roof-lofts were?
Some ruin-bibber, randy for antique,
Or Christmas-addict, counting on a whiff
Of gown-and-bands and organ-pipes and myrrh?
Or will he be my representative,

Bored, uninformed, . . .

Despite, or more likely *because of*, the apparent futility of the quest for a reason to linger in the church, Larkin does indeed linger, because the Church is, or at least it should be, "A serious house on serious earth." Perhaps he speaks for all the Jobs of the world, whose hunger for something more serious than "hectoring large-scale vv." will never be "obsolete."

A serious house on serious earth it is,
In whose blent air all our compulsions meet,
Are recognized, and robed in as destinies.
And that much never can be obsolete,
Since someone will forever be surprising
A hunger in himself to be more serious,
And gravitating with it to this ground,
Which, he once heard, was proper to grow wise in,
If only that so many dead lie around.

P. Larkin, "Church Going," *Philip Larkin, Collected Poems*. Edited with an Introduction by Anthony Thwaite (London: Marvel Press/ Faber and Faber Limited, 1988, 1989), 97-98.

The merits of all the friends' arguments deserve careful consideration, if only because the certainty of their convictions is so universally attractive. Who among us does not yearn to believe that some truths can never be defeated, whatever assaults our personal experiences may mount against them? Surely it is a comfort to believe that we can escape our confused and shattered little worlds by retreating to the sanctuary of church, synagogue, or mosque, where those schooled in the theology of the friends assure us that God will make all things right in the end. And yet, according to this book, God himself suggests that before we settle into the comfort offered by orthodox spokespersons for universal truths, we have permission to ask of them a pointed question: "Have *you* considered my servant Job?"

To be candid, those who have been consigned to the ash heap of suffering may have to concede that they sit in the pews of holy places as discomfited listeners. They may be able to manage little more fidgeting attention, until and unless they hear their named called. If and when this happens, it is likely their flickering faith, rekindled by an honest spark, will burst into full flame. ["Church Going". . . and the Hunger for Something More Serious]

NOTES

[1] C. Newsom, *The Book of Job: A Contest of Moral Imaginations* (Oxford: Oxford University Press, 2003), 575.

[2] Ibid., 576.

[3] The grammar of v. 23 invites different readings, as modern translations make clear. I have followed NJPS here, because it comes closest to R. Gordis's rendering of the verse, which I believe is correct: "'It is not for man to set the time to go to God for judgment,' i.e., man has no right to insist on a given time for God's judgment" (R. Gordis, *The Book of Job: Commentary, New Translation, and Special Studies* [New York: Jewish Theological Seminary of America, 1978], 390).

[4] Gordis, *Book of Job,* 510; N. Habel, *The Book of Job: A Commentary* (OTL; Philadelphia: Westminster Press, 1985), 476.

[5] The object of the verb *māʾas*, "reject," is missing in Hebrew. NRSV supplies the pronoun "it," thus, "because you [Job] reject *it* [repentance]." The same verb *māʾas* "reject," occurs in Job's last words in the book, conventionally interpreted as Job's confession of sin: "therefore I despise myself and repent (*māʾas*) in dust and ashes" (42:6; NRSV). The interpretation rests on understanding the object of Job's repentance. The problem the text presents, here as in 34:33, is that there is no expressed object in Hebrew (see further the commentary on 42:1-6).

[6] Cf. G. Fohrer, *Das Buch Hiob* (KAT; Gütersloh: Gerd Mohn, 1963), 465.

[7] H.-M. Wahl, *Der gerechte Schöpfer: Eine redactions-und theologiegeschichtliche Untersuchung der Elihureden—Hiob 32-37* (BZAW 207; Berlin, New York: Walter de Gruyter, 1993), 89-90.

[8] F. I. Anderson, *Job: An Introduction and Commentary* (TOTC; Downers Grove IL: Inter-Varsity, 1976), 255.

GOD'S DETACHED JUSTICE

Job 35:1-16

At this point in the book, most of what the friends have to say in answer to Job's "Why?" questions has already been said. Thus, when Elihu launches into yet another defense of God's justice, we readers, not to mention Job himself, may roll our eyes and say, "here we go again." Once again, Elihu uses rhetorical questions that suggest he is inviting Job into a genuine dialogue (v. 2; cf. 33:13; 34:7, 13, 16, 17, 29). And once again, his words are little more than a ruse for proving that his answers to these questions are more reasonable and far more important than anything Job might bring to the conversation (v. 16; cf. 33:12; 34:35-37). Once again, Elihu recites what he has heard Job say, thus to convince him that he, unlike the other friends, has carefully considered his arguments (vv. 2-3; cf. 33:8-11; 34:5-6, 9). And once again, his quotations either distort or exaggerate what Job has actually said, leaving us with the impression that his primary objective is to falsify Job's truth in order to make his own more unassailable. [Structure of Job 35:1-16]

Despite the familiar ring of much in this chapter, Elihu's defense of God's justice accents two matters that merit sustained consideration. First, returning to the debate between Job and the friends concerning the place of human beings in the world (4:17-21; 7:17-18; 14:1-12; 15:7-16; 22:1-5; 25:1-6), Elihu instructs Job to measure the smallness of his existence against the vastness of the universe God administers. By any calculation, Job should conclude that nothing he can do, either for ill or for good, makes any difference in God's cosmic plan (vv. 5-8). Secondly, Elihu returns to Job's complaint that God's very exaltedness means that God is too far removed from the concerns of the righteous (9:11; 13:24; 23:1-3, 8-16) and too silent to be heard by those desperately yearning for some word that will

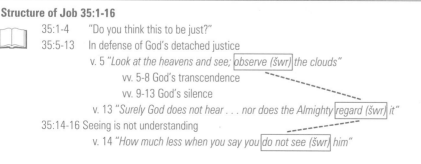

Structure of Job 35:1-16

35:1-4   "Do you think this to be just?"
35:5-13   In defense of God's detached justice
         v. 5 *"Look at the heavens and see; observe (šwr) the clouds"*
             vv. 5-8 God's transcendence
             vv. 9-13 God's silence
         v. 13 *"Surely God does not hear . . . nor does the Almighty regard (šwr) it"*
35:14-16 Seeing is not understanding
         v. 14 *"How much less when you say you do not see (šwr) him"*

"Whatever Is, Is Right"

Alexander Pope (1688–1744), the English satirist and apologist for God, was intent on demonstrating the subordinate role of human reason within the chain of nature. The following excerpt from "Essay on Man" resonates with Elihu's words to Job:

All are but parts of one stupendous whole,
Whose body Nature is, and God the soul . . .

Cease then, nor order imperfection name:
Our proper bliss depends on what we blame.
Know thy own point: this kind, this due degree
Of blindness, weakness, Heaven bestows on
    thee.
Submit, in this, on any other sphere,
Secure to be as blest as thou canst bear:
Safe in the hands of one Disposing Power,
Or in the natal, or mortal hour.
All Nature is but art unknown to thee
All chance, direction, which thou canst not
    see;
All discord, harmony not understood;
All partial evil, universal good:
And spite of pride, in erring reason's spite,
One truth is clear, Whatever is, is right.

A. Pope, "Essay on Man," I, ll. 267-68, 281-94, in *Essay on Man and Other Poems*, Dover Thrift Editions, ed. S. Appelbaum (New York: Dover Publications, 1994), 52-53.

make a difference in their lives (24:1-12). Elihu rebuts this charge by reminding Job that the mysteries of divine justice (vv. 9-12), like the "secrets" of God's wisdom (11:6-12), are necessarily beyond his comprehension. Job may be certain of one thing, however. When God does not answer the cries of the oppressed, it is because God knows that appeals for help motivated more by pain than piety do not deserve to be answered (v. 13).

Job must apply these lessons to his own situation, Elihu insists (vv. 14-16). When and if he does, then he will learn that he has misconstrued both God's transcendence and God's silence. The God who appears to human eyes to be *detached* from the world is in truth a *transcendent Creator* who is ever present in the world but always independent of it. The God whose silence transcends human understanding remains, even in *divine detachment*, the ever-vigilant and *sovereign Judge* of the world. ["Whatever Is, Is Right"]

COMMENTARY

"Do You Think This to Be Just?" 35:1-4

Elihu introduces his speech with a rhetorical question that sets up his summation and critique of what he has heard Job say (vv. 2-3). The question in v. 2a recalls the previous words in 34:4, "Let *us* choose what is right (*mišpāṭ*)." Elihu's "us" referred to the "wise" and the "knowing ones" whom he invited to join him in assessing Job's complaints about God's justice. Toward that end, Elihu focused primarily on the *process* of divine governance, which allowed him to marginalize Job's *personal* complaints about how this process has failed him (see the commentary on 34:1-9). Now that he has proven the reliability of the process, at least to his satisfaction, Elihu's question in this chapter—"Do *you* [Job] think this to be just (*mišpāṭ*)?"—appears to gather up loose ends by addressing the more tangential personal concerns that Job has raised about God's justice. The demonstrative "this" points forward to the summations in vv. 2b-3, where once again the phrasing suggests that Elihu is genuinely interested in Job's particular issues: "*You* say, '*I* am in the right before God'" (v. 2b); "*You* say, 'How does He [God] benefit you?'" (v. 3a); "How am *I* better off than if *I* had sinned?" (v. 3b).[1]

There are several reasons to suspect, however, that Elihu is no more concerned with Job's personal issues now than before. One clue is that here, as in the previous speech, Elihu misrepresents what Job has actually said (see [Quoting or Misquoting Job]). Once again, he alleges that Job has claimed to be more righteous (*ṣādaq*), or more in the right, than God (v. 2a; cf. 34:5). To be sure, Eliphaz has implied that Job is guilty of such arrogance (4:17; 15:14; see further [CD: The Syntax of Job 4:17]), but Job himself has said nothing of the sort. The closest he comes is to question whether any human being can ever expect to be declared "innocent" (*ṣādaq*) in a court of law, when God is both the prosecuting attorney and the judge who renders the verdict (9:1-13).

Elihu also claims once again to have heard Job say that those who seek to be faithful to God gain nothing by avoiding sin (v. 3; cf. 34:6, 9). But here too, it is Eliphaz, not Job, who has reduced the promise of relationship to God to the idea of a business transaction defined by profit-loss margins. By Eliphaz's calculation, the only profit that matters is the dividend God receives when human beings "agree" with God; if individuals incur losses along the way, they must simply accept them as the cost of doing business with God (22:2, 21). [Does Elihu take Eliphaz as His Model?] For his part, Job admits to being faced with only two choices, neither of which is attractive. He may choose to believe either that the way he lives his life is *so important* that God has singled him out for special attention (7:12), or that because his life is *so unimportant*, God should not give him a second thought (7:20). Job ultimately determines that the integrity he brings to the relationship with God is worth whatever it costs him, even if the only return he gets on his investment is death (10:1; 13:13-15; 16:18-19; 27:1-6; 31:35-37). Although neither Job nor Elihu has been privy to the deliberations in the heavenly council as recorded in the prologue, it is Job who seems determined to live his life in accord with their expectations. When the *satan* poses the question, "Does Job fear God for nothing?" (1:9), both God and Job seem to think that the matter is worthy of serious consideration.

Having laid the groundwork for yet another demonstration of his ability to provide what this book requires, Elihu sets out again to "answer" both Job and his friends (v. 4; cf. 32:10, 20; 33:12). Given the

Does Elihu Take Eliphaz as His Model?

Given his apparent reliance on Eliphaz's previous arguments, E. Good has speculated that the younger Elihu may look to his elder as the role model he both emulates and improves upon. If so, he may be a kindred spirit with László, a character in Andrew Miller's novel, *Oxygen*, who justifies being set in his ways by saying, "At my age it's difficult to change the way you see the world. We take on a certain view when we are young then spend the rest of our lives collecting the evidence."

E. M. Good, *In Turns of Tempest: A Reading of Job with a Translation* (Stanford: Stanford University Press, 1990), 329-30.
A. Miller, *Oxygen* (New York: Harcourt, Inc., 2001), 104.

gaps between what Job has said and what Elihu has heard, however, both Job and the friends may have cause to wonder if Elihu is in a position to offer any answer that will resolve the issues at hand. As Good has wryly observed, "If he [Elihu] has no grasp on Job's words, how can he begin to refute them?"[2]

In Defense of God's Detached Justice, 35:5-13

Elihu's answer focuses on two matters, both of which reinforce the suspicion that he remains far less interested in assessing Job's personal questions than with validating the cosmic scales of divine justice on which every human being must be weighed (see ch. 34, and especially the "Connections" there). First, Elihu instructs Job to focus not on himself but instead on the canopy of "heavens" and "clouds" that dwarfs all mere mortals on earth (vv. 5-8). If Job will but measure himself against the expanse of the world God has created, then it should be clear to him that God's concerns are infinitely larger than anything confined to a single person. The inviolable truth encoded within creation itself is this: neither Job's sin nor his righteousness has any bearing on God's ultimate administration of justice (vv. 6-7). No good deed an individual may do adds anything to the sum of God's righteousness; no evil an individual may perpetrate subtracts from the totality of God's justice. To be sure, the way individuals live their lives has consequences, but whether positive or negative, the impact is limited to the human community (v. 8).

Perhaps Elihu's appeal to creation theology intends to comfort Job by assuring him that he is *not* the center of the universe. ["I Promise You: Nobody is Thinking About You"] Once relieved of the burden of thinking that cosmic order succeeds or fails with him, perhaps Job will be moved to praise the God whose cosmic justice cannot be compromised by anything he does. Eliphaz uses a similar strategy in his first response, which models for Job a doxology in praise of God's inscrutable power and providence (5:8-16). If this is Elihu's objective, then his argument may

---

Building Job Up to Justify Cutting Him Down

E. Good observes that Elihu seems to want "to cut Job down, deny him too much stature," not because Job has the power Elihu alleges, but because he fears that if he does not act to stop him, he might attain it. If this is Elihu's strategy, then its seductive appeal is surely not limited to religious debates:

People often overestimate the efficacy of those who differ drastically from them. Americans worry about Russian world empires, and Russians worry about American imperialism, fundamentalists worry that secular humanists will take over the country, and atheists worry that fundamentalists will become the majority they claim they are. For the same reason, Elihu, denying Job's influence, in effect asserts it.

E. M. Good, *In Turns of Tempest: A Reading of Job with a Translation* (Stanford: Stanford University Press, 1990), 330.

"I Promise You: Nobody Is Thinking About You"

In "On Not Being God," Barbara Brown Taylor reflects on God's address to Job in Job 38:16-18. Her lead sentence in the article is, "Humankind's most basic theological problem . . . is that God is God and we are not." Each one of us cannot help but think we are the center of the universe , if only because "the eyes we see with are here in our heads." She concedes that she indulges in the same self-centered perspective. She assumes, instinctively, that "everything begins here," that is, with me. She recalls what a jolt it was to receive in the post one day an issue of the magazine Modern Maturity, with an article by Richard Rosenblatt titled "Rules for Aging." Her following excerpt from Rosenblatt's article underscores the truth Elihu seeks to press on Job.

Nobody is thinking of you. Yes, I know . . . You are certain that your friends are becoming your enemies; that your enemies are acquiring nuclear weapons; that your grocer, garbage man, clergyman, sister-in-law, and dog are all of the opinion that you have put on weight; furthermore, that everyone spends two thirds of the day commenting on your disintegration, denigrating your work, plotting your murder. I promise you: Nobody is thinking about you. They are thinking about themselves, just like you.

To be reminded that we are not the center of the universe is to undergo a radical shrinkage of our egos. It is jolting to know that we are no more than a speck in the vast cosmos; that we may know some of the stars by name, but they neither know nor care about ours. It is also deeply reassuring. As Brown Taylor says,

Thank God they [the stars] ignore me. Can you imagine how awful it would be, if you got into a rage one night and knocked nine or ten stars out of the sky with your wrath? Or if you walked out into your back yard for a good cry and toppled your favorite shade tree with your grief? Some of us dream of being that powerful, but it is a great mercy that such dreams do not come true. (613)

Nevertheless, as she acknowledges, such reassurances can be dangerously evasive, especially when Joban pain strikes at the center of the only universe we can see and touch and feel.

Barbara Brown Taylor, "On Not Being God," *RevExp* 99 (2002), 610.

---

be revealing in ways he does not intend. [Building Job Up to Justify Cutting Him Down] Job has demonstrated that he knows the conventional language of praise, but when he submits its affirmations to a sufferer's critique, he insists that it raises more questions than it answers. The psalmist may look at the vastness of God's world and ask with astonished wonder, "What are human beings that you [God] are so mindful of them?" (Ps 8:4), but the same words on Job's lips (7:17-18) evoke a doxology of terror, not praise (9:5-10).

Elihu's summons to praise and Job's persistent lament are like two ships passing in the night. Neither offers passage to the other, because both are bound for different ports. Elihu's ticket to faith promises transport to a world where the Sovereign's justice overrules every individual's personal concerns. Job's faith seeks to purchase a reserved seat on a journey bound for anywhere in the world where the Sovereign honors every individual's quest for justice. Once again, Elihu and Job seem to be worlds apart.

Elihu's second argument (vv. 9-13) also seeks to move Job away from the egocentricity of his personal issues to larger, more important, cosmic principles of divine justice. In Elihu's view, Job has mistakenly concluded, based on nothing more than his own perception of God's

Watching Job Through Elihu's Eyes

📖 Anita Shreve's novel, *All He Ever Wanted* (New York: Little, Brown, 2003), tracks the vexed courtship and eventual marriage of Nicholas Van Tassel, an undistinguished, insecure, but pompous professor at Thrupp College, and Etna, his repressed wife, who leaves him feeling abandoned as she aggressively but secretly tries to create a haven for herself within a relationship that has no room for her independence. In reviewing the book, the Seattle based literary critic Claire Dederer makes the following observation about Shreve's portrayal of Van Tassel: "Watching Etna through Van Tassel's eyes is like looking at a beautiful bird from a hungry cat's point of view." If we look at Job through Elihu's eyes, the same observation might apply.

Claire Dederer, review of A. Shreve, *All He Ever Wanted*, "Editorial Reviews," Amazon.com, 6 June 2003.

indifference to him, that God never responds to oppressed people who cry out for justice (cf. 24:1-12). Elihu counters by arguing that God does not respond to the appeals for help of some, because God's knows that their petitions are "empty" (v. 13) of the faith they pretend. They cry out in desperation, because the immediacy of pain, not the permanence of faith, has driven them to last resorts. Pushed to the limits, they seek relief wherever it may be found, but never once do they ask the question—"Where is God my Maker?" (v. 19; cf. Jer 2:6, 8)—that confirms their quest is anchored to a sustaining faith in God. No one should be surprised when God does not answer such appeals, least of all Job. With all the subtlety of a predator eyeing a prey too slow or too stupid to avoid capture, Elihu suggests that Job is perilously close to being numbered among the witless victims that do not deserve to be rescued by God. [Watching Job Through Elihu's Eyes]

Elihu's second argument, like his first, appeals to creation theology in the certain conviction that nature itself conveys the larger truths about God's justice that Job seeks. One small detail in this regard merits close inspection, because it anticipates a major line of argumentation that both Elihu (36:26–37:24) and God (38:39–39:30; 40:15–41:34) will model. God may execute justice in ways that seem to the human eye to be detached from the exigencies of everyday life, but Elihu insists that everyday life provides ample evidence for affirming what God is doing. One need only consider the wisdom made available by the "animals (*bahămôt*) of the earth" and the "birds of the air" (v. 11). It is instructive to note that Job has done just this. When Zophar appealed to the extremities of creation's boundaries in order to teach Job that God's wisdom is far beyond his comprehension (11:7-12), Job mocked him by responding that one only has to ask the "animals" (*běhēmôt*) and the "birds of the air" to know that creation reveals as much, if not more, than it conceals about what God is doing (12:7-10).

Elihu actually seems to be in agreement with both Zophar and Job. On the one hand, he endorses Zophar's assertion that God's wisdom, like the distant horizons of the cosmos, is inaccessible to mere creatures like Job. He will elaborate the same point at considerable length in his last speech (36:26–37:24), which he introduces with a thesis statement of his theology of creation's truth: "All people have looked on it; everyone watches it from afar" (36:25). Creation's truth, properly understood, puts human beings in their *place* by *displacing* their presumptive claims to occupy the center of the world. As Elihu will say, "Surely God is great, and we do not know him (36:26) . . . we cannot find him. . . . Therefore mortals fear him" (37:23-24). On this point, he and Zophar do not disagree.

On the other hand, Elihu does not reject Job's invitation to learn what the animals have to teach human beings about living wisely in this world and in relation to the One who created it. On this point, he seems to be in one accord not only with Job but also with God, who will soon invite Job to consider carefully what creation has to teach him. When Job asks the animals to impart to him their wisdom concerning the world, God instructs him to pay special attention to Behemoth (*bĕhēmôt*; the same word occurs in 12:7 and 35:11), "whom I made just as I made you" (40:15; NJPS). God and Elihu speak the same words, but are they saying the same thing?

In the aftermath of God's instructions, the drama of this book will place a critical question before both Job and his readers. Does God seek to teach Job, through Behemoth, that creation's truth *displaces* him from the center of God's attention? If so, then God may be understood as endorsing the creation theology of Zophar and Elihu. Or, does God single out Job for a special lesson on creation in order to *place* (or perhaps, in view of the friends' theology, *replace*) him at the center of the divine plans for the world? If so, then the full truth of the lesson Behemoth and the animals impart to Job, on God's behalf, may disclose more than either Job or his friends has yet to understand. [The Moral Sense of Nature]

Seeing Is Not Understanding, 35:14-16

With but sixteen total occurrences, the verb *šwr*, "look at, regard, see," is both relatively infrequent in the Old Testament and relatively insignificant. Typically the verb provides little more than a generic synonym for other "see" words. Ten of the sixteen occurrences, however, are in the book of Job, six of which are in the speeches of Elihu, three in this chapter alone (33:14, 27; 34:29; 35:5, 13, 14). Where the verb conveys more than the generic meaning "see," it usually adds the nuance "perceive," thus "see *and* understand." This seems to be true of Elihu's use of the word in chapter 35.[3] He calls attention to the difference between what Job sees but fails to understand and what God seems to Job not to understand, even though God sees everything.

Thus far, Elihu has instructed Job to "observe (*šwr*) the clouds, which are higher than you" (v. 5), in the apparently futile hope that what Job sees will help him to understand his relative unimportance in God's

The Moral Sense of Nature

📖 There still is night, down where the long-abandoned wagon road disappears amid the new growth beneath the tumbled dam, deep, virgin darkness as humans had known it through the millennia, between the glowing embers and the stars. Here the dusk comes softly, gathering beneath the hemlocks and spreading out over the clearing, muting the harsh outlines of the day. There is time to listen to the stillness of the forest when the falling light signals the end of the day's labor but the gathering darkness does not yet warrant kindling a lamp. Here time is not of the clock: there is a time of going forth and a time of returning, and there is night, soft, all-embracing, all-reconciling, restoring the soul. On the clear nights of the new moon, the heavens declare the glory of God and the ageless order of the forest fuses with the moral law within. Here a human can dwell at peace with his world, his God, and himself.

With these words, Erazim Kohák, Professor of Philosophy Emeritus at Boston University, begins his wide-ranging and passionate investigation of the moral sense of nature. I cite this opening paragraph, not because it is sufficient to make a point, but because it so elegantly hints at the major issues Kohák will inhabit in the following two hundred plus pages.

The first lines chart the journey, moving from what is primary and first present to what is secondary and appears only later. *First* there is the world of nature—"night," "new growth," "virgin darkness"—*then* there are "humans." *First* there is the order that is intrinsic to nature—the "dusk" that "comes softly," the "time to listen to the stillness of the forest," "the gathering darkness," "the clear nights of the new moon"—*then* there is the "labor" humans exert to create another order—"lamps" to extend light into darkness, "clocks" to *tell time*. The last two lines introduce two new clusters of words, both suggestive of ideas latent in all that has preceded: "the glory of God" and "the ageless order of the forest [that] fuses with the moral law within."

Kohák will exegete these last ideas with argumentation that he hopes will be persuasive enough to secure his readers' agreement. The "glory of God" resides in God's having lovingly crafted and endowed creation with a built-in order of rightness. Nonhuman life does not have to choose to live in accordance with this order; it responds instinctively to its intrinsic rightness. The night does not decide to follow the day; it simply appears when it is time. The forest does not decide to be still and silent; it simply welcomes the tranquility when it arrives. It is different for human beings. While God has also lovingly created us and endowed us with our own refracted capacities to create, we must decide whether to use our "creations"—the "lamps" and "clocks" by which we contribute our own sense of rightness to the intrinsic rhythms of the natural order—for good or for ill, for helpful or hurtful purposes. We may choose to *"fuse"* our morality, our "perception of life in terms of an order of rightness" (72), with creation's intrinsic values as partners, or to *impose* it as tyrants. Kohák hopes to nudge us toward the former, not the latter.

Both Elihu and Job seem attuned to the possibility that creation has something to teach human beings about the moral life that conforms to God's hopes and expectations for the world. Elihu believes the lesson to be learned is that human beings must submit to the just order God has decreed. Job seems to think that creation itself—the "animals" and the "birds of the air"—endowed with instinctive sensitivities hard wired to God's own morality, has something to teach us about the values and purposes that are required if human beings are to live in peace with their world, their God, and themselves.

Both Elihu (36:26–37:24) and God (38:39–39:30; 40:15–41:34) have more to say about creation's moral order and the human being's place within it. This requires that Job and we his readers suspend our final assessment of the merits of the arguments until we have heard what they have to say. We should not be surprised to find that Kohák's contribution to our deliberations will also require further consideration (see further **["Morality . . . Is Not a Human Invention"]**).

E. Kohák, *The Embers and the Stars: A Philosophical Inquiry Into the Moral Sense of Nature* (Chicago: The University of Chicago Press, 1984), ix-x.

---

cosmic design. He has tried to teach Job that when God does not "regard" (*šwr*) the cries of the oppressed (v. 13), it is because God understands that in truth they are without merit. In the closing verses of this speech, Elihu employs the same verb for the third time. Job has complained that God does not "see" him (v. 14), that is, that God has no interest in and no regard for a "case" that requires God's intervening justice (v. 15; cf. 9:1-13; 13:13-28; 31:35-37). This charge, in Elihu's eyes, is further confirmation that Job's vision serves only to blind him to the truth about God's justice. Job will not "see" God in court, Elihu confidently asserts, because God does not ever make an appearance in defense of those who testify before the bar of divine justice with "empty talk" and with "words without knowledge" (v. 16).

With this all-seeing, all-knowing conclusion, Elihu answers his own leading question to Job, "Do you think this to be just?" (v. 2). There is no reason for Elihu to wait while Job muddles his way toward an inadequate response. "Words without knowledge" will never add up to the understanding Elihu already possesses. Until God, Job's too elusive, too present, "Seeing eye" and "Watcher of humanity" (7:8, 20), speaks the words Elihu has claimed as his own (38:2), *perhaps* more as genuine invitation than preemptory rebuke, Elihu the "answerer" will have the last say.

CONNECTIONS

A transcendent judge, at work behind the scenes but inaccessible? A detached justice, bias-free and uncompromisable but also beyond review? Such is the view of God and divine justice that Elihu offers Job. As with all the arguments of the friends, Elihu's speech in this chapter requires close scrutiny. It is unwise to rush to criticism without first considering its appeal.

Elihu commends God's detached justice to Job for several reasons. Because *God*, not Job, is the Judge, Job is free to be who he is, a needful recipient of justice who has no responsibility for defining what it is or for executing it when it is required. Job need not worry that anything he does will compromise God's judgment, because God's infinite wisdom always transcends the limitations of the merely immediate, the merely personal, the merely isolated issues that might otherwise clog up the system and diminish its capacity to serve the larger good. Moreover, should Job doubt that God's justice is operative, perhaps because too many who seem deserving of punishment remain free from its constraints, or perhaps because too many who appeal for help still wait for its arrival, he can be confident that God is withholding or dispensing the required judgments in accordance with a comprehensive strategy beyond his comprehension.

There is considerable evidence to support the merits and the abiding appeal of Elihu's description of divine justice. In the ancient world, the Egyptians depicted the deceased standing before Osiris, the god of the dead, who looked on as the balance of the divine scales of justice inexorably tipped toward the truth about their worthiness for passage into the next life. [Osiris and the Scales of Justice] In the Roman world, Themis, the goddess of justice and law, is depicted with scales in her left hand, symbolizing the fairness of her deliberations, and a sword and chain in her right, symbols for the certainty of her enforcement. In the modern world, and especially here in the United States, we know this image as "Lady Justice," whose statue identifies so many of the court houses across the land. Since the sixteenth century, when artists began depicting a blindfold covering the statue's eye, we have enshrined the promise of fair and impartial justice for all in the credo, "Justice is blind."

For all its merits, however, Elihu's defense of God as a transcendent but inaccessible Judge and God's justice as impartial but detached may require a closer inspection, especially if we are to look on with the eyes of Job. Persons consigned to the ash heap of innocent suffering, for no reason, yearn for more than blind justice. As Martha Nussbaum, Professor of Law and Ethics in both the Law School and Divinity School at the University of Chicago, argues, justice always requires more than simply an assessment of the "facts" of a case. Justice requires the wisdom of a "judicious spectator."[4] It requires the perspective of one who may be called a "spectator," for those who pass judgment on others must surely maintain a level of skeptical *detachment*, that is, judicial neutrality, if they are to render a decision that is uncompromised by personal interests, safety, and happiness.

But justice must also be "judicious," by which she means that justice requires judges who demonstrate more than merely a technical mastery of the law. Judges must have sentiment and imagination. Above all, they must possess the moral capacity that makes possible a *sympathetic identification* with those who are being judged. "To be able to assess judicially another person's pain, to participate in it and then to ask about its significance," she argues, "is a powerful way of learning what the human facts are and of acquiring a motivation to alter them."[5] Conversely, if judges cannot vividly imagine what it feels like to be the persons who come into their courts, if they have no emotional triggers that cause them to flinch in the presence of another person's pain, loss, and desperate need for restitution, then it is unlikely that their verdicts can promise anything more than a passionless assignment of guilt or innocence that alters nothing.

Lady Justice

Osiris and the Scales of Justice

Ptolemaic Period, 332-330 BC. Illustration from the "Book of the Dead."

Osiris and the Scales of Justice

This illustration from the "Book of the Dead," one of several examples of Egyptian funerary literature, depicts the judgment of the deceased before Osiris, the god of the dead (seated to the far left). Osiris looks on as the soul of the deceased is weighed in the balance against the feather of the goddess Maat, who represents truth and justice. To the left of the scales, Thoth, the ibis-headed secretary of the gods, prepares to record the verdict. To the right of the scales, the jackal-god Anubis tips the balance in favor of the deceased's worthiness to pass into the next life, while just behind him an animal-like figure sits poised to spring into action should the scales tip toward a negative judgment. To the right of this creature, the deceased raises his arm to celebrate the judgment, as Maat looks on from behind (see further ["The Protestation of Guiltlessness"]).

For further reading, see E. A. Budge, *The Book of the Dead*. 3 vols. (London, 1910). An abridged version is available: E. A. Budge, *The Book of the Dead* (New York: Grammercy Books/Random House, 1960).

[The Argument for "Poetic" not "Detached" Justice] In short, the problem with the credo "Justice is blind," whether derived from Elihu's theology or from popular iconic images of "Lady Justice," is that blind justice often lacks the requisite vision to change lives. [Is Justice Truly Blind? Or Does she Just Prefer to Ignore the Truth in a Man?"]

One further observation may be factored into our reflections. Elihu fancies himself as the detached "answerer" this Joban story needs (32:21-22; see further the "Connections" at Job 32). He believes he has listened carefully to all the arguments, sifted them impartially for strengths and weaknesses, and can now offer the spectatorial assessment that settles matters once and for all. To return to Walt Whitman's poetic image, Elihu believes he is the "equable man" (see the "Connections" at Job 22):

He bestows on every object or quality its fit proportion, neither more nor less,
He is the arbiter of the diverse, he is the key,
He is the equalizer of his age and land,
He supplies what wants supplying, he checks what wants checking.

The Argument for "Poetic" not "Detached" Justice

M. Nussbaum's thesis is that judges can learn something about the passion required for assessing another person's pain by reading good literature that sharpens their sensitivities and enlarges their imagination. As examples, she discusses Walt Whitman's description of the poet as the "equable man" (see below), Charles Dickens's *Hard Times*, and Richard Wright's *Native Son*. As case in point, she cites the following excerpt from Stephen G. Breyer's confirmation hearings before the Senate Judiciary Committee upon his nomination to the United States Supreme Court:

I read something that moved me a lot not very long ago. I was reading something by Chesterton, and he was talking about one of the Brontes, I think her *Jane Eyre*. He says you go and look out at the city—I think he was looking at London—and he said you, you see all the houses now, even at the end of the nineteenth century, and they look all as if they're the same. And you think all those people are out there going to work and they're all the same. He says, but what Bronte tells us is they're not the same. Each one of those persons in each one of those houses and each one of those families is different, and they each have a story to tell. Each of those stories involves something about human passion. Each of those stories involves a man, a woman, children, families, work, lives—and you get that sense out of the book. And so sometimes I've found literature very helpful as a way out of the tower. (79)

Nussbaum does not mention the book of Job as a possible source of the literary imagination she recommends for "poetic" justice, but she might well have. Job's offering is similar, if considerably more radical. He dares to suggest that not only his friends but also God might learn something about being an advocate for the unjustly accused if God could come down out of the ivory tower and experience what it is like to be treated like them (see, for example, the commentary on 27:13-23).

M. Nussbaum, *Poetic Justice: The Literary Imagination and Public Life* (Boston MS: Beacon Press, 1995).

In short, like Whitman's "equable man," Elihu believes "he *is* judgment." "Nature accepts him absolutely."[6]

If we look carefully at Elihu's defense of God's detached justice, then we may detect the not so faint parallels between his image of God and his image of himself (see further, the "Connections" at Job 33). When he says *God* is transcendent; we hear him say *he* is as well. When he says *God's wisdom* is beyond comprehension, we hear him claim the same for *his own* opinions. When he says *God's justice* is impartial and beyond reproach, we hear him asserting that his own judgments are authoritative. And when he says that *God's indifference* to Job's personal concerns is the truest measure of God's judicious compassion for the world, we hear him justifying *his own retreat* from Job. The most direct route to showing compassion for the Jobs of the world is to leave them alone on the ash heap, until and unless they concede that neither God nor Elihu ever "hear[s] an empty cry" (v. 13).

As we consider how to respond to Elihu's arguments, we do well to ponder these matters. An image is not reality; it can only aim to reflect it. Judges are not justice; they can only determine to serve it. And those who speak for God do not have a special purchase on divine wisdom; they can only hope to be authentic mediators of its elusive truth. ["When I Pray to Him, I Find I'm Talking to Myself"]

"Is Justice Truly Blind? Or Does She Just Prefer to Ignore the Truth in a Man?"

One of the verities of comedy, as often noted by philosophers from Plato to Bergson, is that it requires an absence of feeling or at least a silencing of compassion (see further **[CD: "The Great Reservoir of Comedy"]**). We are able to *laugh at* things with unrestrained gusto when we have enough personal disinterest to protect ourselves against the need to *laugh with*, that is, to *feel compassion for*, whatever is being made fun of. As long as we feel no pity or guilt, we laugh out loud and enjoy the moment without a second thought.

If, however, our experience has been different, other emotional responses might be stirred up. Daryl Horton's poem, "Blind Justice," written from the perspective of the African-American experience, is one such response:

She stands there
Weighing my life in both hands
A cloth covers her eyes
While she tries to see the truth between the two
    men
The scale tilts
Leaning to one side
But for who?
Blind eyes can't see a lie
And further more
Should she be the one making the choice?
The eyes may not see
But the ears can hear the slang in my voice
Is Justice truly blind?
Or does she just prefer to ignore
The truth in a man
Whose country his back bore
My sweat! My blood!
Sun beaten man receiving no respect
Whips rip into my skin, scale tilts
Rope tightens on my neck
I dangle
I kick
But the scale
It still tilts
Can a black man

Receive a fair decision?
Blind Justice
Is there not enough of my people in prison?
I speak loud
And I plead
Justice! remove that cloth
And see the truth in me
The scale tilts
The rope tugs
The whips that rip into my back
Draw forth more blood
So I speak no more
I revert to waving my fist
Now I'll only ask once more
Before the beatings commence.

For further reading on the sources mentioned above, see Aristotle's *Poetics* and Henri Bergson's *Laughter: An Essay on the Meaning of the Comic* (1900). For a recent collection of essays on comedy in literature, which builds on the insights of Aristotle, Bergson, and others, see J. Wood, *The Irresponsible Self: On Laughter and the Novel* (New York: Farrar, Straus and Giroux, 2004).

Daryl Horton is an African-American poet, born in 1976. Some of his work has been published in an anthology of the National Poetry Society, although as far as I am aware this poem, "Blind Justice," is available only on the internet: *http://www.timbookto.com/Horton/blindjus.htm*. That the poem has not been published by any major publishing house may be additional evidence in support of our collective disinterest in the question that lies at the center of his ruminations: "Is Justice truly blind? / Or does she just prefer to ignore/ The truth in a man."

NOTES

[1] The syntax of the question in v. 3a (*mah yiskān lāk*) invites different translations. Several modern translations emend the Hebrew indirect object *lāk*, "you," to *lî*, "me," for example, NIB: "What profit is it to me?" (cf. NRSV, REB, NAB). The emendation is not necessary, however, if one takes the phrase as an indirect or "virtual quotation," as for example in NJPS: "If you ask how it benefits you" (for supporting argumentation, see R. Gordis, *The Book of Job: Commentary, New Translation, and Special Studies* [New York: Jewish Theological Seminary of America, 1978], 400; E. Dhorme, *A Commentary on the Book of Job* [Nashville: Thomas Nelson Publishers, 1967], 530-31). The Hebrew of v. 3b is literally, "What do I gain from my sin?" (*māh 'ō'îl mēḥattā'tî*). If one takes the *mem* (normally, "from") that precedes *ḥattā'tî* as a *mem* of separation, that is, as meaning "without," then Rowley's suggested translation, "How am I better off than if I had not sinned?" is an attractive alternative (H. H. Rowley, *Job* [The Century Bible; Ontario: Thomas Nelson, 1970], 287).

[2] E. M. Good, *In Turns of Tempest: A Reading of Job with a Translation* (Stanford: Stanford University Press, 1990), 329.

[3] Cf. N. Habel, *The Book of Job: A Commentary* (OTL; Philadelphia: Westminster Press, 1985), 489-90.

[4] M. Nussbaum, *Poetic Justice: The Literary Imagination and Public Life* (Boston MS: Beacon Press, 1995), 86-90. The concept of the "judicious spectator" draws upon the work of Adam Smith, an 18th-century British philosopher and economist, who describes such a figure in *The Theory of Moral Sentiments* (1759). For Nussbaum's discussion of Smith, see 72-79.

[5] Ibid., 91.

[6] Whitman, "By Blue Ontario's Shore," *Leaves of Grass*, edited with an introduction by J. Loving (Oxford: Oxford University Press, 1990), 269 (emphasis added).

ELIHU'S WORLD

Job 36:1–37:24

Elihu's last speech is his longest. The length underscores his need to say more (36:2) if he is to fulfill his self-appointed role as the "Answerer" this story needs. It also reflects his conviction that he is singularly suited to stand in between the friends and Job on the one side, and God on the other, and speak *to,* perhaps also *for,* both parties to this conversation at the same time. In the first half of his speech (36:1-21), Elihu continues to address issues Job and the friends have raised, especially God's use of suffering to direct persons like Job toward the faith God requires. In the second half (36:22–37:24), Elihu speaks as one so attuned to what God thinks that neither the friends nor Job has to wait for God's actual words. They need only listen to his representation of what God will say (in the final form of the book, Job 38:1–40:2 and 40:6–41:34) to know the divine truth that settles once and for all every issue that has been raised thus far.

   C. Newsom is therefore correct when she concludes that, "Elihu's final speech faces in two directions."[1] I would press her assessment still further. By facing two audiences at the same time—Job/the friends and God—Elihu provides a suggestive thematic representation of the prologue's depiction of the *satan,* who has one foot in the heavenly council of God and the other on earth (2:7a, 7b). Like his counterpart, Elihu believes his God-given role on earth is to investigate the claims of those who profess fidelity to God, making sure that no potential criticism remains unheard or unanswered. Toward that end, he addresses Job and the friends, "afflicting" them when necessary with objections meant to separate the wheat from the chaff. ["A Barb'd Tongue"] And like his counterpart, Elihu believes his role on earth gives him special access to and potential influence on divine prerogatives. Toward that end, he not only reports *to* God, he also speaks and acts *for* God, ever confident that he too has been divinely commissioned with the words, "Very well, all that they have is in your power" (cf. 1:12).

   Commentators outline the speech in different ways. To accent the emphases of this commentary, I propose a seven-part structure.

"A Barb'd Tongue"

Walt Whitman's poem, "By Blue Ontario's Shore," reflects on the poet's encounter with a "Phantom," who calls for a poem that "comes from the soul of America" (see further the "Connections" at Job 22). The task Whitman sets for himself is the creation of an American literature that is equal to the best of the classical writings that have gone before and at the same time is both fresh and original. The poem's narrator accepts the challenge with these words:

I am he who tauntingly compels men, women, nations,
Crying, Leap from your seats and contend for your lives!

I am he who walks the States with a barb'd tongue, questioning
    every one I meet,
Who are you that wanted only to be told what you knew before?
Who are you that wanted only a book to join you in your nonsense?

W. Whitman, "By Blue Ontario's Shore," *Leaves of Grass*, ed. with an intro. by J. Loving (Oxford: Oxford University Press, 1990), 264.

I. Introduction (36:1-4)
II. *Behold* (*hen*; v. 5) God's power to judge the wicked and the afflicted (36:5-15)
  III. Application to Job: admonition and warning (36:16-21)

> IV. *Behold* (*hen*) God's power and heed Elihu's advance summons to praise (36:22-25)

V. *Behold* (*hen*; vv. 26, 30) and praise the Lord of nature: strophe 1 (36:26-33)
VI. Praise the Lord of nature: strophe 2 (37:1-13)
  VII. Application to Job: rhetorical questions and certain answers (37:14-24)

The arguments that support these demarcations in the speech will be addressed in the respective sections of the commentary. The following general observations set the table for those discussions.

• The heptadic structure invites reflection on Elihu's cosmology, more specifically, on the world as he envisions it and what it requires of his listeners if they are to live happily and well within it. One of the rhetorical building blocks for Elihu's world is the fourfold repetition of the words "Behold/see (God)" (vv. 5, 22, 26, 30). The first occurrence of the phrase addresses Job and the friends. The other three ostensibly address them as well. Even so, because he believes he speaks to and for audiences on earth and in heaven, Elihu is confidant that the world he constructs is identical to the one God has created. God, too, would happily inhabit Elihu's world.

• Elihu's theology of creation defines God's justice as the providential use of suffering to warn and admonish those who, like Job, need the chastening discipline of pain in order to attain the faith God requires (36:5-15).

• In Elihu's world, the Lord of nature, who commands the rain, thunder, and lightning as agents of divine retribution, brooks no response from the faithful except praise (36:26-33; 37:1-13). If Job does not heed the warning (36:16-21), then he will continue to be numbered among those who would rather take comfort "in their own conceit" (37:24). Absent this requisite praise, Job will never be able to answer correctly the questions that Elihu (read God) has determined are the true measure of his fidelity (37:14-24).

• Finally, the structure of Elihu's speech suggests that he places himself and his model for the praise required of Job at the center of his world (36:22-25). Because his words are "perfect" (v. 4: *tāmîm*), they are the equal not only of Job's acclaimed blamelessness and integrity (*tām*; 1:8; 2:3) but also of God's (37:16: *tāmîm*). Like Janus, the Roman god of gates and doors, Elihu looks in opposite directions, towards Job and towards God, at the same time. From his privileged position at the center, he offers the bridge that promises to connect both. Like Janus, Elihu exemplifies the wisdom that promises to tie together the beginnings and endings of this drama.[Janus]

Janus
5th C. BC. Bronze Sculpture, Museo dell'Accademia Etrusca, Cortona, Italy (Credit: Scala/Art Resource, NY)

Janus

Janus, the Roman god of gates and doors, beginnings and endings, is depicted as looking in opposite directions at the same time. Whether familiar with the mythology or not, we sustain its legacy on our calendar. Every January, the month that bears the god's name, we look back to the year that has passed and forward to the next.

COMMENTARY

Elihu's Introduction: "In Praise of Myself," 36:1-4

The introduction returns both to the beginnings of Elihu's first speech (32:6-22), commending the knowledge he brings to this debate, and also, more subtly, to the beginnings mapped out by the prologue. With the deference of one who seems almost to need permission to continue speaking, Elihu asks his audience to be patient as he completes what he has to say on God's behalf (v. 2). He indicates the scope and importance of what he wishes to impart in several ways. His knowledge comes "from far away" (v. 3a: *mērāḥôq*). In its simplest form, the phrase refers to spatial distance; for example, the friends who look on Job "from a distance" (2:12: *mērāḥôq*) also bring their knowledge from places far away. The source of their wisdom can likely be traced to their place of origin in the east. Elihu claims something more than this for his knowledge, for now he prepares to speak "what is right" (NRSV: "ascribe righteousness") about his "Maker" (v. 3b: *pōʿălî*; cf. 32:22, where a parallel word, *ʿōśēnî*, occurs). Unlike the friends, the source of Elihu's knowledge is neither confined to any one place in the world nor limited by any falsity that might inhere in those places (v. 4a). His truth can be traced directly to the Creator of the world.

Elihu's claim to have access to the Creator's wisdom lays the ground for a further assertion. He speaks as one "who is perfect in knowledge" (v. 4b). His use of the word "perfect" (*tāmîm*) may be little more than another rhetorical return to the prologue, which uses the same language to describe Job (*tām*: 1:1, 8;2:3; NRSV: "blameless"). If so, then Elihu claims only that he can stand before God with the same integrity that Job has (cf. the same root in 27:5; 31:6). Here again, however, we may wonder if Elihu's objective is simply to claim parity with Job and his friends.

The gist of this speech suggests otherwise. He seems intent on demonstrating that his knowledge is superior—not just equal—to theirs. Moreover, before this speech is over, Elihu will have come very close to suggesting that the perfection he claims for his knowledge is the *equivalent of,* perhaps even a worthy *substitute for,* the knowledge of God (37:16). While others (read Job and the friends) can only grasp the wonder of God's works "from far away" (36:25b: *mērāḥôq*), Elihu suffers no such limitations. Because he looks in two directions at the same time, Elihu has the capacity not only to know where this story began but also to know where it will inevitably end. Ostensibly, the end comes with God's definitive display of perfect knowledge at the end of the book. By the time God speaks, however, Elihu hints that it will be God who echoes his perfect wisdom rather than the other way round. In short, an introduction that on first impression seems designed to evoke Job's affirmation of *God's* world, seems instead to be summoning forth praise for *Elihu's.* ["I Celebrate Myself"]

"I Celebrate Myself"

📖 In "Song of Myself" (1855), Walt Whitman imagines himself as the best exemplar of divinity and humanity that the world offers (see further **["I Am an Encloser of Things to Be"]**). The first lines of his poem resonate with Elihu's understanding of his position at the center of his/God's world:

I celebrate myself, and sing myself,
And what I assume, you shall assume . . .
I and this mystery here we stand.

W. Whitman, "Song of Myself," *Leaves of Grass,* ed. with an intro. by J. Loving (Oxford: Oxford University Press, 1990), 29, 31.

Behold God's Power to Judge the Wicked and the Afflicted, 36:5-15

Elihu's defense of divine justice begins with the first of four strategically placed appeals for Job (and his friends) to "Behold/see God" (v. 5; cf. vv. 22, 26, 30; NRSV does not clearly reflect the repetition). At the top of Elihu's list of things that all must see and understand is God's power, here specifically equated with God's irresistible display of just force when dealing with the "wicked" and the "afflicted" (v. 6). The terms Elihu chooses to define the range of God's power are somewhat curious. Given the debate between Job and the friends, we might well have expected him to follow their lead by contrasting the fates of the "wicked" and the "righteous."

Elihu uses the word "righteous" (v. 7), but his reference is to kings, who exercise power by virtue of their title and status in society (vv. 7-12). He implies, but does not substantiate, that such persons inevitably succumb to the temptation to use power for arrogant, self-aggrandizing purposes, whereupon God demonstrates superior power by binding them with "fetters" and "cords of affliction" (v. 8) that imprison them in a most un-royal way. [Fetters and Cords] The purpose of their humiliation is pedagogical: God "discloses" (*nāgad*; v. 9a; NRSV: "declares") the arrogance of their deeds, "opens their ears" to disciplining instruction (v. 10; cf. v. 15), and "summons" (*'āmar*; v. 10b) them to a better use of power.[2] Elihu essentially reprises his earlier argument for suffering as a means of divine discipline (33:19-28). [Suffering as Divine Discipline] In this speech, however, he omits both the earlier focus on the auditory part of the revelatory process, which warns individuals without afflicting them (33:15-18), and the interpretive part of the process, in which an angelic mediator translates the experience of suffering into language that can be understood (33:23-28). Now Elihu concentrates only on the experience of suffering itself. Pain, it seems, requires no assistance in communicating its message. If they can *feel* its truth, then no words are necessary. Pain's truth is that God offers the powerful two clear choices. If they "listen" and "serve "/ "obey" (*'ābad*) its claim on them, then life after affliction will be full of "prosperity" and "pleasantness" (v. 11). If they do not, their certain fate is to "die without knowing." REB's trans-

---

Fetters and Cords

As Newsom notes, "this language may be figurative, but it is grounded in an all too familiar social reality." The following texts are illustrative:

Then they captured the king [Zedekiah] and brought him up to the king of Babylon at Riblah, who passed sentence on him. They slaughtered the sons of Zedekiah before his eyes; then put out the eyes of Zedekiah; they bound him in fetters and took him back to Babylon. (2 Kgs 25:6-7)

The Lord spoke to Manasseh and to his people, but they gave no heed. Therefore the Lord brought against them the commanders of the army of the king of Assyria, who took Manasseh captive in manacles, bound him with fetters, and brought him to Babylon. (2 Chr 33:10-11)

Yet she [Jerusalem] became an exile,
she went into captivity;
even her infants were dashed in pieces
at the head of the street:
lots were cast for her nobles,
all her dignitaries were bound in fetters. (Nah 3:10)

C. Newsom, "The Book of Job," in vol. 4 of *NIB* (Nashville: Abingdon Press, 1996), 586.

Suffering as Divine Discipline

Suffering is an inescapable human reality. The challenge for ancient Israel, as for all communities of faith, was to locate the experience of suffering within an understanding of God's moral governance of the world. The Old Testament explores a range of options, which cluster around two major perspectives. Not surprisingly, both occupy center stage in the book of Job.

First, Israel's covenantal theology interprets suffering as the just and expected consequence of disobedience to God. Within a moral calculus that equates suffering with sin, its absence with fidelity, the key to enduring the experience and finding meaning within it is to confess, repent, and trust in God's gracious forgiveness. Eliphaz, Bildad, and Zophar build their theological counsel on the cornerstone of this conviction. A second perspective strongly resists the argument that all suffering can be equated with sin or God's punishment. Authentic faith, this perspective insists, requires that innocent suffering be addressed with lament and complaint, not confession, even when, indeed especially when, the party responsible for the wrongdoing is God. Job himself is the parade example of this approach (for further discussion of these two perspectives, see **[Retribution]**).

Elihu's appeal to suffering as spiritual *discipline* (*mûsār*, 36:10; NRSV: "instruction") represents a subset of the first approach. The verbal root (*yāsar*) from which the noun "discipline" derives, means "chastise." When parents, teachers, and God "chastise," they typically do so for positive effect. The intent is to correct wrongful behavior with punishment that educates, trains, and transforms. Elihu's argument for suffering as the rod of God's corrective discipline is part of a larger trajectory of similar texts, for example:

You shall love the Lord your God, therefore, and keep his charge, his decrees, his ordinances, and his commandments always. Remember today that it was not your children (who have not known or seen the discipline of the Lord your God), but it is you who must acknowledge his greatness, his mighty hand and his outstretched arm . . . . (Deut 11:1-2)

O Lord, in distress they sought you,
they poured out a prayer
when your chastening was upon them. (Isa 26:16)

O Lord, do your eyes not look for truth?
You have struck them down,
but they felt no anguish;
you have consumed them,
but they refused to take correction.
They made their faces harder than rock;
they have refused to turn back. (Jer 5:3)

O Lord, do not rebuke me in your anger,
or discipline me in your anger. (Ps 6:1; cf. Pss 38:1; 39:11; 118:18)

My child, do not despise the Lord's discipline
or be weary of his reproof. (Prov 3:11; cf. Job 5:17)

For further reading, see J. A. Sanders, *Suffering as Divine Discipline in the Old Testament and Post-Biblical Judaism*. Colgate Rochester Divinity School Bulletin 38 (1955); E. S. Gerstenberger, W. Schrage, *Suffering* (Biblical Encounter Series; Nashville: Abingdon, 1977); D. Simundson, *Faith Under Fire: Biblical Interpretations of Suffering* (Minneapolis: Augsburg Fortress, 1980); W. Brueggemann, "Suffering," *Reverberations of Faith: A Theological Handbook of Old Testament Themes* (Louisville, London: Westminster John Knox Press, 2002), 200-204.

lation is apt: they die "with their lesson unlearnt."[3] ["It Is Where We Are Wounded That Is When He Speaks"]

If Elihu equates the "righteous" with arrogant kings, then who are the "afflicted"? He appears to associate the "afflicted" with the "godless in heart" (v. 13: *ḥanpê lēb*), who rather than recognize that God knows what is best for them, become angry when their own plans are thwarted. They would rather stay their own course than admit God is right by calling out for God's help when things go wrong (v. 13). As a result, they die prematurely; their only legacy is the abiding shame that bears witness to a perverted life (v. 14).[4]

"It Is Where We Are Wounded That Is When He Speaks"

"Age of Anxiety," W. H. Auden's Pulitzer Prize-wining poem (1948), follows the conversations of four characters who meet in a bar and try to sort out their lives in the midst of war: Quaint, the son of an Irish immigrant; Malin, a medical intelligence officer on leave from the Canadian Air Force; Rosetta, a buyer for a big department store; and Emble, who enlisted in the Navy during his sophomore year at university. The title of the poem reflects Auden's despair that the quest for meaning is doomed from the start. While we are alive, we can look forward to little more than anxiety. When life ends, we die; there is nothing more.

The four characters end their conversations in a drunken weariness and return to their homes, unable to remember anything they have said. Malin is the last of the characters to speak in the poem.

> For the others, like me, there is only the flash
> Of negative knowledge, the night when, drunk, one
> Staggers to the bathroom and stares at the glass
> To meet one's madness . . .
>
> And, scorned on a scaffold, ensconced in His life
> The human household. In our anguish we struggle
> To elude Him, to lie to Him, yet His love observes
> His appalling promise; His predilection
> As we wander and weep is with us to the end,

> Minding our meanings, our least matter dear to Him,
> His Good ingressant on our gross occasions
> Envisages our advance, valuing for us
> Though our bodies too blind or too bored to examine
> What sorts excite them are slain interjecting
> Their childish Ows and, in choosing how many
> And how much they will love, our minds insist on
> Their own disorder as their own punishment,
> His Question disqualifies our quick senses,
> His Truth makes our theories historical sins,
> It is where we are wounded that is when He speaks
> Our creaturely cry, concluding His children
> In their mad unbelief to have mercy on them all
> As they wait unawares for His World to come.

The narrator, summing up, invites us, as it were, to ponder God's "Truth" and God's "World" *from Elihu's perspective*, and Malin's woundedness *from Job's ash heap*.

> So thinking, he returned to duty, reclaimed by the actual world where time is real and in which, therefore, poetry can take no interest.
>
> Facing another long day of servitude to wilful authority and blind accident, creation lay in pain and earnest, once more reprieved from self-destruction, its adoption, as usual, postponed.

W. H. Auden, "The Age of Anxiety (Part Six: Epilogue)," *W. H. Auden: Collected Poems*, ed. E. Mendelson (New York: Vintage International, 1991), 534-36.

Elihu's identification of the afflicted with the godless invites a number of questions. If, as he argues, it is the destiny of all persons, regardless of title or status, to stand before the God who "does not deprive sufferers of their due" (v. 5; REB), then how is the fate of the "afflicted" different than what awaits the "righteous"? Because this portion of his speech (vv. 13-15) is much briefer than what has preceded, the answer to the question is elusive. Elihu provides no description of the revelatory process, apart from the echoing assertion that God "opens their ear by adversity" (v. 15). Perhaps we are to understand that the whole of the process spelled out above—disclosure, opening the ear, summons to correction (vv. 9-10), and the opportunity to decide whether to hear or not (vv. 11-12)—is implied here. However, given Elihu's confidence in his ability to see both the beginnings and the endings of the story, we may wonder if his omission of any process for the "afflicted" does not indicate that he knows in advance what the outcome will be.

Moreover, we may note that Bildad has used the same word, "godless" (*ḥānēp*; 8:13a), as Elihu to identify the wicked, who abandon ("forget") God in order to pursue their own perverted paths. Job has himself used the word *ḥānēp* to describe those whom God has decided are wicked (27:8) and whose cries for help, therefore, God will not hear (27:9-10). The problem is that shared vocabulary does not automatically insure a consensus of meaning. Elihu would no doubt agree with Bildad's assessment: "the hope of the godless will perish" (8:13b). But if he has listened carefully to Job, then it is hard to believe that he would agree with him. Job's argument is that those whom God has *erroneously* labeled as "godless" may cry out for help all they want, but God will never respond, because God has *preemptively* decided, without benefit of process or deliberation, that they are unworthy (see the commentary on 27:7-12). In sum, Bildad and Elihu agree that God will punish the godless. Job uses their words but speaks a different truth: "It is all one; therefore I say, he destroys the blameless and the wicked" (9:22).

The bottom line, Elihu seems to say, is this. Whether one is righteous or afflicted, whether one has abused power or never had opportunity to exercise power, whether one is arrogant or godless, God demands the same response. The one non-negotiable requirement is absolute submission to God: if we serve obediently the God who decides to bring pain and suffering into life, we will survive; if we do not, we will not. Job has heard this line before (22:21); it is unlikely that he will find it any more persuasive now than it was then. If we listen carefully to Elihu's counsel with the ears of Job, if we are able to wince with something remotely like his pain at being consigned to the ash heap of life "for no reason," then we may wonder if the call to faith in Elihu's world adds up to anything more than a pious justification for slavery. When and if we begin to consider such matters, we may find that we are closer to Job, whose first response to his friends' counsel was to complain that life in relation to God reduces one to slavery (7:1-6), than to Elihu, who seems to think slavery a virtue. ["Careless Seems the Great Avenger"]

Application to Job: Admonition and Warning, 36:16-21

This section of Elihu's speech is so full of textual uncertainties that many commentators consider it virtually unintelligible. ["Enough to Make Their Hair Stand on End"] It is relatively clear that Elihu *admonishes* Job for making the wrong decisions in response to the choices God has put before him, and that he *warns* him there will be no escaping God's judgment if he does not reverse his course. Beyond this, almost all of the details are open to a wide range of interpretations. We may gain some insight into the difficulties in the text, although likely no pur-

---

"Careless Seems the Great Avenger"

James Russell Lowell (1819–1891), an ardent abolitionist, was one of a group of authors, along with Henry Wadsworth Longfellow and John Greenleaf Whittier, who were called the "Fireside Poets." His poem, "The Present Crisis" (1844), was the inspiration for the name of the magazine "The Crisis," the flagship publication of the National Association for the Advancement of Colored People, established in 1910 under the leadership of W. E. B. Du Bois. This excerpt from the poem speaks to the abiding conviction that God has *not* decreed that slavery is the destiny for human beings.

Once to every man and nation comes the moment to decide,
In the strife of Truth with Falsehood, for the good or evil side;
Some great cause, God's new Messiah, offering each thebloom or blight,
Parts the goats upon the left hand, and the sheep upon the right,

And the choice goes by forever 'twixt that darkness and that light . . . .
Careless comes the great Avenger; history's pages but record
One death-grapple in the darkness 'twixt old systems and the Word;
Truth forever on the scaffold, Wrong forever on the throne;
Yet that scaffold sways the future, and behind the dim unknown,
Standeth God within the shadow, keeping watch above His own.

For further reflection, see W. E. B. Du Bois, *The Souls of Black Folk* (New York: Bantam Books, 1989), which uses a portion of this poem as the epigraph for ch. 2, "Of the Dawn of Freedom," 10-29.

James Russell Lowell, "The Present Crisis," *The Complete Poetical Works of James Russell Lowell*, ed. H. E. Scudder (Boston: Houghton Mifflin & Company, 1897, 1925), 67-68.

---

chase on their resolution, by asking two questions that the general sense of Elihu's words invites.

(1) *What choices has God presented to Job?* Elihu appears to focus on the choice between life and death. Verse 16 contrasts the "jaws of distress" (NIV; *mippî ṣār*) with a "spacious place free of restriction" (NIV; *raḥab lōʾ mûṣāq*). The first phrase conveys the imagery of entrapment in a confined place, like a mouth clamping down on food, where no options for escape are available. [The Mouth of Death] Conversely, the second phrase suggests freedom, along with which comes abundant living, here imaged as a table laden with food. Presumably, Elihu believes God has made the choices clear to Job and that Job has freely chosen death over life.

The lead verb in v. 16, however, which NRSV translates "allures," complicates matters. The Hebrew root (*sut*) is the same as that which occurs in 2:3, where God concedes to the *satan*, "you *incited* me." In the vast majority of its occurrences, this verb carries the negative, even

---

"Enough to Make Their Hair Stand on End"

The proposed emendations confronting interpreters, R. Gordis notes (citing A. B. Ehrlich), are "enough to make their hair stand on end." Gordis offers the following "general sense" of the text:

Job has been saved from affliction and actually been granted prosperity (v. 16). Nonetheless, he has not practiced justice for the weak against the evildoers (v. 17). Elihu warns Job against letting his wealth lead him astray (v. 18) in the mistaken belief that his possessions will safeguard him against punishment (v. 19).

R. Gordis, *The Book of Job: Commentary, New Translation, and Special Studies* (New York: Jewish Theological Seminary of America, 1978), 415.

The Mouth of Death

📖 Commentators often note that the idiom "jaws of distress" (36:16; *mippî ṣār*) has parallels in Canaanite mythology, where Baal descends into the mouth of Mot (Death), the god of the underworld, in order to defeat the forces of chaos (e.g., N. Habel, *The Book of Job* [OTL; Philadelphia: Westminster Press, 1985], 508-509).

Baal must enter his innards
(and) go down into his mouth (*bph yrd*).

J. C. L. Gibson, *Canaanite Myths and Legends* (Edinburgh: T & T Clark, 1977), 69.

---

sinister, idea of enticing someone to do something that is almost always harmful or disadvantageous for them, something they would never have chosen for themselves had they not been pressured to do so (e.g., 1 Sam 26:19; 2 Sam 24:1; Isa 36:18; Jer 43:2; the lone exception is 2 Chr 18:31). A straightforward rendering of this verb in v. 16 is, "He [God] has enticed you out of distress." The implication would be that God has in effect baited Job with one option—life—knowing full well that if Job accepts it on God's terms, the outcome will be negative rather than positive.

For obvious reasons, most commentators find such a meaning unacceptable and thus suggest a range of alternate possibilities: perhaps something has been omitted from the text; perhaps God is not the subject of this verb, perhaps the verb does not have its normal negative connotations in this text; perhaps the text is corrupt and should be emended by substituting a different verb.[5] [A Comparison of Translations] Perhaps. But we should probably still acknowledge that any time a "choice" has to do with enticement, whatever its meaning, it will usually be something less than clear and straightforward.

(2) *Why has Job made the wrong choice?* Several possible answers may be teased out from Elihu's speech.

• Verse 17 uses forensic terms (*dîn*, "case/lawsuit" [2x]; *mišpāṭ*, "justice, judgment") that suggest Job's problem has to do with justice issues. The syntax of the verse leaves it unclear, however, whether Job has erred because he has become obsessed with the "judgment *due* the wicked" (NIV; cf. NJPS), or with *his own suit* against God, which is a "wicked case,"[6] or

---

A Comparison of Translations

AΩ A comparison of translations makes clear the difficulties:

He also allured you out of distress
into a broad place where there was no constraint,
and what was set on your table
was full of fatness. (NRSV)

Beware, if you are tempted to exchange hardship for comfort,
with unlimited plenty spread before you and a generous table. (REB)

He is wooing you from the jaws of distress
to a spacious place free from restriction,
to the comfort of your table laden with choice food. (NIV)

Therefore he will give you ample salvation from the narrow mouth
which has no foundations beneath it;
but the repose of your table will be filled with distress.
(NAB, following the Vulgate with a note that the "Hebrew text is in disorder")

Indeed, He draws you away from the brink of distress
To a broad place where there is no constraint;
Your table is laid out with rich food. (NJPS)

God brought you out of trouble,
and let you enjoy security;
your table was piled high with food. (TEV)

perhaps because *Job has failed to offer the justice to others that he demands for himself.*[7]

• Whereas v. 16 may be interpreted to mean that God has tried to lure (*sut*) Job in one direction, vv. 18-19 suggest that Job has been more "enticed" (*sut*) by other, more dangerous, alternatives. Just what these other enticements are, however, is unclear. NRSV's translation of v. 18a indicates that Job's "wrath" or "anger" has seduced him (cf. NJPS); NIV's translation understands the temptation to be "riches" (cf. REB, TEV). The second half of v. 18 adds another possibility. NRSV suggests Job has been tempted to conclude that the "greatness of the ransom (*kōper*)" required for his restoration, namely his confession of sin (cf. *kōper* in 33:24), is too high a price to pay. NIV understands the same word (*kōper*) to mean "bribe," presumably a reference to under-the-table payoffs that tempt people toward wrong judgments (cf. REB, NJPS). Verse 19 offers still another possibility: the temptation for Job to rely on his own "strength" (*kōaḥ*), presumably instead of trusting in the "strength (*kōaḥ*) of [God's] understanding" (v. 5; cf. v. 22; 37:23).

• In v. 20, Elihu alleges that Job "longs for the night," although if this is true, it is unclear why Job is wrong to do so. Job has claimed that the wicked long for the cover of darkness, because it allows them to go about their evil deeds without being seen by anyone, including God (24:13-17). If this claim is the target of Elihu's concern, then he is likely warning Job, as he has done previously (34:20-22), that the night provides no escape from God's judgment for anyone, including Job himself.

Elihu may also be targeting Job's opening words from the ash heap in chapter 3, where his curses and laments seek a rhetorical subversion of light by darkness. Job's objective, however, was to create an avenue of escape from God not because he is wicked but because he believes his blamelessness counts for nothing in God's system of justice. He longs for a place "where light is like darkness" (10:22), because perhaps there God will not be able to torment him any longer. If it is Job's curses and laments that have led him down the wrong path, then the corrective Elihu will soon offer is a summons to praise (36:22–37:13).

• Given so many difficulties, it is tempting to consider that v. 21 offers at least one unambiguous answer to the question we are tracking. NRSV provides a representative translation: "Beware! Do not turn to iniquity; because of that you have been tried by affliction." The words "you have been tried by affliction" are often understood as the capstone of Elihu's argument concerning God's use of suffering to turn

Job away from sin (33:19-28). Here too, unfortunately, the Hebrew text is not quite so clear.

The translation "you have been tried" follows the Syriac version (Peshitta) of the Old Testament, which (1) understands the Hebrew verb *bāḥar*, normally rendered "choose," as having the meaning it acquires in Aramaic, "test, prove" and (2) revocalizes the verb, changing it from an active to a passive form (from *bāḥartāh* to *buḥartāh*). If we follow the MT as it stands, however, the translation would be, "you [Job] have chosen affliction." Such a rendering implies that Job preferred affliction over peace and well being, which to most interpreters rightly sounds both awkward and illogical. It strains the imagination to believe that Elihu accuses Job of knowingly choosing a path that leads not only to his suffering but also to the innocent deaths of his children. Therefore, if one follows the MT at this point, it seems necessary to emend it at another; instead of reading "you have chosen *affliction,*" some have proposed, "you have chosen *iniquity.*"[8]

In view of the difficulties in this verse, the interpreter seems to have two options. One can either shoehorn the text, by emendation, into compliance with Elihu's *theology—God has tried Job with suffering,* because he has sinned. Or, one can shoehorn the text, by different emendations, into compliance with Elihu's *anthropology—Job has chosen affliction* (and/or iniquity), because, like all mortals who inevitably fail to measure up to God's expectations, he is a sinner. With either option, it is likely the interpreter will still end up with more questions than answers about how Elihu's admonishments and warnings in vv. 16-21 apply to Job.

Behold God's Power and Heed Elihu's Advance Summons to Praise, 36:22-25

Whether Job (or we) has (have) understood the import of this speech thus far, Elihu remains focused on God and on what God requires of those who would be faithful. With a second summons to "see/behold God," he returns to his preoccupation with God's power (v. 22a). The first summons (v. 5) addressed Job and the friends. This one does too, while at the same time envisioning a wider audience. Now Elihu stands before Job, but he seems to be looking beyond him to God, who is overhearing his words.

The interrogative "Who?" (*mî*) introduces three rhetorical questions (vv. 22b-23). Each question invites careful reflection on God's incomparable power as Creator: "Who is a teacher like him?" "Who prescribes for him his way?" and "Who can say to him, 'You have done wrong'?" The presumed answer in each case is, "No one." No one can teach God anything, because as Creator of the world God's knowledge is unequalled. No one can map out a course of action for God, because the range of God's concern is cosmic. And no one can hold God accountable, because the sovereign Ruler of the world answers to no other judge. What *one* can and must do, Elihu says, is join with *all people* who, having beheld God's majesty from afar, offer *collective* songs of praise in grateful response (vv. 24-25).[9]

In the outline for chapters 36–37, I have suggested that Elihu places this summons to praise, *and* himself, at the center of the rhetorical world he offers. Perhaps the idea that Elihu builds a world around himself is occasioned by nothing more than a structural formality, in which case, a different outline might negate the suggestion. On the other hand, if there are substantive connections between these rhetorical questions, each of which is ostensibly designed to summon forth *praise for God*, and *Elihu's commendation of himself* as the "answerer" this book requires, then the case for suspecting that Elihu is subtly constructing God's world in his own image becomes stronger. The following probes of his "rhetorical" questions and their presumed answers invite further reflection.

(1) *Who is a "teacher" like God?* The word "teacher" (*môre*) is rarely used in the Hebrew Bible with reference to God. [The "Teacher"] Related forms of the verb Elihu uses (Hiphil of *yārāh*, "instruct"), however, do

---

The "Teacher"

One text that invites comparison is Isa 30:18-26.

Therefore the Lord waits to be gracious to you;
therefore he will rise up to show mercy to you.
For the Lord is a God of justice;
blessed are all those who wait for him.

Truly, O people of Zion, inhabitants of Jerusalem, you shall weep no more. He will surely be gracious to you at the sound of your cry; when he hears it, he will answer you. Though the Lord may give you the bread of adversity and the water of affliction, yet your Teacher (*môrêka*) will not hide himself any more, but your eyes shall see your Teacher (*môrêka*). And when you turn to the right or when you turn to the left, your ears will hear a word behind you, saying, "This is the way, walk in it." Then you will defile your silver-covered idols and your gold-plated images. You will scatter them like filthy rags; you will say to them, "Away with you!"

He will give rain for the seed with which you will sow the ground, and grain, the produce of the ground, which will be rich and plenteous. On that day your cattle will graze in broad pastures; and the oxen and donkeys that till the ground will eat silage, which has been winnowed with shovel and fork. On every lofty mountain and every high hill there will be brooks running with water . . . . Moreover the light of the moon will be like the light of the sun, and the light of the sun will be sevenfold, like the light of the seven days, on the day when the Lord binds up the injuries of his people and heals the wounds inflicted by his blow.

This announcement of salvation echoes several themes found in Elihu's speech: an affirmation of the "God of justice"; a promise that a merciful God will bring healing to those who suffer adversity faithfully; the expectation that the agent of deliverance will be a "Teacher," who will make clear the way that leads a sinful people back to God; and the promise that God's justice and mercy will transform and redeem all creation. It is likely that the historical setting for the promise is the time of the Babylonian exile, although the eschatological imagery (e.g., "On that day") could suggest a still later time. The "Teacher" is not identified explicitly as God, although he is clearly represented as one who speaks with divine authority.

occur seven times in the book of Job, five times in the dialogues between Job and his friends, and twice in Elihu's speeches. In 6:24, Job responds to Eliphaz's first efforts to answer him by saying, "Teach me (*hôrûnî*), and I will be silent." Bildad takes up the challenge by referring Job to the wisdom of the ancestors: "Will they not teach you (*yôrûkâ*)" (8:10). Job finds the teaching of the ancestors to be deficient, and so he appeals to creation itself to disclose the truth about the way the world works that neither his friends nor the ancestors is able to grasp: "Ask the animals, and they will teach you (*tōrekā*), the birds of the air, and they will tell you (*tōrekā*)" (12:7-8). Because creation and its Creator seem unwilling or unable to respond in any way that confirms his trust, Job concludes his response to the friends by stepping into the void and offering his own instruction: "I will teach you (*'ôreh*) concerning the hand of God" (27:11).[10]

Elihu has two contributions to make to this debate about who will teach whom. In 34:31-32, a response obscured by textual difficulties, he makes his initial move toward shifting the debate away from the instruction of human teachers, whether the friends or Job, towards the wisdom that only God can provide: "Has anyone said to God. . . teach me (*hōrēnî*) what I do not see. . . ?" In 36:22, he clarifies what he means: God is the master teacher; God neither seeks nor requires instruction from anyone else. ["Great Universal Teacher"] Elihu appears to transfer to God the final authority for teaching humans what they need to know. It is instructive to note, however, that his words in 36:22 are the last ones that address God's role as "teacher." When God finally speaks from the whirlwind (chs. 38–41), God will not use the word "teach" a single time. The last word on who teaches whom belongs to Elihu, which hints that he believes there may be more than one right answer to the question "Who is a teacher like God?"

(2) *Who prescribes God's way?* Two aspects of this question merit attention. First, the verb "prescribe" (*pāqad*) occurs six times in Job. Three of the six occur in the dialogues between Job and the friends

---

"Great Universal Teacher"

In "Frost at Midnight," Samuel Taylor Coleridge (1772–1834) writes a "conversation poem" to his sixteen-month-old son, Hartley. Reflecting on the "secret ministry" (l. 1) of the frost on a freezing February in 1798, Coleridge returns to memories of his own childhood in the country. The blessings he received from the Lord of nature, the "Great universal teacher," he now seeks to convey and secure for his son.

But *thou*, my babe! shalt wander like a breeze
By lakes and sandy shores, beneath the crags

Of ancient mountains, and beneath the clouds,
Which image in their bulk both lakes and shores
And mountain crags: so shalt thou see and hear
The lovely shapes and sounds intelligible
Of that eternal language, which thy God
Utters, who from eternity doth teach
Himself in all, and all things in himself
Great universal Teacher! he shall mould
Thy spirit, and by giving make it ask.

Coleridge, "Frost at Midnight," ll. 54-64, in *Samuel Taylor Coleridge: Selected Poems*, ed. R. Holmes (London: Penguin Books, 1996), 47.

(5:24; 7:18; 31:14). In each of these cases, *pāqad* conveys the basic meaning "visit" or "inspect," in the sense of examining something or someone closely. Job's two uses of the word are instructive, for he speaks of the way God "visits" human beings in order to examine their fidelity and hold them accountable for their failures: "What are human beings . . . that you *visit* them every morning and test them every moment?" (7:17-16); "When God *visits* (NRSV: "makes inquiry"), what shall I answer him?" (31:14). The other three occurrences of *pāqad* are in Elihu's speeches (34:13; 35:15; 36:23). In two of the three, the syntax (*pāqad* followed by the preposition *ʿal,* "to, upon") extends the basic meaning "visit" to "instruct, order, command." In both instances, Elihu uses rhetorical questions that shift Job away from complaints about how God chooses to "visit" him in order to rebuke Job for presuming that he or anyone else is in a position to give orders to the Creator of the world: "Who gave him *charge over* the earth?" (34:13); "Who has *imposed on* him his way?" (36:23).[11]

The presumptive answer to both Elihu's questions is, of course, "No one." God does not take counsel or instruction from anyone; God gives it. Elihu may only be echoing a familiar appeal to creation theology in order to evoke Job's praise of God (cf. Isa 40:13-14). A second aspect of his language, however, subtly points in another direction. Habel has noted that Elihu's use of the word "way" (*derek*) in the context of an appeal to creation evokes theological metaphors from Israel's wisdom tradition, especially Proverbs 8:22-31.[12] In this hymn, Wisdom, personified as the first and best of God's "ways" (v. 22: *derek*; the parallel term is "his acts"), celebrates its role as the companion who stood at God's side (v. 30) when the world was created. Because Wisdom is involved with God's creativity from the very beginning, it knows the full scope of God's hopes and expectations for the cosmos. Thus, when Wisdom summons human beings to "listen" to its instructions and keep its "ways" (v. 32: *derek*), it speaks as God's privileged mediator between heaven and earth (cf. Sir 24:1-7).

Elihu's use of the word "way" may be nothing more than a coincidental allusion to Wisdom's "way" in Proverbs 8. On the other hand, in view of Elihu's inclination to model his arguments on those of Eliphaz, we should recall that Eliphaz has already introduced the imagery of Proverbs 8 into this debate. In 15:7-8, Eliphaz rebukes Job for presuming that *he* is the first and best of God's creative acts, that *he* has access to the full range of God's wisdom, that *he*, therefore, is privileged to raise questions about God's moral governance of the cosmos. When Eliphaz asks, "Are you the firstborn of the human race?" he expects Job to concede that he is not (see the commentary on 15:7-16). When Elihu draws upon the same imagery to ask his question—"Who has prescribed for him his way?"—we should expect that he too invites Job to answer by saying, "No one, *apart from Wisdom,* has any input into God's ways of governing the world." As we consider both the structure and the substance of Elihu's final speech, however, we may wonder if he would accept a different response. Could Job give the right answer to Elihu's question by responding, "No one, *apart from Elihu,* a k a, Wisdom"?

(3) *Who can say to God, "You have done wrong?"* The verb "done" (*pāʿal*) occurs thirteen times in Job, eight of which are in Elihu's speeches (7:20; 11:8; 22:17; 31:3; 33:29; 34:8, 22, 32; 35:6; 36:3, 23; 37:12). The verbal root *pāʿal,* "to do, make," normally refers to human action; in the book of Job, the referent is almost always "sin, deceit, injustice." Job asks, for example, "If I sin, what do I do to you [God]?" (7:20). The noun "wrong" (*ʿawlāh*) occurs nine times in Job, two of which are in Elihu's speeches (5:16; 6:29-30; 11:14; 13:7; 15:16; 22:23; 27:4; 34:32; 36:23). The word is one of several generic terms for "sin," "iniquity," "falsehood." Throughout the speeches of the friends, the principal debate is about whether Job is the guilty party, whether Job has sinned against God.

Elihu participates in this same debate, but as he is the only speaker in the book to use both words—*pāʿal* + *ʿawlāh*—in the same sentence, he shapes the issue in a distinctive way. In 34:32, he rebukes Job for his complaints about divine justice by asking, "Has anyone said to God. . . 'teach me what I do not see; if I have *done iniquity,* I will do it no more'?" Despite the textual difficulties (see the commentary on 34:31-37), the thrust of this question continues the basic arguments that have preceded: Job must confess the wrong *he* has done; when one stands before the Judge of the world, there is no other option. Elihu's question in 36:23, however, sharpens the debate by giving voice to another option: Is it possible for anyone to turn the tables on God and say, "*You* have *done wrong*"? The possibility has certainly been lurking at the edges of Job's thoughts (e.g., 19:7; 24:12; 27:2), if not the friends, but it is Elihu who introduces the thought in the most direct way. He does so not to encourage exploration of the possibility but instead to dismiss it out of hand as absurd.

One further observation on this matter is in order. The world Elihu envisions seems to have no place for thinking about who or what is "wrong," apart from the mandate that human beings confess they are culpable for everything. But is what Elihu regards as absurd in *his world* consonant with the *world that God has created*? The answer to this question depends on the exegesis of God's own survey of the world (38:1-41:34) in which Job lives. In anticipation of this discussion, we may note that God will address Job with questions that resemble those Elihu seems already to have dismissed (cf. 40:6-8). The words that frame God's questions, however, are different than Elihu's. God asks Job not about what is "wrong" but about what is "just" (*mišpāṭ*) and what is "righteous" (*ṣādeq*). In God's world, if not in Elihu's, the imperative to consider these issues seems anything but absurd. ["Few Things Human Can Stand to Be Rubbed So Long"]

Behold and Praise the Lord of Nature: Strophe 1, 36:26-33

A third summons to "Behold/see God" (v. 26a) introduces the first stanza of Elihu's praise.[13] The two previous summonses (vv. 5, 22) call for consideration of God's *irresistible* and *incomparable power*. The third one has a similar objective, although now Elihu's focus shifts to God's *wondrous* and *purposive mastery* of nature. Regrettably, many of the details in his description of various meteorological phenomena continue to elude us. Even when we do not fully understand what he is saying, however, it is clear that Elihu is mesmerized by the stunning intricacies of God's world. When he summons Job to see the world as he sees it, he trusts that Job will respond with a doxology of praise that is worthy of the awe-inspiring Lord of nature.

He begins with the phenomenon of rain (vv. 27-28). God has designed a two-step process. First, God gathers up drops of water from primordial reservoirs into rain clouds; second, God allows them to trickle down, in carefully calibrated proportions, on "human beings" (*ʾādām*) who cannot survive without the sustenance of water. Next (vv. 29-30), Elihu describes God's delicate spreading of the clouds, so that lightning can zigzag toward earth with its own distinctive testimony to the power of the Creator of the cosmos. [From Heaven to the Roots of the Sea]

When Elihu contemplates the wonder and majesty of these natural phenomena, he discerns that God has endowed creation with a moral purposiveness (vv. 31-33). On the one hand, God uses nature as a means to "govern" (*dîn*; v. 31a) and "command" (*ṣaw*; v. 32b). Although the text is obscure, Elihu associates God's governance with retribution: lightning strikes its targets with God's judgment; thundering storms announce God's arrival. [Textual Difficulties in 36:33] On the other hand, God's control of nature is also beneficent, for the rains provide "food in abundance" (v. 31b).

"Few Things Human Can Stand to Be Rubbed So Long"

I once saw a painter smear black paint on a blue sky,
then rub it in until that lie of hers

was gone. I've seen men polish cars
so hard they've given off light.
As a child I kept a stone in my pocket,

thumb and forefinger in collusion
with water and wind,
caressing it day and night.

I've begun a few things with an eraser,
waited for friction's spark.
I've learned that sometimes severe

can lead to truer, even true.
But few things human can stand
to be rubbed so long—I know this

and can't stop. If beauty comes
it comes startled, hiding scars,
out of what barely can be endured.

S. Dunn, "Rubbing," *Different Hours* (New York, London: W. W. Norton & Company, 2000), 81-82.

From Heaven to the "Roots of the Sea"

AΩ The imagery of 36:30b is obscure, as a comparison of modern translations shows:

See, he scatters his lightning around him
and covers the roots of the sea. (NRSV)

See how he scatters his lightning about him,
bathing the depths of the sea. (NIV)

See how he scatters his light about him,
and its rays cover the sea. (REB)

See, he spreads His lightning over it;
It fills the bed of the sea. (NJPS)

He sends lightning through all the sky,
but the depths of the sea remain dark. (TEV)

At issue is the meaning of the Hebrew phrase "and covers the roots of the sea." Does the verb "cover" mean "cover over," that is, "overlay," perhaps with the extended sense of "overcome"? If so, then the imagery suggests God's control of the primordial waters of chaos (cf. Ps 29:10). Or does this verb (or an emendation of it) mean "uncover," in the sense of "expose," "lay bare"? If so, then the imagery suggests God's use of the lightning to illumine or reveal the mysteries of what is hidden, whether the secrets are positive or negative (cf. Ps 18:15). With either possibility, the basic thrust probably remains the same: God is in full control of the phenomena of nature; the clouds and the lightning serve God's purposes.

Job should praise the Lord of nature, Elihu suggests, because like the rain, the lightning, and the thunder, he too has been created to serve the Creator. And like nature itself, Job becomes most fully who God has created him to be, when he joyfully receives God's gracious provision and obediently responds to God's just commands.

Praise the Lord of Nature: Strophe 2, 37:1-13

This second stanza advances the summons to praise the Lord of nature by elaborating on the meteorological phenomena that have so captured Elihu's imagination: storms (thunder, lightning, wind), rain (snow and ice), and clouds. As he has been inclined to do throughout this speech, Elihu offers himself as the model for the responses of all others (vv. 1-2). When he beholds the majesty and meaning of God's world, his heart "pounds" and "leaps" within his chest. With an impassioned double imperative—"Listen, listen"—he summons all to hear what he hears when God speaks in the tumultuous roaring (*rōgez*: NRSV: "trouble") and rumbling of the thunder. That Job has used the same term (*rōgez*; 3:26) to describe the turmoil rumbling in his heart, gives Elihu no pause. That Job has tracked the source of this turmoil (*rōgez*, 14:1; NRSV: "trouble") to the God who created the world as a place where human beings, like nature itself, simply live and die without hope for anything more, is no obstacle for the praise that Elihu feels and summons from others.

In Elihu's view, everything has its place in the grammar of God's creation. Lightning punctuates the corners of the earth with dazzling illumination (vv. 3, 11b). Thunder bespeaks the unfathomable mysteries of God's power (vv. 4-5). Winter storms bear witness to God's miraculous transformation of rain into ice and snow (vv. 6-7, 10). Clouds laden with moisture move across the sky, constantly changing shape at God's command (vv. 11-12). In every instance, nature responds with unfailing fidelity to God's guidance.

Once again, Elihu sees a moral purposiveness in God's control of creation, which he spells out in v. 13 (cf. 36:31-33). And once again,

Elihu interprets God's intent primarily in terms of retribution. When deciding what message nature should teach the earth, God chooses from two options. The first is "correction" or "punishment," the second, "love." This sequencing of God's priorities echoes Elihu's own message concerning suffering as the pedagogy of redemption. The syntax of v. 13 has invited consideration of a third option. The words "for his land (*'ereṣ*)" may be emended to read "for his pleasure/acceptance (*rāṣah*)."[14] What the emendation gives with one hand, however, it may take back with the other. Elihu has offered his own instructions about the promise of God's "acceptance" (*rāṣah*; 33:26), which he interprets as requiring a confession of sin. However viable this third option may be, it remains the case that Elihu believes the first word in creation's grammar announces God's decision to punish. ["He Who Learns Must Suffer"]

Elihu's hymn of praise to the world God has created is remarkable in several ways, not least because of his attention to details. It is for this same reason therefore curious that what most evokes his adoration is the *world of nature*, not the *world of creatures and human beings*. Different words for thunder, rain, lightning, and clouds occur multiple times throughout this speech.[15] By contrast, there are but three references to living creatures, two to human beings (v. 7: "everyone" [*kol 'ādām*]; "all [*kol 'anṣê*] whom he has made") and one to animals (v. 8: *ḥayyāh*; cf. 36:33). Textual difficulties obscure the meaning in v. 7; about all that is clear is that God uses nature to "seal" or "close up" (*ḥātam*) human beings. NIV's translation stays relatively close to the Hebrew: "he [God] *stops* every man from his labor." Verse 8, likely a parallel statement with reference to animals, provides some clarification. Just as animals seek shelter in their dens when the winter storms arrive, so human beings retreat to the sanctuary of their homes when the weather becomes too severe to carry on with their normal labors. [No More Than "a Passing Glimpse"]

Beyond the frustrating obliqueness of these verses, two aspects of what they contribute to Elihu's view of the world invite reflection. First, Elihu's description of the world is strategically positioned as a segue to God's own summons to Job to look at the world and learn what it has

---

Textual Difficulties in 36:33

AΩ Although the first line of 36:33 is clear, the second is not. The MT reads literally, "the cattle also [tell] of the one coming up" (cf. NIV). The imagery suggests that (even the) cattle can sense the coming storms and instinctively take advantage of the warning to protect themselves. If the text is correct, then it anticipates what Elihu will say in 37:8 concerning the animals that seek shelter from the severity of the winter storms.

A number of translators have thought it better to emend the second line, presumably to offer a closer parallel to the first line. NRSV, for example, emends the word "cattle" (*miqneh*) to "jealousy" (from the verbal root *qn'*) and reads the word "coming up" (*ôleh*) to mean "iniquity" (*'awlāh*).

For a discussion of the problems and possibilities, see, for example, R. Gordis, *The Book of Job. Commentary, New Translation, and Special Studies* (New York: Jewish Theological Seminary of America, 1978), 423-24; E. Dhorme, *A Commentary on the Book of Job* (Nashville: Thomas Nelson, 1984), 557-58; M. Pope, *Job* (AB; Garden City NY: Doubleday & Company, 1965), 276-77.

"He Who Learns Must Suffer"

📖 It is God's law that he who learns must suffer. And even in our sleep, pain that cannot forget, falls drop by drop upon the heart, and in our own despite, against our will, comes wisdom to us by the awful grace of God. (Aeschylus)

No More than "a Passing Glimpse"

I often see the flowers from a passing car
That are gone before I can tell what they
are.

I want to get out of the train and go back
To see what they were beside the track.

I name all the flowers I am sure they weren't:
Not fireweed loving where woods have burnt—

Not bluebirds gracing a tunnel mouth—
Not lupine living on sand and drought.

Was something brushed across my mind
That no one on earth will ever find?

Heaven gives its glimpses only to those
Not in position to look too close.

R. Frost, "A Passing Glimpse," *The Poetry of Robert Frost*, 248.

to teach him about God's moral governance. Unlike Elihu, however, God will direct Job's attention not only to meteorological phenomena (38:19-38), but also specifically and with detail to the world of animals (38:39–39:30). Second, in contrast to Elihu, who suggests that animals (and humans) instinctively seek to escape difficult or unpleasant conditions, God invites Job to consider that while some animals may seek refuge from the forces of nature, others like Behemoth and Leviathan (40:15–41:34) instinctively delight, with God's approval, in confronting and besting the challenge.

The assessment of the differences in the world as Elihu sees it and the world as God sees it must await our consideration of the so-called whirlwind speeches that comprise the next chapter in this book. One preliminary observation may be offered. In Elihu's world, creation summons human beings to praise, while they hide from the danger a Creator's power presents. [God's "Perturbless Plan"] In God's world, some creatures (and perhaps some human beings who may learn from them) can only thrive and celebrate life when they have the chance to wrest from creation's challenges a place to stand that gives purpose and meaning to their existence.

Application to Job: Rhetorical Questions and Certain Answers, 37:14-24

With a final summons to "hear this," now specifically addressed to Job, Elihu uses a series of rhetorical questions (vv. 14-20), clearly imitative

God's "Perturbless Plan"

It's easy to invent a Life—
God does it—every Day—
Creation—but the Gambol
Of His Authority—

It's easy to efface it—
The thrifty Deity
Could scarce afford Eternity
To Spontaneity—

The Perished Patterns murmur—
But His Perturbless Plan
Proceed—inserting Here—a Sun—
There—leaving out a Man—

E. Dickinson, "#724," ed. T. H. Johnson, *The Complete Poems of Emily Dickinson* (Boston/New York: Little, Brown and Company, 1960), 355.

of those God will also soon ask, to solicit the praise he believes God is owed. Does Job know how to make lightning erupt from the clouds (v. 15)? Does Job know how to coerce rain's coolness from the clouds when the south winds of summer scorch the earth (vv. 16-17)? Can he spread out the primordial firmament, then hammer in metal-like windows, so that clouds have a chance to do what clouds do (v. 18)? The only answer to these questions that will conform to Elihu's creation theology is for Job to say, "No, I can do none of these things; only God can. When Elihu asks his last question (vv. 19-20)— Can any human being inform the Creator of the world by trying to answer these questions?—can the invitation to respond be anything other than sarcastic?

The transition to the response Elihu seeks from Job is signaled by the words "and now" (*we'attāh*), which introduce vv. 21-24. He returns to his preoccupation with "light" (*'ôr*), which has repeatedly been his cipher for "lightning" (36:30, 32; 37:3, 11, 15). Now the referent shifts to the sun, whose brilliant rays provide the grammar that bespeaks God's "golden splendor" shining forth from the north. [CD: God's Home in the North] The point of the metaphor is this: One can no more stare at the sun without damaging one's vision, than stand before the awesome glory of God without averting one's eyes. For a final time, Elihu insists that this display of divine power is purposeful, not arbitrary. It is a speech-act that spells out God's hopes and expectations for the world with the words "justice" (*mišpāṭ*) and "righteousness" (*ṣĕdāqāh*; v. 23).

Elihu's last words announce the "therefore" that brings his speech to its long awaited close. Mortals should "fear" (NIV: "revere") God (v. 24a). The meaning of the line is clear and no doubt also strategically placed, for it effectively invites Job to return to an answer he has already seriously considered: "Truly, the fear of the Lord, that is wisdom" (28:28). Given the many obscurities in Elihu's speech thus far, however, we should not be surprised to find that the second half of v. 24 adds yet one more. The Hebrew is, "He [God] does not see any who are wise of heart." Because the phrase "wise of heart" is typically used with a positive meaning (e.g., Prov 10:8; 11:29; 16:21), the idea that God should have no regard for such persons has seemed odd to many. The LXX remedies the problem by reading the negative as an asseverative, "surely, indeed," and taking "wise of heart" to be the subject of the verb rather than its object: "indeed, all the wise of heart see him." A variety of other emendations have been proposed, almost all of them aimed at correcting or avoiding what the MT seems to say. [Alternate Translations]

Alternate Translations

AΩ Therefore men are in awe of Him
Whom none of the wise can perceive. (NJPS)

Therefore mortals pay him reverence,
and all who are wise fear him. (REB)

No wonder, then, that everyone
is awed by him,
and that he ignores those who claim to be wise. (TEV)

Therefore men revere him,
though none can see him, however
wise their hearts. (NAB)

Therefore, men revere him,
for does he not have regard for all the wise in
heart? (NIV)

The safest approach would be to acknowledge that the text is awkward, perhaps corrupt, and simply let it go at that. Nonetheless, it is interesting to speculate on what Elihu might be saying, if the MT has correctly preserved his last words. If Elihu is inviting Job to reconsider his words concerning wisdom, then perhaps he is also aware that Job has used the expression "wise of heart" in 9:4a: "He [God] is wise in heart and mighty in strength." Job's affirmation of God's wisdom and strength is properly deferential; taken at face value, it presumably conforms to Elihu's expectations. But Job's affirmation is offered in the context of his contemplation of taking God to court for an indefensible misuse of divine wisdom and power (9:1-10:22). As far as he can see, the response owed a guilty God is to complain, not praise. Thus, he follows his affirmation of God's putative virtues with a question that he feels compelled to explore, even if Elihu will not: "Who has resisted him, and succeeded?" (9:4b; cf. Elihu's "rhetorical" questions in 36:22-25; 37:14-20). Further, if Elihu has indeed listened carefully to all that Job has said, then he should know that Job's assertion that the pursuit of wisdom begins and ends with "fear" or "reverence" for God leaves him far short of the submissive praise Elihu wants to hear. If anything, Job's affirmation at the end of chapter 28 signals his resolve to pursue the questions he first raises in chapters 9–10, not to turn away from them (see the commentary and "Connections" at Job 28).

If Elihu has all Job's musings concerning wisdom in mind when he closes out his last speech, then perhaps the affirmation that "God has no regard for mortals who claim (or pursue) wisdom" should not be emended after all. In Elihu's world, perhaps this is in fact the last and best word that those who fancy themselves as God's privileged mediators of truth can offer to Job. ["A Man Said to the Universe"]

"A Man Said to the Universe"

A man said to the universe:
"Sir, I exist!"
"However," replied the universe,
"The fact has not created in me
A sense of obligation."

Stephen Crane, "War is Kind and Other Lines: XXI," *The Oxford Book of Short Poems*, ed. P. Kavanagh, J. Michie (New York: Oxford University Press, 1985), 177.

CONNECTIONS

The last speech of Elihu invites our assessment of his contribution to this book. To be sure, readers and commentators alike often conclude that Elihu adds little that is new to what has already been said. Some single out for special attention his defense of suffering as redemptive (33:19-22), but most credit him with little more than simply smoothing over the ragged edges of arguments already advanced by the friends. Almost everyone notes that Elihu's last speech sets the table for God's climatic appearance at the end of the book, and while this no doubt heightens our expectation, Elihu's words are widely regarded as but a poor imitation of the divine speeches; they are not only disappointing but also irritating. By almost any conventional assessment, therefore, Elihu's contribution to what the friends have already said and what God will say seems to add up to nothing more that surplus and redundancy.

We began this survey of Elihu's speeches by accepting Newsom's invitation to approach them with a "deliberately generous curiosity." Such an approach, Newsom suggests, requires that we suspend endorsement of the conventional assessment long enough to consider another question: Might Elihu's words be what he claims they are—"a genuine contribution to and enrichment of the dialogue"?[16] Newsom's question provides the compass that has charted the course for much of the preceding commentary on the separate units of Elihu's speech, including their respective "Connections." We have paused along the way to reflect on a number of loose threads that we may now attempt to weave into the tapestry of an answer to her question.

These last "Connections" begin where Elihu's speeches begin. He has stepped into this story, either because the narrator who speaks through him is angry about what has passed for truth in the debate thus far (32:1-5), or because he is a full-fledged fictionalized character whose convictions are so unsettled by what he has heard that he overcomes a genuine timidity that might otherwise preclude his speaking at all (32:6-22). In either case, we must hear him as a "belated reader/listener to this debate. Job's story existed before he came on the scene. Its issues did not initially address him. While the world that shapes his values and needs is contiguous with the world that shaped the text, it is also different from it.

Just how and why Elihu's world is different depends on the dating of his speeches. Almost everyone agrees that chapters 32–37 are late additions to the text. The evidence available strongly suggests a post-exilic setting, perhaps one more specifically connected with late Persian and early Hellenistic periods (see the commentary at 32:1-5). Although certainty eludes us, we may safely assume that the religious, cultural, and political supports for God's palpable presence, once secured by seemingly inviolable promises, are now but distant memories. We should not be surprised, therefore, that Elihu sifts through the whole of the story before him in order to select specific issues that require attention if they are to be meaningfully transported into his world.

• He accents former convictions about God's indisputable sovereignty, now clouded by the reality of foreign rulers who exercise political control over Israel, with new affirmations of God's irresistible power and might (36:5, 22; 37:22-24).

• He buttresses former certainties about God's moral governance of the world, now called into question by the undeniable injustices the righteous suffer without redress, with new assertions promising the wicked cannot hide from God's punishment (34:10-30).

• He reclaims former beliefs about God's readiness to respond to the sufferer's cry for help, now thinned out from far too many experiences of prolonged silence, by inscribing both God's silence and human suf-

The Book of Job Without Job?

Yehuda Amichai (1924–2000) is a Jewish poet whose love of God found expression in thick irony and thinly veiled skepticism. The poem below speaks of the temptation to filter from the Bible the sediments that may be unwelcomed, unwanted, or simply unimportant for what passes for peace of mind in the present world. When it comes to the book of Job, Amichai suggests, some might well prefer to preserve the book by losing the voice of the one who lent it its name.

From the Book of Esther I filtered the sediment
of vulgar joy, and from the Book of Jeremiah
the howl of pain in the guts. And from
the Song of Songs the endless
search for love, and from Genesis the dreams
and Cain, and from Ecclesiastes
the despair, and from the book of Job: Job.
And with what was left, I pasted myself a new
    Bible.
Now I lived censored and pasted and limited
    and in peace.

A woman asked me last night on the dark
    street
how another woman was
who'd already died. Before her time—and not
In anyone's else's time either.
Out of a great weariness I answered,
"She's fine, she's fine."

Y. Amichai, "From the Book of Esther I Filtered the Sediment," *The Selected Poetry of Yehuda Amichai: Newly Revised and Expanded Edition*, ed. and trans. from the Hebrew by C. Bloch and S. Mitchell (Berkeley, Los Angeles: University of California Press, 1996), 124.

fering into a purposive divine revelatory process. Suffering provides the assurance that God is trying to teach prideful persons a lesson: to save their lives, they must confess their sin (33:14-20). God's silence in the face of petitions for relief is the painful but necessary reminder that the lesson has not yet been learned (35:5-13).

The friends, who have listened to Job's complaints, have tried to import answers from their world into his. Elihu has listened in, and he can see where their answers fail to address satisfactorily both Job's world and his. As a belated reader and interpreter, he has the advantage of twenty-twenty hindsight. In this regard, he is like all readers of this book. He has both the possibility and the burden of recalibrating the truth of this "book" in order to address the demands of the world in which he lives. Toward that end, he reads what has been said, and offers clarifications, modifications, and where necessary, corrections that translate old convictions into words that speak to new audiences. [The Book of Job Without Job?]

Elihu's "contribution" to this story crystallizes in the summons to praise recorded in chapters 36–37. Elihu is not the first speaker in this book to suggest that praise is the antidote to suffering, nor will he be the last. Eliphaz has already modeled for Job the praise he would offer God, should suffering ever tempt him to other responses (5:8-16). Like Elihu, he would sing of God's wondrous acts in creating and sustaining the world, for the God who sends the rain to replenish the dry land is the same God who saves the needy when they falter (5:10-11; cf. 36:26-28; 37:6-12). If Job will only trust this God, then he can happily join his voice to Eliphaz's choir. Elihu has heard this summons to praise, and he no doubt agrees with Eliphaz about its importance for the Jobs of the world. But he seems to think that Eliphaz has missed an opportunity to capitalize on its promise. Eliphaz wants Job to submit to his teaching, as if the mere summons to praise conveys its own persuasion. Elihu wants Job to gaze upon the beauty of God's world and submit to its wonder. Where Eliphaz's discourse is argumentative and rational, Elihu's is contemplative and aesthetic.[17] Like the casual tourist in a gallery filled with beautiful pictures, Eliphaz stops briefly to look at the rain, then moves on to other things. By contrast, Elihu is mesmerized by the rain and so captivated by the larger canvases of related natural phenomena (thunder, lightning, winds, snow, ice, clouds) that he loses himself in reflection. For him, praise is not something that one can be reasoned into; it is a near unutterable gratitude that leaves one fumbling for words.

Newsom has suggested that the template for Elihu's praise is the sapiential nature hymn. While this genre is present in various places within the Old Testament (e.g., Pss 104, 148), the attention to detail that characterizes Elihu's praise to the Lord of nature is perhaps best exemplified by the hymn in Sirach 42:15-43:33.[18] [Sirach 42:15–43:33 and Job 36:27–37:13] When Elihu appropriates this genre, Newsom notes that he is doing more than merely modeling a way of speaking. He is invoking a way of perceiving the world that cultivates a sense of wonder. This observation leads in turn to an important question: What is "the moral significance of wonder" in the life of faith? Newsom offers three discernments: (1) contemplating the wonder of *God's* creation requires

---

Sirach 42:15–43:33 and Job 36:27–37:13

ΑΩ Newsom cautions against reading Ben Sira *into* Job indiscriminately. Nevertheless, she notes a number of general and particular connections that suggest these two texts are invoking the same hymnic genre. The list below does not do justice to the details of her argument, but it will suffice as an overview:

	Sirach	**Job**
Summons to praise	42:15	36:24
Substantiation of praise with *kî* ("for," "because") clause	43:5, 11, etc.	36:27
Recognition that adequate knowledge of God's wonders is impossible	42:16-17; 43:28-29	36:24-26
Attention to cosmological (heavens, sun, moon) and meteorological phenomena (thunder, lightning, wind, rain, snow, ice, clouds)	43:1-22	36:27-33; 37:1-13
Affirmation of creation's moral purposiveness	42:23-25; 43:6, 23	36:31-33; 37:13

Newsom notes that commentators typically analyze the details and the imagery of Elihu's summons to praise the Lord of nature, sometimes recognizing the parallels with Sirach, but do not pay enough attention to how the genre *shapes* and is *shaped by* the world of the speakers who invoke such praise. Her discernments deserve to be quoted in full:

... genres are not just forms of speech but also forms of thought. To invoke a genre is to invoke a way of perceiving the world, a way of arranging values, and a particular stance or set of dispositions. As a way of framing a situation, a genre has a rhetorical and even an ideological force. One must not forget, however, that there are no such things as pure types. Texts invoke or participate in genres, often several at once; they do not belong to them. And with every instantiation of a genre, the performance adds to and thus modifies the generic repertoire, changing the contours of what passes for that genre. (221)

C. Newsom, *The Book of Job: A Contest of Moral Imaginations* (Oxford: Oxford University Press, 2003), 220-33. For a summary of the comparisons, see 228-29.

that we not be self-absorbed by *our* needs; (2) to experience awe and wonder opens us to an encounter with something *other* than ourselves; even things or persons that are familiar may be experienced as new and surprising; and (3) the "gaze of wonder" neutralizes, at least temporarily, the natural inclination to look at the world as if it is primarily designed for our benefit; in sum, "what is gazed upon is seen in its essential goodness."[19] Each of these discernments offers a possible response to the larger question that frames these "Connections." Does Elihu's summons to praise, his invitation to contemplate the wonder of God's creation, make a genuine contribution to this story?

Before finalizing an answer to this question, we should note that Elihu seeks not only to improve upon what Eliphaz *has already said*. As a belated reader who has considered carefully the words of everyone who speaks in this book, he also seems to be trying to improve upon, or at least clarify, what he knows God *will say*. Presumably he knows that God will soon also invite Job to gaze upon the beauty and mystery of the world around him. Given the transmission history of the book, in fact, it is likely that Elihu (or his author) takes his cue from God; both his attentiveness to the intricacies of nature (36:26–37:13) and his use of rhetorical questions to solicit the response he seeks (37:14-20) are imitative of the divine speeches.

A comparison of what evokes Elihu's "gaze of wonder" and the wonder that God seeks to cultivate in Job is instructive. God invites Job to ponder the cosmic boundaries (38:4-18), the meteorological phenomena (38:19-38), and then a variety of creatures from the animal kingdom—some wild, some domesticated (38:39–39:30)—and two —Behemoth and Leviathan (40:15–41:34)—whose extraordinary power, pride, and dominion require Job's special consideration. Both the substance and the tenor of this panoramic review suggest a certain divine mesmerization, as if God, stepping back from the world that God has created, is now enthralled by the wonder of it all. Will Job see what God sees? Will Job be moved, like God is moved, to celebrate the full range of possibilities the world offers? ["Where, Where in Heaven Am I?"]

Elihu's "Ode to Creation" *adds* to the wonder of God's world by *subtracting* from its reality. There is almost no place in Elihu's world for creatures, animal or human. To find them, one must look for the places where they hide (37:7-8). Huddled together in dens and homes, they offer cowered praise to the God whose awesome power seems far more threatening than inviting. Perhaps, given Elihu's reading of creation's grammar, all creatures should be glad to have at least a place to hide. And perhaps in his world, cowering praise is better than no praise at all. But we may ask whether Elihu's summons to wonder does not seek to manage the complexity of God's world by resorting to simplification. [Without Human Beings, Is Anything Possible?] Is a world without creaturely wild-

ness and tameness the world that God celebrates? Is God enthralled with a world that has
no place for creaturely power and pride?
Newsom invites us to frame our answers to these
questions by pondering them not only with
Elihu's "gaze of wonder" but also with Job's eyes,
reddened and darkened by anguish (16:16). Can
Elihu's world "be properly *urged upon* a person
in pain?" Can it "properly be *spoken* by a person
in pain?" Is the displacement of everything else
save a sense of wonder ever "adequate to the
moral demand posed by the presence of Job in
his pain"?[20]

At several points along the way in the commentary on chapters 36-37, we have noted that
Elihu's last words offer a rhetorical invitation to
return to the prologue. There, another of God's
advocates assumed responsibility for mediating
between divine intentions and human aspirations, speaking to and for God on the one hand,
assessing human fidelity on the other. Now, after
159 verses, Elihu completes his role as the self-
appointed "Answerer" who speaks for God and
to Job. If Elihu (or his author) intended his
words to advance the *dialogue*, then in at least
one respect he has failed, for he has neither
invited nor received any response from Job. The
world Elihu envisions is a "soliloquizing world,"
a world of "blocked conversation," where one
person commands the stage while all other participants in the drama become silent listeners.[21]
When Elihu finally brings down the curtain on
his soliloquy, we may wonder not only whether
there is any room for Job to respond. We might
also ask if there is any room for God. After all,
the prologue launches this drama with a question from God that seems
intent on receiving an answer from someone: "Have you considered my
servant Job?" (1:8). [CD: A "Voyeur of His Own Weary Clarities"?]

"Where, Where in Heaven Am I?"

The clouds, the source or rain, one stormy night
Offered an opening to the source of dew;
Which I accepted with impatient sight,
Looking for my old sky-marks in the blue.
But stars were scarce in that part of the sky,
And no two were of the same constellation—
No one was bright of enough to identify;
So 'twas with not ungrateful consternation,

Seeing myself well lost once more, I sighed,
"Where, where in Heaven am I? But don't tell me!
O opening clouds, by opening on me wide,
Let's let my heavenly lostness overwhelm me."

R. Frost, "Lost in Heaven," *The Poetry of Robert Frost*, ed. E. C. Lathem (New York: Henry Holt and Company, 1969), 295-96.

Without Human Beings, Is Anything Possible?

Dostoevsky's *The Brother's Karamazov* provides perhaps the most trenchant cri-
tique in modern literature of conventional theodicies. As his character Ivan effectively argues, "If God does not exist, everything is per-
mitted." Elihu's argument, which preserves the orderliness of God's creation by effectively removing unruly human beings like Job from the equation, invites, perhaps inadvertently, an inversion of the question: without human beings, whether unruly or not, is anything God hopes to achieve in the world really possible?

Job's presenting question in 7:17—"What are human beings, that you [God] make so much of them?"—lingers still over this drama, even if there is no place for it in Elihu's world.

F. Dostoevsky, *The Brothers Karamazov* (New York: Bantam Books, 1981). For a representative selection of Ivan's arguments related to this matter, see bk. 2, ch. 6, p. 80; bk. 2, ch. 7, p. 95; bk. 5, ch. 4, p. 291; bk. 5, ch. 5, p. 317; bk. 11, ch. 4, p. 708

NOTES

[1] C. Newsom, "The Book of Job," in vol. 4 of *NIB* (Nashville: Abingdon Press, 1996), 583.
[2] Cf. N. Habel, *The Book of Job: A Commentary* (OTL; Philadelphia: Westminster Press, 1985), 507.

[3] The Hebrew text at 36:12a is literally, "If they do not listen, *they will cross the channel*" (NRSV: "But if they do listen, *they shall perish by the sword*"). The word translated "channel" likely refers to the "river of death" that marks the passage to the netherworld (cf. 33:18). For alternatives to NRSV, see REB, TEV, and NIV (marginal note).

[4] The Hebrew of 36:14b is literally, "they live their lives among prostitutes (*qĕdišîm*)." The word *qĕdišîm* normally refers to "temple prostitutes," men and women who earn their keep by making themselves available, under the regulatory controls identified with Canaanite fertility cults, for sexual liaisons that were believed to influence the deity. Although likely only a caricature of Canaanite religion, there is no doubt the practice was widely condemned in Israel (e.g., Deut 23:17-18; 1 Kgs 14:24; 15:12; 2 Kgs 23:7). For further reading, see K. van der Toorn, "Prostitution (Cultic)," *ABD*, ed. D. N. Freedman (New York: Doubleday, 1992), vol. 5, 510-13.

[5] For the range of proposals, see, for example, E. Dhorme, *A Commentary on the Book of Job* (Nashville: Thomas Nelson Publishers, 1967), 545; R. Gordis, *The Book of Job: Commentary, New Translation, and Special Studies* (New York: Jewish Theological Seminary of America, 1978), 415-16; S. R. Driver and G. B. Gray, *A Critical and Exegetical Commentary on the Book of Job* (Edinburgh: T and T. Clark, 1921), 277.

[6] Cf. E. M. Good, *In Turns of Tempest: A Reading of Job with a Translation* (Stanford: Stanford University Press, 1990), 151; Habel, *Book of Job*, 509.

[7] So, Gordis: "But you did not plead the cause of the poor or the suit of the orphan" (*The Book of Job*, 416); cf. Pope: "the orphan's justice you belied" (*Job* [AB; Garden City NY: Doubleday, 1979], 267).

[8] Cf. Driver and Gray, *Book of Job*, 313.

[9] Cf. Newsom's comments: "By. . . urging Job to speak the words of praise that all people sing (v. 24), Elihu attempts to silence Job's alienated voice and reintegrate him into the collective voice of universal praise" ("The Book of Job," 589).

[10] Cf. Whal, *Der gerechte Schöpfer*, 119, n. 157.

[11] Cf. Dhorme, *Commentary on the Book of Job*, 551. For further reading on the semantic range of the verb *paqad*, see W. Schottroff, "*pqd*, to visit," in E. Jenni, C. Westermann, *TLOT*, vol. 2, trans. M. E. Biddle (Peabody MS: Hendrikson Publishers, 1997), 1018-31.

[12] Habel, *Book of Job*, 510.

[13] For the suggestion that 36:26–37:24 can be structured as strophes or stanzas in a hymn, see L. Perdue, *Wisdom in Revolt: Metaphorical Theology in the book of Job* (JSOTSup 112; Sheffield: JSOT Press, 1991), 255-57.

[14] Cf. Pope, *Job*, 283; F. I. Anderson, *Job: An Introduction and Commentary* (TOTC; Downers Grove IL: Inter-Varsity, 1976), 266; Newsom, "The Book of Job," 591.

[15] On the rhetorical importance of meteorological imagery in Elihu's speech, see Habel, *Book of Job*, 504.

[16] C. Newsom, *The Book of Job: A Contest of Moral Imaginations* (Oxford: Oxford University Press, 2003), 201.

[17] Ibid., 231-32.

[18] Ibid., 220-33.

[19] Ibid., 226.

[20] Ibid., 232 (emphasis added).

[21] I borrow these suggestive terms from James Wood, who observes that Shakespeare uses soliloquy to enable his characters to indulge in rambling streams of consciousness that ostensibly serve to tell the audience what they need to know. Wood notes, however, that soliloquies serve more than the technical demands of the theater. They also allow both the character and the playwright to remind the audience and themselves that they exist ("Shakespeare and the Pathos of Rambling," *The Irresponsible Self: On Laughter and the Novel* [New York: Farrar, Straus and Giroux, 2004], 33).

GOD'S FIRST ANSWER, JOB'S FIRST RESPONSE

Job 38:1–40:5

God's Answer from the Whirlwind and Job's Response, Job 38:1–42:6

The last time God spoke in this drama was in the prologue: "Very well, he is in your power" (2:6a). With these unsettling words, God handed Job over to the *satan* to do with him as he would. The "fence" (1:10) of divine blessing that once protected Job's world collapses. A porous caveat—"only spare his life" (2:6b)—now leaves God's servant vulnerable to undeserved pain and suffering. In the wake of God's last words, Job has blessed (1:21; cf. 2:10), cursed (3:3-10), and plunged into the abyss of lament's anguished question "Why?" (3:11, 12, 20). Eliphaz, Bildad, and Zophar have offered their answers; Job has refused them. Elihu has corrected the flaws he finds in the friends' answers with his own twenty-twenty hindsight; Job has not responded, his silence a loud declaration that Elihu's answers are no more adequate than anything he has already heard. The answers he yearns for reside with a God he cannot find (23:3). The wisdom he needs to understand why this God is silent is beyond his grasp (28:12, 20). To God's last words in the prologue, Job adds his own last words: "Let the Almighty answer me" (31:35). It is a bold and desperate challenge for God to come out of hiding. If God does not respond, then Job will be forced to conclude that the answers he seeks, like the God he has relentlessly pursued, are nowhere to be found.

["Religion Was a Night-light for Children"]

The words "Then the Lord answered Job out of the whirlwind" (38:1) introduce the answer that Job and we readers have now long awaited. The outline of God's answer is clear. God has two speeches (38:1–39:30; 40:1-34 [MT: 41:26]); Job offers two responses (40:3-5;

> **"Religion Was a Night-light for Children"**
>
> When the discussions and debates between Job and his friends end, Job remains desperately in search of answers for why he suffers so that seem beyond his grasp. His fate and his ebbing faith resonate with Andrew Miller's description of Alice, whose bout with terminal cancer eats away at her every last hope:
>
> The last of her faith had ebbed away during the chemo. A night on her knees by the side of the bed vomiting into a bucket, and above her just miles of emptiness. No gentle Jesus. No saints or angels. Religion was a night-light for children.
>
> A. Miller, *Oxygen* (New York: Harcourt, Inc., 2001), 75.

42:1-6). Both divine speeches begin with the same narrative introduction (38:1; 40:6). In both, God challenges Job to "gird up his loins" and answer questions (38:3; 40:7-14). In the first speech, the questions cluster around the theme of God's "counsel" or "plan" for the world (38:2: *ʿēṣā*), which is then developed with specific attention to the cosmic boundaries (38:4-18), meteorological phenomena (38:19-38), and five pairs of animals (38:39–39:30). In the second speech, the questions focus on God's governance of the world (40:8: *mišpāṭ*), with particular attention to a sixth and final pair of animals, Behemoth (40:9-15) and Leviathan (41:1-34 [MT: 40:25–41:26]). Following the first speech, God specifically invites Job once again to respond (40:1-2). He does so by saying "I am small," then placing his hand over his mouth to indicate that he will speak no further (40:3-5). God's second speech ends without repeating the request for response. Job answers nonetheless, this time with an enigmatic statement of what he now knows and sees about God and about himself (42:1-6). [Structure of Job 38:1–42:6]

God's appearance initiates the last dialogue the book of Job records. From a purely rhetorical standpoint, the balance between God's answers and Job's responses is clearly uneven: God speaks for 123 verses, Job for but nine. Nonetheless, the exchange between these two brings heaven and earth together around the ash heap of human suffering. From Job's perspective, and no doubt from ours as well, it is a conversation fraught with enormous importance and consequence. What is at stake, as J. Hempel suggested, is nothing less than the search by the Jobs of the world for "the last truth about God."[1]

With so much riding on the interpretation of these speeches, it is certainly a frustration, to say the least, to find that their "last truth" remains elusive. What exactly does God's answer teach Job? What do Job's responses disclose about what he has learned? Many commentators, noting that the divine speeches blatantly avoid Job's basic "Why" questions, have concluded that God's answers are no less *evasive* and no less *irritating* than those of all Job's friends. What do words about snow, rain, ice, clouds, and ostriches have to do with Job's suffering? As Clifford Edwards observes, "One is tempted to paraphrase God as saying, 'I may not be much at psychology and human relations, but I am great at meteorology and zoology.'"[2] What do creatures like Behemoth and Leviathan have to do with Job's quest for divine justice? William Safire's quip may be more colorful than others, but it speaks for many, including some highly regarded theologians:

It is as if God appears in a tie-dyed T-shirt emblazoned with the words "Because I'm God, That's Why." The gist of the stormy answer he blew at

Structure of Job 38:1–42:6

I. *God's First Speech: The "Design" of the Cosmos (38:1–40:2)*	***Job's First Response (40:3-5)***
A. Narrative introduction: "Then the Lord answered Job out of the whirlwind" (38:1)	"I am small" (40:4)
Thematic question: "Who is this that darkens counsel . . . without knowledge?" (38:2)	"I have spoken once . . . but will proceed no further" (40:5)
Imperative challenge: "Gird up your loins . . . I will question you, and you shall declare to me" (38:3)	
B. Development of theme 1. The cosmic boundaries (38:4-18) 2. Meteorological phenomena (38:19-38) 3. The animal kingdom (38:39–39:30)	
C. Second invitation to respond (40:1-2)	
II. *God's Second Speech: God's Just Governance of the Cosmos (40:6–41:34 [MT: 41:26])*	***Job's Second Response (42:1-6)***
A. Narrative introduction: "Then the Lord answered Job out of the whirlwind" (40:6)	"I know that you can do all things . . ." (42:2)
Imperative challenge: "Gird up your loins . . . I will question you, and you declare to me" (40:7)	"I had heard . . . but now my eye sees you . . ." (42:5)
Thematic questions: "Will you discredit my justice?" (NIV; 40:8-14)	"therefore I . . ." (42:6)
B. Development of theme 1. Behemoth (40:15-24) 2. Leviathan (41:1-34 [MT: 40:25–41:26])	
God = 123 verses	**Job = 9 verses**

Cf. V. Kubina, *Die Gottesreden im Buche Hiob* (Freiburger theologische Studien 115; Freiburg: Herder, 1979), 121.

Job was fairly summed up by hell-and-brimstone preacher John Calvin in five words: "Who are you to ask?"[3]

Other interpreters discern more substantive answers in what God says, but a survey of the commentary literature makes clear that there is little or no agreement on what these answers are. At one end of the spectrum, some argue that simply by answering Job, whatever that answer may be, God proves that God never forgets or abandons the suffering person.[4] On the other end of the spectrum, some who risk defining God's answer argue that the lesson Job must learn is that God is not confined by human standards of justice. As M. Tzevat puts it, "The God who speaks to man in the book of Job is neither just nor

The Spectrum of Possibilities

L. Perdue offers a representative listing of the major proposals. For the bibliography that supports the various possibilities, readers may consult his notes.

1. Although there is chaos in the world, God acts with freedom to sustain justice in creation and history.
2. God's actions in the world are paradoxical: he nurtures but limits Yam ["the sea"], checks the power of death by the recurring cycle of birth, and feeds the offspring of eagles with the dead flesh of other creatures. In a world of paradoxes, Job's speeches rooted in retribution make no sense and thus are dismissed. Paradox is overcome by community with God.
3. Reality is amoral, while God transcends human standards of justice. Retribution as a vehicle for the operation of God and creation is rejected. Piety is either unrewarded or does not exist.
4. While God's darker side has created evil, he acts to constrain its destructive effects. However, God is limited in power and unable to eradicate evil from the earth.
5. God's wisdom and justice transcends human comprehension. Efforts to impugn divine justice are sheer folly.
6. God's sovereignty as Creator and Lord of history is upheld, leading to the rejection of false questioning and the proper response of confession and praise.
7. The blustery attack by God reveals that he is a capricious, chaotic, and even jealous tyrant whose abuse of power leads to Job's proper renunciation.
8. Creation is nihilistic, possessing no meaning in and of itself. Yet in coming as savior, God offers a new creation.

L. Perdue, *Wisdom in Revolt: Metaphorical Theology in the Book of Job* (JSOTSup 112; Sheffield: JSOT Press, 1991), 197-98.

---

unjust. He is God."[5] [The Spectrum of Possibilities] Still others argue that the "irreducible ambiguities" in the divine speeches are an important clue for Job and all who seek simple, propositional answers to complex questions.[6] When the question has to do with innocent suffering, "*no answer*" may be *the* answer we need to hear from God, even if it is difficult to accept. ["There Is One Thing Worse Than Giving an Answer"]

I am persuaded that L. Alonso-Schökel is correct when he says that every assessment of the meaning of the divine speeches depends on the expectations the interpreter brings to the text.[7] The dynamics of the book require God to intervene, but what do we *expect*—and, we might add, *need*—to happen when God does so? If our expectations and needs align with the friends, then we will be looking for confirmation that Job is wrong: wrong to have claimed innocence before a righteous God; wrong to have refused the discipline of suffering from a God trying to save him; wrong to have challenged God's justice; wrong to have assumed that the Creator of the world owes him an explanation for anything. We will likely find what we are looking for in the suggestion that when God speaks, Job

"There Is One Thing Worse Than Giving an Answer"

In his biography of G. K. Chesterton, Gary Wills adds an appendix that addresses Chesterton's imaginative but baffling Joban parable, *The Man Who Was Thursday* (1907). With commentary that applies both to the end of Chesterton's novel and to the conclusion of its biblical model, Wills offers the following assessment:

[T]here is one thing worse than giving no answer. And that is to give an answer. That would turn God into a theologian, reducing Jehovah to the level of Job's friends. The author of God's speeches in the book of Job is the first person we know of to realize that the only theology worth having is the one that forswears theodicy. The riddling rabbi in the whirlwind obviously has answers, but not any small enough to dispense . . . . Any of God's things is a secret too deep to be fathomed—though Job is rewarded for trying. Because he is the best of God's things.

G. Wills, *Chesterton*, 2nd ed. (New York: Doubleday, 2001), 289.

is first reduced to silence (40:5), then transformed by repentance (42:6). On the other hand, if we have sympathy for Job, we will be looking for some sign that his quest for comfort and consolation is important to God. However extreme Job's words may be, we expect and need God to value those who must speak pain in order to be faithful. From this perspective, we will nod in agreement when God addresses Job by name, when God invites him into a dialogue, however uneven the conversation may be, when God shows him mysteries of the world that few can ever see or imagine.

Between Job and the friends, it is easy to side with Job. Whatever may be the merits of the friends' arguments, they come across as religious ideologues. They are caricatures of persons who care more about being right in their own eyes than being compassionate toward others who challenge their truth. Few readers will find them worthy models for faith. With the friends now removed from center stage, the divine speeches require a recalibration of our expectations. *Between God and Job,* where should we take our stand?[8] To frame the question in either/or terms may seem foolish. Who would side *with* Job, if it means that we must be *against* God? Indeed, God seems to challenge Job in 40:8 to concede that once the issue is framed in such either/or terms, there can be little doubt about the outcome. Before we dismiss the possibility out of hand, however, we should pause to consider whether *our* expectations concerning God's stance towards Job are the same as *God's* expectations of Job's (and our) stance before the Creator of the world. Is it *God* who expects Job to conform to a certain predetermined answer, or *we readers* who expect *and need* this story to confirm that God is a certain kind of God? Much depends, as Alonso-Schökel says, on whether our expectations are open or closed:

> Closed expectation digs out a channel in advance, and refuses to accept any dénouement which follows a different channel. Open expectation looks in a particular direction, but is prepared to do a detour in order to follow the way out suggested by the text. In the first type of expectation, because the author's final response (through the mouth of one of his characters) does not fit in with my preconceptions, I either reject it, or criticise it, or select what I want from it. In the second type of expectation, although the author chooses a route I was not expecting and so at first disorients me, I nevertheless try to follow him and discover where his trail is leading.[9]

The following preliminary observations mark out areas where the text invites readers to keep their expectations open. The first three address the style or the rhetoric of the divine speeches, that is, *how* God speaks when addressing Job. The last addresses the substance of the speeches, that is, *what* God says. In each instance, a case can be made that a good deal of the commentary on these speeches has tended toward closed expectations, either by ignoring possible detours the text suggests or by determining that alternate routes, however attractive or promising, ultimately lead to a cul-de-sac: if one enjoys driving round and round in circles, then the risk may be worth the effort; otherwise, it is usually best to stick to the main roads. I agree that it is always wise to have a precise map if one wishes to arrive at some designated place. Nevertheless, I believe Newsom is right when she says that the ambiguities embedded within the divine speeches "require the reader to assume a more active role in *making meaning* than does a text in which the 'message' is simple and transparent."[10] If there is any truth in the thought that *making* the journey is at least as important as the arriving, then the markers below may prove to be important signposts along the way.

(1) *When God last spoke*, the freight of what was said was conveyed by *prose*. Now, what God has to say about Job's world is articulated in *poetry*. Prose is descriptive language; it reports what is, as accurately and as objectively as possible. God's prose words in the prologue describe Job's world rather matter-of-factly as one in which undeserved suffering happens "for no reason." Poetry is evocative. Its rhetoric is terse and elliptic, leaving blanks that must be filled in by the reader. It is indirect and suggestive, inviting readers to imagine how general principles may be converted into specific truths that can be accessed in concrete circumstances. Prose reduces the mystery of suffering to settled truths that can be stated in simple, unquestioned affirmations: "The Lord has given and the Lord has taken away; blessed be the name of the Lord" (1:21). Poetry opens up settled realities, exposing them to unimagined possibilities for construing the world that may be both daring and daunting. ["It Is Possible, Possible, Possible"] "Plain speech," as the poet Czeslaw Milosz suggests, may be "the mother tongue," but "One clear stanza can take more weight / Than a whole wagon of elaborate prose."[11] ["No Non-poetic View of Reality Can Be Complete"]

(2) *When God last spoke*, the context was depicted as an ordinary conversation. Now, God speaks "out of the whirlwind." Both the rhetoric and the context suggest that God appears to Job in a theophany. Theophanies mark moments of

"It Is Possible, Possible, Possible"

W. Brueggemann, in summoning preachers to truth claims that defy conventional prose, calls upon Wallace Stevens's understanding of poetic speech as the "fiction of an absolute":

It is possible, possible, possible. It must
Be possible. It must be that in time
The real will from its crude compoundings come,

Seeming, at first, a beast disgorged, unlike,
Warmed by a desperate milk. To find the real,
To be stripped of every fiction except one,

The fiction of an absolute.

W. Brueggemann, *Finally Comes the Poet: Daring Speech for Proclamation* (Minneapolis: Fortress, 1989), 5. The citation is from Stevens's poem "Notes Toward a Supreme Fiction"; see *Wallace Stevens: Collected Poetry and Prose* (New York: Library of America, 1997), 349.

"No Non-poetic View of Reality Can Be Complete"

In his essay on "The Theological Significance of Biblical Poetry," Patrick D. Miller concludes by applying his general observations about poetic discourse specifically to the poetic speech of God in Job:

Poetic discourse is thus a mode of speech that is indirect, open, and rooted in imagination . . . . All of this is true *mutates mutandis* about the poetic speech from God. It, too, is indirect, open, universal, and dependent upon the imagination for construction. It is interesting in this regard to compare the prose speech of God in the book of Job with the poetic divine speech. Not to dismiss the former. It has its very important function. But we are clearly drawn to the open, figurative, indirect speech of God, filled with ambiguity, and we are puzzled by the explicit, literal, resolving divine speech of the epilogue. If one thinks that a simply a matter of content, then one has not heard the poetry. Or perhaps one should say that what is happening belongs in one case to imaginative, open poetic speech and in the other to explanatory, bound prose speech.

The last paragraph in Miller's essay calls upon the work of the British cosmologist John D. Barrows (*Theories of Everything: The Quest for Ultimate Explanation* [London, New York: Oxford University Press, 1991]) for an assessment of poetry's contribution to worldviews that may otherwise be tempted to settle for the merely scientific:

In a recent scientific work titled *Theories of Everything*, John Barrows makes the statement at the end of the book that "no non-poetic view of reality can be complete." That is quite a word from one whose speech is, presumably, customarily literal, explanatory, and precise, but it is surely one of the things that we hear also from biblical poetry.

P. D. Miller, "The Theological Significance of Biblical Poetry," *Language, Theology, and the Bible: Essays in Honour of James Barr*, ed. Samuel E. Balentine, J. Barton (Oxford: Clarendon Press, 1994), 229-30.

---

divine disclosure, when the holy God approaches the everyday world in extraordinary ways. For example, God comes riding on storm clouds, symbols of the unassailable power of a king on a throne, or a mighty warrior in a chariot (e.g., Ps 18:10; Ezek 1; Hab 3:8). Thunder often represents God's voice (e.g., Exod 19:16, 19; Ps 18:13), lightning bolts or fire the agents of God's intervention (e.g., Exod 3:2-3; Ps 18:14; Hab 3:11). Such powerful displays of God's presence, which cause nature itself to convulse with divine judgment, often evoke dread and fear in those who would contend with the Almighty (e.g., Judg 5:4-5; Nah 1:3-6; Hab 3:5-12).[12] It is not without reason, therefore, that a majority of commentators interpret God's words out of the whirlwind as a terrifying display of power that is designed to blow Job away, at least rhetorically, if not also literally. Job has in fact feared that should he ever find the God he seeks, God would confront him with such overwhelming force that he could not stand (9:3, 12, 14, 32-35; 13:13-28; 23:6-7, 8-16). After 123 verses from God, most filled with questions that seem impossible for Job to answer, J. L. Crenshaw's observation surely merits careful consideration: "In the face of such a blustering deity, who would not be speechless?"[13]

Theophanies serve more than one purpose, however. In the Old Testament they almost always trigger a tensive combination of responses. Precisely because they are such awesome, up-close, and personal encounters with the holy, they are both frightening and attractive at the same time. On the one hand, people dare not come too close, for the danger is great; on the other, the attraction of such an extraordinary proximity to the sacred is so compelling, people instinctively want to approach as nearly as possible. The theophany Moses experiences in Exodus 3 is perhaps the quintessential example. Standing before a bush that burns without being consumed, Moses hears the voice of God, which both summons him by name—"Moses, Moses!" (Exod 3:4: cf. Exod 19:10-11)—and warns him to take precautions—"Come no closer!. . . for the place on which you are standing is holy ground" (Exod 3:5; cf. Exod 19:12, 21-23). Moses responds by hiding his face, "because he is afraid to look at God" (Exod 3:6), all the while inching himself close enough to hear and respond to the voice that beckons him (Exod 3:7-12; cf. Exod 19:17-19). The precautions are necessary, because theophanic experiences mean that danger is all around. But for Moses and those enslaved in Egypt, this is a danger *not to be avoided*, for the God who speaks to them in the burning bush is the One who wants them to be *close enough* to hear these words: "I have observed the misery of my people who are in Egypt; I have heard their cry. . . I know their sufferings, and I have come down to deliver them." (Exod 3:7-8).[14]

Job's quest for God resonates both thematically and linguistically with the cry of the oppressed slaves in Egypt.[15] When Job complains that his "groaning" is heavy (23:2) and that the God he seeks seems to have no regard for the "cries for help" of those who languish in suffering (24:12; cf. Exod 2:23-25), he is in effect asking, "Where is the God of the burning bush?" If our expectations are closed, then we may conclude that when God speaks to Job out of the whirlwind, the objective is to force him into silent submission, lest he breach the dangerous border between the holy and the merely common. But if our expectations are open, thus permeable to encounters with the holy that expand rather than constrict the range of what is possible, then maybe, just maybe, the God who speaks with whirlwind force is the God of the exodus, who wants Job to come close enough to hear the words, "I am here."

(3) *When God last spoke*, it was in the declarative, a subtle but telling suggestion that all conversations with the Almighty end with God having the last word. Job's initial response was to image God's rhetoric, answering declarative fiats with unfeigned affirmative assertions (1:21). Gradually (2:10), then with increasing intensity, pain drives Job into the hinterland of the interrogative (3:11-26; 10:18-22; 24:1), where the grammar of faith demands God's response to "Why?" questions that threaten to crack open every untested conviction. Now, as if matching the shift in Job's rhetoric, God comes *asking* questions, not answering them.

Most commentators connect God's questions ("Where were you?" "Can you?" "Have you?" "Who?" "Do you know?") with the language of disputation. The setting for this language is usually associated with the prophetic lawsuit, in which God, depicted as both prosecuting attorney and judge, cross-examines defendants in a legal case.[16] The objective in such cases is to probe for weaknesses in a person's arguments by asking questions they cannot answer adequately and/or truthfully without incriminating themselves. If one assumes this is the setting for God's questions, then the intent is not only to dispute Job's charges but also to demonstrate his arrogance and mendacity in having raised them at all. On first impression, Job's responses certainly appear to endorse this understanding. Because he cannot satisfactorily answer God's questions, he first yields in silence (40:5), then, apparently, confesses that he has been wrong (42:6).

Two observations argue against closing off our expectations concerning what God's questions seek to accomplish. First, despite what we might assume, God does not have the last word in this discourse; that belongs, surprisingly, to Job (42:1-6). The meaning of Job's last words constitutes perhaps the most important crux in the book. A full exploration of the matter must await the exegesis that follows, but this much can be said for now. If God's objective is only to silence Job, that is, to prove that he has nothing of merit to say about the world God has created and administers, then God's second speech (40:6–41:34) appears redundant at best. Once Job agrees to speak no further, what reason is there for God to continue, unless silence is *not* what God wants from Job? And if God's sole purpose is to coerce a confession of guilt from Job, then why, in the aftermath of what seems like just such an admission, does the book conclude with God saying to the friends, "You have not spoken of me what is right, as my servant Job has done" (42:7, 8)? God has summoned Job to answer three times (38:3; 40:2, 6). Neither silence nor confession seems fully adequate as the response God seeks.[17]

Second, do rhetorical questions serve only to dispute, rebuke, and dismiss those addressed? Is their sole objective to establish the questioner's superiority by unmasking the poverty of someone else's intellect? Crenshaw raises the question bluntly: "Must 'the greater glory of God' always require a belittling of human beings?"[18] However, when one examines the prophetic trial speeches that are so often compared with Job 38–41, it is apparent that rhetorical questions do not always function to put down persons for failed or flawed understandings. Sometimes, especially in situations where the grim realities of everyday life may have thinned the imagination, they serve to resurrect hope from the ashes of despair.

The questions in Isaiah 40:12-31 are case in point. Addressing an audience whose hope for the future has been trimmed to conform to the bleak truth of life in exile, the prophet asks questions that seek to expand their horizon:

Who has measured the waters in the hollow of his hand
and marked off the heavens with a span?
Who has directed the spirit of the Lord,
or as his counselor has instructed him?
Whom did he consult for his enlightenment,
and who taught him the path of justice?

Have you not known? Have you not heard?
Has it not be told you from the beginning?
Have you not understood from the foundations of the earth?

Lift up your eyes on high and see: Who created these? (Isa 40:12-14, 21, 26)

The objective of such questions is not to condemn persons for their failures. It is to encourage them to believe that the Creator of the world can construct new possibilities where none seem to exist. The objective is not to silence those whose doubts threaten to eclipse faith. It is to summon forth new affirmations that transform brokenness and loss by embracing the unfathomable certainty of God's promise to redeem. These questions *can be* answered; indeed, the purpose in asking them is to open up a space in the imagination that *invites* and *makes possible* an answer that has the capacity to change everything. When God addresses similar questions to Job, we should pause to consider whether the objective is to *belittle* a blatant wrongdoer or to *embolden* a true servant whose faith is faint but worthy. If all poetry is a "raid on the inarticulate," as T. S. Eliot says, then perhaps God's rhetorical questions are a raid on Job's despair about what seems incomprehensible.[19] [God's Speeches and "the Rhetoric of the Sublime"]

(4) Finally, it is not just *how* God speaks—through poetry, in theophany, and with rhetorical questions—that invites readers to keep their expectations open. It is also *what* God says. God's speeches have to do with the "design" (38:2) and moral "governance" (40:8) of the world. In this respect, what God has to say about creation returns to a principal concern that has shaped this book from the outset. Every participant in the drama—Job, the four friends, and not least God—has a stake in the discussion about how to understand what William P. Brown has aptly called the "ethos of the cosmos."[20] [Ethos and Ethics]

God's Speeches and "the Rhetoric of the Sublime"

C. Newsom calls upon Edmund Burke's classic philosophical analysis of the rhetoric of the sublime (*A Philosophical Enquiry into the Origin of Our Ideas of the Sublime and Beautiful*, ed. J. T. Boulton [London: Basil Blackwell, 1987]) to elucidate language that borders on the possible and the impossible, the knowable and the unknowable, in short, the finite and the infinite:

The sublime is classically described in terms of a crisis of understanding. Crucial to the sublime is the perceiving subject's sense of being overwhelmed by something too immense, vast, or powerful to be grasped by the categories available to the mind. More than merely a cognitive crisis, it is a crisis of subjectivity itself. And yet what is in some respects a negative experience is paradoxically accompanied by a sense of "transport" or "elation," or a moment in which the self is "realized" in a new way. Not surprisingly, the divine speeches in Job have often served as parade examples of the sublime . . . .

C. Newsom, *The Book of Job: A Contest of Moral Imaginations* (Oxford: Oxford University Press, 2003), 237.

• The prologue envisions "the land of Uz" as the setting for an imaginative return to the garden of Eden (see the commentary on Job 1–2). God's primordial assessment that the world is "very good" hovers over the narrator's initial description of Job's family and possessions. Everything changes, however, when the *satan* invites God to reconsider the meaning of "very good." Is it possible that God has created a world in which "good" is never challenged by "bad," in which blessing is never threatened by curse, in which faith is always hedged safely away from doubt? When God agrees to take up the question, Job's "very good" world is redefined by "suffering that was *very great*" (2:13). In the presence of such suffering, the discussion of what it means to live obediently in God's world rapidly descends into silence. It is as if no one—not Job, not the friends, not God—dares speak another word until Job's misery can be factored into the rhetoric. It is the first clue that suffering like Job's changes everything in *heaven* and on *earth*.

Ethos and Ethics

William P. Brown, drawing upon the work of Paul Lehmann (*Ethics in a Christian Context* [New York: Harper and Row, 1963]), notes that the word *ethos* derives from a Greek word meaning "stall" or "dwelling," which means the *place* or *environment* "that makes possible and sustains moral living." By extension, "ethics," also derived from the same Greek word, "defines the setting that is conducive for the formation of a community's character." Thus "ethos" refers to a "sphere of moral existence" or "moral ontology," which provides "an account of the meaning of our being in the world and how to orient ourselves in the world."

W. P. Brown, *The Ethos of the Cosmos: The Genesis of Moral Imagination* (Grand Rapids, MI: William B. Eerdmans, 1999), 11.

• After seven days and nights of quiet suffering in a world now turned upside down, Job breaks the silence (see the commentary on Job 3). He speaks as only he can, not as a Creator, who entertains hypothetical questions about the design of the world, not as a friend, who looks upon another's suffering from a safe distance, but as a single individual who must scratch for meaning in the midst of pain too personal for cosmic theories. With a seven-fold "counter-cosmic incantation"[21] that parodies Genesis 1, he curses the day of his beginnings, and by extension the primordial day on which the Creator of the world assumed responsibility for all beginnings (3:3-10). With anguished lament (3:11-26), he questions why life in God's world should be valued if it promises nothing more than randomly distributed misery. Both his curses and his laments are a call for a different world.

• The dialogues between Job and his friends return repeatedly to creation imagery in the search for answers to Job's questions. Eliphaz charts the course that Bildad and Zophar follow (especially in the first cycle, 4-14) by appealing to nature's witness in defense of God's moral governance of the world. Using agricultural metaphors, he argues that there is an organic connection between those who "sow iniquity" and reap "trouble" (4:8-9; cf. 8:11-12). Using animals as ciphers for human beings, he points to the lion as a symbol for the wicked, whose predatory assaults on the righteous are doomed to failure (4:1-11; cf. 8:13-15). In Elihu's world, the Lord of nature commands the rain, thunder, and lightning to serve as agents of divine retribution divine (37:1-13). From his perspective, animals and humans count for little, except to provide the cowering praise due an incomparably powerful Creator (37:7-8).

Job has also looked to creation for instruction about life in God's world. But when he asks the "animals," and the "birds of the air," and the "plants of the earth," and the "fish of the sea" (12:7-8) what they have to teach him, the only truth they convey is that the life of every living creature is in "the hand of the Lord" (12:9). Job yearns for a larger truth than this. What does it mean to be "in the hand of God"? ["The Hand of God"] Is it a curse or a blessing for creatures to be "in the hand of the Lord" (see further [He's Got the Whole World on His Back])? If Job is *merely* a creature, does God regard him as a creature of chaos that must be defeated? Has God concluded that his curses are proof that he has allied himself with the untamable primordial beast Leviathan (3:8)? Are his laments such a threat to cosmic order that God must muzzle him, like the mythological sea monster Yam (7:12)? Are his wailings so unacceptable in an orderly world that God must drive him into the wastelands, where wild jackals and unclean ostriches are the only community he can expect (30:29)? If he is *merely* a human being, which, as his friends keep reminding him, means that his personal fate has little or no bearing on cosmic order (4:17-21; 8:8-10; 11:7-12; 15:14-16; 18:4; 22:1-3), then why does God single him out for such disproportionate attention (14:1-12)?

When the debate between Job and his friends ends, one of Job's most basic questions about God's design for the world remains yet unanswered: "What are human beings, that you [God] make so much of them?" (7:17). In the world of the psalmist (Ps 8:4), perhaps also in the world the friends inhabit, the question may call for humble praise to the Creator. In Job's world, it only evokes terror.

In the wake of such contrasting perspectives concerning creation's design, this story invites, if not requires, that God speak another word about the suffering that defines Job's world. Is the flat concession "for no reason" (2:3) the sum of what God has to say? Both the *how* and the *what* of God's words in chapters 38–41 hold the promise that there is more. As a down payment on the purchase of what this "more" may mean, it is instructive to compare Job's understanding of his place in the world with God's invitation to imagine something different.

When Job looks at his world, he construes its values as a series of tightly bordered concentric circles (see the commentary on Job 29–30 and [Job's Moral World]). At the center is civility, that is, submissive compliance to what God has decreed is acceptable and commendable. At the outer edges, well beyond the borders of what God can barely tolerate, are those who cannot or will not conform to these requirements. When Job tries to make sense of his place in this world, he can only conclude that God has consigned him to live beyond the pale. Like the wild

The Existential Man

Carl Milles, *The Existential Man* ("The Hand of God"). Bronze statue. Millegården, Stockholm.

"The Hand of God"

The Swedish artist Carl Milles (1875–1955), who studied with Auguste Rodin in Paris, sculpted "The Hand of God" (1954) as his last work. He depicts a naked man, two-meters tall, peering towards the heavens. He leans backward, as if overwhelmed by the vastness of his world. His hands are outstretched, the right palm-upward, the left palm-downward, a pose suggesting both entreaty and resolve. His feet, spread apart, provide a base of support, but on what? In whom? The man seems unaware of the oversized hand that holds him suspended in mid-air. It is believed that Milles used his own left hand as the model.

Milles envisions both the precariousness and the promise of any person who struggles to comprehend his or her place in the vast scheme of the cosmos. It is instructive to consider what this person might be thinking if his name were Job. Job knows that the hand of God has touched him, but whether it is for good or for ill is not at all clear (cf. 10:3, 7; 12:9-10; 19:21). If the hand depicted here is the hand of God, then will the fingers remain spread in support of the one vulnerable to the world's assaults? Or will the fingers close and squash this one who has no visible means of escape? Job fears the latter (13:14-15), but he hopes for the former (23:1-7).

For further reading, see S. Terrien, *The Iconography of Job Through the Centuries: Artists as Biblical Interpreters* (University Park PA: The Pennsylvania State University Press, 1996), 269-71.

animals that inhabit the wilderness, his behavior is so extreme that God will not permit him to threaten the peace and tranquility enjoyed by those who play by the rules and stay where they belong (30:29).

When God invites Job to see the world from God's perspective, the view is quite different. God's world is more *canopied than concentric*: the far reaches of the cosmos (38:4-18) overhang (and undergird) meteorological phenomena (38:19-38), which in turn provide the scared canopy under which the animals, almost all numbered among the hostile and wild (38:39–39:30), frolic in the freedom of being exactly who they are. At the center of God's world are two creatures—Behemoth and Leviathan (40:15–41:34)—conventionally regarded as so wild, so hostile, that they must be vigorously confronted and defeated. When God looks at them, however, God sees no cause for opposition. Instead, God celebrates their power, pride, and fierce resistance to domestication, for these are God-given virtues of creatures that instinctively confront all challenges without any fear of a potential defeat. [A "Sacred Canopy"] Moreover, to the extent that there are *boundaries* or borders in God's canopied world, they are far more *porous* and *permeable* than what Job has been able to discern. This is particularly clear in the contrasting views of Job and God concerning the "waste and desolate land" (30:3b; 38:25-27).[22] Job defines this as a place of punishment, where wild animals and "wild" human beings are banished to scavenge for whatever resources a desolate land offers. When God looks on the same desolateness, however, God sees promise and potential, for barren ground can be watered, and where there is no life, green grass can grow.

Job's question—"What are human beings, that you make so much of them?"—lingers still. Neither the friends nor Job himself has thus far arrived at an answer that satisfies all. The only participant yet to have a say is God. Where does God believe Job fits in God's world? Commentators regularly note that God's review of creation includes no explicit mention of Job in particular or human beings in general. This omission is typically interpreted as God's strategic subversion of any assumption that human beings occupy a place of importance in the cosmic scheme of things, whatever their status. Others salvage a more optimistic reading by noting that God's speeches are *addressed to* Job, which is perhaps a clue that God does regard Job as special; he deserves more than only being numbered among a catalogue of other creatures.[23] If we keep our expectations open, however, then we may discern a still more intriguing possibility. When God directs Job's attention to Behemoth, who along with Leviathan stands at the center of God's world, the invitation is to consider a creature whom God has made "just as I made *you*" (40:15). As the only reference, albeit indirect, to the creation of human beings in the divine speeches, this invitation suggest that Behemoth, who displays extraordinary strength and courage (40:16-18) in resisting all forms of aggression and violence (40:23-24), is the one true analogue for humankind that God has placed in the created order.

If rhetorical questions can be invitations to imagine what is otherwise incomprehensible, as I have suggested, then perhaps it is fitting to preface the commentary that follows with yet one more. When God

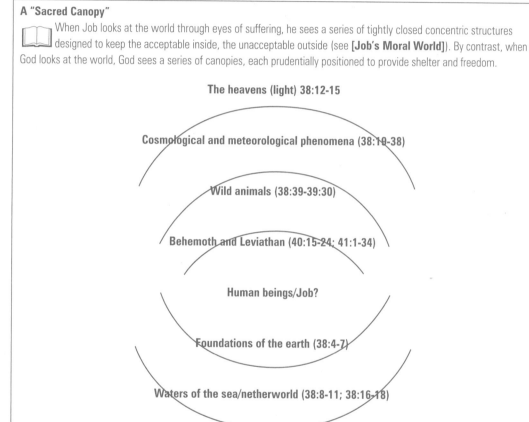

A "Sacred Canopy"

When Job looks at the world through eyes of suffering, he sees a series of tightly closed concentric structures designed to keep the acceptable inside, the unacceptable outside (see **[Job's Moral World]**). By contrast, when God looks at the world, God sees a series of canopies, each prudentially positioned to provide shelter and freedom.

The heavens (light) 38:12-15

Cosmological and meteorological phenomena (38:19-38)

Wild animals (38:39-39:30)

Behemoth and Leviathan (40:15-24; 41:1-34)

Human beings/Job?

Foundations of the earth (38:4-7)

Waters of the sea/netherworld (38:8-11; 38:16-18)

C. Newsom has noted that the divine speeches employ a subtle but important "spatial imagery." With a series of images for borders and boundaries, God invites Job's reflection on "formlessness and structure, order and disorder, life and death, the darkness that harbors violence and the light that dispels it." Such binary "opposites" are conventionally regarded as mutually exclusive; the presence of one member of the pair automatically cancels out the other. And yet, as she discerns, in God's view of the world, this does not seem to be true: "The very oppositions that simultaneously make life possible and threaten it are thus manifested even as they are declared to be unknowable and uncontrollable by human understanding and will. "

God's view of the world invites reflection on what the sociologist Peter Berger calls the "sacred canopy" of structures and beliefs that religion uses to construct a world of meaning. On the one hand, the world is defined by a transcendent sacred order that can at best only be approximated. On the other, human beings, both individually and collectively, have the capacity to construct meaning that keeps life tuned to possibilities that remain inviolable, even when they are ungraspable.

For further reading on P. Berger's views, see *The Sacred Canopy* (New York: Doubleday, 1967).

C. Newsom, *The Book of Job: A Contest of Moral Imaginations* (Oxford: Oxford University Press, 2003), 241-42.

Structure of Job 38:1–40:2

God's first speech: the "design" of the cosmos (38:1–40:2)

I. Introduction (38:1-3)
   A. Formulaic introduction: "The Lord answered Job out of the whirlwind" (v. 1)
   B. Thematic question: "Who is this that darkens counsel . . . without knowledge?" (v. 2)
   C. Imperative challenge: "Gird up your loins . . . I will question you, and you shall declare to me" (v. 3)

II. Development of theme (38:4–39:30)
   A. The cosmic boundaries (38:4-18)
      —the foundations of the *earth* (vv. 4-7)
      —the waters of the *sea* (vv. 8-11)
      —the lights of the *heavens* (vv. 12-15)
      —the depths of the *netherworld* (vv. 16-18)
   B. The meteorological phenomena (38:19-38)
      —light and darkness (vv. 19-21)
      —snow, hail, and wind (vv. 22-24)
      —rain (vv. 25-27)
      —rain, dew, frost, and ice (vv. 28-30)
      —constellations (vv. 31-33)
      —clouds (vv. 34-38)
   C. The animal kingdom (38:39–39:30)
      —lion and raven (vv. 39-41)
      —mountain goat and deer (39:1-4)
      —wild ass and wild ox (vv. 5-12)
      —ostrich and warhorse (vv. 13-25)
      —hawk and eagle/vulture (vv. 26-30)

III. A second summons to answer (40:1-2)

invites the Jobs of this world to look at Behemoth and Leviathan, what are they supposed to *see* and *understand* about their identity and vocation in relation to God? [CD: "I Am a Keeper of the Zoo"]

COMMENTARY

God's answer begins with a *question*, followed by a demand for *Job's response* (38:2-3). It is but the first clue that understanding God's design for the world requires more than one voice. What God has to say is not complete until Job adds his words. If this dialogue is to be meaningful for either party, then both speakers must be joined in an honest exchange of answers that lead to questions, which in turn evoke responses that have the potential to reshape the answers that launched the process.

God's demand for a response begins with an offer to take Job along on a virtual journey through the world that promises more than either he or his friends has thus far been able to see with their limited vision. [Structure of Job 38:1–40:2] Starting with the outermost edges of the cosmos (38:4-18), God invites Job's reflection on the intricacies of meteorological phenomena (38:19-38), like the rain, which mysteriously transforms itself into ice (38:28-30), and the stars and clouds, which mysteriously cluster into constellations with discernible shapes (38:31-33). Then, God directs Job's attention to the mysterious habits of wild animals (38:39–39:30), which not only survive but also thrive in environments no human would consider habitable. At each stage along the journey, God asks questions that Job can only answer by conceding his limitations. "Where were you when I laid the foundation of the earth?" (38:4); Job's only possible answer is, "I was nowhere." "Can you send forth lightnings?" (38:35); Job must admit, "No, I cannot." Or, "Can you hunt the prey for the lion?" (38:39), in response to which Job can only say, "No, only You, God, can do such things." And yet, the journey goes on, the questions continue, and God repeats the demand for Job's response (40:1-2). When Job retreats to silence (40:3-5), this dialogue,

---

"Stay Silent Now"

📖 In *Letter To A Man In The Fire*, Reynolds Price reflects on a letter he received from a young student, who had been forced to withdraw from medical school because of a reoccurrence of cancer. Jim Fox had read Price's account of his own ordeal with cancer (*A Whole New Life*, 1994). Now he was writing to ask Price's response to his questions about the existence of God and the nature of God's care.

Price directs his correspondent's attention to the book of Job, especially to chs. 38–41, which he describes as "the most probing of all human documents I've encountered on the matter" (68). He notes that the tone of God's speech throughout is "sardonic and grandly dismissive."

. . . God flatly refuses to take note of Job's horrific losses and sufferings; he never so much as glances at Job's specific request for a bill of particulars against him, though that's the request which seems to have brought God forward to defend himself. For all his expansive detail and haunting imagery, in fact, God's answer to Job may be reduced to sixteen sublimely unsatisfying words—"If you were not my active partner from the start of creation, then stay silent now." (69)

To offer such an observation to a person dying of cancer hardly seems to encourage trust in a loving God. Price continues with an additional word that suggests his young friend, perhaps like Job himself, may hear more than a counsel to despair, if he will listen carefully.

Yet however unnourishing such a reply may sound initially, it seems to me to constitute a beginning to the best lead we're given in the face of ultimate mystery in all of Hebrew and Christian scripture—the most reliable weather vane through fair skies and foul for any troubled human being. Perhaps Job's God means something as drastic as this— *Observe that all of creation is the vehicle upon which you pursue the Creator's will. Attempt any change of pace at your own dire peril. Relish the journey for however long it lasts and wherever it goes.* (69)

R. Price, *Letter To A Man In The Fire: Does God Exist and Does He Care?* (New York: Scribner, 1999), 68-69.

---

such as it is, seems to be over. ["Stay Silent Now"] It is not, for with a second speech from the whirlwind God will push past Job's silence with still another request for his response (40:7).

First Words: "Gird Up Your Loins," 38:1-3

Imagine the challenge of the poet who tries to translate what God is thinking into human discourse. Even accepting the axiom that every conversion of thought into words leaves some measure of truth unspoken, any attempt to represent God's voice will necessarily be fraught with insurmountable difficulties. Once one chooses the words, what tone is best to convey them? Where should the accents be placed? Should pauses be inserted, and if so, for what purpose? To invite response, however inadequate? Or, to make every response, other than awe, not only unthinkable but also unsayable?[24] Given the enormity of the task, perhaps we should concede at the outset that the poet who risked crafting the words out of the whirlwind *succeeds* in conveying God's truth precisely by *failing* to reduce its ambiguity. [Nicely Ornamenting What Cannot Be Known]

Nicely Ornamenting What Cannot Be Known

In an essay on "Virginia Woolf's Mysticism," James Wood notes that what makes her novels great is her refusal to allow art to remove or reduce the mystery of things. In this respect, the novelist's objective is somewhat like the theologian's. Both use words in an effort to say the unsayable and to describe the indescribable; for both, failure is in effect success.

Art, in this sense, acts like ritual rather than doctrine: it cannot define truth, but it nicely ornaments what cannot be known.

J. Wood, "Virginia Woolf's Mysticism," *The Broken Estate: Essays on Literature and Belief* (New York: Random House, 1999), 100.

The author of God's speeches in Job risks failure by attempting to construe a dialogue between the Creator of the world and a sufferer who has dared to challenge the Almighty's wisdom. Although there is literary precedent in the ancient Near East for describing an innocent sufferer's complaints and appeals to the deity, none of the relevant parallels go so far as to portray the deity appearing and engaging in a face-to-face encounter.[25] [A "Tour de Force"] Going where no one has gone before, the Joban poet sets the stage for this divine-human dialogue with three rhetorical moves: he chooses the lan-

---

A "Tour de Force"

A number of ancient Near Eastern texts provide literary precedent for the book of Job. The most important of these are Mesopotamian texts: for example, the so-called "Babylonian Job," also known by its first line as *Ludlul bel nemiqi* ("I will praise the Lord of Wisdom"), which was probably composed in the fifteenth century; and "The Babylonian Theodicy," composed c. 1000 BCE Both have to do with a righteous sufferer who complains about his misfortune; both depict the complaints as directed to the deity, who has inexplicably abandoned the sufferer; and both conclude with appeals for mercy that have or will lead to restoration. But, as Newsom has noted, "the one thing that is almost completely missing in the Mesopotamian appeals by a sufferer is the dramatic representation of a direct reply by the deity." In *Ludlul bel nemeqi*, Marduk's response comes in dreams that are conveyed to the sufferer (Subshi-meshre-Shakkan) by intermediaries, for example,

> A second time [I saw a dream]
> And [in my night dream which] I [saw]
> A remarkable young [man . . . .]
> Holding in his hand a tamarisk rod of purification—
> "Laluralimma, resident of Nippur,
> Has sent me to cleanse you." (Tablet III, ll. 21-26)
> (Lambert, 49)

In "The Babylonian Theodicy," the sufferer complains to his friend, who offers a series of explanations in defense of the deity. A resolution of sorts is reached in the final lines, when the sufferer thanks his friend for his companionship and asks him to join him in a petition to the gods for

mercy. A positive response is implied, but there is no direct reply from the deity:

> You are kind, my friend; behold my grief.
> Help me; look on my distress; know it.
> I, though humble, wise, and a suppliant,
> Have not seen help and succour for one moment.
> I have trodden the square of my city unobtrusively,
> My voice was not raised, my speech was kept low.
> I did not raise my head, but looked at the ground,
> I did not worship even as a slave in the company of my associates.
> May the god who has thrown me off give help,
> May the goddess who has [abandoned me] show mercy,
> For the shepherd Samas guides the people like a god.
> (Stanza XXVII, ll. 287-97) (Lambert, 89)

Newsom concludes as follows:

So far as one can tell, there is no literary precedent for a pair of speeches that set over against one another the voice of a sufferer and the response of his God. What the author of the book of Job has composed is something of a tour de force.

W. G. Lambert, *Babylonian Wisdom Literature* (Oxford: Clarendon Press, 1960).

C. Newsom, *The Book of Job: A Contest of Moral Imaginations* (Oxford: Oxford University Press, 2003), 238. A caveat is necessary here. Newsom is calling attention to the juxtaposition specifically of the two final speeches of Job and God in chs. 29–31 and 38:1–42:6, respectively. I suggest that her major point is also cogent when one considers the juxtaposition of God's two addresses from the whirlwind (38:1–40:2; 40:6–41:34) and Job's two responses (40:3-5; 42:1-6). As she notes, "When Job replies to God in 40:1-5 and 42:1-6, he does so with words and images that allude back to his own speech in chapters 29-31" (238).

guage of *poetry*, which opens the imagination to possibilities beyond what conventional prose allows; he chooses the context of a *theophany*, in this case a whirlwind (*sĕʿārâ*) or tempest storm, to convey both the danger and the attraction of being in such close proximity to the presence of God; and he chooses to construct God's grammar with *rhetorical questions*, which reveal Job's limitations even as they invite him to reach for answers that are as yet beyond his grasp (for further discussion of these matters, see the preceding "Overview").

The introduction to God's speeches (38:1-3) provides three additional accents that heighten the drama.

• The name of the God who speaks here is "Yahweh" (38:1, hereafter YHWH; NRSV: "the Lord"). Within the book of Job, this name appears elsewhere only in the prologue and epilogue. In the dialogues between Job and his friends, the names for God are "El," "Eloah," "Shaddai," and "Elohim" (see [Names for God]). The use of the name "YHWH" enables the author to reconnect this story with the events in the "garden of Uz," where YHWH's last words, addressed to the *satan*, were, "Very well, he [Job] is in your power; only spare his life" (2:6). The God who addresses Job directly from the whirlwind now has more to say about Job's life and the powers that shape it. Moreover, by identifying these whirlwind words with the voice of YHWH, the author places the revelation to Job within the trajectory of Israel's memory of the life-changing encounters granted to previous paragons of faith, for example, Noah (Gen 8:20-22), Abraham (Gen 15:7-21), Moses (Exod 3:1-6; 19:17-19), and Elijah (1 Kgs 19:8-21).

•The subject of God's first speech is the "design" or "plan" (*ʿēsâ*; 38:2) of the cosmos. From the perspective of life on the ash heap, Job has repeatedly questioned God's design, for it seems to him to be both chaotic and unjust (see especially 12:13-25). If the best God's wisdom can offer is a world programmed for gratuitous suffering, then Job would prefer darkness to light, and death over life (cf. 3:20-23; 10:18-22). God now challenges Job by characterizing his assessment as "words without knowledge." It is surely a challenge that makes clear the limits of Job's understanding, which Job will subsequently acknowledge (40:3). If God's first speech had *ended* with these words, then we should no doubt have to conclude that God's intent is to rebuke and dismiss Job as an unworthy conversation partner. [CD: "You Can't Handle the Truth!"]

The author of these speeches daringly suggests a different purpose. Proving Job's deficiencies is not the *end* of what God has to say. It is only a *beginning*. And this beginning in turn opens the door for Job to

Leaning Into the Winds of God's Challenge

A Greek codex of the book of Job (8th–9th C.), preserved in the Saint John Monastery on Patmos, contains forty-three illuminations. One of them shows Job preparing himself to respond to God's speech from the whirlwind in Job 38–41. Job is robed in a linen garment, the folds of which are blown to the right by the force of God's thunderous speech. His head is twisted in the same direction, as if the winds have caused him to avert his gaze from the Almighty. Job's stance, however, indicates that he refuses to be swept away. His hands grasp the cords of a belt at his waist as he girds up his loins in response to God's command (38:3; 40:7). His feet are braced and set wide apart. His knees are flexed and angled into the wind.

The illumination is damaged and does not show Job's mouth. One can only imagine how the artist understood what Job was prepared to say to God at this climatic moment. Did the artist paint Job's mouth in such a way as to suggest that he was retracting his charges against God in humiliation and contrition? Did the artist think that Job was at last ready to yield to the God he had no chance of resisting? Job's bodied resistance to God's forceful speech suggests that the artist broke with convention by imagining still another possibility: a Job who leaned into the winds of divine justice with words that matched God's, challenge for challenge. S. Terrien invites reflection with the

Job Prepares to Fight with God
Job Prepares to Fight with God. 9th C. Illumination. Saint John Monastery, Patmos. (Credit: Bibliotheque du Monastere St. Jean le Theologien, Patmos)

following comment on this image: "It is told that an ancient rabbi witnessing an instance of Job-like misfortune 'worried God all night in prayer,' shouting to the Almighty, 'Art thou not ashamed of thyself?'" The story is cited by S. Terrien in his discussion of the meaning of this illumination (40). Terrien concludes that Job did not go as far as the rabbi. This is a reasonable judgment, but it seems to rely more on the conventional understanding of the end of the book of Job than on the evocative symbolism of this painting. Perhaps the miniaturist at Patmos imagined Job saying something similar in this scene.

For further reading on the Patmos illuminations, see S. Terrien, *The Iconography of Job Through the Centuries. Artists as Biblical Interpreters* (University Park PA: The Pennsylvania State University Press, 1996), 33-43.

respond with more than a confession of ignorance. Ultimately, Job will answer God's challenge by declaring that he sees and understands more about the design for the cosmos than he did before (40:5). ["Now You Will Uncode All Landscapes"]

• Finally, God's challenge to see and understand more about the design for the world includes a strategic summons. Job must gird up his loins like the *geber* (NRSV: "man") he was born to be (38:3; 40:7; cf. 3:3).[26] The word refers to a "mighty man" or "warrior" (e.g., Judg 5:30; 2 Sam 23:1; Jer 41:16), who prepares for battle by tucking the ends of his robe into his belt, so that he can run without restriction. Commentators often assume that the imagery is negative: God is either mocking Job as

---

"Now You Will Uncode All Landscapes"

Seamus Heaney (1939–), Professor of Poetry at Oxford University (1989–1994) and winner of the Nobel Prize in Literature (1995), was born on a small farm in Mossbawn, about thirty miles northwest of Belfast, Northern Ireland. Although he has lived and taught in places all over the world, including Berkeley and Harvard, Heaney's poetry, especially the example cited below, remains grounded in concrete images of the land and the social and political responsibilities it bequeaths to those who would be its worthy stewards.

When you have nothing more to say, just drive
For a day all round the peninsula.
The sky is tall as over a runway,
The land without marks so you will not arrive

But pass through, though always skirting landfall.
At dusk, horizons drink down sea and hill,
The ploughed field swallows the whitewashed gable
And you're in the dark again. Now recall

The glazed foreshore and silhouetted log,
That rock where breakers shredded into rags,
The leggy birds stilted on their own legs,
Inlands riding themselves out into the fog

And drive back home, still with nothing to say
Except that now you will uncode all landscapes
By this: things founded clean on their own shapes,
Water and ground in their extremity.

Seamus Heaney, "The Peninsula," in *Seamus Heaney: Selected Poems 1966–1987* (New York: Farrar, Straus and Giroux, 1990), 16.

---

a "pretend warrior" or luring him into a battle that he can only lose.[27] Both the context and the tenor of the divine speeches suggest something different. God invites Job to gird up his loins, in advance of what is coming, not because he is destined to be defeated, but because the victory is his for the taking, if only he will make the necessary preparations, which is what God wants and expects (cf. Jer 1:17).[28] [Leaning into the Winds of God's Challenge]

The Cosmic Boundaries, 38:4-18

Job's journey begins with an invitation to consider the four outermost parts of the cosmos: the foundations of the *earth* (vv. 4-7), the waters of the *sea* (vv. 8-11), the lights of the *heavens* (vv. 2-15), and the depths of the *netherworld* (vv. 16-18). The first stop is the earth (vv. 4-7), not the portion Job can see, which is pockmarked by ash heaps of suffering, but the parts he cannot see: the foundations that anchor the earth's pillars; the cornerstone, which stabilizes the structure laid on top. The imagery suggests that God is both the architect and the hands-on builder of a world constructed according to a master plan. The lengths and widths are measured precisely. The heights and depths are plumbed to make certain that everything is straight and sure. God's world is structured not simply as a *safe house* in which one may live without fear of its collapse; it is also envisioned as a *sacred temple* in which one all may seek refuge from hostile forces (e.g., Pss 23:5-6; 46:4-5; 48:1-4).[29] Moreover, because the creation of earth's foundation is a profound liturgical experience, God invites Job to listen in as a choir of morning stars and heavenly beings join their voices in celebration (v. 7; cf. Ezra 3:10-11; Zech 4:7; 2 Chr 5:11-14).

The rhetorical questions that convey this opening vision of the world challenge Job to declare whether he has the discernment to understand what God has designed. The opening question—"Where were you when I laid the foundation of the earth?" (v. 4a)—echoes Eliphaz's question in 15:7-8. Eliphaz assumes that the only legitimate answer Job can offer is to concede that because he was *not* present at creation's primordial beginnings, he cannot possibly claim to understand what God has done. Most commentators assume that God's question has the same purpose. Perhaps this is so, but we may wonder if this is the whole of the matter.

God seems intent on taking Job *where he has not been before* precisely so that he *can understand more* than he has thus far. Now that God has shown Job the foundations of his world, now that Job sees it is a safe place to be, now that he understands it as a temple in which all may seek refuge, will he feel secure enough to add his voice to the chorus that celebrates what God has done? The question is pertinent, because the celestial choir "sings" (*rānān*) for joy. Job's curses and laments, which are tuned to the belief that a world defaced by ash heaps of suffering is one in which "no joyful cry" (*rĕnānāh*; 3:7) should be heard, strike a seemingly discordant note. He has concluded that the only choir in which he might be welcomed consists of ostriches that screech in the wilderness (30:29). It is therefore curious that as this journey through the cosmos continues, God will soon direct Job's attention specifically to the ostrich, whose shrill sounds, now conveyed by its unique name (*rĕnānîm*, "cries of joy"; 39:13), do not seem at all offensive to God. Perhaps the choir that gives God pleasure is the one comprised of voices that sing with harmonic dissonance. If so, then perhaps one objective of this first stop on the cosmic journey is to help Job understand that his mournful lamentation is the intrinsic counterpoint that gives praise definition and resonance. [CD: The Pythagorean Comma and the Music That Echoes Cosmic Harmony]

The second stop on Job's cosmic journey invites him to shift his focus from the earth's stable foundations to the unruly waters of the sea that have the potential to overflow and destroy everything God has so meticulously built (vv. 8-11). The sea is conventionally regarded, both in ancient Near Eastern mythology (see [Ancient Near Eastern Creation Accounts]) and in the Old Testament (e.g., Pss 18:4; 74:13-14; 77:16-20; 89:9-13; Isa 51:9-10), as a hostile force that the deity must defeat if creation is to survive. This conventional view comports with Job's understanding of God's assessment of him. He fears that God considers him to be a dangerous opponent, like the mythical sea-god Yam, who must be muzzled lest his complaints subvert creation's order (7:14). God now invites Job to see and understand something quite different.

What Job regards as "bars and doors" (v. 10) designed to constrict his freedom (v. 11a) are the "swaddling bands" (v. 9b) that God uses to calm a newborn baby, whose instincts are to kick wildly upon exiting the close security of the mother's womb. What Job views as boundaries that prevent his maturation (v. 10a) are in God's eyes the gateways that invite him to pursue proud ambitions as far as he can before something beyond his control forces him to stop (v. 11). In sum, when Job looks upon the surging waters of the sea, God invites him to understand that when any part of creation threatens to exceed the limitations of what is permitted, it may be *constrained*, but it is not *condemned*. ["Swaddled in a Fresh Cosmic Diaper"]

The third stop on this journey offers a view of the light from the heavens (vv. 12-15). Has Job commanded the morning light? Does he know dawn's place and role in God's cosmic scheme? Ironically, Job has claimed to have some insight into such matters. He has cursed the light (3:4-5), because in a world turned upside down by suffering, each new day seems to promise nothing more than an endless cycle of months and years that add misery to misery. He has accused God of not knowing or not caring that the wicked use the cover of dusk and twilight to perpetrate violence against the unsuspecting (24:13-17). Once again, God invites Job to see and understand more. The light is not to be despised because it only brings more of the same; it is to be welcomed as the regular promise of new beginnings. Each time the sun rises, what had seemed shapeless in the dark becomes distinct and recognizable. Just as teachers use a stamp to transform a clump of clay into a document with precise images and words that convey clear messages (v. 14), so God uses the light to vivify the earth and bring forth something new and promising each day. Similarly, the dawn is not a blanket under which the wicked may hide. Instead, v. 13 personifies the dawn

---

"Swaddled in a Fresh Cosmic Diaper"

Although God claims to have rebuked and restrained Yam . . . there is no sense in this passage that their conflict was violent or that Yam was killed. Rather the image here is of God scolding Yam the way a parent would scold a raucous and unruly toddler, after which it is swaddled in a fresh cosmic diaper. . . . Indeed, the image of Yam diapered in clouds suggests that this primordial, chaotic force has been integrated into the present world ecology, like the chaos clothed in the cosmos. And the image of the creator God doing the diapering may even suggest that God and Yam are something like family. . . . In our present turn-of-the-century culture of psychotherapy, oriented toward reflection on family dynamics, some might go so far as to ask whether Yam is in some sense an expression of another, more chaotic aspect within the godhead (i.e., divine family), or whether Yam is a revelation of God's inner child. We need not go that far, however, to see that in this passage the chaos monster Yam is not completely eradicated from the world, nor is it completely dissociated from the creator God. It is a personification of primordial chaos *within* cosmos, intimately related to the divine.

T. K. Beal, *Religion and Its Monsters* (New York, London: Routledge, 2002), 49.

as God's designated housekeeper who sets things in order each day, which includes shaking the corners of the earth like a carpet to rid it of any dust or vermin that might have accumulated overnight.

The vision of the light God offers Job is instructive in several ways. God clearly invites Job not to neglect the promise of the light by being preoccupied only with the threat of the darkness. In God's design for the world, light defines darkness; it is shortsighted of Job to read it the other way round. And God clearly summons him not to conclude that God is indifferent to justice by focusing only on the lawlessness of the wicked. In the world God shows Job, the wicked cannot escape justice; wherever they may hide, however defiant they may be (v. 15), God will find them and deal with them. On the other hand, darkness has a role to play in God's world; without it, there would be no orderly cycle of night and day, no primordial pairing of natural opposites, which according to Israel's creation traditions is essential if all God's creatures are to have a chance to thrive. ["You Make Darkness"] The wicked also have a place in God's world. God does not approve their deeds and will faithfully bring them to justice. Yet, even as God limits their power to hurt and harm the world, when the morning brings everything into light, the damage they have done in the time available to them is clear.

This third stop on the cosmic journey, then, should convince Job that he is wrong to have accused God of harboring a secret creational intent to allow darkness and wickedness free reign to impose chaos on the world (cf. 10:13). On this matter, Job has neither seen nor understood the full truth about God. And yet, Job has persistently complained that God's justice, even if sure and consistent, often comes much too late to do those who need it any good (e.g., 24:1-12). If his discernment on this matter is flawed, then he hopes that someone, if not the friends, then surely God, will show him how he has erred (24:25). At this point in his journey through the world with God, we might imagine that Job sees more than he did before, but it remains unclear whether this "more" is enough. [CD: "It Is Not My Task, Is It, to Decide Which World Would Be More Pleasant to Live In"]

The fourth stop on Job's journey takes him to the edge of the waters of the netherworld, the domain of death (vv. 16-18). Once again, God invites Job to declare what he knows: "Have you entered . . . walked . . . seen . . . comprehended?"[30] If we take the questions literally, then Job must concede that he has not traveled to the primordial waters of

---

"You Make Darkness"

Bless the Lord, O my soul.
O Lord, my God, you are very great. . . .
You make darkness, and it is night,
when all the animals of the forest come creeping
    out.
The young lions roar for their prey,
seeking food from God.
When the sun rises, they withdraw
and lie down in their dens.
People go out to their work
and to their labor until the evening.
(Ps 104:1, 20-23)

the underworld. He has not literally died and made the post-mortem journey to the netherworld of Sheol, from whence no one returns (see [Sheol]). Even so, this particular stop on the journey seems most odd, especially when the traveler is Job. If there is anyone who knows something about death *in* life, surely it is Job. Who is more qualified, by raw experience, than Job to speak with understanding about what it means to look on helplessly while all that gives life meaning dies "for no reason"? Who else can speak about death with a conviction that equals the pained experience of Job (e.g., 3:20-22; 7:20-21; 10:18-22; 16:15-17; 17:1-2, 11-16)? Even though Job has not literally died, surely he has come as close as is humanly possible. The tease of rhetorical questions like God's last to Job in this section—"Have you comprehended?" (v. 18)—is the possibility that the respondent may in fact offer an answer that makes a difference to the questioner. [CD: "Say Yes, Job, Say Yes!"] Once before Job has spoken in ways that invite God to understand suffering and death from his perspective (see the commentary on 27:7-12). Perhaps, now at long last, when God says, "Declare, if you know all this" (v. 18), the invitation signals that God is indeed willing to listen to what Job has to say about suffering and death.

The Meteorological Phenomena, 38:19-38

Turning from the invisible cosmic foundations, God now directs Job's attention to the visible phenomena of nature.[31] This part of the tour comprises six strophes, which provide a suggestive thematic echo of the six days of creation in Genesis 1.[32] Beginning with the first and most basic creative act, the separation of light from darkness (vv. 19-21; cf. Gen 1:3), God describes the storehouses of the snow, hail, lightning, and wind (vv. 22-24), the channels for rain in the desert (vv. 25-27), the mysterious transformations that produce rain, dew, ice, and frost (vv. 28-30), the movement of the constellations (vv. 31-33), and the control of clouds and rain (vv. 34-38). If the rhetorical connection with Genesis were to be followed to its anticipated conclusion, we would expect God to end up by describing the creation of land animals and human beings (Gen 1:24-26). The next section of God's speech will in fact turn to the animal kingdom (38:39–39:30), though, curiously, with no mention of human beings. This omission is a telling clue that the journey God now offers Job will not be simply a repetition of what has already been said about primordial beginnings.

"Where Is the Way to the Dwelling of the Light?" (vv. 19-21)
The question returns Job to day one of the primordial beginnings, when God separated light from darkness and assigned each its proper place in the created order (Gen 1:3-5). Light shepherds the day

through its various activities; when its work is done, darkness appears on cue to provide comparable guidance for the night. It is this divinely crafted rhythm that sustains the whole of the created order. Indeed, according to Genesis 1, God's hopes and expectations for the world rest on the possibility that creation itself will image God's wisdom by engaging in comparable acts of division and separation. Just as God separates the light from the darkness, so the firmament partners with God by dividing the waters above the earth from those below the earth, which enables the dry land to appear (Gen 1:6-9). God separates the dry land from the waters in order that the land may bring forth vegetation, then entrusts to the plants and trees the responsibility to reproduce, each according to its distinctive seed (Gen 1:9-13). God creates man and woman, two distinct creatures who are united by their very differences, and then entrusts to them the stewardship of everything God has made (Gen 1:26-31).[33]

Does Job know the way to the wisdom encoded in creation that images God's? Does he understand and can he sustain the divisions between light and darkness on which creation depends? The answer to these questions depends in large measure on how we read God's statement in v. 21: "Surely you know, for you were born then." Once more, God's words echo Eliphaz's challenge in 15:7-8 (cf. 38:4). If Job knows the way to wisdom, then surely, as Eliphaz insinuates, he must be the "firstborn of the human race," who like Wisdom itself (Prov 8:22-31) is privileged to have participated with God in birthing the world. Eliphaz raises the possibility only to rebuke Job for the hubris of assuming that he was and is God's consultant in building the cosmos. If the tone of God's invitation to Job is sarcastic[34]—Job was *not* present when God created the world, therefore he *cannot* know what God knows—then we should conclude that Eliphaz and God are on the same page.

Nevertheless, even before God invited him on this tour of primordial beginnings, Job has pondered the possibility that his search for wisdom may not be all that different than God's (28:23-28). Might it be that God *acquires* wisdom in the very act of creative engagement with the world (28:25-26)? It is curious, for example, that Genesis 1 does not disclose just where light and darkness reside before they make their appearance on earth. It only reports that having created the light, God enters into a process of separating it from the dark, so that both may function in ways that are mutually beneficial for a "very good" world. [The Dwelling Places of Light and Darkness] Is the wisdom God acquires by actively engaging light and darkness also available to Job? Perhaps one purpose of addressing Job *as if* he were "the firstborn of the human race" is to invite him to understand his creaturely role in the ongoing work of separation that promotes cooperation but not estrangement;

that constructs boundaries without constricting the free and productive interplay of difference. If the objective of this virtual tour is to give Job *genuine insight* into what God was doing in preparing the world for the arrival of human beings, then perhaps the challenge in v. 21 conveys *sincerity*, not *sarcasm*. ["Be Lowly Wise"]

"Have You Entered the Storehouses of the Snow?" (vv. 22-24)

The word "storehouses" (*'ōṣrôt*) refers to places where things of value are carefully kept, for example, the sacred treasures of the temple (e.g., 1 Kgs 7:51 [= 2 Chr 5:1]; 15:18 [= 2 Chr 16:2]), private wealth (Prov 8:21), and food and grain (e.g., Joel 1:17; Mal 3:10; Neh 13:12-13). God invites Job to understand that snow, hail, lightning, and wind are similar treasures kept securely in the heavens (cf. Deut 28:12; Jer 10:13; Ps 135:7; Sir 39:17; 43:14). If such valuables are not protected, they may be plundered and exploited as ill-gotten gain (e.g., Jer 20:5; Hos 13:15; Prov 21:20). Such is not the case with the storehouses for weather that God now shows Job, as the verbs in this pericope make clear. God "reserves" them (v. 23), then "distributes" and "scatters" them purposefully, as needed (v. 24).

"Be Lowly Wise"

In Job 38–40, as in Job 28, a fundamental issue is the acquisition of wisdom. As Job puts it, "Where shall wisdom be found? And where is the place of understanding?" (28:12; cf. v. 20). He articulates the answer he contemplates in two parts: *"Mortals do not know* the way to it" (28:13); *"God understands* the way . . . and *he knows* its place" (28:23). Both in the Bible and beyond, the gap between what God knows and what humans do not or cannot know inserts itself as one of the most persistent and vexing questions of human existence.

The creation stories in Gen 1–3, which have been so enormously influential for Judaism and Christianity, seem to resolve the issue in God's favor, first by *prohibiting* humans from knowing certain things (Gen 2:17), then by *banishing* humans from the Garden of Eden when prohibition does not work (Gen 3:22-24). In the Genesis account, it is the crafty serpent that treats what God seems to forbid with sarcasm: "Did God say, 'You shall not eat from any tree in the garden'?" (Gen 3:1).

Immersing himself in the Genesis story, Milton offered a popular retelling that at once elevated Adam and Eve to epic dimensions and favored their search for knowledge over any rigid forbidding of it. At a critical juncture in Milton's *Paradise Lost*, after Satan determines to tempt Adam and Eve, the Lord sends the Archangel Raphael to describe to them God's creational design, a part of which includes the Genesis caution against transgressing the divine boundaries of forbidden knowledge. In Milton's version, however, Adam responds to Raphael's counsel by saying that he only wants to *know more* of God's world in order to be able to *glorify God more fully* (VII, 94-97). In response to Adam, Raphael discloses that God has instructed him to "to answer thy desire / Of knowledge within bounds" (VII, 119-20).

How then should human creatures pursue "knowledge within bounds"? Raphael counsels caution and humility, for clearly some knowledge will remain forever beyond the reach of humans, but he does not forbid the pursuit. If humans will "be lowly wise," then their search for knowledge will bring God glory:

> Heaven is for thee too high
> To know what passes there; be lowly wise:
> Think only what concerns thee and thy being;
> Dream not of other worlds, what creatures there
> Live, in what state, condition, or degree,
> Contented that thus far hath been revealed
> Not of earth only but of highest Heaven. (VIII, 172-78)

For a wide-ranging and thoughtful exploration of how society deals with the moral questions concerning the promise and the peril of knowledge, see R. Shattuck, *Forbidden Knowledge: From Prometheus to Pornography* (New York: Harcourt Brace and Company, 1996).

The Dwelling Places of Light and Darkness

Although the Bible does not speak of the dwelling places of light and darkness with any specificity (in addition to Job 38:20, see Ps 19:4b-6), the Greek poet Hesiod (8th century BCE), offers a mythic account, which depicts Atlas lifting up the heavens at the edge of the world, there to find "the awful home of murky night." In this account, as in the biblical text, Night and Day live and work in alternate cycles, one coming into the house after having completed its work as the other leaves the house to begin its duties. I am indebted to C. Newsom ("The Book of Job," in vol. 4 of *NIB* [Nashville: Abingdon Press, 1996], 603-604) for this reference.

There stands the awful home of murky Night wrapped in dark clouds. In front of it the son of Iapetus (22)

stands immovably upholding the wide heaven upon his head and unwearying hands, where Night and Day draw near and greet one another they pass the great threshold of bronze: and while the one is about to go down into the house, the other comes out at the door.

And the house never holds them both within; but always one is without the house passing over the earth, while the other stays at home and waits until the time for her journeying come; and the one holds all-seeing light for them on earth, but the other holds in her arms Sleep the brother of Death, even evil Night, wrapped in a vaporous cloud. —*Theogony*, ll. 744-57

Two matters concerning these storehouses merit attention. (1) God's questions to Job—"Have you entered. . . seen?" (v. 22), "What is the way. . . where?" (v. 24)—play off the conventional understanding that human beings have no access to, hence no knowledge of what is hidden in the storehouses of heaven, unless God grants them special privileges (Deut 28:12). There is some precedent for such an extraordinary disclosure of God's cosmic secrets in post-biblical literature. [Enoch's Vision of the Secrets in Heaven] In the Old Testament, however, the possibility exists only in the realm of the imagination. God's *rhetorical* questions seem intent on directing Job's imagination toward just such an impossible possibility. (2) Things that fall from the sky, especially hail and wind, are routinely associated with violence and destruction (hail: Exod 9:22-26; Josh 10:11; Isa 28:17; 30:30-31; Ezek 13:11, 13; Hag 2:17; wind: Gen 41:56; Exod 10:13; Jer 18:17; Jonah 4:8). God often conscripts nature as an agent of divine retribution, as Elihu has already explained to Job at some length (36:31-33; 37:1-13). If Job's tour of the universe were to stop at the storehouses of the weather, then he would no doubt be tempted to conclude that God only opens the treasury in times of "trouble" or to wage "war" against those who risk opposing the Almighty (v. 23). Yet, as the tour continues, God seems intent on teaching Job that nature also yields its treasures in life-giving ways that he has not yet comprehended.[35]

"Who Has Cut a Channel for the Torrents of the Rain?" (vv. 25-27)

The imagery of cutting water channels is instructive for two reasons, first for what it says about God, and second for what it asks of Job. First, ancient Near Eastern gods were revered for their ability to produce rain, and their kings, who ruled by embodying the gods'

Enoch's Vision of the Secrets in Heaven

According to Gen 5:24, "Enoch walked with God; then he was no more, because God took him." The Ethiopic Book of Enoch, also known as *1 En.* (2nd century BCE-1st century CE), embellishes this brief biblical account with an elaborate description of the cosmic secrets God revealed to Enoch in heaven, including the storerooms for the wind and hail.

And there my eyes saw the secrets of lightning and thunder, and the mysteries of the winds, how they are distributed in order to blow upon the earth, and the secrets of the clouds and the dew I saw there from where they proceed in that place and (how) from there they satiate the dust of the earth. At that place, I (also) saw sealed storerooms from which the winds of the storerooms of hail and the winds of the storerooms of the mist are distributed; and these clouds hover over the earth from the beginning of the world. And I saw the storerooms of the sun and the moon, from what place they come out and to which place they return . . . . (*1 En.* 41:3-5; cf. 60:11-23)

For the text and translation of *1 Enoch*, see E. Isaac, "1 (Ethiopic Apocalypse of Enoch," *The Old Testament Pseudepigrapha*, vol. 1: Apocalyptic Literature and Testaments, ed. J. H. Charlesworth (Garden City NY: Doubleday and Company, 1983), 5-89. For a succinct discussion of the critical issues, see G. W. E. Nickelsburg, "Enoch, First Book of," *ABD*, ed. D. N. Freedman (New York: Doubleday, 1992), vol. 2, 508-16.

powers, took pride in cutting the canals and building the irrigation systems that secured the prosperity of their kingdoms. [Adad, Irrigator of Heaven and Earth] It is not surprising, therefore, that the author of these speeches claims similar power for Israel's God. What is striking is that God cuts channels in order to bring rain to a land "where no one lives" (v. 26a) and to the "desert, which is empty of human life" (v. 26b). Such "waste and desolate land" (v. 27) will not support cities or culture; it certainly cannot provide the economic security that sustains kingdoms. By all conventional human assessments, irrigating the desert is at best gratuitous. At worst, it is an irresponsible waste of time and energy, for as these verses imply, in the end the desert will remain the desert; the difficulties it presents for human life may be temporarily staid, but they will never be completely eliminated. Either way, it hardly seems worthy of a Creator's wisdom; unless, of course, what is gratuitous by human standards is an act of unexpected and unwarranted grace from God's perspective.[36] [CD: "There Is a Part of Everything Which Is Unexplored"]

Secondly, why should God ask Job about cutting channels for rain in the desert? Is it only one of a litany of questions designed to show Job that he cannot do what God does, no mater how foolish or irresponsible it may be? Or, might there be another, more positive, objective? Two clues tilt us toward exploration of the latter possibility. The first is a subtle thematic connection between God's question and Job's own ruminations about the human capacity, imaged by the miner's search for buried treasures, to "cut out channels in the rocks" (28:10) to get to the source of water. The task requires extraordinary courage and skill, for miners must work in isolation, daring to enter remote places where ordinary people fear to go (28:4). Job has wondered if his quest for wisdom requires him to follow in the miner's footsteps. Perhaps those

Adad, "Irrigator of Heaven and Earth"

Adad, the Assyrian god of thunderstorms, was petitioned to bring rain for positive purposes, e.g., to nourish earth's vegetation:

> To the god Adad, canal-inspector of heaven (and) underworld, the lofty, lord of all, almighty among the gods, the awesome (god) whose strength is unrivaled, who bears a holy whip which churns up the seas, who controls all the winds, who provides abundant water, who brings down rain, who makes lightning flash, who creates vegetation, at whose shouts the mountains shake (and) the seas are churned up, the compassionate god whose sympathetic concern is life. (A. K. Grayson, ed., *Assyrian Rulers of the Early First Millennium BC II [858–745 BC]* [Toronto: University of Toronto Press, 1996], 59. For discussion of this text with reference to Job, see W. P. Brown, *The Ethos of the Cosmos: The Genesis of Moral Imagination* [Grand Rapids MI: Eerdmans, 1999], 345).

As the "irrigator of heaven and earth," Adad could also use rain and lightning for destructive purposes, e.g., to destroy the wicked and evoke the prayers of the righteous for mercy. The fragmentary prayer below illustrates:

> O lord of [lightning whose she]en illumines [the gloom]
> Might[y] whose [command] cannot be altered,
> Irriga[tor of heaven and earth],
> who rains down [abundance],
>
> Who [destroys the wic]ked, storm unrelenting,
> I cal[l upon, lord], in the midst of [holy] heaven,
> I, [your servant], come before you,
> I seek you out and [kneel be]fore you, . . .
>
> [I come before you this d]ay,
> receive my lamentations, accept my ple[as]!
> Let the [evil] portended by your utterance not come
> near me . . . (For the full text, see B. R. Foster, *Before the Muses: An Anthology of Akkadian Literature, Vol II: Mature, Late* [Bethesda MD: CDL Press, 1993], 547)

Assyrian kings, who embodied both the destructive and nourishing powers of Adad, conceived their god-like responsibilities in similar ways. They could rain down destruction on their enemies, with a force and authority comparable to Adad's. And they could build irrigation systems, which not only secured the prosperity of the land on which all citizens depended but also secured the citizens' loyalty to the king

The Storm-god Adad

The storm-god Adad standing on a bull, brandishing a flash of lightning. Basalt bas-relief on a stele from Arslan-Tash, North Syria. 8th BC.

Louvre, Paris, France (Credit: Erich Lessing/Art Resource, NY)

who provided for them. See, for example, Tikulti-Ninurta I's boast concerning his ability to build water channels that sustained the people of his kingdom:

> I cut straight as a string through rocky terrain, I cleared a way through high difficult mountains with stone chisels, I cut as wide path for a stream which supports life in the land (and) which provides abundance, and I transformed the plains of my city into irrigated fields. (A. K. Grayson, ed., *Assyrian Rulers of the Third and Second Millennia BC [to 1115 BC]* [Toronto: Toronto University Press, 1987], 273).

who risk probing the limits of their world come as close as humanly possible to imaging the work of the Creator. As he considers this option, however, Job seems persuaded that it is a fool's errand. Even if the fearless miner could cut his way to the source of the waters, he would not find the wisdom he seeks, for the waters would rise up and say, "It is not in me" (28:14). Now, God's question invites Job to consider the task once more, this time, perhaps, by accenting the *possibilities* that lie before him, not the *limitations*.

A second clue is the overlap between God's assessment of the "waste and desolate land" and Job's own estimation of what it means to be consigned to live in such places (cf. 38:27 with 30:3). Job equates this land where no one can survive with punishment and banishment. He believes that because he has defied the status quo values of his world, as articulated by his erstwhile friends, he has been exiled to a godforsaken place, where innocent sufferers are labeled as *things* to be despised rather than *persons* worthy of compassion. God's assessment of where Job is is different. "Waste and desolate land" has a place in God's world. Even though it may never produce a "cash crop," even though its strange otherness may never be "civilized" or domesticated, it has a peculiar potential for life (v. 27) that God honors and sustains. Job has complained that God has "filled" (9:18; Hiphil of *śābāʿ*, "satisfy," "satiate") him with destructive suffering "for no reason" (9:17: *ḥinnām*; cf. 1:9; 2:3). But if God also "satisfies" (38:27; Hiphil of *śābāʿ*) life-denying places with water that is essentially wasteful, at least by any calculable reason, then perhaps Job has more to learn about the promise of finding life in the desert, where few would expect to look.

"Has the Rain a Father?" (vv. 28-30)

Once more the poet invokes the language of procreation ("begetting," "womb," "giving birth"; cf. 38:8) to describe God's relationship to water. Here, however, the poet draws upon both mother and father imagery to call attention to the mysterious ways rain, once it takes its first recognizable shape in the womb, may "grow up" and "become" a variety of different and seemingly incongruous things. If it is humid during the day and relatively cool during the night, rain may fall from the heavens as drops of dew (v. 28). If the temperature drops, it may transform itself almost immediately into frost (v. 29). If the cold increases and persists, the rain may hide itself in the earth for an unpredictable period of time, then re-emerge as ice that is as hard as stone (v. 30). Like a parent celebrating the maturation of a child as she makes her way through the changing circumstances of life, God seems genuinely enthralled with these transformations, for each in its own way validates God's hopes and expectations. Habel's discernment suggests the lesson God may wish Job to learn from this part of his tour: "The riddles of nature are pointers . . . to deeper riddles and transformations of life."[37]

"Can You Bind the Chains of the Pleiades?" (vv. 31-33)

This section on the constellations is the only one in the catalogue of meteorological phenomena that does not deal with water. For this reason, it may seem out of place, perhaps even irrelevant to what has preceded. The fact that Job has referred to three of the four constellations mentioned here (9:9) suggests, however, that there is a certain poetic "logic" to God's including them as a necessary stop on the tour (see further [Constellations]). Job has already conceded that God *made* the Pleiades, the Orion, and the Bear (the fourth, Mazzaroth, may be identified with Sirus, but this is uncertain), [38] but he has complained that God's ability to cluster the stars of heaven into discernible shapes is nothing more than testimony to *purposeless power* that has little or nothing to do with what happens on earth. God now invites Job behind the curtain in order to show him the intricate behind-the-scene planning that makes possible what he has seen but not yet understood.

The Pleiades is a "herd" (*kîmā*) of seven stars or chambers in the south that store the winter storms; by "chaining" them, God limits their destructive potential. The Orion (Heb.: *kĕsîl*, "fool"), presumably a northern constellation, associated in Greek mythology with a hunter by the same name who defies the deity and must therefore be "chained," is, by God's decree, "loosed." And finally, God "guides" (*tanḥēm*; lit., "comforts") the "Bear," usually identified with the brightest star in the Ursa Major (commonly known as the "Big Dipper"), which is the lode star that provides orientation to all the constellations. Can Job image God's control of the heavens by translating its directives into meaningful rhythms for life on earth (v. 33)? Like all the previous questions addressed to him on this cosmic tour, these invite Job to contemplate his role in connecting heaven and earth in ways that defy logic by stretching his imagination.

"Can You Lift Up Your Voice to the Clouds?" (vv. 34-38)

The last stop on this tour of meteorological phenomena returns to the theme of water, now explicitly augmented for the first time with a series of questions that challenge Job's wisdom (*ḥokmāh*; vv. 36, 37). Does Job have the power to command the clouds to pour rain or to send forth the lightning that portends a thunderstorm? Does he possess the wisdom to number the clouds, imaged as containers that miraculously fill with water, then tilt them gently so that they pour out their contents on dry ground?[39]

The presumptive answer to these questions is, "No, Job can do none of these things, for they require a wisdom that God alone possesses." Job has indeed thought deeply about God's wisdom and about whether God desires to share it or withhold it from human beings. To the question "where shall wisdom be found?" the only answer Job has been able to produce thus far begins with these words: "Mortals do not know. . . God knows" (28:12, 23; see further the "Connections" at Job 28). There is, however, a suggestive hint that God now seeks to enlarge Job's answer. It is likely that the Hebrew words in v. 36 translated "inward parts" (*ṭuḥôt*) and "mind" (*śekwî*) refer instead to two remarkable birds, "the ibis" and the "the cock."[40] In ancient lore, both birds were noted for their superior wisdom, particularly their ability to announce changes in the weather. The ibis was thought to predict the rising of the Nile; the cock, the coming of the rain and the dawn. [The Egyptian God Thoth, with an Ibis Head]

Thoth

The moon god Thoth.

Detail from the sarcophagus of Buthehamon. Egypt, 21st dynasty. Museo Egizio, Turin, Italy (Credit : Nimatallah/Art Resource, NY)

The Egyptian God Thoth, with an Ibis Head

 In Egyptian lore, the moon god Thoth was often depicted with the head of an ibis to symbolize wisdom.

If God is willing to impart wisdom to some creatures, then perhaps God is also willing to share it with Job. If so, then this last stop on the tour of the meteorological phenomena may be designed to return Job to one of his previous statements. In response to the friends' claim to have a monopoly on wisdom, Job countered with a challenge: "Ask the animals, and they will teach you; the birds of the air, and they will tell you. . . . Who among these does not know that the hand of the Lord has done this?" (12:7-9). Job no doubt spoke these words sarcastically, but if he is indeed willing to ask the animals and learn from what they have to teach him about God's world, then the next stop on this tour suggests that his initial instincts, though limited, were more right than he knew.[41]

Structure of the Animal Discourse

It remains a matter of debate whether the order of the five pairs of animals is intentional or arbitrary. One suggestive proposal comes from James Miller, who discerns both a linear arrangement and a chiastic pattern. The linear arrangement, as outlined below, gives the discourse a loose but recognizable forward movement, which leads the reader to consider the human's role (as the rider, and presumed trainer of the warhorse) in the cycle of animals that scavenge for food:

1. The lion and its scavenger, the raven, in search of prey which includes
2. the mountain goat, the wild ass, the wild ox, and the ostrich which laughs at
3. the war horse which bears its rider off to war where
4. the eagle dines on the corpses (420)

The chiastic pattern also calls attention to the images of scavenging that frame this discourse as a cycle of life serving death (A1, A2 and A1', A2'). But it places the accent elsewhere, specifically on the two animals that stand at the center—the wild ass (C) and the wild ox (C')—both of which refuse to serve the cycle.

A1 the lion in search of prey
A2 and the raven as its scavenger

B The mountain goat bearing young which run off

C The wild ass, free of human service
C' The wild ox, free of human service

B' The ostrich neglecting its own egg

A1' The war horse eager to go off to battle
A2' and the eagle as the battle scavenger (Miller, 421)

Miller reads both the linear and chiastic arrangements of the animal discourse as evidence of the poet's "dark humor" concerning the role of human beings in God's design for the world. Humans have some influence over the horse that carries them into battle, but in the end of the day their primary role is to become corpses for scavenging birds. Either way, Job should not be surprised when disaster comes his way. Why not? Miller answers as follows: "From the perspective of God man may be seen as a bit player in the food chain, and his existence is superfluous to the well being of the other animals" (421).

J. E. Miller, "Structure and Meaning of the Animal Discourse in the Theophany of Job (38, 39-39, 30)," ZAW 103 (1991).

The Animal Kingdom, 38:39–39:30

Like a photographer increasing the magnifying power of the camera's lens, God now singles out five pairs of animals for Job's consideration: lion and raven (38:39-41); mountain goat and deer (39:1-4); wild ass and wild ox (39:5-12); ostrich and warhorse (39:13-25); and hawk and eagle (or vulture; 39:26-30). [Structure of the Animal Discourse] With detailed descriptions that exceed anything found elsewhere in the Old Testament, God brings these animals into such clear focus that they appear near enough for Job to touch. What is God's objective? Why should God include these particular animals on Job's tour of the world? The creation imagery that undergirds the divine speeches provides the beginnings of an answer. The *animals are not brought to Job* so that he can name them and thus define their existence in relation to himself, as in Genesis 2:19-20; instead, *Job is brought to the animals* so that they may teach him something about his own creaturely existence in God's world.[42] But what is Job supposed to learn? If he were to reach out and make contact with these animals, what would he feel. . . and perhaps understand that he has not before?

The conventional answers to these questions typically tilt toward the negative rather than the positive. By and large, most commentators conclude that God's purpose is to coerce from Job the concession that he cannot replicate what God has created. He cannot, for example, hunt the prey for the lion (38:39); he knows nothing about the reproductive habits of the mountain goats (39:1-4); he does not possess the wisdom to create a hawk that soars in flight (39:26). And yet, here again, the lyrical playfulness of the poetry that conveys God's words and the litany of rhetorical questions that invite the contemplation of impossible answers require that we keep our expectations open.

Towards this end, some preliminary observations set the table for the exegesis that follows.

• All but one of the animals God selects for special attention are wild and undomesticated, yet the imagery associated with them—birthing, feeding, and freedom—suggests that God is attentive to their every need. The lone exception is the warhorse (39:19-25), which is closely associated with the rest by its wild lust for battle. Here too, however, God appears to delight in the horse's courage and bravery, its ability to "laugh at fear" (39:22), as if these are virtues more to be commended than condemned.

• Almost all of the animals are understood to be ritually unclean, thus unacceptable, at least from a conventional priestly perspective, as offerings to God. Some however, most notably the lion, which occupies the first position in God's list (38:39-40), appear to have cultic significance.[43] Whereas convention may deny access to the holy to anything associated with the lion (cf. Eliphaz's description in 4:11-12), God's assessment of who or what is welcomed in this "temple-world" (see the comments above on 38:4-18) may be quite different. God's blessing of the tribe of Dan, characterized as a "lion's whelp" (Deut 33:12), is both a caution against premature judgment and an invitation to reflection.

• Ancient Near Eastern iconography and texts depict virtually all of the animals listed here in a variety of ways.[44] Three motifs are particularly instructive. (1) Egyptian and Mesopotamian kings are portrayed as *hunting* wild animals, not only for sport but also as a symbolic demonstration of their *power to defeat* the hostile forces that threaten the land's security. [The Royal Hunt] (2) Royal and divine figures are portrayed as *holding* wild animals in their hands, a gesture that symbolizes their *power to limit and control* the unruly forces that threaten an orderly world. [The Lord of the Animals] (3) Royal and divine figures are represented or associated with the iconic motif of the "world tree," which *provides shelter and vegetation* for the wild animals—often the same ones por-

The Royal Hunt

📖 Mesopotamian texts, for example, often describe the king defeating hostile enemies who are portrayed as wild animals. (For the inscriptional evidence, see W. P. Brown, *The Ethos of the Cosmos: The Genesis of Moral Imagination* [Grand Rapids MI: Eerdmans, 1999], 351-54.) Visual depictions of the royal hunt reinforce the king's claim to absolute sovereignty by showing how easily he targets animals that strike terror in others for defeat. In this visual, a hunter is poised to thrust his spear into three creatures that rise up in futile resistance: a mountain goat or wild deer, a lion, and an ostrich, each of which God singles out for special attention in Job 38–39 (see further [**Royal Sport**]).

O. Keel, *Jahwes Entgegnung an Ijob* (FRLANT 121; Göttingen: Vandenhoeck & Ruprecht, 1978), 86-125.

The Lord of the Animals

📖 The motif, which O. Keel calls "the Lord of the animals," occurs in Mesopotamian iconography that dates from the third millennium to the 5th C. BCE. The motif typically depicts either a human hero (sometimes a king) or a divine figure holding up two wild animals on either side. Various representations show different animals, including the lion, wild bull, wild ass, ostrich, deer, and the ibex or wild goat. The image below, which depicts a royal figure holding two fierce looking winged lions, representative of chaos, is one example.

O. Keel, *Jahwes Entgegnung an Ijob* (FRLANT 121; Göttingen: Vandenhoeck & Ruprecht, 1978), 86-125.

trayed as defeated (1) and/or restrained (2)—that gather round it. [The World Tree]

• In view of the multiple ways animals are depicted in the ancient Near East—as creatures to be *defeated*, *controlled*, and *nurtured*—it is not surprising that animal imagery in the Old Testament, including the book of Job, reflects a similar diversity.[45] Animals provide examples of *wisdom* that humans should learn from (e.g., Prov 6:6-8; 30:24-28; Job 28:7-8; 35:11) and examples of *foolishness* or *wickedness* that humans should avoid (e.g., Jer 2:23-25; Job 11:12; 24:5; 30:29). Some are creatures that are *dependent* on God's provisions (e.g., Pss 104:10-30; 147:9-11) and whose *praise* God gladly receives (Ps 148:7-14). Others exhibit such *opposition* to God and such a *threat* to civilization that they must be banished to ruined and desolate places (e.g., the wild ass: Isa 32:14; Jer 14:6; Job 24:5; 30:7), where their *whelping and screeching cannot be heard* by anyone (e.g., jackals and ostriches: Isa 34:13; 43:20; Mic 1:8; Job 30:29; Lam 4:3). On the one hand, the enmity between animals and humans typifies the *abiding distortion* of God's "very good" world (Gen 9:2). On the other, the promise that God will one day enact a "covenant" with the wild animals that transforms and restores the world remains a *lingering hope* (Gen 9:15-17; Hos 2:18 [MT: 2:20]; Job 5:22-23; for texts that suggests a transformation of the animals, see Isa 11:6-8; 65:25).

The Lion and the Raven (38:39-41)

The first pairing brings together two animals that appear to have little in common. The lion was widely regarded in the ancient Near East and in Israel as the most powerful and fearsome predator in the wild (e.g., Gen 49:9; Num 23:24; Judg 14:18; Ps 17:12; Isa 5:29; Nah 2:12). The raven, also a carnivorous creature, is a relatively small bird that cannot kill its own prey; it survives by scavenging the remains that other predators leave behind (Prov 30:17). What appears to draw them together in God's perspective is a shared vulnerability that may be unseen by those who only fear or disdain them. The lioness hunts not only for herself; she has an instinctive responsibility to her cubs, who cannot survive if she fails to bring them food. Similarly, the raven is not instinctively selfish; it also feeds itself with the "cries" for help of its young—the verb, *śāwā'* (38:41), is also frequently used with reference to human beings, who "cry out" to God for deliverance (e.g., Pss 5:2; 18:6; 41; 72:12; 119:147; Isa 58:9; Hab 1:2; Lam 3:8)—echoing in its ears.

Goddess, Feeding Two Goats.

Mycenean ivory, cover of a pyxis, from Minet-el-Beida. Louvre, Paris, France (Credit: Erich Lessing/Art Resource, NY)

The World Tree

In Mesopotamian art, the "Lord of the animals" motif is sometimes combined with the motif of the "world tree." The tree, frequently stylized as a divine figure, was revered as the creator and provider of the vegetation that sustains life itself. The depiction above is instructive. It depicts a goddess, wearing a necklace and diadem, feeding stalks of grain to two wild goats.

God's questions invite Job to ponder how he would respond to the needs of these two particular creatures. It is likely, based upon his previous statements, that Job would not look favorably on the "needs" of the lion and the raven. He has accused God of hunting him down like a lion that deserves to be killed (10:16). He has complained that God is deaf to his "cries" (19:7: *śāwā'*) for help. Why then, given his understanding of the way the world works, should Job be concerned with whether the lion's pride or the raven's young have enough to eat? One might expect him to answer God's questions about providing for the lion and the raven by saying not only, "No, I *cannot*" but also "No, I *would not*, even if I could." [Is the Well-being of the Lion a Moral Offense?]

But what if God's questions seek a different answer? What if they are designed more to enlarge Job's understanding of the world and his moral sensibilities than to deny them? Job has claimed a sensitivity to and a moral responsibility for the "poor who cry (*śāwā'*)" for help (29:12), which suggests that he would believe more about his place in the world if only he could. He believes his integrity is based on his

Is the Well-being of the Lion a Moral Offense?

Newsom suggests that the choice of the lion to begin the series may be strategically designed as part of a moral discourse that challenges conventional assumptions. In "The Babylonian Theodicy" (composed c.1000 BCE), for example, an innocent sufferer cites the flourishing of the lion and the wild ass as evidence of the moral disorder of the world:

The on[ager], the wild ass, that had its fill of [wild grass?],
Did it carefully ca[rry out?] a god's intentions?
The savage lion that devoured the choicest meat,
Did it bring its offerings to appease a goddess' anger?
The parvenu who multiplies his wealth,
Did he weigh out precious gold to the mother goddess for a family? (ll. 48-53)

Newsom offers the following assessment:

Although there is little likelihood that the Job poet is consciously invoking the Babylonian Theodicy, it is plausible that these animals served as part of a conventional trope in the poetics of the wisdom dialogue tradition or more broadly in poetry that reflected on moral order. Together with the human upstart they are represented as by definition godless and impious; consequently, their well-being is an offense. To single out the lion and the wild ass as objects of providential care, as the divine speeches do, is to issue a radical challenge to the fundamental images that informed moral thought in this tradition.

C. Newsom, *The Book of Job: A Contest of Moral Imaginations* (Oxford: Oxford University Press, 2003), 246. For the excerpt from "The Babylonian Theodicy," Newsom cites the translation in B. R. Foster, *Before the Muses: An Anthology of Akkadian Literature, Vol II: Mature, Late* (Bethesda MD: CDL Press, 1993), 808.

commitment to being a "father to the needy" (29:16), who open their mouths eagerly to receive what he provides (29:23). Nonetheless, he despairs that those he once cared for have now shamelessly abandoned him, leaving him to "cry" (*šāwaʿ*; 30:20) alone in a world where no one is listening. If, however, *God provides for the raven* (cf. Ps 147:9), a bird humans conventionally regard as unclean and detestable (Lev 11:15; Deut 14:14), and if *the raven in turn feeds the prophet Elijah* in a land where there is no food (1 Kgs 17:4-6), then perhaps the "birds of the air" (12:7) do in fact have something to teach Job about God's moral design for the world.

The Mountain Goat and the Deer (39:1-4)

In the Old Testament, the mountain goat and deer are noted for their agility (2 Sam 22:34; Isa 35:6) and beauty (Gen 49:21; Prov 5:19; Song 2:7, 9, 17, 3:5; 4:5). God focuses on neither of these traits, however. Instead, God asks Job to consider the birthing process that produces these two creatures. Does Job know the number of months required for gestation? Does he know the time of birth? Does he know how the parturition happens? The details suggest that God not only knows but also "watches over" and "guards" (v. 1: *šāmar*; NRSV: "observe") every step in the process. That God knows more and cares more about the birthing habits of wild animals than Job may be the point of this stop on the tour. But one suspects there must be something more God wants Job to learn.

As Newsom has noted, mountain goats and wild deer are the "counterimage" to domestic sheep and goats.[46] Because the latter are important economic resources, it is imperative that shepherds know the habits of their flocks and do what is necessary to protect them, especially during the critical birthing season (cf. Gen 30:31-45). The loss of a lamb or a kid not only thins the flock, it also threatens the livelihood of the family and tribe. By contrast, mountain goats and deer roam free in the wild. They give birth without human supervision. When the newborn reach maturity, they instinctively leave their mother's care, never to return (v. 4), with no thought whatsoever to diminishing the livelihood of those left behind. Why should Job know or care about how these creatures reproduce, since they provide no calculable contribution to his personal welfare? That God cares about them suggests that Job should too. Perhaps the lesson Job has yet to learn is that God does not equate any creature's importance in the world with conventional quid pro quo expectations.

The Wild Ass and the Wild Ox (39:5-12)

If God's care for the mountain goat and the wild deer confounds Job's expectations, then God's description of the wild ass and wild ox likely only adds to his wonderment. Job associates the wild ass (or onager, perhaps the ancestor of the domestic donkey), which roams the desolate steppe and salt lands, with the destitute and the outcasts (24:5; 30:7).[47] God describes the wild ass as being comfortably at "home" (v. 6) in places that provide everything it needs to thrive. Job associates its existence beyond the orderly structures of civilization with chaos, rejection, and death (Isa 32:14; Jer 14:6; cf. Gen 16:12). God looks upon the wild ass's life outside the confines of order as a celebration of freedom (v. 5) from all forms of human control or manipulation.[48]

What Job sees as chaos that can only lead to despair and a yearning for death (cf. 3:19; 7:1-2), God sees as the wild ass's reason to "laugh" (*śāḥaq*, v. 7; NRSV: "scorn").

The wild ox (the now extinct aurochs, ancestor of domestic cattle) is known and feared for its strength, particularly its horns, which are used for goring (Num 23:22; 24:8; Deut 33:17; Pss 22:21; 92:10). It was often hunted in the ancient Near East, but it was never successfully domesticated.[49] [Hunting the Aurochs] From a strictly zoological perspective, therefore, anyone, Job included, could reasonably be expected to answer God's questions—Will it spend its nights in the confines of your stable (v. 9); Will it spend its days ploughing your fields? (v. 10)—by saying, "No, of course not." Similarly, if what is at issue

Hunting the Aurochs

The Egyptian king Thutmose III (Dynasty 28), upon hearing of the presence of a herd of aurochs nearby, is reported to have left Memphis to hunt them. In four days, he killed seventy-five out of a herd of 176 aurochs. The killing is commemorated on a hunting scarab. See O. Borowski, *Every Living Thing: Daily Use of Animals in Ancient Israel* [Walnut Creek CA; London; New Delhi: AltaMira Press, 1998], 190-91.

Similarly, a Ugaritic epic recounts the story of the deity Baal hunting for wild ox in the marshes of Lake Huleh, located just north of the Sea of Galilee, according to J. Hartley (*The Book of Job* [NICOT; Grand Rapids MI: William B. Eerdmans, 1988], 508), who cites C. Gordon, *Ugaritic Textbook* (Rome: Pontifical Biblical Institute, 1965), 182: Text 76, II, 9, 12.

here is the economics of domestication, [50] that is, breeding out wildness by offering a steady supply of food and shelter in exchange for forced labor (cf. Isa 1:3), [51] then there is little reason to expect that Job will have to think long about his answer. The wild ox will not "serve" him (v. 9), no matter how long he may train it to do so.

God's rhetoric suggests, however, that there are other matters, beyond zoology and economics, for Job to consider. Can Job imagine "trusting" (*bāṭaḥ*, v. 11; NRSV: "depend") himself to the wild ox's power? Can he imagine "believing" (*ʾāman*; v. 12) that the wild ox might bring nourishment to him? The language of "trust" and "belief" evokes ideas of relationship and reliance. In a religious or theological context, one thinks of the commitment that binds humans to God, often in spite of overwhelming reasons to abandon the relationship. It is curious that Job, whose piety is without equal (according to God: 1:8; 2:3), speaks so seldom of these matters. We may wonder if suffering threatens to erase these words from his vocabulary. The one and only time in the book Job says, "I believe" the words convey more despair than hope: "I do *not* believe that he [God] would listen to my voice" (9:16). The closest he can come to using the verb "trust" is to speak of the thirsty travelers in the desert, whose expectation that water exists somewhere always ends in disappointment: "They [the caravans of Tema] are shamed, because they trusted" (6:20; author's translation). What, then, should Job learn about "trust" and "belief" from the wild ox, a creature that refuses to serve the expectations of others, even if there is some mutual benefit to both parties in its doing so? The question may seem more, not less, absurd than those Job has already heard. Such is the challenge that comes with the invitation to see the world from God's perspective.

The Ostrich and the Warhorse (39:13-25)

For the first and only time in this zoological survey, the poet uses declarative sentences, not rhetorical questions, to describe an animal that merits Job's attention. The shift may be incidental; it may also be a subtle hint that the characteristics of the ostrich, from a conventional perspective at least, do not typically invite questions. Once again, however, God's description turns conventional assumptions on their end.

God challenges Job to reconsider the merits of the ostrich in four ways. (1) Job has used the conventional name for the ostrich, "screechers" (*yaʿănāh*; 30:29; cf. Lev 11:16; Deut 14:15; Isa 13:21; 34:13; 43:20), to convey the unwanted companionship he feels with them; they are both regarded, he believes, as unclean creatures whose wailings make them unfit for the civilized world. God gives the ostrich

Tut-ankh-Amon Hunting Ostriches

Tut-ankh-Amon, standing in his chariot with drawn bow, charges a herd of gazelles and ostriches.Detail from lid of chest of Tutankhamun. The king in his chariot hunts desert animals.

Egyptian, 18th Dynasty, C. 1357-1349 BC. Stuccoed wood. Egyptian Museum, Cairo, Egypt. (Credit: Werner Forman/Art Resource, NY)

a different name, "cries of joy" (*rěnānîm*; 39:13; cf. Lam 4:3), which suggests a very different appraisal of its screeching. (2) The ostrich's wings, which are useless for flying, are conventionally regarded as an anomaly that singles it out for ridicule. The verb God uses to describe the wild but flightless flapping of its wings (so NRSV) is better translated "to be glad" or "rejoice" (39:13a: *ʿālas*; cf. NJPS, NIV). (3) The ostrich is alleged to be cruelly indifferent to its young, leaving its eggs to hatch on top of the ground, forgetting that they may be trampled on or devoured by predators (39:14-16).[52] Remarkably, God takes full credit for the ostrich's lack of "wisdom" and "understanding" (39:17), as if celebrating the very deficiencies that others mock. (4) Finally, the ostrich is widely regarded as the epitome of stupidity, a trait that no doubt made it all the more attractive for hunters who enjoyed the sport of tracking an animal too dumb to elude them. What hunters and others take for stupidity, however, God describes as the ostrich's utterly absurd but admirable disregard for danger. As the horse and rider approach, the ostrich turns and laughs (*śāḥaq*, 39:18; cf. 39:7) in their face, as if mocking warriors who have foolishly underestimated the skills of their opponent (see [Laughing at the Hunt]).

Pairing the ostrich with the horse seems odd on first impression for a variety of reasons. Unlike all the other animals in this list, the horse alone can be domesticated. Yet the reference here is to the horse that has been *trained* by humans for war. However successful such manipulation may be, it seems only to accent instincts the horse already possesses. Its leaping, snorting, pawing, and unrestrained eagerness for the fight can be likened to the lust of a stallion that has scented a mare in heat.[53] Like the wild ass and the ostrich, it too "laughs" (*śāḥaq*, 39:22; cf. 39:7, 18) in the face of any danger that may come from pursuing its objectives. More remarkable still is the description of the horse's lust for battle with terminology that is elsewhere used of God. "Might" (39:19; cf. 12:13), "terror" (39:20b; cf. 9:34; 13:21), "majesty" (39:20b; cf. 37:22), and "thunder" (39:25; cf. 40:9), are characteristics that describe the theophanic appearance of God.[54]

The Hawk and the Vulture (39:26-30)

The poet begins the last grouping with a conventionally positive image, then destabilizes it with an unexpected celebration of something that triggers a quite different thought. The hawk, soaring to heights Job cannot imagine, spreads its wings and instinctively migrates to its wintering domain in the south (39:26; cf. Jer 8:7). The vulture[55] also flies to nests secured on high rocky crags that Job cannot see. What commands Job attention, however, is not the majestic flight of these raptors but instead their capacity to spy out from on high their food, which is the blood of human corpses slain in battle.[56] Just as God provides for the lion and the raven (38:39-41), who feed off other animals, so God has created a world in which human beings are part of a mysterious food chain that sustains the vulture.

To comprehend such things, Job must see the world not only through his own eyes but also through the eyes of other creatures. Some are instinctively courageous, others are naturally shy and timid; some are undeniably strong, some are indisputably weak; some have an uncanny wisdom, others an unchangeable deficit of wisdom. Grouped together in pairs, each animal seems inexplicably bound to the other. All, for different reasons, are mysteriously dependent on God, who celebrates a world teeming with chaos that is sacred, with rebellion that is the mark of freedom, and with horror that God regards as beauty. Can Job create such a world? The first and obvious answer is, "No." Underlying that question is another, "Can Job see, understand, and learn something from this world?" The answer to this question remains as yet unclear.

A Second Summons to Answer and Job's Response, 40:1-5

For a second time in this opening discourse, God summons Job to respond (cf. 38:3). Once again, God addresses Job with language that he has himself used, a subtle clue that for all the differences in their perspectives, God and Job do share, to some extent, a common language. Job has filed a suit (*rîb*; 9:3) against God. God now addresses him as the "faultfinder" (*rōb*; v. 2a) who has dared to engage the Almighty in a court of law. Because he knows that God is no ordinary defendant, Job has sought but despaired of finding an "umpire" (*môkîaḥ*; 9:33), who can mediate the differences between these two unevenly matched litigants. Now God addresses Job as the *môkîaḥ* (v. 2b; NRSV: "who argues with God") who must speak if this "case" is to proceed any further. S. Mitchell has captured nicely the general sense of God's words: "Has God's accuser resigned? Has my critic swallowed his tongue?"[57] It is difficult to judge the tone with which God speaks these words. Most assume that God's challenge is either thinly ironic or heavily disputatious. With either assessment, the presumption is that God intends to convince Job that the inequalities between them cannot and will not be changed. Without dismissing this reading altogether, I suggest that God's tone may convey to Job a genuine invitation to respond. [Parallels Between Job 40:1-2 and Jeremiah 12:1-4]

The substance of Job's initial response is conveyed with but one word in Hebrew, *qallōtî*, "I am small" (v. 4a). Job does *not* say, "I have sinned," which is what the friends have demanded (8:5-7; 11:13-20; 22:21-27). He does *not* say, "I am terrified," as he thought he would be, if he should ever have to face God (9:34; 13:21). He does *not* praise God for the mysterious justice encoded in creation, which wounds some and heals others, as Elihu has urged him to do (33:14-30; 35:5-13; 37:1-13).[58] Instead, he *concedes* that he is of little account in the eyes of God. Elsewhere this verb form (*qll*, Qal) connotes shame and contempt, often in the context of those who *complain* that they have

---

Parallels Between Job 40:1-2 and Jeremiah 12:1-4

With keen discernment, J. Gerald Janzen has noted parallels between God's response to Job and the divine response to Jeremiah in Jer 12:1-4.

"Shall one who argues with the Almighty instruct? Shall one answer as an adjudicator of God?" The first divine speech gathers all the preceding questions into a summary challenge with this parallel pair of questions. Often in the Hebrew Bible, God is said to have a *rib*, a cause for dispute or "argument" with Israel. In Jer 12:1 the situation is reversed: The prophet has a dispute against Yahweh, very much in the same vein as Job (cf. Jer 12:1-4). Interestingly, in that context Yahweh responds to the faithful prophet in the same taunting fashion as in Job chs. 38–41:

J. Gerald Janzen, *Job* (Atlanta: John Knox, 1985), 241-42.

"If you have raced with men on foot, and they have wearied you,
how will you compete with horses?
And if in a safe land you fall down,
how will you do in the jungle of the Jordan?" (Jer 12:5)

The point of this divine response is not to put the prophet down with an impossible question, but to express surprise over the quickness with which the prophet succumbs to discouragement and disillusionment and to challenge the prophet to a deeper loyalty and vocational endurance. Where such endurance founders on mistaken views as to God's ways of working they must be eschewed (cf. Jer 15:15-21). It is the same with Job.

Placing the Hand on the Mouth

Placing the hand on the mouth is conventionally interpreted as a gesture that conveys silence, motivated either by shame or awe. G. Glazov has argued, however, that the gesture connotes a number of different things, for example:

1. It may convey *discretion*, in which case Job may be taking recourse in the modern equivalent of the fifth amendment, lest he incriminate himself with further speech.
2. It may convey *Job's disapproval*, perhaps even his revulsion, concerning the way his encounter with God has proceeded.
3. It may symbolize *Job's futile efforts to silence the anguish* that orthodoxy forbids him to speak.
4. It *may be*, indeed the final form of the book of Job suggests that it *is*, but a *temporary pause*, for ultimately Job will remove the hand; ultimately, he will speak to God (42:1-6).

G. Yuri Glazov, "The Significance of the 'Hand On The Mouth' Gesture in Job XL 4," *Vetus Testamentum* LII (2002): 30-41.

been belittled by others (cf. Gen 16:4-5; 1 Sam 2:30; 2 Sam 6:22) or by God (e.g., Nah 1:14).[59] "Since" (*hen*; NRSV: "See") Job counts for so little, how can he possibly offer any response that will matter to God?[60]

To his first words, Job adds a gesture—placing his hand over his mouth (v. 4b)—that bodies forth the shame he feels.[61] [Placing the Hand on the Mouth] He has said what he dared to say; now he resolves to speak no further. The silence to which Job retreats at the end of this "dialogue" with God thematically returns this drama to the prologue. In the "garden of Uz," where Job's once Edenic world was turned upside down by a God he could neither see nor directly address, he had responded with gestures (1:20), then words (1:21), that eventually gave way to silence (2:13). Now that God has finally appeared and shown him another perspective on his post-Edenic world, Job is certainly more informed than he was before. But if there are words adequate for his place in this world that seems so to enthrall God, Job still does not what they are. ["A Refusal to Speak Can Be Wondrously Inscrutable"] Is silence the only response the Creator will accept from those who dare to question the world's design?[62] When God initiates a second address to Job, both Job and his readers learn that God desires something more than silence. ["Misgiving"]

CONNECTIONS

God's first words from the whirlwind convey questions that invite Job, at least rhetorically, to answer. But when God speaks, how should Job, or any other mere human, respond? What can any creature say to the Creator of the world that has merit, substance? If it is a risky venture for the poet of Job 38:1–40:5 to translate God's thoughts into ordinary human discourse, surely the risk is infinitely greater for the commentator who dares to extract a (or any) meaning from a divine-human

"A Refusal to Speak Can Be Wondrously Inscrutable"

Silence is an ambiguous response, as the two commentators below illustrate.

Instead of confessing his ignorance and, by implication, his presumptuousness, in judging God, Job replies (40:3-5) that he is too insignificant to reply; that he can say no more. This response, as Saadya Gaon observed in the tenth century, is ambiguous: "When one interlocutor says to his partner, 'I can't answer you,' it may mean that he acquiesces in the other's position, equivalent to 'I can't gainsay the truth'; or it may mean he feels overborne by his partner, equivalent to 'How can I answer you when you have the upper hand?'" In order to elicit an unequivocal response, God speaks again. (Moshe Greenberg)

J. Miles, who cites the above opinion favorably, pushes beyond it by noting that "A refusal to speak can be wondrously inscrutable." While Job's silence may be *deferential*, as Greenberg suggests, it may also be *defiant*, as he points out by offering a translation of Job 40:4-5 that accents "a note of recalcitrance," which in turn invites a different interpretation of what this exchange between Job and God entails:

Look, I am of no account. What can I tell you?
My hand is on my mouth.
I have already spoken once: I will not harp.
Why go on? I have nothing to add.

Structurally, the Job writer has created a symmetry in the form of two demands and two refusals. Job speaks at length about justice and demands that God respond. God refuses. God speaks at length about power and demands that Job respond. Job refuses. Sheer silence on Job's part would be, for dramatic purposes, a bit too ambiguous. It is important that Job respond just enough to let us know that he is refusing to respond, enough to answer in the negative our question Will he be taken in? Both of Job's responses to the Lord are refusals to respond. Thus does he prove that he has not been taken in. Thus does he clear the way for the Lord's atonement and for the joy and reconciliation of the conclusion. . . The Lord, by his silence, tortured Job. Job, by his near silence, leaves the Lord in another kind of agony.

M. Greenberg, "Job," *The Literary Guide to the Bible*, ed. R. Alter, F. Kermode (Cambridge MS: The Belknap Press of Harvard University Press, 1987), 298.
J. Miles, *God: A Biography* (New York: Alfred A. Knopf, 1995), 317-18.

---

dialogue that is in and of itself already virtually beyond imagination. Even so, it is dialogue between God and Job that this book imagines. And it is the imperative for reflection upon this dialogue, however it may exceed credulity or comprehension, which emboldens the commentator to throw caution to the wind by reaching for theological connections. Even if our reach exceeds our grasp, perhaps tenuous jabs at ultimate, but ever elusive truths, will nudge us one step closer to the dialogue God seeks.

In the midst of seeking answers for undeserved suffering, Job evokes the witness of creation. "Ask the animals," he says to the friends, "and they will teach you. . . the birds of the air, and they will tell you; ask the plants of the earth. . . the fish of the sea. . . . Who among all these does not know that the hand of the Lord has done this?" (12:7-9). As if overhearing this appeal,

"Misgiving"

All crying, "We will go with you, O Wind!"
The foliage follow him, leaf and stem:
But a sleep oppresses them as they go,
And they end by bidding him stay with them.

Since ever they flung abroad in spring
The leaves had promised themselves this flight,
Who now would fain seek sheltering wall,
Or thicket, or hollow place for the night.
And now they answer hi summoning blast
With an ever vaguer and vaguer stir,
Or at utmost a little reluctant whirl
That drops then no further than where they were.

I only hope that when I am free,
As they are free, to go in quest
Of the knowledge beyond the bounds of life
It may not seem better to me to rest.

R. Frost, "Misgiving," *The Poetry of Robert Frost*, ed. E. C. Lathem (New York: Henry Holt and Company, 1969), 236.

God now invites Job to listen to what the animals have to teach him about the moral design of creation. ["Morality . . . Is Not a Human Invention"] God's review of the animal kingdom essentially reprises and expands upon the creation accounts in Genesis 1–2. There is, however, one important difference. In Genesis 2:19-20, *God brings the animals to man* in order that he may name them, thus defining their existence in relation to himself. In Job 38:39–39:30, *God brings Job to the animals.* Now it is they who will teach him something important about his own creaturely existence in relation to God.[63] If we imagine Job asking the animals what it means to live as creatures in God's world, then what would they say? How might Job respond to what he hears? More importantly, would his response advance the dialogue God seeks or bring it to an end before it starts?

Two stories about the relationship between human beings and animals may seed our reflection on the questions above. Both are fictional, hence evocations—not flat statements—of truth. Neither story is explicitly connected to what we find in Job, but both may be welcomed conversation partners in our reading and thinking. In George Steiner's apt description of fiction's potential, these works offer, perhaps, "a sort of theology passed on by whispers."[64] ["We Seek the Immunities of Indirection"]

The first is Franz Kafka's short story, "A Report for an Academy" (1919).[65] The protagonist is an educated ape, Red Peter, whose name tells part of his story. He was called "Peter," because his captors thought it appropriate to identify him with a recently deceased trained ape by the same name. The name "Red" came from the red scar on his hip, a telltale reminder of the wound he received when he was shot and captured five years ago in the jungles of West Africa. Transported by ship

---

"Morality . . . Is Not a Human Invention"

E. Kohák offers this observation about how the "moral sense of nature" (see further **[The Moral Sense of Nature]**), transforms the human perception of what is "wild" and "chaotic":

Morality, the perception of life in terms of an order of rightness, is not a human invention, a construct imposed by reflection upon unruly passion . . . . We have impressed our self-perception on nature to such an extent that nature now seems to conform to it. The perception, though, changes drastically when we no longer encounter nature as culture's wilderness preserve where reality remains "in the wild"—by our standards, anyway—but rather encounter it in its own being, ordered by its own sense. Accustomed to thinking in terms of an imposed, not of an intrinsic,

order, a citydweller first notes the absence of such an imposed order in nature. He sees mushrooms as growing "wild," not in neat trays, animals range "wild," unrestricted by leashes and cages, the entire forest, untouched by human hands for generations, grows "wild" as neglected garden, devoid of order and waiting to have one imposed on it. At first the newcomer to the land may even try. But the forest is too vast. It absorbs human efforts. What it offers is something else: when humans give up the effort to impose their order and accept instead their place within the forest, they begin to discover beneath the seeming chaos a deep, intrinsic order.

E. Kohák, *The Embers and the Stars: A Philosophical Inquiry Into the Moral Sense of Nature* (Chicago: The University of Chicago Press, 1984), 72-73.

to Europe, Red Peter found himself confined to a crate "too low to stand upright and too narrow for sitting down" (2-3). For the first time in his life, there was no way out, for as he slowly began to realize, in this new world as defined by humans, apes belong in crates. He recalls those first dark days in his new world:

> According to what I was told later, I am supposed to have made remarkably little noise. From that people concluded that either I must soon die or, if I succeeded in surviving the first critical period, I would be very capable of being trained. I survived this period. Muffled sobbing, painfully searching out fleas, wearily licking a coconut, banging my skull against the wall of the crate, sticking out my tongue when anyone came near—these were the first occupations in my new life. In all of them, however, there was one feeling: no way out. (3)

"We Seek the Immunities of Indirection"

George Steiner argues that "real presences," by which he means the transcendent reality of God, ground all human communication, including all genuine artistic forms that attempt to convey something of this reality. Even so, these secondary forms of expression have their necessary place in the journey towards grasping the ungraspable.

> . . . we crave remission from direct encounter with the "real presence" or the "real absence of the presence," the two phenomenologies being rigorously inseparable, which an answerable experience of the aesthetic must enforce on us. We seek the immunities of indirection. In the agency of the critic, reviewer or mandarin commentator, we welcome those who can domesticate, who can secularize the mystery and summons of creation.
>
> G. Steiner, *Real Presences* (Chicago: University of Chicago Press, 1989), 39.

If being an ape in a human world meant that he belonged in confinement, then Red Peter decided that he must cease being an ape and become more like the humans who were, so far as he could tell, free. This he did by imitating their behavior. He learned to spit, without licking his face clean afterwards, to smoke a pipe, and to drink alcohol. It was in mastering this last habit, the one seemingly most valued by humans, that he experienced his biggest breakthrough:

> I grabbed a bottle of alcohol which had been inadvertently left standing in front of my cage, uncorked it just as I had been taught, amid the rising attention of the group, set it against my mouth and, without hesitating, with my mouth making no grimace, like an expert drinker, with my eyes rolling around, splashing the liquid in my throat, I really and truly drank the bottle empty, and then threw it away, no longer in despair, but like an artist. Well, I did forget to scratch my belly. But instead of that, because I couldn't do anything else, because I had to, because my senses were roaring, I cried out a short and good "Hello!" breaking out into human sounds. And with this cry I sprang into the community of human beings, and I felt its echo—"Just listen. He's talking!"—like a kiss on my entire sweat-soaked body. (6)

From the moment he spoke these first drunken words, his journey into the world of humans became much simpler. He moved from trainers to teachers, from the Zoological Garden in Hamburg to the grand Music Hall, along the way attaining a European education that enabled him to become a teacher of humans himself. It is in this capacity that we first meet him in Kafka's story. Standing before the members of a scientific society, Red Peter begins the invited "report" of his life story with these words: "Esteemed Gentlemen of the Academy!"

As with all of Kafka's fiction, these words along with the story they introduce invite decipherment. We read about an ape-turned-human, and we laugh, albeit nervously, for we wonder if the humor comes at our expense. Who is making fun of whom? Once again, George Steiner's words seem instructive, although perhaps now in ways more disconcerting than comforting: "it is not so much we who read Kafka's words, it is they who read us. And find us blank."[66]

The second story is Yann Martel's 2002 Booker Prize-winning novel, *Life of Pi*.[67] The protagonist is a sixteen-year-old Hindu-Christian-Muslim boy named Pi, who emigrates with his family from their South Indian home in Pondicherry to Canada. On their fourth day out, their ship, a Japanese vessel named Tsimtsum, sinks in the Pacific Ocean. Pi is stranded on a lifeboat for 227 days with the only other creature that survives, a Bengali tiger, named (erroneously) in the ship's logs as Richard Parker. As the son of a zoo owner, Pi has grown up with an instinctive appreciation for all animals, but now, adrift with a man-eating tiger, his all-too-theoretical appreciation for this animal yields to the hard reality that survival for either of them likely means that one will become food for the other. As the days pass, the two eye each other warily; the only thing separating them is a tarpaulin that each accept, at least initially, as a territory-marker. Gradually, after various feints and dodges by each creature, Pi begins to realize that Richard Parker is not his enemy. He is, instead, the key to Pi's survival. Martel articulates Pi's moment of discernment as follows:

> It was Richard Parker who calmed me down. It is the irony of this story that the one who had scared me witless to start with was the very same one who brought me peace, I dare say even wholeness.
>
> He was looking at me intently. After a time I recognized the gaze. I had grown up with it. It was the gaze of a contented animal looking out from its cage or pit the way you or I would look out from a restaurant table after a good meal, when the time has come for conversation and people-watching. . . . He was simply taking me in, observing me, in a manner that was sober but not menacing. He kept twitching his ears and varying the sideways turn of his head. It was all, well, *catlike*. . . .
>
> He made a sound, a snort from his nostrils. I picked up my ears. He did it a second time, I was astonished. . . .
>
> Richard Parker did it again, this time with a rolling of the head. He looked exactly as if he were asking me a question.

I looked at him, full of fearful wonder. There being no immediate threat, my breath slowed down, my heart stopped knocking about in my chest, and I began to regain my senses.

I had to tame him. It was at that moment that I realized this necessity. It was not a question of him or me, but of him *and* me. We were, literally and figuratively, in the same boat. We would live—or we would die—together. . . .

But there's more to it. I will come clean. I will tell you a secret: part of me was glad about Richard Parker. A part of me did not want Richard Parker to die at all, because if he died I would be left alone with despair, a foe even more formidable than a tiger. If I still had the will to live, it was thanks to Richard Parker. He kept me from thinking too much about my family and my tragic circumstances. He pushed me to go on living. I hated him for it, yet at the same time I was grateful. I *am* grateful. It's the plain truth: without Richard Parker, I wouldn't be alive today to tell you my story. (162-64)

In an "Author's Note," Martel reports that the genesis of this book was a conversation with an elderly man in Pondicherry, who said to him, "I have a story that will make you believe in God" (x). Yet, Martel's crafting of the book's final chapters invites readers to wonder whether the story does this after all. Eventually, the lifeboat comes safely ashore in Mexico. Richard Parker disappears into the jungle. Pi begins his recovery in a local infirmary. A representative from the Japanese Maritime Department, Mr. Okamoto, comes to interview him in the hope of gaining information about the fate of the ship. As Pi unfolds the story of his long journey with Richard Parker, Mr. Okamoto finds it unbelievable: "Mr. Patel, a tiger is an incredibly dangerous wild animal How could you survive in a lifeboat with one?. . . Come on, Mr. Patel, it's just too hard to believe!" (296-97).

The following excerpts are from Pi's response to Mr. Okamoto, but they might just as well apply to an imaginary conversation between God and Job. . . and perhaps, by extension, to us readers of his incredible journey with God:

"If you stumble at mere believability, what are you living for? Isn't love hard to believe?

"Mr. Patel—"

"Don't bully me with your politeness! Love is hard to believe, ask any lover. Life is hard to believe, ask any scientist. God is hard to believe, ask any believer. What is your problem with hard to believe?"

"We're just being reasonable."

"So am I! I applied my reason at every moment. Reason is excellent for getting food, clothing and shelter. Reason is the very best tool kit. Nothing beats reason for keeping tigers away. But be excessively reasonable and you risk throwing out the universe with the bathwater". . .

Mr. Okamoto: "But for the purposes of our investigation, we would like to know what really happened."

"What really happened?"

"Yes."

"So you want another story?"

"Uhh. . . no. We would like to know what really happened.". . .

"I know what you want. You want a story that won't surprise you. That will confirm what you already know. That won't make you see higher or further or differently. You want a flat story. An immobile story. You want dry, yeastless factuality." (297-98, 302)

After taking Job on an incredible journey through the cosmos, God asks for Job's response. Job responds with silence. Perhaps we would do the same under similar circumstances. After all, when one has seen and experienced what Job has seen, what can or should anyone say to the Creator of the world? If we laugh at the thought of animals as teachers, might we look as foolish as the "esteemed gentlemen of the Academy," who think of an ape-turned-human as the measure of their own accomplishments? If we are too "reasonable" to be taken in by a story that requires us to "see higher or further or differently" than we normally do, if we want "another story," do we really believe in love, or life, or God? In the face of such questions, silence may be the right and best first response. [CD: The Quarrel with Ourselves] But, at least according to the story we read in the book of Job, it cannot be the final word we offer to the Creator of the world. ["When We Run Out of Words"]

"When We Run Out of Words"

Language is the deck of cards we have been given to name our experience. There are hundreds of games we can play with it, but in the end there are only fifty-two cards. We cannot say anything with five aces in it, or win an argument that calls for three red queens. There are limits to our language, and while most of the time the fifty-two cards seem entirely too few, the truth is that more would ruin the game. Because we are limited in what we can say, we know what it is to come to the end of speech—to come to the very edge of language—and to gaze slack-jawed at what still lies beyond. If you have ever stood on a high cliff over the sea and felt that strange, frightening pull toward the brink, then you know what I mean. There is a human fascination with limits that is both holy and chastening at the same time.

Without limits, we should have no feel for the infinite. Without limits, we would be freed from our longing for what lies beyond. It is precisely our inability to say God that teaches us who God is. When we run out of words, we are very near the God whose name is unsayable. The fact that we cannot say it, however, does not mean we may stop trying. The trying is essential to our humanity. It is how we push language to the limit so that we may listen to it as it fails, exploding into scripture, sonnet, story, song. All these may fail in the end to name the living God, but they fail like shooting stars.

Barbara Brown Taylor, *When God Is Silent* (Cambridge, Boston MS: Cowley Publications, 1998), 90-92

NOTES

[1] J. Hempel, "The Contents of the Literature," *Record and Revelation: Essays on the Old Testament by the Members of the Society for Old Testament Study*, ed. H. Wheeler Robinson (Oxford: Clarendon Press, 1938), 73. For reflections on Hempel's discernments, see the essays by R. E. Murphy, J. L. Crenshaw, and J. Gerald Janzen in "Job," *RevExp* 99 (2002): 581-605.

[2] C. Edwards, "Greatest of All People in the East: Venturing East of Uz," *RevExp* 99 (2002): 535.

[3] W. Safire, *The First Dissident: The Book of Job in Today's Politics* (New York: Random House, 1992), 22.

[4] E.g., G. Fohrer, *Das Buch Hiob* (KAT; Gütersloh: Gerd Mohn, 1963), 534; H. H. Rowley, *Job,* (The Century Bible; Ontario: Thomas Nelson, 1970), 18-21; S. R. Driver and G. B. Gray, *A Critical and Exegetical Commentary on the Book of Job* (Edinburgh: T and T. Clark, 1921), lv; W. Eichrodt, *Theology of the Old Testament*, vol. 2 (London: SCM Press, 1964), 491; G. von Rad, *Wisdom in Israel* (Nashville: Abingdon, 1972), 221-26.

[5] M. Tzevat, "The Meaning of the Book of Job," HUCA 37 (1966): 105. From a still wider perspective that interprets Job in the context of ancient Near Eastern thought, see T. Jacobsen, *The Treasures of Darkness: A History of Mesopotamian Religion* (New Haven: Yale University Press, 1976), 163: "The personal, egocentric view of the sufferer—however righteous—is rejected. The self-importance which demands that the universe adjust to his needs. . . is cast aside. . . an individual has no rights, not even to justice."

[6] See, especially, C. Newsom, "The Book of Job," in vol. 4 of *NIB* (Nashville: Abingdon Press, 1996), 595-97; idem, *The Book of Job: A Contest of Moral Imaginations* (Oxford: Oxford University Press, 2003), 234-58.

[7] L. Alonso-Schökel, "God's Answer to Job," *Job and the Silence of God*, ed. C. Duquoc, C. Floristán (Edinburgh: T. & T. Clark, 1983), 45.

[8] Ibid., 46.

[9] Ibid.

[10] Newsom, "The Book of Job," 596 (emphasis added).

[11] C. Milosz, "A Treatise on Poetry: Preface," *New and Collected Poems: 1931–2002* (New York: HarperCollins, 2001), 109.

[12] The classic study by J. Jeremias (*Theophanie: Die Geschichte einer Alttestamentlichen Gattung* [Neukirchen-Vluyn: Neukirchener Verlag, 1965]), argues that the original setting for the theophany is a military context, in which God comes as a divine warrior to celebrate a victory against Israel's enemies (e.g., Exod 15:7-10; Deut 33:2-3, 26-29; Hab 3:3-15; Ps 68:8-9, 32-35). For further discussion, see T. Hiebert, "Theophany in the OT," in *ABD*, ed. D. N. Freedman (New York: Doubleday, 1992), vol. 6, 505-11.

[13] J. L. Crenshaw, *Old Testament Wisdom: An Introduction* (Atlanta: John Knox, 1981), 111.

[14] For further discussion of theophany in the context of Exodus 3-4, see D. Gowan, *Theology in Exodus: Biblical Theology in the Form of a Commentary* (Louisville KY: Westminster John Knox Press, 1994), 26-40.

[15] Cf. J. Gerald Janzen, *Job* (Atlanta: John Knox, 1985), 170.

[16] For discussion of the form, see O. Keel, *Jahwes Entgegnung an Ijob: Eine Deutung von Ijob 38-41* (FRLANT 121; Göttingen: Vandenhoeck & Ruprecht, 1978), 24-35; V. Kubina, *Die Gottesreden im Buche Hiob* (Freiburger theologische Studien 115; Freiburg: Herder, 1979), 131-43.

[17] For a preliminary exploration of these matters, see Samuel E. Balentine, "'What Are

Human Beings, That You Make So Much of Them?' Divine Disclosure from the Whirlwind: 'Look at Behemoth, '" *God in the Fray: A Tribute to Walter Brueggemann*, ed. T. Linafelt, T. K. Beal (Minneapolis: Fortress, 1998), 259-78; idem, "For No Reason," *Int* 57 (2003): 349-69.

[18] J. L. Crenshaw, "When Form and Content Clash: The Theology of Job 38:1–40:5," *Creation in the Biblical Traditions*, ed. R. J. Clifford, J. J. Collins (CBQMS 24; Washington, DC: The Catholic Biblical Association of America, 1992), 84.

[19] T. S. Eliot, "Four Quartets: East Coker, V," *Collected Poems 1909–1962* (New York: Harcourt, Brace & World, Inc., 1970), 189.

[20] W. P. Brown, *The Ethos of the Cosmos: The Genesis of Moral Imagination* (Grand Rapids MI: William B. Eerdmans, 1999). For his discussion of Job, see 317-80.

[21] M. Fishbane, "Jeremiah IV 23-26 and Job III 3-13: A Recovered Use of the Creation Pattern," *VT* 21 (1971): 153.

[22] See Newsom (*Book of Job,* 240), who notes that the reference to "waste and desolate" land is the one point at which Job's description of the world and God's overlaps.

[23] Cf. Janzen, *Job,* 229.

[24] On the "uncertain tonality" of the speeches, see Newsom, *The Book of Job*, 235-36.

[25] Ibid., 238.

[26] On this and other strategic verbal connections between God's first words from the whirlwind and Job's opening words in ch. 3, see Alter, *The Art of Biblical Poetry*, 96-110. With respect to this particular connection, Alter says, "It is as though God were implying: you called yourself man, *gever*, now gird up your loins like a man and see if you can face the truth" (97).

[27] E.g., S. Terrien, "The Yahweh Speeches and Job's Response," *RevExp* 58 (1971): 507.

[28] Cf. G. Janzen, *Job,* 232-33.

[29] Cf. W. P. Brown, *The Ethos of the Cosmos*, 341-42.

[30] See also Brown (ibid., 344), who frames this section in the same way but offers a different interpretation of the intent of the questions.

[31] Y. Hoffman, *A Blemished Perfection: The Book of Job in Context* (JSOTSup 213; Sheffield: Sheffield Academic Press, 1996), 104. For a recent investigation of the astronomical language and imagery in Job, see B. Halpern, "Assyrian and pre-Socratic Astronomies and the Location of the book of Job," *Kein Land für sich allein: Studien zum Kulturkontackt in Kanaan, Israel/Palästina; für Manfred Weippert zum 65 Geburtstag*, ed. U. Hüber, E. A. Knauf (Göttingen: Vandenhoecke & Ruprecht, 2002), 255-64.

[32] The structure of this part of the speech may be outlined in different ways. Some take vv. 19-21, which return to the theme of light (cf. vv. 12-15), as the conclusion of the previous section (e.g., Janzen, *Job,* 236-37; C. Newsom, "The Book of Job," in vol. 4 of *NIB* [Nashville: Abingdon Press, 1996], 603-604). The six-strophe structure proposed here, which takes vv. 19-21 as the beginning of a new section, follows L. Perdue (*Wisdom in Revolt: Metaphorical Theology in the Book of Job* [JSOTSup 112; Sheffield: Almond Press, 1991], 208-10).

[33] See further, Samuel E. Balentine, *The Torah's Vision of Worship* (Minneapolis MN: Fortress Press, 1998), 82-89.

[34] Newsom, "The Book of Job," 603.

[35] Cf. Brown, *Ethos of the Cosmos*, 345.

[36] Cf. Brown's comments on God's assessment of the "desert's intrinsic worth" : "The fall of rain on parched soil is a morally indiscriminate act founded on divine gratuitousness rather than on human merit. Divine attention is warranted not by entitlement but by need, a worth beyond merit" (ibid., 348).

[37] N. Habel, *The Book of Job: A Commentary* (OTL; Philadelphia: Westminster Press, 1985), 543.

[38] So A. De Wilde, *Das Buch Hiob* (Leiden: Brill, 1981), 556.

[39] Brown notes that the image of "clods clinging together" (v. 38b) suggests that water is "imbued with community-binding force." The verb "cling" (*dābaq*) is used elsewhere to convey the intimate bonds of human relationship (e.g., Gen 2:24 and 1 Kgs 11:2 [man and woman]; Ruth 1:14 [mother and daughter-in-law]; Num 36:7, 9 [tribe and land]; 2 Sam 20:2 [king and people]). See *Ethos of the Cosmos*, 350, n. 91. God's challenge to Job, therefore, has to do with whether he possesses the wisdom to use the natural resources of the world (in this case, water) for constructive, not destructive, purposes.

[40] R. Gordis, *The Book of Job: Commentary, New Translation, and Special Studies* (New York: Jewish Theological Seminary of America, 1978), 452-53; E. Dhorme, *A Commentary on the Book of Job* (Nashville: Thomas Nelson Publishers, 1967), 593; G. Fohrer, *Das Buch Hiob* (KAT; Gütersloh: Gerd Mohn, 1963), 508-509; Newsom, "The Book of Job," 605.

[41] Cf. Janzen, *Job,* 239.

[42] Cf. Brown, *Ethos of the Cosmos*, 365.

[43] O. Borowski, *Every Living Thing: Daily Use of Animals in Ancient Israel* (Walnut Creek CA; London; New Delhi: AltaMira Press, 1998), 198-200, 226-27. It is difficult to know what significance, if any, the connection between the lion and the cult has for interpreting God's instructions to Job. On the one hand, the discovery of lion bones at cultic sites in Dan, for example, may indicate nothing more than an appreciation, perhaps bordering on reverence, for the lion's noted strength and courage. On the other, perhaps even oblique connections between the lion and the cult suggest that one of God's objectives in this discourse is to disclose something new to Job about creatures that are conventionally thought to be too wild or too unclean for proximity to the holy. This possibility merits further reflection given Job's priestly profile in the prologue and the epilogue (see the commentary on Job 1–2 and 42:7-17, and [Job's Royal and Priestly Anthropology], [Job as Priest], and [Inside the Priestly Rituals]), which suggests that innocent suffering has some bearing on how or if he can continue to trust in conventional cultic rituals on the other side of his life on the ash heap.

[44] The seminal work on the ancient Near Eastern iconographic parallels is O. Keel, *Jahwehs Entgegnung an Ijob: Eine Deutung von Ijob 38-41 vor dem Hintergrund der zeitgenössischen Bildkunst* (FRLANT 121; Göttingen: Vandenhoeck & Ruprecht, 1978). For a survey of the inscriptional evidence, see Brown, *Ethos of the Cosmos*, 351-60.

[45] Cf. K. Dell, "The Use of Animal Imagery in the Psalms and Wisdom Literature of Ancient Israel," SJT 53 (2000): 275-91; J. H. Eaton, *The Circle of Creation: Animals in the Light of the Bible* (London: SCM Press, 1995).

[46] Newsom, *Book of Job: A Contest of Moral Imaginations*, 246; idem, "The Book of Job," 609-10.

[47] For a detailed taxonomic description of the wild ass, see C. P. Groves, "The Taxonomy, Distribution, and Adaptations of Recent Equids," *Equids in the Ancient World*, ed. R. H. Matthews, H.-P. Uerpmann (Wiesbaden: Ludwig Reichert Verlag, 1986), 42.

[48] Habel (*Book of Job,* 545-46) rightly notes that the verb "set free" (*ḥāpaš*; v. 5a), with its derivatives, is used elsewhere with reference to setting prisoners and slaves free (e.g., Exod 21:2, 5; Deut 15:12, 13, 18; cf. Isa 58:6).

[49] Borowski suggests that efforts to absorb the aurochs into domestic herds caused a "loss of genetic identity," which resulted in its extinction (*Every Living Thing*, 101).

[50] So, for example, Newsom, "The Book of Job," 610; *Book of Job: A Contest of Moral Imaginations*, 246.

[51] On domestication as the physical removal of an animal's wildness for economic profit, see Borowski, *Every Living Thing*, 23-29.

[52] See M. Pope (*Job* [AB; Garden City NY: Doubleday, 1979], 309) for the evidence indicating that ostriches do not in fact abandon their nests.

[53] Newsom, *Book of Job: A Contest of Moral Imaginations*, 247; idem, "The Book of Job," 612.

[54] Habel, *Book of Job,* 547-548; cf. Newsom, *Book of Job: A Contest of Moral Imaginations*, 247; idem, "The Book of Job," 611.

[55] The word *neser* may be translated either "eagle," as in NRSV, or "vulture." The context here suggests the latter translation is more appropriate.

[56] Cf. Newsom ("The Book of Job," 612; following Dhorme, *Commentary on the Book of Job,* 613), who rightly notes that the verb "slain" (v. 30: *hālal*) is used "almost exclusively of humans in biblical Hebrew" (see, for example, Jdg 9:40; 1 Sam 17:52; Jer 14:18; Ezek 31:17).

[57] S. Mitchell, *The Book of Job* (New York: Harper Collins, 1992), 84.

[58] Cf. Habel, *Book of Job,* 549.

[59] For a survey of the verb, see C. A. Keller, "*qll* to be light," in E. Jenni, C. Westermann, eds., *Theological Lexicon of the Old Testament*, vol. 3, trans. M. E. Biddle (Peabody MS: Hendrikson Publishers, 1997), 1141-45.

[60] The prefacing particle in v. 4, *hen*, often means "behold" or "see," as in NRSV, in which case it is the equivalent of an interjection, perhaps even an introduction to an exclamatory statement. When this particle introduces a question, as here, it typically introduces a conditional statement (e.g., Hag 2:12; Prov 11:31): "*Since* (or *if*) I am of small account, how can I answer you?" Cf. Janzen, *Job,* 243; Perdue, *Wisdom in Revolt*, 216.

[61] C. Muenchow, "Dust and Ashes in Job 42:6," JBL 108 (1989): 608; cf. B. Couroyer, "'Mettre sa main sur sa bouche,'" RB 67 (1960): 197-209.

[62] See, for example, J. T. Wilcox, *The Bitterness of Job: A Philosophical Reading* (Ann Arbor: University of Michigan Press, 1969), 99-117, who argues that God's primary objective in the divine speeches is to say "No to Job's No." Wilcox interprets Job's "No" in the Nietzchean sense of a "no-saying" about God's moral governance of the world. When God says "No to Job's No," the objective is to prove that there is something fundamentally wrong with *Job's moral sense*, not *God's*.

[63] Cf. Brown, *Ethos of the Cosmos*, 365.

[64] G. Steiner, *No Passion Spent: Essays 1978–1995* (New Haven, London: Yale University Press, 1996), 249.

[65] The story was first collected in a volume of Kafka's stories titled *Ein Landarzt* (1919) and subsequently published in N. Glatzer, ed., *Franz Kafka: The Complete Stories* (New York: Schocken, 1971). The page references here are from the E-text translation provided by I. Johnston, which may be consulted at http://www.mala.bc.ca/~johnstoi/kafka/reportfora-cademy.htm.

[66] G. Steiner, *No Passions Spent*, 251. Steiner's remarks, which I have cited previously in the commentary on Job 29:1-11, concern Kafka's novel, *The Trial* (New York: Schocken Books, 1937) (on which, see further [Contemplating a Fierce Judge]), but they seem to apply with equal truth to this short story.

[67] Y. Martel, *Life of Pi* (New York, San Diego, London: Harcourt, Inc., 2001).

GOD'S SECOND ANSWER, JOB'S SECOND RESPONSE

Job 40:6–42:6

In the first speech from the whirlwind, God summoned Job to gird up his loins like the mighty *geber* ("man") he was born to be (38:3a; cf. 3:3) and to accompany God on a journey designed to show him more about the design of creation than he had previously understood. At both the beginning and the end of this first speech, God invited Job's response to what he had seen (38:3b; 40:2). Job's response was to retreat to silence (40:4-5). Now God initiates a second speech that indicates Job's journey is not over. Once again, God commands Job to gird up his loins like a *geber*; for a third time, God invites Job's response (40:7). The journey now focuses on God's governance of the world (40:8-14), exemplified in a sixth and final pair of animals—Behemoth (40:15-24) and Leviathan (41:1-34)—which God singles out for Job's special consideration. While silence may be appropriate as an initial response to what God discloses to Job, this second speech suggests that God expects and desires something more. ["There Is Danger in Unnatural Silence"]

> **"There Is Danger in Unnatural Silence"**
> There is danger in unnatural silence
> No less than in excess of lamentation.
> Sophocles, *Antigone*.

COMMENTARY

"Would You Discredit My Justice?" 40:6-14

The prologue envisions two responses Job might offer to undeserved suffering. The *satan* wagers that Job will *curse* God (1:11; 2:4 cf. 2:9). God, presumably, expects Job to prove that he is indeed a faithful servant by continuing to *bless* God, regardless of the suffering that befalls him (2:3). Initially, Job validates God's expectations (1:21), but he gradually begins to explore a third option that neither the *satan* nor God appear to have factored into the possibilities. Blessing gives way to cursing (3:3-10); cursing issues forth in pained lament (3:11-26); and lament escalates into a quest for justice that places *God's* righteousness, not *Job's*, on trial (see [The Trial Metaphor in Job]). Job's lawsuit against God culminates in the rhetorical equivalent of a legal subpoena (31:35-37), which presents God with either-or options that resemble those first suggested by the prologue. God must *either* appear in court to answer Job's charges *or* Job will pronounce God guilty of injustice by default. The opening question in this second challenge— "Would you discredit my justice (*mišpāṭ*)? Would you condemn me to justify yourself?" (40:8; NIV)—suggests that God wants Job to reassess this either-or understanding of what constitutes justice.[1] God too, it seems, desires that Job explore another option—beyond blessing, cursing, lament, *and* silence—that sustains his pursuit of justice in ways he has not yet comprehended.

With a series of rhetorical questions and evocative commands, God invites Job to understand that the justice on which the world relies requires godlike *power* (v. 9a: "an arm like God"; cf. Exod 15:16; Pss 77:15; 89:13; Isa 63:5), *words* (v. 9b: "thunder with a voice like his [God's]; cf. Pss 18:13; 77:18; 104:7), and *majesty, dignity,* and *glory* (v. 10; cf. Exod 15:7; Pss 96:6; 104:1; 138:5; Isa 2:10, 19, 21; 24:14). It also requires righteous anger (vv. 11-13), like that which God displays in bringing down the proud and the wicked, who arrogantly presume they can abuse others without penalty (cf. Job's complaint in 21:28-30; 24:1-12). The last words of God's challenge (v. 14) invite close inspection, for they suggest that *if* Job can image God's power, words, majesty, and anger, *then* God will acknowledge that his quest for justice is not only principled but also effective. [CD: "If You Have Courage . . . Victory Shall Be Yours"]

How are we to interpret God's challenge to Job? Is the objective to show Job that he cannot judge the world in any way that merits God's approval? Is it to embolden Job to pursue justice in creaturely ways that somehow resemble, and perhaps even advance, God's own cosmic responsibilities? Much depends on the assessment of the "pride" language that God uses to convey the challenge. The terms for "majesty" and "dignity" in v. 10a (*gāʾôn* and *gōbah*) and for "proud" in vv. 11b and 12a (*gēʾeh*) derive from a verbal root meaning "to be high" or "exalted." Job has used this language twice before, both times positively as a means of describing the instinctive need of some things in God's creation to stand tall (8:11) or be "proud" (10:16; NRSV: "bold"), if they are to survive. The friends use this language four times. When they associate pride with God, it is always positive (37:4). They equate human pride, however, with the arrogance of evildoers who challenge God's authority (33:17; 35:12; cf. 22:29; see further the commentary on 33:14-30 and [Pride Goes Before Destruction]). These very different perspectives on pride heighten our expectation that what God has to say will resolve the matter one way or the other, either by rebuking Job, like the friends, for his hubris, or by affirming him, against the friends, for his rightful aspiration to a virtue God gladly shares.

The language of pride occurs five times in God's speeches. In two instances, God speaks positively, commending to Job's careful consideration the "proud waves of the sea" (38:11) and the "pride" exemplified in Leviathan's strength (41:15 [MT: 41:7]).[2] The three remaining references occur in this pericope, 40:10, 11, 12. An important clue for evaluating God's purpose in summoning Job to deck himself with "pride and dignity" (v. 10a, REB), then to "look on all who are proud" and bring them down (vv. 11b, 12a), may be found in the coupling expression "glory and splendor" (v. 10b: *hôd wĕhādār*).[3] The latter phrase occurs six times in the Hebrew Bible. Four of the six are used as ascriptions of praise offered to God (Pss 96:6 [paralleled in 1 Chr 16:27]; 104:1; 111:3). Two are used with reference to human beings, once to describe the blessings God bestows upon the king (Ps 21:5 [MT: 21:6]; cf. Ps 45:3 [MT: 45:4]), a second time in Job 40:10, where God summons Job to put on the regalia of "glory and splendor," like a king.[4] The recognition that the endowment with "glory and splendor" is shared in Hebrew scripture, albeit unequally, by a triad of persons—God, king, and Job—invites us to consider that God is not rebuking Job for usurping a virtue that properly belongs only to God. Instead, God may be summoning Job to a royal responsibility that represents the apex of his vocational calling to image God.[5]

We may press this last suggestion a step farther. If God is challenging Job to consider his royal responsibilities for governance, then God may also be addressing Job's lingering, still unanswered question, "What are human beings, that you [God] make so much of them?" (7:17). For the psalmist (Ps 8:4-5; cf. Ps 144:3-4), such a question conveys astonished praise, for who can fathom God's decision to elevate mere human beings to royal status and then to entrust to them a dominion and responsibility for the cosmos that is almost equal to that of the Creator? For Job, however, the question evokes lament, not praise, deep sarcasm, not lofty wonderment. The measure of his suffering has forced him to conclude that if God has lifted him up for special attention, it is only because God delights in making him a better target for destruction (see further [CD: Psalm 8 and Job 7]). Eliphaz has responded to Job by redirecting him to his own version of the psalmist's question—"What are human beings, that they can be clean?" (15:14; cf. 4:17-19; 22:2-3)—to which he offers the only answer his theology of creation permits: Job, like all human beings, is a sinful and flawed creature in whom God places no trust whatsoever. God's challenge in 40:7-14 puts the psalmist's words before Job once more, this time with rhetorical questions—"Have you an arm *like God*?" "Can you thunder with a voice

Behemoth and Leviathan

William Blake depicts Behemoth as a huge land creature, Leviathan as an enormous sea creature. Both creatures are terrifying in their appearance, yet both are safely contained in their world, thus posing no threat to Job, his wife, and the three friends, who huddle safely together under the canopy of a starry heaven shared with God and the angels. Leaning forward upon a cloud at the very top, God extends the left arm past Job, with the index finger pointing downward, almost touching Behemoth. The left border contains a quotation from Job 37:11-12; the top, a quotation from Job 36:29; and the right, quotations from Job 40:19 and 41:34. It is, however, the citation from Job 40:15 in the bottom border that most clearly explicates what God wishes Job to see and understand: "Behold now Behemoth which I made with thee."

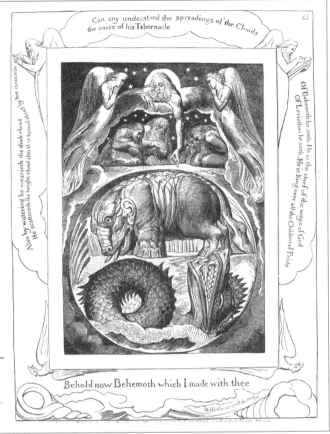

Behemoth and Leviathan

William Blake (1757-1827). *Behemoth and Leviathan.* 1823-1825. Engraving from Blake's *Illustrations of the Book of Job.*

like his?"—that now issue forth in a directive: "Deck yourself with majesty and dignity; clothe yourself with glory and splendor (*hôd wĕhādār*)." The latter part of this imperative is only a slight variation of the psalmist's affirmation of the place of human beings in God's world: "You have made them a little lower than God, and crowned them with glory and honor (*kābôd wĕhādār*)" (Ps 8:5 [MT: Ps 8:6]).

This subtle echo of Psalm 8 suggests that God is not admonishing Job for trying to project "his own brand of justice on the earth as if he were a god."[6] Rather, God appears to be challenging Job to live still more boldly into the role that God has specially created for human beings. To do so, Job must dare to participate in the governance of the world with the pride and courage that derives from being charged with responsibilities that are only a little lower than God's. Such a mandate, however, only begs a further question. What does it mean to pursue justice with dignity, power, and glory that is the near equal of God's?

"Look at Behemoth, Which I Made Just as I Made You," 40:15-24

The answer to the question just posed is embedded in God's invitation to Job to think carefully about the characteristics of a sixth and final pair of animals, Behemoth and Leviathan (see the commentary below on 41:1-34). [Behemoth and Leviathan] The word "Behemoth" (intensive plural of "cattle," "animal") means "super beast." Apart from its occurrence in Job 40:15-24, the use of this term as a name for an animal does not occur elsewhere in the Hebrew Bible, hence the specific identity of this creature is difficult to determine. A wide range of possibilities, mostly drawn from references in Egyptian and Mesopotamian texts, have been proposed, including literal animals such as the hippopotamus and the water buffalo, and mythological creatures that symbolize chaos. [CD: Who or What Is Behemoth?] As Newsom has noted, the debate about whether Behemoth is a real animal or a mythical monster is likely misplaced. The description in Job suggests that both Behemoth and Leviathan are better understood as liminal creatures whose characteristics place them somewhere between mere earthly animals and supernatural figures that belong to the world of myth and legend.[7] In this respect, they are particularly well suited as models that invite Job's continuing exploration of what it means for human beings to be created "in the image of God," i.e.,as mere mortals who are nevertheless "a little lower than God" (Ps 8:5 [MT: Ps 8:6]). [CD: Behemoth and Leviathan in the Garden of Eden]

Most biblical commentators argue that God singles out Behemoth and Leviathan for special mention in order to prove to Job that God alone has the power to control or defeat these hostile forces, which threaten the stability of creation.[8] Although

Behemoth and the Devil

From the Liber Floridus, Ghent. Centraale Bibliotheek van de Rijksuniversiteit, Ghent, Belgium. (Credit: Foto Marburg/Art Resource, NY)

there is substantial support for this approach, [9] the text offers clues that invite a more nuanced understanding. The following observations about God's description of Behemoth reinforce Alonso-Schökel's suggestion: when interpreting the divine speeches, readers should keep their expectations open. [10]

• With the exception of the ostrich (39:13-18), Behemoth is the only creature in this zoological survey that God introduces with affirmations, not questions. God does not ask Job to do or say anything. He must simply listen, look, and learn from this creature that God has made, "just as I made you" (v. 15: *'ăšer 'āśîtî 'immāk*; lit., "whom I made along with you"). Later Jewish apocalyptic literature speculated that God made both Behemoth and Leviathan on the fifth day of creation (2 Bar 29:4; 2 Esd 6:49-52; see [CD: Who or What Is Behemoth?]). The Joban poet may be engaging in a similar kind of speculation. By positioning Behemoth as the first of the *sixth* pair of animals shown to Job, he invokes the creation rhetoric that stipulates God made the land animals, along with human beings, on the *sixth day* of creation (Gen 1:24-27). [11] Moreover, because Behemoth's creation provides the only reference in the divine speeches to human beings, the poet suggests that this creature provides a model by which Job may understand his own identity and vocation in God's world. Though the correspondence is only obliquely stated, Behemoth and Job are in some sense twins. When Job looks at Behemoth, he somehow sees himself.

• Behemoth is a creature with extraordinary strength and power (vv. 16-18). With bones like "tubes of bronze" and limbs like "bars of iron," it can withstand almost any force that may be brought against it. Its strength resides not merely in its ability to protect itself against life-threatening forces; it also has the sexual potency to generate new life out of its own resources. The description of its tail as "stiff like a cedar" (v. 17) is likely a euphemism for the erection of the penis. [12] In sum, Behemoth is a creature peculiarly endowed with a capacity not only for sustaining life but also for creating it. Why should such things matter to Job? What should he learn from looking at this particular example of creaturely strength and power? A clue may be found in Job's lament about his own failing power to withstand God's assault against him. He has asked, "What is my strength?" (6:11). He despairs that his "bones" and "sinews" are not as durable as "bronze" (10:11; 6:12). He complains that the "belly" that birthed him destined him for death (3:10-11; 10:18-19), not life; that even though he has tried to sustain the life of others since the day he emerged from his mother's "belly" (31:18), the end result has been only misery. If God has indeed made Behemoth just like him, then perhaps God has created Job with capacities he has not yet realized.

• Behemoth is described as the "first (*rē'šît*) of the great acts of God" (v. 19a). The word *rē'šît* recalls not only the creation narrative in Genesis 1 (v. 1: *běrē'šît*, "in beginning"), which introduces God's purposive design for the cosmos, but also the description of Wisdom in Prov 8:22, who celebrates its role as the co-creator God called forth at the beginning (*rē'šît*) as part of the master plan for creation. Eliphaz has invoked the same imagery in order to ask Job, "Are you the firstborn of the human race?" (15:7). The question is meant to rebuke Job for daring to imagine that he has some special standing with God. God's description of Behemoth as the "first" of creation's works now offers Job a model of royalty that invites from Job the very self-understanding that Eliphaz would deny. Behemoth is like a king in its own domain: the mountains bring forth tribute; the wild animals play as contented subjects in its realm; nature—plants, trees, marshland, and streams—provides its every need (vv. 20-22).[13] If Job were to respond to Eliphaz with what God has shown him in this comparison with Behemoth, he might be expected to counter by saying, "Yes indeed, I *am* like the primal creature who is a near equal to God; I *am* endowed with royal responsibilities" (see further [King Job]).

• Finally, Behemoth is distinguished by the way it responds to aggression and violence (vv. 23-24). If the river rages against (*ya'ăśaq*, lit., "oppresses") it, it does not flee in fear. If the Jordan bursts forth (*yāgîaḥ*; the same verb describes the bursting forth of the waters in 38:8), it trusts (*yibṭaḥ*) in its own resources. Verse 24 provides an important caveat. No earthly creature (including Job) can dictate Behemoth's movements by leading it around with hooks; no one in its world

---

Textual Problems in 40:19b

AΩ   NRSV's translation of 40:19b—"only its Maker can approach it with the sword"—along with other modern translations (cf. NIV, NJPS) is deceptively straightforward. Its rendering implies a confrontation in which God defeats Behemoth. While such a reading comports with the conventional interpretation of Behemoth as God's hostile opponent, it does not do justice to the complexity of the Hebrew text. C. Newsom spells out succinctly the major issues as follows:

As pointed, the clause reads "his maker brings near his sword." If "his sword" refers to God's sword, the claim would be that *God (alone) is capable of confronting the power of this creature,* thus forming a contrast with v. 24, which implies that no human can. Though plausible, it is not the only possible reading. Given the ambiguity of the pronouns, the words might also be taken to mean that it is *God who has given Behemoth*

his great power (Behemoth's "sword") as a token of his lordship over the other animals as the chief of the works of God. But the word translated "his maker" (*ha 'ōśô*) is grammatically anomalous, being doubly determined. The Hebrew consonants suggests that the word should be pointed *he'aśû,* "made," the same word used to describe Leviathan as "made without fear" (41:25). A modest emendation in 40:19b (from *yaggēš* to *nōgēś*) yields "made to dominate his companions" [cf. NAB: "made the taskmaster of his fellows"], a claim more in keeping with the context. The following description is not at all evocative of violence but describes the peaceful, even stolid pleasures of Behemoth, whose food comes to him as he lies shaded in the water, unmoved even as the river's torrents rush against him.

C. Newsom, *The Book of Job: A Contest of Moral Imaginations* (Oxford: Oxford University Press, 2003), 250 (emphasis added); cf. idem, "The Book of Job," in vol. 4 of *NIB* (Nashville: Abingdon Press, 1996), 619.

Ugaritic Parallels

AΩ In Ugaritic texts, Baal and Anat wage victorious battle against the sea monster Lotan (Leviathan). For example:

> She [Anat] raised her voice and shouted: . . .
> What enemy has risen against Baal,
> What foe against the Rider on the Clouds?
> Didn't I demolish El's Darling, Sea?
> didn't I finish off the divine river, Rabbim?
> didn't I snare the Dragon?
> I enveloped him,
> I demolished the Twisting Serpent,
> the seven headed monster.
>
> When you [Baal] killed Lotan, the Fleeing Serpent,
> finished off the Twisting Serpent,
> the seven-headed monster,
> the heavens withered and drooped
> like the folds of your robes . . . .

For the translation, see M. Coogan, *Stories from Ancient Canaan* (Philadelphia: Westminster, 1978), 92, 106. For further discussion of Ugaritic mythology in relation to Job, see M. Pope, *Job* (AB; Garden City NY: Doubleday, 1979), 329-32.

(including Job) can tame its aggression by piercing "its nose (*'ap*) with a snare."[14] Despite its extraordinary strength and courage, Behemoth is nonetheless only a creature, not a god. God, its "Maker," can wage a victorious battle, if necessary, against this fearless opponent (cf. v. 19b). [Textual Problems in 40:19b]

What is perhaps most striking about all these descriptions of Behemoth is that God does *not* regard this creature as a threat to creation's order or as an opponent that God must defeat in order to be God. Instead, God commends Behemoth to Job as a model for what it means to be a creature worthy of the Creator's pride and praise. The lesson for Job seems to be that those who dare to stand before their maker with exceptional strength, proud prerogatives, and fierce trust come as near to realizing God's primordial design for life in this world as it is humanly possible to do.

Leviathan, 41:1-34 (MT: 40:25–41:26)

Canaanite literature identifies Leviathan (or "Lotan") as the mythological sea serpent (lit., the "twisting one") that the gods must defeat in battle in order to secure creation's stability. [Ugaritic Parallels] Old Testament texts make a similar identification, but they do so in a curiously ambivalent way. On the one hand, they affirm that Israel's God establishes the order of creation by defeating Leviathan (e.g., Ps 74:13-14; Isa 27:1). [Demonizing Leviathan] On the other, they also affirm that Leviathan (along with other water animals) is a valued creature in the "very good" world that offers God both praise and satisfaction (Gen 1:21; cf. Pss 148:7; 104:26). The poet who crafted God's description of Leviathan in Job 41 exploits this ambivalence in a way that summons both Job and his readers to keep their expectations open.

The speech comprises four sections with two interwoven thematic foci. The first (41:1-12 [MT: 40:25–41:4] and third sections (41:25-32 [MT: 41:17-24]) invite reflection on how Leviathan can be hunted, only to conclude that it successfully defies all such efforts by slithering away safely, leaving would-be captors in its

Structure of Job 41:1-34

AΩ
- I. 41:1-12 [MT: 40:25–41:4] "Can you draw out Leviathan with a fishhook?"
  - II. 41:13-24 [MT: 41:5-16] "Who can strip off its outer garment?"
- III. 41:25-32 [MT: 41:17-24] "When it raises itself up the gods are afraid"
  - IV. 41:33-34 [MT: 41:25-26] "On earth it has no equal . . . it is king"

wake. Sections two (41:13-24 [MT: 41:5-16]) and four (41:33-34 [MT: 41:25-26]) provide extensive descriptions of Leviathan's physical characteristics, which serve to justify God's assessment that on earth this remarkable creature "has no equal." [Structure of Job 41:1-34]

"Can You Draw Out Leviathan with a Fishhook? (41:1-12 [MT 40:25–41:4])
Unlike the Behemoth speech, the Leviathan poem begins with a series of rhetorical questions. Can Job capture Leviathan with a hook or a cord? Can he domesticate this creature by forcing it into a "covenant" (v. 4) that reduces it to nothing more than a servant who pleads for mercy from its master? Can he turn this mighty creature into a play toy for children? Can he kill Leviathan with harpoon or spear, then cut up its carcass and sell it for profit in the market place? The expected answer from Job to all these questions is, "No, of course not."

We might assume that the unstated corollary to this

Saint Michael Fighting the Dragon
Albrecht Dürer (1471-1528). *Saint Michael Fighting the Dragon.*
(Credit: Dover Pictorial Archive Series)

Demonizing Leviathan

In the history of interpretation, Leviathan came to be viewed not only as a primordial threat to creation but also, especially in Christian exposition, as the AntiChrist, the quintessential embodiment of the evil that threatens the Church (see especially the eschatological vision of God's defeat of the "beast rising out of the sea" in Rev 12–22; see further the depiction of the AntiChrist riding Leviathan in **[Leviathan]**). The image above, which depicts the angel Michael slaying the Leviathan-like forces of evil, is illustrative of many others in the Christian tradition.

answer is that only God can capture, tame, and/or kill a creature like Leviathan. Textual ambiguities in 41:10-12 (MT: 41:2-4), however, complicate such an assumption. The first half of v. 10, which affirms that no one is fierce enough to rouse up Leviathan, including Job (cf. 3:8), is coupled to a question that may be read in two different ways. NRSV follows some Hebrew manuscripts that read, "Who can stand before *me* (*lĕpānay*, v. 10b [MT: 41:2b])?"—a translation that accents

God's incomparability, i.e., Who can stand against God? NIV follows other textual and versional evidence by translating, "Who can stand before *him* (*lĕpānayw*)?"—a reading that shifts the emphasis to *Leviathan's invincibility*, i.e., Who can contend with Leviathan?

The possible slippage between first person references ("I," "me") and third person references ("it") continues in v. 11 (MT: 41:3). The Hebrew text uses first person language. NJPS's translation suggests that the words refer to what God is saying about *God's* power to confront Leviathan: "Whoever confronts *Me* (*hiqdîmanî*) *I* will requite (*'ăšallēm*)" (cf. NIV).[15] Alternatively, one might interpret the first person pronouns as conveying God's quotation of *Leviathan's boast about its own power*: "Whoever confronts *me*, *I* will repay."[16] NRSV offers a third possibility by substituting third person pronouns, which suggests that God is speaking about the *inability of anyone* to confront *Leviathan*: "Who can confront *it and be safe?*" (cf. REB, TEV, NAB).[17] This change has the advantage of sustaining what God has said in the preceding verses about Leviathan's extraordinary power. At the same time, it invites a rather shocking speculation. Is Leviathan's power so godlike that even God hesitates to engage it in battle (cf. v. 10a [MT: 41:2a])?

Verse 12 (MT: 41:4) presents an array of additional difficulties. The verbal phrase that introduces the verse (*lō' 'ăḥarîš*) may be translated either "I *will not* keep silence" (NRSV, NJPS) or "I *will* silence." The words that NRSV translates "limbs," "mighty strength," and "splendid frame" may refer either to Leviathan's powerful *physical attributes* or to the rhetorical force of its *powerful words*, i.e., "boasting," "heroic words" (*dĕbar gĕburôt*; the second word is semantically related to *geber*, the word God uses to address Job in 38:3 and 40:7), "persuasive argument."[18] The adjudication of these textual ambiguities depends in large measure on how one assesses the overall objective of the divine speeches. If one accepts the conventional interpretation, then God's intention is to prove to Job that *God alone has the power to subdue (silence)* a creature as powerful as Leviathan. If not, then one might consider other options. Perhaps one of the reasons God commends Leviathan to Job's attention is to invite him to understand that *God will not subdue (silence) creatures* that speak heroically about their God-given role in creation. [Considering the Alternatives]

"Who Can Strip Off Its Outer Garments? (41:13-24 [MT: 41:5-16])

The second part of God's speech begins with rhetorical questions (41:13-14 [MT: 41:5-6]), then shifts to declarative sentences (41:15-24 [MT: 41:7-16]). The thematic focus throughout is on Leviathan's

Considering the Alternatives

In considering these alternatives, I concur with C. Newsom, who supports the preference for the latter option as follows:

There is no known tradition of Leviathan's boasting silenced by God. Moreover, the continuation of the passage in fact does begin a detailed description of the physical appearance of Leviathan. And if there is any boast, it is the one that God himself makes on behalf of Leviathan at the end of the speech: "On earth there is no one who can dominate him, made as he is without fear. He looks down upon all that is haughty; he is king over all that are proud [41:32-33]." . . . Far from recounting a confrontation with Leviathan that results in its defeat, humiliation, and abasement, the passage celebrates its rightful pride, based upon its terrifying strength and violence.

C. Newsom, *The Book of Job: A Contest of Moral Imaginations* (Oxford: Oxford University Press, 2003), 251-52.

---

extraordinary physical strength and power. The description begins (vv. 13-17 [MT: 41:5-9]) and ends (vv. 22-24 [MT: 41:14-16]) with Leviathan's body. Its skeleton is protected by a double-coat of mail that weapons of war cannot penetrate (see below, vv. 26-29 [MT: 41:18-21]). The "doors of its face" close over teeth set so tightly together they seal up every opening. Its neck is a tower of strength; its heart is as hard as a millstone. If God wishes Job to gird up his loins "like a warrior" (*geber*, 38:3; 40:7), then there can be no stronger example of what this means than Leviathan.

At the center of God's portrait is a description of Leviathan's mouth (vv. 18-21 [MT: 41:10-13]). If we read this section alongside the previous description of Leviathan's mouth (41:3-4 [MT: 40:27-28]), then two contrasting images emerge: one that emphasizes what *does not come forth* from its mouth; the other, that which *does*. What does not come forth from this creature's mouth are "soft words." In the unlikely event anyone should ever successfully capture it and force it into service, even then it would not conform to any "covenantal" relationship that required it to do or say only what its master permitted. Instead, when it opens its mouth it instinctively speaks like a god. The rhetoric emphasizes fire and light, smoke and flames, phenomena elsewhere associated not only with the strong and compelling appearance of ancient Near Eastern deities but also with YHWH. [Speaking with the Authority of the Gods] Like a god, Leviathan announces its presence with an awesome fierceness that commands attention and defies coercion. In sum, if what does and does not come forth Leviathan's mouth offers a model for Job, then the lesson commends strong words, not soft or gentle ones, speech that demands respect, not disregard.[19]

"When It Raises Itself Up the Gods Are Afraid" (41:25-32 [MT: 41:17-24])

The third section of the poem returns the focus to the impossibility of hunting and capturing Leviathan. Should gods or mortals rouse this

Speaking with the Authority of the Gods

What comes forth from Leviathan's mouth—"light," "flaming torches," "sparks of fire," "smoke," "flame" (41:18-21 [MT: 41:10-13])—resembles the power with which other divine beings, including Israel's God, announce their presence. Thus, when Marduk, the patron god of Babylon, "moved his lips, fire blazed forth" (Pritchard, 62). Elsewhere, when Yam's (the Sea's) messengers present themselves before the divine assembly, they do not prostrate themselves but instead stand proudly and speak with authority:

> The gods lift up their heads
> From upon their knees,
> From upon [their] thrones of prin[ceship].
> Then come the messengers of Yamm,
> The envoys of Judge Nahar,
> At El's feet they do [not] fall down,
> Prostrate themselves not to the Assembled Body.
> *Prou[dly] standing,* [they] say their speech.
> Fire, burning fire, *doth flash*;
> A whetted sword [are their e]yes. (Pritchard, 130)

Israel's poets use similar imagery to describe the awesome appearance of YHWH, for example:

> Then the earth reeled and rocked;
> the foundations also of the mountains trembled

> and quaked because he was angry.
> Smoke went up from his nostrils.
> and devouring fire from his mouth;
> glowing coals flamed forth from him . . . .
> Out of the brightness before him
> there broke through his clouds
> hailstones and coals of fire.
> The Lord thundered in the heavens,
> and the Most High uttered his voice.
> And he sent out arrows, and scattered them;
> he flashed forth lightnings, and routed them.
> Then the channels of the sea were seen,
> and the foundations of the world were laid bare
> at your rebuke, O Lord,
> at the blast of the breath of your nostrils. (Ps 18:7-8, 12-15)

> The voice of the Lord flashes
> forth flames of fire.
> The voice of the Lord shakes the wilderness;
> the Lord shakes the wilderness of Kadesh.
> The voice of the Lord causes the oaks to whirl,
> and strips the forest bare;
> and in his temple all say, "Glory!" (Ps 29:7-9)

ANET, 3rd ed. with supplement, ed. J. B. Pritchard (Princeton: Princeton University Press, 1969).

---

fearsome creature and pursue it with all the weapons at their disposal—swords, spears, darts, javelins, arrows, slingstones, and clubs—Leviathan would simply "laugh" at their foolishness (v. 29, *śāḥaq* [MT: 41:21]; cf. 39:7, 18; 39:22). Eluding their best efforts, it moves along the riverbanks, its weight leaving marks in the mud like a heavy threshing sledge. Diving deep into the abyss, it leaves the waters churning like a boiling cauldron. The rhetoric evokes more than simply fear from those left staring at its wake. A final allusion to the foam glistening like the white hair of an elderly person suggests that Leviathan has transformed the watery chaos with a *mysterious wisdom* that commands respect and an *awesome beauty* that deserves honor.[20] ["Something Beyond Imagining"]

"On Earth It Has No Equal. . . It Is King" (41:33-34 [MT: 41:25-26])

The description of Leviathan's power and presence culminates with an affirmation of its creaturely status in relationship to God. Though it

"Something Beyond Imagining"

By this point God appears to be caught up in the incantation, unable to stop singing Leviathan's praises. . . . This description overwhelms the imagination, piling feature upon feature to create an impossible image, thereby conceiving an inconceivable monstrosity: its coat of mail . . . the doors of its face . . . terror surrounding its teeth . . . its back is made from fusing together rows of shields . . . it sneezes light . . . its eyes glow like the dawn . . . flames and sparks spew forth from its mouth . . . smoke billows from its nostrils . . . terror dances before it . . . it is clad in immovable, hard-cast folds of flesh . . . its heart is hard as stone . . . its belly is covered with sharp potsherds. This description of Leviathan is an impossibly over-determined amalgam of features (fire, water, smoke, armor, weaponry, anamalia, etc.) stitched together in one monstrous body. . . . That is, there is no language for it, no way to represent it. Failing to find adequate words to describe the monster, this text uses language to go beyond language, to conjure something beyond imagining.

T. K. Beal, *Religion and Its Monsters* (New York, London: Routledge, 2002), 52.

---

has no equal on earth, Leviathan, like Behemoth, is a creature "made" by (*ʿāśāh*; cf. 40:15, 19), hence subordinate to, God. And like Behemoth, Leviathan is a "king" (*melek*) in its own domain. Whereas Behemoth's royal status derives from being the "first" of God's works, Leviathan's royalty is manifest in its ability to rule or govern its world: Leviathan "looks on everyone who is proud (*gābōah*)." In this respect, Leviathan offers a model for responding to the very challenge that God has extended to Job. If Job is to govern the world in a way that God can celebrate, he must be able to "look on all who are proud (*gēʾah*)" and deal with them justly (40:11). With this final acclamation of Leviathan as king, God completes the tour that gives Job his best chance to understand what creaturely royalty and justice looks like from God's perspective.

To summarize, God's second speech from the whirlwind challenges Job to understand that Behemoth and Leviathan disclose something important that should enlarge his understanding about creaturely existence. In Behemoth, Job looks on as God praises a creature that displays undaunted trust in its instinctive ability to withstand all oppo-

---

"God Licenses Rage Against God"

Commenting on God's revelation to Job concerning Behemoth and Leviathan, T. K. Beal observes that "God does not squash Job like a monster. Rather, God *out-monsters* him, pushing the theological crisis brought on by Job's unjustifiable suffering to new, horrifying extremes, opening up a vision of the world and its creator God on the edge." He expands upon this observation as follows:

On the one hand, there is some consolation here, in that *God licenses rage against God in the face of undeserved pain*. God licenses theodicy as a questioning and challenging of God's justice against the friends' defensive justifications of God. On the other hand, there is some terror here, insofar as the challenging and questioning that God encourages is a soliciting of chaos against order. Does the child who rages out of control necessarily want the parent to encourage the rage or even to outdo her or him in it? This is a terrifying revelation, affirming Job's theodicy questions that open up abysses and awakens monsters, who turn out to be beloved of God, against the friends' theodic answers that attempt to shut them up and put them back in place. We are left, like Job, in a world that at any moment may crumble into primordial chaos, even at God's bidding.

T. K. Beal, *Religion and Its Monsters* (New York, London: Routledge, 2002), 55.

sition. In Leviathan, Job sees a creature that exemplifies a proud and beautiful dominion that threatens everyone but God, who not only delights in its strength but also praises its refusal to trade its creaturely royalty for lesser crowns. ["God Licenses Rage Against God"] God has now twice summoned Job to gird up his loins like the creature he was born to be, then to look at what God has to show him about the way the world works. Three times now, God has invited Job's response to what he has seen and understood. Job has tried silence, presumably convinced that a sovereign Creator will accept no other response from a mere creature. With this second speech, God seems intent on convincing Job that silence can never be fully adequate as a response to divine revelation. When the Almighty repeats the imperative, "Declare to me" (38:3; 40:7), Job must find the words that constitute an acceptable answer. ["I Am Rowing, I Am Rowing"]

Job's Second Response, 42:1-6

Job's final response pushes beyond his initial silence in ways that both confirm he has listened carefully to what God has said and that he is ready to venture an answer that may be more worthy than what he has offered thus far. On the one hand, he demonstrates that he is willing to relinquish his *many* "Why?" questions for the *one* question that God has convinced him is more important. He begins by quoting God to God—"Who is this that hides counsel without knowledge" (v. 3a; cf. 38:2)—then concedes that he is the one who has questioned divine

---

"I Am Rowing, I Am Rowing"

The journey towards knowing how to respond to God, Anne Sexton suggests in the lead poem to her collection titled "The Awful Rowing Toward God," requires the ardent faith that in the end "there will be a door" that God will open.

I was stamped out like a Plymouth fender
into this world.
First came the crib
wth its glacial bars.
Then dolls
and the devotion to their plastic mouths.
Then there was school,
the little straight rows of chairs,
blotting my name over and over . . .

Then there was life
with its cruel houses
and people who seldom touched—
though touch is all—. . .

but I grew, I grew,
and God was there like an island I had not rowed to . . .

I am rowing, I am rowing
though the oarlocks stick and are rusty
and the sea blinks and rolls
like a worried eyeball,
but I am rowing, I am rowing,
though the wind pushes me back
and I know that that island will not be perfect,
it will have the flaws of life,
the absurdities of the dinner table,
but there will be a door
and I will open it
and I will get rid of the rat inside of me,
the gnawing pestilential rat.
And God will take it with his two hands
and embrace it.

A. Sexton, "Rowing," *The Complete Poems: Anne Sexton*, with a foreword by M. Kumin (Boston, New York: Houghton Mifflin, 1999), 417-18.

purposes that clearly exceed his comprehension (v. 3b). Then, with a second quotation of what God has said, this time the divine imperative to "declare" what he has understood (v. 4; cf. 38:3b; 40:7b), Job offers an answer that indicates he has now not only *heard* but also *seen* (v. 5) something about God, the world, and himself that surpasses anything he has been able to grasp before.

The key to what Job has now heard, seen, and *understood* begins with the "therefore" that introduces v. 6, which by all accounts holds the promise of unlocking *the* meaning of the entire book that bears his name. It is precisely at this point, however, that the book confronts interpreters with its greatest challenge, perhaps strategically so. Although the grammatical issues are widely noted, there are vast differences in how best to resolve them.[21] Moreover, the possible interpretations are so numerous and invite such different, often mutually exclusive, understandings that commentators and readers alike might well be tempted to settle for Job's first response, not his second. Like him, we may conclude that the better course of wisdom is to place our hand on our mouth and speak no more (40:4).[22] Indeed, one of the intractable ironies of the book is that even if we should concede that Job has courageously pushed beyond silence, hearing what he says threatens to render us mute.

NRSV's translation of v. 6 is but one of many that suggest Job's final words should be interpreted as a confession of sin: "therefore I despise myself and repent in dust and ashes." Such a rendering suggests that as Job stands before the God who holds supreme power over frail and flawed human beings, he concedes at last that he has been wrong to attack God's justice. Before such a God as this, humans must necessarily be submissive. The only proper response, Job seems to have concluded, is that which conforms to Eliphaz's counsel: if Job is to have any "peace" at all, then he must simply "agree with God" (22:21). It is clear that this understanding is deeply ingrained in the interpretive history. Textual ambiguities also make it clear, however, that whatever Job's last words may mean, they convey anything but a simple confession of sin.

No less than five different translations deserve consideration as legitimate possibilities. [A Survey of Possible Translations] How readers assess the strengths and weaknesses of these possibilities depends in no small measure, as has been suggested previously, on both the *expectations* and *needs* they bring to this book (see the "Overview" to Job 38:1–42:6). If one construes the objective of the whirlwind speeches in terms of a win-lose proposition, then one will likely incline towards interpretive options that vindicate God at Job's expense. If one is sympathetic to Job's complaints, then options that salvage his integrity by placing

A Survey of Possible Translations

C. Newsom lists five legitimate translation possibilities for Job 42:6 that merit careful consideration (the brackets below cite her footnotes):

(1) "Therefore I despise myself and repent upon dust and ashes" (i.e., in humiliation; cf. NRSV; NIV);

(2) "Therefore I retract my words and repent of dust and ashes" (i.e., the symbols of mourning) [Cf. N. Habel, *The Book of Job* (Philadelphia: Westminster, 1985), 575)];

(3) "Therefore I reject and forswear dust and ashes" (i.e., the symbols of mourning) [Cf. D. Patrick, "The Translation of Job 42.6," VT 26 (1976): 369-70];

(4) "Therefore I retract my words and have changed my mind concerning dust and ashes" (i.e., the human condition) [Cf. J. Gerald Janzen, *Job* (Atlanta: John Knox, 1985), 255-59];

(5) "Therefore I retract my words, and I am comforted concerning dust and ashes" (i.e., the human condition) [Cf. L. Perdue, *Wisdom in Revolt: Metaphorical Theology in the Book of Job* (JSOTSup 112; Sheffield: JSOT, 1991), 232].

In view of these possibilities, Newsom's counsel to interpreters is worth citing in full:

Asking which possibility is correct misses the interpretive significance of the ambiguity that is also part of the divine speeches. A reader who has interpreted the divine speeches as a defense of God's honor and a rebuke to the audacity of a mere human in challenging God will tend to hear Job's words more or less according to the first alternative above . . . . A reader who understands the book largely in terms of the legal metaphor and takes God's speeches as a rebuttal of Job's lawsuit might be inclined to hear Job's words in terms of the second alternative. One who emphasizes the celebratory tone of the divine speeches might hear Job's words according to the third alternative. [For those who understand the divine speeches as] challenging Job's legal paradigm and placing the question of human existence in terms of a world in which the chaotic must be acknowledged, either the fourth or the fifth alternative seems fitting. *The ambiguities inherent in the divine speeches and Job's reply resist every attempt to reduce them to a single, definitive interpretation. That ambiguity does not mean that a reader should refrain from arguing for a particular interpretation of the divine speeches and Job's reply, but only that more than one legitimate interpretation is possible* (emphasis added).

C. Newsom, "The Book of Job," in vol. 4 of *NIB* (Nashville: Abingdon Press, 1996), 629.

God's sovereignty in question become more interesting. Throughout this commentary, I have suggested that the Joban drama consistently resists the simplicity of such either-or options. This is especially true of the dialogue between God and Job. Without resolving the tension between the various alternatives for interpreting v. 6, a case may be made in support of a mediating position. If God's objective in addressing Job is to invite a new understanding of his role in the world, one that is consonant with God's own hopes and expectations, then to the extent that Job attains this understanding, both he and God may claim the victory. Three critical discernments lay the groundwork for exploring this possibility.[23]

(1) The verb NRSV translates as "despise myself" (*mā'as*) means "reject" or "recant." It is ordinarily active, not reflexive, and is almost always followed by a direct object.[24] In 42:6 there is no clearly identified object, although we may reasonably assume that an object is implied. Of the possible objects that have been proposed, the immediate context suggests that the best option is "my words."[25] [What or Whom Does Job Reject?] The specific content of what may be included in

What or Whom Does Job Reject?

AΩ Scholars postulate a number of possible direct objects that convey what or whom Job might be rejecting. (For a discussion of the issues, see E. J. Van Wolde, "Job 42, 1-6: The Reversal of Job," *The Book of Job*, ed. W. A. M. Beuken [Leuven: Leuven University Press, 1994], 242-50.) Thus, Job could be saying, "I reject/ recant":

1. my previous arguments against God (L. Kuyper, "The Repentance of Job," VT 9 [1959]: 91-94)

2. my lawsuit (*mišpāṭ*) against God (cf. 31:13) (N. Habel, *The Book of Job: A Commentary* [OTL; Philadelphia: Westminster Press, 1985], 576)

3. "dust and ashes" (D. Patrick, "The Translation of Job 42.6," VT 26 [1976]: 369-71; cf. W. Morrow, "Consolation, Rejection, and Repentance in Job 42:6," JBL 105 [1986]: 212-15; E. M. Good, *In Turns of Tempest: A Reading of Job with a Translation* [Stanford: Stanford University Press, 1990], 376)

4. God (J. B. Curtis, "On Job's Response to Yahweh," JBL 98 [1979]: 503)

Job's "words" is open to debate, but his previous concession that he has spoken about "things too wonderful for me" (42:3) makes it plausible that Job refers to God's wondrous "design" (cf. 38:2) for creation.[26] Before God addressed him directly, Job had cursed God's design for the world as being inimical and meaningless for innocent sufferers like him (Job 3). God has now countered with a vision of creation teeming with a variety of intricately balanced life forces, including wild creatures Job had presumed were beyond the realm of God's care and concern. In response to this revelation, Job may be understood to recant his limited understanding of creation's design and to acknowledge that he now sees a world that requires him to reassess his place within it.

(2) An initial clue that Job is now ready to reassess his previous understanding occurs in the first half of the phrase, which NRSV translates "repent *in* dust and ashes." The collocation *niḥamti ʿal* is more properly translated "repent *concerning* dust and ashes." Whereas NRSV suggests that Job engages in the traditional ritual of gesturing forth sorrow for wrongdoing by sitting *in* dust (and ashes),[27] the words Job speaks indicate instead that he "repents" or "changes his mind" *about* what "dust and ashes" now means for him.[28] Job's change of mind invites us to understand that God's revelation has persuaded him to give up lamentation for some other (as yet unlear) response that is more congruent with what God desires. [Maimonides on Job]

(3) A second and still more important clue to Job's change of mind is the phrase "dust and ashes." The phrase (*ʿāpār waʾēper*) occurs only three time in the Old Testament: Genesis 18:27; Job 30:19; and Job 42:6. In each case it signifies something about the human condition in relation to God. In Job 30:19, Job laments that God has thrown him into the "mire" (*ḥōmer*, cf. Job 4:19; 10:9; 33:6) of human mortality, where human existence is defined as "dust and ashes." In the context of his suffering, Job understands this to mean that he exemplifies the way afflicted human beings are banished from society (30:1-8), then scorned and terrorized by their peers (30:9-15) and by God (30:16-23).

Maimonides on Job

The suggestion that Job's repentance concerns a change of mind about the meaning of dust and ashes, which a number of modern scholars have pursued (cf. L. J. Kaplan, "Maimonides, Dale Patrick, and Job XLII 6," *VT* 28 [1978]: 356-57), was anticipated by the Jewish philosopher Moses Maimonides (1135–1204) in his classic text, *The Guide to the Perplexed*:

[Job] said all that he says as long as he had no true knowledge and knew the deity only because of his acceptance of authority, just as the multitude adhering to the Law know it. But when he knew God with a certain knowledge, he admitted that true happiness, which is the knowledge of the deity, is guaranteed to all who know Him and that a human being cannot be troubled in any way by any of the misfortunes in question. While he had known God only through traditional stories and not by way of speculation, Job imagined that the things thought to be happiness, such as health, wealth, and children, are the ultimate goal. For this reason he fell into such perplexity as he did. This is the meaning of the dictum: *I had heard of Thee by hearing of the ear; but now mine eye seeth Thee; wherefore I abhor myself and repent of dust and ashes* (Job 42:6). This dictum may be supposed to mean, *Wherefore I abhor all that I used to desire and repent of my being in dust and ashes*—this being the position he was supposed to be in: *And he sat among the ashes* (Job 2:8).

Statue of Maimonides

Statue of Maimonides in the Cordoba Ghetto. Cordoba, Spain.
(Credit: Pronin, Anatoly/Art Resource, NY)

There are numerous studies on Maimonides'reading of Job. For further reading, see, for example, J. S. Levinger, "Maimonides' Exegesis of the Book of Job," *Creative Biblical Exegesis: Christian and Jewish Hermeneutics Throughout the Centuries*, eds. B. Uffenheimer, H. G. Reventlow (Sheffield: Sheffield Academic Press, 1988), 81-88; R. Jospe, "The Book of Job as Biblical *Guide of the Perplexed*," *Revelation, Reason, and Faith: Essays in Honor of Truman G. Madsen*, eds. D. Perry, D. Peterson, S. Ricks (Provo, Utah: Brigham Young University Press, 2002), 566-584; R. Eisen, *The Book of Job in Medieval Jewish Philosophy* (Oxford: Oxford University Press, 2004), 43-77.

M. Maimonides, *The Guide to the Perplexed*, trans. Shlomo Pines (Chicago: Chicago University Press, 1963), 3:23, 492-93.

His experience leads him to conclude that as "dust and ashes" he has been consigned to live in a world where he cries out to a cruel God who does not answer (30:20-21). In Genesis 18:27, the phrase "dust and ashes" applies to Abraham. In the context of arguing with God about matters of justice, Abraham acknowledges that he is a mere creature of "dust and ashes" who has entered into dangerous territory. Abraham's recognition of his status before God is similar to Job's in 30:19, with one important exception: Abraham persists with his questions, and God answers.[29] Indeed, the Hebrew text of Genesis 18:22, without the scribal correction, invites a still more revealing understanding of God's regard for this creaturely interrogator. It says, "YHWH remained standing before Abraham."[30] The image suggests that God, the "Judge of all the earth" (Gen 18:25), stands waiting to hear what "dust and ashes" will say on the subject of divine justice. As E. Ben Zvi has discerned, this picture of Creator and creature locked in dialogue over matters of mutual concern provides a glimpse of how the creaturely pursuit of justice enacts what it means to be made in the image of God: "The text underscores the notion that when the ideal teacher defends the universal order and confronts God with the standards by which God ought to judge the world, *he is in fact fulfilling the role God has chosen for him to fulfill.*"[31]

These two images of "dust and ashes" should inform the interpretation of Job's final response to God. When Job had tried previously to embrace the psalmist's wonderment about God's purpose in creating human beings, his suffering turned conventional words of praise into questions of lament. "What are human beings, that you make so much of them?" (Job 7:17; cf. Ps 8:4). The only answer Job could offer was that to be created in the image of God is more a curse than a blessing. As a creature made "a little lower than God," Job concludes that God has targeted him for death not life. Stripping him of the "glory" and "crown" that would have confirmed his nobility as a human being (Job 19:9), God has placed him instead on a "throne" mired in hopeless servitude. What is the "glory and honor" (Ps 8:5) in being singled out by God for a life of relentless suffering and humiliation? Until and unless someone convinces him otherwise, Job's only answer to this question is that innocent suffering renders "dust and ash" creatures mute before a God who permits neither challenge not confrontation.

God's disclosure invites a transformation in Job's understanding about what it means to be "dust and ashes." By God's design, the world contains unruly natural forces that may "oppress" creatures, like the waters that rage against Behemoth (40:23a). It also contains manufactured weapons that may wound or kill creatures, like those hunters use when pursuing Leviathan (41:1-12 [MT: 40:25–41:4], 25-32 [MT: 41:17-24]). Forces of aggression and violence do not however have the only say in determining the shape of God's world. By God's design and to God's great delight, creatures that will not be subdued or dominated also have something to contribute. Some, like Behemoth, trust in their own indomitable power (40:23b) to shape the world as a place where all live in peaceful and contented fulfillment (40:20-22). Some, like Leviathan, laugh at danger (41:29 [MT: 41:21]) and live like kings who have too much pride to trade nobility for any role that makes them less than the creatures they were created to be (41:34 [MT: 41:26]).

[Transformation *for* Innocent Suffering or *in Opposition* to It?]

Transformation *for* Innocent Suffering or *in Opposition* to It?

📖 J. Gerald Janzen's discerning interpretation of Job's transformed understanding of "dust and ashes" is perhaps closest to the view I am proposing here, although I depart from him in important ways. He suggests that Job's new understanding of "dust and ashes" teaches him that innocent suffering does not belittle humankind. Instead, it is the very condition under which the "royal vocation" to image God can be accepted and embraced. In this respect, Janzen suggests that Job comes to a new understanding of suffering that bears a "family resemblance" to the portrayals of the suffering servant in Second Isaiah and to the role of suffering in the service of God commended in the New Testament by Jesus (e.g., Mark 10:35-45; Matt 16:13-28) and Paul (Phil 2:5-11).

In response to Janzen, one may argue that he invokes the theology of innocent suffering in a way that does not adequately address the primary issue at stake in the book of Job. Job does not suffer on behalf of others. His family does not die on behalf of others. His suffering and their death are, by God's admission, "for no reason" (Job 2:3) and can hardly be construed in any normal sense as redemptive. I am more inclined to say that what Job has learned is that humankind may image God not by acquiescing to innocent suffering but rather by protesting it, contending with the powers that occasion it, and, when necessary, taking the fight directly to God. It is just such power, courage, and resolve that God seems to commend to Job in the figures of Behemoth and Leviathan.

J. Gerald Janzen, *Job* (Atlanta: John Knox, 1985), 254-59.

Having listened in as God celebrates the virtues of Behemoth and Leviathan, Job now understands that there is indeed a place in God's world for creatures that refuse to submit to forces that would rob them of their dignity by reducing them to slaves to wanton misery. Like them, God has endowed human beings with power and responsibility for their domains. They too have been created to be fierce and unbridled opponents of injustice, sometimes *with* God, sometimes *against* God, even if it means they will lose the fight. ["We Thank Thee, Father, for These Strange Minds"] As near equals of God, their destiny is to live at the dangerous intersection between the merely human and the supremely divine. When human beings dare to live out this mandate, their appearance before God as "dust and ashes" confirms their heritage as faithful descendants of Abraham They may be sure that if they dare to live faithfully into their legacy, they will find themselves standing before a Creator who awaits and desires their arrival. They may speak words of praise; they may speak of words of curse. They may also risk moving beyond these levels of discourse to speak words of resistance and protest. ["Job Interrupts God"] But they must not be silent, for silence is unworthy of those who have stood in the divine presence and have learned that creation has been entrusted to them, because they are a "little lower than God." In the end, to learn such a lesson may be the sum and substance of what Job says when he

"We Thank Thee, Father, for These Strange Minds"

📖 We thank thee, Father, for these strange minds that *enamor us against thee.* —
Emily Dickinson

For this quotation, along with discussion of Dickinson's penchant for wrestling with God, see A. Kazin, *God and the American Writer* (New York: Alfred A. Knopf, 1997), 142-60. The quotation (emphasis added) is from p. 155.

"A Man Should Carry Two Stones in His Pocket"

📖 Job's stance before God at the end of Job 42:6 invites reflection on the observation of Rabbi Bunam (19th C.): "A man should carry two stones in his pocket. On one should be inscribed, 'I am but dust and ashes.' On the other, 'For my sake the world was created.' And he should use each stone as he needs it."

Cited in R. Gordis, *The Book of God and Man: A Study of Job* (Chicago/London: The University of Chicago Press, 1965), 131.

Job Interrupts God

Job Interrupts God. Illumination. Vatican Museum, Rome.

"Job Interrupts God"

The idea that faith permits, indeed sometimes requires, one to argue with God is seldom endorsed by the religious establishment. The more orthodox counsel to those who harbor questions for the Almighty usually follows the advice offered by James Russell Lowell (1819–1891), the American essayist who succeeded Henry Wadsworth Longfellow as Professor of Modern Languages at Harvard University: "There is no good arguing with the inevitable. The only argument available with an east wind is to put on your overcoat."

Artists are often less reticent to defy conventional interpretations. One example is this twelfth century illumination from a Greek codex of the book of Job. (A copy of this manuscript is preserved in the Index of Christian Art, which may be consulted in the Dumbarton Oaks Research Library, Washington, DC. I am grateful to Dr. Natalia Teteriatnikov at this institution for her conversations with me concerning this manuscript.) This rendering depicts Job standing face-to-face with God. His head is not turned away; instead he fixes eyes his eyes on God's as the two square off before each other. Job's hands are not raised in the traditional gesture of supplication. Rather, he raises his right hand and points in God's direction with his index finger. Regrettably, the illumination is damaged and does not allow us to see whether Job's mouth is open or closed, but all the signs indicate that he is in the act of speaking directly to God. We may also note that while Job speaks, God does not interrupt but instead looks on with a fixed gaze that suggests attentiveness and interest in what Job has to say.

James R. Lowell, "Democracy: Inaugural Address on Assuming the Presidency of the Birmingham and Midland Institute, Birmingham, England, 6 October, 1884," *Essays: English and American*, vol. 28 (The Harvard Classics; New York: P.F. Collier & Sons, 1909–1914), 7.

responds to God's revelation by saying, "now my eye sees you." ["A Man Should Carry Two Stones in His Pocket"] It remains unclear, however, whether what Job now sees and understands is acceptable in God's eyes. For the answer to this question, if it is to be found, the book directs readers to the epilogue.

CONNECTIONS

Cynthia Ozick begins her insightful essay on "The Impious Impatience of Job "[32] with a series of questions:

> Who among us has not been tempted to ask Job's questions? Which of us has not doubted God's justice? What human creature ever lived in the absence of suffering? If we, ordinary clay that we are, are not equal to Job in the wild intelligence of his cries, or in the unintelligible wilderness of his anguish, we are, all the same, privy to his conundrums. (60)

With these questions, she joins her voice with all those who have sat with Job on the ash heap of suffering, with all those who perforce come to this book with a profound and passionate supplication: "We are driven—we common readers—to approach Job's story with tremulous palms held upward and unladen" (60).

Ozick tracks the basic plotline of the story, ending with reflections on "The Answer" from the whirlwind that silences Job but leaves her with more questions than she had when she began. Her quandary merits citation in full, even though its reach toward the epilogue addresses matters we have yet to explore in this commentary.

> So the poet, through the whirlwind's answer, stills Job.
> But can the poet still the Job who lives in us? God's majesty is eternal, manifest in cell and star. Yet Job's questions toil on, manifest in death camp and hatred, in tyranny and anthrax, in bomb and bloodshed. Why do the wicked thrive? Why do the innocent suffer? In brutal times, the whirlwind's answer tempts, if not atheism, then the sorrowing conviction of God's indifference.
> And if we are to take the close of the tale as given, it is not only Job's protests that are stilled; it is also his inmost moral urge. What has become of raging conscience? What has become of lovingkindness? Prosperity is restored; the dead children are replaced by twice the number of boys, and by girls exceedingly comely. But where now is the father's bitter grief over the loss of those earlier sons and daughters, on whose account he once indicted God? Cushioned again by good fortune, does Job remember nothing, feel nothing, see nothing beyond his own renewed honor? Is Job's lesson from the whirlwind finally no more than the learning of indifference? (72)

An answer that confirms nothing more than "the sorrowing conviction of God's indifference"? Perhaps Ozick overstates the matter. Although conversant with the "torrent of clerical commentary" (60) on Job, she is a novelist, not a biblical scholar. If, as she concedes, she is guilty of turning away from scholarly insight and learning, she does so

"Something to Be Said for Novice Readers"

So there is something to be said for novice readers who come to Job's demands and plaints unaccoutered: we will perceive God's world exactly as Job himself perceives it. Or put it that Job's bewilderment will be ours, and our kinship to his travail fully unveiled, only if we are willing to absent ourselves from the accretion of centuries of metaphysics, exegesis, theological polemics. Of the classical Jewish and Christian theologians (Saadia Gaon, Rashi, ibn Ezra, Maimonides, Gersonides, Gregory, Aquinas, Calvin), each wrote from a viewpoint dictated by his particular religious perspective. But for us to be as (philosophically) naked as Job means to be naked of bias, dogma, tradition. It will mean to imagine Job solely as he is set forth by his own words in his own story . . . .

. . . the more we throw off sectarian sophistries—the more bluntly we attend to the drama as it plays itself out—the more clearly we will see Job as he emerges from the venerable thicket of theodicy into the heat of our own urgency. Or call it our daily breath.

C. Ozick, *Quarrel and Quandary* (New York: Alfred A. Knopf, 2000), 63-64.

only in order to be as naked before the book of Job that English readers encounter as Job was sitting on the ash heap. ["Something to Be Said for Novice Readers"] Whatever the merits of the various scholarly proposals concerning the whirlwind speeches, most readers of the English text will likely conclude that the price for a happy ending to this story is first Job's silence, then his submission. But surely some, if not all, "common readers," as Ozick describes herself, will "raise tremulous palms upward" in the hope of receiving something more from this story than the sanctification of moral indifference.

Ozick's reading of the ending of this book raises two questions that merit reflection. Does the text offer a different model for understanding what God reveals and Job understands about the requisite ethic for living in a world where suffering happens "for no reason"? If the text does offer other models, why do they seem to have such little purchase on the lesson(s) so many readers take from this book?

Joban Models for Piety

From the first mention of the name "Job" in the prologue, this story takes on a certain universal aspect. It is not only that we cannot locate the land of Uz on a map, that we do not know exactly when, where, or in what circumstances the book was written, or that we cannot be certain whether a person named Job is historical or mythical. It is also that the story line of a righteous sufferer is so deeply rooted in all times, places, and cultures that it transcends every attempt to reduce it to any one lesson. There are, however, subtle hints embedded within the text, which are advanced and embellished in the history of both Jewish and Christian interpretive practices, that link Job's piety to a certain spectrum of scriptural models, most notably Noah and Daniel (cf. Ezek 14:14, 20) and Abraham (see [Job and Abraham]). Of these, this commentary had frequently called attention to theological parallels between Job's contention with God and Abraham's questioning of God's justice in Genesis 18:22-33 (see, for example, the commentary above on 42:1-6). In addition to these, one other person should be mentioned: Jacob, the eponymous ancestor of Israel. [33]

The Jacob narratives in Genesis 25–36 depict a multifaceted character. On the one hand he is a rogue and a cheater (Gen 27); on the other, he is a blessed exemplar of heroic proportions (Gen 32). Given this portrait, it is striking that the text introduces Jacob as a "person of *integrity*" (25:27: *'iš tam*; NRSV: "a quiet man"), which is precisely the first attribute that the prologue attributes to Job (Job 1:1; NRSV: "blameless"). Because Job and Jacob are the only two persons in the Old Testament to whom this virtue is explicitly ascribed (cf. Gen 6:9 [Noah]; Gen 17:1 [Abraham]), we may ask how these two characters exemplify the "integrity" that scripture commends.[34]

Jacob's journey to the promised land of Canaan, and to the blessing of God, requires that he pass over the Jabbok. For all his careful planning, he finds himself confronting a mysterious opponent he had not expected (Gen 32:22-32). Through the night he wrestles with this assailant, both physically and rhetorically, trying to secure a victory and if not at least a blessing. With respect to the physical contest, he learns that he cannot overpower his opponent. He cannot win this match, but he will not give up the fight, and in the end, surprisingly, he manages to secure a crippling draw. With respect to the blessing, he discovers, also to his surprise, that what he had tried to secure by force, he receives as a gift. On the other side of this encounter, he is changed. His name is no longer "Jacob"—"heel/trickster/supplanter"—but "Israel"—"the one who fights with God." His last words in this pericope summarize the outcome: "I have seen God face to face, and yet my life is preserved" (Gen 32:30). ["Job, of All People, Lured God Out of Hiding"]

It is possible to read this encounter as Jacob's defeat. To be sure, wrestling with God leaves him wounded, an apt description not only for the physical injury that leaves him limping into the promised land, but also for the spiritual woundedness of the people called Israel who will follow in his footsteps. But if it is a defeat, it is a "magnificent defeat," as Frederick Buechner has put it, for in such encounters with God, brokenness becomes the source and sustenance of blessing.[35] Such is the promise to all those whose

"Job, of All People, Lured God Out of Hiding"

When the dust settles, Job is strangely pacified. In his last short speech to God, Job admits, "I have spoken of the unspeakable and tried to grasp the infinite. I had heard of you with my ears; but now my have seen you. Therefore, I will be quiet, comforted that I am dust." Why quiet, since he never got an answer, and why comforted that he is dust? Because Job, of all people, lured God out of hiding. He saw God face to face—*panim* to *panim*—and lived to tell the tale.

Barbara Brown Taylor, *When God is Silent* (Cambridge, Boston MS: Cowley Publications, 1998), 70-71.

"Unless We Become as Rogues"

J. William Whedbee introduces his chapter, titled "The Adventures of a Wandering Rogue: The Comedy of Jacob (Genesis 25-35)," with this epithet form Emily Dickinson: "Unless we become as rogues, we cannot enter the kingdom of heaven."

J. Whedbee, *The Bible and the Comic Vision* (Cambridge: University Press, 1998), 93.

faith is shaped by the *roguish integrity* of the people called Israel, and the *scandalous integrity* of the one who says to his disciples, "If any want to become my follower, let them deny themselves and take up their cross and follow me. For those who want to save their life will lose it, and those who lose their life for my sake will find it" (Matt 16:24-25 and parallels). ["Unless We Become as Rogues"]

Why Do Joban Models for Piety Have So Little Claim on Us?

Why are the Jobs of this world, whose suffering will not be "stilled" by theological maxims, so often consigned to ash heaps outside the community of the faith? Why do the Jacobs of this world, who foolishly and perhaps arrogantly, risk defeat by stepping into the ring with God, limp towards their blessing alone? The answers to these questions may be many. Perhaps both scholars and "common readers" find Job too unpredictable (or, as we say in the academy, too unreadable), too dangerous, too unorthodox for inclusion in our settled worlds. Perhaps we would prefer a less volatile relationship with God, one that does not require us to follow Job into the whirlwind or Jacob into the Jabbok or Jesus into Gethsemane. Of course, we must also be open to the possibility that this probe into Job and Jacob's integrity is simply wrong. Perhaps the lesson to be learned is that Job does repent of the sin of challenging God. Perhaps Jacob's limp is really more a defeat to be avoided than a victory to be pursued, a scriptural warning that keeps us mindful of the price always required of those who try to steal a blessing. ["About Anyone So Great It Is Probable That We Can Never Be Right"] Each one of us who comes to this ancient story, whether as skilled readers of the ancient text or as common readers of the English versions that provide our only access to it, must decide what its lessons are. [The Art of Belief]

To conclude these reflections, I return to Ozick's last line from the quotation cited above: "Is Job's lesson from the whirlwind finally no more than the learning of indifference?" Ozick does not venture an answer to her own question. Instead, she concludes her quarrel and quandary concerning the book of Job with these words:

"About Anyone So Great It Is Probable That We Can Never Be Right"

Any commentator on the book of Job, including this one, might take encouragement from T. S. Eliot, who in appraising the incomparable Shakespeare, concluded, "About anyone so great it is probable that we can never be right; and if we are never right, it is better from time to time that we should change our way of being wrong."

Cited in T. N. D. Mettinger, "The God of Job: Avenger, Tyrant, or Victor," *The Voice From the Whirlwind: Interpreting the Book of Job*, ed. L. G. Perdue, W. Clark Gilpin (Nashville: Abingdon, 1992), 39.

"The Art of Belief"

In assessing Emily Dickinson's pained journey in the Christian tradition, R. Lundin says she "realized that belief is an art that demands trial and practice." He explains as follows:

In saying Dickinson's poetry was an "art of belief," I intend the phrase in several ways. Her poetry is in large measure about belief—about the objects of belief and its comforts, as well as belief's great uncertainties. With daring tenacity, she explored the full range of human experience in her reflections upon such subjects as God, the Bible, suffering, and immortality. "On subjects of which we know nothing, or should I say *Beings*," she wrote a few years before she died, "we both believe and disbelieve a hundred times an Hour, which keeps Believing nimble."

R. Lundin, *Emily Dickinson and the Art of Belief* (Grand Rapids, MI: William B. Eerdmans, 1998), 3.

So much for the naked text. Perhaps this is why—century after century—we common readers go on clinging to the spiritualizing mentors of traditional faith, who clothe in comforting theologies this God-wrestling and comfortless Book.

Yet how astoundingly up-to-date they are, those ancient sages—redactors and compilers—who opened even the sacred gates of Scripture to philosophic doubt! (73)

NOTES

[1] On the dual connotations of *mišpāṭ* as both a legal act, i.e., "judging," and an administrative procedure, i.e., "governance," see S. Scholnick, "The Meaning of Mispat in the Book of Job," *JBL* 101 (1982): 522-23.

[2] See note 6 in the commentary on Job 33.

[3] Samuel E. Balentine, "'What Are Human Beings, That You Make So Much of Them?' Divine Disclosure from the Whirlwind: 'Look at Behemoth,'" *God in the Fray: A Tribute to Walter Brueggemann*, ed. T. Linafelt, T. K. Beal (Minneapolis: Fortress, 1998), 268-69.

[4] On the royal imagery that is used with reference to Job in 40:10-13, see J. Gerald Janzen, *Job* (Atlanta: John Knox, 1985), 243-44. See further, [King Job] and [Job's Royal and Priestly Anthropology].

[5] Note, for example, that the collocation in Job 40:10, "*clothe* yourself (*tilbāš*) with glory and splendor," occurs also in Ps 104:1, but with reference to God: "You [God] are *clothed* (*lābāštā*) with glory and spendor."

[6] W. P. Brown, *The Ethos of the Cosmos: The Genesis of Moral Imagination* (Grand Rapids MI: Eerdmans, 1999), 368.

[7] C. Newsom, "The Book of Job," in vol. 4 of *NIB* (Nashville: Abingdon Press, 1996), 615; idem, *The Book of Job: A Contest of Moral Imaginations* (Oxford: Oxford University Press, 2003), 248.

[8] J. G. Gammie offers one important dissent from the conventional view by interpreting both Behemoth and Leviathan as positive models for Job. In his view, they serve not only to rebuke Job but also to instruct and console him; "Behemoth and Leviathan: On the Didactic and Theological Significance of Job 40:15–41:26," *Israelite Wisdom: Theological and Literary Essays in Honor of Samuel Terrien*, ed. J. G. Gammie et al. (Missoula MT: Scholars Press, 1978), 217-31.

[9] See, for example, the imagery of God as a "warrior" (e.g., Pss 74, 89; Isa 51) who defeats the forces of chaos in order to establish divine rule over the cosmos. See further [The Warrior God].

[10] The commentary here reprises my earlier discussion of Behemoth in "'What Are Human Beings That You Make So Much of Them?'" 270-71.

[11] Cf. N. Habel, *The Book of Job: A Commentary* (OTL; Philadelphia: Westminster Press, 1985), 565.

[12] As often noted, e.g., M. Pope, *Job* (AB; Garden City NY: Doubleday, 1979), 324; E. Dhorme, *A Commentary on the Book of Job* (Nashville: Thomas Nelson Publishers, 1967), 620; Habel, *Book of Job*, 553; Newsom, "The Book of Job," 618.

[13] Cf. L. Perdue, *Wisdom in Revolt: Metaphorical Theology in the Book of Job* (JSOTSup 112; Sheffield: Almond Press, 1991), 222-23; idem, *Wisdom in Creation*, 177.

[14] The word for "nose" in v. 24b, *'āp*, also means "anger, rage," as in God's summons to

Job to "pour out the overflowing of [his] anger" in the pursuit of justice (38:8).

[15] Cf. Habel, *Book of Job,* J. Hartley, *The Book of Job* (NICOT; Grand Rapids MI: William B. Eerdmans, 1988), 531-32.

[16] Cf. Newsom ("The Book of Job," 623), who reinforces this suggestion by connecting Leviathan's boast with the previous affirmation that it refuses to speak "soft words" (41:3 [MT 40:27]) to any would-be master.

[17] Cf. G. Fohrer, *Das Buch Hiob* (KAT; Gütersloh: Gerd Mohn, 1963), 527; R. Gordis, *The Book of Job: Commentary, New Translation, and Special Studies* (New York: Jewish Theological Seminary of America, 1978), 483; Dhorme, *Commentary on the Book of Job,* 631.

[18] Newsom, *Book of Job,* 251.

[19] Balentine, "'What Are Human Beings, That You Make So Much of Them?'" 273. See further, Gammie ("Behemoth and Leviathan," 223, 225) who also notes that what comes from Leviathan's mouth is a major emphasis in the poem. He suggests that the poet uses this emphasis both to caricature Job's verbal defenses and at the same time to affirm his protests.

[20] Perdue has rightly noted that God's description of Leviathan accents both its power and beauty. This stands in marked contrast with conventional interpretations, which usually depict it as an ugly and terrifying creature (*Wisdom in Revolt*, 230, n. 5). See also Newsom ("The Book of Job," 623-24), who notes that Leviathan's physical attributes have the capacity to "transform the appearance of the sea itself."

[21] The secondary literature on Job 42:6 is vast, as a review of the standard commentaries makes clear. The following works may be singled out for special mention: L. J. Kuyper, "The Repentance of Job," VT 9 (1959): 91-94; D. Patrick, "The Translation of Job XLII 6," VT 26 (1976): 369-71; D. J. O'Connor, "Job's Final Word—I am Consoled," *ITQ* 50 (1983–1984): 181-97; W. Morrow, "Consolation, Rejection, and Repentance in Job 42:6," JBL 105 (1986): 211-25; C. Muenchow, "Dust and Dirt in Job 42:6," JBL 108 (1989); A. Wolters, "A Child of Dust and Ashes (Job 42, 6b)," ZAW 102 (1990): 116-19; P. A. H. de Boer, "Does Job Retract?" *Selected Studies in Old Testament Exegesis*, ed. C. Van Duin (OTS 27; Leiden: Brill, 1991), 179-95; E. J. Van Wolde, "Job 42, 1-6: The Reversal of Job," *The Book of Job,* ed. W. A. M. Beuken (Leuven: Leuven University Press, 1994), 223-50. Two recent book-length treatments offer additional evidence that the debate concerning the meaning of Job's last words continues to be both complex and important: Y. Pyeon, *You Have Not Spoken What Is Right about Me: Intertextuality and the Book of Job* (New York: Peter Lang, 2003); Duck-Woo Nam, *Talking about God: Job 42:7-9 and the Nature of God in the Book of Job* (New York: Peter Lang, 2003).

[22] T. Tilley has noted that the multiple translation possibilities for Job 42:6 mean that Job is often "reduced to silence, if not by God, then by interpreters of the text" ("God and the Silencing of Job," *Modern Theology* 5 [1989]: 261). Tilley elaborates this argument in a subsequent book-length treatment of the issues: *The Evils of Theodicy* (Washington, DC: Georgetown University Press, 1991), 89-112.

[23] What follows draws heavily on my previous discussion in "'What Are Human Beings, That You Make So much of Them?'" 274-78.

[24] Morrow provides the semantic survey, noting that of nearly seventy occurrences of *māʾas* in the Qal stem, all but four are followed by direct objects (Job 7:16; 34:33; 36:5; 42:6); "Consolation , Rejection, and Repentance," 214.

[25] Cf. S. R. Driver and G. B. Gray, *A Critical and Exegetical Commentary on the Book of Job* (Edinburgh: T and T. Clark, 1921), 373; Tsevat, "The Meaning of the Book of Job," 91; Fohrer, *Das Buch Hiob*, 531; Pope, *Job,* 349. See also the following Bible translations: NAB, NJPS, JB, TEV.

[26] So also Newsom, "The Book of Job," 629.

[27] E.g., Josh 7:6; 2 Sam 13:19; Isa 58:5; 61:3; Jer 6:26; Ezek 27:30; cf. Job 2:8, 12). See further, S. Olyan, *Biblical Mourning: Ritual and Social Dimensions* (New York: Oxford University Press, 2004), 111-23.

[28] On *niḥamtî 'al* as "repent concerning/about," see Morrow, "Consolation, Rejection, and Repentance," 215-16; D. Patrick, "The Translation of Job XLII 6," VT 26 (1976): 370; J. B. Curtis, "On Job's Response to Yahweh," JBL 98 (1979): 497-511. See further L. J. Kaplan, who argues that such an interpretation of the phrase was already proposed by the Jewish philosopher Maimonides (1138–1204); "Maimonides, Dale Patrick, and Job XLII 6," VT 28 (1978): 356-58.

[29] For my argument here, it is not necessary to resolve the question of whether Job is dependent on Genesis or vice versa. It is sufficient to note that significant parallels between Abraham and Job suggest the likelihood that both texts reflect acute concerns with questions about divine justice that emerged in the postexilic period (see further [Job and Abraham]). See J. Blenkinsopp, who notes that these connections were already noticed by medieval Jewish commentators ("Abraham and the Righteous of Sodom," JSS 33 [1982]: 126-27; idem, "The Judge of All the Earth: Theodicy in the Midrash on Genesis 18:22-33," JSS 41 [1990]: 1-12. On the postexilic provenance of Gen 18:22-33 and its connections with Job, see further L. Schmidt, *"De Deo" : Studien zur Literarkritik und Theologie des Buches Jona, des Gesprächs zwischen Abraham und Jahwe in Gen 18 22ff. und von Job 1* (BZAW 143; Berlin: Walter de Gruyter, 1976), 131-64.

[30] The scribal correction (*tiqqun sopherim;* see further [*Tiqqune Sopherim*]) of Gen 18:22 is "Abraham remained standing before YHWH."

[31] E. Ben Zvi, "The Dialogue Between Abraham and Yhwh in Gen 18:23-32: A Historical-Critical Analysis," JSOT 53 (1992): 39 (emphasis added). For a similar assessment, see Janzen, *Job,* 257.

[32] C. Ozick, "The Impious Impatience of Job," *Quarrel and Quandary* (New York: Alfred A. Knopf, 2000), 59-73.

[33] The Testament of Job (first century BCE- first century CE) traces Job's lineage to the "sons of Esau, the brother of Jacob" (T. Job 1:6). Curiously, biblical scholars have made little of the connection. Two notable exceptions are E. Davis, "Job and Jacob: The Integrity of Faith," *Reading Between the Texts: Intertextuality and the Hebrew Bible*, ed. D. N. Fewell (Louisville KY: Westminster/ John Knox Press, 1992), 203-24 and E. Van Wolde, "Different Perspectives on Faith and Justice: The God of Jacob and the God of Job," *The Many Voices of the Bible*, ed. S. Freyne, E. Van Wolde (Concilium 2002/1; London: SCM Press, 2002), 17-23.

[34] Davis ("Job and Jacob") has explored this issue in helpful ways, though she draws different conclusions about what Job and Jacob teach us about the "integrity" of faith.

[35] F. Buechner, *The Magnificent Defeat* (San Francisco: Harper and Row, 1966), 10-18.

EPILOGUE: "AS MY SERVANT JOB HAS DONE"

Job 42:7-17

After forty-two chapters and 1,059 verses, the narrator at long last reappears, presumably to bring this Joban drama to its fitting conclusion. The narrator offers two judgments: the first (vv. 7-9) reports God's judgment *against* the friends, "who have not spoken about me what is right"; the second (vv. 10-17), God's judgment *for* Job, which results in the restoration of his wealth, family, and place in society. These two judgments, however, leave readers with neither a simple nor obviously coherent ending for the story.

In part, this is because of the complex transmission history of the book, which by conventional assessment requires that we read the prose prologue and epilogue, without the intervening dialogues and divine speeches, as a set piece (see the Introduction). According to this assessment, the original prose story begins by introducing a righteous person who suffered "once upon a time," then concludes with the conventional affirmation that "they all lived happily ever after." Such a story invites readers to overlook any troubling details—for example, how can ten beloved children who have died "for no reason" simply be replaced with new ones?—by embracing larger truths that minimize or dismiss them. The rationale that undergirds this hermeneutic move is perhaps best expressed in the famous interchange between Shakespeare's widow of Florence and Helena:

> Widow: Lord, how we lose our pains!
> Helena: All's well that ends well yet,
>   Though time seem so adverse and means unfit.
> (*All's Well That Ends Well*, V, i, 24-26)

Even if we can settle into this "all's well that ends well" summation to Job's story, the telltale "yet," followed by the trailer words "adverse" and "unfit," may leave us anxiously waiting for the proverbial other shoe to drop. [CD: "The Pursuit of Utopia Ends Up Licensing Every Form of Success"]

Critical theories about the book's transmission history help with assessing its conclusion but *only* in part. Whatever satisfaction may be gained by reading the prologue and epilogue as one story must be relinquished or at least recalibrated by the recognition that however its various parts may have come together over time, the book's final shape presents 42:7-17 as the conclusion to the *whole* story. Whether this final form is the accidental product of multiple redactors or the skillful work of a single author, the end result is the same: one must read *from* the prologue, then *through* the middle section of dialogues and divine speeches, *in order to arrive at whatever conclusion* the epilogue offers. Reading from front to back, the epilogue does not so much *close* this book with answers as *open* it to further questions. In advance of the commentary below, one such question may be singled out. When the narrator quotes God as saying that Job has spoken "what is right" (vv. 7, 8), is this an affirmation of his *pained acceptance* of suffering as part of *God's inscrutable wisdom* (1:21; 2:10)? Or, is it an affirmation of Job's *pained protest* of suffering, which he insists is part of *God's inscrutable injustice* (e.g., 10:7-8; 16:16-17; 19:6-7; 24:1)? A "yes" answer to the former invites the affirmation that innocent suffering is providential. A "yes" answer to the latter invites us to affirm that innocent suffering can never be congruent with God's will. With either answer, the epilogue hints that understanding "what is right" is rarely simple.

COMMENTARY

"You Have Not Spoken of Me What Is Right," 42:7-9

The first clue that the epilogue may offer something different than we expect occurs in the narrator's opening statement. The words "After the *Lord* had spoken these words to Job " direct us back to the divine speeches in 38:1–40:34, not to Job's final response in 42:1-6.[1] Although readers might have hoped for some authoritative assessment of what Job says he now sees and understands about his place in God's world—however the enigmatic words of 42:6 may be interpreted—the narrator suggests the focus is elsewhere. God has summoned Job to gird up his loins like a mighty warrior, shown him a world teeming with beautiful chaos and proud, indomitable creatures, and has heard both Job's silence and his move beyond silence. Does God accept Job's last words as worthy of the revelation he has been granted, or not? ["The Prosecutor Bursts Out Laughing"]

Without directly addressing that question, the narrator moves immediately to report God's one and only response to the three friends. The friends did not speak in the prologue, hence God's evaluation must refer to the speeches throughout the dialogues, in which they consistently counseled Job to agree with their theology: if Job suffers, then it

"The Prosecutor Bursts Out Laughing"

Y. L. Perets's nineteenth short story, "Bontsye the Silent," looks at the biblical representation of Job through the eyes of Yiddish culture. Bontsye, the Joban-like protagonist of the story, suffers from the day he is born to the day he dies without respite. Throughout his life, he never complains. Instead, he suffers in silence, which in turn builds his moral debit against heaven for allowing his suffering to persist without any redress. When he dies, Bontyse appears before the heavenly council. A Defending Angel makes the case before the Prosecutor for his entry into God's presence. The climax of the heavenly trial comes when the Presiding Judge prepares to render the final verdict.

"My child!" continues the Presiding Judge, "you have always suffered and kept silent! There is not a single member, not a single bone in your body without a wound, without a bloody welt, there is absolutely no secret place in your soul where it shouldn't be bleeding . . . and you always kept silent . . . .

"There, no one understood all this. Indeed, you, yourself, perhaps did not realize that you can cry out; and due to your cry, Jericho's wall can quake and tumble down! You, yourself, did not comprehend the extent of your sleeping power . . . .

"In the other world your silence was not comprehended, but that is the *Realm of Lies*, here in the *Realm of Truth* you will receive your compensation!

"On you, the Supreme Assembly shall pass no judgment; on you, it will make no ruling; for you, it will neither divide nor apportion a share! Take whatever you want! *Everything* is yours!"

Bontsye, for the first time, raises his eyes! He is just about blinded by the light on all sides; everything sparkles, everything flashes, beams shoot out from everything: from the walls, from the vessels, from the angels, from the judges! A kaleidoscope of suns!

He drops his eyes wearily!

"Are you sure?" he asks, doubtful and shamefaced.

"Absolutely!" the Presiding Judge affirms!

"Absolutely, I tell you; for everything is yours; everything in Heaven belongs to you! Choose and take what you wish. You only take what belongs to *you*, alone!

"Are you sure?" asks Bontsye once more with growing confidence in his voice.

"Definitely! Absolutely! Positively! they affirm to him from every side.

"Gee, if you mean it," smiles Bontsye, "what I'd really like is, each and every morning, a hot roll with fresh butter!"

Judges and angels lowered their heads in shame: the Prosecutor burst out laughing. (The full text is cited in B. Zuckerman, *Job the Silent: A Study in Counterpoint* [New York, Oxford: Oxford University Press, 1991], 181-95. The excerpt above is from pp. 193, 195.)

The ending to Perets's story is no less enigmatic than the ending to the book of Job. Why does the Prosecutor laugh? Multiple answers deserve consideration. Perhaps the ending is ironic, a laugh that is really a cry of despair, because suffering has reduced one to long for something so trivial. Perhaps the laugh is an intentional signal of how absurd silence is in the face of suffering, in which case the laugh comes at the expense of anyone who thinks patience is a virtue. Perhaps the Prosecutor laughs to keep from crying, in effect taking the edge off his own defeat, for now he must admit that the world of suffering, and its Creator, are not worth more than a buttered roll (see further **[Does God Laugh or Rage at Human Dissent?]**).

must be because he, not God, needs correcting. Eliphaz, always the lead spokesman for the three, sums up their best thinking in his last speech: "Agree with God, and be at peace; in this way good will come to you" (22:21). It is now Eliphaz whom God singles out for the rebuke that all three friends deserve. None of them has spoken "what is right" (*někônāh*; vv. 7, 8). The term refers to that which is "correct" or "truthful," not merely in an intellectual sense, but with reference to facts that are established and consistent with reality (cf. Deut 17:4; 1 Sam 23:23).[2] With little more than a word, God labels everything the friends have said as wrong. Elihu is not mentioned, perhaps an indication that his words are a later addition to the book. Nevertheless, because God's "wrath is kindled" (*hārāh 'appî*) against the three friends, which is the same emotion that drives Elihu's words (32:2, 3, 5), we may suspect that if Elihu had belonged to the original story, God's anger would have rebuked and corrected him no less than the others.

If the friends are wrong, then in what sense may what Job has said or done be right? Given God's rebuke of the friends' speeches, we may suspect that it is Job's similar rebuke of the friends, spelled out in the countering complaints of chapters 4–27, which merits God's approval. The rhetoric of vv. 7-8, however, refers us instead back to the profile of piety Job exemplified in the prologue. There it is reported that Job lived out his beliefs about God and the world by regularly engaging in conventional cultic rituals. He offered "burnt offerings" (ʿōlôt) on behalf of his children, presumably accompanied by prayers of intercession, in the expectation that he could atone for any inadvertent sins they may have committed (1:5). Now, God instructs Job to receive the "burnt offering" (ʿōlāh) presented by the friends, who require his prayer of intercession if God is to forgive them (v. 8). [Seven Bulls and Seven Rams] In the Edenic, pre-suffering world that defined Job's prologue piety, there

Seven Bulls and Seven Rams

The instruction to the friends to take to Job "seven bulls and seven rams" for a burnt offering is a curious detail. The numbers exceed what is normally required for burnt offerings (cf. Lev 4), hence they may be designed simply to bring the epilogue into rhetorical conformity with the exaggerated numbers used in the prologue. Two other texts use the same numbers, Num 23, which reports Balaam's divination procedures, and Ezek 45:21-25, which describes instructions for the Passover offerings. Of these, the former may be instructive. When Balak, king of Moab, asks the non-Israelite seer Balaam to curse the Israelites, Balaam instructs the king to build seven altars and to "prepare seven bulls and seven rams" for sacrifice (23:2; cf. vv. 4, 14, 29-30). When the sacrifices are completed, however, Balaam delivers an oracle blessing the Israelites, not cursing them. In response to the king's question about why he had not done what he had been asked to do, Balaam answers by saying, "Did I not tell you, whatever the Lord says, that is what I must do?" (v. 24).

Balaam and His Ass Stopped by an Angel
From the Psalter of St. Louis.
Bibliotheque Nationale, Paris, France (Credit: Snark/Art Resource, NY)

was no place, and no need, for any response to God other than blessing. Even when suffering forced its way into Job's world, he clung resolutely to his trust in the mysterious wisdom of a God who uses both good and evil to accomplish divine purposes (2:10). By recalling the prologue's description of Job's extraordinary piety, the epilogue invites us to wonder if this is what God now affirms as the true definition of "what is right."

The Saintly Job

The portrait of Job as a saintly intercessor has no doubt played a largely positive role both socially and religiously in societies that revere this story. *On religious grounds*, the image of one who prays selflessly for the forgiveness of those who wrongfully abuse him endorses a simple piety and an unquestioning belief in God's governance of the world. Moreover, for Christians, the image of the saintly Job has the added attraction of embracing Job as a forerunner of Christ, whose prayer from the cross—"Father, forgive them; for they do not know what they are doing" (Luke 23:24; cf. Stephen's prayer in Acts 7:60)—provides the ultimate model of faith. *On social grounds*, the saintly Job commends obedience instead of rebellion, conformity instead of agitation, and tolerance instead of rigid adherence to nonnegotiable principles of justice.

Artists, no less than biblical interpreters, exegete Job's story with sensitivity to both its religious and social message. One example is this fresco of Job praying for his friends by Taddeo Gaddi (1300–1366), perhaps the most distinguished pupil of the Florentine painter Giotto. Gaddi depicts Job as a royal figure, kneeling in prayer before an ornate chair with a palatial edifice. Painted into the scene are a number of symbols that link Job to Christ. To Job's left, resting on the folds of his garment, is a skull, an allegorical reminder of the skull of Adam, which according to medieval legend, was buried at the foot of the cross of Christ. In front of Job is a crown of thorns, alongside what appears to be an instrument of torture, both symbols of Jesus' passion.

While the religious imagery is prominent, we should note also the events that shaped Gaddi's world and his artistic imagination. In the first half of the fourteenth century, Pisa and the cities of Tuscany had enjoyed unprecedented prosperity. Everything began to change in 1346–1347, when bad weather conditions ravaged harvests and produced famines. In 1348, a bubonic plague known as the Black Death arrived in Sicily and quickly spread inland, ultimately killing between a third and a half of the population in many urban areas, including the Tuscany cities of Florence and Sienna. As personal incomes plummeted and tax revenues

Job Intercedes for His Friends

Taddeo Gaddi. *Job Intercedes for His Friends*. 1355. Fresco. Composanto, Pisa. (Camposanto Monumentale di Pisa Archivio Fotografico Opera Primaziale Pisana)

grew increasingly severe, mercenaries began harassing survivors by raiding their homes and destroying their families. In such a world as this, where prosperity had vanished for reasons beyond control and the graveyards were full of righteous victims, Gaddi's Job no doubt makes both a religious and political statement about where the hope for the future lies.

For further reading on the interpretation of Job's piety in Jewish, Christian, and Muslim traditions, see N. Glatzer, ed., *The Dimensions of Job: A Study and Selected Readings* (New York: Schocken, 1969), 12-16.

There can be little doubt that the Job of the prologue—the selfless intercessor who prays for the forgiveness of those who wrongfully abuse him—is deeply rooted in both Jewish and Christian traditions. [The Saintly Job] That said, A. Brenner speaks for many readers when she observes that although the Job of the prologue is "positively saintly," it is his very piety that forces us to wonder if he is altogether "human."[3] Once Job loses everything for "no reason," most would expect a normal person, regardless of piety and devotion, to be at least somewhat less sanguine. Indeed, one might well expect suffering to transform the grammar of devotion with strong words of curse and complaint, which is precisely what Job's language in chapters 3–31 reflects. Having protested with such passion, can Job really be expected now to return to his previously undisturbed certainties as if nothing has changed? Does God really expect or require Job simply to pray for others, when Job's own prayers for help have proved so utterly useless? Such questions push beyond Brenner's observation. They invite us to wonder not only if the *Job* who returns to prayer in the epilogue is *fully human.* They also invite us to consider if the *God* of the epilogue, to whom he is instructed to pray once more, is *fully God. Has nothing changed for either Job or God* since God spoke the words to the *satan* that left a righteous sufferer sitting on the ash heap, "Very well, he is in your power; only spare his life" (2:6)? [CD:"The Lord Can Never Seem Quite the Same to Himself"]

The epilogist quotes God as saying to Eliphaz and his friends, "My servant Job will pray for you."[4] [CD: "And My Servant Job Shall Pray for You"] There is no record of the words Job prayed. Instead, the text leads up to the edge of the prayer, then skips over it to report that "when he had prayed" (v. 10), the Lord restored Job's fortunes. If Job prayed a conventional prayer of intercession, we may imagine that the words would have been something like, "O Lord, forgive the friends; do not deal with them according to their foolishness."[5] When the text reports that God "accepted Job's prayer" (v. 9b), it suggests that the *friends' relationship to God* is different than it was before he interceded. The friends have *not* spoken the truth about God, and God is angry. Job *has* spoken the truth about God, and after he prays, the threat of judgment that hangs over their heads is lifted. [The Testament of Job 42:4-8]

The Testament of Job 42:4-8

The Testament of Job (1st century BCE-1st century CE) elaborates on the biblical account in 42:7-9 as follows:

After the Lord finished speaking to me, he said to Eliphas, "You there, Eliphas—you and your two friends—why did you sin? You have not spoken truly regarding my servant Job. Arise and have him sacrifice on your behalf so your sin might be taken away. Except for him, I would have destroyed you." So they brought me the things for sacrifice. And I took them and made an offering on their behalf, and the Lord received it favorable and forgave their sin. (T. Job 42:4-8)

"May It Be *My* Will"

In a Talmudic discussion on the efficacy of prayer, Rabbi Yohanan, commenting on Isa 56:7, argues that even God prays that divine mercy will overcome divine anger:

The Almighty Himself prays: May it be My will that My compassion may conquer my anger, and that My compassion may prevail over My other attributes, so that I may deal mercifully with My children and act toward them with charity that goes beyond the requirements of the law. (b. Ber.7a)

"You Are the Emancipator of Your God"

Robert Frost has imagined a forty-third chapter for the book of Job in which God and Job meet again, years after their first encounter, to reflect on the events they experienced together. The reunion is a chance for two old acquaintances to speak candidly about matters that have long been veiled in silence.

God: Oh, I remember you: you're Job, my Patient.
How are you now? I trust you're quite recovered,
And feel no ill effects from what I gave you.

Job: Gave me in truth: I like the frank admission.
I am a name for being put upon.
But, yes, I'm fine, except for now and then
A reminiscent twinge of rheumatism.
The letup's heavenly. You perhaps will tell us
If that's all there is to be of Heaven,
Escape from so great pains of life on earth
It gives a sense of letup calculated
To last a fellow to Eternity.

God: Yes, by and by. But first a larger matter.
I've had you on my mind a thousand years
To thank you someday for the way you helped me
Establish once and for all the principle
There's no connection a man can reason out

Between his just deserts and what he gets.
Virtue may fail and wickedness succeed.
'Twas a great demonstration we put on.
I should have spoken sooner had I found
The word I wanted. You would have supposed
One who in the beginning *was* the Word
Would be in a position to command it.
I have to wait for words like anyone.
Too long I've owed you this apology
For the apparently unmeaning sorrow
You were afflicted with in those old days.
But it was of the essence of the trial
You shouldn't understand it at the time.
It had to seem unmeaning to have meaning . . .
My thanks are to you for releasing me
From moral bondage to the human race.
The only free will there at first was man's,
Who could do good or evil as he chose.
I had no choice but I must follow him.
With forfeits and reward he understood—
Unless I liked to suffer loss of worship.
I had to prosper good and punish evil.
You changed all that. You set me free to reign.
You are the Emancipator of your God,
And as such, I promote you to a saint.

R. Frost, "A Masque of Reason," *The Poetry of Robert Frost*, ed. E. Lathem (New York: Henry Holt and Company, 1969), 474-76.

The text also hints that after Job prays, *God's relationship to the friends* has changed. *Before* Job prays, God is angry, and intent on doing "foolishness" (v. 8: *nĕbālāh*) with the friends. The word *nĕbālāh* normally refers to reprehensible acts of shame that subvert accepted ethical norms and bring dishonor and judgment on the perpetrator.[6] The occurrence in 42:8 is the only instance in the Old Testament where God is said to be the one doing *nĕbālāh*. The conventional view (as suggested by NRSV) is that the *friends'* foolishness, not *God's*, needs changing or forgiving. A straightforward reading, however, suggests that Job may be praying words like these: "O Lord, do not do anything foolish when you deal with the friends."[7] To judge the friends according to conventional standards of retributive justice would, in Job's understanding, subvert and dishonor God's own passion for forgiveness. ["May It Be *My* Will"] Job prays, at God's invitation, and on the other side of his prayer God does not deal foolishly with the friends. In sum, Job's intercession restores *both* the friends *and* God to a relationship that is different than that which existed before Job stepped into the breach between them. ["You Are the Emancipator of Your God"]

John the Baptist as Job
John the Baptist as Job. 1350. Baptistry, San Marco Basilica, Venice.

Job as a Symbol of Rebirth

Job's ultimate restoration has long been associated in Christian tradition with the rebirth and resurrection exemplified and promised by Jesus (for additional discussion and images, see **[Resurrection?]**). One such example is this four-teenth century mosaic, commissioned for the tomb of Andrea Dandolo, Doge of Venice, in the Baptistry of the San Marco basilic. Among several scenes depicting the risen Christ sending out his apostles to preach the gospel, several frescoes feature episodes from the life of John the Baptist. The bearded man in this fresco to whom the angel presents a vestment was long thought to be John the Baptist. But S. Terrien suggests that the inscription just above the angel's head—HIC AGELUS REPRAESETAT VESTE BTO IOBI—has been mistranslated. The last word is not IOHI, "to John," but IOBI, "to Job." Thus the proper translation is, "HERE AN ANGEL PRESENTS A VESTMENT TO THE BLESSED JOB."

In support of his argument for connecting this image with Job, Terrien notes that the bearded man is stepping out of a tomb, his left foot still wrapped in the burial linens. As he accepts new garments from the angel with his right hand, his left hand grasps an open scroll with an inscription. Although he concedes that much of the inscription is indecipherable, Terrien suggests that the words are likely from Job 1:21: "The Lord has given and the Lord has taken away; blessed be the name of the Lord."

S. Terrien, *The Iconography of Job through the Centuries: Artists as Biblical Interpreters* (University Park PA: Pennsylvania State University Press, 1996), 90-92.

"And the Lord Restored the Fortunes of Job," 42:10-17

After Job prays, he and his family are also restored. [Job as a Symbol of Rebirth] In view of what has transpired thus far, we may suspect that this restoration, like that which effects some change in both the friends and God, is more than simply a return to the way life used to be. Two subtle clues invite inspection.

Tobit's Restoration

The apocryphal book of Tobit (probably early 2nd century BCE) is the story of a righteous Jew, now living in exile, who, like Job, had suffered the loss of his property, his standing in the community, and his health. His wife, laboring tirelessly on his behalf, rebuked him from clinging to his righteousness in the midst of such troubles (see further, D. Dimant, "Use and Interpretation of Mikra in the Apocrypha and Pseudepigrpha," *Mikra: Text, Translation, Reading and Interpretation of the Hebrew Bible in Ancient Judaism and Early Christianity*, ed. M. J. Moulder et al. [Van Gorcum: Assen/Maastricht; Philadelphia: Fortress Press, 1998], 417-19).With words echoing those of Job's wife (Job 2:9), she says, "So much for all your acts of charity and all your good works!" (Tob 2:14; REB). Ultimately, Tobit and his family are restored, whereupon Tobit offers a prayer of thanksgiving to the God who has not only prospered him but will one day also rebuild Jerusalem (Tob 13). On the heels of this prayer, the narrator begins the final chapter of the book with these words:

So ended Tobit's thanksgiving. He died peacefully at the age of a hundred and twelve, and was buried in Nineveh with all honour. He was sixty-two years old when his eyes were damaged, and after he recovered his sight he lived in prosperity, doing acts of charity and never ceasing to praise God and to proclaim his majesty. (Tob 14:1-2; REB)

Tobit's Restoration

The Angel Raphael takes leave of old Tobit and his son, after healing Tobit's blindness and providing a rich wife for Tobit's son Tobias.

Pieter Lastman (1583-1633). Statens Museum for Kunst, Copenhagen, Denmark
(Credit: Erich Lessing/Art Resource, NY)

First, Job's possessions are not only restored, they are also doubled: "the Lord gave Job twice as much as much as he had before" (v. 10; cf. v. 12).[8] Perhaps the doubling is only a rhetorical flourish designed to bring the epilogue into conformity with the prologue, which suggests that Job's possessions are a tangible confirmation of his unparalleled piety. Perhaps it is no more than a characteristic feature of conventional stories about the reward that eventually comes to those who remain faithful to God, no matter the hardships they must endure.[9] [Tobit's Restoration] Even so, it is hard to overlook the connection elsewhere in the Old Testament between double compensation and (at least) a tacit admission of guilt. As F. Anderson notes, calling attention to the legislation in Exodus 22:4, "It is a wry touch that the Lord, like any thief who has been found out (Exod 22:4), repays Job double what he took from him."[10] If the epilogist has this legislation in mind, then perhaps we should think of *Job's restoration* as coinciding with, if not effecting,

Subverting the Assumptions of Patriarchy?

Scholars are divided on whether the inheritance of Job's daughters subverts patriarchal convention or represents it. See, for example, the contrasting viewpoints on Job 42:10-17 in D. Bergant, *Israel's Wisdom Literature: A Liberation-Critical Reading* (Minneapolis: Fortress, 1997), 15-49; J. Chittister, *Job's Daughters: Women and Power* (New York: Paulist Press, 1990); and I. Pardes, *Countertraditions in the Bible: A Feminist Approach* (Cambridge: Harvard University Press, 1994), 145-56.

It is instructive to note the expansion upon Job 42:15 in the Testament of Job (1st century BCE-1st century CE), which devotes four chapters (T. Job 46-50) to the inheritance of the daughters. According to this account, Job's estate was distributed initially among only the males. When the daughters complained, Job responded that they were each to receive an inheritance "better than that of your seven brothers" (T. Job 46:4), namely, one cord of the three-corded belt by which God miraculously healed Job. When one of his daughters asks how this inheritance is better, Job explains as follows:

Job and His Daughters

William Blake (1757-1827). *Job and His Daughters*. 1823-1825. Engraving from Blake's *Illustrations of the Book of Job*.

Then the other daughter, named Kasia, said to him, "Father, is this the inheritance which you said was better than that of our brothers? Who has any use for these unusual cords? We cannot gain a living from them, can we?"

And their father said to them, "Not only shall you gain a living from these, but these cords will lead you into the better world, to live in the heavens. Are you then ignorant, my children, of the value of these strings? The Lord considered me worthy of these in the day in which he wished to show me mercy and to rid my body of the plagues and worms . . . .

"Now then, my children, since you have these objects you will not have to face the enemy at all, but neither will you have worries of him in your mind, since it is a protective amulet of the Father. Rise then, gird yourselves with them before I die in order that you may be able to see those who are coming for my soul, in order that you may marvel over the creatures of God." (T. Job 47:1-4, 10-11)

In commenting on this account, P. Machinist notes that it exemplifies the "scripturalization" of biblical concepts that characterized Second Temple and later rabbinic texts. The objective, he concludes, was "to meet the demands of changing social preferences."

P. Machinist, "Job's Daughters and Their Inheritance in the Testament of Job and its Biblical Congeners," *The Echoes of Many Texts: Reflections on Jewish and Christian Traditions: Essays in Honor of Lou H. Silberman*, ed. W. G. Dever, J. E. Wright (Atlanta: Scholars Press, 1997), 80.

God's restoration (on the possibility that Job may be praying not only *to* but also *for* God, see [Can Anyone Summon God to Repentance?]). ["CD: If Job Does Not Repent, then the Lord Must"] At the very least, God's double compensation stands in marked contrast to what is offered by the community of "brothers and sisters and friends" (v. 11) who gather round to impart solidarity and companionship. It is they who offer the "consolation" and "comfort" that Eliphaz, Bildad, and Zophar would not, or could not provide Job (v. 11; cf. 2:11). They comfort him "for all the evil that the Lord had brought upon him," not with words or theology but with active communion. They offer fellowship through the sharing of a meal, and they demonstrate compassion with tangible gifts—a modest amount of money[11] and a gold ring—that contribute to his material needs.

A second clue that Job's restoration constitutes more than a simple return to the status quo occurs in vv. 13-15. The narrator takes care to name Job's daughters but not the sons: Jemimah ("dove"; cf. Song 2:14), Keziah ("cinnamon"; cf. Exod 30:24; Ps 45:8), and Keren-happuch (something like "cosmetics box," presumably a reference to the black powder used to beautify the eyes; cf. 2 Kgs 9:30; Jer 4:30). The narrator then goes a step further by reporting that Job gave the daughters an inheritance along with the sons. In the conventional world of biblical patriarchy, which the book of Job largely assumes, daughters inherit only when there are no sons (Num 26:33; cf. Num 27:1-11; 36:1-12).[12] On the other side of the ash heap, suffering seems to have transformed not only Job's personal situation but also his understanding of what constitutes justice. His decision to bequeath an inheritance to his daughters hints that social conventions that arbitrarily reduce the status of some persons will be turned on their end. [Subverting the Assumptions of Patriarchy?]

"And so," the epilogue reports, "The Lord blessed (*bārāk*) the latter days of Job more than his beginning" (v. 12). Counting the six occurrences in the prologue, this is the seventh and final instance of the verb "bless" in the book (see [Blessing/Cursing in Job]). What, after all Job has experienced since the prologue first introduced this word into the story, does it mean for Job to be blessed by God? As if trying to keep the answer to this question intentionally vexed, the narrator uses the same words Bildad spoke in 8:7. Appealing to the doctrine of retribution (see [Retribution]), Bildad assured Job that *if* he would only confess his guilt, *then* God would make his "beginning" seem small in comparison to the prosperity of his "latter days." In view of God's declaration that the friends "have not spoken what is right" about God, Bildad's assurance now sounds ironic at best. The blessing God gives seems to be Job's reward for *not* conforming to his friends' theology.

"Who Then Will Not Weep Over the Man of God?"

📖 The final chapter of the Testament of Job, most likely the first commentary on the book that bears Job's name, describes the eulogy Job receives upon his death.

> Woe to us today! A double woe!
> Gone today is the strength of the helpless!
> Gone is the light of the blind!
> Gone is the father of the orphans!
> Gone is the host of strangers!
> Gone is the clothing of the widows!
> Who then will not weep over the man of God?
> (T. Job 52:2-4)

"What Remains of Job?"

📖 Elie Wiesel concludes his essay on "Job: Our Contemporary" by suggesting that the end of the book is only an invitation to a new beginning. Reading between the lines of this ancient text, Wiesel suggests that it contains an ever-present, ever-vexing claim on those who find themselves summoned by its "grave and disquieting" message.

> Once upon a time, in a faraway land, there lived a legendary man, a just and righteous man who, in his solitude and despair, found the courage to stand up to God. And to force Him to look at his creation. And to speak to those men who sometimes succeed, in spite of Him and of themselves, in achieving triumphs over Him, triumphs that are grave and disquieting.
>   What remains of Job? A fable? A shadow? Not even a shadow of a shadow? An example, perhaps?

E. Wiesel, "Job: Our Contemporary," *Messengers of God: Biblical Portraits and Legends* (New York: Touchstone, 1976), 235.

The final words concerning Job amount to an epitaph. "And so it was that Job died, *old and full of days*" (v. 17). ["Who Then Will Not Weep Over the Man of God?"] The language "old and full of days" links Job to the memory of some of Israel's most revered ancestors, most notably Abraham (Gen 25:8), Isaac (Gen 25:29), and David (1 Chr 29:28). The reasons these three persons had a special place in the annals of Israel's righteous heroes may be many, but by evoking their memory in association with Job, the narrator invites speculation on particular connections. In Abraham's *insistence* that the "Judge of all the earth do what is just" (Gen 18:25), in Isaac's *trust* in his father's wisdom, even as he offers him for sacrifice on the altar (Gen 22:1-19), in David's *flawed fitness* to serve as God's king (e.g., 2 Sam 7:14-17), *and* also in Job, whose life embodies all their legacies in important ways, the expression "full of days" becomes an invitation to a larger understanding of what it means to live in relationship with God.

It is fitting that the end of the book effectively returns us once more to the beginnings of this drama (see [Endings as Beginnings]). When considering who belongs among the models of faith that best exemplify God's hopes and expectations, the journey begins with the question that God poses at the outset of this book: "Have you considered my servant Job?" (1:8). ["What Remains of Job?"] ["Revery Alone Will Do"]

CONNECTIONS

The epilogue clearly invites us to return to the prologue of this story in order to find its conclusion. "Once upon a time, in the land of Uz, there lived a man named Job". . . "And Job died, old and full of days." Job's restoration holds the promise that there is life on the other side of the ash heap. For that, we give thanks, even as we concede that we do not understand why he has been required to make this journey. Despite the promise of this "all's well that ends well" ending, we must wonder if Job or we can ever find the way back to that far away place where life was once untroubled and blessing God was unquestioned. Perhaps such wonderment is part of the journey with God that faith requires. Perhaps those who find themselves sitting with Job on the ash heap of suffering "for no reason" should know more about life in relation to God than they did before. ["All the Others Translate" but the Poet]

In the introductory comments on the prologue, I suggested the silence that descends over the land of Uz at the end of chapter 2 is a first clue that suffering like Job's changes everything *in heaven and on earth*. The commentary on the epilogue has identified some of the clues that strengthen this suggestion. These last "Connections" invite further reflection on what might have changed in heaven and on earth after Job prayed and the "Lord accepted Job's prayer."

"Revery Alone Will Do"

In considering how to respond to God's inviting question, "Have you considered my servant Job?" readers might consider Emily Dickinson's panged celebration of what the life of faith requires:

> To make a prairie it takes a clover and one bee,
> One clover, and a bee,
> And revery.
> The revery alone will do,
> If bees are few.

Emily Dickinson, "# 1755," in T. H. Johnson, ed., *The Complete Poems of Emily Dickinson* (Boston/New York: Little, Brown and Company, 1960), 710.

He Descended into Hell

Matthew's gospel reports that at the moment Jesus breathed his last breath, "the curtain of the temple was torn into, from top to bottom. The earth shook, and the rocks were split. The tombs also were opened, and many bodies of the saints who had fallen asleep were raised" (Matt 27:51-52).

Matthew's report of the opening of the graves is but one of a few oblique New Testament references to Jesus' descent into hell (cf. 1 Pet 3:19; 4:6). Despite the meager textual witness, early Christian writers from Ignatius to Aquinas explored the meaning of this descent, and at least since the second century, the Apostle's Creed has included its affirmation as a statement of faith. Moreover, numerous artists from the Byzantine period through the Renaissance have offered imaginative visual exegesis by suggesting that during the interval between his death and resurrection, Jesus communed with a variety of saints, including Adam, Moses, David, and the prophets.[13] Of these, I single out Vittore Carpaccio's suggestive fifteenth century depiction of the "Meditation on the Passion."[14]

The background of this painting offers two contrasting views of the landscape. To the left is a dead tree, bending toward a deserted mountain trial, where a leopard is about to devour a doe. The imagery suggests a world of death, unrestrained force, and hapless victims. To

"All the Others Translate" but the Poet

All the others translate: the painter sketches
A visible world to love or reject;
Rummaging into his living, the poet fetches
The images out that hurt and connect . . .

W. H. Auden, "The Composer," in *W. H. Auden: Collected Poems*, ed. E. Mendelson (New York: Vintage International, 1991), 181.

The Meditation on the Passion

Vittore Carpaccio (Italian, Venetian, born c. 1455, died 1523/26). *The Meditation on the Passion*. c. 1510. Oil and tempera on wood. The Metropolitan Museum of Art, New York. John Stewart Kennedy Fund, 1911

the right we see just the opposite: trees and plants full of life; walled villages that are safe and secure; and animals (leopard, doe, and red bird) that inhabit the same world without fear or intimidation. In the foreground, Carpaccio places three figures: Jerome (left), Christ, seated on a dilapidated throne (center), and Job (right). It is the figure of Job who commands our attention.

Carpaccio has placed him on the side where images of life and peace and promise define the landscape of his encounter with the soon-to-be resurrected Christ. Yet he has also surrounded Job with images that suggest the imprint of death on his life is still very real. A shattered human skull along with dried out bones pieces are strewn on the ground beneath his feet. A piece of the granite-like block, which supports him and his hope, is broken off at the bottom. A legible portion of the Hebrew inscription on the block is from Job 19:25: "I know that my redeemer lives." Most intriguing of all is the depiction of Job pointing with his right hand to his feet, as if to suggest that before Jesus ascends to his glory, he should take one last look at where Job's journey has taken him.

The imagery provides a suggestive exegesis of Luke's account of Jesus' post-resurrection appearance to the disciples on the road to Emmaus (Luke 24). *After* the disciples had recognized him, *after* they had broken bread with him, *after* they had proclaimed the post-Easter hallelujah—"The Lord has risen indeed!" (24:35)—Jesus unexpectedly appears and speaks one further word of instruction: "Look at my hands and my feet. . . . Touch me and see" (24:39). It seems a rather odd thing to say to those who have already experienced his resurrection and have already begun to proclaim its promise for others, *unless* perhaps Jesus is concerned to remind them one last time that even in the afterglow of resurrection it is imperative that those who proclaim the gospel be able to touch and feel the raw hurt of brokenness and loss. Job points to his feet, much like Jesus may have done with the disciples. The evocative difference here is that it is *Job who directs Jesus* to take one last look before resurrection becomes a reality. Carpaccio suggests that when Jesus descended into hell, during the crucial interval when he was preparing to ascend, Job was teaching Jesus something important about what it means to live after one has walked through Job's world.[15]

On the other side of death, Jesus commands those who would follow him not only to *look* at him but also to t*ouch* his wounds. The command suggests a tactile proximity, as if the disciples should place their hands and feet on Jesus', bodying up to him as it were, with such closeness that his wounds are impressed on them. Whatever space may be between them now, the disciples no longer have the room to make decisions based on the perspectives of the onlooker (on the perspective of the onlooker, see further the "Connections" at Job 30). Now, when Jesus speaks, his words are so close, they can not only see but also feel his presence. And we ask, no doubt along with them, what are disciples supposed to *see* and *feel* about the God who was in Jesus that we did not before?

Lessons from the Grave

A second exegete of the human condition, like Carpaccio a "common reader" of the biblical text (on this term, see the "Connections" for Job 40:6–42:6), opens a way to find an answer to this question. Near the end of his novel *Crossing to Safety*, Wallace Stegner describes the vacation Sally and her husband took to Italy. They visited the tiny village of San Sepolchro in southern Tuscany, where they happened upon Pierro della Francesca's fifteenth-century fresco of the resurrected Christ. ["The Resurrection"] Sally's husband stopped casually to look at the painting, as tourists often do, and then moved on to the next picture. Sally lingers behind, staring at the face of della Francesca's Christ. Despite the golden halo over Christ's head and the flag of victory in his hand, she sees that his eyes are staring into the foreground with a look that seems to be remembering the pain of crucifixion, as if to suggest that "if resurrection had taken place, it had not yet been comprehended."[16]

Sally's husband sees her staring at the painting, but he cannot at first figure out what has so captured her interest and imagination. He looks at her intently. She is standing there, propped up on the crutches she has needed to walk since a childhood bout with polio crippled her with a lasting lesson about what pain and loss means. His eyes return to the painting and gradually, but with increasing clarity, he sees what Sally sees in the eyes of this one who until moments ago had been horribly dead. The truth and the promise of resurrection, he now understands, is that "those who have been dead understand things that will never be understood by those who have only lived."[17]

"Those who have been dead understand things that will never be understood by those who have only lived." I do not know of any statement that provides more profound explication of the last words in the biblical text of Job—"full of days" (42:17)—than these words from Stegner. And yet, such profundity is nonetheless unsettling, like Job's story itself. Why must the Jobs of this world suffer a virtual (or real) death before someone comes to "console and comfort" them? Why must the Jobs of this world live and die as persons who are abandoned and ignored? Why must they cry out for comfort to "friends" who remain so oblivious to their pain? Why must their fight for justice and redemption be a post-mortem victory? Is this what God desires? Is this what Jesus hoped for when he commanded his disciples, "Look at my hands and feet. Touch me and see"?

We return once more to the end of Luke's account of the disciples' Emmaus journey. After the disciples had encountered the risen Lord, presumably while the words "He has risen indeed!" were still ringing in their ears, they returned to Jerusalem to begin their ministry. While they were in Jerusalem, still taking about these things, Luke reports that Jesus came and stood in their presence one last time. He greeted them with familiar words that should have been put them at ease—"Peace be with you"—but they were "startled and terrified" (Luke 24:36-37). After all they had shared with Jesus on this long day's journey to Emmaus, now they could not recognize the one who spoke to them. Just moments before they had recognized and acclaimed him as the risen Lord; now they thought they were seeing a ghost. For the second

Resurrection of Christ

Piero della Francesca (c. 1420-1492). Fresco. Pinacoteca Comunale, Sansepolcro, Italy. (Credit: Alinari/Art Resource, NY)

"The Resurrection"

On the left, della Francesca depicts a barren landscape with naked trees reaching toward a darkening sky. To the right, the landscape is alive with foliage, human dwellings, and bursts of sunlight. Between these scenes of life and death, he places the resurrected Christ, with one foot still in the tomb, as if he is still in the act of stepping out of the grave. In Christ's right hand is a staff holding a flag of victory. On his left hand and foot we can see the crucifixion scars. His side shows the wound from the soldier's spear, still dripping drops of blood.

time this day, Jesus does something truly remarkable. He says to all of them, "Look at my hands and feet. . . . Touch me and see that it is I myself" (Luke 24:39). And then, while they were "disbelieving and still wondering" (Luke 24:41) what all this meant, Jesus asked them if they had any food to give him. *He* had just given *them* bread, blessed and broken. Now he asked *them* to feed *him*. They gave him a piece of fish, the same food they had once seen him use to feed the five thousand who had followed him into a deserted place outside Bethsaida (Luke 9:10-17). He took the fish and ate in their presence. Luke pauses at just this moment to allow us to take a close look at the scene. Jesus, with scarred hands and feet, asking for food; disciples, disbelieving and wondering, offering him the only thing they have. The scene suggestively reprises the bread broken and shared between Job and "his brothers and sisters and all who had known him before" (Job 42:11).

When we stand before Job at the end of his story, we are in a very real sense standing before Jesus at the end of his. When the question comes, "Do you have anything to eat?" that is, do you have anything to feed people like us, people who may well have died with the unanswered question, "My God, my God, why have you forsaken me" still on their lips, what will we *say*? More importantly, what will we *feel* that compels us to *do* something that will make a difference *in life*, not only *in death*? [CD: "Come Not When I Am Dead"] If the God who was in Jesus truly expects us to touch and feel what it means to be "grieved, even to death" (Matt 26:38), then perhaps answering the question that launches this book— "Have you considered my servant Job?"—is still worthy of our best efforts.

NOTES

[1] E. M. Good, *In Turns of Tempest: A Reading of Job with a Translation* (Stanford: Stanford University Press, 1990), 380.

[2] M. Pope, *Job* (AB; Garden City NY: Doubleday, 1979), 350. For the use of this term and its derivatives elsewhere in the Hebrew Bible and in Job, see Duck-Woo Nam, *Talking about God: Job 42:7-9 and the Nature of God in the Book of Job* (New York: Peter Lang, 2003), 22-24, and Good (*In Turns of Tempest*, 381), who sums up as follows:

> [T]he galaxy of different meanings shows that the word does not signify "truth" in the merely intellectual sense but bears on the satisfaction of what has been established. The basic connotation. . . signifies that Yahweh criticizes the friends and praises Job because they have not, as he has, said something "established," properly prepared. Moreover, the relationship of the word's root *kwn* to creation [e.g., Isa 45:18; Pss 24:2; 119:90; Prov 3:19] connects Yahweh's praise of Job to his perception of the cosmic order about which Yahweh asked in 40:8. The friends, for all their certainty about traditional dogma, have failed to speak satisfactorily of the deity, whereas Job has done so.

[3] A. Brenner, "Job the Pious? The Characterization of Job in the Narrative Framework of the Book," JSOT 43 (1989): 44.

[4] For what follows, see further Samuel E. Balentine, "My Servant Job Shall Pray For You," *Theology Today* 58 (2002): 502-18.

[5] See, for example, J. Gerald Janzen, *Job* (Atlanta: John Knox, 1985), 266; J. Wharton, *Job* (*Westminster Bible Companion*; Louisville KY: Westminster John Knox Press, 1999), 179.

⁶ The idiom *'āśāh nĕbālāh,* "do foolishness," occurs frequently in the Old Testament, always with a strong negative connotation (Gen 34:7; Deut 22:21; Josh 7:15; Judg 20:6; Jer 29:23). See further, M. Saebo, *"nabal* fool," in E. Jenni, C. Westermann, *TLOT,* vol. 2, trans. M. E. Biddle (Peabody MS: Hendrikson Publishers, 1997), 712. The comments by Driver (*A Critical and Exegetical Commentary on the Book of Job* [Edinburgh: T and T. Clark, 1921], 26) are instructive: "[T]he fault of the *nabal* was not weakness of reason, but moral and religious sensibility, an invincible lack of sense or perception, for the claims of either God or man."

⁷ Cf. Pope, *Job,* 347, 350-51; Janzen, *Job,* 266; Good, *In Turns of Tempest,* 383. There is a suggestive echo here of Job's rebuke of his wife in 2:10 for "talking like a shameless fool (*hannĕbālôt*)" by urging him to curse God. Just as Job dismisses his wife's counsel as foolishness, so now he appears to be unwilling to accept God's "foolish anger" toward the friends.

⁸ The doubling may also be reflected in the unusual form of the word for "seven" in v. 13 (*šib'ānāh*), which some interpreters suggest refers to a doubling (fourteen) of sons, and in the reference to the 140 years (twice two normal lifetimes; cf. Ps 19:10) that Job lived after he was restored. See, for example, E. Dhorme, *A Commentary on the Book of Job* (Nashville: Thomas Nelson Publishers, 1967), 651; N. Habel, *The Book of Job: A Commentary* (OTL; Philadelphia: Westminster Press, 1985), 577, 585; C. Newsom, "The Book of Job," in vol. 4 of *NIB* (Nashville: Abingdon Press, 1996), 635.

⁹ Newsom, "The Book of Job," 635.

¹⁰ F. I. Anderson, *Job: An Introduction and Commentary* (TOTC; Leicester, England: Inter-Varsity Press, 1976), 293; cf. Roland E. Murphy, *The Book of Job: A Short Reading* (New York: Paulist Press, 1999), 102; Newsom, "The Book of Job," 636.

¹¹ The amount of money signified by the term *qĕśîtāh* (v. 11) is uncertain. Jacob, for example, pays the sum of one hundred *qĕśîtāhs* to purchase a piece of land (Josh 24:32; l; the only other occurrence of the term is in Gen 33:19; cf. Newsom, "The Book of Job," 635; J. Hartley, *The Book of Job* [NICOT; Grand Rapids MI: William B. Eerdmans, 1988], 541). The LXX uses a word that means "lamb," which perhaps suggests an amount equivalent to the monetary value of such an animal (cf. Good, *In Turns of Tempest,* 170-71, 386-87; Pope, *Job,* 351).

¹² On Job and "the moral world of biblical patriarchy," see C. Newsom, "Job," *The Women's Bible Commentary,* ed. C. Newsom, S. Ringe (Louisville KY: Westminster John Knox, 1992), 133-35.

¹³ For discussion and visuals, see H. Hornik and M. Parsons, "The Harrowing of Hell," BR 19 (June 2003): 18-26.

¹⁴ For commentary on this painting and its significance for Job, see S. Terrien, *The Iconography of Job through the Centuries: Artists as Biblical Interpreters* (University Park PA: Pennsylvania State University Press, 1996), 135-39, and H. Hornik, "The Venetian Images by Bellini and Carpaccio: Job as Intercessor or Prophet?" *RevExp* 99 (2002): 541-68.

¹⁵ The comments here reprise my earlier discussion in Samuel E. Balentine, "Who Will Be Job's Redeemer?" *PRSt* 26 (1999): 280-83.

¹⁶ W. Stegner, *Crossing to Safety* (New York: Random House, 1987), 221.

¹⁷ Ibid., 222.

BIBLIOGRAPHY

I. Commentaries

Anderson, F. I. *Job: An Introduction and Commentary.* Tyndale Old Testament Commentaries. Downers Grove, IL: Inter-Varsity, 1976.

Clines, D. J. A. *Job 1–20.* Word Bible Commentary. Dallas TX: Word, 1989.

Crenshaw, J. L. "Job, Book of," in *The Anchor Bible Dictionary*, ed. D. N. Freedman. Vol. 3 (H-J). New York: Doubleday, 1992. 858-68.

Dhorme, E. *A Commentary on the Book of Job.* Nashville: Thomas Nelson Publishers, 1984.

Driver, S. R. and G. B. Gray. *A Critical and Exegetical Commentary on the Book of Job.* The International Critical Commentary. Edinburgh: T. & T. Clark, 1977.

Fohrer, G. *Das Buch Hiob.* Kommentar zum Alten Testament. Gütersloh: Gütersloher Verlagshuas Gerd Mohn, 1963.

Good, E. *In Turns of Tempest: A Reading of Job with a Translation.* Stanford CA: Stanford University Press, 1990.

Gordis, R. *The Book of Job. Commentary, New Translation and Special Studies.* New York: The Jewish Theological Seminary of America, 1978.

Habel, N. *The Book of Job.* Old Testament Library. Philadelphia: Westminster, 1985.

Hartley, J. *The Book of Job.* New International Commentary of the Old Testament. Grand Rapids MI: William B. Eerdmans, 1988.

Janzen, J. G. *Job.* Interpretation. Atlanta: John Knox, 1985.

Murphy, R. E. *The Book of Job: A Short Reading.* New York: Paulist Press, 1999.

Newsom, C. "The Book of Job." *The New Interpreter's Bible.* Vol. 4. Nashville: Abingdon, 1996. 319-37.

Newsom, C., "Job," in *The Woman's Bible Commentary*, ed. C. Newsom and Sharon H. Ringe. Louisville: Westminster/John Knox, 1992. 130-44.

Pope, M. *Job.* The Anchor Bible. Garden City NY: Doubleday, 1979.

Rowley, H. H. *Job.* The Century Bible (New Series). Nashville: Thomas Nelson and Sons, 1970.

Simundson, D. J. *The Message of Job: A Theological Commentary.* Augsburg Old Testament Studies. Minneapolis MN: Ausgburg Publishing House, 1986.

Wharton, J. A. *Job.* Westminster Bible Companion. Louisville: Westminster John Knox, 1999.

II. Additional Works

Balentine, S. E., ed. "Have You Considered My Servant Job?" Thematic issue of *Review and Expositor* 99 (2002).

Beal, T. K. *Religion and Its Monsters.* New York: Routledge, 2002. 35-70.

Beuken, W. A. M., ed. *The Book of Job.* Leuven: University Press, 1994.

Bloom, H., ed. *The Book of Job.* New York: Chelsea House, 1998.

Bloom, H. *Where Shall Wisdom Be Found?* New York: Riverhead Books, 2004.

Brown, William P. *The Ethos of the Cosmos: The Genesis of Moral Imagination in the Bible.* Grand Rapids MI: William B. Eerdmans, 1999. 317-79.

Cook, S. L., and C. L. Patton, J. W. Watts, eds. *The Whirlwind: Essays on Job, Hermeneutics and Theology in Memory of Jane Morse.* JSOTSup 336. Sheffield: Sheffield Academic Press, 2001.

Crenshaw, J. L. *Defending God: Biblical Responses to the Problem of Evil.* Oxford: University Press, 2005.

Dell, K. *The Book of Job as Skeptical Literature.* BZAW 197. Berlin: Walter de Gruyter, 1991.

Duke, D. N. and S. E. Balentine, eds. "Theodicy at the Turn of Another Century." Thematic issue of *Perspectives in Religious Studies* 26 (1999).

Girard, R. *Job: The Victim of His People.* Trans. Y. Freccero. Stanford: Stanford University Press, 1987.

Glatzer, N. *The Dimensions of Job. A Study and Selected Readings.* New York: Schocken Books, 1969.

Gutiérrez, G. *On Job: God-Talk and the Suffering of the Innocent.* Maryknoll NY: Orbis, 1987.

Hoffman, Y. *A Blemished Perfection: The Book of Job in Context.* JSOTSup 213. Sheffield: Sheffield Academic Press, 1996.

Holbert, John C. *Preaching Job.* St. Louis: Chalis Press, 1999.

Keel, O. *Jahwes Entgegnung an Ijob.* FRLANT 121. Göttingen: Vandenhoeck & Ruprecht, 1978.

Kubina, V. *Die Gottesreden im Buche Hiob.* Freiburger theologischen Studien. Freiburg, Basel, Wien: Herder, 1979.

Miles, J. *God. A Biography.* New York: Alfred A. Knopf, 1995.

Mitchell, S. *The Book of Job.* San Francisco: North Point, 1987.

Nam, Duck-Woo. *Talking About God: Job 42:7-9 and the Nature of God in the Book of Job.* Studies in Biblical Literature 49. Frankfurt NY: Peter Lang, 2003.

Newsom, C. *The Book of Job: A Contest of Moral Imaginations.* Oxford: University Press, 2003.

Newsom, C. and S. E. Schreiner, "Job, Book of," in *Dictionary of Biblical Interpretation*, ed. John H. Hayes. Vol. A-J. Nashville: Abingdon Press, 1999. 587-99.

Perdue, L. G. *Wisdom in Revolt: Metaphorical Theology in the Book of Job.* JSOTSup 112. Sheffield: JSOT Press, 1991.

Perdue, L. G. and W. C. Gilpin, eds. *The Voice From the Whirlwind: Interpreting the Book of Job.* Nashville: Abingdon, 1992.

Pyeon, Y. *You Have Not Spoken What Is Right About Me: Intertextuality and the Book of Job.* Studies in Biblical Literature 45. Frankfurt NY: Peter Lang, 2003.

Safire, W. *The First Dissident: The Book of Job in Today's Politics.* New York: Random House, 1992.

Sutherland, R. *Putting God on Trial: The Biblical Book of Job.* Victoria: Trafford, 2004.

Terrien, S. *The Iconography of Job Through the Centuries. Artists as Biblical Interpreters.* University Park: The Pennsylvania State University Press, 1996.

Tilley, T. W. *The Evils of Theodicy.* Washington, D.C.: Georgetown University Press, 1991. 89-112.

Van Wolde, E., ed. *Job 28: Cognition in Context.* Biblical Interpretation Series. Leiden, Boston: Brill, 2003.

Wahl, H.-M. *Der gerechte Schöpfer: Eine redaktions-und theologischtliche Untersuchung der Elihureden Hiob 32-37.* BZAW 207. Berlin: Walter de Gruyter, 1993.

Westermann, C. *The Structure of the Book of Job: A Form-Critical Analysis.* Philadelphia: Fortress, 1981.

Whedbee, W. J. *The Bible and the Comic Vision.* Cambridge: University Press, 1998. 221-62.

Wilcox, J. T. *The Bitterness of Job: A Philosophical Reading.* Ann Arbor: University of Michigan Press, 1969.

Zukerman, B. *Job the Silent: A Study in Historical Counterpoint.* New York: Oxford University Press, 1991.

INDEX OF AUTHORS

INDEX OF SCRIPTURES

INDEX OF SIDEBARS

Index of Illustrations

INDEX OF TOPICS